United Nations International Comparison Project

PHASE III

WORLD PRODUCT AND INCOME
International Comparisons of Real Gross Product

Produced by The Statistical
Office of The United Nations
and The World Bank

IRVING B. KRAVIS • ALAN HESTON • ROBERT SUMMERS

in collaboration with Alicia R. Civitello,
Samvit P. Dhar, Shigeru Kawasaki,
Hugues Picard, and Martin Shanin

PUBLISHED FOR THE WORLD BANK
THE JOHNS HOPKINS UNIVERSITY PRESS
BALTIMORE AND LONDON

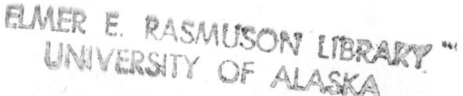

The Johns Hopkins University Press
Baltimore, Maryland 21218, U.S.A.

Editor Ross Bankson
Figures Pensri Kimpitak
Index Ralph Ward and James Silvan
Proofreading Harry Einhorn
Binding and cover design Joyce Eisen

Library of Congress Cataloging in Publication Data

Kravis, Irving B.
  World product and income.

  At head of title: United Nations International Compari-
son Project, phase III.
  Includes index.
  1. National income. 2. Gross national product. 3. Com-
parative economics. I. Heston, Alan W. II. Summers,
Robert. III. United Nations Statistical Office. IV. World
Bank. V. United Nations International Comparison
Project.
VI. Title.
HB141.5.K72   339.3   81–15569
ISBN 0–8018–2359–5   AACR2
ISBN 0–8018–2360–9 (pbk.)

INTERNATIONAL COMPARISON PROJECT
COMPUTER TAPES

A computer tape containing the statistics presented in the
basic tables of chapters 6, 7, and 8 of this volume for the
thirty-four benchmark countries may be purchased from the
International Comparison Unit, Department of Economics,
3718 Locust Walk (CR), University of Pennsylvania, Philadelphia, Pennsylvania 19104, U.S.A. The tape also provides the 1950–80 per capita GDPs of nearly 100 additional
countries, which are presented in chapter 8 only in aggregations of regions and socioeconomic groups of countries.
These latter data are also provided on microfiche that will
accompany the tape.

Of the proportion which the product of any region bears to the people, an estimate is commonly made according to the pecuniary price of the necessities of life, which is never certain, because it supposes what is far from truth, that the value of money is always the same, and so measures an unknown quantity by an uncertain standard. It is competent enough when the markets of the same country, at different times, and those times not too distant, are to be compared; but of very little use for the purpose of making one nation acquainted with the state of another.

Samuel Johnson
*A Journey
to the Western Islands
of Scotland*
1775

Contents

Preface

The International Comparison Project (ICP) has been a far-flung cooperative effort involving many institutions and persons in thirty-four countries. The ICP was a joint responsibility of the United Nations Statistical Office, the World Bank, and the International Comparison Unit of the University of Pennsylvania. The major operational responsibility rested with the United Nations Statistical Office, whose director exercised general supervision over the development of the project. The immediate responsibility for technical guidance and supervision rested with the project director at the University of Pennsylvania, who divided his efforts between the work there and at the United Nations.

The World Bank provided essential financial support from its own resources and organized a consortium of contributors that included the bilateral aid agencies of Denmark, the Federal Republic of Germany, Norway, the Netherlands, and the United States. Hungary and the United Kingdom made technical experts available to assist certain developing countries participating in the ICP.

The responsibility for the collection, collation, and transmission of the required data for each of the participating countries was assumed principally by the following national statistical authorities:

AUSTRIA: Central Statistical Office
BRAZIL: Fundação Getúlio Vargas, Instituto Brasileiro de Economía
COLOMBIA: mainly the Departamento Administrativo Nacional de Estadística (DANE) and also the Centro de Estudios Sobre Desarrollo Económico (CEDE) at the Universidad de los Andes, and the Banco de la República
HUNGARY: Central Statistical Office
INDIA: Central Statistical Organisation of the Department of Statistics
IRAN: Economic Statistics Affairs Directorate of the Bank Markazi
JAMAICA: Department of Statistics

JAPAN: Office of Statistical Standards of the Administrative Management Agency, Statistics Bureau of the Prime Minister's Office, Economic Research Institute of the Economic Planning Agency, Ministry of Education, Ministry of Health and Welfare, Ministry of International Trade and Industry, Ministry of Transport and Society for Contractors Management Research
KENYA: Central Bureau of Statistics of the Ministry of Economic Planning and Development
MALAWI: National Statistical Office of the Office of the President and Cabinet
MALAYSIA: Department of Statistics
MEXICO: Subdirección de Investigación Económica y Bancaria del Banco de México, S.A.
PAKISTAN: Statistics Division of the Ministry of Planning and Development
PHILIPPINES: National Census and Statistics Office of the National Economic and Development Authority and other related government agencies
POLAND: Central Statistical Office
REPUBLIC OF KOREA: Statistics Department of the Bank of Korea and the National Bureau of Statistics of the Economic Planning Board
ROMANIA: Central Statistical Board
SPAIN: Instituto Nacional de Estadística
SRI LANKA: Department of Census and Statistics
SYRIAN ARAB REPUBLIC: Central Bureau of Statistics of the Office of the Prime Minister
THAILAND: National Statistical Office
UNITED STATES: Statistical Policy Division of the Office of Management and Budget in the Executive Office of the President, Bureau of Labor Statistics, and the National Income and Wealth Division of the Bureau of Economic Analysis of the Department of Commerce
URUGUAY: Banco Central del Uruguay
YUGOSLAVIA: Federal Statistical Office
ZAMBIA: Central Statistical Office.

The Statistical Office of the European Communities supplied the data for its nine members: Belgium, Denmark, France, the Federal Republic of Germany, Ireland, Italy, Luxembourg, the Netherlands, and the United Kingdom.

Many persons in the above-mentioned agencies and others made important contributions in providing the data and serving as critics and advisers. At the risk of slighting some whose contribution has not come to the attention of the central staff, the help of the following is gratefully acknowledged: Josef Schmidl, Reinhold Schwarzl, and Christa Voigt of Austria; Laura Kingston and Angelo de Souza of Brazil; Roberto Pinella of Colombia; Ivan Kovacashazi, Peter Pukli, Szabolcs Ráth, György Szilágyi, and Mihály Zafir of Hungary; M. S. Avadhani, Uma Roy Choudhury, Lalit Mohan, Ram Murti, Suraj Prakash, Ved Prakash, S. X. Sharma, and Pritam Singh of India; R. Booth, G. Gunter, A. McKenzie, and D. Walton of Jamaica; Zin Murage, Mariana Ouma, and Parmeet Singh of Kenya; Kwok Kwan Kit and Wong Tat Fook of Malaysia; Aftab Ahmadkhan, Nasim M. Sadiq, and Mohammad Yusof of Pakistan; Lilia H. Constantina and Tito Mijares of the Philippines; Ewa Cwil, Wieslawa Drözdź, Jan Gawronski, Eugenia Krzeczkowska, Aleksandra Kudrewicz, Anna Orlinska, and Antoni Stolarek of Poland; Chae Hwa Lee of the Republic of Korea; W. S. M. Fernando, W. A. A. S. Peiris, and D. S. L. Weeratunga of Sri Lanka; Farid El Boustani of Syria; Prakorb Juangbhamich and Prapan Vonkhorporn of Thailand; Jose R. E. Noguez of Uruguay; and D. Miljkovic and Zoran Plavac of Yugoslavia. The regional commissions of the United Nations have also been very helpful in contacts with the participating countries.

The assistance of Maria Köszegi of the Central Statistical Office of Hungary in the fieldwork in Kenya and Zambia is gratefully acknowledged. Angus Fell did work for the ICP in Sri Lanka and Robert Oswald in Jamaica, Kenya, Malawi, and Syria on behalf of the U.K. Ministry of Overseas Development.

Methodological issues were clarified in discussions with a number of persons not already mentioned, including Sultan Ahmad, Lazlo Drechsler, John Edelman, Hans-Dieter Faerber, Dino Gerardi, Paul Isenman, Hugo Krijnse Locker, A. Kundu, Yoshimasa Kurabayashi, Frank Orlando, Vittorio Paretti, and Lawrence H. Summers. Thanks are due to Colin Clark, a pioneer in the field of international comparisons, for his comments on the treatment of services (see Chapter 5) and also for calling attention to the quotation from Samuel Johnson. Peter Hill and Robin Marris made some particularly valuable suggestions that influenced the final text in a variety of ways, and general discussions with a number of colleagues in the Department of Economics at the University of Pennsylvania were very helpful.

Two conferences held during the gestation period of Phase III made possible a sharing of ideas with many international comparison experts holding diverse views. The Rockefeller Foundation very kindly made its conference center at Bellagio, Italy, available for one of these conferences, and Estudios Conjuntos sobre la Integración Económica Latinamericana (ECIEL) and the Fundação Getúlio Vargas served as hosts in Rio de Janeiro, Brazil, for the other.

It is appropriate to acknowledge once again the contribution of the agencies and people who were indispensable in the preparation of Phases I and II, for the present report builds on the previous ones. From the standpoint of presentation the texts of the previous reports have been freely drawn upon in order to make this volume reasonably complete and freestanding.

Statistical assistance in the work of the central staff was provided by Chad Leechor, Peter Trupia, Alex Carpio, Roshan Trakru, and Alfonso Uong. Myrtle Campbell performed the secretarial duties for the ICP group in the United Nations Statistical Office. The same functions at the University of Pennsylvania were performed by Kathleen Conway, who typed the manuscript in its successive versions with remarkable patience and speed. Robert McPheeters provided liaison with the World Bank.

WORLD PRODUCT AND INCOME
International Comparisons of Real Gross Product

1

Introduction and Summary of Results

THIS VOLUME REPORTS ON THE THIRD PHASE of the United Nations International Comparison Project (ICP). The main results, summarized in this chapter, provide comparisons of real gross domestic product (GDP) per capita for thirty-four countries in 1975. Quantity and price comparisons are given also for personal consumption, capital formation, and public consumption. In subsequent chapters, still further subdivisions of final expenditures on GDP are estimated. These new 1975 benchmark estimates considerably expand the Phase I set covering six countries in 1967 and ten countries in 1970 and the Phase II set covering six additional countries in 1970 and all sixteen in 1973.

Because the benchmark studies provide estimates of detailed components of GDP, they afford insights into comparative economic structure. For example, they show the extent of country-to-country price differences in investment goods and other components of GDP, thus making possible a comparison of the shares of investment goods and other components of GDP in real (price-corrected) terms. A variety of structural relationships involving both quantities and prices are explored at various points in this report. In particular, one of these relationships is exploited to obtain estimates—admittedly approximations—of real GDP per capita for nearly all the countries of the world in 1975 in order to get estimates of real incomes of regions of the world. Finally, some demand analysis applications of the results are presented in the last chapter.

In addition, estimates are provided, on an approximate basis, of real GDP per capita for the thirty-four countries annually for the period 1950 through 1980 in addition to the three available benchmark years, 1970, 1973, and 1975.

The Nature of the Study

The ICP was established at the end of the 1960s to fill an important gap in the world's statistical system. The two previous decades had witnessed a rapid development of national-income accounting all over the world. Great progress had also been made toward standardization of the accounting methods followed by various countries. However, conversion of GDP and other national-accounts estimates of the different countries to a common currency in such a way as to make them directly comparable was not possible. Intercountry comparisons of national-accounts aggregates based on exchange rates as the conversion factors were known from limited earlier studies[1] to deviate substantially from comparisons based on the purchasing power of currencies.[2]

Exchange Rates and Real Purchasing Power

Indeed, Phases I and II of the ICP showed that the purchasing power of the currency of low-income countries relative to that of very high-income countries is often two or three times as great as the exchange rate would indicate. Unfortunately, a twofold or threefold overstatement of the number of currency units required to match the purchasing power of the currency of a high-income numéraire country will lead to a correspondingly large understatement of the low-income country's relative real income.

---

1. Clark (1941), Gilbert and Kravis (1954), and Gilbert and associates (1958).
2. Even the casual observations of travelers verified this. See, for example, Keynes (1930), vol. 1, p. 100.

Income or product comparisons among the high-income countries based on the use of exchange rates are subject to smaller but still notable margins of error. Furthermore, a substantial degree of spurious variability has crept into exchange-rate–derived comparisons under the flexible exchange-rate system adopted in the early 1970s. Year-to-year changes in exchange rates between major currencies of 20 percent or more have been observed.[3] Since most of these large changes have been unrelated to the relative movements of the real national product of the countries concerned, exchange-rate conversions necessarily have at times given quite erroneous measures of the relative real products of pairs of countries.

For countries at all income levels, exchange rates not only obscure the true quantity relationships for GDP as a whole; they also distort certain kinds of structural comparisons. These distortions arise because the deviation of purchasing power parities from exchange rates is not uniform for all kinds of goods. In the price structure of low-income countries, for example, capital goods tend to be more expensive relative to consumer goods than is the case in high-income countries. Exchange-rate conversions thus tend to exaggerate the relative proportion of GDP that is taken in the form of capital goods in poor countries.

The Need for the Comparisons and Their Antecedents

International comparisons of real product and currency purchasing powers are desired for a variety of analytical and policy purposes, at both the national and international levels. They are indispensable, for example, in understanding economic growth, and in helping national economic planners to assess past economic performance and future expansion paths. Their utility is attested to by the many international organizations and countries that have attempted to produce on a relatively small scale and only for selected years their own estimates of per capita income comparisons.

Before the start of the ICP, a number of such efforts had been made, including those by the U.N. Statistical Office, the Organisation for European Economic Co-operation (OEEC),[4] the Council for Mutual Economic Assistance (CMEA),[5] the World Bank, the Economic Commission for Latin America (ECLA),[6] and a number of governments, including those of Canada, the Federal Republic of Germany, Japan, the Soviet Union, and the United States. Some pioneering work in comparisons between socialist and market economies was carried out as well under the auspices of the Conference of European Statisticians (1968).

In addition, estimates were made by individuals, many of them in the public domain. Virtually all the private estimates and some of the official ones were based on armchair calculations. Estimates for which fieldwork was done varied widely in the intensity and quality of the effort. Although many of these came closer to the truth than the simple conversion at official rates of exchange, a more solid and consistent basis for the estimates was clearly needed. The studies were so varied in time and method that they resulted in an incomplete jigsaw puzzle of comparisons. No useful worldwide system of consistent, reliable comparisons covering a substantial number of countries was produced. More than that, no uniform framework was laid down that could be used as the basis for an expanded and continuing coverage of countries over time.

The Methodological Tasks of the ICP

The first task of the ICP was to establish methods that could be used for a system of comparisons of real product and income embracing all the countries of the world. This presented many new challenges.

One challenge arose from the great diversity of countries with respect to levels of income and development and systems of economic organization. Simple methods used in some of the predecessor comparisons could not be readily applied to such a heterogeneous set of countries. It was clear, for example, that price comparisons among all these different countries could not be based on a single common list of items. A list limited to precisely defined items in common supply everywhere would be too small to represent adequately the final expenditures of many or even most countries.

It was considered essential that the system be completely evenhanded among the countries in the sense that the country selected as the reference country would be no more than a numéraire. That is, comparisons between any pairs of countries would be the same regardless of which country was taken as the reference country. This requirement would not be satisfied, for example, by some methods in which one country is

---

3. The yen-dollar exchange rate, for example, declined by 22 percent between 1977 and 1978. Exchange-rate conversions yielded Japan–United States per capita GNP indexes of 69.6 in 1977 and 88.5 in 1978. Since Japan's real GNP per capita grew by 4.7 percent and that of the United States by 3.6 percent during the two years, one or both of the per capita ratios must be far off the mark as a measure of relative GNP per capita.

4. Now the Organisation for Economic Co-operation and Development (OECD). The OEEC works include Gilbert and Kravis (1954) and Gilbert and associates (1958).

5. See Drechsler (1966).

6. U.N. Economic Commission for Latin America (1967), pp. 107–42.

selected as the base country and every other country is compared with it.

It was also desired to establish a unique cardinal scaling of the countries with respect to real-income levels. This could not be achieved by the kind of binary comparisons that were the main focus of the previous studies (namely, those in which each comparison is made independently between a pair of countries). In general, a set of binary comparisons in which each country is compared directly with each other country is unlikely to possess the property of transitivity. That is, except under special conditions, $I_{j/k}$ will not equal $I_{j/l}$ divided by $I_{k/l}$ where $I_{j/k}$ is a price or quantity index for the jth relative to the kth country and l is a third country.[7] To satisfy this transitivity requirement, a method generating multilateral comparisons—those in which all the countries are treated as being interdependent—had to be used.

There was also a need to derive comparisons not only for the national-income aggregate, GDP, but also for its main components, such as capital formation and further subdivisions, such as producer durable goods and construction.

The outcome that was sought, therefore, was a matrix in which the various components of final expenditures on gross domestic product (food, clothing, construction, equipment, producer durable equipment, and the like) are listed on the rows and the countries in the columns. The figures in the cells then are values that are directly comparable along any row. (That is, for any expenditure category, one country's real quantity relative to another's is given by the ratio of the first country's cell entry to that of the second country.) In addition, the entries are directly comparable within a column so the sum of entries for a country over any selected subset of components is the correct real aggregate for the subset. (This combination of properties is referred to below as matrix consistency.)

The Content of the ICP Reports

The second main task of the three initial phases of the ICP was to make a start in providing actual comparisons. First ten, then sixteen, and now thirty-four countries have been covered.

As with the first two reports, this one combines a report on methodological work with actual comparisons. In the Phase I report, *A System of International*

Comparisons of Gross Product and Purchasing Power,[8] the conceptual bases of product and of prices and quantities were laid out, the nature of the data inputs and the method of organizing them were described, and the index number problems were set out. The reasons were given for adopting the aggregation methods employed. The ten countries in this phase had different social systems and were at different levels of development and in different geographical regions: Colombia, France, the Federal Republic of Germany, Hungary, India, Italy, Japan, Kenya, the United Kingdom, and the United States. The reference date was 1970.

In the report on Phase II, *International Comparisons of Real Product and Purchasing Power,*[9] some clarifications and minor modifications of the methodology were presented, and it was shown that the extension of the system to six more countries (Belgium, Iran, the Republic of Korea, Malaysia, the Netherlands, and the Philippines) could be absorbed into the interdependent system without major disturbances to the relationships among the countries covered earlier. Comparisons for 1970 and 1973 were presented for the sixteen countries.

The present report follows the pattern of the earlier ones in describing methods and procedure as well as presenting the detailed empirical results. As with the previous volumes, some extensions of the estimates to other years and applications of the results to demand analysis are included. In addition, some tentative estimates of regional and global aggregates are given for real GDP. A more detailed guide to the materials in this report will be found at the end of this chapter.

ICP Methods in Brief

A summary of ICP procedures is provided here for the reader who does not wish to delve into the fuller treatment presented in Chapters 2 through 5.

The Approach

The basic methodological approach of the ICP is to obtain quantity comparisons by means of price and expenditure comparisons. Expenditures (E), prices (P), and quantities (Q) are linked together in the familiar identity $E = P \cdot Q$. It follows that for any pair of countries, j and k, with respect to commodity i,

$$(1.1) \quad \frac{E_{ij}}{E_{ik}} = \frac{P_{ij}}{P_{ik}} \cdot \frac{Q_{ij}}{Q_{ik}}, \quad \text{so} \quad \frac{Q_{ij}}{Q_{ik}} = \frac{E_{ij}}{E_{ik}} \div \frac{P_{ij}}{P_{ik}}.$$

---

7. As will be seen below, however, binary comparisons can be further processed to produce transitive comparisons. The number of comparisons would be astronomical if there were one for each pair of countries ($n [n-1] / 2$ where n is the number of countries). There are 561 pairs arising from the 34 countries included in the present study.

8. Kravis, Kenessey, Heston, Summers (1975).

9. Kravis, Heston, Summers (1978a).

Thus the quantity ratio can be estimated either directly or indirectly through the ratio of E_{ij}/E_{ik} to P_{ij}/P_{ik}. Direct quantity comparisons—that is, direct estimates of Q_{ij}/Q_{ik}—are difficult to make for many kinds of goods. The ICP category women's clothing, for example, is so heterogeneous that quantity data for each type and quality are difficult to obtain. Also the quantity ratios (Q_{ij}/Q_{ik}) for individual types and qualities can be expected to exhibit wide dispersion relative to the corresponding price ratios. Hence, primary reliance has been placed on indirect estimates of the quantity ratio. Expenditures for detailed categories were available from national accounts data or could be otherwise derived. In addition, direct price comparisons are easier to obtain than quantity comparisons, and the sampling variance of the quantity ratios derived from them will be smaller than that of the direct quantity ratios.

The Data

The comparisons are based on data supplied by the countries on prices and expenditures for 151 "detailed" final-expenditure categories. For a few categories quantity data were supplied either in lieu of prices or as supplementary information. To ensure comparability, the data supplied by the countries were tailored to the precise definitions of the ICP. Each country was asked to classify its final expenditures on GDP into the 151 standard categories.[10] The individual commodities and services for which prices were furnished were selected from ICP lists in which each item was described explicitly. To ensure that the price comparisons related to comparable qualities, the written specifications were supplemented by correspondence, exchanges of samples, and inspections of items in shops by visiting experts.

Multilateral Comparisons

In Phase III, as in the previous phases, both binary and multilateral comparisons have been produced. The Phase III binary methods (some of which differ from traditional binary procedures) are described and their results are presented in Chapter 7. The present chapter summarizes only the multilateral methods and results.

The multilateral comparisons are more appropriate for the general purposes of international political economy than the binary comparisons. For example, transitive comparisons are required by aid donors, whether national or international entities, that want to use relative incomes of potential recipients to de-

termine the allocation of grants or soft loans. Similarly, allocating the burden of the financial support of international organizations requires a unique scaling of all countries rather than comparisons of particular pairs. Analytical studies, particularly those seeking insights into economic development, are often based on cross-section data that require comparative real-product figures for a large number of countries.[11] For these and other situations in which many countries must be considered in relation to each other, the telling disadvantage of binary comparisons is that they will not, if carried out in the traditional way, define a cardinal scaling of countries with respect to real GDP per capita that is independent of the choice of the base country.

Aggregation

The aggregation of purchasing power parities (PPPs) or price-level comparisons[12] in the multilateral comparisons was carried out in two stages. First, at the detailed category level, reported prices for individual items—each conforming to an ICP specification of a good or service falling within the category—were combined to obtain a PPP for each country. Second, these categories' PPPs were averaged to obtain the PPP applicable to various levels of aggregation, such as food and consumption and the overall PPP for GDP.

The need for special multilateral methods at the detailed-category level arises because all items in each category were not priced in every country. Any effort to establish a completely common list for so heterogeneous a set of countries would lead either to the pricing in some countries of items that were not in common use or to so short a list as to make it unrepresentative.

To deal with the fact that the typical tableau of item prices (items on the row stubs and countries in the column headings) has missing entries, the country-product-dummy (CPD) method was developed. CPD is a multiple regression method that uses all the prices available to produce transitive price comparisons that are independent of the choice of base country. It may help to provide an intuitive insight into the method to point out that if the tableau of prices were complete, it would (apart from certain weighting considerations)

10. The classification is given in the appendix to Chapter 2.

11. For ICP purposes, a real product is a final product (that is, something that is bought for own use by the purchaser and not for resale) that is valued at common prices in two or more countries. Valuation at common prices makes it possible to interpret the relative values (real products) as relative quantities.

12. Each country's PPP can be converted into a price-level comparison (with the price level of the numéraire country equal to 100) by dividing it by the exchange rate (own currency per unit of the numéraire currency) and multiplying by 100.

produce a category PPP equal to the geometric mean of the ratios of the country's price to the numeraire country's price.

The PPPs directly obtained from the CPD method are used to derive notional quantities by dividing the PPPs into the expenditures. The method of summing the notional quantities of the detailed categories into higher level aggregates turns on the use of a set of "international prices" for the various categories. The international price for a category is defined as a quantity-weighted average of the detailed category PPPs after they have all been made commensurate by being divided by their respective country PPPs over GDP.

The international prices are used to value the category quantities of each of the countries in international dollars so that the category quantities can be added together to get total GDP or any subaggregate. The international prices and aggregate PPPs have been simultaneously estimated by use of a procedure devised by R. C. Geary and amplified by S. H. Khamis. The ICP inputs for the Geary-Khamis formulas are (1) the category PPPs for the various countries, obtained mainly by the CPD method, and (2) all the category quantities of the countries obtained by dividing these PPPs into the appropriate category expenditures of the countries.

If the quantity weights used in computing the international prices were simply the category quantities of the ICP countries, the international prices and therefore the estimates of per capita GDPs would depend fortuitously on which countries happened to be in the ICP set. If the ICP countries were unrepresentative of all the countries of the world, this would adversely affect the ICP results. Therefore, weights are used that give each ICP country an effect in the calculation of international prices that reflects the prevalence throughout the world of countries with a similar economic structure.

It should be added that an international dollar has the same purchasing power over the U.S. GDP as a whole as the U.S. dollar. However, its purchasing power over individual categories is different because that is determined by the structure of international prices. The price and quantity relationships among the countries would be the same if some other country were taken as the numéraire country, though the results would be scaled differently and would be described in terms of international pounds, international marks, or the like.

The Problem of Regionalization

An important methodological issue had to be faced for the first time because Phase III involved as many

as thirty-four countries. It relates to choosing between the best possible comparisons of countries within a given region (regional comparisons) and the best possible comparisons of countries regardless of location (universal comparisons).[13] The issue arises out of a familiar problem in price and quantity index number construction. In comparing two situations, whether separated in time or space, the valuation of the quantities characterizing either of the situations at prices other than own prices introduces a conceptual difficulty: since each country adapts its quantities to its own existing price structure, its quantities would not be the same if it were confronted with any other set of prices, including those of the other situation. Valuation at other than own prices tends to inflate the aggregate value of the bundle of goods because no allowance is made for the substitutions in quantities toward the goods that are relatively cheap in the other price structure.

The practical importance of this issue is not large when the two situations are very similar, as, for example, in a quantity comparison between two adjoining years for a given country. In international comparisons its significance is likely also to be small for comparisons between countries that have similar relative prices and quantities, but it may loom large in comparisons between countries that have widely divergent price and quantity structures.

It has sometimes been inferred from this that the best possible quantity comparisons between a pair of economically similar neighbors should involve only the price structures of the two countries themselves. Similarly, it has been suggested that when countries in a region are economically similar, the best possible quantity comparisons among themselves would exclude other countries.[14]

The validity of these conclusions depends on the purpose the comparison is intended to serve. If all that is desired is a comparison between a pair of countries, say, France and the Federal Republic of Germany without regard to any other countries, then, indeed, only the French and German price structures should

---

13. Because this methodological issue did not arise in the earlier phases, it is treated more fully here than other technical matters. The reader less interested in methodology may proceed to the next section.

14. In practical work, the choice of the specifications to be used in the price comparisons also is an important consideration. The larger the number of countries included and the more heterogeneous they are, the less the list of specifications can be tailored to represent the goods bought in any one country. The use of specifications, prices, and expenditures conforming closely to those of a given country is referred to as meeting the criterion of "characteristicity." See Chapter 3.

be taken into account. But if the comparison is desired in the context of the European Economic Community, then a Communitywide price structure, not just those of France and the Federal Republic of Germany, is relevant.

A TWO-STAGE APPROACH. Partly because there are some regional groupings for which there is a desire or need for intraregional comparisons, it has been suggested that the worldwide system of comparisons should be built up in stages: first, comparisons should be made between regions. The worldwide system of comparisons would leave unchanged the between-country relationships established by the regional comparisons and would link the countries of one region to those of other regions through comparisons of the regions.

Such a two-stage approach has its obvious attractions. There are regional organizations (for example, the Economic Commission for Latin America) and subregional organizations (for example, the European Economic Community) that have already produced for their member countries indexes that could be incorporated into a world system without altering the relationships among the members. Such a system would have great practical advantages, since the U.N. Statistical Office's very large burden of preparing the comparisons could be shared with regional organizations.

Unfortunately, a two-stage system has compelling disadvantages. The quality of comparisons within regions is improved at the cost of the quality of comparisons between countries in different regions. The results for each pair of countries will depend on the regional classification. A comparison of Japan and France, for example, in a worldwide system built up from intraregional comparisons, would be influenced on each side by the price and quantity structures of the other countries in the region of each.

Another decisive objection to a two-stage procedure is that it is impossible to achieve full consistency between the regional and interregional results. It is possible to distribute a region's total real GDP over the countries in the proper intraregional proportions, and then to allocate the GDP for each country to detailed categories in accordance with the intraregional multilateral comparison. But when the real expenditures for a category are then added across the countries, the regional total will not match the corresponding total given by the interregional comparison. If, however, the expenditures for each category given for the region by the interregional comparison are allocated to the countries according to the proportions indicated by the regional comparison, the relative GDPs of the

countries, each obtained by summing the category expenditures, will not be the same as those produced by the regional comparisons. Thus the comparisons between countries in different regions are inevitably compromised.

A ONE-STAGE APPROACH. An alternative is to follow a one-stage or universal approach—that is, to ignore regions and treat all countries symmetrically.

As was noted above, for some purposes this involves some disadvantages for comparisons involving close neighbors that have similar economic structures. In a universal approach, the comparison for such a pair would be influenced by the price and quantity structures of distant and very different countries. The comparison between France and Italy, for example, would be affected by the prices and quantities of, say, Japan and Thailand, and also by the specifications chosen by these two distant countries. This is in marked contrast to a France-Italy binary comparison, involving only the weights and specifications of the two countries. It differs also from a France-Italy comparison based on a regional multilateral comparison for Europe alone. To be sure, the France-Italy comparison here would not be tailored to just these two countries in the choice of weights and specifications, but the other countries would be more similar to France and Italy than would be the countries in the world at large. The strength of this objection concerning extraneous influences is diminished, however, by the fact that the more similar France and Italy are, the more likely it is that the exotic weights of extraregional countries will have similar effects on the valuation of the quantities of the two countries and thus leave the comparison between them relatively undisturbed.

Partly for this reason, the disadvantage of the universal approach for intraregional comparisons is small compared with the disadvantage of the two-stage approach for comparisons of countries in different regions. That is, estimates of the relative incomes of two countries within the *same* region will, when computed on a universal basis, differ from the estimates when computed on a regional calculation. But they will differ to a lesser degree, on the average, than the estimates for two countries in *different* regions when computed by the universal and regional approaches. The fact that the universal procedure is better for interregional comparisons while intraregional comparisons are altered less by the universal approach adds to the attractiveness of universality.

THE ICP PROCEDURE. The ICP has opted for a procedure that is essentially universal. The Geary-Khamis formula referred to above is applied to all thirty-four countries, yielding a complete set of price and quantity comparisons for GDP and its subaggregates. However, an element of regionalization enters the ICP procedure at the preceding stage when the price inputs for the Geary-Khamis calculation—a PPP for each of the 151 detailed categories for each country—are prepared. The CPD method, described above, was applied in two stages. In the first stage, for each category CPD was applied to the countries of each region. Then through use of the appropriate regional CPD regression equations, all holes in the price tableaux of all the detailed categories were filled. The estimates of the missing prices were thus based on data of countries similar to the countries with the holes. These "augmented" price tableaux were then used in a thirty-four–country CPD, and the resulting PPPs were the inputs for the Geary-Khamis calculation.

The decision to adopt a universal approach, though based largely on technical considerations, is also congenial to the responsibilities of a statistical office functioning at the center of the world statistical system. It is natural for such an office to attempt to produce the most general kind of comparisons—comparisons that treat all countries in an evenhanded way. The important governmental and analytical uses of the international comparisons that such an organization is expected to produce usually cut across regional lines.

The Main Results

Table 1-1 shows the 1975 GDPs of the thirty-four Phase III countries first in national currencies, then in U.S. dollars after conversion by means of exchange rates, and finally in international dollars (I$). Only the last set of figures applies a common measuring rod—a set of international prices—to the quantities constituting the GDPs of the various countries.

GDP in U.S. Dollars

The reader's attention is invited first to the "nominal" (exchange-rate–converted) figures (columns 3 and 4), since comparisons of this type are most usually cited. According to this measure, the GDP of all but five of the countries was less than 10 percent of that of the United States, and for thirteen of the countries it was less than 1 percent. After the United States, Japan had the highest GDP, about one-third of that of the United States, followed by the Federal Republic of Germany and France, the former with more than

one-quarter of the U.S. GDP and the latter with more than one-fifth.

GDP in International Dollars

Of course, the raison d'être of the ICP is to go behind these comparisons of nominal GDPs. Comparisons relying on exchange rates do not explicitly reflect the differing relative purchasing powers of the currencies over all goods and services. They apply quite variable measures of value to the quantities in each country's GDP. The ICP comparisons, however, are obtained by applying a common set of prices, representative of the world price structure, to the quantities of the commodities and services entering into each country's final expenditure on GDP. The quantities valued in international dollars are comparable from country to country for GDP as a whole or for any given subaggregate.

What difference does it make whether the GDPs are in exchange-rate–converted U.S. dollars (column 3) or in PPP-converted international dollars (column 5)? The answer is an important theme of this volume. A glimpse of one facet of the answer can be obtained simply by comparing columns 3 and 5 for the African countries that have low incomes and for the European countries that have high incomes. The ratio of the PPP-converted GDP to the exchange-rate–converted GDP, referred to as the exchange-rate–deviation index, averages 2.00 for the three African countries and 1.13 for the fifteen European countries. There is a clear tendency for the international-dollar figures to be relatively higher for low-income countries. That is, the exchange-rate–converted figures tend to understate the real GDPs of low-income countries relative to high-income countries. (The international-dollar figure for the United States is standardized to be the same as its U.S. dollar figure.)

The key data in Table 1-1 are transformed to per capita terms in Table 1-2. It is in this form that the data will be presented in most of the tables of this volume. For explaining variations of the exchange-rate–deviation index and for most other purposes, it is more useful to consider international comparisons of GDP per capita rather than aggregate GDP. Of course, the ratio between any country's real GDP and its exchange-rate–converted GDP is the same whether expressed in terms of the aggregate figures of Table 1-1 or in terms of the per capita figures of Table 1-2.

The most striking feature of Table 1-2 is the wide diversity in income levels, several countries having real per capita GDPs less than 7 percent that of the United States (column 6). The differences in real terms are, however, considerably smaller than those indicated by the exchange-rate conversions (column 4).

Table 1-1. Gross Domestic Product in National Currencies, in U.S. Dollars at Official Exchange Rates, and in International Dollars, 1975

Country	GDP *in national currency (millions)*[a] (1)	*Official exchange rate (per US$)* (2)	GDP *in U.S. dollars converted at official exchange rate*		GDP *in international dollars (I$)*[b]	
			Millions (3)	*U.S. = 100* (4)	*Millions* (5)	*U.S. = 100* (6)
Africa						
Kenya (shilling)	23,940	7.4113	3,230	0.21	6,304	0.41
Malawi (kwacha)	604	0.8662	697	0.05	1,774	0.12
Zambia (kwacha)	1,585	0.6435	2,463	0.16	3,675	0.24
Asia						
India[c] (rupee)	736,869	8.376	87,974	5.74	284,129	18.5
Iran[d] (rial)	3,512,000	67.639	51,923	3.39	88,554	5.78
Japan (yen)	148,155,000	296.80	499,175	32.6	547,421	35.7
Korea (won)	9,951,703	484.0	20,561	1.34	52,360	3.42
Malaysia (ringgit)	22,332	2.4016	9,299	0.61	18,367	1.20
Pakistan (rupee)	132,044	9.931	13,296	0.87	41,474	2.71
Philippines (peso)	115,082	7.2746	15,820	1.03	39,812	2.60
Sri Lanka (rupee)	26,408	10.600	2,491	0.16	9,011	0.59
Syria (pound)	19,533	3.700	5,279	0.34	13,194	0.86
Thailand (baht)	298,863	20.379	14,665	0.96	39,194	2.56
Europe						
Austria (schilling)	656,256	17.417	37,679	2.46	37,561	2.45
Belgium (franc)	2,270,292	36.781	61,725	4.03	54,632	3.56
Denmark (kroner)	218,021	5.7462	37,942	2.48	29,909	1.95
France (franc)	1,453,467	4.2864	339,088	22.1	309,995	20.2
Germany (DM)	1,034,034	2.4605	420,254	27.4	368,049	24.0
Hungary (forint)	462,678	20.66	22,395	1.46	37,514	2.45
Ireland (pound)	3,762	0.4501	8,358	0.55	9,683	0.63
Italy (lira)	125,378,000	652.85	190,515	12.4	215,565	14.1
Luxembourg (franc)	85,228	36.781	2,317	0.15	2,118	0.14
Netherlands (guilder)	209,420	2.5297	82,801	5.40	73,726	4.81
Poland (zloty)	1,752,268	19.92	87,965	5.74	122,408	7.99
Romania (lei)	444,200	12.00	37,017	2.42	50,708	3.31
Spain (peseta)	6,019,215	57.407	104,851	6.84	142,422	9.29
U.K. (pound)	104,268	0.4501	231,655	15.1	256,835	16.8
Yugoslavia (dinar)	581,937	17.386	33,472	2.18	52,113	3.40
Latin America and Caribbean						
Brazil (cruzeiro)	1,009,602	8.204	123,062	8.03	194,061	12.67
Colombia (peso)	412,828	30.869	13,374	0.87	38,088	2.49
Jamaica (dollar)	2,611	0.9091	2,872	0.19	3,519	0.23
Mexico (peso)	1,101,371	12.50	88,110	5.74	149,599	9.76
Uruguay (new peso)	8,369	2.299	3,640	0.23	7,913	0.52
North America						
U.S. (dollar)	1,532,701	1.00	1,532,701	100.0	1,532,701	100.0

a. Between computation of the indexes in early 1981 and final editing of the text, there were minor revisions in the estimates by countries of their 1975 GDP. The only changes on a *System of National Accounts* (SNA) basis of more than 2 percent were −5.2 percent for Malawi, −10.2 percent for Mexico, 6.0 percent for Syria, and 2.4 percent for Uruguay. These estimates have not been incorporated in this report; however, any extrapolations beyond 1975 are done on the basis of the latest set of data and are consistent with the most recent growth rates reported.

b. The 1975 international dollar has the same purchasing power as the 1975 U.S. dollar.

c. Reference year beginning April 1.

d. Reference year beginning March 21.

Sources: The GDP figures are those reported for ICP purposes by participating countries or, in the case of the member countries of the European Common Market, by the Statistical Office of the European Communities. The exchange rates are annual average market rates (rf rates) as reported in International Monetary Fund, *International Financial Statistics* (February 1977), except that for Sri Lanka a weighted average of export rate (7.704) and import rates (12.72) was used, and for Hungary, Poland, and Romania the noncommercial exchange rate was used.

Figure 1–1.   Exchange-rate–Deviation Index in Relation to Real GDP per Capita, Thirty-four Countries, 1975

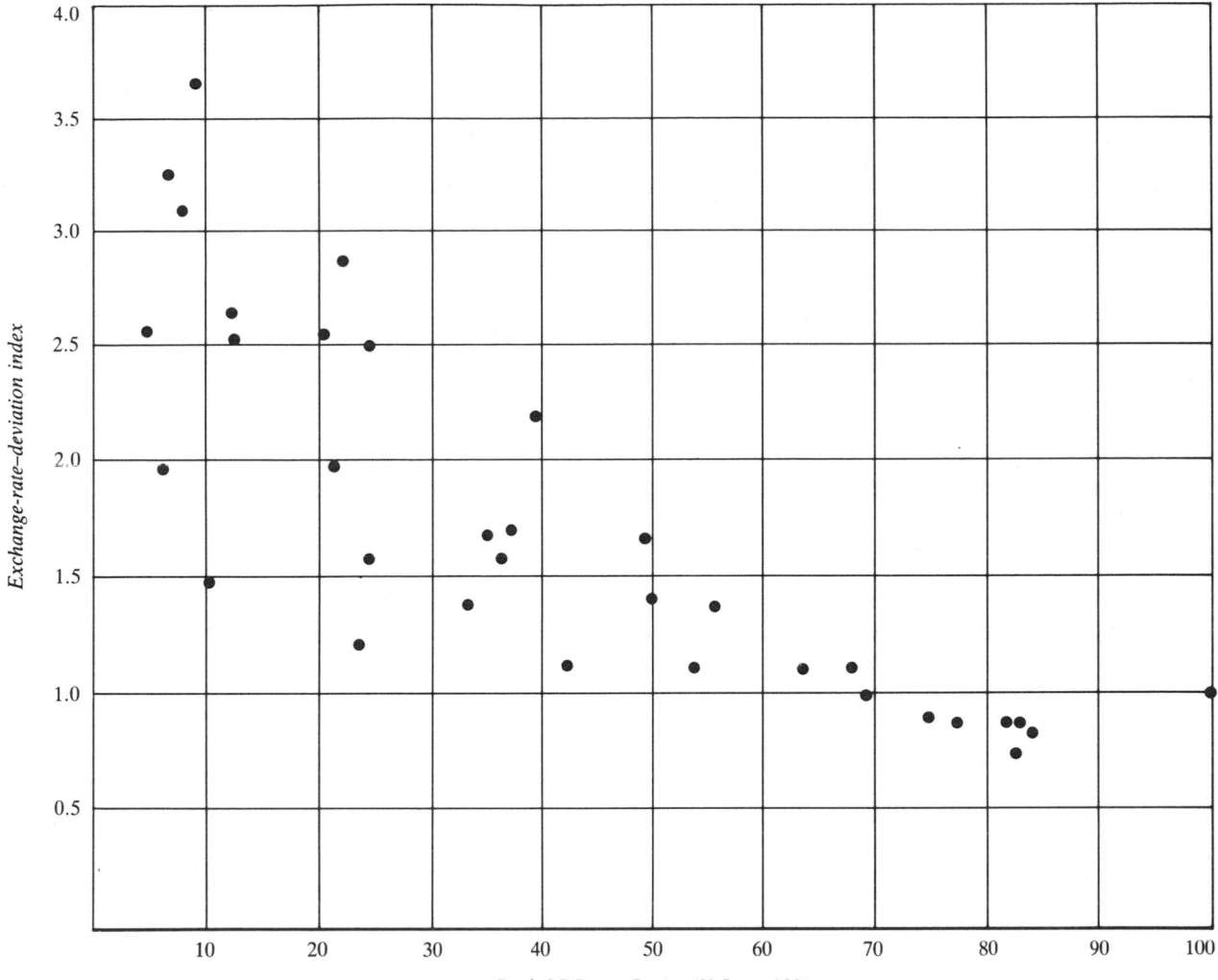

Real GDP per Capita (U.S. = 100)

Exchange-rate–Deviation Index

The systematic relationship between the ICP estimates and the exchange-rate–derived figures can be clearly seen by arranging the countries in order of increasing real GDP per capita: the ratio of real GDP per capita to exchange-rate–converted GDP per capita—the "exchange-rate–deviation index" (column 8)—falls as per capita real GDP rises (see Figure 1-1).[15] One explanation for this phenomenon is provided by the "productivity differential" model set forth in Chapter 8.

The negative association between the exchange-rate–deviation index and the level of real GDP per capita is found in all three ICP reference years. Table 1-3

shows the index of real per capita GDP for 1970, 1973, and 1975 for sixteen Phase II countries.[16] Here the countries are arrayed in order of ascending 1975 real per capita GDP, an arrangement that will be followed in most subsequent tables in this volume.

In 1970 the real GDP per capita of the fifteen countries relative to that of the United States ranged from 20 percent higher than indicated by the exchange-rate–converted figures (Federal Republic of Germany) to more than three times as great (India).

Effect of Varying Exchange Rates

The depreciation of the U.S. dollar relative to European currencies from 1970 through 1973 brought

---

15. In Chapter 8, the structural relationship between the exchange-rate–deviation index and real per capita GDP is exploited to get estimates of real income for countries that have not received full benchmark treatment.

16. The 1970 and 1973 estimates are revised from those presented in the Phase II report. The revisions incorporate data changes that become available after the Phase II estimates had been completed and reflect the new Phase III treatment of services in the areas of medical care and education. See Table 3-5.

Table 1-2. Population and per Capita Gross Domestic Product in National Currencies, in U.S. Dollars at Official Exchange Rates, and in International Dollars, 1975

| | | | Per capita GDP | | | | |
| | | | In U.S. dollar converted at exchange rate | | In international dollars[a] | | Exchange-rate–deviation index |
Country	Population (millions) (1)	In national currency (2)	US$ (3)	U.S. = 100 (4)	International $ (5)	U.S. = 100 (6)	(5) ÷ (3) (7)
Africa							
Kenya (shillings)	13.399	1,787	241	3.36	470	6.56	1.95
Malawi (kwacha)	5.044	119.8	138	1.93	352	4.90	2.55
Zambia (kwacha)	4.981	318.2	495	6.89	738	10.3	1.49
Asia							
India[b] (rupees)	603.887	1,220	146	2.03	470	6.56	3.23
Iran[c] (rials)	32.742	107,265	1,587	22.1	2,705	37.7	1.70
Japan (yen)	111.566	1,327,937	4,474	62.3	4,907	68.4	1.10
Korea (won)	35.281	282,065	583	8.12	1,484	20.7	2.54
Malaysia (ringgit)	11.922	1,873	780	10.9	1,541	21.5	1.98
Pakistan (rupees)	70.260	1,879	189	2.64	590	8.23	3.12
Philippines (pesos)	42.071	2,735	376	5.24	946	13.2	2.51
Sri Lanka (rupees)	13.496	1,957	183	2.55	668	9.30	3.65
Syria (pounds)	7.354	2,656	718	10.0	1,794	25.0	2.50
Thailand (baht)	41.869	7,138	359	5.00	936	13.0	2.61
Europe							
Austria (schillings)	7.520	87,267	5,010	69.8	4,995	69.6	1.00
Belgium (francs)	9.801	231,635	6,298	87.8	5,574	77.7	0.88
Denmark (kroner)	5.060	43,087	7,498	104.5	5,911	82.4	0.79
France (francs)	52.748	27,555	6,428	89.6	5,877	81.9	0.91
Germany (DM)	61.829	16,724	6,797	94.7	5,953	83.0	0.88
Hungary (forint)	10.541	43,893	2,125	29.6	3,559	49.6	1.68
Ireland (pounds)	3.176	1,184	2,673	37.2	3,049	42.5	1.14
Italy (lire)	55.830	2,245,670	3,440	47.9	3,861	53.8	1.12
Luxembourg (francs)	0.360	236,741	6,472	90.2	5,883	82.0	0.91
Netherlands (guilders)	13.660	15,331	6,061	84.5	5,397	75.2	0.89
Poland (zlote)	34.022	51,504	2,586	36.0	3,598	50.1	1.39
Romania (lei)	21.245	20,908	1,742	24.3	2,387	33.3	1.37
Spain (pesetas)	35.515	169,480	2,946	41.0	4,010	55.9	1.36
U.K. (pounds)	55.981	1,863	4,134	57.6	4,588	63.9	1.11
Yugoslavia (dinars)	20.110	28,937	1,664	23.2	2,591	36.1	1.56
Latin America and Caribbean							
Brazil (cruzeiros)	107.145	9,422	1,149	16.0	1,811	25.2	1.58
Colombia (pesos)	23.676	17,436	568	7.92	1,609	22.4	2.83
Jamaica (dollars)	2.043	1,278	1,406	19.6	1,723	24.0	1.23
Mexico (pesos)	60.145	18,312	1,465	20.4	2,487	34.7	1.70
Uruguay (N. pesos)	2.782	3,008	1,308	18.2	2,844	39.6	2.17
North America							
U.S. (dollars)	213.566	7,176	7,176	100.0	7,176	100.0	1.00

a. The 1975 international dollar has the same purchasing power as a 1975 U.S. dollar.
b. Reference year beginning April 1.
c. Reference year beginning March 21.
Sources: Column 1 contains the midyear population estimates in the United Nations *Monthly Bulletin of Statistics* (June 1981), except for a few countries that submitted population estimates matched to their national accounts data. Differences are not above 2 percent in any case. Columns 2 and 3 are calculated from data in column 1 and Table 1-1. Column 5 is taken from Summary Multilateral Table 6-5.

Table 1-3. Per Capita Gross Domestic Product in National Currencies and in International Dollars, Sixteen Countries, 1970, 1973, and 1975

Country	Exchange rates (currency units per U.S. dollar)			Indexes of per capita GDP converted by exchange rates (U.S. = 100)			Indexes of real GDP per capita (U.S. = 100)			Exchange-rate– deviation indexes		
	1970 (1)	1973 (2)	1975 (3)	1970 (4)	1973 (5)	1975 (6)	1970 (7)	1973 (8)	1975 (9)	1970 (10)	1973 (11)	1975 (12)
Kenya	7.1429	7.0012	7.4113	2.97	3.05	3.36	5.88	5.94	6.56	1.98	1.95	1.95
India	7.499	7.742	8.376	2.08	2.14	2.03	6.45	6.05	6.56	3.10	2.83	3.23
Philippines	6.0652	6.7629	7.2746	3.94	4.26	5.24	11.7	12.0	13.2	2.95	2.82	2.52
Korea	310.42	398.54	484.0	5.53	6.21	8.12	11.8	14.6	20.7	2.13	2.35	2.55
Malaysia	3.0797	2.4426	2.4016	6.87	10.9	10.9	15.6	19.7	21.5	2.27	1.81	1.98
Colombia	18.352	23.813	30.869	7.19	7.37	7.92	17.2	17.8	22.4	2.39	2.42	2.83
Iran	76.38	68.72	67.639	7.98	13.9	22.1	19.4	28.1	37.7	2.43	2.02	1.70
Hungary	30.0	24.59	20.66	21.3	25.8	29.6	41.4	44.0	49.6	1.94	1.71	1.68
Italy	627.16	583.0	652.85	35.8	41.5	47.9	48.0	47.3	53.8	1.34	1.14	1.12
U.K.	0.4174	0.4078	0.4501	45.6	51.2	57.6	62.7	60.7	63.9	1.37	1.19	1.11
Japan	358.15	272.19	296.8	39.7	60.5	62.3	58.5	63.7	68.4	1.47	1.05	1.10
Netherlands	3.6166	2.7956	2.5292	50.5	72.1	84.5	68.3	69.3	75.2	1.35	0.96	0.89
Belgium	49.656	38.977	36.781	55.5	75.6	87.8	72.3	76.5	77.7	1.30	1.01	0.89
Germany	3.6465	2.6725	2.4605	63.7	89.4	94.7	76.5	76.0	83.0	1.20	0.85	0.88
France	5.5289	4.454	4.2864	57.9	77.3	89.6	71.9	75.4	81.9	1.24	0.98	0.91
U.S.	1.0	1.0	1.0	100.0	100.0	100.0	100.0	100.0	100.0	1.00	1.00	1.00

Note: 1970 and 1973 data are revised. The per capita U.S. GDPs that are the base values for columns 4 to 9 are 1970, 4,813.9; 1973, 6,204.5; and 1975, 7,177.0.

European-U.S. exchange rates into closer alignment with PPPs; the exchange-rate–deviation index for all the European countries is closer to 1 in 1973 than in 1970. For three of the six lowest income countries in Table 1-3 the 1973 exchange-rate–deviation index differed by less than a few percentage points from that of 1970.[17] All three of these countries depreciated their currencies against the dollar.

Between 1973 and 1975, changes in exchange rates for the developed countries tended to be smaller, and the 1975 exchange-rate–deviation indexes differ very little from those of 1973 for most developed countries in the bottom half of the table.

The large changes in exchange rates in these years underline the unreliability of comparisons based on exchange-rate conversions. The exchange-rate–converted figures for the Federal Republic of Germany, for example, imply that its per capita GDP relative to that of the United States rose from 63.7 percent in 1970 to 89.4 percent in 1973. In fact, the estimates, based on PPPs, of the Federal Republic of Germany's real GDP per capita relative to that of the United States remained almost constant, the indexes showing a slight decline from 76.5 to 76.0 percent. The latter result is much more closely in accord with the relative growth of the real per capita GDP (that is, as measured in constant internal prices) between the two years in the two countries; real GDP per capita increased by 10.0 percent in the Federal Republic of Germany and by 11.7 percent in the United States.[18] (The decline in the German index—from 76.5 to 76.0 percent—does not precisely match the implied 1.7 percent decrease, because international prices are used to derive the real GDP figures for each year while German and U.S. prices, respectively, are used in the growth-rate calculations.)

The variation in the exchange-rate–deviation index from country to country means that the relative per

17. The extent of the dollar depreciation against individual currencies between 1970 and 1973 and between 1973 and 1975 can be seen in columns 1 to 3 of Table 1-3. Against the weighted basket of sixteen currencies constituting the SDR, the dollar depreciated between 1970 and 1973 by 16 percent and by less than 2 percent between 1973 and 1975. (Figures are based on data in *International Financial Statistics*, May 1978.) The SDR is a unit of account in the Special Drawing Rights created by the International Monetary Fund.

18. The figures on GDP in constant prices and the population figures for the two countries are taken from U.N. data.

Table 1-3, by giving the U.S. value of GDP for each year in the footnote, makes it possible for the reader to convert the indexes to per capita GDP in international dollars. However, direct comparisons of the value aggregates (in international dollars) should not be made between the two years. It would be wrong, for example, to think that the real per capita GDP of the Philippines went up by 32.2 percent ($[12.0 \cdot 6,204.5] \div [11.7 \cdot 4,813.9]$) between 1970 and 1973. The reason is that the purchasing powers of the 1973 international dollars and that of 1970 international dollars are not the same.

capita income levels of the countries cannot be inferred from exchange-rate–converted GDP per capita. In several instances even the ordinal ranking based on international prices differs from that based on exchange-rate conversions.[19] For example, in two of the years, the use of international prices produces a slightly higher per capita GDP for India than for Kenya, which is the opposite of the result obtained when exchange rates are used to convert the countries' GDPs to U.S. dollars.

Estimates for Nonbenchmark Years

Table 1-3 was confined to countries for which benchmark estimates are available for 1970, 1973, and 1975. In Table 1-4 real per capita GDP estimates are given for all thirty-four countries for a number of years for which there were no benchmark studies. (The 1970 and 1975 benchmark figures of the preceding table are repeated for the sake of completeness.) The table represents a selection of results, reported more fully in Chapter 8, of techniques of extrapolating the 1975 estimates for the thirty-four benchmark countries to other years. Though the extrapolations place these indexes on a different footing from the much more substantially based benchmark figures, they better trace the changes in the relative standings of different countries than do the exchange-rate–converted figures.

Individual countries' national-accounts aggregates in constant prices are used in the extrapolation process. The extrapolations are carried out in a way that takes account of the effect of changes in the terms of trade. In any one year, a country's income and product, taken at current prices, are the same. But between two given years a country's income may diverge from its production because of changes in its physical volume and terms of international trade. The difference between changes in income and production has been particularly important in recent years for oil exporters and some oil importers.

Even if the domestic output of every single type of product, including petroleum, had remained constant, and even if its exports had remained constant, an oil exporter's real income would have increased because of the rise in the price of petroleum. Some of the gain would show up in the country's increased domestic absorption of consumers goods, public goods, or investment goods, and the rest of its gain would show up in its net foreign balance. Because the figures in

Table 1-4 reflect the terms of trade as they are found in each year, the table has been titled "Gross Domestic Income," GDY. (The simple extrapolation of the ICP benchmark year estimates by each country's change in its GDP would yield a measure of relative physical production at constant base-year prices for petroleum and all other products. Extrapolations based on production alone are given in Chapter 8.)

The figures in Table 1-4 thus are the results of relative changes in production, in the volume of net exports, and in the terms of trade. The role of the last two factors looms large in small countries or low-income countries where international trade is large relative to GDP. The decline in the Zambia index between 1970 and 1975 is attributable mainly to a shift from a positive net foreign balance (exports minus imports) equivalent to 17 percent of GDP in 1970 to a negative one of about 20 percent of GDP in 1975 (both comparisons in Zambian current prices) and to the role played in this deterioration by a 22 percent decline in the price of copper,[20] Zambia's chief export.

Changing Relative Incomes

A striking feature of Table 1-4 is the general tendency for per capita incomes relative to the United States to rise through time for most countries. The European countries found in the last lines had GDYs in the range of 40 to 85 percent of the United States in 1979, compared with a 25 percent to 60 percent range in 1950. Middle-income developing countries also gained, some, like the Republic of Korea and Iran, very rapidly. No other country, however, matched Japan in its catching-up speed. Japan overtook Italy by 1970 and the United Kingdom by 1975. At the opposite extreme, with comparatively little income growth, are the lowest income countries, especially the first half-dozen poorest countries.

Regional and World GDP

A second set of nonbenchmark materials offered in Chapter 8 consists of the extensions of the 1975 estimate of real GDP per capita to other countries. Briefly, estimating equations are formed from the benchmark data by regressing real GDP per capita against nominal GDP per capita and certain other variables. These equations are then used to estimate 1975 real per capita GDP for other countries. The results for individual countries, which, of course, are subject to wider margins of error than the benchmark estimates, are not

---

19. This can be checked by comparing columns 4 and 6 of Table 1-2, but it is more easily seen in Table 1-10, columns 3 and 6, in which the countries are arrayed in ascending order of 1975 real GDP per capita.

20. *International Financial Statistics* (May 1978), p. 423.

Table 1-4. Gross Domestic Income per Capita, Selected Years and Dates

Country	1950	1955	1960	1965	1970	1975	1977	1979
Malawi	3.69	3.97	4.35	4.01	4.40	4.90	4.80	4.43[a]
Kenya	7.77	7.44	6.81	5.20	5.88	6.56	6.90	6.20[a]
India	7.08	6.98	7.50	6.38	6.46	6.56	6.29	5.68[a]
Pakistan	9.03	7.34	7.75	8.99	8.45	8.23	8.08	7.60[a]
Sri Lanka	11.4	10.8	10.2	8.84	9.51	9.30	10.0	9.04[a]
Zambia	11.0	15.0	15.3	15.1	15.5	10.3	8.35	7.55[a]
Thailand	9.89	7.57	9.50	10.1	11.7	13.0	13.0	13.4[a]
Philippines	10.3	11.4	12.3	11.5	11.7	13.2	12.7	13.3[a]
Korea	7.55	7.87	8.15	8.53	11.8	20.7	23.6	24.8[a]
Malaysia	14.6	15.5	16.7	15.9	15.6	21.5	24.1	23.2[a]
Colombia	18.5	18.7	17.5	16.0	17.2	22.4	23.6	22.5[a]
Jamaica	12.6	18.2	23.3	23.0	23.6	24.0	20.3	18.0[a]
Syria	17.1	—	16.5	17.0	17.2	25.0	24.9	23.7[a]
Brazil	15.2	15.5	18.2	16.5	18.7	25.2	25.7	25.6[a]
Mexico	25.5	25.6	29.0	29.8	32.4	34.7	31.1	32.3[a]
Iran	11.9	13.5	16.5	14.9	19.4	37.7	38.3	—
Uruguay	54.9	60.5	54.2	42.9	43.6	39.6	38.0	40.0[a]
Ireland	33.02	32.9	35.5	36.2	41.4	42.5	41.9	40.9[a]
Italy	27.5	31.4	38.5	41.1	48.0	53.8	53.5	52.2
Spain	26.5	31.4	33.7	42.7	49.0	55.9	53.1	50.3[a]
U.K.	59.1	59.6	64.2	62.4	62.7	63.9	62.7	64.0
Japan	17.1	21.2	29.8	38.8	58.5	68.4	69.3	70.9
Austria	37.9	43.4	53.4	54.7	62.2	69.6	69.4	70.0
Netherlands	50.2	53.8	59.3	60.9	68.3	75.2	73.3	71.1[a]
Belgium	54.8	55.9	59.9	63.7	72.3	77.7	76.3	74.9[a]
France	48.2	50.1	59.2	62.6	71.9	81.9	81.3	81.8
Denmark	61.9	58.4	70.2	75.6	81.8	82.4	81.1	80.0[a]
Germany	40.8	53.5	68.0	69.4	76.5	83.0	83.3	85.9
U.S.	100.0	100.0	100.0	100.0	100.0	100.0	100.0	100.0

— Not available

a. The extrapolation refers to GDP, not GDY. Additional years are provided in Chapter 8. Note that estimates for 1979 are subject to revision.

reported. However, aggregations of 1975 world GDP by geographic region are as follows:

	Nominal GDP		Real GDP		
	Billion US$ (1)	Percent (2)	Billion I$ (3)	Percent (4)	Exchange-rate– deviation index (5) = (3) ÷ (1)
Africa	175	3.5	324	5.6	1.85
Asia (including Oceania)	974	19.5	1,471	25.0	1.51
Europe	1,774	35.5	1,757	29.9	0.99
Latin America (including Caribbean)	546	10.9	806	13.7	1.48
North America	1,528	30.6	1,520	25.8	0.99
World	4,997	100.0	5,878	100.0	1.18

If the countries are reclassified according to stage of development,[21] the resulting per capita figures are:

21. Twenty countries are considered to be industrialized; they included all members of OECD except Greece, Portugal, Spain, and Turkey. Australia, New Zealand, and South Africa are also included. The developing countries are ninety-eight market economies: thirty-two with nominal GDP of $250 or less in 1976, nine oil exporters, and fifty-seven middle-income countries.

	Nominal	Real
a. Industrialized	5,734	5,737
b. Developing	534	1,020
c. Ratio (a ÷ b) · 100	10.7	5.6

Other Countries as Numéraire

The discussion so far has focused on indexes based on the United States, and this indeed will remain the standard method of summarizing the results of the ICP. As was explained above, however, the choice of the United States as the numéraire country and the expression of values in terms of international dollars is not critical in determining the per capita quantity relationships either at the detailed-category level, at summary-category levels, or at higher levels of aggregation. Any other country could have been selected as the numéraire without affecting the quantity relationships such as those in column 6 of Tables 1-1 and 1-2. It is true, however, that all the value figures such as those in column 5 of the two tables would be altered by a common factor if expressed in a different currency, and all the index comparisons in column 6

Table 1-5. Relative Gross Domestic Product per Capita, All Pairs of Countries, 1975

	Malawi	Kenya	India	Paki-stan	Sri Lanka	Zambia	Thai-land	Philip-pines	Korea	Malay-sia	Colom-bia	Jamaica	Syria	Brazil	Roma-nia	Mexico	Yugo-slavia
Malawi	100.0	133.8	133.8	167.8	189.9	209.8	266.2	269.0	422.0	438.1	457.4	489.8	510.2	515.0	678.7	707.2	736.8
Kenya	74.8	100.0	100.0	125.5	141.9	156.8	199.0	201.1	315.5	327.5	341.9	366.2	381.4	385.0	507.3	528.7	550.8
India	74.7	100.0	100.0	125.4	141.9	156.8	198.9	201.1	315.4	327.4	341.9	366.1	381.3	384.9	507.3	528.6	550.7
Pakistan	59.6	79.7	79.7	100.0	113.1	125.0	158.6	160.3	251.4	261.0	272.5	291.9	304.0	306.9	404.4	421.4	439.1
Sri Lanka	52.7	70.5	70.5	88.4	100.0	110.5	140.2	141.7	222.3	230.7	240.9	258.0	268.7	271.3	357.5	372.5	388.1
Zambia	47.7	63.8	63.8	80.0	90.5	100.0	126.9	128.3	201.2	208.8	218.0	233.5	243.2	245.5	323.5	337.1	351.2
Thailand	37.5	50.3	50.3	63.1	71.3	78.8	100.0	101.1	158.5	164.6	171.8	184.0	191.7	193.5	255.0	265.7	276.8
Philippines	37.2	49.7	49.7	62.4	70.6	78.0	98.9	100.0	156.8	162.8	170.0	182.0	189.6	191.4	252.2	262.9	273.9
Korea	23.7	31.7	31.7	39.8	45.0	49.7	63.1	63.8	100.0	103.8	108.4	116.1	120.9	122.0	160.8	167.6	174.6
Malaysia	22.8	30.5	30.5	38.3	43.3	47.9	60.8	61.4	96.3	100.0	104.4	111.8	116.5	117.6	154.9	161.4	168.2
Colombia	21.9	29.2	29.3	36.7	41.5	45.9	58.2	58.8	92.3	95.8	100.0	107.1	111.5	112.6	148.4	154.6	161.1
Jamaica	20.4	27.3	27.3	34.3	38.8	42.8	54.3	54.9	86.2	89.4	93.4	100.0	104.2	105.1	138.6	144.4	150.4
Syria	19.6	26.2	26.2	32.9	37.2	41.1	52.2	52.7	82.7	85.9	89.7	96.0	100.0	100.9	133.0	138.6	144.4
Brazil	19.4	26.0	26.0	32.6	36.9	40.7	51.7	52.2	81.9	85.1	88.8	95.1	99.1	100.0	131.8	137.3	143.1
Romania	14.7	19.7	19.7	24.7	28.0	30.9	39.2	39.6	62.2	64.5	67.4	72.2	75.2	75.9	100.0	104.2	108.6
Mexico	14.1	18.9	18.9	23.7	26.8	29.7	37.6	38.0	59.7	61.9	64.7	69.3	72.1	72.8	96.0	100.0	104.2
Yugoslavia	13.6	18.2	18.2	22.8	25.8	28.5	36.1	36.5	57.3	59.5	62.1	66.5	69.2	69.9	92.1	96.0	100.0
Iran	13.0	17.4	17.4	21.8	24.7	27.3	34.6	35.0	54.9	57.0	59.5	63.7	66.3	67.0	88.3	92.0	95.8
Uruguay	12.4	16.5	16.5	20.8	23.5	25.9	32.9	33.3	52.2	54.2	56.6	60.6	63.1	63.7	83.9	87.4	91.1
Ireland	11.5	15.4	15.4	19.4	21.9	24.2	30.7	31.0	48.7	50.5	52.8	56.5	58.9	59.4	78.3	81.6	85.0
Hungary	9.9	13.2	13.2	16.6	18.8	20.7	26.3	26.6	41.7	43.3	45.2	48.4	50.4	50.9	67.1	69.9	72.8
Poland	9.8	13.1	13.1	16.4	18.6	20.5	26.0	26.3	41.2	42.8	44.7	47.9	49.9	50.3	66.3	69.1	72.0
Italy	9.1	12.2	12.2	15.3	17.3	19.1	24.2	24.5	38.4	39.9	41.7	44.6	46.5	46.9	61.8	64.4	67.1
Spain	8.8	11.7	11.7	14.7	16.7	18.4	23.3	23.6	37.0	38.4	40.1	43.0	44.7	45.2	59.5	62.0	64.6
U.K.	7.7	10.3	10.3	12.9	14.6	15.1	20.4	20.6	32.3	33.6	35.1	37.5	39.1	39.5	52.0	54.2	56.5
Japan	7.1	9.6	9.6	12.0	13.6	15.0	19.0	19.2	30.1	31.3	32.7	35.0	36.4	36.8	48.5	50.5	52.6
Austria	7.0	9.4	9.4	11.8	13.4	14.8	18.7	18.9	29.7	30.8	32.2	34.5	35.9	36.3	47.8	49.8	51.9
Netherlands	6.5	8.7	8.7	10.9	12.4	13.7	17.3	17.5	27.5	28.5	29.8	31.9	33.2	33.6	44.2	46.1	48.0
Belgium	6.3	8.4	8.4	10.6	12.0	13.2	16.8	17.0	26.6	27.6	28.9	30.9	32.2	32.5	42.8	44.6	46.5
France	6.0	8.0	8.0	10.0	11.4	12.6	15.9	16.1	25.3	26.2	27.4	29.3	30.5	30.8	40.6	42.3	44.1
Luxembourg	6.0	8.0	8.0	10.0	11.3	12.5	15.9	16.1	25.2	26.2	27.3	29.3	30.5	30.8	40.6	42.3	44.0
Denmark	5.9	8.0	8.0	10.0	11.3	12.5	15.8	16.0	25.1	26.1	27.2	29.1	30.4	30.6	40.4	42.1	43.8
Germany	5.9	7.9	7.9	9.9	11.2	12.4	15.7	15.9	24.9	25.9	27.0	28.9	30.1	30.4	40.1	41.8	43.5
U.S.	4.9	6.6	6.6	8.2	9.3	10.3	13.0	13.2	20.7	21.5	22.4	24.0	25.0	25.2	33.3	34.7	36.1

would be altered by a common factor to make the value figure for the new numéraire country equal to 100. Any one of the thirty-four countries could legitimately be selected as the numéraire country, with the real per capita GDPs of the other countries then being expressed as a ratio to the real per capita GDP of that country. The full matrix of such relationships for the thirty-four benchmark countries is presented in a convenient way in Table 1-5, where each row country is taken in turn as the numéraire country. For example, the table shows that the 1975 real per capita GDP of India was 50.3 percent of that of Thailand, whereas the relationship of Thailand to Malaysia was 60.8 percent. (The corresponding exchange-rate–converted figures can be calculated from column 3 of Table 1-2. In the India-Thailand and Thailand-Malaysia cases, they are 40.7 percent and 46.0 percent, respectively.)

Consumption, Capital Formation, and Government

The three main components of GDP—consumption, capital formation, and government—for the benchmark countries and reference year 1975 are presented in Tables 1-6 and 1-7. Table 1-6 shows the breakdown of the components in national currencies and by percentage shares of GDP. Table 1-7 presents the same breakdown in international dollars, the corresponding percentage shares, and, for each of the three components, per capita quantity indexes, with the United States equal to 100.

Countries Grouped by Income Level

In these and many subsequent tables not only are the countries arrayed in order of increasing real per capita GDP, but also, for certain variables, unweighted average values are given for groups of countries with similar per capita incomes.[22] Not all variables pro-

22. The income groups are:

	Range of real per capita GDP (U.S. = 100)	Number of countries
I	0–14.9	8
II	15.0–29.9	6
III	30.0–44.9	6
IV	45.0–59.9	4
V	60.0–89.9	9
VI	90.0–100.0	1

	Iran	Uru-guay	Ireland	Hun-gary	Poland	Italy	Spain	U.K.	Japan	Austria	Nether-lands	Bel-gium	France	Luxem-bourg	Den-mark	Ger-many	U.S.
Malawi	769.0	808.7	866.9	1,011.9	1,023.0	1,097.9	1,140.3	1,304.5	1,399.8	1,420.2	1,534.6	1,584.9	1,671.0	1,672.9	1,680.7	1,692.6	2,040.4
Kenya	574.9	604.6	648.1	756.5	764.8	820.7	852.4	975.2	1,046.4	1,061.7	1,147.2	1,184.8	1,249.2	1,250.6	1,256.4	1,265.3	1,525.3
India	574.8	604.5	648.0	756.4	764.6	820.6	852.3	975.0	1,046.3	1,061.5	1,147.0	1,184.6	1,249.0	1,250.4	1,256.2	1,265.1	1,525.1
Pakistan	458.2	481.9	516.6	603.0	609.6	654.2	679.4	777.3	834.1	846.3	914.4	944.4	995.7	996.8	1,001.5	1,008.5	1,215.8
Sri Lanka	405.0	426.0	456.6	533.0	538.8	578.2	600.6	687.1	737.3	748.0	808.3	834.8	880.1	881.1	885.2	891.5	1,074.7
Zambia	366.6	385.5	413.3	482.4	487.7	523.4	543.6	621.9	667.3	677.0	731.6	755.5	796.6	797.5	801.2	806.9	972.7
Thailand	288.9	303.8	325.7	380.2	384.3	412.5	428.4	490.1	525.9	533.6	576.6	595.5	627.8	628.5	631.4	635.9	766.6
Philippines	285.8	300.6	322.2	376.1	380.2	408.1	423.8	484.9	520.3	527.9	570.4	589.1	621.1	621.8	624.7	629.1	758.4
Korea	182.2	191.7	205.4	239.8	242.4	260.2	270.2	309.1	331.7	336.6	363.7	375.6	396.0	396.4	398.3	401.1	483.5
Malaysia	175.6	184.6	197.9	231.0	233.5	250.6	260.3	297.8	319.6	324.2	350.3	361.8	381.5	381.9	383.7	386.4	465.8
Colombia	168.1	176.8	189.5	221.2	223.7	240.0	249.3	285.2	306.0	310.5	335.5	346.5	365.3	365.7	367.4	370.0	446.1
Jamaica	157.0	165.1	177.0	206.6	208.9	224.1	232.8	266.3	285.8	290.0	313.3	323.6	341.2	341.5	343.1	345.6	416.6
Syria	150.7	158.5	169.9	198.3	200.5	215.2	223.5	255.7	274.4	278.4	300.8	310.7	327.5	327.9	329.4	331.8	399.9
Brazil	149.3	157.0	168.3	196.5	198.6	213.2	221.4	253.3	271.8	275.8	298.0	307.8	324.5	324.8	326.4	328.7	396.2
Romania	113.3	119.2	127.7	149.1	150.7	161.8	168.0	192.2	206.3	209.3	226.1	233.5	246.2	246.5	247.7	249.4	300.7
Mexico	108.7	114.4	122.6	143.1	144.7	155.2	161.2	184.5	197.9	200.8	217.0	224.1	236.3	236.5	237.6	239.3	288.5
Yugoslavia	104.4	109.8	117.7	137.3	138.8	149.0	154.8	177.0	190.0	192.7	208.3	215.1	226.8	227.0	228.1	229.7	276.9
Iran	100.0	105.2	112.7	131.6	133.0	142.8	148.3	169.6	182.0	184.7	199.6	206.1	217.3	217.5	218.6	220.1	265.3
Uruguay	95.1	100.0	107.2	125.1	126.5	135.8	141.0	161.3	173.1	175.6	189.8	196.0	206.6	206.9	207.8	209.3	252.3
Ireland	88.7	93.3	100.0	116.7	118.0	126.6	131.5	150.5	161.5	163.8	177.0	182.8	192.8	193.0	193.9	195.2	235.4
Hungary	75.0	79.9	85.7	100.0	101.1	108.5	112.7	128.9	138.3	140.3	151.7	156.6	165.1	165.3	166.1	167.3	201.6
Poland	75.2	79.1	84.7	98.9	100.0	107.3	111.5	127.5	136.8	138.8	150.0	154.9	163.3	163.5	164.3	165.4	199.4
Italy	70.0	73.7	79.0	92.2	93.2	100.0	103.9	118.8	127.5	129.4	139.8	144.4	152.2	152.4	153.1	154.2	185.9
Spain	67.4	70.9	76.0	88.7	89.7	96.3	100.0	114.4	122.8	124.6	134.6	139.0	146.5	146.7	147.4	148.4	178.9
U.K.	58.9	62.0	66.5	77.6	78.4	84.2	87.4	100.0	107.3	108.9	117.6	121.5	128.1	128.2	128.8	129.7	156.4
Japan	54.9	57.8	61.9	72.3	73.1	78.4	81.5	93.2	100.0	101.5	109.6	113.2	119.4	119.5	120.1	120.9	145.8
Austria	54.1	56.9	61.0	71.3	72.0	77.3	80.3	91.9	98.6	100.0	108.1	111.6	117.7	117.8	118.3	119.2	143.7
Netherlands	50.1	52.7	56.5	65.9	66.7	71.5	74.3	85.0	91.2	92.5	100.0	103.3	108.9	109.0	109.5	110.3	133.0
Belgium	48.5	51.0	54.7	63.8	64.5	69.3	71.9	82.3	88.3	89.6	96.8	100.0	105.4	105.5	106.0	106.8	128.7
France	46.0	48.4	51.9	60.6	61.2	65.7	68.2	78.1	83.8	85.0	91.8	94.8	100.0	100.1	100.6	101.3	122.1
Luxembourg	46.0	48.3	51.8	60.5	61.2	65.6	68.2	78.0	83.7	84.9	91.7	94.7	99.9	100.0	100.5	101.2	122.0
Denmark	45.8	48.1	51.6	60.2	60.9	65.3	67.8	77.6	83.3	84.5	91.3	94.3	99.4	99.5	100.0	100.7	121.4
Germany	45.4	47.8	51.2	59.8	60.4	64.9	67.4	77.1	82.7	83.9	90.7	93.6	98.7	98.8	99.3	100.0	120.6
U.S.	37.7	39.6	42.5	49.6	50.1	53.8	55.9	63.9	68.6	69.6	75.5	77.0	81.9	82.0	82.4	83.0	100.0

duced in the ICP comparisons are correlated with per capita income, but many are, and this smoothing device aids the reader in observing such an association when it exists. For example, in Table 1-7, the percentage of real GDP (that is, GDP in international dollars) devoted to capital formation rises for Groups I through IV in the sequence 13, 20, 22, and 26, before declining to 20 percent for the United States.

The figures in these tables can be analyzed further in several ways, and for the most part the reader is left to follow his own interests. An illuminating way of thinking through the implications of the two tables, however, is presented in Table 1-8.

Price Structures

Table 1-8 shows the relation of the price structure of each country to the structure of international prices. Specifically, the figures in the table represent for each country the ratio of the share of a given component in expenditure on GDP in national prices (from Table 1-6) to the share of the component in expenditure on GDP in international prices (from Table 1-7). This ratio is written

$$(1.2) \qquad R_{ij} = \frac{p_{ij}q_{ij} \Big/ \sum\limits_{i=1} p_{ij}q_{ij}}{\Pi_i q_{ij} \Big/ \sum\limits_{i=1} \Pi_i q_{ij}}$$

where p_{ij} and q_{ij} are the domestic price and quantity of the ith component in the jth country, and Π_i is the international price of the component. The value of R_{ij} for GDP as a whole is 1 since both the numerator and denominator of the right-hand side would be 1 for all of GDP. A value greater than 1 for a given country and component indicates that, relative to the relationship of the country's prices to international prices for its GDP as a whole, the country's price for that particular component is high. A figure below 1 indicates that the component is cheap in the country's structure of relative prices compared with the world structure of relative prices. (A fuller discussion of the analysis of price structures and a more precise treatment of R_{ij} appears in Chapter 6.)

The deviations of consumption from the overall price relationship for GDP as a whole tend to be smaller than the deviations of either of the other major components. This is to be expected, because consumption is such a large proportion of GDP—generally 55 to 80 percent in own prices. Much larger deviations are found in the capital formation and government components.

The pattern of these deviations for capital formation is particularly interesting, because investment is so strategic for economic development. In relative terms, capital goods are expensive in the lowest income countries ($R_{Cap,I} = 1.19$), and inexpensive in the highest income countries ($R_{Cap,V} = 0.91$ and $R_{Cap,VI} = 0.81$). The countries between these groups tend to have relative prices for capital goods that are intermediate, but there are some exceptions (for example, Malaysia and Uruguay). It should be added that these figures referring to capital formation as a whole mask some

very different relationships for its major components: construction and producer durables. These components will be discussed in Chapter 6.

These characteristics of price structures observed in Table 1-8 can be seen directly in Tables 1-6 and 1-7. A comparison of these tables shows that the share of capital formation of the lowest income countries is reduced—sometimes quite sharply—when the valuation basis is shifted from national to international prices. The Group I average share of capital formation is reduced from 16 percent in national prices (column 6 of Table 1-6) to 13 percent in international prices (column 6 of Table 1-7.). For the highest income countries, the opposite is true; the share of capital for-

Table 1-6. Gross Domestic Product and Its Main Components in National Currencies and by Percentage Distribution, 1975

Country	In national currencies Consumption (1)	Capital formation (2)	Government (3)	GDP (4)	Percentage distribution Consumption (5)	Capital formation (6)	Government (7)	GDP (8)
Group I[a]					74.7	16.0	9.2	100.0
Malawi	482	76	46	604	79.9	12.5	7.7	100.0
Kenya	18,538	3,214	2,372	23,844	76.7	13.4	9.9	100.0
India	530,059	149,444	57,366	736,869	71.9	20.3	7.8	100.0
Pakistan	107,148	12,796	12,100	132,044	81.1	9.7	9.2	100.0
Sri Lanka	22,805	1,915	1,688	26,408	86.4	7.3	6.4	100.0
Zambia	952	333	300	1,585	60.0	21.0	18.9	100.0
Thailand	217,177	59,798	21,888	298,863	72.7	20.0	7.3	100.0
Philippines	79,736	27,787	7,559	115,082	69.3	24.1	6.6	100.0
Group II					70.8	18.8	10.3	100.0
Korea	7,120,527	2,007,291	823,885	9,951,703	71.6	20.2	8.3	100.0
Malaysia	14,364	5,322	2,646	22,332	64.3	23.8	11.8	100.0
Colombia	325,444	75,789	11,595	412,828	78.8	18.4	2.8	100.0
Jamaica	1,877	396	338	2,611	71.9	15.2	13.0	100.0
Syria	13,081	2,770	3,682	19,533	67.0	14.2	18.9	100.0
Brazil	721,011	215,689	72,902	1,009,602	71.4	21.4	7.2	100.0
Group III					64.6	25.3	10.0	100.0
Romania	241,883	180,209	22,108	444,200	54.5	40.6	5.0	100.0
Mexico	815,664	230,633	55,074	1,101,371	74.1	20.9	5.0	100.0
Yugoslavia	345,598	170,835	65,504	581,937	59.4	29.4	11.3	100.0
Iran	1,597,900	1,264,700	649,500	3,512,100	45.5	36.0	18.5	100.0
Uruguay	6,722	807	840	8,369	80.3	9.6	10.0	100.0
Ireland	2,783	584	395	3,762	74.0	15.5	10.5	100.0
Group IV					65.2	27.1	7.7	100.0
Hungary	282,089	144,602	35,987	462,678	61.0	31.3	7.8	100.0
Poland	1,006,030	619,831	126,407	1,752,268	57.4	35.4	7.2	100.0
Italy	86,809,690	23,902,910	14,665,000	125,377,500	69.2	19.1	11.7	100.0
Spain	4,413,848	1,360,801	244,566	6,019,215	73.3	22.6	4.1	100.0
Group V					64.8	24.1	11.1	100.0
U.K.	71,255	16,901	16,112	104,268	68.3	16.2	15.5	100.0
Japan	92,030,670	48,571,870	7,552,000	148,154,500	62.1	32.8	5.1	100.0
Austria	420,075	175,221	60,360	656,256	64.1	26.7	9.2	100.0
Netherlands	133,104	51,463	24,853	209,420	63.6	24.6	11.9	100.0
Belgium	1,495,031	523,314	251,947	2,270,292	65.9	23.1	11.1	100.0
France	950,277	344,461	158,729	1,453,467	65.4	23.7	10.9	100.0
Luxembourg	53,988	22,716	8,524	85,228	63.3	26.7	10.0	100.0
Denmark	142,753	41,540	33,728	218,021	65.5	19.1	15.5	100.0
Germany	670,570	251,275	112,189	1,034,034	64.8	24.3	10.8	100.0
Group VI					72.2	16.5	11.3	100.0
U.S.	1,106,904	253,143	172,654	15,320,701	72.2	16.5	11.3	100.0

a. Group entries are averages for the countries within the group.

Table 1-7. Per Capita Gross Domestic Product and Its Main Components in International Dollars, by Percentage Distribution and in Indexes of Quantity per Capita, 1975

Country	Valuation at international prices (I$)				Distribution of GDP valued at international prices				Per capita quantity indexes based on international dollars			
	Consumption (1)	Capital formation (2)	Government (3)	GDP (4)	Consumption (5)	Capital formation (6)	Government (7)	GDP (8)	Consumption (9)	Capital formation (10)	Government (11)	GDP (12)
Group I	467	90	89	646	73	13	14	100.0	9.4	6.2	12.1	9.0
Malawi	275	34	43	352	78	10	12	100.0	5.5	2.4	5.8	4.9
Kenya	365	48	58	470	78	10	12	100.0	7.3	3.3	7.9	6.6
India	337	74	60	470	72	16	13	100.0	6.8	5.0	8.1	6.6
Pakistan	442	54	94	590	75	9	16	100.0	8.9	3.7	12.8	8.2
Sri Lanka	508	72	87	668	76	11	13	100.0	10.2	5.0	11.9	9.3
Zambia	417	142	179	738	57	19	24	100.0	8.4	9.7	24.3	10.3
Thailand	697	160	79	936	74	17	9	100.0	14.0	11.0	10.8	13.0
Philippines	694	139	114	946	73	15	12	100.0	13.9	9.5	15.5	13.2
Group II	1,171	319	170	1,660	70	20	10	100.0	23.5	21.9	23.2	23.1
Korea	1,015	325	144	1,484	68	22	10	100.0	20.4	22.3	19.7	20.7
Malaysia	948	420	173	1,541	62	27	11	100.0	19.0	28.8	23.6	21.5
Colombia	1,265	291	52	1,609	79	18	3	100.0	25.4	20.0	7.1	22.4
Jamaica	1,285	232	206	1,723	75	14	12	100.0	25.8	15.9	28.0	24.0
Syria	1,295	233	266	1,794	72	13	15	100.0	26.0	16.0	36.2	25.0
Brazil	1,219	414	178	1,811	67	23	10	100.0	24.5	28.4	24.3	25.2
Group III	1,803	583	291	2,679	67	22	11	100.0	36.2	40.0	39.6	37.3
Romania	1,436	810	141	2,387	60	34	6	100.0	28.8	55.6	19.2	33.3
Mexico	1,812	552	123	2,487	73	22	5	100.0	36.4	37.9	16.8	34.7
Yugoslavia	1,692	609	290	2,591	65	24	11	100.0	33.9	41.8	39.5	36.1
Iran	1,345	888	471	2,705	50	33	17	100.0	27.0	61.0	64.1	37.7
Uruguay	2,234	176	434	2,844	79	6	15	100.0	44.8	12.1	59.0	39.6
Ireland	2,299	464	286	3,049	75	15	9	100.0	46.1	31.9	38.8	42.5
Group IV	2,626	956	275	3,757	67	26	7	100.0	50.7	65.6	37.4	52.4
Hungary	2,313	957	289	3,559	65	27	8	100.0	46.4	65.7	39.3	49.6
Poland	2,155	1,143	300	3,598	60	32	8	100.0	43.2	78.5	40.8	50.1
Italy	2,636	824	401	3,861	68	21	10	100.0	52.9	56.5	54.6	53.8
Spain	3,001	900	110	4,010	75	22	3	100.0	60.2	61.8	14.9	55.9
Group V	3,552	1,442	460	5,454	65	26	9	100.0	71.3	99.0	62.6	76.0
U.K.	3,174	711	703	4,588	69	16	15	100.0	63.7	48.8	95.6	63.9
Japan	2,925	1,791	190	4,907	60	37	4	100.0	58.7	123.0	25.9	68.4
Austria	3,444	1,196	355	4,995	69	24	7	100.0	69.1	82.1	48.3	69.6
Netherlands	3,398	1,586	414	5,397	63	29	8	100.0	68.2	108.8	56.3	75.2
Belgium	3,715	1,440	419	5,574	67	26	8	100.0	74.5	98.8	57.0	77.7
France	3,746	1,602	530	5,877	64	27	9	100.0	75.1	110.0	72.1	81.9
Luxembourg	3,935	1,542	407	5,883	67	26	7	100.0	78.9	105.9	55.3	82.0
Denmark	3,887	1,364	660	5,911	66	23	11	100.0	78.0	93.6	89.8	82.4
Germany	3,743	1,745	464	5,953	63	29	8	100.0	75.1	119.8	63.1	83.0
Group VI	4,984	1,457	735	7,176	70	20	10	100.0	100.0	100.0	100.0	100.0
U.S.	4,984	1,457	735	7,176	70	20	10	100.0	100.0	100.0	100.0	100.0

mation rises when international prices replace national prices.

The entries in Table 1-8 indicate that government is relatively inexpensive (figures below 1) in the low-income countries and relatively expensive (figures above 1) in the high-income countries. Once again, these findings are reflected in the shares of expenditure shown in Tables 1-6 and 1-7. When international prices rather than local prices are used for evaluation, government-expenditure shares are on average five percentage points higher in the Group I countries and marginally lower in Groups V and VI. If international prices shrink the share of capital formation in the low-income countries and expand the share in the high-income countries, they must in each case have offsetting effects on the share of one or both of the other components. Most of the accommodation is found in government. Thus the usual finding that the share of government in GDP expands as per capita income rises is not supported when all components of GDP are valued at international prices. In real terms, the share of government is highest in the lowest income countries. (Note, however, that these remarks apply to expenditures on general government. Public expenditures on education, health, and recreation are classified as part of consumption in the ICP system.)

A standard of comparison more commonly used than the international price structure is the U.S. structure of prices. Thus in Table 1-9 PPPs relative to the United States and price-level indexes with the United States as the base country are presented.

Much the same story emerges from this table as the one that came out of Tables 1-6 and 1-7. Capital formation in low-income countries is characterized by PPPs that are high (column 2) relative to the PPPs for GDP as a whole (column 4) and, correspondingly, by price indexes that are high (column 7) relative to price-level indexes for GDP as a whole (column 9). Because the countries are arrayed in order of increasing per capita incomes, one must go well down the table be-

fore finding instances in which capital goods are not very expensive relative to GDP as a whole (the Netherlands, Denmark, and the Federal Republic of Germany).

The paucity of these cases indicates that the prices of capital goods are relatively cheap in the United States compared with the prices in the consumption and government sectors. Since the internal price structures of different countries (each relative to the price structure of the United States) are being compared, it does not contradict the point made earlier to observe that, in terms of a common currency (for example, U.S. dollars), capital goods in very poor countries tend to be low in price relative to the same goods in rich countries. The reason is that the prices of commodities and services in the consumption and government sec-

Table 1-8. Relation of National Price Structure to International Price Structure, 1975

Group and country	Consumption	Capital formation	Government	GDP
Group I	1.04	1.19	0.66	1.00
Malawi	1.02	1.28	0.64	1.00
Kenya	0.99	1.31	0.80	1.00
India	1.00	1.29	0.61	1.00
Pakistan	1.08	1.08	0.72	1.00
Sri Lanka	1.14	0.67	0.56	1.00
Zambia	1.06	1.08	0.78	1.00
Thailand	0.98	1.16	0.86	1.00
Philippines	0.94	1.64	0.55	1.00
Group II	1.01	0.96	0.86	1.00
Korea	1.05	0.92	0.86	1.00
Malaysia	1.04	0.87	1.05	1.00
Colombia	1.00	1.01	0.85	1.00
Jamaica	0.96	1.12	1.08	1.00
Syria	0.93	1.08	1.28	1.00
Brazil	1.06	0.93	0.73	1.00
Group III	0.96	1.13	0.93	1.00
Romania	0.91	1.19	0.85	1.00
Mexico	1.02	0.94	1.00	1.00
Yugoslavia	0.91	1.25	1.01	1.00
Iran	0.92	1.55	1.06	1.00
Uruguay	1.02	1.55	0.66	1.00
Ireland	0.98	1.01	1.12	1.00
Group IV	0.97	1.05	1.04	1.00
Hungary	0.94	1.16	0.96	1.00
Poland	0.96	1.11	0.87	1.00
Italy	1.01	0.89	1.12	1.00
Spain	0.98	1.03	1.48	1.00
Group V	1.00	0.91	1.31	1.00
U.K.	0.99	1.04	1.01	1.00
Japan	1.04	0.90	1.31	1.00
Austria	0.93	1.11	1.30	1.00
Netherlands	1.01	0.84	1.54	1.00
Belgium	0.99	0.89	1.48	1.00
France	1.03	0.87	1.21	1.00
Luxembourg	0.95	1.02	1.45	1.00
Denmark	1.00	0.83	1.38	1.00
Germany	1.03	0.83	1.38	1.00
Group VI	1.03	0.81	1.11	1.00
U.S.	1.03	0.81	1.11	1.00

Table 1-9. Purchasing-power Parities and Price Indexes for Gross Domestic Products Consumption, Capital Formation, and Government, 1975

Country	Purchasing-power parities (currency unit per U.S. dollar)					Price indexes (U.S. = 100)			
	Consumption (1)	Capital formation (2)	Government (3)	GDP (4)	Exchange rates (5)	Consumption (6)	Capital formation (7)	Government (8)	GDP (9)
Group I						40	60	25	40
Malawi	0.335	0.537	0.196	0.341	0.866	39	62	23	39
Kenya	3.61	6.20	2.77	3.80	7.41	49	84	37	51
India	2.50	4.13	1.45	2.59	8.38	30	49	17	31
Pakistan	3.32	4.11	1.67	3.18	9.93	33	41	17	32
Sri Lanka	3.20	2.41	1.30	2.93	10.6	30	23	12	27
Zambia	0.441	0.579	0.306	0.431	0.644	68	90	48	67
Thailand	7.2	11.0	6.0	7.6	20.4	35	54	29	37
Philippines	2.63	5.85	1.43	2.89	7.27	36	80	20	40
Group II						50	64	46	52
Korea	191.0	215.0	147.0	190.0	484.0	40	45	30	39
Malaysia	1.22	1.31	1.17	1.22	6.40	51	54	48	51
Colombia	10.4	13.5	8.5	10.8	30.9	34	44	28	35
Jamaica	0.688	1.027	0.730	0.742	0.909	76	113	80	82
Syria	1.32	1.98	1.71	1.48	3.70	36	54	46	40
Brazil	5.31	5.98	3.46	5.20	8.20	65	73	42	63
Group III						60	92	57	65
Romania	7.6	12.9	6.7	8.8	12.0	64	107	56	73
Mexico	7.2	8.5	6.8	7.4	12.5	58	68	54	59
Yugoslavia	9.8	17.1	10.2	11.2	17.4	56	99	59	64
Iran	34.9	53.3	38.3	39.7	67.6	52	79	57	59
Uruguay	1.04	3.02	0.63	1.06	2.30	45	88	28	46
Ireland	0.366	0.487	0.396	0.388	0.450	83	110	89	88
Group IV						69	93	74	74
Hungary	11.1	17.6	10.7	12.3	20.7	54	85	52	60
Poland	13.2	19.6	11.3	14.3	19.9	66	98	56	72
Italy	567.0	639.0	595.0	582.0	652.8	87	98	91	89
Spain	39.8	52.3	57.1	42.3	57.4	69	91	99	73
Group V						103	122	132	107
U.K.	0.386	0.522	0.372	0.406	0.450	86	116	83	90
Japan	271.0	299.0	323.0	271.0	296.8	91	101	109	91
Austria	15.6	23.9	20.5	17.5	17.4	90	138	118	100
Netherlands	2.76	2.92	4.00	2.84	2.53	109	116	158	112
Belgium	39.5	45.6	55.8	41.6	36.8	107	124	152	113
France	4.63	5.01	5.17	4.69	4.29	108	117	120	109
Luxembourg	36.7	50.3	52.9	40.2	36.8	100	138	145	110
Denmark	6.98	7.40	9.18	7.29	5.75	122	129	160	127
Germany	2.79	2.86	3.55	2.81	2.46	113	116	144	114
Group VI						100	100	100	100
U.S.	1.00	1.00	1.00	1.00	1.00	100	100	100	100

Note: See Table 1-1 for currency units.

tors in poor countries, converted to dollars (by exchange rates), are even further below the corresponding prices in rich countries than are the prices of capital goods. In India, for example, capital goods were priced at 49 percent of the U.S. price level, whereas the price levels for consumption and government were 30 percent and 17 percent, respectively.

The inference drawn from the earlier tables about prices for government services are also reflected in Table 1-9. Government, with its large component of employee compensation, tends to be low in the rela-

tive price structure of low-income countries and high in the upper income countries.

Comparisons for the Commodity and Service Components of GDP

For the most part, an examination of more detailed subaggregations is left to Chapter 6, but the dichotomy between the commodity and service components of GDP is explored briefly here. Table 1-10 shows per capita quantity indexes for these two components, first

Table 1-10. Comparisons of per Capita Quantity Indexes for Commodity and Service Components of Gross Domestic Product Based on Exchange-rate Conversions with Real Indexes Based on International Dollars, 1975
(U.S. = 100 in columns 1–6)

Group and country	Expenditures based on exchange-rate conversion			Quantity indexes based on international dollars			Exchange rate deviation indexes		
	Commodities (1)	Services (2)	GDP (3)	Commodities (4)	Services (5)	GDP (6)	Commodities (7)	Services (8)	GDP (9)
Group I[a]	5.0	2.0	3.7	8.8	9.4	9.0	1.84	5.98	2.64
Malawi	2.8	0.8	1.9	5.1	4.5	4.9	1.83	5.39	2.55
Kenya	4.0	2.5	3.4	5.8	8.1	6.6	1.44	3.25	1.95
India	3.0	0.8	2.0	6.3	7.1	6.6	2.08	9.35	3.22
Pakistan	3.7	1.3	2.6	8.3	8.1	8.2	2.22	6.48	3.12
Sri Lanka	3.7	1.1	2.6	8.7	10.6	9.3	2.33	10.08	3.65
Zambia	8.6	4.7	6.9	9.7	11.4	10.3	1.13	2.43	1.49
Thailand	6.8	2.4	4.9	14.5	10.0	13.0	2.12	4.22	2.61
Philippines	7.6	2.3	5.2	12.3	15.1	13.2	1.62	6.64	2.51
Group II	15.2	8.1	12.1	23.4	22.7	23.1	1.67	3.19	2.11
Korea	11.4	4.0	8.1	22.5	16.8	20.7	1.98	4.23	2.54
Malaysia	13.5	7.5	10.9	21.4	21.6	21.5	1.58	2.90	1.98
Colombia	9.5	5.9	7.9	21.0	25.5	22.4	2.20	4.34	2.83
Jamaica	22.4	16.1	19.6	20.8	30.6	24.0	0.93	1.91	1.23
Syria	13.8	5.2	10.0	28.6	17.3	25.0	2.08	3.33	2.50
Brazil	20.7	9.9	16.0	25.7	24.2	25.2	1.24	2.44	1.58
Group III	31.1	15.5	24.2	37.5	37.0	37.3	1.25	2.60	1.61
Romania	35.3	10.2	24.3	34.4	30.9	33.3	0.97	3.05	1.37
Mexico	26.8	12.2	20.4	36.2	31.4	34.7	1.35	2.58	1.70
Yugoslavia	31.5	12.5	23.2	36.8	34.7	36.1	1.17	2.77	1.56
Iran	30.3	11.6	22.1	43.4	25.7	37.7	1.43	2.21	1.70
Uruguay	20.9	14.8	18.2	34.0	51.4	39.6	1.63	3.47	2.17
Ireland	41.8	31.4	37.2	39.9	47.9	42.5	0.96	1.52	1.14
Group IV	50.6	23.4	38.7	53.8	49.2	52.4	1.07	2.40	1.39
Hungary	42.0	13.7	29.6	51.3	46.0	49.6	1.22	3.35	1.68
Poland	52.2	15.4	36.0	52.8	44.5	50.1	1.01	2.89	1.39
Italy	56.7	36.8	47.9	53.8	53.8	53.8	0.95	1.46	1.12
Spain	51.6	27.5	41.0	57.4	52.6	55.9	1.11	1.91	1.36
Group V	92.7	69.1	82.3	77.4	73.0	76.0	0.85	1.09	1.05
U.K.	58.8	56.0	57.6	55.2	82.1	63.9	0.94	1.47	1.11
Japan	73.0	48.8	62.3	71.6	61.5	68.4	0.98	1.26	1.10
Austria	84.6	50.9	69.8	72.1	64.3	69.6	0.85	1.26	1.00
Netherlands	95.7	70.1	84.5	82.0	61.0	75.2	0.86	0.87	0.89
Belgium	99.8	72.3	87.8	82.6	67.3	77.7	0.83	0.93	0.88
France	103.1	72.3	89.6	85.0	75.4	81.9	0.82	1.04	0.91
Luxembourg	106.0	70.0	90.2	85.4	74.8	82.0	0.81	1.07	0.91
Denmark	107.3	100.9	104.5	76.9	93.9	82.4	0.72	0.95	0.88
Germany	105.6	80.8	94.7	85.9	76.7	83.0	0.81	0.95	0.88
Group VI	100.0	100.0	100.0	100.0	100.0	100.0	1.00	1.00	1.00
U.S.	100.0	100.0	100.0	100.0	100.0	100.0	1.00	1.00	1.00

a. Group entries are averages for the countries within the group.

based on the conversion of each country's expenditures by means of exchange rates, and second in real terms by valuing all the quantities at average international prices. "Services" is defined as including categories in which expenditures are on nonstorable goods. These include the services rendered by household employees, teachers, and government employees; repairs of various kinds; rents; public transport and communication; public entertainment; hotels and restaurants; and household services.[23] All the other categories of

23. See Appendix Table 2-1 for specific categories classified as services.

GDP in this rough classification are regarded as commodities.

When indexes with the United States equal to 100 are based on the use of exchange rates to convert all figures to U.S. dollars, it appears that other countries consume relatively larger quantities of commodities than of services. (Compare columns 1 and 2.) Further, the ratio of the commodity index to the service index (with the United States equal to 100 in both cases) is greatest in the lowest income countries and smallest in the highest income countries. There is a fair amount of variation in between, with the ratio being higher than a regular negative association with real GDP per capita would suggest. Both developing countries and socialist countries are found with high ratios (for example, India and Romania). Generally, however, one would be led to believe by the figures in columns 1 and 2 that low-income countries tend to be even poorer in their flows of services than in their flows of commodities.

VALUATION IN REAL TERMS. These results depend upon the valuation of the goods in each country at its own prices. When all goods in each country, both commodities and services, are valued at a common set of prices—average international prices—a different picture emerges (columns 4 and 5). The indexes reflecting the relative flow of services are larger, especially for the low-income countries. Further, the sharp difference between the per capita absorption of services and commodities virtually disappears. The quantity indexes for services are much closer to those for commodities. Indeed, there is actually a tendency for the relationship to twist around for the lowest income countries; five of the eight Group I countries have higher quantity indexes for services than for commodities. Thus the actual relative composition of GDP quantities between poor and rich countries is quite different from what would be inferred from exchange-rate conversions.

PER CAPITA GDP AND EXPENDITURES ON SERVICES. One notable difference, to be described more fully in Chapter 6, involves the relation between expenditures on services and per capita GDP. The conventional wisdom has it that the share of income spent on services tends to rise as per capita income increases. This indeed tends to be the case for the ICP countries when the share of service expenditures is calculated in each country's own prices. When international prices are used to value each country's quantities, however, the proportion spent on services remains fairly level as per capita GDP rises. As this implies, it is the rise in prices of services and not the rise in quantities that plays the main role in pushing up service expenditures as income increases.

The underlying factors at work can be explained by the productivity differential model referred to earlier and developed more fully in Chapter 8. Services, which are nontraded goods, are cheap in low-income countries; hence exchange-rate conversions greatly understate the true quantities of services in low-income countries relative to those in high-income countries. Indeed, the low prices of services in the price structure of the low-income countries encourage their use and lead to quantities that are high relative to the quantities of the relatively more expensive commodities. In the case of commodities, therefore, although the understatement of real quantities by exchange-rate

conversions is substantial, it is much less than in the case of services. For the Group I countries, the average exchange-rate–deviation index for commodities is 1.84, whereas that for services is 5.98. Both indexes tend to decline with rising income so that for the Group V countries the figures are 0.85 for commodities and 1.09 for services.

An analysis of traded and nontraded goods, and an amplified examination of price relationships, is presented in Chapter 6.

The Future of the ICP

This report brings to an end the initiating and development phases of the International Comparison Project. There has been more than a decade of close collaboration between a unit at the University of Pennsylvania and the U.N. Statistical Office, with the active support of the World Bank during most of the period.

From now on, the U.N. Statistical Office will assume full responsibility for the management and operation of the ICP. The broad aim remains as it was in the beginning: the establishment of an international data base that includes annual estimates of real GDP and its main components, and PPPs of the currencies of all of the countries of the world.

This broad objective, at least for the near future, involves several lines of work:

1. The benchmark estimates will have to be extended beyond the thirty-four countries included in the present study. The U.N. Statistical Office has already embarked on Phase IV of the ICP in which it is tentatively planned to make comparisons for about seventy countries. For the moment, it seems wise to contemplate repetitions of benchmark studies for countries already included in the ICP at five-year intervals.

2. The benchmark comparisons will have to be extrapolated to cover years falling between the benchmarks. This may be done only for GDP as a whole or for GDP and its three main components and perhaps also for major subcomponents.

3. Ways must be found to make comparisons for the countries that cannot be accorded benchmark treatment. It is unrealistic to believe that it will be possible in the near future to carry out benchmark estimates for all of more than 150 countries and areas for which data are included in the recent issues of the U.N. *Yearbook of National Accounts Statistics*. Work is already under way at the U.N. Statistical Office, the EEC, and the World Bank on reduced-information methods—that is, methods that would make it possible to estimate a country's relative GDP with less than the full set of data required for the present benchmark

estimates. Successful development of this work might lead not only to the preparation of estimates that were of second-best quality, *faute de mieux,* for countries that could not otherwise be covered, but also to less burdensome data requirements for the first-best (benchmark) estimates.

In the interim, a less attractive alternative to reduced information methods, but one that is relatively inexpensive, is the further development of shortcut methods. Considerable experience with this approach has shown its feasibility. Indeed, the present report utilizes the approach to provide GDP estimates for many countries other than the thirty-four benchmark countries (see Chapter 8).

A Guide for the Reader

For the reader who wishes to probe beyond the summary of results offered in the preceding pages, a few words of guidance beyond what has already been said may prove helpful.

Chapters 2 through 5 deal with methodological issues. The basic aggregation methods—CPD and Geary-Khamis—are set out in more detail in the Phase I report, but the present chapters illuminate and clarify several methodological issues and present a rounded picture of the gathering and processing of the data. Chapter 4, which deals with regionalization, and Chapter 5, which deals with services, break new ground.

Chapters 6 and 7 present the substantive results of the comparisons, the former dealing with multilateral comparisons and the latter with binary comparisons. The emphasis in Chapter 7 is on what are called "augmented" binary comparisons, which are designed to circumvent the limitations for binary comparisons posed by a data-collection scheme aimed primarily at multilateral comparisons.

Part II goes beyond the basic reporting aspect for ICP Phase III. Chapter 8 extends the benchmark estimates to some other years, in both current and constant prices, and to regional and global aggregates for real GDP. Chapter 9 explores some aspects of the interrelationships among the disaggregated price and quantity data that were presented in Chapter 6.

The need to avoid repeating cumbersome descriptive phrases has led to the selection of labels such as "augmented" binary comparisons, "indirect" price comparisons, and the like. While each is defined at an appropriate point in the text, a glossary is also provided at the end of the volume for the convenience of the reader.

2

The ICP Approach and Its Data Requirements

THIS CHAPTER SETS OUT the basic ICP approach to price and quantity comparisons, and then describes the way in which the necessary data have been collected and organized.

The Question of Taste Differences

Before describing the ICP approach and data collecting and processing, some fundamental questions must be dealt with: What is the role of tastes in making cardinal comparisons of the bundles of goods consumed by the peoples of all the different countries in the world? What possibility is there that peoples with histories and cultures as different as those of India and the Federal Republic of Germany, for example, have the same tastes? If their tastes differ, what is the justification for comparing the welfare values of the collections of goods consumed by each?[1]

Without doubt, the rigorous theory of economic cost-of-living–index numbers narrowly circumscribes the comparisons that can be made. Comparisons of welfare or of the costs of maintaining a given level of welfare are justified in the theory only with respect to a given person at a given moment. It is held legitimate to ask questions about the factor by which that person's money income would have to be changed to leave him indifferent between the price structure he actually faces at a particular moment and some alternative price structure with which he might be confronted at the same moment. The theory does not warrant comparisons of the welfare of the same individual at two different times because of the difficulties in assuming

that his tastes remain identical as he passes through life.[2] Obviously, comparisons of the welfare of an entire nation at two points in time are even more difficult to justify. But if a nation's people cannot be depended upon to have unchanging tastes over time, what meaningful comparisons can be made if at the same time the nations are very different?

Another line of reasoning based on production considerations rather than directly on consumer welfare may provide slightly more leeway for interspatial comparisons. Assume that two countries have identical production functions and each country is characterized by complete mobility of resources among industries and constant returns to scale in each industry (that is, homothetic transformation curves). Given this set of conditions, the ratio of the GDP of the higher income country to that of the lower would correspond to the ratio of (1) the resources that would be required in the lower income country to produce the same output as the higher income country to (2) the resources used in the lower income country to produce its actual level of income. However, this escape from the strictures of welfare theory remains open only if it is not insisted that production in itself has no meaning unless it is validated by consumer satisfactions. Tastes play a background role even in this production orientation.

In practice, the limitations set by the theory of cost-of-living–index numbers are generally ignored in intertemporal comparisons. Problems of interpersonal comparisons are put to one side completely, and money aggregations simply are compared at the two points in time. For example, two aggregates are compared directly even if there has been a redistribution that brought gains to some individuals and losses to others.

1. Hill (1981) contributed to the discussion of this and related questions, dealing specifically with earlier ICP work.

2. See Fisher and Shell (1972).

The universal assumption that tastes remain unchanged is not regarded as unreasonable when the comparison is confined to a short interval, such as one year to the next or even a period of several years. Hemlines may rise or fall and car fenders may change contours, but if one is prepared to accept the desire for change in style as an inherent part of the utility function once a certain level of income is reached, then such changes need not be regarded as changes in taste.

Over a longer period, however, the style of life appears to change in a more fundamental sense. Clothing is apt to be made of different materials. Entertainment may be transmitted in different forms. Travel from home to place of work and to friends' homes may be by a different form of transport. Even the food may be different, at least in the degree of its processing, from that available in an earlier age. The consequences of these changes are captured in the intertemporal indexes of most nations by a choice of new specifications, by the reweighting of different goods from time to time, or both.

How do the assumptions required for international comparisons differ from those now conventionally accepted for intertemporal comparisons? The aggregation assumption that disregards the internal distributional effect on welfare is the same. What is different is that the assumption of similar tastes places a still greater strain on credulity when the comparison is made between situations at distant places at the same time than when it is made between situations at the same place but at different times.

Doubts raised about comparisons between different places and about temporal comparisons within a country can be answered in two ways. On one level, one can stress the differences in the physical forms of the things people consume in different situations. The prevalence of French wine, Japanese sake, German beer, and American cola can be regarded as reflecting different tastes. So, too, can the relatively large quantities of automobiles, refrigerators, and other durable goods consumed by Americans as compared with the quantities consumed by other peoples. In this view, comparisons between such different bundles of goods are not warranted or are, at best, of very limited economic significance.

On the other level, it is possible to regard the basic needs and desires of man as fundamentally the same in different periods and different places. In this view, what changes from time to time and what is different from place to place is not so much what people would like to have but what it is that the economy affords them. What differs is, first, the extent to which the economy is capable of satisfying their wants (differences in factor endowments making consumption pos-

sibility loci different) and, second, the means by which they are satisfied—that is, the physical identity of the goods. Differences in technology and differences in relative factor prices have been mainly responsible for variations in the physical forms in which the economy produces goods that satisfy those basic wants. But the basic wants themselves have remained substantially constant through time and over space.

There are reasons for believing that it is the latter view that, in the main, is the more valid description of the international differences observed in the physical composition of the real income of nations. Support for this view can be found both in ordinary observation and, to a modest degree, in econometric analyses. Any world traveler cannot help but be struck by the similarity of goods found in all major cities. A person could be in a department store in Tokyo or New York and be unable to tell which was which, were it not for the difference in language and appearance of the people. As economic levels rise, plumbing facilities in housing and the possession of automobiles and other durable goods—once regarded as American idiosyncracies[3]—are becoming common in more and more regions of the world.

In Japan, for example, the strong tradition that rooms should be no larger than eight tatamis (about thirteen square meters), has continued—in tatami rooms. However, the average size of rooms and the size of dwellings has tended to increase as the proportion of tatami rooms in houses has decreased in favor of Western-style rooms, which are usually larger. Even in those parts of Asia in which material values were once thought to take a second place to the spiritual, emerging middle classes typically pursue the same patterns of consumption that people with equivalent income levels pursue elsewhere in the world.

These casual empirical remarks suggest that many of the differences in consumption patterns of the peasant and subsistence sectors in less developed countries relative to those of either middle-income urban dwellers in the same countries or of persons in the richer countries can be explained by differences in opportunities.[4] If this is the case, the measurement of rel-

---

3. Some members of the Organisation for European Economic Co-operation (OEEC) staff involved in producing the comparisons of the early 1950s (Gilbert and Kravis, 1954; and Gilbert and associates, 1958) were of the opinion that most Europeans did not want the elaborate bathroom facilities of U.S. houses. The increased use of central heating in the United Kingdom, despite claims that it was not really desirable, is another case in point.

4. The differences in opportunity are mainly attributable to differences in income levels and relative prices. There is also a more literal sense in which "opportunities" are limited by the availability of goods in each situation, but such availabilities are themselves related to the same factors that determine incomes and prices.

ative income levels between the rural and urban sectors of the less developed countries and wealthy countries as a whole is in principle a valid exercise. The problem then becomes one of finding criteria of equivalence between the different physical forms of goods that are used to satisfy similar wants. This is difficult but not objectionable in principle, and, as will be shown, it is manageable in practice.

The limited econometric evidence available, much of it from the ICP itself, supports the working hypothesis that tastes are similar the world over. Several studies indicate that at least for the United States and the countries of Western Europe, great similarities exist in consumption patterns; income elasticities of demand for various categories of goods and ownership patterns for consumer durables seem to be alike.[5] Studies based on both time-series and cross-section data (at both the aggregate and household levels) of developing countries indicate similarities in consumption patterns when income and prices are taken into account.[6] The ICP evidence on the 1970s, first based on ten countries in Phase I, then on sixteen countries in Phase II, and now on thirty-four countries in Phase III, clearly indicates that income levels and relative prices go far toward explaining the relative quantities of different goods consumed in different countries. (Analysis of intercountry data done two decades earlier gave similar results.[7])

The evidence based on thirty-four countries is marshaled in Chapter 9 with the aid of a number of different analytical approaches. Since the Phase III data constitute a single cross-section, the analysis is not as direct as it would be if the effects on consumption patterns could be estimated directly for different countries and then the effects compared. Still, the explanation of the variations in spending patterns across countries provided by relative prices and levels of per capita income is sufficiently high that the hypothesis that tastes are alike cannot be grossly wrong. This conclusion is probably more true the more aggregated the categories of consumption are.

The Approach to the Comparisons

The design of the data collection effort and the plans for organizing the data depended on the broad strategy selected for making the price and quantity comparisons. At the outset two major decisions were required.

One was the decision to work with disaggregation of GDP with respect to final expenditures. This is in accord with a procedure established in the Gilbert and Kravis work carried out at the OEEC shortly after World War II and followed in virtually all other efforts at international product comparisons of GDP, whether in Europe or Latin America.[8]

This is not, of course, the only way of approaching the comparisons. An alternative is to work with a breakdown of GDP in terms of product originating in different industries. This product-originating approach, used by Paige and Bombach in a U.K.-U.S. comparison (1959), makes possible comparisons of the industrial structure and provides the basis for sector-by-sector and even industry-by-industry productivity comparisons. However, the cost of obtaining these interesting and valuable materials is the need to follow a double-deflation procedure. That is, comparisons must be made of input prices as well as output prices for each industry to ensure that the net output of each industry is validly compared. It is also necessary to ensure that the product coverage of each industry be the same and that the degree of integration from raw materials to finished product either be the same or else that suitable adjustments be made for the differences.[9] These difficulties explain why the product-originating approach has been followed so rarely, but the knowledge to be gained from the approach is considerable. It is to be hoped that as comparisons based on the final-expenditure approach become more fully established, a further effort will be made to develop the more difficult industry-by-industry comparisons.

The second major decision was to place the main reliance on price comparisons. Quantity comparisons are derived indirectly even though they are considered as important as—indeed even more important than—price or purchasing power comparisons. For any ho-

---

5. Houthakker and Taylor (1966), pp. 167–72; and Wells (1969), pp. 152–62.

6. Lluch, Powell, Williams (1977), p. 240.

7. Gilbert and associates (1958); and Kravis, Kenessey, Heston, Summers (1975, table 15-9, p. 283.

8. Gilbert and Kravis (1954), pp. 22–23; Paretti, Krijnse Locker, Goybet (1973); and U.N. Economic Commission for Latin America (1967), pp. 107–42.

9. The results of the Paige-Bombach study are compared below with those of the Gilbert-Kravis study for GDP as a whole.

	U.K./U.S. 1950 real per capita GNP valued at the prices of	
	United Kingdom	*United States*
Product-originating approach	56.2	62.2
Expenditure approach	49.0	62.9

The differences, though small, arise in part because the investigators faced different methodological problems (Paige and Bombach, 1959, p. 15). The possible effects of the alternative methodology on the results were probably reduced by the considerable reliance of the Paige-Bombach study on the Gilbert-Kravis price comparisons, which related to final products, because the fieldwork required to gather a more appropriate set of comparative price data could not be undertaken.

mogeneous category of goods or services, the ratio of one country's quantity to another's is obtained by dividing the ratio of category expenditures in the two countries by their price ratios. Thus,

$$(2.1) \qquad \frac{p_{ij}q_{ij}}{p_{ik}q_{ik}} \div \frac{p_{ij}}{p_{ik}} = \frac{q_{ij}}{q_{ik}}$$

where i refers to the ith commodity and j and k refer to countries.

This indirect method of making quantity comparisons for individual categories is followed because direct quantity comparisons are very difficult to make for many types of products. Apparel, for example, is so heterogeneous that quantity data for each type and each quality of product are difficult to obtain. Furthermore, even if the quantity information were available, the quantity ratios of the various types could be expected to exhibit wide dispersion relative to the corresponding price ratios. The approach involving direct price ratios thus has two advantages. First, price ratios for individual products are easier to obtain; second, the sampling variance of the indirect quantity ratios will be smaller than the variance of the direct-quantity ratio.

There are, however, a few kinds of relatively homogeneous products for which quantity data are available on a comprehensive basis. In these cases, primarily in the service sectors where national accounting conventionally measures output by the quantity of input, as in education, it may be better to carry out international comparisons through direct quantity ratios (see Chapter 5).

Direct price comparisons are subject mainly to sampling errors, but the indirect quantity indexes are subject also to possible errors in the expenditure ratios. Unfortunately, expenditures in certain categories are likely to be particularly susceptible to error. For example, the reported distribution of total footwear expenditures among men, women, and children varies significantly among certain countries. Some of the difference may reflect true differences in spending patterns, but a large part probably arises from country-to-country differences in the statistical allocation of the footwear total to the different kinds of users. Noncomparability in expenditure data is likely to be particularly great for residual categories (for example, in the ICP classification system, ICP 8.4, other services, n.e.s.), because it is unlikely that national-income accountants in different countries assigned difficult-to-classify expenditures to those categories in identical ways.

The decisions to work with final-expenditure breakdowns and to rely mainly on price comparisons together determine the nature of the data required and collected for the aggregation process. The data consist of expenditures for each of the categories of final expenditures in the classification selected, and of prices for one or more specifications of goods within each category. Each of these two major types of input is discussed in the following sections.

Concepts of Quantity and Price

It would be too much to claim that the conceptual problems involved in defining GDP so that it constitutes an unduplicated aggregate that distinguishes the results of economic activity from noneconomic activity have been completely resolved. For some questions, to be sure, the outcome has been a clear resolution based on underlying theoretical considerations. For the others, where theory could not resolve the issues, conventions commanding international agreement have been developed. These resolutions and conventions have been set out carefully and systematically in the U.N. publication *A System of National Accounts* (SNA).[10]

When it comes to international comparisons, however, the SNA, detailed and careful as it is, leaves open the possibility that two countries may conform to the SNA and still be left with some incomparabilities in their GDPs. International differences in GDP coverage that may be relatively unimportant for measuring time-to-time changes within countries may have to be taken into account in place-to-place comparisons.

The Meaning of Output

Important areas in which this possibility arises include the differences in environmental conditions, the measurement of capital formation, and what can be termed the "general quality of output."

ENVIRONMENT. The conventions governing the preparation of national accounts do not provide for any deductions from GDP for environmental deterioration, but they do lead to additions for some, but not all, expenditures designed to improve the environment or to prevent further deterioration.

Expenditures by government, households, or businesses on capital account to reduce pollution or otherwise protect the environment are counted as additions to final product. Expenditures for these purposes by businesses on current account, however, are not regarded as final products; they merely increase the prices of output. This means that efforts to offset the deterioration of the environment affect the GDP estimates of different countries according to their extent and

---

10. U.N. Statistical Office (1968).

according to the transactors that carry on these efforts. Consider two countries. One has devoted substantial resources to combating environmental deterioration. The other country has used none of its resources for this purpose. The former—other things being equal—would have a relatively small GDP if its environmental efforts were financed through business expenditures on current account. If, on the other hand, its efforts were conducted through governmental expenditures, the two countries would be shown to have equal GDPs. Nevertheless, given the present stage of international comparisons, no effort has been made in the ICP to deal with these problems.

Differences in environmental conditions raise further questions about the comparisons of real product quite apart from the adverse effects of production. Some of these questions are easy to answer. For example, a cold climate requires people to produce heat for residences and other buildings, but this requirement is absent in a warm climate. Production of heat is an economic activity that adds to welfare and must be counted as a part of the contribution the economy is making to welfare. Thus the income of a country that requires and produces heat is higher than the income of a country in a warm climate that does not require or produce heat, the production of all other products being equal in the two countries. It is equally clear, however, that added inputs or costs to attain a given level of welfare that are necessitated by a harsher environment do not represent more production. A potato remains a potato whether it takes two man-hours of labor to produce in a rich soil in a hospitable climate or four man-hours in a barren soil in an unfavorable climate.

CAPITAL FORMATION. A question arises into which of these two reasonably clear-cut cases—the one representing added outputs necessitated by a cold climate, the other representing merely added costs—the extra inputs and costs that may be required to produce capital goods in an unfavorable environment should be placed. For example, a mountainous country may have to build largely curved highways at a steep incline, whereas a country with a flat terrain may be able to build most of its highways straight and level. Is flat land for highways analogous to fertile land for potatoes and mountainous land analogous to barren land? If so, the unit of output should be one mile of highway, regardless of its inclination. Alternatively, a mile of mountain road may be regarded as more output than a mile of flat road within each country and counted as such in comparisons between countries.

Consider another illustration. Suppose that in a cold climate a steam power plant had to be built with insulating walls around its boiler room and switchhouse, whereas in a warm climate both can be exposed to the weather. Assuming that all other characteristics are identical, should the inputs and costs required for enclosed construction in the cold climate be regarded simply as added costs, or as more output?

One line of reasoning in response to such questions is to regard the future flow of services that each capital good would produce in each country as the basis for evaluating the relative amounts of investment. This implies that an international comparison should be made of the present value of the increases in output—ultimately in the form of consumption goods—that new capital goods would contribute in each economy. In the real world, no dated list is available of consumer goods that eventually will flow from new investment, but only the value of investment and the prices of the capital goods themselves in each country's own currency. Furthermore, knotty problems would arise in isolating the differences in future flow that could be attributed to the input of capital from the differences attributable to other elements, such as other factor inputs and environment. Therefore, it is too difficult to implement the future-flow-of-services approach.

If the capacity of each new machine or other form of investment to contribute to production could be measured in one dimension, the task would be relatively simple. If, for example, the productivity of a steam power plant could be measured solely by the kilowatts it generates, there would be an unambiguous basis for quantity comparisons. However, other things, such as fuel economy, labor requirements, and reliability affect the net contribution of the power plant. A variety of desired qualities also characterizes most other producer durable goods.

For those kinds of producer durables that are marketed in a variety of models, it is possible through statistical analysis to relate observed prices to the various physical characteristics that contribute directly (for example, the horsepower of a tractor) or indirectly (weight as a guide to durability) to the value of the good as an instrument of production. That is, the presumption is that the prices producers are willing to pay for these characteristics reflect their contribution to production. Thus for certain goods that are available in a variety of models, price comparisons have been made between different countries for models defined by certain combinations of these characteristics. These methods, sometimes referred to as "hedonic indexes," are discussed later in this chapter.[11]

For other machinery and for construction, when no empirical evidence existed on the relative productivity of different variants, the price comparisons have been

11. See also Griliches (1971).

based on equivalent physical specifications. In the case of highways, for example, without any basis for assessing productivity, prices have been compared for things with like physical specifications. The cost of a flat road of a given specification in one country was compared with the cost of a road of the same specification in another country, and likewise for a mountainous road. The effect, of course, was to treat the mountainous road as more output than a flat road; in a sense, an adverse environment in this instance required more production, just as low temperatures necessitated the provision of heat and warm clothing. Similarly, insulating walls for power plants in cold climates were regarded as part of output rather than mere additions to cost.

THE GENERAL QUALITY OF OUTPUT. The basic approach to the treatment of differences in quality for specific goods is to avoid such differences between goods for which comparisons are made or to adjust prices where goods of equivalent quality cannot be found. Thus, because quality differences of this type do not affect the output comparisons, they need not be discussed in the definition of output. They are treated below in the section entitled "Matching Methods."

Some kinds of quality differences, however, are associated with the whole aggregate of goods rather than with specific products. For a given aggregate of goods, it is more advantageous to the population to have conveniently located, well-stocked stores with courteous and efficient sales personnel than to be forced to search for supplies and to queue up for service. A similar point applies to such ancillary services as credit, delivery, the right to return merchandise, and repairs and adjustments. Generally, a greater variety of goods also is to be preferred to a lesser variety.

A retail distribution system that provides all these conveniences and services is more expensive and absorbs more real resources than one that does not. The GDP of each country includes the value of such services to the extent that they are rendered. The ICP method of international comparisons, however, does not attempt to measure international differences in their provision. It simply compares the extent to which each economy delivered meat and potatoes, shoes and stockings, and other commodities to its residents without regard to the extent or nature of the accompanying services. The direction and extent of the bias that result from the omission of these general quality factors are difficult to judge.

The Concept of Price

The definition of output and the concept of price are closely related. Thus the decision to ignore all the differences discussed in the previous paragraphs and to define commodities primarily in physical terms has direct implications for the concept of price. The concept used is influenced also by the final expenditure approach followed in the ICP and by SNA definitions.

THE USE OF MARKET PRICES. To start with the latter point, purchasers' values (market prices) are used in valuing the final products that make up GDP.[12] The possibility of systematic factor-cost comparisons either in lieu of, or as supplements to, the market price comparisons was considered and rejected. Even on theoretical grounds, the case for factor prices is not completely without blemish, because the quantities observed are responses to market prices. The operative reason behind the decision against factor prices, however, was the great difficulty of ascertaining true factor costs in many countries.

This difficulty arises out of the extensive distortions of market prices from factor costs that characterize nearly all countries. The industrialized market economies subsidize their domestic agriculture. Developing countries subsidize industrial production directly or through the exchange-rate system.[13] Socialist countries also have price structures reflecting the effect of public policies.

In some sectors in which governments paid for substantial portions of the total social cost of a commodity or service, however, an estimate has been made of the *total* market price or social price: that paid by households plus that paid by governments. This was done, for example, in housing services.

The reason for this treatment is that in some countries the use of prices paid by households alone would lead to a gross underestimation of the relative importance of certain categories of expenditures. In Hungary, for example, tenants paid less than 20 percent of the current costs of housing in 1970. Thus in any aggregation of relative real product, the use of Hungarian weights based on tenant prices or expenditures would assign much less importance to housing than it should.

Although other unusual differences exist between factor costs and market prices, notably in alcoholic beverages, tobacco, and public transportation, expenditures in these categories are much less important. In the OEEC comparisons, such distinctions between factor prices and market prices had little effect on the aggregate results.[14] Recent experiments of the

---

12. Final products are those bought by purchasers for their own use and not for resale.

13. See Balassa and associates (1971); and Little, Scitovsky, Scott (1970).

14. Gilbert and Kravis (1954).

European Economic Community (EEC) with comparisons with and without the value-added tax also found small differences.

THE NATURE OF THE NATIONAL AVERAGE PRICES. The market price sought for each good is the average price for all the units of that product that entered into the nation's GDP in the reference year. Variety and the extent of distributive services have already been ruled out as elements affecting the definition of the product. Apart from the problems of specifying quality (considered below) decisions have to be made also about such aspects of product definition as seasonality, size of transaction, location, and own-account production.

The fundamental approach in all these cases was to define products on the basis of their physical characteristics: a potato with given physical characteristics was treated not only as the same product but also as the same quantity, whether it was purchased in the country or in the city, in January or in June, by the piece or by the bushel, and whether it was purchased at a retail market or consumed out of own production. The price of the potato is apt to vary, of course, from one situation to another. The appropriate price for the present study is an average in which the actual price of each unit entering into GDP is given an equal weight; if the country has followed the recommendations of the SNA, this average will correspond to that implicit in the expenditure figure.

Deviations from this a-potato-is-a-potato rule were permitted only infrequently—when there was clear evidence that physically different products were equivalent in use in two or more countries. The criteria used to identify such cases are described below in the section "Matching Methods."

With respect to the seasonal factor, the ICP takes the view that a country that uses extensive resources to produce fruit out of season is simply obtaining a final product in an expensive way: strawberries in January are not different from strawberries in June—just more expensive. The alternative view, that strawberries in January involve more final product than an equal amount of identical strawberries in June, is, in any case, impractical. Whatever its intellectual merits, it would require the continual determination of the seasonality of production for each final product with a potentially seasonal character before it could be said how much product it really was. Seasonals in different countries would have to be matched.

The treatment of products as identical without regard to international differences in the average quantity purchased per transaction may raise some questions. See also the discussion of treatment of different kinds of packaging below in the section "Matching

Methods." Many items, particularly foods and pharmaceutical products, are more expensive per unit when bought in small quantities. Rice in the United States in 1970, for example, cost 14 percent more per pound when purchased in a sixteen-ounce bag than when purchased in an eighty-ounce bag. The price premium per unit on small purchases can be regarded as the price paid by the consumer for more distributive service, and it can be argued that the additional service should be treated as part of final product. Although this view has some validity, it can be countered that shoppers, especially those with high incomes, sometimes may buy large quantities without any price incentive merely to economize their shopping time.

In Europe a different approach has been considered that in practice will yield the same price ratio as the ICP. Within the European Community, or between two European countries undertaking a binary comparison, the practice is frequently to treat different-size units as different items. For example, French-style bread may be compared for several sizes, such as 50 grams, 200 grams, and 500 grams, and the country-to-country price ratios averaged. In the ICP each country is asked to price the size or sizes that are most frequently purchased. Prices per unit are then compared across countries. In this way prices used for each country will tend to approximate the average price embedded in its expenditure figure. If weights are available for each size, then the weighted average price ratio for bread would approximate the ratio of the average prices.

The national accounting concept of the average transaction price has its clearest justification when viewed from the production side, where every dollar spent can be regarded as a measure of resource absorption. If, for example, aggregate expenditure in a country for oranges and apples are 200 and 100 currency units (dollars, DM, or whatever), respectively, the numbers tell us that (ignoring the imperfections in the price system, such as monopoly and other distortions) twice as much labor and other productive resources was absorbed in the provision of oranges as in the provision of apples.[15]

---

15. From the welfare side, it has sometimes been suggested that the implicit assumption that the marginal utility of each dollar's worth of income is the same to each recipient runs counter to the intuitive observation that a dollar's increment in income for a poor person is apt to have greater personal and social welfare significance than a dollar's increment for a rich person. From this standpoint, an alternative way to evaluate changes in period-to-period national incomes has been suggested—namely, to assign more weight than in the conventional method to the temporal growth in incomes of poor people. Thus Kuznets has proposed that for comparative purposes the growth of regional or world income over time might be calculated by averaging the growth rates of the countries through

PRICING SELF-PRODUCED GOODS. A special problem in the concept of national average price arises with location, because it is closely related to the treatment of consumption of own production. As with the other price problems, this issue is linked directly to the concept of national product.

Under conditions of optimal resource allocation, goods that absorb more resources represent more output than goods that absorb fewer resources. Potatoes consumed in the city count for more output than potatoes consumed on the farm. This valuation, based on the conditions of static equilibrium, is embedded in national-income–accounting practice. Thus, in national accounts statistics as usually prepared, a shift from farm to urban consumption, with farm and urban prices constant, raises real product. If this treatment is matched in international comparisons, own consumption of potatoes and purchased consumption of potatoes will be treated as separate products. This implies pricing the former at producer prices, the latter at retail prices.

This method leads to a lower estimate of the relative product for a country with relatively high own consumption and with a relatively large spread between the producer and retail prices. The following illustration shows how the arithmetic works:

	Urbanized country			Rural country			Extensions	
	p_u	q_u	$p_u q_u$	p_r	q_r	$p_r q_r$	$p_u q_r$	$p_r q_u$
Own consumption of potatoes	5	10	50	2	100	200	500	20
Purchased potatoes	10	100	1,000	8	10	80	100	800
Total			110	1,050		110	280	600	820

Both countries consume 110 units of potatoes, but with very different distributions between own consumption and purchased consumption. The quantity index with the urbanized country's weights is

$$(2.2) \qquad \frac{\sum p_u q_r}{\sum p_u q_u} \cdot 100 = \frac{600}{1,050} \cdot 100 = 57.$$

the use of population weights or even weights that are inversely proportional to per capita income. This is an informative way of illuminating the welfare significance of growth and has obvious applications to the assessment of international differences in GDP per capita. It does not, however, represent (and probably is not intended to represent) a proposal to alter for purposes of the basic estimates the accounting rule that each dollar of transactions have the same significance regardless of the income or location of the transactor. See Kuznets (1972). A similar idea has been applied to the analysis of national growth rates by Ahluwalia and Chenery in Chenery and others (1972).

The quantity index with the rural country's weights is

$$(2.3) \qquad \frac{\sum p_r q_r}{\sum p_r q_u} \cdot 100 = \frac{280}{820} \cdot 100 = 34.$$

If the difference in price spread is eliminated so that the retail price in the rural country is 4 (that is, two times the own-consumption price as in the urbanized country), both indexes come to 57. (Or, if the common spread is four times the own-consumption price—for example, p_u for purchased potatoes is 20—both indexes come to 34.)

Whether it is correct to use a method that results in counting the same quantity of potatoes as less output because they are consumed on the farm depends on the reasons for the different distribution of populations between farm and city. In general, a population living close to its points of production will require less transport and, all other things being equal, will enjoy more final product than a population dwelling at a greater average distance from its points of production. Distance involves a cost, and a greater need to overcome it should not be allowed to count as more output any more than the greater need to wrest production from a less fertile soil.

Someone might wish to argue that urban dwelling (at a distance from production) is a result of choice rather than necessity, and that the greater costs entailed in this preference constitute a contribution to welfare. There may be an element of truth in this view: the attraction of cities seems to be powerful the world over and only partly explicable by the cities' greater economic opportunity. The relative roles of choice and necessity in urban concentration, and the relative utilities and disutilities involved in urban dwelling, are not clear. Counting an urban potato as more product than a rural potato because of the costs of transport and trade margins would be to ascribe more welfare to city than to rural dwelling. It may be slightly more neutral, for international comparison purposes, to regard a potato as a potato.

The way to achieve this is to combine own production and purchased output for each product into a single category. This still leaves open the question of how the national average price will be determined—particularly, how home consumption will be valued for the purpose of estimating the national average price. There are two possibilities for the valuations of own consumption: one is to value it at retail, the other to value it at producer prices. In the latter case, the national price is the weighted average of producer and retail prices, using consumption weights. In either case, once the national average price is determined, both methods treat all units consumed so that they make an equal contribution to each country's relative product: a potato is a potato for comparison purposes, whether consumed on the farm or in the city. What is different is that the relative importance of the product—that is, the price weight assigned to the quantity—will be greater when own consumption is valued at retail prices. The quantity ratio for potatoes will be the same regardless of which prices are used because all potatoes are treated as a single category.

Where there is no quality difference, there is a clear case for valuing own consumption at producer prices and using a weighted average of producer and retail prices. First, the weighted prices more truly reflect the average resource input in each country. Second, they are the prices that are in each country's expenditure data (if the SNA is followed), and, therefore, they are the prices that will produce price ratios consistent with the appropriate quantity and expenditure ratios. Thus in the above example, the ICP would enter as the price for the urbanized country 9.55 (1,050/110), and for the rural country 2.55 (280/110). The resulting price ratio of rural to urban, 0.267 (2.55/9.55), when divided into the expenditure ratio of 0.267 (280/1,050), will yield a quantity ratio of 1, which corresponds to the ICP treatment.

The Expenditure Data

The classification of final expenditures on GDP adopted by the ICP is set out in the appendix to this chapter. This classification follows closely the U.N. *System of National Accounts* (SNA) and is virtually identical with the Phase II classification.[16] (Appendix Table 2-1 shows the classifications of the categories into services and commodities.)

Framework

Two of the three major SNA components of GDP are modified for ICP purposes: first, SNA's private final consumption expenditure (PFCE) is replaced by the ICP's final consumption expenditure of the population (CEP); and, second, SNA's government final consumption expenditure (GFCE) is replaced by the ICP's public final consumption expenditure (PFC). SNA's gross fixed capital formation is unchanged except that in ICP ag-

gregations the term "gross capital formation" (GCF) is used to include net change in stocks and net exports as well as gross domestic fixed capital formation. (To facilitate exposition, the term "consumption" is used for CEP, "government" for PFC, and "capital formation" or sometimes "investment" for GCF.)

The main modifications affecting CEP and PFC relate to government expenditures for health care, education, and recreation. The modifications were made to ensure that comparisons for these groupings were independent of the degree to which a country's expenditures for them are made collectively by the society on the one hand and out of household budgets on the other. Therefore, all public expenditures in health care, education, and recreation other than those of a clearly governmental character (for example, the licensing of physicians) were transferred to ICP consumption. Although this may change the relative sizes of consumption and government, it leaves total SNA gross domestic product unaltered. The summary categories and the per capita amounts involved in these transfers of expenditures are listed in Table 2-1. They correspond approximately to the distinction between public and private goods that is made in the theory of public finance.[17]

Goods that can be subdivided into units that in principle can be sold to individuals (or to individual households) and consumed by them without any benefit accruing to any other individual (or household) are regarded as private goods (for example, a loaf of bread or a tooth extraction). Goods that cannot be so subdivided for exclusive consumption, goods that cannot be consumed by one individual (or household) without having some of the benefits spill over to others, goods the use of which cannot be withheld from those who do not pay—these are all regarded as public or social goods (defense). On this basis, all or most commodities and services in the food, clothing, shelter, education, medical-care, recreation, and transportation categories fall under consumption. By contrast, services provided through the making of laws and their administration, including police protection, fall under government.

"Government" is thus viewed in the ICP as comprising a common set of final products that most societies, regardless of economic and social system, provide through public organizations and finance by tax revenues. These final products take the form largely of services that provide citizens with physical, social, and national security. They include the making of laws, the administration of justice, and the establishment

---

16. The exceptions are the consolidation of house furnishing repairs with household services into a single category (ICP 4.530), and the consolidation of miscellaneous transport into local transport (ICP 6.310). These changes were made because some countries could not break out expenditures for these categories separately and because price comparisons for them are difficult.

17. Musgrave (1969); see also Samuelson (1969).

Table 2-1. Government per Capita Expenditures Transferred to Final Consumption Expenditures of Population, 1975

Country (currency unit)	Health (1)	Recreation and culture (2)	Education (3)	Welfare (4)	Total transfer from SNA government (5)	Rent subsidy (6)
Africa						
Kenya (shillings)	39.70	0.00	112.25	0.00	151.95	0.00
Malawi (kwacha)	1.40	0.37	2.62	0.17	4.56	0.35
Zambia (kwacha)	7.43	1.61	18.27	0.00	27.31	0.40
Asia						
India (rupees)	6.45	1.18	16.20	2.27	26.10	0.00
Iran (rials)	1,258.32	546.70	3,093.89	232.12	5,131.02	0.00
Japan (yen)	5,629.00	2,160.00	51,503.00	6,489.00	65,782.00	1,102.00
Korea (won)	205.24	33.36	5,285.88	167.46	5,691.94	0.00
Malaysia (ringgit)	26.59	1.17	79.43	0.00	107.20	0.00
Pakistan (rupees)	10.82	0.00	21.09	0.00	31.91	0.00
Philippines (pesos)	19.92	3.61	55.50	1.45	80.48	11.31
Sri Lanka (rupees)	23.41	0.59	46.38	4.89	75.28	0.00
Syria (pounds)	5.03	3.81	53.84	0.00	62.68	0.00
Thailand (baht)	25.01	1.17	:186.58	4.01	216.77	0.00
Europe						
Austria (schillings)	3,398.94	329.79	2,740.69	570.48	7,039.90	0.00
Belgium (francs)	0.00	0.00	12,420.97	0.00	12,420.97	381.70
Denmark (kroner)	1,453.75	0.00	3,364.62	0.00	4,818.38	142.49
France (francs)	0.00	0.00	967.77	0.00	967.77	56.29
Germany (DM)	0.00	0.00	606.27	0.00	606.27	13.75
Hungary (forint)	1,401.86	446.73	1,242.48	190.49	3,281.56	332.89
Ireland (pounds)	65.18	0.00	51.64	0.00	116.81	9.45
Italy (lire)	0.00	0.00	95,343.00	0.00	95,343.00	0.00
Luxembourg (francs)	0.00	0.00	10,180.55	0.00	10,180.55	0.00
Netherlands (guilders)	0.00	0.00	973.94	0.00	973.94	68.81
Poland (zlote)	1,462.23	127.95	1,838.37	46.44	3,474.99	378.26
Romania (lei)	507.41	122.24	594.45	24.99	1,249.09	0.00
Spain (pesetas)	4,123.80	344.76	2,333.44	1,961.45	8,763.45	25.90
U.K. (pounds)	72.86	0.00	86.14	0.00	159.00	18.77
Yugoslavia (N. dinars)	1,001.74	515.37	1,010.79	226.85	2,754.75	4.33
Latin America and Caribbean						
Brazil (cruzeiros)	44.61	6.23	196.04	0.00	246.88	2.09
Colombia (pesos)	159.33	12.49	490.48	137.54	799.85	0.00
Jamaica (dollars)	21.71	.29	44.45	2.60	69.05	0.00
Mexico (pesos)	387.11	0.0	584.20	0.00	971.32	21.98
Uruguay (N. pesos)	28.40	7.91	62.94	0.00	99.25	0.00
North America						
U.S. (dollars)	144.67	14.92	367.97	31.45	559.01	3.75

and maintenance of standards where necessary to promote the public welfare, as in foods and drugs, medical practice, and education.

It is less clear where insurance-type expenditures should be classified. Social security was included as part of the level of living by a U.N. expert committee,[18] and some forms of security, such as life and health insurance, can be purchased individually in many Western countries. On the other hand, the largely governmental character of the bulk of these services in most countries points to the classification of private

insurance schemes with government. In ICP practice, household net expenditures on life insurance (estimated service charges) were left in consumption as a matter of expediency; in view of the small magnitude of these expenditures in most countries other than the United States, it did not seem worthwhile to make the necessary adjustments.

The other major ICP modification of the SNA does change total GDP. All rent subsidies extended by government to households have been added to gross rents and to the SNA concept of GDP. The importance of these subsidies in many countries relative to the value of gross rents paid by tenants (or imputed to households) would lead to a distortion in the pattern of final

18. United Nations (1954), p. 80.

expenditure if they were excluded. A corresponding adjustment to rents paid—that is, in the price of housing space—is made in developing the purchasing power parities for the countries affected.

The three major components of GDP—consumption, capital formation, and government—were divided into 36 summary and 151 detailed categories.[19] The 151-category breakdown required a substantial expansion of the detail provided in the SNA. The way in which the detailed categories—108 in consumption, 38 in capital formation, and 5 in government—are combined to constitute summary categories and the content of the detailed categories can be seen by examining the ICP classification in the appendix to this chapter.

Accounting Problems

Before the details of the Phase III expenditure data are considered, some conceptual and accounting problems and difficulties that may diminish the international comparability of the data should be noted.

TREATMENT OF NET PURCHASES OF RESIDENTS ABROAD. In principle, the consumption-expenditures-of-the-population (CEP) total, like the SNA total or private consumption expenditure, should include the consumption expenditure of residents both within and outside the domestic territory and should exclude the consumption expenditure of nonresidents within the domestic territory. In the SNA it is recommended that the breakdown of consumption expenditure refer to purchases within the domestic territory only and that an overall adjustment be made for net purchases of residents abroad.

The data on the CEP supplied by many of the ICP countries are based on the domestic concept of expenditure rather than the national concept recommended in the SNA. As a consequence, there is a certain noncomparability in the consumption concepts between the countries. However, countries for which net purchases of residents abroad is important tend to report it as a separate entry that can be added to total consumption in the territory to give consumption of residents, which is comparable to what countries not reporting net purchases provide.

The main problem is how correctly to add net purchases to consumption. Clearly, one way is to eliminate net purchases as a separate category by distributing it to the detailed consumption categories. However, data on this distribution have been made available only by one or two countries.

The present approach differs somewhat from that followed in Phase II, in which the net purchases were simply added to consumption in international dollars after taking exchange rates as the PPP for this category. The former treatment does not seem symmetrical with the treatment of exports less imports (ICP 19), where the exchange rate is used to provide "notional" quantities,[20] which are then valued at the international price for the exports less imports. The latter is the supercountry weighted exchange-rate–deviation index. In the present report, the international price of exports less imports has been used to value net purchases of residents abroad. This has the advantage of treating these expenditures identically in both categories; it has the drawback that it may not treat consumption comparably between countries that do and do not report net purchases.

TREATMENT OF FINAL CONSUMPTION EXPENDITURES OF PRIVATE NONPROFIT INSTITUTIONS. A similar problem arises in the treatment of final consumption expenditure of private nonprofit institutions serving households.[21] In the SNA there is no provision for an independent breakdown by object of such expenditure or for the distribution of the total to the appropriate categories of private final consumption expenditure. Instead, this expenditure is recorded in the form of an overall addition to the final consumption expenditure of households that for ICP purposes is assigned to "other services, n.e.s." (ICP 08.400). As a result, quantity comparisons for the other services category reported below are not reliable: other categories of consumption are slightly understated in countries with relatively large reported expenditures on the other-services category, and they are probably slightly overestimated in countries with relatively small reported miscellaneous expenditures. Of course, aggregate consumption and GDP are not affected.

TREATMENT OF PURCHASES OF HOTELS, RESTAURANTS, AND THE LIKE. According to the SNA, all expenditures of households in hotels, restaurants, and

---

19. In the Summary Tables of Chapter 6, fifty aggregates are given involving thirty-five summary categories. The excluded category is changes in stocks (ICP 18.000), which is separately provided in the detailed Appendix Tables to Chapter 6; ICP 18.000 can be derived from the Summary Tables by subtracting construction and producer durables from domestic capital formation.

20. See Chapter 3, the section "Aggregation of Category Expenditures and Prices" for an explanation of "notional" quantities and the section "Supercountry Weighting" for an explanation of supercountries.

21. For a description of the composition of the expenditures of these institutions see U.N. Statistical Office (1968), p. 89.

similar establishments should be recorded together as part of the major expenditure category "other goods and services, n.e.s." A footnote in the SNA indicates that it is desirable to have outlays on food, beverages, and tobacco also recorded separately. This is a change from the former SNA, in which the individual elements of such expenditure were to be allocated to the appropriate individual categories. In accordance with the present SNA, the ICP classification provides separate categories for all final (nonbusiness) expenditures in restaurants and cafés (ICP 08.310) and in hotels and similar lodging places (ICP 08.320).

STATISTICAL DISCREPANCY.   When a country places the statistical discrepancy in its income breakdown, the implication is that the expenditure approach provides a better measure of its GDP. No problem is created for the ICP in this instance; the expenditure breakdown is simply used. When the discrepancy is entered in the expenditure breakdown, however, the implication is that the income total is the more reliable measure of its GDP and that the total of expenditures either overstates or understates GDP by the amount of the statistical discrepancy. In these cases, the ICP allocated the statistical discrepancy to the various expenditure categories. Advantage was taken of whatever information was available for the inclusion or exclusion of ICP categories in the prorating. For example, the relatively firm estimates of public final consumption expenditure and of net exports of goods and services were usually maintained at their original values—that is, they were excluded from the prorating.

PROBLEMS CREATED BY BUSINESS AND GOVERNMENT PAYMENTS FOR CONSUMER GOODS.   In some countries radio and television is provided in whole or in part by government. In other countries it is provided by direct listener charges, and in others almost entirely at business cost through advertising. Since no adjustments have been attempted for this in the entertainment category, quantity comparisons may be misleading. However, the effect on overall GDP is apt to be very small. It has been estimated, for example, that the gross benefit of television to U.S. consumers in 1975, as measured by the cost of producing and broadcasting television entertainment, was $3.67 billion[22] ($17.19 per capita). The net benefit, calculated by deducting the cost to consumers of owning and operating their television receivers during commercials, was estimated at $1.88 billion ($8.82 per capita).[23]

22. Throughout this book billion refers to thousand million.
23. These 1975 estimates were provided by John E. Cremeans of the U.S. Department of Commerce. For a discussion of the problems and further estimates see his paper (1979).

In other sectors where consumers do pay part of the cost, as in government-subsidized housing, the detailed quantity comparisons will be correct as long as the price recorded for ICP purposes is the same as that embodied in the expenditures. However, when the detailed categories are aggregated, the use of the subsidized expenditure figure will lead to an underestimate of the social importance of that category. Subsidized commodities and services also create a difference between the relative purchasing power of currency from the standpoint of household and from the standpoint of the nation as a whole. All other things being equal, the purchasing power of money income will be greater for a consumer whose government absorbs a greater share of the total social expenditure on medical and educational services and other consumer goods. If such comparisons are to be made, however, they should be based on money incomes after direct taxes. (The burden of indirect taxes is included in the market prices compared by the ICP.) For the general measure of the relative purchasing power of currencies, it is purchasing power over goods and services for the society as a whole that is generally reported by the ICP. However, measures of purchasing power for households, which treat goods at prices actually paid by households (including zero prices), are offered in Chapter 6.

The Price Data

In principle, an international price comparison would be based on a random sample of the price relatives (that is, the ratio of one country's price to the other's price) of the commodities and services in the overlapping set of products found in the countries. Of course, the character of such a random sample of the population of overlapping items being sampled would be unambiguous only if the different countries had identical products, each of which were purchased in the same frequency from country to country. Identity of goods is extremely unlikely, and the near certainty is that some items in the overlapping set are purchased more often in one country than in the others.

The Sampling of Price Ratios

In the real world, to approximate any such ideal scheme for random sampling would be difficult, if not impossible. In ICP practice the initial choice of the specifications was guided by three considerations.

First, as a matter of practical convenience, a stratified sample based on a traditional final-product classification was chosen. The classification was, however, modified with a view toward reducing the dispersion of international price relatives within categories. Much of this was based on a priori expectations. For example, the category of purchased transport was broken down into local and long-distance transport, and the latter was further disaggregated into train, bus, and airplane transport. However, in a few cases in which similar price relationships seemed likely to prevail, different SNA categories were consolidated. For example, the repair categories in furniture, furnishings, and household equipment and operation, which are included in the SNA separately for each subgroup (that is, for furniture, for appliances, and for other subgroups), were combined into one detailed category, thus reducing the need for pricing work. Experience with the actual dispersion of price relatives in Phases I and II was used to modify some of the classifications. For example, first- and second-level teachers were consolidated into a single category. Also, weights within detailed categories, even very approximate ones if necessary, were introduced. See the Chapter 3 section "Aggregation at the Detailed-Category Level."

Second, a set of minimum targets for the number of specifications to be priced in each detailed category was determined initially on the basis of the relative importance of the categories in the GDPs of five or six countries for which information was available in the early planning stage. The roughly proportional sampling ratios then were modified in light of the expected degree of dispersion of price relatives within the categories. For example, only one or two specifications were provided for relatively homogeneous categories such as eggs and butter, whereas five were called for in a heterogeneous category such as men's and boys' hosiery, underwear, and nightwear.

Third, the selection of specific items within the detailed categories was governed by two principles. The first was the criterion of "concentrated selection"—that is, the selection of the goods with the largest expenditure weights was adopted. The advantage of this rule is that it produces a large coverage of the expenditures within each category at a low cost, and thus it diminishes the likelihood of sampling error attributable to omitted items.

However, concentrated sampling has significant disadvantages for ICP purposes. In the first place, it yields an unambiguous rule for the selection of items only if applied to the expenditure of one country. When used in this fashion, however, it is likely to produce a sample of items some of which will fall outside the overlapping sets referred to above. Even if applied from the standpoint of one country to the items within the overlapping set, concentrated sampling will bias the price comparisons so as to produce lower relative prices

for the country whose expenditures are used as the basis for the selection of items.[24] This is due to the inverse correlation between price relatives and quantity relatives. The second disadvantage of concentrated selection is that it is likely to lead to an underrepresentation of the items of low importance within each group.[25] If the price relatives are markedly different for low- and high-volume items, this will bias the results.

The second principle governing the selection of items was that each specification chosen had to be important or at least in common use in the consumption of each country. The idea is to avoid the selection of items that, although they can be found in a given country, will be so uncommon as to provide an unrepresentative basis for price comparisons for the category in which they fall. This means that each specification should be typical for the category in each of the countries with respect to volume of sales, sources of supply (domestic versus foreign), and any other factors that affect relative price formation. It means also that care must be taken to avoid price gathering in outlets catering to the minority with extremely high or extremely low income in the population.

Although an effort was made to keep the representative goods similar as the price collection was extended to successive countries, the satisfaction of the criteria of concentrated selection and common use, as well as the practical need to make maximal use of data available without special fieldwork, resulted in variations from one country to another in the number and identity of the representative goods chosen for a given detailed category.

In 1970, for example, although four kinds of fish were priced in Japan, the list did not include carp, which was a common fish in Hungary and India, because, with few exceptions, the Japanese consume only sea fish. Again, broadcloth shorts were priced in the European countries, and cotton briefs in Kenya. In this case, both styles were common in both areas, but prices that were already available were used. As a practical matter, countries naturally sought to use as many as possible of the prices available from their regular price work to meet the ICP target number of prices in each category (see Tables 2-3 to 2-6).

The Diversification of the Specifications

The price collection effort in Phase I almost as a matter of practical necessity took specifications and prices available in the United States as a starting point.

---

24. Brady and Hurwitz (1957).
25. Ibid.

As other countries were studied, many specifications were added as a result of their suggestions and some old ones deleted, so that by the end of Phase II less than half of the specifications were based on U.S. descriptions.[26] With the addition of a still larger number of countries in Phase III, it was possible to accelerate the movement toward a world system of price collection having regional lists of items yet retaining substantial overlap across regions so as to make interregional comparisons meaningful. This was accomplished by the exchange of proposed specification lists between regional numéraire countries and the ICP, exchanges of samples, and visits of pricing experts to individual countries.

Some regional meetings of countries were also held. At a meeting in Vienna in 1976, attended by the fifteen Phase III countries in Europe, a preliminary list of consumer-goods specifications was clarified and amended. Smaller meetings were held in Europe on construction and producer-durables specifications. Representatives of ten Asian countries participating in Phase III met in New Delhi in December 1976 and agreed on a number of new specifications for consumption items. In addition, discussions were held on producer durables and construction. It was not feasible to hold meetings of the remaining Phase III countries, but this model is being carried into the Phase IV work, and meetings are planned for other regions, too.

An important consequence of the extensive diversification of the sources of the specifications is that U.S. prices were available for a much smaller proportion of them: less than 50 percent of the consumption items compared with 88 percent in Phases I and II. This is not as true for construction and producer durables, but there has been a substantial movement toward broadening the sources of specifications for these categories, too.

The result of these principles and procedures was that the tableau of prices (items in the rows, countries in the columns) was incompletely filled. This posed a major problem for the production of transitive comparisons involving many countries. The ICP method of comparing prices in these circumstances is described in Chapter 3.

The Matching Problem

After the decisions about the selection of specifications were made, each price collected was subject to close scrutiny to ensure that qualities were really equivalent in the countries being compared.

The specification itself was the focal point for the work of quality matching. An example of a simple specification used in the ICP is the one for eggs: "fresh chicken eggs, large size (weighing at least 680.4 grams per dozen), white or brown shell. Not the best quality, but close to it. The white is less thick and high than the best quality: the yolk must be firm, high, and not easily broken."

Sometimes, as in the case of the egg specifications, it could be assumed that anything meeting the specification in one country could be considered equal in quality to anything meeting the specification in another country. This was true for most foods. For most other goods, no brief specification could define the product with sufficient precision to ensure such a result; each specification narrowed the range of products, to be sure, but it still covered a variety of qualities.

An important means of coping with this problem was for U.N. price experts to visit the participating countries to resolve questions about matching. For consumer goods, the U.N. expert could visit shops with national price experts to identify matching items. The U.N. expert dealing with capital goods could often examine a more extensive set of catalogue materials than it was feasible to send to New York. Experts for both kinds of goods could also benefit from the knowledge of the national experts and sometimes in return offer useful suggestions for the collection of prices that were not readily available. Experts from virtually all of the participating countries also visited the United States or a regional numéraire country.

The visits helped also to clear away misunderstandings arising from differences in terminology. In Japan, for example, "cashmere" refers to a weave rather than to a yarn, as in the United States and Europe. Again, in England, "ox liver" is used rather than "beef liver," the American terminology.

In their meetings, the experts sometimes decided on the substitution of new specifications for the ones that had been tentatively agreed on in advance. After these meetings, further specifications usually had to be prepared and new prices gathered.

The experts often carried samples or sent them ahead, and returned with other samples to aid in the completion of the matching process. The samples usually were for grains, dried vegetables, tobacco, apparel, footwear, textiles, stationery, or small housewares. In the case of consumer and producer durables, the brochures of the producers played a large role. The aid of buyers for large stores, manufacturers, and trade

---

26. Kravis, Heston, Summers (1978a), p. 32.

associations also was obtained in determining matching specifications.

Matching Methods

In the matching process, several different methods were relied upon. They are set out in the following paragraphs.

PHYSICAL IDENTITY. The preferred method was to find goods that were physically identical in each of the countries. This was substantially the situation for many foods. Among nonfoods, also, comparison of prices for physically identical goods sometimes could be made, particularly when the same models of a given brand or trademark were sold in the different countries. It has been possible for the EEC to rely on brand names because there is a wide use of the same brands across the countries, and each imported Community brand receives equal treatment in access to the market of a given member country. Consequently, the variance of price ratios tends to be less within the EEC if, say, an electric mixer is specified as a brand, than if it is described by specifications. For the broader group of ICP countries, the opposite is true, because any particular brand will have very unusual prices for reasons of customs, trade restraints, and the like, while a functional specification will produce price ratios with less variation. For some producer durables (items such as earth-moving equipment), more reliance could be placed in brand names by the ICP than in consumption.

EQUIVALENCE IN QUALITY. More usually, however, identical commodities could not be found. In a number of cases, there were products in different countries that conformed to the same general specification but had small differences in design or composition that seemed to be relatively unimportant or offsetting with respect to cost. If such differences were deemed unlikely to affect the country to country price ratios, they were ignored. For example, a Japanese polyester cotton broadcloth with a thread count of 116 by 72 was taken as comparable to a U.S. one with a thread count of 128 by 72.

REPLICATION OF PRODUCT. In general, the end product was regarded as the touchstone in assessing equivalence in quality, and different prices were compared for equivalent goods even though different means of production were used in different countries. Ready-made men's suits, for example, are most common in the United States and are cheaper than tailor-made garments, whereas in India the opposite was true. In this case, a U.S. ready-made garment equivalent in quality to each Indian tailored garment was identified. This effort involved an exchange of cloth samples and consultations with cloth manufacturers in both countries, tailors in India, and ready-made–clothing manufacturers in the United States.

EQUIVALENCE IN USE. A number of cases were encountered in which things were not physically identical but clearly served the same need or use. For example, in the United States, 120-volt bulbs are common, whereas in many other countries 240-volt bulbs are the norm. It appears that there would be little or no difference in the cost of production were the two types of bulbs produced under similar conditions in the same country, and because no difference exists in the utility afforded by them, they were treated as equivalent products. In some instances, the establishment of equivalence required a larger leap in judgment than in the case of light bulbs. For example, the "tomato" ketchup specification was broadened to cover ketchup sauces from other fruits or vegetables more readily available in certain countries, such as bananas in the Philippines and pumpkins in India.

PRICE ADJUSTMENT. In some cases in which the quality in a given country was not directly comparable to the quality in the reference country, a price adjustment was made to raise or lower the price in one country by the amount appropriate to the difference in quality. The amount of the adjustment was based on differences between the market prices or costs for the two qualities. Ideally, the adjustments should have been made in each country's prices in turn, because the percentage difference in prices or costs between the two specifications would not necessarily be the same in the two countries. The required information generally was easier to obtain for the numéraire country, however, and the adjustments usually were made in terms of that country's prices. Costs were used widely in construction to adjust for such differences as the inclusion of a basement in the price estimated in one country and its absence in that of another country. An analogous treatment was made for many items of producer durables.

REGRESSION METHOD. Regression methods are a means of achieving a broader and more systematic price adjustment to a common set of specifications for complicated products that appear on the market in many different models, each with its own mix of specifications. These methods are described in a later section and need not be discussed here.

Before the subject of matching is dropped, mention should be made of the problems created for price comparisons when the same goods are packaged differently in different countries. Paper containers, for example, are cheaper for distribution of cream in the United States, where high wages make the collection and cleaning of used bottles expensive. Bottles are cheaper for distributions in other countries, where paper products are costly. The solution was to treat cartons and bottles containing the same quality and quantity of cream as equivalent and directly comparable. This could be regarded as an instance of taste equivalency.

Where two types of packaging of a product exist side by side in both countries, with one more expensive than the other in both countries, the different packaging was treated as representing different qualities. Rice, for example, is sold in both boxes and bags in Europe and the United States, with the box packaging consistently the more expensive. In such cases, the packaging was part of the specification, and prices were compared only for similarly packaged products.

Unique Goods and Empty Categories

When price comparisons are made on the basis of a sample of representative goods of equivalent quality, as has been outlined above, expenditures on other goods are in effect transferred to the expenditure on the representative goods in the same category. In direct price comparisons the effect of such transfers is to raise the quantities of the representative goods by the same proportion as their expenditure has been increased. In direct quantity comparisons, the quantities must be increased explicitly by the same proportion as expenditures; otherwise, the implicit price relationships would be distorted.

In an earlier study,[27] "unique" goods were defined as goods available only in one of the countries in a binary comparison. Because unique goods are omitted from the list of representative goods, expenditures on them are transferred to representative items, as described in the previous paragraph.

If unique goods are pervasive, special methods for handling them must be developed. Among the developed countries, few unique products are found that play any major role in consumption, and, from the standpoint of international comparisons, it is fortunate that such goods are becoming less and less frequent—though it may make for a duller world.

When multilateral comparisons—those involving a number of countries at once—are considered, the number of unique goods is relatively small, and they are not likely to be important to the expenditure of

27. Gilbert and Kravis (1954).

any country. Small dwellings (with a floor area of, say, fifteen square meters), not substantially built, and without running water or electricity, are unique in India in a binary comparison with the United States. However, once the comparison is made multilateral and other low-income countries are included, the uniqueness disappears. As has been noted, methods have been developed to include specifications that are common to some countries though absent in others (see Chapter 3).

Country Data Collection

A discussion of the overall consumer price sample follows, but it will be preceded by a brief description of the collection procedures for the different countries. These descriptions of price collection are based on information supplied by the countries or by ICP staff who took part in the work. More space has been given in these descriptions to new ICP countries and to Phase II countries that undertook new methods of item selection or price collection.

AUSTRIA. Austria, which served as the regional numéraire country for Europe, played a central role in drawing up the list of items to be priced in Phase III in Europe. In addition to this work, the Austrian Central Statistical Office carried out a special binary comparison with Poland that was complementary to its ICP participation. Austria made substantial use of its regular consumer-price specifications and undertook a number of special price surveys.

BRAZIL. Brazil served as the Latin American numéraire country. The Getúlio Vargas Foundation, which was the coordinating agency for work in Brazil, obtained most of the prices from the Instituto Brasileiro de Geografía e Estatística (IBGE), the main price-collecting agency in Brazil. In a country as diverse as Brazil, calculation of national average prices is a major task. As part of its regular price collection IBGE in its National Inquiry on Prices collected food prices in twenty-four centers, while in the regional centers of São Paulo, Porto Alegre, Recife, and Belo Horizonte other prices were collected by research institutes. Special collections for the ICP were carried out in November 1975 in eleven cities in Brazil, mostly for nonfood items of consumption, and average national prices were estimated.

COLOMBIA. Price collection for the ICP was carried out by the Departamento Administrativo Nacional de Estadística (DANE) in seven regions of Colombia, where prices were collected in November 1975 for about 230 items in urban areas and 60 items in rural areas. Average rural and urban prices were separately calculated and combined into a national average with the aid of population weights. The prices were adjusted to annual average 1975.

EUROPEAN ECONOMIC COMMUNITY. For consumption the nine countries of the EEC conducted a special price survey in autumn 1975 covering over 660 consumer goods and services in the capital city of each country. The Statistical Office of the European Community (SOEC) provided the ICP with the published and unpublished prices from this survey. Those items provided by national statistical offices were collected by their staff, while prices for special items (about half the total) were collected by an international team organized by SOEC. Generally, one to ten observations were collected for each specification, usually in several outlets. For certain ICP categories, for which it was necessary to fill out the sample, additional prices were specially requested from member countries. Adjustments were made at ICP to bring these prices to annual average national prices. Annual prices were estimated from movements of group price indexes from autumn 1975 for each country. The SOEC, on the basis of special surveys, provided coefficients for all of consumption relating capital-city to national average prices. The price adjustments made with the use of these coefficients by the ICP in New York were sent to SOEC for review.

The method of drawing up price lists in the EEC emphasized obtaining overlapping items for each possible comparison for all the pairs of countries. Prices were not necessarily collected for all EEC countries for each item. Somewhere between 340 and 410 items were priced in each country.

In a number of categories SOEC priced more items than were incorporated in the world ICP list. This was in part because the items were specific to the EEC or Europe and in part because SOEC used narrower specifications than the ICP. One aspect of this was that SOEC treated different sizes and packages as separate items, whereas the ICP did not. The SOEC also treated different brands of appliances meeting the same ICP specifications as separate items. There are other instances in which SOEC treated an ICP specification as consisting of a number of items. For example, SOEC could distinguish four types of apples in its countries.

The ICP could not follow such a practice on a worldwide basis because of the very large number of varieties. It seemed that the greater specification detail involved in intra-EEC prices (compared with EEC-ICP matches) provided a strong reason for their use in comparisons within the EEC. It was decided therefore to use all of the SOEC prices for comparisons within the EEC, and to use a smaller set of these prices to compare with the remaining ICP countries. Even the smaller number used in the comparisons of EEC with other countries tended to be larger than the number of specifications employed for most countries (see Table 2-2).

The procedure used in Phase III for most categories in connection with EEC data may be illustrated in the drugs category (ICP 5.11). The EEC compared prices for forty-five carefully chosen drugs in various package sizes, while the ICP list involved thirty-nine carefully chosen drugs used widely around the world. However, only eight items on the two lists overlapped. This overlap was quite adequate to link the EEC with Europe and the rest of the world, and this was done by the country-product–dummy (CPD) methods discussed in Chapter 3. However, the overlapping EEC-ICP list produced PPPs within the EEC that were different from and probably less reliable than those based on all forty-five EEC items. In these circumstances an average PPP for the SOEC countries was first estimated on the basis of the overlapping EEC-ICP list. (The average PPP for the EEC was derived from a world [thirty-four–country] CPD. See Chapter 3.) The intra-EEC PPPs for the nine EEC countries were computed in a comparable way by SOEC on the basis of all their drug prices. The intra-EEC results were then linked to the world PPPs. Assume, for example, that in the context of the world comparisons the average price level (PPP/exchange rate) of the EEC was 110 relative to 100 for the world numéraire country or area. If within the EEC the price level of Italy relative to the EEC came to 80, Italy relative to the world numéraire would be 88 (110 × 80 ÷ 100).

HUNGARY. As part of the regular price work, the Central Statistical Office in Hungary collected prices for 2,300 items in 6 percent of all outlets twice monthly. In addition to Budapest and ninety cities, one-eighth of the 3,000 communes were covered. This regular survey produced national average annual prices and was sufficient for the majority of ICP prices. Where ICP requirements were not met from the regular collection, a special survey was taken.

INDIA. India served as the numéraire country for Asia. Price collection was more systematic in Phase III than in the earlier phases. There was a larger reliance on the National Sample Survey Organization (NSSO). The NSSO and the Central Statistical Organization are both part of the Department of Statistics of India, which provided all data to the ICP. Prices were collected for 314 items by NSSO in thirty-eight villages and nineteen urban centers, with one quotation per village and three per urban center. The NSSO field staff were not able to locate a number of items (for example, ready-made clothing) in village markets. Further, some cloth specifications had technical characteristics (thread count and weight) that the enumerator could not identify or that were not available in the markets. In these cases, the field staff relied on a smaller number of centers.

Price collection was carried out in May 1978. Simple averages of prices were calculated separately for rural and urban areas, and then adjusted by rural and urban group indexes back to 1975, actually 1975–76. (The Indian fiscal year for national accounts is April 1 through March 30, which contains the major source of annual variation in output—namely, the fall harvest.) The rural and urban prices were then averaged by using quantity weights based on expenditure surveys.

IRAN. For the Phase II comparisons, the Bank Markazi in Iran had made substantial collections of prices that were put on a national-average basis, either by population-weighted averages of thirty-five city prices or, in the case of Teheran items, by group relations of Teheran prices to national averages. New 1975 prices were collected for a few items in October 1975 and adjusted to an annual national average. In the bulk of the cases the 1973 prices of Phase II were updated to 1975 by either item or group indexes.

JAMAICA. Most ICP prices in Jamaica were obtained from prices gathered by the Department of Statistics for its three consumer price indexes relating to Kingston, to twenty-eight other urban centers, and to twenty-seven communities in rural areas. The household expenditure survey of 1971–72 was used as a basis for weights to combine prices from these sources into national averages. Special collection was carried out in 1977 for items not in the consumer price indexes, and these prices were extrapolated back to 1975 by movements of related items between 1977 and 1975.

JAPAN. The Phase III survey has been described in a report of the Study Group on the ICP in Japan in cooperation with the Statistics Bureau, Prime Minister's Office.[28] For those of the 485 regularly priced specifications that could be used by the ICP, the Statistics Bureau computed a national average price from data collected in the 168 cities, towns, and villages constituting the CPI samples. The weights were drawn from data on expenditures by category and number of households.

28. Administrative Management Agency (1977).

Special price surveys for other items were conducted in Tokyo, Nagoya, and Osaka in June and July 1976. A simple average of the prices in these cities was calculated and converted to a national average on the basis of the relation of prices in these cities to the national average for similar items or groups. The national average price was then put on a calendar-1975 basis by appropriate group or item indexes.

KENYA. The Central Bureau of Statistics was able to supply a number of items from its regular collection. Where prices were available in several centers an average was calculated by use of population weights. In many cases these prices represent provincial centers, such as Mombasa and Kusumu, and direct rural prices were not used. For the most important item, cornmeal, regulated prices prevailed in urban and rural areas, and could be used for ICP purposes. But for fresh produce the estimated national price may not reflect rural markets adequately.

Additional prices were collected, largely in Nairobi. Unfortunately, it did not prove possible to obtain as many consumer prices for Kenya as desired, given the use of Kenya as a numéraire country for Africa.

REPUBLIC OF KOREA. Regular consumer price collection in the Republic of Korea was carried out for about 350 items in 1975 in forty-nine centers by the National Bureau of Statistics of the Economic Planning Board. Those items that could be used for the ICP were averaged by use of population weights. Items specially collected for the ICP by the Economic Planning Board were priced in Seoul. The National Accounts Division of the Bank of Korea provided expenditure data and other information.

MALAWI. Regular price collection in Malawi is confined to urban areas and, since the country is highly rural, only a small proportion of the total consumption of basic items is covered. From May through October 1976, rural prices for about 100 items were specially collected in the southern centers and northern regions by the National Statistical Office. About 40 percent of the items were foods, 39 percent clothing and footwear, 20 percent household supplies, and 5 percent items in the remaining ICP categories. These regional rural prices were averaged by use of population weights.

More complete pricing was undertaken in the urban centers of Blantyre, Lilongwe, and Zomba. In addition, average prices of smaller centers were included, their weight being that of other urban places. In computing national average prices for items where both urban and rural prices for an item were available, expenditure weights based on a national expenditure survey were used. These 1976 prices were then moved back to 1975 on the basis of item or group indexes.

MALAYSIA. A very large number of the ICP items were available from the extensive consumer price collection in Malaysia conducted by the Department of Statistics. Prices are collected in forty-nine centers, and a national average price was computed by use of population weights. Special price collections were carried out in Kuala Lumpur.

MEXICO. Consumer price collection in Mexico is conducted by the Dirección General de Estadística in the capital cities of each state and in Mexico City. To obtain national average prices it was necessary to obtain an average of the various urban prices and to take account of rural prices. The adjustment for rural prices was done roughly on the basis of a sample survey of forty common items in rural areas linked to several of the major provincial cities. From these rural and urban prices, adjustment factors were obtained to move from urban average to national average prices.

PAKISTAN. The Statistical Division found that a large number of the ICP items could be obtained from the consumer price index. Prices for the index are collected in twelve large urban centers and twenty-seven smaller centers, all of which are thought to reflect rural markets in Pakistan. For each of these items a simple average was calculated from monthly prices to obtain an annual average. Then the population of each center was used to obtain an average for the large centers and for the small centers. When prices were not reported for a smaller center, the weight of that center was excluded from the calculation, the absence of price being assumed to reflect the lack of importance of the item in expenditures.

Special collection of items was concentrated in Karachi, where the Statistical Division is headquartered. These item prices were collected in 1977 and 1978, and indexed back to 1975.

PHILIPPINES. Beyond those items available for the consumer price index from the National Census and Statistics Office, a special collection of prices in the Philippines was carried out in 189 establishments in the seven cities and municipalities of Metro Manila. At least three establishments were sampled and an average calculated in each city or municipality. A weighted average of these averages was taken as the final price. The Philippines also carried out a special survey for restaurant meals. Forty restaurants were surveyed. They were distributed among third class (five), second class (twenty-five), first class (seven),

and hotel (three), reflecting a concentration appropriate for the ICP.

POLAND. Most prices for the ICP in Poland were based on prices collected by the Central Statistical Office (CSO) for purposes of national statistics of price levels. The Research Center of the CSO prepared weighted averages for items sold in both the socialized and free-trade sectors. For consumption of self-produced items, such as duck, chicken, potatoes, plum brandy, and the like, existing household surveys provided data for estimating producer prices, which were used to value this output. Some prices, particularly for textiles, clothing, footwear, and certain consumer durable goods, were collected by the Research Center in cooperation with experts from industrial or commercial branches.

ROMANIA. All prices in Romania were supplied by the Central Statistical Office. Where prices were available in both the socialized sector and in the private market, the prices were averaged. For some items of fruits and vegetables the price used for comparison was from the private market, because it was judged by the Romanians and ICP staff that the quality there more closely matched the ICP specifications.

SPAIN. Regular price collection of the Instituto Nacional de Estadística involves about 270 locations, including centers less than 2,000 in population, for food items, and 56 locations, including the 50 provincial capitals, for other items. Special pricing, which was done in cooperation with the ICP and the SOEC, was carried out in five cities and usually at least three quotations were obtained per city. Some of the special prices were gathered in 1976; these were deflated back to 1975.

SRI LANKA. The Department of Census and Statistics carried out a special survey of prices for 334 items in the five centers of Colombo (28.1 percent of the population), Galle (9.4 percent), Jafna (10.2 percent), Kandy (39.7 percent), and Anapadhapura (12.6 percent), in March and April 1976. In many cases, 1975 prices could also be collected and were directly used. Otherwise, prices for 1976 were moved back to 1975 by the relation for that item in one of the centers, or by national group indexes.

SYRIA. Syria could match with ICP specifications about 130 items from the prices regularly collected by the Central Bureau of Statistics. Prices were averaged across the thirteen provinces, through use of population weights. In a special ICP collection for about

200 items not in the regular survey, population weights were assigned to the chief center, other urban centers, and rural areas. The special collection was carried out by the regular price survey staff during 1978, and the estimated national average prices were put on a 1975 basis by use of some direct information, as well as price movements of related items or indexes.

THAILAND. A special pricing survey was undertaken in early 1976 in the north, northeast, central east, south, and Bangkok regions by the National Economic and Social Development Board. The survey included about 500 items of consumption, as well as a rent survey. The regional prices were collected in rural and urban areas and a population-weighted average was calculated for all of Thailand.

UNITED STATES. Almost 95 percent of the prices for the United States were provided directly by the Bureau of Labor Statistics (BLS), Office of Prices and Living Conditions. Some were in the form of regularly published CPI prices for food. The rest were based on price information used in the compilation of indexes of consumer prices for urban wage and clerical workers, twice-yearly inventory pricing, and prices specially collected for the ICP. Except for the last category, prices relate to fifty-six standard metropolitan statistical areas. The special price collection was done in four cities: New York, San Francisco, Milwaukee, and Dallas, in June–July 1977. In addition, some prices were collected directly by the ICP, from mail or phone solicitations, from published sources, and from unpublished BLS materials—for example, restaurant menus. The number of prices provided from each source is as follows:

Regular food prices, BLS	90
Regular CPI, BLS	222
LIFO ("last in, first out" inventory accounting), BLS	51
Special BLS collection	103
Prices from BLS mail schedules (water and sewage rates, taxi fares, and the like)	45
Collected by ICP from other published sources (magazine prices, postal rates, and the like)	30
Total	541

BLS expenditure survey weights and U.S. population weights were used to calculate national average prices, and the ICP itself developed a national average sales tax, by expenditure group, from state sales-tax records and population weights. 1977 prices were adjusted to the year 1975 through the use of regularly published indexes.

URUGUAY. The Dirección General de Estadística y Censos (DGEC) in Uruguay undertook the collection of prices. Of the 275 items priced, 94 came from the consumer price index, 72 came from the retail price index, and 109 were specially collected. The special collection in Uruguay was carried out in 1977 within the Montevideo district, and these prices were adjusted to 1975. It is customary in Uruguay to take the price in greater Montevideo as the national average price, but the DGEC carried out a special survey to verify for the ICP that the assumption was appropriate. The coordination and expenditure work was done by the Banco Central del Uruguay.

YUGOSLAVIA. The regular price collection of the Federal Office of Statistics, which is done in fifty-four cities and processed with the use of 1970 quantity weights, yielded about one-third of the ICP prices. For the remaining items, a special survey was conducted in towns with populations over 80,000, where at least five establishments were sampled per item. The prices for the towns were averaged with the use of estimated volume weights. For items such as milk, some alcoholic beverages, and fresh produce, in which substantial own consumption occurred, national average prices were calculated from the weighted average of prices for own-produced consumption and retail prices.

ZAMBIA. Prices regularly collected for the Central Statistical Office were obtained from three centers by correspondence with retailers. This meant that the type of price survey required by the ICP for Zambia was a major undertaking involving considerable experimentation. Because of resource limitations, most of the ICP prices were from Lusaka, and it is not certain that regional differences are fully reflected in the final prices. However, some uniformity of prices throughout the country is maintained by the government for staples, which accounted for a large portion of the transactions.

Prices for Consumption Goods

Table 2-2 summarizes the number of items priced in each country by the major ICP categories. Totals for consumption are given that both exclude and include autos and rents, which, as will be explained, are treated differently from other items. The average number of items priced, excluding autos and rents, was 365 per country. Excluding the United States where the number of priced items was intentionally reduced, the Phase II countries added 48 items per country over 1970 and 1973. Only Kenya and Colombia showed substantial reductions from Phase II.

The target number of items for each expenditure group, intended to help countries achieve what was considered minimum coverage, is also shown in the

Table 2-2. Consumer Goods Specifications Priced by Country, 1975
(number of prices received from ICP countries, excluding autos and rents)

Country	Category[a] 01	02	03	04	05	06	07	08	Total	Total including autos and rents
Target number	67	50	7	37	23	21	22	16	243	
Africa										
Kenya	80	38	8	19	3	14	14	11	187	201
Malawi	112	55	7	48	24	26	37	31	340	355
Zambia	110	59	8	43	27	27	34	16	324	333
Asia										
India	170	90	21	89	54	32	47	40	543	582
Iran	95	59	10	56	26	25	29	27	327	377
Japan	98	59	14	50	37	23	37	26	344	383
Korea	90	38	10	33	17	19	21	21	249	285
Malaysia	109	44	9	45	10	26	31	30	304	354
Pakistan	112	49	12	53	31	24	40	17	338	347
Philippines	116	56	11	55	29	30	35	48	380	421
Sri Lanka	109	56	9	52	26	24	32	29	337	353
Syria	93	47	8	31	23	21	19	21	263	271
Thailand	106	39	14	63	34	29	47	36	368	409
Europe										
Austria	158	106	18	103	35	40	58	36	554	597
Belgium	143	52	19	46	19	28	37	28	372	396
Denmark	132	45	16	43	11	26	36	26	335	354
France	138	49	19	44	17	27	37	29	360	385
Germany	139	73	19	46	17	29	38	47	408	434
Hungary	146	135	24	92	19	32	69	59	576	592
Ireland	126	63	12	32	16	28	35	27	339	360
Italy	133	54	19	43	17	26	35	28	355	376
Luxembourg	143	53	17	45	19	28	35	28	368	391
Netherlands	138	66	19	45	14	29	37	29	377	401
Poland	172	110	18	87	26	30	47	36	526	550
Romania	117	87	15	60	23	27	42	35	406	413
Spain	134	59	13	64	17	26	51	33	397	409
U.K.	136	49	17	39	14	26	34	27	342	363
Yugoslavia	125	80	15	77	37	28	48	38	448	476
Latin America and Caribbean										
Brazil	123	53	12	41	31	22	25	42	349	359
Colombia	66	42	7	34	19	23	21	17	229	280
Jamaica	98	54	10	39	22	17	21	21	282	331
Mexico	75	50	6	42	24	22	23	37	279	284
Uruguay	72	49	11	35	27	21	23	15	253	303
North America										
U.S.	153	93	15	85	33	33	51	71	534	571
Total	4,067	2,111	462	1,779	798	888	1,226	1,062	12,393	13,296
Percent	32.8	17.0	3.7	14.4	6.5	7.2	9.9	8.6	100.0	
Mean	120	62	14	52	24	26	36	31	365	391

a. The categories are: 01, food, beverages, and tobacco; 02, clothing and footwear; 03, gross rent, fuel, and power; 04, house furnishings and operations; 05, medical care; 06, transport and communications; 07, recreation, education; and 08, other goods and services.

table. Most of the countries provided prices in excess of these minimums in all the categories. The only general shortfall was in medical services.

The numbers in Table 2-3 represent the prices judged, after close scrutiny, to meet the ICP specifications. The process began with the conversion of prices to a standard ICP unit for each item (for example, most commonly a kilogram for foods). Each price was coded with ICP identification numbers for item and country and entered on a machine-readable price file. A listing of the coded prices was then sent to each country with the request that the country verify the quality comparison implied by the matching of its item to the ICP code.

Table 2-3 gives the number of consumer-goods specifications priced in each region for each major category of consumption and for total consumption. The number of specifications priced in each region is also shown as a percentage of the total number of ICP specifications. Because Asia and Europe have the largest num-

Table 2-3. Number and Percentage of Consumption Specifications Priced in Each Region

Category	Asia Number	Asia Percent	Latin America Number	Latin America Percent	Africa Number	Africa Percent	Europe Number	Europe Percent	North America Number	North America Percent	Total Number	Total Percent
Food, beverages, tobacco	281	76	192	52	164	44	267	72	151	41	371	100
Clothing, footwear	168	84	124	62	96	48	168	84	92	46	201	100
Gross rent, fuel, power	26	70	21	57	10	27	32	86	15	41	37	100
House furnishings, operations	157	68	92	40	73	31	154	66	82	35	232	100
Medical care	77	94	53	65	42	51	67	82	33	40	82	100
Transport, communications	50	82	42	69	36	59	56	92	33	54	61	100
Recreation, education	93	73	54	42	57	45	112	89	50	39	126	100
Other goods and services	85	79	66	62	39	36	83	78	71	66	107	100
Total	937	77	644	53	517	42	939	77	527	43	1,217	100

ber of countries, their coverage is significantly larger than any of the other regions. However, coverage in all of the regions is large enough to establish a significant overlap between the regions.

The distribution of the entire set of ICP specifications, priced by at least one country (excluding autos and rents) according to the number of countries pricing them is as follows:

Priced by	Number of specifications	Percent
Only 1 country or by none	109	9.0
2–5 countries	335	27.5
6–10 countries	294	24.1
11–20 countries	321	26.4
21–30 countries	124	10.2
31–34 countries	34	2.8
Total	1,217	100.0

After all the editing was completed, there were 38 specifications for which there was no price for any country and 73 for which there was a price for only one country. This left a little over 1,100 specifications for which prices were actually used. A total of 227 specifications were priced by only one region (distributed 101 in Asia, 8 in Latin America, 6 in Africa, 98 in Europe, and 14 in the United States). There were also some instances in which specifications were priced by only one country within a region but also by one or more countries outside the region.

An example of interregional overlapping without intraregional overlapping is provided by Uruguay and Iran; in both countries mattresses are commonly stuffed with wool. As the illustration suggests, a regional ef-

fort to eliminate items that are not common to all or most of the countries within the region may exclude from the list items that are common in one or more of the regional countries and in one or more countries outside the region. This consideration arose at times in the European and Asian meetings referred to earlier. It is important in future ICP work that due account be taken of the need to include in the regional lists specifications available between as well as within the regions.

Readers may be interested to know that five specifications were priced by all countries: toothpaste, tomatoes, eggs, motion-picture admissions, and postage rates.

Three kinds of computer programs were then used to check on the consumer prices. First, a comparison of matching prices for each country was made with the regional numéraire country and with the United States. The output of this Compare program includes price ratios such as yen/rupee or won/dollar, as well as conversion of these price ratios to an index number formed by dividing them by the appropriate exchange rate. Copies of the Compare printouts were sent to the countries for their scrutiny. Compare could not, however, catch all errors. A major reason was that if a country submitted, say, 350 prices, perhaps only 200 to 300 would match with items priced in the regional numéraire country or in the United States. As a consequence, a substantial number of prices would not be subject to checking by this procedure.

A second check was provided by comparing prices from all countries supplying a particular item. In this Cleanser program, each price was expressed as a ratio to the price in a numéraire country and also in price-index form by dividing the ratio by the exchange rate relative to the numéraire country. The numéraire country for an item was simply the first country in the list of the thirty-four that had a price for the item. This technique, which was also used along with Compare in Phases I and II, again proved helpful in spotting errors.

Another program used in Phase III computed average prices and the variance of prices for each item by region and for the world. The prices were normalized either by converting them all to dollars at exchange rates, or at preliminary PPPs. This program was originally designed to suggest possible items for deletion in future comparisons, but, in fact, was useful in making clear why some prices could not be used in Phase III without further clarification from the countries.

When an unusual price ratio was uncovered by these mechanical checks or by old-fashioned scanning of the data, an effort was made to ascertain the reasonableness of the prices that produced it. One of the first avenues of exploration was to ascertain whether similar ratios could be found for another category that might be expected to have similar cost conditions. For example, price ratios for men's woolen clothing might be expected to be similar to those for women's woolen clothing. For the sixteen Phase II countries, ICP 1975 prices could also be checked for consistency with prices in 1970 and 1973. Recourse was sometimes taken to alternative price sources—either national, as with a published price index, or international, such as the ILO reports on food prices, or the U.N. survey of prices paid by officials in different countries.

Many of the problem cases fell into one of several standard categories. Perhaps the most common problem was a misunderstanding about the unit to which the price referred. When no special comment about the unit was made in the country's report to the ICP, the price was assumed to be for the ICP unit (for example, price per 100 aspirins) whereas, in fact, the supplied price may have been for the common national unit (say 40 aspirins). In other cases, a low reported price was a subsidized price, and if it could be established that the expenditures also were based on that price, then it was accepted for ICP purposes. Sometimes, a two-price system existed (for example, domestic and imported butter in Iran) and the expenditures included the quantities at each price. In this case, the ICP sought the weighted average price, which countries could usually provide. In a number of cases where ICP questions were raised about prices, including service items in a number of developing countries,

the prices submitted were verified as correct and appropriate for ICP use.

There were also cases in which prices could not be used. Frequently, when countries drew up their original price list, it was thought a specification could be matched in the country and that the item was indeed commonly consumed. In a number of instances, prices submitted to the ICP turned out upon questioning to relate to items that were not usual in the country's consumption pattern. The criterion of common use in the ICP relates to the ready availability of the item in a large number of outlets in the country. It is possible to purchase almost every ICP item in each of the countries, but if an item is available in only a few outlets in the capital city, it cannot serve as a representative item for price comparisons. Among items eliminated on this criteria are rye bread in France, tonic water in the Federal Republic of Germany, vacuum cleaners in Kenya, and—surprisingly—brussels sprouts in Belgium.

Prices for Construction

For final expenditure on construction, prices are compared for whole projects, such as an office building of a certain size or a kilometer of highway. Each price pertains to a specification that consists of a brief description of the project, usually about a page in length, giving the materials to be used and the major operations to be performed.[29] Prices are compared for units such as square meters of floor area for buildings and linear kilometers for roads.

Table 2-4 summarizes the number of construction projects priced per region, along with the number of ICP specifications for each detailed category of construction. In general, the response of countries in Phase III was much improved over earlier rounds, and most countries achieved the target level of specifications. On average, the number of construction specifications priced per country was thirty-eight, or near the ICP target of two or three per category. Countries in Africa and Asia averaged over thirty specifications per country, and in Latin America and the Caribbean, a very impressive fifty-six per country. Europe averaged only twenty-eight per country, not for lack of effort, but owing to the further development of a method emphasizing the thorough costing of fewer specifications. Several countries, including Brazil, Canada, the Federal Republic of Germany, and the United Kingdom,

---

29. For a fuller exposition of the problems of comparing construction costs and of alternative methods, see Kravis, Kenessey, Heston, Summers (1975), chap. 11.

Table 2-4. Number of Specifications Priced by Detailed Category of Construction by Region

ICP *category*	Africa	Asia	Europe	Latin America	Total including U.S.	Number of ICP specifications	ICP target numbers	Average quotations per specification
10.000 Residential buildings	14	73	79	70	260	24	6	10.8
10.100 One- and two-dwelling buildings	11	40	36	36	134	11	3	12.2
10.200 Multidwelling buildings	3	33	43	34	126	13	3	9.7
11.000 Nonresidential buildings	59	199	204	137	661	62	20	10.7
11.100 Hotels, hostels, etc.	13	31	29	18	100	9	3	11.1
11.200 Industrial buildings	8	30	29	19	94	8	3	11.9
11.300 Commercial buildings	11	26	42	28	120	13	3	9.2
11.400 Office buildings	10	31	25	20	94	8	2	11.8
11.500 Educational buildings	4	26	24	18	77	5	2	15.4
11.600 Hospitals	5	23	15	9	56	4	2	14.0
11.700 Agricultural buildings	6	24	34	20	96	12	3	8.0
11.800 Other buildings	2	8	6	5	24	3	2	8.0
12.000 Other construction	22	91	142	59	339	27	10	12.6
12.100 Roads, etc.	7	24	42	18	96	6	3	16.0
12.200 Utility lines	13	58	74	33	192	15	5	12.8
12.300 Other construction	2	9	26	8	51	6	2	8.5
13.000 Land improvement	2	16	14	13	51	6	3	8.5
Total	95	379	439	279	1,311	119	39	11.0

Table 2-5. Number of Specifications Priced by Detailed Category of Producer Durables by Region

ICP *category*	Africa (1)	Asia (2)	Latin America (3)	Europe (4)	World (includes United States) (5)	Number of specifications distinguished (6)	Average number of quotations per specification (7)
14.00 Transport equipment	25	70	43	103	254	15	14.1
14.10 Railway vehicles	9	22	13	48	96	6	16.0
14.30 Trucks, buses, and trailers	4	15	12	20	54	3	18.0
14.40 Aircraft	4	7	5	12	30	2	15.0
14.50 Ships and boats	0	0	0	0	0	0	0.0
14.60 Other transport equipment	8	26	13	23	74	4	18.5
15.00 Nonelectrical machinery and equipment	136	435	254	1,067	2,016	139	14.5
15.10 Engines and turbines	5	16	7	9	40	3	13.3
15.20 Agricultural machinery and equipment	26	64	36	200	347	24	14.5
15.30 Office machinery	21	71	36	98	238	14	17.0
15.40 Metalworking machinery and equipment	15	66	33	148	279	17	16.4
15.50 Construction and mining machinery	26	75	58	177	354	19	18.6
15.60 Special industry machinery	21	47	31	180	302	30	10.1
15.70 General industry machinery	18	80	39	208	368	25	14.7
15.80 Service industry machinery	4	16	14	47	88	7	12.6
16.00 Electrical machinery and appliances	47	191	106	303	687	44	15.6
16.10 Electric transmission and distribution	13	65	30	115	237	15	15.8
16.20 Communication equipment	11	35	19	71	144	11	13.1
16.30 Other electrical equipment	12	42	30	42	135	9	15.0
16.40 Instruments	11	49	27	75	171	9	19.0
17.00 Other durable furnishings and equipment	17	83	45	143	307	19	16.2
17.10 Furniture and fixtures	12	50	26	69	166	9	18.4
17.20 Other durable goods	5	33	19	74	141	10	14.1
Total	225	779	448	1,616	3,264	217	14.8

have also been working to find better ways to compare construction costs, either intertemporally or interspatially. Both Brazil and the Statistical Office of the European Community (SOEC) came essentially to the same method, which was used by SOEC for the 1975 comparisons. The method is based on breaking construction projects down into modules, some of which, like wiring and foundation work, will enter into different construction projects. The cost of an entire project may then be obtained by summing the costs of its constituent modules.

The method seems to offer somewhat more flexibility to the countries in an area in which it has often been difficult for them to match ICP specifications or to suggest substitute specifications that could be priced elsewhere. It may also simplify the updating of results between benchmark studies by making it possible to use the time-to-time price movements in the costs of the modules, the weights being obtained from the benchmark estimates. The method is being used in the 1979 round of comparisons for nineteen Latin American countries, and present plans call for the approach to be further extended in ICP work in Phase IV.

Prices for Producer Durables

The Phase III price comparisons for producers' durables represent a substantial expansion in numbers owing to an intensification of ICP efforts in this area. More varied and clearer specifications were provided and preparatory meetings served to work out better understandings about the specifications and, in some cases, to contribute to plans for data collection. Further, the expanded international trade in producer durables and less secrecy about prices may also have made it easier for countries to supply more prices in this area.

During Phases I and II, countries priced from 18 to 63 specifications in producer durables, while in Phase III the range by region was 75 per country in Africa to 107 per country in Europe, the total being 3,264 prices for the thirty-four countries. These data and more detailed breakdowns by producer-durable category are given in Table 2-5.

As in the other sectors, a substantial effort was made to move away from the matching of each country's prices with U.S. prices. This objective could be achieved for European countries, where the SOEC established a list of items priced by its members that substantially overlapped with the ICP list, and Austria developed a substantial link with the other European countries. For countries outside of Europe, however, it often remained much simpler to match with the United States than with the regional numéraire. One objective of

Phase IV will be to develop the matching capacities of the other regional numéraire countries.

In practice, however, the effect of the United States on these comparisons is minimal, since most of the linking through the United States occurs at a fine level of detail. This point may be illustrated by a lift hoist, one of the twenty-five specifications in the general industrial machinery category (ICP 15.7). The key measurable characteristics of this item, and the ICP-suggested values, were:

Key measurable characteristic	Unit	ICP-suggested measurements
Diesel motor power/revolutions per minute (RPM)	horsepower/ RPM	50–52/2,400
Pull capacity	tons	2
Distance between center of gravity and heel of load	millimeters	500
Maximum height (telescopic)	meters	3.96
Weight (with battery)	kilograms	3,730

Twenty-six countries provided a total of seventy-two price quotations for nineteen variations of the basic lift hoist. For most of these variations, it was simple to find a U.S. price as a match, though for this item, Austria was also a base for several variations. Since the role of either Austria or the United States in this case is to provide the link for small variations in the five factors given above, their effect on the comparisons is quite marginal. Variants involving major differences were not linked in through the U.S. or Austrian prices, but were treated as separate specifications. (Among the twenty-four other items in the category were specifications for an electric forklift truck, a hand pallet truck, a goods hoist, an electrical industrial tractor, and a diesel industrial tractor.)

An examination of Table 2-5 reveals that, except for ships (ICP 14.5), most of the categories of producer durables are well represented.[30] As in the earlier phases, the PPPs for 14.5 were imputed from PPPs obtained for other transportation categories.

Because of the frequency of minor variations in specifications, it was found convenient in the data processing of producer-durable prices to express each price relative to the United States or to the regional numéraire country for purposes of further processing.

Prices for Government Services

As in the previous phases of the ICP, standard national-accounts practice was followed by valuing the

---

30. Prices representing a fair coverage of the ships category were reported to the ICP. However, it was very difficult to ensure comparability in this category, and the prices were not used to estimate PPPs.

Table 2-6. Automobile Regression Equations for Twenty-two Countries, 1975

Variable	Austria	Belgium	Brazil	Denmark	France	Germany	Hungary	Ireland	Italy
Curb weight (1,000 pounds)	—	0.3767 (0.06)	—	0.3659 (0.012)	0.3405 (0.06)	0.2973 (0.06)	—	0.3696 (0.08)	0.1916 (0.07)
Length (inches)	—	—	0.005378 (0.00467)	0.001727 (0.00153)	—	0.002552 (0.00157)	0.007475 (0.00221)	0.003330 (0.00139)	—
Width (inches)	0.03335 (0.00724)	0.01695 (0.00569)	0.02989 (0.02181)	—	0.02285 (0.00660)	—	—	—	0.02076 (0.00467)
Maximum horsepower	0.003878 (0.00098)	0.003423 (0.00072)	—	—	0.003218 (0.00090)	0.003047 (0.00073)	—	0.003901 (0.00088)	0.006794 (0.00071)
Maximum RPM	—	—	—	—	0.00007116 (0.00002)	—	—	—	—
Maximum speed (kilometers per hour)	—	—	—	—	—	—	0.008198 (0.00149)	—	—
Displacement (cubic inches)	0.004136 (0.00109)	—	0.001129 (0.00087)	0.006578 (0.00195)	—	0.001112 (0.00080)	—	—	—
4-cylinder (dummy variable)	—	—	—	—	—	—	0.06903 (0.04364)	—	—
6-cylinder (dummy variable)	—	0.1457 (0.0751)	—	—	—	—	—	—	—
8-cylinder (dummy variable)	—	—	—	—	—	—	—	—	—
Intercept	8.5551	9.6358	7.6470	9.2389	7.1155	7.7612	8.8960	6.1392	12.5602
R^2	0.8390	0.8876	0.8014	0.8293	0.8658	0.8872	0.9557	0.8598	0.9329
Standard error of estimate	0.1231	0.1090	0.1035	0.1840	0.1012	0.1076	0.0463	0.1323	0.0882
Number of observations	99	132	19	66	109	109	16	96	101
Base of cylinder dummies		4 cylinder					2, 3-cylinder		
Average prices (own currency)									
Arithmetic	81,575	121,848	39,538	54,936	18,805	10,696		2,348	2,132,078
Geometric	77,552	115,044	38,415	49,548	18,023	10,142	72,020	2,186	1,997,397
Standard deviation	29,016	46,996	11,158	27,018	6,634	3,773		1,073	947
Average weight (pounds)	2,029	1,962	2,008	2,131	1,900	2,134	1,875	2,017	1,715
Average horsepower	63	62	62	65	56	71	49	71	54

Notes: Dependent variable: natural logarithm of automobile prices in domestic currency.   Standard errors of coefficients are shown in parentheses.

output of government services by the value of the inputs to government. Compensation was compared for about a score of jobs in four occupational groupings differing mainly in educational requirements. The description of each job was taken from the International Standard Classification of Occupations.[31] The problems encountered in coping with possible differences in the productivity of employees in different countries are treated in Chapter 5, along with a discussion of how allowance was made for different inputs of capital.

Government expenditure on commodities was allocated to thirteen industrial groupings based on the International Standard Industrial Classification (ISIC) of all economic activities.[32] Since no special price comparisons were made for government purchases of commodities, some assumptions had to be made about the PPPs for these groupings. The general approach was to use the most appropriate PPPs computed elsewhere in the study. The manner in which this was accomplished is set out in the next chapter.

Categories Requiring Special Treatment

It is evident that the price comparisons for government had to be treated in ways that differed in at least some respects from the rather straightforward methods that could be used for most commodities. There were a number of other categories—less than a score—that also required special treatment. In five categories PPPs were imputed from a combination of other categories very much like what was done in the case of government expenditure on commodities. The PPP for the increase in stocks (ICP 18) was taken as the weighted average PPP for all other commodities, while the PPP for other services (ICP 8.4) was the weighted PPP for all other services. Each of the PPPs for three detailed education categories—physical facilities for education (ICP 7.42), educational books and supplies (ICP 7.431), and other educational expenditure (ICP 07.432)—was based on a weighted average of the PPPs for a selected set of other detailed categories. For the net expenditure of residents abroad (ICP 08.9) and the net foreign balance (ICP 19), the exchange rate was regarded as the PPP. The special treatment of certain comparison-resistant services—those of medical personnel, hospitals, and teachers—involved the use of direct quantity comparisons; these methods are described in Chapter 5. Two commodity categories—automobiles and rents—also required different treatment; the methods applied to these categories are described in the following paragraphs.

AUTOMOBILES. For most detailed categories a set of reasonably homogeneous items can be defined such

31. International Labour Organisation (1969).
32. U.N. Statistical Office (1968).

Jamaica	Japan	Malawi	Malaysia	Mexico	Nether-lands	Philip-pines	Poland	Spain	Thailand	U.K.	U.S.	Yugoslavia
0.4812 (0.17)	0.2726 (0.06)	0.4530 (0.07)	—	0.7610 (0.07)	0.3411 (0.08)	—	—	0.3302 (0.09)	0.1493 (0.12)	0.4053 (0.05)	0.4217 (0.05)	0.5214 (0.17)
—	—	—	0.02674 (0.00340)	0.0007686 (0.00067)	0.002503 (0.00202)	0.01887 (0.00253)	—	—	—	—	—	—
—	—	—	—	—	—	—	—	—	—	—	—	0.03487 (0.01715)
0.003281 (0.00238)	—	0.003088 (0.00119)	—	—	—	—	0.008866 (0.00246)	0.009305 (0.00147)	0.008069 (0.00233)	0.001252 (0.00077)	0.001359 (0.00106)	—
—	—	—	—	—	0.00004796 (0.00003)	—	—	0.0001616 (0.00003)	—	—	0.0001204 (0.00004)	0.00006679 (0.00006)
—	0.004450 (0.00083)	—	—	0.000395 (0.00024)	0.005026 (0.00092)	—	—	—	0.002332 (0.00069)	—	—	—
—	—	—	—	—	—	—	0.5697 (0.1467)	—	—	—	—	—
—	0.1459 (0.0359)	—	—	—	—	—	—	—	—	—	−0.1297 (0.0765)	—
—	—	0.3158 (0.1289)	—	—	—	—	—	—	—	—	−0.3416 (0.0968)	—
7.5773	12.6536	7.4001	4.8963	10.5659	7.5222	7.4907	10.9874	10.0566	10.8339	6.3436	6.4051	7.4751
0.5984	0.9165	0.7909	0.8711	0.6860	0.8331	0.7039	0.7527	0.9815	0.6958	0.8851	0.7009	0.8122
0.1595	0.0852	0.1668	0.1500	0.0574	0.1363	0.1576	0.2249	0.0290	0.1417	0.1057	0.1891	0.1241
20	97	67	10	14	110	24	19	9	23	130	137	15
		4-cylinder	4, 6-cylinder				2, 3-cylinder				4-cylinder	
6,597	874,971	6,057	12,651	56,340	11,546	—	172,153	190,263	154,071	1,836	4,427	56,524
6,402	834,118	5,592	11,595	56,061	10,849	38,584	157,236	186,186	149,313	1,732	4,117	54,481
1,676	303,302	3,151	6,196	5,916	4,909		72,630	45,520	39,161	833	2,191	15,555
1,952	2,033	2,120	2,100	2,401	1,959	2,434	1,930	1,740	2,131	2,008	3,460	1,806
75	89	84	64	83	62	81	60	55	94	68	125	48

that a subset of items can be priced in each country. The use of the country product-dummy (CPD) method, which is explained in Chapter 3, makes it possible to estimate category PPPs even though each item has not been priced in each country. However, the heterogeneous character of automobile models found in different countries makes impossible the direct pricing everywhere or even nearly everywhere of a standard set of automobiles. There are, to be sure, some models that are found in more than one or even more than a few countries, but confining the sample to such models would often make the sample unrepresentative.

It is, however, relatively easy to gather information about prices and key price-determining characteristics for a representative sample of models or types in each country. Quality matching can be based on the so-called hedonic regression technique, in which price is taken as the dependent variable and the key price-determining characteristics (such as size) as the independent variables.[33] Experience has shown that it is quite possible to find for each country an empirical formula through multiple regression analysis that enables one to estimate what the price would be for any closely specified kind of car. A series of "standard" cars, defined by key price-determining characteristics,

can then be selected and priced on the basis of the equation for each country. In this way the matching of quality is achieved.

Regressions in which price was the dependent variable and physical characteristics such as weight and horsepower were the independent variables were estimated for twenty-two countries. The number of automobile models used in the regressions varied from 9 in Spain to 137 in the United States. Eleven of the thirty-four countries had too few models to make regressions possible. The equation for Belgium was used for Luxembourg.

A summary of these regression results is provided in Table 2-6. The last rows of the table show the characteristics of the samples of automobiles that were used.

The procedures followed in fitting the regressions were unchanged from those described in the Phase I and II reports.[34] The main features were the use of the logarithmic form for the dependent variable and the arithmetic form for the independent variables, and the acceptance of the need to vary the choice of independent variables from one country to another. The criteria for selecting variables for inclusion were statistical significance and expected sign of the coefficients, as well as the estimating ability of the equation,

33. See Kravis, Kenessey, Heston, Summers (1975), chaps. 8 and 9.

34. Ibid., p. 109; Kravis, Heston, Summers (1978a), pp. 36ff.

Table 2-7. Standard Models of Automobiles and Estimated Price in each Country, 1975

Country (currency unit)	Model: Fiat 126	Leyland Mini 850	Renault 4L	VW Golf	Ford Escort 1100
Horsepower class:	0–24	25–49	25–49	50–74	25–49
Weight class (pounds):	0–1400	0–1400	1401–1700	1401–1700	1701–2000
Africa					
Kenya (shillings)	—	—	—	33,270[a]	29,336[a]
Malawi (kwacha)	—	3,413	3,455	4,039	4,272
Sri Lanka (rupees)	—	31,125[a]	35,037[a]	—	—
Zambia (kwacha)	—	2,911[a]	2,675[a]	3,068[a]	—
Asia					
Japan (yen)	—	577,260	—	661,713	—
Korea (won)	—	—	—	—	—
India (rupees)	—	—	—	—	23,825[a]
Iran (rials)	—	—	—	—	—
Malaysia (ringgit)	—	—	—	6,640	8,911
Pakistan (rupees)	—	—	35,617[a]	—	—
Philippines (pesos)	—	17,233	—	28,143	—
Syria (pounds)	—	—	15,396[a]	—	—
Thailand (baht)	—	—	75,484	97,178	94,894
Europe					
Austria (schillings)	39,895	47,366	48,656	67,986	63,715
Belgium (francs)	66,951	74,957	77,937	98,514	100,974
Denmark (kroner)	23,968	27,813	28,566	34,755	36,909
France (francs)	10,189	11,717	11,882	16,420	16,651
Germany (DM)	5,208	5,662	6,004	6,992	7,399
Hungary (forint)	—	50,073	56,571	—	71,082
Ireland (pounds)	1,214	1,319	1,431	1,689	1,819
Italy (lire)	1,305,967	1,490,638	1,511,322	2,032,084	1,972,223
Luxembourg (francs)	66,951	74,957	77,937	98,514	100,974
Netherlands (guilders)	5,938	6,799	7,071	8,746	9,416
Poland (zlote)	72,501	140,050	132,794	—	154,397
Romania (lei)	—	—	—	—	—
Spain (pesetas)	—	122,258	109,069	—	—
U.K. (pounds)	1,069	1,179	1,192	1,384	1,462
Yugoslavia (dinars)	31,919	37,147	39,909	—	—
Latin America and the Caribbean					
Brazil (cruzeiros)	—	—	—	—	33,456
Colombia (pesos)	—	—	111,465[a]	—	153,877[a]
Jamaica (pounds)	—	4,265	4,321	5,101	5,415
Mexico (pesos)	—	—	—	—	51,382
Uruguay (new pesos)	—	—	14,674[a]	—	20,189[a]
North America					
U.S. (dollars)	—	—	—	2,679	2,682

a. Nonregression estimate. The estimated prices in Iran and Zambia for the Chevy Camaro, which was not available in the United Kingdom, were derived with the aid of the U.K./German ratio for the Volvo. The Plymouth Valiant and Chevrolet Camaro estimates for Colombia were done through the United States because the match with the United Kingdom was weak.

where equations with large residuals for particular specifications were judged poorer than equations with more uniform errors. In two countries only one independent variable was used, in one of them because of the paucity of the models available. Nineteen of the twenty-two equations have $\bar{R}^2$'s of 0.70 or higher; the lowest $\bar{R}^2$ (for Jamaica) is around 0.60.

There were, however, some modifications from Phases I and II in the way the results of the regressions were used to make price comparisons. The basic approach of identifying a set of "standard" models that were then priced through the regression equations was

retained, but the details of its implementation were changed.

The first step in identifying the standard models was to construct a grid of seven horsepower classes and seven weight classes. The proportions of sales of automobiles in the forty-nine resulting cells were examined for those countries with sales data. On this basis fourteen cells were chosen as important enough to warrant comparisons among a significant number of countries. For each cell a particular "standard" model actually found on the market of one of the countries was chosen to represent the cell. For each standard

Fiat 128	Simca 1100LS	BMW 1602	Datsun B Bird 1800	Audi 100L	Toyota Mark 2	Volvo 242L	Plymouth Valiant	Chevy Camaro
50–74	50–74	75–99	100–129	75–99	100–129	75–99	75–99	100–129
1701–2000	2001–2300	2001–2300	2001–2300	2001–2300	2301–2600	2301–2600	Above 2600	Above 2600
38,544[a]	40,519[a]	—	—	55,238[a]	52,467[a]	—	—	—
4,247	4,846	5,605	6,082	6,223	6,753	7,271	8,702	—
49,476[a]	—	65,150[a]	—	—	—	—	—	—
—	3,889[a]	4,222[a]	4,233[a]	—	—	6,348[a]	—	9,834[a]
678,764	—	859,285	873,533	—	985,718	—	—	—
1,984,896[a]	2,352,863[a]	—	—	3,446,911[a]	—	—	—	—
24,853	24,853[a]	—	—	—	—	—	—	—
—	—	247,678[a]	558,337[a]	—	537,441[a]	843,987[a]	—	1,681,110[a]
7,590	—	—	—	—	—	23,338	—	24,620
42,178[a]	—	59,427[a]	—	—	—	—	—	—
30,927	33,351	41,042	41,042	54,466	—	68,304	—	—
21,351[a]	26,520[a]	—	—	35,550[a]	—	—	—	—
102,348	106,145	138,569	163,909	—	169,661	—	—	—
69,605	69,335	87,793	95,267	108,550	103,938	109,961	—	—
103,165	115,026	133,314	145,147	158,298	161,050	176,686	—	—
36,196	40,556	51,419	52,599	61,221	62,788	77,777	—	—
17,750	18,898	21,988	23,804	25,918	25,246	28,807	31,704	—
7,365	8,105	9,763	10,527	11,002	11,617	12,722	16,325	19,419
76,231	78,544	100,470	—	—	—	—	—	—
1,802	2,030	2,476	2,720	2,834	3,023	3,335	3,945	—
2,133,553	2,243,649	2,828,656	3,267,796	3,280,038	3,487,349	3,487,349	4,249,703	—
103,165	115,026	133,314	145,147	158,298	161,050	176,686	—	—
9,360	10,217	12,673	12,929	14,760	14,730	18,654	—	—
170,213	168,711	222,073	—	—	265,165	—	—	—
63,118	—	—	—	—	—	—	—	—
196,836	198,479	283,660	346,682	—	—	—	—	—
1,440	1,623	1,883	1,970	2,122	2,230	2,531	3,714	—
60,281	68,076	73,054	74,745	—	—	—	—	—
33,489	34,218	37,468	37,511	47,753	40,506	—	—	—
186,467[a]	139,793[a]	—	—	—	—	—	340,670[a]	457,511[a]
5,381	6,191	7,226	7,881	—	—	—	—	14,298
50,856	—	—	—	—	—	—	61,260	63,639
23,626[a]	23,868[a]	—	—	31,032[a]	—	—	—	—
2,786	3,155	3,324	—	3,409	3,790	3,773	3,364	4,099

model a price was estimated for each country, using the coefficients of its regression equation and the values of independent variables for the model. These prices were estimated only for cells within the range of the sample of models used to estimate the regression equation for that country. The standard models are listed in Table 2-7, along with the estimated prices for each country, wherever the model represents a horsepower-weight combination that is important in the automobile market of the given country.[35]

The twelve nonregression countries are also included in Table 2-7. The price of each automobile important in the market of each nonregression country was compared with the price in the United Kingdom. The United Kingdom was used as the bridge country because the range of models in the U.K. market seemed to provide more overlap with the models common in the nonregression countries.[36] If the same model was available in the United Kingdom, the actual U.K. price of the model was taken for the comparison. If not,

---

35. The earlier phases identified ten standard models from nine weight classes; otherwise the procedures were the same.

36. There were some exceptions, however, in which prices were compared through Germany and the United States. See Table 2-7.

the price of the model was estimated from the U.K. regression.

In Phases I and II the geometric mean of price ratios with the United Kingdom for the models price compared in this way was taken as the PPP for the nonregression country. The PPP was placed on a U.S. base by multiplying it by the U.K. PPP. Thus prices for "standard" models were not estimated for nonregression countries.

In the present (Phase III) work, the nonregression country PPP with respect to the United Kingdom, for each of the fourteen standard automobile cells for which such a PPP was available, was used to estimate the nonregression country's price for the standard model. In Sri Lanka, for example, there were two models in the weight-horsepower cell, where the standard ICP model was the Renault 4L. The ratios of actual Sri Lanka prices to U.K. prices were taken for both models. The geometric mean of these Sri Lanka and U.K. price ratios was then multiplied by the U.K. price for the Renault 4L (from the U.K. regression equation) to provide the Sri Lanka estimate for this standard model.

This method allows the prices for the nonregression countries to be treated like prices for the regression countries in calculating category PPPs for automobiles. (That is, the prices derived in the manner described can be entered in the tableau used to calculate PPPs by the CPD method. See Chapter 3.) Also it permits binary comparisons to be carried out through the standard models, which is likely to increase the extent of comparisons possible while eliminating the possible influence of the weights of intermediary countries. For example, in the present procedure, the U.K. weights would not enter into an India-Syria binary comparison as would have been the case if previous methods had been followed.

HOUSE RENTS.   Space rental for housing, which represents anywhere from 3 to 10 percent of the GDP of the ICP countries, poses special difficulties for international comparisons. The problem of standardization of quality is even more thorny for housing services than for automobiles, because dwelling units are more heterogeneous, both within and between countries. Furthermore, rents or house values are less uniform within a country—even for dwelling units of comparable quality—than are automobile prices. Another complication is that a substantial number of dwelling units are owner-occupied in most countries. Market prices for housing services are available only for rented dwellings, and ICP's price comparisons for housing services are necessarily based on rent comparisons. In this respect, the ICP does not deviate from standard national-accounts practice, in which the intertemporal

estimation of price changes for housing services within individual countries also is based on changes in rents.

A consequence of these difficulties is that considerable margins of error remain in the rent estimates for specified types of dwelling units even though an effort has been made to take account of the key rent-determining qualities of each kind of dwelling unit. However, it may be hoped that aggregation leads to a canceling of errors.

The ICP compares rental prices of the housing stock by estimating prices (rents) per unit of floor space of comparable housing. Comparability is defined by floor area and observable amenities such as availability of water, electricity, and central heating; age and condition of the dwelling, and the like. The basic approach is to relate rents in each country to these physical characteristics through regression analysis—the hedonic method. As in the case of automobiles, specifications for a set of "standard" dwelling units are developed. Prices of the dwellings are estimated from the individual country regression equations and then compared across countries.

An important rent-determining factor that is not taken into account in these specifications is location. Obviously, a dwelling with a given set of physical characteristics in central Paris or Warsaw is more highly valued by consumers than one in a rural area in the same country.

The ICP, however, has deliberately treated location as a price-increasing factor rather than as a quality variable adding to or subtracting from quantity. Although urban rents are universally higher than rural rents, the view adopted here, as in the Phase I report, is that the streams of housing services flowing from two identical dwelling units, one in the country and the other in the city, should be valued the same. Therefore, every housing specification selected for a country is priced at the national average rental for the specification. This has the advantage of simplicity; it avoids the need to match places in different countries having equivalent scarcity values. (With regard to land scarcity, what U.S. cities match London or Budapest?) Furthermore, this is consistent with the a-potato-is-a-potato approach set out earlier. Taking account of the scarcity value of land might lead to the conclusion that, given two countries with identical housing stocks, the country with the more concentrated population has a larger real quantity of housing. Clearly this is not in the spirit of the ICP.

While many countries maintain a sample of rented units for purposes of estimating time-to-time changes of rents, a knowledge of the physical characteristics of the units is not necessary for intertemporal index estimation, so they are often unrecorded. Therefore,

Table 2-8. Rent Specifications Defined by Size, Age, and Facilities

Specification number	Size in square meters	Year built	Facilities	Specification number	Size in square meters	Year built	Facilities
1	15	1946–59	None	32	25	1970–75	Electricity, water
2	25	1946–59	None	33	35	1970–75	Electricity, water
3	35	1946–59	None	34	60	1945 or before	Electricity, water, bath
4	15	1960–69	None	35	60	1946–59	Electricity, water, bath
5	25	1960–69	None	36	60	1960–69	Electricity, water, bath
6	35	1960–69	None	37	60	1970–75	Electricity, water, bath
7	15	1970–75	None	38	35	1945 or before	Electricity, water, bath, toilet
8	25	1970–75	None	39	60	1945 or before	Electricity, water, bath, toilet
9	35	1970–75	None	40	90	1945 or before	Electricity, water, bath, toilet
10	15	1945 or before	Electricity	41	35	1946–59	Electricity, water, bath, toilet
11	25	1945 or before	Electricity	42	60	1946–59	Electricity, water, bath, toilet
12	35	1945 or before	Electricity	43	90	1946–59	Electricity, water, bath, toilet
13	15	1946–59	Electricity	44	35	1960–69	Electricity, water, bath, toilet
14	25	1946–59	Electricity	45	60	1960–69	Electricity, water, bath, toilet
15	35	1946–59	Electricity	46	90	1960–69	Electricity, water, bath, toilet
16	15	1960–69	Electricity	47	35	1970–75	Electricity, water, bath, toilet
17	25	1960–69	Electricity	48	60	1970–75	Electricity, water, bath, toilet
18	35	1960–69	Electricity	49	90	1970–75	Electricity, water, bath, toilet
19	15	1970–75	Electricity	50	35	1945 or before	All including central heat
20	25	1970–75	Electricity	51	60	1945 or before	All including central heat
21	35	1970–75	Electricity	52	90	1945 or before	All including central heat
22	15	1945 or before	Electricity, water	53	35	1946–59	All including central heat
23	25	1945 or before	Electricity, water	54	60	1946–59	All including central heat
24	35	1945 or before	Electricity, water	55	90	1946–59	All including central heat
25	15	1946–59	Electricity, water	56	35	1960–69	All including central heat
26	25	1946–59	Electricity, water	57	60	1960–69	All including central heat
27	35	1946–59	Electricity, water	58	90	1960–69	All including central heat
28	15	1960–69	Electricity, water	59	35	1970–75	All including central heat
29	25	1960–69	Electricity, water	60	60	1970–75	All including central heat
30	35	1960–69	Electricity, water	61	90	1970–75	All including central heat
31	15	1970–75	Electricity, water				

it has been necessary in many countries to conduct special rent surveys for the ICP in order to estimate average rents for specifications defined by floor area and amenities. Often these surveys could be carried out by adding a few questions to an existing survey. For example, information about the specifications of dwelling units was sometimes gathered in conjunction with the regular rent survey for the consumer price index. Some countries specially estimated the rents on certain types of dwellings common in their countries, which also matched ICP specifications. Each EEC country provided rent estimates for ten to twelve different dwelling types.

The ICP method used in Phases I and II was to estimate rents for more than thirty specifications made up of combinations of floor area, age of structure, and the presence or absence of facilities such as electricity and toilet. To illustrate, one specification pertained to a dwelling of sixty square meters built between 1945 and 1960, without central heating, but with gas and electricity. In Phase III a similar procedure was followed, but with a total of sixty-one specifications. These specifications are set out in Table 2-8.[37] An estimated rent was obtained for as many of the specifications as possible from those that correspond to types of dwell-

ings commonly found in each country. In general, specifications falling outside the middle 90 percent range of the stock of dwellings in a particular country were not priced in that country. The distribution of dwellings on which weights were based for each specification was obtained from housing census data. When countries (for example, those of the EEC) provided average rents for a limited number of particular specifications without resorting to regressions, these rents were simply entered directly into the 34 × 61 price tableau for the category.

When countries had available rent surveys, regression estimates were made, by either the country or the ICP staff. The results of these regression equations are summarized in Table 2-9 for thirteen countries. The sample size varied from a few hundred to over 10,000 for countries such as Sri Lanka and India, which linked their rent collections to other surveys in prog-

37. There are 120 potential combinations from the characteristics utilized in Table 2-8 (6 facilities × 4 age groups × 5 size groups = 120). However, many combinations are rare or nonexistent (for example, a dwelling of ninety square meters with no facilities). Weights for excluded combinations, when reported, were assigned to the closest included specification.

Table 2-9. Summary of Effects of Characteristics of Dwellings on Their Estimated Rent as Derived from Rent Regressions for Thirteen Countries in 1975

Characteristics of dwellings	Austria	Brazil	Colombia	India	Iran	Jamaica	Japan	Korea	Malaysia	Sri Lanka	Thailand	U.S.	Uruguay
Base rent (Electricity, 1945–59, 35 square meters)	242.72	406.59[a]	231.80	20.194	742.19	26.44	4,007.4	9,097.0	20.65	28.25	298.78	52.17[b]	8.171
Available facilities													
None	n.a.	n.a.	72.7	57.9	60.3	71.7	n.a.	47.2	49.5	n.a.	n.a.	n.a.	n.a.
Electricity	100.0	n.a.	100.0	100.0	100.0	100.0	100.0	100.0	100.0	62.8	76.8	n.a.	30.2
Electricity and water	118.3	n.a.	233.7	159.2	139.4	136.2	174.3	122.1	138.3	100.0	100.0	n.a.	100.0
Electricity, water, and flush toilet	117.6	n.a.	n.a.	233.1	n.a.	n.a.	n.a.	n.a.	n.a.	n.a.	135.0	100.0	305.8
Electricity, water, flush and bath	146.0	100.0	489.1	n.a.	384.4	272.2	574.9	n.a.	363.4	n.a.	n.a.	163.3	n.a.
Electricity, water, flush, bath and central heating	211.5	n.a.	n.a.	n.a.	n.a.	n.a.	n.a.	n.a.	n.a.	n.a.	n.a.	193.2	635.3
Period of construction													
Before 1945	97.7	n.a.	95.1	85.0	89.6	75.3	67.3	104.2	92.8	99.5	82.6	84.5	79.0
1945–59	100.0	n.a.	100.0	100.0	100.0	100.0	100.0	100.0	100.0	100.0	100.0	100.0	100.0
1960–69	146.9	n.a.	104.5	123.8	116.7	139.7	128.6	97.2	100.0	115.4	110.0	111.1	134.9
1970–75	219.9	n.a.	108.7	171.6	152.0	139.7	166.7	105.8	114.2	n.a.	121.3	123.2	134.9
Floor area													
15 square meters	82.6	n.a.	94.5	73.5	70.2	74.9	74.5	55.4	79.9	82.0	85.4	n.a.	92.9
25 square meters	90.0	n.a.	96.4	88.5	86.9	89.2	88.9	79.0	91.7	90.7	93.1	n.a.	96.9
35 square meters	100.0	100.0	100.0	100.0	100.0	100.0	100.0	100.0	100.0	100.0	100.0	100.0	100.0
60 square meters	126.9	132.4	109.2	121.7	125.2	120.2	120.7	n.a.	126.4	n.a.	n.a.	111.4	122.0
90 square meters	169.1	163.6	117.9	n.a.	148.2	n.a.	139.0	n.a.	157.1	n.a.	n.a.	136.2	169.4
Standard error of estimate	n.a.	0.523	0.555	0.710	0.484	0.644	0.422	0.363	0.591	0.682	0.438	0.311	.218
R^2	n.a.	0.630	0.620	0.441	0.737	0.603	0.624	0.606	0.693	0.554	0.443	0.585	.814
Number of sample dwellings	n.a.	820	2,707	17,326	600	199	4,048	1,970	3,061	11,250	1,814	9,995	1,161
Average rent													
Arithmetic	n.a.	1,864	1,538	n.a.	3,535	50.75	14,059	n.a.	65.47	40.89	454.0	174.7	86.89
Logarithmic		1,282	1,020	18.62	2,349	32.29	11,305	n.a.	36.62	22.44	375.2	156.0	77.63
Number of independent variables	9	12	26	14	14	9	31	15	23	30	20	41	10

n.a. Not available.

Note: The first line and the average-rent lines are in national currencies.

a. Base rent is for 35-square-meter dwellings of average age with electricity, water, flush toilet, and bath.

b. Base rent is for 35-square-meter dwellings built in the period 1945–59 with electricity, water, and flush toilet.

ress. The dependent variable is the natural logarithm of rent of a dwelling in national currency. The characteristics are the independent variables that are included in the questions as a series of dummy variables. Because the surveys varied in the number of housing characteristics sampled, the number of variables entering into the regression equations ranged from nine to forty-one. Since many of these variables are specific to countries, like a dummy variable for a region of a country, their effects have not all been reported. Rather, the principal effects of the regression coefficients are summarized into three groupings: facilities, age, and floor area.

For each country, rent in national currency estimated from the underlying regression equation is given in row 1 of Table 2-9, most usually for the common specification, thirty-five square meters, with electricity, and built in the period 1945 through 1959.[38] The effects of changing the size, amenities, or age from this basic specification are provided in the entries in the table. For example, Japan's base rent of 4,007.4 yen for a dwelling of thirty-five square meters, with electricity and built between 1945 and 1959, would be multiplied by 1.207 to obtain a sixty-square-meter dwelling, and by 0.673 if the dwelling were built before 1945.

In general, the estimated effects of the different elements in each set of dwelling characteristics in Table

38. Where this specification was not important or not available for the country, a different base has been used and described. All blank entries in the table are due either to the lack of underlying detail to allow an estimate in the regression equation or to the unimportance of the dwelling type for the country.

2-9 vary in the expected ways. The six facility combinations are arrayed in order of increasing quality of dwelling, and this is reflected in the increasing effect of the amenities on rent in all of the countries. The age variable, with the exception of Korea, produces higher rents for newer buildings, combining both the effects of quality of building (including perhaps a preference for newness), and probably the effect of rent controls or rent inertia on older buildings.[39] As would be expected, rents are related to size. For most countries the increase in rents is less than proportional to increase in size, so rent per square meter tends to decline with size of dwelling.

On average, rents could be estimated for eighteen specifications per country—a total of 619 for the 34 countries. Weights were assigned to the specifications available for each country on the basis of total number of dwellings, rather than only rented dwellings. The assumption that the housing services of owner-occupied dwellings are the same as those of comparable rented dwellings is standard in national income work. However, this assumption is strained in countries with very thin rental markets, such as Malawi. In such countries the market rent would likely be lowered if the large amount of institutionally provided housing were exchanged on the market. Where consumers do not pay the full social cost of dwellings, countries were asked to provide both the rent charged the tenant and the social cost (rent plus subsidies) for the dwelling. As was discussed earlier in this chapter, under the section "The Expenditure Data," in the ICP treatment of rents both rent and subsidies are included in the price and expenditures, and this represents a modification of the SNA. The PPPs estimated from such rents are appropriate to aggregate GDP comparisons. In Chapter 7, comparisons will be made of PPPs actually faced by consumers, to take account of the fact that consumers do not pay full cost of rents in some countries.

A rough check on the results obtained by these methods was carried out by drawing on international housing statistics giving the number of dwellings, the average number of rooms, and the proportion of dwellings with electricity, piped water, flush toilets, and a bathroom.[40] Direct-quantity ratios derived from these statistics were compared with indirect-quantity ratios obtained by dividing the ICP rent PPPs derived by methods described above into the per capita expenditure ratios.

The ICP per capita quantities are expressed relative to the United States in column 1 of Table 2-10. The other columns of the table contain non-ICP data that are relevant to the assessment of these ratios. Columns 2 and 3 contain direct-quantity indexes based simply on the quantity of rooms per capita and per household from housing censuses. Because the per capita figures from this source are not adjusted for quality, they should not be expected to be the same as column 1. Two attempts have been made to derive independent estimates of the quality of housing from external data.

First, columns 6, 7, 8, and 9 of Table 2-10 give the data on percent of houses with electricity, water, flush toilet, and bath.

The second attempt cannot be fully explained until the ICP's CPD method of deriving PPPs for detailed categories is discussed in Chapter 3. For the moment, the reader is asked to accept that a by-product of the CPD procedure is an estimate of the world average price for each dwelling specification. If these prices are weighted for each country by the quantity of that type of housing, an average rent per square meter can be obtained.[41] This average rent, divided by the same value for the United States and multiplied by 100, is given in column 4 of Table 2-10. Each of the entries can be regarded as an index of housing quality relative to the United States. That is because for any country relative to the United States only the weights used for the given country and for the United States differ, world prices being applied to each specification in both countries. Column 5 of Table 2-10 incorporates a quality adjustment based on column 4 of the quantity index of column 2. The entries of column 5 should be closer to the ICP index in column 1 than the entries of column 2.

Some simple regressions based on the data in Table 2-10, which provide rough checks on the quantity ratios, are reported below. (In this analysis, only results based on the number of rooms per capita have been reported, but the results are substantially the same if rooms per household are used.) The first two equations show that the ICP quantity is more closely correlated with adjusted number of rooms than with number of rooms per capita for the thirty-four countries:

39. In most countries private landlords receive a higher rent on new buildings, in part because the average length of time tenants have been in the newer buildings is less. This effect would occur even without rent control, because there is a cost to turning over tenants which is passed on to new renters. This rent inertia is also reinforced by most systems of rent control.

40. U.N. Statistical Office (1980b).

41. In carrying out this computation it is necessary to allow for the systematic negative relation between rent per square meter and size of dwelling. This was done by weighting the prices for specifications with various amenities and age for only one size of dwelling, thirty square meters.

Table 2-10. Housing Characteristics of ICP Countries
(U.S. = 100)

Country	ICP quantity index (1)	Index of number of rooms from housing census		Quality index of housing from CPDs (4)	Index of rooms adjusted for quality (2) · (4) (5)	Proportion of houses with			
		Per capita (2)	Per household (3)			Electricity (6)	Piped water (7)	Flush toilet (8)	Bathroom (9)
Africa									
Kenya	3.1	24	37	20.6	5	—	—	—	—
Malawi	0.7	32	41	27.6	8	0.157	0.216	0.330	0.201
Zambia	3.8	23	37	25.7	6	0.275	0.124	0.151	—
Asia									
India	3.7	21	39	30.7	6	0.060	0.110	—	0.130
Iran	27.1	26	59	25.7	7	0.254	0.131	—	—
Japan	49.9	60	74	75.0	45	—	0.983	0.314	0.733
Korea	2.8	26	59	23.4	6	0.499	0.352	0.018	—
Malaysia	15.3	23	45	35.1	8	0.434	0.338	0.186	0.513
Pakistan	2.8	20	39	32.4	6	0.179	0.084	0.039	0.240
Philippines	11.1	24	47	23.5	6	0.232	0.240	0.226	—
Sri Lanka	5.2	23	43	18.8	4	0.090	0.044	0.067	0.070
Syria	13.0	26	49	39.9	10	0.417	0.402	0.160	0.250
Thailand	1.2	22	—	23.1	5	0.189	0.086	0.011	—
Europe									
Austria	67.2	67	80	69.2	46	0.980	0.878	0.728	0.595
Belgium	56.7	100	98	94.8	95	1.000	0.880	0.625	0.485
Denmark	99.1	75	69	85.7	64	0.990	0.987	0.962	0.768
France	71.0	67	71	90.7	61	0.988	0.966	0.697	0.469
Germany	75.3	86	82	92.9	80	0.997	0.992	0.942	0.818
Hungary	8.2	55	51	60.0	33	0.943	0.440	0.341	0.397
Ireland	22.3	67	92	75.2	50	0.947	0.732	0.700	0.554
Italy	48.3	67	72	88.5	59	0.990	0.861	0.166	0.645
Luxembourg	71.8	100	104	84.1	84	1.000	0.984	0.930	0.687
Netherlands	57.7	75	100	83.5	63	0.981	0.969	0.999	0.813
Poland	37.3	43	57	54.2	23	0.962	0.473	0.329	0.295
Romania	33.3	43	51	77.1	33	0.486	0.123	0.122	0.096
Spain	55.8	86	86	60.2	52	0.893	0.776	0.706	0.462
U.K.	58.4	100	96	90.6	91	—	0.936	0.989	0.851
Yugoslavia	20.9	43	55	41.9	18	0.879	0.336	0.261	0.246
Latin America and the Caribbean									
Brazil	13.4	55	92	41.5	23	0.556	0.338	0.240	—
Colombia	9.0	32	67	54.7	18	0.581	0.642	0.465	0.426
Jamaica	8.5	33	47	40.3	13	—	0.216	0.313	—
Mexico	14.7	24	45	47.2	11	0.589	0.387	0.415	0.318
Uruguay	33.1	40	33	54.0	22	0.807	0.631	0.627	0.637
North America									
U.S.	100.0	100	100	100.0	100	1.00	0.975	0.960	0.952

— Not available.

$$(2.2) \quad \text{LICPQ} = \begin{array}{cc} -0.1420 & + 1.9240 \ \text{LRM} \\ (0.2537) & (0.2538) \end{array}$$

$$\bar{R}^2 = 0.631 \quad \text{SEE} = 0.810 \quad n = 34$$

$$(2.3) \quad \text{LICPQ} = \begin{array}{cc} -0.0952 & + 1.0674 \ \text{LAJRM} \\ (0.2234) & (0.1196) \end{array}$$

$$\bar{R}^2 = 0.704 \quad \text{SEE} = 0.726 \quad n = 34$$

The symbols LICPQ, LRM, and LAJRM are respectively the logarithms of the ICP per capita quantity, of rooms per capita, and of rooms per capita adjusted for quality (columns 1, 2, and 5 of Table 2-10, respectively). These

equations suggest that ICP results are consistent with the basic data on number of rooms.

Further, when room counts are adjusted for average quality from the CPD regression equations, the coefficients of the intercept and slope terms are not significantly different from 0.0 and 1.0, respectively. This means that the estimates obtained by quality-adjusting the census data are not significantly different in a statistical sense from the ICP estimates.[42]

42. If the hypothesis that the intercept is 0 and the slope is 1 in equation (2.3) is tested by restricting the coefficients to these values,

Another extension of this analysis is shown in equations below, which include variables for electricity and toilet. The two other amenities, water and bath, were not significant individually or in combination. Because the number of observations or included countries may differ in these and in the above equations, neither the $\bar{R}^2$s nor standard errors of estimate (SEE) are necessarily comparable:

(2.4) $\quad$ LICPQ $= \quad -0.3452 \quad + \quad 1.1117$ LRM
$\qquad\qquad (0.2832) \qquad (0.4398)$
$\qquad\qquad + \quad 0.6876$ LEL
$\qquad\qquad\quad (0.3052)$
$\qquad \bar{R}^2 = 0.652 \quad$ SEE $= 0.795 \quad n = 30$

(2.5) $\quad$ LICPQ $= \quad -0.2337 \quad + \quad 0.7713$ LAJRM
$\qquad\qquad (0.2715) \qquad (0.2437)$
$\qquad\qquad + \quad 0.4610$ LEL
$\qquad\qquad\quad (0.3183)$
$\qquad \bar{R}^2 = 0.686 \quad$ SEE $= 0.755 \quad n = 30$

(2.6) $\quad$ LICPQ $= \quad -0.1330 \quad + \quad 1.3757$ LRM
$\qquad\qquad (0.2372) \qquad (0.1832)$
$\qquad\qquad + \quad 0.3830$ LT
$\qquad\qquad\quad (0.1720)$
$\qquad \bar{R}^2 = 0.680 \quad$ SEE $= 0.751 \quad n = 31$

(2.7) $\quad$ LICPQ $= \quad -0.0705 \quad + \quad 0.9060$ LAJRM
$\qquad\qquad (0.2104) \qquad (0.1832)$
$\qquad\qquad + \quad 0.2470$ LT
$\qquad\qquad\quad (0.1628)$
$\qquad \bar{R}^2 = 0.742 \quad$ SEE $= 0.675 \quad n = 31$

(2.8) $\quad$ LICPQ $= \quad -0.3303 \qquad + \quad 0.6722$ LRM
$\qquad\qquad (0.2542) \qquad\qquad (0.4478)$
$\qquad\qquad + \qquad 0.8330$ LEL $+ \quad 0.2936$ LT
$\qquad\qquad\quad (0.3352) \qquad\quad (0.1702)$
$\qquad \bar{R}^2 = 0.729 \quad$ SEE $= 0.708 \quad n = 28$

(2.9) $\quad$ LICPQ $= \quad -0.2278 \qquad + \quad 0.5732$ LAJRM
$\qquad\qquad (0.2507) \qquad\qquad (0.2743)$
$\qquad\qquad + \qquad 0.5944$ LEL $+ \quad 0.2375$ LT
$\qquad\qquad\quad (0.3653) \qquad\quad (0.1682)$
$\qquad \bar{R}^2 = 0.749 \quad$ SEE $= 0.682 \quad n = 28$

The symbols LEL and LT refer to the logarithms of columns 6 and 8 of Table 2-10, the proportions of dwellings with electricity and flush toilet. Equations (2.4) through (2.9) include each of these variables and the combination of the two with both the unadjusted room count and the adjusted housing quantity.[43] In theory, the ICP quality measure should capture the

effects of the amenities; in practice, while these amenities all enter positively in the equation, their coefficients tend not to be significant.

Two points are worth mentioning about these results. First, as stated above, they point out the basic consistency of the ICP quantities with independent observations on housing characteristics. Second, the equations suggest the possibility of using housing census statistics for non-ICP countries as a method of indirectly deriving PPPs. This would be done by using country values in, say, equation 2.3 to estimate a comparable housing quantity relative to the United States. The rental PPP could then be derived by dividing the expenditure ratio by the quantity ratio. Such a procedure might also be developed for any country not in a position to carry out a proper rent survey, or for perhaps rural areas of countries, which often are extremely hard to sample because rentals are very uncommon.

Summary

It has been argued in this chapter that tastes, at least those that affect broader categories of consumption, are similar throughout the world. The desires for food, clothing, shelter, recreation, and so on are sufficiently alike among people everywhere that the physical forms of the goods that satisfy these wants tend to be similar when income levels and supply conditions are the same. Therefore, international comparisons of incomes based on observed consumption patterns (and capital-formation patterns as well) may be regarded as a useful basis for assessing relative levels of welfare. Empirical support for this position is given in Chapter 9.

The ICP approach to international comparisons is to obtain price comparisons that are then used in conjunction with expenditure ratios to derive real quantity comparisons. This procedure takes advantage of the identity price times quantity equals expenditure.

The methods of dealing with the conceptual problems of marking off the production boundary separating economic activity from the rest of life, and of factoring expenditures into prices and quantities, follow the conventional lines laid down in current national accounting practices. No effort is made, for example, to take account of a more deleterious effect on environment of output in one country relative to that in others. National average market prices for

---

the F value is 1.92 with 2 and 32 degrees of freedom. The critical value of F at the 5 percent level is 3.30, so the hypothesis that the intercept is 0, and the slope is 1, can be accepted.

43. When three or four of the facilities are combined in one equation, usually one or two of the variables, such as electricity, is negative in sign, and the equation does not have a higher $\bar{R}^2$ than equations with two amenities. The combination of electricity and toilet is usually better than any other combination of variables.

specified products are compared among the different countries.

The expenditure framework also follows, insofar as possible, a conventional classification of final expenditures. The decision to compare the components of GDP by final expenditure distribution, rather than by goods produced in different industries, was a pragmatic one. It is simpler to make price comparisons for final goods than to compare the prices of the net output of industries.

In the initial design of the sample of specifications for which price comparisons would be made, a stratified sample was based on the chosen expenditure classification. An attempt was made to select goods that were likely to be important in the expenditures of many countries. For any particular country, however, an important principle governing the selection of the items for pricing from the list of the ICP specifications was that the item be in common use in that country. The consequence of the sample design and of this rule was that the price lists of the various countries contained many overlapping specifications, but there was no single common list of goods that all countries priced. This had an important influence on ICP's methodological problems discussed in the next chapter.

Considerable effort was devoted to ensuring that the goods for which prices were compared were equivalent in quality. The various ways in which this effort was carried out are described in the chapter.

The broad outlines of the price collection in each country and summary statistics on the number of prices collected for consumption goods, construction, and producer durables are also given. Two categories—automobiles and house rents—were treated by regression methods, which are described.

The next chapter deals with the ways in which these raw materials—the prices and expenditures supplied by the countries—were processed into price and quantity comparisons among the countries.

Appendix: The ICP Classification System

The classification of final expenditures follows closely the classifications suggested in the U.N. System of National Accounts (SNA; United Nations, *A System of National Accounts*, Studies in Methods, series F, no. 2, rev. 3 [New York: United Nations, 1968]). Some modifications have been necessary to meet the special requirements of the International Comparison Project; these are covered in footnotes (at the end of this appendix) indicated by letter superscripts. Actually, it has been necessary to develop a more detailed classification than that given in the SNA, but in this pro-

cess, the list of items given in the SNA classifications has been used as a guide. For producer durables, use has been made of the International Standard Industrial Classification (ISIC; United Nations, *International Standard Industrial Classification*, Statistical Papers, series M, no. 4, rev. 2 [New York: United Nations, 1968]) in order to obtain more detailed product breakdowns.

The main categories and their code numbers are as follows:

0 Final Consumption Expenditure of the Population[a]
  01. Food, beverages, and tobacco
  02. Clothing and footwear
  03. Gross rent, fuel, and power[b]
  04. Furniture, furnishings, household equipment, and operations
  05. Medical care and health expenses[c]
  06. Transport and communication
  07. Recreation, entertainment, education, and cultural services[d]
  08. Other goods and services[e]
1 Gross Capital Formation[f]
  10. Residential buildings[g]
  11. Nonresidential buildings[h]
  12. Other construction[i]
  13. Land improvement and plantation and orchard development[j]
  14. Transport equipment
  15. Nonelectrical machinery and equipment
  16. Electrical machinery and equipment
  17. Other durable furnishings and equipment
  18. Increase in stocks[k]
  19. Exports less imports of goods and services
2 Public Final Consumption Expenditure
  20. Compensation of employees
  21. Expenditure on commodities

The most disaggregated categories, which together account for the total GDP, constitute what is referred to in the text as the "detailed categories." The more aggregative "summary categories," which also account for the total GDP, are in italics. (Two sets of footnotes are used. The first, using numerical superscripts following category numbers, refers to special groupings of categories in the summary tables in Chapters 6 and 7. The second, using letter superscripts following category titles, refers to more detailed explanations of the categories themselves.)

0 *Final Consumption Expenditure of the Population* (CEP)[a]
  01.000 *Food, beverages, and tobacco*
    01.100 *Food*
    01.100 *Bread and cereals*
      01.101 Rice, glazed or polished but not otherwise worked (including broken rice)

01.102 Maize; meal and flour of wheat, barley, and other cereals

01.103 Bread and rolls

01.104 Biscuits, cake, and other bakery products; tarts and pies other than meat and fish tarts; farinaceous products stuffed with substances other than meat

01.105 Cereal preparations, preparations of flour, starch, or malt extract, used as infant food or for dietetic or culinary purposes

01.106 Macaroni, spaghetti, noodles, vermicelli, and similar products, whether cooked ready for consumption or not; rice cooked ready for consumption; malt, malt flour, malt extract, potato starch, sago, tapioca, and other starches; and the like

01.110 *Meat*

01.111 Fresh beef and veal

01.112 Fresh lamb and mutton

01.113 Fresh pork

01.114 Fresh poultry

01.115 Other fresh meat (sheep, goats, horses, game, edible offal, frog meat, and meat of marine mammals such as seals, walruses, and whales)

01.116 Frozen, chilled, dried, salted, smoked, canned meat, meat preparations, bacon, ham, and other dried, salted, or smoked meat and edible offals; meat extracts and meat juices; sausages, meat pies, meat soups in liquid, solid, or powder form, whether or not containing vegetables, spaghetti, rice, or the like; paste products filled with meat, such as canelloni, ravioli, and tortellini

01.120 *Fish*

01.121 Fresh or frozen fish and other seafood

01.122 Canned and preserved fish and other seafood and fish preparation; tinned fish soup, snails, fish pie

01.130 *Milk, cheese, and eggs*

01.131 Fresh milk

01.132 Milk products (evaporated, condensed, dried milk, cream, buttermilk, whey, yogurt, cheese, curd)

01.133 Eggs, treated eggs, egg products

01.140 *Oils and fats*

01.141 Butter

01.142 Margarine, edible oils, peanut butter, mayonnaise, other edible oils

01.143 Lard and other edible fat

01.150[1] *Fresh fruits and vegetables* (other than potatoes and similar tubers)

01.151 Fresh fruits, tropical and subtropical (oranges, tangerines, lemons, limes, grapefruits, bananas, mangos, pineapples, and the like)

01.152 Fresh fruits, other (apples, pears, cherries, grapes, melons, plums, strawberries, and the like)

01.153 Fresh vegetables (beans, cabbages, carrots, cauliflowers, cucumbers, eggplants, garlic, ginger, onions, peas, pumpkins, squash, spinach, lettuce, tomatoes, edible seeds, herbs, lentils, pulses, mushrooms, rhubarb, truffles, and the like)

01.160[1] *Fruits and vegetables other than fresh* (excluding potatoes and similar tubers)

01.161 Dried, frozen, preserved fruits, juices, fruit peel, nuts, and parts of plants preserved by sugar

01.162 Dried, frozen, preserved vegetables, vegetable juices, vegetable soups without meat or meat extract (or only traces thereof)

01.170[1] *Potatoes, manioc, and other tubers* (potatoes, manioc, arrowroot, cassava, sweet potatoes, and other starchy roots; tinned and other products such as meal, flour, flakes, chips, except starches)

01.180[2] *Sugar* (refined sugar and other products of refining beet and cane sugar, not including syrups)

01.190 *Coffee, tea, and cocoa*

01.191 Coffee

01.192 Tea

01.193 Cocoa

01.200[2] *Other foods*

01.201 Jam, preserves, marmalades, jellies, syrup, honey

01.202 Chocolate, sugar confectionery, ice cream

01.203 Salt, spices, vinegar, prepared baking powders, sauces, mixed condiments and mixed seasonings; yeast; substitutes for coffee, tea, and cocoa; and other food not elsewhere specified

01.300 *Beverages*

01.310 Nonalcoholic beverages (mineral waters and other soft drinks)

01.320 Alcoholic beverages

01.321 Spirits

01.322 Wine and cider (including cider with low alcohol content)

01.323 Beer (including beer with low alcohol content)

01.400 *Tobacco*

01.410 Cigarettes

01.420 Other (cigars, tobacco, snuff, and the like)

02.000 *Clothing and footwear*

02.100 *Clothing other than footwear, including repairs*

02.110[3] Clothing materials: woolen, cotton, silk, synthetic fibers, flax, hemp, and the like; and materials of mixed fibers other than those classified above

02.120[3] Outer clothing (coats, suits, trousers, shirts, blouses, skirts, dresses, sweaters, and the like, both ready made and custom tailored)

02.121 Men's (16 years and over)

02.122 Women's (16 years and over)

02.123 Boys' and girls' (15 years and under)

02.130[3] Hosiery, underwear, and nightwear

02.131 Men's and boys'

02.132 Women's and girls'

02.150[3] Other clothing (haberdashery, millinery, aprons, smocks, bibs, belts, gloves, and mittens other than rub-

---

1. In the summary tables, these categories are combined as fruits and vegetables.

2. In the summary tables, these categories are combined as spices, sweets, and sugar.

3. In the summary tables, these categories are combined as clothing.

ber; handkerchiefs, except paper handkerchiefs; muffs, sleeve protectors, bathing suits, crash helmets, suspenders; accessories for making clothing, such as buckles, buttons, fasteners, patterns, and zippers)

02.160[3] Rental of clothing, repairs to clothing other than footwear

02.200 *Footwear, including repairs*

02.210[4] Footwear (includes rubbers, sport shoes [other than boots and shoes with ice or roller skates attached, gaiters, spats, leggings, puttees])

02.211 Men's (16 years and over)

02.212 Women's (16 years and over)

02.213 Children's (15 years and under)

02.220[4] Repairs to footwear (including shoe cleaning)

03.000 *Gross rent, fuel, and power*

03.100 *Gross rents*

03.110 Gross rents (excluding indoor repair and upkeep).[ac] All gross rent in respect of dwellings, actual and imputed in the case of owner-occupied houses, including ground rents and taxes on the property. In general, house rent will be space rent, covering heating and plumbing facilities, lighting fixtures, fixed stoves, wash basins, and similar equipment that customarily is installed in the house before selling or letting. Also included are payments for garbage and sewage disposal. Rents paid for rooms in boardinghouses, but not in hotels, are included. Rents of secondary dwellings such as summer cottages, mountain chalets, and the like, also are included.

03.120 Expenditures of occupants of dwelling units on indoor repair and upkeep (indoor painting, wallpaper, decorating, and the like)[m]

03.200 *Fuel and power*

03.210 Electricity

03.220 Gas (natural and manufactured gas, including liquefied, petroleum gases [butane, propane, and the like])

03.230 Liquid fuels (heating and lighting oils)

03.240 Other fuels, water charges, and ice (coal, coke, briquettes, firewood, charcoal, peat, purchased heat, hot water, water charges, and ice)

04.000 *Furniture, furnishings, household equipment, and operation*[n]

04.100[5] *Furniture, fixtures, carpets, and other floor coverings*

04.110 Furniture and fixtures (beds, chairs, tables, sofas, storage units, and hallboys; cribs, high chairs, playpens; door and dividing screens; sculptures, carvings, figurines, paintings, drawings, engravings, and other art objects; venetian blinds; fireplace equipment; other furniture and fixtures)

04.120 Floor coverings (carpets, large mats, and linoleum; other floor coverings)

04.200[5] *Household textiles and other furnishings* (curtains, sheets, tablecloths and napkins, towels, tapestries, bedding mattresses, and other coverings, of all materials; furnishings such as ashtrays, candlesticks, and mirrors; awnings, counterpanes, and doormats; flags; garden umbrellas; garment and shoe bags, laundry hampers and bags, and shoe racks; mosquito nets; steamer and traveling rugs; wastepaper baskets and flower and plant boxes and pots)

04.300[5] *Heating and cooking appliances, refrigerators, washing machines, and similar major household appliances, including fittings.*

04.310 Refrigerators, freezers, and cooling appliances (refrigerators, food freezers, ice boxes, room air conditioners, and fans)

04.320 Washing appliances (dishwashers, other washing appliances)

04.330 Cooking appliances (includes reflector ovens, camping stoves, and similar appliances, toasters, electric coffeemakers)

04.340 Heating appliances other than cooking (clothes drying and ironing appliances)

04.350 Cleaning appliances (electric floor-scrubbing, -waxing, and -polishing machines, vacuum cleaners, water-softening machines)

04.360 Other major household appliances (sewing and knitting machines, garden tractors, power-driven lawnmowers, nonportable safes, water pumps)

04.400[6] *Glassware, tableware, and household utensils* (pottery, glassware, cutlery, silverware; hand kitchen and garden tools [not power driven]; all types of kitchen utensils; portable toilet and sanitary utensils for indoor use; electric bulbs, plugs, wire, cable, and switches; heating pads, saucepans, nonelectric coffeemakers; thermos bottles and flasks; watering cans, wheelbarrows, garden hose and sprinkling devices, lawnmowers [not power driven], and other garden appliances; portable money boxes and strong boxes; household scales; ladders; locksmith's wares)

04.500 *Household operation*

04.510[6] Nondurable household goods: household paper products; cleaning supplies (household soap, scourers, polishes, cleaning materials, shoe polish, mops, brooms and brushes, dyes for dyeing clothing and household textile furnishing; insecticides, fungicides, and disinfectants); and other household goods (matches, candles, lamp wicks, clothes hangers, clothespins, rope, string and twine, nails, nuts and bolts, screws, tacks, hooks, knobs, needles, pins, aluminum foil, and the like)

04.520[6] Domestic services (total compensation, including payments in kind to domestic servants, cleaners, and the like; includes payments in cash and in kind to babysitters, chauffeurs, gardeners, governesses, tutors, and the like)

04.530[6] Household services other than domestic (includes cleaning, dyeing, and laundering; hire of furniture, furnishings, and household equipment, including

4. In the summary tables, these categories are combined as footwear.

5. In the summary tables, these categories are combined as furniture and appliances.

6. In the summary tables, these categories are combined as supplies and operations.

payments by subtenants for the use of furniture, and the like; service charges for insurance of household property against fire, theft, and other eventualities; payments for services such as chimney cleaning, window cleaning, snow removal, exterminating, disinfecting, and fumigating, and the like; also all repair of furniture, furnishings, and household equipment)

05.000 *Medical care and health expenses*[aa]

05.100[7] *Medical and pharmaceutical products* (includes medical and pharmaceutical products, whether directly purchased by consumers or by hospitals and independent practitioners, and the like, for use in the care of patients)

05.110 Drugs and medical preparations (medicines, vitamins and vitamin preparations, cod and halibut liver oil)

05.120 Medical supplies (clinical thermometers, hot-water bottles and ice bags; bandage materials, first-aid kits, elastic medical hosiery, and similar goods)

05.200[7] *Therapeutic appliances and equipment* (major appliances and equipment, whether directly purchased by consumers or by hospitals and independent practitioners, and the like, for use in the care of patients: eyeglasses; hearing aids; glass eyes, artificial limbs, orthopedic braces and supports; surgical belts, trusses, and supports; medical massage equipment and health lamps; wheelchairs and invalid carriages, motorized or not)

05.300[7] *Services of physicians, dentists, and nurses and related professional and semiprofessional personnel* (compensation of employed persons and net income of independent practitioners for services performed, both in and out of the hospital)

05.310 Physicians

05.320 Dentists

05.330 Nurses, physiotherapists, technicians, midwives, and so forth

05.400[7] *Current expenditures of hospitals, laboratories, clinics, and medical offices, not elsewhere classified* (including expenditure related to physical facilities and personnel other than medical and related practitioners)

06.000 *Transport and communication*

06.100 *Personal transport equipment*

06.110 Passenger cars

06.120 Other

06.200 *Operation of personal transport equipment*

06.210 Tires, tubes, other parts and accessories

06.220 Repair charges

06.230 Gasoline, oils, and greases

06.240 Other expenditures (parking and garaging; bridge, tunnel, ferry, and road tolls; driving lessons; hire of personal transport equipment, service charges on insurance of personal transport equipment)

06.300 *Purchased transport services*

06.310[8] *Local transport* (fares on trains, buses, and cabs; includes local and long-distance water transport, moving and storage of household goods, service charges for special transport accident insurance)

06.320[8] *Long-distance transport* (fares on transport; fees for transporting personal transportation equipment, for baggage transfer; storage and excess charges; tips to porters; service charges for baggage)

06.321 Rail

06.322 Bus

06.323 Air

06.400 *Communication*

06.410 Postal

06.420 Telephone and telegraph

07.000 *Recreation, entertainment, education, and cultural services*

07.100[9] *Equipment and accessories, including repairs*[o]

07.110 Radios, television sets, and phonographs (includes tape recorders, radio transmitting and receiving sets for amateur radio stations, clock radios)

07.120 Major durables for recreational, entertainment, and cultural purposes (airplanes; boats and outboard motors; cameras, projection equipment, other photographic equipment; binoculars, microscopes, and telescopes; pianos, organs, violins, cornets, and other major musical instruments; typewriters; power-driven equipment for woodworking, metalworking, and the like; horses; swimming pools that are not permanent fixtures)

07.130 Other recreational equipment and goods (semidurable and nondurable goods; harmonicas and other minor musical instruments; records; flowers; all sports equipment and supplies except sports clothing and footwear; camping equipment; films and other photographic supplies; used postage stamps for philatelic purposes; children's outdoor play equipment; pets other than horses; feeding stuffs for pets; exercising equipment)

07.200[9] *Entertainment, religious, recreational, and cultural services* (excluding hotels, restaurants, and cafés)[ad]

07.210 Public entertainment (private and public expenditures on places of public amusement and recreation, including theaters, cinemas, sports, museums, art galleries, historical monuments, botanical and zoological gardens, parks, ski facilities, and the like)

07.220 Other entertainment, religious, recreational, and cultural services (expenditures on private entertainment such as hiring musicians, clowns, and the like for private parties; bridge, dancing, and sports lessons; gambling; portrait and other services such as film developing and print processing furnished by photographers; hire of radio and television sets, airplanes, boats, horses, and other recreational equipment; veterinary and other services for pets; radio and television licenses where government broadcasting stations exist; religious activities)

---

7. In the summary tables, these categories are combined as medical care.

8. In the summary tables, these categories are combined as purchased transport.

9. In the summary tables, these categories are combined as recreation.

07.300[9] *Books, newspapers, magazines, and stationery*[p]

07.310 Books, newspapers, magazines, and other printed matter

07.320 Stationery supplies (ink, paper clips, pens, pencils; typewriter carbon and stencil paper; pencil sharpeners, paper punches, hand stamps and seals; typewriter ribbons; slide rules, drawing sets, and similar instruments)

07.400[10] *Education*[ab]

07.410 Compensation of employees (total expenditure for personnel, whether paid by governments or institutions or directly by households)

07.411 Teachers for primary and secondary schools

07.413 Teachers for colleges and universities

07.420[10] *Expenditures of educational institutions related to physical facilities*

07.430[10] *Other expenditures of educational institutions*

07.431 Books, stationery, and related supplies

07.432 Other

08.000 *Other goods and services*[c]

08.100[11] *Services of barber and beauty shops, baths, and the like*

08.200[11] *Goods for personal care*[q]

08.210 Toilet articles and preparations (including shaving equipment; electric hair dryers; hair clippers, electric or not; permanent wave sets for home use; tooth and toilet brushes)

08.220 Personal effects (jewelry, watches, rings, and precious stones; travel goods, handbags, and similar goods; umbrellas, walking sticks, and canes; pipes, lighters, tobacco pouches; pocket knives, sunglasses; clocks; baby carriages)

08.300[12] *Expenditures in restaurants, cafés, and hotels*

08.310 Restaurants and cafés

08.320 Hotels and similar lodging places

08.400[12] *Other services n.e.s.* (not elsewhere specified)[r] (service charges for life insurance and for insurance against civil responsibility for injuries to other persons or other persons' property not arising from the operation of personal transport equipment; actual charges for bank services; fees and service charges for brokerage, investment counseling, household finance company loans and services of similar financial institutions; charges for money orders and other financial services provided by the post office; fees to tax consultants; administrative charges of private pension schemes; fees for legal services and to employment agencies; dealers' margins on purchases from pawnbrokers; duplicating, blueprinting, photostating, addressing, mailing, and stenographic services; payments for copies of birth, death, and marriage certificates; charges for newspaper notices and advertisements; fees to house agents and the like; welfare services.[ae])

08.900[13] *Net Expenditures of Residents Abroad*

1 *Gross Capital Formation* (GCF)

Construction (10.000 through 13.000)

10.000 *Residential buildings* (value of work put in place on the construction of buildings consisting wholly or primarily of dwellings, excluding the value of the land improvement, if this can be separately estimated; major alterations and improvements in residential buildings; and transfer and similar costs in respect of purchase of existing residential buildings. Includes the cost of external and internal painting of new buildings and of all permanent fixtures such as furnaces, fixed stoves, and central-heating, air-conditioning, and water-supply installations, as well as all equipment customarily installed before dwellings are occupied. Hotels, motels, and similar buildings operated on a purely transient basis are considered as nonresidential.)

10.100 *One- and two-dwelling buildings* (detached, twin, and row houses, including prefabricated units)

10.200 *Multidwelling buildings* (apartment buildings with three or more units)

11.000 *Nonresidential buildings* (value of work put in place on the construction of buildings and structures wholly or primarily for industrial or commercial use; major alterations and improvements in nonresidential buildings; and transfer and similar costs in respect of purchase of existing nonresidential buildings. Includes the construction of factories, warehouses, office buildings, stores, restaurants, hotels, farm buildings such as stables and barns, and buildings for religious, educational, recreational, and similar purposes; and the fixtures and nonmovable equipment that are an integral part of these structures)

11.100 *Hotels and other nonhousekeeping units* (including dormitories)

11.200 *Industrial buildings* (factories, mines, and special buildings for utility industries such as power, communications, and transportation)

11.300 *Commercial buildings* (stores, banks, warehouses, and garages)

11.400 *Office buildings*

11.500 *Educational buildings* (including day nurseries, laboratories, libraries, and museums)

11.600 *Hospital and institutional buildings*

11.700 *Agricultural buildings* (barns and storage facilities)

11.800 *Other buildings* (including buildings for cultural, religious, sports, and social purposes)

12.000 *Other construction* (value of work put in place on new construction and major alterations and renewals of nonmilitary projects such as the permanent ways of railroads; roads, streets, sewers; bridges, viaducts, subways, and tunnels; harbors, piers, and other harbor facilities; car-parking facilities; airports; pipelines, oil wells, and mineshafts; canals and waterways; water-power projects, dams and dikes that are not part of irrigation and flood-control projects; aqueducts; drainage and sanitation projects; athletic fields, electric-transmission lines, gas mains and pipes, telephone

---

10. In the summary tables, these categories are combined as education.

11. In the summary tables, these categories appear as personal care.

12. In the summary tables, these categories appear as miscellaneous services.

13. This category is normally combined with other services.

and telegraph lines, and the like. Includes the cost of raising the surface of future building sites, leveling the sites, and laying out the necessary streets and sewers, but excludes groundwork within the building line, when a start is made on the actual construction, which should be included in residential or nonresidential buildings, as the case may be. Includes as well transfer and similar costs in respect of purchase of existing assets of this type)

12.100 *Roads, streets, and highways* (including road bridges and tunnels)

12.200 *Transport (other than road) and utility lines* (railroad ways; lines for telephone and power; pipes for gas, water, and sewer systems; airplane runways; canals; harbor facilities)

12.300 *Other construction* (including dams for power; petroleum and gas well drilling and exploration)

13.000[14] *Land improvement and plantation and orchard developments*[s] (all land reclamation and land clearance, irrespective of whether it represents an addition to total land availability or not; irrigation and flood-control projects and dams and dikes that are part of these projects; forest clearance and afforestation; and transfer costs in connection with transactions in land, mineral deposits and concessions, forests, fishing and concessions, and the like. Includes planting and cultivation, until they yield products, of new orchards, rubber plantations, and other new holdings of fruit-bearing and sap-bearing plants that require more than a year to become productive)

Producer Durables[t] (14.000 through 17.000)

14.000 *Transport equipment* [384]

14.100[15] *Railway vehicles* [3842] (locomotives of any type or gauge, and railway and tramway cars for freight and passenger service; specialized parts for locomotive, railroad, and tramway cars [3710, 3829, 3819])

   14.110 Locomotives

   14.120 Other

14.200[15] *Passenger cars* [3843] (complete passenger automobiles, commercial cars, taxis; specialized passenger automobile parts [3560] and accessories such as engines, brakes, clutches, axles, gears, transmissions, wheels, and frames)

14.300[15] *Trucks, buses, and trailers* [3843] (complete buses, trucks, and truck trailers, universal carriers, special-purpose motor vehicles [ambulances, fire trucks; trailer and pickup coaches; vehicle-drawn caravans; motorized sleighs]; specialized motor-vehicle parts and accessories, except automobile [3560], such as engines, brakes, clutches, axles, gears, transmission, wheels, and frames)

14.400[15] *Aircraft* [3845] (airplanes, gliders, other aircraft, and parts such as engines, propellers, pontoons, and undercarriages; space vehicles and specialized parts [3560])

14.500[15] *Ships and boats* [3841] (ships, barges, lighters, and boats, except rubber boats, specialized marine engine

and ship parts [3560]; the conversion, alteration, and breaking up of ships [6100])

14.600[15] *Other transport equipment* [3844, 3849] (motorcycles, scooters, bicycles, tricycles, pedicabs, and specialized parts such as motors, saddles, seat posts, frames, gears, and handlebars [3844]; transport equipment not elsewhere classified, such as animal-drawn wagons, carts, and sleighs, hand-drawn pushcarts, wheelbarrows, and baby carriages [3849])

15.000 *Nonelectrical machinery and equipment* [382]

15.100[16] *Engines and turbines* [3821] (steam and gas engines and steam, gas, and hydraulic turbines; petrol, diesel, and other internal-combustion engines. Complete steam, gas, and hydraulic turbine-generator sets are classified as electrical industrial machinery and apparatus in category 16.100. Turbines or engines for a given type of transport equipment are classified in the appropriate transport-equipment category.)

15.200[16] *Agricultural machinery* [3822] (machinery and equipment for use in the preparation and maintenance of the soil, in planting and harvesting of the crop, in preparing crops for market on the farm, or in dairy farming and livestock raising; for use in performing other farm operations and processes such as planting, seeding, fertilizing, cultivating, harvesting, for example, ploughs, harrows, stalk cutters, milking machines, and farm tractors)

   15.210 Tractors

   15.220 Other

15.300[16] *Office machines* [3825] (office machines and equipment, such as calculating machines, adding machines, accounting machines; punchcard-system machines and equipment; digital and analog computers and associated electronic data-processing equipment and accessories; cash registers; typewriters; weighing machines except scientific apparatus for laboratories; duplicating machines except photocopying machines; and the like)

15.400[16] *Metalworking machinery* [3823] (includes lathes and machines for boring, drilling, milling, grinding, shearing, and shaping; drop forges and other forging machines; rolling mills, presses, and drawing machines; extruding, melting, and nonelectrical machines; and machine tools, dies, and jigs, including accessories for metalworking machines)

15.500[16] *Construction, mining, and oil-field machinery* [3824] (cementmaking and other heavy machinery and equipment used by construction industries; oil-refining machinery and equipment and heavy machinery and equipment used by mining industries)

15.600[16] *Special industry machinery, not elsewhere specified* [3824, 3823] (special industrial machinery and equipment except metalworking machinery; for example, machinery used in the food, textile, paper, printing, chemical, and woodworking industries)

15.700[16] *General industry machinery* [3829] (machinery and equipment, except electrical machinery, not elsewhere

---

14. In the summary tables, this category is included with other construction.

15. In the summary tables, these categories are combined as transport equipment.

16. In the summary tables, these categories are combined as nonelectrical machinery.

classified, such as pumps, air and gas compressors; blowers, air-conditioning, and ventilating machinery; fire sprinklers; refrigerators and equipment; mechanical power-transmission equipment; lifting and hoisting machinery, cranes, elevators, moving stairways, industrial trucks, tractors, trailers, and stackers; sewing machines; industrial-process furnaces and ovens. Included are general-purpose parts of machinery such as ball and roller bearings, piston rings, valves; parts and accessories on a job or order basis)

15.800[16] *Service industry machinery* [3829] (automatic merchandising machines; washing, laundry, dry-cleaning, and pressing machines; cooking ranges and ovens; and the like)

16.000 *Electrical machinery and appliances* [383, 385]

16.100[17] *Electrical transmission, distribution, and industrial apparatus* [3831] (electric motors; generators and complete turbine-generator and engine-generator sets; transformers; switchgear and switchboard apparatus; rectifiers; other electrical transmission and distribution equipment; electrical industrial-control devices such as motor starters and controllers, electronic timing and positioning devices, electromagnetic clutches and brakes; electrical welding apparatus; and the like)

16.200[17] *Communications equipment* [3832] (radio and television receiving sets, sound-reproducing and -recording equipment, including public-address systems, phonographs, dictating machines, and tape recorders; phonograph records and prerecorded magnetic tapes; wire and wireless telephone and telegraph equipment; radio and television transmitting, signaling, and detection equipment and apparatus; radar equipment and installations; parts and supplies specifically classified in this group; semiconductor and related sensitive semiconductor devices; fixed and variable electronic capacitors and condensers; radiographic, fluoroscopic, and other X-ray apparatus and tubes)

16.300[17] *Other electrical equipment* [3839] (other electrical apparatus, accessories, and supplies not elsewhere classified, such as insulated wires and cables; storage and primary batteries, wet and dry; electric lamps and tubes; fixtures and lamp sockets and receptacles; snap switches, conductor connectors, and other current-carrying wiring devices; conduits and fittings; electrical insulators and insulation materials, except procelain and glass insulators)

16.400[17] *Instruments* [3851, 3852, 3853] (laboratory and scientific instruments and measuring and controlling equipment not elsewhere classified; cyclotrons, betatrons, and other accelerators; surgical, medical, and dental equipment, instruments, and supplies and orthopedic and prosthetic appliances [3851]; optical instruments and lenses, ophthalmic goods, photographic and photocopying equipment and supplies. Included are optical instruments for scientific and medical use [3852]; clocks and watches

of all kinds; clock and watch parts and cases; and mechanisms for timing devices [3853].)

17.000 *Other durable furnishings and equipment*

17.100[18] *Furniture and fixtures* [3320, 3812, 3851, 3901, 3902, 3909] (equipment, furnishings, and furniture used by businesses, governments, offices, hotels, boardinghouses, restaurants, hospitals, research institutions, schools, and other services)

17.200[18] *Other durable goods* [3813, 3819, 3811] (all durable goods not elsewhere classified, such as containers, tanks, and nonelectrical hand tools)

18.000 *Increase in stocks*[19] (commodity stocks [increase in value of materials and supplies, work in progress, and finished products and goods in the possession of industries; excludes standing timber and crops, but includes logs and harvested crops; excludes partially completed construction works]; and livestock, including breeding stock, dairy cattle, and the like[k] [livestock raised for slaughter; all chicken and other fowl; value of additions to, less disposals of, breeding stocks, draught animals, dairy cattle, sheep, llamas, and the like, raised for wool clipping])

19.000[19] *Exports of goods and services less imports of goods and services* (merchandise exports, f.o.b. [free on board], and imports, c.i.f. [cost, insurance, and freight], include all transactions [sales and purchases] between the residents of a country and the rest of the world in commodities; include new and used ships and aircraft, though they may not cross the customs frontier of the country, and also electricity, gas, and water. Exclude such items as goods in direct transit through the country, goods not owned by residents for purposes of storage and transshipment only, tourists' and travelers' effects, and goods for exhibition or study, samples that are returnable or of no commercial value, returnable containers, and animals for racing or breeding. Data are net of the value of returned goods and in-transit losses. Exports and imports of services cover primarily freight, passenger, and other transport and communication services and insurance services; since merchandise imports are initially valued c.i.f. and may thus include payments of services to resident producers, such payments should be offset by a corresponding entry in exports of services.)

2 *Public Final Consumption Expenditure* (PFC)[u]

20.000 *Compensation of employees*

20.100[20] *Compensation of employees having first level of education*[v]

20.200[20] *Compensation of employees having second level of education*[v]

   20.210 Compensation of blue-collar employees[w]

   20.220 Compensation of white-collar employees[x]

20.300[20] *Compensation of employees having third level of education*[v]

---

18. In the summary tables, these categories are combined as other durables.

19. In the summary tables, these categories are included in capital formation.

20. In the summary tables, these categories are combined as compensation of government employees.

17. In the summary tables, these categories are combined as electrical machinery.

21.000 *Expenditure on commodities*

[a] CEP (Final consumption expenditure of the population) is identical with "household final consumption expenditure" as defined by the SNA except for the following points:

[aa] CEP *includes* certain expenditures on medical and other health services not included in household final consumption expenditure by the SNA. The expenditures to be included are defined in terms of SNA Tables 5-3 and 5-4 (SNA, pp. 87–89), as follows:

[aaa] CEP *includes* government expenditures on "hospitals and clinics" and "individual health services" (items 4.2 and 4.3 in the SNA classification of the purposes of government—SNA Table 5-3). All expenditures of government on these items, which according to the SNA would be recorded as parts of "government final consumption expenditure," should be included in CEP.

[aab] CEP *includes* expenditures of nonprofit bodies serving households—SNA Table 5-4. All expenditures of such nonprofit bodies on these items, which according to the SNA would be recorded as parts of "final consumption expenditure of nonprofit institutions serving households," should be included in CEP.

[ab] CEP *includes* certain expenditures on schools and other educational facilities not included in household final consumption expenditure by the SNA. The expenditures to be included are defined in terms of SNA Tables 5-3 and 5-4 as follows:

[aba] CEP *includes* government expenditures on "schools, universities, and other educational facilities" and "subsidiary services" (items 3.2 and 3.3 in SNA Table 5-3). The inclusion applies to all expenditures of government on these items, which according to the SNA would be recorded as parts of government final consumption expenditure.

[abb] CEP *includes* expenditures of private nonprofit bodies on education (item 2 in SNA Table 5-4). The inclusion affects all expenditures of nonprofit bodies on this item, which according to the SNA would be recorded as parts of final consumption expenditure of nonprofit institutions serving households.

[ac] CEP *includes* current expenditures of government for provision, assistance, or support of housing (for example, government expenditures to meet current costs of dwellings). Insofar as such expenditures of government constitute part of the compensation of employees in the government sector as income in kind, they are already included in household consumption expenditure (and therefore in CEP); and hence the inclusion of this item does not require additional rearrangement between household and government expenditures. However, government expenditure for provision, assistance, or support of housing *other* than that included in the compensation of employees of the government sector should be included in CEP and excluded from public final consumption expenditure.

[ad] CEP *includes* certain expenditures on recreational and related cultural services not included in household final consumption expenditure by the SNA. The expenditures to be *included* are the following:

[ada] Expenditures on recreational and related cultural services and religion and services not elsewhere classified (items 7.1 and 7.2 in SNA Table 5-3), treated as part of final government consumption expenditure in the SNA.

[adb] Expenditures on recreational and related cultural services and religious organizations (items 5 and 6 in SNA Table 5-4), treated as part of final consumption expenditure of nonprofit institutions serving households in the SNA.

[ae] CEP *includes* expenditures on welfare services by government and by nonprofit institutions serving households. The expenditures to be *included* are those described in item 5.2 of SNA Table 5-3 and item 4 of SNA Table 5-4.

[b] Includes government expenditures for housing, as described in note ([ae]), above.

[c] Includes certain expenditures of government and of nonprofit institutions serving households; see note ([aa]), above.

[d] Includes certain expenditures of government and of private nonprofit bodies on educational, recreational, and cultural services; see notes ([ab]) and ([ad]), above.

[e] Includes expenditures of government and of nonprofit institutions serving households on welfare services; see note ([ae]), above.

[f] "Gross capital formation" is identical with "gross capital formation" as defined by the United Nations, *System of National Accounts* (1968), except that it includes "exports of goods and services less imports of goods and services."

[g] For the definition of the scope of this category, see item 1 in Table 6-3 of the SNA (p. 114).

[h] For the definition of the scope of this category, see item 2 in Table 6-3 of the SNA (p. 114).

[i] For the definition of the scope of this category, see item 3 in Table 6-3 of the SNA (p. 114).

[j] For the definition of the scope of this category, see item 4 in Table 6-3 of the SNA (p. 114).

[k] Includes increase in breeding stocks, draught animals, dairy cattle, and the like, though these are in the SNA as part of gross fixed capital formation rather than as increase in stocks.

[l] In the SNA, custom tailoring and hire of clothing are included in the category "clothing other than footwear."

[m] Expenditures on indoor repair and upkeep are included in gross rents in the SNA.

[n] In the SNA, each subcategory of "furniture, furnishings, household equipment, and operation" includes a separate item for repair. The present classification combines all repairs within category 04, into the single subcategory 04.53.

[o] In the SNA, repairs are treated as a separate category rather than being added to each breakdown.

[p] Stationery is placed with miscellaneous goods in the SNA.

[q] Includes SNA categories "goods for personal care," "jewelry, watches, rings and precious stones," and "other personal goods."

[r] Membership dues in professional associations, included in this category by the SNA, here are classified with public final consumption expenditure. Also, the SNA separates financial services from other services, and both of them are included here.

[s] SNA separates "land improvement" and "plantation, orchard, and vineyard development."

[t] Bracketed numbers following categories refer to codes of the International Standard Industrial Classification; see U.N. Statistical Office, *International Standard Industrial Classification of All Economic Activities* (New York: United Nations, 1968). Descriptions, taken over with little or no modification, include some consumer durables that should be excluded, insofar as they are purchased by the consumer. The ISIC codes are used solely to indicate the types of products included in each ICP category. Products used for current repairs rather than for additions or replacements to the stock of capital are excluded, in accordance with the rules of the SNA (see SNA paragraph 6:23).

[u] "Public final consumption expenditure" (PFC) is identical with "government final consumption expenditure," as defined by the SNA, except for the following points:

[ua] PFC *includes*, in addition to the expenditures of government (that is, central government, state and local government, social security agencies, and the like) certain expenditures of private nonprofit institutions serving households. The purposes for which expenditures are included are:

ᵘᵃᵃ Service charges on accident and health insurance (item 5.5 in SNA Table 6-1).

ᵘᵃᵇ Membership dues in professional associations.

ᵘᵃᶜ Research and scientific institutes (item 1 in SNA Table 5-4).

ᵘᵃᵈ Professional, labor, and civic organizations (item 7 in SNA Table 5-4).

ᵘᵇ PFC *excludes* some expenditures classified as government final consumption expenditure in the SNA. The excluded categories are:

ᵘᵇᵃ PFC *excludes* expenditures for provision, assistance, or support of housing (for example, government expenditures to meet current costs of dwellings) unless they are part of the compensation of employees in governments.

ᵘᵇᵇ Hospitals and clinics and individual health services (items 4.2 and 4.3 in the classification of the purposes of government, SNA Table 5-3). All expenditures of government on these items, which according to the SNA would be recorded as part of government final consumption expenditure, should be included in the final consumption expenditure of the population (CEP).

ᵘᵇᶜ PFC *excludes* expenditures on recreation and related cultural services and religion and services not elsewhere classified (items 7.1 and 7.2 in SNA Table 5-3). All expenditures of government on these items, which according to the SNA would be recorded as part of government final consumption expenditure, should be included in CEP.

ᵘᵇᵈ Schools, universities, and other educational facilities and subsidiary services (items 3.2 and 3.3 in SNA Table 5-3). All expenditures of government on these items, which according to the SNA would be recorded as part of government final consumption expenditures, should be included in CEP.

ᵘᵇᵉ PFC *excludes* expenditures on welfare services (item 5.2 in SNA Table 5-3). All expenditures of government on this item, which according to the SNA would be recorded as part of government final consumption expenditures, should be included in CEP.

ᵛ The general definitions of the first, second, and third levels of education—as suggested by UNESCO—are as follows:

ᵛᵃ The first level of education consists of schools such as elementary and primary schools "whose main function is to provide basic instruction in tools of learning."

ᵛᵇ The second level of education consists of schools such as middle, secondary, high, and vocational schools, "which provide general or specialized instruction, or both, based upon at least four years previous instruction at the first level."

ᵛᶜ The third level of education consists of schools such as universities and higher professional schools, "which require, as a minimum condition of admission, completion of ten or more years of previous instruction at the first and second level or equivalent." For the purposes of the present reporting, the three educational levels should be approximated in the following way: (1) first level, seven to nine years of completed education or less; (2) third level, more than twelve years of completed education; and (3) second level, years of completed education above the first level and under the third level. In case of lack of adequate data, the educational qualifications usually required for a given grade in government employment should be used for subdividing government employment (and the related PFC expenditures) according to the categories requested.

ʷ Government employees at the second level of education whose occupations fall within the following ISCO (*International Standard Classification of Occupations,* rev. 1968 [Geneva: International Labour Organisation, 1969]) major groups can be considered as blue-collar employees:

Major group number	*Title*
7/8/9	Production and related workers, transport equipment operators, and laborers
5	Service workers
6	Agricultural, animal husbandry, and forestry workers, fishermen, and hunters
10	Workers not classifiable by occupation

ˣ Government employees at the second level of education whose occupations fall within the following ISCO major groups can be considered as white-collar employees:

Major group number	*Title*
3	Clerical and related workers
2	Administrative and managerial workers
0/1	Professional, technical, and related workers
4	Sales workers

Appendix Table 2-1. Classification of Detailed Categories: Commodities and Services (Priced and Comparison-resistant); Tradables and Nontradables

Code	Commodities	Priced services	Comparison-resistant services
01 Food	All		
02 Clothing, footwear	All but 2.160 and 2.200	2.160 Repair	
		2.200 Footwear repairs	
03 Gross rent, fuel, power	3.200 Gas	3.100 Gross rents	
	3.230 Liquid fuels	3.120 Indoor repairs	
	3.240 Other fuels	3.210 Electricity	
04 House furnishings, operations	All but 4.520 and 4.530	4.520 Domestic services	
		4.530 Other household services	
05 Medical care	5.110 Drugs		5.310 Physicians' services
	5.120 Medical supplies		5.320 Dentists' services
	5.200 Therapeutic appliances		5.330 Nurses' etc. services
			5.410 Hospital services
06 Transportation	6.110 Automobile	6.220 Repair charges	
	6.120 Other personal transport	6.240 Parking, tolls, purchased transport, and communications	
	6.210 Tires, tubes, accessories	6.310 Local transport	
	6.230 Gasoline, oil	6.321 Rail transport	
		6.322 Bus transport	
		6.323 Air transport	
		6.410 Postal communication	
		6.420 Telephone, telegraph	
07 Recreation, education	All recreational equipment	7.210 Public entertainment	7.411 School teachers
	7.310 Books	7.220 Entertainment, other recreation	7.412 College teachers
	7.320 Stationery	7.420 School facilities	
	7.431 School books	7.432 Other educational expenditures	
08 Other services	8.210 Toilet articles	8.100 Barber	
	8.220 Personal goods	8.310 Restaurants	
		8.320 Hotels	
		8.400 Other Services	
		8.900 Expenses of residents abroad	
10–19 Capital formation	All		
20 Government	21.000[a] Commodities		All four compensation categories

Notes: Tradables: All commodity categories except construction (10, 11, 12, and 13). Nontradables: All service categories plus construction (10, 11, 12, and 13).

a. Phase III classification.

3

Methods for the Multilateral Comparisons

THIS CHAPTER EXAMINES the methods of processing the expenditures and price data (described in Chapter 2) into price and quantity indexes for detailed and summary categories and for larger aggregations including consumption, capital formation, government, and GDP itself.[1] First the statistical properties sought in the indexes are considered. Then four alternative sets of methods for producing the desired indexes are briefly described.

Most of the chapter is devoted to an explanation of the particular set of methods used in the ICP. Reasons for the ICP choices are explained, and a description of the application of the methods to aggregation at different levels is given. The first level combines the price comparisons for specific items within each detailed category to derive purchasing power parities (PPPs) and price indexes for the detailed categories themselves. The PPPs are expressed in own currency units per unit of the numéraire currency (for example, francs per dollar),while the price indexes, obtained by dividing each country's PPPs by its exchange rate with the numéraire currency, are expressed relative to the numéraire country, which is set at 100. The second level of aggregation involves the combination of the PPPs for the detailed categories to form PPPs for larger aggregations of expenditures, including the summary categories, the three major divisions of GDP (consumption, capital formation, and government), and GDP itself.

In a final section, the results of the preferred methods are compared with other methods. A brief attempt is made at the end to assess the degree of precision of the estimates.

For ease of exposition, the complications posed by the possible regionalization of the index number calculations will not be considered in this chapter. Chapter 4 will deal with the further problems arising from attempting to apply methods first to calculation of multilateral indexes within regions and then to interregional comparisons.

The Desired Properties

The choice of methods of aggregating these expenditures and price data to form price and quantity indexes should be governed by the statistical and economic properties that are sought. No method of aggregation can satisfy all the desired conditions. The relative importance to be attached to different properties depends upon the purpose to be served and upon the number or types of countries to be compared—whether a single pair of countries, countries in a relatively homogeneous region, or all the countries of the world.

Generally, properties that are apt to be desired, whatever the context, include those that produce consistency and representativeness. The first five of the following properties are concerned with consistency and the next two relate to representativeness. The last one deals with a narrower statistical consideration.

Base-country Invariance

This property calls for symmetrical treatment of all countries so that it makes no difference for the final comparisons which country is chosen as the base. That is, the country selected as the base serves simply as a

---

1. This chapter draws freely in some sections on a paper presented at a joint meeting of the working groups "National Accounts," "Input-Output Tables," and "Price Statistics" organized by the Statistical Office of the European Communities in Luxembourg, March 20–22, 1978. See Kravis, Heston, Summers (1978c).

numéraire.[2] In binary comparisons, involving only two countries, this condition is familiar under the name "country reversal test." (It is more familiar still in connection with intertemporal comparisons where it is known as the time-reversal test.[3]) For a binary comparison the country reversal test is satisfied if $I_{j/k} \cdot I_{k/j} = 1$ where I is a price or quantity index (the subscripts indicating countries) and each index is computed independently.[4]

Factor-reversal Test

Another consistency requirement is that the product of the price and quantity comparisons should equal the expenditure ratio. In the intertemporal comparison literature, this is called the factor-reversal test. In a trivial sense, this test is satisfied whenever a direct (independently computed) price (quantity) index is used with an indirect quantity (price) index, the indirect index being obtained by dividing the former into the expenditure ratio. For the test to be satisfied meaningfully, the relationship must hold when the price and quantity indexes are computed independently.

Transitivity

Each index, whether a price or quantity, should be a number on a continuous scale such that pairwise comparisons between the indexes of members of any group of countries will be transitive in the sense that $I_{j/k} = I_{j/l} \div I_{k/l}$. This property, Fisher's "circularity test," is relevant only to relationships between more than two countries.[5]

Matrix Consistency

Quantities expressed in value terms in matrix form, defined for n countries and m goods categories, should be stated in such a way that (1) the values for any category will be directly comparable between countries, and (2) the values for any country will be directly comparable between categories. The first requirement states that for any category, the value figures must reflect the correct quantity ratios between countries. The second makes it possible to obtain a country's quantity at any level of aggregation simply by summing the quantities of all the categories constituting that aggregate. If the quantities, measured in physical units, were known for all countries and all categories, the quantity numbers would meet requirement 1.[6] Such quantity numbers would not meet requirement 2, however, because they could not be added together meaningfully across categories for a particular country to get the country's aggregate quantity.[7]

Transactions Equality

Closely related to the equal treatment of countries is the requirement that the relative importance of each transaction be dependent only on its magnitude and not on the size of the country in which it occurred. This can be best elucidated by the class of index-number formulas, described below, which involves the valuation of each country's quantities at prices that are averages across all the countries. In the computation of the average international price for eggs, for example, each purchase of a dozen eggs of a given specification should have the same weight whether the

---

2. This distinction in terminology is maintained throughout the report. That is, a numéraire country is one that serves merely as a reference point without any unique influence on the results, while a base country is one the choice of which *does* have a unique influence on the comparisons. This influence stems from the fact that its weights are used to calculate the index numbers, and also from the fact that, at an earlier stage, the selection of items for the price comparisons is governed by the availability of goods on its market. A base country thus imparts its own stamp to the results.

3. Fisher (1922), chap. 13. For a review of index number formulas in the context of international comparisons see Ruggles (1967).

4. An argument can be advanced for not requiring base-country invariance. Saying that A needs k times as much income to enjoy at his prices the level of satisfaction now enjoyed by B is not necessarily the same as saying that if B's prices were left unchanged but his income was reduced by a factor $1/k$ he would enjoy the same level of satisfaction as A enjoys at his original income while facing his original prices. Put in Hicksian terms, the equivalent variation expressed relative to A's income need not be the reciprocal of the compensating variation expressed relative to B's income. If the common tastes of A and B are homothetic—that is, if all income consumption paths of their indifference map are rays emanating from the origin—the two will indeed be the same. See Hicks (1946), pp. 38–41 and 331–33, and note 13 below.

5. An index can produce transitive results that are not base-country invariant. A Laspeyres index, for example, produces transitive comparisons once a given country is selected as the base country, but there will be a different set of transitive comparisons for each base country.

6. The denomination of quantities in physical units would be sufficient to meet requirement 1, but not necessary. See the discussion of notional quantities below.

7. Matrix consistency was called "additive consistency" in the Phase I and II reports. The term was subsequently taken by others to include the requirement that the matrix consistency be achieved by independently computed indexes for any level of aggregation including the detailed category. It was denied, in this view, that an index number system that achieves consistency by a simultaneous calculation of indexes for all categories is "fully additive." (See European Communities Statistical Office, 1977, p. 31.) To avoid any semantic confusion, a new label has been adopted here. A "fully additive" set of index numbers clearly has matrix consistency, with the property of independence for the indexes for detailed categories. It is argued below that this is not necessarily an advantage. See later in this chapter under the section "Aggregation of Category Expenditures and Prices."

purchase is made in a small country or a large one. This kind of symmetrical treatment would not be achieved if the average international prices were computed as a simple (unweighted) average of the national prices (unit-country weighting).[8] There are three facets of the underlying reasons for desiring transactions equality.

CONSISTENCY WITH NATIONAL-ACCOUNTS PRACTICES. Weighted average international prices conform to standard national-accounts practice, in which average transactions prices are the prices implicitly embedded in the expenditures. Such average prices justify the adding up of apples and oranges because they provide an approximate measure of the resources absorbed by each product or, alternatively, an approximate measure of the utilities obtained in consuming each product. To approximate average international prices, total expenditures in all the countries covered should be divided by the total quantity exchanged.

EQUAL TREATMENT OF INDIVIDUAL TRANSACTORS IN DIFFERENT COUNTRIES. The importance attached to this aspect of transactions equality will vary with the purpose. If, for example, the EEC wanted to establish a progressive tax on incomes, it would be important to establish the tax base (individual incomes) in an evenhanded way among all individuals regardless of whether they resided in a small or a large country.[9]

INVARIANCE OF THE INDEXES TO CHANGES IN POLITICAL SUBDIVISION OF THE WORLD AND REGIONS INTO COUNTRIES. If each transaction is given equal treatment regardless of location, changes in political boundaries will not affect the country comparison other than those involving the altered areas. The average international prices used, for example, to value the quantities of India and Sri Lanka in a comparison of Asian countries would remain the same whether Bangladesh and Pakistan were treated as one country or two; consequently, India–Sri Lanka comparisons would be invariant to the political change.[10]

_____

8. Unit-country weighting was used in the recent comparisons of the EEC (European Communities Statistical Office, 1977).

9. Unit-country weighting would increase the influence of small countries' transactions upon the final estimates of relative incomes. For example, unit-country weighting in the recent comparisons of the EEC meant that a dozen eggs purchased in Luxembourg had roughly 150 times the influence on the average Community price as a dozen eggs purchased in the Federal Republic of Germany.

10. However, see the later section "Aggregation of Category Expenditures and Prices" for qualifications with respect to the ICP method actually used.

Country Characteristicity

The term "country characteristicity" was suggested by Drechsler (1975) in a thoughtful paper dealing with the desired properties of formulas for international comparisons, among other things. In constructing price and quantity indexes, the sample of items should be representative of the goods found in the markets of the countries being compared. Similarly the weights assigned to the items should correspond as closely as possible to the relative importance of the items in the countries. This property is, of course, easier to satisfy when only a pair of countries is being compared— particularly if the two are very similar—than when a wider grouping of countries is involved. If the focus is on comparisons between a particular pair of countries, the characteristicity consideration would lead to a comparison based on the sample of most representative items obtainable in each of the countries and on weights based solely on the spending patterns of that pair. As the number of countries grows beyond two, it is increasingly difficult to satisfy both characteristicity and transitivity.

World Representativeness

When countries are to be compared with reference to some worldwide standard, the empirical version of the standard that is actually applied should be representative of the world rather than of the limited set of countries included in the exercise. For example, if the quantities of the countries in the comparison are to be valued at average world prices, the prices should be averaged in a way that reflects, as best it can be estimated, prices all over the world and not simply those of the included countries.

Statistical Efficiency

Because the underlying data collected by the ICP are subject to sampling errors, the multilateral methods used should give quantity and price indexes that are relatively insensitive to these underlying sampling errors. (In formal statistical terms, the aggregation method should give estimates of relative quantities and prices that have minimum variance.)

Overview of the Criteria

Each of these criteria has much to commend it. The representativeness criteria hardly need more comment. The five consistency criteria are important because a single set of unambiguous estimates is desired. In many applications, the utility of the results would be greatly diminished if, for example, the entire set of quantity relationships among the countries varied according to which one was selected as the base country.

The remarks at the beginning of Chapter 2 about the similarity of tastes in different countries suggest that the theory of economic behavior at least in principle has applicability in ICP comparisons. There should be no doubt, however, that the properties described above are not derived explicitly from economic theory. Frisch, in his classic survey of index-number theory, distinguishes between two approaches to the construction of index numbers.[11] The statistical approach compares two situations by a summary number that simply reflects in some sense the average difference between the statistics describing each of the situations. The functional approach, on the other hand, compares two situations on the basis of a theoretical structure derived from economic considerations.

It should be clear that the ICP criteria listed above were devised in the spirit of the statistical approach. In fact, economic theory indicates that all desirable properties cannot be possessed by any single set of indexes. The kinds of restrictions on spending behavior implied by the theory of consumer behavior (for example, Slutsky conditions[12]) in principle should be built into the procedure for making international comparisons. That is, the satisfying of Slutsky conditions should be listed as a criterion. However, few producers of index numbers attempt to impose such requirements on their data.[13] Economic theory in its present form provides limited guidance on aggregation procedures across individual households, business firms, and governmental units and gives virtually none across diverse geographical regions.[14]

Four Sets of Methods

Broadly speaking, there are four sets of methods for the international comparison of prices and quantities. Much of the pioneering work was done with binary comparisons (for pairs of countries). This procedure still has a substantial effect on current work. Binary comparisons are involved in three of these sets of methods. In the first, binary comparisons are aimed solely at comparing prices or quantities for one pair of countries at a time. In the others, binary comparisons are used as building blocks for comparisons involving more than two countries. Of course, many of the methods devised primarily to deal with many countries at once are applicable also to pairs of countries as well.

Comparison between Two Countries

In a binary comparison concerned solely with price and quantity ratios for two countries, transitivity involving third countries need not be considered.

The most commonly used formulas are the place-to-place equivalents of the Laspeyres (LA) and Paasche (PA) indexes. For quantity indexes these are:

$$(3.1) \qquad \mathrm{LA}^q_{j/b} = \frac{\sum\limits_{i=1}^{m} p_{ib} q_{ij}}{\sum\limits_{i=1}^{m} p_{ib} q_{ib}}$$

$$(3.2) \qquad \mathrm{PA}^q_{j/b} = \frac{\sum\limits_{i=1}^{m} p_{ij} q_{ij}}{\sum\limits_{i=1}^{m} p_{ij} q_{ib}}$$

where p and q are prices and quantities, i refers to goods, and country j is being compared with b, the base country.

The Laspeyres formula values the quantity of each product in both countries at the base country's price. In the Paasche formula the quantities are valued at the partner country's own prices. Under either formula, the values in the numerator and denominator for any i are comparable between the countries, and they may be added to yield aggregates for each country that are also comparable. However, no simple average of subaggregate indexes can be formed to give the index for the aggregate.

For country j the use of its own price weights in the Paasche formula is likely to produce a lower quantity index relative to the base country than will the use of the base country's prices in the Laspeyres formula. This widely noted outcome is due to the negative correlation that generally prevails between price ratios and quantity ratios for individual products or for detailed categories.[15] Compared with the base country,

---

11. Frisch (1936). Frisch's terminology differs slightly from that used here; his term for the "statistical" concept was "atomistic."

12. Phlips (1974), pp. 40–56.

13. While one usually thinks of the theory of consumer behavior imposing restrictions on index-number construction, the reverse may be the case too. For example, insistence upon base-country invariance is equivalent to requiring for consumption that the underlying function is homothetic, an assumption not usually made in consumer behavior research.

14. The force of proposals to select an index number based on the utility function (see, for example, Phlips, 1974, pp. 92–94) is weakened by the doubtful applicability of such a function to a nation rather than to an individual (see, for example, Debreu, 1974; Mantel, 1977; and Sonnenschein, 1973), and to GDP rather than to consumption. However, for an experiment with an aggregation method for consumption only based on a utility function, see the account in Chapter 9 of the application of the linear expenditure system to ICP data.

15. This is a usual, but not necessary, consequence of negatively sloped demand curves. These notions arise again in more rigorous terms in Chapter 9 in a discussion of revealed preference.

a country will usually absorb relatively large quantities of goods that are comparatively cheap and relatively small quantities of those that are comparatively expensive. This observed tendency for Paasche quantity indexes to be lower than Laspeyres indexes is referred to here as the own-weight effect. (This is directly analogous to the so-called Gerschenkron effect in intertemporal indexes.) The Paasche-Laspeyres spread, as the ratio of the Paasche to Laspeyres indexes is denoted, varied among the fifteen binary comparisons included in Phase II of the ICP from around 0.5 in the binary comparisons of Kenya, India, Philippines, the Republic of Korea, and Colombia with the United States to around 0.85 in the binary comparisons of France and the Federal Republic of Germany with the United States.[16]

Neither of these indexes satisfies the country-reversal test, but the geometric mean of the two, Fisher's "ideal" index (F), does:[17]

$$(3.3) \qquad F_{jb} = (\mathrm{LA}_{jb} \cdot \mathrm{PA}_{jb})^{1/2}.$$

This index is rarely justified in theoretical terms, but is a widely used compromise between the indexes reflecting relative prices in the two countries.[18] However, the Fisher index, unlike each of its two component indexes, does not produce matrix consistency. Nor does it, without special treatment, produce transactions equality.

A frequently cited advantage of binary comparisons is that they can embody more characteristicity than any others simply by virtue of their exclusion of third countries in the choice of items to be price-compared and in the selection of weights. However, this is not necessarily an advantage if it is desired to compare two countries in some broader context, as, for example, France and the Federal Republic of Germany in connection with some issue within the European Community. A binary comparison of these two countries that takes no account of the other member countries might be of less interest in the Community context than, for example, a comparison in which the quantities of both countries were valued at average Community prices.[19]

Methods of binary comparisons are considered further in Chapter 7. A method is developed there for producing better binary comparisons than traditional binary procedures would normally permit from the use of the ICP data base.

Comparisons among Three or More Countries

Aggregation methods that produce a unique cardinal scaling for three or more countries that meet many or most of the conditions outlined above—multilateral methods—are relatively new. A truly multilateral set of comparisons among countries has the characteristic that at least some aspect of *every* country's prices or quantities enters into comparisons of *all* pairs of countries. While procedures representing a step in this direction were used at least as early as the 1950s,[20] the first major multilateral approaches have appeared only in the last decade or two.

Three classes of methods may be distinguished: (1) selective sets of binary comparisons, (2) multilateral methods utilizing binary comparisons, and (3) multilateral methods not dependent upon binary comparisons. In the first two, binary comparisons produced by the methods described above are usually taken as the starting point.

SELECTIVE SETS OF BINARY COMPARISONS. In this class of methods a selected set of binary comparisons is used as the basis for inferring the comparisons for the other pairs. The simplest procedure falling into this category is the star system of binary comparisons. In the star system, each country (a point of the star) is compared in a binary way with a base country (the center of the star). Comparisons between point countries are given by the ratio of the corresponding point-to-center comparisons. Matrix consistency and transitivity can be produced if the prices of the center are used to value the quantities of all the point countries. Of course, this would detract from the characteristicity of the binary comparisons. More important, however, neither this nor any other way of using the star-system comparisons can satisfy the base-country–invariance requirement.

An alternative way of selecting a basic set of binary comparisons that can be used to infer comparisons for the other pairs is suggested by a Divisia-type index.[21] Such an index could be adapted to international comparisons by ordering countries according to some similarity criterion and then selecting as the basic binary comparisons successive contiguous countries. Unfor-

16. Kravis, Heston, Summers (1978a), table 5-31.

17. Henceforth, the subscripts indicating the countries in the comparison will be written without the slash; that is, *jb* instead of *j/b*.

18. While there is a utility function for which *F* is the appropriate true cost-of-living index, it is not one that has commanded attention in the theoretical literature.

19. See Hill (1981), chap. 5, on this point. Hill's report on international comparison methods contains an insightful discussion of many of the choices that are treated only briefly here.

20. European weights were used in the OEEC studies of Gilbert and Kravis (1954) and Gilbert and associates (1958).

21. The Divisia index is particularly suited to intertemporal comparisons. See, for example, a series of studies by Jorgenson, Christensen, and others. The citations can be found in Christensen, Cummings, Jorgenson (1980).

tunately, in international comparisons there is no natural arrangement of pairs of situations for constructing the chain (the empirical form that the Divisia idea takes) as is so unequivocally provided by time in intertemporal comparisons. (Ordering is important. I_{14}, a comparison of the first and fourth country, can be estimated by either $F_{12} \cdot F_{23} \cdot F_{34}$ or $F_{13} \cdot F_{32} \cdot F_{24}$, but these two estimates would not necessarily be the same.) It is not even clear that the underlying theoretical notion of cumulative change through time in a given place measured by the Divisia integral index has a proper analogue in interspatial comparisons. Nevertheless, the use of a chain index has been suggested by a number of writers, and indeed the ICP has experimented with the procedure with Phase II data.[22] Ideally, countries should be ordered according to the similarity of their relative prices and output compositions. This might most practically be carried out by ordering them by real per capita income. This ordering would not be known precisely until the exercise was completed, but the results probably would be insensitive to minor changes in the ordering of countries. For the relatively small number of countries included in the ICP Phase II comparisons, the chain had several large, discrete jumps in per capita income levels. The largest two in 1970 were both 22 percentage points. If all the countries in the world were included, however, contiguous countries would be much more similar. (In Phase III, the two largest gaps for thirty-four countries are seventeen and eight percentage points.) With small gaps arbitrariness of the choice of a basis for chaining would be less serious.

MULTILATERAL METHODS UTILIZING BINARY COMPARISONS. This class of methods differs from the preceding ones in two ways. First, the data set bearing on the set of all countries being compared is summarized in the form of a collection of binary indexes for all possible pairs. Second, a comparison between any two countries is computed in a way that depends on all the binary indexes that involve either country. Methods of this type, which produce transitive comparisons, include those of Elteto, Koves, and, Szulc (EKS)[23] and Van Yzeren.[24] Both of these methods are discussed at length in the Phase I report,[25] so only the essential features of each are described here.

In the case of EKS, which has been used in Eastern Europe, the notion of a binary comparison is gener-

alized to make the index for two countries depend not only on the original country binary index for the two countries but also on the ratio of the two countries' original-country binary indexes with all other countries.[26] If the original-country indexes are Fisher binaries, EKS's comparison of country j's output relative to country k's (for all j and k) is the transitive index that deviates "minimally" (in an appropriate logarithmic least-squares sense) from what would be obtained if Fisher ideal indexes were used. The underlying principle of quadratic minimization leads to this formula for execution:

$$(3.4) \qquad \text{EKS}_{jk} = \left[F_{jk}^2 \cdot \prod_{\substack{l=1 \\ l \neq j,k}}^{n} \frac{F_{jl}}{F_{kl}} \right]^{\frac{1}{n}}$$

where F_{jk} is the Fisher quantity index for country j relative to country k.[27] The Fisher indexes themselves are not transitive, but the EKS agglomeration of Fisher indexes is. The EKS method is a multilateral method because a quantity or price comparison of any two countries make use of the prices and quantities in all other countries.

The Van Yzeren approach, used in the mid-1950s in comparisons made by the European Coal and Steel Community (1960), also builds up multilateral comparisons out of binary ones. The criterion for combining the binary indexes, however, is based on Van Yzeren's concept of a complicated set of market baskets. Thus it avoids the special and arbitrary quadratic minimization principle. (But in the limiting case of two countries, both EKS and Van Yzeren reduce to the Fisher index.) In essence, the method calls for pricing the goods and services of each of a number of countries in each of the other countries. A set of price indexes is computed on the basis of minimizing what Van Yzeren calls a "discordance function"—that is, "a yardstick for the degree to which the currency ratios are adapted to the price and quantity patterns of the different countries."

A drawback of both the EKS and Van Yzeren methods, and indeed of the selective set of binaries of the

---

22. It was considered, for example, though rejected by Keynes (1930). For the ICP experiments see Kravis, Heston, Summers (1978c).

23. The original publications describing these methods are not in English, but see Drechsler (1975), pp. 17–34.

24. Van Yzeren (1946), pp. 3–34.

25. Kravis, Kenessey, Heston, Summers (1975), pp. 66–68.

26. An original country binary index is one derived directly from the data of the two countries being compared. It is in contrast to a bridge country comparison, which is illustrated by the comparison of point countries in a star system by the ratio of the corresponding point-to-center comparisons.

27. A symmetric representation of EKS_{jk} is

$$\text{EKS}_{jk} = \prod_{l=1}^{n} \left[\frac{F_{jl}}{F_{kl}} \right]^{\frac{1}{n}} \quad \text{where} \quad F_{ll} = 1.$$

The representation of equation 3.4 shows how the index gives greater weight to the original country (j,k) Fisher index than to the ratios involving each of the other countries.

previous section, is they do not directly prescribe procedures for making product comparisons at levels of aggregation below the full set of categories to which the methods are applied. Unfortunately, applying these methods to GDP and subaggregates does not produce matrix consistency.

Multilateral methods that use binaries as building blocks sometimes seem to be preferred because binary comparisons are regarded as inherently superior. The reason for this assessment of binary comparisons is that each depends exclusively on the prices and quantities of the two countries involved. However, if, as was suggested above, this exclusiveness is no advantage in a multilateral context, then neither is there any inherent advantage in multilateral comparison methods that are based on binaries or that are constructed so as to produce results that deviate minimally from the results of binary comparisons.[28]

MULTILATERAL METHODS NOT DEPENDENT UPON BINARY COMPARISONS. A third set of methods does not involve the calculation of binary indexes at all. In making quantity comparisons among many countries, there are two basic choices. The first involves averaging quantity ratios[29] (or price ratios) while the second calls for averages of quantities (or prices) not in ratio form. When quantity or price ratios are averaged, expenditures are used as weights; when quantities (or prices) are averaged, prices (or quantities) are used as weights.

The first alternative takes two forms. The real GDP of the jth country relative to that of the numéraire, r_{jb}, can be obtained by computing a weighted average of the ratios of category quantities (q_{ij}/q_{ib}) for all categories, using as weights average category *expenditure shares* for all n countries. Alternatively, PPP_{jb} can be obtained first by the equivalent weighted averaging of p_{ij}/p_{ib} values. The r_{jb} can then be obtained by converting the domestic currency GDP$_j$ to a value expressed in base-country currency units, which can be compared directly with GDP$_b$. If weighted *geometric* means are used (that is, the averaging process is multiplicative), then

$$(3.5) \quad r_{jb} = \prod_{i=1}^{m} (q_{ij}/q_{ib})^{w_i}; \; w_i = \frac{1}{n} \sum_{j=1}^{n} \left(e_{ij} \bigg/ \sum_{i=1}^{m} e_{ij} \right)$$

$$(3.6) \quad \text{PPP}_{jb} = \prod_{i=1}^{m} \left(\frac{p_{ij}}{p_{ib}} \right)^{w_i} ; \; w_i = \frac{1}{n} \sum_{j=1}^{n} \left(e_{ij} \bigg/ \sum_{i=1}^{m} e_{ij} \right)$$

where e represents expenditures. Indexes formulated in this way are known as Walsh indexes.[30] The fact that the two indexes satisfy the factor-reversal test ensures that the application of equation 3.5 gives the same result as is obtained from the indirect method of applying the PPP of equation 3.6 to domestic currency GDP$_j$. The formula for computing w_i calls for an arithmetic rather than a geometric mean of expenditure proportions across all the countries being compared. A geometric average procedure has the major disadvantage of assigning a negligible weight to any category that is unimportant in any single country.

The second approach to quantity comparisons also has two variants, one a direct comparison and the other an indirect one involving estimates of PPPs. However, an arithmetic rather than a geometric averaging process is used, and category quantities (or prices) rather than quantity ratios (or price ratios) are the inputs to the averaging.

The direct comparison between any country and any other is given by the ratio of their GDPs as obtained by valuing their category quantities at *prices* that are in an appropriate sense the average of prices in all countries ($\bar{p}_i$ in equation 3.7):

$$(3.7) \quad r_{jb} = \frac{\sum_{i=1}^{m} \bar{p}_i q_{ij}}{\sum_{i=1}^{m} \bar{p}_i q_{ib}} .$$

The precise definition of the $\bar{p}_i$'s, to be thought of as "international prices," is left intentionally vague at this point. They must be averaged for each category from country prices denominated in domestic currency units. Therefore, as will be discussed below, they can be obtained only from the p_{ij} after applying some sort of conversion factors. No such vagueness is necessary in defining a PPP here. In equation 3.8 the quantity

---

28. This point is due to Hill (1981), chap. 5. Hill says about multilateral methods that take the Fisher indexes produced by binary comparisons as the starting point: "The construction of a multilateral set of measurements at a later stage has then to be regarded as a process whereby an initial set of perfectly good binary measures has to be distorted, rather in the manner practised by Procrustes, in the interests of securing transitivity" (p. 5-38). Beyond that Hill argues: "In general, not much confidence can be placed on arguments which rely heavily on the special case of two countries when trying to appraise methodologies designed for large groups of countries" (p. 5-21).

29. It should be remembered that the methods described in Chapter 2 lead to information about relative q's rather than the q's themselves. Methods outlined here drawing on knowledge of the q's in practice must be modified to take account of this feature of the ICP data.

30. Walsh (1910). A Walsh index, with geometric weights, was used in comparisons reported by Salazar-Carillo (1973).

weights are simply the aggregate of the observed quantities in the various countries.

$$(3.8) \quad \text{PPP}_{jb} = \frac{\sum_{i=1}^{m} p_{ij} Q_j}{\sum_{i=1}^{m} p_{ib} Q_j} \qquad Q_j = \sum_{j=1}^{m} q_{ij} \, .$$

The methods represented in equation 3.7 may be referred to as the "average price" approach. The specific formula adopted by the ICP, it will be seen, falls within this group.

The Walsh quantity index of equation 3.5 and the average-price-weight index of equation 3.7 are both transitive and base-country invariant, but only the latter has the property of matrix consistency.[31] Use of a Walsh index would necessitate some sort of manipulation to produce a table in which values are provided for the components of GDP that are consistent with GDP totals. The inevitable arbitrariness of such a procedure should be avoided unless there are compelling compensating advantages.

The average price approach of equation 3.7 lends itself to a relatively simple and clear-cut basis for evaluating each country's comparative GDP and components thereof. In principle, it calls for the determination of the average international price of each final product that is consumed in the world. The average price is simply the total amount spent divided by the quantity consumed. The average price of each of the products is the basis for valuing the quantities of the product consumed in each country.

One type of average-price approach, developed by Dino Gerardi, was used by the Common Market in its 1975 comparisons.[32] It is referred to here as the unit-country weighting method. The average price (in practice, an average PPP) used to value quantities (or detailed expenditure categories) is a simple geometric mean of the PPPs in each country. The weight of each country is equal for each item, or category, hence the term unit-country weighting. The average price is separately estimated for each item or category. Expenditures obtained by multiplying each category quantity by the category average price can be aggregated to make real quantity comparisons between the countries, and purchasing power parities can be derived.

Any average-price method, whether based on unit-country weighting or not, will produce the same relative quantities for a given detailed category, since each country's quantities are being multiplied by the same category price. Average-price methods will differ in their relative valuations between items, say, eggs and shoes. In the unit-country weighting system, each country is treated equally in determining the relative prices of eggs and shoes, no matter what relative (or absolute) quantities are consumed in the two countries. This formulation violates the fundamental definitions of average price developed in national accounting, described above under the criterion of transactions equality. It has for this reason been unacceptable to the ICP. The attraction of unit-country weighting is its simplicity in calculation of average prices and in subsequent aggregations, but this simplicity is achieved by avoiding the fundamental problem of developing average prices that are commensurable across items and countries.[33]

If transactions equality is to be preserved, the averaging of the prices of different countries requires finding a way to cope with the lack of commensurability of prices quoted in different currency units. The appropriate procedure is to convert the prices to a common currency through PPPs, but, of course, those are unknown. An obvious practical possibility would be to use exchange rates as the conversion factors, and this was the procedure followed in the earlier Common Market study in calculating average European prices.[34] This procedure assumes that exchange rates are equal to PPPs, and the disbelief that this assumption is warranted is the raison d'être of the whole ICP exercise. In the ICP it was found—to take an extreme example—

31. One might wish to choose among aggregation procedures on the basis of what they individually imply about the consuming behavior of the residents of the countries. Walsh (in the geometric mean weighting form) can be regarded as being the proper "true cost of living" index associated with a utility function of the Cobb-Douglas form. Therefore, it assumes unitary price and income elasticities. No corresponding statement about elasticities can be made about the average-price-weight methods, however, because they do not have a specific utility function counterpart. Thus it is not possible to compare them with Walsh in terms of consumer behavior.

32. See European Communities Statistical Office (1977), chap. 2.

33. It has been suggested that an appropriate criterion for judging comparison methods is this: if a country's total GDP and population were to double, then because its per capita GDP did not change, its relative standing among nations as estimated by a comparison method should not change. The unit-country method would give identical estimates in the two situations, but the method adopted by the ICP, discussed in detail below, would not. The ICP view is that this is *not* an appropriate criterion, because it violates the requirement of transactions equality. The ICP estimate would be different because in the doubling case the country's weight in determining world average prices would be increased. The set of average prices would be closer to the structure of the country's estimated relative GDP per capita. The EKS and Van Yzeren methods, like the unit-country method, all give unchanged estimates. So too does the Walsh index unless the expenditure shares of the countries are weighted.

34. Paretti, Krijnse Locker, Goybet (1974), p. 666. In this study, the average prices were computed with the aid of quantity weights.

that the purchasing power of the Indian rupee over all GDP relative to the U.S. dollar in 1973 was more than three times as great as the exchange rate indicated. Of course, the deviations between purchasing power and exchange rates were smaller among European nations, so the probable distortion in average prices was correspondingly smaller. Judging from price indexes computed with the use of European quantity weights, the use of 1970 exchange rates to make German and Dutch prices commensurable for the calculation of overall average prices made the influence of German prices too small by 8 percent and the influence of Dutch prices nearly 6 percent too large.[35] That is, use of exchange rate conversions gave German prices too little weight and Dutch prices too much in the process of averaging country prices.

The ICP's treatment of this problem is described later in the discussion of the second level of aggregation. Before that, though, the methods applied at the first level of aggregation must be presented. However, a consideration arising at both levels of aggregation, the matter of representativeness of the thirty-four countries of the ICP set, logically requires discussion ahead of both.

Supercountry Weighting

If an average-price method proceeded simply by someone's calculating a set of average relative prices of the countries included in the study at a particular stage, then the average set—and therefore the estimate of the relative per capita GDPs derived from it—would depend fortuitously on just which countries happened to be included in the ICP. To avoid this, in the averaging process the prices of each of the included countries were weighted in accordance with the degree to which each ICP country's price structure could be regarded as representative of the price structure of the various countries of the world as a whole. A set of "supercountries" was defined, each of which had the same price and expenditure *structure* as a corresponding representative (ICP) country but with a GDP *total* equal to the sum of the nominal (exchange-rate–converted) GDPs of all the countries regarded as having the same price and quantity structures. That is, all non-ICP countries were allocated to supercountries corresponding to the thirty-four ICP representative countries.

The starting point of this procedure was the cross-classification of all the countries of the world by region and by per capita nominal (exchange-rate–converted)

GDP. The aggregate populations and GDPs resulting from this cross-classification are shown in Table 3-1.[36] The table shows how the initially chosen narrow income classes were consolidated into eight broader classes. These classes were selected in the light of the resulting distribution of the thirty-four Phase III countries, shown in Table 3-2, through use of the following criteria:

1. Countries with large enough differences in levels of income to make likely differences in price and quantity structures were placed in different classes.
2. Marginal adjustments in category limits were made to minimize the extent to which any one ICP country would end up bearing an unduly large or unduly small supercountry weight.

Once the income classes shown in Table 3-2 were selected, the aggregate population and nominal GDP of each cell were assigned to one of the thirty-four Phase III countries. Following the principle used in the Phase II report, where there was more than one Phase III country in a cell, the aggregate GDP was divided evenly among the countries, with the provision that no country would receive less than its own GDP as a weight. India, Italy, the United Kingdom, the Federal Republic of Germany, France, Netherlands, Belgium, and Brazil are the countries for which equal within-cell shares would have produced weights that were smaller than their actual GDPs. The population and GDP of cells in which there were no Phase III countries were assigned to the nearest cell in which there was one.

In the case of the African countries, the undeviating application of these rules would have produced a very large supercountry GDP for Zambia relative to Kenya and Malawi. The total GDP for Africa in Table 3-3 would have been distributed as follows:

Zambia	141,813
Kenya	12,210
Malawi	12,210
Total	166,233

It was arbitrarily decided to waive the rules and to assign half the total African weight to Zambia and to divide the other half between the other two countries.

Another anomaly, but one that was allowed to stand, involved the five ICP countries in the European region

---

35. Based on the Laspeyres parity index, ibid., p. 712.

36. The basic data consisted of exchange-rate–converted GDP for more than 180 countries obtained either from the U.N. Economic Commission for Europe (1976), vol. 2, table 1A, or from World Bank (1977). Minor differences between these GDP figures and those in Table 1-1 are attributable to different sources used and reflect mainly the different dates at which the countries provided the estimates.

Table 3-1. Distribution of World Population and of World (Nominal GDP) by per Capita Nominal GDP and Region, 1975

Per capita nominal GDP (US$)	Population (in millions)						GDP (in millions of US$)					
	Africa	Asia	Europe	North America	Latin America and Caribbean	World	Africa	Asia	Europe	North America	Latin America and Caribbean	World
0 – 99	9.90	34.55				44.45	860	3,374				4,234
100 – 199	114.75	780.53			4.58	899.86	14,951	109,189			850	124,990
200 – 249	38.89	155.49				194.38	8,609	33,990				42,599
Subtotal	163.54	970.57			4.58	1,138.69	24,420	146,553			850	171,823
250 – 299	62.73	1.87				64.60	16,370	460				16,830
300 – 399	82.80	967.44			8.49	1,058.73	28,380	345,279			3,206	378,865
400 – 499	27.00	21.41			4.10	52.51	11,785	9,597			1,866	23,248
Subtotal	172.53	990.72			12.59	1,175.84	56,535	355,336			5,072	416,943
500 – 599	25.98	35.28	2.40		42.10	105.76	14,505	19,089	1,220		23,714	58,528
600 – 649					13.98	13.98					8,443	8,443
650 – 699	0.86				10.25	11.11	567				7,083	7,650
700 – 799	5.61	19.53			7.00	32.14	4,346	14,962			5,268	24,576
800 – 899	15.75	1.45			9.40	26.60	13,680	1,250			7,520	22,450
900 – 999	0.88	16.12	39.18		1.97	58.15	860	15,010	35,659		1,926	53,455
Subtotal	49.08	72.38	41.58		84.70	247.74	33,958	50,311	36,879		53,954	175,102
1,000 – 1,499	25.50	14.90	22.21		173.49	236.10	35,290	17,590	27,573		197,745	278,198
1,500 – 1,999	0.60	37.39	30.86		26.20	95.05	1,160	61,346	47,367		50,106	159,979
Subtotal	26.10	52.29	53.07		199.69	331.15	36,450	78,936	74,940		247,851	438,177
2,000 – 2,499		1.03	31.44		13.39	45.86		2,370	69,768		31,895	104,033
2,500 – 2,999	0.54	2.39	324.04	3.12		330.09	1,360	6,057	838,913	8,735		855,065
Subtotal	0.54	3.42	355.48	3.12	13.39	375.95	1,360	8,427	908,681	8,735	31,895	959,098
3,000 – 3,499			55.96	0.20		56.16			172,484	630		173,114
3,500 – 3,999		3.39	31.67			35.06		12,157	119,280			131,437
4,000 – 4,499		123.75	55.96			179.71		543,023	228,820			771,843
4,500 – 4,999			7.57			7.57			37,794			37,794
Subtotal		127.14	151.16	0.20		278.50		555,180	558,378	630		1,114,188
5,000 – 5,499		0.03	0.04	0.10	0.04	0.21		160	200	480	230	1,070
5,500 – 5,999	2.44	0.11	18.58			21.13	13,510	610	109,034			123,154
6,000 – 6,499		0.16	62.95			63.11		950	400,186			401,136
6,500 – 6,999		13.70	61.83	22.88		98.41		92,062	424,835	160,067		676,964
Subtotal	2.44	14.00	143.40	22.98	0.04	182.86	13,510	93,782	934,255	160,547	230	1,202,324
7,000 – 7,499			9.07	213.54		222.61			63,753	1,513,828		1,577,581
7,500 – 8,000												
8,000 – 9,999			69.60			69.60			123,532			123,532
Over 10,000		1.85	78.67			1.85		26,350				26,350
Subtotal		1.85	78.67	213.54		294.06		26,350	187,285			1,727,463
Total	414.23	2,232.37	823.36	239.84	314.99	4,024.79	166,233	1,314,875	2,700,418	1,683,740	339,852	6,205,118

in the per capita income class between $5,000 and $7,000. Four of these countries had to be assigned their actual incomes, and this left Luxembourg as the only country receiving more than its actual weight.

The results of this assignment of world GDP and world population to the thirty-four Phase III countries are shown in Table 3-3. The supercountry weighting procedure then creates a set of thirty-four new entities, each of which will be treated as a country in the computations described below. The populations and GDPs assigned to the thirty-four supercountries in Table 3-3 can be summarized as follows:

Country	Population	GDP
Malawi	103.5	41,559
India	608.2	89,560
Kenya	103.5	41,558
Pakistan	181.2	30,297
Sri Lanka	181.2	30,296
Zambia	207.2	83,116
Thailand	330.2	118,445
Philippines	330.2	118,446
Korea	330.2	118,445
Syria	43.6	33,950
Romania	63.5	64,018
Colombia	52.3	31,702
Malaysia	43.6	33,951
Brazil	106.2	109,166
Uruguay	52.3	31,703
Iran	40.6	69,773
Yugoslavia	31.2	47,801
Mexico	60.1	83,640
Jamaica	44.1	83,641
Hungary	88.8	227,170
Ireland	88.8	227,170

Table 3-2. Population and Nominal GDP of Phase III Countries, by per Capita Nominal GDP and Region, 1975

Per capita nominal GDP (US$)	Country	Population (in millions)					GDP (in millions of US$)				
		Africa	Asia	Europe	North America	Latin America and the Caribbean	Africa	Asia	Europe	North America	Latin America and the Caribbean
Under 250	Malawi	5.04					659				
	India		608.07					85,960			
	Pakistan		69.23					11,270			
	Kenya	13.40					3,139				
	Sri Lanka		13.51					3,407			
250–499	Thailand		41.87					14,318			
	Philippines		42.52					15,624			
	Korea		35.28					19,089			
	Zambia	4.98					2,429				
500–1,249	Colombia					23.64					13,574
	Syria		7.35					5,469			
	Malaysia		11.90					9,283			
	Brazil					106.23					109,166
	Uruguay					2.78					3,529
	Romania			21.24					26,450		
1,250–1,999	Mexico					60.15					79,016
	Jamaica					2.04					2,919
	Yugoslavia			21.35					33,080		
	Iran		33.02					53,985			
2,000–2,999	Hungary			10.54					22,690		
	Ireland			3.13					7,800		
	Poland			34.02					88,320		
	Spain			35.60					101,033		
3,000–4,999	Italy			55.83					172,104		
	U.K.			55.96					228,820		
	Japan		111.57					490,634			
	Austria			7.52					35,754		
5,000–6,999	Netherlands			13.65					81,202		
	Luxembourg			.36					2,197		
	Belgium			9.80					62,245		
	France			52.79					335,744		
	Germany			61.83					424,835		
Over 7,000	Denmark			5.06					35,451		
	U.S.				213.54					1,513,828	

Source: U.N. *Statistical Office* (1976), vol. 2, table 1A; and World Bank (1977).

Country	Population	GDP
Poland	88.8	227,170
Spain	88.8	227,170
Japan	143.4	675,312
Italy	55.8	172,104
United Kingdom	56.0	228,820
Austria	39.3	157,454
Netherlands	13.6	81,202
Luxembourg	5.3	30,229
Belgium	9.8	62,245
France	52.8	335,744
Germany	61.8	424,835
Denmark	78.7	187,285
United States	239.8	1,683,740

The effect of the method is usually to assign any two Phase III countries in the same cell, the same supercountry population and same supercountry GDP.

This leads, of course, to the same per capita GDP, which is the average for all countries in that group.[37] The fact that two or more of these new entities are sometimes assigned the same exchange-rate–converted per capita income does not in any way imply that the per capita incomes of the two corresponding representative countries will be estimated to be the

37. There are two exceptions to this statement. One, already noted in the text, is that a country that would not receive at least its own GDP under the assignment rules was assigned its own population and income. The other is that where in a given region there is no ICP country in a particular income class, the population and GDP of that income class are assigned to another income class with the consequence that the per capita supercountry GDP for that income class may be raised or lowered.

Table 3-3. Supercountry Populations and Nominal GDPs, 1975
(34 Countries)

Per capita nominal GDP (US$)	Supercountry population					Supercountry GDP (in millions of US$)				
	Africa	Asia	Europe	North America	Latin America and the Caribbean	Africa	Asia	Europe	North America	Latin America and the Caribbean
Under 250 Malawi	103.5					41,559				
India		608.2					85,960			
Kenya	103.5					41,558				
Pakistan		181.2					30,297			
Sri Lanka		181.2					30,296			
250–499 Zambia	207.2					83,116				
Thailand		330.2					118,445			
Philippines		330.2					118,446			
Korea		330.2					118,445			
500–1,249 Syria		43.6					33,950			
Romania			63.5					64,018		
Colombia					52.3					31,702
Malaysia		43.6					33,951			
Brazil					106.2					109,166
Uruguay					52.3					31,703
1,250–1,999 Iran		40.6					69,773			
Yugoslavia			31.2					47,801		
Mexico					60.1					83,640
Jamaica					44.1					83,641
2,000–2,999 Hungary			88.8					227,170		
Ireland			88.8					227,170		
Poland			88.8					227,170		
Spain			88.8					227,170		
3,000–4,999 Japan		143.4					675,312			
Italy			55.8					172,104		
U.K.			56.0					228,820		
Austria			39.3					157,454		
5,000–6,999 Netherlands			13.6					81,202		
Luxembourg			5.3					30,229		
Belgium			9.8					62,245		
France			52.8					335,744		
Germany			61.8					424,835		
Over 7,000 Denmark			78.7					187,285		
U.S.				239.8					1,683,740	

same. The analysis of the supercountry entities is for the purpose of estimating average prices only. Each country's own quantities (obtained from its expenditures and prices) are then valued at these supercountry-based average prices.

If the GDPs of countries not included in the ICP set have been appropriately assigned to ICP countries, the "true" world average price structure will be obtained. Then if more countries are subsequently added to the ICP set, the reassignment of supercountry weights should leave the average prices essentially unchanged. Thus the extent to which the multilateral comparisons of the ten countries of Phase I remained approximately the same after six countries were added in Phase II provides some reassurance about the success of su-

percountry weighting.[38] The immediately following sections include descriptions of the use of supercountry weights at each level of aggregation.

Aggregation at the Detailed-category Level

In most index-number work, particularly in international comparisons, attention centers on overall formulas for aggregation such as those discussed earlier.

38. Kravis, Heston, Summers (1978a), pp. 78–79. See also in this chapter the section "Measures of Precision of Income Comparisons."

If a common list of items is priced in all countries and weights are available for each item, these methods apply directly to the most detailed items, and no further consideration is required.

In binary comparisons, there is no choice but to use a list of items common to the two countries.[39] If weights for individual items are lacking, the usual procedure is to form an unweighted geometric mean of the price relatives.[40]

The Two Levels of Aggregation

If in a comparison involving three or more countries the available price information related to only one particular item[41] (that is, one closely specified good or service) within each detailed expenditure category, aggregation would consist simply of combining the information for the different categories for each country—the single prices and expenditures—to produce aggregate price and quantity indexes for GDP as a whole or for subsets of categories.

But normally more price information is available for detailed expenditure categories. There are categories that are relatively homogeneous in their product composition and for which reliable price relationships can be obtained by comparing prices for only a single specification. Eggs are a good example. But usually items falling within a category are much more heterogeneous (women's outer clothing, for example), so it is desirable to compare prices for a larger group of specifications—as many as twenty. For such categories there is an averaging problem at the detailed category level. If individual expenditures were available for each specification and each specification were priced in every participating country, each individual specification could be regarded as a separate category and aggregation could be accomplished in one pass.

More commonly, however, satisfactory weights are available at the category level only—not at the level of individual specifications within categories.[42] Also, prices are usually not available for all items from all countries. Therefore, it is preferable to aggregate at successive levels rather than in a single pass. A way

must be found first to produce average price ratios (p_{ij}/p_{ib}, where i is now a detailed category) for the detailed categories, which can then be aggregated at a second level with the use of the category weights. The problem of missing prices for some specifications should be coped with at the first level before proceeding to a higher level of aggregation.

The Problems of Within-category Aggregation

Three main problems must be resolved in obtaining a PPP or a price index for each category: (1) determining the type of average, (2) deciding whether a simple or a weighted average should be employed, and (3) making a judgment about what provision, if any, should be made for transitivity.

The first problem is the easiest to resolve. A geometric mean is to be preferred because, as has been noted, it meets the country-reversal test. The arithmetic mean, its chief rival, does not.

WEIGHTING WITHIN DETAILED CATEGORIES. The weighting question is more difficult. Of course, if the within-category dispersion of price ratios were small, the decision would not be of great consequence. In fact, experience in the ICP indicates that the highest price ratio for a pair of countries (p_i/p_k) is not uncommonly two or three times the lowest one within a detailed category. Thus a simple average can be misleading in cases in which two or more specifications are of significantly different importance in the countries being compared. Demand curves being negatively sloped, this circumstance can easily arise if an item is expensive relative to a substitute in one country, but relatively cheap in the other.

Weighting of price ratios for the different specifications within detailed categories is thus desirable in principle. The appropriate weights would be the expenditure shares devoted to the different specifications in the countries. However, such weighting requires a knowledge in each country of final expenditures for each specification priced. It calls, for example, for expenditure data on dresses, skirts, jackets, blouses, sweaters, and so forth, rather than merely for women's outer clothing. Data in this degree of detail simply are not available in many countries.

In most developing countries, the estimate of final expenditure by households is derived as a residual from GDP after public consumption expenditures (government) and capital formation are estimated directly. Because the consumption total is not built up from data on individual categories, it is already a major task in these countries to estimate final expenditures for the more than 100 categories of consumption expen-

---

39. This statement is true for traditional binaries, but the augmented binaries presented in Chapter 7 relax this requirement to some degree. Also, see note 62 below about imputations in the traditional binaries.

40. A geometric mean meets the country-reversal test; an arithmetic mean does not.

41. In this discussion the terms "item" and "specification" are used interchangeably.

42. This is partly because the degree of disaggregation in the classification was chosen with a view to the likely degree of detail for which expenditure data would be available in most countries.

ditures used in the ICP. Even where some of the underlying data are available, they often are not processed and published in a way that matches the national-accounts concepts.

An additional complication often arises even when the necessary expenditure data are available in sufficient detail: not all of the major items in a category are priced, and it is very difficult to impute the weights of the omitted items to those that are included. Ideally, the weights for the missing items should be assigned to the included items on the basis of similar price relationships, but it is not known what these similarities are.[43]

There are, however, cases in which the detailed categories contain different subgroups that have very different price relationships and for which the relative importance of the items is known at least in a general way. In the category gasoline, oil, and grease (ICP 06.230), for example, motor oil and gasoline, each with one specification usually priced, differ sharply in their relative prices from country to country. The use of a simple geometric average of the price ratios to form a PPP for the category—that is, using equal weights—would clearly be unsatisfactory in view of the substantially greater importance of gasoline in expenditures in all countries.

Thus despite the lack of data and the inherent difficulties, subcategory weights were introduced on a limited scale for some categories. In Phase I they were used in six categories (rents, potatoes, automobiles, gasoline and oil, local transport, and purchased meals). In Phase III they were used in nine (the initial six plus flour and meal, spirits, and telephone and telegraph). In most of these cases weights were not broken down to the item level but only to subcategories. Thus corn meal was weighted separately from wheat flour; yams and sweet potatoes from white potatoes; taxis from local bus transport; telephone from telegraph; and alcoholic and other beverages from food in restaurants. Where there was more than one item compared in a subcategory, the weight of the subcategory was divided equally among the items. In a few instances, such as potatoes, and meal and flour, the weights were actually applied at the item level.

Some of the more detailed expenditures that provided the subcategory weights were obtained from published information for some countries; this was the case, for example, for meal and flour and for telephone and telegraph. In other instances the expenditures were supplied by countries in response to a questionnaire. In many cases, however, the weights

had to be guessed on the basis of data for other countries. It was thought better, for example, in a country for which there were no data, to divide the weight for gasoline, oil, and grease between gasoline and motor oil on a 0.95 to 0.05 basis, the ratio observed in other countries, than to assume implicitly a fifty-fifty division.

Table 3-4 gives the rough weights in seven categories used in the different regions when individual country data were not available.[44] The weights for rents and automobiles were described in Chapter 2.

In its own comparisons for 1970 the European Economic Community made extensive use of item weighting. These comparisons for France, the Federal Republic of Germany, and Italy set alongside the corresponding ones for Phase I of the ICP where item weights were used sparingly make possible a judgment about how sensitive the results are to item weighting. The comparison of the two, reported on in the Phase I volume in more detail,[45] revealed only very small differences at the aggregative level. Of the three possible pairings of the countries, the largest difference between comparisons of personal consumption per capita obtained from weighted and unweighted averages within detailed categories level was 2.2 percent. However, price comparisons at the detailed-category level *are* affected; in about a tenth of the nearly 100 detailed categories, the weighted and unweighted results differed by more than 10 percent.

TRANSITIVITY. The third problem, that of transitivity, does not, of course, arise unless more than two countries are considered simultaneously. In multilateral comparisons transitivity both at the category level and at higher levels of aggregation can be achieved simply if two conditions are met: (1) an identical list of goods is priced in each country, and (2) the same weight is applied to an item price ratio regardless of the country.

The second requirement will be discussed in the next section, which deals with aggregation at the second level, because the same considerations are involved at both levels.

A list confined to specifications commonly found in as heterogeneous a group of countries as in the ICP set would be so small that it could hardly be expected to be representative of the commodities found on the

---

43. For a practical illustration of the problem see Kravis, Kenessey, Heston, Summers (1975), p. 48.

44. The weights in Table 3-4 were also used in the estimates of interregional CPDs. See Chapter 4.

45. Kravis, Kenessey, Heston, Summers (1975), pp. 52–53. In its subsequent benchmark study for 1975, the EEC used unweighted averages of price relatives to obtain category PPPs. European Communities Statistical Office (1977), p. 33.

Table 3-4. Expenditure Weights for Subcategories by Region

ICP category and subcategory	Africa	Asia	Europe	Latin America	U.S.
1.102 Meal					
Wheat	5	50	90	25	60
Corn	85	30	5	50	10
Oats, barley and millet	10	20	5	25	30
1.170 Potatoes					
English	20	40	100	40	96
Sweet, yams, etc.	80	60	0	60	4
1.321 Spirits					
Whiskies	10	10	20	10	50
Vodka, gin	20	20	50	20	30
Other	70	70	30	70	20
6.230 Gas and oil					
Gas	95	90	95	95	95
Oil	5	10	5	5	5
6.310 Local transport					
Bus, trolley, etc.	80	80	80	80	67
Taxi	20	20	20	20	33
6.420 Telephone, telegraph					
Telephone	97	95	99	97	99
Telegraph	3	5	1	3	1
8.310 Restaurants					
Food	85	85	60	70	70
Alcoholic beverages	5	5	20	15	20
Nonalcoholic beverages	10	10	20	15	10

markets of most of the countries. Even for the countries within a region, a common list that is representative for all the countries will usually be difficult to define. The relatively homogeneous European Common Market used a common list for its 1970 comparisons involving six member countries but had to allow for variations in the list in its later comparisons when its membership was expanded to nine countries.[46]

If a common list is not possible, what then? One possibility is to overlook the transitivity criterion and to produce a series of binary comparisons. In the comparisons made by the socialist economies of Eastern Europe and in the binary comparisons made in the first two phases of the ICP, this choice is carried out through the star pattern of comparisons referred to earlier. That is, one country is selected as the base (the center of the star) and the others (points of the star) are compared with it. (For a further discussion of the star system, see Chapter 4.) In the Phase I and II binary comparisons of the ICP, the unweighted geometric means of the price ratios for each detailed cat-

egory were calculated for all of the specifications priced in both the base country and the given partner country. That is, for category i,

$$(3.9) \qquad \left(\frac{p_j}{p_b}\right)_i = \prod_{\alpha=1}^{A_i} \left(\frac{p_{\alpha j}}{p_{\alpha b}}\right)^{1/A_i}$$

where $(p_j / p_b)_i$ is the average PPP of the jth country relative to the base country b for the ith category; $p_{\alpha j}$ is the price of the αth specification in the jth country in its currency; $p_{\alpha b}$ is the price of the same specification in the base country in its currency; and A_i is the number of items within the category priced in both the jth country and the base country. The corresponding PPP for another country relative to the base country for the same category, $(p_k/p_b)_i$, would more often than not be based on a different set of specifications. In such a case, $(p_j / p_b)_i \div (p_k/p_b)_i$ would not necessarily equal $(p_j / p_k)_i$ as the latter would probably be calculated from a different set of items. Of course, this anomaly could be ignored; any two partner countries could be compared simply by using the base country as a "bridge." In place of the original country comparisons, $(p_j / p_k)_i$ could always be taken as the ratio of the j and k comparisons with the base country. This

---

46. Indeed, only around 40 percent of the consumer goods specifications were priced in all the countries. European Communities Statistical Office (1977), p. 12.

would achieve transitivity, but only in a superficial way: it would be a result of simply ignoring the original-country estimates. The objection to this procedure is that it would not give comparisons that were base-country invariant. The reason is that the use of a bridge country interposes its sample of specifications (and where weights are used, as will be the case for higher levels of aggregation, its weights), which is not necessarily characteristic of either j or k. The comparison of Kenya and India, for example, by way of the United States or the United Kingdom may exclude goods the two countries have in common but are not found in the bridge country. (For a further discussion of bridging, see Chapter 4.)

The Country-Product-Dummy Method (CPD)

To deal with representative price lists not necessarily identical from country to country, and to ensure base-country invariance, the ICP estimated category PPPs for each country by using a somewhat specialized regression technique. The problem to be resolved is created by missing entries in a tableau of prices for each category in which items are on the row stubs and countries in the column headings. The question was how to treat the $p_{\alpha j}$'s in a way that took systematic account of the absence of price entries for particular items in particular countries. The ICP procedure is a generalized bridge-country technique, called the country-product-dummy (CPD) method.

As usually employed, a bridge-country method links two countries together on the basis of the relationship of each to a third (base) country. For example, if prices in country j were found to be 15 percent higher than in country b (on the basis of one subset of vegetable prices), while prices in country k were found to be 10 percent higher than prices in country b (on the basis of a different subset of vegetable prices), the use of country b as the bridge country would lead to the conclusion that prices in j were approximately 5 percent higher than prices in k. That is:

$$(3.10) \quad \left(\frac{p_j}{p_k}\right)_{veg.} = \left(\frac{p_j}{p_b}\right)_{veg.} \div \left(\frac{p_k}{p_b}\right)_{veg.}$$

$$= 1.15 \div 1.10 = 1.045.$$

The CPD method takes advantage of all such information in the tableau (for example, price comparisons of j and k with all other countries) in estimating the PPP for each country. It draws upon the comparisons available from all possible bridge countries.

The basic view of the price universe underlying this method is that each price can be regarded as dependent on the country in which it is observed and on the item to which it refers. Accordingly, the natural log-

arithm of price is taken as the dependent variable in a linear regression equation in which the independent variables consist of two sets of dummy variables, one relating to the various countries (excluding the numéraire country) and the other to the various items. The equation that embodies the CPD method is

$$(3.11) \quad \ln p = \beta_1 X_1 + \beta_2 X_2 + \ldots + \beta_{n-1} X_{n-1} + \gamma_1 Z_1 + \gamma_2 Z_2 + \ldots + \gamma_A Z_A + u$$

where $\ln p$ is the natural logarithm of the price of a particular item in a particular country. Each of the $n-1$ countries being compared other than the base country is represented by an X dummy variable and each of the A items in the category is represented by a Z dummy variable.

The symbol u represents a normally distributed variable with mean zero and variance σ^2. The X's and Z's are called dummy variables because they can take on only the values zero or one. Assume, for example, that in the category fresh vegetables X_3 represents the country France and Z_4 the item lettuce. For this price observation, the variables X_3 and Z_4 will equal one and all the other dummy variables will be equal to zero. In general, an observation used as an input to the regression consists of a vector of $(n + A)$ numbers: $\ln p$, $(n-1)$ individual X values, and A individual Z values. Specifically, the vector in the French-lettuce case would be $(\ln p_{34}; 0, 0, 1, 0, \ldots, 0; 0, 0, 0, 1, 0, \ldots, 0)$ where p_{34} is the price of lettuce in France measured in francs.

The regression coefficient of each country's dummy variable (the β's) may be interpreted as the logarithms of the PPP of that country's currency relative to that of the numéraire country for the category.

For reasons of computational convenience, a slightly different variant of the CPD method was applied to the twenty-two categories of producer durables. For these categories each country's item price was expressed as a ratio of the corresponding U.S. price.[47] These standardized item prices—including all U.S. prices set equal to one—were regressed against the same set of country and item dummy variables.[48]

47. Because of widespread product differentiation in this sector, more extensive matching of specifications with the numéraire country was required. Each price quotation was adjusted to allow for identifiable quality differences between models used in individual countries and the United States.

48. The use of standardized prices changes only slightly the interpretation of the regression coefficient estimates as given in equation 3.11: the β's will be the same, but each item $\hat{\gamma}$ here will be equal to the corresponding $\hat{\gamma}$ there divided by the U.S. item price. In Phases I and II the omission of item dummies in the producer-durables categories led to slight (stochastic) differences in the estimates of the β's.

In both versions, the individual observations were weighted by the supercountry expenditure on the category and by the reciprocal of the number of items priced by the country. The function of the supercountry weights, as was explained earlier, is to assign to each country's price structure a weight that reflects the importance not only of its own GDP but also that of all the countries in the world not included in the ICP for which the ICP country's price structure can be regarded as representative. Although it is usual to employ quantities as weights for prices, the relative importance assigned to different items within a detailed category would not be units invariant with the use of quantity weights. Supercountry expenditures rather than quantities were therefore used.

The reciprocal weighting was to allow for differences among countries in the numbers of items priced. Where a country priced more than one item in a category, the weight was distributed evenly over the items. Thus the importance assigned to a country in the regression computation is the same whether it has supplied prices for few or many items in the category (except for the nine detailed categories, mentioned earlier, in which within-category weights were used).

The CPD method is a way of obtaining transitive, base-country invariant PPPs that are based on geometric averages of price relatives for the individual items. Indeed, if there are no missing observations in the price tableau, the PPP produced by the CPD method for each country is simply the weighted geometric mean of the PPPs of the individual items. When there are missing prices the CPD method has the advantage of providing transitivity and of making full use of all the information in the price tableau. It makes it unnecessary to compare each country's prices exclusively with those of any particular base country; as long as at least two countries price a specification, prices for that specification can be usefully included.[49]

CPD was used to obtain PPPs for the large preponderance of categories, but there were a few categories for which other procedures were followed. The PPPs for six categories (other educational expenditures [ICP 07.432], physical facilities for education [ICP 7. 420], educational books and supplies [ICP 7.431], other services [ICP 8.400], increase in stocks [ICP 18], and government expenditures on commodities [ICP 20]) were derived from the PPPs of other categories.[50] The PPPs for certain comparison-resistant services (health, education, and government employees) were calculated

by special procedures in which CPD sometimes played a role, but not always (see Chapter 5).

CPD as "Filler"

Thus far the CPD method has been described as a means of overcoming the handicap posed by missing prices within a detailed category. It also provides a way of dealing with situations in which no items have been priced for an entire category for a particular country. In the binary comparisons the problems posed when neither country provided a price in a detailed category were resolved by imputing prices from other categories or by reassigning expenditures.[51] Application of the CPD method provides a less arbitrary, though still ad hoc, imputation that is useful for multilateral comparisons—and useful in the augmented binaries described in Chapter 7. The problem now is one of holes, but they are holes in the matrix of category PPPs rather than the tableau of item prices within a category. Here CPD is applied to the matrix of PPPs for a group of categories, just as in its application to a detailed category it is applied to the tableau of prices In this case, the weight assigned to each PPP present consists of the supercountry expenditure on the category. The basic assumption of this Filler technique is that a missing PPP for a country can be inferred from its PPPs for related categories by relying on the relation of the PPPs in the missing category to the related categories in other countries. Where the factors determining prices are apt to be similar to those that are operating in other categories, the Filler technique seems appropriate. For example, a missing PPP for hospital construction may be inferred from the country's PPP for other construction categories on the basis of the relation between hospital construction PPPs and PPPs for other construction categories (that is, for educational, commercial, or manufacturing buildings) in other countries. Thus in the Filler approach the CPD method was applied to the entire set of nonresidential-building categories to estimate missing PPPs in the matrix of PPPs (the eight nonresidential-building categories in the rows and the thirty-four countries in the columns).

The hole-filling procedure for missing PPPs was carried out in a more uniform way in Phases II and III than in Phase I. In Phase III it was applied separately to twenty-nine sets of categories, twenty-four in consumption, two in construction, and three in producer durables.[52]

49. For a fuller discussion of the CPD, see Kravis, Kenessey, Heston, Summers (1975), pp. 55–65; and Summers (1973), pp. 1–16.

50. See Chapter 2 under the section "The Price Data."

51. See Kravis, Kenessey, Heston, Summers (1975), p. 63.

52. Most of the sets of categories corresponded to the grouping of detailed categories into summary categories, but service categories in consumption other than rents and educational and medical services were grouped together.

Of the more than 3,000 consumption cells (34 countries times 96 categories) for which PPPs were desired, about 100 were empty and were estimated by the Filler version of CPD. Among the 1,200 capital formation cells, about 120 required the use of Filler.

Filler was less frequently used in Phase III than in the previous phases because the participating countries supplied more prices than in the earlier phases (see Chapter 2).

The rationale for hole-filling with Filler lies in the ICP's conception of why PPPs were missing, just as CPD's justification depended on the ICP's conceptions of why item prices were missing. The heart of the matter is the notion of random influences governing the selection of items for a country's regular pricing and its special ICP pricing: missing PPPs bear the same relationship to others in the same category in other countries or to those in other categories in the same country, as the PPPs that have been observed.

But perhaps a category PPP may be missing for systematic reasons such that the proportionalities assumed by Filler are not realized. It is possible that no price is reported because the quantity consumed is very small, and the small quantity is an endogenous response to a high price. If the low quantities are generally a result of high prices, then the absence of prices should be an indication that the missing prices are unusually high or are not in the same relationship to available prices in other categories and other countries as is implied by the Filler rationale.

This suggests that some sort of reverse demand function—that is, a relationship between price as the dependent variable and quantity and income as independent variables—should be used to infer a missing PPP. This possibility has been rejected, however, for both a priori and empirical reasons.

First, the possibility of error in this way of estimating a missing PPP is very large, since one of the independent variables, quantity, can be estimated only at the risk of large margins of error. The price that must be divided into the expenditure to get quantity is unknown. In addition, expenditures for categories for which no prices have been provided are, as hypothesized, apt to be small, and therefore these estimates are also likely to be error-ridden.

Second, reverse-demand equations could be used only selectively, since there are a number of categories for which the ordinary demand model does not apply on a cross-country basis. For example, expenditures on pork and lard are low in several countries in Phase III, for religious rather than economic reasons. In the case of capital formation, reverse-demand functions may be inapplicable because the composition of new capital goods in any given year may depend more on the priorities assigned to housing, education, medical care, transport, and so forth, in the current policies or plans of the government than on relative prices and incomes.

An attempt was made to see if indeed Filler-produced PPPs tended to be lower than PPPs based on direct price comparisons as estimated from reverse-demand curves, but no empirical support emerged for this hypothesis.[53] The ICP conclusion then was that this objection to the use of Filler in estimating missing PPPs could be set aside. There is, in any case, considerable consolation in the fact that Filler-estimated PPPs were in categories with small expenditures, and therefore errors in the estimates were likely to have minimal effects on the overall estimates of GDP.[54]

CPD versus EKS

CPD has sometimes been criticized for providing estimates of missing prices, the implication being that there is something spurious about such estimates. A basic difference between CPD and other methods in this respect is that the assumptions made by the CPD about the missing prices are explicit and easy to understand. Other methods that seem to evade the need to deal with missing prices cannot avoid making some assumptions about them also. Ignoring them does not remove their influence.

The only systematic alternative that has been offered for coping with missing data is the Elteto, Koves, and Szulc (EKS) method, which has been used in European work on international comparisons. The rationale for EKS is based in part on the conjecture that countries with similar quantity structures within categories will exhibit similar pricing patterns. That is, there will be some tendency for the same items to be priced or be left unpriced. If this were so, binary price

53. The ratio of the PPP for a detailed category to the PPP for the summary category was taken as the dependent variable in a regression in which the independent variables were real per capita income, quantity, and a dummy variable that was assigned a value of 1 when the detailed-category PPP had been estimated by Filler and a value of zero in other cases. Quantities were computed by dividing the expenditure by the PPP; in view of the often dubious nature of that PPP, expenditures were sometimes used instead of quantities. The trials covered woolen clothing materials (ICP 2.111), clothing repairs (ICP 2.160), washing appliances (ICP 3.320) and the pooling of six detailed categories of meats (ICP 1.110). The coefficient of the dummy variable was not significantly different from zero in any of the regressions, and in two, including the only one (clothing repairs) that was larger than its standard error, the coefficients were positive instead of negative.

54. This judgment is based on the ICP use of the Geary-Khamis formula, presently to be described. It is possible that the effects might not be minimal if the Paasche or the Laspeyres formula were used.

indexes, upon which EKS depends, would be characteristic in the sense of that term set out earlier in this chapter in the section "The Desired Properties." This case is buttressed by the argument that EKS produces results that deviate minimally in a logarithmic least-squares sense from Fisher indexes.

However, EKS suffers from a distinct disadvantage relative to the CPD. This may be seen by considering the properties of the prices of PPPs that would be estimated by the two methods if hole-filling were undertaken. The prices or PPPs that are obtained by hole-filling through CPD[55] have an attractive property: if CPD is applied to the synthesized complete tableau consisting of all the observed prices plus the prices estimated by application of CPD to the original incomplete tableau, the PPPs estimated from the full synthesized tableau will be the same as those obtained by applying CPD to the observed incomplete tableau. The same would *not* be true of EKS. With EKS, there is no unique price that implicitly or explicitly is assigned to a missing observation.[56]

In contrast, the CPD method models the stochastic process, which generates the item price data. The empirically observed prices recorded in the price tableau (items in the rows, countries in the columns) can be regarded as at least in some sense sample observations from a world in which each underlying category PPP is the location parameter at the middle of the distribution of price ratios of the items of that category. CPD simply makes the most plausible assumptions about the character of the sampling process.

Further, the CPD method lends itself to additional uses in the full sweep of international comparison work. Later in this chapter the estimates of standard errors of the $\hat{\beta}$'s produced by the CPD regression equation will be drawn upon to provide at least a crude basis for assessing the reliability of the PPP estimates. Another feature, of which less use has been made, is that the item dummy coefficients (the $\hat{\gamma}$'s) obtained from CPD represent, after exponentiation, average prices of the items. These can be used in a number of applications, including making more limited comparisons for countries not included in the original CPD estimates.[57]

Aggregation of Category Expenditures and Prices

As was indicated earlier, the basic ICP method of aggregating the price and quantity indexes for the detailed categories involves the use of a set of average international prices to provide a common measuring rod for the evaluation of each country's quantities.[58] The price inputs to this process are the detailed category PPPs derived in the manner described in the previous section, and the detailed category quantities are obtained from the expenditures provided by the countries. Since country PPPs for each category are denominated in their own currency units per unit of the numéraire country's currency, they cannot be combined directly to obtain average world prices. To make the country PPPs commensurate, each country's category PPPs are divided by the country PPP for GDP as a whole. Then the international price for a category is simply the quantity-weighted average of the category PPPs expressed relative to the country overall PPPs. (Incidentally, dividing by the overall PPPs makes the international price invariant with respect to the choice of country currency units.) The category quantities for the countries when valued by the international prices can be aggregated to get GDP. While quantities are not actually available, so-called notional quantities (defined later in this section) can be calculated as the ratio of category expenditures to category PPPs. The category expenditures used in this connection are, for reasons given above, supercountry expenditures.

Implementing the Geary-Khamis System

Computing the international prices is easy if the overall PPPs are known. Conversely, since the PPP for a country is defined as the ratio of the country's GDP

55. The CPD estimate of p_{aj} is $e^{\beta j + \gamma_\alpha}$ where $\hat{\beta}_j$ and $\hat{\gamma}_\alpha$ are the regression estimates of the parameters of equation 3.11.

56. Suppose the only missing price is the one for the third item in the fourth country. The EKS estimates of PPP$_4$ would be a function of a number of geometric means of item price ratios. Among these would be a set in which the fourth country's available item prices are expressed relative to the corresponding item prices of each of the other countries. Consider the number that could be inserted into the (third item–fourth country) hole that would give the same geometric mean in a comparison of the fourth country with the jth one. If G_{4j} is the geometric mean, then this number would simply be $P_{3j} \cdot G_{4j}$. But the fact that this expression carries a subscript $_j$ means that the hole-filler would have to be different for each different geometric mean entering into the EKS estimate of PPP$_4$.

57. For an example of this use see Kravis (1980).

58. EKS is also a contender at this level of aggregation. If the PPPs of all the detailed categories are available (Filler having been used to eliminate all holes), EKS is a transitive index that exhibits more characteristicity than its competitors. This is because EKS is a function of Fisher indexes. Of course, this is an advantage only if it is thought that the original Fisher indexes are superior to "true" multilateral price indexes for the countries involved. For reasons to doubt such a superiority, see the section "Four Sets of Methods" above. Also, EKS lacks a clear economic interpretation such as that provided by the approach originated by Geary which is discussed in detail later.

valued at its own price to its GDP valued at international prices, the PPPs are easily computed if the international prices are known. In a seminal paper[59] Geary observed that it is possible to solve a set of equations, the number being equal to one less than the number of countries plus the number of categories, to get simultaneously all the international prices and all the PPPs. Khamis later amplified this basic idea.[60]

Specifically, the Geary-Khamis equation system divides into two subsets: the first, equation 3.12, defines m category international prices (Π_i) and the second, 3.13, defines the overall PPPs for n countries (PPP$_j$):

$$(3.12) \quad \Pi_i = \sum_{j=1}^{n} \frac{p_{ij}}{\text{PPP}_j} \left[\frac{q_{ij}}{\sum_{j=1}^{n} q_{ij}} \right] \qquad i = 1, \ldots, m.$$

$$(3.13) \quad \text{PPP}_j = \frac{\sum_{i=1}^{m} p_{ij} q_{ij}}{\sum_{i=1}^{m} \Pi_i q_{ij}} \qquad j = 1, \ldots, n.$$

Each of the two subsystems has a clear economic interpretation. Equation 3.12 says that the international price of the ith category is the quantity-weighted average of the purchasing-power–adjusted prices of the ith category in the n countries.[61] Equation 3.13 says that the purchasing power of a country's currency is equal to the ratio of the cost of its total bill of goods at national prices to the cost at international prices.

In implementing the Geary-Khamis system, the ICP has had to adapt it to ICP data. This has an important consequence for the interpretation of ICP international prices. The inputs required by the Geary method as originally propounded were prices and physical quantities for the sets of goods and services to be covered. The ICP inputs into Geary-Khamis are different. The ICP price input for each category is 1 for the numéraire country, and it is the category PPPs vis-à-vis the numéraire country for the other countries. The ICP quantity input for each category is the set of notional quantities ($Q_{ij} = E_{ij}/\text{PPP}_{ij}$) referred to above, each obtained as the ratio of expenditure to PPP. If the international

prices and purchasing power parities obtained using ICP inputs are denoted $\overline{\Pi}$ and $\overline{\text{PPP}}$, then their values are determined by equations 3.14 and 3.15.

$$(3.14) \quad \overline{\Pi}_i = \sum_{j=1}^{n} \frac{\text{PPP}_{ij}}{\text{PPP}_j} \cdot \frac{Q_{ij}}{\sum_{j=1}^{m} Q_{ij}} \qquad i = 1, \ldots, m$$

$$(3.15) \quad \overline{\text{PPP}}_i = \frac{\sum_{i=1}^{m} \text{PPP}_{ij} Q_{ij}}{\sum_{i=1}^{m} \overline{\Pi}_i Q_{ij}} \qquad j = 1, \ldots, (n - 1)$$

where the United States is assumed to be the numéraire country, $\text{PPP}_{ij} = p_{ij}/p_{i,US}$ and

$$Q_{ij} = \frac{p_{ij} \cdot q_{ij}}{p_{ij}/p_{i,US}} = p_{i,US} \cdot q_{ij}.$$

Note that p and q refer to Geary's inputs and PPP and Q to ICP inputs. It is easy to show that $\overline{\Pi}_i = \Pi_i/p_{i,US}$ and $\overline{\text{PPP}}_j = \text{PPP}_j$. Thus, the PPP produced by the ICP version of Geary-Khamis is indeed correct.

Further adaptations required by the nature of the data led to the calculation of the Geary-Khamis formula over 143 categories rather than the full set of 151. Six of the remaining eight categories covered composite, heterogeneous goods and services for which no direct or indirect PPPs were available,[62] or goods covered by one of the other 143 more "elementary" categories; and two were national-income–accounting categories that had no proper interpretation in the Geary system.[63] The expenditures for each of the six were allocated to one or another of the 143 elementary categories, so that the Geary-Khamis GDP and sub-

59 Geary (1958), pp. 97–99.

60. Khamis (1967), pp. 213–320; Khamis (1970), pp. 81–98; Khamis (1972), pp. 96–121. For an early application of Geary's suggestion, see Kawakatsu (1970). Brady and Hurwitz (1957), operating in the spirit of the Geary conception, devised an iterative scheme that leads to the Geary computational result.

61. The original Geary notion can be restated easily in terms of weighted geometric averages instead of weighted arithmetic ones (Rao, 1972). This alternative version does not provide matrix consistency.

62. In the binary comparisons, analogous imputation methods were used; for example, the Paasche and Laspeyres PPPs from other commodity categories were used as the PPP for stocks. The general method of imputation for binary categories in which two countries had no overlapping prices in a detailed category was to use the PPP from the next higher level of aggregation. For example, if no pork comparison was possible between Syria and the United States, the PPP for all other meats would receive the pork expenditure weight. The binary procedure, unlike Geary-Khamis, is not simultaneous, so it was relatively simple to impute a PPP for one category from a computation involving other categories, and then to calculate the total of all categories. However, in the case of the commodity and service purchases of government, the imputation was made through the use of the multilateral PPP. The expenditure breakdowns of government purchases were approximated for several countries, so no real characteristicity was lost by using imputations involving weights of third countries.

63. Though increase in stocks (ICP 19) can also be negative, this category is treated with the imputed set. When the change in stocks is distributed, in accordance with the explanation that follows, among other categories, the changes will only reduce the expenditures on these categories, not make them negative.

aggregate comparisons were based on price and expenditure comparisons for the more elementary goods and services. (In effect, it was assumed that the prices paid for each of the items in the six categories by the purchasers standing behind the categories were the same as the equivalent item prices collected for the more elementary categories.) After the Geary-Khamis calculations, appropriate proportions of the expenditures of the 143 categories were reallocated back to the six categories.

The procedure followed can be illustrated by government expenditure on commodities (ICP 21). The starting point was a distribution of such expenditures, very approximate, for a number of countries, among thirteen groupings based on divisions of the International Standard Industrial Classification.[64] The expenditure of each of the thirteen groupings was assigned to the appropriate ICP category or categories. For example, government expenditures on food, beverages, and tobacco were spread proportionately across all food, beverages, and tobacco categories, and government expenditures on wood and wood products were divided between the categories of furniture and fixtures in the consumption sector (ICP 04.11) and furniture and fixtures in the producer-durables sector (ICP 17.1). A Geary-Khamis calculation was then made to determine the real value of expenditure—that is, measured in international prices—of each of the 143 ICP categories, the latter now inclusive of whatever government expenditure was allocated to the category. Following this, government commodity expenditures were reconstructed by taking from each ICP category the prorated share of government. This gave a total for government expenditure on commodities in international prices. Finally, the PPP for government expenditure on commodities was obtained as the quotient of two ratios: (1) a given country's government expenditure on commodities in own currency divided by the corresponding total in international prices and (2) the corresponding ratio for the United States.[65]

The category exports less imports (ICP 19) required special treatment in two respects. As a national-income–accounting category that can take on negative values, it must be handled outside the Geary-Khamis system, and its international price is best inferred from the exchange rates of the individual countries. The beginning point for each country was the ratio of its

exchange rate to its PPP, as estimated from the initial Geary-Khamis calculation for GDP excluding the foreign balance. The exchange rate (national currency units per U.S. dollar) was a natural way to view the national price of the foreign balance. A glance at the Geary formulas will indicate that it was quite in the spirit of the calculations for the other categories to divide these national prices by the PPPs. The next issue was how to weight these ratios to obtain an average international price. For the other categories, the weights used in calculating average international prices were the category quantities. Because that was not feasible here, the weights were based on the relative importance of the supercountry that each of the thirty-four countries represented. The prices being averaged correspond to the exchange-rate–deviation index (that is, the exchange rate divided by the PPP).

The value of the category exports less imports for each country measured in international dollars was obtained in the usual way, by dividing the own-currency value by the exchange rate and then multiplying by the international price obtained as just described. Of course, an excess of imports over exports makes this number negative, but just as a negative net foreign balance representing a reduction in GDP in ordinary national-income accounting is added to the domestic part of GDP, here too the negative exports less imports is simply added to the values in international prices of all the other GDP categories.

There is, however, one slight complication arising from the ICP treatment of this category and another category handled in the same way, net expenditures of residents abroad (ICP 8.9). Because the estimate of the average international price turns out to be greater than unity, the valuation of the U.S. foreign balance at the international price makes it larger than the original U.S. dollar figure. When it is added to the other U.S. categories (those derived through Geary-Khamis), valued at international prices, the U.S. total GDP exceeds the original dollar figure for U.S. GDP. Because as a matter of convenience it is desirable to retain the original U.S. GDP total, all international prices were scaled downward so that the total GDP of the United States at international prices equaled the U.S. GDP at U.S. prices. This adjustment does not affect the relation of the GDP of other countries to the United States at international prices, because the aggregates and subaggregates for all countries are adjusted in the same proportion.

Assessment of the Geary-Khamis system

The fact that the ICP international price for each country ($\bar{\Pi}_i$) deviates from the Geary concept (Π_i) by

---

64. See Kravis, Kenessey, Heston, Summers (1975), p. 163.

65. That is $p_j q_j /\Pi q_j \div p_{US} q_{US}/\Pi q_{US} = p_j/p_{US} = \text{PPP}_j$, where p refers to national prices, Π to international prices, and q to quantities, all referring to the composite grouping of commodities purchased by government, and j is a given country.

a factor equal to the numéraire-country price for that category would appear to be a source of concern. In view of the stress that was put on the desirability of base-country invariance, it may seem surprising that the absolute values of the international prices used in ICP computations do not possess the property. Since $\overline{\Pi}_i = \Pi_i/p_{i,US}$, it is clear that the $\overline{\Pi}$s are not base invariant but rather are expressed relative to the prices of the numéraire country. This occurs because the CPD method produces for each category in each country a PPP that is expressed as a value with the numéraire country price equal to one. Thus, if another country were used as the numéraire, its price in each category would equal one. The effect would be not only to change the whole level of the PPPs emerging from the CPD regressions, but also to change their relative magnitudes. Since a different set of category PPPs would be fed into the Geary-Khamis equations, it is to be expected that international prices emerging from the solution of the equations would be different.

This poses a crucial question: if the international prices themselves are not base-country invariant, how then can it be claimed that the GDP comparisons produced by valuing each country's quantities at international prices are base-country invariant?

The answer is that the international prices are never used alone. They are used only to value notional quantities that are themselves derived as the ratio of expenditures in national currency to PPPs. They appear only as part of terms of the form $\overline{\Pi}_i Q_{ij}$. Because this product, $(\Pi_i/p_{i,US}) \cdot (q_{ij}p_{i,US})$, is equal to $\Pi_i q_{ij}$, the ICP real quantity values coming from Geary-Khamis are correct, even though the quantity input was notional rather than physical.

A further implication of this lack of independent economic significance of the ICP international prices ($\overline{\Pi}_i$) is that they cannot be interpreted in themselves as reflections of the relative resource absorption of different categories of goods. Such an interpretation, inherent in Geary's formulation, is lost in the ICP because it has been necessary to move from a simple and concrete definition of price as observable physical units to the abstraction of PPP for categories of goods. However, when $\overline{\Pi}_i$ is used to value quantities, the resulting real expenditure ($\Pi_i q_{ij}$) embodies Π_i and thus aggregations are the same as if the Geary Π's were used.

Furthermore, the fact that ICP international prices cannot be used by themselves does not mean that they do not facilitate international comparisons of price structure. The choice of the numéraire country does indeed determine the structure of the international prices; simultaneously, however, it determines in a precisely matching way the structure of each country's PPPs. In Chapter 9 price-structure comparisons are made that draw on the Geary-Khamis estimates of international prices.

There are other objections to the Geary-Khamis system that have been put forward since the Phase I report. It has been said that the Geary equations as originally set out in equations 3.12 and 3.13 will not be "fully additive." That is, if the equations are applied separately to different sectors (for example, consumption, capital formation, and government), the sum of the components for a country will not be the same as the country's GDP estimate obtained by applying the Geary equations to all sectors at once. This is indeed true; the question, however, is whether it is a disadvantage. The view taken in the ICP is that it is not. The matrix consistency produced by the ICP version of Geary-Khamis meets the needs of international comparisons, and nothing is lost by the fact that calculations for separate categories would yield slightly different results.

However, an important property of the comparisons *would* be lost if "full additivity" were insisted upon. There is no way to derive average relative prices for different categories while preserving transactions equality without accepting the interdependence of categories. The use of an overall PPP for GDP as a whole to make the own-currency prices of the different countries commensurate (that is, dividing each country's price in each category by the PPP for GDP) is the ICP method of coping with this problem, and it is what makes the interdependence necessary—and desirable.[66]

The main drawback of interdependence is that an error in the price data for one category will affect the entire system of results. Under any aggregation formula, such an error will affect aggregations including the category in which the error occurs. In an interdependent system, however, a price error in one category will affect not only aggregate results but also the results for other categories. Fortunately, ICP ex-

66. There are, in principle, two ways of obtaining a country's GDP expressed relative to a numéraire country: (1) by dividing its total expenditure by its PPP and (2) by valuing each of its category quantities at the appropriate international price and then summing these values over all categories. The salient feature of Geary-Khamis is that it generates international prices and PPPs simultaneously in a way that ensures that these two totals will be equal. Though international prices could be obtained by inserting PPPs from Walsh for some other method of aggregation in equation 3.12 or 3.14, such international prices would *not* lead to a total valuation of category quantities that equals the PPP-derived GDP. The simple (unweighted) averaging of each country's prices would satisfy the requirement but would not meet the transaction-equality condition.

periments with Geary-Khamis make it clear that the quantitative magnitudes of such effects are small and may be safely ignored.[67]

A careful analysis by Orlando, however, concluded that Geary-Khamis is more sensitive to errors than Walsh indexes,[68] but he found the differences between the methods small. He carried out Monte Carlo experiments in which randomly distributed errors with a coefficient of variation of 10 percent were inserted into the data of fifteen Latin American countries. The coefficient of variation of the Geary-Khamis GDP comparisons for these countries was less than one percentage point higher than the coefficient of variation for the Walsh indexes when the shocks were assumed to originate from price or prices and expenditures, and a little over one percentage point higher when they were assumed to originate from expenditures alone.

A small caveat should also be added regarding the invariability of the Geary-Khamis results to the way in which national boundaries are drawn. "Insensitivity" is a more accurate term than "invariability." The qualification is necessary because the way in which

each region's prices contribute to the formation of the average international prices (π's) differs slightly according to whether regions are taken separately or are consolidated into a single country. The source of the difference is that each entity's price for each category enters into the averaging process only after being divided by the entity's overall PPP (see equation 3.14). The π's will differ slightly if a country, C, is treated as a single entity in the averaging, with all its prices relative to its overall PPP, from the π's obtained if the country is divided into, say, two regions, C_1 and C_2, with C_1 prices taken relative to its PPP (PPP_1) and C_2 prices relative to PPP_2. It will remain true, however, that under either treatment the transactions of each region enter into the calculation with their appropriate weights; that is, the principle of transactions equality is satisfied. While the two treatments will not yield identical π's, the differences clearly will be a second order magnitude.

It has been pointed out that the ICP version of Geary-Khamis is computationally complex.[69] This might be a serious drawback for individual scholars, but not for international organizations such as the United Nations and its regional organizations, which can be expected to bear the main burden of future international comparison work.

The outcome of these considerations is that the Geary-Khamis formula retains its claim to preferred status over its rivals for ICP use. No other formula has the twin advantages of corresponding to a satisfactory economic interpretation of a world price structure and of satisfying as many of the desired statistical properties. Conceptually, the Geary-Khamis equations come very close to matching the way the problem is posed when international comparisons are made: it assumes that there is a unique price level for each country, and that this can be measured by the weighted average deviation of its prices from average international prices.

The conception of an interdependent price system also is mirrored in the Geary-Khamis equations. From a purely sampling standpoint, too, there is something

---

67. For example, in one trial it was assumed that an error had been made in the 1970 Phase II calculations in which the French PPP for rent was four times its correct value. It was found that French real per capita GDP would be 5.3 percent less but no other country's GDP would be affected by more than 0.2 of 1 percent. As for the other categories, the average international prices, which are the keys to the effects on real quantities, were changed in most cases by less than 1 percent and in no case by more than 2 percent. This illustration of the possible effect of an error is an extreme one, because rent was the most important expenditure category and the French real expenditure on rent was the largest of any country other than the United States. Also, automated techniques of error search, described in Chapter 2, make it unlikely that so large an error would escape detection. The expansion of the system to more countries will further diminish the effect of any error.

68. Orlando (1979). The averages over the fifteen countries were as follows:

	Average σ/m		Differences in σ/m between Geary-Khamis and Walsh	
	Geary-Khamis	Walsh	Average	Largest
Random errors in				
Prices	1.96	1.26	0.68	2.44
Expenditures	1.36	0.17	1.18	2.37
Prices and expenditures	2.24	2.24	0.86	3.41

Standard deviation (σ) divided by mean (m)

The version of Walsh employing arithmetically averaged weights is used above. Orlando also shows results for a version in which weights are averaged geometrically but the arithmetic version seems preferable (see the earlier section in this chapter entitled "Four Sets of Methods"). In any case, the coefficient of variation of the version chosen is usually smaller than that of the geometric form.

69. Though the system as written consists of an equation for each of the n countries and each of the m categories with $(n+m)$ unknowns, one of the equations is redundant. After suitable manipulation, the sum over i of equation 3.14 can be shown to be equal to the sum over j of equation 3.15, since the system is homogeneous. By setting the PPP for the numéraire country equal to one and dropping the numéraire-country equation of 3.14, a system of 176 linear equations in 176 unknowns (33 $\overline{\text{PPP}}_j$'s and 143 $\overline{\pi}_i$'s) is obtained for the Phase III data. Thus, the index $_j$ in equations 3.14 and 3.15 runs from 1 to $(n-1)$; that is, 1 to 33. The special block-diagonal structure of the computational version of equations 3.13 and 3.14 makes the matrix inversion and solution of the system an easy task.

to be said for welcoming the notion of an interdependent system and allowing the prices of, say, dairy products, to influence international meat prices. The prices collected and compared for each category represent such a small sample of those that exist that it increases the reliability of the comparisons if each price may reflect relationships in other categories and be influenced in turn by other prices in the system. Of the statistical properties sought, the ICP version of Geary-Khamis satisfies base-country invariance, transitivity, matrix consistency, transactions equality, and world representativeness. Its disadvantages lie in its failure to meet the factor-reversal test and its slightly greater vulnerability to error-ridden data than the Walsh index.

Measures of Precision of Income Comparisons

How accurate are the relative GDP per capita estimates the ICP presents in Table 1-2? The figures clearly are subject to error, and this section attempts to quantify the magnitude of error. Possible sources of inaccuracy include (1) errors or incomparabilities in the raw data on expenditures and item prices reported by the countries, (2) possible misspecification of the proper aggregation procedures, (3) stochastic variations resulting from the use of sample data, and (4) computational mistakes in processing the data. The last source is, by its nature, unquantifiable. Any known mistakes would have been eliminated.[70]

Source (1) and an aspect of source (2) are best illuminated by referring to the ICP's experience with data revisions in its successive phases. The estimates of 1970 real per capita GDP for the ten Phase I countries were first revised in the Phase II report on the basis of later information.[71] Expenditure and price revisions in 1970 data in the three years that followed the date of preparation of the Phase I report changed real per capita GDP on average by about half of 1 percent; the average of the percentage changes ignoring signs was 3.3 percent.[72] The sensitivity of the real per capita GDP estimates to the change in the system of supercountry weights between Phases I and II and to the consequence of adding six countries to the ten of Phase I was measured by upward revisions in GDP per capita estimates ranging from 2 percent to 10 percent.[73] The overall effect of data revisions and weighting changes averaged +3.6 percent with the smallest and largest changes being −5 percent and 11 percent, respectively.[74]

A similar analysis of the revisions of the 1970 estimates between the Phase II and Phase III work is offered in Table 3-5. First, the three sets of 1970 per capita GDP estimates are given in columns 1 to 3, and the extent of the changes are indicated in the form of ratios in columns 4 and 5. The changes in the estimates between the Phase II report and the present one, shown in column 5, are for most countries quite modest. They tend to be smaller than the revisions made between the Phase I and Phase II versions of the 1970 estimates. (Compare columns 4 and 5.)

The revisions in the estimates are attributable to the following factors:

● Revisions in the country's own estimate of its GDP. The extent of the changes, which are shown in ratio form in column 8, was substantial in Malaysia, owing to an improved estimate for the nonpeninsular part of the country.

● Revisions in the country's estimate of its population. The 1970 population figure was reduced by 1 percent in Iran and the United States, and there were a number of smaller changes. The population data are not shown separately in the table, but the effects of the revisions are included when all sources of differences are taken into account (column 11).

● Effect of new treatment of medical care, education, and government. In Phase III, the assumption of equal productivity of medical, government, and educational personnel was dropped. The effect on the Phase II estimates, column (2), of this change alone is shown in column 9; it is presented in ratio form in column 10. The effect is to reduce the estimate of real per capita GDP of low-income countries by 2 to 6 percent.

● Effects of U.S. revisions in 1970 government employees' compensation and of an ICP shift to the use of the international price of the net foreign balance to value the net expenditure of residents abroad.[75] These produced slight downward changes in the estimates, none over 1 percent; the effects are not shown separately.

The combined effects of these changes are shown in column 11. The success of this effort to account for the change in the 1970 estimates between the Phase II and Phase III report may be measured by the cor-

70. See, however, note 68 above reporting the results of simulation experiments on the effects of errors.

71. See table 3-2 of Kravis, Heston, Summers (1978b), "Factors Accounting for Differences between Phase I and Phase II Indexes of GDP per Capita, 1970."

72. Ibid., column 7.

73. Ibid., columns 10 and 11.

74. Ibid., column 12.

75. See Chapter 2 in the section "The Expenditure Data."

Table 3-5. Reconciliation of Phase II and Phase III Estimates of 1970 Real GDP per Capita

| | Real GDP per capita (U.S. = 100) | | | | | GDP in national currencies[b] | | | Effect of new medical, educational and government service PPPs (with Phase III expenditures) | | |
| | Indexes estimated in | | | Ratios | | | | | | | |
Country[a]	Phase I (1)	Phase II (2)	Phase III (3)	(4) = (2) ÷ (1)	(5) = (3) ÷ (2)	Phase II (6)	Phase III (7)	Ratio (8) = (7) ÷ (6)	1970 GDP per capita[c] (9)	Ratio (10) = (9) ÷ (3)	Cumulative changes[d] (11)
Kenya	5.72	6.33	5.88	1.11	0.93	11,499	11,453	1.00	6.25	0.94	0.94
India	7.12	6.92	6.46	0.97	0.93	403,749	404,601	1.00	6.90	0.94	0.94
Philippines[e]	—	12.0	11.7	—	0.98	41,363	42,447	1.03	12.3	0.95	0.97
Korea[e]	—	12.1	11.8	—	0.98	2,577,402	2,671,737	1.04	12.4	0.95	0.99
Malaysia[e]	—	19.1	15.6	—	0.82	12,404	10,588	0.85	16.3	0.96	0.81
Colombia	15.9	18.1	17.2	1.14	0.95	130,872	130,361	1.00	17.9	0.96	0.96
Iran[e]	—	20.3	19.4	—	0.96	884,100	841,486	0.95	19.8	0.98	0.92
Hungary	40.3	42.7	41.4	1.06	0.97	321,056	317,916	0.99	41.6	1.00	0.99
Italy	45.8	49.7	48.0	1.09	0.97	57,937	57,937	1.00	48.5	0.99	0.98
Japan	61.5	59.2	58.5	0.96	0.99	70,894	70,868	1.00	59.0	0.99	0.99
U.K.	60.3	63.5	62.7	1.05	0.99	50,772	50,798	1.00	63.0	0.99	0.99
Netherlands[e]	—	68.7	68.3	—	1.00	114,573	114,571	1.00	68.1	1.00	1.00
France	75.0	73.2	71.9	0.98	0.99	783,248	782,557	1.00	72.2	1.00	0.99
Belgium[e]	—	72.0	72.3	—	1.01	1,263,310	1,280,899	1.01	72.3	1.00	1.01
Germany	74.7	78.2	76.5	1.05	0.98	679,407	678,739	1.00	76.7	1.00	1.00
U.S.	100.0	100.0	100.0	1.00	1.00	981,209	981,200	1.00	100.0	1.00	1.00

a. Countries listed in order of 1970 real per capita GDP (column 3).

b. In millions of currency units, except for Italy and Japan, which are in billions. See Table 1-1 for lists of currency units.

c. Phase II methods applied to Phase III data. Columns 9 and 10 from columns 12 and 13, Table 5-11.

d. Product of columns 8 and 10 and of similar columns showing (1) ratios of new to old population estimates and (2) ratios of estimates reflecting new and old PPPs for U.S. government employees and new and old treatment of net foreign balance.

e. Not included in Phase I.

respondence between the figures in columns 11 and 5. The correspondence is, in general, fairly high, with the largest failure, 4 percent, for Iran. Of course, the test may not be a very demanding one, since most of the revisions between the Phase II and Phase III estimates of real GDP are so small. The biggest change, for Malaysia, is explicable almost entirely by the expenditure revision.

An assessment of the effects of another facet of source (2) inaccuracies and of those arising from source (3) is set out in Table 3-6. The table compares the results of the alternative ways of aggregating the detailed price and expenditure data of the thirty-four Phase III countries that were discussed above. The Geary-Khamis estimates are compared with those of four multilateral methods, the Fisher binary method, and the exchange-rate–conversion method.[76] (Only 143 categories entered into the aggregation to GDP in the implementation of the four multilateral methods (columns 1B to 1E), so 143-category versions of Geary-

76. In Chapter 9 still another aggregation procedure is contrasted with the Geary-Khamis method. Because the linear expenditure system that is estimated there covers consumption alone, the comparisons derived from it are not introduced into Table 3-6.

Khamis and Fisher are presented for direct comparability.) The countries are arrayed and grouped in order of ascending real GDP per capita as estimated by Geary-Khamis.

The Geary-Khamis estimates are highest of all for twenty-one of the countries, Walsh gives the highest in eight of the others, and the two are tied for one country. Fisher is highest in the remaining three. Unit-country weighting estimates are lowest in nearly two-thirds of the comparisons; Fisher and Walsh are lowest in nearly all the rest. (The Walsh lows are all concentrated in Groups I and II, while the Walsh highs are in Groups IV and V.) Column 2C shows that the differences among the methods are small at the high end of the income range, averaging only 6 percent in Group V, but the spread increases as one moves to lower income groups. In Group I the differences for Kenya and Malawi are 36 percent and 26 percent. This is only indicative of the possible error. In the worst case, if Kenya is compared with Poland bridging through the United States, the variability of the methods is greater: Kenya is 9 percent of Poland according to Walsh but 13 percent according to Geary-Khamis. This 43 percent difference exceeds the 36 percent difference indicated by the column 2C entry for Kenya. For most

Table 3-6. Estimates of per Capita Quantity Indexes for Gross Domestic Product, 1975: A Comparison of Alternative Estimating Methods, and Estimates of Degree of Accuracy

	1. Method[a]								
Country	A. Geary-Khamis (151 categories) (1A)	A'. Geary-Khamis (143 categories) (1A')	B. Walsh (143 categories) (1B)	C. EKS (143 categories) (1C)	D. Van Yzeren (143 categories) (1D)	E. Unit-country weighting (143 categories) (1E)	F'. Fisher ideal (143 categories) (1F')	F. Fisher ideal (151 categories) (1F)	G. Exchange-rate conversion (151 categories) (1G)
Group I									
Malawi	4.90	4.55	3.62	3.82	3.80	4.04	3.74	4.1	1.93
Kenya	6.56	6.47	4.76	5.44	5.44	5.84	5.80	6.1	3.36
India	6.56	6.56	6.38	5.74	5.73	5.74	6.00	6.0	2.03
Pakistan	8.23	7.91	6.86	6.62	6.60	6.99	6.44	5.9	2.64
Sri Lanka	9.30	8.87	8.79	7.84	7.83	7.79	7.82	8.0	2.55
Zambia	10.3	10.1	8.33	·9.09	9.08	9.29	9.23	9.9	6.89
Thailand	13.0	12.7	10.3	10.9	10.9	11.5	10.5	10.8	4.88
Philippines	13.2	12.8	12.1	11.1	11.0	11.3	12.0	12.0	5.24
Group II									
Korea	20.7	19.9	17.6	17.8	17.7	18.5	17.2	17.9	8.12
Malaysia	21.5	21.6	21.2	20.5	20.5	19.7	20.6	20.2	10.9
Colombia	22.4	22.6	19.5	19.9	19.9	20.4	19.7	19.4	7.87
Jamaica	24.0	24.2	23.5	23.9	23.9	22.7	25.2	25.1	19.6
Syria	25.0	23.6	20.3	20.7	20.7	21.6	20.6	20.9	10.0
Brazil	25.2	25.1	24.1	24.7	24.6	23.5	23.9	24.3	16.0
Group III									
Romania	33.3	33.4	33.0	30.3	30.3	30.2	30.4	30.8	24.3
Mexico	34.7	34.4	32.7	33.2	33.1	32.1	33.6	35.6	20.4
Yugoslavia	36.1	35.8	37.3	35.6	35.6	33.3	36.5	36.8	32.2
Iran	37.7	38.7	34.3	34.8	34.7	35.5	34.1	33.2	22.1
Uruguay	39.6	39.2	32.0	33.5	33.4	35.4	32.1	33.2	18.2
Ireland	42.5	42.9	42.8	41.9	41.8	39.9	42.2	43.4	37.2
Group IV									
Hungary	49.6	48.9	51.1	48.7	48.6	45.6	48.1	48.9	29.6
Poland	50.1	50.1	52.9	49.4	49.3	46.2	46.2	46.7	36.0
Italy	53.8	54.1	55.0	54.5	54.3	50.5	54.9	55.3	47.9
Spain	55.9	55.9	54.4	54.8	54.8	52.6	53.9	54.1	41.0
Group V									
U.K.	63.9	64.3	66.7	64.1	64.0	60.6	64.8	66.8	57.6
Japan	68.4	68.6	66.1	65.3	65.3	66.6	67.5	66.6	62.3
Austria	69.6	70.5	70.6	70.6	70.4	67.0	71.0	70.4	69.8
Netherlands	75.2	74.1	74.8	73.8	73.7	71.8	72.1	71.4	84.5
Belgium	77.7	77.5	78.4	77.6	77.3	74.8	76.4	76.5	87.8
France	81.9	81.9	80.0	81.1	81.0	77.8	80.2	81.1	89.6
Luxembourg	82.0	82.9	83.8	82.1	81.8	79.9	81.6	79.4	90.2
Denmark	82.4	83.3	85.4	81.4	80.9	78.6	82.7	80.9	104.5
Germany	83.0	81.8	81.8	81.4	81.1	78.5	81.7	80.8	94.4
Group VI									
U.S.	100.0	100.0	100.0	100.0	100.0	100.0	100.0	100.0	100.0

a. See text for a description of the methods. Except for column 1F, the category PPPs inputs were obtained mainly by the CPD method.
b. This is the same as the exchange-rate–deviation index appearing in Table 1-2, column 7.
Sources: Column 1A; Table 1-2, column 6.
    Columns 1A'–1F': calculations made for this table.
    Column 1F: Table 7-1.
    Column 1G: Table 1-2, column 4.
    Column 4: A System, Table 5-8, line 4. Entries for non–Phase I countries are imputed as follows: Groups 1 and 2—the average of Colombia, India, and Kenya; Group 3—the average of all 10 Phase I countries; Groups 4 and 5—the average of Hungary, Italy, the United Kingdom, Japan, France, and the Federal Republic of Germany.

2. Range of 1A', 1B, 1C, 1D, 1E, 1F'			3. Geary-Khamis as a ratio of		4. Possible deviation of Geary-Khamis at 0.95 level (percent)	5. Confidence interval limits of Geary-Khamis (col.4) at 0.95 level		6. Precision interval limits of Geary-Khamis (col. 4) at 0.95 level		7. Average deviation of Geary-Khamis taking account of aggregation differences (percent)
A. Low	B. High	C. High/Low	A. Exchange-rate conversion[b] (1A/1G)	B. Fisher ideal (1A/1F)		A. Lower	B. Upper	A. Lower	B. Upper	
(2A)	(2B)	(2C)	(3A)	(3B)	(4)	(5A)	(5B)	(6A)	(6B)	(7)
3.62	4.55	1.26	2.54	1.20	7.30	4.54	5.26	3.61	5.26	16.8
4.76	6.47	1.36	1.95	1.08	9.50	5.94	7.18	4.37	7.18	21.4
5.73	6.55	1.14	3.23	1.09	7.59	6.06	7.06	5.37	7.05	12.8
6.44	7.91	1.23	3.12	1.39	7.30	7.62	8.82	6.20	8.82	15.9
7.79	8.87	1.14	3.65	1.16	7.30	8.62	9.98	7.57	9.89	12.5
8.33	10.1	1.21	1.49	1.04	7.30	9.55	11.1	7.87	11.0	15.2
10.3	12.7	1.23	2.66	1.20	7.30	12.1	13.9	9.77	13.9	15.9
11.0	12.8	1.16	2.52	1.10	7.30	12.2	14.2	10.5	14.2	14.0
17.2	19.9	1.16	2.55	0.91	7.30	19.2	22.2	16.6	22.2	13.5
19.7	21.6	1.10	1.97	1.06	7.30	19.9	23.1	18.2	23.1	11.4
19.5	22.6	1.16	2.85	1.15	4.81	21.3	23.5	17.9	23.5	12.5
22.7	25.2	1.11	1.22	0.96	7.30	22.2	25.8	20.9	25.8	10.2
20.3	23.6	1.16	2.50	1.20	7.30	23.2	26.8	19.9	26.8	13.8
23.5	25.1	1.07	1.58	1.04	7.30	23.4	27.0	21.9	27.0	10.1
30.2	33.4	1.10	1.37	0.83	6.23	31.2*	35.4	28.2	35.4	10.8
32.1	34.4	1.07	1.70	0.97	6.23	32.5	36.9	30.4	36.9	9.36
33.3	37.3	1.12	1.56	0.98	6.23	33.9	38.3	31.5	40.0	11.8
34.1	38.7	1.13	1.70	1.14	6.23	35.4	40.0	31.0	40.0	11.8
32.0	39.2	1.22	2.18	1.19	6.23	37.1	42.1	30.3	42.1	14.9
39.9	42.9	1.06	1.14	0.98	6.23	39.9	45.1	37.1	45.1	7.16
45.6	51.1	1.12	1.68	1.01	5.47	46.9	52.3	43.7	54.7	11.1
46.2	52.9	1.14	1.39	1.07	5.50	47.3	52.9	43.7	55.8	12.1
50.5	55.0	1.09	1.12	0.97	5.48	50.9	56.7	47.5	57.7	9.48
52.6	55.9	1.06	1.36	1.03	5.50	52.8	59.0	49.7	59.0	8.32
60.6	66.7	1.10	1.11	0.96	5.17	60.6	67.2	57.1	69.7	9.86
65.3	68.6	1.05	1.10	1.03	6.13	64.2	72.6	61.1	72.6	8.41
67.0	71.0	1.06	1.00	0.99	5.50	65.8	73.4	62.5	73.9	8.49
71.8	74.8	1.04	0.89	1.05	5.50	71.1	79.3	68.8	80.1	7.51
74.8	78.4	1.05	0.88	1.02	5.50	73.4	82.0	70.9	82.8	7.66
77.8	81.9	1.05	0.91	1.01	5.30	77.6	86.2	73.7	86.2	7.63
79.9	83.8	1.05	0.91	1.03	5.42	77.6	86.4	74.7	87.4	7.74
78.6	85.4	1.09	0.79	1.02	5.50	77.9	86.9	74.7	89.1	8.74
78.5	81.8	1.04	0.88	1.03	5.50	78.4	87.4	75.3	87.6	7.41
100.0	100.0	1.00	1.00	1.00	1.00	100.0	100.0	100.0	100.0	1.00

(*Sources continued*)

Column 5A: Column 1A entry times (1.0 − column 4 entry/100).
Column 5B: Column 1A entry times (1.0 + column 4 entry/100).
Column 6A: Minimum (lower limits of 0.95 confidence intervals of Geary-Khamis, Walsh, EKS, Van Yzeren, unit-country weighing, and Fisher) · (column 2A entry) · (1.0 − column 4 entry/100) · (column 1A entry/column 1A' entry).
Column 6B: Maximum (upper limits of 0.95 confidence intervals of Geary-Khamis, Walsh, EKS, Van Yzeren, unit-country weighing, and Fisher) · (column 2B entry) · (1.0 + column 4 entry/100) · (column 1A entry/column 1A' entry).
Column 7: (100 [column 6B − column 6A]/2 ÷ column 1A).

comparisons, however, the differences would not be so extreme.

The variability of these estimates is large for all Group I countries and good-sized for most countries in Groups II and III. However, for each of these countries even the smallest per capita real GDP estimate substantially exceeds the estimate obtained through use of the exchange rate. According to Geary-Khamis (151 categories), Kenya's per capita GDP was 6.6 percent of that of the United States. Walsh on a comparable basis[77] gives an estimate 26 percent lower (4.8 percent), but the exchange-rate–conversion procedure gives only 3.4 percent (see column 1G). Every one of the aggregation methods applied to countries in Groups I–III shows the exchange-rate–conversion estimate to be far too low. (Note that the countries where the variability of estimates is greatest are just the countries for which the exchange-rate–conversion method gives the greatest understatement.)

Further, with respect to the stochastic variations (source 3), the ICP aggregation procedure is partly stochastic and partly nonstochastic.[78] When regression analysis is applied at the subcategory level, CPD generates standard errors that can be used in assessing sampling variation in the ICP income comparisons. However, since Geary-Khamis is a nonstochastic method, it does not provide a basis for judging how sensitive its results are to variations in the price and expenditure input data. In Phase I a complicated simulation experiment was devised to estimate the underlying variability of the ICP results arising from the sampling process used in collecting item prices.[79] The outcome took the form of an estimate for each of the ten Phase I countries of one-half the width of a 0.95 confidence interval, stated in percentages, of the Geary-Khamis estimate (see column 4 of Table 3-6). The experiment was not repeated with Phase III data, but for column 4, values were imputed on the basis of income to each of the twenty-four countries of Phase III not included in Phase I.[80] (Observe that the entries are larger for developing countries than developed countries.) Estimates of the 0.95 confidence limits for the Geary-Khamis comparison for each country appear in columns 5A and 5B. (The pattern of column 4 entries leads, of course, to larger intervals in per-

centages for the developing countries than for the developed ones.)

The variability of estimates in columns 1A′ through 1F′ suggests it would be useful to construct an interval estimate for each country, centered on Geary-Khamis, that takes account of the differences in estimates resulting from the use of alternative choices of estimating procedures. A so-called precision interval has been defined as a range based on the regular confidence intervals computed for all six of the methods. Specifically, the low end of the range is the minimum of the six lower confidence interval limits, and the top of the range is the maximum of the six upper confidence interval limits. (This concept, put in set-theory jargon, says a 0.95 precision interval is the *union* of the 0.95 confidence intervals of the six methods.) Needless to say, this synthetic interval is not really founded on principles of statistical inference. As presented in columns 6A and 6B, it is simply a heuristic device designed to help convey the uncertainties associated with each country comparison arising from both stochastic and misspecification considerations.[81] Column 7 provides a single summary number, the average percentage "plus or minus" around the Geary-Khamis estimate within which the truth lies—subject to the critical caveat that it does not incorporate the uncertainties conveyed by the review of the data revisions and the supercountry sensitivities from Phase II.

What stands out most prominently in Table 3-6 is that all methods give very similar GDP per capita comparisons. The arguments presented in the early part of this chapter in support of Geary-Khamis give the concept of international prices a central role, but Table 3-6 makes clear that even if this very useful concept is denied a role in the comparison process, the estimates of comparative affluence are not greatly affected.

Summary

The chapter began with a review of the desired properties of international comparisons, including base-country invariance, transitivity, matrix consistency, transactions equality, and country characteristicity. These sought-after properties were helpful in assessing the pros and cons of four broad sets of methods for carrying out international comparisons of price and quantity. The methods chosen by the ICP fall within the category of multilateral methods that are not de-

77. That is, adjusting the Walsh result based on 143 categories to a 151-category index by the ratio of the Geary-Khamis 151 to 143 indexes.

78. The linear-expenditure-system analysis of Chapter 9 with its explicitly stochastic estimating procedure automatically provides standard errors to accompany its per capita consumption comparisons.

79. See Kravis, Kenessey, Heston, Summers (1975), pp. 77–79.

80. The imputations are described in the notes to Table 3-6.

81. These intervals refer to comparisons with the United States. The table as it stands does not provide enough information to calculate precision intervals applicable to other base countries.

pendent on binary comparisons. At the first stage of aggregation, within detailed categories, the ICP relies on the country-product-dummy (CPD) method. At the second stage of aggregation, the ICP has adopted a method devised by Geary that uses a concept of international average prices. The method combines the data on prices and quantities for detailed categories to obtain comparisons for aggregates, such as consumption and GDP. At both levels of aggregation the ICP introduces supercountry weighting to approximate the world price structure in deriving the average prices. Some of the alternative methods are briefly discussed, and the GDP estimates produced by them are compared with those of Geary-Khamis. Rough measures of precision with the ICP comparisons are also presented.

4

The Regionalization Problem

PREVIOUS COMPARISONS OF REAL PRODUCT have been confined to relatively homogeneous groups of countries or to a limited number of heterogeneous countries.[1] Thus one set of studies compared Western European countries with the United States, another set compared the countries of Eastern Europe, and still another compared Latin American countries.[2] More heterogeneous countries were included in the previous ICP comparisons: ten in Phase I and sixteen in Phase II.[3]

The larger number of countries included in Phase III and their wide geographical distribution presented new problems and opportunities for applying the methods described in Chapter 3. When only ten or even sixteen countries were under study, there was little point in considering whether comparisons could be improved by identifying relatively homogeneous subsets of countries. The Geary-Khamis method (described in Chapter 3), which achieves transitivity by making the estimate of GDP per capita of each country interdependent with the estimate for every other country, was applied to the entire set of countries without any effort to distinguish such subsets and to take them into account in the index number calculations. (For simplicity, the problem of aggregating item prices ac-

cording to CPD to get category PPPs is ignored in this section.) This completely symmetrical treatment of all countries will be called the universal approach. It can readily be applied to thirty-four countries or indeed to all the countries of the world.

With as many as thirty-four countries, however, it becomes necessary to consider whether some advantage might not be gained by employing the Geary-Khamis method in successive stages, first applying it to sets of relatively homogeneous countries and then using it to link the sets. An obvious basis for identifying homogeneous sets of countries is geographical propinquity. Though there are analytical criteria that might more appropriately be used in the grouping of countries, it is convenient for the moment to think of each set of homogeneous countries as constituting a region. The choice being posed, then, is between a one-stage, universal comparison, one that includes all countries, and a two-stage comparison in which comparisons are first made among the countries in each region, and then among the regions. In the latter system, countries in different regions are compared through the regional linkings.

Characteristicity versus Universality

The great advantage claimed for working with a first stage of intraregional comparisons is that it allows more scope for characteristicity for countries within regions than does a universal comparison. Of course, the greatest degree of characteristicity is achieved in a binary comparison, particularly when the countries compared are very similar. In a binary comparison it is possible to choose a sample of items that closely represents the consumption pattern of both countries

---

1. The issues discussed in this chapter were treated earlier in a paper by Kravis, Heston, Summers (1979). Some of the material in this chapter is taken from that paper, but subsequent research has led to a clearer understanding of the issues and to a revision of some of the conclusions.

2. Gilbert and Kravis (1954); Gilbert and associates (1958); Paretti, Krijnse Locker, Goybet (1973); European Communities Statistical Office (1977). The Eastern European studies have not been published, but see Drechsler (1975), pp. 17–34. For the Latin American studies see Salazar-Carrillo (1978).

3. Phase I: Kravis, Kenessey, Heston, Summers (1975); Phase II: Kravis, Heston, Summers (1978a).

and to use weights based solely on the spending patterns of the pair. When the comparison goes beyond a binary one and more countries are included, both the sample of item prices and the weights entering into the comparison of any pair of countries are influenced by the presence of the other countries. As was pointed out in Chapter 3, if a comparison between a pair of countries is desired in an isolated context, then the exclusion of third-country influences is clearly an advantage. If, however, the comparison is desired in a broader context, say, of a region (for example, France-Italy in the European Community), then the exclusions may not be advantageous.

An important issue is how the result of a comparison between a pair of countries is altered when one or more third countries are added. Analysis of this question starts with the simple fact that the structure of each country's quantities adapts to its own price structure. That is, expensive commodities are consumed in relatively small amounts, and cheap ones are consumed in relatively large amounts. Consequently, when a country's quantities are valued at its own prices the aggregate produced by such a valuation is likely to be smaller relative to the aggregate for another country (also valued at the first-country prices) than when both countries' quantities are valued at the prices of the second country. (See the comments on the own-weight effect in the Chapter 3 section entitled "Four Sets of Methods.")

Operation of the own-weight effect when third countries are added can be more easily seen if it is assumed that the index-number method used is an average-price method. (See Chapter 3, under "Four Sets of Methods.") When one or more countries are added to a comparison that formerly involved only a pair of countries, the average prices used to value the quantities of the included countries, including the original pair, are apt to be less closely correlated with the prices of either member of the original pair than the average prices derived from the prices of the two countries alone. As between the two countries in the original pair, the own-weight effect will tend to raise the relative quantity index of the country whose prices are less closely correlated with the new and broader set of average prices.

If neither country's prices are closely correlated with the prices of the newcomer(s), the original comparison between them may not be much affected by the addition(s). In such a case, not much is lost by giving up some characteristicity.

Furthermore, a system of binary comparisons, one for each possible pair of countries, has some substantial practical and theoretical disadvantages. Opera-

tionally, the task of designing an adequate binary sample of goods for price comparison for each pair of countries would place an enormous burden on both the ICP center and the individual countries. This disadvantage could be sharply reduced by confining the binary comparisons to pairs of countries within the same homogeneous region, but even then the average country would have to find comparable specifications for comparisons with 10 to 25 other countries, depending on the number of regions into which the eventual 80 to 120 countries of the ICP are divided.

But even if these practical problems could be circumvented,[4] a system of binary comparisons will not satisfy some of the important properties sought in a system of real-product comparisons. In particular, the failure of such a system to produce index numbers that have the properties of transitivity and base country invariance is, as was argued in Chapter 3, a compelling objection. It is true that binary comparisons can be processed to produce multilateral comparisons that have these properties and still possess characteristicity to some degree, but third-country information then enters into any pairwise comparison. Also, the resulting system does not meet the requirement of matrix consistency.

Finally, any improvement in characteristicity in comparisons of countries within regions is obtained only by sacrificing characteristicity in comparisons of countries in different regions. If intraregional comparisons were made in a first stage and interregional comparisons in a second stage, the U.K./Japan comparison—to take one example—would be influenced from one side by the prices and expenditures of all the European countries included in the Europe calculations, and from the other side by the prices and expenditures of all the Asian countries included in the Asia calculations.

The criterion labeled here as "universality" requires that all countries, regardless of location, income level, social system, or any other consideration, be compared by a common standard. This is the approach that must be followed, if, for example, it is desired to ensure that a banana eaten in Japan is not counted as more real product relative to an orange than a banana eaten in Germany is counted relative to an orange. What rationale can be offered—and particularly what rationale consistent with national-accounting practice can be offered—for counting a pound of bananas as less product than a pound of oranges in Europe and as more product in Asia? How can the legitimacy of

---

4. See the proposal for "augmented binaries" in Chapter 7.

a Germany/Japan comparison be defended?[5] The adoption of a two-stage procedure involves a willingness to abandon this common-yardstick approach in a search for more characteristicity in the intraregional comparisons. The adoption of the universal approach forgoes this search in order to keep a uniform yardstick.

Since on almost any basis for identifying homogeneous sets of countries there will be some between-set comparisons that seem important, the interests of within-set comparisons must be balanced against those of between-set comparisons. If a geographical classification is used, for example, the natural interest in peer comparisons will require some interregional comparisons. The Federal Republic of Germany may be as interested in comparisons with the United States and Japan as in comparisons with Luxembourg and Spain—or more interested. Since a substantial part of world trade is interregional[6]—indeed the trade of some major trading countries outside their region actually dominates their intraregional trade[7]—considerations of international competition lead to a desire for interregional comparisons. There are also political and governmental reasons for interregional comparisons. For example, comparisons among developing countries, regardless of region, are often needed in the distribution of aid or of lending on concessional terms. Sacrificing the quality of interregional comparisons in an effort to produce characteristic intraregional comparisons thus has its limitations.

5. These rhetorical questions might take on a different cast if it were possible to work empirically with consumer indifference curves. Even then, the assumption that every individual in every country had the same indifference map would be required to take account of differing marginal rates of substitution at different levels of income or in different supply situations. However, even in the pragmatic, statistically oriented approach followed in the ICP and other major international-comparison studies, such uniform marginal rates of substitution across all countries are not insisted upon in the case of a good that is not in common consumption in a given country. The treatment of such a good is equivalent to assuming that it can be transformed to a commonly consumed good at the prevailing relative prices of the exceptional good and the commonly consumed goods in the same final consumption category. (See Chapter 2, under the section "The Price Data.")

6. According to the eleven-area classification used by GATT (1976), table F, 58 percent of world trade was interregional in 1975. Though the classification is partly a regional and partly a type-of-country (for example, OPEC) categorization, a purely geographical classification would not radically alter the indicated proportion.

7. This is true of the United States and Japan, but the interregional trade of other countries, such as the Federal Republic of Germany, the United Kingdom, and France is also substantial. See the next section, under "Trade Ties."

Multilateral comparisons—those in which the quantity or price indexes for all countries are determined with the complete interdependence of all included countries—are clearly best for universality. The optimum scope of the multilateral comparisons depends on the purpose at hand. For general-purpose use by universal agencies such as the United Nations and the World Bank and for general economic analysis, all the countries should be treated symmetrically. When all countries are included in a single multilateral comparison, each country has an influence in fashioning the common yardstick that measures the product of all. Thus the prices and quantities of India and Japan, for example, influence the measured relationship between distant France and Germany. Of course, the effect of these distant influences is apt to be very similar for countries that are as alike as France and Germany. To the extent this is true, the effect of remote influences on the comparison of similar neighbors will be limited.

Nevertheless, there may be special needs for comparisons involving only a pair of countries or some group of countries for which it may seem desirable to exclude such outside influences. The operational purposes of the European Economic Community, for example, may call for multilateral comparisons confined to the countries of the Community. A multilateral comparison including only Community countries permits the France-Germany relationship to be affected by other Community members but not non-Community countries.

However, there is danger that a large number of special-purpose comparisons will cast doubt on the credibility of the entire set of international comparisons. If for each practical use there is a choice of estimates to be made for individual pairs of countries, all the estimates may be thrown into question. It is important, therefore, to avoid proliferation of estimates; this can be accomplished by confining the production of such special comparisons for subsets of countries to cases in which they are required to meet important practical operating needs.

It would, of course, be helpful if a single general-purpose set of estimates could be devised that would serve all or at least most uses. The simplest solution would be to use the comprehensive universal approach, in which all countries are included in a single multilateral calculation. The alternative is to develop a worldwide system that uses regional or even binary comparisons as building blocks. Ways would have to be sought in the latter case to minimize the resulting disadvantages: the multiplicity of countries with which each country would have to make price comparisons, the use of different yardsticks, and certain undesirable statistical properties.

Identifying Homogeneous Sets of Countries

A regional approach can be implemented in several ways. The chief variations turn on how countries are grouped into regions and how countries in different regions are linked together. Here alternatives are assessed.

Geographical Propinquity

Geographical propinquity is a basis for grouping countries that has the sanction of custom and, often, of close political and cultural ties. "Europe" and "Latin America," for example, are familiar ways of classifying countries in the daily business of coping with the political, social, and economic events and trends of the world. The matching U.N. organizations covering these regions (the Economic Commission for Europe and the Economic Commission for Latin America) take an active interest in price and real-product comparisons among their member countries. Within regions, too, important subregional organizations engage in international comparisons, organizations such as the Council for Mutual Economic Assistance (CMEA), Programa de Estudos Conjuntos de Integracão Económica da América Latina (ECIEL), and the European Economic Community (EEC). Thus there are strong practical reasons for considering grouping of countries by geographic region.

If continents were used as the main basis for defining regions, one classification of the thirty-four Phase III countries that is suggested is as follows:

Africa	Asia	Europe	Latin America and the Caribbean	North America
Kenya	India	Austria	Brazil	U.S.
Malawi	Iran	Belgium	Colombia	
Zambia	Japan	Denmark	Jamaica	
	Korea	France	Mexico	
	Malaysia	Germany	Uruguay	
	Pakistan	Hungary		
	Philippines	Ireland		
	Sri Lanka	Italy		
	Syria	Luxembourg		
	Thailand	Netherlands		
		Poland		
		Romania		
		Spain		
		U.K.		
		Yugoslavia		

Two points might be made about such a classification. First, there is nothing sacrosanct about the use of continents as the sole basis of geographical classification. Some regional groupings cut across continental lines, and others subdivide continents. The former set includes regions composed of littoral countries, such as the Pacific basin, the Atlantic Community, or the Mediterranean area. Classifications involving continental subsets are represented by political groupings such as the CMEA and the EEC.

The second point is that classifications based on geography or on geography with an admixture of political considerations may not warrant treatment as regions on the basis of the characteristicity considerations (discussed in the previous section) that provide the analytical case for a two-stage approach. Unless the countries of a geographic or political region are relatively homogeneous in a relevant economic sense, there are no advantages—and there may be some disadvantages—in segregating them, from the technical statistical standpoint.

The justification for such groupings on purely political grounds may be sufficient. There may be important political uses of comparisons that make it worthwhile grouping certain countries together regardless of considerations of homogeneity. It would not, for example, undermine this basis for treating the nine countries of the European Community as a region if it turned out that Ireland, a member of the nine, were less similar to the other eight than nonmembers, such as Norway and Sweden. But the reasons for the grouping would be political and not grounded in economics or in statistical considerations.

Analytic Criteria

What are the appropriate economic and statistical criteria to be used in identifying homogeneous groups of countries? The purposes at hand—price, quantity and income comparisons— plainly suggest similarity in price structure (that is, in relative prices), similarity in quantity structures, and perhaps similarity in income levels as criteria.

The raw materials for the calculation of price similarities are available in the form of the item prices submitted by the countries. Neither quantities nor incomes are initially available; relative quantities for each of the 151 detailed categories and per capita incomes are available only as outputs of the ICP. The outputs also include prices (PPPs) for the detailed categories. Incomes and category quantities and prices, unlike the item prices, thus cannot be known until the method of processing the raw data is decided upon, and an aspect of that methodology—whether it should be applied universally or initially to regions—is at issue. Some kind of iterative procedure could be worked out in which tentative classifications of countries were used to produce an initial set of incomes, category quantities, and prices. These would then be used to revise the country classification, and the new country classification would then be used to obtain a second set of approximations of incomes, category quantities and prices, and so on. Such a process, however, would be cumbersome.

Instead, primary reliance has been placed on two sets of data that come in a form that makes unnecessary even a preliminary judgment about the classification of countries. One data set consists of the item prices, which, as was noted above, are available without any processing that prejudges the issue. A similarity index, described below, is used to measure the similarity of the price vectors of each pair of countries. Countries with very similar price structures are then grouped together.

The other set of data consists of the Paasche-Laspeyres spread (PLS, the ratio of the former to the latter index)[8] as obtained from binary comparisons for each possible pair of countries.[9] PLS takes into account not only the similarity of prices, as does the index based on item prices, but the similarity of quantities as well. This is because the size of the spread depends on the degree of correlation between the price and quantity ratios of the two countries, and on the dispersions of their price ratios and their quantity ratios.[10]

For any given binary comparison, the smaller the spread (that is, the closer the PLS is to unity) the more similar the price and quantity structures of the two countries.

Very similar price structures in two countries imply that average prices computed from the prices of the two countries would be highly correlated with the prices of each. Very similar quantity structures imply that the weights for preparing the price comparisons drawn from each country would be similar to those of the partner country. The PLS thus serves as an indicator of the degree of characteristicity in a comparison involving a particular pair of countries. The closer the PLS is to unity, the greater the characteristicity.

While the main reliance will be placed on similarity of item prices and on the PLS, attention will also be paid to groupings based on the similarity of their real per capita GDPs (income). The circularity referred to earlier (that is, the necessity to decide on the classification of countries before being able to calculate incomes) could be reduced by ranking the countries according to their per capita GDPs as estimated, in some cases very approximately, in earlier work.[11] Since the earlier rankings too could be obtained only after a decision on country classifications (the universal approach was used), this would still involve a certain degree of circularity, although the insensitivity of income rankings to the starting classification makes this no problem. In fact, the final Phase III estimates from Table 1-2 have been used. The classification of countries according to income similarity desired here is in any case only illustrative.

Finally, the closeness of trading ties will be considered as a basis for grouping. This classification is not, of course, aimed at homogeneity, but is based rather on the notion that particular interests might attach to comparisons with countries that are important trading partners.

Homogeneity Based on Item Prices

The measure of similarity between the vectors of item prices for any pair of countries is their weighted raw correlation coefficient.[12] This is defined as the ratio of the weighted cross moment to the square root

---

8. Which set of weights in a binary comparison should be regarded as yielding the equivalent of a Paasche (PA) index and which set as producing the equivalent of a Laspeyres (LA) index must be determined arbitrarily. The convention adopted here is to regard the higher income country as the base country; the use of its weights thus produces what is referred to here as the Laspeyres index.

9. In view of what has been said about the difficulty of making all the price comparisons required for all possible binary comparisons, it may seem surprising that the Paasche-Laspeyres spreads are available. The Paasche and Laspeyres indexes used in what follows are taken from "augmented" binary comparisons. These binaries depart from the traditional ones in that they include some prices estimated by the CPD method. As is explained in Chapter 7, the augmented binary approach was designed to offset the disadvantage of relatively small numbers of overlapping prices for some pairs of countries in the ICP data set. The limited overlapping arises because each country's price collection was designed primarily for comparisons within a region and focused particularly on the regional numéraire country. As compared with Paasche and Laspeyres indexes based on the overlapping items in the ICP data set, it is believed that augmented binaries yield better approximations to the results that would have been produced by traditional binaries based on data especially selected for the two countries.

10. The price and quantity ratios are (P_{ij}/P_{ck}) and (Q_{ij}/Q_{ck}), respectively. The Paasche-Laspeyres spread is

$$\text{PLS} = P_{PA}/P_{LA} = 1 + r \frac{\sigma_P}{P_j/P_k} \frac{\sigma_Q}{Q_j/Q_k}$$

where r is the coefficient of the correlation between the price and quantity ratios, the σ's are weighted standard deviations of price and quantity ratios, and the bars over P_j/P_k and Q_j/Q_k refer to weighted means. The derivation of this relationship, which is attributable to Bortkiewicz, is given in Allen (1975), p. 62f.

11. Summers, Kravis, Heston (1980).

12. The similarity concept is used extensively in Chapter 9 as well as here. A detailed description of the similarity measure is given in both places to serve the needs of readers interested in only particular chapters.

Table 4-1. Index of Item Price Similarity for GDP, Based on Overlapping Item Prices for Pairs of Countries, 1975

	Malawi	Kenya	India	Paki-stan	Sri Lanka	Zambia	Thai-land	Philip-pines	Korea	Malay-sia	Colom-bia	Jamaica	Syria	Brazil	Roma-nia	Mexico	Yugos-lavia
Malawi	1,000	671	798	680	747	877	751	752	776	785	726	833	692	770	639	812	746
Kenya	671	1,000	720	783	774	901	711	687	736	779	733	868	717	573	498	846	748
India	798	720	1,000	747	798	809	736	807	752	807	760	646	701	707	704	775	701
Pakistan	680	783	747	1,000	731	778	759	682	778	703	784	715	761	595	633	593	530
Sri Lanka	747	774	798	731	1,000	802	683	715	671	790	726	665	640	666	677	723	659
Zambia	877	901	809	778	802	1,000	807	792	778	824	769	788	697	794	749	791	771
Thailand	751	711	736	759	683	807	1,000	805	782	770	818	816	574	754	704	793	669
Philippines	752	687	807	682	715	792	805	1,000	740	748	719	676	696	786	749	810	780
Korea	776	736	752	778	671	778	782	740	1,000	816	733	792	653	722	671	758	678
Malaysia	785	779	807	703	790	824	770	748	816	1,000	797	751	784	847	805	823	744
Colombia	726	733	760	784	726	769	818	719	733	797	1,000	783	738	739	701	820	757
Jamaica	833	868	646	715	665	788	816	676	792	751	783	1,000	757	648	658	816	757
Syria	692	717	701	761	640	697	574	696	653	784	738	757	1,000	740	680	641	704
Brazil	770	573	707	595	666	794	754	786	722	847	739	848	740	1,000	750	876	791
Romania	639	498	704	633	677	749	704	749	671	805	701	658	680	750	1,000	777	809
Mexico	812	846	775	593	723	791	793	810	758	823	820	816	641	876	777	1,000	809
Yugoslavia	746	748	701	530	659	771	609	780	678	744	757	757	704	791	809	809	1,000
Iran	622	705	706	686	633	664	704	760	776	833	701	703	742	764	744	712	740
Uruguay	755	725	725	733	753	792	700	782	680	719	790	694	713	797	737	773	795
Ireland	777	799	752	747	703	840	703	770	729	819	759	838	727	809	744	764	857
Hungary	761	673	757	711	681	338	423	315	382	384	390	804	707	823	815	396	821
Poland	760	731	738	664	692	780	664	755	785	738	704	751	670	767	702	725	758
Italy	772	533	721	631	618	831	714	814	769	819	798	789	648	855	719	812	855
Spain	676	528	633	558	581	804	701	790	666	791	788	689	641	846	765	813	872
U.K.	788	321	714	691	606	830	652	789	680	850	797	815	735	841	763	768	869
Japan	740	605	662	508	623	747	713	732	764	750	636	726	725	756	743	759	796
Austria	682	743	644	578	596	688	661	746	660	818	643	723	724	773	784	752	829
Netherlands	745	830	695	748	598	835	709	679	681	823	758	816	743	808	697	823	874
Belgium	725	837	711	750	602	817	643	630	648	804	756	794	712	796	665	817	881
France	748	799	721	757	607	812	649	700	680	808	788	771	701	838	682	818	860
Luxembourg	787	666	734	666	658	833	687	776	722	849	807	818	727	846	711	830	891
Demmark	738	691	714	706	612	837	742	732	682	808	723	787	691	813	741	758	847
Germany	721	671	672	650	535	789	701	721	696	820	774	715	691	802	796	763	858
U.S.	729	773	646	649	672	789	703	753	708	754	764	774	679	807	716	748	758

Note: Countries are ordered by relative income, as given in Table 1-2, column 6.

of the product of the two weighted second moments, each moment being computed relative to the origin rather than the mean. It is the same as the cosine of the angle between the n dimensional vectors, where n is the number of item prices. The formula is:

$$(4.1) \quad S_{jk}^P = \frac{\sum_{\alpha=1}^{A} W_\alpha P_{\alpha j} P_{\alpha k}}{\sqrt{\sum_{\alpha=1}^{A} W_\alpha P_{\alpha j}^2 \cdot \sum_{\alpha=1}^{A} W_\alpha P_{\alpha k}^2}}$$

where S_{jk}^P is the item price similarity index between countries j and k, and α is a running index over A items. $P_{\alpha j}$ is an item price, converted to dollars through an exchange rate, and then expressed as a ratio to the geometric mean price across the countries. This scaling was adopted to make the similarity index units invariant; otherwise, the indexes would have been unduly influenced by items that came with big price tags in all countries (for example, automobiles) and would

not have reflected adequately items with small price tags (for example, pencils). W_α is the weight assigned to the αth item. The W's were obtained by dividing world expenditures on each detailed category evenly among the items in the category.[13]

Note that the similarity indexes are based on the overlapping item prices in each pair of countries; the number varies from 118 (Pakistan/Luxembourg) to 582 (Austria/Poland), and the average number is about 250. The prices cover all of GDP.

The S_{jk}^P's are shown in Table 4-1 where the countries are arrayed in order of rising per capita incomes. Although the S_{jk}^P's as defined may vary between 0 and

13. World expenditures for each category were obtained by converting each country's per capita expenditure in its own currency to dollars by dividing by PPPs derived from Summers, Kravis, Heston (1980), multiplying this dollar expenditure by the supercountry population, and summing these products.

	Iran	Uru-guay	Ireland	Hun-gary	Poland	Italy	Spain	U.K.	Japan	Austria	Nether-lands	Bel-gium	France	Luxem-bourg	Den-mark	Ger-many	U.S.
Malawi	622	755	777	761	760	772	676	788	740	682	745	725	748	787	738	721	729
Kenya	705	725	799	673	731	533	528	821	605	743	830	837	799	666	691	671	773
India	706	725	752	757	738	721	633	714	662	644	695	711	721	734	714	672	646
Pakistan	686	733	747	711	664	631	558	691	508	578	748	750	767	666	706	650	649
Sri Lanka	633	753	703	681	692	618	581	606	623	596	598	602	607	658	612	535	672
Zambia	664	792	840	338	780	831	804	830	747	688	835	817	812	833	837	789	789
Thailand	704	700	703	423	664	714	701	652	713	661	709	643	649	687	742	701	703
Philippines	760	732	770	315	755	814	790	789	732	746	679	630	700	776	732	721	753
Korea	776	680	729	382	785	769	666	680	764	660	681	648	680	722	682	696	708
Malaysia	833	719	819	384	738	819	791	850	750	818	823	804	808	849	808	820	754
Colombia	701	790	759	390	704	798	788	797	636	643	758	756	788	807	723	774	764
Jamaica	703	694	838	804	751	789	689	815	726	723	816	794	771	818	787	715	774
Syria	742	713	727	707	670	648	641	735	725	724	743	712	701	727	691	691	679
Brazil	764	797	809	823	767	855	846	841	756	773	808	796	838	846	813	802	807
Romania	744	737	744	815	702	719	765	763	743	784	697	665	682	711	741	796	716
Mexico	712	773	764	396	725	612	813	768	759	752	823	817	818	830	758	763	748
Yugoslavia	740	795	857	821	758	855	872	869	796	829	874	881	860	891	847	858	758
Iran	1,000	620	823	751	726	848	802	824	754	803	829	808	828	835	809	803	739
Uruguay	620	1,000	772	726	780	776	751	765	693	659	757	726	747	768	743	728	754
Ireland	823	772	1,000	770	706	858	837	956	822	807	915	915	893	913	929	910	846
Hungary	751	726	770	1,000	846	772	837	768	254	426	746	736	750	778	735	732	415
Poland	726	780	706	846	1,000	706	813	711	759	750	704	697	717	723	705	677	688
Italy	848	776	858	772	706	1,000	885	888	877	812	891	898	928	918	877	909	848
Spain	802	751	837	837	813	885	1,000	850	729	845	865	855	867	896	821	832	790
U.K.	824	765	956	768	711	888	850	1,000	809	836	914	929	917	925	913	916	868
Japan	754	693	822	254	759	827	729	809	1,000	770	803	785	803	821	794	833	838
Austria	803	659	807	426	750	812	845	836	770	1,000	847	829	833	839	799	858	804
Netherlands	829	757	915	746	704	891	865	914	803	847	1,000	958	941	946	927	944	889
Belgium	808	726	915	736	697	898	855	929	785	829	958	1,000	960	972	921	956	880
France	828	747	893	750	717	928	867	917	803	833	941	960	1,000	947	916	936	875
Luxembourg	835	768	913	778	723	918	896	925	821	839	946	972	947	1,000	916	946	891
Denmark	809	743	929	735	705	877	821	913	794	799	927	921	916	916	1,000	935	851
Germany	803	728	910	732	677	909	832	916	833	858	944	956	936	946	935	1,000	866
U.S.	739	754	846	415	688	848	790	868	838	804	889	880	875	891	851	866	1,000

1, to save space in printing decimal points, they have been multiplied by 1,000. The full matrix has been printed as a matter of convenience for the reader, even though the triangle on either side of the main diagonal contains all the information.

The results suggest some tendency for the price similarity index to be correlated with the similarity of incomes. In Table 4-1 this can be seen in the tendency for the indexes to decline in each column as the rows become more remote from the principal diagonal. Regression analysis confirms and quantifies this relationship (standard errors appear in parentheses):

$$(4.2) \qquad S^P_{jk} = 0.669 + 0.144 \ S^Y_{jk}$$
$$(0.009) \quad (0.015)$$

$$\overline{R}^2 = 0.15 \quad n = 561$$

where S^Y_{jk}, the index of income similarity, is defined as $2 \cdot \text{Minimum} \ (Y_j, Y_k)/(Y_j + Y_k)$, where Y refers to the measure of real per capita GDP of countries j and

k (taken from Table 1-2). (Like S^P_{jk}, the values of S^Y_{jk} range from 0 to 1.)

Close inspection of the table also suggests that while price similarity often is high between countries in the same region, there are many cases of similar price structures between countries in different regions. The similarity of Italian prices to those of Brazil and the United States, for example, is not significantly less than the similarity of Italian prices to those of Ireland and Yugoslavia, and is actually greater than the similarity of Italian prices to those of some other European countries, such as Austria, Hungary, and Poland. Even more striking cases of greater interregional similarity can be found for other countries, especially for some, such as Japan, that are outside Europe.

The inference that can be drawn is that a grouping of countries by a criterion other than geographical propinquity may increase the average within-group similarity. Accordingly, clustering techniques were applied to obtain a grouping of countries based on ho-

Figure 4–1.   Clustering of Countries according to Similarity Indexes for Item Prices (S^p) for All Components of GDP

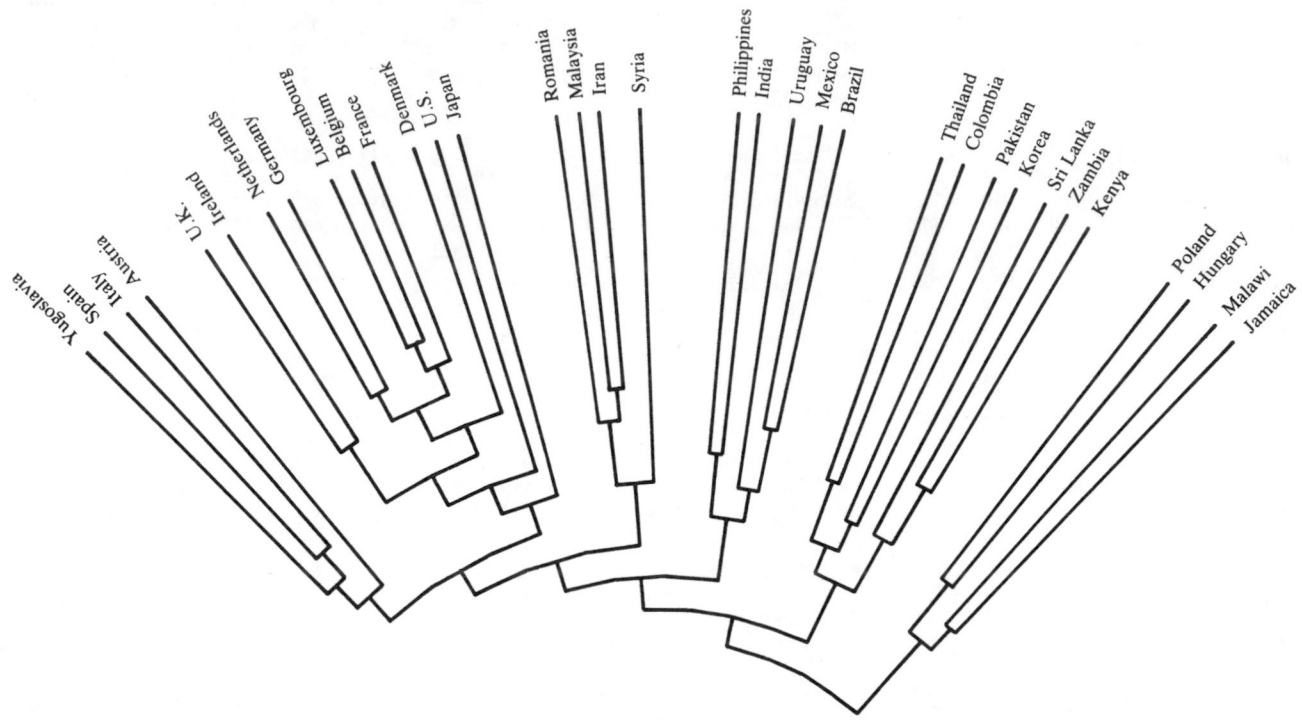

mogeneity of relative item prices. The similarity tree of Figure 4-1, based on a computing algorithm of Johnson (1967), shows such a grouping. On the basis of these results, the following classification of countries into regions—really "homogeneity groups"—was chosen. The average similarity index ($\overline{S^p}$) and the standard deviation (σ_{SP}) of the indexes for each of the five new homogeneity groups are shown below each list of constituent countries.

	I	II	III	IV	V
	Hungary	Colombia	Brazil	Iran	Austria
	Jamaica	Kenya	India	Malaysia	Belgium
	Malawi	Korea	Mexico	Romania	Denmark
	Poland	Pakistan	Philippines	Syria	France
		Sri Lanka	Uruguay		Germany
		Thailand			Ireland
		Zambia			Italy
					Japan
					Luxembourg
					Netherlands
					Spain
					U.K.
					U.S.
					Yugoslavia
$\overline{S^p}$	793	764	784	765	872
σ_{SP}	38	49	44	50	52

How much more homogeneous is this grouping than the geographical one? How much greater is the ho-

mogeneity achieved by each of these groupings than is observed when the world is treated as a single region? The answers to these questions are reflected in the average similarity indexes for all pairs of countries within the regions, within the homogeneity groups, and within the group of thirty-four countries as a whole.

Classification scheme	Number of pairs	Mean index of price similarity	Standard deviation
Price homogeneity[14]	134	840	50
Geographical[15]	165	803	82
Universal	561	754	96

Thus it is true that the continental classification achieves more than half (57 percent) of the improvement in price-structure homogeneity that can be obtained by

14. See the immediately preceding classification. The mean of 840 is the average of the intragroup averages, weighted by the number of pairs within each group.

15. The classification is given above in the subsection "Geographical Propinquity." The average-price similarity indexes (and standard deviations) for pairs within geographical regions are Africa 816 (103), Asia 727 (65), Europe 833 (91), Latin America and the Caribbean 794 (49). The average index for all intraregional pairs is 802 (82). (See previous footnote for the method of calculating this average.) The average of 803 in the text table was calculated by arbitrarily assuming a similarity index for the North American region (which here contains only the United States) of 950. The standard deviation (82) in the text table excludes North America.

using price-structure homogeneity as a criterion of grouping;[16] that is, $(803 - 754)/(840 - 754)$.

The Paasche-Laspeyres Spread

The conclusions just discussed are based on the similarity of price structures. Will similar conclusions be reached when one takes account of similarity in both prices and quantity structures?

To answer this question, one can examine the ratios of the Paasche (own-weight) to Laspeyres (base-country weight) indexes. These Paasche-Laspeyres spreads (PLS) are presented in Table 7-3 of Chapter 7, where binary indexes are more fully dealt with.

Inspection of Table 7-3 indicates that countries in rows or columns close together have higher PLS indexes than those farther apart. This association of the PLS with income difference is shown to be much stronger than that of price similarity by equation 4.3 (standard errors in parentheses):

$$(4.3) \qquad \text{PLS}_{jk} = \underset{(0.104)}{0.4536} + \underset{(0.0163)}{0.3668} \, S_{jk}^{Y}$$

$$\overline{R^2} = 0.47 \qquad n = 561$$

The similarity tree depicting the clustering of countries by PLS is given in Figure 4-2. The selection of five groups of countries is necessarily more arbitrary here than in Figure 4-1, because of the relative separation of Zambia and Kenya from the other countries in Group I. The grouping selected is:

I	II	III	IV	V
India	Colombia	Austria	Brazil	Belgium
Kenya	Jamaica	Hungary	Korea	Denmark
Malawi	Philippines	Iran	Malaysia	France
Pakistan	Thailand	Poland	Mexico	Germany
Sri Lanka		Romania		Ireland
Zambia		Spain		Italy
		Syria		Japan
		Uruguay		Luxembourg
		Yugoslavia		Netherlands
				U.K.
				U.S.
PLS 766	748	730	714	884
σ_{PLS} 51	78	101	91	63

16. A five-category division of countries into homogeneity groups was chosen to facilitate the comparison with the geographical grouping. Increasing the number of groups in either set would tend to raise the average intragroup similarity indexes. Five groups rather than six or eight or some other number is an arbitrary choice, but it seems likely that the comparative results obtained would not differ substantially. For example, with six groups, the geographical regions (the sixth is formed by splitting Hungary, Poland, Romania, and Yugoslavia off from the rest of Europe) have a mean similarity

The degree of homogeneity, as measured by PLS, for the different classifications of countries is:

Classification scheme	Number of pairs	Mean PLS	Standard deviation
PLS homogeneity	118	805	79
Geographical[17]	165	779	85
Universal	561	669	136

On the PLS basis the five-continent geographical grouping goes further in achieving the highest possible homogeneity than it achieves in item-price similarity; the geographical grouping achieves 81 percent of the possible improvement in homogeneity:

$$(779 - 669) \, / \, (805 - 669).^{[18]}$$

Income Similarity

The use of the index of income similarity, S_{jk}^{Y}, as the criterion of similarity between pairs of countries, produced very similar results with respect to the relative improvement in homogeneity achieved by the geographical grouping. The groups were:

I	II	III	IV	V
Malawi	Korea	Romania	Hungary	U.K.
Kenya	Malaysia	Mexico	Poland	Japan
India	Colombia	Yugoslavia	Italy	Austria
Pakistan	Jamaica	Iran	Spain	Netherlands
Sri Lanka	Syria	Uruguay		Belgium
Zambia	Brazil	Ireland		France
Thailand				Luxembourg
Philippines				Denmark
				Germany
				U.S.
$\overline{S^Y}$ 795	949	944	964	928
σ_Y 121	29	30	19	52

The average between-pair S_{jk}^{Y} within groups is as follows:

Classification scheme	Number of pairs	Mean income similarity index	Standard deviation
Income homogeneity	109	901	72
Geographical[19]	165	781	145
Universal	561	588	255

index of 817 (818 if the United States is counted in as 950), and the homogeneity groups a mean index of 850. Here, the geographical grouping produces 66 percent of the possible improvement in homogeneity.

17. The standard deviation refers to an average of 777, excluding North America. The average of 779 includes North America with an assumed average of 950.

18. The same conclusion is reached when groupings of six are used both for the geographical and the homogeneity classifications. The mean within-group PLSs are 767 and 829, respectively.

19. S^Y includes North America as 950. Average excluding North America is 780 (145).

Figure 4–2.   Clustering of Countries according to Spreads between Paasche and Laspeyres Indexes of GDP per Capita

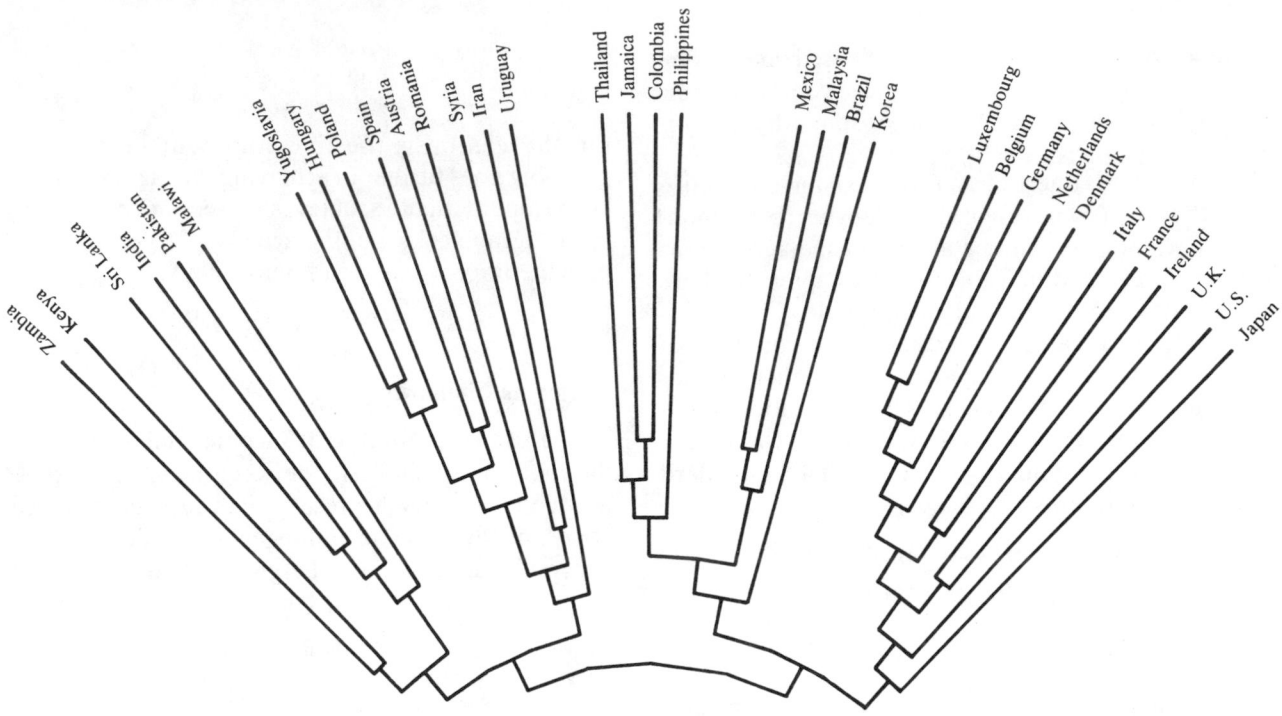

Thus the geographical grouping accounts for 60 percent of the increase in income homogeneity that could be achieved.

In other chapters in which income-homogeneity groups are used to facilitate the presentation of the substantive results of Phase III, the grouping produced by the clustering technique has been modified. Large income gaps were used to demarcate six income groups.

Trade Ties

The important interregional aspect of international trading ties referred to earlier can be seen when the share of each country's 1975 total trade (exports plus imports) with each of the other thirty-three countries is examined. Most of the developing countries have much stronger trading ties to the developed countries than to other developing countries, whether within the same region or not. For example, the ten most important partners of Zambia among the Phase III countries include countries in Europe, Asia, North America, and Latin America but none in Africa. An analogous statement can be made about Brazil with respect to Latin America. For European countries, intraregional trade links tend to be much more substantial, but even there important extraregional ties

are found. The United States is the most important trading partner of the United Kingdom. For the other members of the European Community, the United States ranks third, fourth, or fifth in importance, ahead in every instance of at least some other Community members.

No grouping is suggested here on the basis of trade ties because of the difficulty of constructing a satisfactory index of trade ties that meets the country-reversal test. The problem is that for any pair of trading partners the importance of one to the other may differ greatly for each member of the pair. For example, the United States accounted for 59 percent of Jamaica's trade with the other Phase III countries, but Jamaica accounted for less than 1 percent of U.S. trade with the other Phase III countries. It is clear, however, that any such classification would deviate in some important respect from one based on geographical propinquity.

The Choice of Regional Groupings

Though the geographical classification defines homogeneity rather less satisfactorily than price, price-and-quantity, or income similarity, still it seems clear, in view of the important political considerations alluded to earlier, that if any subsets of more homogeneous countries are to be used in international comparison work, the grouping of countries should be based on geographical propinquity.

The continental classification used in the above comparisons is retained for the subsequent analysis of regionalization. This version of a geographical grouping could doubtless be improved upon. The average intraregional homogeneity, by any of the measures used above, might be increased if, for example, Europe and Asia were subdivided into subregions. These possibilities can be investigated more fully when there are more countries in the ICP data set.

However, it should be pointed out that the improved homogeneity shown by the geographical classification may be influenced by the particular constellation of countries included in the ICP set of thirty-four. A very high proportion of the European countries are in the group, while the proportion of the African, Asian, and Latin American states included is much lower. If, as the data suggest, Europe is a more homogeneous area than the other continents, the results obtained here may give an unduly high average homogeneity for the geographical classification.

The following sections examine ways in which the methods discussed in Chapter 3 can be altered to take account of regional groupings. They also report on experiments designed to illuminate the effects of different approaches.

Since the possibilities for incorporating a regional element vary somewhat with the overall index-number method chosen, it is convenient to organize the subsequent discussion around the broad classes of methods distinguished in Chapter 3: (1) selected sets of binary comparisons, (2) multilateral methods that rely on binary comparisons, and (3) multilateral methods not dependent upon binary comparisons. The main attention to the problems of regionalization is given in what follows to the first and third kinds of methods.

Selective Sets of Binary Comparisons

In this group of methods a selected set of binary comparisons is used as the basis for inferring the comparisons for the other pairs. The most common procedure, employed, for example, in the OEEC and CMEA comparisons, is the star system described above.[20]

Even when the choice of the base country seems obvious (the United States in the OEEC and Russia in the CMEA) the star system has serious disadvantages. For one, the transitivity requirement is not satisfied. In general, a comparison between two countries at points of the star using a bridge country will not yield the same result as an original-country binary comparison between the two.[21] That is, if I_{kl} is computed from data relating only to the kth and lth countries, the relationship $I_{kl} = I_{kb} \div I_{lb}$ will not hold. The equality can be made to hold, to be sure, by pricing a common list of items in all countries and then valuing all countries' quantities using a common set of prices—most plausibly those of the base country. A common list can, however, be very unrepresentative for some or most countries, and the use of one country's prices involves a significant departure from characteristicity.[22]

Most important, a star system is not base-country invariant. The choice of the base country influences the results for both conceptual and practical reasons. Conceptually, a quantity index such as I_{jb} will be determined by the price structure used in valuing each country's quantities. When the center (b) serves as the bridge to link two points of the star (such as k and l) the resulting quantity index (I_{kl}) no longer depends solely on the prices of k and l but is influenced by the prices of b. Thus the index will depend on which country is selected as the base. In addition, as a practical matter, the sample of items selected for comparisons involving different pairs of countries will be affected by the choice of base country. A comparison between the kth and lth countries should involve items in common use in these countries, but in fact the degree of characteristicity will be reduced by the inclusion of items important in the base country. The particular "irrelevant" items will vary with the choice of base country. The special influence of the bridge country can be reduced but not eliminated by bridging at the most detailed category level rather than at the level of GDP as a whole.[23] However, bridging at the GDP level produces transitivity for total GDP, while bridging at the detailed level does not.

20. For a discussion of the star system in a regionalization context, see Krzeczkowska (1978), pp. 203–23.

21. As was noted earlier, the term "original-country comparison" is used to refer to a comparison between countries derived directly from an index-number calculation involving their data. Such comparisons are in contrast to bridge-country comparisons in which I_{kl} is derived by dividing I_{kb} by I_{lb}.

22. Somewhat greater characteristicity can be obtained by using as the set of comparisons from which all others are derived, the Fisher or "ideal" index of the center and each point of the star. However, this will not produce transitivity.

23. The reason is that with detailed-category bridging the weights of the bridge country influence only the price comparisons at the detailed category level; the bridge country's weights are not used to aggregate the detailed categories. See Krzeczkowska (1967), pp. 353–66.

A star system for a world of very heterogeneous countries hardly seems attractive, but the system's simplicity and familiarity make the possibilities of its practical implementation for many countries in different regions worth considering here.

The star system can be applied directly to all the countries on the world level. The present set of comparisons could, for example, have been carried out by using the United States or the Federal Republic of Germany or some other country as the center of the set of binary comparisons involving each of the other thirty-three countries as a partner country. The points of the star, such as France and Italy or Thailand and India, would be compared with each other through the use of the center country as a bridge.

A way of using the star system in regionalization would be to apply it first within each region and subsequently use it to link the regions. European countries such as France and the Federal Republic of Germany would be compared with one another, Austria serving as bridge. Similarly, in Asia, India would serve as a bridge for comparisons of other pairs such as Sri Lanka and Malaysia. On the assumption that Austria is more similar to Germany and France than each is to the United States and that India is more similar to Sri Lanka and Malaysia than either is to the United States, the use of different bridge countries for intra-Europe and intra-Asia comparisons is preferable to the use of a single bridge, the United States. (As has been noted, the assumption of greater intraregional similarity is not always warranted.) This leaves the question of how to link the regions so that European and Asian countries can be compared.

A natural extension of the star system of binary comparisons, moving from several sets of regional comparisons to world comparisons, is to choose a base country for the world and do a binary comparison for each regional base country with the world base country. If the United States were selected as the base country for the world as well as for the North American region, binary comparisons would be required between the United States and the base countries of the other regions. The United States would provide the bridge through which other regional base countries would be linked. For example, $I_{Brazil/India}$ would be derived by dividing $I_{Brazil/U.S.}$ by $I_{India/U.S.}$. A comparison between nonbase countries in different regions would thus require the intermediation of two or three bridge countries.[24] A U.K./Japan comparison would require linking the United Kingdom to the United States through Austria, Japan to the United States through India, and then finally the United Kingdom to Japan through the United States: $I_{U.K./Japan} = (I_{U.K./Austria} \times I_{Austria/U.S.}) \div (I_{Japan/India} \times I_{India/U.S.})$.

Unfortunately, the results of such a structure of comparisons depends critically on the choice of base countries. As an illustration of the sensitivity of the star system to the choice of regional base country, an experiment with Phase III binary data is reported in Table 4-2.[25] In column 1 the Fisher quantity index for per capita GDP produced by the original-country binary comparison of each country with the United States is presented as a reference point.[26] In the following columns the results of various bridging procedures are compared with the results of original-country comparisons and with each other. In columns 2 and 3 the comparisons rest on bridging at the GDP level and in columns 4 and 5 on bridging at the detailed category level. In columns 2 and 4 the regional base countries are Kenya, India, Austria, and Brazil, and in columns 3 and 5 the regional bases are Malawi, Malaysia, France, and Mexico. The entry of 1.21 for Thailand in column 2, for example, indicates that the Thailand/U.S. per capita GDP ratio obtained by bridging at the GDP level through India (that is, Thailand/U.S. derived from Thailand/India times India/U.S.) was 21 percent higher than the Thailand/U.S. result of an original-country comparison. When a different regional base country, Malaysia, was used as the bridge, the entry of 0.91 in column 3 shows the bridged estimate was 9 percent lower than the original-country result. The entries in columns 4 and 5 indicate that bridging when done at the detailed category level is 13 percent over the mark or 7 percent under the mark, respectively, according to whether Thailand is bridged to the United States through India or Malaysia.

The following conclusions can be drawn from the table:

1. Bridging produces results that can differ from the original-country results by 20 to 25 percent (Malaysia, Philippines, Jamaica).

2. The choice of the bridge country can make a difference of 20 to 25 percent—or even more. See the ratios for India, Malaysia, and Thailand in column 6. This difference can be notable even in a relatively homogeneous region such as Western Europe, where bridging effects tend to be smaller than in other regions. For example, when Denmark and Luxembourg are bridged to the United States through Austria (column 4), Denmark's real per capita GDP, 88.2 with the

---

24. Two if one of the nonbase countries is in the region of the world base country; three otherwise.

25. Only actual prices are used here; that is, these are traditional binaries, not the augmented binaries referred to in note 9 above.

26. A more extensive experiment might have been to examine each country in a region as a base country.

Table 4-2. Comparisons of Fisher Estimates of Real GDP per Capita, 1975, Based on Original-country Binaries and on Bridging at Different Levels and through Different Regional Base Countries
(U.S. = 100)

Country	Original-country binary (1)	Ratio of bridged index to original-country index, with bridging at level of base country				Ratio of set A to set B, bridged indexes with bridging at level of	
		GDP		Detailed categories			
		Set A (2)	Set B (3)	Set A (4)	Set B (5)	GDP (6)	Detailed categories (7)
Africa							
Kenya	6.5	*1.00*	0.86	*1.00*	0.89	1.16	1.12
Malawi	4.0	1.15	*1.00*	1.05	*1.00*	1.15	1.05
Zambia	9.9	0.97	0.95	0.98	1.00	1.02	0.98
Asia							
India	5.9	*1.00*	0.81	*1.00*	0.86	1.23	1.16
Iran	34.6	0.99	0.88	1.03	0.91	1.12	1.13
Japan	64.6	1.06	0.92	1.08	0.99	1.15	1.09
Korea	18.8	0.98	0.81	0.96	0.84	1.21	1.14
Malaysia	19.5	1.23	*1.00*	1.23	*1.00*	1.23	1.23
Pakistan	7.1	0.94	1.13	1.02	1.13	0.83	0.90
Philippines	11.4	1.14	1.01	1.26	1.08	1.13	1.17
Sri Lanka	8.2	1.10	1.01	1.09	0.97	1.09	1.12
Syria	20.3	0.99	0.98	0.93	0.94	1.01	0.99
Thailand	10.0	1.21	0.91	1.13	0.93	1.33	1.22
Europe							
Austria	74.6	*1.00*	0.89	*1.00*	0.92	1.12	1.09
Belgium	77.2	1.11	1.01	1.04	1.04	1.01	1.03
Denmark	84.0	1.06	0.96	1.05	0.97	1.10	1.08
France	80.6	1.13	*1.00*	1.07	*1.00*	1.13	1.07
Germany	81.1	1.10	1.01	1.04	1.01	1.09	1.03
Hungary	49.3	1.06	0.95	0.98	0.95	1.12	1.03
Ireland	43.5	1.05	1.00	1.04	1.04	1.05	1.00
Italy	55.7	1.09	1.02	1.05	1.01	1.07	1.04
Luxembourg	81.3	1.10	1.07	1.05	1.06	1.03	0.99
Netherlands	72.1	1.08	0.99	1.07	0.99	1.09	1.08
Poland	47.0	1.07	0.87	0.99	0.88	1.23	1.12
Romania	29.6	1.08	0.98	1.06	1.02	1.10	1.04
Spain	55.0	1.02	0.92	0.99	0.94	1.11	1.05
U.K.	66.6	1.07	1.00	1.08	1.01	1.07	1.07
Yugoslavia	37.2	1.03	0.94	0.99	0.99	1.10	1.00
Latin America and the Caribbean							
Brazil	24.0	*1.00*	1.09	*1.00*	1.02	0.92	0.98
Colombia	19.0	1.18	1.12	1.14	1.14	1.05	1.00
Jamaica	24.6	1.04	0.98	1.23	1.08	1.06	1.14
Mexico	35.5	0.92	*1.00*	0.96	*1.00*	0.92	0.96
Uruguay	33.2	0.91	1.02	0.94	0.96	0.89	0.98
North America							
U.S.	100.0	1.00	1.00	1.00	1.00	1.00	1.00

Notes: Both the original-country indexes and the bridged indexes for each country listed in the table are related to the United States. The regional base countries used for sets A and B are italicized in columns 2 through 5.

For purposes of columns 2 and 3, original-country binary comparisons were initially calculated for each country vis-à-vis the indicated base country. The indexes were then shifted to a U.S. base with the regional base country used as a bridge.

For purposes of columns 4 and 5, the original-country binary indexes were shifted to a U.S. base category by category.

The ratios in columns 2 to 7 are based on preliminary data although the indexes shown in column 1 are based on final data.

United States equaling 100, is 3.3 percent higher than Luxembourg's 85.4, but when both are bridged through France (column 5), Denmark's per capita is 81.5, which is 5.5 percent lower than Luxembourg's 86.2.

3. The choice between bridging at the GDP level or at the detailed-category level can produce a 10 to 15 percent variation in the results (compare columns 2 and 4 in the cases of Malawi, Philippines, and Jamaica).

4. Bridging at the detailed-category level usually, but not always, produces per capita Fisher indexes that are closer to the original-country estimates than does bridging at the GDP level. There are thirty-seven entries in columns 4 and 5 that are closer than the entries

Table 4-3. Comparisons for Countries in Different Regions of Fisher Index Estimates of Real per Capita GDP, 1975, Based on Original-country Binaries and on Bridging through Regional and World Base Countries

| Countries compared | Original country (1) | Detailed category bridging bridge country for[a] | | Ratio of result by bridging to original-country binary (4) |
		Numerator country (2)	Denominator country (3)	
Kenya–U.K.	9.2	Malawi	Austria	0.84
Sri Lanka–France	10.1	India	Austria	0.82
Zambia–Italy	16.3	Kenya	Austria	1.09
Colombia–Germany	23.0	Brazil	Austria	1.15
Malaysia–Netherlands	25.2	India	Austria	1.24
Zambia–Mexico	27.2	Kenya	Brazil	1.03
Malawi–Thailand	38.2	Kenya	India	1.17
Uruguay–Germany	44.6	Brazil	Austria	0.87
Jamaica–Hungary	47.3	Brazil	Austria	1.07
Korea–Uruguay	49.3	India	Brazil	1.04
Syria–Mexico	50.6	India	Brazil	1.15
Philippines–Colombia	57.1	India	Brazil	0.91
Iran–Italy	57.9	India	Austria	1.10
U.K.–Japan	97.6	Austria	India	0.96
Germany–Japan	122.2	Austria	India	0.96

Note: The ratios in column 4 are based on preliminary data, but the figures in column 1 are based on final data.

a. The two regional bridge countries were in turn bridged through the United States. The Malawi–Thailand comparison, for example, was thus derived as follows: Malawi/Thailand = (Malawi/Kenya) · (Kenya/United States) ÷ (Thailand/India) · (India/United States).

of columns 2 and 3 to the original-country figures in column 1, and only thirteen in which the opposite is true, excluding ties and comparisons involving base countries. However, this advantage of the comparisons bridged at the detailed-category level is offset by the fact that they are not transitive. Those bridged at the GDP level are transitive, since they represent transformation of a single column of numbers, but neither set of bridged comparisons is base invariant.

The experiments reported in Table 4-2 relate to bridging countries at the ends of regional stars to a single base country (the center of a world star) so that transitive, though not base-invariant, comparisons could be made. More extensive bridging would be required to link two countries, each of which was one of the points of a different regional star system. Fourteen examples of such bridging are compared in Table 4-3 with original-country binaries. Although the largest difference is not greater than that found in the simple bridging of Table 4-2, differences of 10 or 15 percent are more numerous. The mean absolute deviation from 100.0 of the detailed category bridgings in Table 4-2 is 5.5 (on the basis of 66 observations in columns 4 and 5), while it is 11.2 in Table 4-3 (column 4).

In all these comparisons, it is likely that some of the large differences between original-country and the various bridged GDP estimates reflect the erratic effects of samples of prices that were not collected with a view to making some of the original-country comparisons. This factor probably plays a smaller role in comparisons involving the European countries for which the possibility of comparisons with both Austria and

the United States was taken into account in planning the fieldwork.

Nevertheless, it is hard to escape the conclusion that the lack of base-country invariance in the star system is not simply a theoretical disadvantage but a substantial empirical reality that produces substantial differences in the estimates of real per capita GDP when different regional and world countries are selected to play the role of center for the stars.

There are, however, some variants of a star system that would serve to reduce the degree of sensitivity of the comparisons to the base-country choices, at least with regard to the second-stage star, in which the regions would be linked to the center of a world star. They involve shifting the interregional comparisons from those utilizing particular base countries in each region toward comparisons between whole regions.

One possibility would be to retain the base-country prices in the interregional comparisons but to weight the price relatives with average regional expenditures in lieu of base-country expenditures. For example, Austrian and U.S. prices would be used in the Europe/North America (Austrian/U.S.) comparison, but the expenditures would be all-European rather than Austrian and all-North American rather than U.S.[27] Eu-

27. The price comparisons would be computed as an expenditure-weighted average of price relatives. For European weights, the formula would be

$$I_{A/US} = \sum_i^m \frac{p_{i,A}}{p_{i,US}} \cdot w_{i,Eur}; \quad w_{i,Eur} = \frac{p_{i,Eur}q_{i,Eur}}{\sum_i^m p_{i,Eur}q_{i,Eur}}.$$

ropean expenditures would be obtained by adding up expenditures at the lowest level of aggregation across all the European countries. For example, the expenditures for France at each detailed-category level would be converted to Austrian schillings by the PPP between Austria and France for each item or category. The advantage of this method is that it allows the regional distribution of expenditures to influence the interregional links, though, of course, the aggregate regional expenditure distribution will still depend on the choice of the base country.

The logical extension of this line of reasoning is to abandon interregional base-country comparisons and substitute comparisons between the regions themselves. These require the use of prices as well as expenditures that pertain to an entire region, rather than merely to a single country within the region. Regional expenditures could be obtained as above by summation at the lowest level of aggregation after converting to the base country's currency through the PPPs from the intraregional binaries. A set of regional prices would be estimated by converting the price in each country to the base country's currency at the exchange rate. In Europe, for example, these prices would then be averaged through the use of quantity weights[28] across all the European countries to obtain a European price for each item denominated in Austrian schillings. It is this average European price that would become the input to a binary comparison between Europe and the world base region, North America. The advantage of this technique would be that the linking of Europe to the world would not depend so critically on just which country was chosen as the European base. It would, however, still be dependent because the aggregation of expenditure would not be base-country invariant.

Thus a star system for the regions would consist of a set of either base-country or interregional comparisons. The number of regions is sufficiently small to make it possible to carry out binary comparisons for each pair of base countries or regions rather than to make it necessary to rely on the star system in linking the regions. However, the choice of a single region as the basis for the bridging of all the other regions with one another has the advantage of making it possible to produce a unique cardinal scaling of the countries. This would not be possible if each regional entity were compared directly with each other regional entity. However, the results would not in any case be invariant to the choice of the base region.

Once the comparison of each regional entity with the base regional entity was completed, a way would have to be found to link the countries in each region to the region as a whole to make possible comparisons between countries in different regions.

Whatever the merits of binary comparisons when only pairs of countries are compared, it would not be right to use the results of such comparisons as the standard against which the accuracy of the results of multilateral comparisons should be judged. What is wanted in multilateral comparisons is different: the establishment of a set of indexes that is equally valid and consistent for all pairs of countries.[29]

From the standpoint of such a set of comparisons, whether for a regional grouping or for the world, the limitations of a star system of binary comparisons, particularly the problems with respect to transitivity and matrix consistency, are difficult to overcome. At the regional level, the estimates of the relative per capita GDPs of the countries could be significantly affected. Ways have been suggested to minimize the sensitivity of the results to the choice of base countries for interregional linking. But the pursuit of these methods would lead to further difficulties of consistency between retaining the regional control totals for GDP produced by the interregional comparison (and allocating these totals to the countries in proportions indicated by the intraregional star system), or retaining the regional control totals for the categories (and allocating these to the countries in the proportion shown by the intraregional comparisons). As shown below, the sum of a country's expenditures obtained by the latter method will not equal the GDP obtained by the former method.

All things considered, the case against the use of a star system in international comparisons is compelling.

Multilateral Methods Based on Binary Comparisons

The essential feature of multilateral comparison methods is that the price and quantity indexes for all

28. Each country's quantities expressed in Austrian schillings (derived from the binary comparisons) might serve as the quantity weights. Alternatively, the Fisher quantity indexes might be used for this purpose.

29. On this point Hill (1981), pp. 2–18, writes: "When the group approach is used no special significance is to be attached to the results obtained from isolated binaries: in particular, the binary results are not to be elevated to the status of norms by which to evaluate or appraise the multilateral results. From a theoretical point of view there is no sense in describing a particular multilateral index as biased because it happens to be close to a Laspeyres index. The attribution of bias in these circumstances is equivalent to asserting that the index should have been defined with respect to a typical consumer from one or other of the two countries in question instead of a representative group consumer. But this is merely to reassert the difference in value judgments from which the two different approaches stem."

countries are treated as completely interdependent; the index for each country depends on and influences all the others. The essence of regionalization from the standpoint of multilateral comparisons is the partitioning of the countries into subsets, each of which receives multilateral treatment but with inputs coming from only the countries within the subset. If regionalization were ignored and universality opted for, all countries would be considered together in a single multilateral calculation.

The various subsets of countries can be linked together many ways, ranging from a simple binary approach for each of the regional base countries (though this would be incongruous with the multilateral approach at the regional level) to a full multilateral treatment of the aggregations of the individual subsets.

One group of multilateral methods that might be used for calculation, either at the regional or interregional level, consists of those that achieve a multilateral character by generalizing the binary comparisons. These include the methods suggested by Elteto, Koves, and Szulc (EKS) and by Van Yzeren, which produce a transitive set of comparisons between all the countries that takes into account the relationships between all possible pairs. (See Chapter 3 for a brief description of these methods.) They can be used within each region to produce a unique cardinal scaling of countries so that the relationship of each country to the regional average can easily be computed. These regional averages could also be used for interregional comparisons so as to produce a unique cardinal scaling of per capita GDPs for the regions. By means considered in the next section, a unique cardinal scaling of the countries of the world with respect to per capita GDP could be achieved. However, procedures have not been developed for either method, at least as of this writing, for making product comparisons at levels of aggregation below the aggregate level. EKS and Van Yzeren could, of course, be used to compare the subaggregates directly, but the results of their application in this way would not yield matrix consistency. The failure would arise from a lack of column additivity; that is, the sum of expenditures in real terms over the detailed categories would not be the same as those produced by EKS and Van Yzeren for the total GDP.

Multilateral Methods Not Dependent on Binary Comparisons

It was seen in Chapter 3 that the multilateral methods that do not rely on the calculation of binary indexes achieve transitivity by aggregating each country's quantities or prices by using a common set of weights that represent averages for all the countries. Before further amplification of this, it is necessary to return to a step in the data processing that was set aside above. All the discussion of this chapter so far has been directed at the aggregation of detailed category PPPs and expenditures to get GDP and overall PPPs. Now the determination of the category PPPs from item prices will be discussed in a regionalization context.

Aggregation at the Detailed-category Level

At the first level of aggregation—obtaining average PPPs for each detailed category from the price comparison for individual specifications—the CPD method can be readily adapted to the needs of regionalization. Of course, the way in which it is applied will depend on the degree of emphasis on regionalization. If the aim is a full two-stage approach, CPD will be used in a somewhat different way than if the aim is a set of universal comparisons in which account is taken of regions merely as a means of dealing with the differences in the list of goods priced in different countries and regions.

The CPD method, as described in Chapter 3, makes each estimated price a function of the country and the item to which it refers. The equation (3.11) that embodies the method is repeated here as 4.4 for convenience of reference.

$$(4.4) \quad \ln p = \beta_1 X_1 + \beta_2 X_2 + \ldots + \beta_{n-1} X_{n-1} + \gamma_1 Z_1 + \gamma_2 Z_2 + \ldots + \gamma_A Z_A + u$$

where $\ln p$ is the natural logarithm of the price of a particular item in a particular country; there are n countries being compared and A items in the category; and u is a normally distributed variable with mean zero and variance σ^2. The X's are dummy variables, each of which represents one of the n countries (other than the numéraire) and the Z's are dummy variables, each of which represents one of the A items.

The reader will recall that the β coefficients when exponentiated are estimates of the PPPs. These were the PPPs that were used in Phases I and II of the ICP. This is still the use made of the β coefficient in the various multilateral comparisons presented in this report, including the intraregional and universal (that is, thirty-four–country) versions.

From the standpoint of regional estimation, the disadvantage of the use of the CPD in the universal approach is that prices from outside the region influence PPPs of the countries in the region (unless the price matrix is complete). If there were no missing prices, the CPD method (without item weighting) would produce the geometric means of the price relatives, as would the EKS method.

The assignment of a high priority to intraregional characteristicity leads to a two-stage system in which multilateral comparisons are produced first for countries in relatively homogeneous sets and subsequently for the sets as entities. In what follows, the use of CPD is considered first in this setting of two-stage comparisons. For reasons given earlier, the first-stage sets of countries used in the empirical illustrations are those selected on the basis of geographical propinquity rather than homogeneity of prices, quantities, or incomes.

The Use of the CPD in a Two-stage Approach to Regionalization

Intraregional characteristicity can be promoted by deriving the intraregional PPPs from a first-stage CPD and subsequently linking the regions in a second stage. The first-stage CPDs pose no critical problems;[30] the CPD method is applied for each category in each region to derive intraregional category PPPs vis-à-vis the currency of the regional numéraire country.[31] These Stage I PPPs serve directly as the detailed-category price inputs for a regional Geary-Khamis or other aggregation method that combines the detailed categories to obtain price and quantity comparisons for GDP and other aggregates.

But how should the price inputs for the Geary-Khamis or other aggregation method be obtained for the comparison of regions? This requires a PPP for each detailed category for each region relative to the world numéraire. Such a link can also serve to convert the PPPs of the countries of each region from their expression in the currency units of the regional numéraire country (derived in Stage I) to PPPs relative to the currency units of the world numéraire country.

Several approaches to the estimation of these regional PPPs were considered. One approach, obviously, is to link the different regions by comparisons of the regional numéraire countries. CPDs using only prices of the regional numéraire countries would be estimated to get the regional PPPs relative to the world numéraire for each category, and then a Geary-Khamis for the regional numéraire countries (including, of course, the world numéraire country) could be run. This method, as was shown in the discussion of binary comparisons, has the disadvantage of producing results that are dependent on the selection of the numéraire countries.

A number of ways have been considered that aim at achieving base-country invariance or at least allowing all countries within each region to influence the world comparisons while still retaining the intraregional (Stage I) PPPs and quantity relationships for the detailed categories and for GDP as a whole.[32] Some of these methods involve the use of what will be referred to as an augmented price tableau. An augmented price tableau is one in which the holes—the missing prices—have been filled in by estimating each from the Stage I CPD equation. The augmented price tableau for each region contains a full vector of prices for each country for all items priced by two or more countries in the region. Note that if a CPD were run on the augmented price tableau for a given region, it would yield the same PPPs as those produced by the original incomplete tableau of prices. In this sense the augmented price tableau retains the characteristicity of the original regional tableau.

There are two ways the augmented price tableau can be used for the purpose at hand. Both ways call for a second-stage CPD in which all thirty-four countries are entered, each with its full regional price vector.[33] The method that most fully preserves the in-

---

30. A practical problem that arose in computing regional CPDs was how to treat a price supplied by only one country in a region when the price of the same item was available for one or more countries outside of the region. This was a not-infrequent occurrence in Africa, for which there were only three ICP countries. For the calculation of intraregional PPPs, such an item was excluded, but it was included in the calculation of the interregional CPDs.

When intraregional PPPs were required for a regional Geary-Khamis, use was sometimes made of information outside of the region. For example, in a few cases in which a country did not have enough overlapping items for a regional CPD but did have sufficient overlaps for inclusion in a universal CPD, its PPP relative to the regional numéraire country was derived by the formula $PPP_{A/R} = PPP_{A/W} \div PPP_{R/W}$, where A represents the country and R and W the regional and the world numéraires, respectively.

31. More strictly, the CPD method was applied to fewer than 151 detailed categories because of special treatment of a number of categories, including health, education, rents, automobiles, net expenditures of residents abroad, commodities of government, exports less imports, and change in stocks.

32. The Gamma method, which is not discussed in the text but is presented in Kravis, Heston, Summers (1979), utilizes the average regional prices produced by the regional CPDs. The prices are the exponentiated γ coefficients of equation 4.4; since the numéraire country's PPP is, by definition, 1, an estimate of the average price of a particular item denominated in the numéraire country's currency is simply the exponential of the coefficient of that item's dummy variable. These prices form the inputs to a second-stage CPD in which PPPs for regions are derived. Note that none of this depends upon the choice of the numéraire country within each region, except in the trivial sense of affecting the scaling.

33. If, for example, items A, B, and C have been priced in all three countries of a region, but item D in only two of the countries, the first-stage CPD for the region will be used to estimate the price

traregional relative PPPs given by Stage I CPDs utilizes only the PPPs for the regional numéraire country produced by this Stage II CPD. (Note that the PPPs generated by the Stage II CPD are all expressed relative to the world numéraire.)

These PPPs for the regional numéraire country provide the basis for forming the price inputs for the second-stage Geary-Khamis, the latter being required as a means of linking the intraregional quantity comparisons to the world numéraire country and thus to other countries outside the region.

The required regional PPP for each category, needed as an input for a Stage II Geary-Khamis, is obtained by multiplying each regional numéraire country PPP (from the second CPD) by the regional (international) price ($\overline{\Pi}^R$) obtained from the regional Geary-Khamis calculation.

The regional PPPs derived in this way are in the spirit of Geary's original concept of international prices. That is, the price input for the Stage II Geary-Khamis calculation for category i is

$$(4.5) \qquad \overline{\Pi}_i^R \cdot \text{PPP}_{iw} = \frac{\Pi_i^R}{p_{ib}} \cdot \frac{p_{ib}}{p_{iw}} = \frac{\Pi_i^R}{p_{iw}}$$

where

Π_i^R = Geary type average regional price for commodity i

$\overline{\Pi}_i^R$ = ICP version of Geary average regional price

PPP_{iw} = PPP of regional numéraire relative to world numéraire

p_{ib} = price in regional numéraire country

p_{iw} = price in world numéraire country.

In this method, which utilizes the augmented price tableau, the intraregional PPPs will not be exactly the same as those produced by a CPD applied to the region alone. The reason is that the CPD makes each country PPP equal to the weighted geometric mean of the ratio of country prices to exponentiated item (γ) coefficients, and the γ coefficients will differ in the two sets of CPDs because the Stage II CPDs may contain some items not in the price tableau of a particular region. If it is desired to leave the intraregional relative PPPs

unchanged from those produced by the Stage I CPDs, the PPP for each category in each country can be linked to the world numéraire country through the regional PPP for the category. Thus, if absolute priority is to be given to regional comparisons, this method should be chosen.[34]

The other method of using the augmented price tableaux utilizes the PPPs produced by the Stage II CPDs for all the countries rather than merely the PPP of the regional numéraire countries. The PPPs of the thirty-four countries are the direct price inputs for a Geary-Khamis calculation covering all the countries. In this approach, a regional element is embodied in deriving the category PPPs, but the aggregation of the PPPs across categories is in a universal mode. More will be said later about this combination of a two-stage CPD and a single-stage Geary-Khamis.

Relative to a universal CPD based on the direct price inputs of all countries regardless of region, the augmented-price-tableau methods give enhanced influence to intraregional price relationships. Missing prices are explicitly filled in on the basis of intraregional price relationships; in the universal CPD, the missing prices are implicitly estimated on the basis of price relationships in all the countries.

An illustrative set of PPPs produced by alternative methods, for fresh vegetables, is set out in Table 4-4. In column 2 PPPs produced by the first-stage CPDs are shown for each country relative to the currency of the regional numéraire country. In column 3 the PPPs are converted to price indexes, with regional numéraire country prices taken as 100.

The next three columns show the results of different procedures for moving from these intraregional PPPs or price indexes to worldwide PPPs or price indexes, each related to a single world numéraire currency. In column 4 the underlying second-stage (worldwide) PPPs for the regional numéraire countries are the exponentiated β coefficients from a thirty-four–country CPD, into which an augmented tableau of prices was entered for the countries in each region. These PPPs relative to the United States (the world numéraire country) are converted to price indexes and are entered in column 4. For Asia, for example, India's PPP is 1.61 ru-

---

of item D in the third country. Then in the second-stage CPD, all four items will be entered for each of the three countries. Similarly, if items B, D, and F constitute the list of items priced by at least two countries in a second region, any missing prices will be estimated by a regional CPD. Thus, while each regional price tableau that is fed into the interregional CPD is without holes (except where only one country in a region prices an item, in which case just that price is entered), the list of items priced need not be identical from one region to another.

34. The Gamma method (see note 32) also leaves intraregional price indexes unchanged. The choice between the Gamma method and the regional numéraire version of the augmented-price-tableau method is not a clear-cut one, but the augmented-tableau approach is marginally preferable from the standpoint of worldwide comparisons because it makes fuller use of overlapping prices for different regions. Also, since the United States is treated as a region and its arithmetic average prices are entered directly, the Gamma method has the complication that the average regional prices it produces are in the nature of geometric means.

Table 4-4. Alternative Estimates of PPPs and Price Levels for Fresh Vegetables Relative to Regional and World Numéraire Countries, 1975

Region/country currency unit	Within region			World price indexes (world numéraire = 100.0)			Ratios to one-stage universal CPD	
	Exchange rate with regional numéraire currency (1)	*PPPs national currency/ regional currency* (2)	*Price index (regional numéraire =100.0)* (3)	*Stage II CPD is direct source of PPPs for*		*One stage (universal) CPD* (6)	*Numéraire country method* (7) = (4) ÷ (6)	*Thirty-four country method* (8) = (5) ÷ (6)
				Numéraire country (4)	*All countries* (5)			
Africa								
Kenya (shillings)	numéraire[a]	1.00	100.0	39.5	39.5	44.4	0.89	0.89
Malawi (kwacha)	0.117	0.069	59.1	23.4	23.3	22.8	1.02	1.02
Zambia (kwacha)	0.007	0.152	174.6	69.0	72.6	73.2	0.94	0.99
Asia								
India (rupees)	numéraire[a]	1.00	100.0	19.2	19.2	20.6	0.93	0.93
Iran (rials)	8.08	18.48	228.8	43.9	43.9	45.6	0.96	0.96
Japan (yen)	35.43	142.78	402.9	77.4	77.3	85.0	0.91	0.91
Korea (won)	57.48	87.63	151.7	29.1	29.1	30.4	0.96	0.96
Malaysia (ringgit)	0.287	0.601	209.7	40.2	40.3	42.8	0.94	0.94
Pakistan (rupees)	1.19	1.32	111.7	21.4	21.4	20.8	1.03	1.03
Philippines (pesos)	0.89	2.06	237.1	45.5	45.5	45.1	1.01	1.01
Sri Lanka (rupees)	1.27	1.26	172.7	33.1	33.2	34.6	0.96	0.96
Syria (pounds)	0.442	0.437	98.9	18.9	19.3	20.6	0.92	0.94
Thailand (baht)	2.43	5.48	225.2	43.2	43.2	44.4	0.97	0.97
Europe								
Austria (schillings)	numéraire[a]	1.00	100.0	62.7	62.7	62.3	1.01	1.01
Belgium (francs)	2.11	2.11	100.1	62.8	62.8	67.5	0.93	0.93
Denmark (kroner)	0.330	0.618	187.2	117.4	117.4	126.5	0.93	0.93
France (francs)	0.246	0.242	98.4	61.7	61.7	66.4	0.93	0.93
Germany (DM)	0.141	0.148	104.9	65.8	65.8	70.8	0.93	0.93
Hungary (forint)	1.19	0.756	63.7	39.9	38.7	40.7	0.98	0.95
Ireland (pounds)	0.026	0.030	116.9	73.3	73.3	79.5	0.92	0.92
Italy (lire)	37.48	29.75	79.4	49.8	53.6	53.6	0.93	0.93
Luxembourg (francs)	2.11	2.72	128.9	80.8	80.8	87.0	0.93	0.93
Netherlands (guilders)	0.145	0.173	119.1	74.7	74.7	80.4	0.93	0.93
Poland (zlote)	1.14	0.909	79.5	49.8	52.8	54.5	0.91	0.97
Romania (lei)	0.69	0.441	64.0	40.1	40.1	40.7	0.98	0.98
Spain (pesetas)	3.30	1.84	55.9	35.0	35.1	37.7	0.93	0.93
U.K. (pounds)	0.026	0.026	98.9	62.0	62.1	67.1	0.92	0.93
Yugoslavia (dinars)	1.000	0.694	69.5	43.6	43.6	45.0	0.97	0.97
Latin America and Caribbean								
Brazil (cruzeiros)	numéraire[a]	1.00	100.0	59.6	59.6	67.0	0.89	0.89
Colombia (pesos)	3.76	1.73	46.0	27.4	26.8	29.3	0.94	0.91
Jamaica (pounds)	0.11	0.222	200.1	119.3	117.1	120.3	0.99	0.97
Mexico (pesos)	1.52	0.783	51.4	34.1	32.3	38.7	0.88	0.83
Uruguay (N. pesos)	0.280	0.176	62.9	37.5	36.6	38.2	0.98	0.96
North America								
U.S. (dollars)	numéraire[a]	1.00	100.0	100.0	100.0	100.0	1.00	1.00

a. Dollar exchange rates of numéraire currencies:
   8.204 Brazilian cruzeiros
   7.4113 Kenyan shillings
   8.376 Indian rupees
   17.417 Austrian schillings

Notes: Col. 3: Regional PPP for each country relative to regional numéraire country (column 2) divided by the exchange rate in column 1. (Columns 3 to 6 are placed in index form by multiplying by 100.) Each PPP is the exponentiated β coefficient from a regional CPD. Col. 4: PPP of each country relative to world numéraire divided by exchange rate relative to the dollar. For numéraire countries the PPP is the exponentiated β coefficient of a thirty-four-country CPD in which an augmented tableau of prices is entered for each region. For the other countries, the PPP is the product of the numéraire country PPP relative to the dollar and the country's PPP relative to the numéraire currency (in column 2). Col. 5: PPP of each country relative to the U.S. dollar, divided by exchange rate relative to the U.S. dollar. The PPP is the exponentiated β coefficient from a thirty-four-country CPD in which an augmented tableau of prices is entered for each region. Col. 6: PPP of each country relative to dollar divided by the exchange rate relative to the U.S. dollar. The PPP is the exponentiated β coefficient from a thirty-four-country CPD in which the inputs are the prices reported by each country.

pees per dollar. When divided by the exchange rate (8.376 rupees per dollar) and expressed as a percentage, this becomes 19.2, the number found in column 4. For a country that does not serve as a regional numéraire, the column 4 entry for the price index relative to the United States is simply the product of the country's price index relative to the regional numéraire times the price index of the regional numéraire vis-à-vis the United States. For example, the Iranian price index of 43.9 given in column 4 is the product of the Iranian price index relative to India and the Indian price index relative to the United States (228.8 × 19.2 ÷ 100 = 43.9).

Note that these computations are independent of which Asian country is the numéraire country. If Iran were the numéraire country, the entries in column 2 would have been 1/18.48 of the values shown, and the stage II CPD would have produced a PPP of 29.71 rials to the dollar. When divided by the rial/dollar exchange rate (67.68 rials to the dollar) and expressed as a percentage, this comes again to the column 4 entry of 43.9. (The Indian entry in column 2 would be 0.0541—the reciprocal of 18.48—which when multiplied by the Iranian PPP of 29.71 rials to the dollar would yield 1.61 rupees to the dollar, and thus 19.2 as in column 4.)

The results of the other way of using the augmented price tableaux—that is, taking *all* of the PPPs directly from the thirty-four countries—are set out in column 5.

Finally, the results of a universal, one-stage CPD, using the original prices provided by all thirty-four countries as the inputs, are presented in column 6.

Ratios comparing the results of the different methods of deriving the PPPs are shown in columns 7 and 8. These differences refer to the PPPs for a single category, fresh vegetables. In this case, the differences between one-stage, universal CPD and the numéraire country and thirty-four–country methods range from −17 percent to +3 percent, but the latter two differ by less than 8 percent, at most. What is most important, however, is how large the average difference is across categories. The Geary-Khamis calculations reported in the next section are a means of calculating such an average.

Aggregation of the Categories

It is assumed now that price comparisons have been produced for each detailed category for the entire set of countries. The remaining problem is that of aggregating categories to get price comparisons for GDP and its major components for various countries and various regions.

If universality is favored and no effort is made to take account of regions, all countries can be included

in a single straightforward aggregation procedure like the Geary-Khamis formula followed in the ICP or one of the other methods mentioned in Chapter 3. The logical price inputs for such a procedure would be provided by the universal CPD.

Two-stage Comparisons

If maximum characteristicity in the regional sense is desired, a two-stage approach, analogous to that considered above in connection with binary comparisons and in the discussion of CPD, is indicated.

As in the two-stage procedure at the detailed-category level, the first step is to carry out the Stage I comparisons by applying the Geary-Khamis formulas to each of the regions. This will yield price and quantity comparisons of the countries within each region with the regional numéraire country.

Once again, the question arises whether to link the regions through comparisons of the numéraire countries alone or through comparisons of the regional entities. In the discussion of the binary comparisons, linkage through the base countries alone was shown to yield results that were sensitive to the selection of the base countries. In a multilateral context, in which the search for base-country invariance is stressed, comparisons of entire regions seem clearly indicated.

The data needed for such comparisons are, as in the case of comparisons involving nations, price comparisons between regional entities and each regional entity's expenditures. Both the price comparisons and the expenditures are required not only for GDP but also for each of the detailed categories. The PPPs for the regions can be obtained by (1) applying a Stage II CPD to the augmented price tableaux and (2) multiplying the regional numéraire country's PPP produced by this CPD by the regional price ($\overline{\overline{\Pi}}^R$) obtained from the Stage I Geary-Khamis calculation. The aggregate expenditures for each regional entity can be obtained from the Geary-Khamis calculation for the region. The regional Geary-Khamis output produces expenditures for each category in commensurate terms (that is, valued at regional prices, denominated in the numéraire currency), so they need only be summed.[35]

The output of the second-stage Geary-Khamis provides the value in international currency (dollars or other world numéraire) of each region's quantity of each detailed category.

The point has now been reached at which there are comparisons between countries in each region (the

---

35. The actual outputs in the ICP computations are on a per capita basis. For the purpose of getting regional expenditures, each ICP country's real per capita expenditure must be multiplied by its supercountry population.

Table 4-5. Numerical Examples Showing the Difference between Two Ways of Integrating Regional and World Product Comparisons

	A. Region 1 (first stage) Real GDP in currency of regional numéraire country				
	Countries			Regional total	Proportion of total regional GDP
Category	A	B	C		
Food	2	6	1	9	(0.257)
Clothing	1	7	1	9	(0.257)
Shelter	3	2	2	7	(0.200)
Other	4	3	3	10	(0.285)
Total GDP	10	18	7	35	(1.000)
Proportion of total regional GDP	0.286	0.514	0.200	1.000	

	B. World (second stage) Real GDP in currency of world numéraire country			Distribution of regional GDPs among categories		
Category	Region 1	Region 2	World total	Region 1	Region 2	World total
Food	80	. . .	. . .	0.381	. . .	. . .
Clothing	100	. . .	. . .	0.476	. . .	. . .
Shelter	10	. . .	. . .	0.048	. . .	. . .
Other	20	. . .	. . .	0.095	. . .	. . .
Total GDP	210			1.000		

first-stage Geary-Khamis results) and comparisons between the regional entitites (the second-stage Geary-Khamis results). How should these two sets of results be combined to produce comparisons between countries in different regions? Ideally, the comparisons should preserve both (1) the intraregional quantity relationships among the countries of each region for GDP and each of its components as these were estimated in the regional Geary-Khamis calculation and (2) the quantity relationships among the regions for GDP and each of its components as these were estimated in the interregional Geary-Khamis calculation.

These consistency objectives cannot both be satisfied at once. One must choose between the final selection of consistent relative quantity estimates for total GDP on the one hand (the GDP-consistency method) and of consistent relative quantity estimates for each category on the other (the category-control-total method).

These alternatives and the need for choosing between them are set out in a simple hypothetical example in Table 4-5. Section A of the table gives the real GDP resulting from a Geary-Khamis comparison for one particular region of the world and section B the results of an interregional comparison that bears on that region. Section A is based on only the data of the selected region; section B is based on quantity and average price inputs for the world composed of the several regions.

The GDP-consistency method integrates the regional and world results by distributing each region's total GDP (as obtained from the second stage) among the countries of the region in accordance with the proportions indicated by the Stage I results.

Region 1's GDP of 210, produced by the world (second-stage) comparison, is distributed to the countries in proportion to the countries' shares in regional real GDP indicated by the first stage (0.286, 0.514, and 0.200 for countries A, B, and C, respectively).

	A	B	C	Total	Proportion of total regional GDP
Food	12	36	6	54	0.257
Clothing	6	42	6	54	0.257
Shelter	18	12	12	42	0.200
Other	24	18	18	60	0.285
Total GDP	60	108	42	210	1.000
Proportion of total regional GDP	0.286	0.514	0.200	1.000	

The resulting GDP figures (60, 108, and 42), now expressed in world numéraire currency, are used as control totals to apportion the country's GDP obtained among its subcomponents (food and the like) in accordance with the relative importance of the categories in real terms as measured by the results of the regional Geary-Khamis. Observe, however, that aggregation of the category quantities across countries does not yield regional totals for food, clothing, shelter, and other categories that are in the same proportions as those produced by the second-stage calculation. (That is, the series 0.257, 0.257, 0.200, 0.285 differs from the series 0.381, 0.476, 0.048, 0.095.)

This method can also be implemented by the use of the PPP between the regional and world numéraires to convert the GDP of each country as calculated in the regional Geary-Khamis, where it is denominated in the regional numéraire currency, into a value expressed in the world currency.[36]

The category-control-total method integrates the regional and world results by distributing each region's quantity for each category (as obtained from the second stage) among the countries of the region in accordance with the proportions indicated by the Stage I results.

The total regional quantity of each category (in the world numéraire currency) indicated by the Stage II calculation is distributed to the countries in proportion to the countries' shares in the regional total for that category indicated by Stage I. Region I's total of 80 for food, for example, is used as a control total and allocated to the countries in the proportion indicated by the Stage I results (2/9, 6/9, and 1/9 for countries A, B, and C, respectively).

	A	B	C	Total	Proportion of total regional GDP
Food	17.78	53.33	8.89	80	0.381
Clothing	11.11	77.78	11.11	100	0.476
Shelter	4.29	2.86	2.86	10	0.048
Other	8.0	6.0	6.0	20	0.095
Total GDP	41.18	139.97	28.86	210	1.000
Proportion of total regional GDP	0.196	0.667	0.137	1.000	

36. Another way of explaining the GDP-consistency method is to suppose the GDP of France is to be estimated in the world numéraire currency, say, dollars. The second-stage Geary-Khamis gives a GDP for Europe in dollars, and the European Geary-Khamis gives GDP for France in the European currency, say, European schillings. The formula below shows how the French GDP in dollars can be obtained. The first term on the right-hand side is the ratio of French to total European GDP, and the second is total European GDP in international dollars.

$$(A) \quad \text{GDP}_F^{I\$} = \frac{\text{GDP}_F^{ES} \cdot Pop_F}{\sum_j \text{GDP}_j^{ES} \cdot Pop_j} \cdot \frac{\Sigma \text{GDP}_j^{ES} \cdot Pop_j}{\text{PPP}_{ES/US}} = \frac{\text{GDP}_F^{ES} \cdot Pop_F}{\text{PPP}_{ES/US}}$$

where all GDPs are per capita values; *Pop* is population, the subscript *F* refers to France, and *US* to the United States; the superscript *I\$* represents international dollars; and *ES* represents European schillings. The GDP_j^{ES}'s are obtained from the first-stage Geary-Khamis while $\text{PPP}_{ES/US}$ is from the second-stage Geary-Khamis.

Alternatively, the second term on the right side, the European per capita GDP quantity, could have been obtained from the second-stage Geary-Khamis. That is,

$$(B) \quad \frac{\sum_j \text{GDP}_j^{ES} \cdot Pop_j}{\text{PPP}_{ES/US}} = \text{GDP}_E^{I\$} \cdot Pop_j$$

where *E* refers to Europe.

This method can also be implemented by converting each category valued in the currency of the numéraire country to the currency of the world numéraire (through the category PPP of the regional numéraire country's PPP relative to the world numéraire currency).[37] World average prices (that is, international prices), obtained in the interregional (second-stage) Geary-Khamis, are used in effect to value the real quantities in each category in each country from the regional Geary-Khamis.[38] However, when the regional quantity in *each category* is distributed in accord with the proportions indicated in the first stage, the aggregation of the categories for each country does not yield GDPs that are in the same proportions as the Stage I results.

The two approaches each rescale the individual countries' category quantities of a region so that (1) in the first case, their column totals add up to the total regional GDP obtained from the second-stage Geary-Khamis, or (2) in the second case, their row sums equal the total regional quantities from the second-stage Geary-Khamis. To illustrate the difference these

37. Again using France and Europe as an illustration, for the *i*th category:

$$(C) \quad Q_{iF}^{I\$} = \frac{Pop_F \cdot \frac{P_{iF}Q_{iF}}{\text{PPP}_{F/A}} \cdot \Pi_i^{ES}}{\sum_j Pop_j \frac{P_{ij}Q_{ij}}{\text{PPP}_{ij/A}} \cdot \Pi_i^{ES}} \cdot \frac{\sum_j Pop_j \cdot \frac{P_{ij}Q_{ij}}{\text{PPP}_{j/A}} \cdot \Pi_i^{ES}}{\text{PPP}_{i\ ES/US}} \cdot \Pi_i^{I\$}$$

where Q_{ij} is the quantity of the *i*th category; Π_i^{ES} is the European schilling price of the *i*th category; $\Pi_i^{I\$}$ is the international dollar price of the *i*th category; $\text{PPP}_{i,j/A}$ is the *j*th country PPP for the *i*th category expressed relative to Austrian schillings; $\text{PPP}_{i\ ES/US}$ is the PPP of the European schilling relative to the dollar for the *i*th category; and the other symbols are as above.

The first term on the right side represents the French share in the European absorption of category *i*, which can be found in the output of the regional Geary-Khamis. The next term is the value of the total fifteen-country absorption, converted to U.S. dollars; the numerator again is from the regional Geary-Khamis, while the denominator is from the second stage. The product of these two terms would leave the relative importance of the categories unchanged from the regional Geary-Khamis; that is, regional prices are used to value the quantities. The valuation of the categories in the region is adjusted to world prices by multiplying by the final term, $\Pi_i^{I\$}$, world prices, from the second-stage Geary-Khamis. (Note that the $\Pi_i^{I\$}$'s are distributed around the value of one for the world.) The expression to the right of the equal sign reduces to

$$(D) \quad Q_{iF}^{I\$} = \left(Pop_F \cdot \frac{\frac{P_{iF}Q_{iF}}{\text{PPP}_{F/A}} \cdot \Pi_i^{ES}}{\text{PPP}_{i\ ES/US}} \right) \Pi_i^{I\$}.$$

38. It would also be possible to value the notional quantities in each country by the international prices from the interregional (second-stage) Geary-Khamis. However, this procedure preserves neither row-to-row or country-to-country consistency with the regional results.

alternatives can make, the resulting proportions of the regional GDP allocated to the countries by the two methods are shown below:

	A	B	C	B/C
GDP-consistency method	0.286	0.514	0.200	2.57
Category-control-total method	0.196	0.667	0.137	4.87

Since it is not possible to make the individual countries' quantities consistent with *both* the column totals and row totals—requiring conformity with either necessarily is distorting for the other—a choice must be made. It should be emphasized that this is a choice imposed by the notion of full regionalization rather than the particular methods that have been discussed.

The GDP-consistency method seems to have two important advantages. (1) From a worldwide standpoint, it preserves regional and interregional consistency for GDP as a whole. This is apt to be more important for most users than consistency for subcomponents. (2) It preserves the composition of real product within each country (that is, the relative importance of food and other products) as produced by the regional calculations. This is an advantage because intraregional comparisons tend to be more characteristic for the countries within the region.

From another standpoint, however, this second advantage seems to be more liability than asset. It means, in effect, that different average international prices are used to value the same categories of goods in different regions. Comparisons of any subaggregates, such as food or capital formation, between countries in different regions would thus be impugned, because the valuation of each category of the aggregate is done at different prices in each region. Even GDP itself does not escape this objection. The total GDPs of different regions are compared at a set of world prices. Then these regional GDPs are allocated to the countries of the regions on the basis of the intraregional GDP comparisons, each of which is based on the "international" prices of the region, which differ both from those of the world and from those of other regions. Thus while the intraregional relationships for GDP would be protected, the cost would be dubious comparisons at the GDP and subaggregate levels for countries in different regions.[39] Consequently, the category-control-total method seems the less objectionable of the two.

39. Even the category-control-total method does not value apples relative to oranges in the same way in all regions. This is because even though the same Stage II Geary-Khamis prices are used for all countries they are applied to quantities that involve relative valuation of apples and oranges that may be different in each region as determined in the regional Geary-Khamis computation.

The Method Adopted by the ICP

The universal (one-stage CPD and one-stage Geary-Khamis) and the full two-stage (two-stage CPD and two-stage Geary-Khamis) represent extreme ways of dealing with the regional problem. The universal approach ignores regional ties and treats all countries together in a single set of calculations. The full two-stage approach gives priority to regional calculations.

In the course of preparing this report, a serious effort was made to find a compromise solution, one that would both produce transitive, base-country–invariant comparisons and take account of regional characteristicity, and yet at the same time somehow preserve the quality of comparisons between countries in different regions.

A compromise solution has emerged from this work, but it is a compromise that has only a modest element of regionality in it. It is justifiable as much on grounds of producing better universal comparisons as on the basis of regionalization. Before this solution is described, it may be well to set out the factors that led to a decision veering so much toward universality.

1. From the standpoint of a world statistical office, it seems appropriate to produce the most general kind of comparisons treating all countries symmetrically—that is, without regard to location and in a way that does not favor reliability of comparisons for some pairs or groups over other pairs or groups.

2. For many important analytical and policy purposes, comparisons are needed between countries in a given economic category or level of development (industrialized, developing, and so forth) regardless of their location. The fact that countries are in different continents is for many purposes irrelevant.

3. The technical improvement in the quality of comparisons achieved by the greater intraregional homogeneity of countries is notable, especially for Europe, but if homogeneity were the main criterion for the grouping of countries, countries in different geographical regions would often be in the same group. For example, the quantity structure of the GDP of Denmark is more like that of the United States than it is like that of Spain. (See the Paasche-Laspeyres spreads in Table 7-3.)

4. A two-stage comparison in which countries within regions were compared first and then linked through comparisons of the regions would substantially impair comparisons between countries in different regions.

The methods adopted for the preferred estimates in this report combine a two-stage CPD with a single-stage Geary-Khamis. Only one Geary-Khamis calculation is made, and it includes all thirty-four countries. The two-stage CPD procedure is designed to obtain as price inputs country PPPs that, while primarily uni-

Table 4-6. Comparisons of Multilateral Estimates of Real GDP per Capita, 1975, Produced by Various Treatments of Regionalization

| | | Ratios to two-stage, one-stage of | | |
| | | | Full two-stage[b] | |
Region/country	Two-stage, one-stage (1)	Universal[a] (2)	GDP consistency (3)	Category control totals (4)
Africa				
Kenya	6.56	1.02	0.90	0.87
Malawi	4.90	1.06	0.88	0.91
Zambia	10.3	1.04	0.83	0.83
Asia				
India	6.56	1.03	0.95	0.90
Iran	37.7	1.02	1.05	0.97
Japan	68.4	1.01	1.04	1.07
Korea	20.7	1.04	0.93	0.99
Malaysia	21.5	0.98	1.03	0.96
Pakistan	8.23	0.96	0.91	0.83
Philippines	13.2	1.07	0.98	0.97
Sri Lanka	9.30	1.03	0.99	0.96
Syria	25.0	1.02	1.05	1.02
Thailand	13.0	1.01	0.94	0.93
Europe				
Austria	69.6	1.02	1.00	1.01
Belgium	77.7	1.04	1.00	1.02
Denmark	82.4	1.04	1.04	1.03
France	81.9	1.02	0.97	1.00
Germany	83.0	1.03	1.00	1.01
Hungary	49.6	1.03	1.02	0.98
Ireland	42.5	1.03	0.99	1.00
Italy	53.8	1.03	1.01	1.01
Luxembourg	82.0	1.01	0.98	0.99
Netherlands	75.2	1.03	0.97	1.00
Poland	50.1	1.02	1.02	0.97
Romania	33.3	1.01	1.01	1.03
Spain	55.9	1.02	0.97	1.01
U.K.	63.9	1.02	0.98	0.98
Yugoslavia	36.1	1.02	1.01	0.98
Latin America and Caribbean				
Brazil	25.2	1.03	0.98	0.96
Colombia	22.4	0.96	0.91	0.95
Jamaica	24.0	1.02	0.93	0.91
Mexico	34.7	1.01	0.94	0.95
Uruguay	39.6	1.01	0.92	0.93
North America				
U.S.	100.0	1.00	1.00	1.00

Note: In the headings the first reference to stage refers to the number of CPDs and the second to the number of Geary-Khamis calculations. In both cases "one-stage" means that all thirty-four countries have been treated together in a single calculation while "two-stage" means that calculations have been made first for countries within each region, and the regions linked in a second calculation. The ratios are based on preliminary data, but the figures in column 1 represent final data.

a. One-stage, one-stage.

b. Two-stage, two-stage.

versal, have benefited from regional characteristicity of price structures.

The CPD method used is the second version of the augmented tableau approach described above. Stage I CPDs are used to fill holes in the regional price matrices. These full regional tableaux, including a complete price vector for each of the thirty-four countries, become the price inputs for a second-stage CPD. The PPPs produced by the set of second-stage CPDs, one for each detailed category, are the price inputs for a universal (thirty-four–country) Geary-Khamis calculation.

The price inputs are superior to those of a one-stage CPD, including all countries at once, owing to the tendency, demonstrated earlier in this chapter, for price structures to be more homogeneous within regions than among countries generally. Filling out the tableau of prices at the regional level before proceeding to a worldwide comparison takes advantage of these regional similarities. It should be stressed again that the use of CPD to estimate missing prices in this way is an explicit method of coping with the missing-price problem; the assumptions about these gaps are out in the open. Every method of aggregation makes some assumption about missing prices, but they are rarely spelled out. The CPD method should not be faulted for manufacturing artificial prices where other methods do not.

The incorporation of these price inputs in a one-stage Geary-Khamis calculation means that regional similarities in price structure have been taken into account, but without sacrifice of the desirable properties of the universal approach. A single set of average international prices is used to value the quantities of all the countries. Any country can be legitimately compared with any other country at the detailed-category level or at any level of aggregation up to total GDP. There is within-region and across-region consistency in the senses of base-country invariance, transitivity, and matrix consistency.

Comparison of Results

The estimates of 1975 real per capita GDP produced by the two-stage, one-stage method, adopted for Phase III, are entered in column 1 of Table 4-6. The results of other methods of meeting the regionalization problem discussed in the previous section are presented in columns 2 through 4 in the form of ratios to the preferred result in column 1. The ratios for the universal method are in column 2, and those for the two-stage, two-stage approach—which stands fully on an initial stage of intraregional comparisons and a subsequent stage of linking the regions—are shown in columns 3 and 4.

As expected, the universal and two-stage, one-stage method yield very similar results, usually within 2 or 3 percent. The largest difference for any country relative to any other country is 11 percent (the Philippines relative to Pakistan or Colombia). Because the imputations for missing prices are carried out in a better way, the column 1 estimates are considered more reliable.

The better of the two variants of the full two-stage procedures is, on the basis of the arguments offered earlier, the one in which the regional and interregional results are integrated by the use of category-control totals. These estimates, expressed as ratios of the two-stage, one-stage estimates, are entered in column 4. Once again, for most of the countries (twenty-four out of thirty-three) the results are within 5 percent of the two-stage, one-stage results, but there are three that

are off by 13 to 17 percent relative to the United States. The largest difference for any country relative to another is 29 percent (Japan relative to Pakistan or Zambia). Much the same can be said about the estimates produced when the GDP-consistency method is used to integrate the intraregional and interregional results (column 3). The largest difference from the two-stage, one-stage estimate of the per capita GDP for any country relative to any other country is 22 percent (Syria or Iran, and Zambia).

Reasons have been given earlier in this section for preferring the two-stage, one-stage approach over any of the versions of the two-stage, two-stage approach. Another important reason can be found in the results in Table 4-6. In understanding this, it must be first recalled that the two-stage, one-stage approach is clearly superior for comparisons of pairs of countries in different regions, while the claims that can be made for the two-stage, two-stage approach are based on better comparisons of pairs of countries within regions. Suppose it can be shown that either (1) the two-stage, one-stage approach not only produces superior interregional comparisons but at the same time produces intraregional comparisons that do not differ much from those yielded by the two-stage, two-stage approach or (2) the two-stage, two-stage approach produces its better intraregional comparisons while at the same time yielding interregional comparisons that are not very different from those of the two-stage, one-stage approach. If the first proposition could be shown to be more nearly true than the second, that would be an argument for the two-stage, one-stage approach, while if the reverse were the case, the two-stage, two-stage approach would be favored.

There is an a priori reason for believing that the first proposition is a more likely outcome. From the standpoint of two countries within a region, say, France and the Federal Republic of Germany, a comparison between them is less characteristic as a consequence of the addition of prices of distant countries, say, India and Thailand. The new average prices, including the effects of the very different price structures of the remote countries, will have a similar effect on the valuation of the quantities of France and Germany if these two countries are indeed similar.[40] That is, if France and Germany really have similar quantity

---

40. First, to the extent France and Germany have priced the same item in a detailed category, the franc/DM relation for the category will be unchanged, so their relative quantities will remain unchanged. Further, if their relative quantity structure between categories is really similar, then whatever set of category valuations (international prices) is used, the French/German comparison would not be altered.

structures and incomes, raising some prices in the set of average international prices and lowering others will not greatly alter their *relative* (France/Germany) per capita GDP from what it would be if only intra-regional average prices had been used in the valuation of their quantities. There is no similar influence at work keeping the interregional comparisons in the two-stage, two-stage approach from wandering off from the relationships produced in the two-stage, one-stage approach.

These expectations have been examined in light of the results reported in Table 4-6. Each of the two-stage, two-stage approaches has been compared with the one-stage, one-stage method in the following way. (The reference calculations were one-stage, one-stage only because the exercise was carried out before the final decision in favor of a two-stage, one-stage approach was made.) Any pair of countries, say, the *j*th and the *k*th, may be compared either through one-stage, one-stage (y_{jk}^1) or through one of the two-stage, two-stage methods, GDP-consistency (y_{jk}^2) or category-control totals (y_{jk}^3). The "absolute relative" differences between each of the latter methods and the first are given by $\Delta_{jk}^i = |y_{jk}^1 - y_{jk}^i|/\sqrt{y_{jk}^1 y_{jk}^i}$, $i=2$ referring to the GDP consistency, and $i=3$ to the category totals.[41] The 561 possible pairs that can be formed from the 34 Phase III countries divide into two sets, 163 intraregional pairs (for example, Malawi-Zambia or Colombia-Mexico), and 398 interregional pairs (for example, Malawi-Colombia or Zambia-Mexico). The averages of both the Δ^2's and Δ^3's have been calculated

for each set to see if the means for the 163-pair set are significantly different statistically from the means for the 398-pair set. Table 4-7 shows that in each case the intraregional mean is about half the interregional mean (lines 1 and 2). Since the average Δ^i is obtained through sampling without replacement, the *t* statistic must reflect a standard error of the mean in this case about five-sixths as great as the conventional one.[42] As line 4 of Table 4-7 indicates, the means of the intraregional Δ's are indeed significantly smaller than the mean Δ's for all pairs, whether the GDP-consistency or the category-control-total method is used, while the means of the interregional Δ's are significantly larger in both cases. Since the one-stage, one-stage comparisons are very close to the regionalized ones for intraregional comparisons, the universal method may be regarded as quite attractive: it gives results that are not so very different from those obtained from the two-stage methods that are thought to provide more characteristic intraregional comparisons, and results that are better for interregional comparisons. Since the results of the universal approach are so similar to those of the two-stage, one-stage approach finally selected, there is a strong presumption that the same conclusion would emerge if the latter were taken as the reference point for the exercise.

Further Considerations

Before closing this chapter, two other aspects of the regionalization problem are considered. One relates to leeway for some variation in data collection by different regions. The other concerns aggregation formulas other than those used by the ICP.

Flexibility Provided for Different Regional Data Inputs

All the methods of treating the regionalization problems outlined above afford complete flexibility for regional and subregional groups of countries to include price specifications of their own choosing (as long as they also price a reasonable number of specifications used by countries in other regions), and to subdivide detailed ICP categories as finely as they wish. At the CPD level additional item prices present no problem. The further subdivision of detailed categories can be

41. As indicated above, the actual comparisons reported in Table 4-7 used a one-stage, one-stage comparison as a base. (There was also a two-stage, one-stage based on the same preliminary data for comparison.) Since the two-stage, one-stage and universal comparisons are very close (see column 2 of Table 4-6), the tests in Table 4-7 reflect accurately what would have been the results if two-stage, one-stage had been used instead of one-stage, one-stage. The income comparisons may be illustrated for Malawi and Zambia.

	Malawi	Zambia	Malawi/Zambia
Two-stage, one-stage (derived from Table 4-6)	4.90	10.3	$y^1 = 0.476$
Universal (one-stage, one-stage)	5.19	10.7	$(y^1) = 0.485$
Two-stage			
GDP-consistency	4.31	8.5	$y^2 = 0.507$
Category-control total	4.46	8.5	$y^3 = 0.525$

Δ^2 and Δ^3 therefore are:

$$\Delta^2 = |0.476 - 0.507| / \sqrt{(0.476) \cdot (0.507)} = 0.063$$

$$\Delta^3 = |0.476 - 0.525| / \sqrt{(0.476) \cdot (0.525)} = 0.098$$

The values for Δ^2 and Δ^3 using one-stage, one-stage would have been 0.044 and 0.079, and the same would be true for other pairs.

42. The standard error of the mean for sampling without replacement equals $\sigma/\sqrt{n} \cdot \sqrt{N-n}/\sqrt{N-1}$ where N is the population size and n is the sample size ($\sqrt{561-163}/\sqrt{561-1} = 0.84$).

Table 4-7. Comparison of Two Variants of the Two-stage, Two-stage Regionalization Method with the One-stage, One-stage Method: Comparisons within Regions versus Comparisons between Regions

Average absolute relative difference	*Number of pairs*	One-stage, one-stage compared with two-stage, two-stage	
		GDP *consistency*	*Category-control total*
1. Within regions $\bar{\Delta}$	163	0.035	0.037
2. Between regions $\bar{\Delta}$	398	0.069	0.075
3. Overall $\bar{\Delta}$	561		
Mean		0.059	0.064
Standard deviation		0.046	0.075
4. t [a]			
Within-regions		-7.92 [b]	-5.46 [b]
Between-regions		$+7.92$ [b]	$+5.46$ [b]

a. $t = \dfrac{(\bar{\Delta}_{ni}^{i} - \mu^{i})}{\bar{\sigma}_{\Delta_{ni}}}$ where $\bar{\sigma}_{\Delta_{ni}} = \dfrac{\sigma_i}{\sqrt{n_i}} \cdot \dfrac{\sqrt{N-n_i}}{\sqrt{N-1}}$.

b. Statistically significant at the 0.01 level. The fact that the between-regions t-values are the exact negatives of the within-regions ones is not a coincidence. That is, the two individual statistical tests for GDP consistency ($t = \pm 7.92$) are equivalent; and the same is true for category-control total.

accepted if all the countries in a region supply the expenditures for the new subdivisions. No difficulty arises if only some countries give these additional weights. Then a single CPD can be run with assignment of weights to items or groups of items for countries that have supplied this additional detail, and the usual frequency weighting of the items for countries that have not subdivided the expenditures.

At the Geary-Khamis level, also, if most but not all countries have provided the added breakdown of expenditures, it is still possible to use the additional information. Geary-Khamis can still be run with the enlarged set of categories with entries for all the categories. For the countries that have not provided the added detail, the PPP for the ICP-detailed category can be entered for each of the breakdowns and the expenditure of the ICP-detailed category divided evenly among the subdivisions.[43]

Other Aggregation Formulas

While the basic notion of the two-stage approach to the regionalization question can be adapted to aggregation formulas other than CPD and Geary-Khamis, each formula is likely to require some tailoring of the procedure to the task at hand.[44] Possible substitutes for CPD are less systematic in their treatment of the missing prices except for the EKS method. For a given

set of prices, a systematic approach, whether CPD or EKS, seems clearly superior to an ad hoc method of bridging on the basis of individual countries. (The ICP preference for CPD over EKS was discussed in Chapter 3.)

When it comes to combining the categories, any aggregation method that produces base-invariant, transitive real expenditures for each category and matrix consistency for combinations of categories will lend itself to virtually the same regionalization procedures discussed in connection with the two-stage Geary-Khamis. Where an aggregation formula does not produce expenditures for individual countries that can be aggregated for a region as part of its regular output (the Walsh formula, for example), a way must be found to devise them.[45]

Summary

Despite the apparent appeal of a system in which comparisons are made initially at a regional level and subsequently integrated without alteration into a world system, such a course has compelling disadvantages. For example, a series of star-system binary comparisons—one for each region—with the regions, too, linked in a star system, has been ruled out because of the sensitivity of the results to the choice of the regional base countries (and to the choice of the world base country, as well).

One problem, not in itself decisive, relates to the arrangement of all the countries of the world into re-

43. Or if it seems clear that an even division does violence to the likely facts, the average breakdown of the countries that have provided the data can be used.

44. See Kravis, Kenessey, Heston, Summers (1975), p. 66, for a discussion of various alternatives including EKS and Walsh. Gerardi's unit-country–weighting formula is referred to in Chapter 3 above.

45. See Kravis, Heston, Summers (1979) for some suggestions regarding the Walsh index.

gional groups that are meaningful and acceptable to the countries. In Europe, for example, there are major political and economic groupings of countries that leave a number of nonmember countries that are difficult to classify into groups. From a technical point of view, the case for an initial stage of regional comparisons rests on the argument that greater homogeneity of countries within a region will make it possible to produce more characteristic comparisons for them than will be the case when interdependent comparisons are produced for the whole range of countries in the world. However, the groupings of countries on the basis of geographical propinquity or political affiliation will often include some economically dissimilar countries in a given group and exclude some similar countries from it. It has been shown, indeed, that classifications of countries based solely on criteria of similarity of economic structure (prices, quantities, incomes) usually group together some countries from different geographical regions and from different political groups. Nevertheless, it remains true that the usual geographical groupings of countries into regions such as "Europe" and "Latin America" produce greater homogeneity within the classification than is found in the world at large.

The compelling case against an initial stage in which regional comparisons are made and a second stage in which comparisons linking the regions are made is that there is no satisfactory way in such a system to preserve the integrity of comparisons between countries in different regions. Furthermore, it turns out that the universal approach is more compatible with intraregional comparisons than the two-stage approach is with interregional comparisons. A universal comparison yields results that are relatively closer to the results of a purely intraregional comparison. In contrast, the results of a two-step, interregional comparison differ to a larger degree from those of a universal comparison. To put it another way, the costs of regionalization are large in worldwide comparisons, while the damage done to intraregional comparisons when they are derived as a part of worldwide comparisons is relatively small.

The ICP has therefore opted for a universal solution modified with an admixture of regionalization in organizing the price inputs for the one-stage Geary-Khamis calculation. The inputs required include a PPP for each of the 151 detailed categories in the ICP clas-

sification. In the method adopted by the ICP in Phase III, advantage is taken of regional similarities in price structures to cope with a major problem in deriving the needed set of PPPs—namely, incompletely overlapping sets of price comparisons among the participating countries. The solution involved the application of the CPD method first at a regional level to fill in for each country any missing entries in the vector of item prices consisting of all items for which at least two countries in the region have provided prices. After each country's price vector has been completed to match those of other countries in the same region, a second-stage CPD covering all thirty-four countries is calculated. The resulting PPPs are the inputs for a single-stage Geary-Khamis calculation performed for all thirty-four countries.

This decision in favor of a solution veering heavily toward a universal approach is congenial to the responsibilities of a statistical office functioning at the center of the world statistical system. It is natural for such an office to attempt to produce the most general kind of comparisons that treat all countries in an even-handed way—that is, a way that avoids any attempt to improve comparisons between some pairs or groups at the expense of comparison between others. The important governmental and analytical uses of the international comparisons that such an organization is expected to produce will usually cut across regional lines.

Of course, operational needs may be encountered by pairs or groups of countries that require special comparisons confined to members of the group. Where such a need exists, special-purpose comparisons will doubtless be produced by the interested countries for their own purposes. This has the disadvantage that there will be more than one set of comparisons, since the ICP system will, of course, continue to cover all countries.

None of this means that the future work in the International Comparison Project can be carried out without the active support and cooperation of the regional organizations. Identifying appropriate specifications, ensuring that comparability does indeed exist for the items that are priced, and organizing the collection of the expenditure and quantity data required—all this can better be performed at the regional level in close collaboration with the U.N. Statistical Office.

5

The Treatment of Services

THIS CHAPTER EXAMINES THE METHODS of comparisons for the service components of final expenditure on GDP.[1] The discussion concentrates on those service categories for which outputs are difficult to measure, such as medical care, education, and government services. The methods used in Phases I and II are described and assessed for possible error. Alternative methods of forming the price and quantity comparisons for the problematic services are canvassed, and the sensitivity of the overall comparisons of real GDP per capita to different methods is shown.

Although some improvements in the methods of comparing outputs for medical care, education, and government services proved feasible in Phase III, the problems remain great. The Phase I and II methods had the serious disadvantage of assuming equal productivity across countries for equally qualified personnel engaged in the provision of the problem services. It has proved possible to modify this assumption in Phase III for medical care by making an adjustment for the differences in the productivity of inputs for broad groups of countries and by making a simple adjustment for capital per worker in medical care and in government services. For educational services the modifications of earlier work were to improve the estimates of teacher inputs by education level, and to introduce the number of students as a further dimension of output.

The Problems Posed by Services

The nature of services, their distinction from commodities, and the question of how to value them in relation to the total production of the economy are all issues that have been debated since the beginning of modern economics and, indeed, in some respects, through the ages. A commodity can be defined as a physical object that is transferable between economic transactors, but a satisfactory definition of services is harder to arrive at.

Seeking a Definition

In the final expenditure framework of the ICP, services constitute a heterogeneous collection of final products. Unlike commodities, the production of each is necessarily simultaneous with its consumption and, consequently, no service can be stocked.[2] Some services affect goods in the possession of consumers, such as the repair and refurbishing of a variety of objects including clothing, dwellings, and automobiles. Some—such as medical, educational, recreational, and cultural services, and the services of barber shops, beauty parlors, and restaurants—affect the individual directly. Still other types, such as those provided by household employees and transportation enterprises, may affect either objects in the possession of consumers or may affect their persons. Housing space, treated as a service in the ICP and most other classification systems, presumably affects the condition of consumers directly. The same is true of the services of government.

2. The attributes and distinctions set out in this and the following paragraph draw freely on the article by Hill (1977). Two other papers dealing with the treatment of services in international comparisons came to hand after the basic work of this chapter had been completed. See Hungarian Central Statistical Office (1980) and Marris (1980). Also, the treatment in this chapter has taken into account the Report of the Expert Working Group, U.N. Statistical Office (1980a).

1. The detailed categories classified as services are identified in Appendix Table 2-1 at the end of Chapter 2.

Services are not necessarily distinguishable from commodities on technological grounds. Some, such as domestic services, are extremely labor intensive, while others, such as air travel, are more capital intensive. However, labor-intensive services tend to be a greater proportion of total expenditures than capital-intensive ones.[3]

Technology fails as a distinguishing characteristic also because the production of services sometimes duplicates operations performed in commodity production. For example, the painting of a new house is considered as part of construction and, therefore, as commodity production, while the identical operation applied to an old owner-occupied house is treated as a service.

Nor can services be distinguished from commodities because in the act of consumption they are transitory while commodities are permanent. Many commodities are more transitory than many services. For example, the consumption of a banana involves a more transitory effect than the painting of a house.

Lastly, the distinction between services and commodities cannot turn on the foreign-trade possibilities. Services are mainly nontradable, but they can be and often are purchased by a foreign visitor. Some, such as those provided by airlines, hotels, and restaurants, may even cater especially to foreign customers.

The Special Problems of Service Comparisons

The special problems services present in intertemporal comparisons of real product take on an especially difficult aspect in interspatial comparisons. This is not true of all final-product services. Some, such as barbershop and laundry services, are rendered by individual producers to individual customers in exchange for payment. There is no difficulty in identifying the nature of the transaction or about defining the units of output involved in terms such as a man's haircut or the laundering of a cotton sheet for a double bed. International price comparisons must be based on units of similar quality in different countries, but the quality problems are not essentially different from those encountered in price comparisons for commodities. Some commodities—eggs are an example—are easier to price on a standard-quality basis across countries than are haircuts or the laundering of sheets, but others, such as freight cars and women's dresses, are harder.[4]

There are, however, some final-product services for which units of output and the quality thereof are much less unambiguous. These services are found mainly in the health, education, and government sectors. They are characterized by one or both of two features: (1) The transaction is one in which the buyer pays for the time devoted by a person, usually a professional or other specialist, to the furtherance of an end sought by the buyer. The ends themselves—such as the favorable outcome of a legal proceeding, better health, more knowledge, or safety on the streets—cannot be bought and sold directly. (2) In many cases the persons who supply these services and the equipment they use in their work are paid for out of the public purse, and the individuals for whom the services are designed are not involved in any market transaction at all.[5] The kinds of questions that arise for such services can be illustrated by educational services. What is the appropriate unit of output for the international comparison of the prices or quantities of educational services? Pupil-hours spent in receiving instruction? The number of teacher-hours of instruction provided? Or is it some measure of learning, such as improved pupil performance in internationally comparable examinations?

National-income statisticians, seeking to avoid arbitrary decisionmaking, regard that which is actually exchanged between a buyer and seller as the touchstone for defining a transaction and the unit in which it should be measured.[6] A client may hire a lawyer in the hope of an acquittal, and a patient may go to a physician for a cure, but whether the acquittal or the cure is actually achieved depends on many factors that go beyond the service of the lawyer or doctor. Neither the acquittal nor the cure has been exchanged in the marketplace. They are ultimate objectives for which economic transactions take place, just as satisfying hunger is the objective in the purchase of food, but the production boundary does not extend to these ultimate satisfactions whether derived from the services or from commodities. Potatoes may be bought to satisfy hunger, but what is measured in national-income accounting is the kilograms of potatoes purchased, not the utilities derived from them in satisfying hunger. The efficiency of the consumer in transforming goods he buys on the market into satisfactions is not part of

---

3. Kravis, Heston, Summers (1982).

4. The factoring of price and quantity of commodities is not without problems. For a controversy about the treatment of quality changes in producers' durable goods as changes in prices or as

changes in quantities see Denison (1957) and *Survey of Current Business* (May 1969), pp. 1–27, and (May 1972), pp. 95–115 and 69–94. See also Jorgenson and Griliches (1967), pp. 249–83.

5. Marris (1980) has discussed the public good aspect of these services. On this point see also Kravis, Kenessey, Heston, Summers (1975), p. 27.

6. For a recent forceful and clear statement of this view, from which the illustrations in this paragraph are drawn, see European Communities Statistical Office (1979).

the production process of the economy. Utilities are not anyhow measurable.

Of course, there is nothing in this general view that precludes defining transactions in terms that come closer to approximating human motivations and satisfactions where market-based alternatives present themselves. Dentist-hours spent in patient care are a better output indicator than the number of dentists, and specific dental services, such as extractions and the making of dentures, are preferable to dentist-hours as measures of output.

Largely because such alternatives are not readily available for services of general medical practitioners, educators, and government employees, the most usual practice in national accounting is to use inputs, and particularly labor inputs, as the measure of intertemporal changes in prices and quantities for these sectors. The rationale is that the inputs are one and the same as the outputs. When there are private purchasers, as often is the case for the services of general medical practitioners, it is the time of the physicians with their supporting aides and equipment that enters into the value of both input and output. For services provided out of the public purse without direct charges to the users, the only actual market transactions are those in which the government purchases the labor and other inputs. Of course, where the service is provided by the government at or near cost, as in a government-owned and -operated transport system, the principle of measuring as close to the consumption point as possible clearly leads away from input-oriented measures such as the number of trains run or available passenger seat–kilometers. It leads instead toward the choice of the number of passengers or passenger-kilometers as the unit of output.

Whatever the merits of the standard national-accounting view of these matters, it is difficult at certain points to maintain its strict adherence to market criteria. This is clear in intertemporal comparisons in which, in at least some countries, national-income statisticians apply arbitrarily assumed rates of productivity increase to the labor inputs in preference to the unrealistic assumption of zero productivity changes. In international comparisons, the simplest application of the market approach is to regard an hour's service by a teacher or physician or civil servant as making the same contribution to output in every country. An obvious and easily made improvement is to stratify the persons in each sector by their quality with regard to years of education, training, and experience. With this alteration, it would be, for example, a teacher with a given number of years of education working with pupils at a given level of education who would be assumed to have the same productivity in every country.

This is essentially the method that was followed in Phases I and II of the ICP for medical, educational, and government personnel. Before the disadvantages of this approach are considered, its ICP use will be described more fully.

The Treatment of Services in Phases I and II of the ICP

Where there was a clearly defined unit of service output available, the ICP constructed price and quantity indexes in Phases I and II like those for commodities. A purchasing power parity (PPP) for each detailed category was calculated[7] and the quantity ratio was obtained by dividing the PPP into the expenditure ratio.[8] Services treated in this way—referred to hereafter as priced services—included repairs to a variety of consumer-owned assets, such as clothing, dwellings, household appliances, and automobiles; the services of household employees; other household services (including dry cleaning and laundering); transport services; entertainment and cultural services; services of barber and beauty shops; services of restaurants, cafés, and hotels; space rental of housing; and miscellaneous services (including those of financial and insurance institutions). Spending on these priced services accounted for 58 percent of all services and 16 percent of GDP per capita (in own prices) for the aggregate of the sixteen Phase II countries in 1970.

Direct price comparisons of service outputs were not made for ten detailed categories in the three problem sectors—health care, education, and government services—because of the great difficulty in obtaining satisfactory measures of output. In 1970 these categories—referred to hereafter as comparison-resistant services—accounted for the remaining 42 percent of all service expenditures of the Phase II countries and 11 percent of total GDP.[9] Comparison-resistant services include services of physicians, dentists, hospitals, nurses, teachers, and government employees. (Medical care, education, and government include other

7. If prices were compared for only one specification in the category, the PPP was the ratio of the domestic currency price in the given country to the domestic currency price in the numéraire country. If prices were compared for more than one specification, the PPP was estimated by the CPD method.

8. The quantity ratio obtained by such a division is referred to as an indirect quantity ratio, just as a PPP derived by dividing a directly estimated quantity ratio into an expenditure ratio is referred to as an indirect PPP.

9. The term comparison-resistant was suggested by György Syilágyi. The share of these services in the real GDP of each of the Phase II countries is shown below in Table 5-2.

detailed categories in the commodities classification.) In the comparison-resistant categories it was assumed that outputs were proportional to inputs; this is equivalent to assuming equal productivity of inputs in different countries. The output comparisons were derived directly from quantities of relatively homogeneous inputs or indirectly by means of price comparisons of such inputs. Methods followed in Phases I and II for these three groups of comparison-resistant services are further described in the following sections.

It may be useful to summarize the way in which the 151 detailed expenditure categories have been classified for purposes of the following discussion:[10]

	Number of categories	Share of expenditures
Commodities	120	73
Services	31	27
Priced services	21	16
Comparison-resistant services	10	11

The share of expenditures refers to average shares in 1970 for sixteen Phase II countries in own-currency GDP.

Medical Care and Health Services

Quantity comparisons for three categories, physicians (ICP 5.31), dentists (ICP 5.32), and nurses, physiotherapists, technicians, midwives, and the like (ICP 5.33) were based on direct comparisons of the numbers of physicians, dentists, and nurses respectively. For hospitals (ICP 5.41) the number of bed-days was generally used as a basis for quantity comparisons, but in a few cases where bed-days were not available, the number of beds was used.[11]

Since it is plausible to assume that the output of health-care personnel would be greater the larger the amount of capital the average doctor or dentist has to work with, a crude adjustment for each of the four categories was made on the basis of some limited data to take account of the amount of cooperating capital. Among the ten Phase I countries, the smallest of these adjustments reduced the France/U.S. quantity ratio by 4 percent, while the largest reduced the Kenya/U.S. ratio by 14 percent. The PPP for each category was then derived by dividing the expenditure ratio by the quantity ratio.

Experiments with price comparisons based both on the prices of certain services (for example, tonsillectomies) and on annual earnings of labor inputs were also carried out in Phase I. Because the extent to which medical services were paid for out of public funds varied among the countries, being very limited, for example, in the United States and substantial in the United Kingdom and Hungary, price comparisons based on full social-cost prices were difficult to make. Furthermore, the unavailability of data on the total earnings of medical personnel in some countries made the approach unfeasible. Thus direct quantity comparisons based on inputs were used in Phases I and II.

Education

For educational personnel—teachers of students at the first and second levels (ICP 07.411) and at the third level (ICP 07.412)—the quantity comparisons were based on the number of standardized persons engaged in providing the services.[12] The quantity comparisons for primary and secondary education were based on the number of "standard" teachers who have completed two years of college or university studies. This involved reductions of the raw quantity ratios relative to the United States in Phase I of 16 percent for Colombia and India and 33 percent for Kenya. Quantity comparisons for the third level of education were based simply on the number of teachers. The indirect PPPs were obtained by dividing the expenditure ratios by the quantity ratios. Various alternative calculations based on direct price (salary) comparisons and on the use of numbers of pupils as quantity indicators were also presented in Phase I, but they were not used in the aggregations to obtain GDP and other totals.

Compensation of Government Employees

The final expenditure breakdown in the national accounts of each country reports the services of government in terms of expenditures for two categories of inputs: the compensation of employees and purchases of commodities. The commodity inputs were compared among countries in Phase I and II by means of price comparisons for the various categories of government purchases of commodities and has been treated as a commodity category.[13]

---

10. Three health categories, drugs and medical preparations (ICP 5.11), medical supplies (ICP 5.12), and therapeutic equipment (ICP 5.20), consisted of commodities and were treated in the conventional way by means of direct price comparisons.

11. In what follows, the hospitals category is treated as a comparison-resistant service, since units of output closer to ultimate consumer satisfaction such as the removal of an appendix or the delivery of a baby might be used.

12. As in the case of health care, some education categories were composed of commodities and price comparisons were imputed from other categories—for example, books. These included expenditures related to physical facilities (ICP 07.42) and other expenditures of educational institutions (ICP 07.43).

13. See Kravis, Kenessey, Heston, Summers (1975), pp. 163ff. In this chapter, and in the remainder of this volume, Phase I and II definitions of services have been used. Government purchases

The employee-compensation part of government final expenditure was treated through a direct price comparison for government employees. Expenditures on the compensation of employees were divided among four categories of government personnel based on skill and education: unskilled blue collar (ICP 20.1), skilled blue collar (ICP 20.21), white collar (ICP 20.22), and professional (ICP 20.3). Within each of these categories a PPP was established relative to the United States and based on comparisons of compensation per employee for each of a number of occupations (most often four or five). For each occupation a specific job description was the basis of the price comparison. The indirect quantity comparisons relative to the United States were then derived by dividing the relative expenditure in each category by the PPP.

Input Indicators for Comparison-resistant Services

The following sections explore the use of inputs as indicators of output for comparison-resistant services. The simplest assumption of equal productivity of inputs in all countries is evaluated first. Subsequent sections examine the arguments for and quantitative importance of several alternative assumptions for valuing comparison-resistant services.

Inputs as Measures of Outputs

The use of inputs as output indicators in international comparisons in these three important sets of comparison-resistant services involves the underlying assumption that the productivity of professional personnel is equal across countries in each of the services. This may lead to inaccuracy in the measurement of quantity ratios for several reasons.

RELATIVE ATTRACTION OF PROFESSIONS. The quality of the inputs of professional labor may not be the same from country to country. The relative attraction of the different professions and occupations is not the same in the various countries. It is commonly believed, for example, that in France the most talented young people elect government careers, while in the United States their peers choose medicine. The knowledge and skill imparted by education and training in preparation for each profession may also differ from country to country. Certainly there are substantial differences in the length of training involved in professional preparation in different countries, particularly for medicine, and it is questionable that the quantity of preparation resulting from a given number of years of education is the same in different countries. Thus the quality problem is not completely resolved by standardizing on number of years of training, as was done in Phases I and II with primary and secondary school teachers.

DIFFERENCES IN PRODUCTIVITY. Inputs with comparable ability and training would not necessarily result in equal output per unit of input; the efficiency with which given inputs produce services may vary internationally. These differences in productivity cannot be judged solely from differences in the number of patients seen by physicians and dentists per hour or per day, or in the number of students taught by a teacher.[14] It is difficult to say whether twenty minutes of the physician's time devoted to a single patient is more or less output than two minutes of his time devoted to each of ten patients, assuming the same facilities and assistance in each situation. Is short time per patient an indicator of inadequate care or of high productivity? Doubtless the answer will vary with the circumstances. It is complicated by the fact that there is a service element in the personal attention enjoyed by the patient or student that must be taken into account in addition to the direct effect on the patient's health or the pupil's knowledge.

There probably is no escape in international comparisons from the assumption that the number of patients seen in an hour is not an adequate indicator of productivity. But this does not mean that the productivity of an hour's treatment by a dentist or physician is the same in every country. For one thing, the mix of services provided may differ widely from one country to another, with procedures requiring relatively little skill playing a larger role in treatment hours in some countries than in others. More generally, international differences in work habits may permeate all

---

of commodities, ICP 21, is treated as a commodity even though in principle these purchases are the means to providing a service. For most purposes, including analyses of services, it turns out to make little difference in the empirical results whether government commodity purchases are treated as a commodity or service. The PPP for this category is derived from direct price comparisons of like goods (for example, the PPP for government purchases of food is assumed to be the same as the PPP for household purchases of food). Thus, the ICP does not make a direct price comparison of the government services that occasion the purchase of these commodities. This means that if ICP 21 were placed in the service category it would have been classified as a priced service, not a comparison-resistant service, despite the lack of specific price comparisons for it.

14. There may be less objection to the use of the number of patients and the number of pupils as time-to-time quantity indicators within a given country. Year-to-year differences in the teacher/pupil ratio and in the average physician time per patient are apt to be smaller than the country-to-country differences.

economic sectors so that an hour's work by persons of equal ability and training in a given profession may be performed with different degrees of efficiency in different countries. The general milieu may be affected also in some countries by the existence of substantial unemployment and underemployment. Efficiency may be adversely affected by the presence of disguised unemployment in certain low-income countries where alternative employment opportunities are limited.[15]

OMITTED INPUTS. A third reason why output measures based on ratios of labor inputs may be unreliable is that some inputs will not be taken into account. The health care that a physician or a dentist can deliver in an hour is very much influenced by the way his practice is organized. For example, American dentists working with two full-time auxiliaries (including both secretaries and technicians) were able to handle two-thirds more patient visits than dentists working alone,[16] and the dentist who uses high-speed equipment and sends intricate laboratory work out to specialized firms will be able to treat more patients than the one who does not. It is particularly difficult to obtain complete data on inputs of auxiliary personnel and on the use of specialist firms in the practices of independent doctors and dentists.

The most important input omitted or inadequately treated in the Phase I and II estimates was capital. Clearly, a government secretary with a word-processing machine will be more productive than a secretary with an old-fashioned typewriter, just as a government accountant with fine computer facilities will be more effective than another who must perform all accounting operations manually. In education, particularly at the second and third levels, learning will be enhanced by better libraries and better laboratories. Similarly, the use of superior classroom space may be presumed to play a useful role in education. Furthermore, even if it could not be shown that the superior space adds to learning but only to enjoyment,[17] a pleasant and spacious environment for learning should no more be omitted from the measurement of output and income than a pleasant and spacious environment for dwelling.

As in the case of government and education services, the availability of equipment may add to the productivity of health-care professionals. It may be true that in very low-income countries medical practice is concerned mainly with easily diagnosed diseases, and that medical capital may not be critical in diagnosis and treatment of such diseases. Still, this difference in the nature of medical problems is hardly a reason for omitting the contribution of capital to medical practice to whatever extent it is employed in a given country. The objections to the inclusion of capital are not based on principle but, as will soon be discussed, on measurement problems. On net, it seemed that despite the measurement problems, some allowance for capital was warranted.

Input Quantities versus Input Prices in Output Comparisons

Even if it is deemed necessary, in spite of all the disadvantages, to proceed with quantity comparisons based on input ratios, the question still arises whether the best approach is through a direct comparison of input quantities, or through a direct comparison of input prices and the corresponding indirect comparison of input quantities. In general, where at all possible, the ICP approach is to make direct salary comparisons and indirect quantity comparisons on the ground that the sampling variability of direct price ratios between countries is likely to be smaller than the sampling variability of direct quantity ratios. With some kinds of inputs, however, it is easier to get reliable data on quantities than on prices. This often is true, for example, of government workers and independent medical practitioners for whom it may be difficult to obtain accurate estimates of incomes.[18]

Assessment of Input-based Measures of Output

The confidence that may be placed in the input approach in international comparisons is diminished by the evidence clearly indicating that reliance on input indicators of output is sometimes defective even in an intertemporal context. Such an output proxy is misleading when, as is often the case, there are changes in the productivity of service industries over time. In the United States, for example, a study of employees

---

15. Denison and Fuchs have suggested that disguised unemployment is likely to affect productivity in the service industries generally. Fuchs (1968), pp. 97–98, tested the relation proposed by Denison (1965) that increases in productivity tend to be larger in industries where self-employment declines. Fuchs found some support of this proposition for the U.S. service industry during the 1939–63 period.

16. Feldsteen (1974).

17. Extensive empirical work on educational production functions has failed to unearth any clear connection between improvement in student achievement and quality and quantity of education capital for the range of facilities in the United States. See Summers and Wolfe (1977), p. 645; and DeAmico and Ingle (1969), pp. 237–40.

18. When data difficulties arise for government workers, the problems usually relate to the salaries of state and local employees.

in more than 100 federal agencies from 1967 through 1971 showed an increase in output per man-year of 7.1 percent, ranging from 5.2 percent for public services such as customs and social security to 23.3 percent for industrial services such as the mint. The report found that the main causes of the productivity improvements were investments in structures and machinery and equipment in which technological advances were embodied.[19] Other studies have suggested that the diminution of underemployment in service industries has often been responsible for increasing productivity.

These considerations make it clear that the disadvantages of input-based measures of output are considerably greater for international comparisons than for relatively short intertemporal comparisons. In intertemporal comparisons, the problems just reviewed are apt to have relatively modest effects on the measurement of output per unit of input in successive years. But in international comparisons wide differences from one country to another in the quality of inputs, in their working efficiency, and in the degree to which auxiliary inputs can be completely accounted for may have major effects. It is much more tempting in international comparisons, therefore, to consider the possibility of moving closer to outcome-oriented measures of output. Some attention is given to this possibility in what follows, but, in the end, the Phase III comparisons rely mainly on market-based measures of input and output.

The prospects of success in a search for better measures of output vary from sector to sector. For health services, output-oriented measures are more readily available, and some of them are considered below. Education and government services are more difficult cases. Further research in comparative education might eventually make it possible to produce an alternative output measure based on improvements in achievement levels. For government, there are a number of attempts to develop output-related criteria to judge efficiency.

The Sensitivity of the Results to Methods of Treating Comparison-resistant Services

Even if output comparisons for certain services can be based only on input ratios, the way in which inputs

were used to measure outputs in Phases I and II is not the only way. Assumptions other than equal productivity, which underlies the method used in Phases I and II, could be made. As has been suggested, it seems unreasonable to expect the productivity of, say, physicians, even for physicians of equal training and experience, to be equal in two countries when in other industries output per person in one country may be ten times that of the other. It is important, therefore, to consider alternative assumptions about the productivity of inputs and to investigate how sensitive the overall output comparisons are to the alternatives.

Assessing the PPPs for Comparison-resistant Services

A method of assessing the effects of the equal-productivity assumption, originally suggested by Colin Clark (1979),[20] is to compare the PPPs produced by the equal-productivity assumption for comparison-resistant services with the PPPs for priced services (that is, those, such as barbershops and dry cleaners, for which price comparisons for outputs were made). Table 5-1, using 1970 data for the Phase II countries, shows this comparison. PPPs for the combined service sectors, for commodities, and for GDP as a whole are also presented.

The PPPs for comparison-resistant services are generally lower than the PPPs for priced services. (Compare columns 4 and 6 and note the ratios in column 8.) Furthermore, since the countries are arrayed in ascending order of real GDP per capita, it can be seen that the differences are systematically related to income.[21] For the lowest income countries the comparison-resistant PPPs are as low as a third of the PPPs for priced services; and for the highest income countries the ratio is closer to but usually still less than 1.[22]

19. U.S. Congress, Joint Economic Committee (1972), pp. 98–101. See also the reference to the increased productivity of dentists in the United States, Kravis, Kenessey, Heston, Summers (1975), p. 95. For further evidence of the importance of productivity changes in service industries, see Kendrick (1973), and for a survey of evidence in different countries see Clark (1979).

20. See also Isenman (1980) and Marris (1980).

21. The high prices for Iran's comparison-resistant services arise because the salaries of skilled government employees and of medical and educational personnel are high relative to the salaries of unskilled workers. Many priced services use unskilled labor, so the prices of such services tend to be low. The fact that Iran was using imported medical personnel from other countries may be a further reason for the relatively high cost of these services within the Iranian price structure.

22. If it were desired to take the PPPs for commodities as the standard for assessing the comparison-resistant PPPs, matters would look worse. The PPPs for priced services are below those for commodities by substantial amounts in some low-income countries. However, it seems more plausible to assume that the position of physicians, dentists, and government employees in a country's relative price structure is better approximated by other service prices that also represent goods with low degrees of tradability than by the more tradable commodities. (See Kravis, Heston, Summers, 1978b, pp. 219ff.) This point is also argued below.

Table 5-1. Comparison of PPP for Comparison-resistant Services with PPPs for Other Sectors and for GDP, 1970

Country (currency unit)	GDP (1)	Commodities (2)	All services (3)	Priced services (4)	Commodities and priced services (5)	Comparison-resistant services (6)	All services to commodities (3) ÷ (2) (7)	Comparison-resistant to priced services (6) ÷ (4) (8)	Priced services to commodities (4) ÷ (2) (9)
Kenya (shillings)	3.38	4.44	1.97	3.41	4.17	1.13	0.44	0.33	0.77
India (rupees)	2.25	3.31	0.83	1.46	3.08	0.46	0.25	0.32	0.44
Philippines (pesos)	1.95	2.83	0.82	1.18	2.47	0.50	0.29	0.43	0.42
Korea (won)	137.99	184.65	69.84	113.97	170.45	39.29	0.38	0.34	0.62
Colombia (pesos)	7.32	9.40	4.50	6.00	9.18	2.77	0.48	0.46	0.64
Malaysia (ringgit)	1.30	1.59	0.87	1.08	1.60	0.63	0.55	0.58	0.68
Iran (rials)	31.51	40.78	18.31	17.12	35.87	20.66	0.45	1.21	0.42
Hungary (forint)	15.22	20.93	7.13	9.37	17.58	4.31	0.34	0.46	0.45
Italy (lire)	458.26	544.51	326.97	358.92	514.43	273.86	0.60	0.76	0.66
Japan (yen)	241.10	296.48	154.86	193.20	263.43	105.83	0.52	0.55	0.65
U.K. (pounds)	0.30	0.34	0.24	0.28	0.33	0.19	0.72	0.69	0.82
Netherlands (guilders)	2.67	3.01	2.22	2.08	2.91	2.25	0.74	1.08	0.69
Belgium (francs)	37.99	45.27	26.92	29.35	41.90	23.14	0.59	0.79	0.65
France (francs)	4.40	4.93	3.65	3.75	4.69	3.41	0.74	0.91	0.76
Germany (DM)	2.99	3.37	2.49	2.66	3.33	2.18	0.74	0.82	0.79
U.S. (dollars)	1.00	1.00	1.00	1.00	1.00	1.00	1.00	1.00	1.00

Source: Column 1 taken from Kravis, Heston, Summers (1978a); other columns derived from data in same source.

Furthermore, the lower average PPPs for comparison-resistant services are representative of the group; the PPPs for the ten detailed categories of comparison-resistant services are rather consistently smaller than the average PPPs for priced services in the low-income countries (nine categories for India and Korea, and eight for the Philippines).[23]

A possible inference is that the very low PPPs for the comparison-resistant services in the poor countries are simply a consequence of the exaggeration of the quantities of such services in these countries. That is, the direct quantity ratios for inputs may be biased upward as indicators of output ratios, and thus the PPPs, derived from the division of the expenditure ratios by the quantity ratios, may be biased downward.[24]

The assessment of this possible bias turns on expectations about country-to-country differences in the relative prices of services and commodities—and of comparison-resistant and priced services—when the countries are arrayed from low to high according to per capita real GDP.

According to the productivity-differential model of price levels, suggested by several writers ranging from Ricardo to Balassa, commodities, owing to their more tradable character, are likely to be more nearly equal in price in different countries than services, which are less tradable.[25] With commodity prices equal or nearly equal, wages in commodity industries will depend on productivity; they will be low in low-productivity countries and high in high-productivity countries. Productivity differences depend in turn on differences in technology; they tend to be small in most service industries, where the production technologies in use are relatively similar across countries. Since wages in the service and other nontradables industries will be similar to those in the commodity-goods industries and since international differences in productivity in the service industries are smaller, country-to-country differences in prices of services will be greater than those of commodities, and they will be positively correlated with real per capita income.

This model has not been fully tested empirically, but there are two sets of empirical evidence that support its predictions about service/commodity relation-

23. See Kravis, Heston, Summers (1978a), appendix table 4-3.

24. The comparison-resistant services can be divided into those where PPPs were based strictly on salary comparisons, and those where PPPs were derived from quantity ratios. The former, which are the four government-employee categories, have higher PPPs than the other comparison-resistant services, but otherwise display the same pattern as the other categories.

25. See Kravis, Heston, Summers (1978b), pp. 219–20, for a fuller exposition of the model and for references. Note that both the commodities and the services referred to in this context are final products.

ships, one found in ICP results and the other in external data.

The ICP evidence consists of the relationship of the priced-services PPPs, which are not controversial, to commodity PPPs. Although the ratios of the priced service to the commodity PPPs, shown in column 9 of Table 5-1, cannot be said to be monotonically related to per capita income, they are in general lower for the low-income countries than for the high-income countries. The relationships can be further examined after conversion of the PPPs to price indexes based on the United States as 100. (The price indexes are obtained from the PPPs by dividing them by each country's exchange rate with the U.S. dollar.)The simple relationships between the price indexes of commodities (P_C) and of priced services (P_P) with real per capita GDP (r), again taking the United States as 100,[26] are:

$$(5.1) \quad \ln P_C = \begin{array}{cc} 3.3172 & + \quad 0.2662 \ln r \\ (0.1281) & (0.0359) \end{array}$$
$$\bar{R}^2 = 0.78 \quad \text{SEE} = 0.129 \quad n = 16$$

$$(5.2) \quad \ln P_P = \begin{array}{cc} 2.3510 & + \quad 0.4139 \ln r \\ (0.3209) & (0.0899) \end{array}$$
$$\bar{R}^2 = 0.57 \quad \text{SEE} = 0.322 \quad n = 16$$

$$(5.3) \quad \ln P_P/P_C = \begin{array}{cc} -0.9662 & + \quad 0.1477 \ln r \\ (0.2274) & (0.0637) \end{array}$$
$$\bar{R}^2 = 0.23 \quad \text{SEE} = 0.125 \quad n = 16$$

Priced-service prices rise relative to commodity prices, without overtaking them, as per capita income increases. Also, the range of variation of price levels is smaller for commodities than for priced services.[27]

The external evidence can be found in Kuznets-type sectoral productivity ratios,[28] indicating that productivity in the service industries relative to productivity in commodity industries tends to be substantially higher in low-income than in high-income countries. Chenery and Syrquin (1975) and Chenery (1979) have offered a "stylized" presentation of the relationships, based on 101 countries and covering the period 1950–70. It shows that productivity per person is more than twice as high in the service industries as in the commodity industries in the range of incomes of the first six countries in Table 5-1. As income per capita rises and reaches the range in which Italy and Japan are found, service-industry productivity is little higher than commodity

productivity.[29] All other things being equal, one therefore would expect that in the low-income countries the PPPs for services would be less than half—actually 45 percent—of those for commodities. This compares with an actual average of 40 percent (for the first six entries in column 7). However, this seemingly remarkable verification of the ICP PPPs is marred by the fact that the Chenery and Syrquin "services" refer to all service-producing industries rather than the end-use or final-product services to which the PPPs refer. There is considerable overlap, but there are also substantial differences.

However, the crucial question relates to the expected PPPs for the comparison-resistant services (P_X) relative to those of the priced services (P_P) and commodities (P_C). The productivity model does not address this question directly, but suggests that the evidence should be sought in the tradability and productivity of comparison-resistant services relative to those of commodities and priced services.[30] On tradability grounds, it has been suggested, there is ample reason to expect lower PPPs for services in poor countries relative to their PPPs for commodities. Since both priced and comparison-resistant services share this characteristic, both should have relatively low PPPs in poor countries. Tradability considerations provide little basis for arguing that the PPPs for the comparison-resistant services should be lower than those for priced services.

Relative productivity in priced and comparison-resistant services can be approached only in a still less

29. Chenery and Syrquin do not offer data for countries with incomes beyond this range since the focus of their work is on the less developed countries. See Kravis, Heston, Summers (1982) for confirmation of this behavior of sectoral productivity indexes based on more recent data and also on earlier work by Kuznets.

30. In addition to tradability and productivity, account must be taken of market structure. Most of the priced services are sold in markets that include the same gamut of large- and small-scale enterprises as is found in commodity markets. While government intervention in markets is hardly unknown both for commodities (for example, agricultural products) and for priced services (for example, transportation), the effect of government policies on prices and quantities is probably greater on average in health care, education, and government employment than in either of the former sectors. An important consequence is that while priced services and commodities are generally sold at prices that include full cost or at least a substantial part of costs, comparison-resistant services are often available at zero cost to the final consumer.

Again, this is an uninvestigated issue, but it is surmised here that the extent and direction of the relatively greater effect of government on comparison-resistant services is not systematically related to per capita income levels. However, a study of twelve areas in seven countries led to the conclusion that health services tended to be more structured when per capita health expenditures were low. Even so, the effect on PPPs would not be predictable. Kohn and White (1976), p. 392.

26. Standard errors are in parentheses.

27. For a real per capita GDP level of 90 percent of that of the United States ($r = 90$), service prices are 3.3 times service prices; at a GDP level of 5 percent of the United States ($r = 5$), the corresponding multiplier for commodity prices is 2.2.

28. Sectoral share in output divided by sectoral share in employment.

satisfactory way. Relatively high productivity in poor countries in education and government would not be surprising, if it is true generally, as some evidence indicates for manufacturing,[31] that the size of international productivity differences is inversely correlated with the dispersion of technology. Relative to the production of commodities and many priced services, the technology used in education and government must be very similar in different countries, although that cannot be claimed for health care. On productivity grounds, the probable inference is that the PPPs for comparison-resistant services should be lower than the PPPs for priced services in the poor countries.[32]

It is, of course, possible that the higher productivity of personnel in comparison-resistant services may be offset by higher incomes. In that case the "true" PPPs in comparison-resistant services would be no lower than the PPPs in priced services. There is, indeed, reason to believe that relative incomes may be higher in low-income countries for producers of comparison-resistant services. Although each of the two sets of services (priced and comparison-resistant) contains industries that differ from one another in the education and skill of their personnel, it seems likely that comparison-resistant services involve a higher mix of professional personnel, while the priced services require a higher mix of white-collar and artisan personnel.

The literature on income distribution makes it clear that the differentials between skilled and unskilled, between white-collar and manual, and between professional and other employees are subject to many complex market and institutional factors.[33] Subject to some exceptions, the general trend in these differentials within countries has been downward in an inverse association with rising real per capita incomes. Less information is available about international differences in these differentials, but what analyses have

been made suggest that the differentials are higher in low-income countries.[34]

Thus there are reasons to believe that both productivity and earnings are higher in comparison-resistant services than in priced services in poor countries. Is there any reason to believe that productivity will be larger by a greater margin than earnings? In that case the presumption of lower "true" PPPs for comparison-resistant services may be accepted. The answer is yes: it has been found that the ratio of productivity in one country to another, industry by industry, is likely to deviate from the ratio of the national averages more than will the corresponding wage ratios.[35]

The inference is that the difference between the PPPs for comparison-resistant and priced services are in the right direction, though this does not necessarily carry with it support for a graduation from low- to high-income countries in the ratio of P_X to P_P as steep as is produced by the equal-productivity assumption (see column 8, Table 5-1).

In summary, tradability and productivity considerations point to PPPs for comparison-resistant services closer to those for priced services than to those for commodities. Further, there are grounds for thinking that the P_X's for poor countries should be lower than the P_P's, but there is no basis for determining whether they should or should not be as much lower as the equal-productivity assumption indicates.

The Sensitivity of GDP Results

If the PPPs for priced services are therefore taken as representing the upward boundary of the possible error introduced by the equal-productivity assumption, it is possible to estimate the maximum effect of the assumption on the Phase II estimates of real GDP per capita. The results of a recalculation of the 1970 real per capita GDPs of the Phase II countries, incorporating the assumption that the PPPs for comparison-resistant services are the same as those for priced ser-

---

31. Kravis (1976), pp. 35ff.

32. Of course, lower PPPs for comparison-resistant services might conceivably be due also to the use of more capital or to cheaper intermediate inputs, but poor countries are unlikely to be heavy users of capital in service industries, and intermediate inputs are important only in a few of the final-product services considered here.

33. For example, higher salaries in comparison-resistant services relative to those of priced services might characterize poorer countries, owing to the heritage of a colonial past or to international social pressures that lead to more comparable salaries for professionals than for others. In these cases the differentials would be attributable to nonmarket forces. To accept this nonmarket hypothesis, it would have to be assumed that institutionally determined wage patterns are generally more prevalent among poor than among rich countries.

34. See Phelps-Brown (1977), chap. 3. There is also a scrap of evidence in the ICP data set that seems to indicate relatively higher incomes in comparison-resistant services in poor countries. This is the fact that the ratio of compensation of government-employed professionals to the compensation of government-employed skilled workers declines with country income. The 1970 ratios are 2.4, 2.8, 1.7, 1.7, and 1.4 for five sets of countries grouped by rising per capita income level. (Kravis, Heston, Summers, 1978a, pp. 150–52, lines 150 and 152. For the grouping of the countries, see ibid., p. 116). The comparison is relevant because the personnel in most of the comparison-resistant categories are largely white collar and educated while the personnel in the priced services tend to be more artisan.

35. Kravis (1956).

vices, are shown in column 3 of Table 5-2. Alternative recalculations based on the less plausible assumptions that the PPPs for comparison-resistant services are equal to commodity PPPs and to the PPPs for commodities plus priced services are also given (columns 3 and 4).[36] The size of the difference between recalculated GDP and the original GDP estimates (column 2) depends on both the size of the differences between the two sets of PPPs and the share of comparison-resistant services in real GDP per capita as measured by Phase II methods. The largest effect is for Kenya, with comparison-resistant services accounting for 24 percent of 1970 real GDP (see column 1) and the average PPP for comparison-resistant services only one-third of that for priced services. The substitution of the PPPs for priced services triples the PPPs for the comparison-resistant sectors and thus reduces their measured output to one-third of what constituted 24 percent of real per capita GDP. This reduces the overall estimates of real per capita GDP by 16 percent, from 6.33 percent of the United States as reported in Phase II to 5.31. The effects for all the countries are shown in columns 3 and 7. For high-income countries like France and Germany, which spend about 10 percent on comparison-resistant services, the reduction in overall GDP per capita comes to only 1 or 2 percent (since for such countries there is only a 10 or 20 percent difference in the PPPs for priced and problem services). A similar point applies to the middle-income countries such as Hungary and Italy.

The comparison-resistant service PPPs used in these calculations are, as has been noted, probably too high. The comparison-resistant service PPPs based on the equal-productivity assumption may be too low. Is there a way to estimate comparison-resistant service PPPs that are closer to the true ones? A recent suggestion by Colin Clark, made in correspondence with the authors, is worth investigating.

If the PPP for priced services (PPP_P) is regarded as a composite of the PPPs for commodities (PPP_C) and pure (comparison-resistant) services (PPP_X), the PPPs for comparison-resistant services can be estimated from the PPPs for commodities and priced services if the mix of commodities and comparison-resistant services

making up the priced service PPPs is known.[37] Recognizing the difficulties of ascertaining this mix, Clark made some sample calculations assuming the commodity inputs to be one-third.[38] He concluded that there was some overevaluation of the real per capita GDP of low-income countries, but in no case did it exceed 5 percent.

When Clark's method, including his assumption about the mix of commodities and comparison-resistant services, is applied to the PPPs in Table 5-1, the estimated PPPs for comparison-resistant services sometimes differ markedly from those reported in column 6, but on average they are only 3 percent higher. The results of recalculating 1970 real per capita GDPs with these PPPs are shown in columns 6 and 8 of Table 5-2. With a few exceptions, this rough application of Clark's idea yields per capita GDPs that are closer to the estimates based on the equal-productivity assumption than are the estimates that assume PPPs for comparison-resistant and priced services to be the same.

To apply this method in a more than illustrative way, it would be necessary to take account of the commodity component of priced services in each country rather than apply an across-the-board proportion to all the countries. Also, allowance probably should be made for intraindustry transactions within the priced-services sector. Thus the PPP for priced services should be regarded as a weighted average of the PPPs for commodities, priced services, and comparison-resistant services. The weights would be the relative importance of each of the three in the value of output of the priced-services sector in the given country, taking the compensation of employees as the weight for comparison-resistant services. For countries for which the necessary information can be obtained, the Clark approach, modified in this way, would provide a useful check on the PPPs obtained by other methods, preferably methods that derive the PPP directly from data for the comparison-resistant services.

Another check on the sensitivity of the GDP results to alternative assumptions was carried out by Marris (1980).[39] Marris excluded the services of doctors, den-

---

36. Replacing the PPPs for comparison-resistant services with PPPs for commodities and priced services combined is equivalent to omitting the comparison-resistant services from the calculations and taking the resulting quantity ratio for commodities and priced services as the ratio for GDP as a whole. For an exercise of this kind, see the reference to Marris's work (1980) later in this section. This method would understate the income of low-income countries, since the average PPP for the rest of the economy that would be implicitly assigned to comparison-resistant services would clearly be too high. Using the commodity PPPs would introduce a still greater bias.

37. The formula is (commodity share $\times$ PPP_C) + (comparison-resistant service share $\times$ PPP_X) = PPP_P, which can be solved for PPP_X.

38. The mix might be obtained from input-output tables, but as Clark observes, the categories used in national input-output tables seldom correspond closely to the detailed final-product categories that constitute priced services. Also, many services are sold both to final consumers and to business firms and governments as intermediate products, and the characteristics of these two sets of sales may not be the same.

39. Another possible procedure is to examine the effects of the Phase II results if some assumption about productivity other than

Table 5-2. Estimates of 1970 Real GDP per Capita on Alternative Assumptions for Comparison-resistant Services

| | | | Real GDP per capita (U.S. = 100) | | | | | |
| | | | With PPP for comparison-resistant services same as | | | | Ratios | |
Country	Share of comparison-resistant services in real GDP (1)	Productivity of inputs same for all countries (2)	Priced services (3)	Commodities (U.S. = 100) (4)	Rest of economy (5)	By Clark method (6)	3 ÷ 2 (7)	6 ÷ 2 (8)
Kenya	24.1	6.33	5.31	5.19	5.22	5.39	0.84	0.85
India	21.0	6.92	5.93	5.67	5.68	6.70	0.86	0.97
Philippines	18.6	12.0	10.7	10.2	10.2	12.9	0.89	1.07
Korea	17.9	12.1	10.7	10.4	10.4	11.0	0.88	0.91
Colombia	15.5	18.1	16.6	16.1	16.1	17.1	0.92	0.94
Malaysia	14.0	19.1	18.0	17.5	17.6	18.5	0.94	0.97
Iran	9.8	20.3	20.7	19.3	19.5	26.1	1.02	1.28
Hungary	11.7	42.7	40.0	38.7	38.9	43.7	0.94	1.02
Italy	11.8	49.2	47.8	46.3	46.5	49.3	0.97	1.00
Japan	9.8	59.2	56.6	55.5	55.7	57.7	0.96	0.98
U.K.	10.8	63.5	61.3	60.5	60.6	61.8	0.97	0.97
Netherlands	9.7	68.7	69.2	67.0	67.2	71.3	1.01	1.04
Belgium	11.7	72.0	70.2	67.9	68.2	73.0	0.98	1.01
France	9.5	73.2	72.6	71.1	71.3	73.8	0.99	1.01
Germany	9.1	78.2	76.9	75.7	75.7	77.7	0.98	0.99
U.S.	9.2	100.0	100.0	100.0	100.0	100.0	1.00	1.00

tists, nurses, and government employees and shifted the basis for comparison for the quantity of educational services (teachers) to a quantity index based on the number of pupils. The exclusion of the omitted services is equivalent to assuming that they are consumed in different countries in the same proportion to the rest of GDP in real terms. An alternative interpretation of the exclusion, discussed by Marris, is that health and government services are intermediate products. In any case, Marris found that the quantitative effect of the exclusion and of the shift to a pupil index on GDP per capita was "negligible at all levels of development."[40]

---

that of equality were made for the inputs of physicians and the like. It might be assumed, for example, that the relative productivity in the production of comparison-resistant services is the same as in the priced services. This assumption has a similar underlying rationale to the use of the PPP for priced services, but it could serve as a useful check, since it involves the use of a different body of data. Unfortunately, as was noted earlier, some of the basic data necessary to implement this approach—the number of persons engaged in producing commodities in each of the two types of services—are not available. If crude labor figures obtained from the ILO *Yearbook of Labor Statistics* are used, and if productivity in the comparison-resistant sector is set equal to that in priced services, estimated real GDP per capita is decreased by proportions ranging from 20 to 25 percent for the four lowest income countries to less than 10 percent for the four highest income countries. Not much weight can be attached to these results, however, since they are sensitive to errors in the number of workers assigned to these sectors.

40. Marris also offered an alternative calculation that differed from the main one in that it assumed that exchange-rate–converted

The upshot of these different approaches seems to be that the results for middle- and high-income countries are insensitive to differences in the treatment of comparison-resistant services. More is at stake for the low-income countries, but here also even radically different approaches often made a difference of only a few percent in the estimated real GDP per capita. However, there are exceptional cases in which some approaches produce differences of 15 percent or even more in estimated real per capita GDP for one or two low-income countries. Also, the accuracy of the education and health comparison is in itself important. Consequently, further efforts have been made in Phase III to grapple with the problem of producing comparisons that are superior to those based on the equal-productivity assumption. These attempts and the methods finally adopted for Phase III are described in the following sections.

Medical Care

Before the discussion of issues dealing directly with the medical care quantity ratios, some problems relating to expenditure data need attention.

---

teachers' salaries of different countries reflected differences in teacher productivity. The effects of these adjustments were "moderate." For example, the real per capita GDP of India was reduced from the Phase II estimate by 10 percent and that of Japan by 0.5 percent.

The Expenditure Breakdown

Experience indicates that it is difficult for countries to provide the breakdown between expenditures on nurses (ICP 5.33) and expenditures on hospitals (ICP 5.41) because expenditures on nurses in hospitals are not easily separated from those on other staff. The problem is further complicated by the lack of standardized definitions and classifications of nurses across countries. Consequently, it is often impossible to determine whether a doubtful PPP for nurses derived by dividing the direct quantity ratio into the expenditure ratio is in error because of faulty expenditures, or poor quantity data, or both. Because the PPPs seem to differ substantially, nurses and hospitals have been kept as separate categories in the Phase III calculation, even though very rough estimates of the separate expenditures had to be used for some countries.

Another expenditure area that presents problems is the services of dentists. Many countries in which dentistry is not important are not able to provide reliable data on the number of dentists. In some countries, the census category for dentists may include persons occasionally pulling teeth who report themselves as dentists, while in other countries the number of dentists may very well have been underestimated. Some of the Phase III countries have not been able to distinguish between expenditures on physicians and expenditures on dentists, even though they are able to report fairly accurately the number of practitioners in each category. The available data on prices of services of physicians and dentists indicate that the PPPs of the two categories are typically different, but not in any obvious pattern. Dentists are relatively less expensive in some low-income countries and relatively more expensive in others. The same is true for dentists in more affluent countries. Whether these differences reflect quality differences or institutional differences is not known. The existence of the differences made it seem preferable here, too, to keep the two categories separate even though the expenditure division between them had to be very roughly approximated.

The Effects of Capital Inputs

The use of input-based indicators of output gives rise to three kinds of problems in forming quantity ratios for medical care: making adequate allowance for capital inputs, determining an appropriate kind of quantity indicator for the labor inputs, and adjusting the labor inputs to take account of quality differences. In this section, data on capital stocks available for eight Phase III countries are used to assess the differences between input-based estimates of relative outputs derived from labor inputs alone and those derived from labor and capital inputs. In the former case a country's index is given by the ratio of its labor input to that of the numéraire country; in the latter it is a weighted average of labor and capital inputs relative to those of the numéraire country.

In any effort to incorporate capital, two major statistical difficulties must be resolved. First, statistics on capital stocks, especially for specific service sectors, are sparse, and those that are available may not be comparable among countries. Second, the proper incorporation of capital inputs requires a knowledge of each country's production function. The methods adopted here cope with these problems in a way that can be described only as extremely crude. However, they do provide some notion of the possible quantitative significance that might be associated with the incorporation of capital inputs.

The basic framework for experimenting with combining labor and capital inputs is a Cobb-Douglas production function: $Q_j = A L_j^\alpha K_j^\beta$ where Q is quantity, A is a constant, K the stock of capital, L the amount of labor, and the subscript j refers to a country. This ancient (for modern empirical economics) generalization seems to have survived the advent of several more sophisticated production functions, and its simplicity seems appropriate here in view of the uncertainties surrounding the data and their applicability to the countries.

The simplifying assumptions are made that A, α and β are equal for all countries and that $\alpha + \beta = 1$, the latter not an uncommon finding in empirical work. Thus, for a particular detailed category, such as the services of physicians,

$$(5.4) \qquad \left(\frac{Q_j}{Q_b}\right)_{L,K} = \left(\frac{L_j}{L_b}\right)^\alpha \left(\frac{K_j}{K_b}\right)^{1-\alpha}$$

where b refers to the numéraire country.

If a country's Q_j/Q_b is estimated on the basis of its labor input alone—that is, the ratio of its number of physicians to the numéraire country's number—$(Q_j/Q_b) = (L_j/L_b)$. The size of the difference between (L_j/L_b) and $[(L_j/L_b)^\alpha \cdot (K_j/K_b)^{1-\alpha}]$ will measure the effect on Q_j/Q_b of the inclusion of capital. The ratio of the quantity ratio based on labor only to that based on both inputs is

$$(5.5) \qquad \frac{(Q_j/Q_b)_L}{(Q_j/Q_b)_{L,K}} = \frac{(L_j/L_b)}{\left(\dfrac{L_j}{L_b}\right)^\alpha \cdot \left(\dfrac{K_j}{K_b}\right)^{1-\alpha}}$$

$$= \left(\frac{L_j/L_b}{K_j/K_b}\right)^{1-\alpha}.$$

For the purpose of this exercise, the value of α has been set at 0.85, the proportion of labor income to income from labor and capital in nine developed countries.[41]

In the raw data with which the ICP starts, the labor ratios L_j/L_b are category specific; that is, there is an L_j/L_b for each detailed service category (physicians, dentists, and the like). The ratios are formed directly from the numbers of workers in the given category in the jth and nth countries. Where necessary, as, for example, in the case of teachers, the numbers are adjusted before the formation of the ratio to allow for quality differences (see below).

The greatest data problem was posed by the capital ratios K_j/K_b. Both of the two possible sources of information, capital-consumption allowances and capital-stock estimates, are fraught with perils. Since capital-consumption allowances are derived from capital-stock estimates, the latter were selected for use here because they involve one step less exposure to possible distortion from the incomparability of methods used in the different ICP countries. Reliance on capital stock data in the present context requires the Herculean assumption that the quantities of input of the services of capital in the various countries were proportional to their capital stocks.

Data on capital stock devoted to health care in 1975 were available for eight countries, some consisting of very crude estimates. The figures were placed on a per capita basis and converted to dollars through the exchange rate. A rough correction was then made for price differences on the basis of the association shown in Phase II data for 1973 between the prices of capital goods and real GDP per capita.[42] (The estimates of real GDP per capita, necessary to apply this relationship to the eight countries, were obtained from earlier short-cut estimates.[43])

In the first attempt, no allocation of capital to the detailed category was made. In a second version, a rough allocation was made between hospital capital and other health capital, where only the latter was assumed to augment the productivity of physicians, dentists, and nurses. Since the L_j/L_b ratios were category specific, the choice was either to combine all three labor categories or to assume that the K_j/K_b ratio

was the same for each of them. A combined L_j/L_b ratio was used with the weights for physicians, dentists, and nurses based on the aggregate per capita expenditures of the thirty-four Phase III countries.[44]

Hospital bed–days were omitted from the calculation since, with professional workers fully accounted for, the main source of hospitals' contribution to output is the capital employed. This means that non-professional personnel are omitted from explicit treatment (a choice that was imposed by the unavailability of data); implicitly, their relative quantities are assumed to vary with included labor and capital.

The results are set out in Table 5-3. The first column shows the relative inputs and outputs of services of physicians, dentists, and nurses as measured by labor inputs. The second and third columns give capital, the former including hospital capital and the latter excluding it. Column 4 presents output based on labor alone, while columns 5 and 6 present output estimates where labor and capital are combined (with weights of 0.85 and 0.15); and columns 7 and 8 the ratios of these to the labor-based estimates in column 4. Since the countries are arrayed in order of ascending real GDP per capita, it can be seen that the ratios suggest that the effect of the inclusion of capital is somewhat correlated with per capita income levels. As is indicated by equation 5.5, the effect on the output ratio depends on whether a country has a larger number of doctors and other health-care workers relative to the numéraire country than it has a stock of capital employed in the health sector. One would presume that the shortfalls of capital in poor countries relative to rich ones would be greater than for personnel. However, the personnel involved here are highly skilled, and the relative investment in human and physical capital in this area often turns on government policies. It cannot be assumed therefore that the failure of the ratios to support strongly the expected positive association with real GDP per capita necessarily results from the crudeness of the data, though data defects could easily account for the outcome.[45]

How important quantitatively can the omission of capital be if the results are taken at face value? The largest change is a reduction in the health-services quantity ratio for Jamaica of 31 percent. It should be remembered, however, that there are also three detailed categories in the health sector consisting of commodities (drugs, medical supplies, and therapeutic ap-

41. Average of Denison's 1950–62 figures (the figures are similar for various subperiods that he shows). The income of capital is the income from nonresidential structures and equipment. Income from housing, land, property abroad, and inventories has been excluded for the present purpose. See Denison (1967), p. 38.

42. See Kravis, Heston, Summers (1978a), p. 120.

43. See Summers, Kravis, Heston (1980). The Phase III estimates of real GDP per capita were not available when the work on capital goods was done.

44. This is equivalent to entering each specific L_j/L_b ratio in the production function with exponents proportional to their weights, with the weights normalized to sum to 0.85.

45. Specifically, the data in Table 5-3 would give a very different impression if the Malawi entry in column 4 were much higher.

Table 5-3. Comparison of Estimates of Real 1975 Output of Health Services per Capita Based on Labor Inputs with Estimates Based on Inputs of Labor and Capital

	Relative per capita inputs			Output estimates				
		Health-care capital			Labor and capital			
							Ratios	
Country	Labor (1)	Excluding hospital (2)	Total (3)	Labor alone[a] (4)	All health capital (5)	Health excluding hospital (6)	(7) = (5) ÷ (4)	(8) = (6) ÷ (4)
Malawi	1.50	1.17	0.5	1.50	1.4	1.3	0.96	0.85
Jamaica	19.6	1.42	1.7	19.6	13.2	13.6	0.67	0.69
Yugoslavia	60.4	34.7	25.9	60.4	55.6	53.2	0.92	0.88
Romania	53.0	33.6	21.9	53.0	49.5	46.4	0.93	0.88
Hungary	100.6	51.3	38.2	100.6	90.9	87.0	0.90	0.86
Poland	73.6	22.0	15.6	73.6	58.7	55.2	0.80	0.75
U.K.	89.9	75.1	56.0	89.9	83.7	89.4	0.97	0.93
U.S.	100.0	100.0	100.0	100.0	100.0	100.0	1.00	1.00

a. $Q_j/Q_b = L_j/L_b$.

pliances) that accounted for an average of 40 percent of expenditures in health care for the sixteen Phase II countries. The downward adjustment for Jamaica's health-care relative quantity owing to the inclusion of capital would be around 19 percent ($0.31 \cdot 0.60 = 0.19$).

This calculation is based on the implicit assumption that the productivity of capital invested in health care is the same in all countries. It is very difficult to obtain any convincing empirical evidence on the relative productivity of health-care capital. It seems clear that the marginal return on capital invested in health care varies widely from country to country. A recent U.S. study, after analyzing the diffusion through American hospitals of a number of new technologies, including postoperative diagnostic radioisotopes, cobalt therapy, open-heart surgery, and renal dialysis, suggested a strong tendency toward the investment of resources in care that produced benefits that were small relative to costs.[46] The rising importance of third-party payments was seen as an important factor pushing investment toward the zero marginal benefit level for patients for whom marginal costs were zero. In the United Kingdom, by contrast, where national policy placed a closer limit on medical investment, the marginal social return was presumably higher.[47]

In comparisons across countries, it is the average output of capital that is relevant in assessing the productivity of medical-care inputs. However, the simple model used here assumes that the coefficients of capital and labor are the same everywhere, and this implies a fixed relationship between the marginal and average returns to capital. In the real world, it seems

more likely than not that differences in the average productivity of capital are smaller across countries, and the enormous international differences in the availability of health-care capital should not be ignored.

Rough as the data are in Table 5-3, including the implausible result for Malawi, they support a treatment of capital similar to that of Phase I, in which direct labor ratios were reduced relative to the United States for countries in which the capital stock per worker was much lower. The ratios for health-care output inclusive of capital inputs to output based on labor alone (column 8) are averaged for low-income (Malawi and Jamaica), middle-income (Hungary, Poland, Romania, and Yugoslavia), and high-income (United Kingdom and United States) countries; the results may be stylized as yielding divisors of 1.30, 1.15, and 1. Though admittedly a slender basis for adjustment, these results have been used to divide the direct labor quantities of nurses, physicians, and dentists by 1.15 for middle-income countries (with per capita GDPs 30 to 50 percent of that of the United States) and 1.30 for lower income countries. This treatment has been based on the data excluding hospital capital from other medical capital. A capital adjustment has also been made for hospitals, since capital per bed ratios are uniformly related to income across the ICP countries for which data are available.

Relative to the United States, the hospital-capital/bed-day ratios (not shown in the table) are about 10 percent for Jamaica and Malawi, 30 to 45 percent for the middle-income countries of Table 5-3, and 83 percent for the United Kingdom. If the Cobb-Douglas exercise underlying Table 5-3 is applied to hospital capital and bed-days instead of medical capital and personnel, again assuming a capital coefficient of 0.15, the results are similar. The ratio of output taking ac-

46. Russell (1979), p. 157. For a similar point with respect to intensive care units, see Relman (1980).

47. Russell (1979), p. 146.

count of hospital capital to that based on bed-days alone is 0.715 for Jamaica and Malawi, 0.875 for Hungary, Poland, Romania, and Yugoslavia, and 0.97 for the United Kingdom.

Thus, the final decision for Phase III ICP comparisons was to divide the direct quantity ratios for physicians, dentists, nurses, and hospital beds by 1.30 for low-income countries (those with real per capita GDPs of less than 30 percent of the United States), and by 1.15 for middle-income countries (real per capita GDPs of 30 to 50 percent of the United States).[48]

No adjustment for capital per worker has been attempted for education where the role of capital is even less clear, but for general government, an adjustment has been made. This is discussed below.

Labor Inputs as Output Indicators for Medical Services

As was indicated earlier, the ICP chose the number of doctors per capita as the output indicator in Phases I and II. (The total number of hours per capita spent in patient care by physicians would have been preferred had it been available.) Studies that have appeared since the Phase II report was prepared throw light on the use of the number of doctors for this purpose.

A major cross-national study of health care, surveying 15,000 households in six countries,[49] examined the use of physician, dentist, hospital, and other health services in relation to the health status, distance from health service, education, income, and other variables apt to affect patient demand and access to medical treatment. In general, multivariate analysis exhibited weak but expected relationships between physician use and income variables, education, perceived availability of health-care services, and age, and a strong relationship between severity of need and contacts with a physician. However, comparisons of situations with different mixes of services (for example, physicians, nurses, hospital beds) revealed a tendency for users to rely on the services that were more readily available. For example, hospital use tended to be higher where physicians were less available.

The relevant data from this study on stock of physicians and visits are given in Table 5-4 in columns 1 through 5. The data are not ideal for the purposes at hand, since they refer to communities rather than to countries and since some are medical centers in which the proportions of physicians in research, in teaching and in specialized practice are apt to be higher than in other places.[50] If the figures are taken at face value, however, there is little or no correlation between numbers of physicians and patient contacts.[51] This implies that a very different output relationship would emerge if relative outputs were based on patient contacts rather than on numbers of physicians.

The number of physicians presents a problem, too, because of the possible diversity in the degree of specialization in different countries. The total number of physicians in practice (column 2) and in general practice (column 3) are not significantly correlated. The difference in the degree of specialization between the United States and Europe has been reported as follows:[52]

	Twelve European countries	United States
Nonspecialists	133,649	77,363
Internists	62,154	76,283
Surgeons	41,127	67,166
All specialists	163,314	233,482
Percentage of specialists to total	55.0	75.1

The figures must be interpreted with caution, since specialists not infrequently provide patients with primary care. This seems to be particularly true in the United States, where it was recently reported that about a fifth of the population received continuing general medical care from a specialist.[53] In Europe there is a greater tendency for specialists to see patients only as referrals, so the number of contact points with the medical system may be less than in North America.[54] It might be possible to resolve these international incomparabilities if studies were available indicating the

---

50. This undoubtedly accounts for the dramatic difference between columns 2 and 3 for Baltimore, as compared with other centers.

51. The coefficients of determination, adjusted for degrees of freedom, are:

	Contacts of	
	All patients	Ill patients (nonchronic)
All physicians	0.05	−0.06
In practice	0.10	−0.02
In general practice	0.03	−0.07

The range of countries represented falls in the upper half of the ICP income distribution.

52. These figures are from Doan (1977), pp. 207–26, tables on pp. 212 and 216.

53. See Aiken and others (1970).

54. Kohn and White (1976), p. 394.

---

48. Real per capita GDPs for 1975 for this purpose were taken from Summers, Kravis, Heston (1980).

49. Kohn and White (1976), p. 29 and table 2-4. The survey period was June 1968 to May 1969 and coverage included twelve rural and urban places.

Table 5-4. Number of Physician and Patient Contacts

| Location [d] | Physicians per 10,000 [a] | | | Contact with physicians [b] | | Hospital comparisons [c] | | |
	Total (1)	In practice (2)	In general practice (3)	All (4)	With illness non-chronic (5)	Beds per 10,000 (6)	Stays per 1,000 in 1 year (7)	Length stay in days (8)
Canada								
Grand-Prairie (R)	6.9	6.5	6.1	127	340	120	156	10.9
Saskatchewan (U)	16.0	9.9	5.9	152	308	102	125	11.9
Fraser (U)	11.6	11.4	10.1	146	345	97	139	11.6
Jersey (U)	9.1	8.9	7.9	150	377	144	150	10.5
United States								
Northwest Vermont (U&R)	27.7	9.6	1.4	157	383	92	142	7.9
Baltimore (U)	21.6	11.7	2.3	204	444	138	99	11.9
South America								
Buenos Aires (U)	21.6	19.7	4.5	198	458	46	65	10.9
United Kingdom								
Liverpool (U)	10.9	7.6	4.1	183	444	125	79	14.8
Denmark								
Helsinki (U)	18.1	12.2	4.2	123	225	119	114	13.6
Poland								
Lodz (U&R)	16.1	10.1	2.0	157	314	73	101	23.6
Yugoslavia								
Barnat (U&R)	10.1	7.3	4.4	166	341	56	86	17.5
Rijeka (U)	15.1	9.9	4.1	140	374	80	95	15.4
Median	15.1	9.9	4.3	155	360	100	108	11.9

a. Columns 1, 2, and 3 from Kohn and White (1976), tables 6-5A, B, and C, p. 109.

b. Column 4 gives crude rates per 1,000 of physician contact of sample persons within a two-week period from Kohn and White (1976), table 7-2D, p. 145; and column 5 for persons with illness, not chronic, table 7-16.6, p. 160.

c. Column 6 from Kohn and White (1976), table 6.11, p. 123; column 7 from table 8.1D, p. 201; and column 8 from table 8.4A, p. 205.

d. R = rural, U = Urban.

relative values of the contributions of each type of practitioner in each country.[55]

Reliance on the number of physicians, as either generalists or specialists, is further complicated by wide international differences in the tasks performed by persons holding a given occupational title. "In the United Kingdom, for instance, midwives deliver almost all babies, but anesthetics are given by anesthesiologists, who in fact outnumber general surgeons and are paid as much; whereas in other countries, obstetricians deliver babies and specially trained nurses give anesthetics."[56]

In addition, the data on the number of physicians are subject to incomparabilities arising out of the possibility that they may not be equally well matched with

55. For an effort to produce a relative scale for valuing the services of different types of U.S. practitioners based on resource cost, see Hsiao and Stason (1979). The article gives references to earlier studies in the field.

56. Kohn and White (1976), p. 121.

the expenditure data in all countries. For ICP purposes, research physicians should be excluded both from the count of the number of physicians and from the expenditure figures; although it is doubtful that the figures available uniformly reflect this rule, the resulting errors are not likely to be large. Of greater consequence, possibly, is the number of physicians and nurses who are employed by firms and institutions to provide medical care to other employees. If the rules of *A System of National Accounts* (SNA) are followed, the expenditures in running such medical dispensaries will be regarded as intermediate rather than final product and will not show up in ICP health-care expenditures. If the personnel are not counted in the ICP numbers of physicians and nurses in the given country, the indirectly derived PPP will not be distorted on this account, but the quantity of medical care rendered in the country will be understated. If the personnel are counted in the numbers but not in the expenditures, a directly computed quantity ratio would be correct, but the indirectly derived PPP would be distorted. Of course, the extent of error in the PPPs and the country-to-country quantity ratios—and, indeed, even their direction—will also depend on the treatment of the numbers and the expenditures in the numéraire country. All this assumes that the quantity comparisons in this sector are based on quantities of inputs (physicians) and that the PPPs are derived by dividing the quantity ratio into the expenditure ratio.

It is important to note here that where the expenditures are wrong or where they do not embody the prices used in a direct price comparison, the indirect quantity ratios obtained by dividing the expenditure ratios by the price ratios will also be wrong.

The Productivity of Medical Inputs

Another major disadvantage of using the number of physicians as an international indicator of the relative quantity of medical services is that it embodies the assumption that physicians are equally productive in all countries. In principle, the validity of this assumption could be tested in different ways.

QUALITY OF ENTRANTS AND THEIR TRAINING. One test would be a careful international comparison of the qualifications of beginning medical students and of the quality of medical training. This might produce a series of specifications, each pertaining to a physician with a given degree of skill, for which price comparisons could be made. (The CPD method could easily handle problems posed by the lack of complete overlapping in the specifications found in the various countries.) A procedure approximating this was in fact used for education, where skill was judged simply by the years of education of teachers. This approach, it was felt, could not be applied to health care without a great deal more information about medical education and training in the various countries.

PERFORMANCE ON COMMON EXAMINATIONS. Another way to measure productivity is through the qualifications of physicians as revealed through their performance on common examinations given in all countries. This assumes, of course, that a practitioner's skill and his productivity can be measured through examinations. Obviously, one would have to find an existing examination taken by physicians in many countries. It happens that there is such an examination, one administered every year to foreign medical-school graduates wishing to practice in the United States. This examination is considered in a later section. It is rejected for ICP use as a quality indicator because of its orientation to medical conditions in the United States and because the examinees may not constitute a representative sample of the physicians in each country.

CONTRIBUTION TO HEALTH. Still another way to evaluate the productivity of medical practitioners would rest on an effort to measure the contribution of each country's medical services to the health of the population. This would be an ambitious undertaking, requiring that proper measures of "health" be identified and that account be taken fully of the contribution of all factors to health so that the role of medical services could be accurately estimated.[57] Further, it would seem to contradict the mainstream of national-accounting practice by going beyond observable market transactions to effects on welfare.

Still, there is some evidence that health-care inputs across countries are correlated with what can be regarded as indicators of the output of health services, such as life expectancy and maternal and infant mortality.[58] A rough check indicates that such relation-

57. Experts sometimes doubt the possibility of measuring the net contribution of medical services in within-country intertemporal comparisons. The reason is that the extension of health services in modern countries has proceeded to the point where the marginal contribution of medical care to health is very small, when medical technology and the other influences on health are held constant. See Fuchs (1979). It may, however, be feasible to gauge the contribution of medical services when cross-country data are analyzed.

58. In one study the simple correlation between life expectancy and number of physicians across sixty-eight countries was reported as 0.88; that between life expectancy and hospital beds per capita was 0.79. The coefficients of determination, adjusted for degree of freedom, come to 0.77 and 0.62, respectively (Gilliand and Galland, 1977, pp. 227–42).

Income per capita produced a simple correlation coefficient with life expectancy of 0.71, less than was produced by either medical input. However, only the difference between 0.88 and 0.71 is significant at the 5 percent level. Gilliand and Galland computed the correlations separately for countries in three different per capita income classes:

	All countries			Below $250		
	Income	Beds	Life expectancy	Income	Beds	Life expectancy
Physicians	0.82	0.82	0.88	0.64	0.46	0.84
Income		0.81	0.71		0.46	0.62
Beds			0.79			0.61
	$250–$1,000			Above $1,000		
Physicians	0.90	0.47	0.79	−0.01	0.08	0.48
Income		0.47	0.44		0.05	0.23
Beds			0.37			0.27

The implication is that gross differences in medical facilities between developed and developing countries produce most of the correlations across countries, and that differences between more homogeneous groups of countries are more complex. Further confirmation is found in Morris (1979), pp. 54–56. He reports that a complete index of life quality involving literacy, life expectancy, and infant mortality correlates across 150 countries with GDP moderately well ($R^2 = 0.53$) but within groups of countries the correlation is much lower (from 1 to 16 percent). Nevertheless, in each

ships are found also among the thirty-four ICP countries. When income per capita is taken as a surrogate for the variables other than medical care that influence health, such as nutrition and adequate housing, the simple correlation coefficient of life expectancy with real per capita GDP is 0.78, with the per capita number of physicians is 0.82, and with the number of hospital beds is 0.77. When all three variables are used to explain life expectancy, the coefficients of the numbers of physicians and beds contribute statistically more to the explanation of cross-country variations in life expectancy than income does.

$$(5.6) \quad \ln LE = \begin{array}{cc} 4.1078 & + \quad 0.0825 \ln MD \\ (0.1833) & (0.0272) \end{array}$$
$$\begin{array}{cc} + \quad 0.0336 \ln BEDS + 0.0396 \ln r \\ (0.0264) \qquad (0.0451) \end{array}$$

$$\overline{R}^2 = 0.76 \quad \text{SEE} = 0.0827 \quad n = 34$$

where LE is life expectancy, MD the number of physicians, $BEDS$ the number of hospital beds per capita, and r real GDP per capita (all 1975 or close to it). However, fairly strong multicollinearity among the independent variables (correlation coefficients in the 0.70s) makes the standard errors of the coefficients large and consequently makes the confidence intervals of the coefficients very wide. Nevertheless, in similar exercises involving maternal and infant mortality, the coefficients of the medical inputs also show up statistically more significant than the coefficient of income.[59]

Even if the objections arising from the standpoint of traditional national-income accounting could be set aside, the possibilities for the conversion of these associations into measures of medical output seem small. It would require a much better understanding of the interplay of the variables involved, far beyond what can be obtained from the present state of knowledge.

At the same time, recent work on international comparisons of medical care offers little reassurance about the use of the number of physicians and other medical inputs as output indicators. However, there is some consolation in the tendency toward substitutability between physicians and other medical inputs found in some of the work, since this suggests that comparisons for health-care services as a whole (that is, the summary category medical care) based on the entire range of inputs may be less subject to error than input-based comparisons for individual types of services.

COMPARISON OF DIRECT AND INDIRECT PPPS. A much simpler way to deal with the productivity problem is to abandon the use of inputs as output indicators and rely instead on direct price comparisons for specified medical services. As will be described in the next section, this was attempted in Phase III with reasonable success for more than half the countries. However, the direct PPP or price comparison results could not be used across the board because they could not be satisfactorily carried out for some countries, while for others rather implausible quantity ratios were obtained when the direct price ratios were divided into the expenditure ratios. The reasons for the untoward quantity results will be discussed later; for now it can be said that one factor is the possibility that the prices embodied in the national-accounts expenditures are not even approximately the same as those used in the price comparisons.

Thus a dilemma was posed. Direct quantity comparisons based on personnel inputs are biased because of productivity differences for which no satisfactory means of correction has thus far been suggested. The alternative of direct price comparisons is available in a satisfactory way only for some countries.

The ICP resolves this dilemma by using the input indicators of output, but applying a productivity correction based on the relationship between the direct and the indirect price comparisons (the latter derived from the input indicators) for the countries for which both types of comparisons are available. The reasons for reading a productivity dimension into this rela-

---

59. The equation for maternal mortality (MM) is:

$$(5.6') \quad MM = \begin{array}{cccc} 189.7 - & 86.45\,MD - & 33.69\,BEDS - & 0.7005\,r. \\ (15.8) & (31.7) & (19.9) & (0.423) \end{array}$$

$$\overline{R}^2 = 0.78 \quad \text{SEE} = 30.48 \quad \overline{MM} = 55.76 \quad n = 24$$

A log-log regression with the same variables yielded an $\overline{R}^2$ of 0.68 and negative signs for the coefficients of the three independent variables, but only the coefficient of r was larger than its standard error.

A similar equation for infant mortality (in the logs) yielded a positive coefficient for the number of physicians with a t-ratio of 1.8 ($\overline{R}^2 = 0.51$). Hospital beds and r both had negative coefficients with t-ratios of 2.7 and 1.7, respectively. When the physician variable was dropped, beds and r remained negative, with t-ratios of 2.1 and 0.7 respectively ($\overline{R}^2 = 0.46$). Beds as the sole independent variable had a negative coefficient with a t-ratio of 4.8 ($\overline{R}^2 = 0.47$).

There is a strong negative relation between the level of education of the mother or parents and infant mortality for most of the seventeen developing countries analyzed. (See Cochrane, O'Hara, Leslie, 1980.) This report also reviews a number of the relationships discussed in the text above. While this contribution of education to health status is noted, there seems no satisfactory way to value this type of output of the educational system.

---

of the above correlations matrices the higher correlation of life expectancy with physicians persists though the same cannot be said of hospital beds.

tionship are given below. First, though, a discussion of the direct PPPs or price comparisons is in order.

Directly Priced Medical Services

As a result of a more extensive effort to price medical services in Phase III, significantly more countries provided prices for a wide range of medical services, including consultations, tests, operations, and hospitalization.[60] Direct price comparisons for physicians' services (PPPs divided by the exchange rate), based on a CPD calculation incorporating these kinds of prices, are set out in column 1 of Table 5-5, in which the countries are arrayed in order of rising real per capita GDP. Column 2 presents the indirect quantity ratio obtained by dividing the price indexes into the expenditure ratios. The latter can be compared with the direct quantity ratios in column 3, which are based on the relative number of physicians providing health care, without any adjustment for international variations in the amount of capital with which physicians work or in the productivity of the inputs.

The results of modifying these quantity ratios to take capital inputs into account, through use of the adjustment ratios described in an earlier section, are given in column 4. Column 6 divides the quantity ratios based on inputs of labor and capital into the expenditure ratios to derive indirect price comparisons. These price comparisons vary widely relative to the direct price comparisons, as the ratios in column 7 clearly indicate. In virtually all the low- and middle-income countries, however, the equal productivity assumption underlying

the indirect price comparisons produces lower price indexes than those obtained from direct price comparisons. To this extent, the data seem to support the view that the low PPPs for comparison-resistant services as a whole reported in Phase II (see column 6, Table 5-1) are lower than warranted.

In determining whether this is the case, one must weigh errors in both kinds of price comparisons. The sources of error in the equal-productivity–based price indexes have already been discussed. The price indexes based on direct price comparisons are also subject to errors.

First, it is difficult to be sure that the quality of a given service being price-compared—for example, a tonsillectomy—is the same in different countries. Second, it is not certain that auxiliary services, such as intensive-care units and pathology, are priced in the same way in different countries. Some of these support services may enter into the prices of tonsillectomies and other operations as overhead cost in some countries and be charged separately in others.

Third, a country may not be able to provide the full price or even an estimate of the cost for a specific service where most of the costs of medical care are borne by the state and the practice of medicine is largely socialized.[61] Even when private health services are available side by side with publicly supported services, the prices of private services are likely to be higher than average, in part because the purchasers usually have relatively high incomes.

Finally, the wide differences between urban and rural prices of private medical practices make it difficult to estimate the average national price. It is possible that the national average prices provided by some countries, in which the private medical sector is predominantly urban, may not take sufficient account of the tendency for rural prices to be lower.[62]

---

60. The number of specifications in each category and the average number priced per country were as follows:

	Number of specifications	Average number per country
Physicians	15	4.0
Dentists	5	1.9
Hospitals	8	2.3

The physicians' specifications included office visits to general practitioners and to several kinds of specialists and some surgical procedures, such as a tonsillectomy and a prostatectomy. The dentists' specifications included a filling and an extraction, both of which were reported by most countries. Hospital specifications included room charges, lab fees, X-ray charges, and operating-room fees. Room charges were assigned a weight of 70 percent; the other 30 percent was allocated to the other hospital specifications. For nurses and the like, the only specification was average income, which was available for sixteen countries. Note that the number of specifications priced per country above is an average taken over the thirty-four countries, even though only thirty-one countries provided prices for physicians' and dentists' services and only sixteen for nurses'. For reasons in the text in discussing Tables 5-5 and 5-7, usable price estimates were not available for all countries.

61. A related consideration is that under socialized medicine the estimated cost price may fail to include a return to capital, and thus may be too low when compared with the price of that service in a country with largely private medicine. To the extent this is true, it would make PPPs incorrect. However, assuming, as is likely, that the capital return is excluded also from the expenditure estimate, the derived quantity ratio, obtained by dividing the PPP into the expenditure ratio, would be correct.

62. There are no extensive data on the rural/urban price spread for medical services, but the Philippines has reported rural/urban price ratios of 0.45 for physicians' visits and 0.58 for hospital rooms. For the United States a survey shows that the ratio of surgical fees in nonmetropolitan areas to those in metropolitan areas with over 3 million people is 0.71. (Data of the Health Insurance Association of America reported in Dyckman [1978]. Simple averages of the cost index for twelve nonmetropolitan areas and for seven metropolitan areas with populations over 3 million were compared to obtain the ratio.) Data provided to the ICP on Brazilian provincial

Table 5-5. Alternative Price and Quantity Comparisons for Services of Physicians, 1975
(U.S. = 100)

Country	Direct price comparisons (1)	Indirect quantity comparison (2)	Direct quantity comparison — Labor inputs only (3)	Direct quantity comparison — Labor and capital — Unadjusted for productivity (4)	Direct quantity comparison — Labor and capital — Adjusted for productivity (5)	Indirect price comparison derived from column 4 (6)	Indirect/ direct prices (7) = (6) ÷ (1)	Final quantity comparison relative to comparison based in inputs of — Labor (8) = (5) ÷ (3)	Final quantity comparison relative to comparison based in inputs of — Labor and capital (9) = (5) ÷ (4)
Malawi	15.0	0.33	1.20	0.92[a]	0.39[c]	5.39	0.36	0.32	0.42
Kenya	81.6	2.30	3.58	2.75[a]	1.16[c]	68.1	0.84	0.32	0.42
India	5.77	3.97	18.2	14.0[a]	5.92[c]	1.63	0.28	0.32	0.42
Pakistan	8.87	4.38	15.0	11.5[a]	4.87[c]	3.37	0.38	0.32	0.42
Sri Lanka	13.7	7.00	13.6	10.5[a]	4.42[c]	9.13	0.67	0.32	0.42
Zambia	37.6	3.16	7.22	5.55[a]	2.34[c]	21.4	0.57	0.32	0.42
Thailand	12.0	7.83	6.96	5.35[a]	2.26[c]	17.5	1.46	0.32	0.42
Philippines	27.6	3.82	51.3	39.5[a]	16.7[c]	2.67	0.10	0.32	0.42
Korea	13.8	16.8	32.4	24.9[a]	16.2[d]	9.33	0.67	0.50	0.65
Malaysia	20.8	18.3	13.2	10.1[a]	6.57[d]	37.7	1.81	0.50	0.65
Colombia	45.4	8.83	26.2	20.1[a]	13.1[d]	19.9	0.44	0.50	0.65
Jamaica	37.4	21.7	16.3	12.5[a]	8.12[d]	64.8	1.73	0.50	0.65
Syria	28.3	3.80	19.0	14.6[a]	9.50[d]	7.36	0.26	0.50	0.65
Brazil	135.7	3.89	34.1	26.2[a]	17.0[d]	20.1	0.15	0.50	0.65
Romania	121.3	6.11	76.8	66.8[b]	53.9[e]	11.1	0.09	0.70	0.81
Mexico	83.9	9.31	32.9	28.3[b]	23.1[e]	27.3	0.33	0.70	0.81
Yugoslavia	21.5	11.3	76.1	66.2[b]	53.4[e]	3.67	0.17	0.70	0.81
Iran	65.6	7.77	25.7	22.4[b]	18.0[e]	22.8	0.35	0.70	0.81
Uruguay	82.1	16.8	67.9	59.1[b]	47.6[e]	22.5	0.27	0.70	0.81
Ireland	38.5	36.3	69.2	60.2[b]	48.5[e]	23.2	0.60	0.70	0.81
Hungary	—	—	118.7	103.2[b]	98.3[f]	5.68	0.00	0.83	0.95
Poland	42.0	10.4	83.2	72.4[b]	68.9[f]	6.00	0.14	0.83	0.95
Italy	48.3	52.1	96.5	83.9[b]	79.9[f]	30.0	0.62	0.83	0.95
Spain	72.0	44.5	87.0	75.6[b]	72.0[f]	42.4	0.59	0.83	0.95
U.K.	—	—	78.7	78.7	78.7	17.0	0.00	1.00	1.00
Japan	18.0	263.8	69.2	69.2	69.2	68.6	3.81	1.00	1.00
Austria	44.3	126.4	109.4	109.4	109.4	51.2	1.16	1.00	1.00
Netherlands	64.6	112.1	93.1	93.1	93.1	77.8	1.20	1.00	1.00
Belgium	50.4	129.5	97.5	97.5	97.5	66.9	1.33	1.00	1.00
France	77.8	88.0	86.1	86.1	86.0	79.5	1.02	1.00	1.00
Luxembourg	56.4	69.4	60.2	60.2	60.2	65.0	1.15	1.00	1.00
Denmark	—	—	108.2	108.2	108.2	19.9	0.00	1.00	1.00
Germany	55.9	158.0	111.9	111.9	111.9	78.9	1.41	1.00	1.00
U.S.	100.0	100.0	100.0	100.0	100.0	100.0	1.00	1.00	1.00

a. Column 3 ÷ 1.30.
b. Column 3 ÷ 1.15.
c. Column 4 ÷ 2.37.
d. Column 4 ÷ 1.54.
e. Column 4 ÷ 1.24.
f. Column 4 ÷ 1.05.

capitals displayed a range of doctor-visit fees from 120 cruzeiros in Recife and Porto Alegre to 200 cruzeiros in São Paulo, Brasília, and Salvador in 1975. These examples suggest that the Philippine differential of about 100 percent between rural and urban areas is not an unreasonable indicator of the differences that may prevail in other developing countries. They also provide insight to the possible size of the errors when it has not been possible for a country to supply a true national average.

The prices for medical services available to the ICP were subject to these drawbacks to varying degrees for different countries. For some of the countries for which no direct price indexes are reported in column 1, these problems seemed too great to permit the use of the prices. Other omissions were due to the lack of prices altogether.

The price indexes presented in column 1 have no obvious deficiencies, and they have the attractive property of coming closer to referring to the same quality of physicians' services than do simple comparisons of the number of physicians.

However, the price comparisons seem usable for only twenty-four of the thirty-one countries that provided them. Even correct PPPs will not necessarily produce correct indirect quantity comparisons. Direct price comparisons will produce correct indirect quantity comparisons only if the expenditures embody both the correct quantities and, at least on average, the prices used in the price comparison. (These conditions are simply a consequence of the identity *price* × *quantity* = *expenditure*.) Sometimes it seems rather clear that these conditions are not met, though it is usually difficult to identify the source of the error. For example, the direct price comparison for physicians in Iran yields an index of 0.656 with the United States as 1. When this is divided into the Iran/U.S. expenditure ratio, 0.051,[63] the indirect quantity comparison comes to 7.8 percent of the United States. The direct quantity comparison based on the number of physicians in each country before any adjustment for capital puts Iran at 25.7 percent of the United States. The direct quantity comparison seems more plausible than the indirect one, even though the direct price comparison used to derive the latter is also plausible. In these circumstances, since the quantity-comparison objective of the ICP dominates its price-comparison objective, the ICP has accepted the plausible quantity comparison and the indirect price comparison associated with it.

An alternative procedure might have been to accept both the direct price index and the direct quantity index. Since their product would exceed the expenditure ratio, the convenience of having the product of the price and quantity ratios produced by the ICP equal the expenditure ratio either would have to be abandoned or the ICP would have had to make adjustments in the national accounts of one or both countries. The latter course would open a Pandora's box, and the inaccuracy introduced into the price comparisons by the former course, though not always small for the detailed categories at issue, is not consequential for GDP as a whole.

The combination of missing or unsatisfactory direct price comparisons for about a third of the countries and of suspect indirect quantity comparisons for some of the others makes it difficult to rely on the direct price comparisons. Yet the alternative of relying on the direct quantity comparisons based on inputs without quality correction is unattractive. The way out is to use the direct quantity comparisons as the starting point, but then to make a rough productivity adjustment on the basis of the observed relationship between direct and indirect price comparisons.

A Productivity Adjustment for the Direct Quantity Ratios

It has already been suggested that the differences between the direct and the indirect price comparisons may be related to their different treatment of the productivity problem. When prices are compared for specific services rendered by physicians, as in column 1 of Table 5-5, the results—with all their imperfections—are more likely to refer to equivalent outputs than price comparisons derived simply by dividing the ratio of the number of practitioner-days (or the ratio of the number of physicians) into the corresponding expenditure ratio. The regression equation linking the two sets of price-level estimates for physicians is as follows:

$$(5.7) \quad \ln P_D = \begin{array}{cc} -0.4430 & + 0.4810 \ln P_{QA} \\ (0.1643) & (0.0873) \end{array}$$

$$\overline{R}^2 = 0.56 \quad \text{SEE} = 0.502 \quad n = 24$$

where P_D is the direct price comparison for outputs, and P_{QA} is the indirect price comparison based on the inputs of labor and capital.[64]

If the difference between the two measures of comparative price levels is attributable to the fact that one relates to prices for comparable services while the other to prices for inputs that are not comparable, the addition of a productivity measure for the inputs should help explain the difference.

The difficulty is to find a measure of productivity. An approach explored here is to assume that productivity is directly related to the quality of physicians in different countries. The quality of physicians is in turn

---

63. That is, 0.519 rials in Iran divided by the exchange rate (67.639 rials per U.S. dollar) relative to $150.10 for the United States.

64. The equation with the indirect price comparison based on labor inputs alone is as follows:

$$(5.7') \quad \ln P_D = -0.4207 + 0.4490 \ln P_Q.$$
$$(0.1653) \quad (0.0802)$$

$$\overline{R}^2 = 0.57 \quad \text{SEE} = 0.497 \quad n = 24$$

Equation 5-7 produces higher direct price levels than indirect ones when the indirect estimate of the price level is below 0.43 of the U.S. level, and lower direct price levels when the indirect estimate is above 0.43. For equation 5.7' the dividing point is 0.47, where P_Q is the indirect price level derived from a direct comparison of labor inputs.

examined on the basis of the results of an examination taken by graduates of foreign medical schools wishing to practice in the United States. In 1975, the examination was taken by over 36,000 applicants from 92 countries and 721 medical schools.[65]

Table 5-6 gives the number and success rate of examinees for the Phase III ICP countries except for Luxembourg and Malawi, which do not have medical schools and thus have no examinees attributed to them.[66]

When this measure of physician quality is added to the variables in equation 5.7 the results are:

$$(5.8) \quad \ln P_D = -0.7974 + 0.5877 \ln P_{QA}$$
$$(0.2135) \quad (0.0984)$$
$$- 0.5981 \ln MT$$
$$(0.2428)$$
$$\bar{R}^2 = 0.63 \quad \text{SEE} = 0.477 \quad n = 21$$

where MT is the percent passing the examination.[67] As between two countries with the same P_{QA}, the one with better trained physicians can be expected to have

a lower P_D. The negative sign and statistical significance of the coefficient of MT is consistent with the hypothesis that the quality similarity across countries for priced medical services is greater than the similarity across countries for physician inputs.

The percentage passing has limitations as a measure of the quality of a country's physicians or of physicians' services. The language of the examination, English, is the language of instruction in only a few of the countries.[68] The sample taking the examination may not represent the population of physicians in the country, although there is no obvious reason to suppose that on average persons of higher or lower ability or learning will take the exams. More important is the possibility that the examination stresses aspects of medical preparation that reflect U.S. practices and needs while medical curriculums in other countries may stress different aspects of medicine to varying degrees; the percentage passing in this case would simply be an indicator of the similarity of other medical curriculums to that of the United States.

Since the use of this exam is discarded on these grounds, it is worth considering real GDP per capita (r) as a possible alternative proxy for quality or more directly as an indicator of physician productivity. This has the advantage of providing a potential productivity variable that may be used not only for physicians but also for other medical-service categories and for education as well. However, it is to be expected that r will have a more complicated relationship to the direct PPPs and to the PPPs derived from the quantity comparisons for inputs.

The association between the two sets of price-level estimates and the r's is influenced both by linkage between r and the output prices, particularly of service outputs, and the connection between r and the productivity of inputs. A schematic portrayal of the relationship is found in Figure 5-1. It may be hypothesized that both the price of a medical service and the productivity of the personnel and related inputs providing medical services are likely to be higher in a high-income country than in a low-income country. The price effect of r, which influences both the direct and indirect price levels, is attributable to the tendency of the relative prices of labor-intensive goods, such as these services are in the main, to rise as real-income increases.

The other influence of r, the productivity effect, operates differentially on the two sets of price-level

65. Before World War II, it was common procedure to approve foreign-trained physicians for practice in the United States on the basis of the quality of the medical school they had attended as determined by a board of evaluation. With the rapid growth of new medical facilities and changes in old facilities, this method became unworkable, and so an objective examination by the Educational Commission for Foreign Medical Graduates (ECFMG) was instituted in 1958. Physicians with four years of training may take the exam. Under AMA guidelines, a grade of 75 makes the applicant eligible for internships in U.S. hospitals. The examination is a multiple-choice type given in English and is used in some medical schools as an internal testing device for all of their students rather than simply an exam to meet U.S. qualifications. Further, many take the exam more than once, but the distribution by country is not available, so it is not known how this affects the results. Educational Commission for Foreign Medical Graduates (1977), pp. 11–12. All of the information about ECFMG has been obtained from annual reports and annual publications called "Results of the ECFMG Examinations."

66. Two clarifications about Table 5-6: First, about 1,500 U.S. citizens (about 4 percent of the total taking the exams) who have had medical training in foreign countries take the exam each year. On average their failure rate is the same as non–U.S. citizens taking the exam, and they have been included in the totals of Table 5-6. Although these U.S. citizens have not obtained admission into a U.S. medical school of their choice, their preparation can usually be considered adequate. Second, the figures given for the United States in the table relate to the success rate on Parts I, II, and III of the National Board of Medical Examiners examinations for students in accredited medical schools in Canada and the United States. These examinations are considered comparable to the ECFMG exams.

67. The equation using P_Q, the indirect price based on the input of labor alone, is:

$$(5.8') \quad \ln P_D = -0.7607 + 0.5439 \ln P_Q - 0.5769 \ln MT.$$
$$(0.2139) \quad (0.0904) \quad (0.2398)$$
$$\bar{R}^2 = 0.63 \quad \text{SEE} = 0.475 \quad n = 21$$

68. A dummy variable for non–English-speaking countries introduced into 5.8 did not have a significant coefficient, but a variable reflecting the examinees' average level of proficiency in English might have been more successful.

Table 5-6. Performance of Medical Graduates of Different Countries in Examinations for Admission to Practice in the United States

Country	Number taking exams 1972–75 (1)	Number passing exams 1972–75 (2)	Percent passing (2) ÷ (1) × 100 (3)	Number taking exams 1972–75 as percent of 1975 physicians (4)
Austria	569	203	36	4.0
Belgium	1,674	1,093	65	10.2
Brazil	2,843	953	34	4.6
Colombia	1,730	456	26	16.3
Denmark	1,397	1,131	81	14.9
France	1,620	722	45	2.1
Germany	4,223	1,816	43	3.6
Hungary	436	117	27	1.8
India	29,060	11,198	39	19.9
Iran	5,105	1,219	24	35.4
Ireland	1,615	1,118	69	42.8
Italy	4,767	1,692	35	5.2
Jamaica	536	383	71	94.0
Japan	5,582	2,451	44	4.2
Kenya	141	103	73	18.4
Korea	5,211	3,207	62	26.6
Malaysia	484	472	98	18.0
Mexico	12,498	3,641	29	38.7
Netherlands	847	614	72	3.9
Pakistan	5,858	1,371	23	32.5
Philippines	25,458	4,864	19	68.7
Poland	1,169	252	22	2.4
Romania	620	172	28	2.2
Spain	7,201	1,466	20	13.6
Sri Lanka	360	225	62	11.4
Syria	1,922	568	30	80.1
Thailand	2,649	1,234	47	53.0
U.K.	5,565	5,145	92	7.4
U.S.	37,684	34,678	92	10.8
Uruguay	153	94	61	4.7
Yugoslavia	996	219	22	3.8
Zambia	40	30	75	6.5

estimates. Because the productivity of inputs is higher in high-income countries, the quantity ratio obtained by simply dividing the undifferentiated (for productivity) number of physicians in each given country by the number in the numéraire country will (since the numéraire country is the highest income country) exaggerate the relative quantities of the other countries, with the exaggeration being the greater the lower the income of the country. The overestimated quantity ratios, when divided into the expenditure ratios to derive the indirect price levels, will yield underestimated price levels, the underestimations being the greater the lower the income of the country. Thus when the indirect price level is taken as the dependent variable in a regression in which r is the independent variable, the productivity effect will tend to exaggerate the extent of the positive relation with r.

This productivity effect can be expected to be absent or to operate with less force when the direct price level is correlated with r. The direct price levels, estimated from the prices of outputs (a tonsillectomy, for example), also may be subject to a productivity bias in the same direction, but it can be anticipated that the bias will be smaller because similar or nearly similar qualities of services are being priced in the different countries.

These expectations are put to the test in equations 5.9 and 5.10, in which the direct and indirect price levels, P_D and P_{QA}, respectively, are regressed against real GDP per capita (r).[69]

69. The r is from a preliminary run of the Phase III data. P_{QA} is the indirect price index derived from the inputs of labor and capital. The equation for the indirect price level derived from labor inputs alone is:

$$(5.10') \quad \ln P_Q = -0.1632 + 1.2338 \ln r.$$
$$(0.2064) \quad (0.1382)$$

$$\overline{R}^2 = 0.77 \quad \text{SEE} = 0.614 \quad n = 24$$

Figure 5–1. Relation of Direct and Indirect Price-level Estimates to Real per Capita GDP

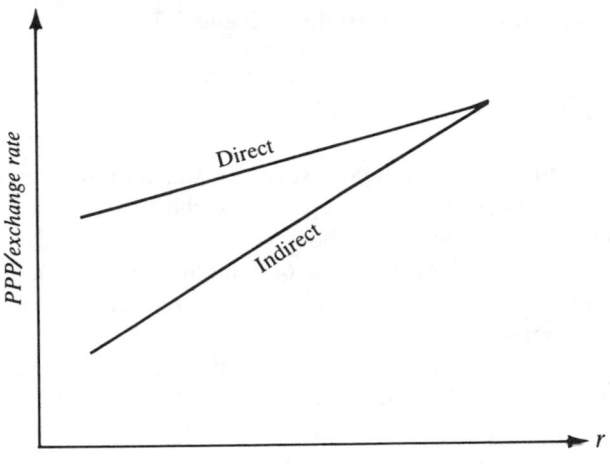

(5.9) $\ln P_D = \begin{matrix} -0.3756 \\ (0.1557) \end{matrix} + \begin{matrix} 0.6538 \ln r \\ (0.1043) \end{matrix}$

$\overline{R}^2 = 0.62$ SEE $= 0.463$ $n = 24$

(5.10) $\ln P_{QA} = \begin{matrix} -0.1466 \\ (0.207) \end{matrix} + \begin{matrix} 1.118 \ln r. \\ (0.138) \end{matrix}$

$\overline{R}^2 = 0.74$ SEE $= 0.615$ $n = 24$

The coefficient of r in 5.10 is 1.7 times the coefficient in 5.9, thus confirming the expected relationship; that is, prices rise less with income (r) for the direct-price-level estimate for which quality is more constant than for the indirect estimate based on numbers of personnel that are not differentiated for quality and productivity effects.

When r is used in lieu of MT in equation 5.8, the results are as follows:[70]

(5.11) $\ln P_D = \begin{matrix} -0.3502 \\ (0.1569) \end{matrix} + \begin{matrix} 0.1728 \ln P_{QA} \\ (0.1600) \end{matrix}$

$\qquad\qquad + \begin{matrix} 0.4607 \ln r. \\ (0.2067) \end{matrix}$

$\overline{R}^2 = 0.63$ SEE $= 0.462$ $n = 24$

If it is accepted that the difference in the relationship of P_D and P_{QA} to r reflects a more valid treatment of productivity in the P_D measure, a basis is provided for adjusting P_{QA}, the indirect price comparison, for its failure to reflect productivity differences. For this purpose it is convenient to rearrange the variables in equation 5.11 as follows:

70. The equation with P_Q as the independent variable is:

(5.11′) $\ln P_D = \begin{matrix} -0.3501 \\ (0.1581) \end{matrix} + \begin{matrix} 0.1559 \ln P_Q \\ (0.1611) \end{matrix}$

$\qquad\qquad + \begin{matrix} 0.4614 \ln r. \\ (0.2245) \end{matrix}$

$\overline{R}^2 = 0.62$ SEE $= 0.464$ $n = 24$

(5.12) $\ln (P_D / P_{QA}) = \begin{matrix} -0.2290 \\ (0.2285) \end{matrix} - \begin{matrix} 0.4637 \ln r. \\ (0.1530) \end{matrix}$

$\qquad R^2 = 0.26$ SEE $= 0.680$ $n = 24$

Equation 5.12 provides a direct estimate of the average difference between the direct and the indirect price comparisons, the former holding quality of output constant and the latter including variations in the productivity of inputs. The relationship, though clearly statistically significant, is not a tight one. It has been drawn upon in making price and quantity comparisons in Phase III in the following way:

1. For middle- and high-income countries (Groups V and VI in the classification in Chapter 6), the input-based measures of output, inclusive of capital as well as labor, have been accepted without adjustment for productivity. For countries such as Hungary and Italy, at the upper end of the middle-income scale, it is not clear that the quality of physicians and their productivity are substantially different from that found in higher income countries, but the adjustment described below is in any event small.

2. For countries in each of four income classes (Groups I, II, III, and IV) the average of r for the class was inserted in equation 5.12, and the estimated value of the dependent variable was taken as the multiplier for raising the indirect price to make the productivity correction. The average r's and resulting multipliers are:

		Average r[71]	Estimated ratio of direct to indirect PPP
Group I	(Malawi, Kenya, India, Pakistan, Sri Lanka, Zambia, Thailand, Philippines)	0.095	2.37
Group II	(Republic of Korea, Malaysia, Colombia, Jamaica, Syria, Brazil)	0.239	1.54
Group III	(Romania, Mexico, Yugoslavia, Iran, Uruguay, Ireland)	0.387	1.24
Group IV	(Hungary, Poland, Italy, Spain)	0.545	1.05

If, as in ICP practice, the identity *price ratio × quantity ratio = expenditure ratio* is maintained, a multiplier for the price comparisons can serve equally as the divisor for the quantity ratios. The ratios in the right-hand column of the preceding text table were in fact applied to the direct quantity ratios of countries in-

71. These averages were based on preliminary ICP results and differ slightly from the averages that are produced by the final estimates in Table 1-2.

dicated to make the desired productivity adjustment. For example, the ratio of the inputs of physicians and associated capital for India relative to the United States, shown as 14 in column 4 of Table 5-5, was divided by 2.37 to yield 5.92, the final (productivity-adjusted) quantity ratio given in column 5.

The basic data for the other health services—dentists (ICP 5.32), nurses (ICP 5.33), and hospitals (ICP 5.41)—are set out in Table 5-7. In columns 1–3 direct price comparisons are presented. They are based on a comparison of average earnings of nurses and on prices of various services treated through CPDs for the other two categories. The unadjusted direct quantity comparisons, based on numbers of dentists, nurses, and bed-days, are presented in the next three columns.[72] These are followed in columns 7–9 by indirect PPPs obtained by dividing the direct quantity comparisons after adjustment for capital inputs into expenditure ratios.[73]

No direct productivity measure could be found for these three categories, and *r* was again used as a proxy. Table 5-8 summarizes the relevant regressions and includes the results presented earlier for physicians in equations 5.9 and 5.10 for comparison. Dentists conform to the earlier hypothesis that the coefficient of *r* associated with the direct price level should be smaller than the coefficient of *r* when the indirect price-level estimate is the dependent variable. The failure of the nurses and hospital equations to conform may reflect errors in the expenditure breakdowns for both nurses and hospitals that have been approximated for one-third of the countries. In addition, the direct quantity comparisons are based on definitions that are not always standard for hospitals and that, for nurses, are neither standard across countries nor always consistent with the expenditure data.

In view of these data problems for the three health-care categories other than physicians, it was decided to use the same productivity adjustment factors for all three categories as for physicians. The final quantity

comparisons for dentists, nurses, and hospitals, based on productivity-adjusted inputs of labor and capital, are shown in columns 10–12 of Table 5-7.

Educational Services

In education as in health services, substantial comparative work has been reported in the professional literature. This work has been drawn on to aid in the reassessment of ICP methods of comparing the output of educational services by teachers and related professional personnel.

In Phases I and II the assumption was made that teacher inputs (and nonteacher inputs) were equally productive across countries in producing educational output. An adjustment was made to the quantities of first- and second-level teachers for differences in the level of their education. Specifically, the raw quantities were adjusted to represent the number of "standard" teachers, defined as those having sixteen or more years of education. The assumptions underlying this standardization were that the productivity of a teacher within a country was related to his or her years of education, and that internal salary differences largely reflect the magnitude of this difference in productivity.[74]

Measuring the Contribution of Educational Inputs

As in the case of health services there have been cross-country studies designed in part to assess the effectiveness with which inputs are used to achieve output goals—learning, in this case.[75]

Tests of mathematical achievement across twelve high-income countries in the 1960s revealed little relation between educational inputs and student performance.[76] Even when standardized for the percentage of students in each age cohort, these studies showed rather similar achievement levels, though those of Japan were higher than others. There appeared to be no relation of performance to inputs across the countries.[77]

However, subsequent analysis of these mathematical tests involving cross-country comparisons and of

72. The number of hospital beds was used for Brazil, India, Kenya, the Republic of Korea, Mexico, and Pakistan. The method for comparison of hospitals used by the European Communities Statistical Office in its 1975 comparisons, while based on input costs, explicitly deflated each cost component of hospitals by PPPs from other appropriate categories. This approach, which should be an improvement over simply comparing expenditures per bed or bed-day, was attempted in a crude form in Phase I of the ICP, but not enough countries provided the cost breakdown. However, the method clearly warrants further exploration.

73. The direct quantity comparisons based on labor and capital are not shown in Table 5-7, but the adjustments for the inclusion of capital are described in a previous section. The figures in columns 4–6 thus may easily be shifted to the labor and capital basis.

74. See Kravis, Kenessey, Heston, Summers (1975), pp. 101–02.

75. There have also been a large number of production-function–type studies for particular countries. For a skeptical view of these studies, particularly one questioning the validity of standardized achievement as a concept of educational output, see Levin (1976). For a review of the educational production-function literature, see Hanushek (1979). Also see Cohn (1972), chap. 8.

76. See Anderson (1969), pp. 67–83.

77. See Postlethwaite (1973), pp. 9–10.

Table 5-7. Alternative Price and Quantity Comparisons for Services of Dentists, Nurses, and Hospitals, 1975

Country	Direct price comparisons			Direct quantity comparisons based on labor inputs			Indirect price comparisons derived from quantity indexes based on inputs of labor and capital			Final quantity comparisons based on inputs of labor and capital, adjusted		
	Dentists (1)	Nurses (2)	Hospitals (3)	Dentists (4)	Nurses (5)	Hospitals (6)	Dentists (7)	Nurses (8)	Hospitals (9)	Dentists (10)	Nurses (11)	Hospitals (12)
Malawi	45.6	n.a.	3.19	0.27	3.55	35.6	11.2	20.7	5.18	0.09	1.15	11.6
Kenya	50.8	20.3	10.3	1.03	6.29	20.1	110.6	112.3	13.8	0.33	2.04	6.52
India	9.14	n.a.	3.61	2.96	7.09	11.3	1.04	15.6	2.17	0.96	2.30	3.68
Pakistan	26.1	3.91	1.92	1.97	3.33	8.12	1.56	57.2	24.2	0.64	1.08	2.63
Sri Lanka	21.9	n.a.	5.47	3.13	11.1	55.7	5.88	15.4	6.50	1.02	3.61	18.1
Zambia	90.3	n.a.	n.a.	1.22	5.76	49.4	42.7	151.9	32.1	0.40	1.87	16.0
Thailand	15.8	n.a.	9.56	3.06	10.3	19.0	70.2	30.5	4.04	0.99	3.33	6.17
Philippines	11.5	n.a.	6.15	60.9	33.3	25.7	3.88	15.6	11.8	19.8	10.8	8.34
Korea	50.9	6.30	5.60	14.5	26.6	9.54	13.2	10.9	57.1	7.22	13.3	4.76
Malaysia	25.4	n.a.	7.66	7.83	32.9	51.2	56.5	13.0	8.96	3.91	16.4	25.6
Colombia	17.8	7.61	8.50	26.2	15.5	24.5	30.3	21.8	23.6	13.1	7.74	12.2
Jamaica	76.9	n.a.	4.82	9.9	31.3	56.9	30.4	56.3	11.6	4.95	15.6	28.4
Syria	70.3	9.65	10.8	20.5	4.52	12.0	11.2	15.0	39.1	10.2	2.26	6.0
Brazil	84.9	n.a.	22.0	4.61	19.0	58.0	431.8	15.2	19.1	2.30	9.47	29.0
Romania	27.9	15.0	31.3	56.0	34.2	126.5	9.3	15.3	10.7	39.3	24.0	88.7
Mexico	58.4	n.a.	40.9	6.72	19.2	20.1	27.1	32.7	84.6	4.71	13.5	14.1
Yugoslavia	21.0	n.a.	11.0	46.9	51.3	114.2	8.22	15.5	30.2	38.9	36.0	80.1
Iran	66.5	n.a.	14.3	12.1	10.0	20.8	51.5	14.3	90.5	8.48	7.04	14.6
Uruguay	73.2	23.8	14.0	40.7	38.0	102.7	18.8	31.0	5.94	39.3	26.7	72.0
Ireland	58.3	33.2	59.6	12.4	108.6	188.3	206.3	1.96	48.4	8.68	76.2	132.0
Hungary	n.a.	n.a.	n.a.	52.6	91.5	145.1	4.83	12.7	12.0	43.6	75.8	120.1
Poland	25.5	n.a.	n.a.	80.8	62.0	111.2	4.33	31.4	19.7	66.9	51.4	92.0
Italy	179.3	33.4	124.3	45.8	40.6	165.9	32.7	34.0	43.8	37.9	33.6	137.4
Spain	62.3	n.a.	25.6	19.4	41.3	73.0	51.0	67.4	21.5	16.0	34.2	60.5
U.K.	n.a.	32.5	n.a.	55.9	125.3	141.2	32.7	0.90	43.2	55.9	125.3	141.2
Japan	49.1	n.a.	8.22	76.8	56.1	171.0	42.7	80.6	2.6	76.8	56.1	171.0
Austria	49.9	n.a.	34.5	41.5	56.2	197.6	84.1	68.8	33.0	41.5	56.2	197.6
Netherlands	78.2	81.0	n.a.	62.6	51.0	128.4	26.6	68.5	92.8	62.6	50.9	128.4
Belgium	51.3	80.7	84.3	38.3	49.0	146.1	65.2	77.6	31.4	38.3	49.0	146.1
France	97.2	77.3	84.5	94.2	106.6	134.7	33.1	67.8	54.6	94.2	106.6	134.7
Luxembourg	91.9	68.5	38.6	62.3	55.6	174.1	65.0	65.6	14.5	62.3	55.6	174.1
Denmark	n.a.	62.6	n.a.	90.0	56.0	145.8	32.0	52.9	45.0	90.0	56.0	145.8
Germany	211.0	63.7	83.8	101.1	64.9	195.7	22.3	57.1	68.6	101.1	64.9	195.7
U.S.	100.0	100.0	100.0	100.0	100.0	100.0	100.0	100.0	100.0	100.0	100.0	100.0

n.a. Not available.

Note: To calculate the indirect indexes in columns 7 through 9, the direct quantity indexes in columns 4 through 6 were adjusted by the factors noted for column 4 of Table 5-5. The quantity indexes in columns 10 through 12 were derived from those in columns 4 through 6 by applying the adjustments noted for columns 4 and 5 of Table 5-5.

tests in other subjects for groups of countries more varied in income level present a richer and somewhat more complex picture.[78] While across countries there was but limited support for the hypothesis that per capita educational inputs were associated with higher test performance, within countries it was found that student performance in mathematics was correlated with years of training of teachers when teachers were grouped according to the extent of their postsecondary education (less than three years; four years; more than four years).

78. Ibid., p. 59.

The performance of students in the four developing countries (Chile, India, Iran, and Thailand) included in the cross-country study of reading comprehension and science (the testing being carried out in local languages) was significantly lower than in developed countries. For science for ten-year-olds, the four countries averaged correct answers for fewer than eight out of forty questions, compared with sixteen for the twelve developed countries. For reading comprehension the differences in results were even more marked.

Teacher-student ratios for the four developing countries were lower, particularly in Iran, than for the developed countries. This difference taken in conjunc-

Table 5-8. Effect of Real GDP per Capita on Direct and Indirect Price Levels for Health Services

Health service	Regression coefficient for real per capita GDP (r) for [a]			Ratio of indirect to direct coefficient [b]		Coefficient of determination			Number of observations (9)
	Direct price level (1)	Indirect price level		Unadjusted for capital (4)	Adjusted for capital (5)	Direct (6)	Indirect		
		Unadjusted for capital (2)	Adjusted for capital (3)				Unadjusted for capital (7)	Adjusted for capital (8)	
1. Physicians (5.31)	0.654 (0.104)	1.234 (0.138)	1.118 (0.138)	1.78	1.59	0.625	0.774	0.736	24
2. Dentists (5.32)	0.573 (0.138)	1.444 (0.213)	1.328 (0.216)	2.39	2.13	0.415	0.662	0.615	24
3. Hospitals (5.41)	1.203 (1.156)	1.176 (0.224)	1.063 (0.228)	0.97	0.87	0.737	0.558	0.497	22
4. Nurses (5.33)	1.439 (0.103)	0.900 (0.538)	0.751 (0.534)	0.58	0.50	0.938	0.122	0.070	14

a. The dependent variables in log regressions were the direct and indirect price-level estimates. The independent variable was the level of real GDP (r) as computed in preliminary Phase III calculations. Standard errors in parentheses.

b. Exponentiated value of (column 2 − column 1) and (column 3 − column 1).

tion with lower test performance in the developing countries is consistent with the view that teachers and other inputs may make a difference in educational achievement when per capita income levels are low, but that once a certain income level is achieved there is no longer a correlation.

Further analysis indicated that the variance of student test performance within countries was related to variables gathered into several clusters: home environment, type of school, type of teaching, and attitudes of student.[79] In general these clusters explained a fairly moderate proportion of the variance between students (30 to 60 percent), but the relative importance of the clusters differed. In particular the home variables were relatively less important and the school variables (relating to inputs such as teachers and library facilities) more important in explaining variation in student performance in the developing countries than in the developed countries. In the developing countries, home variables accounted for less than one-fourth of the explained variation among students, while in the developed countries they accounted for over one-half of the explained variation. The inference is that educational inputs make a larger difference in poor countries than they do in rich ones.

Whatever the future development of work on comparative education, it seems clear that the present state of knowledge does not afford the opportunity to use comparative achievement levels in ICP output comparisons. The number of countries covered is too limited. More important, the factors that account for different achievement levels are not well enough identified.

79. Ibid., app. 7 and 8, pp. 60–61.

General Approach to Phase III Comparisons

Several alternatives remain. One is to stay with the idea of an output-oriented measure, choosing a simpler one than educational achievement—namely, the number of pupils.[80] Another is to follow the procedure of Phases I and II by relying on an input type of indicator such as the number of teachers.[81] In the latter case an adjustment might conceivably be made for the quality of teachers and for inputs of physical capital into education.

That adjustment, incorporating capital inputs, was ruled out. Capital stock figures for education were available for only three countries, and it was not possible to match even the tenuous kind of estimates made for medical-care capital. Further, the contribution of capital per teacher to educational output seems likely to be less important than in health or even in government services.

Direct-quantity indexes for first- and second-level education based on the number of teachers per capita and on the number of students per capita are shown in columns 2 and 4 of Table 5-9. The countries are arrayed in ascending order of per capita real GDP. It is easy to see that the low-income countries tend to have higher quantity indexes when pupils—and not teachers—are used as the indicator, while the opposite

80. An alternative student measure that has been recommended is grades completed. See Duncan and Moore (1968), pp. 664–70. It has not been possible to examine empirically the use of grades completed as a quantity indicator for ICP purposes, but it deserves investigation.

81. See the discussion of these alternative indicators in Kravis, Kenessey, Heston, Summers (1975), p. 102.

Table 5-9. Alternative Price and Quantity Comparisons for First- and Second-level Teachers, 1975
(U.S. = 100)

Country	Direct-price (salary) indexes for teachers (1)	Number of teachers		Number of students	Combined teachers and students	
		Direct quantity index (2)	Direct quantity adjusted for quality (3)	Direct quantity index (4)	Quantity index $\sqrt{(3) \cdot (4)}$ (5)	Indirect price index (6)
Malawi	14.4	19.8	11.1	53.7	24.4	2.3
Kenya	18.6	63.6	35.6	100.7	59.8	8.0
India	6.3	41.1	23.0	65.0	38.6	2.4
Pakistan	n.a.	28.5	15.9	43.8	36.4	2.7
Sri Lanka	9.0	64.4	36.0	80.4	53.8	3.3
Zambia	41.4	35.9	20.1	82.5	40.7	15.3
Thailand	n.a.	48.9	27.3	79.3	46.6	7.7
Philippines	5.1	70.4	39.4	101.1	63.1	4.5
Korea	81.9	50.5	38.4	109.4	64.8	7.5
Malaysia	43.3	69.4	52.7	101.8	73.3	14.9
Colombia	17.8	77.1	58.6	97.7	75.7	7.0
Jamaica	47.7	82.1	62.4	138.1	92.8	15.2
Syria	n.a.	70.1	53.3	99.0	72.6	7.6
Brazil	n.a.	98.1	74.5	87.9	80.9	7.0
Romania	n.a.	78.9	70.4	77.9	74.1	14.3
Mexico	n.a.	56.6	50.5	97.2	70.1	20.8
Yugoslavia	33.3	84.3	75.3	80.1	77.6	18.0
Iran	43.2	52.2	46.6	87.4	63.8	13.6
Uruguay	0.0	105.8	94.5	83.4	88.8	9.9
Ireland	84.5	84.8	75.7	93.9	84.3	42.4
Hungary	16.6	80.8	80.8	69.9	75.2	15.5
Poland	23.2	78.9	78.9	90.7	84.6	17.2
Italy	67.9	109.7	109.7	74.4	90.3	46.7
Spain	35.3	67.4	67.4	80.5	73.7	20.1
U.K.	79.0	93.4	93.4	84.5	88.8	60.4
Japan	92.2	69.2	69.2	75.5	72.3	60.3
Austria	91.4	92.8	92.8	83.2	87.8	43.5
Netherlands	145.4	80.9	80.9	86.8	83.8	102.4
Belgium	125.9	134.7	134.7	77.7	102.3	89.0
France	97.0	112.1	112.1	80.1	94.8	62.9
Luxembourg	163.5	90.2	90.2	67.7	78.1	106.6
Denmark	134.3	86.1	86.1	72.9	79.2	132.9
Germany	136.9	68.5	68.5	72.2	70.3	86.2
U.S.	100.0	100.0	100.0	100.0	100.0	100.0

n.a. Not available.

tends to be true for the high-income countries. The low-income countries, it is clear, tend to have larger class sizes than the high-income countries.

Which is the better measure of relative output? Is a teacher with fifty pupils twice as productive as one with twenty-five? Even if, as some studies have shown, small classes add little or nothing to educational achievement, the greater personal attention of the teacher is likely to be valued by the parent if not by the child. The value placed on smaller class size, for whatever reason, is suggested by the fact that high-income countries choose it even though teachers are

relatively more expensive in such countries (see column 1). More about this shortly.

Use of teacher inputs as the quantity indicator for educational output is more in keeping with the national-accounting practice of most countries. The teacher indicator conforms better to the notion of adhering to the criterion of a market transaction in measuring output. Neither the pupils nor, in the case of public schools, their parents, are involved in any economic transaction; for public schools, the only market transaction is the payment for the teacher's services. However, the number of pupils taught has been recommended as the preferred quantity measure for intertemporal comparisons, and a U.N. expert committee has affirmed this choice for use in interspatial comparisons.[82]

In the face of these conflicting considerations the ICP has decided to adopt a compromise in which both pupil and teacher indicators are used. In principle, the geometric mean of the quantity indexes based on pupils and on teachers is used, but first a quality adjustment is made in the teacher-based index. An alternative way to view this compromise is to regard it as a teacher-based quantity index adjusted for teacher productivity where the latter is measured by the number of pupils taught.

The method actually used is set forth below, but first the adjusted teacher-input measure is described. As with medical care, price comparisons were used as a basis for quality adjustments for teachers in low-income countries.

Direct Price (Salary) Comparisons for First- and Second-level Teachers

The method followed in Phase III classified first- and second-level teachers about whom the countries supplied salary data into five categories according to their years of education: (1) fewer than twelve years, (2) twelve and thirteen years, (3) fourteen and fifteen years, (4) sixteen years, and (5) more than sixteen years. Price comparisons were then made by applying the CPD method to these data. The results, shown in column 1 of Table 5-9, do not differ much from rough estimates of those that would have been obtained by the method used in Phase I (not shown), which converted all salaries to that of a "standard" teacher (see above, the section "The Treatment of Services in Phases I and II of the ICP"). The biggest difference, that for Iran, is attributable to the premium on highly trained personnel that existed in that country; the Iranian price level would have been much lower had the former method been employed to standardize salaries on teachers with, say, twelve years of education instead of sixteen. The CDP method is more neutral on this choice; it makes relatively direct use of all the information available for each country.

Although there are no obvious deficiencies in these direct price comparisons, there are some problems about the indirect quantity indexes that are derived from the division of the direct price indexes into the expenditure ratios. For example, the direct price index places Austrian teachers' salaries at 91.4 percent of

those of the United States, which yields an indirect quantity index of 45.2 percent (not shown in the table). Given that Austria has about 93 percent of the number of teachers that the United States has, a quantity index of 45 percent seems implausible. To the various factors that might produce such results[83] (set forth in the preceding discussion of medical services) should be added the possibly distorting influences arising from differences in the importance of part-time teachers and their treatment in the statistics of different countries.

A Productivity Adjustment for the Teacher Quantity Ratios

The relationship between the two measures of price levels for primary and secondary school teachers is:

$$(5.13) \quad \ln T_D = 1.4257 + 0.7663 \ln T_Q$$
$$(0.2124) \quad (0.0641)$$
$$\bar{R}^2 = 0.85 \quad \text{SEE} = 0.391 \quad n = 27$$

where T_D represents the direct price comparisons (column 1) and T_Q those based on quantities (column 2).[84]

By a line of reasoning similar to that followed in the case of physicians, a productivity correction factor for the quantity ratio of first- and second-level teachers has been based on the following equation:

$$(5.14) \quad \ln T_D / T_Q = 0.3538 - 0.3326 \ln r$$
$$(0.1110) \quad (0.0810)$$
$$\bar{R}^2 = 0.38 \quad \text{SEE} = 0.374 \quad n = 27$$

where the ratio of direct to indirect price levels is the dependent variable. As in medical services, adjustments were deemed necessary for only low-income countries. In education, however, no adjustment was made for countries in Group IV or above, whereas a small adjustment was made in health services for Group IV countries. This variation in treatment is based on

---

82. U.N. Statistical Commission (1979); U.N. Statistical Office (1980a).

83. Another apparent inconsistency in Europe is Luxembourg, where the direct price index is over twice the indirect.

84. When both r and T_Q are used to explain T_D, the result is:

$$(5.13') \quad \ln T_D = -0.4649 + 0.9745 \ln T_Q$$
$$(0.6727) \quad (0.1521)$$
$$- 0.3018 \ln r.$$
$$(0.2010)$$
$$\bar{R}^2 = 0.85 \quad \text{SEE} = 0.381 \quad n = 27$$

The negative sign of the coefficient of r is in contrast to the positive signs of the coefficients of r in the analogous equation 5-11 for physicians. Perhaps the reason is that the direct price-level estimates for medical services were based on price comparisons of outputs and thus, by shifting away from an input-based measure of comparative price levels for outputs, better captured the quality differences. The direct price-level estimate for teachers, T_D, refers to a quality-adjusted *input*, and the negative coefficient of r may reflect the tendency for the skill premium to decline as income rises.

the surmise that there are fewer quality differences across income levels in education than there are in health care. The average *r* for four groups of countries, classified by per capita GDP, is shown in the following text table in column 1. These averages were based on preliminary ICP results and differ slightly from the averages that are produced by the final estimates in Table 1-2. The next column shows the values of T_D/T_Q calculated from *r* through use of the equation. The third column shows the multipliers for indirect price levels derived by normalizing the column 2 figures on the multiplier for the Group IV countries.

	r (1)	Estimated ratio of direct to indirect price levels (2)	Multipliers for indirect PPPs (3)
Group I	0.095	3.116	1.788
Group II	0.239	2.293	1.316
Group III	0.387	1.953	1.120
Group IV	0.545	1.743	1.000

Here, too, the adjustments were actually made to the direct-quantity ratios (column 2 of Table 5-9), so the figures labeled as multipliers were actually used as divisors for quantity ratios. The final input-quantity ratios for teachers are shown in column 3.

Column 4 of Table 5-9 shows the direct-quantity ratio based on the number of students. A geometric mean of the adjusted quantity ratio for teachers, and the pupil output ratio is given in column 5, which is the final quantity ratio that was adopted for the category. The indirect price index based on column 5 is presented in column 6. This is the PPP used for this category in both the binary and multilateral comparisons.

Third-level Education

For third-level teachers, quantities reported by the countries were used without adjustment since comparable salary data were not available. Table 5-10 presents direct-quantity indexes for college teachers in column 1 and for students in column 2. The geometric mean of columns 1 and 2 is given in column 3; it and the indirect price index in column 4 were used in the Phase III aggregations. This treatment of third-level education is parallel to that of the first and second levels.

Compensation of Government Employees

In Phases I and II, both education and government relied on salary comparisons of comparable employees

to generate a PPP from which a quantity index was derived. In Phase III, a capital adjustment is also made for government compensation because of the earlier cited evidence suggesting the growth of productivity in government employees in presently developed countries that was accompanied by more capital per employee. Introduction of the quantity of capital may also be warranted from the standpoint of the position in some developing countries, where there has been a large recent expansion of government employment often serving a training function and without much accompanying capital.

It proved impossible to gather satisfactory data on government capital per employee, but it seemed likely that even an extremely rough approximation would be better than omitting any allowance for capital inputs in government. The ICP decided, therefore, to use the same capital adjustment that was used for health care—namely, 15 percent for countries with per capita income (from a preliminary ICP estimate) of 30 to 50 percent of that of the United States, and 30 percent for countries with incomes less than 30 percent of that of the United States.

The Effect of the Phase III Method Changes

The effects of these changes in methods—the different basis for the adjustments by capital inputs in medical care and government, the adjustments for productivity differences in medical care and education, and the use of pupils in education—are shown in terms of 1970 data in Table 5-11. The PPPs for the comparison-resistant services are still lower than those for priced services, though their ratios to priced services have risen by 25 to 40 percent for the low-income countries (column 3). The effect of the changes has been greater in medical care than education; the new quantity ratios for low-income countries are down by proportions ranging from one-half to one-fourth (column 6). The effect on education is smaller in part because the introduction of students tended to offset any downward adjustments; the quantity ratios decline by 19 and 21 percent in the Philippines and in India, but otherwise the changes were less than 10 percent.

The overall changes in the estimates of real per capita GDP are small (column 13).[85] These results af-

85. Column 13 shows the ratios for GDP for the Phase III treatment of comparison-resistant services to the Phase II treatment, when both use revised 1970 data. If column 12 is compared with column 10, the effect of the data revisions can be seen. As was discussed in Chapter 3, these were substantial for Malaysia and one

Table 5-10. Quantity and Price Comparisons for Third-level Education, 1975

| | Direct quantity index based on the number of | | | |
Country	Teachers (1)	Students (2)	Teachers and students (3)	Indirect price index[a] (4)
Malawi	2.1	1.8	1.9	13.0
Kenya	1.7	0.8	1.2	28.7
India	9.4	10.9	10.1	5.6
Pakistan	2.5	3.2	2.8	15.9
Sri Lanka	4.5	3.2	3.8	10.9
Zambia	2.1	3.2	2.6	67.2
Thailand	8.2	3.6	5.4	22.2
Philippines	24.8	37.4	30.5	8.7
Korea	13.4	16.1	14.7	18.1
Malaysia	10.2	10.6	10.4	11.2
Colombia	30.4	15.7	21.8	20.1
Jamaica	10.5	12.7	11.5	14.4
Syria	10.7	16.0	13.1	10.8
Brazil	20.9	17.7	19.2	25.3
Romania	22.1	13.8	17.5	22.8
Mexico	15.6	14.4	15.0	35.8
Yugoslavia	35.2	37.6	36.4	21.5
Iran	13.8	8.9	11.1	126.9
Uruguay	27.9	22.5	25.1	17.1
Ireland	44.5	19.1	29.2	50.0
Hungary	31.0	19.6	24.1	19.9
Poland	77.9	26.4	45.3	19.0
Italy	25.6	30.8	28.1	37.7
Spain	28.1	24.5	26.2	6.2
U.K.	30.3	17.0	22.7	87.6
Japan	33.1	36.7	34.9	61.3
Austria	22.3	20.9	21.6	62.5
Netherlands	32.1	31.0	31.5	202.7
Belgium	37.8	29.8	35.6	58.3
France	24.6	32.4	28.2	108.4
Luxembourg	13.1	13.4	13.2	45.9
Denmark	69.8	37.6	51.2	169.4
Germany	54.3	31.1	41.1	70.5
U.S.	100.0	100.0	100.0	100.0

a. Derived by dividing the quantity index in column 3 into the expenditure data.

firm the view that what is at stake is the medical care, education, and government quantity estimates themselves. The overall GDP estimates do not seem to be greatly affected by the alternative treatments of comparison-resistant services that are likely to be serious candidates for adoption.

Summary

This review of the methodological choices for the different comparison-resistant services—those for which satisfactory output measures are not available—sug-

gests that the scope for improved methods of international quantity comparisons is limited. A wide range of alternatives, including some fairly radical ones, have been considered, both on an across-the-board basis and for specific services. For example, the possibility of comparing the output of services by assessing outcomes (for example, physicians' cures) rather than inputs (for example, physicians' hours) or treatments (for example, office visit to internist) was considered for both medical and educational services. Aside from running counter to national-accounting practices, there are enormous problems of separating the contribution of medical services to health and of educational services to knowledge (and social attitudes?) from other broad influences affecting health and learning. Thus the ICP has settled for relatively conventional improvements in the Phase III treatment over what was done in the earlier phases.

or two other countries. However, the 1970 data revisions were very small for medical and health categories, and they would not affect the comparisons in columns 1, 2, and 3. Thus the remainder of the table has been based on the original Phase II results, and the final Phase III treatment of the revised data.

Table 5-11. Effect on 1970 PPP and per Capita Quantity Indexes of Changes in Methods for Medical Care, Education, and Government

Country	Ratio of PPPs for comparison-resistant services to PPPs for priced services[a] A (1)	B (2)	Ratio (2)/(1) (3)	Medical care A (4)	B (5)	Ratio (5)/(4) (6)	Education A (7)	B (8)	Ratio (8)/(7) (9)	GDP A (10)	B (11)	(12)[b]	Ratio (11)/(12) (13)
Kenya	0.34	0.42	1.24	7.06	3.46	0.49	14.5	13.0	0.93	6.33	5.18	6.25	0.94
India	0.32	0.44	1.38	6.15	3.51	0.57	17.1	13.5	1.79	6.92	6.46	6.90	0.94
Korea	0.35	0.44	1.26	12.7	8.65	0.68	22.3	21.1	0.95	12.1	11.8	12.4	0.95
Philippines	0.43	0.59	1.37	6.55	3.66	0.56	37.0	30.1	0.81	12.0	11.7	12.3	0.95
Malaysia	0.58	0.71	1.22	18.5	10.9	0.59	30.1	28.1	0.93	19.1	15.6	16.3	0.96
Colombia	0.47	0.59	1.26	17.3	10.5	0.61	30.5	29.2	0.96	18.1	17.2	17.9	0.96
Iran	1.20	1.44	1.20	14.9	11.3	0.76	19.5	18.9	0.97	20.3	19.4	19.8	0.98
Hungary	0.46	0.47	1.02	72.7	69.0	0.95	59.8	61.2	1.02	42.7	41.4	41.6	1.00
Italy	0.83	0.79	0.95	77.6	73.0	0.94	55.1	56.3	1.02	49.2	48.0	48.5	0.99
Japan	0.55	0.54	0.98	119.1	111.5	0.94	63.4	62.7	0.99	59.2	58.5	59.0	0.99
U.K.	0.71	0.67	0.94	78.6	75.0	0.95	78.5	76.8	0.98	63.5	62.7	63.0	1.00
Netherlands	1.09	1.13	1.04	97.1	91.7	0.94	61.4	62.9	1.02	68.7	68.3	68.1	1.00
France	0.95	0.91	0.96	120.7	112.6	0.93	46.8	47.7	1.02	73.2	71.9	72.2	1.00
Belgium	0.80	0.82	1.02	77.4	75.3	0.97	122.5	120.1	0.98	72.0	72.3	72.3	1.00
Germany	0.85	0.84	0.99	106.3	98.8	0.93	55.2	55.5	1.01	78.2	76.5	76.7	1.00
U.S.	1.00	1.00	1.00	100.0	100.0	1.00	100.0	100.0	1.00	100.0	100.0	100.0	1.00

a. The same classification of priced and comparison-resistant services as was used in Phase II is used in this table. Column 1: Table 5-1, column 8, derived from Kravis, Heston, Summers (1978a). Column 2: See sources, below, for data from which derived.

b. Column 12 uses 1970 revised data, Phase II treatment of comparison-resistant services, and five-tier supercountry weights.

Sources: A uses 1970 data, Phase II treatment of comparison-resistant services, and five-tier supercountry weights from Kravis, Heston, Summers (1978a), pp. 94–95. B uses revised 1970 data, Phase III treatment of comparison-resistant services, and five-tier supercountry weights.

The position with respect to Phase III methods for services can be summarized as follows:

1. The commodity components of health, education, and government services were treated, as in Phases I and II, by direct price comparisons.

2. An adjustment for accompanying capital was made for physicians, dentists, nurses, hospitals, and government employees. Though data on health capital could be obtained for only eight countries, of which only two were low-income countries, there was some support for a linkage between the amount of medical-care capital and the level of real income. To allow for smaller inputs of capital, the direct quantity indicators (personnel inputs) were divided by 1.30 for low-income countries (those with per capita real GDPs below 30 percent of that of the United States) and by 1.15 for middle-income countries (30 to 50 percent of that of the United States). No capital adjustment was attempted for capital in education, where the contribution seemed much less clear than for general government or health services.

3. Direct price data for health services (a tonsillectomy, for example) and salary data for nurses and teachers were available for many more countries in Phase III than in Phases I and II. These data seemed to produce plausible PPPs for about two-thirds of the countries. However, because the expenditure data in these fields are weak for many countries at all economic levels, the direct PPPs, when divided into expenditures, did not always yield reliable quantity estimates.

4. Direct salary comparisons for teachers were available for twenty-seven countries for the comparison at the first and second levels of education. The method used in the price comparisons was improved somewhat over Phases I and II in that salaries for teachers with five different levels of training were taken into account more fully. However, for some countries in Europe and other regions these salary-based PPPs were not consistent with expenditures and, therefore, could not be directly used.

5. Since the direct PPPs for medical and educational personnel would not consistently produce plausible indirect quantity ratios, it seemed necessary to go back to direct quantity comparisons based on personnel inputs. However, the quantity-of-input method suffers the disadvantage that it assumes that a given professional group has the same productivity in all countries. It seems more likely that the productivity of such a group varies, at least to some degree, with the productivity of the rest of economy and thus with the level of real per capita income. Consequently, quantity-of-input comparisons and their associated indirect price comparisons tend to bias quantity and price com-

parisons systematically with income levels; quantities tend to be biased upward and prices downward for lower income countries. These biases seemed especially important for very low-income countries.

6. Although these biases do not have large effects on GDP as a whole for most countries, different assumptions produced very different quantity indexes for medical care and education.

7. It was thus felt necessary to search further for a measure of the productivity differences. An indicator of the productivity differences was found in the relationship between the direct price-level estimate and the indirect price-level estimate. (This relationship had to be based, of course, on countries for which both price measures were available.) The former, being based on prices of specified medical services, comes closer to reflecting similar quality of outputs than the latter, which is based on the undifferentiated numbers of professional personnel. The interpretation of the ratio of the direct to indirect PPP as an indicator of the country-to-country differences in the productivity of personnel inputs is supported by its negative association with real per capita GDP (r) in the cases of physicians, dentists, and first- and second-level teachers.

8. The result of these investigations was that the direct quantity ratios for medical care and teachers in education were adjusted downward for some lower-middle-income and low-income countries. Thus the quantity ratios finally used for comparison-resistant medical services in Phase III are a mixture of direct unadjusted quantity ratios for high-income countries and direct quantity ratios for middle- and low-income countries adjusted for differences in the productivity of the inputs (and as noted above for differences in capital inputs).

9. These adjusted quantity ratios for teachers were combined with those of pupils to derive a final quantity index. The present treatment can be looked upon as taking the number of teachers as an output measure, modified by the quality of teachers and their productivity, the latter measured by the number of students.

10. The PPPs finally used for medical-care services and teachers are the indirect ones derived by dividing the adjusted quantity ratios into the expenditure ratios.

11. Comparisons for third-level teachers were based on the number of teachers and pupils, with no other adjustments.

12. For the services rendered by government employees, the quantity ratios derived from price (salary) comparisons were adjusted for capital per worker on the same basis as the medical-care adjustments.

13. These adjustments have a substantial effect on the quantity ratios for medical care and education of the low-income countries, but the effect on overall real GDP generally is not very great.

It is very difficult to establish satisfactory methods for comparison-resistant services, but it is believed that those followed here, however tenuous their statistical basis, move the estimates closer to their true values than the uncorrected figures. In view of the uncertainties involved, however, it is fortunate that for the large preponderance of countries the GDP estimates are rather insensitive to alternatives that seem to present the strongest claims for use.

6

Results of the Multilateral Comparisons

RESULTS OF THE MULTILATERAL COMPARISONS for thirty-four countries in 1975 are presented in this chapter. The treatment here is descriptive; a more analytical discussion is given in Chapter 9.

The expenditure, price, and quantity comparisons are presented in a series of summary multilateral tables:

6-1. Per capita expenditures in national currencies

6-2. Percentage distribution of per capita expenditures in national currencies

6-3. Purchasing power parities per U.S. dollar

6-4. Real per capita quantities relative to the United States

6-5. Per capita quantities in international dollars.

Each table contains entries for GDP, its three major components, and thirty-five summary categories.[1] A set of three appendix tables, found at the end of this chapter, are similar in numbering and content to Tables 6-1, 6-3, and 6-5, but they provide the data for 151 detailed categories. (The appendix tables corresponding to Summary Multilateral Tables 6-2 and 6-4 can easily be derived from Appendix Tables 6-1 and 6-5, respectively. However, in the case of Appendix Table 6-1, only the details provided by the countries are shown; the rough breakdowns of expenditures for the other categories made by the ICP staff are not presented.) The data in the detailed tables are presented as worksheet materials for the convenience of users

who wish to create aggregates other than those provided in the tables. They are not to be regarded as statistics of publishable quality.

In addition to these basic tables, Tables 6-6 through 6-13 are derived to facilitate analysis of the results. An unnumbered table in the second section below groups the thirty-four countries into six per capita GDP classes as an aid to describing the way in which the composition of expenditures, the structure of prices, and relative quantities change as real income rises. Next are several tables that set out the expenditure, price, and quantity comparisons for two composite groupings of interest: (1) commodities and services, and (2) tradable and nontradable goods. In each case the two classifications are defined so that the detailed categories assigned to the groupings exhaust GDP. Finally, purchasing power parities (PPPs) for private households are presented.

An Explanation of the Tables

Chapters 3 and 4 described the methods by which the ICP comparisons have been made. The key steps in the methodology are (1) the production of transitive, base-invariant PPPs at the detailed-category level through the country-product-dummy (CPD) method, and (2) the aggregation of category quantities by means of the Geary-Khamis procedure, which also gives transitive and base-invariant results. The methods can be illuminated further by setting out the mechanical operations by which the tables are derived.

The detailed expenditure data of the thirty-four countries are presented in Appendix Table 6-1 and the aggregates in Summary Multilateral Table 6-1. These

---

1. Each table has fifty lines, of which fifteen are aggregations of entries on other lines. The thirty-five summary categories add up to GDP except for the omission of increase in stocks (ICP 18.00). This item, which can be found in the appendix tables (line 145), is included in the entries for domestic capital formation, capital formation, and GDP in Tables 6-1–6-5.

(Text continues on page 172.)

Category	Line numbers[a]	Malawi (kwacha)	Kenya (shillings)	India (rupees)	Pakistan (rupees)	Sri Lanka (rupees)	Zambia (kwacha)	Thailand (baht)
Consumption, ICP[b,c]	1–108	95.663	1370.08	877.73	1525.01	1689.75	191.107	5187.0
Food, beverages, tobacco	1– 39	55.543	602.13	565.34	905.50	1161.00	77.434	2670.8
Food	1– 33	50.571	505.10	531.96	866.27	1022.08	72.255	2240.1
Bread, cereals	1– 6	19.589	201.96	240.56	289.70	521.26	15.599	690.4
Meat	7– 12	3.386	30.15	11.23	52.04	17.34	18.831	352.7
Fish	13– 14	2.759	2.98	10.78	18.74	48.61	9.938	270.2
Milk, cheese, eggs	15– 17	2.091	95.68	57.49	191.39	45.42	3.151	145.0
Oils, fats	18– 20	0.875	15.07	54.77	122.36	9.93	4.296	55.9
Fruits, vegetables	21– 26	19.739	109.26	84.64	101.72	191.54	14.937	388.0
Coffee, tea, cocoa	27– 29	0.304	7.61	8.27	20.23	22.15	1.024	22.8
Spices, sweets, sugar	30– 33	1.828	42.39	64.23	70.10	165.83	4.478	315.1
Beverages	34– 37	4.199	63.74	7.68	2.12	44.01	4.095	298.3
Tobacco	38– 39	0.774	33.29	25.69	37.12	94.92	1.084	132.3
Clothing, footwear	40– 51	6.704	94.04	66.32	164.29	106.85	12.889	411.4
Clothing	40– 47	6.149	80.45	61.45	133.99	101.66	11.383	386.6
Footwear	48– 51	0.555	13.58	4.86	30.30	5.19	1.506	24.8
Gross rent, fuel	52– 57	5.916	154.79	53.80	175.85	84.10	18.510	302.8
Gross rent	52– 53	3.388	124.49	24.07	104.33	51.65	12.567	154.1
Fuel, power	54– 57	2.527	30.30	29.73	71.52	32.45	5.942	148.7
House furnishings, operations	58– 70	9.000	115.38	24.43	63.36	48.31	11.163	248.9
Furniture, appliances	58– 66	3.013	50.15	6.73	5.44	12.08	3.153	96.8
Supplies, operations	67– 70	5.987	65.23	17.70	57.93	36.23	8.010	152.1
Medical care	71– 77	1.834	65.68	28.40	71.95	43.57	10.661	302.1
Transport, communications	78– 89	7.194	100.01	57.20	29.38	104.33	12.388	360.2
Equipment	78– 79	1.617	10.60	3.20	0.11	1.93	6.283	57.0
Operation costs	80– 83	4.113	42.54	8.97	4.19	29.12	3.936	70.0
Purchased transport	84– 87	1.334	42.39	41.92	23.40	65.35	1.626	222.1
Communications	88– 89	0.130	4.48	3.11	1.68	7.93	0.542	11.1
Recreation and education	90–101	6.267	160.76	46.48	77.77	94.40	26.482	578.0
Recreation	90– 96	2.549	28.81	14.64	48.49	45.05	6.044	293.5
Education	97–101	3.717	131.95	31.83	29.28	49.35	20.438	284.6
Other expenditures	102–107	3.206	77.32	39.74	36.92	61.28	20.980	354.7
Personal care	102–104	0.481	30.30	16.06	15.90	21.41	1.225	112.3
Miscellaneous services	105–107	2.725	47.02	23.68	21.02	39.86	19.755	242.4
Capital formation	109–146	14.968	239.87	247.47	182.12	141.89	66.916	1428.2
Domestic capital formation	109–145	35.587	323.60	250.71	324.06	288.97	128.952	1757.4
Construction	109–122	13.270	204.04	112.55	200.68	165.90	67.859	680.0
Residential	109–110	4.358	63.29	27.59	37.83	42.90	15.117	184.3
Nonresidential	111–118	4.939	46.87	41.85	63.42	51.20	29.674	314.7
Other	119–122	3.973	93.89	43.11	99.43	71.80	23.068	181.0
Producer durables	123–144	19.144	156.58	88.08	123.38	96.40	53.062	847.6
Transport equipment	123–129	8.076	47.76	16.57	29.99	30.16	18.993	243.6
Nonelectrical machinery	130–138	8.709	74.04	32.42	72.67	47.20	19.574	309.2
Electrical machinery	139–142	2.145	26.87	27.00	17.09	17.93	11.523	107.7
Other	143–144	0.214	7.91	12.10	3.63	1.11	2.972	187.1
Exports minus imports	146–146	–20.619	–83.74	–3.25	–141.94	–147.08	–62.036	–329.1
Government	147–151	9.169	177.03	94.99	172.22	125.07	60.228	522.8
Compensation	147–150	4.347	100.01	55.31	91.52	78.62	22.184	293.3
Commodities	151–151	4.822	77.02	39.69	80.70	46.46	38.044	229.5
Gross domestic product	1–151	119.800	1786.97	1220.19	1879.34	1956.71	318.247	7137.9
Aggregates								
ICP concepts[e]								
Consumption (CEP)[b,c]	1–108	95.664	1370.08	877.73	1525.01	1689.75	191.109	5187.0
Capital formation (GCF)[d]	109–146	14.965	239.86	247.47	182.12	141.89	66.917	1428.2
Government (PFC)	147–151	9.169	177.03	94.99	172.22	125.07	60.228	522.8
Gross domestic product	1–151	119.798	1786.97	1220.19	1879.35	1956.71	318.251	7137.9
SNA concepts[e]								
Consumption (PFCE)	1–108	90.759	1218.13	851.64	1493.10	1614.47	163.403	4970.2
Capital formation (GCF)	109–146	14.965	239.36	247.47	182.12	141.89	66.917	1428.2
Government (GFCE)	147–151	13.723	328.98	121.09	204.13	200.35	87.533	739.5
Gross domestic product	1–151	119.451	1786.97	1220.19	1879.35	1956.71	317.851	7137.9

Philippines (pesos)	Korea (won)	Malaysia (ringgit)	Colombia (pesos)	Jamaica (dollars)	Syria (pounds)	Brazil (cruzeiros)	Romania (lei)	Mexico (pesos)	Yugoslavia (dinars)
1895.26	201820.	1204.82	13745.6	918.791	1778.74	6729.19	11385.3	13561.4	17185.2
1154.02	109486.	478.57	5368.9	384.016	914.87	2476.68	4724.1	5306.1	6117.6
1025.98	90434.	406.31	4655.4	300.145	844.98	2283.74	4003.8	5093.9	4955.5
350.24	47229.	117.42	720.2	87.631	125.92	506.19	716.5	1217.5	962.0
189.99	6614.	70.70	1613.3	36.836	101.03	617.70	1258.1	1293.9	1274.6
210.43	5582.	47.95	95.0	24.476	5.85	72.63	47.7	86.6	85.4
25.65	3553.	49.16	513.2	35.896	107.15	231.09	597.9	927.1	780.5
27.00	756.	15.44	210.4	8.856	89.20	159.19	139.8	382.0	285.4
143.83	13369.	52.41	766.1	83.155	333.83	464.38	659.9	738.6	822.8
17.66	416.	8.53	199.6	2.653	8.30	102.70	58.9	147.7	222.1
61.18	12916.	44.70	537.6	20.642	73.70	129.85	525.0	300.6	522.6
73.95	10904.	27.28	531.3	43.840	8.29	40.36	518.6	116.7	733.3
54.10	8148.	44.98	182.1	40.032	61.60	152.59	201.7	95.5	428.9
128.02	19097.	70.25	1266.0	36.966	206.01	629.43	1659.6	1366.7	1620.2
110.03	17703.	62.17	947.7	18.468	173.10	526.73	1365.5	1034.6	1280.3
17.99	1393.	8.08	318.3	18.498	32.91	102.69	294.0	332.1	339.9
170.24	15677.	122.93	1064.2	97.715	214.99	717.36	777.0	1312.6	1421.6
126.12	6342.	99.09	830.0	73.897	127.01	454.73	492.8	704.7	746.6
44.12	9335.	23.85	234.2	23.818	87.98	262.63	284.2	607.9	675.0
86.57	6323.	71.35	854.6	52.907	111.10	558.27	822.6	1489.9	1651.8
40.81	3902.	29.39	280.5	26.229	56.02	297.83	457.0	548.8	1117.9
45.76	2422.	41.96	574.2	26.677	55.07	260.44	365.6	941.1	533.9
63.20	7912.	50.74	716.7	39.875	61.06	362.27	576.4	803.9	1262.7
39.70	13889.	158.06	1272.9	106.335	67.58	721.02	748.6	1096.0	1603.2
13.72	633.	36.51	131.5	10.786	12.92	194.31	157.6	296.3	450.1
3.83	32.	65.75	80.3	48.989	3.53	322.79	72.0	386.5	652.1
19.06	12339.	49.31	973.2	40.739	47.46	173.12	460.6	344.2	2435.6
3.09	885.	6.48	87.9	5.821	3.67	30.81	58.4	69.0	65.3
133.04	15777.	146.47	1605.1	80.662	109.46	593.74	1090.4	1205.2	2058.0
28.86	5775.	58.35	485.3	33.285	35.90	346.63	472.5	408.0	950.3
104.18	10002.	88.12	1119.8	47.378	73.57	247.10	617.9	797.2	1107.7
120.49	15387.	91.13	1597.4	154.600	93.69	670.52	986.7	1251.4	1732.5
36.06	6272.	18.74	309.1	39.881	39.71	152.58	131.6	395.4	325.2
84.43	9114.	72.40	1288.3	114.719	53.99	517.94	855.1	855.9	1407.3
660.48	56894.	446.40	3201.1	193.716	376.66	2013.05	8482.4	3834.6	8495.0
845.52	81389.	437.93	3108.6	331.895	749.79	2388.38	8600.1	4413.6	10345.4
277.39	38465.	252.80	1913.6	146.330	392.17	1183.77	3507.7	2354.5	4615.1
95.50	12567.	69.07	396.1	89.023	114.63	249.05	748.0	1146.1	1760.3
78.46	12867.	79.41	121.8	45.874	56.30	297.86	1516.7	477.6	1633.5
103.42	13031.	104.32	1395.7	11.433	221.24	636.87	1243.1	730.8	1221.3
380.95	33381.	217.09	1362.8	155.252	357.63	1204.61	3501.2	1625.2	3457.3
111.79	15248.	52.63	467.9	47.421	132.85	249.34	592.9	397.8	538.6
181.15	14991.	129.69	236.8	65.706	163.45	550.77	2517.2	566.8	2130.7
59.78	2061.	27.72	593.5	20.897	42.97	191.64	247.2	315.3	545.8
28.24	1082.	7.05	64.5	21.228	18.36	212.87	143.9	345.3	242.2
−185.04	−24495.	8.47	92.5	−138.179	−373.13	−375.32	−117.7	−579.0	−1850.4
179.67	23352.	221.94	489.7	165.508	500.67	680.40	1040.6	915.7	3257.3
96.84	11152.	138.49	400.7	104.345	217.98	468.79	569.0	707.8	1434.1
82.84	12200.	83.45	89.1	61.163	282.70	211.61	471.6	207.9	1823.2
2735.40	282065.	1873.16	17436.3	1278.012	2656.08	9422.57	20908.2	18311.6	28937.4
1895.26	201820.	1204.82	13745.6	918.792	1778.74	6729.19	11385.3	13561.4	17185.2
660.48	56894.	446.40	3201.1	193.716	376.66	2013.06	8482.4	3834.6	8495.0
179.67	23352.	221.94	489.7	165.508	500.67	680.40	1040.6	915.7	3257.3
2735.40	282065.	1873.16	17436.3	1278.012	2656.08	9422.56	20908.2	18311.6	28937.4
1803.46	196128.	1097.62	12950.3	849.745	1716.06	6480.23	10136.2	12568.1	14426.2
660.48	56894.	446.40	3201.1	193.716	376.66	2013.06	8482.4	3834.6	8495.0
260.15	29044.	329.14	1285.1	234.556	563.36	927.28	2289.7	1887.0	6012.0
2724.09	282065.	1873.16	17436.3	1278.012	2656.08	9420.48	20908.2	18289.7	28933.1

(Table continues on the following page.)

165

Category	Line numbers[a]	Iran (rials)	Uruguay (N. pesos)	Ireland (pounds)	Hungary (forint)	Poland (zlotys)	Italy (lire)	Spain (pesetas)
Consumption, ICP[b,c]	1–108	48802.5	2416.26	876.251	26760.9	29569.8	1554882.	124279.3
Food, beverages, tobacco	1– 39	16601.3	1012.85	258.186	9798.6	11604.8	530126.	40652.9
Food	1– 33	15778.4	769.63	202.142	7049.9	8479.3	451297.	37034.8
Bread, cereals	1– 6	4597.0	127.51	27.394	777.7	1007.1	60165.	3486.9
Meat	7– 12	3379.8	203.64	69.583	2008.5	2526.4	150689.	11891.8
Fish	13– 14	182.9	2.40	5.668	62.0	165.7	15458.	2928.8
Milk, cheese, eggs	15– 17	1700.7	105.89	26.763	948.1	1356.9	57693.	5728.1
Oils, fats	18– 20	1200.1	43.90	11.021	565.5	782.4	35536.	3497.1
Fruits, vegetables	21– 26	3103.7	161.90	33.375	1241.5	1340.3	102364.	6178.8
Coffee, tea, cocoa	27– 29	558.8	12.27	4.409	389.2	288.2	7917.	739.1
Spices, sweets, sugar	30– 33	1055.3	112.12	23.929	1057.2	1012.2	21476.	2584.3
Beverages	34– 37	169.7	169.94	14.798	2152.9	2540.1	45262.	2114.0
Tobacco	38– 39	653.2	73.28	41.246	595.8	585.4	33566.	1504.2
Clothing, footwear	40– 51	5082.8	172.54	63.602	2850.3	3777.0	130163.	11780.2
Clothing	40– 47	4109.4	129.49	52.898	2330.9	3229.4	106681.	8952.9
Footwear	48– 51	973.5	43.06	10.704	519.4	547.6	23482.	2827.3
Gross rent, fuel	52– 57	8216.1	266.20	88.476	1985.2	2309.5	194232.	15386.4
Gross rent	52– 53	6620.0	163.69	49.434	1117.7	1749.5	149704.	11914.9
Fuel, power	54– 57	1596.1	102.51	39.043	867.5	560.0	44528.	3471.5
House furnishings, operations	58– 70	3772.3	191.45	59.825	2436.0	2605.8	91599.	9816.8
Furniture, appliances	58– 66	2528.6	72.01	34.321	1351.3	1604.5	49382.	6272.9
Supplies, operations	67– 70	1243.7	119.44	25.504	1084.7	1001.2	42217.	3543.9
Medical care	71– 77	3274.2	152.54	78.715	1576.1	1719.7	124646.	10475.8
Transport, communications	78– 89	3342.2	234.39	75.566	1964.8	1871.4	158606.	12126.7
Equipment	78– 79	1386.3	34.08	25.189	651.0	612.8	38349.	3771.4
Operation costs	80– 83	908.1	60.93	33.061	566.3	380.7	83056.	5674.2
Purchased transport	84– 87	862.3	119.03	12.595	633.7	716.3	22067.	2130.0
Communications	88– 89	185.5	20.36	4.723	113.8	161.6	15135.	551.1
Recreation and education	90–101	5106.4	203.98	114.293	3360.2	3555.5	181354.	11109.1
Recreation	90– 96	1439.7	127.77	48.488	1897.0	1717.1	81085.	6204.2
Education	97–101	3666.7	76.21	65.805	1463.2	1838.4	100269.	4904.9
Other expenditures	102–107	3407.4	182.32	137.594	2789.9	2126.3	144170.	12933.2
Personal care	102–104	974.5	41.91	13.224	716.8	504.3	51245.	2095.6
Miscellaneous services	105–107	2432.9	140.41	124.370	2073.0	1622.0	92925.	10837.6
Capital formation	109–146	38626.1	290.07	183.877	13718.0	18218.5	428138.	38316.1
Domestic capital formation	109–145	29069.6	396.11	253.777	17101.3	21216.5	455345.	44978.1
Construction	109–122	16599.4	276.78	164.674	8529.3	10273.0	281425.	24355.9
Residential	109–110	7189.5	92.45	72.103	2598.2	1848.8	139584.	10381.6
Nonresidential	111–118	5314.3	43.79	44.083	3165.6	4622.6	87856.	5585.7
Other	119–122	4095.7	140.54	48.489	2765.5	3801.6	53985.	8388.6
Producer durables	123–144	13908.7	115.02	101.067	6628.5	7983.1	180225.	15072.4
Transport equipment	123–129	4880.6	31.38	24.872	1273.4	2109.5	46713.	4550.2
Nonelectrical machinery	130–138	6774.2	57.11	56.360	3827.3	4182.9	80226.	5766.2
Electrical machinery	139–142	1475.2	8.50	9.130	770.4	1534.7	34515.	3714.4
Other	143–144	778.8	18.04	10.705	757.3	156.1	18771.	1041.7
Exports minus imports	146–146	9556.5	− 106.04	− 69.899	− 3383.3	− 2998.1	− 27208.	− 6662.0
Government	147–151	19836.8	301.90	124.370	3414.0	3715.4	262669.	6886.3
Compensation	147–150	6636.7	241.74	75.567	917.8	1123.2	161311.	4914.7
Commodities	151–151	13200.1	60.17	48.803	2496.1	2592.2	101358.	1971.6
Gross domestic product	1–151	107264.8	3008.24	1184.494	43892.9	51503.7	2245670.	169480.3
Aggregates								
ICP concepts[e]								
Consumption (CEP)[b,c]	1–108	48802.5	2416.27	876.249	26760.9	29569.8	1554882.	124279.3
Capital formation (GCF)[d]	109–146	38626.1	290.07	183.879	13718.0	18218.5	428138.	38316.1
Government (PFC)	147–151	19836.8	301.90	124.370	3414.0	3715.4	262669.	6886.3
Gross domestic product	1–151	107264.7	3008.24	1184.493	43892.9	51503.7	2245670.	169480.4
SNA concepts[e]								
Consumption (PFCE)	1–108	43671.5	2317.02	749.990	23146.5	25716.6	1459540.	115489.9
Capital formation (GCF)	109–146	38626.1	290.07	183.879	13718.0	18218.5	428138.	38316.1
Government (GFCE)	147–151	24967.8	401.15	241.182	6695.5	7190.4	358012.	15649.7
Gross domestic product	1–151	107264.9	3008.24	1175.047	43560.0	51125.4	2245670.	169454.4

a. Line numbers refer to Appendix Table 6-1 and show the detailed categories that are included in each aggregation.

b. Consumption, ICP, includes both household and government expenditures. The latter are shown separately in Table 2-1. Consumption, SNA, excludes these governmental expenditures.

c. The consumption aggregate (lines 1–108) includes net expenditure of residents abroad (line 108), not shown separately here.

U.K. (pounds)	Japan (yen)	Austria (schillings)	Netherlands (guilders)	Belgium (francs)	France (francs)	Luxembourg (francs)	Denmark (kroner)	Germany (DM)	U.S. (dollars)
1272.834	824898.	55940.6	9743.95	152536.7	18015.27	149964.7	28211.89	10845.43	5182.93
287.044	214787.	13873.3	2110.39	34401.5	4118.37	33419.3	6627.44	2164.80	818.24
208.713	183120.	9957.3	1623.57	28668.1	3402.34	28169.4	4452.75	1650.05	658.25
29.206	34840.	1294.0	212.30	3630.6	434.94	3977.8	595.25	297.95	94.81
61.449	24721.	3098.7	447.29	11250.5	1162.09	9127.8	1362.45	439.68	163.79
6.520	35566.	147.9	51.98	1214.6	181.37	755.6	208.89	25.80	25.96
29.474	12853.	1467.8	273.72	3101.6	451.83	4080.6	544.66	189.23	82.52
8.968	2008.	694.7	74.67	1957.7	211.02	2258.3	248.02	161.88	32.30
39.478	29229.	1936.6	320.64	4360.2	578.22	4877.8	574.90	250.43	147.83
5.609	4446.	244.9	83.38	870.7	85.67	1030.6	272.53	129.66	17.18
28.010	39456.	1072.7	159.59	2282.3	297.21	2061.1	646.05	155.41	93.86
28.796	20320.	2707.3	284.04	3150.4	525.53	3180.6	1237.75	319.87	91.02
49.535	11348.	1208.8	202.78	2583.0	190.49	2069.4	936.96	194.89	68.97
97.050	61264.	6078.4	800.95	11738.8	1344.15	12405.5	1510.67	940.40	336.33
80.813	55223.	5059.6	683.82	9916.3	1090.32	10638.9	1283.20	786.69	284.83
16.237	6041.	1018.9	117.13	1822.5	253.83	1766.7	227.47	153.71	51.50
219.557	118701.	6743.3	1203.51	22203.2	2579.21	25402.8	5515.60	1587.28	903.84
167.003	103669.	4641.0	833.09	13937.9	1951.50	18122.2	4038.54	1177.58	717.46
52.553	15031.	2102.4	370.42	8265.4	627.70	7280.6	1477.07	409.70	186.38
83.332	47989.	4898.8	898.83	17559.8	1796.58	15002.7	2162.25	1045.61	343.14
48.891	27374.	3716.6	597.44	8991.1	1017.48	8405.5	1299.80	600.65	222.06
34.441	20616.	1182.2	301.39	8568.7	779.10	6597.2	862.45	444.95	121.09
75.224	73400.	5603.6	1002.27	12290.3	1903.94	9022.2	1453.75	1371.48	653.69
150.516	72110.	7383.0	941.65	15936.4	2055.79	18302.7	3359.09	1321.35	692.17
33.226	14261.	1583.8	324.30	5056.3	481.80	6363.9	1050.59	331.28	221.44
63.325	18043.	4142.3	432.72	8009.2	1142.94	8236.1	1646.64	628.41	338.12
37.228	33021.	1014.6	68.23	1722.9	304.86	2366.7	423.52	196.02	40.37
16.738	6785.	642.3	116.40	1148.0	126.18	1336.1	238.34	165.63	92.24
187.599	119830.	6332.4	1797.51	20373.5	2112.63	16197.2	5446.23	1398.08	783.74
95.532	59821.	3400.3	804.47	7656.0	1098.79	5627.8	2007.90	731.78	323.24
92.067	60009.	2932.2	993.04	12717.5	1013.84	10569.4	3438.34	666.30	460.50
172.523	113870.	8819.0	988.95	18034.9	2104.74	20213.9	2136.96	1016.54	628.47
32.868	27006.	1658.1	202.93	4065.8	577.44	4905.6	600.20	237.02	136.90
139.654	86863.	7160.9	786.02	13969.1	1527.30	15308.3	1536.76	779.52	491.57
301.902	435364.	23300.6	3767.42	53393.8	6530.27	63099.8	8209.42	4064.03	1185.31
340.647	434809.	22739.4	3157.61	50894.1	6341.22	67666.4	8771.48	3448.94	1128.56
195.725	283787.	14379.1	1768.01	32412.2	4038.56	47849.9	6300.37	2099.53	680.36
75.614	100864.	5183.2	728.70	13178.8	2094.22	18519.4	2916.99	863.57	235.05
77.149	72047.	5484.0	645.90	13323.4	1309.42	20316.6	2346.24	441.62	210.33
42.961	110876.	3711.8	393.41	5910.0	634.92	9013.9	1037.15	794.33	234.99
169.861	146594.	8942.8	1421.82	19740.2	2371.76	18755.5	3061.66	1370.44	491.75
52.071	33424.	1460.1	396.19	4318.6	559.43	4522.2	1000.40	290.53	122.69
72.971	46744.	4683.6	555.49	8819.1	1440.03	8138.9	1343.28	558.41	203.26
34.101	35531.	1936.3	319.99	5272.0	240.01	4866.7	394.27	420.34	118.24
10.718	30897.	862.8	150.15	1330.5	132.29	1227.8	323.72	101.17	47.56
− 38.745	556.	561.2	609.81	2499.7	189.05	−4566.7	−562.05	615.08	56.75
287.810	67691.	8026.6	1819.39	25706.1	3009.18	23677.5	6665.59	1814.49	808.42
192.904	53672.	6157.3	1294.66	18271.4	1969.44	15305.5	5513.43	1419.61	419.96
94.906	14018.	1869.3	524.73	7434.7	1039.74	8372.0	1152.16	394.89	388.46
1862.543	1327937.	87266.7	15330.68	231635.3	27554.67	236740.9	43086.89	16723.87	7176.59
1272.837	824898.	55940.6	9743.95	152536.7	18015.27	149964.8	28211.89	10845.43	5182.93
301.906	435364.	23300.6	3767.42	53393.8	6530.27	63099.8	8209.43	4064.02	1185.31
287.810	67691.	8026.6	1819.39	25706.1	3009.18	23677.5	6665.59	1814.49	808.42
1862.551	1327937.	87266.7	15330.68	231635.4	27554.67	236741.0	43086.89	16723.87	7176.58
1095.060	758014.	48900.7	8701.20	139734.1	16991.22	139784.4	23251.04	10225.41	4620.17
301.906	435364.	23300.6	3767.42	53393.8	6530.27	63099.8	8209.43	4064.02	1185.31
446.812	133472.	15066.4	2793.33	38127.0	3976.95	33858.1	11483.96	2420.76	1367.43
1843.776	1326837.	87267.1	15261.87	231253.8	27498.39	236741.1	42944.41	16710.13	7172.83

d. The capital formation aggregate (lines 109–146) includes increase in stocks (line 145) not shown separately in these summary multilateral tables.

e. Letters in parentheses are: CEP, consumption expenditures of the population; GCF, gross capital formation; PFC, public final consumption expenditure; PFCE, private final consumption expenditure; GFCE, government final consumption expenditure. See Glossary for definitions.

Category	Line numbers[a]	Malawi	Kenya	India	Pakistan	Sri Lanka	Zambia	Thailand
Consumption, ICP[b,c]	1–108	79.9	76.7	71.9	81.1	86.4	60.0	72.7
Food, beverages, tobacco	1– 39	46.4	33.7	46.3	48.2	59.3	24.3	37.4
Food	1– 33	42.2	28.3	43.6	46.1	52.2	22.7	31.4
Bread, cereals	1– 6	16.4	11.3	19.7	15.4	26.6	4.9	9.7
Meat	7– 12	2.8	1.7	0.9	2.8	0.9	5.9	4.9
Fish	13– 14	2.3	0.2	0.9	1.0	2.5	3.1	3.8
Milk, cheese, eggs	15– 17	1.7	5.4	4.7	10.2	2.3	1.0	2.0
Oils, fats	18– 20	0.7	0.8	4.5	6.5	0.5	1.3	0.8
Fruits, vegetables	21– 26	16.5	6.1	6.9	5.4	9.8	4.7	5.4
Coffee, tea, cocoa	27– 29	0.3	0.4	0.7	1.1	1.1	0.3	0.3
Spices, sweets, sugar	30– 33	1.5	2.4	5.3	3.7	8.5	1.4	4.4
Beverages	34– 37	3.5	3.6	0.6	0.1	2.2	1.3	4.2
Tobacco	38– 39	0.6	1.9	2.1	2.0	4.9	0.3	1.9
Clothing, footwear	40– 51	5.6	5.3	5.4	8.7	5.5	4.0	5.8
Clothing	40– 47	5.1	4.5	5.0	7.1	5.2	3.6	5.4
Footwear	48– 51	0.5	0.8	0.4	1.6	0.3	0.5	0.3
Gross rent, fuel	52– 57	4.9	8.7	4.4	9.4	4.3	5.8	4.2
Gross rent	52– 53	2.8	7.0	2.0	5.6	2.6	3.9	2.2
Fuel, power	54– 57	2.1	1.7	2.4	3.8	1.7	1.9	2.1
House furnishings, operations	58– 70	7.5	6.5	2.0	3.4	2.5	3.5	3.5
Furniture, appliances	58– 66	2.5	2.8	0.6	0.3	0.6	1.0	1.4
Supplies, operations	67– 70	5.0	3.7	1.5	3.1	1.9	2.5	2.1
Medical care	71– 77	1.5	3.7	2.3	3.8	2.2	3.4	4.2
Transport, communications	78– 89	6.0	5.6	4.7	1.6	5.3	3.9	5.0
Equipment	78– 79	1.4	0.6	0.3	0.0	0.1	2.0	0.8
Operation costs	80– 83	3.4	2.4	0.7	0.2	1.5	1.2	1.0
Purchased transport	84– 87	1.1	2.4	3.4	1.2	3.3	0.5	3.1
Communications	88– 89	0.1	0.3	0.3	0.1	0.4	0.2	0.2
Recreation and education	90–101	5.2	9.0	3.8	4.1	4.8	8.3	8.1
Recreation	90– 96	2.1	1.6	1.2	2.6	2.3	1.9	4.1
Education	97–101	3.1	7.4	2.6	1.6	2.5	6.4	4.0
Other expenditures	102–107	2.7	4.3	3.3	2.0	3.1	6.6	5.0
Personal care	102–104	0.4	1.7	1.3	0.8	1.1	0.4	1.6
Miscellaneous services	105–107	2.3	2.6	1.9	1.1	2.0	6.2	3.4
Capital formation	109–146	12.5	13.4	20.3	9.7	7.3	21.0	20.0
Domestic capital formation	109–145	29.7	18.1	20.5	17.2	14.8	40.5	24.6
Construction	109–122	11.1	11.4	9.2	10.7	8.5	21.3	9.5
Residential	109–110	3.6	3.5	2.3	2.0	2.2	4.8	2.6
Nonresidential	111–118	4.1	2.6	3.4	3.4	2.6	9.3	4.4
Other	119–122	3.3	5.3	3.5	5.3	3.7	7.2	2.5
Producer durables	123–144	16.0	8.8	7.2	6.6	4.9	16.7	11.9
Transport equipment	123–129	6.7	2.7	1.4	1.6	1.5	6.0	3.4
Nonelectrical machinery	130–138	7.3	4.1	2.7	3.9	2.4	6.2	4.3
Electrical machinery	139–142	1.8	1.5	2.2	0.9	0.9	3.6	1.5
Other	143–144	0.2	0.4	1.0	0.2	0.1	0.9	2.6
Exports minus imports	146–146	− 17.2	− 4.7	− 0.3	− 7.6	− 7.5	− 19.5	− 4.6
Government	147–151	7.7	9.9	7.8	9.2	6.4	18.9	7.3
Compensation	147–150	3.6	5.6	4.5	4.9	4.0	7.0	4.1
Commodities	151–151	4.0	4.3	3.3	4.3	2.4	12.0	3.2
Gross domestic product	1–151	100.0	100.0	100.0	100.0	100.0	100.0	100.0
Aggregates								
ICP concepts[e]								
Consumption (CEP)[b,c]	1–108	79.9	76.7	71.9	81.1	86.4	60.0	72.7
Capital formation (GCF)[d]	109–146	12.5	13.4	20.3	9.7	7.3	21.0	20.0
Government (PFC)	147–151	7.7	9.9	7.8	9.2	6.4	18.9	7.3
Gross domestic product	1–151	100.0	100.0	100.0	100.0	100.0	100.0	100.0
SNA concepts[e]								
Consumption (PFCE)	1–108	76.0	68.2	69.8	79.4	82.5	51.4	69.6
Capital formation (GCF)	109–146	12.5	13.4	20.3	9.7	7.3	21.1	20.0
Government (GFCE)	147–151	11.5	18.4	9.9	10.9	10.2	27.5	10.4
Gross domestic product	1–151	100.0	100.0	100.0	100.0	100.0	100.0	100.0

Philippines	Korea	Malaysia	Colombia	Jamaica	Syria	Brazil	Romania	Mexico	Yugoslavia
69.3	71.6	64.3	78.8	71.9	67.0	71.4	54.5	74.1	59.4
42.2	38.8	25.5	30.8	30.0	34.4	26.3	22.6	29.0	21.1
37.5	32.1	21.7	26.7	23.5	31.8	24.2	19.1	27.8	17.1
12.8	16.7	6.3	4.1	6.9	4.7	5.4	3.4	6.6	3.3
6.9	2.3	3.8	9.3	2.9	3.8	6.6	6.0	7.1	4.4
7.7	2.0	2.6	0.5	1.9	0.2	0.8	0.2	0.5	0.3
0.9	1.3	2.6	2.9	2.8	4.0	2.5	2.9	5.1	2.7
1.0	0.3	0.8	1.2	0.7	3.4	1.7	0.7	2.1	1.0
5.3	4.7	2.8	4.4	6.5	12.6	4.9	3.2	4.0	2.8
0.6	0.1	0.5	1.1	0.2	0.3	1.1	0.3	0.8	0.8
2.2	4.6	2.4	3.1	1.6	2.8	1.4	2.5	1.6	1.8
2.7	3.9	1.5	3.0	3.4	0.3	0.4	2.5	0.6	2.5
2.0	2.9	2.4	1.0	3.1	2.3	1.6	1.0	0.5	1.5
4.7	6.8	3.8	7.3	2.9	7.8	6.7	7.9	7.5	5.6
4.0	6.3	3.3	5.4	1.4	6.5	5.6	6.5	5.7	4.4
0.7	0.5	0.4	1.8	1.4	1.2	1.1	1.4	1.8	1.2
6.2	5.6	6.6	6.1	7.6	8.1	7.6	3.7	7.2	4.9
4.6	2.2	5.3	4.8	5.8	4.8	4.8	2.4	3.8	2.6
1.6	3.3	1.3	1.3	1.9	3.3	2.8	1.4	3.3	2.3
3.2	2.2	3.8	4.9	4.1	4.2	5.9	3.9	8.1	5.7
1.5	1.4	1.6	1.6	2.1	2.1	3.2	2.2	3.0	3.9
1.7	0.9	2.2	3.3	2.1	2.1	2.8	1.7	5.1	1.8
2.3	2.8	2.7	4.1	3.1	2.3	3.8	2.8	4.4	4.4
1.5	4.9	8.4	7.3	8.3	2.5	7.7	3.6	6.0	5.5
0.5	0.2	1.9	0.8	0.8	0.5	2.1	0.8	1.6	1.6
0.1	0.0	3.5	0.5	3.8	0.1	3.4	0.3	2.1	2.3
0.7	4.4	2.6	5.6	3.2	1.8	1.8	2.2	1.9	1.5
0.1	0.3	0.3	0.5	0.5	0.1	0.3	0.3	0.4	0.2
4.9	5.6	7.8	9.2	6.3	4.1	6.3	5.2	6.6	7.1
1.1	2.0	3.1	2.8	2.6	1.4	3.7	2.3	2.2	3.3
3.8	3.5	4.7	6.4	3.7	2.8	2.6	3.0	4.4	3.8
4.4	5.5	4.9	9.2	12.1	3.5	7.1	4.7	6.8	6.0
1.3	2.2	1.0	1.8	3.1	1.5	1.6	0.6	2.2	1.1
3.1	3.2	3.9	7.4	9.0	2.0	5.5	4.1	4.7	4.9
24.1	20.2	23.8	18.4	15.2	14.2	21.4	40.6	20.9	29.4
30.9	28.9	23.4	17.8	26.0	28.2	25.3	41.1	24.1	35.8
10.1	13.6	13.5	11.0	11.4	14.8	12.6	16.8	12.9	15.9
3.5	4.5	3.7	2.3	7.0	4.3	2.6	3.6	6.3	6.1
2.9	4.6	4.2	0.7	3.6	2.1	3.2	7.3	2.6	5.6
3.8	4.6	5.6	8.0	0.9	8.3	6.8	5.9	4.0	4.2
13.9	11.8	11.6	7.8	12.1	13.5	12.8	16.7	8.9	11.9
4.1	5.4	2.8	2.7	3.7	5.0	2.6	2.8	2.2	1.9
6.6	5.3	6.9	1.4	5.1	6.2	5.8	12.0	3.1	7.4
2.2	0.7	1.5	3.4	1.6	1.6	2.0	1.2	1.7	1.9
1.0	0.4	0.4	0.4	1.7	0.7	2.3	0.7	1.9	0.8
−6.8	−8.7	0.5	0.5	−10.8	−14.0	−4.0	−0.6	−3.2	−6.4
6.6	8.3	11.8	2.8	13.0	18.9	7.2	5.0	5.0	11.3
3.5	4.0	7.4	2.3	8.2	8.2	5.0	2.7	3.9	5.0
3.0	4.3	4.5	0.5	4.8	10.6	2.2	2.3	1.1	6.3
100.0	100.0	100.0	100.0	100.0	100.0	100.0	100.0	100.0	100.0
69.3	71.6	64.3	78.8	71.9	67.0	71.4	54.5	74.1	59.4
24.1	20.2	23.8	18.4	15.2	14.2	21.4	40.6	20.9	29.4
6.6	8.3	11.8	2.8	13.0	18.9	7.2	5.0	5.0	11.3
100.0	100.0	100.0	100.0	100.0	100.0	100.0	100.0	100.0	100.0
66.2	69.5	58.6	74.3	66.5	64.6	68.8	48.5	68.7	49.9
24.2	20.2	23.8	18.4	15.2	14.2	21.4	40.6	21.0	29.4
9.6	10.3	17.6	7.4	18.4	21.2	9.8	11.0	10.3	20.8
100.0	100.0	100.0	100.0	100.0	100.0	100.0	100.0	100.0	100.0

(*Table continues on the following page.*)

Category	Line numbers[a]	Iran	Uruguay	Ireland	Hungary	Poland	Italy	Spain
Consumption, ICP[b,c]	1–108	45.5	80.3	74.0	61.0	57.4	69.2	73.3
Food, beverages, tobacco	1– 39	15.5	33.7	21.8	22.3	22.5	23.6	24.0
Food	1– 33	14.7	25.6	17.1	16.1	16.5	20.1	21.9
Bread, cereals	1– 6	4.3	4.2	2.3	1.8	2.0	2.7	2.1
Meat	7– 12	3.2	6.8	5.9	4.6	4.9	6.7	7.0
Fish	13– 14	0.2	0.1	0.5	0.1	0.3	0.7	1.7
Milk, cheese, eggs	15– 17	1.6	3.5	2.3	2.2	2.6	2.6	3.4
Oils, fats	18– 20	1.1	1.5	0.9	1.3	1.5	1.6	2.1
Fruits, vegetables	21– 26	2.9	5.4	2.8	2.8	2.6	4.6	3.6
Coffee, tea, cocoa	27– 29	0.5	0.4	0.4	0.9	0.6	0.4	0.4
Spices, sweets, sugar	30– 33	1.0	3.7	2.0	2.4	2.0	1.0	1.5
Beverages	34– 37	0.2	5.6	1.2	4.9	4.9	2.0	1.2
Tobacco	38– 39	0.6	2.4	3.5	1.4	1.1	1.5	0.9
Clothing, footwear	40– 51	4.7	5.7	5.4	6.5	7.3	5.8	7.0
Clothing	40– 47	3.8	4.3	4.5	5.3	6.3	4.8	5.3
Footwear	48– 51	0.9	1.4	0.9	1.2	1.1	1.0	1.7
Gross rent, fuel	52– 57	7.7	8.8	7.5	4.5	4.5	8.6	9.1
Gross rent	52– 53	6.2	5.4	4.2	2.5	3.4	6.7	7.0
Fuel, power	54– 57	1.5	3.4	3.3	2.0	1.1	2.0	2.0
House furnishings, operations	58– 70	3.5	6.4	5.1	5.5	5.1	4.1	5.8
Furniture, appliances	58– 66	2.4	2.4	2.9	3.1	3.1	2.2	3.7
Supplies, operations	67– 70	1.2	4.0	2.2	2.5	1.9	1.9	2.1
Medical care	71– 77	3.1	5.1	6.6	3.6	3.3	5.6	6.2
Transport, communications	78– 89	3.1	7.8	6.4	4.5	3.6	7.1	7.2
Equipment	78– 79	1.3	1.1	2.1	1.5	1.2	1.7	2.2
Operation costs	80– 83	0.8	2.0	2.8	1.3	0.7	3.7	3.3
Purchased transport	84– 87	0.8	4.0	1.1	1.4	1.4	1.0	1.3
Communications	88– 89	0.2	0.7	0.4	0.3	0.3	0.7	0.3
Recreation and education	90–101	4.8	6.8	9.6	7.7	6.9	8.1	6.6
Recreation	90– 96	1.3	4.2	4.1	4.3	3.3	3.6	3.7
Education	97–101	3.4	2.5	5.6	3.3	3.6	4.5	2.9
Other expenditures	102–107	3.2	6.1	11.6	6.4	4.1	6.4	7.6
Personal care	102–104	0.9	1.4	1.1	1.6	1.0	2.3	1.2
Miscellaneous services	105–107	2.3	4.7	10.5	4.7	3.1	4.1	6.4
Capital formation	109–146	36.0	9.6	15.5	31.3	35.4	19.1	22.6
Domestic capital formation	109–145	27.1	13.2	21.4	39.0	41.2	20.3	26.5
Construction	109–122	15.5	9.2	13.9	19.4	19.9	12.5	14.4
Residential	109–110	6.7	3.1	6.1	5.9	3.6	6.2	6.1
Nonresidential	111–118	5.0	1.5	3.7	7.2	9.0	3.9	3.3
Other	119–122	3.8	4.7	4.1	6.3	7.4	2.4	4.9
Producer durables	123–144	13.0	3.8	8.5	15.1	15.5	8.0	8.9
Transport equipment	123–129	4.6	1.0	2.1	2.9	4.1	2.1	2.7
Nonelectrical machinery	130–138	6.3	1.9	4.8	8.7	8.1	3.6	3.4
Electrical machinery	139–142	1.4	0.3	0.8	1.8	3.0	1.5	2.2
Other	143–144	0.7	0.6	0.9	1.7	0.3	0.8	0.6
Exports minus imports	146–146	8.9	−3.5	−5.9	−7.7	−5.8	−1.2	−3.9
Government	147–151	18.5	10.0	10.5	7.8	7.2	11.7	4.1
Compensation	147–150	6.2	8.0	6.4	2.1	2.2	7.2	2.9
Commodities	151–151	12.3	2.0	4.1	5.7	5.0	4.5	1.2
Gross domestic product	1–151	100.0	100.0	100.0	100.0	100.0	100.0	100.0
Aggregates								
ICP concepts[e]								
Consumption (CEP)[b,c]	1–108	45.5	80.3	74.0	61.0	57.4	69.2	73.3
Capital formation (GCF)[d]	109–146	36.0	9.6	15.5	31.3	35.4	19.1	22.6
Government (PFC)	147–151	18.5	10.0	10.5	7.8	7.2	11.7	4.1
Gross domestic product	1–151	100.0	100.0	100.0	100.0	100.0	100.0	100.0
SNA concepts[e]								
Consumption (PFCE)	1–108	40.7	77.0	63.8	53.1	50.3	65.0	68.2
Capital formation (GCF)	109–146	36.0	9.6	15.6	31.5	35.6	19.1	22.6
Government (GFCE)	147–151	23.3	13.3	20.5	15.4	14.1	15.9	9.2
Gross domestic product	1–151	100.0	100.0	100.0	100.0	100.0	100.0	100.0

a. Line numbers refer to Appendix Table 6-1 and show the detailed categories that are included in each aggregation.

b. Consumption, ICP, includes both household and government expenditures. The latter are shown separately in Table 2-1. Consumption, SNA, excludes these governmental expenditures.

c. The consumption aggregate (lines 1–108) includes net expenditure of residents abroad (line 108), not shown separately here.

U.K.	Japan	Austria	Netherlands	Belgium	France	Luxembourg	Denmark	Germany	U.S.
68.3	62.1	64.1	63.6	65.9	65.4	63.3	65.5	64.8	72.2
15.4	16.2	15.9	13.8	14.9	14.9	14.1	15.4	12.9	11.4
11.2	13.8	11.4	10.6	12.4	12.3	11.9	10.3	9.9	9.2
1.6	2.6	1.5	1.4	1.6	1.6	1.7	1.4	1.8	1.3
3.3	1.9	3.6	2.9	4.9	4.2	3.9	3.2	2.6	2.3
0.4	2.7	0.2	0.3	0.5	0.7	0.3	0.5	0.2	0.4
1.6	1.0	1.7	1.8	1.3	1.6	1.7	1.3	1.1	1.1
0.5	0.2	0.8	0.5	0.8	0.8	1.0	0.6	1.0	0.5
2.1	2.2	2.2	2.1	1.9	2.1	2.1	1.3	1.5	2.1
0.3	0.3	0.3	0.5	0.4	0.3	0.4	0.6	0.8	0.2
1.5	3.0	1.2	1.0	1.0	1.1	0.9	1.5	0.9	1.3
1.5	1.5	3.1	1.9	1.4	1.9	1.3	2.9	1.9	1.3
2.7	0.9	1.4	1.3	1.1	0.7	0.9	2.2	1.2	1.0
5.2	4.6	7.0	5.2	5.1	4.9	5.2	3.5	5.6	4.7
4.3	4.2	5.8	4.5	4.3	4.0	4.5	3.0	4.7	4.0
0.9	0.5	1.2	0.8	0.8	0.9	0.7	0.5	0.9	0.7
11.8	8.9	7.7	7.9	9.6	9.4	10.7	12.8	9.5	12.6
9.0	7.8	5.3	5.4	6.0	7.1	7.7	9.4	7.0	10.0
2.8	1.1	2.4	2.4	3.6	2.3	3.1	3.4	2.4	2.6
4.5	3.6	5.6	5.9	7.6	6.5	6.3	5.0	6.3	4.8
2.6	2.1	4.3	3.9	3.9	3.7	3.6	3.0	3.6	3.1
1.8	1.6	1.4	2.0	3.7	2.8	2.8	2.0	2.7	1.7
4.0	5.5	6.4	6.5	5.3	6.9	3.8	3.4	8.2	9.1
8.1	5.4	8.5	6.1	6.9	7.5	7.7	7.8	7.9	9.6
1.8	1.1	1.8	2.1	2.2	1.7	2.7	2.4	2.0	3.1
3.4	1.4	4.7	2.8	3.5	4.1	3.5	3.8	3.8	4.7
2.0	2.5	1.2	0.4	0.7	1.1	1.0	1.0	1.2	0.6
0.9	0.5	0.7	0.8	0.5	0.5	0.6	0.6	1.0	1.3
10.1	9.0	7.3	11.7	8.8	7.7	6.8	12.6	8.4	10.9
5.1	4.5	3.9	5.2	3.3	4.0	2.4	4.7	4.4	4.5
4.9	4.5	3.4	6.5	5.5	3.7	4.5	8.0	4.0	6.4
9.3	8.6	10.1	6.5	7.8	7.6	8.5	5.0	6.1	8.8
1.8	2.0	1.9	1.3	1.8	2.1	2.1	1.4	1.4	1.9
7.5	6.5	8.2	5.1	6.0	5.5	6.5	3.6	4.7	6.8
16.2	32.8	26.7	24.6	23.1	23.7	26.7	19.1	24.3	16.5
18.3	32.7	26.1	20.6	22.0	23.0	28.6	20.4	20.6	15.7
10.5	21.4	16.5	11.5	14.0	14.7	20.2	14.6	12.6	9.5
4.1	7.6	5.9	4.8	5.7	7.6	7.8	6.8	5.2	3.3
4.1	5.4	6.3	4.2	5.8	4.8	8.6	5.4	2.6	2.9
2.3	8.3	4.3	2.6	2.6	2.3	3.8	2.4	4.7	3.3
9.1	11.0	10.2	9.3	8.5	8.6	7.9	7.1	8.2	6.9
2.8	2.5	1.7	2.6	1.9	2.0	1.9	2.3	1.7	1.7
3.9	3.5	5.4	3.6	3.8	5.2	3.4	3.1	3.3	2.8
1.8	2.7	2.2	2.1	2.3	0.9	2.1	0.9	2.5	1.6
0.6	2.3	1.0	1.0	0.6	0.5	0.5	0.8	0.6	0.7
−2.1	0.0	0.6	4.0	1.1	0.7	−1.9	−1.3	3.7	0.8
15.5	5.1	9.2	11.9	11.1	10.9	10.0	15.5	10.8	11.3
10.4	4.0	7.1	8.4	7.9	7.1	6.5	12.8	8.5	5.9
5.1	1.1	2.1	3.4	3.2	3.8	3.5	2.7	2.4	5.4
100.0	100.0	100.0	100.0	100.0	100.0	100.0	100.0	100.0	100.0
68.3	62.1	64.1	63.6	65.9	65.4	63.3	65.5	64.8	72.2
16.2	32.8	26.7	24.6	23.1	23.7	26.7	19.1	24.3	16.5
15.5	5.1	9.2	11.9	11.1	10.9	10.0	15.5	10.8	11.3
100.0	100.0	100.0	100.0	100.0	100.0	100.0	100.0	100.0	100.0
59.4	57.1	56.0	57.0	60.4	61.8	59.0	54.1	61.2	64.4
16.4	32.8	26.7	24.7	23.1	23.7	26.7	19.1	24.3	16.5
24.2	10.1	17.3	18.3	16.5	14.5	14.3	26.7	14.5	19.1
100.0	100.0	100.0	100.0	100.0	100.0	100.0	100.0	100.0	100.0

d. The capital formation aggregate (lines 109–146) includes increase in stocks (line 145) not shown separately in these summary multilateral tables.

e. Letters in parentheses are: CEP, consumption expenditures of the population; GCF, gross capital formation; PFC, public final consumption expenditure; PFCE, private final consumption expenditure; GFCE, government final consumption expenditure. See Glossary for definitions.

basic data are recast into percentages of GDP for the convenience of the reader in Summary Multilateral Table 6-2.

The starting point for the preparation of the tables was the PPPs for the detailed categories. Most of these were obtained by means of the two-stage CPD method through use of an augmented-price tableau as outlined in Chapter 4 under the section "Multilateral Methods Not Dependent on Binary Comparisons." The PPPs for the detailed categories appear in Appendix Table 6-3. They are expressed in national currency units per U.S. dollar, but, as was brought out in the presentation of the method, the United States serves merely as a numéraire country in this procedure. The relative purchasing powers would be the same if another country had been chosen for this role.

Once the PPPs are in hand, the quantity comparisons for the detailed categories are obtained by dividing the PPPs into corresponding expenditure ratios. That is, for each category and for each country the ratio of the country's expenditure on the category to the U.S. expenditure, each taken from Appendix Table 6-1, is divided by the country's PPP for the category obtained from Appendix Table 6-3. For example, the Denmark quantity index for bread was obtained by dividing the ratio of Danish to U.S. expenditures on bread (320.75 kroner ÷ \$49.52 = 6.48) by the PPP for bread (6.00). The result (6.48 ÷ 6.00 = 1.080) is entered (multiplied by 100 to place it in percentage form) in the appendix table that corresponds to Table 6-4.[2] Each entry in a row of this table shows a country's real quantity for a detailed category as a percentage of the U.S. quantity. Observe that these comparisons for the detailed categories are independent of the method chosen to combine the detailed categories into higher aggregates.

The next step is to combine the PPPs and the quantity comparisons for these detailed categories into the desired levels of aggregation ("rice," "bread," and so on, into "bread and cereals"; then "bread and cereals," "meat," and so on, into "food"—and so on to "consumption" and "GDP").

The procedures used to produce the aggregations in Summary Multilateral Tables 6-3 and 6-4 are based on the Geary-Khamis method described in Chapter 3. The inputs for the estimation of the Geary-Khamis equations are the expenditures of Appendix Table 6-1 rescaled by the supercountry weights and the PPPs

of Appendix Table 6-3. A set of "notional" quantities is obtained by dividing the PPPs into expenditures for each detailed category in each country, the expenditures being denominated in each country's own currency. (The quotation marks around "notional" are meant to indicate that these are not strictly quantities but rather values of quantities at numéraire country [U.S.] prices. That is, $E_{ij}/\text{PPP}_{ij} = [p_{ij}q_{ij}]/[p_{ij}/p_{i,US}] = p_{i,US} \cdot q_{ij}$. These notional quantities are not shown in the table because they represent only intermediate data.) The notional quantity for bread in Denmark (53.46, or, strictly speaking, \$53.46), for example, was obtained by dividing the Danish expenditures on bread (320.75 kroner) from Appendix Table 6-1 by the PPP for bread (6.00) from Appendix Table 6-3. It can now be seen that in a strict sense the inputs for Geary-Khamis are the category PPPs and the category notional quantities.

The international prices for the detailed categories, obtained as part of the solution of the Geary-Khamis equations, are entered in the last column of Appendix Table 6-3. The U.S. PPPs are all unity by definition, so they are not given. This set of prices is used to value each country's nominal quantities to get a set of real expenditures. For example, in the Danish bread illustration the notional quantity (53.46) is multiplied by the international price of bread (0.719) to obtain the value of Danish bread consumption at the international price of bread. This turns out to be 38.4 and is entered in Appendix Table 6-5.[3]

Appendix Table 6-5 is in a form that makes it possible to aggregate real quantities valued in international prices over any particular selection of categories simply by adding the corresponding Appendix Table 6-5 entries. This is because the quantities for the detailed categories have been made commensurate from row to row as well as from column to column by valuing them at international prices (that is, matrix consistency has been achieved). The column additivity is the key to the derivation of Summary Multilateral Tables 6-3 and 6-4.

To explain the PPP and the quantity comparisons in the summary tables, it is convenient to start with Sum-

---

2. What would be Appendix Table 6-4 is omitted to save space. However, the bread index can be calculated from Appendix Table 6-5, since, as explained below, both the Danish and U.S. quantities are valued at the international price of bread. That is, the entry for Denmark on line 3 of Appendix Table 6-5 (38.4), divided by the U.S. entry (35.6), equals, with allowance for rounding, 108.0.

3. A category's international price is easily seen to be the ratio of the U.S. entry for the category in Appendix Table 6-5 to the U.S. entry in Appendix Table 6-1. The latter entry is simply $p_{i,US} \cdot q_{i,US}$; the former is the international price, $\bar{\pi}_i$ times the notional quantity. The notional quantity is $(p_{i,US} \cdot q_{i,US}/\text{PPP}_{i,US})$. Since $\text{PPP}_{i,US} = 1$, the U.S. notional quantity is $(p_{i,US} \cdot q_{i,US})$. Therefore, $\bar{\pi}_i \cdot p_{i,US} q_{i,US}/p_{i,US} q_{i,US} = \bar{\pi}_i$. In the case of bread, 35.6 (from Appendix Table 6-5) divided by 49.52 (from Appendix Table 6-1) equals 0.719. An international price is also provided in Summary Table 6-3; it is defined in the same way as above for a detailed category—that is, it is the U.S. entry in Summary Table 6-5 divided by that entry in Summary Table 6-1.

mary Multilateral Table 6-5. The values in this table are aggregates obtained by summing appropriate entries within columns of Appendix Table 6-5. The "line numbers" column gives the appendix table lines over which the aggregation takes place. For example, an entry for residential construction in Summary Multilateral Table 6-5 is the sum of the entries for the same country in line 109, one- and two-dwelling buildings, and line 110, multidwelling buildings, of Appendix Table 6-5. Thus Zambia's entry for residential construction (35.9) is the sum of Zambia's line 109 (32.6) and line 110 (3.3) entries in Appendix Table 6-5. The values are expressed in international dollars (I$), which have the same purchasing power over total U.S. GDP as a U.S. dollar (US$). For subaggregates and for the detailed categories, however, the purchasing power of an international dollar differs from that of a U.S. dollar because it depends on the structure of average international prices rather than on the U.S. relative price structure.

Since the aggregations of Summary Multilateral Table 6-5 are summations at international prices of the quantities of goods and services consumed by the different countries, they can be recast in index-number form. This has been done with the United States taken as 100 in Summary Multilateral Table 6-4. For example, the expenditure of the United Kingdom on meat at international prices is I$179.1, whereas that of the United States is I$185.2 (Summary Multilateral Table 6-5). The ratio between the two is 0.967, which is entered in percentage form in Summary Multilateral Table 6-4. Particularly noteworthy are the lines that contain country comparisons with the United States at the level of consumption, capital formation, government, and GDP. These ICP aggregates may also be found along with the corresponding *System of National Accounts* (SNA) aggregates at the bottom of the table. (The latter, it will be recalled, include public expenditures on health, education, and recreation in government expenditures.)

The category PPPs are given in Appendix Table 6-3. Their counterparts for aggregated categories are placed in Summary Multilateral Table 6-3. They are obtained by dividing the quantity ratios in Summary Multilateral Table 6-4 into expenditure ratios taken from Summary Multilateral Table 6-1. For example, when the U.K./U.S. expenditure ratio for meat derived from Summary Multilateral Table 6-1 (61.449 ÷ 163.79) is divided by the quantity ratio (0.967), the result is a PPP of 0.388 pounds per dollar, which is entered in Summary Multilateral Table 6-3.[4]

---

4. An alternative way of deriving entries in Summary Multilateral Table 6-3 is to divide the ratio of entries in Table 6-1 to entries in Table 6-5 by the corresponding ratios for the United States.

Comparisons of the Structure of Expenditures, Prices, and Quantities for Six Groups of Countries

Results of the comparisons at the level of GDP and its three major components have already been discussed in Chapter 1. This section focuses on the more salient features of the comparisons at a lower level of aggregation—namely, the summary categories. It concentrates on the search for patterns associated with the large differences in real per capita GDP that exist among these thirty-four countries; for the most part, each reader is left to study differences among individual countries according to his own interest.

It will have been noticed that, as a means of facilitating the perusal of the data, the countries are arrayed in columns from left to right in order of ascending 1975 real GDP per capita in all the basic tables in this chapter (Summary Multilateral Tables 6-1 to 6-5 and Appendix Tables 6-1, 6-3, and 6-5). (For a Romanian reservation about the results of that country, see note 2 in Chapter 7.)

To make the data still more manageable for discussion purposes, some summary categories and aggregations of summary categories from the basic tables have been selected and have been presented as averages for six groups of countries classified according to real per capita GDP. The groups of countries are arrayed according to real per capita GDP. The dividing line was placed at points where there were notable gaps between the real per capita GDPs of countries with successive ranks. The groupings are as follows:

Group	Real GDP per capita (U.S. = 100)	Country
I	Less than 15 percent	Malawi
		Kenya
		India
		Pakistan
		Sri Lanka
		Zambia
		Thailand
		Philippines
II	15–30 percent	Korea
		Malaysia
		Colombia
		Jamaica
		Syria
		Brazil
III	30–45 percent	Romania
		Mexico
		Yugoslavia
		Iran
		Uruguay
		Ireland

Group	Real GDP per capita (U.S. = 100)	Country
IV	45–60 percent	Hungary
		Poland
		Italy
		Spain
V	60–90 percent	U.K.
		Japan
		Austria
		Netherlands
		Belgium
		France
		Luxembourg
		Denmark
		Germany
VI	More than 90 percent	U.S.

Shares of Expenditures in Own Currencies

Table 6-6 examines the percentage distribution in own currency for each of the six groups of countries. The figures are simple averages of the percentages from Summary Multilateral Table 6-2 for the countries included in each group. (The same method of averaging will be followed in the subsequent tables in which data for the six groups are presented.)

One of the most striking aspects of these data is the sharp decline in the proportion of GDP that is accounted for by expenditure on food. The food share drops from 38 percent for Group I to 9 percent for Group VI. A substantial part of this is accounted for by the decline in the relative importance of expenditures on bread and cereals, particularly in the transition from the very lowest group to the next lowest. Expenditures on bread and cereals accounted for about 15 percent of GDP per capita for Group I, only 7 percent for Group II, 4 percent for Group III, and 1 or 2 percent for the other groups. A tendency for declines is evident also for other food components. However, the share accounted for by meat rises from Group I through Group IV and then falls. The falling food shares for the higher income levels is offset by steady, or almost steady, increases in shares for gross rents, furniture and appliances, medical care, personal-transport equipment, personal-transport operation cost, communications, recreation, and personal care. In addition to meat, expenditures on clothing and footwear, purchased transport, and capital formation initially rise and then fall.

Relative Quantities

Underlying these differences in expenditures are differences in both prices and quantities. The behavior of the quantities is shown for each of the six groups in Table 6-7. The figures are averages of the real per capita quantity indexes, with the United States equal to 100, from Summary Multilateral Table 6-4. The quantity indexes tend to rise steadily from one GDP group to another for many more categories than are indicated in the figures in Table 6-6; that is, there are fewer instances of declining figures for the higher income groups. This reflects the fact that higher incomes tend to be used to buy more of all kinds of final products. There are, however, a few groups for which real per capita quantities decline (after initial increases); these include bread and cereals, meat, oils and fats, and purchased transport. Bread and cereals and purchased transport are hardly surprising, since it is clear that substitutes are preferred as income rises. The reasons for the other exceptions have not been researched, but it might be worthwhile to determine whether domestic agricultural policies have a role in producing some of these results. There are, to be sure, other instances of declines in average real quantities between one group and the next higher one, but they tend to be exceptional and often reflect the particular circumstances of a given country. For example, the high per capita consumption of fish in Group V relative to Groups IV and VI results almost entirely from the very large fish consumption of Japan. High fish consumption in the Philippines and to a lesser degree in Thailand accounts for the high average quantity ratio for Group I and high consumption in Malaysia, Jamaica, and the Republic of Korea for the high Group II average. (See Summary Multilateral Table 6-4 for the individual country ratios.) Geography—particularly long coast lines—rather than real per capita income explains these consumption levels.

For food as a whole, per capita quantity averages range from 28 percent of the United States for Group I to 96 percent for Groups IV and V. For individual categories of food and beverages levels of per capita consumption above those of the United States (that is, numbers over 100) are found for Groups IV and V, and in the case of bread and cereals for the lower income groups.

Outside of food and beverages, instances in which the indexes exceed 100 are found, except for purchased transport, only in Group V.[5]

Price Levels

Table 6-8 compares price levels for each category with those of the United States. The figures in the table are derived by dividing the PPPs of Summary Multilateral Table 6-3 by the appropriate exchange rate and then combining these individual country price

5. Another exception is exports minus imports, but here the quantity indexes represent relationships between residuals that are usually small relative to GDP and quite variable from year to year.

indexes to obtain group averages. The general pattern of the table can be seen by examining the last row of figures pertaining to GDP as a whole. In the lowest income countries, the price level for GDP is about 40 percent of that of the United States. It rises in successive stages to nearly 75 percent of the United States for Group IV. It reaches a peak for Group V, where it is slightly higher than the U.S. price level. However, not all countries in Group V have prices higher than those of the United States. The GDP price level (U.S. = 100) for the countries in this group can be seen by checking back to Table 1-9 (column 9) to vary from 90.1 for the United Kingdom to 126.9 for Denmark.

The exception represented by the United States to the general tendency for price levels to be positively correlated with real per capita GDP, evident for 1975 in Table 6-9, was not found in 1970. Most of the change had, however, occurred by 1973. The price-level comparisons for the Group V countries for which data for the earlier years are available are as follows:

	GDP *price level (U.S. = 100)*		
	1970	1973	1975
U.K.	72.8	84.4	90.1
Japan	67.6	95.0	91.2
Netherlands	73.8	104.1	112.3
Belgium	76.2	98.9	113.0
Germany	82.9	117.6	114.2
France	80.1	102.6	109.4
Mean of above	75.6	100.4	105.0
U.S.	100.0	100.0	100.0

In a purely mechanical sense, the changes from one year to another could occur either as a result of changes in the relative internal purchasing power of the currency or as result of changes in the exchange rate. (This stems from the definition of the price level: PPP ÷ exchange rate.) In this case, most of the changes came from the depreciation of the U.S. dollar. The dollar depreciated by varying amounts against the individual currencies and by 16 percent against the weighted average represented by the SDR[6] between 1970 and 1973 but less than 2 percent between 1973 and 1975.[7] Between 1970 and 1973, the PPPs, reflecting the relationships between the internal prices of the various countries, changed by only a few percentage points or not at all for the United States relative to Belgium, the Federal Republic of Germany, and France; by less than 10 percent relative to Japan and the Netherlands; and by 13 percent relative to the United Kingdom. The relationships between the results for these three benchmark years are discussed further in Chapter 8, but the causes and the structural significance of

the changed position of the United States with respect to the price level–real income relationship is left for investigation elsewhere.

In any case, the same pattern of rising prices from Groups I through V and then a decline in Group VI (the United States) is found in the large majority of the individual summary categories in Table 6-8. Price levels for beverages and tobacco tend to seesaw in the progression of the groups from I through VI, probably reflecting different excise-tax policies.

For a few categories, notably consumer transport equipment (mainly automobiles) and, more erratically, producer durable goods, prices are actually higher in low-income countries than in high-income countries. In the United States, the highest income country, the prices of these goods tended to be the lowest.

Although producer durables prices tend to tilt downward against the rising income scale, the price differences among countries are smaller for those goods on average than is the case for other goods. Producer durable goods come closer to carrying world price tags in all countries than do other goods. This is affirmed by the coefficients of variation (calculated by using the data of all thirty-four countries rather than simply the six groups) in the last column of Table 6-8; the coefficient for nonelectrical machines (lines 130–38) is the lowest in the column, and the entry for electrical machinery (lines 139–42) one of the lowest.[8] The similarity in prices of machinery can probably be attributed to the high proportion of its production that enters into international trade.

The greater dispersion of transport equipment prices probably reflects the existence of relatively segregated markets for automobiles. (Compare the coefficients of variation for lines 123–129 and 78–79 with the coefficients for the other types of machinery.) It seems likely that the domestic prices of automobiles are affected by high costs of home production in some low-income countries where markets are small and protected, and sometimes also by high taxes, while some high-income countries have low costs attributable to the economies of large-scale production.

At the other extreme, prices in labor-intensive categories such as the compensation of government employees and medical care tend to be very low in the low-income countries. Construction, unlike producer durables, tends to follow the same price pattern as GDP as a whole.

The dispersion of prices (the coefficient of variation again) is highest in education, purchased transport, and compensation of government employees. These

(Text continues on page 191.)

6. Special drawing rights of the International Monetary Fund are a unit consisting of a basket of currencies.

7. Data from *International Financial Statistics* (May 1978).

8. Excluding exports minus exports, for which the exchange rate is taken as the PPP.

Category	Line numbers[a]	Malawi (kwacha)	Kenya (shillings)	India (rupees)	Pakistan (rupees)	Sri Lanka (rupees)	Zambia (kwacha)	Thailand (baht)
Consumption, ICP[b,c]	1–108	0.335	3.61	2.50	3.32	3.20	0.441	7.2
Food, beverages, tobacco	1– 39	0.373	4.48	3.78	4.34	5.27	0.474	8.2
Food	1– 33	0.356	4.32	3.65	4.29	5.07	0.450	8.0
Bread, cereals	1– 6	0.334	3.17	2.73	2.68	4.93	0.192	4.1
Meat	7– 12	0.444	3.19	2.79	2.98	2.75	0.510	9.0
Fish	13– 14	0.786	8.58	2.09	4.47	4.05	0.710	11.4
Milk, cheese, eggs	15– 17	0.632	4.72	6.66	7.69	5.01	0.584	14.0
Oils, fats	18– 20	0.893	8.09	5.55	6.24	4.44	0.704	16.3
Fruits, vegetables	21– 26	0.264	5.06	3.06	4.05	3.98	0.822	11.3
Coffee, tea, cocoa	27– 29	0.653	6.93	5.08	4.60	4.33	0.775	23.8
Spices, sweets, sugar	30– 33	0.439	4.70	4.36	6.14	5.64	0.487	11.5
Beverages	34– 37	0.587	7.62	6.76	10.21	7.12	0.964	7.7
Tobacco	38– 39	0.420	3.37	5.43	3.87	6.39	1.192	15.7
Clothing, footwear	40– 51	0.606	5.88	4.54	3.51	3.68	0.644	7.0
Clothing	40– 47	0.653	5.70	4.90	3.67	3.80	0.710	7.1
Footwear	48– 51	0.340	7.55	2.36	2.81	2.67	0.367	7.4
Gross rent, fuel	52– 57	0.672	5.56	1.85	5.79	1.91	0.410	7.6
Gross rent	52– 53	0.590	6.14	1.07	4.84	1.45	0.523	9.2
Fuel, power	54– 57	0.935	4.31	4.59	8.84	3.75	0.335	7.9
House furnishings, operations	58– 70	0.508	2.55	3.53	3.47	2.16	0.574	9.1
Furniture, appliances	58– 66	0.628	4.94	7.67	7.12	5.80	0.840	13.0
Supplies, operations	67– 70	0.433	1.73	2.71	3.05	1.65	0.473	7.1
Medical care	71– 77	0.112	4.61	1.05	2.24	0.99	0.387	5.5
Transport, communications	78– 89	1.020	6.64	2.59	2.14	4.51	0.986	10.5
Equipment	78– 79	1.854	13.90	6.33	14.39	14.59	1.582	40.4
Operation costs	80– 83	1.164	7.77	10.99	14.27	10.05	0.946	16.8
Purchased transport	84– 87	0.306	2.69	1.04	0.89	1.90	0.292	4.0
Communications	88– 89	0.473	5.30	4.40	3.82	2.10	0.434	8.0
Recreation and education	90–101	0.128	1.65	0.69	1.19	0.93	0.289	5.6
Recreation	90– 96	0.397	4.57	2.93	2.55	2.57	0.643	14.1
Education	97–101	0.067	1.07	0.38	0.54	0.46	0.187	2.8
Other expenditures	102–107	0.391	4.13	1.83	2.47	2.17	0.476	8.7
Personal care	102–104	0.723	2.82	2.63	3.41	3.18	0.613	9.1
Miscellaneous services	105–107	0.352	7.01	1.55	2.10	1.86	0.453	8.7
Capital formation	109–146	0.537	6.20	4.14	4.11	2.41	0.579	11.0
Domestic capital formation	109–145	0.676	6.40	4.15	5.46	3.94	0.597	11.9
Construction	109–122	0.387	4.15	2.61	3.76	2.47	0.450	7.8
Residential	109–110	0.479	4.50	2.12	2.90	2.60	0.455	9.1
Nonresidential	111–118	0.480	3.51	2.83	3.14	2.66	0.807	10.2
Other	119–122	0.255	4.09	2.84	4.99	2.16	0.263	4.9
Producer durables	123–144	1.412	12.18	9.61	11.30	11.35	0.887	21.1
Transport equipment	123–129	2.352	16.29	8.98	19.80	9.51	0.830	21.8
Nonelectrical machinery	130–138	1.196	11.06	9.07	9.98	12.40	0.960	19.4
Electrical machinery	139–142	0.901	11.78	10.36	9.87	14.51	0.978	24.5
Other	143–144	1.010	9.48	9.69	15.38	21.28	0.755	20.5
Exports minus imports	146–146	0.866	7.41	8.37	9.93	10.60	0.643	20.4
Government	147–151	0.196	2.77	1.45	1.66	1.31	0.306	6.0
Compensation	147–150	0.091	1.72	0.90	0.97	0.91	0.147	4.0
Commodities	151–151	0.624	5.15	2.82	3.37	2.02	0.597	9.3
Gross domestic product	1–151	0.341	3.80	2.59	3.18	2.93	0.431	7.6
Exchange rate[f]		0.866	7.41	8.38	9.93	10.60	0.644	20.4
Aggregates								
ICP concepts[e]								
Consumption (CEP)[b,c]	1–108	0.335	3.61	2.50	3.32	3.20	0.441	7.2
Capital formation (GCF)[d]	109–146	0.537	6.20	4.13	4.11	2.41	0.579	11.0
Government (PFC)	147–151	0.196	2.77	1.45	1.67	1.30	0.306	6.0
Gross domestic product	1–151	0.341	3.80	2.59	3.18	2.93	0.431	7.6
SNA concepts[e]								
Consumption (PFCE)	1–108	0.386	4.02	2.83	3.60	3.77	0.470	7.6
Capital formation (GCF)	109–146	0.537	6.20	4.13	4.11	2.41	0.579	11.0
Government (GFCE)	147–151	0.133	2.18	1.01	1.35	0.95	0.278	4.9
Gross domestic product	1–151	0.340	3.80	2.59	3.18	2.93	0.431	7.6

Philippines (pesos)	Korea (won)	Malaysia (ringgit)	Colombia (pesos)	Jamaica (dollars)	Syria (pounds)	Brazil (cruzeiros)	Romania (lei)	Mexico (pesos)	Yugoslavia (dinars)
2.63	191.	1.22	10.4	0.688	1.32	5.31	7.6	7.2	9.8
3.95	283.	1.58	13.0	0.930	1.60	5.51	10.7	8.5	12.5
4.01	309.	1.50	13.1	0.924	1.57	5.31	10.2	8.7	12.2
3.26	255.	1.18	23.1	0.742	0.85	4.89	8.1	8.5	8.3
3.54	353.	1.64	10.8	0.906	2.79	4.31	10.9	10.6	14.0
4.90	280.	1.57	21.6	1.032	2.24	6.38	11.3	7.9	11.7
10.73	422.	1.72	15.0	0.844	2.75	5.37	9.1	7.7	11.1
3.22	527.	1.53	19.4	0.898	1.64	7.30	9.5	12.1	12.3
5.09	250.	1.47	16.2	1.280	1.38	8.80	9.7	7.3	12.0
7.29	1151.	2.68	13.3	1.371	3.43	6.15	37.0	12.7	38.4
2.79	333.	1.47	9.2	0.530	2.23	3.11	11.1	5.7	14.8
2.78	351.	2.23	15.4	0.867	3.03	5.75	11.7	7.6	14.3
4.74	131.	2.02	6.9	1.084	1.70	8.10	39.4	3.3	12.2
2.76	173.	1.15	10.7	0.832	1.74	7.96	13.3	9.3	13.2
2.91	180.	1.30	10.5	0.788	1.74	8.35	13.3	9.7	13.2
2.05	125.	0.59	10.7	0.798	1.75	6.19	13.0	7.7	13.0
2.19	191.	1.13	9.5	0.991	1.24	6.44	2.8	5.5	7.1
1.72	310.	0.93	12.5	0.963	1.20	5.06	2.0	4.2	4.7
5.73	191.	3.00	6.0	1.111	1.51	11.95	7.6	9.4	16.0
2.93	235.	1.28	12.5	0.703	1.87	7.75	12.9	7.5	13.9
5.03	337.	1.78	22.4	1.282	2.47	10.16	15.0	10.6	16.1
1.99	150.	1.01	9.5	0.454	1.42	5.77	10.5	6.0	10.5
0.98	105.	0.63	9.6	0.380	0.73	3.12	2.4	5.9	4.3
3.17	215.	2.25	12.8	0.977	1.94	8.86	19.2	8.1	16.3
10.45	470.	4.36	82.5	1.992	2.09	13.10	26.4	20.0	20.6
5.82	381	2.64	20.2	1.151	4.22	10.23	19.2	10.3	18.2
1.00	111.	0.76	6.4	0.589	0.94	3.23	11.0	2.7	7.4
2.94	84.	1.98	3.8	0.179	1.82	4.69	5.8	3.4	7.2
1.05	102.	0.81	7.2	0.354	0.75	3.05	5.1	6.5	6.8
3.93	164.	1.21	14.7	0.576	1.69	8.59	9.7	11.8	9.5
0.64	68.	0.56	4.6	0.232	0.46	1.29	3.1	4.2	4.9
2.26	142.	0.94	10.5	0.538	1.21	5.51	8.9	9.0	9.7
3.52	193.	1.07	20.1	0.724	1.94	6.81	14.4	9.2	10.4
1.95	123.	0.91	9.2	0.491	0.95	5.17	8.2	9.1	9.4
5.85	215.	1.31	13.5	1.027	1.99	5.98	12.9	8.5	17.1
6.06	256.	1.29	13.3	0.956	2.54	6.21	12.8	8.9	17.0
4.85	191.	0.82	8.0	0.805	2.30	5.18	8.6	6.0	17.0
4.78	173.	0.69	8.3	0.799	1.95	4.58	12.4	6.6	17.3
4.53	204.	1.02	7.9	0.983	2.08	6.22	6.2	7.3	20.0
5.18	202.	0.75	6.9	0.635	2.37	4.60	16.0	4.5	14.0
9.92	369.	2.92	42.5	1.157	2.88	7.63	22.2	16.8	19.4
10.87	338.	3.35	45.7	1.222	2.77	9.04	24.6	15.6	17.2
11.32	472.	2.74	41.6	1.241	2.69	7.63	23.0	17.5	21.3
7.64	351.	3.76	41.1	1.235	5.03	7.68	22.3	18.8	15.9
6.60	215.	2.76	34.9	0.793	5.32	5.84	12.8	14.0	21.1
7.27	484.	2.40	30.9	0.909	3.70	8.20	12.0	12.5	17.4
1.43	147.	1.16	8.5	0.730	1.71	3.46	6.7	6.8	10.2
0.79	101.	0.98	6.3	0.601	1.95	2.32	4.9	5.2	7.5
3.49	206.	1.30	13.8	0.832	1.70	6.79	9.0	8.5	13.2
2.89	190.	1.22	10.8	0.742	1.48	5.20	8.8	7.4	11.2
7.27	484.	2.40	30.9	0.909	3.70	8.20	12.0	12.5	17.4
2.63	191.	1.22	10.4	0.688	1.32	5.31	7.6	7.2	9.8
5.85	215.	1.31	13.5	1.027	1.99	5.98	12.9	8.5	17.1
1.43	147.	1.17	8.5	0.730	1.71	3.46	6.7	6.8	10.2
2.89	190.	1.22	10.8	0.742	1.48	5.20	8.8	7.4	11.2
2.92	204.	1.31	11.2	0.754	1.41	5.78	8.8	7.5	10.9
5.85	215.	1.31	13.5	1.027	1.99	5.98	12.9	8.5	17.1
1.12	119.	0.92	6.7	0.513	1.30	2.68	4.3	6.2	7.3
2.90	190.	1.22	10.8	0.742	1.48	5.20	8.8	7.4	11.2

(Table continues on the following page.)

Category	Line numbers[a]	Iran (rials)	Uruguay (N. pesos)	Ireland (pounds)	Hungary (forint)	Poland (zlotys)	Italy (lire)	Spain (pesetas)
Consumption, ICP[b,c]	1–108	34.9	1.04	0.366	11.1	13.2	567.	39.8
Food, beverages, tobacco	1– 39	44.0	1.06	0.402	14.5	19.1	665.	43.1
Food	1– 33	43.3	0.98	0.350	13.4	16.6	671.	44.7
Bread, cereals	1– 6	27.1	0.76	0.328	6.5	11.0	516.	38.3
Meat	7– 12	49.7	0.63	0.358	13.5	17.3	839.	52.9
Fish	13– 14	72.7	0.58	0.489	11.7	24.9	1105.	42.0
Milk, cheese, eggs	15– 17	63.0	0.94	0.304	15.0	17.3	673.	51.7
Oils, fats	18– 20	50.9	3.06	0.360	15.4	23.7	693.	44.5
Fruits, vegetables	21– 26	51.2	1.38	0.405	13.8	13.5	535.	37.5
Coffee, tea, cocoa	27– 29	116.2	2.67	0.393	60.0	98.9	1502.	70.5
Spices, sweets, sugar	30– 33	31.0	1.69	0.307	15.2	16.4	602.	40.8
Beverages	34– 37	59.2	1.29	0.568	21.3	37.4	595.	29.9
Tobacco	38– 39	41.2	2.12	0.921	13.9	18.6	651.	30.7
Clothing, footwear	40– 51	29.7	1.64	0.463	18.9	22.7	670.	54.1
Clothing	40– 47	30.7	1.59	0.454	19.3	23.9	684.	65.3
Footwear	48– 51	25.1	1.70	0.513	16.8	16.9	590.	32.0
Gross rent, fuel	52– 57	32.3	0.96	0.394	11.2	7.8	543.	35.7
Gross rent	52– 53	32.6	0.77	0.310	9.6	6.7	484.	29.8
Fuel, power	54– 57	30.8	1.64	0.652	16.1	13.6	802.	73.1
House furnishings, operations	58– 70	44.0	2.37	0.408	16.1	16.8	617.	63.4
Furniture, appliances	58– 66	57.6	2.17	0.432	17.2	18.8	595.	63.4
Supplies, operations	67– 70	28.6	2.38	0.368	14.4	13.8	627.	63.3
Medical care	71– 77	35.5	0.61	0.202	3.4	4.3	314.	26.8
Transport, communications	78– 89	41.8	2.04	0.623	19.4	22.7	700.	66.3
Equipment	78– 79	203.9	8.93	0.756	27.5	49.7	889.	75.0
Operation costs	80– 83	38.8	2.19	0.516	27.9	41.1	677.	93.4
Purchased transport	84– 87	9.6	0.85	0.619	7.4	7.4	342.	24.6
Communications	88– 89	48.2	1.25	0.527	8.3	11.7	628.	21.3
Recreation and education	90–101	30.3	0.80	0.309	7.5	8.6	547.	30.3
Recreation	90– 96	59.3	1.63	0.345	10.2	13.4	721.	48.6
Education	97–101	19.6	0.38	0.274	5.6	5.7	415.	18.9
Other expenditures	102–107	30.5	0.92	0.345	8.8	11.8	577.	33.6
Personal care	102–104	36.7	2.18	0.403	13.4	17.0	718.	41.0
Miscellaneous services	105–107	28.7	0.77	0.330	7.8	10.6	530.	31.8
Capital formation	109–146	53.4	2.02	0.487	17.6	19.6	639.	52.3
Domestic capital formation	109–145	50.4	2.07	0.470	18.0	19.5	637.	52.6
Construction	109–122	33.7	1.64	0.443	14.9	16.1	534.	45.5
Residential	109–110	23.1	2.10	0.457	13.6	15.6	517.	42.6
Nonresidential	111–118	44.3	1.12	0.562	21.5	17.3	682.	41.4
Other	119–122	88.5	1.51	0.342	11.2	15.3	439.	53.7
Producer durables	123–144	90.3	3.26	0.491	23.2	24.2	800.	62.7
Transport equipment	123–129	125.9	5.25	0.621	14.4	23.8	811.	63.9
Nonelectrical machinery	130–138	81.7	3.32	0.460	29.8	26.6	806.	59.5
Electrical machinery	139–142	86.8	3.52	0.546	27.0	20.9	967.	63.4
Other	143–144	56.4	1.69	0.416	19.4	29.8	566.	95.6
Exports minus imports	146–146	67.6	2.30	0.450	20.7	19.9	653.	57.4
Government	147–151	38.3	0.63	0.396	10.7	11.3	595.	57.1
Compensation	147–150	49.7	0.44	0.342	5.8	6.0	514.	51.9
Commodities	151–151	39.4	1.41	0.426	15.8	17.4	640.	52.5
Gross domestic product	1–151	39.7	1.06	0.388	12.3	14.3	582.	42.3
Exchange rate[f]		67.6	2.30	0.450	20.7	19.9	653.	57.4
Aggregates								
ICP concepts[e]								
Consumption (CEP)[b,c]	1–108	34.9	1.04	0.366	11.1	13.2	567.	39.8
Capital formation (GCF)[d]	109–146	53.5	2.02	0.487	17.6	19.6	639.	52.3
Government (PFC)	147–151	38.3	0.63	0.396	10.7	11.3	595.	57.1
Gross domestic product	1–151	39.7	1.06	0.388	12.3	14.3	582.	42.3
SNA concepts[e]								
Consumption (PFCE)	1–108	35.9	1.10	0.381	12.8	15.3	584.	41.6
Capital formation (GCF)	109–146	53.5	2.02	0.487	17.6	19.6	639.	52.3
Government (GFCE)	147–151	32.9	0.56	0.326	6.9	7.9	535.	39.1
Gross domestic product	1–151	39.7	1.06	0.389	12.3	14.4	582.	42.3

a. Line numbers refer to Appendix Table 6-1 and show the detailed categories that are included in each aggregation.

b. Consumption, ICP, includes both household and government expenditures. The latter are shown separately in Table 2-1. Consumption, SNA, excludes these governmental expenditures.

c. The consumption aggregate (lines 1–108) includes net expenditure of residents abroad (line 108), not shown separately here.

U.K. (pounds)	Japan (yen)	Austria (schillings)	Netherlands (guilders)	Belgium (francs)	France (francs)	Luxembourg (francs)	Denmark (kroner)	Germany (DM)	International price (Π)
0.386	271.	15.6	2.76	39.5	4.63	36.7	6.98	2.79	0.96
0.430	317.	16.5	2.68	38.9	4.76	38.7	8.14	3.01	1.16
0.371	319.	16.7	2.64	38.9	4.84	39.9	7.44	2.90	1.14
0.323	274.	15.9	2.38	33.4	4.62	36.0	6.78	2.72	0.92
0.388	574.	20.0	3.00	43.5	5.58	44.2	7.39	3.31	1.13
0.474	334.	19.4	3.05	53.3	6.08	54.2	9.16	3.26	1.33
0.322	352.	15.0	2.47	35.2	3.93	37.5	6.01	2.54	1.22
0.295	397.	17.0	3.44	43.6	5.35	42.5	7.94	3.10	1.34
0.451	412.	14.6	2.49	34.3	4.51	35.9	9.44	2.41	1.12
0.441	705.	33.0	4.02	68.0	6.80	71.3	12.94	7.05	1.84
0.352	208.	14.1	2.13	29.6	4.09	32.7	6.80	2.24	1.07
0.510	374.	14.9	2.47	34.3	4.18	30.3	8.77	3.05	1.26
0.966	220.	22.0	3.74	44.9	5.26	39.0	13.63	4.43	1.23
0.472	264.	17.7	3.13	52.3	6.74	51.9	8.49	3.11	1.14
0.464	267.	18.0	3.16	52.2	6.66	52.8	8.48	3.11	1.16
0.514	251.	16.0	2.97	52.8	6.92	46.6	8.57	3.09	1.01
0.432	329.	12.2	2.42	44.0	4.68	41.2	5.85	2.76	0.94
0.402	319.	9.5	2.12	37.2	4.05	37.6	5.17	2.41	0.87
0.542	321.	27.8	3.59	67.6	7.71	55.0	8.65	4.24	1.22
0.412	313.	16.2	2.38	39.0	4.30	35.9	5.95	2.50	1.07
0.437	319.	16.7	2.28	32.9	3.74	33.5	5.35	2.27	1.12
0.372	298.	15.2	2.64	47.9	5.32	38.9	7.26	2.89	0.98
0.141	134.	10.6	2.45	23.6	3.02	18.6	3.03	2.10	0.61
0.603	309.	26.6	3.53	46.0	5.85	42.9	10.26	3.63	1.22
0.500	272.	27.2	3.89	43.3	6.90	43.4	15.75	3.36	1.40
0.499	420.	28.8	3.16	44.7	5.10	41.5	8.17	3.31	1.27
0.606	169.	17.5	3.41	50.3	5.80	46.6	10.55	3.78	0.61
0.517	159.	14.5	4.52	82.7	7.49	36.2	8.16	4.33	0.89
0.346	226.	14.5	2.81	43.2	4.47	44.3	7.62	2.52	0.74
0.372	259.	19.0	2.73	43.2	5.25	37.7	7.40	2.85	1.03
0.361	208.	11.2	3.16	41.1	4.05	48.4	7.39	2.47	0.53
0.364	302.	15.5	3.33	42.9	5.05	34.3	8.09	2.90	0.92
0.416	256.	15.0	3.26	47.6	5.43	44.7	8.81	3.15	1.06
0.350	326.	15.5	3.34	41.6	4.96	31.6	7.92	2.84	0.89
0.522	299.	23.9	2.92	45.6	5.01	50.3	7.40	2.86	1.23
0.509	298.	24.2	3.03	46.1	5.03	48.8	7.23	2.97	1.23
0.485	334.	24.1	2.69	43.1	4.63	45.8	6.86	2.65	1.07
0.483	458.	28.2	2.25	43.1	4.44	45.6	7.34	3.18	1.08
0.582	392.	23.2	4.03	50.9	6.19	57.5	8.06	3.40	1.22
0.397	228.	22.6	2.33	35.7	3.59	33.7	4.89	1.85	0.91
0.539	245.	23.3	3.48	48.8	5.43	48.8	7.46	3.35	1.45
0.541	342.	27.1	3.41	47.8	5.86	48.3	9.28	2.85	1.54
0.545	214.	22.2	3.34	45.8	5.40	45.9	6.23	3.14	1.48
0.605	222.	23.5	4.48	59.4	6.52	59.3	8.37	4.34	1.39
0.418	222.	23.4	2.75	42.0	4.14	42.0	9.13	3.37	1.22
0.450	297.	17.4	2.53	36.8	4.29	36.8	5.75	2.46	1.28
0.372	323.	20.5	4.00	55.8	5.17	52.9	9.18	3.55	0.91
0.294	277.	18.4	4.30	56.1	4.85	58.4	7.96	3.20	0.71
0.452	298.	18.0	2.96	44.5	4.85	42.7	7.72	2.98	1.12
0.406	271.	17.5	2.84	41.6	4.69	40.2	7.29	2.81	1.00
0.450	297.	17.4	2.53	36.8	4.29	36.8	5.75	2.46	—
0.386	271.	15.6	2.76	39.5	4.63	36.7	6.98	2.79	0.96
0.522	299.	23.9	2.92	45.6	5.01	50.3	7.40	2.86	1.23
0.372	323.	20.5	4.00	55.8	5.17	52.9	9.18	3.55	0.91
0.406	271.	17.5	2.84	41.6	4.69	40.2	7.29	2.81	1.00
0.410	278.	16.0	2.73	39.7	4.74	36.8	7.05	2.85	1.01
0.522	299.	23.9	2.92	45.6	5.01	50.3	7.40	2.86	1.23
0.303	281.	16.1	3.79	51.4	4.73	51.3	7.50	3.20	0.78
0.406	271.	17.5	2.84	41.6	4.69	40.2	7.31	2.81	1.00

d. The capital formation aggregate (lines 109–146) includes increase in stocks (line 145) not shown separately in these summary multilateral tables.

e. Letters in parentheses are: CEP, consumption expenditures of the population; GCF, gross capital formation; PFC, public final consumption expenditure; PFCE, private final consumption expenditure; GFCE, government final consumption expenditure. See Glossary for definitions.

f. Exchange rates have been rounded; for the unrounded rates, see Table 1-1.

Category	Line numbers[a]	Malawi	Kenya	India	Pakistan	Sri Lanka	Zambia	Thailand
Consumption, ICP[b,c]	1–108	5.5	7.3	6.8	8.9	10.2	8.4	14.0
Food, beverages, tobacco	1– 39	18.2	16.4	18.3	25.5	26.9	20.0	39.6
Food	1– 33	21.6	17.8	22.2	30.7	30.6	24.4	42.3
Bread, cereals	1– 6	61.8	67.2	92.8	114.0	111.6	85.9	175.8
Meat	7– 12	4.7	5.8	2.5	10.7	3.8	22.5	24.0
Fish	13– 14	13.5	1.3	19.8	16.2	46.3	53.9	91.6
Milk, cheese, eggs	15– 17	4.0	24.6	10.5	30.2	11.0	6.5	12.5
Oils, fats	18– 20	3.0	5.8	30.6	60.7	6.9	18.9	10.6
Fruits, vegetables	21– 26	50.6	14.6	18.7	17.0	32.5	12.3	23.3
Coffee, tea, cocoa	27– 29	2.7	6.4	9.5	25.6	29.8	7.7	5.6
Spices, sweets, sugar	30– 33	4.4	9.6	15.7	12.2	31.3	9.8	29.3
Beverages	34– 37	7.9	9.2	1.2	0.2	6.8	4.7	42.6
Tobacco	38– 39	2.7	14.3	6.9	13.9	21.5	1.3	12.2
Clothing, footwear	40– 51	3.3	4.8	4.3	13.9	8.6	5.9	17.5
Clothing	40– 47	3.3	5.0	4.4	12.8	9.4	5.6	19.2
Footwear	48– 51	3.2	3.5	4.0	20.9	3.8	8.0	6.5
Gross rent, fuel	52– 57	1.0	3.1	3.2	3.4	4.9	5.0	4.4
Gross rent	52– 53	0.8	2.8	3.1	3.0	5.0	3.4	2.3
Fuel, power	54– 57	1.4	3.8	3.5	4.3	4.6	9.5	10.1
House furnishings, operations	58– 70	5.2	13.2	2.0	5.3	6.5	5.7	8.0
Furniture, appliances	58– 66	2.2	4.6	0.4	0.3	0.9	1.7	3.4
Supplies, operations	67– 70	11.4	31.2	5.4	15.7	18.2	14.0	17.7
Medical care	71– 77	2.5	2.2	4.2	4.9	6.7	4.2	8.5
Transport, communications	78– 89	1.0	2.2	3.2	2.0	3.3	1.8	5.0
Equipment	78– 79	0.4	0.3	0.2	0.0	0.1	1.8	0.6
Operation costs	80– 83	1.0	1.6	0.2	0.1	0.9	1.2	1.2
Purchased transport	84– 87	10.8	39.1	99.8	64.9	85.3	13.8	136.1
Communications	88– 89	0.3	0.9	0.8	0.5	4.1	1.4	1.5
Recreation and education	90–101	6.3	12.5	8.6	8.3	13.0	11.7	13.1
Recreation	90– 96	2.0	2.0	1.5	5.9	5.4	2.9	6.4
Education	97–101	12.1	26.8	18.2	11.7	23.3	23.7	22.2
Other expenditures	102–107	1.3	3.0	3.5	2.4	4.5	7.0	6.5
Personal care	102–104	0.5	7.8	4.5	3.4	4.9	1.5	9.0
Miscellaneous services	105–107	1.6	1.4	3.1	2.0	4.4	8.9	5.7
Capital formation	109–146	2.4	3.3	5.0	3.7	5.0	9.7	11.0
Domestic capital formation	109–145	4.7	4.5	5.3	5.3	6.5	19.1	13.1
Construction	109–122	5.0	7.2	6.3	7.9	9.9	22.2	12.8
Residential	109–110	3.9	6.0	5.5	5.5	7.0	14.1	8.6
Nonresidential	111–118	4.9	6.3	7.0	9.6	9.1	17.5	14.6
Other	119–122	6.6	9.8	6.5	8.5	14.2	37.3	15.6
Producer durables	123–144	2.8	2.6	1.9	2.2	1.7	12.2	8.1
Transport equipment	123–129	2.8	2.4	1.5	1.2	2.6	18.7	9.1
Nonelectrical machinery	130–138	3.6	3.3	1.8	3.6	1.9	10.0	7.8
Electrical machinery	139–142	2.0	1.9	2.2	1.5	1.0	10.0	3.7
Other	143–144	0.4	1.8	2.6	0.5	0.1	8.3	19.2
Exports minus imports	146–146	−41.9	−19.9	−0.7	−25.2	−24.5	−169.9	−28.5
Government	147–151	5.8	7.9	8.1	12.8	11.9	24.3	10.8
Compensation	147–150	11.3	13.9	14.7	22.5	20.5	35.9	17.4
Commodities	151–151	2.0	3.8	3.6	6.2	5.9	16.4	6.3
Gross domestic product	1–151	4.9	6.6	6.6	8.2	9.3	10.3	13.0
Aggregates								
ICP concepts[e]								
Consumption (CEP)[b,c]	1–108	5.5	7.3	6.8	8.9	10.2	8.4	14.0
Capital formation (GCF)[d]	109–146	2.4	3.3	5.0	3.7	5.0	9.7	11.0
Government (PFC)	147–151	5.8	7.9	8.1	12.8	11.9	24.3	10.8
Gross domestic product	1–151	4.9	6.6	6.6	8.2	9.3	10.3	13.0
SNA concepts[e]								
Consumption (PFCE)	1–108	5.1	6.6	6.5	9.0	9.3	7.5	14.1
Capital formation (GCF)	109–146	2.4	3.3	5.0	3.7	5.0	9.7	11.0
Government (GFCE)	147–151	7.6	11.1	8.8	11.1	15.5	23.0	11.1
Gross domestic product	1–151	4.9	6.6	6.6	8.2	9.3	10.3	13.1

Philippines	Korea	Malaysia	Colombia	Jamaica	Syria	Brazil	Romania	Mexico	Yugoslavia
13.9	20.4	19.0	25.4	25.8	26.0	24.5	28.8	36.3	33.9
35.7	47.3	37.0	50.6	50.5	69.7	54.9	53.7	75.9	60.0
38.8	44.5	41.2	53.9	49.3	81.9	65.3	59.7	88.7	61.6
113.3	195.6	105.2	32.9	124.6	157.2	109.2	92.9	150.3	121.9
32.8	11.4	26.4	91.4	24.8	22.1	87.4	70.7	74.2	55.7
165.5	76.9	117.6	17.0	91.3	10.1	43.8	16.2	42.4	28.1
2.9	10.2	34.6	41.5	51.5	47.2	52.1	79.5	145.9	85.3
26.0	4.4	31.3	33.7	30.5	168.2	67.5	45.5	97.5	71.9
19.1	36.1	24.2	32.0	43.9	164.0	35.7	45.8	68.8	46.5
14.1	2.1	18.5	87.3	11.3	14.1	97.2	9.3	68.0	33.7
23.3	41.4	32.4	62.3	41.5	35.3	44.4	50.6	56.1	37.5
29.2	34.1	13.5	38.0	55.5	3.0	7.7	48.9	16.9	56.2
16.6	90.0	32.2	38.5	53.6	52.7	27.3	7.4	42.6	51.0
13.8	32.8	18.2	35.2	13.2	35.1	23.5	37.1	43.9	36.4
13.3	34.6	16.8	31.6	8.2	34.9	22.1	36.1	37.6	34.1
17.0	21.7	26.5	57.9	45.0	36.4	32.2	44.0	84.1	50.8
8.6	9.1	12.1	12.4	10.9	19.2	12.3	30.3	26.5	22.2
10.2	2.8	14.9	9.3	10.7	14.8	12.5	34.0	23.4	22.0
4.1	26.2	4.3	21.0	11.5	31.3	11.8	20.2	34.9	22.7
8.6	7.9	16.2	19.9	21.9	17.3	21.0	18.6	57.9	34.7
3.7	5.2	7.4	5.6	9.2	10.2	13.2	13.7	23.4	31.2
19.0	13.4	34.5	49.8	48.5	32.1	37.3	28.7	129.9	42.0
9.9	11.5	12.4	11.4	16.0	12.9	17.7	37.4	20.7	44.7
1.8	9.3	10.1	14.4	15.7	5.0	11.8	5.6	19.5	14.2
0.6	0.6	3.8	0.7	2.4	2.8	6.7	2.7	6.7	9.9
0.2	0.0	7.4	1.2	12.6	0.2	9.3	1.1	11.1	10.6
47.5	274.4	159.9	379.3	171.2	125.7	133.0	103.8	317.8	145.2
1.1	11.4	3.6	25.2	35.4	2.2	7.1	10.9	21.8	9.8
16.2	19.7	23.0	28.4	29.1	18.6	24.8	27.3	23.8	38.7
2.3	10.9	14.9	10.2	17.9	6.6	12.5	15.1	10.7	30.8
35.2	31.8	34.0	53.1	44.3	35.0	41.6	43.9	41.6	49.4
8.5	17.2	15.4	24.2	45.7	12.4	19.4	17.7	22.2	28.5
7.5	23.7	12.8	11.2	40.2	14.9	16.4	6.7	31.5	22.9
8.8	15.0	16.2	28.6	47.5	11.5	20.4	21.3	19.1	30.3
9.5	22.3	28.8	20.0	15.9	16.0	28.4	55.6	37.9	41.8
12.4	28.1	30.0	20.7	30.8	26.1	34.1	59.4	44.2	53.8
8.4	29.6	45.5	35.2	26.7	25.1	33.6	60.2	57.5	39.8
8.5	31.0	42.5	20.2	47.4	25.0	23.1	25.7	74.4	43.2
8.2	30.0	37.1	7.3	22.2	12.8	22.8	117.0	31.3	38.9
8.5	27.5	59.2	86.3	7.7	39.7	59.0	33.1	68.8	37.0
7.8	18.4	15.1	6.5	27.3	25.3	32.1	32.1	19.7	36.3
8.4	36.8	12.8	8.3	31.6	39.1	22.5	19.6	20.7	25.5
7.9	15.6	23.3	2.8	26.0	29.9	35.5	54.0	15.9	49.3
6.6	5.0	6.2	12.2	14.3	7.2	21.1	9.4	14.2	29.0
9.0	10.6	5.4	3.9	56.3	7.3	76.7	23.7	51.7	24.2
−44.8	−89.2	6.2	5.3	−267.9	−177.7	−80.6	−17.3	−81.6	−187.6
15.5	19.7	23.6	7.1	28.0	36.2	24.3	19.2	16.8	39.5
29.2	26.2	33.8	15.1	41.4	26.6	48.1	27.5	32.1	45.4
6.1	15.2	16.6	1.7	18.9	42.7	8.0	13.5	6.3	35.5
13.2	20.7	21.5	22.4	24.0	25.0	25.2	33.3	34.7	36.1
13.9	20.4	19.0	25.4	25.8	26.0	24.5	28.8	36.3	33.9
9.5	22.3	28.8	20.0	15.9	16.0	28.4	55.6	37.9	41.8
15.5	19.7	23.6	7.1	28.0	36.2	24.3	19.2	16.8	39.5
13.2	20.7	21.5	22.4	24.0	25.0	25.2	33.3	34.7	36.1
13.4	20.8	18.1	25.1	24.4	26.3	24.3	25.0	36.4	28.7
9.5	22.3	28.8	20.0	15.9	16.0	28.4	55.6	37.9	41.8
16.9	17.9	26.2	14.0	33.4	31.6	25.3	38.7	22.3	60.5
13.1	20.7	21.5	22.4	24.0	25.0	25.2	33.3	34.6	36.1

(Table continues on the following page.)

Category	Line numbers[a]	Iran	Uruguay	Ireland	Hungary	Poland	Italy	Spain
Consumption, ICP[b,c]	1–108	27.0	44.8	46.1	46.4	43.2	52.9	60.2
Food, beverages, tobacco	1– 39	46.1	116.3	78.6	82.3	74.4	97.4	115.2
Food	1– 33	55.3	119.3	87.8	80.2	77.6	102.1	126.0
Bread, cereals	1– 6	179.2	177.7	88.1	126.4	96.6	123.1	95.9
Meat	7– 12	41.5	197.5	118.7	91.1	89.1	109.7	137.3
Fish	13– 14	9.7	16.0	44.6	20.5	25.6	53.9	268.9
Milk, cheese, eggs	15– 17	32.7	135.8	106.8	76.8	95.2	103.9	134.3
Oils, fats	18– 20	73.0	44.4	94.7	113.9	102.4	158.9	243.1
Fruits, vegetables	21– 26	41.0	79.6	55.8	61.1	67.1	129.5	111.4
Coffee, tea, cocoa	27– 29	28.0	26.8	65.3	37.7	17.0	30.7	61.0
Spices, sweets, sugar	30– 33	36.2	70.6	83.0	74.3	65.9	38.0	67.5
Beverages	34– 37	3.1	145.1	28.6	111.2	74.6	83.5	77.7
Tobacco	38– 39	23.0	50.1	64.9	62.0	45.6	74.8	70.9
Clothing, footwear	40– 51	50.8	31.3	40.9	44.8	49.5	57.8	64.8
Clothing	40– 47	47.0	28.5	40.9	42.4	47.4	54.7	48.1
Footwear	48– 51	75.4	49.1	40.5	60.0	62.9	77.3	171.4
Gross rent, fuel	52– 57	28.2	30.6	24.9	19.7	32.7	39.6	47.7
Gross rent	52– 53	28.3	29.6	22.2	16.3	36.5	43.1	55.7
Fuel, power	54– 57	27.8	33.5	32.1	28.9	22.1	29.8	25.5
House furnishings, operations	58– 70	25.0	23.5	42.8	44.0	45.3	43.3	45.1
Furniture, appliances	58– 66	19.8	15.0	35.8	35.3	38.3	37.4	44.5
Supplies, operations	67– 70	35.9	41.4	57.3	62.2	59.7	55.6	46.3
Medical care	71– 77	14.1	38.5	59.7	71.4	61.1	60.8	59.9
Transport, communications	78– 89	11.5	16.6	17.5	14.6	11.9	32.8	26.4
Equipment	78– 79	3.1	1.7	15.0	10.7	5.6	19.5	22.7
Operation costs	80– 83	6.9	8.2	19.0	6.0	2.7	36.3	18.0
Purchased transport	84– 87	222.8	345.5	50.4	213.4	240.2	159.7	214.5
Communications	88– 89	4.2	17.7	9.7	14.8	15.0	26.1	28.1
Recreation and education	90–101	21.5	32.5	47.2	57.3	52.6	42.3	46.7
Recreation	90– 96	7.5	24.2	43.5	57.6	39.6	34.8	39.5
Education	97–101	40.6	43.8	52.2	56.9	70.3	52.5	56.5
Other expenditures	102–107	17.8	31.4	63.5	50.2	28.7	39.8	61.3
Personal care	102–104	19.4	14.1	24.0	39.2	21.6	52.1	37.3
Miscellaneous services	105–107	17.3	37.2	76.7	53.9	31.0	35.7	69.3
Capital formation	109–146	61.0	12.1	31.9	65.7	78.5	56.5	61.8
Domestic capital formation	109–145	51.1	17.0	47.8	84.2	96.4	63.3	75.7
Construction	109–122	72.4	24.9	54.6	84.3	93.7	77.4	78.7
Residential	109–110	132.3	18.8	67.2	81.4	50.5	114.9	103.7
Nonresidential	111–118	57.1	18.6	37.3	69.9	126.8	61.2	64.2
Other	119–122	19.7	39.6	60.4	104.9	105.4	52.4	66.5
Producer durables	123–144	31.3	7.2	41.8	58.1	67.2	45.8	48.9
Transport equipment	123–129	31.6	4.9	32.7	72.1	72.4	46.9	58.1
Nonelectrical machinery	130–138	40.8	8.5	60.3	63.2	77.5	48.9	47.7
Electrical machinery	139–142	14.4	2.0	14.1	24.1	62.2	30.2	49.5
Other	143–144	29.1	22.5	54.2	82.1	11.0	69.7	22.9
Exports minus imports	146–146	249.0	−81.3	−273.7	−288.6	−265.2	−73.4	−204.5
Government	147–151	64.1	59.0	38.8	39.3	40.8	54.6	14.9
Compensation	147–150	31.8	129.2	52.6	37.5	44.3	74.8	22.6
Commodities	151–151	86.2	11.0	29.5	40.6	38.4	40.7	9.7
Gross domestic product	1–151	37.7	39.6	42.5	49.6	50.1	53.8	55.9
Aggregates								
ICP concepts[e]								
Consumption (CEP)[b,c]	1–108	27.0	44.8	46.1	46.4	43.2	52.9	60.2
Capital formation (GCF)[d]	109–146	61.0	12.1	31.9	65.7	78.5	56.5	61.8
Government (PFC)	147–151	64.1	59.0	38.8	39.3	40.8	54.6	14.9
Gross domestic product	1–151	37.7	39.6	42.5	49.6	50.1	53.8	55.9
SNA concepts[e]								
Consumption (PFCE)	1–108	26.3	45.4	42.6	39.2	36.5	54.1	60.2
Capital formation (GCF)	109–146	61.0	12.1	31.9	65.7	78.5	56.5	61.8
Government (GFCE)	147–151	55.6	52.3	54.1	70.6	66.3	49.0	29.3
Gross domestic product	1–151	37.7	39.7	42.1	49.2	49.4	53.8	55.9

a. Line numbers refer to Appendix Table 6-1 and show the detailed categories that are included in each aggregation.

b. Consumption, ICP, includes both household and government expenditures. The latter are shown separately in Table 2-1. Consumption, SNA, excludes these governmental expenditures.

c. The consumption aggregate (lines 1–108) includes net expenditure of residents abroad (line 108), not shown separately here.

U.K.	Japan	Austria	Netherlands	Belgium	France	Luxembourg	Denmark	Germany	U.S.
63.7	58.7	69.1	68.2	74.5	75.1	78.9	78.0	75.1	100.0
81.6	82.9	102.8	96.2	108.1	105.7	105.6	99.5	87.9	100.0
85.5	87.3	90.5	93.5	112.0	106.8	107.4	91.0	86.4	100.0
95.4	134.1	85.6	94.0	114.5	99.2	116.7	92.6	115.6	100.0
96.7	26.3	94.7	91.0	157.8	127.2	126.1	112.6	81.0	100.0
52.9	409.6	29.4	65.8	87.8	114.8	53.7	87.8	30.5	100.0
111.0	44.2	118.9	134.2	106.8	139.2	131.9	109.9	90.2	100.0
94.0	15.6	126.6	67.2	139.1	122.1	164.5	96.7	161.4	100.0
59.2	48.0	89.5	87.2	86.0	86.8	91.8	41.2	70.4	100.0
74.1	36.7	43.3	120.8	74.6	73.4	84.1	122.7	107.1	100.0
84.7	202.3	80.9	79.7	82.1	77.5	67.2	101.2	73.9	100.0
62.0	59.7	199.7	126.4	100.8	138.3	115.2	155.1	115.4	100.0
74.4	75.0	79.7	78.6	83.3	52.5	77.0	99.7	63.9	100.0
61.2	69.0	102.2	76.0	66.7	59.3	71.1	52.9	89.9	100.0
61.2	72.5	98.9	76.0	66.7	57.4	70.7	53.1	88.8	100.0
61.3	46.7	123.5	76.6	67.0	71.3	73.6	51.5	96.6	100.0
56.3	39.9	60.9	55.0	55.8	61.0	68.2	104.3	63.7	100.0
57.8	45.3	68.3	54.9	52.2	67.2	67.2	108.9	68.0	100.0
52.0	25.2	40.6	55.4	65.6	43.7	71.0	91.6	51.8	100.0
58.9	44.6	88.3	110.3	131.2	121.9	121.9	105.8	121.8	100.0
50.4	38.6	100.0	117.9	123.2	122.4	113.1	109.5	119.2	100.0
76.5	57.2	64.1	94.5	147.8	120.9	140.2	98.2	127.2	100.0
81.8	83.5	80.7	62.7	79.6	96.3	74.0	73.4	99.8	100.0
36.1	33.7	40.1	38.5	50.0	50.7	61.6	47.3	52.6	100.0
25.0	23.7	26.3	37.7	52.5	31.5	66.3	30.1	44.6	100.0
37.6	12.7	42.6	40.5	53.0	66.3	58.7	59.6	56.2	100.0
152.1	484.0	143.7	49.5	84.8	130.2	125.8	99.4	128.6	100.0
35.1	46.3	47.9	27.9	15.1	18.3	40.1	31.7	41.4	100.0
69.2	67.7	55.9	81.5	60.1	60.4	46.7	91.2	70.6	100.0
79.4	71.4	55.3	91.2	54.9	64.8	46.2	83.9	79.5	100.0
55.3	62.6	56.7	68.2	67.2	54.3	47.4	101.0	58.6	100.0
75.4	59.9	90.7	47.3	66.9	66.3	93.9	42.0	55.7	100.0
57.7	77.0	80.5	45.5	62.4	77.6	80.1	49.8	54.9	100.0
81.2	54.2	94.1	47.9	68.4	62.6	98.4	39.5	55.9	100.0
48.8	123.0	82.1	108.8	98.8	110.0	105.9	93.6	119.8	100.0
59.3	129.2	83.4	92.3	97.7	111.6	122.8	107.5	103.0	100.0
59.3	124.9	87.9	96.5	110.5	128.1	153.7	135.0	116.2	100.0
66.6	93.6	78.2	137.8	130.1	200.6	173.0	169.1	115.6	100.0
63.0	87.4	112.5	76.2	124.6	100.5	167.9	138.5	61.7	100.0
46.0	207.0	69.9	72.0	70.5	75.3	113.8	90.2	182.3	100.0
64.1	121.6	77.9	83.0	82.3	88.8	78.1	83.4	83.1	100.0
78.5	79.6	43.9	94.8	73.7	77.8	76.3	87.8	83.1	100.0
65.8	107.5	103.9	81.7	94.7	131.1	87.3	106.1	87.5	100.0
47.7	135.6	69.6	60.4	75.1	31.2	69.4	39.8	82.0	100.0
53.9	292.8	77.4	114.9	66.6	67.2	61.5	74.5	63.1	100.0
−151.7	3.3	56.8	424.9	119.8	77.7	−218.8	−172.4	440.5	100.0
95.6	25.9	48.3	56.3	57.0	72.1	55.3	89.8	63.1	100.0
156.4	46.1	79.9	71.8	77.6	96.7	62.4	165.0	105.6	100.0
54.0	12.1	26.8	45.7	43.0	55.2	50.5	38.4	34.1	100.0
63.9	68.4	69.6	75.2	77.7	81.9	82.0	82.4	83.0	100.0
63.7	58.7	69.1	68.2	74.5	75.1	78.9	78.0	75.1	100.0
48.8	123.0	82.1	108.8	98.8	110.0	105.9	93.6	119.8	100.0
95.6	25.9	48.3	56.3	57.0	72.1	55.3	89.8	63.2	100.0
63.9	68.4	69.6	75.2	77.7	81.9	82.0	82.4	83.0	100.0
57.8	59.0	66.0	68.9	76.3	77.6	82.3	71.4	77.7	100.0
48.8	123.0	82.1	108.8	98.8	110.0	105.9	93.6	119.8	100.0
107.8	34.8	68.6	53.9	54.2	61.5	48.2	112.0	55.3	100.0
63.4	68.4	69.6	74.8	77.6	81.8	82.0	81.9	82.9	100.0

d. The capital formation aggregate (lines 109–146) includes increase in stocks (line 145) not shown separately in these summary multilateral tables.

e. Letters in parentheses are: CEP, consumption expenditures of the population; GCF, gross capital formation; PFC, public final consumption expenditure; PFCE, private final consumption expenditure; GFCE, government final consumption expenditure. See Glossary for definitions.

Category	Line numbers[a]	Malawi	Kenya	India	Pakistan	Sri Lanka	Zambia	Thailand
Consumption, ICP[b,c]	1–108	274.9	364.8	337.4	441.7	508.3	417.0	696.6
Food, beverages, tobacco	1– 39	172.7	155.5	173.1	241.8	255.3	189.1	375.6
Food	1– 33	161.4	132.8	165.8	229.8	229.3	182.7	316.5
Bread, cereals	1– 6	53.9	58.7	81.0	99.4	97.3	74.9	153.4
Meat	7– 12	8.6	10.7	4.6	19.8	7.1	41.7	44.5
Fish	13– 14	4.7	0.5	6.9	5.6	16.0	18.7	31.7
Milk, cheese, eggs	15– 17	4.0	24.7	10.5	30.3	11.1	6.6	12.6
Oils, fats	18– 20	1.3	2.5	13.2	26.2	3.0	8.2	4.6
Fruits, vegetables	21– 26	83.5	24.1	30.9	28.0	53.8	20.3	38.5
Coffee, tea, cocoa	27– 29	0.9	2.0	3.0	8.1	9.4	2.4	1.8
Spices, sweets, sugar	30– 33	4.5	9.7	15.8	12.3	31.6	9.9	29.5
Beverages	34– 37	9.0	10.5	1.4	0.3	7.8	5.3	48.8
Tobacco	38– 39	2.3	12.1	5.8	11.8	18.3	1.1	10.4
Clothing, footwear	40– 51	12.6	18.2	16.6	53.3	33.0	22.8	67.1
Clothing	40– 47	11.0	16.4	14.6	42.5	31.1	18.6	63.7
Footwear	48– 51	1.6	1.8	2.1	10.8	2.0	4.1	3.4
Gross rent, fuel	52– 57	8.3	26.2	27.4	28.6	41.5	42.5	37.5
Gross rent	52– 53	5.0	17.6	19.5	18.8	30.9	20.9	14.6
Fuel, power	54– 57	3.3	8.6	7.9	9.9	10.5	21.6	22.9
House furnishings, operations	58– 70	19.0	48.5	7.4	19.6	24.0	20.8	29.4
Furniture, appliances	58– 66	5.4	11.3	1.0	0.9	2.3	4.2	8.3
Supplies, operations	67– 70	13.6	37.1	6.4	18.7	21.6	16.6	21.1
Medical care	71– 77	10.0	8.7	16.7	19.7	27.0	16.9	34.0
Transport, communications	78– 89	8.6	18.4	27.0	16.8	28.3	15.4	42.0
Equipment	78– 79	1.2	1.1	0.7	0.0	0.2	5.5	2.0
Operation costs	80– 83	4.5	7.0	1.0	0.4	3.7	5.3	5.3
Purchased transport	84– 87	2.7	9.6	24.6	16.0	21.0	3.4	33.6
Communications	88– 89	0.2	0.8	0.6	0.4	3.4	1.1	1.2
Recreation and education	90–101	36.1	71.9	49.7	48.1	74.8	67.5	75.6
Recreation	90– 96	6.6	6.5	5.2	19.6	18.0	9.7	21.4
Education	97–101	29.5	65.4	44.5	28.6	56.8	57.8	54.2
Other expenditures	102–107	7.6	17.3	20.1	13.8	26.1	40.8	37.9
Personal care	102–104	0.7	11.4	6.5	4.9	7.1	2.1	13.1
Miscellaneous services	105–107	6.9	6.0	13.6	8.9	19.0	38.7	24.8
Capital formation	109–146	34.2	47.6	73.6	54.5	72.3	142.0	160.2
Domestic capital formation	109–145	64.6	62.0	74.1	72.8	90.0	265.0	180.8
Construction	109–122	36.6	52.4	45.9	56.9	71.6	160.8	92.8
Residential	109–110	9.8	15.2	14.0	14.1	17.8	35.9	21.9
Nonresidential	111–118	12.6	16.3	18.0	24.7	23.5	44.9	37.6
Other	119–122	14.2	20.9	13.9	18.2	30.3	79.9	33.3
Producer durables	123–144	19.6	18.6	13.3	15.8	12.3	86.6	58.0
Transport equipment	123–129	5.3	4.5	2.8	2.3	4.9	35.3	17.3
Nonelectrical machinery	130–138	10.8	9.9	5.3	10.8	5.6	30.2	23.6
Electrical machinery	139–142	3.3	3.2	3.6	2.4	1.7	16.3	6.1
Other	143–144	0.3	1.0	1.5	0.3	0.1	4.8	11.1
Exports minus imports	146–146	−30.4	−14.4	−0.5	−18.2	−17.7	−123.0	−20.6
Government	147–151	42.6	58.1	59.6	94.0	87.2	178.9	79.4
Compensation	147–150	33.9	41.3	43.8	67.1	61.3	107.3	51.8
Commodities	151–151	8.7	16.8	15.8	26.9	25.9	71.6	27.6
Gross domestic product	1–151	351.7	470.5	470.5	590.3	667.7	737.8	936.1
Aggregates								
ICP concepts[e]								
Consumption (CEP)[b,c]	1–108	274.9	364.8	337.4	441.7	508.3	417.0	696.6
Capital formation (GCF)[d]	109–146	34.2	47.6	73.6	54.5	72.3	142.0	160.2
Government (PFC)	147–151	42.6	58.1	59.6	94.0	87.2	178.9	79.4
Gross domestic product	1–151	351.7	470.5	470.5	590.2	667.7	737.8	936.1
SNA concepts[e]								
Consumption (PFCE)	1–108	236.5	305.2	303.4	417.8	430.9	350.4	657.5
Capital formation (GCF)	109–146	34.2	47.6	73.6	54.5	72.3	142.0	160.2
Government (GFCE)	147–151	80.5	117.8	93.6	117.9	164.5	244.8	118.5
Gross domestic product	1–151	351.2	470.5	470.5	590.2	667.7	737.1	936.1

Philippines	Korea	Malaysia	Colombia	Jamaica	Syria	Brazil	Romania	Mexico	Yugoslavia
693.6	1014.6	947.6	1265.2	1284.8	1295.4	1219.0	1435.6	1811.8	1692.0
338.1	448.0	350.8	479.6	478.2	660.7	520.4	509.0	719.1	569.0
290.6	332.6	308.1	403.4	369.2	612.6	488.4	446.7	663.6	461.3
98.8	170.7	91.8	28.7	108.7	137.1	95.3	81.1	131.1	106.4
60.7	21.2	48.8	169.3	46.0	41.0	161.9	131.0	137.4	103.1
57.3	26.6	40.7	5.9	31.6	3.5	15.2	5.6	14.7	9.7
2.9	10.3	34.8	41.7	51.8	47.5	52.4	79.9	146.7	85.8
11.2	1.9	13.5	14.5	13.2	72.6	29.2	19.7	42.1	31.0
31.6	59.6	40.0	52.9	72.6	271.0	59.0	75.7	113.6	76.9
4.5	0.7	5.9	27.6	3.6	4.5	30.7	2.9	21.5	10.6
23.5	41.7	32.6	62.8	41.8	35.5	44.8	51.0	56.5	37.8
33.5	39.1	15.4	43.5	63.6	3.4	8.8	56.0	19.4	64.4
14.0	76.3	27.3	32.7	45.4	44.6	23.1	6.3	36.1	43.2
52.8	125.8	69.5	134.8	50.6	134.6	90.0	142.2	168.1	139.3
43.9	114.5	55.8	104.8	27.2	115.7	73.3	119.4	124.5	113.0
8.8	11.2	13.7	30.0	23.3	18.9	16.7	22.8	43.6	26.3
73.2	77.2	102.6	105.5	92.9	163.4	105.0	258.2	225.4	188.8
63.8	17.8	92.9	57.8	66.8	92.3	78.2	212.5	146.3	137.3
9.4	59.4	9.7	47.7	26.1	71.1	26.8	45.7	79.2	51.5
31.7	28.9	59.5	73.3	80.6	63.5	77.2	68.2	212.7	127.6
9.1	12.9	18.4	14.0	22.9	25.3	32.8	34.1	58.0	77.6
22.6	15.9	41.1	59.3	57.7	38.2	44.4	34.1	154.7	50.1
39.7	46.3	49.7	45.9	64.4	51.7	71.2	150.2	83.1	179.4
15.3	79.1	85.7	121.6	133.0	42.5	99.4	47.6	164.7	120.0
1.8	1.9	11.7	2.2	7.6	8.6	20.7	8.3	20.7	30.5
0.8	0.1	31.6	5.0	54.1	1.1	40.1	4.8	47.7	45.6
11.7	67.7	39.4	93.5	42.2	31.0	32.8	25.6	78.4	35.8
0.9	9.4	2.9	20.8	29.2	1.8	5.9	9.0	18.0	8.1
93.6	113.9	132.4	163.8	167.6	107.2	143.2	157.4	137.2	223.1
7.6	36.2	49.5	34.0	59.4	21.9	41.5	50.1	35.7	102.5
86.0	77.7	82.9	129.7	108.2	85.3	101.7	107.3	101.5	120.6
49.3	100.1	89.3	140.9	265.7	71.8	112.6	102.6	129.1	165.5
10.8	34.4	18.5	16.2	58.3	21.6	23.7	9.7	45.6	33.1
38.4	65.6	70.7	124.7	207.3	50.2	88.8	93.0	83.4	132.4
138.8	324.8	419.8	291.0	231.8	233.0	413.7	810.3	552.2	608.9
171.3	389.4	415.3	287.2	425.7	361.7	472.0	822.8	611.4	744.8
61.0	214.4	330.1	254.9	193.8	181.6	243.5	436.7	416.8	288.9
21.6	78.7	108.1	51.4	120.4	63.6	58.7	65.4	189.0	109.7
21.1	76.9	95.2	18.7	57.0	33.0	58.5	300.5	80.4	99.9
18.2	58.8	126.8	184.8	16.4	85.0	126.3	70.8	147.4	79.3
55.6	131.0	107.7	46.5	194.4	180.1	228.5	228.8	140.5	258.2
15.9	69.7	24.3	15.8	59.9	74.0	42.5	37.1	39.2	48.3
23.7	47.1	70.1	8.4	78.4	90.0	107.0	162.5	48.0	148.3
10.8	8.1	10.2	20.0	23.4	11.8	34.6	15.4	23.2	47.6
5.2	6.1	3.1	2.3	32.6	4.2	44.5	13.7	30.0	14.0
−32.5	−64.6	4.5	3.8	−194.0	−128.7	−58.4	−12.5	−59.1	−135.8
113.9	144.6	173.2	52.4	206.1	265.9	178.6	140.8	123.3	290.4
87.3	78.2	100.9	45.2	123.4	79.3	143.6	82.0	95.9	135.4
26.6	66.4	72.3	7.2	82.6	186.5	35.0	58.8	27.4	155.0
946.3	1484.1	1540.6	1608.7	1722.6	1794.2	1811.2	2386.8	2487.3	2591.4
693.6	1014.6	947.6	1265.2	1284.8	1295.4	1219.0	1435.6	1811.8	1692.0
138.8	324.8	419.8	291.0	231.3	233.0	413.7	810.3	552.2	608.9
113.9	144.6	173.2	52.4	206.0	265.9	178.6	140.8	123.3	290.4
946.3	1484.1	1540.6	1608.7	1722.6	1794.2	1811.2	2386.8	2487.3	2591.4
621.1	968.5	842.0	1168.9	1134.9	1224.7	1128.2	1163.9	1693.5	1337.1
138.8	324.8	419.8	291.0	231.8	233.0	413.7	810.3	552.2	608.9
180.4	190.8	278.8	148.8	355.9	336.5	269.0	412.5	237.0	644.5
940.3	1484.1	1540.6	1608.7	1722.6	1794.2	1810.9	2386.8	2482.7	2590.5

(Table continues on the following page.)

Category	Line numbers[a]	Iran	Uruguay	Ireland	Hungary	Poland	Italy	Spain
Consumption, ICP[b,c]	1–108	1345.2	2234.2	2299.3	2313.2	2154.8	2636.4	3000.8
Food, beverages, tobacco	1– 39	437.3	1101.8	744.6	780.1	704.9	923.2	1091.7
Food	1– 33	414.2	893.0	656.8	600.1	580.8	764.1	942.5
Bread, cereals	1– 6	156.3	155.1	76.9	110.3	84.3	107.4	83.7
Meat	7– 12	76.9	365.7	219.8	168.7	165.0	203.1	254.3
Fish	13– 14	3.4	5.5	15.4	7.1	8.9	18.7	93.1
Milk, cheese, eggs	15– 17	32.9	136.6	107.4	77.2	95.7	104.4	135.1
Oils, fats	18– 20	31.5	19.2	40.9	49.2	44.2	68.6	105.0
Fruits, vegetables	21– 26	67.8	131.4	92.1	100.9	110.9	213.9	184.1
Coffee, tea, cocoa	27– 29	8.9	8.5	20.7	11.9	5.4	9.7	19.3
Spices, sweets, sugar	30– 33	36.5	71.1	83.5	74.8	66.4	38.3	68.0
Beverages	34– 37	3.6	166.3	32.8	127.4	85.5	95.7	89.0
Tobacco	38– 39	19.5	42.5	55.0	52.5	38.6	63.4	60.1
Clothing, footwear	40– 51	194.6	119.9	156.5	171.6	189.7	221.2	248.2
Clothing	40– 47	155.5	94.5	135.5	140.5	157.1	181.2	159.3
Footwear	48– 51	39.1	25.5	21.0	31.1	32.6	40.0	88.9
Gross rent, fuel	52– 57	239.7	260.9	211.7	167.5	278.1	336.8	405.8
Gross rent	52– 53	176.6	184.7	138.8	101.8	228.0	269.2	348.0
Fuel, power	54– 57	63.0	76.1	72.9	65.7	50.1	67.6	57.8
House furnishings, operations	58– 70	91.9	86.5	157.1	161.8	166.3	159.0	165.7
Furniture, appliances	58– 66	49.1	37.1	88.9	87.8	95.2	92.8	110.6
Supplies, operations	67– 70	42.7	49.3	68.2	74.0	71.1	66.2	55.1
Medical care	71– 77	56.7	154.5	239.7	286.4	245.1	244.0	240.3
Transport, communications	78– 89	97.6	140.5	148.3	123.7	100.6	277.1	223.5
Equipment	78– 79	9.5	5.3	46.5	33.1	17.2	60.2	70.3
Operation costs	80– 83	29.8	35.4	81.4	25.8	11.8	155.9	77.2
Purchased transport	84– 87	54.9	85.2	12.4	52.6	59.2	39.4	52.9
Communications	88– 89	3.4	14.6	8.0	12.2	12.4	21.6	23.2
Recreation and education	90–101	124.1	187.4	272.2	330.4	303.5	244.0	269.4
Recreation	90– 96	25.0	80.5	144.8	191.5	131.7	115.7	131.4
Education	97–101	99.1	106.9	127.5	138.9	171.8	128.3	138.0
Other expenditures	102–107	103.4	182.8	369.2	291.8	166.6	231.1	356.4
Personal care	102–104	28.1	20.4	34.8	56.8	31.4	75.5	54.1
Miscellaneous services	105–107	75.3	162.4	334.4	235.0	135.2	155.5	302.3
Capital formation	109–146	888.2	176.3	464.0	956.6	1143.1	823.6	899.9
Domestic capital formation	109–145	707.9	235.2	662.2	1165.6	1335.2	876.8	1048.0
Construction	109–122	524.8	180.2	395.7	610.9	679.7	561.4	570.7
Residential	109–110	336.1	47.7	170.7	206.7	128.3	292.0	263.5
Nonresidential	111–118	146.5	47.7	95.7	179.4	325.6	157.2	164.8
Other	119–122	42.2	84.8	129.4	224.7	225.9	112.2	142.4
Producer durables	123–144	223.0	51.1	297.8	413.7	478.5	326.0	347.9
Transport equipment	123–129	59.8	9.2	61.8	136.4	136.9	88.8	109.9
Nonelectrical machinery	130–138	122.8	25.5	181.5	190.3	233.3	147.4	143.7
Electrical machinery	139–142	23.5	3.3	23.2	39.5	101.9	49.4	81.1
Other	143–144	16.8	13.0	31.4	47.6	6.4	40.4	13.3
Exports minus imports	146–146	180.3	−58.9	−198.2	−209.0	−192.1	−53.2	−148.1
Government	147–151	471.2	433.7	285.5	289.1	300.0	401.1	109.6
Compensation	147–150	94.9	385.8	156.9	112.0	132.3	223.2	67.4
Commodities	151–151	376.3	47.9	128.6	177.1	167.7	177.9	42.2
Gross domestic product	1–151	2704.6	2844.3	3048.8	3558.9	3597.9	3861.1	4010.2
Aggregates								
ICP concepts[e]								
Consumption (CEP)[b,c]	1–108	1345.2	2234.2	2299.3	2313.2	2154.8	2636.4	3000.8
Capital formation (GCF)[d]	109–146	888.2	176.3	464.0	956.6	1143.1	823.6	899.9
Government (PFC)	147–151	471.2	433.7	285.5	289.1	300.0	401.1	109.6
Gross domestic product	1–151	2704.6	2844.3	3048.8	3558.9	3597.9	3861.1	4010.3
SNA concepts[e]								
Consumption (PFCE)	1–108	1224.8	2111.4	1979.7	1821.9	1695.7	2516.1	2798.0
Capital formation (GCF)	109–146	888.2	176.3	464.0	956.6	1143.1	823.6	899.9
Government (GFCE)	147–151	591.6	556.6	576.0	751.7	706.1	521.3	311.5
Gross domestic product	1–151	2704.6	2844.3	3019.7	3530.1	3544.9	3861.1	4009.4

a. Line numbers refer to Appendix Table 6-1 and show the detailed categories that are included in each aggregation.

b. Consumption, ICP, includes both household and government expenditures. The latter are shown separately in Table 2-1. Consumption, SNA, excludes these governmental expenditures.

c. The consumption aggregate (lines 1–108) includes net expenditure of residents abroad (line 108), not shown separately here.

U.K.	Japan	Austria	Netherlands	Belgium	France	Luxembourg	Denmark	Germany	U.S.
3174.0	2925.2	3443.7	3398.1	3715.2	3745.5	3934.7	3887.2	3743.2	4984.3
773.5	785.2	974.0	911.2	1024.4	1001.9	1000.7	943.0	832.7	947.6
639.5	653.3	677.5	699.8	838.3	799.0	803.4	680.8	646.4	748.3
83.2	117.0	74.7	82.0	99.9	86.6	101.8	80.8	100.9	87.2
179.1	48.7	175.4	168.6	292.2	235.5	233.5	208.5	150.0	185.2
18.3	141.9	10.2	22.8	30.4	39.8	18.6	30.4	10.6	34.6
111.6	44.4	119.5	134.9	107.3	139.9	132.6	110.5	90.7	100.5
40.6	6.8	54.7	29.0	60.0	52.7	71.0	41.8	69.7	43.2
97.9	79.2	147.9	144.0	142.1	143.3	151.6	68.0	116.3	165.2
23.4	11.6	13.7	38.2	23.6	23.2	26.6	38.8	33.9	31.6
85.3	203.8	81.5	80.2	82.7	78.0	67.7	102.0	74.4	100.7
71.0	68.4	228.8	144.8	115.5	158.4	132.0	177.7	132.2	114.6
63.0	63.5	67.6	66.7	70.6	44.5	65.2	84.5	54.1	84.8
234.3	264.3	391.5	291.3	255.5	227.1	272.4	202.6	344.3	383.0
202.5	240.1	327.5	251.6	220.8	190.2	234.2	175.8	294.2	331.2
31.8	24.2	64.0	39.7	34.7	36.9	38.1	26.7	50.1	51.8
479.1	340.0	518.6	468.5	475.0	519.0	581.0	888.1	542.1	851.3
361.1	282.9	426.5	342.7	326.0	419.8	419.8	680.1	424.4	624.3
118.0	57.1	92.2	125.8	149.0	99.1	161.2	208.0	117.6	226.9
216.4	164.0	324.5	405.3	482.0	447.9	447.8	388.8	447.5	367.4
125.3	95.9	248.2	292.8	306.0	304.0	280.9	271.9	296.1	248.3
91.1	68.1	76.3	112.5	176.0	143.9	166.9	116.9	151.4	119.1
328.3	335.3	323.9	251.6	319.6	386.6	297.1	294.7	400.4	401.3
305.2	285.3	339.1	325.5	423.3	429.3	521.1	399.9	445.3	845.9
77.4	73.2	81.3	116.5	162.4	97.4	204.9	93.1	137.8	309.2
161.4	54.6	182.9	173.8	227.5	284.7	252.1	256.2	241.6	429.6
37.5	119.3	35.4	12.2	20.9	32.1	31.0	24.5	31.7	24.7
29.0	38.1	39.5	23.0	12.4	15.1	33.0	26.1	34.2	82.5
399.2	390.2	322.4	469.9	346.7	348.2	269.3	525.8	407.5	576.8
264.1	237.3	184.1	303.4	182.6	215.5	153.5	279.1	264.3	332.6
135.1	152.9	138.3	166.5	164.2	132.7	115.7	246.6	143.1	244.2
438.0	348.3	527.4	274.8	388.6	385.6	545.4	244.4	323.6	581.2
83.6	111.7	116.7	65.9	90.4	112.6	116.1	72.2	79.6	145.0
354.4	236.6	410.7	208.9	298.2	273.0	429.3	172.2	244.0	436.2
711.3	1791.3	1195.9	1585.6	1439.8	1601.8	1542.2	1363.6	1745.4	1456.8
821.2	1788.9	1154.8	1277.9	1353.1	1545.5	1700.6	1488.5	1426.4	1384.4
429.7	905.7	637.1	699.9	801.4	929.0	1114.4	978.5	842.7	725.1
169.1	237.9	198.6	350.0	330.6	509.7	439.5	429.7	293.7	254.1
161.9	224.4	288.8	195.7	319.9	258.1	431.2	355.5	158.5	256.8
98.6	443.4	149.6	154.2	151.0	161.2	243.7	193.3	390.6	214.2
456.1	866.1	555.0	591.1	586.1	632.0	556.3	594.2	591.6	712.1
148.5	150.6	83.1	179.3	139.4	147.1	144.3	166.2	157.2	189.2
198.3	323.7	313.1	246.2	285.1	394.9	262.8	319.5	263.6	301.2
78.1	222.0	114.0	99.0	123.0	51.0	113.6	65.2	134.2	163.8
31.2	169.7	44.8	66.6	38.6	39.0	35.6	43.2	36.5	58.0
−109.9	2.4	41.1	307.7	86.7	56.3	−158.4	−124.8	319.0	72.4
702.6	190.3	355.3	413.5	419.1	529.6	406.6	660.2	464.2	735.0
466.8	137.5	238.5	214.2	231.5	288.6	186.3	492.4	315.2	298.5
235.8	52.8	116.8	199.3	187.6	241.0	220.4	167.8	149.0	436.5
4587.9	4906.7	4994.8	5397.2	5574.1	5876.9	5883.4	5910.9	5952.7	7176.0
3174.0	2925.2	3443.7	3398.1	3715.2	3745.5	3934.7	3887.2	3743.2	4984.3
711.3	1791.3	1195.9	1585.6	1439.8	1601.8	1542.2	1363.6	1745.4	1456.8
702.6	190.3	355.3	413.5	419.1	529.6	406.6	660.2	464.2	735.0
4587.9	4906.7	4994.8	5397.2	5574.1	5876.9	5883.4	5910.9	5952.7	7176.0
2687.1	2742.6	3068.5	3206.4	3547.8	3607.6	3827.9	3321.5	3613.9	4651.4
711.3	1791.3	1195.9	1585.6	1439.8	1601.8	1542.2	1363.6	1745.4	1456.8
1147.3	370.0	730.5	573.9	577.3	654.5	513.5	1192.9	588.4	1064.7
4545.8	4903.8	4994.9	5365.8	5564.8	5863.8	5883.4	5878.0	5947.7	7172.8

d. The capital formation aggregate (lines 109–146) includes increase in stocks (line 145) not shown separately in these summary multilateral tables.

e. Letters in parentheses are: CEP, consumption expenditures of the population; GCF, gross capital formation; PFC, public final consumption expenditure; PFCE, private final consumption expenditure; GFCE, government final consumption expenditure. See Glossary for definitions.

Table 6-6. Average Percentage Distribution of Expenditures in National Currencies for Groups of Countries by Real per Capita GDP, 1975

Category	Line numbers[a]	Group I	Group II	Group III	Group IV	Group V	Group VI
Consumption, ICP [b]	1–108	74.7	70.8	64.6	65.2	64.8	72.2
Food, beverages, tobacco	1–39	42.2	31.0	23.9	23.1	14.8	11.4
Food	1–33	38.0	26.7	20.2	18.6	11.5	9.2
Bread, cereals	1–6	14.6	7.4	4.0	2.1	1.7	1.3
Meat	7–12	3.4	4.8	5.5	5.8	3.4	2.3
Fish	13–14	2.7	1.3	0.3	0.7	0.6	0.4
Milk, cheese, eggs	15–17	3.5	2.7	3.0	2.7	1.5	1.1
Oils, fats	18–20	2.0	1.3	1.2	1.6	0.7	0.5
Fruits, vegetables	21–26	7.5	6.0	3.5	3.4	1.9	2.1
Coffee, tea, cocoa	27–29	0.6	0.6	0.5	0.6	0.4	0.2
Spices, sweets, sugar	30–33	3.7	2.6	2.1	1.7	1.3	1.3
Beverages	34–37	2.3	2.1	2.1	3.3	1.9	1.3
Tobacco	38–39	2.0	2.2	1.6	1.2	1.4	1.0
Clothing, footwear	40–51	5.6	5.9	6.1	6.6	5.1	4.7
Clothing	40–47	5.0	4.8	4.9	5.4	4.4	4.0
Footwear	48–51	0.6	1.1	1.3	1.2	0.8	0.7
Gross rent, fuel	52–57	6.0	6.9	6.6	6.7	9.8	12.6
Gross rent	52–53	3.8	4.6	4.1	4.9	7.2	10.0
Fuel, power	54–57	2.2	2.3	2.5	1.8	2.6	2.6
House furnishings, operations	58–70	4.0	4.2	5.5	5.1	5.7	4.8
Furniture, appliances	58–66	1.3	2.0	2.8	3.0	3.4	3.1
Supplies, operations	67–70	2.7	2.2	2.7	2.1	2.3	1.7
Medical care	71–77	2.9	3.1	4.4	4.7	5.6	9.1
Transport, communications	78–89	4.2	6.5	5.4	5.6	7.3	9.6
Equipment	78–79	0.7	1.1	1.4	1.7	2.0	3.1
Operation costs	80–83	1.3	1.9	1.7	2.3	3.4	4.7
Purchased transport	84–87	2.0	3.2	1.9	1.3	1.2	0.6
Communications	88–89	0.2	0.3	0.4	0.4	0.7	1.3
Recreation, education	90–101	6.0	6.6	6.7	7.3	9.2	10.9
Recreation	90–96	2.1	2.6	2.9	3.7	4.2	4.5
Education	97–101	3.9	4.0	3.8	3.6	5.0	6.4
Other expenditures	102–107	3.9	7.0	6.4	6.1	7.7	8.8
Personal care	102–104	1.1	1.9	1.2	1.5	1.8	1.9
Miscellaneous services	105–107	2.8	5.2	5.2	4.6	6.0	6.8
Capital formation	109–146	16.0	18.8	25.3	27.1	24.1	16.5
Domestic capital formation	109–145	24.6	24.9	27.1	31.7	23.6	15.7
Construction	109–122	11.5	12.8	14.0	16.6	15.1	9.5
Residential	109–110	3.1	4.1	5.3	5.5	6.2	3.3
Nonresidential	111–118	4.1	3.1	4.3	5.8	5.2	2.9
Other	119–122	4.3	5.7	4.5	5.3	3.7	3.3
Producer durables	123–144	10.7	11.6	10.5	11.9	8.9	6.9
Transport equipment	123–129	3.4	3.7	2.4	2.9	2.2	1.7
Nonelectrical machinery	130–138	4.7	5.1	5.9	6.0	3.9	2.8
Electrical machinery	139–142	1.8	1.8	1.2	2.1	1.9	1.6
Other	143–144	0.8	1.0	0.9	0.9	0.9	0.7
Exports minus imports	146–146	−8.5	−6.1	−1.8	−4.7	0.5	0.8
Government	147–151	9.2	10.3	10.0	7.7	11.1	11.3
Compensation	147–150	4.7	5.8	5.4	3.6	8.1	5.9
Commodities	151–151	4.6	4.5	4.7	4.1	3.0	5.4
Gross domestic product	1–151	100.0	100.0	100.0	100.0	100.0	100.0

a. Line numbers refer to Appendix Table 6-1 and show the detailed categories that are included in each aggregation.

b. Consumption, ICP, includes both household and government expenditures. The latter are shown separately in Table 2-1. It also includes net expenditure of residents abroad.

Table 6-7. Average Quantities per Capita for Groups of Countries Classified by Real per Capita GDP, 1975

Category	Line numbers[a]	Group I	Group II	Group III	Group IV	Group V	Group VI
Consumption, ICP [b]	1–108	9.4	23.5	36.2	50.7	71.3	100.0
Food, beverages, tobacco	1–39	25.1	51.7	71.8	92.3	96.7	100.0
Food	1–33	28.5	56.0	78.7	96.5	95.6	100.0
Bread, cereals	1–6	102.8	120.8	135.0	110.5	105.3	100.0
Meat	7–12	13.3	43.9	93.1	106.8	101.5	100.0
Fish	13–14	51.0	59.4	26.2	92.2	103.6	100.0
Milk, cheese, eggs	15–17	12.8	39.5	97.7	102.5	109.6	100.0
Oils, fats	18–20	20.3	55.9	71.2	154.6	109.7	100.0
Fruits, vegetables	21–26	23.5	56.0	56.2	92.3	73.3	100.0
Coffee, tea, cocoa	27–29	12.7	38.4	38.5	36.6	81.9	100.0
Spices, sweets, sugar	30–33	17.0	42.9	55.7	61.4	94.4	100.0
Beverages	34–37	12.7	25.3	49.8	86.8	119.2	100.0
Tobacco	38–39	11.2	49.1	39.8	63.3	76.0	100.0
Clothing, footwear	40–51	9.0	26.3	40.1	54.2	72.0	100.0
Clothing	40–47	9.1	24.7	37.4	48.2	71.7	100.0
Footwear	48–51	8.4	36.6	57.3	92.9	74.2	100.0
Gross rent, fuel	52–57	4.2	12.7	27.1	34.9	62.8	100.0
Gross rent	52–53	3.8	10.8	26.6	37.9	65.6	100.0
Fuel, power	54–57	5.2	17.7	28.5	26.6	55.2	100.0
House furnishings, operations	58–70	6.8	17.4	33.7	44.4	100.5	100.0
Furniture, appliances	58–66	2.1	8.5	23.1	38.9	99.4	100.0
Supplies, operations	67–70	16.6	35.9	55.9	55.9	102.9	100.0
Medical care	71–77	5.4	13.7	35.9	63.3	81.3	100.0
Transport, communications	78–89	2.5	11.1	14.2	21.4	45.6	100.0
Equipment	78–79	0.5	2.8	6.5	14.6	37.5	100.0
Operation costs	80–83	0.8	5.1	9.5	15.7	47.5	100.0
Purchased transport	84–87	62.2	207.3	197.6	207.0	155.4	100.0
Communications	88–89	1.3	14.1	12.4	21.0	33.7	100.0
Recreation, education	90–101	11.2	23.9	31.8	49.7	67.0	100.0
Recreation	90–96	3.6	12.2	22.0	42.9	69.6	100.0
Education	97–101	21.6	40.0	45.2	59.1	63.5	100.0
Other expenditures	102–107	4.6	22.4	30.2	45.0	66.5	100.0
Personal care	102–104	4.9	19.9	19.7	37.6	65.1	100.0
Miscellaneous services	105–107	4.5	23.2	33.7	47.5	66.9	100.0
Capital formation	109–146	6.2	21.9	40.0	65.6	99.0	100.0
Domestic capital formation	109–145	8.9	28.3	45.6	79.9	100.8	100.0
Construction	109–122	10.0	32.6	51.6	83.5	112.5	100.0
Residential	109–110	7.4	31.5	60.3	87.6	129.4	100.0
Nonresidential	111–118	9.7	22.0	50.0	80.5	103.6	100.0
Other	119–122	13.4	46.5	43.1	82.3	103.0	100.0
Producer durables	123–144	4.9	20.8	28.1	55.0	84.7	100.0
Transport equipment	123–129	5.8	25.2	22.5	62.4	77.3	100.0
Nonelectrical machinery	130–138	5.0	22.2	38.1	59.3	96.2	100.0
Electrical machinery	139–142	3.6	11.0	13.9	41.5	67.9	100.0
Other	143–144	5.2	26.7	34.2	46.4	96.9	100.0
Exports minus imports	146–146	− 44.4	− 100.6	− 65.4	− 207.9	64.5	100.0
Government	147–151	12.1	23.1	39.6	37.4	62.6	100.0
Compensation	147–150	20.7	31.9	53.1	44.8	95.7	100.0
Commodities	151–151	6.3	17.2	30.3	32.3	40.0	100.0
Gross domestic product	1–151	9.0	23.1	37.3	52.4	76.0	100.0

a. Line numbers refer to Appendix Table 6-1 and show the detailed categories that are included in each aggregation.
b. Consumption, ICP, includes both household and government expenditures. The latter are shown separately in Table 2-1. It also includes net expenditure of residents abroad.

Table 6-8. Average Price Indexes for Groups of Countries Classified by Real per Capita GDP, 1975

Category	Line numbers[a]	Group I	Group II	Group III	Group IV	Group V	Group VI	Coefficient of variation[c]
Consumption, ICP [b]	1–108	40.1	50.1	59.2	69.1	102.8	100.0	0.416
Food, beverages, tobacco	1–39	51.3	63.2	71.7	85.8	109.9	100.0	0.347
Food	1–33	49.8	62.9	68.2	82.2	107.2	100.0	0.345
Bread, cereals	1–6	35.3	56.7	55.0	58.1	97.2	100.0	0.439
Meat	7–12	44.4	67.3	72.7	93.2	127.2	100.0	0.460
Fish	13–14	68.5	74.1	77.7	106.0	130.6	100.0	0.410
Milk, cheese, eggs	15–17	81.0	73.3	67.2	88.1	96.8	100.0	0.257
Oils, fats	18–20	77.1	77.9	89.2	94.2	117.3	100.0	0.301
Fruits, vegetables	21–26	58.3	75.1	72.3	70.4	108.9	100.0	0.402
Coffee, tea, cocoa	27–29	81.8	118.5	167.7	285.1	192.5	100.0	0.605
Spices, sweets, sugar	30–33	56.4	52.7	68.5	79.7	87.5	100.0	0.283
Beverages	34–37	80.9	77.1	85.0	108.5	108.0	100.0	0.352
Tobacco	38–39	73.2	66.2	130.4	78.5	147.8	100.0	0.660
Clothing, footwear	40–51	55.7	59.0	79.8	100.5	126.0	100.0	0.422
Clothing	40–47	58.6	60.1	79.9	108.0	126.3	100.0	0.414
Footwear	48–51	43.1	49.3	78.2	78.1	123.8	100.0	0.514
Gross rent, fuel	52–57	47.8	56.4	47.6	59.7	103.1	100.0	0.471
Gross rent	52–53	47.0	57.2	38.0	51.5	91.2	100.0	0.484
Fuel, power	54–57	64.4	82.1	81.9	99.1	151.7	100.0	0.471
House furnishings, operations	58–70	45.5	60.8	84.3	91.8	99.2	100.0	0.350
Furniture, appliances	58–66	77.6	91.4	96.3	94.9	93.8	100.0	0.218
Supplies, operations	67–70	35.9	43.7	70.6	86.4	108.7	100.0	0.486
Medical care	71–77	27.5	29.7	35.9	33.2	62.0	100.0	0.577
Transport, communications	78–89	68.8	74.6	101.3	107.7	137.2	100.0	0.418
Equipment	78–79	168.4	163.5	226.2	162.4	149.1	100.0	0.412
Operation costs	80–83	114.8	103.3	102.4	152.0	130.3	100.0	0.261
Purchased transport	84–87	23.7	34.1	57.4	42.0	129.2	100.0	0.791
Communications	88–89	48.0	39.7	60.0	58.0	138.5	100.0	0.694
Recreation, education	90–101	19.1	29.1	46.9	54.0	102.7	100.0	0.671
Recreation	90–96	51.9	57.6	77.5	77.9	108.2	100.0	0.386
Education	97–101	11.0	17.7	32.2	38.0	100.7	100.0	0.887
Other expenditures	102–107	39.4	43.6	60.6	62.2	109.9	100.0	0.497
Personal care	102–104	50.7	60.8	81.9	82.9	117.0	100.0	0.411
Miscellaneous services	105–107	41.5	39.3	57.4	57.0	108.5	100.0	0.531
Capital formation	109–146	60.4	63.7	91.5	93.2	121.4	100.0	0.342
Domestic capital formation	109–145	67.6	66.6	90.7	93.6	121.6	100.0	0.300
Construction	109–122	46.0	52.2	72.8	78.5	115.8	100.0	0.421
Residential	109–110	47.0	48.0	80.4	74.3	123.8	100.0	0.480
Nonresidential	111–118	53.9	58.4	77.2	92.0	141.3	100.0	0.484
Other	119–122	40.7	47.5	87.1	73.0	91.1	100.0	0.442
Producer durables	123–144	130.1	105.6	135.8	116.4	125.8	100.0	0.189
Transport equipment	123–129	159.1	112.8	163.6	106.1	133.5	100.0	0.333
Nonelectrical machinery	130–138	126.7	108.1	136.8	126.2	118.2	100.0	0.196
Electrical machinery	139–142	125.0	121.3	138.3	123.5	146.4	100.0	0.218
Other	143–144	128.1	95.7	98.1	124.2	114.7	100.0	0.278
Exports minus imports	146–146	100.0	100.0	100.0	100.0	100.0	100.0	0.002
Government	147–151	25.4	45.9	56.8	74.8	132.0	100.0	0.641
Compensation	147–150	14.5	38.2	49.2	56.9	125.2	100.0	0.782
Commodities	151–151	51.9	60.3	72.3	88.4	114.1	100.0	0.373
Gross domestic product	1–151	40.7	51.7	64.5	73.6	107.4	100.0	0.415

a. Line numbers refer to Appendix Table 6-1 and show the detailed categories that are included in each aggregation.

b. Consumption, ICP, includes both household and government expenditures. The latter are shown separately in Table 2-1. It also includes net expenditure of residents abroad.

c. Based on thirty-four countries.

are predominantly categories for which differing institutional factors and governmental policies are apt to have a large influence on prices.

Relative Price Structures

A different standard for assessing price structures is employed in Table 6-9. In this table, the relative price of a summary category in a country is given by the ratio of the share of expenditures in national currencies (from Summary Multilateral Table 6-2) to the corresponding share of expenditures in international dollars (the share in international dollars being derived from the data in Summary Multilateral Table 6-5).[9] The ratios are calculated for individual countries, and to facilitate the exposition the ratios are averaged for the countries in each group. For example, one component of the average Group I ratio for fish (1.18) was the ratio for Kenya, 1.58, which was derived by dividing the share of fish in GDP at national prices, 0.167, by the share of fish in GDP valued at international prices, 0.106, the shares being calculated from Summary Multilateral Tables 6-1 and 6-3, respectively. The ratios computed in this way for the other countries in Group I were averaged with the Kenyan ratio to obtain the group figure.

The significance of the ratio is brought out by examining its formula:

$$(6.1) \quad R_{ij} = \frac{p_{ij}q_{ij} \Big/ \sum_{i=1}^{m} p_{ij}q_{ij}}{\Pi_i q_{ij} \Big/ \sum_{i=1}^{m} \Pi_i q_{ij}} = \frac{p_{ij}q_{ij}}{\Pi_i q_{ij}} \text{PPP}_j = \frac{p_{ij}/\text{PPP}_j}{\Pi_i}.$$

The last term on the right indicates that R_{ij} is equal to the ratio of the domestic price converted to dollars by the PPP[10] and the international price, the latter being the average of such PPP-converted prices for all the countries. Therefore, it provides a means of comparing the price structures of different countries.[11]

9. This way of exploring relative price structures was suggested by Benjamin B. King of the World Bank.
10. $\Sigma p_{ij}q_{ij}/\Sigma \Pi_i q_{ij} = \text{PPP}_j$ by definition.
11. The ICP implementation of the calculation of R_{ij} produces $\overline{R}_{ij}$, which is defined by (6.1').

$$(6.1') \quad \overline{R}_{ij} = \frac{p_{ij}q_{ij} \Big/ \sum_{i=1}^{m} p_{ij}q_{ij}}{\overline{\Pi}_i Q_{ij} \Big/ \sum_{i=1}^{m} \overline{\Pi}_i Q_{ij}}$$

where $\overline{\Pi}_i = \Pi_i/p_{i,US}$ and Q_{ij} (the notional quantity) $= p_{i,US} q_{ij}$ (see Chapter 3, the section "Aggregation of Category Expenditures and Prices"). $Q_{ij} = p_{ij}q_{ij}/\text{PPP}_j = (p_{ij}q_{ij}) \div (p_{ij}/p_{i,US}) = p_{i,US}q_{ij}$. Therefore,

The value of R_{ij} for GDP as a whole is 1 since both the numerator and the denominator of the defining expression are both 1 for all of GDP. Consequently, a value of more than 1 for a given country in a given category indicates that, relative to the relationship of the country's prices to international prices for its GDP as a whole, its prices for that particular category are high. A figure below 1, however, indicates the category is cheap in the country's structure of relative prices compared with the world structure of relative prices.

Chapter 1 discussed the relative prices of the broad categories consumption, investment, and government. Here attention is directed to the summary categories. The most expensive items in the relative price structure of the lowest income countries (Groups I and II), compared with the world relative price structure, are personal-transport equipment and operation costs, and producer durable goods. Another category relatively high in price is furniture and equipment. The least expensive categories tend to be those dominated by personal services, such as education.

In the highest income countries (Groups V and VI), however, education, purchased transport, and the compensation of government employees are among the most expensive categories. In the United States, medical care joins this high-priced group. Food is relatively cheap in the high-income countries and dear in the low-income countries. Within capital formation, construction is cheap relative to producer durables in the three lowest income groups and more expensive in the two highest income groups.

Comparisons for Commodities and Services and for Tradable and Nontradable Goods

Thus far, the results of the ICP have been analyzed through the familiar functional classification of final expenditures (that is, food, clothing, and so forth). For some analytical purposes, it is useful to distinguish between commodities and services and between tradable and nontradable goods. Accordingly, in this sec-

$$(6.2') \quad \overline{R}_{ij} = \frac{p_{ij}q_{ij}}{\dfrac{\Pi_i}{p_{i,US}} \cdot P_{i,US}q_{ij}} \cdot \frac{\sum_i \dfrac{\Pi_i}{p_{i,US}} \cdot p_{i,US}q_{ij}}{\sum_i p_{ij}q_{ij}}$$

$$= \frac{p_{ij}}{\Pi_i} \cdot \frac{\sum \Pi_i q_{ij}}{\sum p_{ij}q_{ij}} = \frac{p_{ij}/\text{PPP}_j}{\Pi_i}$$

since the last expressions on the right of equations 6.2' and 6.1 are the same, the ICP's $\overline{R}_{ij}$ is indeed the same as R_{ij}.

Table 6-9. Average Relation of National Price Structures to International Price Structures for Groups of Countries Classified by Real per Capita GDP, 1975

Category	Lines numbers[a]	Group I	Group II	Group III	Group IV	Group V	Group VI
Consumption, ICP [b]	1–108	1.03	1.01	0.96	0.97	0.99	1.04
Food, beverages, tobacco	1–39	1.13	1.06	0.95	1.00	0.88	0.86
Food	1–33	1.12	1.07	0.92	0.98	0.88	0.88
Bread, cereals	1–6	1.03	1.15	0.91	0.82	0.99	1.09
Meat	7–12	1.00	0.99	0.88	1.11	0.99	0.88
Fish	13–14	1.18	1.04	0.85	0.89	0.92	0.75
Milk, cheese, eggs	15–17	1.57	1.14	0.81	0.99	0.72	0.82
Oils, fats	18–20	1.42	0.96	1.05	0.92	0.78	0.75
Fruits, vegetables	21–26	1.03	1.11	1.01	0.85	0.87	0.89
Coffee, tea, cocoa	27–29	0.95	0.78	1.17	1.84	0.94	0.54
Spices, sweets, sugar	30–33	1.44	1.01	1.02	1.03	0.75	0.93
Beverages	34–37	1.16	1.17	1.00	1.23	0.78	0.79
Tobacco	38–39	1.31	0.87	1.28	0.86	1.14	0.81
Clothing, footwear	40–51	1.10	0.95	1.06	1.21	1.01	0.88
Clothing	40–47	1.13	0.95	1.05	1.27	0.99	0.86
Footwear	48–51	0.94	0.95	1.13	0.99	1.12	0.99
Gross rent, fuel	52–57	1.13	1.07	0.76	0.85	1.01	1.06
Gross rent	52–53	1.08	1.15	0.65	0.79	0.96	1.15
Fuel, power	54–57	1.23	0.95	1.05	1.10	1.15	0.82
House furnishings, operations	58–70	0.95	1.10	1.17	1.18	0.85	0.93
Furniture, appliances	53–66	1.50	1.59	1.30	1.18	0.76	0.89
Supplies, operation	67–70	0.81	0.87	1.06	1.17	1.04	1.02
Medical care	71–77	0.91	0.96	0.82	0.69	0.92	1.63
Transport, communications	78–89	1.23	1.15	1.21	1.17	1.04	0.82
Equipment	78–79	2.93	2.05	1.92	1.40	0.94	0.72
Operation costs	80–83	2.14	1.46	1.17	1.29	0.94	0.79
Purchased transport	84–87	0.83	1.03	1.03	0.93	1.69	1.64
Communications	88–89	1.17	0.49	0.92	0.86	1.27	1.12
Recreation, education	90–101	0.58	0.79	0.98	0.95	1.28	1.36
Recreation	90–96	1.14	1.06	1.09	0.97	0.97	0.97
Education	97–101	0.46	0.67	0.91	0.92	1.75	1.89
Other expenditures	102–107	1.01	0.90	1.00	0.89	1.07	1.08
Personal care	102–104	0.99	1.08	1.14	1.06	1.00	0.94
Miscellaneous services	105–107	1.01	0.85	0.98	0.84	1.10	1.13
Capital formation	109–146	1.20	0.97	1.14	1.06	0.92	0.81
Domestic capital formation	109–145	1.34	1.05	1.13	1.07	0.92	0.82
Construction	109–122	1.02	0.89	0.99	1.02	1.02	0.94
Residential	109–110	1.04	0.83	0.93	0.93	1.04	0.93
Nonresidential	111–118	1.06	0.38	0.86	1.05	1.08	0.82
Other	119–122	0.98	0.94	1.29	1.10	0.91	1.10
Producer durables	123–144	2.11	1.32	1.40	1.13	0.80	0.69
Transport equipment	123–129	2.19	1.29	1.52	0.93	0.80	0.65
Nonelectrical machinery	130–138	2.07	1.30	1.37	1.24	0.74	0.67
Electrical machinery	139–142	2.08	1.71	1.40	1.17	0.93	0.72
Other	143–144	2.11	1.08	1.27	1.20	0.81	0.82
Exports minus imports	146–146	1.71	1.43	1.06	1.15	0.66	0.78
Government	147–151	0.66	1.02	0.94	1.04	1.31	1.10
Compensation	147–150	0.48	1.02	0.93	1.00	1.53	1.41
Commodities	151–151	1.09	1.01	0.96	1.07	0.95	0.89
Gross domestic product	1–151	1.00	1.00	1.00	1.00	1.00	1.00

a. Line numbers refer to Appendix Table 6-1 and show the detailed categories that are included in each aggregation.

b. Consumption, ICP, includes both household and government expenditures. The latter are shown separately in Table 2-1. It also includes net expenditure of residents abroad.

tion the detailed categories are aggregated to obtain expenditure, quantity, and price comparisons for commodities and services and for tradable and nontradable goods. Services are defined as including categories in which expenditures are on goods that cannot be stored. These include categories in which personal services are being engaged (for example, domestic services, teachers, and government employees), repairs of various kinds (footwear, auto), rents, public transport and communication, public entertainment, and restaurants and hotels. All the other categories of GDP are regarded as commodities. (See Appendix Table 2-1 for the assignment of detailed categories to the service and commodity classifications.) The distinction between the services/commodities and tradable/nontradable classification lies in the treatment of construction. Tradables consist of all commodities except construction; nontradables consist of all services plus construction.

The distribution of expenditures between services and commodities and between tradable and nontradable goods is shown in Table 6-10. These are expressed both at national prices and at international prices. As before, the countries are ranked in order of increasing real per capita GDP, and averages are provided for the six groups of countries to show more readily the structural changes associated with rising income levels.

An often expressed generalization is that the share of expenditures on services tends to rise as per capita incomes increase.[12] Does this hold true on a cross-section basis for the thirty-four ICP countries?

Expressed in each country's own prices, the share of services in GDP (column 2) does tend to be positively correlated with per capita GDP, but the association is an irregular one, with the clearest increases occurring from Group I to Group II and after Group IV. When international prices are used, however, the share of services in GDP (column 7) of the low-income countries expands and that of the high-income countries contracts. With international prices, the share is slightly higher in Group I than for the others, but there is very little variation in the average service share. In real terms, Uruguay, the United Kingdom, Jamaica, and Kenya devote the highest proportion of their incomes to services (40–42 percent) while Iran and Syria devote the lowest (22 percent).

Nontradable goods, which overlap services to a great extent, exhibit the same behavior when expressed in own currencies: a rise in the share from Group I to II and again after Group IV. Expressed in international prices, however, there is again relatively little variation in the group averages.

The ratios (R_{ij}'s) depicting the differences in price structures producing these alternative sets of results are set out in Table 6-11. The R_{ij}'s provide a measure of each country's or group's own price structure relative to an international price structure, with the figures for each country or group being normalized around the ratio of 100 for GDP as a whole.

The price of services in this relative sense rises with per capita income sharply but somewhat irregularly, with the largest increases from Group I to II and after Group IV. The socialist countries tend to have low service prices relative to their income levels.[13] The relative price of commodities moves in the opposite direction: down from Group I to Group II and again after Group IV. The rise in relative prices for services is an important factor pushing up the share of expenditures on services expressed in own currency in the higher income countries.

The addition of construction to the service categories to form the aggregate of nontradable goods narrows the difference between relative prices for low- and high-income countries, but not by much. Relative prices for nontradable goods rise from approximately 75 for Group I to over 125 for the United States. The relative prices of tradable goods, however, decline from around 120 to 80 for the two extreme income groups.

A similar story emerges in columns 6 through 10 of Table 6-12, in which the prices of services and of nontradable goods are compared with the U.S. relative price structure rather than the international structure. The prices of services (column 7) rise from 20 percent of the U.S. prices for Group I to 95 percent of the U.S. level for Group V, and nontradable goods (column 9) rise from 25 percent to more than 95 percent. The prices of commodities (column 6) and for traded goods (column 8) are also positively associated with income levels at least through Group V. Even the Group I prices, however, were well over half the U.S. levels for commodities and tradable goods (compared with a level of one-fifth or one-fourth for services and nontradable goods). Thus the dispersion of price levels is smaller for commodities than for services and for tradable goods than for nontradable goods. As was

12. Clark (1951). The results presented here use the Phase III treatment of comparison-resistant services described in Chapter 5. The conclusions are not, however, dependent on these methods. They remain the same for Phase III data if the equal productivity assumption is made or if the PPPs for comparison-resistant services are assumed to be the same as PPPs for priced services. For a fuller discussion, see Kravis, Heston, Summers (1982).

13. This is in part because more services are provided free in these countries. The availability of free services may make wages be less at the same real income; this in turn would produce lower prices for labor-intensive goods, such as services.

Table 6-10. Division of Expenditures between Commodities and Services, Tradable and Nontradable Goods, 1975

Country	National prices					International prices			
	Commodities (1)	Services (2)	Tradable goods (3)	Nontradable goods (4)	GDP (5)	Commodities (6)	Services (7)	Tradable goods (8)	Nontradable goods (9)
Group I	77.8	22.2	66.3	33.7	100	66.2	33.8	54.9	45.1
Malawi	81.2	18.8	70.1	29.9	100	70.7	29.3	60.3	39.7
Kenya	67.3	32.7	55.9	44.1	100	59.9	40.1	48.8	51.2
India	83.7	16.3	74.5	25.5	100	65.2	34.8	55.5	44.5
Pakistan	79.1	20.9	68.4	31.6	100	68.0	32.0	58.4	41.6
Sri Lanka	81.9	18.1	73.4	26.6	100	63.1	36.9	52.4	47.6
Zambia	70.0	30.0	48.7	51.3	100	64.1	35.9	42.3	57.7
Thailand	78.6	21.4	69.1	30.9	100	75.2	24.8	65.3	34.7
Philippines	80.9	19.1	70.8	29.2	100	63.0	37.0	56.5	43.5
Group II	71.6	28.4	58.8	41.2	100	68.3	31.7	53.9	46.1
Korea	78.5	21.5	64.9	35.1	100	73.7	26.3	59.3	40.7
Malaysia	69.9	30.1	56.4	43.6	100	67.5	32.5	46.1	53.9
Colombia	67.4	32.6	56.5	43.5	100	63.3	36.7	47.4	52.6
Jamaica	64.0	36.0	52.6	47.4	100	58.8	41.2	47.5	52.5
Syria	77.1	22.9	62.4	37.6	100	77.6	22.4	67.5	32.5
Brazil	72.7	27.3	60.2	39.9	100	69.0	31.0	55.5	44.5
Group III	72.7	27.3	58.6	41.4	100	68.2	31.8	54.1	45.9
Romania	81.6	18.4	64.9	35.1	100	70.0	30.0	51.7	48.3
Mexico	73.8	26.2	60.9	39.1	100	70.7	29.3	54.0	46.0
Yugoslavia	76.3	23.7	60.3	39.7	100	69.0	31.0	57.8	42.2
Iran	76.9	23.1	61.4	38.6	100	78.0	22.0	58.5	41.5
Uruguay	64.4	35.6	55.2	44.8	100	58.1	41.9	51.8	48.2
Ireland	62.9	37.1	49.0	51.0	100	63.6	36.4	50.7	49.3
Group IV	74.4	25.6	57.9	42.1	100	69.7	30.3	53.5	46.5
Hungary	79.6	20.4	60.2	39.8	100	70.0	30.0	52.9	47.1
Poland	81.2	18.8	61.3	38.7	100	71.3	28.7	52.4	47.6
Italy	66.3	33.7	53.8	46.2	100	67.7	32.3	53.2	46.8
Spain	70.6	29.4	56.2	43.8	100	69.6	30.4	55.4	44.6
Group V	63.2	36.8	48.1	51.9	100	68.8	31.2	54.0	46.0
U.K.	57.3	42.7	46.8	53.2	100	58.5	41.5	49.2	50.8
Japan	65.7	34.3	44.3	55.7	100	70.9	29.1	52.5	47.5
Austria	68.0	32.0	51.5	48.5	100	70.2	29.8	57.4	42.6
Netherlands	63.5	36.5	52.0	48.0	100	73.8	26.2	60.9	39.1
Belgium	63.8	36.2	49.8	50.3	100	72.0	28.0	57.6	42.4
France	64.6	35.4	49.9	50.1	100	70.3	29.7	54.5	45.5
Luxembourg	65.9	34.1	45.7	54.3	100	70.5	29.5	51.6	48.4
Denmark	57.6	42.4	43.0	57.0	100	63.2	36.8	46.6	53.4
Germany	62.5	37.5	50.0	50.0	100	70.2	29.8	56.0	44.0
Group VI	56.1	43.9	46.6	53.4	100	67.7	32.3	57.6	42.4
U.S.	56.1	43.9	46.6	53.4	100	67.7	32.3	57.6	42.4

noted in Chapter 5, the behavior of service prices and more generally nontradable goods across countries at different levels of income is consistent with the predictions of the productivity differential model.

In view of these sharp differences in price relationships for commodities versus services and for tradable versus nontradable goods, it is of interest to note from columns 1 and 2 that the quantity indexes for services are marginally larger than the quantity indexes for commodities for Group I countries. Their average quantity indexes were 9.4 and 8.8, respectively.

Beginning with Group II, the service indexes begin to fall below the commodity indexes. The ratio of the quantity indexes for nontradable goods to the quantity indexes for tradable goods rises from Group I to II and remains fairly constant through Group V.

Thus the positive association between the share of services in expenditures and per capita income reflects mainly a tendency for services to become more expensive as income rises rather than a tendency toward the absorption of relatively greater quantities of services. This absorption does increase with rising in-

Table 6-11. Relation of the National Price Structure to the International Price Structure, 1975

Group and country	Commodities	Services	Tradable goods	Nontradable goods	GDP
Group I	118.0	66.1	121.1	74.5	100
Malawi	114.9	64.2	116.3	75.3	100
Kenya	112.3	81.6	114.6	86.1	100
India	128.3	46.9	134.3	57.3	100
Pakistan	116.2	65.5	117.1	76.0	100
Sri Lanka	129.6	49.2	140.0	55.9	100
Zambia	109.3	83.4	115.2	88.9	100
Thailand	104.5	86.2	105.8	89.0	100
Philippines	128.5	51.6	125.2	67.3	100
Group II	105.1	89.6	110.3	91.0	100
Korea	106.4	81.9	109.4	86.4	100
Malaysia	103.6	92.6	122.4	80.8	100
Colombia	106.6	88.7	119.0	82.8	100
Jamaica	108.9	87.3	110.5	90.4	100
Syria	99.4	102.1	92.4	115.7	100
Brazil	105.4	88.0	108.3	89.6	100
Group III	106.5	86.5	108.5	90.2	100
Romania	116.6	61.2	125.5	72.7	100
Mexico	104.3	89.6	112.9	84.9	100
Yugoslavia	110.6	76.5	104.3	94.1	100
Iran	97.7	104.7	104.9	93.0	100
Uruguay	110.7	85.1	106.5	93.0	100
Ireland	98.9	101.9	96.8	103.3	100
Group IV	106.7	83.7	108.3	90.7	100
Hungary	113.7	68.0	113.8	84.5	100
Poland	113.9	65.5	116.9	81.4	100
Italy	97.9	104.4	101.1	98.7	100
Spain	101.4	96.8	101.5	98.2	100
Group V	92.0	119.2	89.2	113.2	100
U.K.	97.9	102.9	95.2	104.7	100
Japan	92.5	118.2	84.4	117.3	100
Austria	96.9	107.3	89.7	113.9	100
Netherlands	86.1	139.3	85.5	122.6	100
Belgium	88.6	129.3	86.4	118.5	100
France	91.9	119.1	91.7	110.0	100
Luxembourg	93.5	115.6	88.6	112.1	100
Denmark	91.1	115.2	92.1	106.9	100
Germany	89.1	125.5	89.3	113.7	100
Group VI	82.8	136.0	80.9	126.0	
U.S.	82.8	136.0	80.9	126.0	100

comes, but so does the absorption of commodities. The relatively sharper rise in the prices of services (column 7 of Table 6-12) presumably inhibits the increase in their use, but not so much that their share of expenditures falls very much in real terms.

Thus, in real terms, purchases of commodities and services are more alike in different countries than is indicated by the own-currency shares shown in Table 6-10. The coefficient of variation for the service shares in the expenditures of the thirty-four countries is 0.161 in real terms (that is, shares in column 7 of Table 6-10) and 0.277 expressed in own currency (column 2 shares).

PPPs for Private Households

The discussion of price levels and PPPs to this point has focused on the full social cost of the final products that make up the GDPs of different countries. Of course, there is no transactor or even a clearly defined class of transactors whose purchases are spread over all the goods in the GDP, let alone in the proportions among them found in GDP. A question often asked but not answered by the PPPs that have so far been presented relates to the relative purchasing power of different currencies from the standpoint of private consumers.

Table 6-12. Quantity and Price Indexes for Commodities and Services and for Tradable and Nontradable Goods, 1975

Country	Quantity ratios					Price indexes					Shares in GDP	
	Commodities (1)	Services (2)	Tradable goods (3)	Nontradable goods (4)	GDP (5)	Commodities (6)	Services (7)	Tradable goods (8)	Nontradable goods (9)	GDP (10)	Services (11)	Nontradables (12)
Group I	8.83	9.38	8.63	9.52	9.01	57.2	20.7	60.0	24.9	40.6	33.8	45.1
Malawi	5.11	4.45	5.13	4.59	4.90	54.5	18.6	56.5	23.5	39.3	29.3	39.7
Kenya	5.80	8.14	5.55	7.92	6.56	69.5	30.7	72.6	35.0	51.2	40.1	51.2
India	6.31	7.06	6.31	6.89	6.56	48.0	10.7	51.4	14.1	31.0	34.8	44.5
Pakistan	8.26	8.15	8.33	8.08	8.23	45.0	15.4	46.4	19.3	32.1	32.0	41.6
Sri Lanka	8.68	10.6	8.47	10.4	9.30	42.9	9.9	47.5	12.2	27.4	36.9	47.6
Zambia	9.73	11.4	7.55	14.0	10.3	88.5	41.1	95.5	47.3	67.0	35.9	57.7
Thailand	14.5	10.0	14.8	10.7	13.0	47.2	23.7	48.9	26.4	37.4	24.8	34.7
Philippines	12.3	15.1	12.9	13.5	13.2	61.6	15.1	61.5	21.2	39.7	37.0	43.5
Group II	23.3	22.7	21.7	25.1	23.1	65.9	34.1	70.7	37.2	51.7	31.7	46.1
Korea	22.5	16.8	21.3	19.9	20.7	50.5	23.7	53.1	26.9	39.3	26.3	40.7
Malaysia	21.4	21.6	17.2	27.3	21.5	63.3	34.5	76.6	32.5	50.6	32.5	53.9
Colombia	21.0	25.5	18.5	27.8	22.4	45.4	23.0	52.0	23.2	35.3	36.7	52.6
Jamaica	20.8	30.6	19.8	29.7	24.0	107.3	52.4	111.5	58.6	81.6	41.2	52.5
Syria	28.6	17.3	29.3	19.2	25.0	48.0	30.0	45.7	36.7	40.0	22.4	32.5
Brazil	25.7	24.2	24.3	26.5	25.2	80.7	41.0	84.9	45.1	63.4	31.0	44.5
Group III	37.4	37.0	35.0	40.5	37.3	83.1	41.2	86.6	46.5	64.7	31.8	45.9
Romania	34.4	30.9	29.8	37.9	33.3	102.8	32.8	113.2	42.2	73.0	30.0	48.3
Mexico	36.2	31.4	32.5	37.6	34.7	74.2	38.8	82.2	39.7	58.9	29.3	46.0
Yugoslavia	36.8	34.7	36.3	35.9	36.1	85.7	36.1	82.8	48.0	64.2	31.0	42.2
Iran	43.4	25.7	38.3	36.9	37.7	69.9	45.2	76.1	43.3	58.7	22.0	41.5
Uruguay	34.0	51.4	35.6	45.0	39.6	61.5	28.8	60.5	34.0	46.0	41.9	48.2
Ireland	39.9	47.8	37.4	49.4	42.5	104.7	65.7	104.9	71.9	87.7	36.4	49.3
Group IV	53.8	49.2	48.6	57.4	52.4	94.0	46.3	97.9	53.4	73.5	30.3	46.5
Hungary	51.3	46.0	45.5	55.1	49.6	81.9	29.9	84.0	40.0	59.7	30.0	47.1
Poland	52.8	44.5	45.6	56.3	50.1	98.8	34.6	103.8	46.4	71.9	28.7	47.6
Italy	53.8	53.8	49.6	59.4	53.8	105.3	68.4	111.3	69.8	89.1	32.3	46.8
Spain	57.4	52.6	53.7	58.8	55.9	89.9	52.3	92.1	57.2	73.4	30.4	44.6
Group V	77.4	73.0	71.2	82.4	76.0	119.0	94.6	118.5	96.7	107.5	31.2	46.0
U.K.	55.2	82.1	54.5	76.7	63.9	106.5	68.2	106.0	74.9	90.1	41.5	50.8
Japan	71.6	61.5	62.3	76.6	68.4	101.9	79.2	95.1	84.9	91.2	29.1	47.5
Austria	72.1	64.3	69.4	69.9	69.6	117.3	79.1	111.2	90.7	100.3	29.8	42.6
Netherlands	82.0	61.0	79.5	69.4	75.2	116.7	115.0	118.6	109.3	112.3	26.2	39.1
Belgium	82.6	67.3	77.7	77.6	77.7	120.9	107.4	120.7	106.2	113.0	28.0	42.4
France	85.0	75.4	77.4	88.0	81.9	121.4	95.8	123.9	95.5	109.4	29.7	45.6
Luxembourg	85.4	74.8	73.4	93.6	82.0	124.1	93.5	120.5	97.9	110.0	29.5	48.4
Denmark	76.9	93.9	66.7	103.7	82.4	139.6	107.4	144.5	107.6	126.8	36.8	53.4
Germany	85.9	76.6	80.6	86.1	83.0	122.9	105.4	126.0	103.0	114.2	29.8	44.0
Group VI	100.0	100.0	100.0	100.0	100.0	100.0	100.0	100.0	100.0	100.0	32.3	42.4
U.S.	100.0	100.0	100.0	100.0	100.0	100.0	100.0	100.0	100.0	100.0	32.3	42.4

The spending of households largely overlaps the composition of ICP consumption, but household spending is smaller because ICP consumption includes all housing, medical care, and education whether paid for by private households or out of the public purse. Furthermore, the identity of the commodities and services and the proportions of total national expenditures paid for out of public funds varies from one country to another. Thus the scope of the bundle of goods paid for by private households varies among different countries.

If PPPs for private households are nevertheless de-

sired, there are two possible ways to provide them. One is to form a common denominator of categories of goods completely paid for by households in all the countries. This would not be a narrow or unimportant list of goods, but it would exclude some important categories—namely, housing, education, medical care, and recreation.

The alternative is to count in all the free or publicly subsidized goods received by consumers, assigning them the zero or subsidized prices at which they were transferred to consumers. This can be accomplished by either of two simple procedures. The private household expenditures for ICP consumption goods in each country in the country's own currency can be divided by the country's expenditure for ICP consumption in international dollars, and the result divided by the corresponding ratio for the United States. An alternative procedure producing the same result is to multiply the regular ICP PPPs by the proportion of (1) private to total (private plus public) own-currency expenditures on ICP consumption goods in each country to (2) the corresponding ratio for the numéraire country (United States).[14]

As the latter alternative implies, the relationship between these private-household PPPs and the full-coverage-of-GDP PPPs is a measure of the importance of government subsidies to consumption. It is a very rough measure because the ICP has made an effort to obtain the subsidy component of prices only for the main categories for which such subsidies were obviously important in many countries. There may be some omissions—public transport, for example—for which public subsidies loom large in some or many countries.

The resulting private-household PPPs are set out in column 3 of Table 6-13. The standard ICP PPPs for consumption, the "full price" PPPs, are included for comparison. The differences between the two sets of PPPs, shown in ratio form in column 4, are not so large as might have been expected from the wide range of institutions and policies found among the thirty-four Phase III countries. The largest deviation, that for Pakistan, was less than 10 percent above the private PPP. Almost half were within 5 percent of the full-price PPP. However, in over two-thirds of the cases the private PPP is higher than the standard PPP. This is because the relative importance of public contributions to the cost of the bundle of goods that is included in ICP consumption is higher in the United States than in most other countries. In the United States nearly 11 percent of the consumption bill is paid out of public funds. Among the limited number of countries for which the proportion is lower are Austria, Denmark, Hungary, Ireland, Poland, the United Kingdom, Yugoslavia, and Zambia.

The private-household PPPs are more suitable than the ICP's standard PPPs for consumption when one wishes to derive real wage comparisons from the money wages of different countries. They are, however, subject to important limitations. For wage or salary earners as a whole and even more for any subset of them,

one must consider the possibility that the benefits of free or subsidized goods may accrue to the group in proportions larger or smaller than the average proportions for the nation. Also, the relative importance of different kinds of goods in the expenditures of particular groups may vary from that of the nation as a whole.[15] For employees generally or for other groups of income recipients, the use of private-household PPPs to derive comparative real income must take account also of the nature of taxation in different countries. If no direct taxes were paid by the groups whose real incomes were being compared, the costs of government would have to be recouped through indirect taxes. Such taxes are included in the goods prices used in the comparisons; thus no further corrections are required on this account. If direct taxes are paid, then the real-income comparisons must be based on after-tax incomes.

Summary

Tables 6-1 through 6-5 of this chapter are the basic tables presenting the results of the Phase III price and quantity comparisons for thirty-four countries with a 1975 reference date. The tables give data for GDP, consumption, investment, and government and for thirty-five further breakdowns of expenditures on GDP (summary categories). Appendix tables give the essential data for a finer though less reliable breakdown of expenditures into 151 detailed categories. Appendix tables corresponding to Tables 6-1, 6-3, and 6-5 are included. They give own-currency expenditures, PPPs, and international-dollar expenditures. Appendix tables corresponding to Tables 6-2 and 6-4 are not given but are easily derivable from Appendix Tables 6-1 and 6-

15. The reader can recompute household PPPs with alternative weights by making use of the data in Tables 2-1, 6-1, and 6-3. The private-household PPPs presented here should be distinguished from a PPP calculated only for items directly purchased by consumers. This latter PPP has been calculated in the Austria-Poland comparison and is there termed the "real" PPP. See Central Statistical Offices of Austria and Poland (1980). In these comparisons categories were treated as direct consumer purchases if there were private purchases in at least one of the two countries. The relation between the "real" PPP and the private PPP will depend on the relative shares in total consumption of the direct purchases by consumers in the given country and the base country. When the base country has a smaller share of freely provided services in consumption, then the private PPP will be less than the real PPP, and vice versa. In the ICP framework the relation between the real and private PPPs is directly proportional to the relative shares of directly purchased consumption to total consumption in international dollars. In symbols: $PPP_{A/B}$ *(private)* $= PPP_{A/B}$ *(real)* $\cdot S_A/S_B$ where S equals private household expenditures on the included categories as a percentage of total ICP consumption.

14. The total expenditures in own currency are given in Table 6-1 and in international dollars in Table 6-5. The public expenditures are the sum of total transfers from SNA government (column 5) and rent subsidies (column 6) in Table 2-1.

Table 6-13. Private Household PPPs, 1975

Country	Full price PPP (1)	Ratio of household to total ICP consumption expenditure (2)	Private household PPP[a] (3)	Ratio (4) = (3) ÷ (1)
Malawi	0.335	0.948	0.356	1.064
Kenya	3.612	0.889	3.602	0.997
India	2.502	0.970	2.723	1.088
Pakistan	3.320	0.979	3.647	1.098
Sri Lanka	3.197	0.955	3.427	1.072
Zambia	0.441	0.855	0.423	0.959
Thailand	7.161	0.958	7.697	1.075
Philippines	2.628	0.952	2.805	1.067
Korea	191.285	0.972	208.533	1.090
Malaysia	1.223	0.911	1.250	1.022
Colombia	10.448	0.942	11.042	1.057
Jamaica	0.688	0.925	0.714	1.038
Syria	1.320	0.965	1.429	1.082
Brazil	5.309	0.963	5.735	1.080
Romania	7.626	0.890	7.617	0.999
Mexico	7.198	0.927	7.484	1.040
Yugoslavia	9.767	0.839	9.198	0.942
Iran	34.889	0.895	35.023	1.004
Uruguay	1.040	0.959	1.119	1.076
Ireland	0.366	0.856	0.352	0.960
Hungary	11.125	0.865	10.795	0.970
Poland	13.197	0.870	12.875	0.976
Italy	567.178	0.939	597.249	1.053
Spain	39.827	0.929	41.519	1.042
U.K.	0.386	0.860	0.372	0.965
Japan	271.187	0.919	279.553	1.031
Austria	15.622	0.874	15.319	0.981
Netherlands	2.758	0.893	2.762	1.002
Belgium	39.484	0.916	40.575	1.028
France	4.625	0.943	4.894	1.058
Luxembourg	35.856	0.932	37.492	1.046
Denmark	6.979	0.824	6.453	0.925
Germany	2.786	0.943	2.947	1.058
U.S.	1.000	0.891	1.000	1.000

a. Column 1 times the ratio of column 2 for country *i* to column 2 for the United States.

5, respectively. The construction of the basic tables is explained; each follows the methods set out in Chapters 3 and 4.

As a means of describing the structure of expenditure prices and quantities, the thirty-four countries are arrayed in order of increasing real GDP per capita and divided into six groups. Among the notable features of the averages calculated for the six groups are these:

1. When the shares of the thirty-five expenditure categories in total own-currency GDP are examined, the most striking change is a decline of the food share from 38 percent for Group I (countries with per capita GDP less than 15 percent of the United States) to 9 percent for Group VI (the United States).

2. Underlying these differences in expenditures are differences in both prices and quantities. When the data are examined in terms of real expenditures (that is, at international prices), quantities per capita for most categories tend to rise monotonically, indicating the tendency of higher income countries to absorb more of all goods. A few categories, including bread and cereals, and purchased transport, are exceptions, showing lower per capita quantities at high incomes.

3. Price levels are positively correlated with real GDP per capita, rising from 40 percent of the U.S. level in Group I to slightly above the U.S. level in Group V.

4. This gradation of prices with income level varies from category to category. Producer durable goods tend to have more nearly uniform prices in all countries than do other kinds of goods.

5. Closely related to this finding is the conclusion that producer durables are expensive relative to other things in low-income countries and cheap relative to other things in high-income countries. The opposite is true of categories dominated by personal services, such as education.

6. The share of spending on services seems to rise sharply with the level of income when expressed in own-currency expenditures. However, the valuation of each country's services and commodities at a common set of international prices shows that in real terms the poor and rich allocate their expenditures between these two broad categories of product in roughly similar proportions. The correlation between the service share and per capita income found in own-price data is attributable to higher prices of services in the high-income countries rather than to larger quantities relative to their absorption of commodities.

In a final section of the chapter, PPPs faced by private households are calculated. Unlike the basic ICP PPPs reported elsewhere in this volume, the private household PPPs do not take into account the full social cost of goods but only the price (whether zero, subsidized, or full cost) paid by the household.

Appendix Table 6-1. Per Capita Expenditures in National Currencies, 1975

Line no.	Code	Category	Malawi (kwacha)	Kenya (shillings)	India (rupees)	Pakistan (rupees)	Sri Lanka (rupees)	Zambia (kwacha)	Thailand (baht)
1.	1.101	Rice	1.037	9.10	125.52	39.67	332.10	0.321	658.2
2.	1.102	Meal, other cereals	17.624	—	—	—	118.78	11.624	5.8
3.	1.103	Bread	0.838	16.72	0.27	3.20	60.31	3.112	14.4
4.	1.104	Biscuits, cakes, etc.	0.051	4.63	1.40	—	8.67	0.442	0.5
5.	1.105	Cereal preparations	0.023	—	—	0.93	1.33	0.081	11.6
6.	1.106	Macaroni, spaghetti	0.016	—	—	—	0.07	0.020	0.0
7.	1.111	Fresh beef, veal	1.242	—	1.05	24.96	11.34	13.331	53.2
8.	1.112	Fresh lamb, mutton	0.523	—	1.24	22.03	1.33	0.040	0.0
9.	1.113	Fresh pork	0.202	—	0.94	0.00	2.52	0.200	176.5
10.	1.114	Fresh poultry	1.369	1.49	3.83	4.97	0.74	3.915	88.8
11.	1.115	Other fresh meat	0.014	2.98	—	0.07	0.07	0.081	24.0
12.	1.116	Frozen and salted meat	0.036	—	—	0.00	1.33	1.265	10.2
13.	1.121	Fresh and frozen fish	0.845	—	6.08	18.33	38.68	3.253	265.5
14.	1.122	Canned fish	1.915	—	4.70	0.41	9.93	6.686	4.6
15.	1.131	Fresh milk	0.881	—	42.26	113.16	17.19	2.068	2.7
16.	1.132	Milk products	0.773	—	11.66	56.63	18.45	0.442	41.5
17.	1.133	Eggs, egg products	0.437	10.60	3.57	21.59	9.78	0.642	100.8
18.	1.141	Butter	0.120	1.49	3.38	80.47	0.59	0.281	0.2
19.	1.142	Margarine, edible oil	0.742	12.09	35.27	41.89	—	0.382	16.6
20.	1.143	Lard, edible fat	0.013	1.49	16.13	0.00	—	3.634	39.1
21.	1.151	Fresh tropical fruits	3.183	—	25.41	—	40.01	0.663	256.0
22.	1.152	Other fresh fruits	0.120	—	0.75	—	1.63	0.161	0.4
23.	1.153	Fresh vegetables	11.644	—	43.51	46.14	72.24	8.914	108.6
24.	1.161	Fruit other than fresh	0.341	1.49	—	0.60	1.04	0.100	12.3
25.	1.162	Vegetables other than fresh	0.045	—	—	27.18	0.59	1.787	7.8
26.	1.170	Tubers, including potatoes	4.407	15.23	10.52	10.56	76.02	3.312	2.8
27.	1.191	Coffee	0.123	—	0.64	0.04	7.93	0.342	10.8
28.	1.192	Tea	0.177	—	7.63	19.90	—	0.482	8.1
29.	1.193	Cocoa	0.004	—	0.00	0.29	—	0.200	4.0
30.	1.180	Sugar	1.232	37.91	41.76	36.85	85.14	3.132	49.5
31.	1.201	Jam, syrup, honey	0.052	—	4.48	0.23	0.52	0.301	0.1
32.	1.202	Chocolate, ice cream	0.082	—	1.88	2.76	2.59	0.342	2.4
33.	1.203	Salt, spices, sauces	0.463	1.49	16.10	30.26	77.58	0.703	263.1
34.	1.310	Nonalcoholic beverages	1.116	12.09	0.56	1.68	4.37	0.883	114.8
35.	1.321	Spirits	0.752	9.10	—	—	36.01	0.180	142.8
36.	1.322	Wine, cider	0.091	1.49	—	—	0.15	0.060	0.7
37.	1.323	Beer	2.240	41.05	—	—	3.48	2.971	40.1
38.	1.410	Cigarettes	0.515	30.30	7.85	—	51.20	0.783	123.5
39.	1.420	Cigars, tobacco, snuff	0.259	2.98	17.84	—	43.72	0.301	8.8
40.	2.110	Clothing materials	0.185	—	54.01	108.23	80.02	0.723	160.5
41.	2.121	Men's clothing	2.113	—	—	—	18.08	4.618	32.4
42.	2.122	Women's clothing	1.570	—	—	—	1.78	2.931	20.3
43.	2.123	Boys' and girls' clothing	1.766	—	—	—	0.37	1.385	39.8
44.	2.131	Men's and boys' underwear	0.159	—	—	—	0.07	0.442	11.1
45.	2.132	Women's and girls' underwear	0.172	—	—	—	0.15	0.582	25.9
46.	2.150	Haberdashery, millinery	0.175	—	—	0.75	—	0.642	1.5
47.	2.160	Clothing rental and repair	0.010	—	—	6.31	—	0.060	95.1
48.	2.211	Men's footwear	0.235	—	—	10.43	—	0.743	9.6
49.	2.212	Women's footwear	0.107	2.98	1.92	5.85	—	0.462	4.2
50.	2.213	Children's footwear	0.177	1.49	0.96	2.59	—	0.141	10.5
51.	2.220	Footwear, repairs	0.036	—	0.06	11.43	0.52	0.160	0.5
52.	3.110	Rents	2.693	122.99	—	91.66	—	12.467	106.7
53.	3.120	Indoor repair and upkeep	0.695	1.49	—	12.67	—	0.100	47.4
54.	3.210	Electricity	0.386	—	2.64	7.54	3.48	0.944	25.5
55.	3.220	Gas	0.005	—	0.75	0.67	0.59	—	11.8
56.	3.230	Liquid fuels	0.524	4.63	10.38	9.95	11.56	—	16.7
57.	3.240	Other fuels, ice	1.612	21.20	15.97	53.36	16.82	4.898	94.7
58.	4.110	Furniture, fixtures	0.943	—	2.70	0.38	8.00	1.405	28.4
59.	4.120	Floor coverings	0.157	—	0.16	0.04	0.74	0.040	0.6
60.	4.200	Household textiles, etc.	0.986	7.61	0.38	2.19	1.11	1.004	26.4
61.	4.310	Refrigerators, freezers	0.089	1.49	1.16	—	0.67	0.361	4.5
62.	4.320	Washing appliances	0.058	0.00	0.00	—	0.00	0.020	1.6
63.	4.330	Cooking appliances	0.321	2.99	0.02	—	—	—	—
64.	4.340	Heating appliances	0.030	0.00	0.10	—	—	—	—
65.	4.350	Cleaning appliances	0.039	0.00	0.00	—	0.00	0.020	0.3
66.	4.360	Other household appliances	0.389	0.00	2.20	—	1.19	0.081	32.7
67.	4.400	Household utensils	2.352	10.60	—	0.50	13.63	1.044	52.0
68.	4.510	Nondurable household goods	1.083	16.72	4.44	28.91	8.15	2.851	54.3
69.	4.520	Domestic services	1.102	36.42	1.72	15.07	5.63	3.935	34.4
70.	4.530	Household services	—	1.49	2.49	13.45	8.82	0.181	11.4
71.	5.110	Drugs, medical preparations	0.322	—	—	—	11.34	1.426	116.6
72.	5.120	Medical supplies	0.183	—	—	—	2.15	0.201	77.7
73.	5.200	Therapeutic equipment	0.153	0.00	—	—	1.04	0.081	34.3
74.	5.310	Physicians' services	0.069	—	—	—	10.23	1.144	28.6
75.	5.320	Dentists' services	0.006	—	—	—	0.22	0.060	7.8

— Country did not supply the expenditure breakdown for this category. In the calculations, the ICP estimated a rough breakdown for such categories, which underlies the entries in Appendix Table 6-5.

Philippines (pesos)	Korea (won)	Malaysia (ringgit)	Colombia (pesos)	Jamaica (dollars)	Syria (pounds)	Brazil (cruzeiros)	Romania (lei)	Mexico (pesos)	Yugoslavia (dinars)	Line no.
221.48	34078.	86.42	2.0	25.353	8.97	209.81	29.1	47.5	51.4	1.
66.89	8190.	8.92	384.8	17.717	68.40	97.57	244.6	303.1	—	2.
36.06	1156.	4.93	237.7	33.767	37.12	138.65	372.6	686.7	401.1	3.
13.17	2687.	8.45	28.7	6.404	1.36	19.82	54.3	102.3	115.8	4.
5.68	—	2.58	11.5	4.123	6.39	1.47	0.3	23.1	13.1	5.
6.97	—	6.11	55.5	0.266	3.67	38.88	15.6	54.8	64.4	6.
22.72	3645.	1.69	858.1	17.872	20.80	323.52	99.4	555.1	386.8	7.
0.00	—	1.34	9.3	3.496	66.09	13.93	58.9	41.4	57.8	8.
83.72	1573.	34.00	373.0	3.608	0.00	62.36	434.5	216.1	191.5	9.
63.75	859.	30.76	309.0	6.799	10.20	118.85	450.3	278.2	84.8	10.
12.50	—	—	—	—	—	29.34	7.0	13.5	28.2	11.
7.30	213.	—	—	—	—	69.69	208.1	189.6	525.5	12.
168.67	3601.	37.11	61.8	13.176	3.13	41.82	24.9	27.8	42.1	13.
41.76	1980.	10.84	33.3	11.301	2.72	30.81	22.8	58.8	43.3	14.
15.33	644.	4.33	322.6	4.477	26.79	102.70	196.5	344.9	401.3	15.
1.57	1223.	23.54	—	24.091	55.07	76.30	217.0	301.3	222.8	16.
8.75	1687.	21.29	101.5	7.328	25.29	52.09	184.4	280.9	156.3	17.
1.52	—	1.12	—	2.024	2.99	12.47	33.3	86.3	33.4	18.
3.35	—	—	142.0	6.832	81.72	92.43	93.4	191.4	202.9	19.
22.13	200.	—	47.3	0.000	4.49	54.29	13.2	104.3	49.1	20.
26.17	26.	19.39	87.1	9.509	36.85	73.36	106.7	217.5	72.6	21.
6.97	3670.	6.95	37.3	0.001	69.89	10.27	136.7	92.6	262.4	22.
72.38	—	17.13	192.1	26.306	179.49	148.19	187.6	311.4	331.4	23.
1.26	357.	1.54	13.6	8.662	14.69	11.01	9.4	20.2	13.8	24.
0.62	—	5.36	97.9	1.458	17.95	160.66	66.7	61.3	36.1	25.
36.44	3879.	2.03	338.1	37.219	14.96	60.89	152.7	35.6	106.7	26.
13.90	374.	5.95	60.5	1.164	3.81	94.64	53.4	118.9	205.3	27.
—	24.	2.47	25.9	0.120	—	7.44	0.5	2.2	11.4	28.
—	18.	0.12	113.2	1.369	0.27	0.63	5.0	26.6	5.4	29.
25.31	1989.	27.23	304.7	12.306	37.12	91.70	126.4	101.9	216.5	30.
7.20	228.	0.45	69.9	2.745	1.36	5.61	52.3	74.7	64.4	31.
5.56	81.	5.40	116.4	4.987	33.45	6.13	159.7	42.3	84.5	32.
23.10	10619.	11.62	46.6	0.604	1.77	26.41	186.6	81.7	157.2	33.
31.73	1579.	6.79	114.5	11.417	5.44	16.15	38.5	44.1	88.0	34.
20.30	6106.	7.15	171.3	15.948	1.90	2.19	196.2	28.8	231.6	35.
0.33	381.	1.64	17.5	1.554	0.68	9.55	201.6	1.4	140.0	36.
21.58	2838.	11.70	228.0	14.921	0.27	12.47	82.2	42.3	273.6	37.
52.53	8148.	41.43	127.5	37.353	60.92	151.12	191.3	95.0	426.3	38.
1.57	0.	3.56	54.6	2.679	0.68	1.47	10.4	0.6	2.6	39.
65.87	3523.	35.81	497.8	3.259	72.34	62.36	343.9	228.6	250.2	40.
11.20	—	6.84	96.8	—	25.70	129.12	—	291.0	—	41.
6.70	—	5.47	49.4	—	31.00	165.07	—	187.6	—	42.
2.45	—	1.37	38.3	—	26.65	29.34	—	57.3	99.6	43.
3.16	1686.	2.80	75.8	1.175	2.72	7.33	—	98.1	100.8	44.
3.23	961.	1.86	123.2	2.702	3.13	8.80	—	123.3	150.6	45.
15.55	308.	—	—	0.248	9.38	108.57	140.6	24.3	121.3	46.
1.88	87.	—	—	0.246	2.18	16.15	4.7	24.3	3.7	47.
7.44	446.	3.24	106.9	6.793	8.16	27.87	—	159.1	132.6	48.
5.40	388.	—	122.7	6.954	10.06	35.21	—	96.7	139.3	49.
3.04	551.	1.60	72.6	4.092	13.46	23.48	—	48.4	57.8	50.
2.11	8.	—	16.1	0.659	1.22	16.13	14.6	27.9	10.2	51.
—	5983.	88.38	—	65.752	102.80	428.31	359.0	639.9	538.7	52.
—	359.	10.70	—	8.145	24.20	26.42	133.8	64.8	207.9	53.
10.20	2321.	11.97	78.5	10.677	15.50	118.85	62.6	231.0	266.8	54.
3.47	—	2.03	10.3	1.336	5.03	68.95	37.2	163.5	4.0	55.
11.57	568.	3.82	96.0	1.125	44.33	17.60	75.9	41.9	189.6	56.
18.87	—	6.03	49.3	10.680	23.12	57.23	108.5	171.4	214.6	57.
7.30	416.	6.55	—	18.539	16.59	137.18	291.5	216.0	538.7	58.
0.14	0.	0.87	—	1.680	6.80	18.34	30.0	18.8	83.0	59.
15.14	468.	11.06	42.7	0.785	8.70	52.09	34.7	23.1	172.5	60.
6.77	707.	3.82	—	2.688	4.35	27.87	35.3	37.8	62.6	61.
0.95	233.	0.24	—	0.059	1.77	8.80	10.7	25.2	66.6	62.
5.47	518.	1.64	—	1.556	1.50	18.34	23.4	21.7	100.6	63.
0.50	209.	0.36	—	0.121	1.63	8.07	22.3	4.2	25.9	64.
0.81	144.	0.33	—	0.432	3.53	13.94	2.3	34.1	16.3	65.
3.73	1207.	4.53	—	0.370	11.15	13.21	6.8	167.9	51.8	66.
7.84	685.	13.77	126.0	0.000	14.69	26.42	149.2	145.5	361.9	67.
23.15	861.	16.57	—	7.096	19.58	129.10	102.0	313.5	124.0	68.
10.72	202.	—	130.3	17.110	2.04	89.51	2.5	295.2	18.4	69.
4.04	673.	—	—	2.471	18.76	15.41	111.9	187.0	29.5	70.
15.38	2380.	—	—	—	—	118.92	139.0	253.5	359.0	71.
2.19	453.	—	—	—	—	23.49	21.2	29.2	6.5	72.
2.57	95.	—	11.7	—	—	22.61	18.5	55.6	13.7	73.
11.58	1685.	—	—	—	—	65.12	—	146.6	63.5	74.
3.07	253.	—	—	—	—	44.58	—	8.7	25.7	75.

(Table continues on the following page.)

Line no.	Code	Category	Malawi (kwacha)	Kenya (shillings)	India (rupees)	Pakistan (rupees)	Sri Lanka (rupees)	Zambia (kwacha)	Thailand (baht)
76.	5.330	Nurses' services	0.292	—	—	—	5.56	2.570	29.2
77.	5.410	Hospitals	0.810	10.90	—	—	13.04	5.180	7.9
78.	6.110	Personal automobiles	1.100	9.10	0.29	0.04	—	6.143	44.8
79.	6.120	Other personal transport	0.517	1.49	2.92	0.07	—	0.140	12.2
80.	6.210	Tires, tubes, accessories	0.230	1.49	1.69	0.04	9.71	0.502	29.8
81.	6.220	Automobile repairs	0.887	15.23	—	1.28	0.37	1.426	5.7
82.	6.230	Gasoline, oil, grease	2.456	19.70	—	2.85	18.45	1.687	34.2
83.	6.240	Parking, tolls, etc.	0.539	6.12	0.22	0.01	0.59	0.321	0.2
84.	6.310	Local transport	—	—	12.73	—	—	0.522	148.1
85.	6.321	Rail transport	0.046	—	6.89	—	—	0.241	13.3
86.	6.322	Bus transport	1.069	—	22.12	—	—	0.823	56.0
87.	6.323	Air transport	0.026	—	0.18	—	—	0.040	4.8
88.	6.410	Postal communication	0.056	2.99	1.08	—	5.78	0.442	4.5
89.	6.420	Telephone, telegraph	0.074	1.49	2.03	—	2.15	0.100	6.6
90.	7.110	Radios, televisions, phonographs	0.351	—	3.51	0.16	1.70	—	21.2
91.	7.120	Durable recreational equipment	0.004	—	0.18	—	0.89	—	19.8
92.	7.130	Other recreational equipment	0.001	—	0.25	—	4.00	0.261	69.7
93.	7.210	Public entertainment	0.203	—	—	—	5.04	1.466	26.4
94.	7.220	Other recreation, culture	1.619	—	—	—	19.78	2.369	88.9
95.	7.310	Books, papers, magazines	0.229	—	5.13	—	5.19	0.180	58.1
96.	7.320	Stationery	0.142	—	1.54	—	8.45	0.643	9.4
97.	7.411	First- and second-level teachers	1.435	—	—	—	36.83	11.765	213.5
98.	7.412	College teachers	0.195	—	—	—	2.67	1.024	22.3
99.	7.420	Physical facilities for education	0.343	—	—	—	0.44	0.522	15.0
100.	7.431	Educational books, supplies	0.567	—	—	—	0.81	2.228	28.4
101.	7.432	Other educational expenditures	1.177	—	—	—	8.60	4.899	5.4
102.	8.100	Barber and beauty shops	0.061	2.98	1.83	—	3.78	0.020	27.6
103.	8.210	Toilet articles	0.219	—	4.45	—	14.23	0.923	53.8
104.	8.220	Other personal care goods	0.201	—	9.78	0.77	3.41	0.281	31.0
105.	8.310	Restaurants, cafes	—	—	—	—	—	18.751	210.6
106.	8.320	Hotels, lodgings	—	—	—	—	—	0.301	24.1
107.	8.400	Other services	1.854	—	11.64	—	13.86	0.703	—
108.	8.900	Expenditures of residents abroad	0.000	0.00	−3.96	0.00	−14.08	0.602	−41.7
109.	10.100	One- and two-family dwellings	3.970	52.99	—	—	35.05	—	—
110.	10.200	Multifamily dwellings	0.388	10.30	—	—	7.85	—	—
111.	11.100	Hotels	0.193	—	—	—	5.63	0.261	11.2
112.	11.200	Industrial buildings	0.724	9.10	—	—	2.52	—	9.6
113.	11.300	Commercial buildings	0.579	2.99	—	—	10.82	4.618	175.0
114.	11.400	Office buildings	1.931	—	—	—	5.56	3.735	41.1
115.	11.500	Educational buildings	0.482	4.48	—	—	—	2.871	72.3
116.	11.600	Hospital buildings	0.724	6.12	—	—	—	0.462	4.1
117.	11.700	Agricultural buildings	0.208	2.99	—	—	—	0.602	—
118.	11.800	Other buildings	0.097	—	—	—	—	—	—
119.	12.100	Roads, streets, highways	0.306	25.52	5.78	—	18.01	3.213	48.0
120.	12.200	Transport and utility lines	1.694	43.29	—	—	24.82	7.850	—
121.	12.300	Other construction	1.127	16.42	—	—	0.00	8.011	—
122.	13.000	Land improvement	0.846	8.66	9.63	—	28.97	3.995	59.9
123.	14.110	Locomotives	0.177	—	1.12	—	4.37	0.844	8.0
124.	14.120	Other railway vehicles	0.122	—	2.76	—	4.07	1.847	2.5
125.	14.200	Passenger automobiles	0.260	—	0.82	—	7.04	3.754	39.1
126.	14.300	Trucks, buses, trailers	6.845	—	9.29	—	13.11	9.757	108.3
127.	14.400	Aircraft	0.216	—	0.50	—	0.22	2.530	39.8
128.	14.500	Ships, boats	0.335	—	1.24	—	0.59	0.000	7.7
129.	14.600	Other transport equipment	0.121	—	0.84	—	0.74	0.261	38.2
130.	15.100	Engines, turbines	0.863	3.13	8.36	—	2.15	0.361	—
131.	15.210	Tractors	0.563	—	2.11	—	5.70	1.224	22.3
132.	15.220	Other agricultural machinery	0.939	—	1.40	—	0.67	0.441	4.0
133.	15.300	Office machinery	0.313	6.27	0.49	—	0.37	0.522	—
134.	15.400	Metalworking machinery	0.190	6.27	2.92	—	1.11	0.884	—
135.	15.500	Construction, mining machinery	1.433	1.64	1.36	—	2.37	5.200	—
136.	15.600	Special industrial machinery	1.497	6.27	4.12	—	17.56	1.867	—
137.	15.700	General industrial machinery	2.789	—	11.48	—	16.67	8.914	—
138.	15.800	Service industrial machinery	0.121	—	0.19	—	0.59	0.161	—
139.	16.100	Electrical transmission equipment	1.045	11.05	16.58	—	11.19	4.858	—
140.	16.200	Communications equipment	0.372	4.78	4.51	—	5.63	2.469	—
141.	16.300	Other electrical equipment	0.231	3.13	5.45	—	0.07	3.212	—
142.	16.400	Instruments	0.497	7.91	0.46	—	1.04	0.984	—
143.	17.100	Furniture, fixtures	0.179	1.64	0.38	—	1.04	—	—
144.	17.200	Other durable goods	0.035	6.27	11.72	—	0.07	—	—
145.	18.000	Increase in stocks	3.172	−37.02	50.09	0.00	26.67	8.031	229.7
146.	19.000	Exports minus imports	−20.619	−83.74	−3.25	−141.94	−147.08	−62.036	−329.1
147.	20.100	Unskilled blue collar	0.796	25.67	25.86	—	34.23	15.117	—
148.	20.210	Skilled blue collar	0.538	—	3.02	—	5.04	0.944	—
149.	20.220	White collar	1.922	—	12.21	—	30.01	4.537	—
150.	20.300	Professional	1.091	52.84	14.22	—	9.34	1.586	—
151.	21.000	Commodities of government	4.822	77.02	39.69	80.70	46.46	38.044	—

— Country did not supply the expenditure breakdown for this category. In the calculations, the ICP estimated a rough breakdown for such categories, which underlies the entries in Appendix Table 6-5.

Philippines (pesos)	Korea (won)	Malaysia (ringgit)	Colombia (pesos)	Jamaica (dollars)	Syria (pounds)	Brazil (cruzeiros)	Romania (lei)	Mexico (pesos)	Yugoslavia (dinars)	Line no.
17.21	989.	—	—	—	—	16.70	—	77.5	136.3	76.
11.22	2057.	—	—	—	—	70.84	178.3	232.7	658.1	77.
12.36	428.	33.78	—	—	9.52	158.11	145.4	261.7	398.6	78.
1.35	205.	2.73	—	—	3.40	36.19	12.2	34.7	51.6	79.
0.81	—	16.77	—	8.818	0.95	75.56	23.1	24.7	37.4	80.
0.26	—	5.65	—	8.328	0.95	25.68	12.2	121.7	79.9	81.
1.71	—	40.37	—	22.045	1.36	176.06	36.1	173.1	443.4	82.
1.05	—	2.96	—	9.798	—	45.49	0.7	66.9	91.4	83.
10.60	5479.	14.75	342.5	18.411	—	127.64	123.1	243.3	181.9	84.
0.19	1335.	1.27	5.4	0.386	7.48	16.15	163.1	9.2	46.4	85.
4.21	5300.	22.75	418.7	18.317	9.43	22.01	167.9	46.3	149.3	86.
4.06	225.	10.54	206.6	3.625	0.68	7.33	6.6	45.4	57.9	87.
0.40	171.	2.15	10.2	1.258	1.50	7.33	20.5	8.8	19.6	88.
2.69	714.	4.34	77.7	4.563	2.18	23.48	37.9	60.3	45.7	89.
7.32	1562.	—	46.9	0.067	4.90	97.57	119.6	150.1	146.5	90.
2.90	597.	—	—	0.312	2.99	26.42	10.9	19.6	32.1	91.
1.69	150.	—	—	0.769	1.36	22.01	73.0	12.0	27.7	92.
10.65	33.	—	—	18.928	—	37.42	—	113.4	507.9	93.
2.66	1856.	—	—	4.748	—	95.72	—	43.9	83.8	94.
3.19	1053.	—	—	8.444	4.62	30.81	61.0	53.1	125.1	95.
0.45	522.	—	—	0.016	7.75	36.69	41.3	15.9	27.1	96.
61.28	6926.	—	—	37.769	—	136.65	373.7	536.9	715.2	97.
17.49	1174.	—	—	1.373	—	36.33	43.6	61.1	123.7	98.
13.95	881.	—	—	1.155	—	11.12	54.1	102.5	75.9	99.
5.87	402.	—	—	0.941	—	18.53	16.1	57.0	82.8	100.
5.59	620.	—	—	6.140	—	44.48	130.4	39.9	110.0	101.
8.18	2794.	2.45	—	7.652	7.75	39.61	28.3	74.8	55.4	102.
—	—	8.14	—	25.254	28.56	85.10	—	176.7	—	103.
—	—	8.14	—	6.976	3.40	27.87	—	144.0	—	104.
—	5645.	29.03	—	26.110	22.30	264.85	699.6	456.4	652.5	105.
8.56	466.	14.30	—	39.915	23.80	66.02	63.8	288.2	447.8	106.
53.43	—	—	265.8	48.694	7.89	187.07	91.8	111.4	307.0	107.
0.00	−1720.	—	0.0	−34.275	0.00	0.00	0.0	−270.3	−282.2	108.
42.02	8370.	—	—	—	50.18	63.70	227.4	803.4	875.2	109.
53.48	4197.	—	—	—	—	185.35	520.5	342.7	885.1	110.
1.66	360.	3.97	1.4	—	—	16.32	151.5	23.9	119.7	111.
5.87	4671.	20.01	14.7	—	—	74.24	855.9	109.8	943.3	112.
35.37	3159.	15.01	44.0	—	—	73.62	59.4	124.1	128.0	113.
8.63	965.	15.01	25.0	—	—	65.29	28.5	100.3	108.5	114.
18.75	1282.	10.40	16.9	—	—	35.82	90.7	57.3	16.7	115.
4.16	206.	7.07	3.6	—	—	16.28	49.4	23.9	94.6	116.
3.54	1042.	3.98	—	—	—	0.00	240.2	14.3	116.9	117.
0.48	1183.	3.97	—	—	—	16.28	41.0	23.9	105.7	118.
28.02	2079.	11.97	—	—	—	245.83	215.1	142.6	442.5	119.
41.33	5053.	39.51	—	—	—	209.86	405.9	530.1	514.8	120.
29.02	5368.	8.66	—	—	—	143.90	452.0	29.1	192.0	121.
5.04	530.	44.17	260.4	—	—	37.29	170.1	29.1	72.1	122.
0.93	1209.	—	—	0.763	3.13	0.89	88.9	1.4	14.4	123.
2.61	418.	—	—	0.256	0.54	34.52	112.9	55.1	48.3	124.
30.45	2301.	11.57	146.4	11.187	9.11	36.65	10.8	58.5	27.9	125.
65.06	4097.	26.36	219.5	21.496	16.59	132.64	254.6	211.7	349.3	126.
7.56	3009.	—	71.5	0.451	1.50	26.18	115.4	41.8	30.8	127.
5.09	4009.	12.00	—	0.120	0.27	11.47	0.0	18.3	—	128.
0.10	204.	—	—	13.147	101.71	6.98	10.3	11.1	—	129.
27.57	1046.	11.02	—	6.003	21.62	34.15	54.0	35.1	87.6	130.
19.23	59.	10.95	—	0.466	15.64	29.39	166.0	30.2	169.3	131.
3.09	466.	1.63	—	16.002	6.12	34.49	134.7	35.5	175.1	132.
4.99	451.	5.44	19.9	5.839	2.45	47.37	88.2	48.7	49.6	133.
12.67	2175.	6.10	—	1.212	4.76	68.85	547.6	70.9	367.8	134.
43.85	796.	29.31	—	9.080	25.97	60.03	600.9	61.8	166.4	135.
27.76	4263.	30.87	—	7.593	18.22	74.91	763.9	77.1	610.0	136.
31.47	4751.	27.76	—	16.639	—	112.90	144.4	116.2	458.2	137.
10.51	983.	6.62	—	2.872	—	88.67	17.7	91.3	46.7	138.
16.99	968.	9.98	—	6.478	22.71	91.79	141.6	151.0	350.3	139.
21.96	297.	11.26	—	5.963	4.08	33.15	42.2	54.6	125.5	140.
14.86	724.	0.05	—	3.434	12.78	36.60	15.7	60.2	43.8	141.
5.97	72.	6.43	—	5.023	3.40	30.09	47.6	49.5	26.3	142.
0.86	211.	6.41	19.9	2.375	13.60	75.57	118.2	122.6	227.6	143.
27.38	871.	0.64	44.7	18.853	4.76	137.30	25.7	222.7	14.6	144.
187.18	9543.	−31.96	−167.8	30.313	0.00	0.00	1591.2	433.9	2273.1	145.
−185.04	−24495.	8.47	92.5	−138.179	−373.13	−375.32	−117.7	−579.0	−1850.4	146.
25.72	—	—	—	25.913	112.73	159.39	—	53.1	125.0	147.
11.01	—	—	—	1.768	17.54	82.51	—	260.5	71.6	148.
12.41	—	—	—	52.844	53.44	123.77	—	237.1	544.4	149.
47.71	—	—	—	23.820	34.27	103.13	—	157.1	693.2	150.
82.84	12200.	83.45	89.1	61.163	282.70	211.61	471.6	207.9	1823.2	151.

(Table continues on the following page.)

Line no.	Code	Category	Iran (rials)	Uruguay (N. pesos)	Ireland (pounds)	Hungary (forint)	Poland (zlotys)	Italy (lire)	Spain (pesetas)
1.	1.101	Rice	1678.0	7.76	0.315	54.8	9.2	1558.	338.2
2.	1.102	Meal, other cereals	178.3	10.58	4.093	143.4	207.1	3242.	83.7
3.	1.103	Bread	2586.4	54.17	12.595	421.5	503.9	27333.	2015.4
4.	1.104	Biscuits, cakes, etc.	138.6	31.14	8.501	97.6	215.0	13308.	833.3
5.	1.105	Cereal preparations	3.9	0.63	1.575	11.4	47.1	394.	80.2
6.	1.106	Macaroni, spaghetti	11.7	23.22	0.315	49.0	24.8	14329.	136.0
7.	1.111	Fresh beef, veal	450.8	130.97	17.632	62.5	245.5	76016.	3008.6
8.	1.112	Fresh lamb, mutton	2350.6	18.23	9.445	10.8	11.4	2561.	1545.9
9.	1.113	Fresh pork	3.4	5.85	2.833	768.4	480.6	10836.	1391.4
10.	1.114	Fresh poultry	522.6	8.75	5.983	514.4	271.1	18771.	1950.2
11.	1.115	Other fresh meat	35.9	—	2.833	52.8	75.1	11571.	380.5
12.	1.116	Frozen and salted meat	16.5	—	30.856	599.6	1442.7	30933.	3615.1
13.	1.121	Fresh and frozen fish	175.4	1.99	4.723	39.9	45.2	10604.	2378.2
14.	1.122	Canned fish	7.5	0.41	0.944	22.1	120.5	4854.	550.6
15.	1.131	Fresh milk	240.8	71.95	17.003	380.8	540.0	15941.	2984.3
16.	1.132	Milk products	1000.4	20.46	2.833	243.0	382.0	31256.	1088.3
17.	1.133	Eggs, egg products	459.5	13.49	6.927	324.4	434.8	10496.	1655.4
18.	1.141	Butter	393.2	13.48	9.131	77.1	458.8	6341.	132.9
19.	1.142	Margarine, edible oil	601.5	28.86	1.575	80.6	152.8	28067.	—
20.	1.143	Lard, edible fat	205.5	1.55	.0.315	407.7	170.8	1128.	430.1
21.	1.151	Fresh tropical fruits	657.1	26.21	3.464	128.4	125.4	12180.	1045.9
22.	1.152	Other fresh fruits	1004.3	40.92	3.464	399.6	247.1	22963.	1265.3
23.	1.153	Fresh vegetables	1070.8	40.55	7.241	373.6	493.8	45244.	1606.1
24.	1.161	Fruit other than fresh	157.1	1.47	3.148	90.2	41.5	6162.	267.1
25.	1.162	Vegetables other than fresh	0.8	12.80	5.668	78.2	108.5	8956.	981.0
26.	1.170	Tubers, including potatoes	213.5	39.95	10.391	171.5	324.0	6860.	1013.3
27.	1.191	Coffee	1.1	5.62	0.315	362.5	208.0	7290.	576.5
28.	1.192	Tea	555.6	3.48	3.779	15.0	67.0	376.	25.9
29.	1.193	Cocoa	2.1	3.17	0.315	11.8	13.2	251.	136.8
30.	1.180	Sugar	819.8	35.41	4.408	279.3	272.1	9081.	917.7
31.	1.201	Jam, syrup, honey	40.4	26.08	4.093	27.8	40.7	878.	472.7
32.	1.202	Chocolate, ice cream	54.2	24.18	11.649	474.6	559.4	8812.	237.3
33.	1.203	Salt, spices, sauces	140.9	26.46	3.779	275.5	139.9	2705.	956.7
34.	1.310	Nonalcoholic beverages	74.7	53.65	5.037	201.3	127.2	4514.	487.9
35.	1.321	Spirits	52.9	42.52	3.148	705.3	1800.4	7809.	284.6
36.	1.322	Wine, cider	18.4	49.28	1.259	593.4	390.7	28461.	1079.8
37.	1.323	Beer	23.6	24.49	5.352	652.9	221.8	4478.	261.8
38.	1.410	Cigarettes	486.0	62.38	37.468	591.4	583.4	32384.	1308.6
39.	1.420	Cigars, tobacco, snuff	167.2	10.91	3.778	4.4	2.0	1182.	195.6
40.	2.110	Clothing materials	1284.5	9.03	1.575	252.0	708.7	4675.	429.7
41.	2.121	Men's clothing	1306.6	47.81	11.649	616.0	716.3	20061.	2933.2
42.	2.122	Women's clothing	990.3	34.41	11.335	388.0	598.0	27405.	2497.9
43.	2.123	Boys' and girls' clothing	185.1	4.99	5.982	305.7	264.2	11625.	1265.7
44.	2.131	Men's and boys' underwear	94.1	7.54	9.131	136.9	200.3	18592.	521.3
45.	2.132	Women's and girls' underwear	112.8	10.12	10.076	240.0	391.3	19631.	705.3
46.	2.150	Haberdashery, millinery	133.0	—	2.519	339.8	334.6	3618.	411.9
47.	2.160	Clothing rental and repair	2.7	—	0.630	52.6	15.9	1075.	188.0
48.	2.211	Men's footwear	447.6	4.02	4.093	182.2	142.6	6591.	958.2
49.	2.212	Women's footwear	443.6	19.32	4.408	232.0	266.5	12180.	1007.9
50.	2.213	Children's footwear	49.9	15.80	1.889	77.1	107.4	3314.	651.9
51.	2.220	Footwear, repairs	32.3	3.91	0.315	28.1	31.0	1397.	209.2
52.	3.110	Rents	5637.8	—	39.358	820.5	1461.2	146480.	8467.1
53.	3.120	Indoor repair and upkeep	982.2	—	10.076	297.2	288.3	3224.	3447.8
54.	3.210	Electricity	403.9	33.69	13.539	245.7	177.4	17643.	1583.0
55.	3.220	Gas	130.4	8.55	5.668	144.9	83.2	11410.	1239.3
56.	3.230	Liquid fuels	645.9	48.22	3.778	146.5	0.2	13452.	236.1
57.	3.240	Other fuels, ice	415.9	12.05	16.058	330.4	299.1	2024.	413.1
58.	4.110	Furniture, fixtures	291.6	16.46	10.390	650.8	667.7	24288.	2857.3
59.	4.120	Floor coverings	1222.2	0.89	4.723	104.0	153.4	1522.	382.3
60.	4.200	Household textiles, etc.	470.3	15.28	9.446	292.7	392.4	10281.	1423.4
61.	4.310	Refrigerators, freezers	224.5	13.51	1.890	106.1	169.6	2149.	520.0
62.	4.320	Washing appliances	57.6	1.70	2.519	63.8	53.9	5230.	302.7
63.	4.330	Cooking appliances	164.4	8.36	1.575	49.0	86.0	1755.	505.5
64.	4.340	Heating appliances	58.8	8.64	1.890	50.2	37.7	573.	75.7
65.	4.350	Cleaning appliances	12.7	1.84	0.315	19.4	24.4	1308.	161.0
66.	4.360	Other household appliances	26.5	5.34	1.575	15.5	19.5	2275.	—
67.	4.400	Household utensils	293.3	21.46	8.816	390.9	479.9	7881.	294.5
68.	4.510	Nondurable household goods	575.6	29.39	10.076	470.7	302.4	17177.	1702.7
69.	4.520	Domestic services	216.6	67.49	3.149	52.2	16.1	9959.	1342.0
70.	4.530	Household services	158.2	1.10	3.463	170.9	202.9	7200.	204.7
71.	5.110	Drugs, medical preparations	1067.2	53.96	13.224	594.3	572.6	21762.	2278.9
72.	5.120	Medical supplies	12.3	3.66	2.204	18.0	60.5	788.	2032.2
73.	5.200	Therapeutic equipment	27.7	0.29	3.463	12.0	51.0	1164.	102.8
74.	5.310	Physicians' services	516.9	—	9.446	181.8	130.1	24682.	2770.3
75.	5.320	Dentists' services	161.4	—	4.408	23.7	31.6	4352.	257.7

— Country did not supply the expenditure breakdown for this category. In the calculations, the ICP estimated a rough breakdown for such categories, which underlies the entries in Appendix Table 6-5.

U.K. (pounds)	Japan (yen)	Austria (schillings)	Netherlands (guilders)	Belgium (francs)	France (francs)	Luxembourg (francs)	Denmark (kroner)	Germany (DM)	U.S. (dollars)	Line no.
0.250	19863.	31.1	7.32	53.6	7.93	61.1	8.50	4.84	3.70	1.
1.125	242.	207.6	3.66	80.4	5.93	86.1	50.20	20.93	—	2.
12.361	5019.	576.7	109.81	1929.2	183.27	2350.0	320.75	166.69	49.52	3.
12.593	2429.	387.8	79.79	1393.3	194.04	1291.7	192.88	90.18	16.37	4.
2.536	2546.	23.7	6.59	80.4	22.69	88.9	14.62	1.62	5.15	5.
0.340	4742.	67.2	5.13	93.8	21.08	100.0	8.30	13.70	3.40	6.
14.630	6463.	645.1	153.95	4082.1	432.70	3294.4	206.92	72.46	61.75	7.
3.804	63.	11.2	1.46	50.1	61.54	52.8	3.76	3.22	1.54	8.
4.752	11097.	891.2	87.04	1069.9	103.40	916.7	195.45	58.76	31.43	9.
1.519	2895.	236.2	27.38	995.7	127.19	744.4	30.63	7.26	22.99	10.
1.715	878.	157.8	16.54	448.2	149.05	358.3	51.78	15.32	3.04	11.
35.029	3325.	1157.2	160.91	4604.4	288.22	3761.1	873.91	282.67	43.03	12.
5.198	27634.	60.9	27.74	639.4	87.47	402.8	71.34	15.32	16.22	13.
1.322	7933.	87.0	24.23	575.1	93.90	352.8	137.55	10.48	9.74	14.
14.594	6785.	663.7	78.40	999.7	92.99	1322.2	186.56	61.20	35.26	15.
7.788	3254.	505.9	163.25	1486.8	288.47	1950.0	259.88	86.16	34.27	16.
7.092	2814.	298.3	32.07	615.1	70.37	808.3	98.22	41.87	12.99	17.
6.324	798.	273.4	15.30	1187.3	141.69	1425.0	143.68	88.60	4.33	18.
1.322	1201.	319.4	58.71	744.9	67.77	808.3	94.86	71.67	26.62	19.
1.322	9.	101.9	0.66	25.4	1.55	25.0	9.49	1.62	1.34	20.
4.966	2752.	267.3	46.71	711.0	79.76	827.8	72.33	33.04	9.07	21.
3.984	6606.	558.1	55.64	1077.4	130.64	1025.0	67.59	42.65	17.39	22.
9.253	16188.	604.1	69.84	1206.5	188.58	1450.0	139.92	45.90	33.79	23.
3.877	1371.	101.9	41.36	204.7	27.77	236.1	101.19	42.68	24.40	24.
7.556	1147.	172.7	52.20	452.4	90.20	513.9	107.90	46.71	53.99	25.
9.843	1165.	232.4	54.90	708.1	61.27	825.0	85.97	39.45	9.18	26.
2.358	1506.	202.7	73.57	825.5	71.24	972.2	252.57	108.70	14.79	27.
3.054	2850.	17.4	8.05	33.7	4.53	36.1	15.61	12.10	2.06	28.
0.196	90.	24.9	1.76	11.5	9.90	22.2	4.35	8.86	0.33	29.
4.680	2062.	155.3	24.16	332.7	45.54	388.9	78.66	54.76	31.04	30.
1.858	860.	131.8	17.79	262.7	35.60	222.2	60.28	9.67	18.41	31.
16.952	1766.	586.7	93.92	1438.2	188.10	1230.6	348.81	72.44	29.35	32.
4.520	34769.	198.9	23.72	248.6	27.96	219.4	158.30	18.54	15.06	33.
8.664	6292.	389.6	65.15	671.2	88.23	644.4	180.04	38.12	18.00	34.
8.020	3756.	391.0	30.01	818.3	65.35	855.6	270.55	86.63	15.26	35.
7.217	6579.	1114.6	87.77	694.1	339.03	702.8	255.14	73.90	11.35	36.
4.895	3693.	812.1	101.10	966.8	32.93	977.8	532.01	121.22	46.41	37.
42.872	11321.	1179.5	141.22	2046.3	167.10	1641.7	695.06	175.97	61.56	38.
6.663	27.	29.3	61.57	536.7	23.40	427.8	241.90	18.92	7.41	39.
1.107	14404.	446.5	56.81	470.8	64.67	525.0	39.33	23.10	4.51	40.
14.755	2151.	806.0	144.14	2028.7	170.28	2236.1	225.49	111.50	84.79	41.
25.741	3397.	1282.4	246.85	2500.5	223.10	2644.4	385.77	144.12	102.02	42.
7.842	1344.	616.5	73.50	833.5	86.70	916.7	115.61	101.88	28.67	43.
8.860	3110.	—	42.97	1606.3	237.75	1700.0	145.85	125.05	4.12	44.
13.236	2841.	—	64.79	1425.5	177.62	1497.2	230.24	161.61	20.55	45.
8.736	27634.	518.0	50.29	978.7	108.61	1052.8	131.03	108.30	19.05	46.
0.536	341.	120.7	4.47	72.5	21.59	66.7	9.88	11.13	21.12	47.
3.823	2106.	285.5	33.97	559.3	74.13	538.9	65.22	30.94	20.79	48.
9.699	2546.	390.7	56.88	746.3	101.63	727.8	110.08	39.32	21.71	49.
1.768	1264.	283.0	22.25	402.1	66.52	391.7	43.48	51.59	7.83	50.
0.947	125.	59.7	4.03	114.8	11.55	108.3	8.70	31.86	1.17	51.
141.387	100747.	3250.0	696.56	12786.6	1676.02	16508.3	2363.04	1115.64	649.40	52.
25.616	2922.	1391.0	136.53	1151.2	275.48	1613.9	1675.49	61.95	68.06	53.
25.080	8336.	817.8	158.27	2729.4	208.25	2408.3	460.47	174.71	94.38	54.
15.791	3738.	226.1	147.88	1758.0	172.88	1586.1	132.01	68.14	43.76	55.
2.894	2501.	482.7	54.76	2066.3	149.50	1825.0	643.87	74.24	31.46	56.
8.789	457.	575.8	9.52	1711.7	97.07	1461.1	240.71	92.61	16.78	57.
12.200	3998.	1848.7	279.87	4816.7	560.11	4597.2	450.79	240.91	87.89	58.
12.898	2519.	384.0	140.70	616.9	59.05	591.7	315.81	63.92	28.68	59.
9.557	11186.	381.6	52.64	1241.9	157.47	1155.6	235.97	140.13	49.08	60.
3.609	2142.	230.5	24.60	445.1	39.62	402.8	84.19	40.95	12.94	61.
4.162	690.	181.5	36.31	674.3	81.07	608.3	47.04	46.74	9.74	62.
1.947	3765.	321.8	23.79	343.7	42.52	300.0	51.98	8.22	8.96	63.
1.751	1013.	263.0	17.42	305.4	22.12	288.9	34.78	23.76	0.87	64.
1.196	359.	67.4	7.10	178.1	16.25	141.7	24.70	13.91	3.82	65.
1.572	1703.	38.0	15.01	368.9	39.26	319.4	54.54	22.13	20.08	66.
14.309	6014.	391.0	131.85	3303.0	268.64	3097.2	281.22	131.12	27.08	67.
7.842	6131.	537.6	92.90	1192.1	215.61	1066.7	259.68	155.69	54.07	68.
5.234	287.	73.1	14.06	2666.0	174.58	1202.8	150.00	82.55	23.67	69.
7.056	8183.	180.5	62.59	1407.6	120.27	1230.6	171.54	75.60	16.26	70.
12.808	13992.	899.6	88.21	2996.0	420.00	2350.0	280.63	330.99	113.15	71.
2.233	5342.	35.1	3.29	108.6	8.47	86.1	10.08	11.87	14.96	72.
3.001	6588.	151.2	16.84	470.9	34.49	272.2	58.10	27.41	23.77	73.
9.075	21180.	—	275.04	3605.0	440.23	2161.1	185.57	326.19	150.19	74.
4.502	5324.	—	23.06	502.8	72.91	813.9	90.51	30.34	54.66	75.

(Table continues on the following page.)

Appendix Table 6-1 *(continued)*

Line no.	Code	Category	Iran (rials)	Uruguay (N. pesos)	Ireland (pounds)	Hungary (forint)	Poland (zlotys)	Italy (lire)	Spain (pesetas)
76.	5.330	Nurses' services	95.1	—	0.945	279.0	307.9	10478.	1863.2
77.	5.410	Hospitals	1393.6	15.36	45.025	467.3	566.0	61419.	1170.7
78.	6.110	Personal automobiles	1310.8	25.64	23.929	559.2	504.3	35357.	3677.1
79.	6.120	Other personal transport	75.5	8.44	1.260	91.7	108.5	2991.	94.3
80.	6.210	Tires, tubes, accessories	230.0	5.96	3.463	96.8	75.8	3690.	132.3
81.	6.220	Automobile repairs	332.7	22.60	4.408	114.8	98.7	21440.	1221.2
82.	6.230	Gasoline, oil, grease	290.3	25.45	22.985	337.6	174.7	45209.	3422.9
83.	6.240	Parking, tolls, etc.	55.2	6.92	2.204	17.1	31.5	12717.	897.8
84.	6.310	Local transport	430.0	87.71	6.927	175.5	336.6	6394.	1384.5
85.	6.321	Rail transport	66.0	3.10	1.574	161.3	142.8	7774.	521.8
86.	6.322	Bus transport	228.0	24.04	2.519	246.7	217.1	5391.	111.8
87.	6.323	Air transport	138.4	4.18	1.574	50.3	19.9	2508.	111.8
88.	6.410	Postal communication	47.1	0.81	1.259	56.9	66.0	3636.	38.6
89.	6.420	Telephone, telegraph	138.4	19.54	3.463	56.9	95.6	11499.	512.5
90.	7.110	Radios, televisions, phonographs	257.9	12.50	3.778	317.0	429.3	6591.	741.9
91.	7.120	Durable recreational equipment	11.2	0.99	0.945	17.9	31.1	2508.	94.0
92.	7.130	Other recreational equipment	129.9	8.85	6.927	186.2	180.9	15923.	812.8
93.	7.210	Public entertainment	260.5	17.79	7.242	610.5	208.5	12914.	2845.8
94.	7.220	Other recreation, culture	685.9	50.82	10.705	320.7	591.4	18879.	245.2
95.	7.310	Books, papers, magazines	93.6	28.95	17.632	299.8	190.3	21243.	1244.8
96.	7.320	Stationery	0.7	7.86	1.259	144.8	85.6	3027.	219.7
97.	7.411	First- and second-level teachers	1701.2	59.37	46.599	708.4	850.9	79241.	2506.4
98.	7.412	College teachers	867.4	8.99	5.982	90.1	155.9	6305.	84.4
99.	7.420	Physical facilities for education	611.1	—	10.076	415.4	594.1	8633.	309.8
100.	7.431	Educational books, supplies	446.6	—	1.574	37.9	21.4	1451.	1027.2
101.	7.432	Other educational expenditures	40.4	—	1.574	211.4	216.1	4639.	977.2
102.	8.100	Barber and beauty shops	497.1	8.56	2.519	103.3	71.9	12825.	847.9
103.	8.210	Toilet articles	214.8	23.18	4.723	215.0	239.1	9636.	1178.1
104.	8.220	Other personal care goods	262.6	10.17	5.983	398.5	193.3	28784.	69.6
105.	8.310	Restaurants, cafes	960.2	109.35	87.532	1438.1	1398.9	63102.	3043.9
106.	8.320	Hotels, lodgings	273.5	27.59	15.113	128.1	67.0	16031.	4570.5
107.	8.400	Other services	1199.2	3.47	21.725	506.9	156.1	13792.	3223.2
108.	8.900	Expenditures of residents abroad	0.0	0.00	0.000	0.0	0.0	0.	0.0
109.	10.100	One- and two-family dwellings	6850.5	50.86	22.985	1234.1	369.8	91384.	1256.2
110.	10.200	Multifamily dwellings	339.0	41.58	49.118	1364.1	1479.0	48200.	9125.4
111.	11.100	Hotels	85.5	—	0.945	242.6	184.9	3672.	419.6
112.	11.200	Industrial buildings	1209.5	—	11.965	1374.8	2496.2	38169.	744.8
113.	11.300	Commercial buildings	192.4	—	9.761	309.4	462.3	4764.	818.2
114.	11.400	Office buildings	1945.5	—	8.501	168.3	184.9	15798.	834.0
115.	11.500	Educational buildings	479.5	—	3.779	272.0	231.1	8293.	980.9
116.	11.600	Hospital buildings	106.9	—	3.464	97.5	184.9	6072.	865.5
117.	11.700	Agricultural buildings	1044.5	—	4.409	642.2	785.8	6556.	387.8
118.	11.800	Other buildings	250.4	—	1.260	58.9	92.4	4532.	535.0
119.	12.100	Roads, streets, highways	1215.6	43.93	21.411	532.1	591.5	22139.	2769.4
120.	12.200	Transport and utility lines	943.7	25.13	19.521	1532.1	1811.5	29500.	2014.2
121.	12.300	Other construction	—	58.55	3.149	523.7	—	2346.	3084.2
122.	13.000	Land improvement	—	12.94	4.409	177.6	104.6	0.	520.9
123.	14.110	Locomotives	58.0	0.04	0.314	103.2	131.7	2705.	175.1
124.	14.120	Other railway vehicles	48.9	0.03	0.314	272.4	554.3	2364.	207.2
125.	14.200	Passenger automobiles	922.4	5.03	10.075	67.3	50.4	13523.	436.8
126.	14.300	Trucks, buses, trailers	2904.5	12.40	9.131	744.4	740.3	16819.	1533.4
127.	14.400	Aircraft	33.6	4.43	0.630	77.2	168.0	2723.	477.8
128.	14.500	Ships, boats	106.9	9.12	4.093	6.7	418.7	7397.	—
129.	14.600	Other transport equipment	806.3	0.33	0.314	2.2	46.1	1182.	—
130.	15.100	Engines, turbines	934.6	1.97	4.093	126.1	343.3	5194.	593.9
131.	15.210	Tractors	690.2	13.76	7.556	216.2	133.2	4550.	472.1
132.	15.220	Other agricultural machinery	610.8	6.19	5.038	360.4	558.9	6538.	173.7
133.	15.300	Office machinery	134.4	4.47	6.298	217.9	249.9	8114.	472.8
134.	15.400	Metalworking machinery	366.5	1.75	1.260	553.9	1007.1	5123.	743.9
135.	15.500	Construction, mining machinery	2125.7	0.25	11.335	383.6	539.0	15780.	836.1
136.	15.600	Special industrial machinery	1206.4	19.68	9.131	1174.6	725.3	14078.	1164.8
137.	15.700	General industrial machinery	394.0	—	8.186	732.5	503.7	10424.	957.2
138.	15.800	Service industrial machinery	311.5	—	3.463	62.0	122.4	10424.	351.7
139.	16.100	Electrical transmission equipment	311.5	4.84	4.408	104.5	157.8	11087.	757.7
140.	16.200	Communications equipment	723.8	1.17	2.204	215.6	667.9	10639.	1281.5
141.	16.300	Other electrical equipment	85.5	0.47	1.574	38.0	588.4	10227.	1392.9
142.	16.400	Instruments	354.3	2.02	0.944	412.2	120.5	2561.	282.3
143.	17.100	Furniture, fixtures	51.9	1.59	1.889	640.0	91.5	4281.	336.5
144.	17.200	Other durable goods	726.9	16.45	8.816	117.4	64.5	14490.	705.2
145.	18.000	Increase in stocks	-1438.5	4.31	-11.965	1943.5	2960.5	-6305.	5549.7
146.	19.000	Exports minus imports	9556.5	-106.04	-69.899	-3383.3	-2998.1	-27208.	-6662.0
147.	20.100	Unskilled blue collar	3118.3	—	8.186	233.8	178.1	51657.	560.3
148.	20.210	Skilled blue collar	656.6	—	11.650	20.6	61.7	18968.	447.5
149.	20.220	White collar	803.3	—	46.285	312.8	539.2	71718.	2968.2
150.	20.300	Professional	2058.5	—	9.446	350.7	344.2	18968.	938.7
151.	21.000	Commodities of government	13200.1	60.17	48.803	2496.1	2592.2	101358.	1971.6

— Country did not supply the expenditure breakdown for this category. In the calculations, the ICP estimated a rough breakdown for such categories, which underlies the entries in Appendix Table 6-5.

U.K. (pounds)	Japan (yen)	Austria (schillings)	Netherlands (guilders)	Belgium (francs)	France (francs)	Luxembourg (francs)	Denmark (kroner)	Germany (DM)	U.S. (dollars)	Line no.
0.715	18868.	—	124.09	1965.9	435.31	1886.1	239.13	128.26	—	76.
42.890	2106.	1773.9	471.74	2640.4	492.53	1452.8	589.72	516.41	—	77.
32.315	12091.	1425.5	251.68	4652.8	432.81	5858.3	934.78	313.64	190.53	78.
0.911	2169.	158.2	72.62	403.5	48.99	505.6	115.81	17.65	30.91	79.
8.556	627.	453.5	24.60	958.3	94.24	983.3	123.12	92.63	35.11	80.
11.646	8139.	1296.5	160.91	2381.5	416.56	2447.2	503.75	135.49	81.91	81.
37.155	8291.	2087.8	193.85	3757.2	455.71	3863.9	836.76	326.01	180.44	82.
5.967	986.	304.5	53.37	912.3	176.42	941.7	183.00	74.29	40.66	83.
22.704	8390.	325.8	19.62	430.7	126.51	591.7	136.96	49.26	19.00	84.
2.573	18895.	291.2	20.57	546.9	66.87	733.3	187.15	125.94	1.14	85.
3.859	4724.	226.1	9.37	559.0	72.02	788.9	26.88	5.50	2.93	86.
8.092	1013.	171.5	18.67	186.3	39.47	252.8	72.53	15.32	17.31	87.
4.180	798.	142.3	16.62	368.9	53.14	436.1	16.80	79.20	10.42	88.
12.558	5987.	500.0	99.78	779.1	73.05	900.0	221.54	86.43	81.82	89.
13.380	8910.	614.6	194.51	2176.0	169.83	1333.3	436.17	77.20	58.27	90.
7.413	1604.	291.0	80.24	203.0	36.48	122.2	98.02	57.79	36.90	91.
23.168	9116.	506.2	220.94	2176.0	348.87	1383.3	541.70	236.88	63.10	92.
7.288	5181.	384.2	58.49	423.5	80.59	286.1	97.83	55.59	48.95	93.
24.580	24846.	1076.6	63.03	1127.6	173.73	777.8	348.02	153.57	58.07	94.
16.970	8542.	458.4	168.45	1381.2	253.49	1516.7	455.33	119.21	45.30	95.
2.733	1622.	69.3	18.81	168.7	35.81	208.3	30.83	31.54	12.66	96.
71.096	38013.	1956.1	637.99	9852.7	751.12	8958.3	1779.45	438.48	294.05	97.
6.109	5781.	214.1	147.07	694.8	119.28	202.8	453.75	64.97	91.05	98.
7.270	8076.	364.4	157.98	1648.8	108.91	1069.4	915.61	115.87	50.67	99.
2.715	2752.	98.4	24.30	255.0	16.76	161.1	143.68	5.42	4.56	100.
4.877	5387.	299.2	25.70	266.2	17.76	177.8	145.85	41.57	20.17	101.
6.877	7924.	450.3	48.17	1758.8	62.50	2033.3	193.28	69.08	22.68	102.
11.504	13337.	474.6	72.69	820.1	248.56	1027.8	179.05	59.92	—	103.
14.487	5745.	733.2	82.07	1486.9	266.38	1844.4	227.87	108.02	—	104.
89.727	41966.	4199.1	214.49	10249.9	846.71	12966.7	1013.24	355.85	—	105.
25.473	13257.	1661.3	52.42	782.7	240.71	991.7	108.10	107.91	—	106.
31.155	31640.	1300.5	519.11	2936.3	455.88	1330.0	413.42	313.76	238.18	107.
0.000	2949.	—	0.00	0.0	0.00	0.0	0.00	0.00	23.33	108.
17.917	64661.	2747.9	209.08	3126.6	541.06	9825.0	1137.94	209.71	162.62	109.
57.698	36203.	2435.4	519.62	10052.1	1553.16	8694.4	1779.05	653.87	72.43	110.
1.733	3451.	552.5	3.22	158.8	32.84	322.2	78.66	17.66	5.34	111.
16.148	19549.	1209.2	146.71	5804.4	230.42	6425.0	490.91	167.83	41.71	112.
15.541	7852.	804.4	118.08	2110.7	227.27	3213.9	442.09	52.97	37.38	113.
15.541	11957.	493.1	127.60	1979.1	220.98	6694.4	490.91	61.80	24.57	114.
10.325	12029.	859.7	79.65	791.0	202.00	644.4	245.45	66.26	39.07	115.
5.805	3236.	788.6	58.93	1002.0	94.70	963.9	196.44	44.14	23.45	116.
6.859	3236.	545.9	16.03	1055.3	13.33	769.4	284.78	22.13	10.59	117.
5.198	10738.	230.7	95.68	422.1	287.90	1283.3	117.00	8.83	28.22	118.
15.541	26433.	1678.6	108.93	2110.7	284.01	3852.8	433.99	270.16	—	119.
14.237	30350.	1918.5	127.16	2638.4	268.90	4497.2	433.99	413.01	—	120.
3.465	41115.	18.5	54.54	316.6	63.13	536.1	86.76	87.23	—	121.
9.718	12979.	96.3	102.78	844.3	18.88	127.8	82.41	23.94	—	122.
0.340	134.	176.1	4.54	49.8	25.27	133.3	24.70	3.91	3.62	123.
0.500	735.	181.4	7.54	210.4	44.65	141.7	32.81	10.43	8.74	124.
17.398	11607.	605.1	150.59	919.9	208.96	1305.6	107.12	113.83	39.27	125.
15.362	16080.	418.2	100.44	1005.2	210.62	708.3	94.47	104.97	51.35	126.
2.948	601.	47.6	48.46	1561.0	26.22	1636.1	7.11	3.59	10.82	127.
15.113	3567.	21.1	81.63	520.4	34.98	544.4	719.76	50.20	6.25	128.
0.411	699.	10.6	3.00	52.0	8.74	52.8	14.43	3.59	2.65	129.
3.252	2053.	185.1	43.78	551.8	35.22	511.1	35.38	39.85	9.07	130.
1.626	403.	239.5	19.62	536.6	35.95	461.1	133.00	18.70	15.26	131.
1.715	1882.	449.1	22.91	547.4	81.54	538.9	71.34	27.35	19.63	132.
16.095	5423.	359.2	29.36	640.8	112.69	591.7	7.11	49.10	28.61	133.
7.663	7386.	352.4	35.87	493.1	83.26	455.6	393.68	58.26	23.93	134.
20.775	4679.	523.9	127.45	2562.1	146.93	2363.9	168.77	116.60	33.74	135.
12.254	12289.	806.9	101.39	1280.5	803.41	1183.3	393.68	88.96	23.32	136.
6.521	11599.	1747.2	87.55	1103.5	70.52	1016.7	70.16	79.80	35.49	137.
3.072	1031.	20.3	87.55	1103.5	70.52	1016.7	70.16	79.80	14.22	138.
12.362	12441.	744.3	101.24	1478.2	39.19	1363.9	63.44	52.14	21.90	139.
17.434	12791.	366.1	130.53	1921.3	137.16	1775.0	239.33	217.84	49.82	140.
2.965	3549.	557.8	55.49	1527.1	44.06	1408.3	70.35	141.10	11.57	141.
1.340	6749.	268.1	32.72	345.4	19.60	319.4	21.15	9.25	34.95	142.
2.680	20087.	351.1	35.87	640.8	44.06	591.7	260.28	58.26	24.42	143.
8.038	10810.	511.7	114.27	689.7	88.23	636.1	63.44	42.91	23.14	144.
-24.937	4428.	-582.4	-32.21	-1258.2	-69.06	1061.1	-590.51	-21.03	-43.55	145.
-38.745	556.	561.2	609.81	2499.7	189.05	-4566.7	-562.05	615.08	56.75	146.
27.402	18249.	1323.7	358.20	4833.5	99.04	3144.4	1361.26	141.46	83.95	147.
27.402	17210.	193.0	170.57	1450.2	401.40	1677.8	1088.93	224.81	61.03	148.
109.805	4311.	3655.6	545.83	8942.0	818.80	8386.1	2382.41	906.50	154.26	149.
28.295	13902.	985.1	220.06	3045.7	650.21	2097.2	680.83	146.84	120.73	150.
94.906	14018.	1869.3	524.73	7434.7	1039.74	8372.0	1152.16	394.89	388.46	151.

Line no.	Code	Category	Malawi (kwacha)	Kenya (shillings)	India (rupees)	Pakistan (rupees)	Sri Lanka (rupees)	Zambia (kwacha)	Thailand (baht)
1.	1.101	Rice	0.494	2.30	3.28	3.73	6.62	0.744	4.7
2.	1.102	Meal, other cereals	0.373	3.66	3.06	2.92	5.48	0.195	13.9
3.	1.103	Bread	0.320	2.57	2.67	3.03	2.34	0.201	25.5
4.	1.104	Biscuits, cakes, etc.	1.426	9.67	6.85	6.36	12.91	1.392	19.7
5.	1.105	Cereal preparations	1.082	4.51	3.29	0.90	4.68	1.206	17.5
6.	1.106	Macaroni, spaghetti	1.806	5.93	7.65	3.58	6.34	0.707	14.6
7.	1.111	Fresh beef, veal	0.354	2.47	1.35	1.96	1.93	0.394	6.1
8.	1.112	Fresh lamb, mutton	0.393	2.83	2.78	3.71	3.01	0.550	0.0
9.	1.113	Fresh pork	0.389	3.63	2.54	0.00	3.81	0.550	8.1
10.	1.114	Fresh poultry	0.669	8.13	7.37	5.15	7.51	0.798	14.9
11.	1.115	Other fresh meat	0.586	3.99	2.97	3.92	6.81	0.648	17.9
12.	1.116	Frozen and salted meat	0.617	7.19	5.26	0.00	5.77	0.849	14.8
13.	1.121	Fresh and frozen fish	0.654	14.77	1.57	4.82	4.61	0.600	12.3
14.	1.122	Canned fish	0.773	5.34	4.28	6.93	2.95	0.702	14.2
15.	1.131	Fresh milk	0.530	4.34	6.44	8.47	5.57	0.530	30.1
16.	1.132	Milk products	0.991	8.35	6.23	6.11	3.95	0.634	20.8
17.	1.133	Eggs, egg products	0.558	4.88	6.41	7.83	7.35	0.753	15.6
18.	1.141	Butter	1.008	5.73	7.55	8.20	8.95	0.707	38.7
19.	1.142	Margarine, edible oil	0.876	8.56	6.40	5.52	4.17	0.683	26.4
20.	1.143	Lard, edible fat	0.798	7.85	3.78	0.00	0.00	0.673	13.0
21.	1.151	Fresh tropical fruits	0.178	4.84	4.81	6.84	3.73	0.471	11.6
22.	1.152	Other fresh fruits	0.485	15.20	6.11	4.86	4.30	1.360	10.3
23.	1.153	Fresh vegetables	0.202	2.93	1.61	2.13	2.34	0.467	8.8
24.	1.161	Fruit other than fresh	1.126	13.08	12.69	9.93	10.95	1.129	22.5
25.	1.162	Vegetables other than fresh	1.470	6.46	5.16	5.21	13.03	1.268	25.6
26.	1.170	Tubers, including potatoes	0.266	8.99	3.19	4.62	4.99	1.300	14.8
27.	1.191	Coffee	1.195	7.49	6.12	21.08	8.94	0.875	27.6
28.	1.192	Tea	0.302	3.66	3.03	2.76	2.05	0.479	10.9
29.	1.193	Cocoa	0.841	6.81	2.10	2.54	0.00	0.381	23.8
30.	1.180	Sugar	0.353	4.26	4.46	6.35	5.58	0.390	6.8
31.	1.201	Jam, syrup, honey	0.566	9.11	6.27	6.77	7.40	0.774	14.5
32.	1.202	Chocolate, ice cream	0.960	7.12	6.94	7.37	6.34	0.983	10.2
33.	1.203	Salt, spices, sauces	0.757	9.01	3.61	6.03	5.89	0.931	14.2
34.	1.310	Nonalcoholic beverages	0.608	6.64	10.88	15.37	8.67	0.767	20.0
35.	1.321	Spirits	0.733	12.00	8.00	5.98	8.92	1.809	6.5
36.	1.322	Wine, cider	1.587	13.62	27.71	7.40	8.41	2.953	7.6
37.	1.323	Beer	0.538	7.06	10.20	6.72	7.00	0.952	8.3
38.	1.410	Cigarettes	0.309	2.84	4.41	6.47	8.26	0.821	14.3
39.	1.420	Cigars, tobacco, snuff	1.373	16.14	10.70	5.90	8.83	9.957	24.4
40.	2.110	Clothing materials	0.784	10.43	8.67	6.45	6.35	0.604	14.0
41.	2.121	Men's clothing	0.729	8.14	4.79	4.12	3.98	0.783	9.6
42.	2.122	Women's clothing	0.930	4.61	4.80	5.32	3.03	0.894	5.6
43.	2.123	Boys' and girls' clothing	0.557	5.48	3.81	3.60	3.84	0.850	9.1
44.	2.131	Men's and boys' underwear	1.014	8.87	5.05	4.11	5.05	0.947	12.2
45.	2.132	Women's and girls' underwear	0.574	6.67	3.30	4.47	3.70	0.559	12.0
46.	2.150	Haberdashery, millinery	0.520	4.80	3.91	3.05	3.30	0.441	10.2
47.	2.160	Clothing rental and repair	0.141	1.35	1.11	0.89	0.00	0.216	2.4
48.	2.211	Men's footwear	0.358	7.90	2.94	3.11	2.91	0.396	12.2
49.	2.212	Women's footwear	0.376	6.73	2.23	2.34	2.15	0.315	8.4
50.	2.213	Children's footwear	0.240	5.30	1.85	2.39	3.37	0.283	4.6
51.	2.220	Footwear, repairs	0.423	7.57	1.49	2.46	3.38	0.490	5.0
52.	3.110	Rents	0.582	5.92	1.03	4.96	1.41	0.507	16.1
53.	3.120	Indoor repair and upkeep	0.711	15.60	1.50	4.49	0.00	0.727	5.9
54.	3.210	Electricity	0.664	20.32	5.51	3.98	4.30	0.276	11.4
55.	3.220	Gas	3.263	14.00	9.05	3.18	10.67	2.067	19.4
56.	3.230	Liquid fuels	1.173	15.56	9.14	6.79	6.62	0.690	22.0
57.	3.240	Other fuels, ice	0.659	2.21	2.31	8.17	1.94	0.228	4.2
58.	4.110	Furniture, fixtures	0.576	2.56	3.88	3.25	2.90	0.486	6.9
59.	4.120	Floor coverings	0.958	6.22	2.94	3.24	6.42	0.901	30.8
60.	4.200	Household textiles, etc.	0.411	12.43	4.02	5.01	7.66	0.782	8.8
61.	4.310	Refrigerators, freezers	2.442	14.02	14.06	18.89	30.29	1.939	38.1
62.	4.320	Washing appliances	1.107	0.00	0.00	0.00	0.00	1.268	8.2
63.	4.330	Cooking appliances	0.776	7.61	4.97	12.42	14.95	1.772	27.3
64.	4.340	Heating appliances	1.142	0.00	8.62	3.00	0.00	1.613	63.1
65.	4.350	Cleaning appliances	1.114	0.00	0.00	0.00	0.00	1.511	52.0
66.	4.360	Other household appliances	2.887	0.00	25.19	33.97	68.65	3.582	59.1
67.	4.400	Household utensils	0.859	5.86	4.37	6.66	4.17	0.683	11.0
68.	4.510	Nondurable household goods	0.923	7.59	4.71	5.70	5.87	0.916	13.6
69.	4.520	Domestic services	0.079	0.33	0.33	1.10	0.17	0.106	1.2
70.	4.530	Household services	0.275	4.41	1.63	1.54	1.27	0.508	4.0
71.	5.110	Drugs, medical preparations	0.490	3.49	2.47	3.58	1.50	0.578	9.1
72.	5.120	Medical supplies	0.819	11.51	3.92	6.31	7.93	0.786	12.1
73.	5.200	Therapeutic equipment	0.608	0.00	0.67	0.88	1.18	0.555	5.9
74.	5.310	Physicians' services	0.110	11.97	0.33	0.79	1.52	0.325	8.4
75.	5.320	Dentists' services	0.107	8.22	0.09	0.16	0.42	0.275	14.3

Philippines (pesos)	Korea (won)	Malaysia (ringgit)	Colombia (pesos)	Jamaica (dollars)	Syria (pounds)	Brazil (cruzeiros)	Romania (lei)	Mexico (pesos)	Yugoslavia (dinars)	Line no.
2.98	326.	1.31	9.6	0.810	1.25	5.90	16.4	10.9	25.1	1.
9.75	238.	1.52	33.3	0.907	1.44	5.87	9.4	8.6	10.0	2.
5.78	243.	1.30	19.7	0.566	0.40	3.77	6.5	8.6	5.3	3.
5.76	363.	2.20	26.6	1.098	1.92	6.28	8.5	6.1	13.7	4.
3.18	133.	1.12	41.8	1.239	0.79	8.44	2.9	15.0	25.2	5.
7.34	180.	1.98	10.8	1.497	1.19	5.47	8.8	7.3	13.5	6.
2.46	339.	2.10	7.6	0.817	3.13	2.91	8.5	8.8	11.7	7.
0.00	309.	1.88	9.9	0.848	2.43	4.07	4.8	9.3	10.7	8.
2.93	280.	1.72	12.1	0.926	0.00	6.52	11.7	9.8	13.6	9.
5.80	430.	2.06	19.8	1.002	3.66	6.10	16.4	15.7	16.3	10.
10.08	580.	3.12	21.9	1.315	8.18	9.19	13.8	20.5	19.0	11.
6.17	261.	1.84	18.1	0.953	2.28	9.59	11.3	10.7	15.2	12.
5.99	286.	1.84	27.6	1.450	3.06	7.68	8.2	11.7	12.2	13.
2.89	270.	1.08	14.4	0.695	1.54	4.80	21.3	5.9	10.4	14.
15.50	632.	3.99	13.8	0.975	2.27	4.74	6.1	10.5	8.8	15.
4.94	401.	1.60	23.8	0.747	2.83	8.63	9.3	5.4	11.9	16.
9.69	479.	2.06	14.8	1.309	3.53	4.68	18.2	10.2	20.5	17.
7.78	875.	2.74	27.3	0.871	3.12	9.14	19.5	20.6	23.8	18.
4.48	505.	1.42	17.3	0.946	1.61	6.63	8.2	9.9	11.8	19.
2.80	457.	1.58	22.2	0.000	0.98	7.62	7.5	12.9	9.3	20.
4.72	1313.	1.29	12.4	0.488	2.66	7.61	26.7	7.0	19.3	21.
6.68	239.	2.51	22.9	1.121	1.65	15.55	8.4	15.0	10.8	22.
3.31	141.	0.97	8.3	1.065	0.71	4.89	4.8	4.0	7.6	23.
7.17	822.	2.12	23.2	1.358	2.83	18.33	11.1	17.5	15.9	24.
8.35	436.	2.18	32.0	1.620	1.61	12.51	12.6	14.6	14.9	25.
5.58	302.	2.67	18.5	2.028	2.69	9.85	10.4	7.9	12.5	26.
7.03	1209.	3.16	9.3	1.295	7.75	6.35	41.0	12.4	54.9	27.
16.63	649.	1.32	12.7	0.722	1.40	6.06	17.7	39.6	5.9	28.
5.38	1072.	1.30	9.5	0.891	1.69	5.06	15.2	10.4	4.8	29.
2.23	663.	1.70	7.3	0.405	1.69	2.40	11.0	3.1	15.2	30.
3.48	578.	1.84	8.3	0.733	3.13	6.40	9.6	10.6	10.7	31.
3.83	443.	2.40	15.2	0.874	3.15	7.42	16.1	5.4	12.4	32.
3.31	328.	1.01	16.8	1.130	2.12	7.89	9.7	13.2	19.3	33.
5.61	1407.	2.20	9.7	1.012	3.16	5.67	10.6	6.2	14.5	34.
1.88	315.	3.25	32.8	1.217	3.94	3.80	20.6	14.1	16.0	35.
2.38	556.	1.84	23.3	1.127	3.54	5.98	7.8	28.1	13.9	36.
3.02	584.	2.00	14.3	0.668	2.17	6.04	11.3	7.7	14.2	37.
4.28	117.	1.81	10.2	1.072	1.51	7.22	40.6	2.9	10.9	38.
6.74	0.	3.75	6.7	0.873	5.32	27.13	21.8	14.8	31.4	39.
5.69	178.	2.87	13.2	1.458	2.57	9.23	27.7	24.8	21.9	40.
2.23	168.	0.87	16.2	0.814	1.50	8.06	10.3	8.1	13.1	41.
2.20	277.	1.47	17.8	0.760	2.86	10.80	16.7	9.9	18.1	42.
1.94	447.	0.86	16.1	1.172	2.47	8.91	14.8	8.1	18.8	43.
3.89	308.	1.19	23.9	0.954	1.20	9.12	14.1	11.7	18.2	44.
2.17	122.	0.85	23.0	0.803	1.39	7.48	12.8	10.8	9.2	45.
2.63	152.	1.31	16.0	0.905	1.52	9.00	11.5	12.7	9.5	46.
0.78	103.	0.28	3.4	0.177	0.97	2.24	3.7	2.3	5.4	47.
2.39	90.	0.59	9.7	0.687	1.72	5.35	13.3	7.1	10.9	48.
1.49	250.	0.75	10.2	1.100	2.05	7.23	16.1	8.2	15.9	49.
1.99	99.	0.33	12.8	0.575	1.64	6.27	8.3	7.5	12.4	50.
3.82	151.	1.34	12.5	0.708	0.58	4.44	8.2	6.6	8.7	51.
1.61	335.	0.90	12.9	1.232	1.22	4.95	1.7	4.0	4.0	52.
3.57	148.	1.24	10.8	0.419	1.27	5.75	5.0	6.0	10.0	53.
2.06	497.	2.86	2.7	0.803	3.76	11.36	6.6	11.7	13.7	54.
8.48	1221.	3.77	5.2	1.358	0.49	10.86	4.4	7.6	14.8	55.
13.81	491.	1.79	27.0	1.697	1.38	18.30	10.4	14.2	33.8	56.
7.69	86.	4.33	5.5	1.001	3.03	10.07	6.9	6.3	8.3	57.
.23	124.	0.75	11.9	0.833	2.56	7.57	9.7	5.6	11.7	58.
2.53	0.	1.90	24.1	1.141	1.63	11.28	13.9	10.0	14.5	59.
4.37	244.	1.76	17.5	0.877	1.29	9.54	14.1	8.8	17.0	60.
11.34	810.	3.71	47.7	1.702	5.68	9.93	24.2	21.1	18.8	61.
3.63	218.	1.19	67.3	2.323	1.94	12.88	30.9	23.7	17.0	62.
12.11	420.	3.22	30.1	1.716	3.45	8.38	9.3	10.7	12.4	63.
36.05	411.	5.25	48.8	1.357	16.44	17.85	20.8	13.4	19.0	64.
5.23	314.	1.71	66.1	0.860	2.79	12.19	31.5	13.7	26.4	65.
25.45	997.	8.19	105.1	3.503	9.64	21.90	47.5	22.8	41.8	66.
5.78	151.	1.11	12.8	0.892	2.07	4.77	14.5	8.6	10.9	67.
4.04	241.	1.63	20.8	0.855	3.00	7.88	12.7	11.4	15.6	68.
0.27	39.	0.22	2.0	0.112	1.14	1.60	6.4	1.1	6.3	69.
1.48	129.	0.80	4.3	0.824	0.83	8.15	8.5	7.2	10.6	70.
3.46	158.	1.58	13.8	0.390	0.96	4.87	13.6	8.1	7.8	71.
5.30	254.	1.45	17.9	1.462	2.08	8.01	13.2	10.2	18.8	72.
1.48	78.	0.38	11.4	1.372	1.26	5.35	2.9	4.5	6.5	73.
0.46	70.	1.40	9.5	0.907	0.42	2.54	1.6	4.2	0.8	74.
0.28	64.	1.36	9.4	0.276	0.42	35.41	1.1	3.4	1.4	75.

(Table continues on the following page.)

Line no.	Code	Category	Malawi (kwacha)	Kenya (shillings)	India (rupees)	Pakistan (rupees)	Sri Lanka (rupees)	Zambia (kwacha)	Thailand (baht)
76.	5.330	Nurses' services	0.179	8.32	1.31	5.68	1.09	0.977	6.2
77.	5.410	Hospitals	0.045	1.02	0.18	2.40	0.46	0.207	0.8
78.	6.110	Personal automobiles	1.843	14.91	9.57	18.20	20.04	1.642	47.5
79.	6.120	Other personal transport	1.679	9.26	5.19	10.92	10.65	0.874	23.2
80.	6.210	Tires, tubes, accessories	1.048	9.49	11.06	9.40	9.95	0.758	15.6
81.	6.220	Automobile repairs	0.865	4.30	3.65	15.53	2.03	0.455	8.0
82.	6.230	Gasoline, oil, grease	1.387	12.01	20.79	15.01	17.32	1.532	22.5
83.	6.240	Parking, tolls, etc.	0.785	3.31	4.55	4.01	0.88	0.476	6.0
84.	6.310	Local transport	0.293	2.37	0.72	0.77	1.57	0.255	3.5
85.	6.321	Rail transport	0.094	1.60	0.34	0.35	1.05	0.096	1.9
86.	6.322	Bus transport	0.139	1.09	0.56	0.42	0.38	0.137	1.4
87.	6.323	Air transport	0.380	4.13	3.10	1.10	2.93	0.296	5.3
88.	6.410	Postal communication	0.420	4.85	3.24	2.51	1.73	0.609	9.5
89.	6.420	Telephone, telegraph	0.550	7.84	5.73	4.45	9.09	0.209	7.3
90.	7.110	Radios, televisions, phonographs	1.296	6.02	10.92	15.27	19.77	1.377	25.1
91.	7.120	Durable recreational equipment	2.460	23.16	7.27	17.22	13.11	1.623	23.2
92.	7.130	Other recreational equipment	1.247	9.34	3.78	4.51	10.64	1.000	14.8
93.	7.210	Public entertainment	0.147	1.75	0.71	1.63	0.76	0.239	8.4
94.	7.220	Other recreation, culture	0.293	2.56	1.93	1.97	1.52	0.572	18.5
95.	7.310	Books, papers, magazines	0.552	5.44	2.52	3.39	4.04	0.223	7.9
96.	7.320	Stationery	0.789	7.39	3.13	4.39	8.99	0.961	17.4
97.	7.411	First- and second-level teachers	0.020	0.59	0.20	0.27	0.23	0.098	1.6
98.	7.412	College teachers	0.113	2.87	0.47	1.58	0.77	0.433	4.5
99.	7.420	Physical facilities for education	0.820	15.23	4.99	4.88	5.46	0.330	9.1
100.	7.431	Educational books, supplies	0.605	5.88	2.66	3.65	5.70	0.513	9.0
101.	7.432	Other educational expenditures	0.475	5.36	4.60	5.65	6.36	0.578	10.4
102.	8.100	Barber and beauty shops	0.303	3.66	0.43	0.80	0.61	0.753	2.6
103.	8.210	Toilet articles	0.952	4.65	5.11	7.11	6.55	0.705	19.8
104.	8.220	Other personal care goods	0.715	2.22	3.64	5.65	3.66	0.566	8.7
105.	8.310	Restaurants, cafes	0.648	11.07	2.79	1.13	6.32	0.493	9.4
106.	8.320	Hotels, lodgings	0.453	6.53	1.38	1.97	2.35	0.379	8.2
107.	8.400	Other services	0.275	1.15	1.05	2.00	0.79	0.320	3.7
108.	8.900	Expenditures of residents abroad	0.000	0.00	8.37	0.00	10.60	0.643	20.4
109.	10.100	One- and two-family dwellings	0.472	4.76	1.95	2.66	2.45	0.440	8.1
110.	10.200	Multifamily dwellings	0.589	3.54	2.57	3.51	3.68	0.616	12.0
111.	11.100	Hotels	0.514	5.81	2.16	2.91	2.50	0.820	8.7
112.	11.200	Industrial buildings	0.583	5.84	2.75	3.75	3.78	1.909	18.1
113.	11.300	Commercial buildings	0.867	3.76	2.64	3.60	4.33	1.119	10.3
114.	11.400	Office buildings	0.441	4.64	2.06	2.81	1.60	0.527	7.9
115.	11.500	Educational buildings	0.251	2.71	2.19	2.96	1.64	0.242	7.7
116.	11.600	Hospital buildings	1.044	3.20	1.90	2.60	1.73	0.779	6.8
117.	11.700	Agricultural buildings	0.211	5.77	5.15	7.02	3.89	0.572	13.8
118.	11.800	Other buildings	0.621	2.22	3.15	4.29	3.07	0.402	17.6
119.	12.100	Roads, streets, highways	0.542	4.04	2.62	3.57	2.51	0.196	4.6
120.	12.200	Transport and utility lines	0.299	3.34	3.25	14.73	1.89	0.324	4.9
121.	12.300	Other construction	0.278	7.97	5.90	8.05	0.00	0.260	3.0
122.	13.000	Land improvement	0.105	5.67	1.14	1.56	1.81	0.122	4.2
123.	14.110	Locomotives	1.905	0.00	10.85	19.69	13.36	0.835	4.5
124.	14.120	Other railway vehicles	0.891	15.65	6.07	12.80	11.37	0.615	7.6
125.	14.200	Passenger automobiles	1.934	15.57	10.09	19.98	21.03	1.662	50.7
126.	14.300	Trucks, buses, trailers	2.497	21.62	9.15	21.78	5.85	0.877	21.3
127.	14.400	Aircraft	1.206	8.94	11.58	17.18	6.95	0.452	20.8
128.	14.500	Ships, boats	2.567	0.00	9.46	17.17	10.73	0.000	24.1
129.	14.600	Other transport equipment	1.559	10.38	6.58	17.26	12.25	0.977	24.2
130.	15.100	Engines, turbines	1.168	13.03	10.77	19.62	20.87	2.137	26.6
131.	15.210	Tractors	1.065	7.65	9.90	7.76	9.15	0.708	18.4
132.	15.220	Other agricultural machinery	1.224	10.38	10.81	9.82	6.76	0.905	18.4
133.	15.300	Office machinery	1.373	14.01	18.97	20.68	10.98	1.188	37.2
134.	15.400	Metalworking machinery	1.089	6.03	8.19	22.48	17.30	0.916	23.6
135.	15.500	Construction, mining machinery	1.448	13.52	15.29	21.61	5.32	0.952	30.0
136.	15.600	Special industrial machinery	1.102	11.63	9.63	9.57	9.84	1.053	16.1
137.	15.700	General industrial machinery	1.217	11.99	8.59	8.08	19.26	0.886	20.1
138.	15.800	Service industrial machinery	1.011	12.37	11.22	14.46	20.87	1.303	20.6
139.	16.100	Electrical transmission equipment	0.868	11.07	10.94	16.53	20.24	0.982	23.2
140.	16.200	Communications equipment	1.073	16.27	9.13	12.00	8.38	0.897	43.0
141.	16.300	Other electrical equipment	0.559	16.42	10.63	7.90	12.92	1.121	9.5
142.	16.400	Instruments	1.211	9.29	7.77	20.20	29.17	1.100	33.8
143.	17.100	Furniture, fixtures	0.949	9.39	9.10	10.80	16.34	0.764	12.4
144.	17.200	Other durable goods	0.622	11.30	12.22	38.58	19.08	0.819	28.0
145.	18.000	Increase in stocks	0.457	4.95	4.09	0.00	5.30	0.552	9.3
146.	19.000	Exports minus imports	0.866	7.41	8.37	9.93	10.60	0.643	20.4
147.	20.100	Unskilled blue collar	0.029	0.92	0.52	0.63	0.64	0.080	2.1
148.	20.210	Skilled blue collar	0.052	1.25	0.56	0.60	0.72	0.165	2.6
149.	20.220	White collar	0.119	2.02	0.83	0.88	0.89	0.204	3.6
150.	20.300	Professional	0.372	2.17	1.67	1.41	1.13	0.346	9.5
151.	21.000	Commodities of government	0.624	5.15	2.82	3.37	2.02	0.597	9.3

Philippines (pesos)	Korea (won)	Malaysia (ringgit)	Colombia (pesos)	Jamaica (dollars)	Syria (pounds)	Brazil (cruzeiros)	Romania (lei)	Mexico (pesos)	Yugoslavia (dinars)	Line no.
1.14	53.	0.31	6.7	0.512	0.56	1.26	1.8	4.1	2.7	76.
0.86	276.	0.22	7.3	0.105	1.45	1.57	1.3	10.6	5.3	77.
12.95	906.	4.69	84.7	2.357	9.77	13.50	27.7	19.8	23.7	78.
3.44	201.	2.32	45.8	1.063	0.56	10.83	18.0	23.3	9.4	79.
6.44	530.	2.14	27.5	1.094	5.82	7.44	21.4	12.4	14.6	80.
2.77	193.	0.88	14.1	0.407	5.69	5.68	6.5	6.5	7.5	81.
7.02	1290.	4.00	13.7	1.561	3.49	18.56	27.3	22.4	31.1	82.
4.48	126.	1.86	22.3	1.182	2.14	4.64	7.5	3.1	7.2	83.
0.68	85.	0.94	3.2	0.517	0.51	2.47	5.4	1.8	7.7	84.
0.63	26.	0.55	3.3	0.147	5.24	1.33	10.5	1.0	3.1	85.
0.49	65.	0.26	4.5	0.279	0.69	1.31	5.1	1.8	3.7	86.
1.67	111.	1.37	9.8	0.465	2.48	4.98	3.1	5.1	5.1	87.
3.07	174.	1.70	6.9	0.776	2.99	6.44	4.1	6.4	7.3	88.
2.92	75.	2.22	3.6	0.147	1.45	4.35	8.0	3.2	7.3	89.
8.92	329.	2.08	41.0	1.693	4.13	11.95	20.2	26.2	26.9	90.
3.11	542.	2.97	25.6	1.327	5.86	15.38	52.3	18.2	23.2	91.
4.61	198.	1.24	20.1	0.943	2.91	8.36	13.0	17.3	16.6	92.
1.63	100.	0.52	5.5	0.217	0.35	4.79	3.2	3.9	3.6	93.
2.36	76.	0.58	11.1	0.887	1.39	6.18	5.9	7.2	11.9	94.
4.85	318.	2.09	15.4	0.722	1.16	11.23	8.3	9.5	8.7	95.
4.92	260.	1.31	19.4	1.103	3.13	8.75	18.5	13.1	12.4	96.
0.33	36.	0.36	2.2	0.138	0.28	0.57	1.7	2.6	3.1	97.
0.63	88.	0.27	6.2	0.131	0.40	2.08	2.7	4.5	3.7	98.
4.08	479.	1.91	6.7	0.662	1.26	10.35	6.0	8.8	15.2	99.
5.04	279.	1.86	16.6	0.785	1.81	8.52	10.6	10.3	9.5	100.
4.95	348.	1.83	17.0	1.015	1.75	6.58	12.6	10.5	14.3	101.
1.16	101.	0.26	5.9	0.430	0.98	5.14	6.7	3.6	4.3	102.
4.21	266.	2.20	31.3	0.885	2.16	6.53	21.5	15.4	12.9	103.
5.33	178.	1.06	19.2	0.535	2.33	7.72	14.9	8.0	11.7	104.
4.17	119.	1.13	11.0	0.510	1.20	5.34	9.2	11.0	11.1	105.
2.02	159.	0.82	7.3	0.440	0.51	3.87	7.3	7.4	5.7	106.
1.45	136.	0.67	6.1	0.376	0.92	4.90	5.1	4.2	7.7	107.
0.00	484.	2.40	0.0	0.909	0.00	0.00	0.0	12.5	17.4	108.
4.00	172.	0.76	8.1	0.685	1.89	4.21	16.1	6.3	19.0	109.
5.61	175.	0.58	10.6	1.050	1.99	4.69	11.2	7.3	15.9	110.
4.38	182.	0.63	9.0	1.076	1.78	7.27	9.0	7.4	15.6	111.
4.99	222.	1.67	11.5	1.132	2.18	7.40	5.4	7.4	26.8	112.
4.89	195.	1.54	9.2	0.815	2.24	7.32	21.9	8.2	15.6	113.
3.82	167.	0.76	8.3	1.173	1.38	4.27	8.7	6.2	18.5	114.
3.17	188.	0.47	4.6	0.627	2.04	4.92	10.3	6.2	17.6	115.
3.09	282.	0.89	8.6	1.103	1.16	7.82	15.6	6.6	16.5	116.
8.58	358.	2.26	7.2	2.076	6.48	0.00	18.7	10.4	23.7	117.
4.48	253.	1.38	8.9	1.098	2.67	6.99	15.6	8.1	20.6	118.
3.38	336.	0.64	5.6	0.688	3.60	5.62	14.4	4.3	15.1	119.
6.01	157.	0.80	9.3	0.637	4.65	4.92	13.3	4.7	12.7	120.
4.71	175.	0.44	4.7	0.440	1.96	2.28	12.6	7.0	11.1	121.
12.53	192.	0.62	5.3	0.343	0.90	3.91	23.5	11.6	23.6	122.
13.62	30.	2.61	21.4	1.379	0.50	10.04	27.2	12.7	31.8	123.
6.71	462.	3.31	52.1	1.696	2.47	16.66	14.5	10.0	18.0	124.
13.77	934.	4.78	84.1	2.492	10.08	14.26	27.8	20.5	25.1	125.
10.17	584.	3.03	33.7	0.917	4.13	6.90	20.6	16.5	15.3	126.
10.79	454.	2.48	59.8	1.403	3.31	12.99	40.3	14.1	26.2	127.
11.19	356.	3.46	49.1	1.425	3.65	9.99	0.0	16.4	18.0	128.
6.96	553.	2.63	49.1	1.590	3.10	12.52	28.9	20.8	15.0	129.
20.22	648.	5.28	52.1	2.259	7.15	15.26	38.5	39.9	28.4	130.
13.36	577.	3.95	47.2	0.731	3.17	5.50	15.8	15.2	10.9	131.
9.60	858.	5.03	70.0	1.654	4.09	7.51	25.4	24.0	18.6	132.
14.72	693.	3.69	49.6	1.230	6.48	18.93	44.2	23.3	39.8	133.
9.25	572.	3.08	38.5	1.455	2.94	6.10	30.6	14.7	24.5	134.
11.25	495.	2.57	39.8	1.000	4.43	9.48	28.8	14.7	22.4	135.
14.87	353.	2.01	57.8	1.161	1.46	4.45	15.5	16.4	25.0	136.
7.02	425.	2.99	28.3	0.975	1.82	9.72	27.8	14.0	18.7	137.
17.52	478.	1.93	44.0	1.714	5.73	6.46	24.7	18.4	12.8	138.
8.37	610.	4.04	42.7	1.272	5.53	6.11	23.1	32.7	13.1	139.
11.81	352.	4.49	57.8	0.940	7.39	11.22	18.7	18.9	22.2	140.
6.09	267.	3.06	43.8	1.597	4.47	8.06	24.8	10.1	21.5	141.
5.39	356.	2.46	40.5	1.535	5.27	12.56	19.9	21.4	24.8	142.
6.25	294.	2.19	36.7	1.127	4.58	8.93	8.2	14.4	16.9	143.
8.32	246.	2.14	39.2	0.949	4.87	5.77	68.7	15.5	12.4	144.
4.15	263.	1.72	14.3	0.977	0.00	0.00	12.2	9.7	13.9	145.
7.27	484.	2.40	30.9	0.909	3.70	8.20	12.0	12.5	17.4	146.
0.65	86.	0.38	4.2	0.328	1.47	1.04	5.1	4.5	6.3	147.
0.54	93.	0.37	4.2	0.410	1.73	1.27	5.3	4.2	7.1	148.
0.71	113.	0.86	6.0	0.698	1.77	4.87	5.8	5.5	8.9	149.
0.91	121.	1.63	8.9	0.782	1.83	4.93	4.9	7.3	8.1	150.
3.49	206.	1.30	13.8	0.832	1.70	6.79	9.0	8.5	13.2	151.

(Table continues on the following page.)

Line no.	Code	Category	Iran (rials)	Uruguay (N. pesos)	Ireland (pounds)	Hungary (forint)	Poland (zlotys)	Italy (lire)	Spain (pesetas)
1.	1.101	Rice	67.6	0.81	0.357	28.6	11.9	870.	42.5
2.	1.102	Meal, other cereals	30.9	1.39	0.269	7.9	9.8	452.	38.8
3.	1.103	Bread	15.6	0.55	0.348	4.1	8.3	426.	31.2
4.	1.104	Biscuits, cakes, etc.	53.0	1.00	0.376	13.9	21.4	803.	47.1
5.	1.105	Cereal preparations	210.1	1.40	0.334	9.5	22.5	1258.	156.1
6.	1.106	Macaroni, spaghetti	34.7	1.06	0.994	13.7	10.6	551.	47.0
7.	1.111	Fresh beef, veal	46.5	0.45	0.306	8.1	11.5	797.	63.1
8.	1.112	Fresh lamb, mutton	44.0	0.59	0.305	8.0	7.4	774.	57.4
9.	1.113	Fresh pork	39.8	1.03	0.438	11.2	15.0	775.	53.1
10.	1.114	Fresh poultry	82.6	2.18	0.590	20.3	29.2	1150.	54.1
11.	1.115	Other fresh meat	98.9	0.57	0.332	16.3	18.6	973.	58.6
12.	1.116	Frozen and salted meat	88.1	1.36	0.372	17.6	19.3	705.	49.6
13.	1.121	Fresh and frozen fish	79.9	0.55	0.500	9.5	12.6	1177.	46.3
14.	1.122	Canned fish	51.6	1.81	0.631	25.4	37.5	990.	33.9
15.	1.131	Fresh milk	79.2	0.86	0.243	11.4	12.4	488.	47.2
16.	1.132	Milk products	60.5	0.97	0.414	12.8	15.9	747.	82.2
17.	1.133	Eggs, egg products	71.6	1.29	0.547	30.0	37.4	896.	54.3
18.	1.141	Butter	95.9	3.05	0.426	26.5	30.6	1206.	94.7
19.	1.142	Margarine, edible oil	46.8	3.59	0.526	14.0	22.5	626.	39.3
20.	1.143	Lard, edible fat	31.7	1.34	0.358	13.9	20.7	660.	81.0
21.	1.151	Fresh tropical fruits	69.6	1.43	0.728	38.5	70.3	814.	44.4
22.	1.152	Other fresh fruits	50.2	1.06	0.549	12.1	19.8	425.	46.6
23.	1.153	Fresh vegetables	29.7	0.84	0.290	8.0	10.5	324.	20.1
24.	1.161	Fruit other than fresh	56.3	2.49	0.385	23.6	35.0	775.	50.2
25.	1.162	Vegetables other than fresh	35.9	2.35	0.590	16.0	25.7	1061.	47.3
26.	1.170	Tubers, including potatoes	59.4	2.03	0.306	12.8	6.8	551.	34.6
27.	1.191	Coffee	103.3	2.48	0.548	65.9	119.5	1600.	79.9
28.	1.192	Tea	70.0	2.41	0.232	34.3	46.6	1088.	47.4
29.	1.193	Cocoa	47.9	1.37	0.217	18.7	38.8	673.	31.6
30.	1.180	Sugar	29.3	1.60	0.328	12.1	12.6	475.	37.7
31.	1.201	Jam, syrup, honey	56.1	1.09	0.241	9.7	14.0	663.	45.6
32.	1.202	Chocolate, ice cream	50.2	3.96	0.308	16.1	19.2	834.	33.2
33.	1.203	Salt, spices, sauces	27.7	1.82	0.421	20.7	18.1	551.	45.7
34.	1.310	Nonalcoholic beverages	57.9	1.53	0.468	13.7	15.1	449.	35.6
35.	1.321	Spirits	86.2	2.58	0.698	56.5	59.1	692.	27.8
36.	1.322	Wine, cider	90.5	0.79	0.587	16.9	46.0	519.	26.4
37.	1.323	Beer	41.0	1.05	0.709	15.0	16.0	867.	28.2
38.	1.410	Cigarettes	30.7	1.69	0.831	12.4	16.6	577.	26.6
39.	1.420	Cigars, tobacco, snuff	185.0	12.97	1.583	36.9	33.3	1574.	73.9
40.	2.110	Clothing materials	56.0	3.05	0.501	38.1	43.1	1103.	89.6
41.	2.121	Men's clothing	21.2	1.27	0.429	17.5	23.6	674.	55.1
42.	2.122	Women's clothing	47.0	1.94	0.566	24.9	29.1	778.	78.0
43.	2.123	Boys' and girls' clothing	58.2	2.02	0.570	19.5	23.0	702.	87.8
44.	2.131	Men's and boys' underwear	37.0	2.36	0.566	18.9	21.9	977.	79.2
45.	2.132	Women's and girls' underwear	41.5	1.69	0.393	19.6	27.9	602.	74.2
46.	2.150	Haberdashery, millinery	29.7	1.49	0.431	16.6	17.0	507.	51.4
47.	2.160	Clothing rental and repair	12.8	1.05	0.284	8.1	7.6	609.	38.0
48.	2.211	Men's footwear	30.4	1.60	0.420	14.7	14.2	553.	30.0
49.	2.212	Women's footwear	22.1	2.65	0.754	21.7	24.7	620.	33.5
50.	2.213	Children's footwear	26.5	1.30	0.381	12.2	11.0	804.	30.3
51.	2.220	Footwear, repairs	30.0	0.76	0.265	12.2	10.2	399.	28.0
52.	3.110	Rents	32.0	0.71	0.274	9.8	6.0	469.	24.5
53.	3.120	Indoor repair and upkeep	39.7	2.35	0.645	10.7	13.7	634.	68.9
54.	3.210	Electricity	68.1	1.41	0.463	20.1	13.6	686.	67.7
55.	3.220	Gas	51.6	3.23	0.960	14.6	16.6	820.	78.5
56.	3.230	Liquid fuels	20.1	2.30	0.710	32.2	67.5	1098.	71.7
57.	3.240	Other fuels, ice	49.0	0.64	0.548	8.5	8.6	1139.	75.1
58.	4.110	Furniture, fixtures	31.4	1.19	0.270	9.3	11.3	307.	51.3
59.	4.120	Floor coverings	64.6	2.64	0.538	20.2	27.0	830.	56.4
60.	4.200	Household textiles, etc.	45.9	1.89	0.456	20.9	18.9	773.	61.0
61.	4.310	Refrigerators, freezers	93.0	2.80	0.340	30.8	30.5	613.	55.7
62.	4.320	Washing appliances	122.7	4.23	0.726	30.8	37.9	1189.	79.3
63.	4.330	Cooking appliances	85.1	1.88	0.556	19.2	16.1	760.	55.4
64.	4.340	Heating appliances	139.8	7.44	0.456	23.3	21.3	916.	77.9
65.	4.350	Cleaning appliances	101.3	11.62	0.864	27.6	23.7	1347.	124.2
66.	4.360	Other household appliances	191.3	5.18	1.078	56.0	64.1	2182.	126.3
67.	4.400	Household utensils	31.6	2.15	0.397	16.8	14.8	570.	49.0
68.	4.510	Nondurable household goods	39.6	1.72	0.417	18.4	18.1	662.	65.3
69.	4.520	Domestic services	8.8	1.18	0.231	10.6	7.1	526.	31.9
70.	4.530	Household services	20.6	1.73	0.335	10.7	14.0	515.	48.8
71.	5.110	Drugs, medical preparations	44.3	1.41	0.308	11.0	10.0	419.	37.2
72.	5.120	Medical supplies	28.3	1.91	0.776	18.8	14.8	1486.	53.2
73.	5.200	Therapeutic equipment	15.6	1.70	0.448	4.4	5.0	688.	38.5
74.	5.310	Physicians' services	19.1	0.64	0.130	1.2	1.3	206.	25.5
75.	5.320	Dentists' services	34.8	0.43	0.929	1.0	0.9	210.	29.3

U.K. (pounds)	Japan (yen)	Austria (schillings)	Netherlands (guilders)	Belgium (francs)	France (francs)	Luxembourg (francs)	Denmark (kroner)	Germany (DM)	International price (Π)	Line no.
0.402	309.	14.1	2.19	41.8	3.96	42.2	7.59	3.05	1.09	1.
0.263	251.	14.6	1.77	32.4	4.53	28.3	5.27	2.29	1.05	2.
0.323	280.	15.3	1.84	25.2	3.70	28.1	6.00	2.14	0.72	3.
0.377	428.	19.8	3.34	48.1	6.28	50.5	8.81	3.94	1.27	4.
0.351	214.	31.6	4.00	51.2	8.03	57.5	6.42	3.52	1.04	5.
0.583	420.	16.4	4.20	44.5	4.63	41.0	10.07	3.86	1.17	6.
0.418	1046.	14.3	3.24	43.8	4.91	42.6	8.55	3.51	0.93	7.
0.334	219.	9.7	2.49	44.7	6.97	41.7	7.63	3.40	1.06	8.
0.419	552.	16.7	2.85	36.9	4.72	35.4	7.12	2.96	1.10	9.
0.512	503.	21.9	3.39	52.4	6.86	51.6	10.34	3.90	1.59	10.
0.464	1148.	16.9	3.82	57.9	7.74	66.9	11.20	4.32	1.52	11.
0.367	378.	32.1	2.66	41.3	5.52	43.7	7.11	3.32	1.17	12.
0.501	375.	22.2	2.93	60.9	6.24	63.5	9.93	3.39	1.45	13.
0.463	259.	15.9	3.05	43.0	5.49	42.7	7.80	2.97	1.13	14.
0.275	502.	12.8	1.81	26.0	3.04	31.9	4.48	1.98	1.13	15.
0.352	251.	14.8	2.75	38.4	3.92	37.9	6.75	2.87	1.17	16.
0.435	317.	22.5	3.10	52.3	5.80	49.9	8.49	3.20	1.57	17.
0.333	562.	23.6	4.27	59.4	7.15	55.8	8.93	4.17	1.68	18.
0.543	355.	17.6	3.32	37.5	4.55	38.5	9.38	2.78	1.28	19.
0.293	415.	10.8	2.70	32.1	6.23	26.6	6.73	2.14	1.25	20.
0.554	402.	19.5	3.22	65.4	7.46	70.0	14.09	4.24	1.29	21.
0.505	545.	12.0	2.39	32.6	5.10	42.9	12.77	2.23	1.12	22.
0.297	230.	10.9	1.72	25.8	2.53	22.8	6.16	1.89	0.71	23.
0.321	590.	17.7	2.91	42.2	5.04	45.8	7.23	2.29	1.23	24.
0.550	701.	22.8	2.97	46.0	5.34	44.6	10.53	2.96	1.29	25.
0.493	732.	12.0	2.08	20.6	3.60	21.8	10.98	1.86	1.14	26.
0.565	434.	36.1	4.23	72.6	7.15	76.4	13.65	7.77	1.96	27.
0.236	680.	27.6	2.88	47.2	6.99	53.7	9.48	5.51	1.11	28.
0.230	550.	13.3	1.83	24.1	3.52	25.7	6.70	2.33	1.05	29.
0.403	454.	10.8	1.91	25.4	2.74	25.0	4.54	2.05	1.02	30.
0.269	469.	12.7	2.29	31.4	3.59	29.6	7.33	2.26	1.03	31.
0.348	438.	14.2	2.47	34.0	4.83	36.8	9.38	2.39	1.10	32.
0.419	212.	22.2	1.60	20.9	4.18	35.9	5.35	2.35	1.17	33.
0.408	670.	14.0	2.14	22.8	2.86	20.7	5.63	2.25	1.35	34.
0.618	392.	16.7	3.16	45.5	5.96	40.6	14.91	3.30	1.61	35.
0.577	292.	16.7	2.80	36.6	3.96	34.2	9.20	2.70	1.06	36.
0.686	259.	11.3	2.12	41.7	4.47	33.0	8.10	3.68	1.16	37.
0.840	196.	21.1	3.31	39.8	4.59	33.3	17.67	4.04	1.10	38.
2.208	484.	11.0	7.19	87.6	12.17	90.1	13.54	6.92	2.31	39.
0.584	529.	42.9	4.77	54.7	8.98	75.8	13.99	4.88	1.97	40.
0.405	283.	17.1	2.62	47.3	5.82	44.8	7.61	2.71	1.10	41.
0.542	253.	22.3	3.89	57.6	7.70	61.4	10.45	3.58	1.29	42.
0.425	431.	18.5	3.16	52.4	7.89	57.8	8.13	2.94	1.32	43.
0.642	303.	16.5	4.34	77.6	8.98	69.0	11.22	4.24	1.48	44.
0.457	257.	14.8	3.04	49.7	5.92	49.2	6.89	2.84	1.13	45.
0.447	210.	17.3	3.10	59.8	6.29	57.5	9.33	3.28	0.97	46.
0.266	147.	16.4	2.99	44.5	5.57	50.1	6.76	3.23	0.57	47.
0.376	226.	12.2	2.28	43.0	6.09	37.9	6.72	2.45	0.93	48.
0.754	274.	19.8	3.58	63.1	8.71	54.7	11.78	3.99	1.14	49.
0.300	265.	14.6	2.96	52.7	5.49	43.4	6.09	2.70	0.86	50.
0.310	135.	16.6	2.77	37.4	5.20	45.7	8.25	2.53	0.85	51.
0.376	319.	7.5	1.85	34.8	3.65	35.8	3.66	2.29	0.85	52.
0.656	203.	26.2	6.08	81.8	9.50	59.9	13.88	5.55	1.11	53.
0.466	270.	20.7	3.85	71.6	6.89	53.6	7.56	3.53	1.14	54.
0.670	770.	30.6	3.57	73.7	9.49	61.9	14.11	6.93	1.40	55.
0.715	248.	38.5	4.18	65.3	8.38	64.4	9.44	4.20	1.43	56.
0.393	445.	24.7	3.07	51.4	5.69	35.1	6.88	3.37	0.81	57.
0.232	389.	10.9	1.07	16.0	1.85	16.8	1.99	1.01	0.69	58.
0.560	149.	14.7	4.18	60.4	7.56	57.2	10.50	5.13	1.17	59.
0.460	466.	19.9	3.23	57.8	5.70	54.3	8.78	3.88	1.26	60.
0.387	529.	22.9	2.41	39.8	4.90	40.0	6.52	2.22	1.44	61.
0.885	232.	22.1	4.72	75.9	9.42	80.2	14.08	4.43	1.49	62.
0.501	277.	17.2	2.32	42.6	4.67	44.0	8.03	2.56	1.24	63.
0.425	222.	19.6	3.61	49.7	6.29	48.8	8.50	2.76	1.33	64.
0.831	344.	20.7	4.91	84.7	9.42	77.7	13.74	4.43	1.58	65.
1.288	892.	32.3	7.40	113.7	12.23	99.2	19.09	6.35	2.01	66.
0.400	307.	17.5	2.56	38.5	4.56	34.9	6.18	2.30	1.11	67.
0.375	218.	16.2	3.24	42.7	5.69	43.8	8.58	3.32	1.23	68.
0.303	166.	13.6	2.59	51.1	5.34	36.0	7.70	3.27	0.29	69.
0.326	692.	19.0	3.21	42.7	5.13	40.5	6.97	3.14	0.96	70.
0.298	226.	22.6	3.23	34.8	3.65	34.3	8.42	3.49	0.93	71.
0.698	343.	27.2	5.60	122.6	12.72	120.2	21.23	9.02	1.32	72.
0.264	246.	14.8	2.46	32.1	4.20	41.5	6.28	2.65	0.83	73.
0.077	204.	8.9	1.97	24.6	3.41	23.9	1.14	1.94	0.54	74.
0.147	127.	14.6	0.67	24.0	1.42	23.9	1.84	0.55	0.54	75.

(Table continues on the following page.)

Line no.	Code	Category	Iran (rials)	Uruguay (N. pesos)	Ireland (pounds)	Hungary (forint)	Poland (zlotys)	Italy (lire)	Spain (pesetas)
76.	5.330	Nurses' services	9.7	0.71	0.009	2.6	4.3	222.	38.7
77.	5.410	Hospitals	61.2	0.14	0.218	2.5	3.9	286.	12.3
78.	6.110	Personal automobiles	238.5	9.04	0.776	29.8	67.6	915.	77.2
79.	6.120	Other personal transport	54.9	7.86	0.632	17.6	19.6	716.	54.3
80.	6.210	Tires, tubes, accessories	58.4	3.37	0.396	23.4	29.0	562.	45.5
81.	6.220	Automobile repairs	18.5	2.09	0.133	16.4	27.0	165.	51.7
82.	6.230	Gasoline, oil, grease	40.1	6.03	0.925	37.3	63.4	1778.	134.2
83.	6.240	Parking, tolls, etc.	35.9	0.34	0.244	11.4	17.4	564.	52.0
84.	6.310	Local transport	5.5	0.77	0.481	4.2	3.7	267.	18.9
85.	6.321	Rail transport	10.0	0.25	0.273	3.3	7.0	132.	10.1
86.	6.322	Bus transport	4.5	0.40	0.303	6.1	5.8	135.	13.0
87.	6.323	Air transport	35.7	0.28	0.681	4.6	7.2	1191.	27.3
88.	6.410	Postal communication	69.7	0.89	0.360	7.0	10.6	493.	21.1
89.	6.420	Telephone, telegraph	43.8	1.26	0.657	11.2	13.2	702.	21.2
90.	7.110	Radios, televisions, phonographs	93.1	4.18	0.535	26.6	35.7	794.	83.5
91.	7.120	Durable recreational equipment	160.8	5.13	0.624	30.1	26.9	1160.	89.3
92.	7.130	Other recreational equipment	64.9	2.38	0.571	25.0	23.9	899.	77.5
93.	7.210	Public entertainment	13.0	0.42	0.099	3.0	4.0	672.	20.7
94.	7.220	Other recreation, culture	79.2	1.53	0.398	11.2	11.7	576.	44.4
95.	7.310	Books, papers, magazines	63.3	2.32	0.298	8.0	6.6	552.	42.0
96.	7.320	Stationery	58.1	1.06	0.408	24.2	14.6	687.	44.1
97.	7.411	First- and second-level teachers	9.2	0.23	0.191	3.2	3.4	298.	11.5
98.	7.412	College teachers	85.8	0.39	0.225	4.1	3.8	246.	3.6
99.	7.420	Physical facilities for education	31.4	1.89	0.605	15.6	14.8	775.	72.6
100.	7.431	Educational books, supplies	68.5	1.75	0.323	10.5	8.1	591.	43.5
101.	7.432	Other educational expenditures	51.2	1.36	0.412	16.2	21.3	697.	53.6
102.	8.100	Barber and beauty shops	21.1	0.68	0.219	3.1	4.3	347.	19.8
103.	8.210	Toilet articles	39.9	2.49	0.309	17.7	18.8	703.	48.4
104.	8.220	Other personal care goods	35.2	4.92	0.658	19.4	31.2	854.	56.5
105.	8.310	Restaurants, cafes	25.5	0.72	0.338	8.4	11.2	570.	42.7
106.	8.320	Hotels, lodgings	40.9	0.95	0.188	3.7	14.3	288.	13.9
107.	8.400	Other services	28.3	2.20	0.429	8.1	10.3	602.	49.7
108.	8.900	Expenditures of residents abroad	0.0	0.00	0.000	0.0	0.0	0.	0.0
109.	10.100	One- and two-family dwellings	22.8	1.94	0.525	12.0	21.0	557.	60.9
110.	10.200	Multifamily dwellings	33.9	2.32	0.427	15.3	14.5	453.	40.6
111.	11.100	Hotels	33.0	1.93	0.764	17.7	13.6	918.	35.3
112.	11.200	Industrial buildings	90.5	0.85	0.924	25.4	19.3	1013.	60.3
113.	11.300	Commercial buildings	75.7	1.69	0.386	28.7	21.7	336.	47.7
114.	11.400	Office buildings	27.5	1.23	1.049	12.6	14.7	864.	28.8
115.	11.500	Educational buildings	32.0	0.82	0.398	17.4	16.2	395.	31.1
116.	11.600	Hospital buildings	24.4	1.49	0.638	10.6	20.7	702.	36.5
117.	11.700	Agricultural buildings	109.8	0.83	0.416	41.8	31.2	548.	72.9
118.	11.800	Other buildings	59.3	1.31	0.613	27.9	10.8	674.	48.7
119.	12.100	Roads, streets, highways	65.6	0.79	0.285	11.7	19.5	406.	41.8
120.	12.200	Transport and utility lines	81.1	2.09	0.510	12.0	14.3	573.	83.6
121.	12.300	Other construction	112.4	2.76	0.108	7.7	13.0	112.	33.0
122.	13.000	Land improvement	66.5	0.78	0.386	8.8	7.4	0.	104.0
123.	14.110	Locomotives	72.3	4.47	0.989	23.2	42.0	1276.	105.7
124.	14.120	Other railway vehicles	52.9	2.49	0.344	20.0	16.2	763.	58.7
125.	14.200	Passenger automobiles	237.9	9.35	0.816	31.4	71.2	951.	80.7
126.	14.300	Trucks, buses, trailers	138.0	5.82	0.516	10.8	21.7	673.	59.6
127.	14.400	Aircraft	117.6	3.01	0.785	21.7	37.8	1350.	50.0
128.	14.500	Ships, boats	144.9	5.65	0.621	15.8	25.1	805.	66.0
129.	14.600	Other transport equipment	83.8	5.10	0.305	20.2	17.6	463.	69.0
130.	15.100	Engines, turbines	128.8	5.41	0.622	34.2	32.9	1072.	111.8
131.	15.210	Tractors	77.2	3.79	0.310	32.0	16.9	602.	43.8
132.	15.220	Other agricultural machinery	97.3	3.63	0.637	24.4	25.6	930.	68.5
133.	15.300	Office machinery	91.7	5.63	0.524	22.7	35.1	789.	54.9
134.	15.400	Metalworking machinery	64.9	4.11	0.352	25.2	32.5	707.	53.6
135.	15.500	Construction, mining machinery	87.4	2.57	0.527	39.7	28.1	970.	105.4
136.	15.600	Special industrial machinery	69.1	2.27	0.454	29.3	23.3	671.	53.9
137.	15.700	General industrial machinery	106.2	4.12	0.415	32.8	22.4	778.	37.1
138.	15.800	Service industrial machinery	86.4	1.95	0.473	15.7	28.4	836.	94.3
139.	16.100	Electrical transmission equipment	120.0	4.88	0.443	24.9	19.5	675.	63.0
140.	16.200	Communications equipment	65.5	2.15	0.423	22.8	27.6	901.	69.2
141.	16.300	Other electrical equipment	103.5	1.95	2.542	14.7	20.2	1981.	68.9
142.	16.400	Instruments	138.8	3.01	0.653	33.2	19.2	1177.	70.6
143.	17.100	Furniture, fixtures	76.6	2.94	0.487	15.0	35.4	644.	58.2
144.	17.200	Other durable goods	69.3	2.03	0.489	20.6	24.8	652.	135.7
145.	18.000	Increase in stocks	43.6	1.34	0.462	16.7	20.3	721.	52.0
146.	19.000	Exports minus imports	67.6	2.30	0.450	20.7	19.9	653.	57.4
147.	20.100	Unskilled blue collar	27.5	0.41	0.310	5.7	3.9	461.	30.5
148.	20.210	Skilled blue collar	39.0	0.38	0.270	4.2	4.7	406.	35.6
149.	20.220	White collar	53.8	0.46	0.369	7.0	7.3	509.	62.5
150.	20.300	Professional	72.3	0.41	0.443	5.3	6.4	489.	58.6
151.	21.000	Commodities of government	39.4	1.41	0.426	15.8	17.4	640.	52.5

U.K. (pounds)	Japan (yen)	Austria (schillings)	Netherlands (guilders)	Belgium (francs)	France (francs)	Luxembourg (francs)	Denmark (kroner)	Germany (DM)	International price (Π)	Line no.
0.004	239.	12.0	1.73	28.5	2.91	24.1	3.04	1.40	0.57	76.
0.194	8.	5.7	2.35	11.5	2.34	5.3	2.59	1.69	0.42	77.
0.614	278.	28.6	3.99	43.9	7.21	43.9	16.25	3.42	1.43	78.
0.526	232.	18.8	3.26	44.8	5.03	43.3	12.67	3.14	1.18	79.
0.395	400.	18.8	2.96	43.5	5.47	37.2	7.63	2.38	1.20	80.
0.163	172.	16.7	1.17	15.7	1.65	14.7	3.31	1.20	0.65	81.
0.907	732.	38.8	5.89	82.9	10.87	70.1	12.68	5.45	1.64	82.
0.262	284.	19.0	2.48	30.9	5.48	40.8	5.88	3.05	0.96	83.
0.440	175.	21.4	3.05	44.7	4.05	32.0	9.31	3.70	0.46	84.
0.286	68.	6.3	1.30	19.4	2.37	19.4	3.96	1.46	0.26	85.
0.331	71.	7.0	1.18	21.7	3.09	21.7	5.37	1.76	0.28	86.
0.840	134.	20.2	5.51	84.2	8.64	88.2	15.32	5.71	0.86	87.
0.413	274.	12.9	3.92	56.8	6.27	20.6	4.78	3.49	0.95	88.
0.576	150.	15.3	4.66	110.9	9.28	62.2	8.63	6.12	0.89	89.
0.452	208.	16.6	2.85	46.2	6.19	41.2	8.18	2.47	1.26	90.
0.548	342.	19.3	3.65	56.7	6.98	50.9	8.26	3.30	1.23	91.
0.477	338.	22.2	3.49	57.4	6.72	53.0	8.79	3.61	1.25	92.
0.186	337.	10.2	1.22	23.6	4.29	11.8	3.39	1.94	0.49	93.
0.355	221.	22.2	3.03	47.1	4.89	36.9	8.51	2.60	0.90	94.
0.267	287.	17.4	2.52	35.2	3.91	35.2	6.53	2.60	0.93	95.
0.403	305.	22.5	3.55	49.4	5.80	44.2	9.19	3.51	1.30	96.
0.272	179.	7.6	2.59	32.7	2.70	39.2	7.64	2.12	0.33	97.
0.394	182.	10.9	5.13	21.4	4.65	16.9	9.73	1.73	0.61	98.
0.589	294.	26.8	4.08	68.2	8.34	57.5	11.28	4.28	1.22	99.
0.293	297.	18.8	2.75	38.3	4.28	37.8	7.10	2.80	1.01	100.
0.419	325.	19.6	2.88	40.8	5.06	40.7	8.27	3.04	1.20	101.
0.295	163.	15.3	2.10	27.8	3.11	27.5	5.56	1.94	0.56	102.
0.319	282.	15.3	2.93	40.9	4.91	39.9	8.19	3.00	1.17	103.
0.586	228.	13.2	3.93	54.7	7.26	47.7	9.68	3.42	1.15	104.
0.345	343.	16.5	2.79	42.1	5.02	33.8	8.26	2.71	0.96	105.
0.230	327.	8.0	1.30	18.0	2.23	14.2	2.93	1.26	0.55	106.
0.452	273.	20.3	3.84	59.2	7.01	46.2	10.08	3.71	0.04	107.
0.000	297.	17.4	0.00	0.0	0.00	0.0	0.00	0.00	1.28	108.
0.565	500.	30.8	2.60	50.3	5.17	50.3	8.33	3.71	1.09	109.
0.459	397.	25.6	2.12	40.9	4.20	40.9	6.77	3.02	1.07	110.
0.967	428.	14.4	7.30	73.5	8.40	73.5	15.27	5.40	1.16	111.
1.015	393.	23.2	6.32	83.1	10.49	106.8	13.46	5.19	1.49	112.
0.361	400.	29.4	2.49	30.1	3.86	30.2	5.18	1.76	1.15	113.
0.810	353.	14.6	5.70	65.8	9.40	65.9	11.03	5.05	1.12	114.
0.447	324.	26.9	2.67	32.9	3.78	32.9	5.35	2.48	0.96	115.
0.641	329.	41.5	4.26	54.4	6.72	54.4	8.83	3.70	1.15	116.
0.554	832.	38.3	3.76	41.9	5.30	44.8	8.40	2.49	1.78	117.
0.616	496.	14.5	4.09	52.2	6.45	52.2	8.47	3.55	1.23	118.
0.382	211.	37.0	2.45	28.7	3.58	28.7	4.60	1.61	0.86	119.
0.562	289.	18.2	2.88	48.0	5.24	48.2	6.15	2.85	1.02	120.
0.093	131.	15.3	0.78	11.4	1.03	10.7	1.78	0.59	0.62	121.
0.444	247.	24.5	2.47	38.9	4.24	38.9	5.44	2.17	0.68	122.
0.868	43.	50.2	5.23	79.0	9.19	79.0	15.41	4.53	0.62	123.
0.463	215.	24.0	2.84	49.7	4.33	49.7	5.06	2.38	1.29	124.
0.644	296.	25.5	4.17	45.7	7.51	45.7	16.92	3.49	1.64	125.
0.435	415.	26.0	2.71	31.2	4.74	31.2	6.41	2.40	1.53	126.
1.167	288.	14.6	4.02	81.8	7.38	81.8	13.76	4.63	1.71	127.
0.540	359.	27.5	3.36	49.3	5.77	39.0	9.04	2.84	1.49	128.
0.308	548.	20.0	2.09	33.5	4.66	33.5	6.47	2.10	1.87	129.
0.716	255.	31.9	4.47	60.5	7.34	60.5	8.67	4.20	2.30	130.
0.408	278.	21.1	2.85	36.9	4.53	37.0	5.43	3.02	1.38	131.
0.693	348.	28.0	4.30	63.6	6.89	63.6	9.36	3.82	1.60	132.
0.647	304.	30.1	3.28	47.2	5.01	47.1	6.73	3.40	1.39	133.
0.448	289.	18.6	2.94	40.8	4.66	40.8	5.35	2.99	1.47	134.
0.624	299.	24.3	3.86	56.3	7.10	56.3	9.65	3.98	1.67	135.
0.464	184.	20.9	2.51	36.9	4.64	36.8	5.20	2.18	1.31	136.
0.477	129.	17.8	3.03	40.3	4.80	40.3	6.53	2.91	1.29	137.
0.404	520.	32.7	4.14	42.6	6.24	42.6	7.86	3.21	1.42	138.
0.544	167.	23.4	3.25	51.7	4.35	51.7	7.72	2.85	1.30	139.
0.586	302.	33.3	4.15	48.9	6.54	48.9	7.31	4.30	1.39	140.
1.089	306.	22.1	30.87	110.2	11.26	110.0	19.34	6.54	1.70	141.
0.728	193.	24.5	3.72	60.2	7.47	60.2	10.00	3.74	1.32	142.
0.491	146.	27.7	3.27	54.5	5.25	54.5	8.98	4.46	0.91	143.
0.473	372.	23.7	3.12	38.2	4.35	38.2	5.81	2.69	1.55	144.
0.467	313.	18.9	3.00	44.2	5.42	43.0	8.50	3.19	1.21	145.
0.450	297.	17.4	2.53	36.8	4.29	36.8	5.75	2.46	1.28	146.
0.263	223.	12.9	3.70	48.4	4.46	51.0	7.31	3.00	0.43	147.
0.221	192.	11.8	3.04	40.3	4.19	44.8	6.35	2.70	0.61	148.
0.299	201.	20.4	4.16	55.9	5.55	60.6	8.10	3.47	0.81	149.
0.479	382.	21.1	5.72	68.9	5.32	70.5	8.18	3.77	0.83	150.
0.452	298.	18.0	2.96	44.5	4.85	42.7	7.72	2.98	1.12	151.

Line no.	Code	Category	Malawi	Kenya	India	Pakistan	Sri Lanka	Zambia	Thailand
1.	1.101	Rice	2.3	4.3	41.9	11.6	54.8	0.5	151.8
2.	1.102	Meal, other cereals	49.7	48.4	38.6	82.7	22.8	62.8	0.4
3.	1.103	Bread	1.9	4.7	0.1	0.8	18.5	11.1	0.4
4.	1.104	Biscuits, cakes, etc.	0.0	0.6	0.3	3.2	0.9	0.4	0.0
5.	1.105	Cereal preparations	0.0	0.3	0.1	1.1	0.3	0.1	0.7
6.	1.106	Macaroni, spaghetti	0.0	0.3	0.1	0.1	0.0	0.0	0.0
7.	1.111	Fresh beef, veal	3.3	8.0	0.7	11.9	5.5	31.5	8.1
8.	1.112	Fresh lamb, mutton	1.4	0.6	0.5	6.3	0.5	0.1	0.0
9.	1.113	Fresh pork	0.6	0.5	0.4	0.0	0.7	0.4	24.0
10.	1.114	Fresh poultry	3.3	0.3	0.8	1.5	0.2	7.8	9.5
11.	1.115	Other fresh meat	0.0	1.1	2.1	0.0	0.0	0.2	2.0
12.	1.116	Frozen and salted meat	0.1	0.2	0.0	0.0	0.3	1.7	0.8
13.	1.121	Fresh and frozen fish	1.9	0.1	5.6	5.5	12.2	7.9	31.4
14.	1.122	Canned fish	2.8	0.3	1.2	0.1	3.8	10.8	0.4
15.	1.131	Fresh milk	1.9	20.2	7.4	15.2	3.5	4.4	0.1
16.	1.132	Milk products	0.9	1.1	2.2	10.9	5.5	0.8	2.3
17.	1.133	Eggs, egg products	1.2	3.4	0.9	4.3	2.1	1.3	10.1
18.	1.141	Butter	0.2	0.4	0.8	16.5	0.1	0.7	0.0
19.	1.142	Margarine, edible oil	1.1	1.8	7.1	9.8	2.9	0.7	0.8
20.	1.143	Lard, edible fat	0.0	0.2	5.4	0.0	0.0	6.8	3.8
21.	1.151	Fresh tropical fruits	23.1	3.2	6.8	3.2	13.8	1.8	28.4
22.	1.152	Other fresh fruits	0.3	0.1	0.1	0.1	0.4	0.1	0.0
23.	1.153	Fresh vegetables	40.8	16.9	19.2	15.4	21.9	13.5	8.7
24.	1.161	Fruit other than fresh	0.4	0.1	0.1	0.1	0.1	0.1	0.7
25.	1.162	Vegetables other than fresh	0.0	1.8	1.0	6.7	0.1	1.8	0.4
26.	1.170	Tubers, including potatoes	18.9	1.9	3.8	2.6	17.4	2.9	0.2
27.	1.191	Coffee	0.2	0.4	0.2	0.0	1.7	0.8	0.8
28.	1.192	Tea	0.7	1.4	2.8	8.0	7.7	1.1	0.8
29.	1.193	Cocoa	0.0	0.2	0.0	0.1	0.0	0.6	0.2
30.	1.180	Sugar	3.6	9.1	9.6	5.9	15.6	8.2	7.5
31.	1.201	Jam, syrup, honey	0.1	0.2	0.7	0.0	0.1	0.4	0.0
32.	1.202	Chocolate, ice cream	0.1	0.2	0.3	0.4	0.5	0.4	0.3
33.	1.203	Salt, spices, sauces	0.7	0.2	5.2	5.9	15.5	0.9	21.8
34.	1.310	Nonalcoholic beverages	2.5	2.5	0.1	0.1	0.7	1.6	7.7
35.	1.321	Spirits	1.7	1.2	1.3	0.1	6.5	0.2	35.4
36.	1.322	Wine, cider	0.1	0.1	0.0	0.0	0.0	0.0	0.1
37.	1.323	Beer	4.8	6.7	0.1	0.0	0.6	3.6	5.6
38.	1.410	Cigarettes	1.8	11.7	2.0	2.1	6.8	1.0	9.5
39.	1.420	Cigars, tobacco, snuff	0.4	0.4	3.9	9.7	11.4	0.1	0.8
40.	2.110	Clothing materials	0.5	4.9	12.3	33.1	24.8	2.4	22.6
41.	2.121	Men's clothing	3.2	2.7	0.2	1.4	5.0	6.5	3.7
42.	2.122	Women's clothing	2.2	5.1	0.4	1.7	0.8	4.2	4.6
43.	2.123	Boys' and girls' clothing	4.2	1.1	0.1	0.3	0.1	2.2	5.8
44.	2.131	Men's and boys' underwear	0.2	0.2	0.2	1.0	0.0	0.7	1.3
45.	2.132	Women's and girls' underwear	0.3	0.3	0.2	0.7	0.0	1.2	2.4
46.	2.150	Haberdashery, millinery	0.3	1.5	0.6	0.2	0.3	1.4	0.1
47.	2.160	Clothing rental and repair	0.0	0.6	0.6	4.1	0.0	0.2	23.1
48.	2.211	Men's footwear	0.6	0.9	0.6	3.1	0.6	1.7	0.7
49.	2.212	Women's footwear	0.3	0.5	1.0	2.9	1.0	1.7	0.6
50.	2.213	Children's footwear	0.6	0.2	0.4	0.9	0.2	0.4	2.0
51.	2.220	Footwear, repairs	0.1	0.2	0.0	3.9	0.1	0.3	0.1
52.	3.110	Rents	3.9	17.5	17.9	15.6	30.9	20.8	5.6
53.	3.120	Indoor repair and upkeep	1.1	0.1	1.6	3.1	0.0	0.2	9.0
54.	3.210	Electricity	0.7	0.2	0.5	2.2	0.9	3.9	2.5
55.	3.220	Gas	0.0	0.1	0.1	0.3	0.1	0.0	0.8
56.	3.230	Liquid fuels	0.6	0.4	1.6	2.1	2.5	0.2	1.1
57.	3.240	Other fuels, ice	2.0	7.8	5.6	5.3	7.0	17.5	18.4
58.	4.110	Furniture, fixtures	1.1	9.1	0.5	0.1	1.9	2.0	2.9
59.	4.120	Floor coverings	0.2	0.9	0.1	0.0	0.1	0.1	0.0
60.	4.200	Household textiles, etc.	3.0	0.8	0.1	0.6	0.2	1.6	3.8
61.	4.310	Refrigerators, freezers	0.1	0.2	0.1	0.1	0.0	0.3	0.2
62.	4.320	Washing appliances	0.1	0.0	0.0	0.0	0.0	0.0	0.3
63.	4.330	Cooking appliances	0.5	0.5	0.0	0.0	0.0	0.1	0.1
64.	4.340	Heating appliances	0.0	0.0	0.0	0.0	0.0	0.0	0.0
65.	4.350	Cleaning appliances	0.1	0.0	0.0	0.0	0.0	0.0	0.0
66.	4.360	Other household appliances	0.3	0.0	0.2	0.1	0.0	0.0	1.1
67.	4.400	Household utensils	3.0	2.0	2.3	0.1	3.6	1.7	5.2
68.	4.510	Nondurable household goods	1.4	2.7	1.2	6.2	1.7	3.8	4.9
69.	4.520	Domestic services	4.1	32.1	1.5	4.0	9.7	10.8	8.2
70.	4.530	Household services	5.1	0.3	1.5	8.4	6.6	0.3	2.8
71.	5.110	Drugs, medical preparations	0.6	1.2	6.9	10.9	7.0	2.3	11.8
72.	5.120	Medical supplies	0.3	0.2	0.6	0.8	0.4	0.3	8.4
73.	5.200	Therapeutic equipment	0.2	0.0	0.2	1.3	0.7	0.1	4.8
74.	5.310	Physicians' services	0.3	1.0	4.7	4.0	3.6	1.9	1.8
75.	5.320	Dentists' services	0.0	0.1	0.1	0.1	0.3	0.1	0.3

Philippines	Korea	Malaysia	Colombia	Jamaica	Syria	Brazil	Romania	Mexico	Yugoslavia	Line no.
81.3	114.4	72.0	0.2	34.2	7.8	38.9	1.9	4.7	2.2	1.
7.2	36.2	6.2	12.1	20.5	50.0	17.5	27.3	37.2	33.3	2.
4.5	3.4	2.7	8.7	42.9	66.4	26.5	41.5	57.4	54.0	3.
2.9	9.4	4.9	1.4	7.4	0.9	4.0	8.1	21.4	10.7	4.
1.9	0.2	2.4	0.3	3.5	8.4	0.2	0.1	1.6	0.5	5.
1.1	7.1	3.6	6.0	0.2	3.6	8.3	2.1	8.7	5.6	6.
8.6	10.0	0.8	105.4	20.4	6.2	103.4	11.0	58.5	30.9	7.
0.0	0.1	0.8	1.0	4.4	28.9	3.6	13.1	4.7	5.7	8.
31.4	6.2	21.7	33.9	4.3	0.0	10.5	40.9	24.2	15.5	9.
17.5	3.2	23.8	24.8	10.8	4.4	31.0	43.7	28.2	8.3	10.
1.9	0.8	0.1	0.9	1.2	0.4	4.9	0.8	1.0	2.3	11.
1.4	1.0	1.7	3.3	5.0	1.0	8.5	21.5	20.8	40.5	12.
40.9	18.3	29.4	3.3	13.2	1.5	7.9	4.4	3.4	5.0	13.
16.4	8.3	11.4	2.6	18.4	2.0	7.3	1.2	11.2	4.7	14.
1.1	1.2	1.2	26.6	5.2	13.4	24.5	36.6	37.4	51.8	15.
0.4	3.6	17.3	4.4	37.8	22.8	10.4	27.4	65.8	21.9	16.
1.4	5.5	16.3	10.8	8.8	11.3	17.5	15.9	43.5	12.0	17.
0.3	0.1	0.7	1.3	3.9	1.6	2.3	2.9	7.0	2.4	18.
1.0	1.2	11.7	10.6	9.3	65.3	17.9	14.6	24.9	22.0	19.
9.9	0.6	1.1	2.7	0.0	5.7	8.9	2.2	10.2	6.6	20.
7.2	0.0	19.4	9.1	25.1	17.9	12.4	5.2	40.0	4.8	21.
1.2	17.2	3.1	1.8	0.0	47.5	0.7	18.3	6.9	27.1	22.
15.5	27.1	12.6	16.5	17.5	178.5	21.5	27.6	54.7	31.0	23.
0.2	0.5	0.9	0.7	7.9	6.4	0.7	1.0	1.4	1.1	24.
0.1	0.2	3.2	3.9	1.2	14.3	16.5	6.8	5.4	3.1	25.
7.5	14.6	0.9	20.8	20.9	6.3	7.1	16.7	5.2	9.7	26.
3.9	0.6	3.7	12.8	1.8	1.0	29.2	2.6	18.7	7.3	27.
0.1	0.0	2.1	2.3	0.2	3.3	1.4	0.0	0.1	2.1	28.
0.5	0.0	0.1	12.6	1.6	0.2	0.1	0.3	2.7	1.2	29.
11.6	3.1	16.4	42.4	31.0	22.4	39.0	11.7	33.3	14.5	30.
2.1	0.4	0.3	8.7	3.9	0.4	0.9	5.6	7.3	6.2	31.
1.6	0.2	2.5	8.4	6.3	11.7	0.9	10.9	0.7	7.3	32.
8.2	38.0	13.5	3.2	0.6	1.0	3.9	22.7	7.3	9.5	33.
7.6	1.5	4.2	15.9	15.2	2.3	3.8	4.9	9.6	8.2	34.
17.4	31.2	3.5	8.4	21.1	0.8	0.9	15.4	3.3	23.3	35.
0.1	0.7	0.9	0.8	1.5	0.2	1.7	27.4	0.1	10.7	36.
8.3	5.6	6.8	18.4	25.9	0.1	2.4	8.4	6.4	22.3	37.
13.5	76.3	25.1	13.8	38.3	44.4	23.0	5.2	36.0	43.1	38.
0.5	0.0	2.2	18.9	7.1	0.3	0.1	1.1	0.1	0.2	39.
22.8	38.9	24.6	74.3	4.4	55.5	13.3	24.5	18.2	22.5	40.
5.5	31.6	8.6	6.5	5.9	18.8	17.6	29.4	39.6	31.3	41.
3.9	16.2	4.8	3.6	8.9	14.0	19.7	13.8	24.3	12.7	42.
1.7	8.3	2.1	3.1	1.4	14.3	4.4	9.5	9.4	7.0	43.
1.2	8.1	3.5	4.7	1.8	3.4	1.2	12.0	12.4	8.2	44.
1.7	8.9	2.5	6.0	3.8	2.5	1.3	17.6	12.9	18.4	45.
5.8	2.0	3.8	2.7	0.3	6.0	11.7	11.9	1.9	12.4	46.
1.4	0.5	6.0	3.8	0.8	1.3	4.1	0.7	5.9	0.4	47.
2.9	4.6	5.1	10.3	9.2	4.4	4.8	6.9	20.9	11.3	48.
4.1	1.8	4.2	13.8	7.2	5.6	5.6	9.3	13.5	10.0	49.
1.3	4.8	4.1	4.9	6.1	7.1	3.2	5.2	5.6	4.0	50.
0.5	0.0	0.3	1.1	0.8	1.8	3.1	1.5	3.6	1.0	51.
60.2	15.1	83.3	48.6	45.1	71.1	73.1	182.8	134.2	114.2	52.
3.6	2.7	9.6	9.2	21.7	21.2	5.1	29.7	12.1	23.2	53.
5.6	5.3	4.8	32.6	15.1	4.7	11.9	10.8	22.4	22.1	54.
0.6	1.2	0.8	2.8	1.4	14.4	8.9	11.8	30.3	0.4	55.
1.2	1.6	3.0	5.1	0.9	45.8	1.4	10.4	4.2	8.0	56.
2.0	51.3	1.1	7.3	8.7	6.2	4.6	12.7	22.3	21.0	57.
2.3	2.3	6.0	7.3	15.5	4.5	12.6	20.9	26.6	32.1	58.
0.1	0.0	0.5	0.4	1.7	4.9	1.9	2.5	2.2	6.7	59.
4.4	2.4	7.9	3.1	1.1	8.5	6.9	3.1	3.3	12.8	60.
0.9	1.3	1.5	0.4	2.3	1.1	4.1	2.1	2.6	4.8	61.
0.4	1.6	0.3	0.4	0.0	1.4	1.0	0.5	1.6	5.8	62.
0.6	1.5	0.6	1.5	1.1	0.5	2.7	3.1	2.5	10.1	63.
0.0	0.7	0.1	0.2	0.1	0.1	0.6	1.4	0.4	1.8	64.
0.2	0.7	0.3	0.4	0.8	2.0	1.8	0.1	3.9	1.0	65.
0.3	2.4	1.1	0.2	0.2	2.3	1.2	0.3	14.8	2.5	66.
1.5	5.0	13.8	10.9	0.0	7.9	6.1	11.4	18.7	36.7	67.
7.1	4.4	12.6	14.9	10.2	8.0	20.2	9.9	34.0	9.8	68.
11.4	1.5	7.4	18.6	44.6	0.5	16.3	0.1	77.0	0.9	69.
2.6	5.0	7.3	14.9	2.9	21.8	1.8	12.7	25.0	2.7	70.
4.1	13.9	9.3	14.8	23.1	33.6	22.6	9.5	28.9	42.6	71.
0.5	2.4	1.0	1.7	1.1	0.4	3.9	2.1	3.8	0.5	72.
1.4	1.0	2.7	0.8	0.7	1.2	3.5	5.2	10.2	1.7	73.
13.6	13.0	5.3	10.5	6.6	7.7	13.8	43.6	18.6	42.7	74.
5.8	2.1	1.1	3.8	1.4	3.0	0.7	11.5	1.4	9.7	75.

(Table continues on the following page.)

Line no.	Code	Category	Malawi	Kenya	India	Pakistan	Sri Lanka	Zambia	Thailand
76.	5.330	Nurses' services	0.9	1.7	1.8	0.9	2.9	1.5	2.7
77.	5.410	Hospitals	7.6	4.5	2.4	1.8	12.1	10.6	4.1
78.	6.110	Personal automobiles	0.9	0.9	0.0	0.0	0.1	5.4	1.4
79.	6.120	Other personal transport	0.4	0.2	0.7	0.0	0.1	0.2	0.6
80.	6.210	Tires, tubes, accessories	0.3	0.2	0.2	0.0	1.2	0.8	2.3
81.	6.220	Automobile repairs	0.7	2.3	0.4	0.1	0.1	2.0	0.5
82.	6.230	Gasoline, oil, grease	2.9	2.7	0.4	0.3	1.7	1.8	2.5
83.	6.240	Parking, tolls, etc.	0.7	1.8	0.0	0.0	0.6	0.6	0.0
84.	6.310	Local transport	0.3	0.6	8.1	3.6	15.3	0.9	19.3
85.	6.321	Rail transport	0.1	0.2	5.3	3.1	1.2	0.7	1.8
86.	6.322	Bus transport	2.2	4.7	11.2	6.3	3.6	1.7	11.6
87.	6.323	Air transport	0.1	4.1	0.1	2.9	0.9	0.1	0.8
88.	6.410	Postal communication	0.1	0.6	0.3	0.1	3.2	0.7	0.4
89.	6.420	Telephone, telegraph	0.1	0.2	0.3	0.3	0.2	0.4	0.8
90.	7.110	Radios, televisions, phonographs	0.3	1.9	0.4	0.0	0.1	0.9	1.1
91.	7.120	Durable recreational equipment	0.0	0.1	0.0	0.0	0.1	0.1	1.1
92.	7.130	Other recreational equipment	0.0	0.2	0.1	0.0	0.5	0.3	5.9
93.	7.210	Public entertainment	0.7	0.8	0.8	1.8	3.2	3.0	1.5
94.	7.220	Other recreation, culture	5.0	2.2	1.4	15.3	11.7	3.7	4.3
95.	7.310	Books, papers, magazines	0.4	1.1	1.9	2.1	1.2	0.8	6.9
96.	7.320	Stationery	0.2	0.3	0.6	0.3	1.2	0.9	0.7
97.	7.411	First- and second-level teachers	24.0	61.9	37.4	26.0	52.8	39.9	45.4
98.	7.412	College teachers	1.1	1.3	5.6	1.6	2.1	1.4	3.0
99.	7.420	Physical facilities for education	0.5	0.6	0.4	0.2	0.1	1.9	2.0
100.	7.431	Educational books, supplies	0.9	0.5	0.6	0.3	0.1	4.4	3.2
101.	7.432	Other educational expenditures	3.0	1.1	0.5	0.6	1.6	10.2	0.6
102.	8.100	Barber and beauty shops	0.1	0.5	2.4	3.0	3.5	0.0	5.9
103.	8.210	Toilet articles	0.3	3.0	1.0	1.8	2.5	1.5	3.2
104.	8.220	Other personal care goods	0.3	7.9	3.1	0.2	1.1	0.6	4.1
105.	8.310	Restaurants, cafes	1.0	3.0	3.3	0.2	3.4	36.4	21.5
106.	8.320	Hotels, lodgings	0.3	0.8	1.0	0.0	0.9	0.4	1.6
107.	8.400	Other services	5.6	2.2	9.3	8.7	14.8	1.8	1.7
108.	8.900	Expenditures of residents abroad	0.0	0.0	−0.6	0.0	−1.7	1.2	−2.6
109.	10.100	One- and two-family dwellings	9.1	12.1	10.2	10.1	15.5	32.6	16.2
110.	10.200	Multifamily dwellings	0.7	3.1	3.8	4.0	2.3	3.3	5.7
111.	11.100	Hotels	0.4	0.3	0.9	0.0	2.6	0.4	1.5
112.	11.200	Industrial buildings	1.8	2.3	2.0	10.4	1.0	11.8	0.8
113.	11.300	Commercial buildings	0.8	0.9	4.4	0.5	2.9	4.8	19.6
114.	11.400	Office buildings	4.9	2.2	2.2	12.9	3.9	7.9	5.9
115.	11.500	Educational buildings	1.8	1.6	1.1	0.0	1.0	11.4	9.0
116.	11.600	Hospital buildings	0.8	2.2	1.0	0.0	2.6	0.7	0.7
117.	11.700	Agricultural buildings	1.8	0.9	5.1	0.3	8.2	1.9	0.0
118.	11.800	Other buildings	0.2	5.9	1.4	0.6	1.2	6.1	0.1
119.	12.100	Roads, streets, highways	0.5	5.5	1.9	7.0	6.2	14.2	8.9
120.	12.200	Transport and utility lines	5.8	13.2	5.1	2.7	13.3	24.6	5.4
121.	12.300	Other construction	2.5	1.3	1.2	1.2	0.0	19.0	9.5
122.	13.000	Land improvement	5.4	1.0	5.7	7.4	10.8	22.1	9.5
123.	14.110	Locomotives	0.1	0.0	0.1	0.0	0.2	0.6	1.1
124.	14.120	Other railway vehicles	0.2	0.1	0.6	0.1	0.5	3.9	0.4
125.	14.200	Passenger automobiles	0.2	1.3	0.1	1.4	0.5	3.7	1.3
126.	14.300	Trucks, buses, trailers	4.2	2.0	1.6	0.7	3.4	17.0	7.8
127.	14.400	Aircraft	0.3	0.5	0.1	0.0	0.1	9.6	3.3
128.	14.500	Ships, boats	0.2	0.0	0.2	0.0	0.1	0.0	0.5
129.	14.600	Other transport equipment	0.1	0.7	0.2	0.1	0.1	0.5	2.9
130.	15.100	Engines, turbines	1.7	0.6	1.8	0.1	0.2	0.4	8.0
131.	15.210	Tractors	0.7	1.4	0.3	1.7	0.9	2.4	1.7
132.	15.220	Other agricultural machinery	1.2	1.0	0.2	1.7	0.2	0.8	0.3
133.	15.300	Office machinery	0.3	0.6	0.0	0.0	0.0	0.6	0.4
134.	15.400	Metalworking machinery	0.3	1.5	0.5	0.0	0.1	1.4	1.6
135.	15.500	Construction, mining machinery	1.7	0.2	0.1	0.1	0.7	9.1	0.8
136.	15.600	Special industrial machinery	1.8	0.7	0.6	4.2	2.3	2.3	8.2
137.	15.700	General industrial machinery	3.0	3.7	1.7	2.8	1.1	13.0	2.1
138.	15.800	Service industrial machinery	0.2	0.2	0.0	0.2	0.0	0.2	0.5
139.	16.100	Electrical transmission equipment	1.6	1.3	2.0	0.7	0.7	6.4	1.6
140.	16.200	Communications equipment	0.5	0.4	0.7	0.0	0.9	3.8	0.6
141.	16.300	Other electrical equipment	0.7	0.3	0.9	1.7	0.0	4.9	1.9
142.	16.400	Instruments	0.5	1.1	0.1	0.0	0.0	1.2	2.0
143.	17.100	Furniture, fixtures	0.2	0.2	0.0	0.3	0.1	1.4	3.2
144.	17.200	Other durable goods	0.1	0.9	1.5	0.0	0.0	3.4	7.9
145.	18.000	Increase in stocks	8.4	−9.1	14.8	0.0	0.0	6.1	30.0
146.	19.000	Exports minus imports	−30.4	−14.4	−0.5	−18.2	−17.7	−123.0	−20.6
147.	20.100	Unskilled blue collar	12.1	12.1	21.5	29.6	23.0	82.0	12.8
148.	20.210	Skilled blue collar	6.3	2.1	3.3	5.0	4.2	3.5	12.5
149.	20.220	White collar	13.1	6.9	11.9	18.7	27.2	18.1	17.6
150.	20.300	Professional	2.4	20.2	7.1	13.8	6.8	3.8	9.0
151.	21.000	Commodities of government	8.7	16.8	15.8	26.9	25.9	71.6	27.6

Philippines	Korea	Malaysia	Colombia	Jamaica	Syria	Brazil	Romania	Mexico	Yugoslavia	Line no.
8.7	10.8	13.4	6.2	12.6	1.8	7.7	19.4	10.9	29.1	76.
5.5	3.2	16.9	8.1	18.8	4.0	19.2	58.9	9.3	53.2	77.
1.4	0.7	10.3	2.2	5.3	1.4	16.8	7.5	18.9	24.0	78.
0.5	1.2	1.4	0.0	2.2	7.2	3.9	0.8	1.8	6.5	79.
0.2	0.0	9.4	0.6	9.7	0.2	12.2	1.3	2.4	3.1	80.
0.1	0.0	4.2	1.2	13.3	0.1	2.9	1.2	12.2	7.0	81.
0.4	0.0	16.5	2.4	23.1	0.6	15.5	2.2	12.6	23.3	82.
0.2	0.1	1.5	0.9	8.0	0.1	9.4	0.1	20.4	12.2	83.
7.1	29.4	7.1	49.0	16.3	26.3	23.6	10.5	61.2	10.8	84.
0.1	13.3	0.6	0.4	0.7	0.4	3.2	4.0	2.4	4.0	85.
2.4	23.2	25.1	26.1	18.6	4.1	4.7	9.3	7.1	11.4	86.
2.1	1.7	6.6	18.0	6.7	0.2	1.3	1.9	7.7	9.7	87.
0.1	0.9	1.2	1.4	1.5	0.5	1.1	4.8	1.3	2.6	88.
0.8	8.5	1.7	19.4	27.6	1.3	4.8	4.2	16.7	5.6	89.
1.0	6.0	8.5	1.4	0.1	1.5	10.3	7.5	7.2	6.9	90.
1.1	1.4	1.8	0.3	0.3	0.6	2.1	0.3	1.3	1.7	91.
0.5	0.9	2.7	0.8	1.0	0.6	3.3	7.0	0.9	2.1	92.
3.2	0.2	14.9	16.8	42.3	5.6	3.8	13.7	14.0	69.2	93.
1.0	22.0	15.3	3.0	4.8	6.6	14.0	11.9	5.5	6.3	94.
0.6	3.1	4.2	10.8	10.9	3.7	2.6	6.8	5.2	13.4	95.
0.1	2.6	2.0	0.9	0.0	3.2	5.5	2.9	1.6	2.8	96.
62.4	63.6	71.8	73.5	91.2	70.8	79.4	72.6	68.9	76.2	97.
16.9	8.2	5.8	12.1	6.4	7.3	10.7	9.7	8.3	20.2	98.
4.2	2.2	2.6	14.1	2.1	4.7	1.3	10.9	14 1	6.1	99.
1.2	1.5	0.9	7.9	1.2	1.6	2.2	1.5	5.6	8.8	100.
1.4	2.1	1.9	22.1	7.3	0.9	8.1	12.4	4.6	9.3	101.
4.0	15.6	5.4	5.4	10.1	4.5	4.4	2.4	11.8	7.3	102.
3.9	7.7	4.3	7.1	33.4	15.5	15.2	1.6	13.4	7.0	103.
3.0	11.2	8.8	3.7	14.9	1.7	4.1	5.7	20.5	18.9	104.
5.1	45.5	24.6	82.9	49.0	17.7	47.5	73.1	39.8	56.2	105.
2.3	1.6	9.5	5.4	49.6	25.3	9.3	4.8	21.3	42.7	106.
31.0	18.5	36.6	36.4	108.7	7.2	32.0	15.0	22.3	33.4	107.
0.0	−4.6	8.1	0.0	−48.1	0.0	0.0	0.0	−27.6	−20.7	108.
11.4	52.9	64.6	46.8	83.1	28.8	16.4	15.4	138.5	50.0	109.
10.2	25.8	43.5	4.6	37.3	34.8	42.3	50.0	50.5	59.7	110.
0.4	2.3	7.3	0.2	2.5	1.2	2.6	19.6	3.8	8.9	111.
1.8	31.2	17.8	1.9	13.9	7.5	14.9	235.8	22.0	52.3	112.
8.3	18.6	11.3	5.5	16.9	7.1	11.6	3.1	17.4	9.5	113.
2.5	6.5	22.0	3.4	9.2	7.9	17.1	3.7	18.1	6.6	114.
5.7	6.5	21.0	3.5	8.4	3.8	7.0	8.5	8.9	0.9	115.
1.5	0.8	9.1	0.5	2.4	2.2	2.4	3.6	4.2	6.6	116.
0.7	5.2	3.1	3.4	1.2	1.7	0.0	22.9	2.5	8.8	117.
0.1	5.7	3.5	0.4	2.6	1.7	2.9	3.2	3.6	6.3	118.
7.2	5.3	16.2	72.8	7.1	12.3	37.7	12.8	28.4	25.3	119.
7.0	32.7	50.3	43 0	7.4	9.2	43.3	31.0	114.8	41.3	120.
3.8	18.9	12.1	36.0	0.8	23.6	38.8	22.1	2.5	10.7	121.
0.3	1.9	48.2	32.9	1.1	40.0	6.4	4.9	1.7	2.1	122.
0.0	24.9	0.0	0.0	0.3	3.9	0.1	2.0	0.1	0.3	123.
0.5	1.2	0.0	0.2	0.2	0.3	2.7	10.0	7.1	3.5	124.
3.6	4.0	4.0	2.9	7.4	1.5	4.2	0.6	4.7	1.8	125.
9.8	10.7	13.3	10.0	35.9	6.1	29.4	18.9	19.6	34.8	126.
1.2	11.4	0.9	2.0	0.6	0.8	3.5	4.9	5.1	2.0	127.
0.7	16.8	5.2	0.6	0.1	0.1	1.7	0.0	1.7	5.0	128.
0.0	0.7	0.9	0.1	15.4	61.3	1.0	0.7	1.0	0.9	129.
3.1	3.7	4.8	0.4	6.1	6.9	5.1	3.2	2.0	7.1	130.
2.0	0.1	3.8	0.3	0.9	6.8	7.4	14.5	2.7	21.3	131.
0.5	0.9	0.5	0.3	15.5	2.4	7.4	8.5	2.4	15.1	132.
0.5	0.9	2.1	0.6	6.6	0.5	3.5	2.8	2.9	1.7	133.
2.0	5.6	2.9	1.0	1.2	2.4	16.5	26.2	7.1	22.0	134.
6.5	2.7	19.1	1.6	15.2	9.8	10.6	34.9	7.0	12.4	135.
2.4	15.8	20.1	1.1	8.6	16.4	22.1	64.6	6.2	31.9	136.
5.8	14.4	12.0	3.1	22.0	42.7	15.0	6.7	10.7	31.6	137.
0.8	2.9	4.9	0.1	2.4	2.1	19.4	1.0	7.0	5.1	138.
2.6	2.1	3.2	5.8	6.6	5.3	19.6	8.0	6.0	34.8	139.
2.6	1.2	3.5	1.1	8.8	0.8	4.1	3.1	4.0	7.9	140.
4.1	4.6	0.0	9.2	3.7	4.9	7.7	1.1	10.1	3.5	141.
1.5	0.3	3.5	3.9	4.3	0.9	3.2	3.2	3.1	1.4	142.
0.1	0.6	2.7	0.5	1.9	2.7	7.7	13.2	7.7	12.2	143.
5.1	5.5	0.5	1.8	30.7	1.5	36.8	0.6	22.3	1.8	144.
54.7	44.0	−22.5	−14.2	37.6	0.0	0.0	157.4	54.1	197.7	145.
−32.5	−64.6	4.5	3.8	−194.0	−128.7	−58.4	−12.5	−59.1	−135.8	146.
17.2	2.7	9.3	0.6	34.2	33.2	66.2	6.9	5.1	8.6	147.
12.4	3.5	6.0	12.2	2.6	6.1	39.4	3.1	37.8	6.1	148.
14.2	60.5	46.3	11.6	61.4	24.5	20.6	30.8	35.2	49.7	149.
43.5	11.5	39.4	20.8	25.2	15.5	17.3	41.3	17.8	71.0	150.
26.6	66.4	72.3	7.2	82.6	186.5	35.0	58.8	27.4	155.0	151.

(Table continues on the following page.)

Line no.	Code	Category	Iran	Uruguay	Ireland	Hungary	Poland	Italy	Spain
1.	1.101	Rice	27.1	10.5	1.0	2.1	0.8	2.0	8.7
2.	1.102	Meal, other cereals	6.1	8.0	16.0	19.1	22.2	7.5	2.3
3.	1.103	Bread	119.4	71.1	26.0	74.8	43.6	46.1	46.4
4.	1.104	Biscuits, cakes, etc.	3.3	39.5	28.7	8.9	12.7	21.0	22.4
5.	1.105	Cereal preparations	0.0	0.5	4.9	1.2	2.2	0.3	0.5
6.	1.106	Macaroni, spaghetti	0.4	25.5	0.4	4.2	2.7	30.4	3.4
7.	1.111	Fresh beef, veal	9.0	271.7	53.7	7.2	19.9	88.9	44.4
8.	1.112	Fresh lamb, mutton	57.0	32.7	33.0	1.4	1.6	3.5	28.7
9.	1.113	Fresh pork	0.1	6.2	7.1	75.1	35.2	15.3	28.7
10.	1.114	Fresh poultry	10.1	6.4	16.1	40.3	14.8	26.0	57.3
11.	1.115	Other fresh meat	0.6	21.3	13.0	4.9	6.1	18.1	9.9
12.	1.116	Frozen and salted meat	0.2	27.4	96.9	39.8	87.4	51.3	85.3
13.	1.121	Fresh and frozen fish	3.2	5.3	13.8	6.1	5.2	13.1	74.7
14.	1.122	Canned fish	0.2	0.3	1.7	1.0	3.6	5.6	18.4
15.	1.131	Fresh milk	3.4	95.3	79.5	38.0	49.2	37.0	71.6
16.	1.132	Milk products	19.4	24.8	8.0	22.2	28.2	49.0	15.5
17.	1.133	Eggs, egg products	10.1	16.5	19.9	17.0	18.3	18.4	48.0
18.	1.141	Butter	6.9	7.4	36.0	4.9	25.2	8.8	2.4
19.	1.142	Margarine, edible oil	16.5	10.3	3.8	7.4	8.7	57.6	95.9
20.	1.143	Lard, edible fat	8.1	1.5	1.1	36.9	10.3	2.1	6.7
21.	1.151	Fresh tropical fruits	12.2	23.7	6.1	4.3	2.3	19.3	30.4
22.	1.152	Other fresh fruits	22.4	43.4	7.1	37.1	14.0	60.6	30.4
23.	1.153	Fresh vegetables	25.6	34.2	17.7	33.2	33.3	99.1	56.6
24.	1.161	Fruit other than fresh	3.4	0.7	10.1	4.7	1.5	9.8	6.6
25.	1.162	Vegetables other than fresh	0.0	7.0	12.4	6.3	5.4	10.9	26.7
26.	1.170	Tubers, including potatoes	4.1	22.4	38.7	15.3	54.4	14.2	33.4
27.	1.191	Coffee	0.0	4.4	1.1	10.8	3.4	8.9	14.1
28.	1.192	Tea	8.8	1.6	18.0	0.5	1.6	0.4	0.6
29.	1.193	Cocoa	0.0	2.4	1.5	0.7	0.4	0.4	4.6
30.	1.180	Sugar	28.6	22.6	13.7	23.6	22.1	19.5	24.8
31.	1.201	Jam, syrup, honey	0.7	24.7	17.5	2.9	3.0	1.4	10.7
32.	1.202	Chocolate, ice cream	1.2	6.7	41.8	32.6	32.2	11.7	7.9
33.	1.203	Salt, spices, sauces	6.0	17.0	10.5	15.6	9.1	5.8	24.6
34.	1.310	Nonalcoholic beverages	1.7	47.1	14.5	19.8	11.3	13.6	18.4
35.	1.321	Spirits	1.0	26.6	7.3	20.1	49.1	18.2	16.5
36.	1.322	Wine, cider	0.2	65.6	2.3	37.2	9.0	58.0	43.3
37.	1.323	Beer	0.7	26.9	8.7	50.3	16.1	6.0	10.8
38.	1.410	Cigarettes	17.4	40.5	49.5	52.3	38.5	61.7	54.0
39.	1.420	Cigars, tobacco, snuff	2.1	1.9	5.5	0.3	0.1	1.7	6.1
40.	2.110	Clothing materials	45.2	5.8	6.2	13.0	32.4	8.4	9.4
41.	2.121	Men's clothing	67.7	41.4	29.8	38.6	33.3	32.7	58.4
42.	2.122	Women's clothing	27.1	22.9	25.8	20.1	26.5	45.3	41.3
43.	2.123	Boys' and girls' clothing	4.2	3.3	13.9	20.7	15.2	21.9	19.1
44.	2.131	Men's and boys' underwear	3.8	4.7	23.9	10.7	13.5	28.2	9.8
45.	2.132	Women's and girls' underwear	3.1	6.7	28.9	13.8	15.8	36.8	10.7
46.	2.150	Haberdashery, millinery	4.4	7.1	5.7	19.9	19.1	6.9	7.8
47.	2.160	Clothing rental and repair	0.1	2.6	1.3	3.7	1.2	1.0	2.8
48.	2.211	Men's footwear	13.7	2.3	9.1	11.5	9.3	11.1	29.7
49.	2.212	Women's footwear	22.9	8.3	6.7	12.2	12.3	22.4	34.3
50.	2.213	Children's footwear	1.6	10.4	4.3	5.4	8.4	3.5	18.5
51.	2.220	Footwear, repairs	0.9	4.4	1.0	1.9	2.6	3.0	6.3
52.	3.110	Rents	149.0	177.3	121.4	70.8	204.6	263.6	292.2
53.	3.120	Indoor repair and upkeep	27.6	7.4	17.4	31.0	23.4	5.7	55.8
54.	3.210	Electricity	6.7	27.2	33.2	13.9	14.8	29.2	26.6
55.	3.220	Gas	3.5	3.7	8.3	13.9	7.0	19.5	22.1
56.	3.230	Liquid fuels	45.9	29.9	7.6	6.5	0.0	17.5	4.7
57.	3.240	Other fuels, ice	6.9	15.3	23.9	31.5	28.3	1.4	4.5
58.	4.110	Furniture, fixtures	6.4	9.6	26.7	48.3	41.0	54.9	38.6
59.	4.120	Floor coverings	22.1	0.4	10.3	6.0	6.7	2.1	7.9
60.	4.200	Household textiles, etc.	12.9	10.2	26.2	17.6	26.2	16.8	29.5
61.	4.310	Refrigerators, freezers	3.5	7.0	8.0	5.0	8.0	5.1	13.5
62.	4.320	Washing appliances	0.7	0.6	5.2	3.1	2.1	6.5	5.7
63.	4.330	Cooking appliances	2.4	5.5	3.5	3.2	6.6	2.9	11.3
64.	4.340	Heating appliances	0.6	1.5	5.5	2.9	2.3	0.8	1.3
65.	4.350	Cleaning appliances	0.2	0.2	0.6	1.1	1.6	1.5	2.0
66.	4.360	Other household appliances	0.3	2.1	2.9	0.6	0.6	2.1	0.7
67.	4.400	Household utensils	10.3	11.1	24.5	25.7	35.9	15.3	6.6
68.	4.510	Nondurable household goods	17.9	21.0	29.7	31.6	20.6	32.0	32.2
69.	4.520	Domestic services	7.2	16.6	4.0	1.4	0.7	5.5	12.3
70.	4.530	Household services	7.4	0.6	9.9	15.3	13.9	13.4	4.0
71.	5.110	Drugs, medical preparations	22.3	35.4	39.8	50.1	53.1	48.1	56.8
72.	5.120	Medical supplies	0.6	2.5	3.7	1.3	5.4	0.7	50.4
73.	5.200	Therapeutic equipment	1.5	0.1	6.4	2.2	8.4	1.4	2.2
74.	5.310	Physicians' services	14.6	38.5	39.2	78.8	55.7	64.5	58.3
75.	5.320	Dentists' services	2.5	8.3	2.5	12.8	19.7	11.1	4.7

U.K.	Japan	Austria	Netherlands	Belgium	France	Luxembourg	Denmark	Germany	U.S.	Line no.
0.7	70.3	2.4	3.6	1.4	2.2	1.6	1.2	1.7	4.0	1.
4.5	1.0	14.9	2.2	2.6	1.4	3.2	10.0	9.6	17.5	2.
27.5	12.9	27.0	42.8	55.1	35.6	60.1	38.4	55.9	35.6	3.
42.3	7.2	24.8	30.3	36.7	39.2	32.4	27.8	29.0	20.8	4.
7.5	12.4	0.8	1.7	1.6	2.9	1.6	2.4	0.5	5.4	5.
0.7	13.2	4.8	1.4	2.5	5.3	2.9	1.0	4.1	4.0	6.
32.6	5.8	42.1	44.3	86.8	82.2	72.0	22.5	19.2	57.5	7.
12.1	0.3	1.2	0.6	1.2	9.4	1.3	0.5	1.0	1.6	8.
12.4	22.0	58.6	33.5	31.8	24.1	28.4	30.1	21.8	34.5	9.
4.7	9.1	17.2	12.8	30.2	29.5	23.0	4.7	3.0	36.6	10.
5.6	1.2	14.2	6.6	11.8	29.3	8.2	7.0	5.4	4.6	11.
111.5	10.3	42.1	70.8	130.3	61.0	100.6	143.5	99.6	50.3	12.
15.1	107.1	4.0	13.8	15.3	20.4	9.2	10.5	6.6	23.6	13.
3.2	34.7	6.2	9.0	15.1	19.4	9.4	20.0	4.0	11.0	14.
60.1	15.3	58.8	49.1	43.5	34.7	46.9	47.2	35.0	40.0	15.
25.9	15.2	39.9	69.5	45.3	86.2	60.2	45.1	35.1	40.2	16.
25.6	14.0	20.8	16.3	18.5	19.1	25.5	18.2	20.6	20.4	17.
31.8	2.4	19.4	6.0	33.5	33.3	42.9	27.0	35.6	7.3	18.
3.1	4.3	23.4	22.7	25.5	19.2	27.0	13.0	33.1	34.2	19.
5.7	0.0	11.9	0.3	1.0	0.3	1.2	1.8	0.9	1.7	20.
11.6	8.8	17.6	18.7	14.0	13.8	15.2	6.6	10.1	11.7	21.
8.8	13.6	52.1	26.1	37.1	28.7	26.8	5.9	21.5	19.5	22.
22.1	50.0	39.2	28.9	33.1	52.9	45.2	16.1	17.2	24.0	23.
14.9	2.9	7.1	17.5	6.0	6.8	6.4	17.3	23.0	30.1	24
17.7	2.1	9.7	22.6	12.6	21.7	14.8	13.2	20.3	69.4	25.
22.8	1.8	22.0	30.2	39.3	19.4	43.2	8.9	24.2	10.5	26.
8.2	6.8	11.0	34.1	22.3	19.5	25.0	36.3	27.4	29.0	27.
14.4	4.6	0.7	3.1	0.8	0.7	0.7	1.8	2.4	2.3	28.
0.9	0.2	2.0	1.0	0.5	3.0	0.9	0.7	4.0	0.3	29.
11.9	4.6	14.6	12.9	13.4	17.0	15.8	17.7	27.2	31.7	30.
7.1	1.9	10.7	8.0	8.6	10.2	7.7	8.5	4.4	19.0	31.
53.7	4.4	45.7	41.9	46.7	43.0	36.9	41.1	33.5	32.4	32.
12.7	192.8	10.5	17.4	14.0	7.9	7.2	34.8	9.3	17.7	33.
28.6	12.6	37.4	41.0	39.6	41.6	41.9	43.1	22.8	24.2	34.
20.9	15.4	37.7	15.3	29.0	17.7	34.0	29.2	42.3	24.6	35.
13.2	23.8	70.4	33.2	20.1	90.6	21.8	29.3	28.9	12.0	36.
8.3	16.5	83.3	55.3	26.8	8.5	34.3	76.1	38.1	53.7	37.
56.1	63.4	61.4	46.9	56.5	40.0	54.2	43.2	47.8	67.6	38.
7.0	0.1	6.1	19.8	14.2	4.4	11.0	41.3	6.3	17.1	39.
3.7	53.6	20.5	23.4	16.9	14.2	13.6	5.5	9.3	8.9	40.
40.0	8.4	51.6	60.3	47.1	32.1	54.8	32.5	45.1	93.0	41.
61.2	17.3	74.2	81.6	55.9	37.3	55.5	47.5	51.9	131.4	42.
24.4	4.1	44.1	30.8	21.0	14.5	21.0	18.8	45.9	37.9	43.
20.5	15.2	45.5	14.7	30.7	39.2	36.5	19.3	43.7	6.1	44.
32.7	12.5	58.2	24.1	32.3	33.9	34.3	37.7	64.2	23.2	45.
19.0	127.7	29.2	15.8	15.9	16.8	17.8	13.7	32.1	18.5	46.
1.2	1.3	4.2	0.9	0.9	2.2	0.8	0.8	2.0	12.1	47.
9.4	8.7	21.8	13.9	12.1	11.3	13.2	9.0	11.7	19.3	48.
14.7	10.6	22.6	18.1	13.5	13.3	15.2	10.7	11.3	24.8	49.
5.1	4.1	16.6	6.5	6.6	10.4	7.8	6.1	16.4	6.7	50.
2.6	0.8	3.0	1.2	2.6	1.9	2.0	0.9	10.7	1.0	51.
317.5	266.9	367.4	317.7	310.3	387.5	389.8	545.6	412.0	548.5	52.
43.6	16.0	59.1	25.0	15.7	32.3	30.0	134.6	12.4	75.9	53.
61.1	35.1	45.0	46.7	43.3	34.3	51.1	69.2	56.3	107.2	54.
33.0	6.8	10.3	57.9	33.4	25.5	35.8	13.1	13.8	61.2	55.
5.8	14.4	17.9	18.7	45.1	25.4	40.4	97.3	25.2	44.9	56.
18.2	0.8	19.0	2.5	27.1	13.9	33.9	28.5	22.4	13.7	57.
36.6	7.1	118.0	181.1	209.5	210.3	190.4	157.1	166.2	61.0	58.
27.0	19.8	30.6	39.4	12.0	9.1	12.1	35.2	14.6	33.6	59.
26.2	30.3	24.2	20.6	27.1	34.8	26.9	33.9	45.6	62.0	60.
13.5	5.8	14.6	14.7	16.2	11.7	14.5	18.7	26.7	18.7	61.
7.0	4.4	12.2	11.5	13.2	12.8	11.3	5.0	15.7	14.5	62.
4.8	16.9	23.3	12.7	10.0	11.3	8.5	8.0	4.0	11.1	63.
5.5	6.0	17.8	6.4	8.1	4.7	7.8	5.4	11.4	1.2	64.
2.3	1.6	5.1	2.3	3.3	2.7	2.9	2.8	5.0	6.0	65.
2.4	3.8	2.4	4.1	6.5	6.4	6.5	5.7	7.0	40.3	66.
39.6	21.7	24.7	56.9	94.9	65.2	98.0	50.3	63.1	29.9	67.
25.8	34.6	40.9	35.3	34.4	46.7	30.0	37.3	57.8	66.6	68.
5.0	0.5	1.6	1.6	15.2	9.5	9.7	5.7	7.4	6.9	69.
20.7	11.3	9.1	18.7	31.6	22.5	29.2	23.6	23.1	15.6	70.
39.8	57.3	36.9	25.3	79.7	106.7	63.4	30.9	87.9	104.8	71.
4.2	20.6	1.7	0.8	1.2	0.9	0.9	0.6	1.7	19.7	72.
9.4	22.2	8.5	5.6	12.1	6.8	5.4	7.6	8.5	19.6	73.
63.4	55.8	88.3	75.1	78.7	69.4	48.6	87.2	90.3	80.7	74.
16.4	22.5	12.1	18.4	11.2	27.5	18.2	26.4	29.6	29.3	75.

(Table continues on the following page.)

Line no.	Code	Category	Iran	Uruguay	Ireland	Hungary	Poland	Italy	Spain
76.	5.330	Nurses' services	5.7	21.5	60.4	61.2	41.6	27.2	27.7
77.	5.410	Hospitals	9.7	48.1	87.7	80.0	61.2	91.1	40.3
78.	6.110	Personal automobiles	7.9	4.1	44.1	26.9	10.7	55.3	68.2
79.	6.120	Other personal transport	1.6	1.3	2.4	6.2	6.5	4.9	2.0
80.	6.210	Tires, tubes, accessories	4.7	2.1	10.5	5.0	3.1	7.9	3.5
81.	6.220	Automobile repairs	11.7	7.0	21.6	4.6	2.4	84.8	15.4
82.	6.230	Gasoline, oil, grease	11.8	6.9	40.6	14.8	4.5	41.6	41.7
83.	6.240	Parking, tolls, etc.	1.5	19.4	8.7	1.4	1.7	21.7	16.6
84.	6.310	Local transport	35.6	52.3	6.6	19.3	41.0	11.0	33.5
85.	6.321	Rail transport	1.7	3.3	1.5	12.5	5.3	15.3	13.5
86.	6.322	Bus transport	14.3	17.0	2.3	11.5	10.5	11.3	2.4
87.	6.323	Air transport	3.3	12.6	2.0	9.3	2.4	1.8	3.5
88.	6.410	Postal communication	0.6	0.9	3.3	7.7	5.9	7.0	1.7
89.	6.420	Telephone, telegraph	2.8	13.7	4.7	4.5	6.4	14.5	21.4
90.	7.110	Radios, televisions, phonographs	3.5	3.8	8.9	15.1	15.2	10.5	11.2
91.	7.120	Durable recreational equipment	0.1	0.2	1.9	0.7	1.4	2.7	1.3
92.	7.130	Other recreational equipment	2.5	4.6	15.1	9.3	9.4	22.1	13.1
93.	7.210	Public entertainment	9.7	20.6	35.4	97.7	25.5	9.3	66.7
94.	7.220	Other recreation, culture	7.8	29.9	24.3	25.8	45.5	29.6	5.0
95.	7.310	Books, papers, magazines	1.4	11.6	55.2	35.1	27.0	35.9	27.6
96.	7.320	Stationery	0.0	9.7	4.0	7.8	7.7	5.7	6.5
97.	7.411	First- and second-level teachers	61.7	87.0	81.4	73.8	82.8	88.6	72.4
98.	7.412	College teachers	6.2	14.0	16.2	13.4	25.2	15.6	14.5
99.	7.420	Physical facilities for education	23.7	1.1	20.3	32.5	48.9	13.6	5.2
100.	7.431	Educational books, supplies	6.6	1.1	4.9	3.7	2.7	2.5	23.9
101.	7.432	Other educational expenditures	0.9	3.7	4.6	15.6	12.2	8.0	21.9
102.	8.100	Barber and beauty shops	13.3	7.1	6.5	19.0	9.4	20.9	24.2
103.	8.210	Toilet articles	6.3	10.9	17.9	14.2	14.9	16.0	28.5
104.	8.220	Other personal care goods	8.5	2.4	10.4	23.6	7.1	38.6	1.4
105.	8.310	Restaurants, cafes	36.0	145.2	247.9	163.7	120.0	105.9	68.1
106.	8.320	Hotels, lodgings	3.7	15.8	44.1	19.1	2.6	30.4	179.8
107.	8.400	Other services	35.6	1.3	42.5	52.2	12.7	19.2	54.4
108.	8.900	Expenditures of residents abroad	0.0	0.0	0.0	0.0	0.0	0.0	0.0
109.	10.100	One- and two-family dwellings	325.4	28.4	47.5	111.4	19.1	178.0	22.4
110.	10.200	Multifamily dwellings	10.7	19.2	123.2	95.4	109.2	114.0	241.1
111.	11.100	Hotels	3.0	1.3	1.4	15.9	15.8	4.6	13.8
112.	11.200	Industrial buildings	19.9	17.6	19.2	80.6	191.8	56.0	18.4
113.	11.300	Commercial buildings	2.9	7.8	29.2	12.4	24.6	16.4	19.8
114.	11.400	Office buildings	79.2	8.3	9.1	14.9	14.1	20.5	32.4
115.	11.500	Educational buildings	14.4	6.1	9.1	15.0	13.7	20.1	30.2
116.	11.600	Hospital buildings	5.0	1.7	6.2	10.5	10.3	9.9	27.2
117.	11.700	Agricultural buildings	17.0	2.8	18.9	27.4	44.9	21.4	9.5
118.	11.800	Other buildings	5.2	2.1	2.5	2.6	10.5	8.3	13.5
119.	12.100	Roads, streets, highways	16.0	48.3	64.9	39.2	26.2	47.0	57.1
120.	12.200	Transport and utility lines	11.8	12.2	38.9	130.0	128.8	52.3	24.5
121.	12.300	Other construction	6.2	13.1	17.9	41.9	61.3	12.9	57.5
122.	13.000	Land improvement	8.2	11.2	7.7	13.7	9.5	0.0	3.4
123.	14.110	Locomotives	0.5	0.0	0.2	2.8	1.9	1.3	1.0
124.	14.120	Other railway vehicles	1.2	0.0	1.2	17.6	44.2	4.0	4.5
125.	14.200	Passenger automobiles	6.4	0.9	20.2	3.5	1.2	23.3	8.9
126.	14.300	Trucks, buses, trailers	32.2	3.3	27.0	105.6	52.2	38.2	39.3
127.	14.400	Aircraft	0.5	2.5	1.4	6.1	7.6	3.5	16.4
128.	14.500	Ships, boats	1.1	2.4	9.8	0.6	24.9	13.7	34.6
129.	14.600	Other transport equipment	18.0	0.1	1.9	0.2	4.9	4.8	5.1
130.	15.100	Engines, turbines	16.7	0.8	15.1	8.5	24.0	11.1	12.2
131.	15.210	Tractors	12.3	5.0	33.6	9.3	10.9	10.4	14.8
132.	15.220	Other agricultural machinery	10.1	2.7	12.7	23.7	35.0	11.3	4.1
133.	15.300	Office machinery	2.0	1.1	16.7	13.4	9.9	14.3	12.0
134.	15.400	Metalworking machinery	8.3	0.6	5.2	32.3	45.5	10.6	20.4
135.	15.500	Construction, mining machinery	40.7	0.2	36.0	16.2	32.1	27.2	13.3
136.	15.600	Special industrial machinery	22.9	11.4	26.4	52.6	40.9	27.5	28.3
137.	15.700	General industrial machinery	4.8	2.2	25.5	28.9	29.0	17.3	33.3
138.	15.800	Service industrial machinery	5.1	1.5	10.4	5.6	6.1	17.7	5.3
139.	16.100	Electrical transmission equipment	3.4	1.3	12.9	5.5	10.5	21.4	15.7
140.	16.200	Communications equipment	15.4	0.8	7.3	13.2	33.6	16.4	25.8
141.	16.300	Other electrical equipment	1.4	0.4	1.1	4.4	49.4	8.8	34.4
142.	16.400	Instruments	3.4	0.9	1.9	16.4	8.3	2.9	5.3
143.	17.100	Furniture, fixtures	0.6	0.5	3.5	38.8	2.4	6.0	5.2
144.	17.200	Other durable goods	16.2	12.5	27.9	8.8	4.0	34.4	8.0
145.	18.000	Increase in stocks	−39.9	3.9	−31.4	141.0	177.0	−10.6	129.4
146.	19.000	Exports minus imports	180.3	−58.9	−198.2	−209.0	−192.1	−53.2	−148.1
147.	20.100	Unskilled blue collar	49.0	84.7	11.4	17.9	20.0	48.5	8.0
148.	20.210	Skilled blue collar	10.2	62.2	26.2	3.0	7.9	28.4	7.6
149.	20.220	White collar	12.1	46.3	101.7	36.2	60.1	114.3	38.5
150.	20.300	Professional	23.6	192.5	17.7	55.0	44.3	32.1	13.3
151.	21.000	Commodities of government	376.3	47.9	128.6	177.1	167.7	177.9	42.2

Appendix Table 6-5 (continued)

U.K.	Japan	Austria	Netherlands	Belgium	France	Luxembourg	Denmark	Germany	U.S.	Line no.
101.5	45.4	45.4	41.2	39.6	86.1	45.0	45.3	52.5	80.9	76.
93.6	111.5	131.0	85.2	97.0	89.3	115.6	96.8	129.8	66.4	77.
75.4	62.1	71.3	90.2	151.8	85.9	191.1	82.3	131.1	272.7	78.
2.0	11.1	9.9	26.3	10.6	11.5	13.8	10.8	6.6	36.5	79.
26.0	1.9	29.0	10.0	26.5	20.7	31.7	19.4	46.8	42.1	80.
46.5	30.9	50.6	89.3	98.5	164.5	108.1	99.0	73.5	53.4	81.
66.9	18.5	87.9	53.8	74.1	68.6	90.1	107.8	97.8	295.0	82.
21.9	3.3	15.4	20.7	28.4	31.0	22.2	29.9	23.4	39.1	83.
23.6	22.0	7.0	2.9	4.4	14.3	8.5	6.7	6.1	8.7	84.
2.3	72.2	12.0	4.1	7.3	7.3	9.9	12.3	22.4	0.3	85.
3.3	18.7	9.2	2.2	7.3	6.6	10.3	1.4	0.9	0.8	86.
8.3	6.5	7.3	2.9	1.9	3.9	2.5	4.1	2.3	14.8	87.
9.6	2.8	10.5	4.0	6.2	8.1	20.2	3.4	21.7	9.9	88.
19.3	35.4	29.0	19.0	6.2	7.0	12.8	22.8	12.5	72.5	89.
37.4	54.3	46.7	86.3	59.5	34.7	40.9	67.4	39.5	73.7	90.
16.6	5.8	18.5	27.1	4.4	6.4	3.0	14.6	21.5	45.4	91.
60.6	33.6	28.5	78.9	47.3	64.7	32.6	76.9	81.8	78.7	92.
19.0	7.5	18.2	23.3	8.7	9.1	11.8	14.0	13.9	23.7	93.
62.5	101.5	43.7	18.8	21.6	32.0	19.0	36.9	53.2	52.4	94.
59.2	27.8	24.5	62.2	36.6	60.5	40.2	65.0	42.8	42.2	95.
8.8	6.9	4.0	6.9	4.5	8.1	6.1	4.4	11.7	16.5	96.
87.2	70.8	86.1	82.2	100.4	92.9	76.2	77.7	69.0	98.1	97.
9.5	19.4	12.0	17.5	19.8	15.7	7.3	28.5	22.9	55.6	98.
15.0	33.4	16.5	47.1	29.4	15.9	22.6	98.8	32.9	61.6	99.
9.4	9.4	5.3	9.0	6.8	4.0	4.3	20.5	2.0	4.6	100.
14.0	19.9	18.4	10.7	7.8	4.2	5.2	21.2	16.4	24.2	101.
13.2	27.5	16.6	13.0	35.8	11.4	41.8	19.7	20.1	12.8	102.
42.2	55.3	36.4	29.0	23.5	59.2	30.1	25.6	23.4	66.3	103.
28.3	28.9	63.8	23.9	31.1	42.0	44.2	26.9	36.2	65.9	104.
248.5	117.2	242.9	73.5	232.9	161.3	366.7	117.4	125.6	228.4	105.
60.5	22.2	114.1	22.1	23.7	59.0	38.1	20.2	46.9	8.0	106.
45.4	97.2	53.7	113.3	41.6	52.7	24.5	34.6	71.4	199.8	107.
0.0	12.7	−277.8	0.0	0.0	0.0	0.0	0.0	0.0	29.8	108.
34.4	140.3	96.7	87.1	67.4	113.6	211.8	148.2	61.3	176.4	109.
134.7	97.7	101.9	262.9	263.2	396.1	227.7	281.5	232.3	77.6	110.
2.1	9.4	44.7	0.5	2.5	4.5	5.1	6.0	3.8	6.2	111.
23.7	74.0	77.4	34.5	103.8	32.7	89.4	54.2	48.1	62.0	112.
49.7	22.7	31.6	54.8	80.8	68.0	122.9	98.5	34.6	43.1	113.
21.5	38.0	37.7	25.1	33.7	26.3	113.8	49.8	13.7	27.5	114.
22.1	35.5	30.6	28.5	23.0	51.1	18.7	43.9	25.6	37.4	115.
10.4	11.3	21.8	15.9	21.2	16.2	20.4	25.6	13.7	26.9	116.
22.1	6.9	25.4	7.6	44.9	4.5	30.6	60.5	15.8	18.9	117.
10.4	26.6	19.6	28.8	9.9	54.8	30.2	17.0	3.1	34.7	118.
35.1	108.3	39.2	38.3	63.4	68.4	116.0	81.3	145.1	47.2	119.
25.8	106.9	107.1	44.9	55.8	52.1	94.8	71.7	147.3	139.6	120.
23.0	192.6	0.7	42.9	17.1	37.7	30.7	30.1	90.7	16.3	121.
14.8	35.6	2.7	28.1	14.6	3.0	2.2	10.2	7.5	11.1	122.
0.2	1.9	2.2	0.5	0.4	1.7	1.0	1.0	0.5	2.2	123.
1.4	4.4	9.8	3.4	5.5	13.3	3.7	8.4	5.7	11.3	124.
44.3	64.2	38.9	59.2	33.0	45.6	46.8	10.4	53.4	64.4	125.
54.0	59.3	24.6	56.6	49.2	67.9	34.7	22.5	66.7	78.5	126.
4.3	3.6	5.6	20.7	32.7	6.1	34.3	0.9	1.3	18.6	127.
41.8	14.8	1.1	36.2	15.8	9.0	20.8	118.9	26.4	9.3	128.
2.5	2.4	1.0	2.7	2.9	3.5	2.9	4.2	3.2	4.9	129.
10.4	18.5	13.3	22.5	20.9	11.0	19.4	9.4	21.8	20.8	130.
5.5	2.0	15.7	9.5	20.0	10.9	17.2	33.7	8.5	21.0	131.
4.0	8.7	25.6	8.5	13.8	18.9	13.6	12.2	11.4	31.4	132.
34.7	24.9	16.6	12.5	18.9	31.3	17.5	1.5	20.2	39.9	133.
25.1	37.4	27.7	17.9	17.7	26.2	16.4	107.8	28.6	35.1	134.
55.7	26.2	36.1	55.3	76.2	34.6	70.3	29.3	49.0	56.4	135.
34.6	87.4	50.7	52.9	45.5	226.8	42.1	99.2	53.6	30.6	136.
17.6	115.9	126.4	37.2	35.4	19.0	32.6	13.9	35.3	45.8	137.
10.8	2.8	0.9	29.9	36.7	16.0	33.8	12.6	35.2	20.1	138.
29.6	97.1	41.3	40.5	37.2	11.7	34.3	10.7	23.8	28.5	139.
41.4	58.9	15.3	43.7	54.7	29.2	50.5	45.6	70.5	69.3	140.
4.6	19.7	42.9	3.1	23.5	6.7	21.8	6.2	36.7	19.7	141.
2.4	46.2	14.5	11.7	7.6	3.5	7.0	2.8	3.3	46.3	142.
5.0	124.7	11.5	10.0	10.7	7.6	9.9	26.3	11.9	22.2	143.
26.3	45.0	33.3	56.6	27.9	31.3	25.8	16.9	24.7	35.8	144.
−64.6	17.1	−37.3	−13.0	−34.4	−15.4	29.9	−84.2	−8.0	−52.8	145.
−109.9	2.4	41.1	307.7	86.7	56.3	−158.4	−124.8	319.0	72.4	146.
45.0	35.5	44.6	41.9	43.2	9.6	26.7	80.6	20.4	36.3	147.
75.1	54.5	9.9	34.1	21.8	58.2	22.7	104.0	50.5	37.0	148.
297.8	17.4	145.4	106.4	129.9	119.7	112.2	238.8	212.1	125.2	149.
48.9	30.1	38.6	31.9	36.6	101.1	24.6	68.9	32.2	100.0	150.
235.8	52.8	116.8	199.3	187.6	241.0	220.4	167.8	149.0	436.5	151.

7

Binary Comparisons

THIS CHAPTER DEALS WITH COMPARISONS between pairs of countries in which each comparison takes account only of the data of the pair of countries to which it refers—that is, binary comparisons. A binary comparison differs from a multilateral comparison for a given pair of countries in that the weights used in the latter—and to some degree the identity of the specifications priced—are influenced by third countries. Thus binary comparisons have more characteristicity but they do not, without further processing, yield a unique cardinal scaling of the GDPs of more than two countries.

In the reports of Phase I and Phase II, binary comparisons were presented for each country with respect to the United States. These comparisons followed the traditional pattern of binary studies in that they relied on overlapping samples of prices provided by each member of each pair of countries. The United States was used as the base country in part because it provided a broad range of prices that yielded substantial overlapping of priced specifications with most other countries.

In the initial plans for Phase III, traditional binary comparisons were proposed for each country with a regional base country as well as with the United States. As was pointed out in Chapter 2, this conformed with the aim of making the position of the United States less central to the comparisons, and of having the regional base countries take on a more important role.

As countries began to supply prices to the ICP, and preliminary price comparisons were prepared, two conclusions became evident. First, the reduced price collection in the United States meant that the number of overlapping items of some countries with the United States was smaller than in Phases I and II. Indeed, there often were a number of detailed categories in which no items matched, even though both the United States and the other country had priced some specifications in the category. Second, while several of the

regional base countries had specially undertaken price collection considerably beyond that of typical participating countries, the binary comparisons within regions did not generally provide enough overlap. Notable exceptions are the binary comparisons between Austria and Hungary and between Austria and Poland, where all categories were covered in each binary.

While the aggregate results of the traditional binary comparisons are reported in this chapter, it was felt that the comparisons—those based solely on the overlapping prices provided by the pair of countries—for individual categories were not sufficiently reliable to warrant publication of price and quantity comparisons for the subcomponents of GDP. A major consideration in this decision is the availability of the results of an alternative binary technique that attempts to overcome the handicap of inadequate overlapping of priced specifications. Comparisons by this method, referred to as augmented binaries, were suggested by Hugues Picard. They are first described and then their results for GDP and its three major components presented. More detailed results are given in the appendix tables. The augmented binary comparisons for the countries are in alphabetical order with reference to the United States in Appendix Tables 7-1 through 7-33. Augmented binary comparisons of each country with its regional reference country follow for countries in Africa, Asia, Europe, and Latin America and the Caribbean in Appendix Tables 7-34 through 7-62. A final set of binaries for all pairs of these regional numéraire countries follows in Tables 7-63 to 7-68.

The Method of Augmented Binaries

The method of augmented binaries includes in the price comparisons made for a pair of countries any item that either of the countries has priced. In the case of an item priced by one country but not the other, the missing price is estimated by the CPD method.

The method of augmented binaries can be illustrated and further explained in this simple example. Consider the following price tableau for a region for a category in which there are five items (1, . . ., 5) and four countries (j, . . ., m). An X indicates that a price was supplied by the country, and a dash is entered if no price was supplied.

Item	Country			
	j	k	l	m
1	X	X	—	X
2	X	—	X	X
3	—	X	—	X
4	X	—	X	—
5	X	—	—	—

For this category, the items that are included in the price comparison in a traditional binary and in an augmented binary are:

Comparison	Types of binary	
	Traditional	Augmented
j/k	1	1, 2, 3, 4, 5
j/l	2, 4	1, 2, 4, 5
j/m	1, 2	1, 2, 3, 4, 5
k/l	none	1, 2, 3, 4
k/m	1, 3	1, 2, 3
l/m	2	1, 2, 3, 4

It is, of course, inherent in the augmented-binary method that it will usually yield more price comparisons for a pair of countries than the traditional method. The source of the added prices that make the extra matchings possible is the country-product-dummy (CPD) method, which has been described in principle in Chapter 3 and as actually used in Phase III in Chapter 4. In the particular example, if the four countries constituted a region, a CPD would be estimated over the items 1, 2, 3, and 4. Item 5 would not be included because only country j has priced it and no information on PPPs would be added by its inclusion. However, as was explained in Chapter 4, country j's price for item 5 is still used if at least one other country in the world has priced it. The full tableau of prices of items 1, 2, 3, and 4 for countries j, k, l, and m is first filled in by using the regional CPD to supply missing prices (for example, item 3 in country j).[1] A new second-stage CPD is then estimated over all thirty-four countries. It includes for countries j, k, l, and m the actual prices for items 1–5 where they have been supplied and the estimated prices for items 1–4 where they have not been reported. From this world CPD, which includes

prices of item 5 from other regions, estimates of item 5 prices for countries k, l, and m would be obtained.

The disadvantage of augmented binaries is that there is some loss of characteristicity. That is, missing prices are estimated for purposes of an augmented binary on the basis of price relationships in third countries, though, to be sure, these are in the main intraregional countries. The method is with respect to characteristicity, intermediate between the traditional binary and the full multilateral approaches. It is not a full multilateral method because the comparison between two countries never includes an item unless its price has been reported in at least one of the two countries. For example, item 3 would not be included in the comparison of countries j and l.

When adequate resources are available to ensure a significant overlap of prices, traditional binaries are preferable to the augmented ones. However, if binary comparisons are desired in a worldwide setting in which there are sharp data limitations, augmented binaries have much to be said in their favor. In the Phase III ICP data set overlap is sometimes skimpy or altogether absent in several categories, but the augmented binaries reduce the dependence of the results on the chance inclusions in and exclusions from the two samples of prices in hand relative to the prices that would be used in a traditional type of comparison. Further, where two countries do have overlaps for most items, the augmented binaries introduce little modification in the traditional result. In the limiting case in which each item priced in one of the countries is also priced in the other, there would be no modification. Thus the augmented binaries help where there is little overlap and do not affect the result much where there is much overlap.

For each pair of countries a purchasing power parity (PPP) for each detailed category was formed as the unweighted geometric mean of price relatives of the items priced by either or both countries. However, in a few categories, such as teachers (ICP 7.411 and 7.412), health personnel (ICP 5.31, 5.32, 5.33) and hospitals (ICP 5.41), the multilateral and binary comparisons use the same indirect PPPs derived by the methods described in Chapter 5. The detailed-category PPPs between each pair of countries were then weighted by expenditures of each country to form the equivalent of Laspeyres and Paasche price indexes, and a corresponding set of quantity indexes was computed in a similar way.

The Results of the Augmented Binaries

Augmented binaries for the 561 pairs of countries are presented in Table 7-1. The Fisher price indexes

---

1. That is, an equation of the form of equation 3.11 is estimated on the basis of whatever prices are available, and then used as an estimating equation to fill in the missing prices.

for GDP are found in the upper right triangle and the Fisher quantity indexes for GDP are found in the lower left triangle for all possible pairs of countries. In this and subsequent tables, the countries are arrayed in ascending order of real GDP per capita used in Chapters 1 and 6, and the convention is adopted of taking the higher income country as the base country. It may be noted in this connection that on any row the entries to the left of the main diagonal represent quantity comparisons of countries with lower incomes to the row country, while the entries to the right of the main diagonal represent price comparisons of countries with higher incomes to the row country.[2]

The use of Table 7-1 can be illustrated by some examples. The Malawi column, for instance, falls entirely in the lower left triangle. The column gives the Fisher indexes of Malawi's real per capita GDP relative to each of the row countries, ranging from 74.1 percent of Kenya's real GDP per capita to 4.1 percent of that of the United States. This decline in the columns is a feature of the lower right triangle, since the GDP of the column country is being compared with successively higher income countries.

For Pakistan, a few columns to the right, the quantity indexes in the lower left triangle begin with Sri Lanka. Pakistan's real GDP per capita, as measured by the Fisher index, is 87.3 percent of Sri Lanka's, 78.3 percent of Zambia's, and so on. To find Pakistan's real GDP per capita for a country arrayed in the table before Pakistan, one has to go to that (lower income) country's column. To find the Pakistan/India relative, for example, reference to the column for India shows that the Indian GDP per capita is 84.4 percent of that of Pakistan; the Pakistan/India index is 118.5 (the reciprocal of 0.844 times 100).

The entries in the upper right triangle, which refer to Fisher price indexes, also adhere to the convention of taking the higher income country as the base. However, these entries are to the right of the main diagonal, and thus for any given cell the column country has a higher income than the row country. For the price indexes, therefore, the column country is the base country. The price indexes were derived from the Fisher PPPs by dividing them by the exchange rate

between the currencies of the numerator (row) and denominator (column) countries.

The Zambia column, for example, indicates that Malawi's price level for GDP was 63.2 percent of Zambia's,[3] Kenya's 83.3 percent of Zambia's, and so on down to Sri Lanka's 39.6 percent. To find Zambia's price level relative to any one of the foregoing involves taking the reciprocal; for example, Zambia's price level relative to that of Malawi's is 158 (the reciprocal of 0.632 times 100). The price comparison of Zambia with countries that have higher incomes than it has requires reference to the columns for those countries. For example, the Zambia/U.S. price comparison, 69.8, can be read from the U.S. column in the Zambia row. The tendency for the price indexes to rise in the U.S. column in the progression from the low- to high-income countries is characteristic of the figures in the upper right triangle. It is, however, less regular than the tendency of the quantity indexes in the lower left triangle to decline.

Table 7-2 presents the Laspeyres and Paasche quantity indexes from which the Fisher quantity indexes of Table 7-1 were derived. As in Table 7-1, the countries are arrayed by increasing GDP per capita as obtained in multilateral comparisons with respect to the United States. Throughout the table the convention of treating the higher income country in each pair as the base country is retained. The upper right triangle gives analogues of the Laspeyres indexes—that is, the quantity indexes weighted by the (higher income) base country's prices. Each cell in the triangle represents a quantity index of the row country with the column country as the base and the column country's prices as weights. For example, the India entry in the Japan column indicates that India's per capita GDP is 12.1 percent of Japan's when Japan price weights are used. The India index relative to other countries, calculated with their price weights, can be read along the part of the row that is to the right of the main diagonal. The indexes of other countries relative to Japan at Japan's price weights may be read in the part of the Japan column that is above the main diagonal.

In the lower left triangle of Table 7-2, the analogues of the Paasche indexes are presented—that is, quantity indexes relative to a higher income country, with own rather than the higher income (base) country's price weights. Each cell here contains a quantity index with the row country as the base and with the use of the column country's prices as weights. Thus the Paasche-

2. The Central Statistical Office of Romania feels that because of the difficulties faced in completing the exchange of product specifications and prices in ample time, the binary PPP reported in Appendix Table 7-25 between Romania and the United States of 9.44 lei per dollar is low, and that a result closer to 11 lei per dollar is more probable. A PPP of 11 lei would produce a price index of 91.7 instead of the 78.7 entered on the Romanian row of the U.S. column in Table 7-1. The Romanian-U.S. quantity ratio would change in a corresponding proportion, and of course the GDP of Romania relative to other countries would also be lower.

3. The Malawi/Zambia PPP was 0.851 Malawi kwacha per Zambia kwacha. When this PPP is divided by the exchange rate, 1.346 Malawi kwacha per Zambia kwacha, the Malawi/Zambia price index of 63.2 is obtained (after multiplication by 100).

Table 7-1. Augmented Binary Comparisons for GDP, All Pairs of Countries; Price and Quality Indexes, 1975

Country	Malawi	Kenya	India	Pakistan	Sri Lanka	Zambia	Thailand	Philippines	Korea	Malaysia	Colombia	Jamaica	Syria	Brazil	Romania	Mexico	Yugoslavia
Malawi		77.4	137.4	121.7	135.6	63.2	110.6	90.3	105.0	91.4	114.7	51.6	104.3	75.1	60.9	80.4	73.9
Kenya	74.1		176.6	152.1	179.6	83.3	132.7	129.0	133.7	112.6	158.0	71.0	129.9	99.1	81.2	103.6	103.8
India	69.1	93.8		91.2	98.6	40.9	79.3	68.2	81.2	65.4	88.4	37.2	73.5	57.7	44.3	55.4	51.6
Pakistan	60.0	83.8	84.4		117.5	48.8	81.8	72.3	104.1	81.2	95.2	40.9	80.5	61.9	52.4	62.5	61.0
Sri Lanka	55.2	72.7	80.0	87.3		39.6	80.7	72.1	81.9	61.0	92.5	36.0	72.7	54.0	40.5	52.1	50.0
Zambia	44.2	58.5	72.0	78.3	94.2		183.0	159.7	183.6	144.5	184.1	87.4	146.0	111.8	101.1	119.2	117.1
Thailand	35.7	51.9	52.5	66.1	65.3	77.1		99.6	87.7	83.8	112.3	52.7	99.6	70.7	54.5	73.5	64.9
Philippines	40.7	49.7	56.8	69.6	68.1	82.4	93.6		101.9	86.5	117.5	47.9	109.7	71.8	59.9	73.7	72.5
Korea	22.6	30.9	30.8	31.2	38.7	46.2	68.5	63.3		80.1	119.3	47.5	97.2	75.2	49.5	74.9	60.5
Malaysia	19.4	27.4	28.6	29.9	38.8	43.9	53.6	55.7	93.3		140.3	60.6	103.3	85.6	66.3	88.3	83.6
Colombia	21.4	27.0	29.2	35.2	35.3	47.6	55.2	56.7	86.4	98.4		45.4	81.1	59.5	49.9	62.8	59.8
Jamaica	19.1	24.1	27.8	32.9	36.5	40.2	47.3	55.9	87.3	91.6	88.4		203.0	130.3	104.9	146.4	136.9
Syria	18.5	25.9	27.6	32.7	35.4	47.2	49.0	47.8	83.5	105.3	97.0	96.4		74.4	56.7	82.2	71.8
Brazil	16.0	21.2	22.0	26.6	29.7	38.5	43.2	45.6	67.5	79.4	82.6	93.9	84.0		78.9	103.2	100.0
Romania	13.0	17.0	18.9	20.7	26.2	28.1	36.9	36.0	67.6	67.6	65.0	76.9	72.7	83.5		130.9	117.2
Mexico	11.7	15.9	18.0	20.7	24.2	28.3	32.5	34.8	53.1	60.3	61.4	65.6	59.6	75.9	90.8		95.8
Yugoslavia	11.2	14.0	17.0	18.7	22.2	25.4	32.4	31.2	57.9	56.1	56.8	61.7	60.1	69.0	89.3	91.9	
Iran	11.5	14.8	16.6	20.0	25.0	28.3	30.6	33.0	54.6	62.7	55.6	63.1	60.8	75.1	91.6	93.9	101.2
Uruguay	12.0	16.2	16.0	20.1	22.4	26.1	28.3	31.5	51.1	57.3	57.4	67.6	61.5	75.4	90.3	96.4	104.9
Ireland	9.4	12.9	14.5	16.1	18.5	22.5	26.3	26.1	43.5	49.0	47.6	56.8	48.4	56.9	73.4	76.6	85.1
Hungary	7.9	10.5	11.8	12.9	16.8	17.5	24.9	22.9	42.0	43.3	40.2	47.4	42.3	49.5	63.1	68.0	70.8
Poland	8.3	10.2	11.4	12.3	15.9	17.3	23.2	21.8	40.8	41.5	39.9	46.3	44.0	50.2	62.4	70.1	72.4
Italy	7.1	10.4	10.6	12.8	15.2	17.5	20.2	22.1	31.6	38.4	35.8	44.3	35.9	44.6	56.2	61.6	66.3
Spain	6.9	9.8	10.2	12.5	14.1	17.1	19.0	20.2	32.8	38.0	36.7	41.6	38.7	44.2	55.1	64.8	65.9
U.K.	5.8	8.6	9.2	10.0	12.3	14.4	16.2	18.1	27.9	32.1	30.8	37.0	30.0	36.1	49.1	50.9	55.8
Japan	6.4	8.5	8.8	9.6	11.8	15.6	16.4	18.0	27.2	33.1	32.4	38.6	29.8	40.3	43.4	51.3	55.4
Austria	5.4	7.7	8.1	9.7	11.1	13.1	15.8	16.4	27.4	29.1	29.3	34.2	29.4	35.1	42.8	49.2	52.3
Netherlands	5.2	8.2	8.0	8.9	10.8	13.7	14.4	16.2	23.5	28.5	26.3	33.9	27.0	33.4	41.7	46.4	49.2
Belgium	4.9	7.9	7.6	8.5	10.3	12.7	13.8	14.9	22.9	26.8	24.7	31.8	25.1	31.2	39.2	45.1	45.5
France	4.6	7.1	7.0	8.3	9.9	11.5	12.8	14.0	21.7	25.4	23.4	30.0	24.0	29.2	38.2	41.5	43.5
Luxembourg	4.9	7.6	7.8	8.6	10.3	12.5	13.8	15.0	22.4	26.9	24.6	30.4	25.2	30.7	38.2	43.9	44.1
Denmark	5.2	7.6	8.0	8.5	11.1	12.4	14.3	15.4	23.4	26.6	25.6	31.4	26.4	30.7	39.1	44.2	44.8
Germany	4.8	7.3	7.3	8.0	10.1	12.2	13.4	14.3	21.5	25.7	23.4	30.9	23.6	29.2	37.3	42.6	44.0
U.S.	4.1	6.1	6.0	6.6	8.0	9.9	10.8	12.0	17.9	20.2	19.4	25.1	20.9	24.3	30.8	35.6	36.8

Note: Upper right triangle: Fisher price indexes of row country with column country = 100. Lower left triangle: Fisher quantity indexes of column country with row country = 100.

type companion of the Laspeyres-type India/Japan comparison can be found here in the India column of the Japan row: India's real per capita GDP is 6.3 percent of Japan's when India's prices are used as weights. The Paasche-type indexes of other countries relative to Japan are found along the row until the main diagonal is reached and the Paasche-type indexes of Japan relative to other countries in the part of the column below the diagonal.

In Chapter 4 the Paasche-Laspeyres spread (PLS) was used as a measure of the similarity of the two countries. The PLS, which is defined as the ratio of the Paasche index to the Laspeyres index, will be closer to unity the more similar are the price and quantity structures of the pair of countries being compared (see Chapter 4 under the section "Identifying Homogeneous Sets of Countries"). The PLS's presented in Table 7-3 are derived directly from Table 7-2. For example, the PLS for Thailand/Mexico, 0.60, is the ratio of the Thailand/Mexico quantity index of 25.2 at Thai prices

and the index of 42.0 at Mexican prices (25.2/42.0 = 0.60).

Two points about Table 7-3 deserve mention. One is that all of the entries are less than unity, meaning that the familiar negative relation between prices and quantities is consistently found between the 561 pairs of countries.[4] The other reaffirms the finding in Chapter 4 that countries with similar real per capita incomes tend to have PLSs close to unity while those with dis-

4. It would be possible for the entries in Table 7-3 to be greater than 1 if a country had a higher GDP at its own prices than when valued at base-country prices. Unlike the similarity indexes of Chapter 9, this index is not constrained to be less than 1, but countries can be considered closer in price and quantity structure the closer is the Table 7-3 value to 1. A PLS greater than 1 indicates that price and quantity structures are different, and that relative quantities are positively correlated with relative prices for some of the categories in at least one of the two countries. The relation of these results to consistency of consumer preference ordering are disussed in Chapter 9.

Table 7-1 *(continued)*

Country	Iran	Uruguay	Ireland	Hungary	Poland	Italy	Spain	U.K.	Japan	Austria	Netherlands	Belgium	France	Luxembourg	Denmark	Germany	U.S.
Malawi	75.8	88.2	56.0	82.4	64.6	57.0	68.2	57.5	48.7	50.7	43.8	44.5	46.7	43.6	35.8	42.8	46.8
Kenya	102.6	113.7	71.1	108.0	91.0	67.3	83.0	67.7	63.3	62.2	48.7	48.7	52.8	49.2	42.5	48.8	54.7
India	55.2	69.7	38.1	57.9	49.2	39.9	48.6	38.3	37.2	36.0	29.9	30.3	32.4	28.9	24.2	29.5	33.6
Pakistan	59.7	72.1	44.7	69.0	59.4	43.1	51.3	45.7	44.1	39.1	35.0	35.1	35.5	34.2	29.5	35.0	40.1
Sri Lanka	46.6	62.9	37.8	51.6	44.8	35.4	44.5	36.3	34.8	33.3	28.3	28.5	29.1	27.9	22.3	27.0	32.0
Zambia	110.0	144.9	83.6	132.7	110.3	82.1	98.0	82.7	70.7	75.4	59.5	61.8	66.9	61.4	53.1	59.7	69.8
Thailand	72.0	94.6	50.7	66.1	58.4	50.4	62.6	52.2	47.8	44.3	40.1	40.2	42.6	39.3	32.7	38.6	45.1
Philippines	71.8	91.2	54.7	77.4	66.6	49.4	63.2	50.4	46.8	45.7	38.4	39.9	41.9	39.1	32.5	38.7	43.7
Korea	67.2	87.1	51.0	65.3	55.3	53.6	60.1	50.5	47.8	42.5	41.0	40.4	41.8	40.4	33.3	39.9	45.3
Malaysia	78.4	104.1	60.4	84.8	72.7	59.1	69.5	58.7	52.6	53.6	45.2	46.1	47.7	45.0	39.1	44.6	53.8
Colombia	64.1	75.2	45.1	66.2	54.8	45.8	52.2	44.3	38.9	38.5	35.4	36.3	37.6	35.7	29.4	35.5	40.6
Jamaica	140.5	158.9	94.1	139.5	117.4	92.2	114.6	91.7	81.4	82.1	68.3	70.2	72.8	71.8	59.6	66.9	78.0
Syria	74.3	89.2	56.3	79.8	63.2	58.2	62.8	57.8	53.7	48.7	43.8	45.5	46.6	44.3	36.3	44.8	47.8
Brazil	96.4	116.5	76.7	109.1	88.6	74.8	88.0	76.8	63.7	65.4	56.8	58.4	61.2	58.1	49.8	57.9	65.8
Romania	119.8	147.5	90.2	129.9	108.0	90.1	107.2	85.7	89.7	81.3	68.9	70.7	70.9	70.9	59.4	68.7	78.7
Mexico	98.4	116.0	72.7	101.3	80.8	69.2	76.6	69.6	63.8	59.4	52.1	51.6	54.8	51.9	44.2	50.6	57.4
Yugoslavia	103.6	121.3	74.4	110.7	88.9	73.0	85.5	72.0	67.2	63.5	55.9	58.0	59.5	58.6	49.5	55.7	63.0
Iran		124.5	77.4	107.1	89.1	73.5	84.3	74.3	71.5	63.3	57.7	57.9	58.9	57.8	50.2	57.4	66.6
Uruguay	97.5		61.0	94.1	74.3	59.9	72.2	61.3	52.9	54.2	46.8	46.9	49.7	47.1	39.9	46.7	54.8
Ireland	77.9	81.5		143.8	118.9	98.5	112.4	97.8	86.4	85.9	73.0	76.1	76.8	78.0	65.1	72.9	84.5
Hungary	69.8	65.5	86.2		81.8	69.3	78.6	69.0	62.1	59.6	53.8	55.6	56.4	56.3	47.3	53.1	60.4
Poland	68.9	68.1	85.6	100.5		87.9	101.4	84.1	77.4	75.2	64.2	67.7	70.2	69.3	57.9	66.0	77.2
Italy	62.7	63.5	77.6	89.0	85.6		115.2	98.9	85.7	87.5	73.5	76.6	78.3	76.8	66.3	73.7	86.6
Spain	63.8	61.4	79.3	91.6	86.4	101.2		88.1	75.1	75.1	67.0	68.7	70.1	69.1	59.3	66.3	76.1
U.K.	51.7	51.6	65.0	74.4	74.3	84.1	81.0		90.6	87.6	73.2	75.8	77.7	78.0	67.2	73.0	86.3
Japan	49.6	55.3	68.1	76.4	74.7	89.7	87.9	102.1		95.9	82.8	88.3	91.6	88.5	75.8	82.4	93.6
Austria	50.1	48.2	61.2	71.1	68.6	78.4	78.4	94.3	93.0		83.2	88.4	91.2	90.8	78.1	86.1	99.2
Netherlands	45.4	46.1	59.5	65.1	66.4	77.2	72.7	93.2	89.2	99.4		104.9	105.9	105.6	93.0	101.5	118.1
Belgium	43.5	44.3	54.9	60.7	60.6	71.3	68.3	86.7	80.5	90.0	91.7		102.9	101.4	88.8	96.7	114.7
France	41.9	41.0	53.3	58.6	57.3	68.4	65.5	82.8	76.0	85.4	89.0	95.2		98.7	87.1	94.1	110.3
Luxembourg	42.7	43.2	52.4	58.6	58.0	69.6	66.4	82.4	78.6	85.8	89.1	96.4	101.2		87.6	94.5	112.9
Denmark	42.2	43.8	53.9	59.9	59.5	69.2	66.3	82.2	78.7	85.6	87.0	94.5	98.4	98.0		106.7	129.1
Germany	40.7	41.2	53.1	58.8	57.6	68.7	65.5	83.3	79.9	85.6	87.9	95.9	100.5	100.2	103.4		117.0
U.S.	33.2	33.2	43.4	49.0	46.7	55.4	54.1	66.8	66.6	70.4	71.5	76.5	81.2	79.5	80.9	80.9	

similar incomes tend to have PLS's well below unity (see Chapter 4 under the section "Identifying Homogeneous Sets of Countries"). Here, this can be seen in the tendency of the PLS to diminish down each column and to increase from left to right along each row. The significance of this arises from the fact that in the columns the country in the heading is compared first with the country that has the next highest income and then with successively higher incomes, while in the rows, the country in the stub is compared with all countries with lower incomes beginning with the lowest income country first. The progressions are not always smooth; some countries, such as Uruguay, tend to have low PLS's for their position in the income array. This suggests that such countries have price or quantity structures that are unusual relative to those of other countries at the same income level.

In the interest of saving space, the Paasche and Laspeyres price indexes are not presented. The reader can easily calculate the Paasche price index by dividing the Laspeyres quantity index given in Table 7-2 into the expenditure ratio taken from the data provided in Table 6-1, taking care to convert the currency of the numerator country to the currency of the base country. The Laspeyres price index can be obtained in a similar way by starting with the Paasche quantity index.[5] The dollar exchange rates given in Table 1-1 can be used to derive the exchange rates between any pair of countries.

The three tables presented above for GDP are matched by sets for consumption (Tables 7-4 to 7-6), capital formation (Tables 7-7 to 7-9) and government (Tables

5. Alternatively, the Paasche price index can be derived by multiplying the Fisher price index by the ratio of the Paasche to the Fisher quantity index. The Laspeyres price index can be obtained by multiplying the Fisher price index by the ratio of the Laspeyres to the Fisher quantity index. This procedure takes advantage of the property that the PLS is the same whether calculated from price or quantity indexes.

Table 7-2. Augmented Binary Quantity Comparisons for GDP

Country	Malawi	Kenya	India	Pakistan	Sri Lanka	Zambia	Thailand	Philippines	Korea	Malaysia	Colombia	Jamaica	Syria	Brazil	Romania	Mexico	Yugoslavia
Malawi		88.7	77.0	71.9	64.7	54.1	46.4	58.0	36.0	24.8	29.0	24.8	25.1	21.0	18.1	15.1	14.6
Kenya	61.8		107.0	103.0	85.3	68.0	66.6	69.6	41.2	34.2	35.7	29.0	36.9	26.1	24.4	19.5	17.1
India	62.0	82.3		92.3	84.2	76.7	62.1	68.4	40.8	33.5	34.8	30.6	34.7	25.7	24.5	20.9	20.7
Pakistan	50.1	68.2	77.2		98.4	96.2	89.6	97.6	48.9	42.4	46.3	37.7	38.4	33.9	27.4	27.9	23.6
Sri Lanka	47.2	62.0	76.0	77.4		116.1	85.8	81.7	54.4	43.4	42.3	43.7	46.1	36.8	31.8	29.0	26.4
Zambia	36.2	50.3	67.7	63.8	76.3		97.3	109.4	62.4	51.7	57.5	48.2	66.5	45.5	40.3	34.3	31.2
Thailand	27.5	40.4	44.3	48.7	49.7	61.1		110.2	87.0	64.8	64.0	54.8	69.3	52.2	53.3	42.0	45.0
Philippines	28.6	35.5	47.2	49.7	56.7	62.0	79.4		79.8	65.5	66.9	62.2	65.8	55.7	46.1	41.9	37.3
Korea	14.2	23.3	23.2	19.9	27.5	34.3	54.0	50.3		121.5	116.1	111.4	108.9	83.8	99.5	65.7	79.2
Malaysia	15.2	22.0	24.3	21.1	34.7	37.2	44.3	47.4	71.6		116.7	101.8	141.0	88.4	81.9	65.6	65.5
Colombia	15.7	20.4	24.5	26.8	29.5	39.3	47.6	48.1	64.3	82.9		95.3	130.0	98.6	85.5	72.2	69.3
Jamaica	14.7	20.1	25.3	28.7	30.4	33.6	40.8	50.2	68.4	82.2	82.0		116.1	101.7	96.9	71.1	65.9
Syria	13.6	18.1	21.9	27.9	27.1	33.5	34.7	34.7	64.0	78.6	72.4	80.1		112.9	93.7	76.1	71.4
Brazil	12.2	17.2	18.8	20.9	24.0	32.6	35.7	37.3	54.3	71.2	69.3	86.7	62.6		110.0	88.0	79.5
Romania	9.4	11.9	14.6	15.7	21.5	19.5	25.5	28.1	46.0	55.8	49.4	60.9	56.4	63.4		112.8	100.9
Mexico	9.1	13.0	15.5	15.3	20.2	23.4	25.2	29.0	42.9	55.4	52.3	60.4	46.7	65.5	73.1		103.8
Yugoslavia	8.7	11.4	13.9	14.8	18.6	20.6	23.4	26.0	42.4	48.0	46.4	57.8	50.6	59.8	79.1	81.4	
Iran	8.3	11.8	13.6	15.7	21.5	22.8	22.3	25.1	40.8	52.3	44.0	57.0	51.3	61.2	74.3	84.6	84.2
Uruguay	8.2	10.8	12.4	15.8	18.6	18.6	20.7	26.1	34.2	41.0	46.2	52.1	43.0	59.5	76.5	71.6	87.7
Ireland	6.8	8.8	11.5	13.0	14.3	17.0	19.6	19.9	33.4	40.9	39.1	49.7	38.9	49.5	61.6	61.8	79.9
Hungary	6.0	7.5	9.5	10.0	13.6	14.3	18.3	18.3	32.6	37.1	34.3	44.1	36.1	43.2	54.7	58.3	67.9
Poland	6.2	7.8	10.2	9.6	13.5	14.0	18.2	18.3	32.1	36.2	33.9	40.1	36.3	43.0	56.7	60.9	67.4
Italy	5.1	7.2	8.4	9.9	11.9	13.0	15.4	17.8	25.9	33.7	30.2	37.8	28.8	39.0	50.3	52.2	62.9
Spain	5.0	6.9	8.2	9.6	11.2	12.5	14.8	16.5	24.6	32.1	29.6	36.2	31.9	38.0	48.2	55.3	62.0
U.K.	4.1	5.7	7.2	8.1	9.5	10.8	12.1	14.6	21.9	26.7	24.6	31.5	23.3	31.1	41.7	41.4	52.5
Japan	4.3	5.3	6.3	6.1	7.7	11.0	11.9	13.0	21.5	28.2	22.5	31.1	20.4	31.2	33.2	39.3	47.0
Austria	3.9	5.3	6.2	7.2	8.1	9.3	12.0	13.7	19.8	25.1	22.6	29.4	22.9	29.3	38.1	40.6	49.1
Netherlands	3.4	5.2	5.3	6.1	7.5	9.4	10.4	11.8	17.8	23.6	19.6	27.3	20.3	26.8	34.6	37.4	44.0
Belgium	3.4	5.1	5.5	6.2	7.4	8.9	10.2	11.2	18.0	22.4	19.2	25.4	19.1	26.1	33.7	36.7	41.8
France	3.1	4.7	5.0	6.1	7.4	8.1	9.7	10.7	17.3	22.0	18.1	24.4	18.2	24.8	32.8	33.5	39.3
Luxembourg	3.3	4.9	5.7	6.2	7.3	8.7	10.2	11.2	17.6	22.8	19.7	25.0	19.0	25.7	32.7	36.8	40.7
Denmark	3.4	4.7	5.8	6.2	8.1	8.9	10.2	11.8	17.3	22.9	20.0	24.7	20.0	25.2	34.9	36.9	41.1
Germany	3.2	4.6	5.0	5.5	7.1	8.7	9.6	10.8	16.1	21.7	17.5	24.6	17.2	23.6	31.7	34.0	39.8
U.S.	2.5	3.7	4.1	4.6	5.2	6.8	7.7	9.1	12.9	16.5	14.0	19.9	15.6	19.3	26.1	30.0	32.9

Note: Upper right triangle: Laspeyres-type indexes of row country with column country as the base, with column country prices as weights. Lower left triangle: Paasche-type indexes of column country with row country as the base, with column country prices as weights.

7-10 to 7-12). Each of these tables is to be read in the same way as its analogue in the initial set.

In general, the entries in the consumption tables tend to behave in much the same way as the entries in the corresponding tables for GDP. This is not nearly so true for the entries in the tables for capital formation and for government. The ordering of the numbers is much less regular. For example, in Table 7-7 the row of entries for Uruguay is higher than those of its neighbors in the income array until the main diagonal is reached; that is, Uruguay's real quantity of capital formation is lower and its price level for capital goods a little higher than would be expected for a country with its per capita income. Similarly, while there is a tendency for the PLS's to decrease down the columns and to increase rightward along the rows in Table 7-9, there are more reversals. Also about 5 percent of the PLS's are above unity. The same points apply even more strongly to the tables for government.

These findings are not surprising, since expenditures in these sectors are heavily influenced or even determined by social policy and are not necessarily in response to relative prices or incomes.

Comparisons of Augmented and Traditional Binary and Multilateral Results

Two obvious questions might be asked about the augmented binaries: How do they compare in their results with those of the traditional binaries? How do the results of both sets of binaries compare with those of the multilateral comparisons?

The Fisher index estimates of real GDP per capita, with the United States as the base country, produced by the augmented binaries are in column 2 of Table 7-13, those produced by traditional binaries in column

Table 7-2 *(continued)*

Country	Iran	Uruguay	Ireland	Hungary	Poland	Italy	Spain	U.K.	Japan	Austria	Netherlands	Belgium	France	Luxembourg	Denmark	Germany	U.S.
Malawi	15.8	17.5	13.0	10.4	11.0	9.7	9.5	8.2	9.4	7.5	8.0	7.2	6.9	7.3	7.9	7.1	6.8
Kenya	18.5	24.4	18.8	14.6	13.5	15.0	14.0	13.0	13.6	11.3	12.8	12.2	10.8	11.8	12.3	11.5	10.3
India	20.4	20.6	18.4	14.7	12.9	13.4	12.6	11.8	12.1	10.6	12.0	10.7	9.7	10.7	11.1	10.6	9.0
Pakistan	25.4	25.5	19.9	16.7	15.8	16.4	16.3	12.4	15.1	13.0	13.1	11.8	11.3	11.9	11.7	11.5	9.3
Sri Lanka	29.0	27.1	24.0	20.7	18.8	19.3	17.7	15.9	18.1	15.2	15.5	14.3	13.1	14.4	15.1	14.2	12.4
Zambia	35.2	36.5	29.7	21.6	21.5	23.7	23.5	19.3	22.1	18.4	20.1	18.1	16.3	17.9	17.3	17.0	14.4
Thailand	42.2	38.8	35.3	34.0	29.6	26.5	24.4	21.7	22.5	20.7	19.9	18.8	16.8	18.8	20.0	18.6	15.1
Philippines	43.4	38.0	34.3	28.6	26.0	27.5	24.7	22.3	24.8	19.7	22.1	19.9	18.2	20.0	20.2	18.9	15.9
Korea	73.1	76.5	56.5	54.3	51.8	38.6	43.8	35.5	34.5	37.8	31.0	29.1	27.2	28.5	31.6	28.7	24.8
Malaysia	75.2	80.1	58.9	50.5	47.6	43.7	44.9	38.6	38.9	33.6	34.2	32.1	29.4	31.8	30.9	30.5	24.8
Colombia	70.1	71.4	57.9	47.0	46.9	42.6	45.5	38.5	46.7	37.9	35.3	31.8	30.2	30.6	32.9	31.4	26.7
Jamaica	69.8	87.6	64.8	51.0	53.4	51.9	47.7	43.5	48.0	39.8	42.3	39.7	37.0	37.1	40.0	38.8	31.7
Syria	72.1	88.0	60.3	49.6	53.2	44.6	47.0	38.7	43.7	37.7	35.9	32.9	31.5	33.4	34.9	32.3	28.2
Brazil	92.0	95.5	65.4	56.9	58.5	51.1	51.5	42.1	52.0	41.9	41.6	37.4	34.4	36.8	37.5	36.2	30.7
Romania	113.0	106.7	87.6	72.9	68.6	62.8	62.9	57.9	56.8	48.0	50.4	45.6	44.6	44.6	43.9	43.8	36.4
Mexico	104.1	129.9	95.0	79.4	80.6	72.5	75.9	62.5	67.1	59.6	57.5	55.4	51.5	52.3	53.1	53.3	42.2
Yugoslavia	121.7	125.4	90.5	73.7	77.8	69.7	70.1	59.4	65.2	55.7	54.9	49.6	48.2	47.9	48.8	48.6	41.2
Iran		129.2	92.8	82.4	84.2	72.4	76.5	63.0	65.5	60.8	55.4	53.4	49.7	52.3	50.2	52.0	39.7
Uruguay	73.5		108.1	78.0	81.9	80.8	81.9	69.1	91.2	63.1	67.8	61.7	55.1	59.9	60.0	59.5	49.9
Ireland	65.5	61.5		92.3	96.0	84.0	88.9	67.5	80.4	68.8	64.7	58.8	56.9	56.0	59.1	58.0	48.5
Hungary	59.1	55.0	80.5		108.0	94.0	99.8	80.6	90.1	78.9	73.7	67.0	65.6	63.2	66.3	66.0	56.3
Poland	56.4	56.6	76.3	93.5		94.1	97.5	83.1	85.7	77.4	78.1	67.9	65.7	65.5	66.4	65.4	54.2
Italy	54.3	49.9	71.8	84.4	77.8		108.9	89.0	100.2	82.0	81.3	73.7	69.2	71.5	72.5	71.5	60.7
Spain	53.2	46.1	70.7	84.0	76.6	94.0		91.6	102.8	84.6	81.0	74.0	72.9	70.8	73.6	74.0	62.0
U.K.	42.4	38.5	62.7	68.7	66.3	79.5	71.5		114.8	103.3	100.1	92.4	86.8	88.0	88.0	88.7	73.5
Japan	37.6	33.5	57.6	64.8	65.1	80.2	75.1	90.8		106.0	99.9	89.2	85.7	86.6	86.8	86.5	75.5
Austria	41.3	36.8	54.4	64.1	60.9	75.0	72.7	86.1	81.7		108.2	95.3	92.1	90.6	92.9	91.8	76.5
Netherlands	37.2	31.4	54.7	57.5	56.5	73.3	65.3	86.8	79.6	91.3		93.4	91.1	90.7	90.4	90.8	77.5
Belgium	35.5	31.7	51.3	54.9	54.2	69.0	63.0	81.4	72.6	85.1	90.1		96.8	97.0	98.8	96.5	81.9
France	35.4	30.4	50.0	52.4	49.9	67.5	58.9	79.0	67.4	79.2	87.1	93.7		103.6	100.9	102.7	89.5
Luxembourg	34.8	31.1	49.0	54.3	51.3	67.8	62.3	77.3	71.3	81.1	87.7	96.0	98.8		101.5	101.3	83.2
Denmark	35.5	31.9	49.2	54.2	53.3	66.1	59.8	76.7	71.4	78.9	83.5	90.5	96.0	94.5		105.9	87.4
Germany	31.8	28.5	48.6	52.4	50.8	66.0	58.0	78.3	73.8	79.8	85.1	95.2	98.4	99.2	100.9		88.3
U.S.	27.8	22.1	38.9	42.7	40.2	50.5	47.2	60.8	58.7	64.8	66.0	71.5	73.7	75.9	75.0	74.1	

3, and the ratio of the latter to the former in column 4. In twenty-nine out of the thirty-three comparisons with the United States the augmented binaries are within 5 percent of the traditional ones; the largest deviations are 7 to 8 percent (for Pakistan and Thailand).

Table 7-13 also contains, in column 1, the multilateral estimates of real GDP per capita for comparison with the binary estimates. It might be expected that the augmented results will be the closer than the traditional results to the multilateral ones, since the augmented binaries use some of the prices that are generated for the multilateral comparisons, while the traditional binaries do not. These effects are not evident, however, at least for this set of comparisons; the augmented estimates are closer to the multilateral in about half the cases. Both sets of binaries are highly correlated with the multilateral results,[6] the augmented an insignificant shade more highly:

$$(7.1) \quad M = -0.0057 + 0.945\,AB$$
$$ (0.0166) \quad (0.011)$$
$$\overline{R}^2 = 0.996 \quad \text{SEE} = 0.057$$

$$(7.2) \quad M = -0.0127 + 0.941\,TB$$
$$ (0.0189) \quad (0.012)$$
$$\overline{R}^2 = 0.994 \quad \text{SEE} = 0.065$$

where M is the multilateral quantity index (column 1), AB the augmented binary (column 2), and TB the traditional binary (column 3), with all variables in natural logarithms.

These high correlations, however, conceal very substantial differences between both sets of binaries on

6. There is a difference between the binary and multilateral valuation of the net foreign balance and the net expenditures of residents abroad that will tend to reduce the difference between the multilateral and binary results for countries with negative foreign balance and vice versa. This statement applies equally to traditional and augmented binaries.

Table 7-3. Paasche-Laspeyres Spread for GDP from Augmented Binary Comparisons, 1975

Country	Malawi	Kenya	India	Pakistan	Sri Lanka	Zambia	Thailand	Philippines	Korea	Malaysia	Colombia	Jamaica	Syria	Brazil	Romania	Mexico	Yugoslavia
Malawi																	
Kenya	0.70																
India	0.81	0.77															
Pakistan	0.70	0.66	0.84														
Sri Lanka	0.73	0.73	0.90	0.79													
Zambia	0.67	0.74	0.88	0.66	0.66												
Thailand	0.59	0.61	0.71	0.54	0.58	0.63											
Philippines	0.49	0.51	0.69	0.51	0.69	0.57	0.72										
Korea	0.39	0.57	0.57	0.41	0.51	0.55	0.62	0.63									
Malaysia	0.61	0.64	0.73	0.50	0.80	0.72	0.68	0.72	0.59								
Colombia	0.54	0.57	0.70	0.58	0.70	0.68	0.74	0.72	0.55	0.71							
Jamaica	0.59	0.69	0.82	0.76	0.70	0.70	0.74	0.81	0.61	0.81	0.86						
Syria	0.54	0.49	0.63	0.73	0.59	0.50	0.50	0.53	0.59	0.56	0.56	0.69					
Brazil	0.58	0.66	0.73	0.62	0.65	0.72	0.68	0.67	0.65	0.81	0.70	0.85	0.55				
Romania	0.52	0.49	0.59	0.58	0.68	0.48	0.48	0.61	0.46	0.68	0.58	0.63	0.60	0.58			
Mexico	0.60	0.67	0.74	0.55	0.70	0.68	0.60	0.69	0.65	0.84	0.72	0.85	0.61	0.74	0.65		
Yugoslavia	0.60	0.66	0.67	0.63	0.71	0.66	0.52	0.70	0.53	0.73	0.67	0.88	0.71	0.75	0.78	0.78	
Iran	0.53	0.64	0.67	0.62	0.74	0.65	0.53	0.58	0.56	0.70	0.63	0.82	0.71	0.67	0.66	0.81	0.69
Uruguay	0.47	0.44	0.60	0.62	0.68	0.51	0.53	0.69	0.45	0.51	0.65	0.60	0.49	0.62	0.72	0.55	0.70
Ireland	0.52	0.47	0.62	0.65	0.60	0.57	0.56	0.58	0.59	0.69	0.68	0.77	0.65	0.76	0.70	0.65	0.88
Hungary	0.58	0.51	0.65	0.60	0.66	0.66	0.54	0.64	0.60	0.73	0.73	0.86	0.73	0.76	0.75	0.73	0.92
Poland	0.57	0.57	0.79	0.61	0.72	0.65	0.61	0.70	0.62	0.76	0.72	0.75	0.68	0.73	0.83	0.76	0.87
Italy	0.53	0.48	0.63	0.60	0.62	0.55	0.58	0.65	0.67	0.77	0.71	0.73	0.65	0.76	0.80	0.72	0.90
Spain	0.53	0.49	0.65	0.59	0.63	0.53	0.61	0.67	0.56	0.72	0.65	0.76	0.68	0.74	0.77	0.73	0.88
U.K.	0.50	0.44	0.61	0.65	0.60	0.56	0.56	0.65	0.62	0.69	0.64	0.72	0.60	0.74	0.72	0.66	0.88
Japan	0.46	0.39	0.52	0.40	0.43	0.50	0.53	0.52	0.62	0.72	0.48	0.65	0.47	0.60	0.58	0.59	0.72
Austria	0.52	0.47	0.58	0.55	0.53	0.51	0.58	0.70	0.52	0.75	0.60	0.74	0.61	0.70	0.79	0.68	0.88
Netherlands	0.42	0.41	0.44	0.47	0.48	0.47	0.52	0.53	0.57	0.69	0.56	0.65	0.57	0.64	0.69	0.65	0.80
Belgium	0.47	0.42	0.51	0.53	0.52	0.49	0.54	0.56	0.62	0.70	0.61	0.64	0.58	0.70	0.74	0.66	0.84
France	0.45	0.44	0.52	0.54	0.56	0.50	0.58	0.59	0.64	0.75	0.60	0.66	0.58	0.72	0.74	0.65	0.82
Luxembourg	0.45	0.42	0.53	0.52	0.51	0.49	0.54	0.56	0.62	0.72	0.64	0.67	0.57	0.70	0.73	0.70	0.85
Denmark	0.43	0.38	0.53	0.53	0.54	0.51	0.51	0.58	0.55	0.74	0.61	0.62	0.57	0.67	0.79	0.69	0.84
Germany	0.45	0.40	0.47	0.48	0.50	0.51	0.52	0.57	0.56	0.71	0.56	0.63	0.53	0.65	0.72	0.64	0.82
U.S.	0.37	0.36	0.46	0.49	0.42	0.47	0.51	0.57	0.52	0.67	0.52	0.63	0.55	0.63	0.72	0.71	0.80

Note: The Paasche-Laspeyres spread is the ratio of own-price weighted quantity index to quantity index weighted by base country prices.

the one hand and the multilaterals on the other. As was noted in Chapter 2, the difference is systematic, with the multilateral method tending to yield a higher quantity index relative to the binary method the lower the income of the country. As column 5 shows, per capita quantity indexes are often 10 to 20 percent higher for low-income countries on a multilateral than on a binary basis.

This systematic difference can be explained by relative price structures. The multilateral weighting scheme is based on the world economy as a whole; the larger transactions of the rich countries produce a set of international prices that are closer to the price structure of the high-income countries than to that of the low-income countries. In each Fisher index relative to the United States, however, the price structure of a given low-income country in effect gets half the weight (and the United States the other half). The "own-weight effect" (described in Chapter 3 under the section "Four Sets of Methods") thus accounts for the lower esti-

mates for low-income countries produced by the binary results.

The view taken here is that the multilaterals offer the most useful general-purpose indexes. They are, as was argued in Chapter 3, based on a conception of the world economy that is relevant for international comparisons and on procedures that make the influence of each country on the results proportionate to the country's role in the world economy. The difference between binary and multilateral results sometimes is very large and seems to cast doubt on both. However, most general uses of international comparisons could hardly be met through the binary indexes in Table 7-13 or even through those in Table 7-1. How, for example, could those indexes be relevant for a national or international agency wishing to take per capita income into account in distributing aid among the low-income countries in Table 7-13? Malawi, the agency would learn from the Malawi column of Table 7-1, had a per capita income 74.1 percent of Kenya

Table 7-3 *(continued)*

Country	Iran	Uruguay	Ireland	Hungary	Poland	Italy	Spain	U.K.	Japan	Austria	Netherlands	Belgium	France	Luxembourg	Denmark	Germany	U.S.
Uruguay	0.57																
Ireland	0.71	0.57															
Hungary	0.72	0.71	0.87														
Poland	0.67	0.69	0.80	0.87													
Italy	0.75	0.62	0.85	0.90	0.83												
Spain	0.70	0.56	0.80	0.84	0.79	0.86											
U.K.	0.67	0.56	0.93	0.85	0.80	0.89	0.78										
Japan	0.57	0.37	0.72	0.72	0.76	0.80	0.73	0.79									
Austria	0.68	0.58	0.79	0.81	0.79	0.91	0.86	0.83	0.77								
Netherlands	0.67	0.46	0.85	0.78	0.72	0.90	0.81	0.87	0.80	0.84							
Belgium	0.66	0.51	0.87	0.82	0.80	0.94	0.85	0.88	0.81	0.89	0.96						
France	0.71	0.55	0.88	0.80	0.76	0.98	0.81	0.91	0.79	0.86	0.96	0.97					
Luxembourg	0.67	0.52	0.88	0.86	0.78	0.95	0.88	0.88	0.82	0.90	0.97	0.99	0.95				
Denmark	0.71	0.53	0.83	0.82	0.80	0.91	0.81	0.87	0.82	0.85	0.92	0.92	0.95	0.93			
Germany	0.61	0.48	0.84	0.79	0.78	0.92	0.78	0.88	0.85	0.87	0.94	0.99	0.96	0.98	0.95		
U.S.	0.70	0.44	0.80	0.76	0.74	0.83	0.76	0.83	0.78	0.85	0.85	0.87	0.82	0.91	0.86	0.84	

and 44.2 percent of Zambia, but these two indexes would not be comparable one to the other. The Malawi/Kenya Fisher index would reflect Malawi and Kenya price weights, while the Malawi/Zambia index would be based on the prices of Malawi and Zambia. Only the multilateral indexes apply a single set of prices to the quantities in each country's GDP.

mented upon, but a more extensive investigation of its implication, first alluded to in Chapter 4, is reserved for Chapter 9, where applications of ICP results are presented.

Summary

Augmented price tableaux are used to obtain binary comparisons for all 561 possible pairs of the Phase III countries. Where these augmented binaries for GDP can be compared with corresponding traditional ones, a close correspondence is found. Tables displaying quantity and price comparisons and also Paasche-Laspeyres spreads are given for consumption, capital formation, government, and all of GDP. The observed pattern of the Paasche-Laspeyres spreads is com-

Table 7-4. Augmented Binary Comparisons for Consumption, All Pairs of Countries; Price and Quantity Indexes, 1975

Country	Malawi	Kenya	India	Pakistan	Sri Lanka	Zambia	Thailand	Philippines	Korea	Malaysia	Colombia	Jamaica	Syria	Brazil	Romania	Mexico	Yugoslavia
Malawi		78.5	133.8	121.3	125.5	62.2	106.2	91.8	92.1	86.0	109.7	53.1	117.5	70.9	68.7	83.0	81.7
Kenya	76.1		171.5	147.1	166.5	81.1	131.0	131.4	132.0	109.4	158.1	73.5	140.6	92.4	90.3	105.0	117.4
India	78.7	102.8		93.6	93.6	42.1	77.7	69.9	71.5	61.4	87.3	39.8	82.8	53.1	47.2	56.0	56.7
Pakistan	59.2	81.8	72.9		108.7	47.6	75.9	72.9	79.5	68.7	92.3	44.9	93.3	57.1	57.1	59.9	69.4
Sri Lanka	55.2	69.7	70.2	88.7		42.8	83.7	79.0	78.8	63.6	96.9	39.6	86.3	56.0	46.1	54.5	57.3
Zambia	59.8	76.7	83.8	108.7	125.3		176.9	161.5	173.4	136.4	179.0	95.2	178.5	113.2	116.8	120.9	138.7
Thailand	40.8	55.4	53.0	79.5	74.9	66.0		105.8	83.0	80.4	114.7	54.6	114.9	69.4	59.1	74.8	70.3
Philippines	46.2	54.0	57.6	80.9	77.5	70.6	92.3		92.1	75.6	110.2	46.6	117.4	63.4	59.8	69.6	74.2
Korea	28.8	33.6	35.1	46.3	48.6	41.0	73.6	67.8		83.0	126.0	55.9	109.1	75.2	58.7	81.4	76.6
Malaysia	25.6	33.7	34.0	44.6	50.0	43.4	63.1	68.7	100.1		151.5	66.0	135.1	85.9	76.1	91.7	94.7
Colombia	22.6	26.3	27.0	37.4	37.0	37.3	49.8	53.1	74.3	74.4		47.1	91.1	57.6	55.5	63.2	67.8
Jamaica	20.6	24.9	26.0	33.8	39.8	30.9	46.1	55.3	73.9	75.2	93.6		212.4	121.8	112.0	142.8	144.2
Syria	19.5	27.3	26.3	34.2	38.4	34.6	46.1	46.2	79.5	77.2	101.6	99.0		63.1	59.6	77.4	72.0
Brazil	19.0	24.4	24.1	32.8	34.7	32.0	44.7	50.1	67.6	71.2	94.3	101.1	92.9		95.4	110.5	114.6
Romania	16.9	21.6	23.4	28.4	36.4	26.8	45.4	45.9	74.9	69.5	84.6	95.1	85.0	90.7		115.7	125.0
Mexico	12.3	16.2	17.2	23.6	26.9	22.6	31.4	34.5	47.2	50.4	64.9	65.3	57.3	68.4	75.6		106.1
Yugoslavia	13.7	15.9	18.7	22.4	28.1	21.7	36.6	35.5	55.1	53.6	66.4	70.9	67.6	72.5	76.8	103.5	
Iran	17.9	21.1	24.6	32.6	39.5	30.6	43.3	49.4	69.1	75.0	85.1	89.0	90.1	93.6	111.6	137.1	137.6
Uruguay	11.6	15.2	13.7	19.2	22.0	18.5	24.7	26.8	39.0	40.6	54.6	62.5	53.6	61.2	64.2	87.1	81.7
Ireland	9.7	13.0	13.6	16.0	19.5	16.1	25.4	25.0	41.2	38.5	50.4	57.1	48.1	51.9	58.7	73.7	74.5
Hungary	10.1	12.8	13.4	16.4	21.4	15.2	28.8	27.6	41.8	41.2	49.8	56.4	48.4	52.7	56.4	78.8	72.8
Poland	11.2	13.1	14.3	16.7	21.7	16.5	27.7	27.8	43.6	42.6	52.7	58.7	55.9	56.9	63.1	86.8	82.5
Italy	7.7	11.3	10.5	14.2	17.3	13.5	21.1	23.6	31.4	33.5	41.1	47.3	37.0	43.8	48.4	65.0	63.0
Spain	6.8	9.8	9.2	12.8	14.5	12.1	17.8	19.4	27.5	28.6	36.2	40.1	35.6	39.8	43.4	62.7	56.4
U.K.	6.4	9.3	9.4	10.8	13.8	11.0	16.8	18.8	27.9	27.2	35.2	39.9	31.6	35.7	40.9	52.9	51.9
Japan	8.3	10.9	11.4	14.2	17.2	14.8	19.9	23.6	32.9	33.8	44.1	46.8	37.0	46.2	47.4	63.9	61.8
Austria	6.0	8.3	8.4	11.1	13.2	10.1	16.6	17.6	26.0	25.7	33.7	36.1	30.8	33.4	37.5	52.5	49.7
Netherlands	6.1	9.6	9.1	10.5	13.3	10.9	16.4	18.8	25.5	26.9	33.6	38.4	30.6	34.5	39.2	53.9	50.1
Belgium	5.5	8.8	8.1	9.6	11.9	9.9	15.1	16.4	23.7	24.0	29.9	35.0	26.9	31.7	34.4	49.9	44.0
France	5.4	8.2	7.5	9.6	11.9	9.3	14.1	16.4	23.1	23.4	29.5	34.3	25.8	30.2	35.1	47.2	44.8
Luxembourg	5.6	8.6	8.2	9.7	12.0	9.9	15.1	16.6	23.3	24.1	29.5	34.0	27.6	31.6	34.6	48.6	43.8
Denmark	6.0	8.7	8.7	9.6	13.4	10.4	15.9	17.8	25.1	25.3	31.8	36.2	29.4	32.1	37.1	50.8	46.2
Germany	5.6	8.7	8.4	9.7	12.5	10.0	15.3	17.0	23.9	24.5	30.0	35.4	27.1	31.3	35.3	49.4	45.6
U.S.	4.5	6.7	6.2	7.3	9.0	7.9	11.2	12.7	17.6	18.3	21.8	26.7	22.0	23.1	27.6	38.5	35.3

Note: Upper right triangle: Fisher price indexes of row country with column country = 100. Lower left triangle: Fisher quantity indexes of column country with row country = 100.

Table 7-4 (continued)

Country	Iran	Uruguay	Ireland	Hungary	Poland	Italy	Spain	U.K.	Japan	Austria	Netherlands	Belgium	France	Luxembourg	Denmark	Germany	U.S.
Malawi	85.5	90.8	58.4	84.5	66.3	60.2	75.1	61.2	48.0	57.7	47.4	48.4	49.1	48.7	37.3	44.7	47.2
Kenya	121.2	115.6	73.2	111.8	95.0	68.8	87.1	70.4	61.1	69.0	50.2	50.4	53.4	52.5	43.5	48.5	53.3
India	59.0	72.9	39.5	60.3	49.4	41.7	52.5	39.6	33.2	39.0	30.0	31.2	33.1	31.2	24.6	28.4	32.7
Pakistan	65.2	76.0	49.2	72.1	61.9	45.6	55.6	50.3	38.8	43.3	37.8	38.7	38.0	39.0	32.6	36.0	40.8
Sri Lanka	55.9	69.0	42.0	57.4	49.5	38.7	50.7	40.9	33.3	37.6	31.1	32.2	31.9	32.7	24.3	29.0	34.1
Zambia	134.3	152.8	94.8	151.0	121.0	92.4	113.0	95.7	72.4	91.2	70.6	72.0	75.8	73.2	58.4	67.1	72.7
Thailand	81.4	98.0	51.4	68.2	61.8	50.6	66.1	53.7	45.9	47.6	40.2	40.6	42.8	41.3	32.5	37.8	43.7
Philippines	73.1	92.6	53.6	72.9	63.1	46.4	62.2	48.9	39.7	46.2	35.9	38.3	37.7	38.4	29.8	34.7	39.6
Korea	83.5	101.6	52.0	77.0	64.4	55.8	70.1	52.9	45.6	49.9	42.4	42.3	43.0	44.0	33.9	39.6	45.8
Malaysia	92.6	117.4	67.0	93.9	79.3	62.8	80.9	65.3	53.4	60.8	48.3	50.5	51.1	51.0	40.3	46.4	52.8
Colombia	72.5	77.6	45.4	69.0	56.9	45.4	56.8	44.8	36.3	41.2	34.4	35.9	36.0	37.0	28.5	33.6	39.4
Jamaica	157.3	153.9	91.0	138.4	116.1	89.6	116.5	89.7	77.8	87.2	68.3	69.7	70.2	72.9	56.9	64.7	72.9
Syria	73.9	85.4	51.3	76.7	57.9	54.5	62.5	53.7	46.7	48.5	40.7	43.1	44.3	42.6	33.3	40.2	42.3
Brazil	121.4	127.6	81.2	120.1	97.0	78.6	95.2	81.3	63.9	76.4	61.7	62.5	64.7	63.6	52.0	59.5	68.5
Romania	117.7	140.6	83.0	129.8	101.3	82.3	100.9	82.0	71.9	78.9	62.8	66.5	64.4	67.2	52.1	61.0	66.4
Mexico	109.6	118.6	75.7	106.4	84.2	70.1	80.0	72.5	61.1	64.3	52.3	52.4	54.7	54.8	43.5	49.9	54.4
Yugoslavia	99.5	115.1	68.1	104.9	80.7	65.9	81.0	67.3	57.5	62.0	51.2	54.2	52.5	55.4	43.6	49.1	54.1
Iran		116.4	70.2	102.6	82.6	67.4	81.3	68.4	60.5	63.2	51.8	53.0	52.4	54.0	43.3	49.9	57.0
Uruguay	59.1		61.3	92.2	71.9	59.9	74.1	62.6	46.6	58.6	48.5	49.7	49.6	51.4	39.9	46.2	55.6
Ireland	52.8	88.0		152.3	121.0	97.3	114.8	98.3	83.7	91.7	73.3	76.7	75.4	79.7	63.0	71.0	81.7
Hungary	54.3	88.0	98.7		78.7	65.4	78.0	68.1	57.0	60.7	50.7	53.1	52.1	55.4	43.7	49.2	54.4
Poland	58.9	98.4	108.3	110.9		86.7	103.4	85.8	70.3	79.1	64.6	68.0	68.8	71.1	55.2	62.8	70.8
Italy	45.0	73.7	83.9	83.1	71.9		121.6	100.6	83.9	94.8	75.2	78.8	78.7	80.3	65.3	73.2	83.1
Spain	41.0	65.5	78.3	76.7	66.3	90.5		86.0	68.7	78.7	66.1	67.3	67.5	68.9	56.0	62.1	70.7
U.K.	37.3	59.4	70.1	67.2	61.2	83.7	89.0		86.4	92.1	73.9	75.9	75.6	79.5	65.4	70.9	81.9
Japan	43.0	81.1	83.6	81.7	75.9	102.1	113.4	117.8		108.4	86.2	90.8	91.9	91.9	72.8	81.8	91.0
Austria	35.6	55.8	66.1	66.4	58.4	78.2	85.6	95.6	79.8		79.4	83.9	83.5	86.2	69.5	77.7	88.1
Netherlands	36.2	56.2	68.9	66.4	59.6	82.2	85.0	99.3	83.7	104.9		104.2	103.6	105.9	88.0	97.2	112.1
Belgium	32.9	51.0	61.2	58.9	52.6	72.9	77.5	89.8	73.9	92.3	89.2		100.9	102.9	84.0	93.9	108.2
France	32.8	50.4	61.4	59.1	51.4	72.0	76.3	89.0	71.9	91.6	88.5	97.8		101.8	84.7	93.4	107.0
Luxembourg	32.8	50.2	59.9	57.4	51.2	72.7	77.0	87.3	74.2	91.3	89.2	98.9	101.3		81.4	90.1	104.2
Denmark	34.0	53.7	63.0	60.3	54.7	74.3	78.7	88.1	77.7	94.1	89.2	100.5	101.0	102.0		108.8	128.6
Germany	32.8	51.6	62.2	59.8	53.7	73.8	79.1	90.4	77.1	93.8	89.9	100.2	102.0	102.7	102.3		114.7
U.S.	24.4	36.5	46.0	45.9	40.4	55.3	59.1	66.6	58.9	70.4	66.3	74.0	75.8	75.5	73.7	74.1	

Table 7-5. Augmented Binary Quantity Comparisons for Consumption, 1975

Country	Malawi	Kenya	India	Pakistan	Sri Lanka	Zambia	Thailand	Philippines	Korea	Malaysia	Colombia	Jamaica	Syria	Brazil	Romania	Mexico	Yugoslavia
Malawi		90.0	92.7	70.6	65.4	75.0	56.2	67.8	43.7	32.9	32.1	27.1	26.5	25.2	23.8	15.7	17.8
Kenya	64.4		122.2	100.4	82.4	89.8	75.2	83.1	46.9	43.1	36.6	30.4	40.4	29.2	34.1	20.3	20.7
India	66.9	86.5		79.5	75.0	97.0	64.7	70.9	43.5	39.7	32.9	30.4	34.0	26.6	30.6	19.9	23.4
Pakistan	49.7	66.7	66.9		95.9	129.0	104.1	114.0	54.9	53.8	47.7	38.8	38.8	37.4	35.5	29.0	27.0
Sri Lanka	46.6	58.9	65.7	82.0		164.2	100.9	93.3	63.0	55.7	44.5	46.6	45.8	40.9	43.7	31.4	32.8
Zambia	47.7	65.6	72.4	91.6	95.6		93.8	104.1	56.5	55.2	49.8	36.8	46.4	37.4	34.7	27.8	26.0
Thailand	29.7	40.9	43.4	60.7	55.5	46.4		111.2	97.3	78.4	59.2	56.1	69.8	55.3	70.2	42.9	57.1
Philippines	31.4	35.1	46.8	57.4	64.3	47.9	76.7		87.7	75.2	62.8	63.7	63.1	59.0	58.5	41.4	44.7
Korea	18.9	24.1	28.4	39.1	37.4	29.8	55.6	52.4		131.8	95.2	94.6	108.6	85.3	114.2	57.8	72.1
Malaysia	19.9	26.3	29.1	36.9	44.8	34.1	50.9	62.8	76.0		90.0	83.2	94.4	79.6	84.1	56.5	63.5
Colombia	15.9	18.8	22.0	29.3	30.7	27.9	42.0	44.9	58.0	61.4		103.5	134.6	105.7	108.8	77.6	80.2
Jamaica	15.6	20.3	22.3	29.5	34.1	25.9	37.9	48.0	57.6	67.9	84.6		128.2	112.0	123.5	71.1	78.9
Syria	14.4	18.5	20.4	30.2	32.2	25.8	30.4	33.8	58.2	63.1	76.7	76.4		124.7	108.3	70.1	81.8
Brazil	14.3	20.4	21.7	29.5	29.5	27.3	36.2	42.6	53.6	63.8	84.0	91.3	69.3		114.0	76.7	85.5
Romania	12.0	13.7	17.9	22.7	30.4	20.7	29.3	36.1	49.0	57.4	65.8	73.4	66.7	72.1		96.5	85.0
Mexico	9.6	13.0	14.9	19.2	23.1	18.4	22.9	28.8	38.6	44.9	54.3	59.9	46.8	61.1	59.2		118.5
Yugoslavia	10.5	12.2	14.9	18.5	24.1	18.0	23.5	28.2	42.1	45.2	55.1	63.7	55.9	61.3	69.3	90.3	
Iran	13.0	16.4	20.6	28.1	34.6	25.2	28.8	37.9	54.4	64.2	69.7	75.5	81.4	78.5	91.9	125.4	115.7
Uruguay	7.7	9.5	10.2	14.8	18.3	13.0	17.6	21.4	28.3	31.3	43.6	48.2	38.4	51.9	54.6	66.1	69.0
Ireland	7.2	8.6	10.9	14.7	15.7	13.0	17.9	18.8	30.3	32.7	41.0	49.6	37.0	45.8	50.4	58.6	68.6
Hungary	7.5	8.4	10.3	13.1	17.2	12.4	18.9	21.5	32.0	34.3	41.0	49.9	39.9	44.2	50.4	63.7	70.2
Poland	8.0	9.3	12.7	13.4	18.5	13.7	19.9	23.1	34.8	36.0	43.9	48.5	44.7	46.9	57.5	72.8	76.6
Italy	5.6	7.4	8.3	12.0	14.1	10.3	15.2	18.7	24.6	29.0	33.9	38.7	28.8	37.5	43.6	53.4	58.8
Spain	5.3	6.9	7.9	10.9	12.8	9.5	13.6	16.4	21.8	25.7	30.8	34.7	30.2	35.0	38.7	54.9	53.7
U.K.	4.5	5.8	7.3	9.5	10.8	8.4	11.8	14.7	21.0	23.4	27.9	32.9	23.6	30.1	35.3	42.7	48.3
Japan	5.8	6.8	9.2	11.3	13.2	10.3	14.3	18.5	26.6	30.2	31.3	36.5	25.8	34.5	37.7	50.3	52.5
Austria	4.4	5.4	6.4	9.1	10.5	7.6	12.2	14.8	19.3	23.0	27.0	30.4	23.7	28.4	33.1	42.6	46.1
Netherlands	4.1	6.0	6.4	8.5	10.0	8.1	11.9	14.6	19.2	23.3	26.1	30.4	23.3	27.9	33.2	44.1	45.2
Belgium	3.9	5.4	5.9	7.9	9.1	7.5	10.7	12.4	18.1	20.4	23.1	27.1	20.1	26.2	29.4	39.8	40.1
France	3.6	5.2	5.5	7.7	9.5	6.9	10.4	13.1	17.8	20.5	23.0	27.1	18.7	25.2	30.5	37.4	40.6
Luxembourg	3.7	5.2	5.9	7.6	8.6	7.4	10.3	12.2	17.2	20.0	22.6	27.1	19.9	25.8	29.5	39.1	40.2
Denmark	3.9	4.8	6.0	7.2	9.8	7.5	10.4	13.3	17.0	20.9	23.7	27.2	20.9	24.9	32.8	40.8	41.5
Germany	3.9	5.3	6.0	7.7	9.3	7.5	10.5	13.4	17.6	21.0	22.4	27.6	19.7	25.0	30.1	39.1	41.4
U.S.	2.7	3.8	4.1	5.7	6.0	5.4	7.8	9.6	12.4	14.7	16.1	20.2	16.4	18.4	21.9	32.5	30.0

Note: Upper right triangle: Laspeyres-type indexes of row country with column country as the base, with column country prices as weights. Lower left triangle: Paasche-type indexes of column country with row country as the base, with column country prices as weights.

Table 7-5 *(continued)*

Country	Iran	Uruguay	Ireland	Hungary	Poland	Italy	Spain	U.K.	Japan	Austria	Netherlands	Belgium	France	Luxembourg	Denmark	Germany	U.S.
Malawi	24.5	17.5	13.1	13.7	15.7	10.6	8.7	9.1	11.9	8.1	8.8	7.7	7.9	8.3	9.4	8.0	7.5
Kenya	27.2	24.5	19.7	19.4	18.6	17.3	14.0	15.0	17.4	12.9	15.2	14.3	13.1	14.3	15.5	14.1	11.9
India	29.3	18.4	17.0	17.6	16.1	13.4	10.7	12.1	14.0	10.9	12.9	11.1	10.3	11.6	12.6	11.7	9.3
Pakistan	37.8	24.9	17.5	20.6	21.0	16.7	14.9	12.3	18.0	13.5	13.0	11.6	11.9	12.2	12.7	12.2	9.2
Sri Lanka	45.0	26.5	24.2	26.7	25.4	21.3	16.5	17.6	22.6	16.7	17.6	15.8	14.9	16.6	18.2	16.7	13.5
Zambia	37.3	26.3	19.9	18.5	19.9	17.7	15.5	14.3	21.1	13.5	14.7	13.2	12.6	13.3	14.2	13.5	11.5
Thailand	65.1	34.6	36.1	43.8	38.6	29.3	23.3	23.7	27.7	22.6	22.7	21.3	19.2	22.1	24.4	22.1	16.2
Philippines	64.3	33.4	33.3	35.3	33.5	29.8	22.8	24.1	30.2	20.8	24.3	21.7	20.6	22.7	23.8	21.6	16.9
Korea	87.8	53.8	55.9	54.6	54.6	40.0	34.6	37.0	40.7	35.1	33.9	31.1	30.0	31.5	37.0	32.4	24.9
Malaysia	87.6	52.8	45.3	49.6	50.5	38.8	31.9	31.5	37.8	28.6	31.2	28.2	26.7	29.1	30.7	28.6	22.7
Colombia	104.0	68.4	62.0	60.4	63.3	49.9	42.6	44.3	62.2	42.1	43.3	38.8	37.6	38.6	42.6	40.2	29.6
Jamaica	104.9	81.0	65.7	63.6	70.9	57.9	46.3	48.3	59.9	42.8	48.5	45.1	43.3	42.7	48.2	45.5	35.5
Syria	99.8	74.7	62.5	58.7	70.0	47.6	41.8	42.4	53.2	40.1	40.3	36.0	35.6	38.4	41.2	37.3	29.4
Brazil	111.6	72.2	58.8	62.8	69.2	51.2	45.3	42.3	61.9	39.3	42.7	38.3	36.1	38.7	41.5	39.0	29.1
Romania	135.6	75.5	68.5	63.1	69.3	53.8	48.7	47.4	59.8	42.4	46.3	40.3	40.3	40.6	41.9	41.4	34.7
Mexico	149.8	114.8	92.6	97.4	103.5	79.1	71.5	65.6	81.3	64.8	65.9	62.7	59.6	60.2	63.1	62.2	45.7
Yugoslavia	163.6	96.7	80.9	75.5	88.8	67.5	59.2	55.9	72.9	53.5	55.6	48.3	49.4	47.7	51.4	50.3	41.4
Iran		73.5	65.7	64.6	72.1	54.4	48.4	45.4	53.2	43.3	44.4	41.7	40.3	42.6	43.1	42.3	31.1
Uruguay	47.5		109.6	103.8	118.1	89.7	80.1	77.6	118.6	69.8	74.0	66.9	63.3	66.2	71.2	69.0	53.3
Ireland	42.5	70.7		107.9	121.4	92.5	85.8	71.9	99.9	72.6	75.1	65.3	65.2	63.7	69.5	67.4	51.9
Hungary	45.7	74.7	90.2		118.5	91.5	83.5	74.7	97.8	74.1	75.8	66.2	67.8	63.3	70.8	68.8	56.0
Poland	48.1	82.0	96.7	103.7		82.0	75.3	69.8	88.9	69.3	69.6	61.0	60.2		65.4	63.1	50.6
Italy	37.2	60.6	76.2	75.5	63.0		97.0	88.5	115.9	80.5	86.3	75.6	73.2	75.4	79.6	76.4	62.1
Spain	34.8	53.6	71.6	70.4	58.4	84.5		99.1	129.3	91.1	92.8	85.2	85.8	83.8	87.9	88.3	67.7
U.K.	30.7	45.5	68.3	60.6	53.6	79.2	79.9		133.8	103.3	104.1	94.3	91.3	90.6	95.1	94.8	73.0
Japan	34.7	55.4	70.0	68.3	64.8	89.9	99.4	103.8		92.2	95.0	84.8	83.8	84.7	88.3	86.4	68.6
Austria	29.2	44.6	60.2	59.6	49.3	76.1	80.5	88.5	69.2		110.0	97.3	97.4	94.2	100.8	98.2	78.9
Netherlands	29.5	42.7	63.3	58.0	51.1	78.3	77.8	94.8	73.7	100.1		90.3	91.1	90.1	92.8	91.7	72.1
Belgium	25.9	38.8	57.3	52.3	45.4	70.3	70.5	85.7	64.2	87.7	88.0		99.8	99.7	105.9	100.8	81.2
France	26.7	40.2	57.8	51.5	43.2	70.9	67.8	86.8	61.8	86.1	86.0	95.9		104.1	104.9	104.6	85.4
Luxembourg	25.3	38.0	56.3	52.0	43.6	70.2	70.8	84.0	65.1	88.7	88.3	98.1	98.6		105.6	103.3	81.2
Denmark	26.8	40.5	57.0	51.4	45.8	69.4	70.5	81.6	68.4	87.8	85.8	95.2	97.3	98.6		105.2	80.8
Germany	25.5	38.6	57.4	51.9	45.6	71.3	71.0	86.3	68.7	89.5	88.2	99.5	99.7	102.0	99.5		81.8
U.S.	19.2	25.0	40.8	37.7	32.3	49.2	51.6	60.7	50.6	62.8	61.0	67.4	67.2	70.2	67.2	67.2	

Table 7-6. Paasche-Laspeyres Spread for Consumption from Augmented Binary Comparisons, 1975

Country	Malawi	Kenya	India	Pakistan	Sri Lanka	Zambia	Thailand	Philippines	Korea	Malaysia	Colombia	Jamaica	Syria	Brazil	Romania	Mexico	Yugoslavia
Malawi																	
Kenya	0.72																
India	0.72	0.71															
Pakistan	0.70	0.66	0.84														
Sri Lanka	0.71	0.71	0.88	0.85													
Zambia	0.64	0.73	0.75	0.71	0.58												
Thailand	0.53	0.54	0.67	0.58	0.55	0.49											
Philippines	0.46	0.42	0.66	0.50	0.69	0.46	0.69										
Korea	0.43	0.51	0.65	0.71	0.59	0.53	0.57	0.60									
Malaysia	0.60	0.61	0.73	0.69	0.80	0.62	0.65	0.84	0.58								
Colombia	0.50	0.51	0.67	0.61	0.69	0.56	0.71	0.71	0.61	0.68							
Jamaica	0.58	0.67	0.74	0.76	0.73	0.70	0.68	0.75	0.61	0.82	0.82						
Syria	0.54	0.46	0.60	0.78	0.70	0.56	0.44	0.54	0.54	0.67	0.57	0.60					
Brazil	0.57	0.70	0.82	0.77	0.72	0.73	0.65	0.72	0.63	0.80	0.79	0.82	0.56				
Romania	0.51	0.40	0.58	0.64	0.70	0.60	0.42	0.62	0.43	0.68	0.60	0.59	0.62	0.63			
Mexico	0.61	0.64	0.75	0.66	0.74	0.66	0.53	0.70	0.67	0.80	0.70	0.84	0.67	0.80	0.61		
Yugoslavia	0.59	0.59	0.64	0.69	0.74	0.69	0.41	0.63	0.58	0.71	0.69	0.81	0.68	0.72	0.81	0.76	
Iran	0.53	0.60	0.70	0.74	0.77	0.68	0.44	0.59	0.62	0.73	0.67	0.72	0.82	0.70	0.68	0.84	0.71
Uruguay	0.44	0.39	0.56	0.59	0.69	0.49	0.51	0.64	0.53	0.59	0.64	0.60	0.51	0.72	0.72	0.58	0.71
Ireland	0.55	0.43	0.64	0.84	0.65	0.65	0.50	0.56	0.54	0.72	0.66	0.75	0.59	0.78	0.74	0.63	0.85
Hungary	0.55	0.43	0.59	0.64	0.64	0.67	0.43	0.61	0.59	0.69	0.68	0.78	0.68	0.70	0.80	0.65	0.93
Poland	0.51	0.50	0.79	0.64	0.73	0.69	0.52	0.69	0.64	0.71	0.69	0.68	0.64	0.68	0.83	0.70	0.86
Italy	0.53	0.43	0.62	0.72	0.66	0.58	0.52	0.63	0.61	0.75	0.68	0.67	0.61	0.73	0.81	0.68	0.87
Spain	0.61	0.49	0.74	0.73	0.78	0.61	0.58	0.72	0.63	0.81	0.72	0.75	0.72	0.77	0.80	0.77	0.91
U.K.	0.49	0.39	0.60	0.77	0.61	0.59	0.50	0.61	0.57	0.74	0.63	0.68	0.56	0.71	0.74	0.65	0.86
Japan	0.49	0.39	0.66	0.63	0.58	0.49	0.52	0.61	0.65	0.80	0.50	0.61	0.48	0.56	0.63	0.62	0.72
Austria	0.54	0.42	0.59	0.67	0.63	0.56	0.54	0.71	0.55	0.80	0.64	0.71	0.59	0.72	0.78	0.66	0.86
Netherlands	0.47	0.40	0.49	0.65	0.57	0.55	0.52	0.60	0.57	0.75	0.60	0.63	0.58	0.65	0.72	0.67	0.81
Belgium	0.51	0.38	0.53	0.68	0.58	0.57	0.50	0.57	0.58	0.72	0.60	0.60	0.56	0.68	0.73	0.63	0.83
France	0.46	0.40	0.53	0.65	0.64	0.55	0.54	0.64	0.59	0.77	0.61	0.63	0.53	0.70	0.76	0.63	0.82
Luxembourg	0.45	0.36	0.51	0.62	0.52	0.56	0.47	0.53	0.54	0.69	0.59	0.63	0.52	0.67	0.73	0.65	0.84
Denmark	0.41	0.31	0.47	0.57	0.54	0.53	0.43	0.56	0.46	0.68	0.56	0.56	0.51	0.60	0.78	0.65	0.81
Germany	0.49	0.38	0.51	0.63	0.56	0.56	0.48	0.62	0.54	0.73	0.56	0.61	0.53	0.64	0.73	0.63	0.82
U.S.	0.36	0.32	0.44	0.62	0.44	0.47	0.48	0.57	0.50	0.65	0.54	0.57	0.56	0.63	0.63	0.71	0.72

Note: The Paasche-Laspeyres spread is the ratio of own-price weighted quantity index to quantity index weighted by base country price.

Table 7-6 *(continued)*

Country	Iran	Uruguay	Ireland	Hungary	Poland	Italy	Spain	U.K.	Japan	Austria	Netherlands	Belgium	France	Luxembourg	Denmark	Germany	U.S.
Uruguay	0.65																
Ireland	0.65	0.65															
Hungary	0.71	0.72	0.84														
Poland	0.67	0.69	0.80	0.88													
Italy	0.68	0.68	0.82	0.83	0.77												
Spain	0.72	0.67	0.83	0.84	0.78	0.87											
U.K.	0.68	0.59	0.95	0.81	0.77	0.09	0.81										
Japan	0.65	0.47	0.70	0.70	0.73	0.78	0.77	0.78									
Austria	0.67	0.64	0.83	0.80	0.71	0.95	0.88	0.86	0.75								
Netherlands	0.66	0.58	0.84	0.77	0.73	0.91	0.84	0.91	0.78	0.91							
Belgium	0.62	0.58	0.88	0.79	0.74	0.93	0.83	0.91	0.76	0.90	0.97						
France	0.66	0.64	0.89	0.76	0.71	0.97	0.79	0.95	0.74	0.88	0.94	0.96					
Luxembourg	0.59	0.57	0.88	0.82	0.72	0.93	0.84	0.93	0.77	0.94	0.98	0.98	0.95				
Denmark	0.62	0.57	0.82	0.73	0.70	0.87	0.80	0.86	0.77	0.87	0.92	0.90	0.93	0.93			
Germany	0.60	0.56	0.85	0.75	0.72	0.93	0.80	0.91	0.80	0.91	0.96	0.99	0.95	0.99	0.95		
U.S.	0.62	0.47	0.79	0.67	0.64	0.79	0.76	0.83	0.74	0.80	0.85	0.83	0.79	0.86	0.83	0.82	

Table 7-7. Augmented Binary Comparisons for Capital Formation, All Pairs of Countries; Price and Quantity Indexes, 1975

Country	Malawi	Kenya	India	Pakistan	Sri Lanka	Zambia	Thailand	Philippines	Korea	Malaysia	Colombia	Jamaica	Syria	Brazil	Romania	Mexico	Yugoslavia
Malawi		70.9	185.9	114.0	207.2	77.0	201.1	74.2	214.1	177.0	192.2	62.8	107.7	138.7	45.7	90.8	64.4
Kenya	75.3		207.8	159.5	230.1	96.6	170.6	112.4	159.4	184.9	175.0	85.1	145.6	154.4	65.8	129.9	87.6
India	31.5	52.7		74.5	108.3	34.8	94.6	58.2	129.8	96.7	100.9	35.9	77.3	82.6	41.2	65.0	47.9
Pakistan	82.6	110.6	216.5		181.3	54.6	129.7	62.0	194.9	168.7	125.9	39.7	85.6	89.0	41.4	88.5	48.5
Sri Lanka	62.3	105.0	203.7	75.6		36.2	95.5	46.9	111.2	81.8	99.7	33.1	61.9	54.7	27.2	57.8	38.0
Zambia	21.6	32.2	81.8	32.3	35.5		229.5	129.3	269.6	244.8	219.0	93.5	129.4	115.0	81.5	155.7	102.8
Thailand	12.3	27.1	44.6	20.2	20.0	64.7		68.4	109.3	106.7	99.9	53.7	72.4	78.4	45.4	73.5	56.4
Philippines	25.6	31.7	55.9	32.6	31.4	88.6	112.9		167.2	154.8	166.1	72.8	147.0	123.1	64.3	110.2	87.0
Korea	6.9	17.3	19.4	8.0	10.2	32.8	54.6	46.2		77.4	100.5	24.9	79.2	78.9	32.5	58.9	35.6
Malaysia	5.3	9.4	16.4	5.9	8.8	22.9	35.3	31.6	81.7		90.9	46.3	55.6	82.6	46.5	75.9	60.4
Colombia	8.7	17.8	28.2	14.0	12.9	45.8	67.6	52.7	112.8	197.2		44.3	67.9	64.4	37.8	64.6	44.2
Jamaica	12.9	17.9	38.6	21.6	19.0	52.2	61.3	58.5	221.2	188.3	109.9		215.0	156.6	77.7	159.1	115.3
Syria	15.8	21.8	37.6	21.0	21.3	78.9	95.1	60.7	145.8	327.9	149.9	97.4		101.9	38.5	83.6	61.3
Brazil	5.1	8.5	14.6	8.4	10.0	36.9	36.4	30.0	60.7	91.7	65.7	55.4	40.7		53.4	90.5	74.3
Romania	5.3	7.0	10.2	6.3	7.0	18.1	21.8	20.0	51.2	56.6	38.8	38.8	37.4	65.0		177.6	113.7
Mexico	6.2	8.1	14.8	6.8	7.5	21.8	31.0	26.9	65.1	79.8	52.3	43.6	39.7	88.4	129.7		74.0
Yugoslavia	5.5	7.6	12.6	7.7	7.2	20.7	25.4	21.4	67.6	63.0	48.0	37.8	34.0	67.6	127.2	84.9	
Iran	4.1	5.9	8.3	5.4	6.5	18.5	17.9	16.7	42.6	53.4	34.4	30.6	28.8	62.1	90.6	65.0	72.8
Uruguay	20.5	28.6	45.9	25.1	26.8	81.1	91.4	74.7	210.1	377.4	161.3	141.0	130.7	285.7	342.5	326.8	331.7
Ireland	6.2	9.1	15.7	9.7	9.4	31.0	31.4	27.0	57.8	106.7	51.5	48.8	34.1	82.0	138.8	115.1	124.0
Hungary	2.8	4.1	7.3	4.0	4.9	12.6	16.4	13.3	42.0	45.1	25.8	23.5	19.0	42.3	78.3	52.2	60.7
Poland	2.7	3.9	6.1	3.6	4.4	11.3	14.6	11.9	33.8	36.1	22.6	21.0	16.3	38.0	63.8	47.2	52.3
Italy	3.4	5.1	8.6	5.0	5.3	16.8	16.8	16.1	32.2	53.8	28.2	27.9	19.4	45.8	86.2	64.0	71.8
Spain	3.9	5.3	8.6	5.2	5.8	16.9	17.2	15.0	41.2	55.1	36.1	26.0	25.1	44.9	78.6	64.8	67.3
U.K.	3.8	5.8	9.1	5.7	6.2	20.2	17.8	16.7	36.1	60.2	30.7	32.8	21.1	50.5	96.1	70.9	81.9
Japan	1.9	2.5	3.7	2.1	2.5	8.5	8.1	7.3	14.6	25.2	14.3	15.5	10.2	22.6	36.3	29.7	35.5
Austria	2.9	4.2	5.8	3.8	3.9	11.9	12.5	11.2	28.6	32.3	22.4	22.4	16.7	36.4	55.3	45.1	50.8
Netherlands	2.1	3.0	4.4	2.9	3.0	10.6	8.9	9.1	17.1	27.5	15.5	17.4	11.6	26.1	49.6	34.9	41.1
Belgium	2.1	3.2	4.7	3.0	3.2	10.1	9.2	8.8	18.6	30.3	15.5	16.8	11.5	25.2	52.3	37.5	42.0
France	1.9	2.8	4.4	2.9	3.0	9.2	8.7	7.8	16.8	28.6	13.7	15.4	11.4	24.1	48.7	33.0	37.4
Luxembourg	2.0	2.9	4.7	2.8	3.1	9.1	8.9	8.3	17.7	29.5	15.3	14.9	10.4	22.8	45.9	35.4	37.1
Denmark	2.2	3.3	5.5	3.5	3.6	10.7	10.4	9.7	20.7	32.4	16.7	18.1	13.6	28.2	54.5	39.8	44.1
Germany	1.8	2.6	3.9	2.4	2.7	9.0	7.9	7.5	14.6	25.3	12.5	15.5	9.4	20.8	44.1	31.6	36.3
U.S.	2.1	2.9	4.5	2.6	3.0	9.3	9.2	8.5	19.8	26.1	16.7	15.7	12.4	28.5	45.2	34.5	39.8

Note: Upper right triangle: Fisher price indexes of row country with column country = 100. Lower left triangle: Fisher quantity indexes of column country with row country = 100.

Table 7-7 *(continued)*

Country	Iran	Uruguay	Ireland	Hungary	Poland	Italy	Spain	U.K.	Japan	Austria	Netherlands	Belgium	France	Luxembourg	Denmark	Germany	U.S.
Malawi	73.1	66.8	68.0	92.5	69.8	77.3	65.6	67.9	60.8	45.0	55.8	56.6	60.1	51.2	54.3	58.0	70.7
Kenya	96.3	89.7	86.8	119.0	90.8	96.4	91.3	82.8	89.7	57.8	71.9	70.4	76.1	64.7	69.3	76.8	93.3
India	62.2	51.1	46.1	60.7	52.8	52.1	51.5	48.6	54.0	38.3	44.7	43.0	44.0	36.4	37.3	46.3	55.4
Pakistan	59.5	57.9	46.1	69.0	55.5	55.8	53.2	48.4	60.3	36.4	42.4	42.7	41.0	38.0	37.1	45.8	59.5
Sri Lanka	36.2	39.6	34.7	40.9	33.6	38.8	34.6	32.1	35.9	25.8	30.4	28.7	29.7	25.4	26.2	30.0	38.1
Zambia	98.4	101.6	82.0	124.3	100.2	94.2	92.2	76.8	83.0	65.5	65.8	71.0	74.1	66.5	67.9	69.9	94.8
Thailand	68.4	60.7	54.6	64.3	52.6	63.8	61.0	58.8	59.0	42.0	52.9	52.6	52.9	46.0	47.2	54.0	64.1
Philippines	94.8	96.3	82.4	102.4	83.3	86.1	90.5	81.2	84.4	60.8	67.3	70.8	76.5	63.7	65.8	73.6	90.0
Korea	48.3	44.4	49.7	42.1	38.1	55.6	42.8	48.5	54.9	30.7	46.1	43.5	45.9	38.7	39.8	48.6	50.0
Malaysia	60.9	39.0	42.7	62.1	56.3	52.7	50.6	46.1	50.2	43.0	45.3	42.3	42.7	36.8	40.1	44.4	60.1
Colombia	52.7	51.0	49.3	60.6	50.2	56.0	43.1	50.4	49.5	34.6	44.8	46.0	49.7	39.6	43.6	50.4	52.5
Jamaica	121.9	119.7	106.9	136.7	111.1	116.3	122.6	96.7	93.7	71.0	82.1	87.1	90.9	83.1	82.6	83.5	114.3
Syria	61.8	61.7	73.1	80.7	68.4	79.8	60.8	72.0	67.9	45.6	58.7	61.2	58.8	56.9	52.6	65.3	69.4
Brazil	69.1	68.0	73.2	87.4	70.6	81.6	81.9	72.5	74.1	50.3	63.2	67.1	66.8	62.7	61.0	71.4	72.6
Romania	136.5	163.7	124.6	136.0	121.2	125.1	134.9	109.7	132.6	95.5	95.6	93.1	95.3	89.8	90.8	97.1	131.9
Mexico	82.6	74.3	65.2	88.6	71.0	73.1	71.0	64.5	70.4	50.8	59.0	56.3	61.0	50.5	53.9	58.8	75.0
Yugoslavia	117.4	116.7	96.4	121.3	102.2	103.7	108.7	89.0	93.9	71.8	79.8	80.1	85.7	76.7	77.5	81.6	103.4
Iran		105.1	89.7	111.2	93.3	90.1	94.2	84.4	87.8	62.7	75.9	73.3	73.3	68.7	68.7	75.7	95.1
Uruguay	431.0		101.3	114.9	87.9	107.4	96.3	93.9	95.6	57.7	81.1	77.0	83.2	71.5	77.4	85.4	89.2
Ireland	156.0	30.5		119.8	106.8	116.3	114.0	90.4	93.5	72.1	84.6	86.9	88.7	86.5	80.8	87.4	104.9
Hungary	77.4	16.5	51.3		85.9	89.0	86.4	78.0	76.1	62.0	71.8	72.0	75.0	66.9	68.5	71.6	86.9
Poland	67.0	15.7	41.8	84.5		102.7	106.0	90.7	96.7	73.9	74.8	78.6	82.6	75.9	78.0	84.2	105.1
Italy	96.7	17.9	53.5	113.8	135.7		99.8	79.4	85.1	69.9	74.9	76.4	78.2	73.8	70.9	77.1	99.1
Spain	90.9	19.6	53.7	115.2	129.4	98.5		81.6	89.1	64.0	71.6	75.2	77.4	71.8	70.5	78.9	95.2
U.K.	100.9	20.0	67.4	126.9	150.3	123.1	121.9		105.2	83.1	92.1	97.4	97.3	97.0	90.2	96.0	117.7
Japan	44.4	9.0	29.8	59.5	64.5	52.5	51.0	43.4		74.9	83.6	90.3	95.1	88.7	90.8	89.1	103.7
Austria	68.2	16.3	42.4	80.0	92.5	70.1	78.0	60.3	146.4		98.6	108.5	114.8	110.1	109.6	112.7	143.4
Netherlands	50.5	10.4	32.4	62.2	82.1	58.8	62.5	48.9	117.8	91.1		106.5	102.9	106.4	97.7	107.4	125.9
Belgium	53.7	11.3	32.4	63.5	80.2	59.1	61.1	47.4	112.0	84.9	96.4		101.4	100.0	95.8	99.8	126.3
France	51.2	9.9	30.2	58.1	72.7	55.1	56.6	45.2	101.2	76.5	95.0	94.0		98.6	94.4	97.5	117.3
Luxembourg	48.5	10.3	27.5	57.9	70.3	51.8	54.2	40.3	96.4	70.8	81.6	84.6	90.0		95.4	99.3	129.7
Denmark	58.2	11.4	35.4	67.8	82.1	64.7	66.3	52.1	113.1	85.4	106.7	106.0	113.0	125.8		102.9	127.1
Germany	45.7	8.9	28.3	56.2	65.7	51.5	51.2	42.3	99.7	71.8	84.0	88.1	94.6	104.5	84.1		118.8
U.S.	50.7	11.9	32.8	64.4	73.4	55.8	59.2	48.1	119.4	78.7	99.8	97.0	109.5	111.6	94.8	117.3	

Table 7-8. Augmented Binary Quantity Comparisons for Capital Formation, 1975

Country	Malawi	Kenya	India	Pakistan	Sri Lanka	Zambia	Thailand	Philippines	Korea	Malaysia	Colombia	Jamaica	Syria	Brazil	Romania	Mexico	Yugoslavia
Malawi		96.7	24.0	109.1	69.6	24.2	9.4	34.5	9.4	4.7	7.3	16.6	21.7	4.8	8.2	7.3	7.2
Kenya	58.6		48.6	156.0	134.4	36.3	25.7	34.1	19.3	8.8	17.6	20.5	32.4	9.7	9.1	7.9	8.4
India	41.2	57.2		225.7	208.3	62.3	48.3	64.4	29.3	18.5	29.7	33.3	44.0	18.8	13.3	16.2	14.7
Pakistan	62.6	78.5	207.0		124.5	47.8	26.8	53.4	18.5	8.4	18.8	25.6	26.0	13.1	10.5	10.4	12.5
Sri Lanka	55.8	82.2	199.2	45.9		44.0	22.2	46.2	17.8	8.9	12.5	30.3	51.6	15.1	11.3	8.9	11.3
Zambia	19.2	28.6	107.2	21.8	28.7		52.6	88.4	39.3	18.5	33.0	60.4	116.0	45.8	31.7	20.2	23.8
Thailand	16.1	28.5	41.2	15.2	18.1	79.5		116.6	62.0	40.5	70.8	63.2	109.5	42.4	30.1	33.1	27.0
Philippines	19.0	29.5	48.5	19.9	21.4	88.7	109.4		50.6	36.9	59.0	58.9	95.1	35.4	25.2	29.2	21.8
Korea	5.0	15.5	12.8	3.5	5.9	27.4	48.0	42.2		117.2	183.2	228.3	180.5	70.9	81.0	84.4	106.8
Malaysia	5.9	10.0	14.6	4.1	8.7	28.2	30.8	27.0	57.0		197.1	205.3	454.5	104.0	75.4	80.1	73.5
Colombia	10.2	18.1	26.9	10.5	13.5	63.6	64.6	47.1	69.5	197.4		114.9	249.4	95.1	60.3	59.2	67.4
Jamaica	10.0	15.5	44.7	18.3	11.9	45.1	59.4	58.1	214.6	172.7	104.9		96.1	51.5	55.4	47.3	38.1
Syria	11.5	14.7	32.0	17.0	8.8	53.7	82.6	38.7	117.5	237.0	90.3	98.7		52.3	64.2	66.4	45.1
Brazil	5.4	7.5	11.3	5.4	6.6	29.7	31.3	25.5	52.0	81.0	45.3	59.7	31.7		98.6	108.9	71.2
Romania	3.5	5.3	7.8	3.7	4.3	10.3	15.9	15.9	32.4	42.5	25.0	27.1	21.8	42.8		166.7	152.0
Mexico	5.3	8.3	13.5	4.4	6.4	23.5	29.1	24.7	50.2	79.5	46.2	40.3	23.7	71.8	100.9		97.6
Yugoslavia	4.2	6.8	10.8	4.8	4.6	18.0	24.0	21.0	42.8	54.0	34.2	37.5	25.6	64.1	106.4	73.8	
Iran	2.9	4.8	6.7	3.5	4.1	14.5	13.9	14.2	25.0	39.3	22.0	30.1	18.3	45.2	68.8	53.3	60.0
Uruguay	17.6	25.2	48.2	20.7	20.5	71.5	91.1	63.8	143.5	411.5	162.9	112.2	81.5	242.1	268.8	297.6	270.4
Ireland	4.5	7.8	12.6	5.6	6.0	23.9	27.9	22.8	48.9	91.9	42.2	44.7	28.0	79.4	94.9	95.4	115.4
Hungary	2.4	3.7	6.8	2.8	3.5	11.4	15.5	12.1	31.2	38.8	22.7	23.8	16.2	39.8	62.3	48.9	57.0
Poland	2.4	3.3	5.5	2.4	2.9	8.7	13.1	10.8	23.3	30.8	18.8	18.5	13.8	33.7	56.6	41.9	49.4
Italy	2.9	4.9	7.5	3.4	3.7	14.1	14.9	14.9	28.2	46.3	23.7	27.8	16.9	46.0	67.1	56.2	68.0
Spain	2.6	4.3	6.9	3.3	3.5	13.4	15.1	13.5	28.3	44.4	24.1	24.6	17.0	40.0	64.4	50.6	63.2
U.K.	2.6	4.5	6.7	3.2	3.6	14.6	13.8	14.4	28.2	44.1	21.8	29.8	16.5	48.2	68.2	54.3	75.3
Japan	1.4	1.9	2.6	1.1	1.2	6.9	6.4	6.3	11.0	18.3	10.1	13.4	6.7	20.3	27.1	21.2	31.9
Austria	1.9	3.2	4.5	2.1	1.9	8.5	9.7	10.0	17.9	25.0	14.1	18.8	11.4	30.4	47.8	36.4	48.1
Netherlands	1.4	2.4	3.0	1.5	1.6	7.3	6.5	7.0	12.5	19.8	10.0	14.6	8.3	22.4	36.8	25.6	37.0
Belgium	1.6	2.7	3.7	1.8	2.0	7.5	7.6	8.0	15.2	23.1	11.9	15.0	9.0	24.3	41.8	30.3	39.2
France	1.4	2.4	3.4	1.8	1.8	7.0	7.3	6.6	13.9	22.8	10.2	13.8	9.5	23.5	37.4	26.6	33.5
Luxembourg	1.6	2.8	4.3	1.9	2.1	7.2	8.3	8.2	16.2	26.0	13.6	13.9	8.8	23.5	37.7	31.7	35.6
Denmark	1.6	2.9	4.8	2.3	2.3	8.2	9.0	8.4	17.3	27.3	13.7	15.6	11.6	28.4	42.2	33.7	39.9
Germany	1.3	2.1	2.7	1.3	1.6	7.0	6.4	6.4	10.9	18.9	9.4	13.3	7.0	18.9	34.6	24.3	32.8
U.S.	1.5	2.5	3.4	1.5	1.7	7.6	7.2	7.6	13.7	19.8	10.4	15.6	8.0	24.0	37.4	28.2	38.1

Note: Upper right triangle: Laspeyres-type indexes of row country with column country as the base, with column country prices as weights. Lower left triangle: Paasche-type indexes of column country with row country as the base, with column country prices as weights.

Table 7-8 *(continued)*

Country	Iran	Uruguay	Ireland	Hungary	Poland	Italy	Spain	U.K.	Japan	Austria	Netherlands	Belgium	France	Luxembourg	Denmark	Germany	U.S.
Malawi	5.9	23.9	8.6	3.2	3.1	4.0	5.9	5.5	2.8	4.2	3.2	2.8	2.6	2.4	3.0	2.6	2.9
Kenya	7.2	32.4	10.7	4.5	4.6	5.4	6.6	7.6	3.2	5.5	3.9	3.7	3.2	3.1	3.6	3.2	3.5
India	10.3	43.6	19.5	7.9	6.8	9.9	10.7	12.3	5.3	7.5	6.6	6.0	5.7	5.1	6.4	5.5	5.9
Pakistan	8.4	30.4	16.9	5.7	5.3	7.4	8.1	10.1	4.0	6.8	5.7	4.9	4.9	4.1	5.2	4.4	4.5
Sri Lanka	10.3	35.1	14.9	7.0	6.6	7.5	9.7	10.8	5.6	8.0	5.4	5.2	4.7	4.4	5.5	4.5	5.2
Zambia	23.5	91.9	40.3	14.0	14.8	20.1	21.4	28.0	10.5	16.6	15.3	13.6	12.2	11.6	14.1	11.6	11.3
Thailand	23.2	91.7	35.4	17.4	16.2	18.8	19.7	22.9	10.3	16.0	12.1	11.1	10.4	9.5	11.9	9.7	11.8
Philippines	19.7	87.5	32.0	14.8	13.1	17.4	16.7	19.4	8.5	12.4	11.6	9.7	9.2	8.4	11.1	8.8	9.5
Korea	72.5	307.7	68.4	56.6	49.0	36.8	59.8	46.3	19.4	45.5	23.5	22.8	20.3	19.4	24.7	19.8	28.7
Malaysia	72.6	346.0	123.8	52.3	42.3	62.5	68.4	82.1	34.8	41.9	38.3	39.6	35.7	33.4	38.5	33.9	34.4
Colombia	53.7	159.5	62.8	29.2	27.1	33.6	54.0	43.2	20.2	35.6	24.1	20.3	18.4	17.1	20.2	16.5	26.6
Jamaica	31.1	177.6	53.3	23.1	23.7	28.0	27.6	36.2	17.9	26.8	20.8	18.9	17.1	16.1	20.9	18.0	15.8
Syria	45.4	209.6	41.5	22.2	19.1	22.4	37.1	26.9	15.7	24.3	16.3	14.5	13.5	12.3	15.9	12.7	19.1
Brazil	85.4	336.7	84.7	44.9	42.9	45.6	50.4	52.8	25.1	43.8	30.4	26.1	24.8	22.1	27.9	22.9	33.8
Romania	119.4	434.8	203.1	98.3	71.9	110.6	95.8	135.4	48.7	64.0	67.0	65.3	63.4	55.8	70.3	56.1	54.7
Mexico	79.2	359.7	138.9	55.6	53.3	72.9	83.0	92.5	41.6	56.0	47.7	46.5	40.9	39.6	47.0	41.0	42.2
Yugoslavia	88.4	406.9	133.3	64.5	55.3	75.8	71.7	89.1	39.4	53.8	45.6	45.0	41.8	38.7	48.9	40.1	41.6
Iran		561.8	200.0	92.7	84.2	110.9	117.0	134.8	67.6	85.9	66.4	67.4	60.7	56.9	68.4	63.3	62.6
Uruguay	330.0		37.4	18.6	17.9	19.0	25.7	26.6	12.5	22.9	13.5	12.8	11.8	10.8	13.3	10.9	15.8
Ireland	121.7	24.8		55.9	50.3	53.2	63.1	70.3	34.2	54.5	34.6	34.2	31.6	28.9	36.8	30.6	36.1
Hungary	64.6	14.7	47.2		92.3	116.3	126.7	141.6	68.6	92.7	71.9	70.7	65.2	60.3	74.7	63.0	70.0
Poland	53.2	13.7	34.8	77.3		149.8	141.0	177.9	72.0	97.2	104.9	88.1	83.0	75.1	92.8	74.7	79.4
Italy	84.3	16.9	53.8	111.2	123.0		107.3	124.8	59.6	79.8	63.6	61.3	55.7	51.9	65.0	55.5	58.4
Spain	70.7	15.0	45.7	104.7	118.5	90.3		132.9	60.5	88.2	76.2	65.1	60.7	55.5	72.3	58.9	68.2
U.K.	75.6	15.1	64.6	113.6	126.9	121.4	111.8		46.4	69.9	50.4	47.0	45.7	39.6	53.1	42.6	50.6
Japan	29.1	6.5	25.9	51.6	57.8	46.3	43.1	40.7		158.0	134.8	120.0	111.1	101.6	128.2	105.2	133.6
Austria	54.1	11.7	33.0	69.1	88.1	61.6	68.9	52.1	135.9		110.4	92.1	85.9	77.8	99.3	80.8	81.2
Netherlands	38.4	8.1	30.3	53.7	64.2	54.3	51.3	47.5	103.0	75.2		100.5	95.1	85.0	109.8	90.3	112.0
Belgium	42.8	10.0	30.7	57.0	73.0	56.9	57.5	47.8	104.5	78.3	92.5		94.6	84.5	107.3	88.7	98.6
France	43.2	8.4	28.9	51.8	63.7	54.4	52.8	44.7	92.3	68.0	94.9	93.3		90.7	113.6	96.3	118.0
Luxembourg	41.3	9.8	26.3	55.5	65.7	51.7	52.9	41.0	91.5	64.4	78.4	84.7	89.4		127.4	105.6	110.2
Denmark	49.6	9.8	34.0	61.6	72.6	64.4	60.7	51.0	99.8	73.4	103.7	104.8	112.4	124.3		86.2	100.0
Germany	33.0	7.4	26.2	50.1	57.8	47.7	44.5	41.9	94.5	63.9	78.1	87.5	92.9	103.4	82.0		129.3
U.S.	41.1	9.0	29.9	59.4	67.9	53.4	51.4	45.7	106.7	76.3	88.9	95.4	101.6	112.9	89.9	106.4	

Table 7-9. Paasche-Laspeyres Spread for Capital Formation from Augmented Binary Comparisons, 1975

Country	Malawi	Kenya	India	Pakistan	Sri Lanka	Zambia	Thailand	Philippines	Korea	Malaysia	Colombia	Jamaica	Syria	Brazil	Romania	Mexico	Yugoslavia
Malawi																	
Kenya	0.61																
India	1.72	1.18															
Pakistan	0.57	0.50	0.92														
Sri Lanka	0.80	0.61	0.96	0.37													
Zambia	0.80	0.79	1.72	0.46	0.65												
Thailand	1.72	1.11	0.85	0.57	0.81	1.51											
Philippines	0.55	0.86	0.75	0.37	0.46	1.00	0.94										
Korea	0.53	0.80	0.44	0.19	0.33	0.70	0.77	0.83									
Malaysia	1.26	1.14	0.79	0.49	0.98	1.52	0.76	0.73	0.49								
Colombia	1.40	1.03	0.91	0.56	1.08	1.93	0.91	0.80	0.38	1.00							
Jamaica	0.60	0.76	1.34	0.71	0.39	0.75	0.94	0.99	0.94	0.84	0.91						
Syria	0.53	0.45	0.73	0.65	0.17	0.46	0.75	0.41	0.65	0.52	0.36	1.03					
Brazil	1.12	0.78	0.60	0.41	0.44	0.65	0.74	0.72	0.73	0.78	0.48	1.16	0.61				
Romania	0.43	0.58	0.59	0.35	0.38	0.32	0.53	0.63	0.40	0.56	0.41	0.49	0.34	0.43			
Mexico	0.73	1.04	0.83	0.42	0.72	1.16	0.88	0.85	0.59	0.99	0.78	0.85	0.36	0.66	0.61		
Yugoslavia	0.59	0.82	0.74	0.38	0.41	0.76	0.89	0.96	0.40	0.73	0.51	0.98	0.57	0.90	0.70	0.76	
Iran	0.49	0.66	0.65	0.42	0.40	0.62	0.60	0.72	0.34	0.54	0.41	0.97	0.40	0.53	0.58	0.67	0.68
Uruguay	0.73	0.78	1.11	0.68	0.58	0.78	0.99	0.73	0.47	1.19	1.02	0.63	0.39	0.72	0.62	0.83	0.66
Ireland	0.52	0.73	0.64	0.33	0.40	0.59	0.79	0.71	0.71	0.74	0.67	0.84	0.67	0.94	0.47	0.69	0.87
Hungary	0.75	0.82	0.86	0.49	0.50	0.81	0.89	0.82	0.55	0.74	0.78	1.03	0.73	0.89	0.63	0.88	0.88
Poland	0.78	0.72	0.82	0.46	0.44	0.59	0.81	0.83	0.47	0.73	0.69	0.78	0.72	0.78	0.79	0.79	0.89
Italy	0.72	0.91	0.76	0.46	0.49	0.70	0.79	0.86	0.77	0.74	0.71	0.99	0.75	1.01	0.61	0.77	0.90
Spain	0.45	0.65	0.64	0.41	0.36	0.63	0.77	0.81	0.47	0.65	0.45	0.89	0.46	0.79	0.67	0.61	0.88
U.K.	0.47	0.59	0.54	0.32	0.33	0.52	0.60	0.74	0.61	0.54	0.50	0.82	0.61	0.91	0.50	0.59	0.85
Japan	0.50	0.59	0.49	0.27	0.21	0.66	0.62	0.74	0.57	0.53	0.50	0.75	0.43	0.81	0.56	0.51	0.81
Austria	0.45	0.59	0.60	0.31	0.24	0.51	0.61	0.81	0.39	0.60	0.40	0.70	0.47	0.69	0.75	0.65	0.89
Netherlands	0.44	0.61	0.46	0.26	0.30	0.48	0.54	0.60	0.53	0.52	0.41	0.70	0.51	0.74	0.55	0.54	0.81
Belgium	0.57	0.75	0.62	0.37	0.38	0.55	0.68	0.82	0.67	0.58	0.59	0.79	0.62	0.93	0.64	0.65	0.87
France	0.54	0.75	0.60	0.37	0.38	0.57	0.70	0.72	0.68	0.64	0.55	0.81	0.70	0.95	0.59	0.65	0.80
Luxembourg	0.67	0.90	0.84	0.46	0.48	0.62	0.87	0.98	0.83	0.78	0.79	0.86	0.72	1.06	0.68	0.80	0.92
Denmark	0.53	0.81	0.74	0.44	0.42	0.58	0.76	0.75	0.70	0.71	0.68	0.75	0.73	1.02	0.60	0.72	0.82
Germany	0.50	0.66	0.49	0.30	0.36	0.60	0.66	0.73	0.55	0.56	0.57	0.74	0.55	0.83	0.62	0.59	0.82
U.S.	0.52	0.71	0.58	0.33	0.33	0.67	0.61	0.80	0.48	0.58	0.39	0.99	0.42	0.71	0.68	0.67	0.92

Note: The Paasche-Laspeyres spread is the ratio of own-price weighted quantity index to quantity index weighted by base country price.

Table 7-9 *(continued)*

Country	Iran	Uruguay	Ireland	Hungary	Poland	Italy	Spain	U.K.	Japan	Austria	Netherlands	Belgium	France	Luxembourg	Denmark	Germany	U.S.
Uruguay	0.59																
Ireland	0.61	0.66															
Hungary	0.70	0.79	0.84														
Poland	0.63	0.77	0.69	0.84													
Italy	0.76	0.89	1.01	0.96	0.82												
Spain	0.60	0.58	0.72	0.83	0.84	0.84											
U.K.	0.56	0.57	0.92	0.80	0.71	0.97	0.84										
Japan	0.43	0.52	0.76	0.75	0.80	0.78	0.71	0.88									
Austria	0.63	0.51	0.61	0.75	0.91	0.77	0.78	0.75	0.86								
Netherlands	0.58	0.60	0.88	0.75	0.61	0.85	0.67	0.94	0.76	0.68							
Belgium	0.64	0.78	0.90	0.81	0.83	0.93	0.88	1.02	0.87	0.85	0.92						
France	0.71	0.71	0.91	0.79	0.77	0.98	0.87	0.98	0.83	0.79	1.00	0.99					
Luxembourg	0.73	0.91	0.91	0.92	0.87	1.00	0.95	1.04	0.90	0.83	0.92	1.00	0.99				
Denmark	0.72	0.74	0.92	0.82	0.78	0.99	0.84	0.96	0.78	0.74	0.95	0.98	0.99	0.98			
Germany	0.52	0.68	0.86	0.79	0.77	0.86	0.76	0.98	0.90	0.79	0.86	0.99	0.96	0.98	0.95		
U.S.	0.66	0.57	0.83	0.85	0.86	0.91	0.75	0.90	0.80	0.94	0.79	0.97	0.86	1.02	0.90	0.82	

Table 7-10. Augmented Binary Comparisons for Government, All Pairs of Countries; Price and Quantity Indexes, 1975

Country	Malawi	Kenya	India	Pakistan	Sri Lanka	Zambia	Thailand	Philippines	Korea	Malaysia	Colombia	Jamaica	Syria	Brazil	Romania	Mexico	Yugoslavia
Malawi		78.1	136.8	145.3	196.7	59.2	86.6	133.8	79.1	60.4	94.3	30.9	50.4	47.5	49.5	41.3	48.9
Kenya	56.7		189.6	199.4	298.5	81.8	110.3	169.7	116.1	73.0	118.2	43.4	72.5	71.6	68.8	60.5	66.2
India	68.2	111.0		102.5	144.6	44.4	60.1	88.0	54.6	40.0	62.1	22.1	34.5	37.8	33.0	29.2	32.7
Pakistan	42.0	69.1	63.8		143.8	44.0	58.2	82.8	54.5	38.3	55.8	21.2	35.5	35.9	32.1	27.7	32.0
Sri Lanka	45.6	67.8	66.5	102.2		29.7	40.9	57.0	35.9	25.7	41.9	14.7	22.4	26.2	21.5	20.9	20.7
Zambia	19.1	31.2	27.3	42.1	42.5		145.7	195.1	127.5	99.3	154.7	53.1	81.9	93.2	78.3	74.5	76.9
Thailand	47.7	84.4	73.6	116.1	112.4	250.3		156.9	92.2	68.9	115.7	37.2	58.0	62.6	59.6	53.0	56.9
Philippines	32.0	57.0	52.2	84.8	83.9	194.3	66.2		67.4	41.7	62.9	25.5	44.9	41.6	40.9	33.4	40.0
Korea	27.8	42.6	43.0	65.9	68.1	152.2	57.7	75.9		67.0	111.5	39.8	66.6	66.6	63.1	60.2	58.4
Malaysia	18.9	35.4	30.7	49.0	49.7	102.0	40.3	64.1	77.8		179.0	58.1	92.3	90.2	98.9	84.7	90.3
Colombia	70.8	127.4	115.1	195.9	177.6	381.3	139.8	247.4	272.7	325.4		33.7	55.3	58.1	55.4	48.7	52.1
Jamaica	18.8	30.2	28.2	44.9	44.1	96.9	37.9	53.2	66.6	87.4	25.9		156.0	167.9	153.8	147.8	144.2
Syria	15.5	24.3	24.3	36.1	38.9	84.5	32.7	40.7	53.6	74.1	21.2	86.3		121.7	93.6	98.3	85.7
Brazil	26.9	40.2	36.2	58.2	54.3	121.1	49.4	71.6	87.3	123.5	32.9	130.7	134.1		83.9	79.2	82.4
Romania	24.7	40.0	39.7	62.3	63.4	137.8	49.6	69.7	88.3	107.8	33.0	136.4	166.8	113.9		99.1	91.0
Mexico	35.0	53.9	53.0	85.4	77.0	171.4	66.0	100.8	109.3	148.8	44.4	168.1	187.9	143.1	119.5		94.8
Yugoslavia	11.6	19.3	18.5	28.9	30.5	64.9	24.1	32.9	44.1	54.6	16.2	67.3	84.2	53.7	50.9	41.2	
Iran	8.3	14.0	12.8	19.2	21.4	42.7	17.9	23.3	31.0	44.0	13.1	50.4	55.0	40.3	37.0	31.6	71.2
Uruguay	9.2	15.6	14.7	24.5	22.6	51.7	17.6	28.6	33.9	39.6	11.2	49.0	59.7	40.7	35.5	26.9	74.7
Ireland	12.5	19.6	19.6	29.8	30.4	65.0	25.2	32.7	40.2	56.4	17.4	66.4	73.1	56.2	47.2	41.7	90.2
Hungary	10.8	17.9	17.4	26.8	29.1	65.2	23.0	29.1	42.7	53.5	13.8	65.7	87.1	50.2	49.0	36.7	98.9
Poland	10.5	17.6	16.5	25.7	27.7	61.5	22.9	28.8	42.8	54.2	14.3	63.4	84.6	46.3	48.6	36.7	99.2
Italy	10.7	16.1	16.4	25.2	25.0	56.6	21.1	26.9	33.9	46.0	13.4	54.5	62.3	46.5	37.5	32.7	74.6
Spain	35.5	55.0	53.4	84.8	82.9	175.1	69.9	97.1	122.4	158.0	48.7	183.8	205.1	144.1	133.7	113.9	263.6
U.K.	5.7	9.0	8.8	13.9	13.1	29.3	11.3	15.7	18.2	25.2	7.6	28.3	32.9	23.1	20.9	17.2	41.6
Japan	21.0	33.3	32.0	50.0	46.1	104.4	39.4	59.9	62.4	91.1	27.3	102.9	105.9	95.5	69.8	59.2	141.9
Austria	11.4	17.3	17.0	27.1	25.6	56.5	21.7	31.3	36.5	47.8	14.8	56.0	61.8	45.1	39.9	33.8	79.0
Netherlands	10.0	15.8	15.5	23.9	23.3	51.1	19.6	26.5	30.9	43.8	13.6	50.9	54.5	43.9	35.7	31.0	69.5
Belgium	9.8	15.2	15.1	23.4	22.8	50.3	19.1	25.7	30.5	42.0	13.0	49.3	54.1	41.8	34.7	30.0	67.9
France	7.5	11.9	11.8	18.5	18.5	39.3	14.7	20.2	25.4	32.6	10.1	39.6	45.3	33.4	28.6	24.6	55.6
Luxembourg	10.3	16.0	16.0	24.4	24.6	53.3	20.5	26.8	32.8	45.4	13.9	53.5	59.1	45.4	37.7	33.2	73.0
Denmark	6.6	9.4	9.7	15.4	14.0	31.8	12.0	16.7	18.8	25.4	7.8	29.5	31.8	26.0	20.0	17.9	40.0
Germany	9.3	13.6	14.1	22.1	20.6	45.8	17.6	24.2	27.7	37.2	11.7	43.3	48.0	36.8	30.5	27.2	59.7
U.S.	5.3	8.3	8.5	12.7	13.5	28.8	10.8	14.2	17.9	23.7	7.1	28.7	33.3	25.2	20.1	18.0	39.0

Note: Upper right triangle: Fisher price indexes of row countries with column country = 100. Lower left triangle: Fisher quantity indexes of column country with row country = 100.

Table 7-10 *(continued)*

Country	Iran	Uruguay	Ireland	Hungary	Poland	Italy	Spain	U.K.	Japan	Austria	Netherlands	Belgium	France	Luxembourg	Denmark	Germany	U.S.
Malawi	43.5	87.5	30.7	59.5	54.0	24.6	24.9	28.9	22.1	20.2	14.7	15.5	20.2	16.0	13.9	15.4	24.9
Kenya	58.3	116.5	44.0	80.5	72.8	36.9	36.2	41.4	31.5	30.0	21.1	22.5	28.7	23.2	22.0	23.8	35.7
India	30.1	58.9	20.9	39.3	36.8	17.1	17.7	20.1	15.5	14.4	10.2	10.7	13.7	11.0	10.0	10.9	16.6
Pakistan	30.7	53.9	21.1	39.2	36.1	17.2	17.0	19.6	15.2	13.9	10.1	10.6	13.3	11.0	9.7	10.6	16.9
Sri Lanka	18.8	39.8	14.1	24.5	22.9	11.7	11.9	14.1	11.2	10.0	7.0	7.4	9.1	7.5	7.3	7.8	10.8
Zambia	74.7	137.8	52.1	86.9	81.6	41.1	44.6	49.9	39.3	35.9	25.5	26.6	33.9	27.3	25.4	27.8	40.2
Thailand	48.9	110.9	36.8	67.6	60.0	30.2	30.6	35.5	28.5	25.6	18.2	19.2	24.8	19.4	18.4	19.7	29.3
Philippines	36.0	65.8	27.4	51.5	46.0	22.9	21.2	24.6	18.1	17.1	13.0	13.7	17.4	14.3	12.8	13.8	21.5
Korea	53.1	108.5	43.4	68.4	60.4	35.4	32.9	41.5	33.9	28.7	21.7	22.6	27.0	22.8	22.2	23.6	33.4
Malaysia	71.5	177.9	59.3	104.5	91.4	50.0	48.8	57.3	44.5	42.0	29.4	31.5	40.4	31.6	31.4	33.7	48.2
Colombia	41.1	107.8	33.1	69.3	59.7	29.4	27.2	32.5	25.5	23.3	16.3	17.5	22.4	17.7	17.6	18.4	27.6
Jamaica	123.0	282.9	99.2	167.7	154.0	83.1	82.5	100.5	77.6	70.5	49.7	52.8	65.5	52.8	53.2	57.0	78.5
Syria	83.9	172.5	67.0	94.1	85.7	54.0	55.0	64.3	56.0	47.5	34.5	35.8	42.5	35.6	36.6	38.3	50.3
Brazil	70.1	155.0	53.4	100.0	96.1	44.3	48.0	56.2	38.1	39.9	26.3	28.4	35.4	28.4	27.5	30.6	40.8
Romania	79.9	186.2	66.5	107.1	95.6	57.5	54.1	64.9	54.5	47.2	33.7	35.7	43.2	35.7	37.4	38.6	53.3
Mexico	78.8	207.6	63.7	120.7	107.0	55.6	53.6	66.7	54.3	47.0	32.8	34.9	42.5	34.3	35.3	36.5	50.5
Yugoslavia	89.6	191.1	75.2	114.6	101.2	62.4	59.2	70.4	57.9	51.5	37.5	39.5	48.0	39.9	40.4	42.5	59.5
Iran		222.6	88.2	115.4	105.4	68.5	74.1	83.5	69.1	63.4	45.3	47.3	57.5	46.8	48.3	51.9	64.2
Uruguay	100.4		33.6	69.4	63.0	29.8	28.3	32.5	25.3	23.6	16.3	17.5	22.1	17.9	17.4	18.3	27.6
Ireland	120.5	141.3		146.8	132.6	85.0	84.0	103.6	89.5	75.6	53.9	56.6	66.3	54.5	59.4	61.0	76.9
Hungary	153.9	114.5	113.9		87.7	53.9	50.9	59.2	47.3	43.8	33.0	34.4	40.8	35.5	32.9	35.5	53.0
Poland	149.3	111.8	111.7	101.0		58.9	55.8	66.3	51.7	47.4	36.2	37.6	45.6	39.0	35.5	39.0	58.7
Italy	106.4	109.7	80.8	76.3	78.7		98.1	120.2	100.8	86.3	61.4	64.6	75.8	63.5	66.1	68.5	91.0
Spain	330.0	387.3	274.0	271.0	278.6	342.5		125.7	97.5	88.0	61.1	65.4	79.1	64.2	67.7	71.8	93.5
U.K.	54.9	63.1	41.7	43.7	44.0	52.4	14.9		84.2	70.0	50.3	53.1	64.5	52.1	53.7	55.4	77.9
Japan	186.3	227.7	135.3	153.3	158.0	175.1	54.0	333.0		88.1	58.8	62.9	77.7	61.0	64.9	65.7	87.2
Austria	100.5	121.1	79.3	81.9	85.4	101.2	29.6	198.0	56.2		68.9	73.8	89.0	72.0	76.5	80.2	105.6
Netherlands	90.1	111.7	71.3	69.6	71.7	91.1	27.3	176.7	53.9	93.0		106.3	127.2	102.0	111.8	114.0	146.3
Belgium	88.8	107.1	69.8	68.8	71.1	89.2	26.3	172.1	51.9	89.4	96.9		119.4	96.6	104.7	107.3	139.9
France	72.8	84.7	59.4	57.6	58.2	75.5	21.6	141.0	41.8	73.8	80.6	83.4		81.9	88.3	90.8	118.9
Luxembourg	97.5	113.8	78.7	72.3	74.2	98.5	29.0	190.8	58.1	99.5	109.6	112.4	133.2		108.4	111.4	142.5
Denmark	52.4	64.9	40.1	43.3	45.4	52.5	15.3	102.7	30.3	51.9	55.5	57.5	68.6	51.2		102.0	132.9
Germany	76.7	97.4	61.4	63.1	64.9	79.6	22.6	156.5	47.1	78.0	85.6	88.3	104.8	78.3	154.2		130.2
U.S.	56.6	59.0	44.4	38.6	39.3	54.7	15.9	101.5	32.3	54.0	60.8	61.8	73.0	55.9	108.0	70.1	

Table 7-11. Augmented Binary Quantity Comparisons for Government, 1975

Country	Malawi	Kenya	India	Pakistan	Sri Lanka	Zambia	Thailand	Philippines	Korea	Malaysia	Colombia	Jamaica	Syria	Brazil	Romania	Mexico	Yugoslavia
Malawi		68.5	69.8	44.0	49.4	20.9	50.8	40.0	34.0	21.6	84.3	21.7	22.3	28.4	36.4	39.1	16.5
Kenya	47.0		116.1	70.1	68.4	34.2	93.1	59.0	44.9	37.2	128.1	31.0	28.0	43.7	44.1	55.2	21.0
India	66.7	106.0		64.1	67.4	28.3	73.8	57.4	46.2	30.5	118.8	28.9	30.5	37.2	49.2	54.8	22.1
Pakistan	40.1	68.0	63.4		103.8	45.9	118.2	88.3	70.6	48.6	187.2	46.0	46.2	61.0	75.2	85.2	34.3
Sri Lanka	42.1	67.2	65.5	100.6		43.6	109.5	88.9	68.6	45.8	175.9	43.6	43.3	60.4	69.7	77.8	32.2
Zambia	17.5	28.5	26.4	38.7	41.4		254.5	243.2	169.1	99.1	434.6	97.7	100.5	124.4	172.8	189.2	77.6
Thailand	44.7	76.5	73.3	114.2	115.2	246.2		77.3	59.0	40.0	153.8	37.9	37.0	51.8	58.8	66.3	27.6
Philippines	25.7	55.1	47.4	81.4	79.1	155.2	56.7		82.0	70.7	233.1	57.9	53.7	83.1	81.0	102.1	38.8
Korea	22.7	40.4	40.0	61.4	67.6	137.0	56.4	70.3		74.5	264.9	67.3	56.3	107.5	89.0	105.3	44.8
Malaysia	16.6	33.7	30.9	49.4	53.9	105.0	40.5	58.1	81.4		342.2	84.5	71.1	129.7	110.5	138.3	55.3
Colombia	59.4	126.7	111.6	205.1	179.4	334.6	127.1	262.6	280.7	309.6		26.8	24.2	38.2	35.4	44.5	17.3
Jamaica	16.4	29.6	27.6	43.7	44.6	96.0	37.8	48.9	65.8	90.4	24.9		88.7	147.9	145.8	170.4	69.9
Syria	10.8	21.1	19.3	28.2	35.0	71.0	28.8	30.8	50.9	77.2	18.6	83.9		175.8	173.5	204.9	85.0
Brazil	25.4	37.1	35.2	55.6	48.8	117.8	47.1	61.6	70.9	117.5	28.4	115.5	102.2		157.7	168.4	69.3
Romania	16.8	36.3	31.9	51.7	57.7	109.9	41.9	60.0	87.5	105.2	30.8	127.6	160.3	82.2		128.5	50.6
Mexico	31.3	52.5	51.3	85.7	76.1	155.3	65.8	99.5	113.6	160.3	44.4	166.1	172.2	121.5	111.2		42.7
Yugoslavia	8.1	17.6	15.5	24.4	28.8	54.4	21.0	28.0	43.3	53.9	15.2	64.9	83.5	41.6	51.1	39.8	
Iran	5.0	10.2	9.2	13.2	17.4	34.6	14.0	14.3	25.3	39.0	9.1	43.2	53.7	28.9	30.3	25.3	60.8
Uruguay	7.1	15.4	13.0	23.5	20.6	41.1	14.7	29.7	32.1	36.2	11.3	44.4	46.0	33.2	30.8	24.6	65.7
Ireland	8.2	15.4	14.6	21.8	25.7	51.2	21.5	23.9	37.5	54.7	14.0	58.7	73.1	38.0	43.0	36.8	85.7
Hungary	8.2	17.6	15.5	23.8	29.0	55.8	21.7	26.8	43.2	56.9	15.3	67.2	85.6	43.6	51.1	40.5	100.9
Poland	8.8	17.9	16.2	25.0	29.1	57.3	22.7	27.8	43.1	58.0	15.6	66.4	82.4	43.3	49.4	40.4	98.6
Italy	8.3	15.0	14.1	21.7	23.6	49.2	20.2	23.8	34.5	50.1	13.0	53.4	61.7	36.1	37.0	32.1	76.3
Spain	29.7	54.0	51.2	81.9	83.3	172.2	69.8	91.9	123.8	166.7	46.9	183.5	214.6	121.4	132.1	112.9	269.4
U.K.	4.8	8.1	8.0	12.7	12.6	26.3	11.1	14.2	18.5	26.0	7.2	27.1	31.3	18.0	19.2	17.0	39.5
Japan	19.2	33.0	30.9	49.3	47.1	100.0	40.6	56.2	69.6	105.4	26.7	109.2	104.6	88.1	66.6	59.9	145.1
Austria	9.9	17.1	16.4	26.5	25.7	55.4	22.2	29.8	38.0	51.4	14.6	56.1	64.2	37.3	39.4	34.1	81.6
Netherlands	7.4	13.5	12.8	19.6	21.3	44.2	18.2	21.6	31.3	45.4	11.8	48.3	55.8	32.8	33.6	29.2	69.1
Belgium	7.6	13.6	12.9	20.1	21.3	44.5	18.2	22.2	31.3	44.2	11.9	47.6	55.5	31.7	33.5	28.9	68.8
France	5.3	10.7	9.8	15.6	17.0	32.7	13.1	17.6	25.5	32.9	9.3	37.3	45.4	24.7	28.3	23.2	56.5
Luxembourg	7.3	13.5	12.8	19.4	21.9	44.6	18.5	21.3	32.1	46.3	12.0	49.7	60.1	32.6	35.6	30.6	72.1
Denmark	5.9	9.5	9.3	15.3	13.9	29.9	12.4	17.1	20.5	29.0	8.0	29.8	32.0	21.2	20.1	18.0	42.5
Germany	7.7	12.9	12.8	20.6	19.8	41.4	17.6	23.1	29.2	40.5	11.4	42.1	48.9	27.7	30.2	26.8	61.9
U.S.	3.4	6.9	6.3	9.5	11.5	22.1	9.0	10.6	17.0	23.5	6.1	26.3	32.9	17.2	19.5	16.0	38.8

Note: Upper right triangle: Laspeyres-type indexes of row country with column country as the base, with column country prices as weights. Lower left triangle: Paasche-type indexes of column country with row country as the base, with column country prices as weights.

Table 7-11 *(continued)*

Country	Iran	Uruguay	Ireland	Hungary	Poland	Italy	Spain	U.K.	Japan	Austria	Netherlands	Belgium	France	Luxembourg	Denmark	Germany	U.S.
Malawi	13.7	11.9	19.1	14.1	12.5	13.9	42.5	6.8	23.1	13.1	13.4	12.7	10.5	14.6	7.4	11.3	8.2
Kenya	19.1	15.8	25.0	18.3	17.3	17.3	56.1	10.1	33.5	17.5	18.3	16.9	13.1	19.0	9.2	14.4	10.0
India	17.9	16.6	26.4	19.6	16.9	19.0	55.6	9.7	33.1	17.7	18.8	17.7	14.3	20.0	10.1	15.4	11.4
Pakistan	28.0	25.5	40.6	30.2	26.5	29.1	87.8	15.1	50.7	27.7	29.0	27.2	21.9	30.8	15.5	23.7	17.1
Sri Lanka	26.1	24.6	35.9	29.2	26.4	26.6	82.6	13.6	45.1	25.5	25.5	24.3	20.1	27.5	14.0	21.3	15.7
Zambia	52.7	65.0	82.5	76.1	66.0	65.1	178.1	32.6	109.0	57.6	59.0	56.9	47.3	63.8	33.8	50.5	37.5
Thailand	22.8	21.1	29.6	24.3	23.1	22.0	70.0	11.5	38.3	21.2	21.0	20.0	16.6	22.7	11.6	17.7	13.1
Philippines	38.2	27.5	44.7	31.5	29.8	30.3	102.6	17.5	63.8	32.8	32.6	29.9	23.2	33.7	16.2	25.5	19.0
Korea	37.9	35.7	43.2	42.1	42.5	33.2	120.9	18.0	55.9	34.9	30.6	29.8	25.4	33.6	17.2	26.2	18.8
Malaysia	49.7	43.3	58.1	50.2	50.6	42.2	149.5	24.4	78.8	44.4	42.2	39.9	32.2	44.6	22.1	34.3	24.0
Colombia	18.9	11.1	21.6	12.5	13.0	13.8	50.6	8.1	27.8	14.9	15.6	14.1	11.0	16.1	7.5	12.0	8.3
Jamaica	58.9	54.1	75.2	64.2	60.5	55.5	184.5	29.6	97.0	55.9	53.6	51.1	42.1	57.7	29.2	44.6	31.3
Syria	56.2	77.6	73.1	88.6	86.9	62.8	196.1	34.5	107.2	59.5	53.2	52.8	45.3	58.1	31.7	47.0	33.8
Brazil	56.3	50.1	83.2	57.8	49.5	60.0	170.9	29.6	103.5	54.5	58.7	55.1	45.0	63.1	32.0	48.8	36.8
Romania	45.1	40.8	51.9	47.0	47.9	38.0	135.5	22.7	73.1	40.3	38.1	36.0	28.9	40.0	19.9	30.7	20.8
Mexico	39.7	29.4	47.2	33.3	33.4	33.4	115.1	17.3	58.4	33.6	33.0	31.1	26.0	35.9	17.7	27.6	20.2
Yugoslavia	83.5	84.8	94.8	97.0	99.8	73.0	257.9	43.9	138.7	76.5	69.9	66.9	54.6	73.8	37.6	57.6	39.1
Iran		160.3	124.8	180.5	180.8	116.6	357.1	65.6	201.3	109.2	92.2	93.7	82.2	101.4	57.6	84.0	60.9
Uruguay	62.9		201.6	115.0	108.1	128.7	426.1	75.5	263.7	133.4	147.1	132.9	100.4	150.4	70.4	111.9	78.5
Ireland	116.1	99.0		116.0	117.8	83.7	289.0	45.3	140.0	84.0	71.4	71.0	62.1	79.2	42.4	63.5	44.9
Hungary	131.2	114.0	111.8		101.5	72.2	244.5	42.6	133.7	73.2	66.0	64.1	53.1	70.3	36.8	55.6	38.4
Poland	123.3	115.7	105.9	100.5		74.8	255.8	42.5	134.3	76.0	68.6	66.6	55.7	73.8	38.4	58.2	40.4
Italy	97.0	93.5	78.0	80.6	82.8		332.2	53.1	170.4	99.2	91.2	88.5	74.9	99.5	51.8	78.3	55.7
Spain	304.9	352.1	260.4	300.3	304.0	352.1		15.3	49.5	29.4	27.2	26.1	21.8	29.6	14.9	22.9	16.0
U.K.	46.0	52.7	38.4	44.8	45.5	51.6	14.6		322.4	199.6	182.1	175.4	149.0	200.4	101.5	155.5	109.6
Japan	172.4	196.6	130.7	175.6	185.9	179.8	58.9	344.0		52.4	54.4	51.2	42.1	58.4	29.5	45.3	34.3
Austria	92.5	110.0	74.9	91.7	96.0	103.3	29.7	196.9	60.3		94.2	89.9	74.4	102.0	51.2	78.6	54.6
Netherlands	88.0	84.8	71.2	73.4	74.9	91.1	27.3	171.2	53.3	91.8		97.1	82.4	109.3	56.8	86.1	61.3
Belgium	84.0	86.4	68.6	73.9	75.8	89.8	26.4	168.9	52.5	88.9	96.6		84.2	112.7	57.9	88.1	62.0
France	64.4	71.5	56.9	62.5	60.9	76.2	21.4	133.5	41.6	73.1	78.9	82.6		135.9	68.4	105.4	73.3
Luxembourg	93.6	86.1	78.3	74.3	74.7	97.5	28.5	181.8	57.7	97.0	110.0	112.0	130.4		52.6	79.3	56.0
Denmark	47.7	59.8	37.9	51.0	53.5	53.2	15.7	104.0	31.1	52.7	54.1	57.1	68.8	49.8		154.4	110.6
Germany	70.0	84.8	59.3	71.5	72.4	81.0	22.4	157.5	48.9	77.4	85.1	88.5	104.3	77.4	153.9		70.1
U.S.	52.5	44.3	43.9	38.9	38.2	53.6	15.8	94.0	30.5	53.4	60.3	61.6	72.7	55.7	105.4	70.0	

Table 7-12. Paasche-Laspeyres Spread for Government from Augmented Binary Comparisons, 1975

Country	Malawi	Kenya	India	Pakistan	Sri Lanka	Zambia	Thailand	Philippines	Korea	Malaysia	Colombia	Jamaica	Syria	Brazil	Romania	Mexico	Yugoslavia
Malawi																	
Kenya	0.69																
India	0.96	0.91															
Pakistan	0.91	0.97	0.99														
Sri Lanka	0.85	0.98	0.97	0.97													
Zambia	0.84	0.83	0.93	0.84	0.95												
Thailand	0.88	0.82	0.99	0.97	1.05	0.97											
Philippines	0.64	0.93	0.83	0.92	0.89	0.64	0.73										
Korea	0.67	0.90	0.87	0.87	0.99	0.81	0.96	0.86									
Malaysia	0.77	0.91	1.01	1.02	1.18	1.06	1.01	0.82	1.09								
Colombia	0.70	0.99	0.94	1.10	1.02	0.77	0.83	1.13	1.06	0.90							
Jamaica	0.76	0.96	0.95	0.95	1.02	0.98	1.00	0.84	0.98	1.07	0.93						
Syria	0.48	0.75[a]	0.63	0.61	0.81	0.71	0.78	0.57	0.90	1.09	0.77	0.95					
Brazil	0.89	0.85	0.95	0.91	0.81	0.95	0.91	0.74	0.66	0.91	0.74	0.78	0.58				
Romania	0.46	0.82	0.65	0.69	0.83	0.64	0.71	0.74	0.98	0.95	0.87	0.87	0.92	0.52			
Mexico	0.80	0.95	0.94	1.01	0.98	0.82	0.99	0.97	1.08	1.16	1.00	0.98	0.84	0.72	0.87		
Yugoslavia	0.49	0.84	0.70	0.71	0.89	0.70	0.76	0.72	0.97	0.98	0.88	0.93	0.98	0.60	1.01	0.93	
Iran	0.36	0.53	0.51	0.47	0.67	0.66	0.61	0.37	0.67	0.78	0.48	0.73	0.96	0.51	0.67	0.64	0.73
Uruguay	0.60	0.98	0.78	0.92	0.84	0.63	0.70	1.08	0.90	0.84	1.02	0.82	0.59	0.66	0.76	0.84	0.77
Ireland	0.43	0.62	0.55	0.54	0.72	0.62	0.73	0.53	0.87	0.94	0.65	0.78	1.00	0.46	0.83	0.78	0.90
Hungary	0.58	0.96	0.79	0.79	0.99	0.73	0.89	0.85	1.03	1.13	1.22	1.05	0.97	0.75	1.09	1.22	1.04
Poland	0.71	1.03	0.96	0.94	1.10	0.87	0.98	0.93	1.01	1.15	1.20	1.10	0.95	0.88	1.03	1.21	0.99
Italy	0.60	0.87	0.74	0.75	0.89	0.76	0.92	0.79	1.04	1.19	0.94	0.96	0.98	0.60	0.97	0.96	1.05
Spain	0.70	0.96	0.92	0.93	1.01	0.97	1.00	0.90	1.02	1.11	0.93	0.99	1.09	0.71	0.97	0.98	1.04
U.K.	0.71	0.80	0.82	0.84	0.93	0.81	0.97	0.81	1.03	1.07	0.89	0.92	0.91	0.61	0.85	0.98	0.90
Japan	0.83	0.99	0.93	0.97	1.04	0.92	1.06	0.88	1.25	1.34	0.96	1.13	0.98	0.85	0.91	1.03	1.05
Austria	0.76	0.98	0.92	0.96	1.01	0.96	1.05	0.91	1.09	1.16	0.98	1.00	1.08	0.68	0.98	1.01	1.07
Netherlands	0.55	0.74	0.68	0.68	0.84	0.75	0.87	0.66	1.02	1.08	0.76	0.90	1.05	0.56	0.88	0.88	0.99
Belgium	0.60	0.80	0.73	0.74	0.88	0.78	0.91	0.74	1.05	1.11	0.84	0.93	1.05	0.58	0.93	0.93	1.03
France	0.50	0.82	0.69	0.71	0.85	0.69	0.79	0.76	1.00	1.02	0.85	0.89	1.00	0.55	0.98	0.89	1.03
Luxembourg	0.50	0.71	0.64	0.63	0.80	0.70	0.81	0.63	0.96	1.04	0.75	0.86	1.03	0.52	0.89	0.85	0.98
Denmark	0.80	1.03	0.92	0.99	0.99	0.88	1.07	1.05	1.19	1.31	1.07	1.02	1.01	0.66	1.01	1.02	1.13
Germany	0.68	0.90	0.83	0.87	0.93	0.82	0.99	0.91	1.11	1.18	0.95	0.94	1.04	0.57	0.98	0.97	1.07
U.S.	0.41	0.69	0.55	0.56	0.73	0.59	0.69	0.56	0.90	0.98	0.73	0.84	0.97	0.47	0.94	0.79	0.99

Note: The Paasche-Laspeyres spread is the ratio of own-price weighted quantity index to quantity index weighted by base country price.

Table 7-12 *(continued)*

Country	Iran	Uruguay	Ireland	Hungary	Poland	Italy	Spain	U.K.	Japan	Austria	Netherlands	Belgium	France	Luxembourg	Denmark	Germany	U.S.
Uruguay	0.39																
Ireland	0.93	0.49															
Hungary	0.73	0.99	0.96														
Poland	0.68	1.07	0.90	0.99													
Italy	0.83	0.73	0.93	1.12	1.11												
Spain	0.85	0.83	0.90	1.23	1.19	1.06											
U.K.	0.70	0.70	0.85	1.05	1.07	0.97	0.95										
Japan	0.86	0.75	0.93	1.31	1.38	1.06	1.19	1.07									
Austria	0.85	0.82	0.89	1.25	1.26	1.04	1.01	0.99	1.15								
Netherlands	0.95	0.58	1.00	1.11	1.09	1.00	1.00	0.94	0.98	0.97							
Belgium	0.90	0.65	0.97	1.15	1.14	1.02	1.01	0.96	1.03	0.99	0.99						
France	0.78	0.71	0.92	1.18	1.09	1.02	0.98	0.90	0.99	0.98	0.96	0.98					
Luxembourg	0.92	0.57	0.99	1.06	1.01	0.98	0.96	0.91	0.99	0.95	1.01	0.99	0.96				
Denmark	0.83	0.85	0.89	1.39	1.39	1.03	1.05	1.02	1.06	1.03	0.95	0.99	1.01	0.95			
Germany	0.83	0.76	0.93	1.29	1.24	1.03	0.98	1.01	1.08	0.98	0.99	1.00	0.99	0.98	1.00		
U.S.	0.86	0.56	0.98	1.01	0.95	0.96	0.99	0.86	0.89	0.98	0.98	0.99	0.99	0.99	0.95	1.00	

Table 7-13. Comparison of Binary and Multilateral Estimates of Real GDP per Capita, 1975

| Country | Quantity indexes | | | Ratios | |
| | | Binary | | Augmented to | |
	Multilateral (1)	Augmented (2)	Traditional (3)	Traditional (4) = (2) ÷ (3)	Multilateral (5) = (2) ÷ (1)
Malawi	4.9	4.1	4.0	1.02	0.84
Kenya	6.6	6.1	6.5	0.94	0.92
India	6.6	6.0	5.9	1.02	0.91
Pakistan	8.2	6.6	7.1	0.93	0.80
Sri Lanka	9.3	8.0	8.2	0.98	0.86
Zambia	10.3	9.9	9.9	1.00	0.96
Thailand	13.0	10.8	10.0	1.08	0.83
Philippines	13.2	12.0	11.4	1.05	0.91
Korea	20.7	17.9	18.8	0.95	0.86
Malaysia	21.5	20.2	19.5	1.04	0.94
Colombia	22.4	19.4	19.0	1.02	0.87
Jamaica	24.0	25.1	24.6	1.02	1.05
Syria	25.0	20.9	20.3	1.03	0.84
Brazil	25.2	24.3	24.0	1.01	0.96
Romania	33.3	30.8	29.6	1.04	0.92
Mexico	34.7	35.6	35.5	1.00	1.03
Yugoslavia	36.1	36.8	37.2	0.99	1.02
Iran	37.7	33.2	34.6	0.96	0.88
Uruguay	39.6	33.3	33.2	1.00	0.84
Ireland	42.5	43.4	43.5	1.00	1.02
Hungary	49.6	49.0	49.3	0.99	0.99
Poland	50.1	46.7	47.0	0.99	0.93
Italy	53.8	55.4	55.7	0.99	1.03
Spain	55.9	54.1	55.0	0.98	0.97
U.K.	63.9	66.8	66.6	1.00	1.05
Japan	68.4	66.6	64.6	1.03	0.97
Austria	69.6	70.4	74.6	0.94	1.01
Netherlands	75.2	71.5	72.1	0.99	0.95
Belgium	77.7	76.5	77.2	0.99	0.98
France	81.9	81.2	80.6	1.01	0.99
Luxembourg	82.0	79.5	81.3	0.98	0.97
Denmark	82.4	80.9	84.0	0.96	0.98
Germany	83.0	80.9	81.1	1.00	0.97
U.S.	100.0	100.0	100.0	1.00	1.00

Category	Line numbers[a]	Per capita expenditure		Purchasing power parities (schillings/dollars)			Quantity per capita (U.S. = 100)		
		Austria (schillings)	U.S. (dollars)	U.S. weight	Austria weight	Geometric mean	U.S. weight	Austria weight	Geometric mean
Consumption, ICP[b,c]	1–108	55940.8	5182.96	17.19	13.68	15.34	78.9	62.8	75.4
Food, beverages, tobacco	1– 39	13873.4	818.24	17.53	16.17	16.83	104.9	96.7	100.7
Food	1– 33	9957.3	658.25	17.89	16.33	17.09	92.6	84.6	88.5
Bread, cereals	1– 6	1294.0	94.81	16.95	16.85	16.90	81.0	80.5	80.8
Meat	7– 12	3098.7	163.79	20.48	19.87	20.18	95.2	92.4	93.8
Fish	13– 14	147.9	25.96	20.31	18.24	19.24	31.2	28.0	29.6
Milk, cheese, eggs	15– 17	1467.8	82.52	15.21	14.82	15.02	120.0	116.9	118.4
Oils, fats	18– 20	694.7	32.30	18.18	17.76	17.97	121.1	118.3	119.7
Fruits, vegetables	21– 26	1936.6	147.83	17.10	13.13	14.98	99.8	76.6	87.4
Coffee, tea, cocoa	27– 29	244.9	17.18	34.64	30.18	32.34	47.3	41.2	44.1
Spices, sweets, sugar	30– 33	1072.7	93.86	14.07	14.30	14.19	79.9	81.2	80.6
Beverages	34– 37	2707.3	91.02	13.10	14.27	13.68	208.4	227.0	217.5
Tobacco	38– 39	1208.8	68.97	19.93	20.55	20.24	85.3	87.9	86.6
Clothing, footwear	40– 51	6078.5	336.33	18.82	18.22	18.52	99.2	96.0	97.6
Clothing	40– 47	5059.6	284.83	19.35	18.90	19.12	94.0	91.8	92.9
Footwear	48– 51	1018.9	51.50	15.88	15.46	15.67	127.9	124.6	126.3
Gross rent, fuel	52– 57	6743.4	903.84	12.86	11.41	12.11	65.4	58.0	61.6
Gross rent	52– 53	4641.0	717.46	9.36	9.14	9.25	70.8	69.1	70.0
Fuel, power	54– 57	2102.4	186.38	26.35	25.31	25.82	44.6	42.8	43.7
House furnishings, operations	58– 70	4898.8	343.14	16.94	14.51	15.68	98.4	84.3	91.1
Furniture	58– 60	2614.4	165.64	14.43	12.21	13.27	129.3	109.4	118.9
Appliances	61– 66	1102.3	56.41	24.84	20.22	22.41	96.6	78.6	87.2
Supplies, operations	67– 70	1182.2	121.09	16.69	17.14	16.91	56.9	58.5	57.7
Medical care	71– 77	5603.6	653.69	12.23	8.94	10.46	95.9	70.1	82.0
Transport, communications	78– 89	7383.0	692.17	29.99	19.32	24.07	55.2	35.6	44.3
Equipment	78– 79	1583.8	221.44	27.63	25.38	26.48	28.2	25.9	27.0
Operation costs	80– 83	4142.3	338.12	29.01	24.19	26.49	50.6	42.2	46.2
Purchased transport	84– 87	1014.6	40.37	18.92	9.93	13.71	253.2	132.8	183.4
Communications	88– 89	642.3	92.24	44.12	13.86	24.73	50.2	15.8	28.2
Recreation, education	90–101	6332.4	783.74	13.93	12.52	13.21	64.5	58.0	61.2
Recreation	90– 96	3400.3	323.24	18.19	17.59	17.89	59.8	57.8	58.8
Education	97–101	2932.2	460.50	10.94	9.39	10.13	67.8	58.2	62.8
Other expenditures	102–107	8819.0	628.47	17.39	13.14	15.12	106.8	80.7	92.8
Personal care	102–104	1658.1	136.90	14.48	14.36	14.42	84.3	83.6	84.0
Miscellaneous services	105–107	7160.9	491.57	18.20	12.89	15.32	113.0	80.1	95.1
Capital formation	109–146	23300.7	1185.32	25.78	24.20	24.98	81.2	76.2	78.7
Domestic capital formation	109–145	22739.5	1128.57	26.20	24.43	25.30	82.5	76.9	79.6
Construction	109–122	14379.1	680.37	26.40	25.46	25.92	83.0	80.0	81.5
Residential	109–110	5183.2	235.05	29.22	28.14	28.67	78.4	75.5	76.9
Nonresidential	111–118	5484.0	210.33	26.89	23.92	25.36	109.0	97.0	102.8
Other	119–122	3711.8	234.99	23.15	24.51	23.82	64.4	68.2	66.3
Producer durables	123–144	8942.8	491.75	25.41	22.68	24.00	80.2	71.6	75.8
Transport equipment	123–129	1460.1	122.69	25.35	25.00	25.18	47.6	46.9	47.3
Nonelectrical machinery	130–138	4683.6	203.26	23.99	21.02	22.45	109.6	96.1	102.6
Electrical machinery	139–142	1936.3	118.24	27.76	24.54	26.10	66.7	59.0	62.7
Other	143–144	862.8	47.56	25.78	25.21	25.49	72.0	70.4	71.2
Exports minus imports	146–146	561.2	56.75	17.42	17.42	17.42	56.8	56.8	56.8
Government	147–151	8026.6	808.43	18.61	18.19	18.40	54.6	53.4	54.0
Compensation	147–150	6157.3	419.96	17.85	17.84	17.85	82.2	82.1	82.1
Commodities	151–151	1869.3	388.47	19.42	19.42	19.42	24.8	24.8	24.8
Gross domestic product	1–151	87268.1	7176.71	18.77	15.89	17.27	76.5	64.8	70.4
Aggregates									
ICP concepts[e]									
Consumption (CEP)[b,c]	1–108	55940.8	5182.96	17.19	13.68	15.34	78.9	62.8	70.4
Capital formation (GCF)[d]	109–146	23300.7	1185.32	25.78	24.20	24.98	81.2	76.2	78.7
Government (PFC)	147–151	8026.6	808.43	18.61	18.19	18.40	54.6	53.4	54.0
Gross domestic product	1–151	87268.1	7176.71	18.77	15.89	17.27	76.5	64.8	70.4
SNA concepts[e]									
Consumption (PFCE)	1–108	48900.9	4620.20	17.75	14.81	16.22	71.4	59.6	65.3
Capital formation (GCF)	109–146	23300.7	1185.32	25.78	24.20	24.98	81.2	76.2	78.7
Government (GFCE)	1–151	15066.5	1367.45	16.17	12.26	14.08	89.9	68.1	78.2
Gross domestic product	1–151	87268.1	7172.96	18.78	15.89	17.27	76.6	64.8	70.4

Note: See the end of Appendix Table 7-68 for notes.

Category	Line numbers[a]	Per capita expenditure		Purchasing power parities (francs/dollars)			Quantity per capita (U.S. = 100)		
		Belgium (francs)	U.S. (dollars)	U.S. weight	Belgium weight	Geometric mean	U.S. weight	Belgium weight	Geometric mean
Consumption, ICP[b,c]	1–108	152538.6	5182.96	43.68	36.23	39.78	81.2	67.4	74.0
Food, beverages, tobacco	1– 39	34401.6	818.24	37.71	36.94	37.32	113.8	111.5	112.7
Food	1– 33	28668.2	658.25	38.02	37.12	37.57	117.3	114.5	115.9
Bread, cereals	1– 6	3630.7	94.81	35.72	36.07	35.90	106.2	107.2	106.7
Meat	7– 12	11250.5	163.79	40.89	40.00	40.44	171.7	168.0	169.8
Fish	13– 14	1214.6	25.96	48.75	47.25	47.99	99.0	96.0	97.5
Milk, cheese, eggs	15– 17	3101.6	82.52	34.92	34.53	34.73	108.9	107.6	108.2
Oils, fats	18– 20	1957.7	32.30	39.32	47.06	43.02	128.8	154.2	140.9
Fruits, vegetables	21– 26	4360.2	147.83	39.22	30.75	34.72	95.9	75.2	84.9
Coffee, tea, cocoa	27– 29	870.7	17.18	66.75	67.48	67.11	75.1	76.0	75.5
Spices, sweets, sugar	30– 33	2282.3	93.86	27.50	29.08	28.28	83.6	88.4	86.0
Beverages	34– 37	3150.4	91.02	34.12	33.58	33.85	103.1	101.4	102.2
Tobacco	38– 39	2583.0	68.97	39.52	39.52	39.52	94.8	94.8	94.8
Clothing, footwear	40– 51	11738.8	336.33	51.97	52.98	52.47	65.9	67.2	66.5
Clothing	40– 47	9916.3	284.83	52.35	54.01	53.17	64.5	66.5	65.5
Footwear	48– 51	1822.5	51.50	49.87	48.03	48.94	73.7	71.0	72.3
Gross rent, fuel	52– 57	22203.2	903.84	46.27	42.42	44.30	57.9	53.1	55.4
Gross rent	52– 53	13937.9	717.46	40.50	35.85	38.11	54.2	48.0	51.0
Fuel, power	54– 57	8265.4	186.38	68.45	61.42	64.84	72.2	64.8	68.4
House furnishings, operations	58– 70	17559.8	343.14 ·	45.17	29.45	36.47	173.8	113.3	140.3
Furniture	58– 60	6675.5	165.64	35.09	18.64	25.57	216.3	114.8	157.6
Appliances	61– 66	2315.6	56.41	71.19	55.87	63.07	73.5	57.7	65.1
Supplies, operations	67– 70	8568.7	121.09	46.84	43.59	45.19	162.3	151.1	156.6
Medical care	71– 77	12290.3	653.69	27.71	22.16	24.78	84.8	67.8	75.9
Transport, communications	78– 89	15936.4	692.17	60.04	41.03	49.63	56.1	38.3	46.4
Equipment	78– 79	5056.3	221.44	44.63	40.78	42.66	56.0	51.2	53.5
Operation costs	80– 83	8009.2	338.12	59.03	43.69	50.79	54.2	40.1	46.6
Purchased transport	84– 87	1722.9	40.37	64.16	25.84	40.71	165.2	66.5	104.8
Communications	88– 89	1148.0	92.24	98.93	79.51	88.69	15.7	12.6	14.0
Recreation, education	90–101	20373.5	783.74	39.16	37.21	38.17	69.9	66.4	68.1
Recreation	90– 96	7656.1	323.24	43.34	42.61	42.97	55.6	54.7	55.1
Education	97–101	12717.5	460.50	36.23	34.58	35.39	79.9	76.2	78.0
Other expenditures	102–107	18034.9	628.47	46.95	40.31	43.51	71.2	61.1	66.0
Personal care	102–104	4065.8	136.90	42.61	35.19	38.72	84.4	69.7	76.7
Miscellaneous services	105–107	13969.1	491.57	48.16	42.10	45.03	67.5	59.0	63.1
Capital formation	109–146	53393.9	1185.32	47.23	45.67	46.44	98.6	95.4	97.0
Domestic capital formation	109–145	50894.2	1128.57	47.76	46.22	46.98	97.6	94.4	96.0
Construction	109–122	32412.2	680.37	47.06	44.56	45.79	106.9	101.2	104.0
Residential	109–110	13178.8	235.05	50.41	43.53	46.84	128.8	111.2	119.7
Nonresidential	111–118	13323.4	210.33	52.34	54.76	53.54	115.7	121.0	118.3
Other	119–122	5910.0	234.99	38.98	32.60	35.65	77.1	64.5	70.5
Producer durables	123–144	19740.2	491.75	48.37	49.02	48.69	81.9	83.0	82.4
Transport equipment	123–129	4318.6	122.69	42.73	47.04	44.83	74.8	82.4	78.5
Nonelectrical machinery	130–138	8819.1	203.26	45.98	45.34	45.66	95.7	94.4	95.0
Electrical machinery	139–142	5272.0	118.24	59.05	60.91	59.98	73.2	75.5	74.3
Other	143–144	1330.5	47.56	46.55	44.61	45.57	62.7	60.1	61.4
Exports minus imports	146–146	2499.7	56.75	36.78	36.78	36.78	119.8	119.8	119.8
Government	147–151	25706.3	808.43	51.66	51.27	51.46	62.0	61.6	61.8
Compensation	147–150	18271.4	419.96	54.59	52.50	53.53	82.9	79.7	81.3
Commodities	151–151	7434.9	388.47	48.49	48.49	48.49	39.5	39.5	39.5
Gross domestic product	1–151	231638.8	7176.71	45.17	39.39	42.18	81.9	71.5	76.5
Aggregates									
ICP concepts[e]									
Consumption (CEP)[b,c]	1–108	152538.6	5182.96	43.68	36.23	39.78	81.2	67.4	74.0
Capital formation (GCF)[d]	109–146	53393.9	1185.32	47.23	45.67	46.44	98.6	95.4	97.0
Government (PFC)	147–151	25706.3	808.43	51.66	51.27	51.46	62.0	61.6	61.8
Gross domestic product	1–151	231638.8	7176.71	45.17	39.39	42.18	81.9	71.5	76.5
SNA concepts[e]									
Consumption (PFCE)	1–108	139736.0	4620.20	44.42	36.43	40.23	83.0	68.1	75.2
Capital formation (GCF)	109–146	53393.9	1185.32	47.23	45.67	46.44	98.6	95.4	97.0
Government (GFCE)	1–151	38127.2	1367.45	45.91	44.11	45.00	63.2	60.7	62.0
Gross domestic product	1–151	231257.1	7172.96	45.17	39.40	42.19	81.8	71.4	76.4

Note: See the end of Appendix Table 7-68 for notes.

Appendix Table 7-3. Augmented Summary Binary Table: Brazil/United States, 1975

Category	Line numbers[a]	Per capita expenditure — Brazil (cruzeiros)	Per capita expenditure — U.S. (dollars)	Purchasing power parities (cruzeiros/dollars) — U.S. weight	Purchasing power parities — Brazil weight	Purchasing power parities — Geometric mean	Quantity per capita (U.S. = 100) — U.S. weight	Quantity per capita — Brazil weight	Quantity per capita — Geometric mean
Consumption, ICP[b,c]	1–108	6729.29	5182.96	7.061	4.468	5.617	29.1	18.4	23.1
Food, beverages, tobacco	1– 39	2476.69	818.24	7.157	5.072	6.025	59.7	42.3	50.2
Food	1– 33	2283.74	658.25	7.133	4.963	5.950	69.9	48.6	58.3
Bread, cereals	1– 6	506.19	94.81	4.653	4.926	4.788	108.4	114.7	111.5
Meat	7– 12	617.70	163.79	5.896	3.909	4.801	96.5	64.0	78.6
Fish	13– 14	72.63	25.96	6.563	6.101	6.328	45.9	42.6	44.2
Milk, cheese, eggs	15– 17	231.09	82.52	6.346	5.551	5.935	50.4	44.1	47.2
Oils, fats	18– 20	159.20	32.30	7.004	7.094	7.049	69.5	70.4	69.9
Fruits, vegetables	21– 26	464.38	147.83	11.593	7.264	9.176	43.2	27.1	34.2
Coffee, tea, cocoa	27– 29	102.70	17.18	6.289	6.316	6.303	94.7	95.1	94.9
Spices, sweets, sugar	30– 33	129.85	93.86	5.823	3.006	4.184	46.0	23.8	33.1
Beverages	34– 37	40.36	91.02	5.694	5.679	5.687	7.8	7.8	7.8
Tobacco	38– 39	152.59	68.97	9.315	7.229	8.206	30.6	23.8	27.0
Clothing, footwear	40– 51	629.43	336.33	8.413	7.866	8.135	23.8	22.2	23.0
Clothing	40– 47	526.73	284.83	8.802	8.420	8.609	22.0	21.0	21.5
Footwear	48– 51	102.69	51.50	6.260	5.882	6.068	33.9	31.9	32.9
Gross rent, fuel	52– 57	717.36	903.84	6.772	6.328	6.546	12.5	11.7	12.1
Gross rent	52– 53	454.73	717.46	5.046	4.927	4.986	12.9	12.6	12.7
Fuel, power	54– 57	262.63	186.38	13.414	12.467	12.932	11.3	10.5	10.9
House furnishings, operations	58– 70	558.27	343.14	8.799	5.009	6.639	32.5	18.5	24.5
Furniture	58– 60	207.61	165.64	8.494	7.892	8.187	15.9	14.8	15.3
Appliances	61– 66	90.22	56.41	14.448	11.436	12.854	14.0	11.1	12.4
Supplies, operations	67– 70	260.44	121.09	6.585	3.371	4.712	63.8	32.7	45.6
Medical care	71– 77	362.27	653.69	5.421	3.100	4.099	17.9	10.2	13.5
Transport, communications	78– 89	721.02	692.17	11.332	5.008	7.534	20.8	9.2	13.8
Equipment	78– 79	194.31	221.44	13.020	11.720	12.353	7.5	6.7	7.1
Operation costs	80– 83	322.79	338.12	12.934	9.640	11.166	9.9	7.4	8.5
Purchased transport	84– 87	173.12	40.37	3.457	2.009	2.636	213.4	124.1	162.7
Communications	88– 89	30.81	92.24	4.859	3.976	4.395	8.4	6.9	7.6
Recreation, education	90–101	593.74	783.74	4.991	1.936	3.109	39.1	15.2	24.4
Recreation	90– 96	346.63	323.24	9.462	8.351	8.889	12.8	11.3	12.1
Education	97–101	247.10	460.50	1.853	0.932	1.314	57.6	29.0	40.8
Other expenditures	102–107	670.52	628.47	5.217	4.605	4.901	23.2	20.4	21.8
Personal care	102–104	152.58	136.90	6.800	6.268	6.529	17.8	16.4	17.1
Miscellaneous services	105–107	517.94	491.57	4.777	4.271	4.517	24.7	22.1	23.3
Capital formation	109–146	2013.05	1185.32	7.070	5.018	5.956	33.8	24.0	28.5
Domestic capital formation	109–145	2388.38	1128.57	7.013	5.344	6.122	39.6	30.2	34.6
Construction	109–122	1183.77	680.37	5.029	4.123	4.554	42.2	34.6	38.2
Residential	109–110	249.05	235.05	4.358	4.561	4.459	23.2	24.3	23.8
Nonresidential	111–118	297.86	210.33	6.395	5.966	6.177	23.7	22.1	22.9
Other	119–122	636.86	234.99	4.479	3.488	3.952	77.7	60.5	68.6
Producer durables	123–144	1204.61	491.75	9.889	7.539	8.634	32.5	24.8	28.4
Transport equipment	123–129	249.33	122.69	10.848	8.797	9.769	23.1	18.7	20.8
Nonelectrical machinery	130–138	550.77	203.26	9.399	7.392	8.335	36.7	28.8	32.5
Electrical machinery	139–142	191.64	118.24	10.740	7.758	9.128	20.9	15.1	17.8
Other	143–144	212.87	47.56	7.395	6.602	6.987	67.8	60.5	64.1
Exports minus imports	146–146	− 375.32	56.75	8.204	8.204	8.204	− 80.6	− 80.6	− 80.6
Government	147–151	680.40	808.43	4.899	2.285	3.346	36.8	17.2	25.2
Compensation	147–150	468.79	419.96	3.598	1.774	2.527	62.9	31.0	44.2
Commodities	147–151	680.40	808.43	4.899	2.285	3.346	36.8	17.2	25.2
Gross domestic product	1–151	9422.75	7176.71	6.819	4.273	5.398	30.7	19.3	24.3
Aggregates									
ICP concepts[c]									
Consumption (CEP)[b,c]	1–108	6729.29	5182.96	7.061	4.468	5.617	29.1	18.4	23.1
Capital formation (GCF)[d]	109–146	2013.05	1185.32	7.070	5.018	5.956	33.8	24.0	28.5
Government (PFC)	147–151	680.40	808.43	4.899	2.285	3.346	36.8	17.2	25.2
Gross domestic product	1–151	9422.75	7176.71	6.819	4.273	5.398	30.7	19.3	24.3
SNA concepts[c]									
Consumption (PFCE)	1–108	6480.32	4620.20	7.568	5.067	6.192	27.7	18.5	22.7
Capital formation (GCF)	109–146	2013.05	1185.32	7.070	5.018	5.956	33.8	24.0	28.5
Government (GFCE)	1–151	927.28	1367.45	4.074	1.768	2.684	38.4	16.6	25.3
Gross domestic product	1–151	9420.66	7172.96	6.820	4.273	5.398	30.7	19.3	24.3

Note: See the end of Appendix Table 7-68 for notes.

Category	Line numbers[a]	Per capita expenditure		Purchasing power parities (pesos/dollars)			Quantity per capita (U.S. = 100)		
		Colombia (pesos)	U.S. (dollars)	U.S. weight	Colombia weight	Geometric mean	U.S. weight	Colombia weight	Geometric mean
Consumption, ICP[b,c]	1–108	13745.7	5182.96	16.50	8.95	12.15	29.6	16.1	21.8
Food, beverages, tobacco	1– 39	5368.9	818.24	16.77	12.19	14.30	53.8	39.1	45.9
Food	1– 33	4655.4	658.25	17.39	12.06	14.48	58.6	40.7	48.8
Bread, cereals	1– 6	720.2	94.81	21.66	19.42	20.51	39.1	35.1	37.0
Meat	7– 12	1613.3	163.79	13.28	9.77	11.39	100.8	74.1	86.4
Fish	13– 14	95.0	25.96	22.71	20.92	21.80	17.5	16.1	16.8
Milk, cheese, eggs	15– 17	513.2	82.52	18.55	15.15	16.76	41.1	33.5	37.1
Oils, fats	18– 20	210.4	32.30	18.71	18.88	18.80	34.5	34.8	34.7
Fruits, vegetables	21– 26	766.1	147.83	21.90	14.23	17.65	36.4	23.7	29.4
Coffee, tea, cocoa	27– 29	199.6	17.18	9.71	9.75	9.73	119.2	119.7	119.5
Spices, sweets, sugar	30– 33	537.6	93.86	11.59	8.98	10.20	63.8	49.4	56.1
Beverages	34– 37	531.3	91.02	17.65	15.77	16.68	37.0	33.1	35.0
Tobacco	38– 39	182.1	68.97	9.76	8.78	9.26	30.1	27.0	28.5
Clothing, footwear	40– 51	1266.0	336.33	15.42	13.51	14.43	27.9	24.4	26.1
Clothing	40– 47	947.7	284.83	16.32	14.89	15.59	22.3	20.4	21.3
Footwear	48– 51	318.3	51.50	10.42	10.58	10.50	58.4	59.3	58.8
Gross rent, fuel	52– 57	1064.2	903.84	11.65	9.95	10.77	11.8	10.1	10.9
Gross rent	52– 53	830.0	717.46	12.64	12.39	12.52	9.3	9.2	9.2
Fuel, power	54– 57	234.2	186.38	7.83	5.86	6.77	21.5	16.1	18.6
House furnishings, operations	58– 70	854.6	343.14	24.78	12.17	17.37	20.5	10.1	14.3
Furniture	58– 60	176.5	165.64	15.49	12.93	14.15	8.2	6.9	7.5
Appliances	61– 66	104.0	56.41	69.84	44.74	55.90	4.1	2.6	3.3
Supplies, operations	67– 70	574.2	121.09	16.49	10.59	13.21	44.8	28.8	35.9
Medical care	71– 77	716.7	653.69	9.30	9.54	9.42	11.5	11.8	11.6
Transport, communications	78– 89	1272.9	692.17	35.44	4.76	12.99	38.6	5.2	14.2
Equipment	78– 79	131.5	221.44	83.23	78.51	80.84	0.8	0.7	0.7
Operation costs	80– 83	80.3	338.12	16.28	17.18	16.72	1.4	1.5	1.4
Purchased transport	84– 87	973.2	40.37	6.47	4.10	5.15	588.0	372.8	468.2
Communications	88– 89	87.9	92.24	3.66	3.71	3.68	25.7	26.1	25.9
Recreation, education	90–101	1605.1	783.74	11.27	4.95	7.47	41.4	18.2	27.4
Recreation	90– 96	485.3	323.24	20.29	9.35	13.77	16.1	7.4	10.9
Education	97–101	1119.8	460.50	4.94	4.11	4.51	59.1	49.2	54.0
Other expenditures	102–107	1597.4	628.47	11.79	10.11	10.92	25.1	21.6	23.3
Personal care	102–104	309.1	136.90	22.27	16.43	19.12	13.7	10.1	11.8
Miscellaneous services	105–107	1288.3	491.57	8.87	9.26	9.07	28.3	29.5	28.9
Capital formation	109–146	3201.1	1185.32	25.86	10.15	16.20	26.6	10.4	16.7
Domestic capital formation	109–145	3108.6	1128.57	25.61	9.95	15.96	27.7	10.8	17.3
Construction	109–122	1913.6	680.37	8.61	6.53	7.50	43.1	32.7	37.5
Residential	109–110	396.1	235.05	8.90	8.36	8.62	20.2	18.9	19.5
Nonresidential	111–118	121.8	210.33	8.37	7.76	8.06	7.5	6.9	7.2
Other	119–122	1395.7	234.99	8.54	6.07	7.20	97.8	69.6	82.5
Producer durables	123–144	1362.8	491.75	48.10	43.32	45.65	6.4	5.8	6.1
Transport equipment	123–129	467.9	122.69	56.09	45.64	50.60	8.4	6.8	7.5
Nonelectrical machinery	130–138	236.8	203.26	45.40	40.07	42.65	2.9	2.6	2.7
Electrical machinery	139–142	593.5	118.24	48.54	43.59	46.00	11.5	10.3	10.9
Other	143–144	64.5	47.56	37.92	38.40	38.16	3.5	3.6	3.6
Exports minus imports	146–146	92.5	56.75	30.87	30.87	30.87	5.3	5.3	5.3
Government	147–151	489.7	808.43	9.99	7.29	8.53	8.3	6.1	7.1
Compensation	147–150	400.7	419.96	6.22	6.58	6.40	14.5	15.3	14.9
Commodities	151–151	89.1	388.47	14.07	14.07	14.07	1.6	1.6	1.6
Gross domestic product	1–151	17436.6	7176.71	17.31	9.09	12.54	26.7	14.0	19.4
Aggregates									
ICP concepts[e]									
Consumption (CEP)[b,c]	1–108	13745.7	5182.96	16.50	8.95	12.15	29.6	16.1	21.8
Capital formation (GCF)[d]	109–146	3201.1	1185.32	25.86	10.15	16.20	26.6	10.4	16.7
Government (PFC)	147–151	489.7	808.43	9.99	7.29	8.53	8.3	6.1	7.1
Gross domestic product	1–151	17436.6	7176.71	17.31	9.09	12.54	26.7	14.0	19.4
SNA concepts[e]									
Consumption (PFCE)	1–108	12950.4	4620.20	17.72	9.79	13.17	28.6	15.8	21.3
Capital formation (GCF)	109–146	3201.1	1185.32	25.86	10.15	16.20	26.6	10.4	16.7
Government (GFCE)	1–151	1285.1	1367.45	8.55	4.58	6.25	20.5	11.0	15.0
Gross domestic product	1–151	17436.6	7172.96	17.32	9.09	12.54	26.7	14.0	19.4

Note: See the end of Appendix Table 7-68 for notes.

Category	Line numbers[a]	Per capita expenditure Denmark (kroner)	Per capita expenditure U.S. (dollars)	Purchasing power parities (kroner/dollars) U.S. weight	Purchasing power parities (kroner/dollars) Denmark weight	Purchasing power parities (kroner/dollars) Geometric mean	Quantity per capita (U.S. = 100) U.S. weight	Quantity per capita (U.S. = 100) Denmark weight	Quantity per capita (U.S. = 100) Geometric mean
Consumption, ICP[b,c]	1–108	28212.05	5182.96	8.106	6.733	7.388	80.8	67.2	73.7
Food, beverages, tobacco	1– 39	6627.47	818.24	9.177	8.724	8.948	92.8	88.3	90.5
Food	1– 33	4452.77	658.25	8.076	7.685	7.878	88.0	83.8	85.9
Bread, cereals	1– 6	595.26	94.81	6.794	6.949	6.871	90.3	92.4	91.4
Meat	7– 12	1362.45	163.79	8.470	7.694	8.072	108.1	98.2	103.0
Fish	13– 14	208.89	25.96	9.452	8.660	9.047	92.9	85.1	88.9
Milk, cheese, eggs	15– 17	544.66	82.52	6.279	6.164	6.221	107.1	105.1	106.1
Oils, fats	18– 20	248.02	32.30	9.295	9.156	9.225	83.9	82.6	83.2
Fruits, vegetables	21– 26	574.90	147.83	9.070	8.650	8.858	45.0	42.9	43.9
Coffee, tea, cocoa	27– 29	272.53	17.18	13.333	13.425	13.379	118.2	119.0	118.6
Spices, sweets, sugar	30– 33	646.05	93.86	6.938	7.152	7.044	96.2	99.2	97.7
Beverages	34– 37	1237.75	91.02	9.887	9.502	9.693	143.1	137.5	140.3
Tobacco	38– 39	936.96	68.97	18.744	18.744	18.744	72.5	72.5	72.5
Clothing, footwear	40– 51	1510.67	336.33	9.227	9.105	9.166	49.3	48.7	49.0
Clothing	40– 47	1283.20	284.83	9.205	9.088	9.146	49.6	48.9	49.3
Footwear	48– 51	227.47	51.50	9.353	9.201	9.277	48.0	47.2	47.6
Gross rent, fuel	52– 57	5515.61	903.84	5.694	5.533	5.613	110.3	107.2	108.7
Gross rent	52– 53	4038.54	717.46	4.683	4.867	4.774	115.7	120.2	117.9
Fuel, power	54– 57	1477.07	186.38	9.584	8.839	9.204	89.7	82.7	86.1
House furnishings, operations	58– 70	2162.25	343.14	7.739	5.139	6.307	122.6	81.4	99.9
Furniture	58– 60	1002.57	165.64	6.263	3.690	4.808	164.0	96.6	125.9
Appliances	61– 66	297.23	56.41	10.950	9.256	10.068	56.9	48.1	52.3
Supplies, operations	67– 70	862.45	121.09	8.262	7.375	7.806	96.6	86.2	91.2
Medical care	71– 77	1453.75	653.69	3.785	2.576	3.122	86.3	58.8	71.2
Transport, communications	78– 89	3359.09	692.17	11.785	7.937	9.671	61.1	41.2	50.2
Equipment	78– 79	1050.59	221.44	16.911	14.737	15.787	32.2	28.1	30.1
Operation costs	80– 83	1646.64	338.12	9.322	6.619	7.855	73.6	52.2	62.0
Purchased transport	84– 87	423.52	40.37	11.217	5.958	8.175	176.1	93.5	128.3
Communications	88– 89	238.34	92.24	8.757	7.425	8.063	34.8	29.5	32.0
Recreation, education	90–101	5446.24	783.74	8.711	8.779	8.745	79.2	79.8	79.5
Recreation	90– 96	2007.90	323.24	8.499	8.342	8.420	74.5	73.1	73.8
Education	97–101	3438.34	460.50	8.860	9.055	8.957	82.5	84.3	83.4
Other expenditures	102–107	2136.96	628.47	9.556	8.946	9.246	38.0	35.6	36.8
Personal care	102–104	600.20	136.90	9.487	8.382	8.918	52.3	46.2	49.2
Miscellaneous services	105–107	1536.76	491.57	9.575	9.187	9.379	34.0	32.7	33.3
Capital formation	109–146	8209.49	1185.32	7.700	6.925	7.302	100.0	89.9	94.8
Domestic capital formation	109–145	8771.54	1128.57	7.798	6.835	7.301	113.7	99.7	106.5
Construction	109–122	6300.39	680.37	7.231	6.840	7.033	135.4	128.1	131.7
Residential	109–110	2917.00	235.05	7.662	7.224	7.440	171.8	162.0	166.8
Nonresidential	111–118	2346.24	210.33	8.839	8.141	8.483	137.0	126.2	131.5
Other	119–122	1037.15	234.99	5.361	4.528	4.927	97.5	82.3	89.6
Producer durables	123–144	3061.66	491.75	8.626	7.062	7.805	88.2	72.2	79.8
Transport equipment	123–129	1000.40	122.69	10.881	8.228	9.462	99.1	74.9	86.2
Nonelectrical machinery	130–138	1343.28	203.26	7.092	5.957	6.500	110.9	93.2	101.7
Electrical machinery	139–142	394.27	118.24	9.400	8.466	8.921	39.4	35.5	37.4
Other	143–144	323.72	47.56	7.438	8.114	7.769	83.9	91.5	87.6
Exports minus imports	146–146	− 562.06	56.75	5.746	5.746	5.746	− 172.4	− 172.4	− 172.4
Government	147–151	6665.61	808.43	7.820	7.453	7.634	110.6	105.4	108.0
Compensation	147–150	5513.44	419.96	7.532	7.326	7.428	179.2	174.3	176.7
Commodities	151–151	1152.17	388.47	8.130	8.130	8.130	36.5	36.5	36.5
Gross domestic product	1–151	43087.15	7176.71	8.007	6.872	7.418	87.4	75.0	80.9
Aggregates									
ICP concepts[e]									
Consumption (CEP)[b,c]	1–108	28212.05	5182.96	8.106	6.733	7.388	80.8	67.2	73.7
Capital formation (GCF)[d]	109–146	8209.49	1185.32	7.700	6.925	7.302	100.0	89.9	94.8
Government (PFC)	147–151	6665.61	808.43	7.820	7.453	7.634	110.6	105.4	108.0
Gross domestic product	1–151	43087.15	7176.71	8.007	6.872	7.418	87.4	75.0	80.9
SNA concepts[e]									
Consumption (PFCE)	1–108	23251.18	4620.20	8.128	7.245	7.674	69.5	61.9	65.6
Capital formation (GCF)	109–146	8209.49	1185.32	7.700	6.925	7.302	100.0	89.9	94.8
Government (GFCE)	1–151	11483.99	1367.45	7.872	6.267	7.024	134.0	106.7	119.6
Gross domestic product	1–151	42944.66	7172.96	8.009	6.897	7.432	86.8	74.8	80.6

Note: See the end of Appendix Table 7-68 for notes.

Category	Line numbers[a]	Per capita expenditure France (francs)	Per capita expenditure U.S. (dollars)	Purchasing power parities (francs/dollars) U.S. weight	Purchasing power parities (francs/dollars) France weight	Purchasing power parities (francs/dollars) Geometric mean	Quantity per capita (U.S. = 100) U.S. weight	Quantity per capita (U.S. = 100) France weight	Quantity per capita (U.S. = 100) Geometric mean
Consumption, ICP[b,c]	1–108	18015.41	5182.96	5.171	4.069	4.587	85.4	67.2	75.8
Food, beverages, tobacco	1– 39	4118.37	818.24	4.594	4.516	4.555	111.5	109.6	110.5
Food	1– 33	3402.35	658.25	4.652	4.659	4.655	110.9	111.1	111.0
Bread, cereals	1– 6	434.94	94.81	4.268	4.338	4.303	105.8	107.5	106.6
Meat	7– 12	1162.09	163.79	5.321	5.504	5.411	128.9	133.3	131.1
Fish	13– 14	181.37	25.96	5.728	5.783	5.756	120.8	122.0	121.4
Milk, cheese, eggs	15– 17	451.83	82.52	3.789	3.854	3.822	142.1	144.5	143.3
Oils, fats	18– 20	211.02	32.30	4.911	5.957	5.409	109.7	133.0	120.8
Fruits, vegetables	21– 26	578.22	147.83	4.754	3.973	4.346	98.4	82.3	90.0
Coffee, tea, cocoa	27– 29	85.67	17.18	7.255	6.552	6.895	76.1	68.8	72.3
Spices, sweets, sugar	30– 33	297.21	93.86	3.605	3.898	3.749	81.2	87.8	84.5
Beverages	34– 37	525.54	91.02	4.178	3.746	3.956	154.1	138.2	145.9
Tobacco	38– 39	190.49	68.97	4.596	4.596	4.596	60.1	60.1	60.1
Clothing, footwear	40– 51	1344.15	336.33	6.974	7.127	7.050	56.1	57.3	56.7
Clothing	40– 47	1090.32	284.83	6.925	7.138	7.031	53.6	55.3	54.4
Footwear	48– 51	253.83	51.50	7.245	7.079	7.162	69.6	68.0	68.8
Gross rent, fuel	52– 57	2579.21	903.84	5.022	4.454	4.730	64.1	56.8	60.3
Gross rent	52– 53	1951.51	717.46	4.329	3.945	4.132	69.0	62.8	65.8
Fuel, power	54– 57	627.70	186.38	7.690	7.442	7.565	45.3	43.8	44.5
House furnishings, operations	58– 70	1796.58	343.14	5.398	3.399	4.283	154.1	97.0	122.2
Furniture	58– 60	776.64	165.64	4.013	2.226	2.989	210.6	116.8	156.9
Appliances	61– 66	240.84	56.41	9.133	7.073	8.037	60.4	46.7	53.1
Supplies, operations	67– 70	779.10	121.09	5.554	5.348	5.450	120.3	115.8	118.1
Medical care	71– 77	1903.94	653.69	3.152	2.841	2.993	102.5	92.4	97.3
Transport, communications	78– 89	2055.79	692.17	7.510	3.924	5.428	75.7	39.5	54.7
Equipment	78– 79	481.80	221.44	7.321	6.408	6.849	34.0	29.7	31.8
Operation costs	80– 83	1142.94	338.12	7.312	3.265	4.886	103.5	46.2	69.2
Purchased transport	84– 87	304.86	40.37	6.177	3.738	4.805	202.0	122.3	157.2
Communications	88– 89	126.18	92.24	9.272	7.384	8.274	18.5	14.8	16.5
Recreation, education	90–101	2112.63	783.74	4.613	3.968	4.278	67.9	58.4	63.0
Recreation	90– 96	1098.79	323.24	5.545	5.256	5.398	64.7	61.3	63.0
Education	97–101	1013.84	460.50	3.958	3.135	3.523	70.2	55.6	62.5
Other expenditures	102–107	2104.74	628.47	5.301	4.270	4.758	78.4	63.2	70.4
Personal care	102–104	577.44	136.90	5.352	5.245	5.298	80.4	78.8	79.6
Miscellaneous services	105–107	1527.30	491.57	5.286	3.990	4.593	77.9	58.8	67.7
Capital formation	109–146	6530.31	1185.32	5.421	4.667	5.030	118.0	101.6	109.5
Domestic capital formation	109–145	6341.26	1128.57	5.478	4.680	5.063	120.1	102.6	111.0
Construction	109–122	4038.56	680.37	5.153	4.419	4.772	134.3	115.2	124.4
Residential	109–110	2094.22	235.05	4.711	4.371	4.538	203.8	189.1	196.3
Nonresidential	111–118	1309.41	210.33	6.684	5.549	6.090	112.2	93.1	102.2
Other	119–122	634.92	234.99	4.226	3.192	3.673	84.6	63.9	73.6
Producer durables	123–144	2371.77	491.75	5.902	5.219	5.550	92.4	81.7	86.9
Transport equipment	123–129	559.43	122.69	6.040	5.442	5.733	83.8	75.5	79.5
Nonelectrical machinery	130–138	1440.04	203.26	5.498	5.023	5.255	141.1	128.9	134.8
Electrical machinery	139–142	240.01	118.24	6.892	6.619	6.754	30.7	29.5	30.1
Other	143–144	132.29	47.56	4.813	4.616	4.714	60.3	57.8	59.0
Exports minus imports	146–146	189.05	56.75	4.286	4.286	4.286	77.7	77.7	77.7
Government	147–151	3009.19	808.43	5.120	5.075	5.098	73.3	72.7	73.0
Compensation	147–150	1969.44	419.96	4.954	4.964	4.959	94.5	94.7	94.6
Commodities	151–151	1039.76	388.47	5.300	5.300	5.300	50.5	50.5	50.5
Gross domestic product	1–151	27554.92	7176.71	5.207	4.292	4.727	89.5	73.7	81.2
Aggregates									
ICP concepts[e]									
Consumption (CEP)[b,c]	1–108	18015.41	5182.96	5.171	4.069	4.587	85.4	67.2	75.8
Capital formation (GCF)[d]	109–146	6530.31	1185.32	5.421	4.667	5.030	118.0	101.6	109.5
Government (PFC)	147–151	3009.19	808.43	5.120	5.075	5.098	73.3	72.7	73.0
Gross domestic product	1–151	27554.92	7176.71	5.207	4.292	4.727	89.5	73.7	81.2
SNA concepts[e]									
Consumption (PFCE)	1–108	16991.35	4620.20	5.321	4.150	4.699	88.6	69.1	78.3
Capital formation (GCF)	109–146	6530.31	1185.32	5.421	4.667	5.030	118.0	101.6	109.5
Government (GFCE)	1–151	3976.97	1367.45	4.638	4.369	4.501	66.6	62.7	64.6
Gross domestic product	1–151	27498.63	7172.96	5.207	4.294	4.729	89.3	73.6	81.1

Note: See the end of Appendix Table 7-68 for notes.

Category	Line numbers[a]	Per capita expenditure Germany (DM)	Per capita expenditure U.S. (dollars)	Purchasing power parities (DM/dollars) U.S. weight	Purchasing power parities (DM/dollars) Germany weight	Purchasing power parities (DM/dollars) Geometric mean	Quantity per capita (U.S. = 100) U.S. weight	Quantity per capita (U.S. = 100) Germany weight	Quantity per capita (U.S. = 100) Geometric mean
Consumption, ICP[b,c]	1–108	10845.56	5182.96	3.115	2.558	2.823	81.8	67.2	74.1
Food, beverages, tobacco	1– 39	2164.81	818.24	3.136	3.089	3.112	85.6	84.4	85.0
Food	1– 33	1650.05	658.25	2.962	2.968	2.965	84.5	84.6	84.5
Bread, cereals	1– 6	297.95	94.81	2.882	2.930	2.906	107.2	109.0	108.1
Meat	7– 12	439.68	163.79	3.377	3.235	3.305	83.0	79.5	81.2
Fish	13– 14	25.80	25.96	3.340	3.343	3.341	29.7	29.8	29.7
Milk, cheese, eggs	15– 17	189.23	82.52	2.542	2.562	2.552	89.5	90.2	89.8
Oils, fats	18– 20	161.88	32.30	3.066	3.484	3.268	143.9	163.5	153.4
Fruits, vegetables	21– 26	250.43	147.83	2.626	2.440	2.531	69.4	64.5	66.9
Coffee, tea, cocoa	27– 29	129.66	17.18	7.323	6.440	6.867	117.2	103.1	109.9
Spices, sweets, sugar	30– 33	155.41	93.86	2.282	2.302	2.292	71.9	72.6	72.2
Beverages	34– 37	319.87	91.02	3.493	3.208	3.347	109.5	100.6	105.0
Tobacco	38– 39	194.89	68.97	4.318	4.318	4.318	65.4	65.4	65.4
Clothing, footwear	40– 51	940.40	336.33	3.164	3.160	3.162	88.5	88.4	88.4
Clothing	40– 47	786.69	284.83	3.176	3.238	3.207	85.3	87.0	86.1
Footwear	48– 51	153.71	51.50	3.100	2.816	2.954	106.0	96.3	101.0
Gross rent, fuel	52– 57	1587.28	903.84	3.334	2.564	2.924	68.5	52.7	60.1
Gross rent	52– 53	1177.59	717.46	3.068	2.290	2.650	71.7	53.5	61.9
Fuel, power	54– 57	409.69	186.38	4.358	3.911	4.129	56.2	50.4	53.2
House furnishings, operations	58– 70	1045.61	343.14	3.090	2.129	2.565	143.1	98.6	118.8
Furniture	58– 60	444.95	165.64	2.614	1.527	1.998	175.9	102.8	134.5
Appliances	61– 66	155.70	56.41	4.602	3.466	3.994	79.6	60.0	69.1
Supplies, operations	67– 70	444.95	121.09	3.037	2.876	2.955	127.8	121.0	124.3
Medical care	71– 77	1371.48	653.69	2.244	1.928	2.080	108.8	93.5	100.9
Transport, communications	78– 89	1321.35	692.17	4.276	2.772	3.443	68.9	44.6	55.4
Equipment	78– 79	331.28	221.44	3.665	3.152	3.399	47.5	40.8	44.0
Operation costs	80– 83	628.41	338.12	3.828	2.723	3.228	68.3	48.6	57.6
Purchased transport	84– 87	196.02	40.37	4.242	1.867	2.815	260.0	114.5	172.5
Communications	88– 89	165.63	92.24	7.404	4.640	5.861	38.7	24.3	30.6
Recreation, education	90–101	1398.08	783.74	2.610	2.608	2.609	68.4	68.3	68.4
Recreation	90– 96	731.78	323.24	2.799	2.862	2.831	79.1	80.9	80.0
Education	97–101	666.31	460.50	2.478	2.376	2.427	60.9	58.4	59.6
Other expenditures	102–107	1016.55	628.47	3.038	2.499	2.755	64.7	53.2	58.7
Personal care	102–104	237.02	136.90	3.202	2.926	3.061	59.2	54.1	56.6
Miscellaneous services	105–107	779.52	491.57	2.993	2.393	2.676	66.3	53.0	59.3
Capital formation	109–146	4064.03	1185.32	3.222	2.652	2.923	129.3	106.4	117.3
Domestic capital formation	109–145	3448.95	1128.57	3.260	2.689	2.961	113.6	93.7	103.2
Construction	109–122	2099.53	680.37	3.126	2.389	2.733	129.2	98.7	112.9
Residential	109–110	863.58	235.05	3.722	3.214	3.459	114.3	98.7	106.2
Nonresidential	111–118	441.62	210.33	3.489	3.387	3.438	62.0	60.2	61.1
Other	119–122	794.34	234.99	2.204	1.656	1.911	204.1	153.4	176.9
Producer durables	123–144	1370.44	491.75	3.428	3.338	3.383	83.5	81.3	82.4
Transport equipment	123–129	290.53	122.69	3.076	2.733	2.900	86.6	77.0	81.7
Nonelectrical machinery	130–138	558.41	203.26	3.213	3.056	3.133	89.9	85.5	87.7
Electrical machinery	139–142	420.34	118.24	4.097	4.542	4.314	78.3	86.8	82.4
Other	143–144	101.17	47.56	3.597	3.485	3.541	61.0	59.1	60.1
Exports minus imports	146–146	615.08	56.75	2.460	2.460	2.460	440.5	440.5	440.5
Government	147–151	1814.50	808.43	3.206	3.201	3.204	70.1	70.0	70.1
Compensation	147–150	1419.61	419.96	3.275	3.221	3.248	104.9	103.2	104.1
Commodities	151–151	394.90	388.47	3.132	3.132	3.132	32.5	32.5	32.5
Gross domestic product	1–151	16724.10	7176.71	3.143	2.638	2.880	88.3	74.1	80.9
Aggregates									
ICP concepts[e]									
Consumption (CEP)[b,c]	1–108	10845.56	5182.96	3.115	2.558	2.823	81.8	67.2	74.1
Capital formation (GCF)[d]	109–146	4064.03	1185.32	3.222	2.652	2.923	129.3	106.4	117.3
Government (PFC)	147–151	1814.50	808.43	3.206	3.201	3.204	70.1	70.0	70.1
Gross domestic product	1–151	16724.10	7176.71	3.143	2.638	2.880	88.3	74.1	80.9
SNA concepts[e]									
Consumption (PFCE)	1–108	10225.54	4620.20	3.162	2.578	2.855	85.8	70.0	77.5
Capital formation (GCF)	109–146	4064.03	1185.32	3.222	2.652	2.923	129.3	106.4	117.3
Government (GFCE)	1–151	2420.77	1367.45	3.011	2.903	2.957	61.0	58.8	59.9
Gross domestic product	1–151	16710.35	7172.96	3.143	2.639	2.880	88.3	74.1	80.9

Note: See the end of Appendix Table 7-68 for notes.

Category	Line numbers[a]	Per capita expenditure		Purchasing power parities (forint/dollars)			Quantity per capita (U.S. = 100)		
		Hungary (forint)	U.S. (dollars)	U.S. weight	Hungary weight	Geometric mean	U.S. weight	Hungary weight	Geometric mean
Consumption, ICP[b,c]	1–108	26761.1	5182.96	13.70	9.22	11.24	56.0	37.7	46.0
Food, beverages, tobacco	1– 39	9798.6	818.24	15.64	13.65	14.61	87.7	76.6	82.0
Food	1– 33	7049.9	658.25	14.89	12.55	13.67	85.3	71.9	78.3
Bread, cereals	1– 6	777.7	94.81	8.03	5.80	6.82	141.5	102.1	120.2
Meat	7– 12	2008.5	163.79	13.01	14.25	13.62	86.0	94.2	90.0
Fish	13– 14	62.0	25.96	15.75	12.74	14.17	18.8	15.2	16.9
Milk, cheese, eggs	15– 17	948.1	82.52	14.96	15.07	15.02	76.2	76.8	76.5
Oils, fats	18– 20	565.5	32.30	15.72	14.86	15.29	117.8	111.4	114.5
Fruits, vegetables	21– 26	1241.5	147.83	16.03	11.78	13.74	71.3	52.4	61.1
Coffee, tea, cocoa	27– 29	389.2	17.18	61.20	59.28	60.23	38.2	37.0	37.6
Spices, sweets, sugar	30– 33	1057.2	93.86	14.24	15.35	14.79	73.4	79.1	76.2
Beverages	34– 37	2152.9	91.02	21.51	19.93	20.70	118.7	110.0	114.2
Tobacco	38– 39	595.8	68.97	14.99	12.42	13.64	69.5	57.6	63.3
Clothing, footwear	40– 51	2850.3	336.33	19.68	18.88	19.27	44.9	43.1	44.0
Clothing	40– 47	2330.9	284.83	20.13	19.56	19.84	41.8	40.6	41.2
Footwear	48– 51	519.4	51.50	17.16	16.33	16.74	61.8	58.8	60.3
Gross rent, fuel	52– 57	1985.2	903.84	11.97	10.82	11.38	20.3	18.3	19.3
Gross rent	52– 53	1117.7	717.46	9.94	9.52	9.73	16.4	15.7	16.0
Fuel, power	54– 57	867.5	186.38	19.80	13.14	16.13	35.4	23.5	28.9
House furnishings, operations	58– 70	2436.0	343.14	19.31	14.72	16.86	48.2	36.8	42.1
Furniture	58– 60	1047.4	165.64	14.68	11.78	13.15	53.7	43.1	48.1
Appliances	61– 66	303.9	56.41	37.57	27.06	31.89	19.9	14.3	16.9
Supplies, operations	67– 70	1084.7	121.09	17.14	16.58	16.86	54.0	52.3	53.1
Medical care	71– 77	1576.1	653.69	4.10	3.02	3.52	79.9	58.9	68.6
Transport, communications	78– 89	1964.8	692.17	24.18	9.33	15.02	30.4	11.7	18.9
Equipment	78– 79	651.0	221.44	28.19	24.73	26.40	11.9	10.4	11.1
Operation costs	80– 83	566.3	338.12	28.83	25.40	27.06	6.6	5.8	6.2
Purchased transport	84– 87	633.7	40.37	4.85	4.30	4.56	365.3	323.7	343.9
Communications	88– 89	113.8	92.24	5.97	7.89	6.86	15.7	20.7	18.0
Recreation, education	90–101	3360.2	783.74	10.14	5.67	7.59	75.6	42.3	56.5
Recreation	90– 96	1897.0	323.24	17.63	6.46	10.68	90.8	33.3	55.0
Education	97–101	1463.2	460.50	4.88	4.90	4.89	64.9	65.1	65.0
Other expenditures	102–107	2789.9	628.47	10.00	7.73	8.79	57.4	44.4	50.5
Personal care	102–104	716.8	136.90	16.03	10.81	13.16	48.4	32.7	39.8
Miscellaneous services	105–107	2073.0	491.57	8.32	7.04	7.65	59.9	50.7	55.1
Capital formation	109–146	13718.1	1185.32	19.50	16.54	17.96	70.0	59.3	64.4
Domestic capital formation	109–145	17101.3	1128.57	19.44	17.22	18.30	88.0	77.9	82.8
Construction	109–122	8529.4	680.37	15.41	14.91	15.16	84.1	81.4	82.7
Residential	109–110	2598.2	235.05	12.22	12.81	12.51	86.3	90.4	88.4
Nonresidential	111–118	3165.6	210.33	22.17	23.53	22.84	64.0	67.9	65.9
Other	119–122	2765.5	234.99	12.53	11.79	12.16	99.8	93.9	96.8
Producer durables	123–144	6628.5	491.75	24.81	21.60	23.15	62.4	54.3	58.2
Transport equipment	123–129	1273.4	122.69	19.99	13.26	16.28	78.3	51.9	63.7
Nonelectrical machinery	130–138	3827.3	203.26	29.01	28.62	28.81	65.8	64.9	65.4
Electrical machinery	139–142	770.4	118.24	25.46	26.87	26.15	24.2	25.6	24.9
Other	143–144	757.3	47.56	17.72	15.64	16.65	101.8	89.9	95.7
Exports minus imports	146–146	− 3383.3	56.75	20.66	20.66	20.66	− 288.6	− 288.6	− 288.6
Government	147–151	3414.0	808.43	10.87	11.01	10.94	38.4	38.8	38.6
Compensation	147–150	917.8	419.96	5.83	5.84	5.83	37.4	37.5	37.5
Commodities	151–151	2496.2	388.47	16.32	16.32	16.32	39.4	39.4	39.4
Gross domestic product	1–151	43893.2	7176.71	14.34	10.86	12.48	56.3	42.7	49.0
Aggregates									
ICP concepts[e]									
Consumption (CEP)[b,c]	1–108	26761.1	5182.96	13.70	9.22	11.24	56.0	37.7	46.0
Capital formation (GCF)[d]	109–146	13718.1	1185.32	19.50	16.54	17.96	70.0	59.3	64.4
Government (PFC)	147–151	3414.0	808.43	10.87	11.01	10.94	38.4	38.8	38.6
Gross domestic product	1–151	43893.2	7176.71	14.34	10.86	12.48	56.3	42.7	49.0
SNA concepts[e]									
Consumption (PFCE)	1–108	23146.7	4620.20	14.68	11.73	13.12	42.7	34.1	38.2
Capital formation (GCF)	109–146	13718.1	1185.32	19.50	16.54	17.96	70.0	59.3	64.4
Government (GFCE)	1–151	6695.6	1367.45	8.70	5.56	6.96	88.0	56.3	70.4
Gross domestic product	1–151	43560.3	7172.96	14.34	10.87	12.49	55.9	42.4	48.6

Note: See the end of Appendix Table 7-68 for notes.

Category	Line numbers[a]	Per capita expenditure		Purchasing power parities (rupees/dollars)			Quantity per capita (U.S. = 100)		
		India (rupees)	U.S. (dollars)	U.S. weight	India weight	Geometric mean	U.S. weight	India weight	Geometric mean
Consumption, ICP[b,c]	1–108	877.75	5182.96	4.114	1.824	2.739	9.3	4.1	6.2
Food, beverages, tobacco	1– 39	565.34	818.24	5.736	3.422	4.431	20.2	12.0	15.6
Food	1– 33	531.97	658.25	4.783	3.308	3.978	24.4	16.9	20.3
Bread, cereals	1– 6	240.56	94.81	3.847	3.062	3.432	82.9	65.9	73.9
Meat	7– 12	11.23	163.79	3.495	3.215	3.352	2.1	2.0	2.0
Fish	13– 14	10.78	25.96	2.588	2.169	2.369	19.1	16.0	17.5
Milk, cheese, eggs	15– 17	57.49	82.52	6.346	6.392	6.369	10.9	11.0	10.9
Oils, fats	18– 20	54.77	32.30	6.339	6.244	6.291	27.2	26.8	27.0
Fruits, vegetables	21– 26	84.64	147.83	5.505	2.194	3.475	26.1	10.4	16.5
Coffee, tea, cocoa	27– 29	8.27	17.18	5.742	3.153	4.255	15.3	8.4	11.3
Spices, sweets, sugar	30– 33	64.23	93.86	5.362	4.339	4.823	15.8	12.8	14.2
Beverages	34– 37	7.68	91.02	13.121	8.127	10.326	1.0	0.6	0.8
Tobacco	38– 39	25.69	68.97	5.083	7.451	6.154	5.0	7.3	6.1
Clothing, footwear	40– 51	66.32	336.33	3.905	6.205	4.922	3.2	5.0	4.0
Clothing	40– 47	61.45	284.83	4.169	7.133	5.453	3.0	5.2	4.0
Footwear	48– 51	4.87	51.50	2.442	2.346	2.394	4.0	3.9	3.9
Gross rent, fuel	52– 57	53.80	903.84	2.231	1.763	1.983	3.4	2.7	3.0
Gross rent	52– 53	24.07	717.46	1.076	1.087	1.081	3.1	3.1	3.1
Fuel, power	54– 57	29.73	186.38	6.680	3.550	4.869	4.5	2.4	3.3
House furnishings, operations	58– 70	24.43	343.14	5.926	2.306	3.697	3.1	1.2	1.9
Furniture	58– 60	3.23	165.64	3.712	3.885	3.797	0.5	0.5	0.5
Appliances	61– 66	3.50	56.41	16.922	18.445	17.667	0.3	0.4	0.4
Supplies, operations	67– 70	17.70	121.09	3.833	1.849	2.662	7.9	3.8	5.5
Medical care	71– 77	28.40	653.69	0.921	1.058	0.987	4.1	4.7	4.4
Transport, communications	78– 89	57.20	692.17	10.475	0.696	2.699	11.9	0.8	3.1
Equipment	78– 79	3.20	221.44	8.938	5.365	6.925	0.3	0.2	0.2
Operation costs	80– 83	8.97	338.12	13.776	7.736	10.323	0.3	0.2	0.3
Purchased transport	84– 87	41.92	40.37	2.040	0.526	1.036	197.4	50.9	100.3
Communications	88– 89	3.11	92.24	5.754	4.026	4.813	0.8	0.6	0.7
Recreation, education	90–101	46.48	783.74	2.231	0.356	0.891	16.6	2.7	6.7
Recreation	90– 96	14.64	323.24	4.507	2.543	3.385	1.8	1.0	1.3
Education	97–101	31.83	460.50	0.633	0.255	0.402	27.1	10.9	17.2
Other expenditures	102–107	39.74	628.47	2.342	1.572	1.918	4.0	2.7	3.3
Personal care	102–104	16.06	136.90	3.684	2.083	2.770	5.6	3.2	4.2
Miscellaneous services	105–107	23.68	491.57	1.968	1.347	1.628	3.6	2.4	3.0
Capital formation	109–146	247.47	1185.32	6.094	3.532	4.639	5.9	3.4	4.5
Domestic capital formation	109–145	250.72	1128.57	5.979	3.559	4.613	6.2	3.7	4.8
Construction	109–122	112.55	680.37	2.577	2.283	2.426	7.2	6.4	6.8
Residential	109–110	27.59	235.05	2.144	2.124	2.134	5.5	5.5	5.5
Nonresidential	111–118	41.85	210.33	2.281	2.223	2.252	9.0	8.7	8.8
Other	119–122	43.11	234.99	3.274	2.467	2.842	7.4	5.6	6.5
Producer durables	123–144	88.08	491.75	10.519	9.876	10.193	1.8	1.7	1.8
Transport equipment	123–129	16.57	122.69	9.572	8.427	8.981	1.6	1.4	1.5
Nonelectrical machinery	130–138	32.42	203.26	11.837	9.618	10.670	1.7	1.3	1.5
Electrical machinery	139–142	27.00	118.24	9.199	10.459	9.809	2.2	2.5	2.3
Other	143–144	12.10	47.56	10.612	12.089	11.326	2.1	2.4	2.2
Exports minus imports	146–146	−3.25	56.75	8.376	8.376	8.376	−0.7	−0.7	−0.7
Government	147–151	94.99	808.43	1.871	1.030	1.388	11.4	6.3	8.5
Compensation	147–150	55.31	419.96	0.970	0.706	0.828	18.6	13.6	15.9
Commodities	151–151	39.69	388.47	2.846	2.846	2.846	3.6	3.6	3.6
Gross domestic product	1–151	1220.21	7176.71	4.189	1.896	2.818	9.0	4.1	6.0
Aggregates									
ICP concepts[e]									
Consumption (CEP)[b,c]	1–108	877.75	5182.96	4.114	1.824	2.739	9.3	4.1	6.2
Capital formation (GCF)[d]	109–146	247.47	1185.32	6.094	3.532	4.639	5.9	3.4	4.5
Government (PFC)	147–151	94.99	808.43	1.871	1.030	1.388	11.4	6.3	8.5
Gross domestic product	1–151	1220.21	7176.71	4.189	1.896	2.818	9.0	4.1	6.0
SNA concepts[e]									
Consumption (PFCE)	1–108	851.65	4620.20	4.511	2.174	3.131	8.5	4.1	5.9
Capital formation (GCF)	109–146	247.47	1185.32	6.094	3.532	4.639	5.9	3.4	4.5
Government (GFCE)	1–151	121.09	1367.45	1.458	0.666	0.985	13.3	6.1	9.0
Gross domestic product	1–151	1220.21	7172.96	4.190	1.896	2.818	9.0	4.1	6.0

Note: See the end of Appendix Table 7-68 for notes.

Category	Line numbers[a]	Per capita expenditure Iran (rials)	Per capita expenditure U.S. (dollars)	Purchasing power parities (rials/dollars) U.S. weight	Purchasing power parities (rials/dollars) Iran weight	Purchasing power parities (rials/dollars) Geometric mean	Quantity per capita (U.S. = 100) U.S. weight	Quantity per capita (U.S. = 100) Iran weight	Quantity per capita (U.S. = 100) Geometric mean
Consumption, ICP[b,c]	1–108	48847.5	5182.96	49.05	30.31	38.56	31.1	19.2	24.4
Food, beverages, tobacco	1– 39	16616.6	818.24	54.63	36.72	44.79	55.3	37.2	45.3
Food	1– 33	15792.9	658.25	54.41	36.50	44.56	65.7	44.1	53.8
Bread, cereals	1– 6	4601.2	94.81	38.19	23.13	29.72	209.8	127.1	163.3
Meat	7– 12	3382.9	163.79	67.32	48.27	57.01	42.8	30.7	36.2
Fish	13– 14	183.1	25.96	68.98	77.64	73.18	9.1	10.2	9.6
Milk, cheese, eggs	15– 17	1702.3	82.52	69.55	64.25	66.85	32.1	29.7	30.9
Oils, fats	18– 20	1201.2	32.30	53.83	58.85	56.29	63.2	69.1	66.1
Fruits, vegetables	21– 26	3106.5	147.83	43.60	43.54	43.57	48.3	48.2	48.2
Coffee, tea, cocoa	27– 29	559.3	17.18	97.83	69.95	82.72	46.6	33.3	39.4
Spices, sweets, sugar	30– 33	1056.3	93.86	40.20	30.07	34.77	37.4	28.0	32.4
Beverages	34– 37	169.8	91.02	61.17	57.42	59.27	3.2	3.0	3.1
Tobacco	38– 39	653.8	68.97	48.16	38.98	43.33	24.3	19.7	21.9
Clothing, footwear	40– 51	5087.5	336.33	32.88	32.05	32.46	47.2	46.0	46.6
Clothing	40– 47	4113.1	284.83	34.09	34.02	34.05	42.4	42.4	42.4
Footwear	48– 51	974.4	51.50	26.20	25.74	25.97	73.5	72.2	72.9
Gross rent, fuel	52– 57	8223.6	903.84	36.23	32.38	34.25	28.1	25.1	26.6
Gross rent	52– 53	6626.1	717.46	31.50	32.31	31.90	28.6	29.3	29.0
Fuel, power	54– 57	1597.5	186.38	54.46	32.66	42.17	26.2	15.7	20.3
House furnishings, operations	58– 70	3775.8	343.14	54.32	44.73	49.29	24.6	20.3	22.3
Furniture	58– 60	1985.9	165.64	39.64	48.76	43.97	24.6	30.2	27.3
Appliances	61– 66	545.0	56.41	133.44	99.27	115.10	9.7	7.2	8.4
Supplies, operations	67– 70	1244.9	121.09	37.54	32.60	34.98	31.5	27.4	29.4
Medical care	71– 77	3277.2	653.69	32.49	35.64	34.03	14.1	15.4	14.7
Transport, communications	78– 89	3345.3	692.17	97.00	17.82	41.58	27.1	5.0	11.6
Equipment	78– 79	1387.5	221.44	224.37	183.62	202.97	3.4	2.8	3.1
Operation costs	80– 83	908.9	338.12	36.06	28.57	32.09	9.4	7.5	8.4
Purchased transport	84– 87	863.1	40.37	18.39	6.00	10.50	356.6	116.2	203.6
Communications	88– 89	185.7	92.24	49.04	42.48	45.64	4.7	4.1	4.4
Recreation, education	90–101	5111.1	783.74	48.98	19.99	31.29	32.6	13.3	20.8
Recreation	90– 96	1441.0	323.24	75.50	40.88	55.55	10.9	5.9	8.0
Education	97–101	3670.1	460.50	30.37	16.65	22.49	47.9	26.2	35.4
Other expenditures	102–107	3410.5	628.47	29.78	26.91	28.31	20.2	18.2	19.2
Personal care	102–104	975.4	136.90	34.76	26.91	30.58	26.5	20.5	23.3
Miscellaneous services	105–107	2435.1	491.57	28.40	26.91	27.64	18.4	17.4	17.9
Capital formation	109–146	38661.6	1185.32	79.39	52.13	64.33	62.6	41.1	50.7
Domestic capital formation	109–145	29096.4	1128.57	79.98	48.48	62.27	53.2	32.2	41.4
Construction	109–122	16614.7	680.37	56.13	34.24	43.84	71.3	43.5	55.7
Residential	109–110	7196.1	235.05	26.26	23.20	24.68	132.0	116.6	124.0
Nonresidential	111–118	5319.1	210.33	57.84	43.35	50.08	58.3	43.7	50.5
Other	119–122	4099.4	234.99	84.47	78.35	81.35	22.3	20.7	21.4
Producer durables	123–144	13921.5	491.75	110.16	96.12	102.90	29.5	25.7	27.5
Transport equipment	123–129	4885.1	122.69	169.37	129.19	147.92	30.8	23.5	26.9
Nonelectrical machinery	130–138	6780.4	203.26	88.44	86.04	87.23	38.8	37.7	38.2
Electrical machinery	139–142	1476.5	118.24	100.97	86.62	93.52	14.4	12.4	13.4
Other	143–144	779.5	47.56	73.05	69.74	71.37	23.5	22.4	23.0
Exports minus imports	146–146	9565.3	56.75	67.64	67.64	67.64	249.2	249.2	249.2
Government	147–151	19855.1	808.43	46.77	40.31	.43.42	60.9	52.5	56.6
Compensation	147–150	6642.8	419.96	51.71	38.26	44.48	41.3	30.6	35.6
Commodities	151–151	13212.3	388.47	41.43	41.43	41.43	82.1	82.1	82.1
Gross domestic product	1–151	107364.3	7176.71	53.80	37.73	45.05	39.7	27.8	33.2
Aggregates									
ICP concepts[e]									
Consumption (CEP)[b,c]	1–108	48847.5	5182.96	49.05	30.31	38.56	31.1	19.2	24.4
Capital formation (GCF)[d]	109–146	38661.6	1185.32	79.39	52.13	64.33	62.6	41.1	50.7
Government (PFC)	147–151	19855.1	808.43	46.77	40.31	43.42	60.9	52.5	56.6
Gross domestic product	1–151	107364.3	7176.71	53.80	37.73	45.05	39.7	27.8	33.2
SNA concepts[e]									
Consumption (PFCE)	1–108	43711.8	4620.20	51.84	32.60	41.11	29.0	18.2	23.0
Capital formation (GCF)	109–146	38661.6	1185.32	79.39	52.13	64.33	62.6	41.1	50.7
Government (GFCE)	1–151	24990.8	1367.45	38.30	32.74	35.41	55.8	47.7	51.6
Gross domestic product	1–151	107364.3	7172.96	53.81	37.73	45.06	39.7	27.8	33.2

Note: See the end of Appendix Table 7-68 for notes.

Category	Line numbers[a]	Per capita expenditure		Purchasing power parities (pounds/dollars)			Quantity per capita (U.S. = 100)		
		Ireland (pounds)	U.S. (dollars)	U.S. weight	Ireland weight	Geometric mean	U.S. weight	Ireland weight	Geometric mean
Consumption, ICP[b,c]	1–108	876.260	5182.96	0.4146	0.3259	0.3676	51.9	40.8	46.0
Food, beverages, tobacco	1– 39	258.186	818.24	0.4637	0.3960	0.4285	79.7	68.0	73.6
Food	1– 33	202.141	658.25	0.4038	0.3519	0.3769	87.3	76.1	81.5
Bread, cereals	1– 6	27.393	94.81	0.3474	0.3297	0.3384	87.6	83.2	85.4
Meat	7– 12	69.584	163.79	0.4042	0.3697	0.3866	114.9	105.1	109.9
Fish	13– 14	5.668	25.96	0.4878	0.4863	0.4871	44.9	44.7	44.8
Milk, cheese, eggs	15– 17	26.763	82.52	0.3717	0.3094	0.3391	104.8	87.3	95.6
Oils, fats	18– 20	11.020	32.30	0.5036	0.4459	0.4739	76.5	67.7	72.0
Fruits, vegetables	21– 26	33.375	147.83	0.4614	0.4028	0.4311	56.0	48.9	52.4
Coffee, tea, cocoa	27– 29	4.408	17.18	0.5118	0.2078	0.3261	123.5	50.1	78.7
Spices, sweets, sugar	30– 33	23.929	93.86	0.3198	0.3141	0.3169	81.2	79.7	80.4
Beverages	34– 37	14.798	91.02	0.6536	0.5906	0.6213	27.5	24.9	26.2
Tobacco	38– 39	41.247	68.97	0.7857	0.7857	0.7857	76.1	76.1	76.1
Clothing, footwear	40– 51	63.602	336.33	0.5128	0.4883	0.5004	38.7	36.9	37.8
Clothing	40– 47	52.897	284.83	0.5056	0.4884	0.4970	38.0	36.7	37.4
Footwear	48– 51	10.705	51.50	0.5524	0.4875	0.5190	42.6	37.6	40.1
Gross rent, fuel	52– 57	88.476	903.84	0.3741	0.3899	0.3819	25.1	26.2	25.6
Gross rent	52– 53	49.433	717.46	0.2967	0.2982	0.2975	23.1	23.2	23.2
Fuel, power	54– 57	39.043	186.38	0.6719	0.6386	0.6550	32.8	31.2	32.0
House furnishings, operations	58– 70	59.824	343.14	0.4602	0.4040	0.4312	43.1	37.9	40.4
Furniture	58– 60	24.559	165.64	0.4058	0.3955	0.4006	37.5	36.5	37.0
Appliances	61– 66	9.761	56.41	0.7653	0.5258	0.6343	32.9	22.6	27.3
Supplies, operations	67– 70	25.504	121.09	0.3925	0.3783	0.3854	55.7	53.7	54.7
Medical care	71– 77	78.715	653.69	0.2362	0.1725	0.2019	69.8	51.0	59.7
Transport, communications	78– 89	75.567	692.17	0.6876	0.4509	0.5568	24.2	15.9	19.6
Equipment	78– 79	25.189	221.44	0.8613	0.7135	0.7839	15.9	13.2	14.5
Operation costs	80– 83	33.060	338.12	0.6002	0.3539	0.4608	27.6	16.3	21.2
Purchased transport	84– 87	12.594	40.37	0.5433	0.4218	0.4787	74.0	57.4	65.2
Communications	88– 89	4.723	92.24	0.6546	0.5251	0.5863	9.7	7.8	8.7
Recreation, education	90–101	114.295	783.74	0.3052	0.2304	0.2652	63.3	47.8	55.0
Recreation	90– 96	48.489	323.24	0.3965	0.2523	0.3163	59.5	37.8	47.4
Education	97–101	65.806	460.50	0.2412	0.2165	0.2285	66.0	59.2	62.5
Other expenditures	102–107	137.594	628.47	0.3515	0.3344	0.3429	65.5	62.3	63.9
Personal care	102–104	13.224	136.90	0.4311	0.3424	0.3842	28.2	22.4	25.1
Miscellaneous services	105–107	124.370	491.57	0.3294	0.3336	0.3315	75.8	76.8	76.3
Capital formation	109–146	183.879	1185.32	0.5189	0.4299	0.4723	36.1	29.9	32.8
Domestic capital formation	109–145	253.778	1128.57	0.5224	0.4352	0.4768	51.7	43.0	47.2
Construction	109–122	164.673	680.37	0.4827	0.4092	0.4445	59.1	50.1	54.5
Residential	109–110	72.103	235.05	0.4095	0.4188	0.4142	73.2	74.9	74.1
Nonresidential	111–118	44.081	210.33	0.6462	0.5923	0.6187	35.4	32.4	33.9
Other	119–122	48.489	234.99	0.4096	0.3112	0.3570	66.3	50.4	57.8
Producer durables	123–144	101.071	491.75	0.5722	0.4896	0.5293	42.0	35.9	38.8
Transport equipment	123–129	24.874	122.69	0.6534	0.5921	0.6220	34.2	31.0	32.6
Nonelectrical machinery	130–138	56.360	203.26	0.4658	0.4485	0.4571	61.8	59.5	60.7
Electrical machinery	139–142	9.131	118.24	0.7047	0.5420	0.6180	14.2	11.0	12.5
Other	143–144	10.705	47.56	0.4880	0.4888	0.4884	46.0	46.1	46.1
Exports minus imports	146–146	−69.899	56.75	0.4501	0.4501	0.4501	−273.7	−273.7	−273.7
Government	147–151	124.370	808.43	0.3501	0.3426	0.3463	44.9	43.9	44.4
Compensation	147–150	75.567	419.96	0.4094	0.3929	0.4011	45.8	44.0	44.9
Commodities	151–151	48.804	388.47	0.2859	0.2859	0.2859	43.9	43.9	43.9
Gross domestic product	1–151	1184.509	7176.71	0.4246	0.3404	0.3802	48.5	38.9	43.4
Aggregates									
ICP concepts[e]									
Consumption (CEP)[b,c]	1–108	876.260	5182.96	0.4146	0.3259	0.3676	51.9	40.8	46.0
Capital formation (GCF)[d]	109–146	183.879	1185.32	0.5189	0.4299	0.4723	36.1	29.9	32.8
Government (PFC)	147–151	124.370	808.43	0.3501	0.3426	0.3463	44.9	43.9	44.4
Gross domestic product	1–151	1184.509	7176.71	0.4246	0.3404	0.3802	48.5	38.9	43.4
SNA concepts[e]									
Consumption (PFCE)	1–108	750.000	4620.20	0.4347	0.3645	0.3980	44.5	37.3	40.8
Capital formation (GCF)	109–146	183.879	1185.32	0.5189	0.4299	0.4723	36.1	29.9	32.8
Government (GFCE)	1–151	241.184	1367.45	0.3090	0.2515	0.2788	70.1	57.1	63.3
Gross domestic product	1–151	1175.063	7172.96	0.4247	0.3412	0.3806	48.0	38.6	43.0

Note: See the end of Appendix Table 7-68 for notes.

Category	Line numbers[a]	Per capita expenditure Italy (lire)	Per capita expenditure U.S. (dollars)	Purchasing power parities (lire/dollars) U.S. weight	Purchasing power parities Italy weight	Purchasing power parities Geometric mean	Quantity per capita (U.S. = 100) U.S. weight	Quantity per capita (U.S. = 100) Italy weight	Quantity per capita (U.S. = 100) Geometric mean
Consumption, ICP[b,c]	1–108	1554899.	5182.96	609.3	483.4	542.7	62.1	49.2	55.3
Food, beverages, tobacco	1– 39	530127.	818.24	692.5	597.0	643.0	108.5	93.6	100.8
Food	1– 33	451299.	658.25	713.2	602.5	655.5	113.8	96.1	104.6
Bread, cereals	1– 6	60165.	94.81	613.5	553.2	582.6	114.7	103.4	108.9
Meat	7– 12	150690.	163.79	767.8	771.0	769.4	119.3	119.8	119.6
Fish	13– 14	15458.	25.96	990.9	983.2	987.0	60.6	60.1	60.3
Milk, cheese, eggs	15– 17	57693.	82.52	627.0	635.1	631.1	110.1	111.5	110.8
Oils, fats	18– 20	35536.	32.30	689.1	671.8	680.4	163.8	159.7	161.7
Fruits, vegetables	21– 26	102364.	147.83	708.2	424.3	548.2	163.2	97.8	126.3
Coffee, tea, cocoa	27– 29	7917.	17.18	1456.4	1428.9	1442.6	32.3	31.6	32.0
Spices, sweets, sugar	30– 33	21476.	93.86	597.7	556.5	576.8	41.1	38.3	39.7
Beverages	34– 37	45262.	91.02	618.3	549.7	583.0	90.5	80.4	85.3
Tobacco	38– 39	33566.	68.97	593.3	593.3	593.3	82.0	82.0	82.0
Clothing, footwear	40– 51	130163.	336.33	665.6	674.0	669.8	57.4	58.1	57.8
Clothing	40– 47	106681.	284.83	684.9	708.0	696.4	52.9	54.7	53.8
Footwear	48– 51	23482.	51.50	558.6	553.2	555.9	82.4	81.6	82.0
Gross rent, fuel	52– 57	194232.	903.84	539.7	508.4	523.8	42.3	39.8	41.0
Gross rent	52– 53	149704.	717.46	484.4	461.5	472.8	45.2	43.1	44.1
Fuel, power	54– 57	44528.	186.38	752.6	771.8	762.2	31.0	31.7	31.3
House furnishings, operations	58– 70	91599.	343.14	704.3	523.2	607.0	51.0	37.9	44.0
Furniture	58– 60	36092.	165.64	544.1	371.9	449.8	58.6	40.0	48.4
Appliances	61– 66	13290.	56.41	1222.5	1012.6	1112.6	23.3	19.3	21.2
Supplies, operations	67– 70	42217.	121.09	681.9	650.5	666.0	53.6	51.1	52.3
Medical care	71– 77	124646.	653.69	318.7	274.4	295.7	69.5	59.8	64.5
Transport, communications	78– 89	158606.	692.17	959.8	441.6	651.1	51.9	23.9	35.2
Equipment	78– 79	38349.	221.44	927.6	841.5	883.5	20.6	18.7	19.6
Operation costs	80– 83	83056.	338.12	1101.2	511.2	750.3	48.0	22.3	32.7
Purchased transport	84– 87	22067.	40.37	638.2	175.0	334.2	312.4	85.6	163.6
Communications	88– 89	15135.	92.24	659.4	605.6	632.0	27.1	24.9	26.0
Recreation, education	90–101	181354.	783.74	509.5	411.4	457.8	56.2	45.4	50.5
Recreation	90– 96	81085.	323.24	744.0	640.8	690.5	39.1	33.7	36.3
Education	97–101	100269.	460.50	344.8	319.1	331.7	68.2	63.1	65.6
Other expenditures	102–107	144170.	628.47	558.1	444.5	498.1	51.6	41.1	46.1
Personal care	102–104	51245.	136.90	630.9	552.6	590.5	67.7	59.3	63.4
Miscellaneous services	105–107	92925.	491.57	537.8	401.2	464.5	47.1	35.1	40.7
Capital formation	109–146	428139.	1185.32	676.8	618.2	646.9	58.4	53.4	55.8
Domestic capital formation	109–145	455347.	1128.57	678.0	620.2	648.5	65.1	59.5	62.2
Construction	109–122	281426.	680.37	549.7	545.4	547.6	75.8	75.2	75.5
Residential	109–110	139584.	235.05	535.3	524.5	529.9	113.2	110.9	112.1
Nonresidential	111–118	87856.	210.33	640.8	708.4	673.7	59.0	65.2	62.0
Other	119–122	53985.	234.99	482.6	429.2	455.1	53.5	47.6	50.5
Producer durables	123–144	180226.	491.75	855.4	792.0	823.1	46.3	42.8	44.5
Transport equipment	123–129	46713.	122.69	847.1	756.3	800.4	50.3	44.9	47.6
Nonelectrical machinery	130–138	80226.	203.26	795.9	786.9	791.4	50.2	49.6	49.9
Electrical machinery	139–142	34515.	118.24	1049.8	986.9	1017.8	29.6	27.8	28.7
Other	143–144	18771.	47.56	648.2	650.4	649.3	60.7	60.9	60.8
Exports minus imports	146–146	– 27208.	56.75	652.9	652.9	652.9	– 73.4	– 73.4	– 73.4
Government	147–151	262672.	808.43	605.8	583.1	594.4	55.7	53.6	54.7
Compensation	147–150	161311.	419.96	538.0	535.6	536.8	71.7	71.4	71.6
Commodities	151–151	101361.	388.47	679.1	679.1	679.1	38.4	38.4	38.4
Gross domestic product	1–151	2245710.	7176.71	620.1	515.1	565.2	60.7	50.5	55.4
Aggregates									
ICP concepts[e]									
Consumption (CEP)[b,c]	1–108	1554899.	5182.96	609.3	483.4	542.7	62.1	49.2	55.3
Capital formation (GCF)[d]	109–146	428139.	1185.32	676.8	618.2	646.9	58.4	53.4	55.8
Government (PFC)	147–151	262672.	808.43	605.8	583.1	594.4	55.7	53.6	54.7
Gross domestic product	1–151	2245710.	7176.71	620.1	515.1	565.2	60.7	50.5	55.4
SNA concepts[e]									
Consumption (PFCE)	1–108	1459556.	4620.20	635.1	501.5	564.4	63.0	49.7	56.0
Capital formation (GCF)	109–146	428139.	1185.32	676.8	618.2	646.9	58.4	53.4	55.8
Government (GFCE)	1–151	358015.	1367.45	520.5	473.0	496.1	55.4	50.3	52.8
Gross domestic product	1–151	2245710.	7172.96	620.1	515.1	565.2	60.8	50.5	55.4

Note: See the end of Appendix Table 7-68 for notes.

Appendix Table 7-13. Augmented Summary Binary Table: Jamaica/United States, 1975

Category	Line numbers[a]	Per capita expenditure Jamaica (dollars)	Per capita expenditure U.S. (dollars)	Purchasing power parities (dollars/dollars) U.S. weight	Purchasing power parities (dollars/dollars) Jamaica weight	Purchasing power parities (dollars/dollars) Geometric mean	Quantity per capita (U.S. = 100) U.S. weight	Quantity per capita (U.S. = 100) Jamaica weight	Quantity per capita (U.S. = 100) Geometric mean
Consumption, ICP[b,c]	1–108	918.799	5182.96	0.8791	0.4999	0.6629	35.5	20.2	26.7
Food, beverages, tobacco	1– 39	384.013	818.24	0.9749	0.8088	0.8879	58.0	48.1	52.9
Food	1– 33	300.143	658.25	0.9823	0.7723	0.8710	59.0	46.4	52.3
Bread, cereals	1– 6	87.629	94.81	0.7939	0.6734	0.7311	137.3	116.4	126.4
Meat	7– 12	36.837	163.79	0.9075	0.8853	0.8963	25.4	24.8	25.1
Fish	13– 14	24.476	25.96	1.1489	0.9589	1.0496	98.3	82.1	89.8
Milk, cheese, eggs	15– 17	35.896	82.52	0.9328	0.8458	0.8883	51.4	46.6	49.0
Oils, fats	18– 20	8.857	32.30	0.9353	0.9276	0.9315	29.6	29.3	29.4
Fruits, vegetables	21– 26	83.154	147.83	1.3187	0.8605	1.0652	65.4	42.7	52.8
Coffee, tea, cocoa	27– 29	2.653	17.18	1.2177	1.0207	1.1148	15.1	12.7	13.9
Spices, sweets, sugar	30– 33	20.642	93.86	0.7439	0.5145	0.6186	42.7	29.6	35.5
Beverages	34– 37	43.838	91.02	0.8641	0.9083	0.8859	53.0	55.7	54.4
Tobacco	38– 39	40.031	68.97	1.0500	1.0553	1.0527	55.0	55.3	55.1
Clothing, footwear	40– 51	36.965	336.33	0.8222	0.8126	0.8174	13.5	13.4	13.4
Clothing	40– 47	18.467	284.83	0.8182	0.8697	0.8435	7.5	7.9	7.7
Footwear	48– 51	18.497	51.50	0.8446	0.7625	0.8025	47.1	42.5	44.8
Gross rent, fuel	52– 57	97.715	903.84	1.1505	0.9838	1.0639	11.0	9.4	10.2
Gross rent	52– 53	73.897	717.46	1.1487	0.9813	1.0617	10.5	9.0	9.7
Fuel, power	54– 57	23.818	186.38	1.1577	0.9917	1.0715	12.9	11.0	11.9
House furnishings, operations	58– 70	52.905	343.14	1.1322	0.2776	0.5606	55.5	13.6	27.5
Furniture	58– 60	21.003	165.64	0.9335	0.8748	0.9037	14.5	13.6	14.0
Appliances	61– 66	5.225	56.41	2.3597	1.6833	1.9930	5.5	3.9	4.6
Supplies, operations	67– 70	26.677	121.09	0.8320	0.1632	0.3685	135.0	26.5	59.8
Medical care	71– 77	39.875	653.69	0.5136	0.3681	0.4348	16.6	11.9	14.0
Transport, communications	78– 89	106.338	692.17	1.3908	0.4700	0.8085	32.7	11.0	19.0
Equipment	78– 79	10.786	221.44	2.3331	1.8096	2.0547	2.7	2.1	2.4
Operation costs	80– 83	48.990	338.12	1.2055	1.0243	1.1112	14.1	12.0	13.0
Purchased transport	84– 87	40.740	40.37	0.4532	0.3741	0.4117	269.8	222.7	245.1
Communications	88– 89	5.822	92.24	0.2179	0.0916	0.1413	68.9	29.0	44.7
Recreation, education	90–101	80.664	783.74	0.5379	0.2028	0.3303	50.7	19.1	31.2
Recreation	90– 96	33.285	323.24	0.9960	0.3176	0.5624	32.4	10.3	18.3
Education	97–101	47.379	460.50	0.2164	0.1617	0.1871	63.6	47.5	55.0
Other expenditures	102–107	154.601	628.47	0.4974	0.4639	0.4804	53.0	49.5	51.2
Personal care	102–104	39.883	136.90	0.6625	0.6718	0.6671	43.4	44.0	43.7
Miscellaneous services	105–107	114.719	491.57	0.4514	0.4189	0.4348	55.7	51.7	53.7
Capital formation	109–146	193.717	1185.32	1.0460	1.0330	1.0395	15.8	15.6	15.7
Domestic capital formation	109–145	331.896	1128.57	1.0529	0.9775	1.0145	30.1	27.9	29.0
Construction	109–122	146.331	680.37	0.8669	0.8298	0.8481	25.9	24.8	25.4
Residential	109–110	89.023	235.05	0.7977	0.7991	0.7984	47.4	47.5	47.4
Nonresidential	111–118	45.874	210.33	0.9965	0.9368	0.9662	23.3	21.9	22.6
Other	119–122	11.434	234.99	0.8202	0.7153	0.7659	6.8	5.9	6.4
Producer durables	123–144	155.252	491.75	1.3044	1.1723	1.2366	26.9	24.2	25.5
Transport equipment	123–129	47.420	122.69	1.6475	1.2494	1.4347	30.9	23.5	26.9
Nonelectrical machinery	130–138	65.707	203.26	1.1993	1.1848	1.1920	27.3	27.0	27.1
Electrical machinery	139–142	20.897	118.24	1.2350	1.2258	1.2304	14.4	14.3	14.4
Other	143–144	21.228	47.56	1.0402	0.9662	1.0025	46.2	42.9	44.5
Exports minus imports	146–146	−138.179	56.75	0.9091	0.9091	0.9091	−267.9	−267.9	−267.9
Government	147–151	165.510	808.43	0.7786	0.6547	0.7140	31.3	26.3	28.7
Compensation	147–150	104.346	419.96	0.6064	0.5509	0.5780	45.1	41.0	43.0
Commodities	151–151	61.164	388.47	0.9648	0.9648	0.9648	16.3	16.3	16.3
Gross domestic product	1–151	1278.025	7176.71	0.8954	0.5609	0.7087	31.7	19.9	25.1
Aggregates									
ICP concepts[e]									
Consumption (CEP)[b,c]	1–108	918.799	5182.96	0.8791	0.4999	0.6629	35.5	20.2	26.7
Capital formation (GCF)[d]	109–146	193.717	1185.32	1.0460	1.0330	1.0395	15.8	15.6	15.7
Government (PFC)	147–151	165.510	808.43	0.7786	0.6547	0.7140	31.3	26.3	28.7
Gross domestic product	1–151	1278.025	7176.71	0.8954	0.5609	0.7087	31.7	19.9	25.1
SNA concepts[e]									
Consumption (PFCE)	1–108	849.750	4620.20	0.9467	0.5795	0.7407	31.7	19.4	24.8
Capital formation (GCF)	109–146	193.717	1185.32	1.0460	1.0330	1.0395	15.8	15.6	15.7
Government (GFCE)	1–151	234.558	1367.45	0.5903	0.3756	0.4709	45.7	29.1	36.4
Gross domestic product	1–151	1278.025	7172.96	0.8952	0.5609	0.7086	31.8	19.9	25.1

Note: See the end of Appendix Table 7-68 for notes.

265

Category	Line numbers[a]	Per capita expenditure Japan (yen)	Per capita expenditure U.S. (dollars)	Purchasing power parities (yen/dollars) U.S. weight	Purchasing power parities (yen/dollars) Japan weight	Purchasing power parities (yen/dollars) Geometric mean	Quantity per capita (U.S. = 100) U.S. weight	Quantity per capita (U.S. = 100) Japan weight	Quantity per capita (U.S. = 100) Geometric mean
Consumption, ICP[b,c]	1–108	824902.	5182.96	314.6	232.0	270.1	68.6	50.6	58.9
Food, beverages, tobacco	1– 39	214788.	818.24	448.4	311.9	374.0	84.2	58.5	70.2
Food	1– 33	183120.	658.25	482.7	320.5	393.3	86.8	57.6	70.7
Bread, cereals	1– 6	34840.	94.81	306.7	313.0	309.8	117.4	119.8	118.6
Meat	7– 12	24721.	163.79	693.6	587.3	638.2	25.7	21.8	23.6
Fish	13– 14	35566.	25.96	335.2	344.7	339.9	397.3	408.7	403.0
Milk, cheese, eggs	15– 17	12853.	82.52	360.5	356.1	358.3	43.7	43.2	43.5
Oils, fats	18– 20	2008.	32.30	373.6	404.3	388.7	15.4	16.6	16.0
Fruits, vegetables	21– 26	29229.	147.83	527.4	306.4	402.0	64.5	37.5	49.2
Coffee, tea, cocoa	27– 29	4446.	17.18	466.2	568.5	514.8	45.5	55.5	50.3
Spices, sweets, sugar	30– 33	39456.	93.86	410.8	231.4	308.3	181.6	102.3	136.3
Beverages	34– 37	20320.	91.02	366.1	340.6	353.1	65.5	61.0	63.2
Tobacco	38– 39	11348.	68.97	229.3	197.0	212.6	83.5	71.7	77.4
Clothing, footwear	40– 51	61264.	336.33	268.0	255.3	261.6	71.3	68.0	69.6
Clothing	40– 47	55223.	284.83	271.9	256.6	264.2	75.5	71.3	73.4
Footwear	48– 51	6041.	51.50	246.6	244.0	245.3	48.1	47.6	47.8
Gross rent, fuel	52– 57	118701.	903.84	326.1	318.4	322.2	41.3	40.3	40.8
Gross rent	52– 53	103670.	717.46	306.8	318.2	312.4	45.4	47.1	46.2
Fuel, power	54– 57	15031.	186.38	400.5	319.4	357.7	25.2	20.1	22.5
House furnishings, operations	58– 70	47990.	343.14	371.1	340.9	355.7	41.0	37.7	39.3
Furniture	58– 60	17703.	165.64	361.7	329.4	345.2	32.4	29.5	31.0
Appliances	61– 66	9671.	56.41	556.8	360.1	447.8	47.6	30.8	38.3
Supplies, operations	67– 70	20616.	121.09	297.4	342.7	319.3	49.7	57.2	53.3
Medical care	71– 77	73400.	653.69	165.1	122.4	142.2	91.7	68.0	79.0
Transport, communications	78– 89	72110.	692.17	363.0	127.4	215.0	81.8	28.7	48.4
Equipment	78– 79	14261.	221.44	271.5	256.0	263.6	25.2	23.7	24.4
Operation costs	80– 83	18043.	338.12	506.6	280.7	377.1	19.0	10.5	14.2
Purchased transport	84– 87	33021.	40.37	151.5	82.0	111.4	997.6	539.9	733.9
Communications	88– 89	6785.	92.24	148.6	157.1	152.8	46.8	49.5	48.2
Recreation, education	90–101	119830.	783.74	230.1	221.7	225.9	69.0	66.4	67.7
Recreation	90– 96	59821.	323.24	287.7	259.7	273.3	71.3	64.3	67.7
Education	97–101	60009.	460.50	189.7	193.5	191.6	67.3	68.7	68.0
Other expenditures	102–107	113870.	628.47	326.2	285.9	305.4	63.4	55.5	59.3
Personal care	102–104	27006.	136.90	235.2	220.1	227.5	89.6	83.9	86.7
Miscellaneous services	105–107	86863.	491.57	351.6	315.2	332.9	56.1	50.3	53.1
Capital formation	109–146	435366.	1185.32	344.3	274.9	307.7	133.6	106.7	119.4
Domestic capital formation	109–145	434810.	1128.57	346.7	274.9	308.7	140.1	111.1	124.8
Construction	109–122	283787.	680.37	375.1	285.9	327.5	145.9	111.2	127.4
Residential	109–110	100864.	235.05	468.6	457.8	463.1	93.7	91.6	92.7
Nonresidential	111–118	72047.	210.33	406.9	391.4	399.1	87.5	84.2	85.8
Other	119–122	110876.	234.99	253.1	188.5	218.4	250.3	186.4	216.0
Producer durables	123–144	146595.	491.75	303.5	255.2	278.3	116.8	98.2	107.1
Transport equipment	123–129	33424.	122.69	369.0	339.7	354.0	80.2	73.8	76.9
Nonelectrical machinery	130–138	46744.	203.26	282.9	207.6	242.3	110.8	81.3	94.9
Electrical machinery	139–142	35531.	118.24	243.4	211.9	227.1	141.8	123.5	132.3
Other	143–144	30897.	47.56	371.7	371.7	371.7	174.8	174.8	174.8
Exports minus imports	146–146	556.	56.75	296.8	296.8	296.8	3.3	3.3	3.3
Government	147–151	67691.	808.43	274.6	244.2	258.9	34.3	30.5	32.3
Compensation	147–150	53672.	419.96	256.1	233.8	244.7	54.7	49.9	52.2
Commodities	151–151	14019.	388.47	294.6	294.6	294.6	12.3	12.3	12.3
Gross domestic product	1–151	1327958.	7176.71	315.0	245.2	277.9	75.5	58.7	66.6
Aggregates									
ICP concepts[e]									
Consumption (CEP)[b,c]	1–108	824902.	5182.96	314.6	232.0	270.1	68.6	50.6	58.9
Capital formation (GCF)[d]	109–146	435366.	1185.32	344.3	274.9	307.7	133.6	106.7	119.4
Government (PFC)	147–151	67691.	808.43	274.6	244.2	258.9	34.3	30.5	32.3
Gross domestic product	1–151	1327958.	7176.71	315.0	245.2	277.9	75.5	58.7	66.6
SNA concepts[e]									
Consumption (PFCE)	1–108	758018.	4620.20	328.2	236.2	278.4	69.5	50.0	58.9
Capital formation (GCF)	109–146	435366.	1185.32	344.3	274.9	307.7	133.6	106.7	119.4
Government (GFCE)	1–151	133473.	1367.45	245.1	214.9	229.5	45.4	39.8	42.5
Gross domestic product	1–151	1326856.	7172.96	315.0	245.1	277.9	75.5	58.7	66.6

Note: See the end of Appendix Table 7-68 for notes.

Category	Line numbers[a]	Per capita expenditure		Purchasing power parities (shillings/dollars)			Quantity per capita (U.S. = 100)		
		Kenya (shillings)	U.S. (dollars)	U.S. weight	Kenya weight	Geometric mean	U.S. weight	Kenya weight	Geometric mean
Consumption, ICP[b,c]	1–108	1370.10	5182.96	7.036	2.220	3.952	11.9	3.8	6.7
Food, beverages, tobacco	1– 39	602.13	818.24	6.348	3.391	4.640	21.7	11.6	15.9
Food	1– 33	505.11	658.25	6.282	3.193	4.478	24.0	12.2	17.1
Bread, cereals	1– 6	201.96	94.81	4.385	2.431	3.265	87.6	48.6	65.2
Meat	7– 12	30.15	163.79	4.803	2.833	3.689	6.5	3.8	5.0
Fish	13– 14	2.99	25.96	11.221	7.839	9.379	1.5	1.0	1.2
Milk, cheese, eggs	15– 17	95.68	82.52	6.219	4.577	5.335	25.3	18.6	21.7
Oils, fats	18– 20	15.08	32.30	8.148	8.089	8.118	5.8	5.7	5.7
Fruits, vegetables	21– 26	109.26	147.83	7.488	3.617	5.204	20.4	9.9	14.2
Coffee, tea, cocoa	27– 29	7.61	17.18	7.021	4.524	5.636	9.8	6.3	7.9
Spices, sweets, sugar	30– 33	42.39	93.86	6.791	4.488	5.521	10.1	6.7	8.2
Beverages	34– 37	63.74	91.02	8.403	7.487	7.932	9.4	8.3	8.8
Tobacco	38– 39	33.29	68.97	4.268	3.069	3.619	15.7	11.3	13.3
Clothing, footwear	40– 51	94.04	336.33	6.211	6.671	6.437	4.2	4.5	4.3
Clothing	40– 47	80.45	284.83	5.909	6.506	6.201	4.3	4.8	4.6
Footwear	48– 51	13.58	51.50	7.883	7.847	7.865	3.4	3.3	3.4
Gross rent, fuel	52– 57	154.79	903.84	8.823	4.929	6.595	3.5	1.9	2.6
Gross rent	52– 53	124.49	717.46	6.854	5.852	6.334	3.0	2.5	2.7
Fuel, power	54– 57	30.30	186.38	16.404	2.990	7.003	5.4	1.0	2.3
House furnishings, operations	58– 70	115.38	343.14	6.006	0.862	2.275	39.0	5.6	14.8
Furniture	58– 60	45.68	165.64	6.105	3.139	4.378	8.8	4.5	6.3
Appliances	61– 66	4.48	56.41	9.970	0.0	0.0	0.0	0.0	0.0
Supplies, operations	67– 70	65.23	121.09	5.842	0.571	1.827	94.3	9.2	29.5
Medical care	71– 77	65.68	653.69	6.912	3.995	5.255	2.5	1.5	1.9
Transport, communications	78– 89	100.01	692.17	10.315	2.895	5.464	5.0	1.4	2.6
Equipment	78– 79	10.60	221.44	14.393	12.671	13.505	0.4	0.3	0.4
Operation costs	80– 83	42.54	338.12	9.295	4.724	6.627	2.7	1.4	1.9
Purchased transport	84– 87	42.39	40.37	2.955	1.775	2.290	59.2	35.5	45.8
Communications	88– 89	4.48	92.24	7.482	5.435	6.377	0.9	0.6	0.8
Recreation, education	90–101	160.76	783.74	5.108	0.866	2.103	23.7	4.0	9.8
Recreation	90– 96	28.81	323.24	7.302	4.241	5.565	2.1	1.2	1.6
Education	97–101	131.95	460.50	3.567	0.738	1.623	38.8	8.0	17.7
Other expenditures	102–107	77.32	628.47	5.272	3.277	4.157	3.8	2.3	3.0
Personal care	102–104	30.30	136.90	3.464	2.947	3.195	7.5	6.4	6.9
Miscellaneous services	105–107	47.02	491.57	5.776	3.533	4.517	2.7	1.7	2.1
Capital formation	109–146	239.87	1185.32	8.183	5.838	6.912	3.5	2.5	2.9
Domestic capital formation	109–145	323.61	1128.57	8.222	6.177	7.127	4.6	3.5	4.0
Construction	109–122	204.05	680.37	4.363	4.381	4.372	6.8	6.9	6.9
Residential	109–110	63.29	235.05	4.394	4.519	4.456	6.0	6.1	6.0
Nonresidential	111–118	46.87	210.33	4.242	4.187	4.215	5.3	5.3	5.3
Other	119–122	93.89	234.99	4.440	4.391	4.416	9.1	9.0	9.0
Producer durables	123–144	156.58	491.75	13.287	12.010	12.632	2.7	2.4	2.5
Transport equipment	123–129	47.76	122.69	17.645	16.319	16.969	2.4	2.2	2.3
Nonelectrical machinery	130–138	74.04	203.26	11.374	10.507	10.932	3.5	3.2	3.3
Electrical machinery	139–142	26.87	118.24	13.251	11.511	12.350	2.0	1.7	1.8
Other	143–144	7.91	47.56	10.311	10.838	10.571	1.5	1.6	1.6
Exports minus imports	146–146	− 83.74	56.75	7.411	7.411	7.411	− 19.9	− 19.9	− 19.9
Government	147–151	177.03	808.43	3.188	2.197	2.647	10.0	6.9	8.3
Compensation	147–150	100.01	419.96	1.729	1.553	1.638	15.3	13.8	14.5
Commodities	151–151	77.02	388.47	4.766	4.766	4.766	4.2	4.2	4.2
Gross domestic product	1–151	1787.00	7176.71	6.792	2.419	4.053	10.3	3.7	6.1
Aggregates									
ICP concepts[e]									
Consumption (CEP)[b,c]	1–108	1370.10	5182.96	7.036	2.220	3.952	11.9	3.8	6.7
Capital formation (GCF)[d]	109–146	239.87	1185.32	8.183	5.838	6.912	3.5	2.5	2.9
Government (PFC)	147–151	177.03	808.43	3.188	2.197	2.647	10.0	6.9	8.3
Gross domestic product	1–151	1787.00	7176.71	6.792	2.419	4.053	10.3	3.7	6.1
SNA concepts[e]									
Consumption (PFCE)	1–108	1218.15	4620.20	7.438	2.662	4.450	9.9	3.5	5.9
Capital formation (GCF)	109–146	239.87	1185.32	8.183	5.838	6.912	3.5	2.5	2.9
Government (GFCE)	1–151	328.98	1367.45	3.407	1.370	2.160	17.6	7.1	11.1
Gross domestic product	1–151	1787.00	7172.96	6.792	2.419	4.053	10.3	3.7	6.1

Note: See the end of Appendix Table 7-68 for notes.

Appendix Table 7-16. Augmented Summary Binary Table: Korea/United States, 1975

Category	Line numbers[a]	Per capita expenditure Korea (won)	Per capita expenditure U.S. (dollars)	Purchasing power parities (won/dollars) U.S. weight	Purchasing power parities (won/dollars) Korea weight	Purchasing power parities (won/dollars) Geometric mean	Quantity per capita (U.S. = 100) U.S. weight	Quantity per capita (U.S. = 100) Korea weight	Quantity per capita (U.S. = 100) Geometric mean
Consumption, ICP[b,c]	1–108	201823.	5182.96	314.8	156.6	222.0	24.9	12.4	17.5
Food, beverages, tobacco	1– 39	109486.	818.24	430.7	258.2	333.5	51.8	31.1	40.1
Food	1– 33	90435.	658.25	423.0	281.1	344.8	48.9	32.5	39.8
Bread, cereals	1– 6	47229.	94.81	256.8	305.6	280.1	163.0	194.0	177.8
Meat	7– 12	6614.	163.79	322.9	334.8	328.8	12.1	12.5	12.3
Fish	13– 14	5582.	25.96	289.1	288.9	289.0	74.4	74.4	74.4
Milk, cheese, eggs	15– 17	3553.	82.52	499.1	464.7	481.6	9.3	8.6	8.9
Oils, fats	18– 20	756.	32.30	496.0	485.4	490.6	4.8	4.7	4.8
Fruits, vegetables	21– 26	13369.	147.83	457.8	161.9	272.3	55.9	19.8	33.2
Coffee, tea, cocoa	27– 29	416.	17.18	1139.8	1146.8	1143.3	2.1	2.1	2.1
Spices, sweets, sugar	30– 33	12916.	93.86	524.6	358.8	433.9	38.4	26.2	31.7
Beverages	34– 37	10904.	91.02	724.2	334.8	492.4	35.8	16.5	24.3
Tobacco	38– 39	8148.	68.97	116.9	116.9	116.9	101.1	101.1	101.1
Clothing, footwear	40– 51	19097.	336.33	212.8	201.5	207.1	28.2	26.7	27.4
Clothing	40– 47	17703.	284.83	222.4	215.1	218.7	28.9	27.9	28.4
Footwear	48– 51	1393.	51.50	159.5	111.9	133.6	24.2	17.0	20.3
Gross rent, fuel	52– 57	15677.	903.84	381.9	185.3	266.0	9.4	4.5	6.5
Gross rent	52– 53	6342.	717.46	317.6	306.4	312.0	2.9	2.8	2.8
Fuel, power	54– 57	9335.	186.38	629.5	146.0	303.2	34.3	8.0	16.5
House furnishings, operations	58– 70	6323.	343.14	274.1	222.3	246.9	8.3	6.7	7.5
Furniture	58– 60	884.	165.64	165.6	168.1	166.8	3.2	3.2	3.2
Appliances	61– 66	3017.	56.41	804.4	673.7	736.1	7.9	6.6	7.3
Supplies, operations	67– 70	2422.	121.09	175.4	129.5	150.7	15.4	11.4	13.3
Medical care	71– 77	7913.	653.69	132.8	107.6	119.5	11.3	9.1	10.1
Transport, communications	78– 89	13889.	692.17	671.1	63.4	206.2	31.7	3.0	9.7
Equipment	78– 79	633.	221.44	826.3	411.1	582.8	0.7	0.3	0.5
Operation costs	80– 83	32.	338.12	796.7	304.8	492.7	0.0	0.0	0.0
Purchased transport	84– 87	12339.	40.37	94.9	60.2	75.5	508.1	322.2	404.6
Communications	88– 89	885.	92.24	90.3	71.2	80.2	13.5	10.6	12.0
Recreation, education	90–101	15777.	783.74	146.3	63.7	96.6	31.6	13.8	20.8
Recreation	90– 96	5775.	323.24	247.4	166.2	202.8	10.7	7.2	8.8
Education	97–101	10002.	460.50	75.3	47.0	59.5	46.2	28.8	36.5
Other expenditures	102–107	15387.	628.47	145.3	127.7	136.2	19.2	16.9	18.0
Personal care	102–104	6272.	136.90	198.6	143.2	168.6	32.0	23.1	27.2
Miscellaneous services	105–107	9114.	491.57	130.4	118.9	124.5	15.6	14.2	14.9
Capital formation	109–146	56894.	1185.32	350.8	167.3	242.2	28.7	13.7	19.8
Domestic capital formation	109–145	81389.	1128.57	344.1	208.3	267.7	34.6	21.0	26.9
Construction	109–122	38465.	680.37	202.5	191.9	197.1	29.5	27.9	28.7
Residential	109–110	12567.	235.05	172.6	172.6	172.6	31.0	31.0	31.0
Nonresidential	111–118	12867.	210.33	216.9	212.1	214.5	28.8	28.2	28.5
Other	119–122	13031.	234.99	219.6	194.6	206.7	28.5	25.3	26.8
Producer durables	123–144	33381.	491.75	531.2	220.4	342.1	30.8	12.8	19.8
Transport equipment	123–129	15248.	122.69	736.9	140.9	322.3	88.2	16.9	38.6
Nonelectrical machinery	130–138	14991.	203.26	548.7	445.4	494.3	16.6	13.4	14.9
Electrical machinery	139–142	2061.	118.24	392.1	385.2	388.6	4.5	4.4	4.5
Other	143–144	1082.	47.56	271.0	254.2	262.4	9.0	8.4	8.7
Exports minus imports	146–146	– 24495.	56.75	484.0	484.0	484.0	– 89.2	– 89.2	– 89.2
Government	147–151	23352.	808.43	170.0	153.9	161.8	18.8	17.0	17.9
Compensation	147–150	11152.	419.96	106.8	111.0	108.9	23.9	24.9	24.4
Commodities	151–151	12201.	388.47	238.3	238.3	238.3	13.2	13.2	13.2
Gross domestic product	1–151	282070.	7176.71	304.5	158.4	219.6	24.8	12.9	17.9
Aggregates									
ICP concepts[c]									
Consumption (CEP)[b,c]	1–108	201823.	5182.96	314.8	156.6	222.0	24.9	12.4	17.5
Capital formation (GCF)[d]	109–146	56894.	1185.32	350.8	167.3	242.2	28.7	13.7	19.8
Government (PFC)	147–151	23352.	808.43	170.0	153.9	161.8	18.8	17.0	17.9
Gross domestic product	1–151	282070.	7176.71	304.5	158.4	219.6	24.8	12.9	17.9
SNA concepts[e]									
Consumption (PFCE)	1–108	196131.	4620.20	341.8	168.9	240.3	25.1	12.4	17.7
Capital formation (GCF)	109–146	56894.	1185.32	350.8	167.3	242.2	28.7	13.7	19.8
Government (GFCE)	1–151	29044.	1367.45	137.9	103.8	119.6	20.5	15.4	17.8
Gross domestic product	1–151	282070.	7172.96	304.4	158.4	219.6	24.8	12.9	17.9

Note: See the end of Appendix Table 7-68 for notes.

Appendix Table 7-17. Augmented Summary Binary Table: Luxembourg/United States, 1975

Category	Line numbers[a]	Per capita expenditure Luxembourg (francs)	Per capita expenditure U.S. (dollars)	Purchasing power parities (francs/dollars) U.S. weight	Purchasing power parities (francs/dollars) Luxembourg weight	Purchasing power parities (francs/dollars) Geometric mean	Quantity per capita (U.S. = 100) U.S. weight	Quantity per capita (U.S. = 100) Luxembourg weight	Quantity per capita (U.S. = 100) Geometric mean
Consumption, ICP[b,c]	1–108	149966.7	5182.96	41.19	35.64	38.32	81.2	70.2	75.5
Food, beverages, tobacco	1– 39	33419.4	818.24	40.13	39.60	39.87	103.1	101.8	102.4
Food	1– 33	28169.4	658.25	41.82	41.27	41.55	103.7	102.3	103.0
Bread, cereals	1– 6	3977.8	94.81	38.42	38.83	38.62	108.0	109.2	108.6
Meat	7– 12	9127.8	163.79	44.58	44.79	44.69	124.4	125.0	124.7
Fish	13– 14	755.6	25.96	55.28	53.37	54.32	54.5	52.6	53.6
Milk, cheese, eggs	15– 17	4080.6	82.52	38.44	38.65	38.54	127.9	128.6	128.3
Oils, fats	18– 20	2258.3	32.30	40.62	48.37	44.33	144.6	172.1	157.7
Fruits, vegetables	21– 26	4877.8	147.83	43.16	36.03	39.43	91.6	76.5	83.7
Coffee, tea, cocoa	27– 29	1030.6	17.18	74.36	73.87	74.11	81.2	80.7	81.0
Spices, sweets, sugar	30– 33	2061.1	93.86	32.07	34.00	33.02	64.6	68.5	66.5
Beverages	34– 37	3180.6	91.02	32.07	31.34	31.71	111.5	108.9	110.2
Tobacco	38– 39	2069.4	68.97	34.62	34.62	34.62	86.7	86.7	86.7
Clothing, footwear	40– 51	12405.6	336.33	53.60	54.33	53.97	67.9	68.8	68.3
Clothing	40– 47	10638.9	284.83	55.19	56.82	56.00	65.7	67.7	66.7
Footwear	48– 51	1766.7	51.50	44.82	43.01	43.91	79.8	76.5	78.1
Gross rent, fuel	52– 57	25402.8	903.84	42.30	39.64	40.95	70.9	66.4	68.6
Gross rent	52– 53	18122.2	717.46	38.44	36.17	37.29	69.8	65.7	67.7
Fuel, power	54– 57	7280.6	186.38	57.15	52.06	54.55	75.0	68.4	71.6
House furnishings, operations	58– 70	15002.8	343.14	44.89	31.60	37.67	138.3	97.4	116.1
Furniture	58– 60	6344.4	165.64	36.79	23.44	29.37	163.4	104.1	130.4
Appliances	61– 66	2061.1	56.41	70.08	57.55	63.51	63.5	52.1	57.5
Supplies, operations	67– 70	6597.2	121.09	44.24	39.22	41.65	138.9	123.1	130.8
Medical care	71– 77	9022.2	653.69	25.45	16.68	20.60	82.8	54.2	67.0
Transport, communications	78– 89	18302.8	692.17	51.51	37.66	44.05	70.2	51.3	60.0
Equipment	78– 79	6363.9	221.44	45.28	41.04	43.11	70.0	63.5	66.7
Operation costs	80– 83	8236.1	338.12	53.87	41.67	47.38	58.5	45.2	51.4
Purchased transport	84– 87	2366.7	40.37	59.58	24.44	38.16	239.8	98.4	153.6
Communications	88– 89	1336.1	92.24	54.32	36.64	44.61	39.5	26.7	32.5
Recreation, education	90–101	16197.2	783.74	37.65	38.03	37.84	54.3	54.9	54.6
Recreation	90– 96	5627.8	323.24	38.14	35.62	36.86	48.9	45.7	47.2
Education	97–101	10569.4	460.50	37.31	39.45	38.36	58.2	61.5	59.8
Other expenditures	102–107	20213.9	628.47	41.90	35.64	38.64	90.3	76.8	83.2
Personal care	102–104	4905.6	136.90	42.18	37.47	39.76	95.6	85.0	90.1
Miscellaneous services	105–107	15308.3	491.57	41.82	35.08	38.31	88.8	74.5	81.3
Capital formation	109–146	63100.0	1185.32	47.14	48.29	47.71	110.2	112.9	111.6
Domestic capital formation	109–145	67666.7	1128.57	47.66	47.29	47.47	126.8	125.8	126.3
Construction	109–122	47850.0	680.37	47.06	46.54	46.80	151.1	149.4	150.3
Residential	109–110	18519.4	235.05	50.41	47.22	48.79	166.9	156.3	161.5
Nonresidential	111–118	20316.7	210.33	52.34	56.64	54.45	170.5	184.5	177.4
Other	119–122	9013.9	234.99	38.98	32.51	35.60	118.0	98.4	107.8
Producer durables	123–144	18755.6	491.75	48.37	49.38	48.87	77.2	78.9	78.0
Transport equipment	123–129	4522.2	122.69	42.73	48.50	45.52	76.0	86.3	81.0
Nonelectrical machinery	130–138	8138.9	203.26	45.98	45.44	45.71	88.1	87.1	87.6
Electrical machinery	139–142	4866.7	118.24	59.05	60.90	59.97	67.6	69.7	68.6
Other	143–144	1227.8	47.56	46.55	44.62	45.57	57.9	55.5	56.6
Exports minus imports	146–146	−4566.7	56.75	36.78	36.78	36.78	−218.8	−218.8	−218.8
Government	147–151	23677.8	808.43	52.54	52.32	52.43	56.0	55.7	55.9
Compensation	147–150	15305.6	419.96	57.89	55.97	56.92	65.1	63.0	64.0
Commodities	151–151	8372.2	388.47	46.75	46.75	46.75	46.1	46.1	46.1
Gross domestic product	1–151	236744.4	7176.71	43.45	39.67	41.52	83.1	75.9	79.5
Aggregates									
ICP concepts[e]									
Consumption (CEP)[b,c]	1–108	149966.7	5182.96	41.19	35.64	38.32	81.2	70.2	75.5
Capital formation (GCF)[d]	109–146	63100.0	1185.32	47.14	48.29	47.71	110.2	112.9	111.6
Government (PFC)	147–151	23677.8	808.43	52.54	52.32	52.43	56.0	55.7	55.9
Gross domestic product	1–151	236744.4	7176.71	43.45	39.67	41.52	83.1	75.9	79.5
SNA concepts[e]									
Consumption (PFCE)	1–108	139786.1	4620.20	41.55	35.41	38.36	85.4	72.8	78.9
Capital formation (GCF)	109–146	63100.0	1185.32	47.14	48.29	47.71	110.2	112.9	111.6
Government (GFCE)	1–151	33858.3	1367.45	46.70	47.47	47.09	52.2	53.0	52.6
Gross domestic product	1–151	236744.4	7172.96	43.46	39.67	41.52	83.2	76.0	79.5

Note: See the end of Appendix Table 7-68 for notes.

Category	Line numbers[a]	Per capita expenditure Malawi (kwacha)	Per capita expenditure U.S. (dollars)	Purchasing power parities (kwacha/dollars) U.S. weight	Purchasing power parities (kwacha/dollars) Malawi weight	Purchasing power parities (kwacha/dollars) Geometric mean	Quantity per capita (U.S. = 100) U.S. weight	Quantity per capita (U.S. = 100) Malawi weight	Quantity per capita (U.S. = 100) Geometric mean
Consumption, ICP[b,c]	1–108	95.660	5182.96	0.6757	0.2477	0.4091	7.5	2.7	4.5
Food, beverages, tobacco	1– 39	55.543	818.24	0.6695	0.2654	0.4215	25.6	10.1	16.1
Food	1– 33	50.571	658.25	0.6899	0.2524	0.4173	30.4	11.1	18.4
Bread, cereals	1– 6	19.590	94.81	0.6417	0.2622	0.4102	78.8	32.2	50.4
Meat	7– 12	3.385	163.79	0.4788	0.4521	0.4653	4.6	4.3	4.4
Fish	13– 14	2.759	25.96	0.6987	0.7322	0.7152	14.5	15.2	14.9
Milk, cheese, eggs	15– 17	2.091	82.52	0.7262	0.6484	0.6862	3.9	3.5	3.7
Oils, fats	18– 20	0.875	32.30	0.8915	0.8907	0.8911	3.0	3.0	3.0
Fruits, vegetables	21– 26	19.739	147.83	0.8696	0.1876	0.4039	71.2	15.4	33.1
Coffee, tea, cocoa	27– 29	0.304	17.18	1.0842	0.4375	0.6887	4.0	1.6	2.6
Spices, sweets, sugar	30– 33	1.829	93.86	0.6482	0.4278	0.5266	4.6	3.0	3.7
Beverages	34– 37	4.199	91.02	0.7089	0.5896	0.6465	7.8	6.5	7.1
Tobacco	38– 39	0.773	68.97	0.4227	0.4169	0.4198	2.7	2.7	2.7
Clothing, footwear	40– 51	6.702	336.33	0.6625	0.6309	0.6465	3.2	3.0	3.1
Clothing	40– 47	6.148	284.83	0.7193	0.6941	0.7066	3.1	3.0	3.1
Footwear	48– 51	0.554	51.50	0.3485	0.3140	0.3308	3.4	3.1	3.3
Gross rent, fuel	52– 57	5.915	903.84	0.7907	0.6410	0.7119	1.0	0.8	0.9
Gross rent	52– 53	3.388	717.46	0.5971	0.5892	0.5932	0.8	0.8	0.8
Fuel, power	54– 57	2.527	186.38	1.5358	0.7265	1.0563	1.9	0.9	1.3
House furnishings, operations	58– 70	8.999	343.14	0.9217	0.3233	0.5458	8.1	2.8	4.8
Furniture	58– 60	2.085	165.64	0.5927	0.4965	0.5425	2.5	2.1	2.3
Appliances	61– 66	0.926	56.41	2.2764	1.3562	1.7570	1.2	0.7	0.9
Supplies, operations	67– 70	5.987	121.09	0.7406	0.2608	0.4395	19.0	6.7	11.3
Medical care	71– 77	1.835	653.69	0.2081	0.0854	0.1333	3.3	1.3	2.1
Transport, communications	78– 89	7.193	692.17	1.2434	0.5199	0.8040	2.0	0.8	1.3
Equipment	78– 79	1.618	221.44	1.9167	1.7036	1.8070	0.4	0.4	0.4
Operation costs	80– 83	4.113	338.12	1.1548	1.1080	1.1312	1.1	1.1	1.1
Purchased transport	84– 87	1.333	40.37	0.3159	0.1500	0.2177	22.0	10.5	15.2
Communications	88– 89	0.130	92.24	0.3579	0.4484	0.4006	0.3	0.4	0.4
Recreation, education	90–101	6.266	783.74	0.4436	0.0742	0.1814	10.8	1.8	4.4
Recreation	90– 96	2.548	323.24	0.8635	0.3280	0.5322	2.4	0.9	1.5
Education	97–101	3.717	460.50	0.1489	0.0485	0.0849	16.7	5.4	9.5
Other expenditures	102–107	3.206	628.47	0.5342	0.3430	0.4281	1.5	1.0	1.2
Personal care	102–104	0.481	136.90	0.7448	0.6752	0.7091	0.5	0.5	0.5
Miscellaneous services	105–107	2.725	491.57	0.4756	0.3156	0.3874	1.8	1.2	1.4
Capital formation	109–146	14.968	1185.32	0.8549	0.4390	0.6126	2.9	1.5	2.1
Domestic capital formation	109–145	35.587	1128.57	0.8543	0.6146	0.7246	5.1	3.7	4.4
Construction	109–122	13.272	680.37	0.4788	0.3518	0.4104	5.5	4.1	4.8
Residential	109–110	4.358	235.05	0.5081	0.4806	0.4942	3.9	3.6	3.8
Nonresidential	111–118	4.940	210.33	0.5941	0.4737	0.5305	5.0	4.0	4.4
Other	119–122	3.973	234.99	0.3463	0.2180	0.2748	7.8	4.9	6.2
Producer durables	123–144	19.143	491.75	1.3393	1.4349	1.3863	2.7	2.9	2.8
Transport equipment	123–129	8.075	122.69	2.0491	2.2908	2.1666	2.9	3.2	3.0
Nonelectrical machinery	130–138	8.710	203.26	1.2222	1.2103	1.2162	3.5	3.5	3.5
Electrical machinery	139–142	2.144	118.24	1.0247	0.9028	0.9618	2.0	1.8	1.9
Other	143–144	0.214	47.56	0.7905	0.8754	0.8319	0.5	0.6	0.5
Exports minus imports	146–146	−20.619	56.75	0.8662	0.8662	0.8662	−41.9	−41.9	−41.9
Government	147–151	9.169	808.43	0.3368	0.1379	0.2155	8.2	3.4	5.3
Compensation	147–150	4.347	419.96	0.1638	0.0759	0.1115	13.6	6.3	9.3
Commodities	151–151	4.822	388.47	0.5238	0.5238	0.5238	2.4	2.4	2.4
Gross domestic product	1–151	119.797	7176.71	0.6671	0.2461	0.4052	6.8	2.5	4.1
Aggregates									
ICP concepts[e]									
Consumption (CEP)[b,c]	1–108	95.660	5182.96	0.6757	0.2477	0.4091	7.5	2.7	4.5
Capital formation (GCF)[d]	109–146	14.968	1185.32	0.8549	0.4390	0.6126	2.9	1.5	2.1
Government (PFC)	147–151	9.169	808.43	0.3368	0.1379	0.2155	8.2	3.4	5.3
Gross domestic product	1–151	119.797	7176.71	0.6671	0.2461	0.4052	6.8	2.5	4.1
SNA concepts[e]									
Consumption (PFCE)	1–108	90.753	4620.20	0.7331	0.3151	0.4806	6.2	2.7	4.1
Capital formation (GCF)	109–146	14.968	1185.32	0.8549	0.4390	0.6126	2.9	1.5	2.1
Government (GFCE)	1–151	13.728	1367.45	0.2815	0.0837	0.1535	12.0	3.6	6.5
Gross domestic product	1–151	119.450	7172.96	0.6671	0.2457	0.4049	6.8	2.5	4.1

Note: See the end of Appendix Table 7-68 for notes.

Category	Line numbers[a]	Per capita expenditure Malaysia (ringgit)	Per capita expenditure U.S. (dollars)	Purchasing power parities (ringgit/dollars) U.S. weight	Purchasing power parities (ringgit/dollars) Malaysia weight	Purchasing power parities (ringgit/dollars) Geometric mean	Quantity per capita (U.S. = 100) U.S. weight	Quantity per capita (U.S. = 100) Malaysia weight	Quantity per capita (U.S. = 100) Geometric mean
Consumption, ICP[b,c]	1–108	1204.83	5182.96	1.576	1.023	1.269	22.7	14.8	18.3
Food, beverages, tobacco	1– 39	478.57	818.24	1.991	1.568	1.767	37.3	29.4	33.1
Food	1– 33	406.31	658.25	1.955	1.510	1.718	40.9	31.6	35.9
Bread, cereals	1– 6	117.42	94.81	1.524	1.302	1.409	95.1	81.2	87.9
Meat	7– 12	70.70	163.79	2.033	1.900	1.966	22.7	21.2	22.0
Fish	13– 14	47.94	25.96	1.566	1.598	1.582	115.6	117.9	116.7
Milk, cheese, eggs	15– 17	49.16	82.52	2.612	1.871	2.211	31.8	22.8	26.9
Oils, fats	18– 20	15.44	32.30	1.544	1.419	1.480	33.7	31.0	32.3
Fruits, vegetables	21– 26	52.41	147.83	1.921	1.290	1.574	27.5	18.5	22.5
Coffee, tea, cocoa	27– 29	8.53	17.18	2.901	2.220	2.538	22.4	17.1	19.6
Spices, sweets, sugar	30– 33	44.70	93.86	1.803	1.483	1.635	32.1	26.4	29.1
Beverages	34– 37	27.28	91.02	2.227	2.243	2.235	13.4	13.5	13.4
Tobacco	38– 39	44.98	68.97	2.029	1.884	1.955	34.6	32.2	33.4
Clothing, footwear	40– 51	70.25	336.33	0.979	1.190	1.079	17.5	21.3	19.4
Clothing	40– 47	62.17	284.83	1.041	1.397	1.206	15.6	21.0	18.1
Footwear	48– 51	8.08	51.50	0.633	0.556	0.593	28.2	24.8	26.4
Gross rent, fuel	52– 57	122.93	903.84	1.395	1.051	1.211	12.9	9.7	11.2
Gross rent	52– 53	99.09	717.46	0.970	0.911	0.940	15.2	14.2	14.7
Fuel, power	54– 57	23.85	186.38	3.030	2.897	2.963	4.4	4.2	4.3
House furnishings, operations	58– 70	71.35	343.14	2.044	1.317	1.641	15.8	10.2	12.7
Furniture	58– 60	18.48	165.64	1.195	1.171	1.183	9.5	9.3	9.4
Appliances	61– 66	10.91	56.41	5.776	4.792	5.261	4.0	3.3	3.7
Supplies, operations	67– 70	41.96	121.09	1.467	1.162	1.306	29.8	23.6	26.5
Medical care	71– 77	50.74	653.69	0.855	0.566	0.696	13.7	9.1	11.2
Transport, communications	78– 89	158.06	692.17	3.203	1.036	1.822	22.0	7.1	12.5
Equipment	78– 79	36.51	221.44	4.577	4.024	4.292	4.1	3.6	3.8
Operation costs	80– 83	65.75	338.12	2.789	2.520	2.651	7.7	7.0	7.3
Purchased transport	84– 87	49.31	40.37	0.994	0.435	0.658	280.6	122.9	185.7
Communications	88– 89	6.48	92.24	2.391	1.567	1.936	4.5	2.9	3.6
Recreation, education	90–101	146.47	783.74	0.953	0.504	0.693	37.1	19.6	27.0
Recreation	90– 96	58.35	323.24	1.527	0.962	1.212	18.8	11.8	14.9
Education	97–101	88.12	460.50	0.550	0.383	0.459	49.9	34.8	41.7
Other expenditures	102–107	91.13	628.47	1.060	0.880	0.966	16.5	13.7	15.0
Personal care	102–104	18.74	136.90	1.399	0.903	1.124	15.2	9.8	12.2
Miscellaneous services	105–107	72.40	491.57	0.965	0.874	0.919	16.8	15.3	16.0
Capital formation	109–146	446.40	1185.32	1.905	1.094	1.444	34.4	19.8	26.1
Domestic capital formation	109–145	437.93	1128.57	1.880	1.083	1.427	35.8	20.6	27.2
Construction	109–122	252.80	680.37	0.818	0.722	0.769	51.4	45.4	48.3
Residential	109–110	69.07	235.05	0.707	0.690	0.699	42.6	41.5	42.1
Nonresidential	111–118	79.41	210.33	1.146	0.925	1.029	40.8	32.9	36.7
Other	119–122	104.32	234.99	0.636	0.636	0.636	69.8	69.8	69.8
Producer durables	123–144	217.09	491.75	3.317	2.884	3.093	15.3	13.3	14.3
Transport equipment	123–129	52.63	122.69	3.641	3.267	3.449	13.1	11.8	12.4
Nonelectrical machinery	130–138	129.69	203.26	3.210	2.691	2.939	23.7	19.9	21.7
Electrical machinery	139–142	27.72	118.24	3.630	3.577	3.604	6.6	6.5	6.5
Other	143–144	7.05	47.56	2.165	2.185	2.175	6.8	6.8	6.8
Exports minus imports	146–146	8.47	56.75	2.402	2.402	2.402	6.2	6.2	6.2
Government	147–151	221.94	808.43	1.170	1.146	1.158	24.0	23.5	23.7
Compensation	147–150	138.49	419.96	0.915	1.019	0.965	32.4	36.1	34.2
Commodities	151–151	83.45	388.47	1.446	1.446	1.446	14.9	14.9	14.9
Gross domestic product	1–151	1873.18	7176.71	1.584	1.052	1.291	24.8	16.5	20.2
Aggregates									
ICP concepts[e]									
Consumption (CEP)[b,c]	1–108	1204.83	5182.96	1.576	1.023	1.269	22.7	14.8	18.3
Capital formation (GCF)[d]	109–146	446.40	1185.32	1.905	1.094	1.444	34.4	19.8	26.1
Government (PFC)	147-151	221.94	808.43	1.170	1.146	1.158	24.0	23.5	23.7
Gross domestic product	1–151	1873.18	7176.71	1.584	1.052	1.291	24.8	16.5	20.2
SNA concepts[e]									
Consumption (PFCE)	1–108	1097.63	4620.20	1.682	1.208	1.425	19.7	14.1	16.7
Capital formation (GCF)	109–146	446.40	1185.32	1.905	1.094	1.444	34.4	19.8	26.1
Government (GFCE)	1–151	329.14	1367.45	0.978	0.711	0.834	33.9	24.6	28.9
Gross domestic product	1–151	1873.18	7172.96	1.585	1.052	1.291	24.8	16.5	20.2

Note: See the end of Appendix Table 7-68 for notes.

Appendix Table 7-20. Augmented Summary Binary Table: Mexico/United States, 1975

Category	Line numbers[a]	Per capita expenditure Mexico (pesos)	Per capita expenditure U.S. (dollars)	Purchasing power parities (pesos/dollars) U.S. weight	Purchasing power parities (pesos/dollars) Mexico weight	Purchasing power parities (pesos/dollars) Geometric mean	Quantity per capita (U.S. = 100) U.S. weight	Quantity per capita (U.S. = 100) Mexico weight	Quantity per capita (U.S. = 100) Geometric mean
Consumption, ICP[b,c]	1–108	13561.6	5182.96	8.06	5.73	6.80	45.6	32.5	38.5
Food, beverages, tobacco	1– 39	5306.2	818.24	9.53	7.70	8.56	84.2	68.1	75.7
Food	1– 33	5093.9	658.25	9.89	7.94	8.86	97.5	78.2	87.3
Bread, cereals	1– 6	1217.5	94.81	8.28	7.24	7.74	177.4	155.0	165.8
Meat	7– 12	1293.9	163.79	10.71	10.37	10.54	76.2	73.7	75.0
Fish	13– 14	86.6	25.96	9.87	7.10	8.37	47.0	33.8	39.8
Milk, cheese, eggs	15– 17	927.1	82.52	8.29	7.94	8.11	141.5	135.5	138.5
Oils, fats	18– 20	382.0	32.30	11.23	11.94	11.58	99.1	105.3	102.2
Fruits, vegetables	21– 26	738.6	147.83	11.85	6.05	8.47	82.6	42.1	59.0
Coffee, tea, cocoa	27– 29	147.7	17.18	15.77	12.60	14.10	68.3	54.5	61.0
Spices, sweets, sugar	30– 33	300.6	93.86	6.88	5.58	6.20	57.4	46.6	51.7
Beverages	34– 37	116.7	91.02	10.94	7.89	9.29	16.3	11.7	13.8
Tobacco	38– 39	95.5	68.97	4.18	2.91	3.49	47.5	33.2	39.7
Clothing, footwear	40– 51	1366.7	336.33	8.95	9.21	9.08	44.1	45.4	44.8
Clothing	40– 47	1034.6	284.83	9.19	10.01	9.59	36.3	39.5	37.9
Footwear	48– 51	332.1	51.50	7.59	7.37	7.48	87.5	85.0	86.2
Gross rent, fuel	52– 57	1312.6	903.84	5.72	5.94	5.83	24.4	25.4	24.9
Gross rent	52– 53	704.7	717.46	4.16	4.17	4.16	23.6	23.6	23.6
Fuel, power	54– 57	607.9	186.38	11.71	11.71	11.71	27.8	27.8	27.8
House furnishings, operations	58– 70	1489.9	343.14	9.63	3.81	6.05	114.1	45.1	71.7
Furniture	58– 60	257.8	165.64	7.07	6.05	6.54	25.7	22.0	23.8
Appliances	61– 66	291.0	56.41	18.79	17.08	17.91	30.2	27.5	28.8
Supplies, operations	67– 70	941.1	121.09	8.87	2.84	5.02	274.1	87.6	155.0
Medical care	71– 77	803.9	653.69	6.50	6.50	6.50	18.9	18.9	18.9
Transport, communications	78– 89	1096.0	692.17	10.08	3.71	6.11	42.7	15.7	25.9
Equipment	78– 79	296.4	221.44	19.08	18.53	18.81	7.2	7.0	7.1
Operation costs	80– 83	386.5	338.12	7.02	5.21	6.05	21.9	16.3	18.9
Purchased transport	84– 87	344.2	40.37	3.21	1.95	2.50	437.8	265.9	341.2
Communications	88– 89	69.0	92.24	2.69	2.42	2.55	30.9	27.8	29.3
Recreation, education	90–101	1205.2	783.74	7.85	4.04	5.63	38.0	19.6	27.3
Recreation	90– 96	408.0	323.24	13.77	8.24	10.65	15.3	9.2	11.8
Education	97–101	797.2	460.50	3.69	3.21	3.44	54.0	46.9	50.3
Other expenditures	102–107	1251.4	628.47	7.65	5.70	6.60	34.9	26.0	30.2
Personal care	102–104	395.4	136.90	10.36	7.88	9.04	36.6	27.9	32.0
Miscellaneous services	105–107	855.9	491.57	6.90	5.05	5.90	34.5	25.2	29.5
Capital formation	109–146	3834.6	1185.32	11.48	7.66	9.38	42.3	28.2	34.5
Domestic capital formation	109–145	4413.7	1128.57	11.43	8.07	9.60	48.5	34.2	40.7
Construction	109–122	2354.5	680.37	6.30	5.85	6.07	59.1	55.0	57.0
Residential	109–110	1146.1	235.05	6.60	6.56	6.58	74.3	73.9	74.1
Nonresidential	111–118	477.6	210.33	7.33	7.17	7.25	31.7	31.0	31.3
Other	119–122	730.8	234.99	5.07	4.54	4.80	68.5	61.3	64.8
Producer durables	123–144	1625.2	491.75	18.35	16.53	17.42	20.0	18.0	19.0
Transport equipment	123–129	397.8	122.69	16.33	15.07	15.69	21.5	19.9	20.7
Nonelectrical machinery	130–138	566.8	203.26	18.26	16.95	17.59	16.5	15.3	15.8
Electrical machinery	139–142	315.3	118.24	21.96	20.27	21.10	13.2	12.1	12.6
Other	143–144	345.3	47.56	14.93	15.08	15.01	48.1	48.6	48.4
Exports minus imports	146–146	−579.0	56.75	12.50	12.50	12.50	−81.6	−81.6	−81.6
Government	147–151	915.7	808.43	7.08	5.62	6.31	20.2	16.0	18.0
Compensation	147–150	707.8	419.96	5.62	5.09	5.35	33.1	30.0	31.5
Commodities	151–151	207.9	388.47	8.66	8.66	8.66	6.2	6.2	6.2
Gross domestic product	1–151	18311.9	7176.71	8.51	6.05	7.17	42.2	30.0	35.6
Aggregates									
ICP concepts[e]									
Consumption (CEP)[b,c]	1–108	13561.6	5182.96	8.06	5.73	6.80	45.6	32.5	38.5
Capital formation (GCF)[d]	109–146	3834.6	1185.32	11.48	7.66	9.38	42.3	28.2	34.5
Government (PFC)	147–151	915.7	808.43	7.08	5.62	6.31	20.2	16.0	18.0
Gross domestic product	1–151	18311.9	7176.71	8.51	6.05	7.17	42.2	30.0	35.6
SNA concepts[e]									
Consumption (PFCE)	1–108	12568.3	4620.20	8.50	5.94	7.11	45.8	32.0	38.3
Capital formation (GCF)	109–146	3834.6	1185.32	11.48	7.66	9.38	42.3	28.2	34.5
Government (GFCE)	1–151	1887.0	1367.45	5.99	4.63	5.27	29.8	23.0	26.2
Gross domestic product	1–151	18289.9	7172.96	8.51	6.05	7.18	42.2	29.9	35.5

Note: See the end of Appendix Table 7-68 for notes.

Category	Line numbers[a]	Per capita expenditure		Purchasing power parities (guilders/dollars)			Quantity per capita (U.S. = 100)		
		Netherlands (guilders)	U.S. (dollars)	U.S. weight	Netherlands weight	Geometric mean	U.S. weight	Netherlands weight	Geometric mean
Consumption, ICP[b,c]	1–108	9744.07	5182.96	3.081	2.609	2.835	72.1	61.0	66.3
Food, beverages, tobacco	1– 39	2110.40	818.24	2.718	2.639	2.678	97.7	94.9	96.3
Food	1– 33	1623.57	658.25	2.716	2.627	2.671	93.9	90.8	92.4
Bread, cereals	1– 6	212.30	94.81	2.321	2.273	2.297	98.5	96.5	97.5
Meat	7– 12	447.29	163.79	3.091	2.969	3.029	92.0	88.3	90.1
Fish	13– 14	51.98	25.96	2.976	3.002	2.989	66.7	67.3	67.0
Milk, cheese, eggs	15– 17	273.72	82.52	2.498	2.522	2.510	131.5	132.8	132.1
Oils, fats	18– 20	74.67	32.30	3.387	3.412	3.399	67.8	68.3	68.0
Fruits, vegetables	21– 26	320.64	147.83	2.722	2.438	2.576	89.0	79.7	84.2
Coffee, tea, cocoa	27– 29	83.38	17.18	4.073	3.970	4.021	122.3	119.2	120.7
Spices, sweets, sugar	30– 33	159.59	93.86	2.089	2.163	2.125	78.6	81.4	80.0
Beverages	34– 37	284.04	91.02	2.437	2.439	2.438	127.9	128.1	128.0
Tobacco	38– 39	202.78	68.97	3.116	3.116	3.116	94.4	94.4	94.4
Clothing, footwear	40– 51	800.95	336.33	3.276	3.317	3.296	71.8	72.7	72.2
Clothing	40– 47	683.82	284.83	3.361	3.447	3.404	69.7	71.4	70.5
Footwear	48– 51	117.13	51.50	2.808	2.718	2.762	83.7	81.0	82.3
Gross rent, fuel	52– 57	1203.51	903.84	2.619	2.366	2.490	56.3	50.8	53.5
Gross rent	52– 53	833.09	717.46	2.354	2.050	2.197	56.6	49.3	52.9
Fuel, power	54– 57	370.42	186.38	3.640	3.624	3.632	54.8	54.6	54.7
House furnishings, operations	58– 70	898.83	343.14	2.988	1.922	2.396	136.3	87.7	109.3
Furniture	58– 60	473.21	165.64	2.248	1.437	1.797	198.8	127.1	159.0
Appliances	61– 66	124.23	56.41	4.832	3.492	4.107	63.1	45.6	53.6
Supplies, operations	67– 70	301.39	121.09	3.141	2.936	3.036	84.8	79.3	82.0
Medical care	71– 77	1002.27	653.69	2.407	2.113	2.255	72.6	63.7	68.0
Transport, communications	78– 89	941.65	692.17	4.290	3.033	3.607	44.9	31.7	37.7
Equipment	78– 79	324.30	221.44	4.029	3.554	3.784	41.2	36.4	38.7
Operation costs	80– 83	432.72	338.12	4.212	2.709	3.378	47.2	30.4	37.9
Purchased transport	84– 87	68.23	40.37	3.965	2.015	2.827	83.9	42.6	59.8
Communications	88– 89	116.40	92.24	5.344	4.539	4.925	27.8	23.6	25.6
Recreation, education	90–101	1797.51	783.74	3.251	2.923	3.083	78.5	70.5	74.4
Recreation	90– 96	804.47	323.24	2.881	2.724	2.801	91.4	86.4	88.8
Education	97–101	993.05	460.50	3.511	3.107	3.303	69.4	61.4	65.3
Other expenditures	102–107	988.95	628.47	3.338	3.114	3.224	50.5	47.1	48.8
Personal care	102–104	202.93	136.90	3.400	3.138	3.266	47.2	43.6	45.4
Miscellaneous services	105–107	786.02	491.57	3.320	3.108	3.212	51.4	48.2	49.8
Capital formation	109–146	3767.42	1185.32	3.574	2.838	3.185	112.0	88.9	99.8
Domestic capital formation	109–145	3157.61	1128.57	3.627	2.907	3.247	96.3	77.1	86.2
Construction	109–122	1768.01	680.37	3.241	2.574	2.888	101.0	80.2	90.0
Residential	109–110	728.70	235.05	2.915	2.357	2.621	131.5	106.3	118.3
Nonresidential	111–118	645.90	210.33	4.270	3.855	4.057	79.7	71.9	75.7
Other	119–122	393.41	234.99	2.646	1.873	2.226	89.4	63.3	75.2
Producer durables	123–144	1421.82	491.75	4.102	3.464	3.769	83.5	70.5	76.7
Transport equipment	123–129	396.19	122.69	3.425	3.284	3.354	98.3	94.3	96.3
Nonelectrical machinery	130–138	555.49	203.26	3.334	3.265	3.299	83.7	82.0	82.8
Electrical machinery	139–142	319.99	118.24	6.487	4.438	5.365	61.0	41.7	50.4
Other	143–144	150.15	47.56	3.198	3.157	3.177	100.0	98.7	99.4
Exports minus imports	146–146	609.81	56.75	2.529	2.529	2.529	424.9	424.9	424.9
Government	147–151	1819.40	808.43	3.732	3.669	3.700	61.3	60.3	60.8
Compensation	147–150	1294.66	419.96	4.254	3.921	4.084	78.6	72.5	75.5
Commodities	151–151	524.74	388.47	3.166	3.166	3.166	42.7	42.7	42.7
Gross domestic product	1–151	15330.89	7176.71	3.236	2.758	2.987	77.4	66.0	71.5
Aggregates									
ICP concepts[e]									
Consumption (CEP)[b,c]	1–108	9744.07	5182.96	3.081	2.609	2.835	72.1	61.0	66.3
Capital formation (GCF)[d]	109–146	3767.42	1185.32	3.574	2.838	3.185	112.0	88.9	99.8
Government (PFC)	147–151	1819.40	808.43	3.732	3.669	3.700	61.3	60.3	60.8
Gross domestic product	1–151	15330.89	7176.71	3.236	2.758	2.987	77.4	66.0	71.5
SNA concepts[e]									
Consumption (PFCE)	1–108	8701.32	4620.20	3.064	2.573	2.808	73.2	61.5	67.1
Capital formation (GCF)	109–146	3767.42	1185.32	3.574	2.838	3.185	112.0	88.9	99.8
Government (GFCE)	1–151	2793.34	1367.45	3.524	3.442	3.483	59.3	58.0	58.6
Gross domestic product	1–151	15262.08	7172.96	3.236	2.765	2.991	77.0	65.7	71.1

Note: See the end of Appendix Table 7-68 for notes.

Category	Line numbers[a]	Per capita expenditure Pakistan (rupees)	Per capita expenditure U.S. (dollars)	Purchasing power parities U.S. weight	Purchasing power parities Pakistan weight	Purchasing power parities Geometric mean	Quantity per capita U.S. weight	Quantity per capita Pakistan weight	Quantity per capita Geometric mean
Consumption, ICP[b,c]	1–108	1525.02	5182.96	5.149	3.186	4.050	9.2	5.7	7.3
Food, beverages, tobacco	1– 39	905.51	818.24	6.492	4.248	5.252	26.0	17.0	21.1
Food	1– 33	866.27	658.25	5.272	4.187	4.698	31.4	25.0	28.0
Bread, cereals	1– 6	289.70	94.81	3.492	3.208	3.347	95.2	87.5	91.3
Meat	7– 12	52.04	163.79	2.907	2.657	2.779	12.0	10.9	11.4
Fish	13– 14	18.74	25.96	5.584	4.822	5.189	15.0	12.9	13.9
Milk, cheese, eggs	15– 17	191.39	82.52	7.388	7.538	7.463	30.8	31.4	31.1
Oils, fats	18– 20	122.36	32.30	5.766	6.948	6.330	54.5	65.7	59.8
Fruits, vegetables	21– 26	101.72	147.83	5.329	3.210	4.136	21.4	12.9	16.6
Coffee, tea, cocoa	27– 29	20.22	17.18	18.282	2.768	7.113	42.5	6.4	16.6
Spices, sweets, sugar	30– 33	70.10	93.86	6.608	6.294	6.449	11.9	11.3	11.6
Beverages	34– 37	2.12	91.02	15.382	15.382	15.382	0.2	0.2	0.2
Tobacco	38– 39	37.12	68.97	6.410	6.076	6.241	8.9	8.4	8.6
Clothing, footwear	40– 51	164.29	336.33	3.844	4.132	3.986	11.8	12.7	12.3
Clothing	40– 47	133.99	284.83	4.058	4.756	4.393	9.9	11.6	10.7
Footwear	48– 51	30.30	51.50	2.661	2.616	2.638	22.5	22.1	22.3
Gross rent, fuel	52– 57	175.85	903.84	4.824	5.567	5.182	3.5	4.0	3.8
Gross rent	52– 53	104.33	717.46	4.868	4.853	4.860	3.0	3.0	3.0
Fuel, power	54– 57	71.52	186.38	4.655	7.089	5.745	5.4	8.2	6.7
House furnishings, operations	58– 70	63.36	343.14	7.561	2.337	4.203	7.9	2.4	4.4
Furniture	58– 60	2.62	165.64	3.739	4.423	4.067	0.4	0.4	0.4
Appliances	61– 66	2.82	56.41	24.236	23.894	24.064	0.2	0.2	0.2
Supplies, operations	67– 70	57.93	121.09	5.020	2.194	3.319	21.8	9.5	14.4
Medical care	71– 77	71.95	653.69	2.806	2.676	2.740	4.1	3.9	4.0
Transport, communications	78– 89	29.38	692.17	9.182	1.699	3.950	2.5	0.5	1.1
Equipment	78– 79	0.11	221.44	17.088	12.700	14.732	0.0	0.0	0.0
Operation costs	80– 83	4.18	338.12	6.755	4.571	5.557	0.3	0.2	0.2
Purchased transport	84– 87	23.40	40.37	2.148	1.500	1.795	38.6	27.0	32.3
Communications	88– 89	1.68	92.24	2.180	2.202	2.191	0.8	0.8	0.8
Recreation, education	90–101	77.77	783.74	4.114	0.746	1.752	13.3	2.4	5.7
Recreation	90– 96	48.49	323.24	8.084	2.090	4.110	7.2	1.9	3.7
Education	97–101	29.28	460.50	1.328	0.361	0.693	17.6	4.8	9.2
Other expenditures	102–107	36.92	628.47	2.361	1.977	2.161	3.0	2.5	2.7
Personal care	102–104	15.90	136.90	5.390	2.277	3.503	5.1	2.2	3.3
Miscellaneous services	105–107	21.02	491.57	1.517	1.799	1.652	2.4	2.8	2.6
Capital formation	109–146	182.12	1185.32	10.298	3.385	5.904	4.5	1.5	2.6
Domestic capital formation	109–145	324.07	1128.57	10.317	4.759	7.007	6.0	2.8	4.1
Construction	109–122	200.68	680.37	5.607	3.543	4.457	8.3	5.3	6.6
Residential	109–110	37.83	235.05	2.914	2.894	2.904	5.6	5.5	5.5
Nonresidential	111–118	63.42	210.33	3.100	3.154	3.127	9.6	9.7	9.6
Other	119–122	99.43	234.99	10.544	4.240	6.686	10.0	4.0	6.3
Producer durables	123–144	123.38	491.75	16.637	10.766	13.383	2.3	1.5	1.9
Transport equipment	123–129	29.99	122.69	18.848	18.743	18.795	1.3	1.3	1.3
Nonelectrical machinery	130–138	72.67	203.26	14.940	9.114	11.669	3.9	2.4	3.1
Electrical machinery	139–142	17.09	118.24	14.191	10.839	12.403	1.3	1.0	1.2
Other	143–144	3.63	47.56	24.265	11.722	16.865	0.7	0.3	0.5
Exports minus imports	146–146	− 141.94	56.75	9.931	9.931	9.931	− 25.2	− 25.2	− 25.2
Government	147–151	172.22	808.43	2.252	.1.245	1.675	17.1	9.5	12.7
Compensation	147–150	91.52	419.96	0.940	0.787	0.860	27.7	23.2	25.3
Commodities	151–151	80.70	388.47	3.670	3.670	3.670	5.7	5.7	5.7
Gross domestic product	1–151	1879.36	7176.71	5.674	2.802	3.987	9.3	4.6	6.6
Aggregates									
ICP concepts[e]									
Consumption (CEP)[b,c]	1–108	1525.02	5182.96	5.149	3.186	4.050	9.2	5.7	7.3
Capital formation (GCF)[d]	109–146	182.12	1185.32	10.298	3.385	5.904	4.5	1.5	2.6
Government (PFC)	147–151	172.22	808.43	2.252	1.245	1.675	17.1	9.5	12.7
Gross domestic product	1–151	1879.36	7176.71	5.674	2.802	3.987	9.3	4.6	6.6
SNA concepts[e]									
Consumption (PFCE)	1–108	1493.11	4620.20	5.563	3.603	4.477	9.0	5.8	7.2
Capital formation (GCF)	109–146	182.12	1185.32	10.298	3.385	5.904	4.5	1.5	2.6
Government (GFCE)	1–151	204.13	1367.45	2.040	1.007	1.433	14.8	7.3	10.4
Gross domestic product	1–151	1879.36	7172.96	5.674	2.802	3.987	9.4	4.6	6.6

Note: See the end of Appendix Table 7-68 for notes.

Category	Line numbers[a]	Per capita expenditure		Purchasing power parities (pesos/dollars)			Quantity per capita (U.S. = 100)		
		Philippines (pesos)	U.S. (dollars)	U.S. weight	Philippines weight	Geometric mean	U.S. weight	Philippines weight	Geometric mean
Consumption, ICP[b,c]	1–108	1895.27	5182.96	3.816	2.170	2.878	16.9	9.6	12.7
Food, beverages, tobacco	1– 39	1154.03	818.24	5.489	3.807	4.571	37.0	25.7	30.9
Food	1– 33	1025.98	658.25	5.767	3.858	4.717	40.4	27.0	33.0
Bread, cereals	1– 6	350.24	94.81	6.372	3.834	4.943	96.3	58.0	74.7
Meat	7– 12	189.99	163.79	4.197	3.680	3.930	31.5	27.6	29.5
Fish	13– 14	210.43	25.96	4.918	5.017	4.967	161.5	164.8	163.2
Milk, cheese, eggs	15– 17	25.65	82.52	9.886	11.357	10.596	2.7	3.1	2.9
Oils, fats	18– 20	27.00	32.30	4.705	3.040	3.782	27.5	17.8	22.1
Fruits, vegetables	21– 26	143.83	147.83	6.612	3.153	4.566	30.9	14.7	21.3
Coffee, tea, cocoa	27– 29	17.66	17.18	8.146	6.988	7.545	14.7	12.6	13.6
Spices, sweets, sugar	30– 33	61.18	93.86	3.104	2.813	2.955	23.2	21.0	22.1
Beverages	34– 37	73.95	91.02	4.198	3.002	3.550	27.1	19.4	22.9
Tobacco	38– 39	54.10	68.97	4.544	4.309	4.425	18.2	17.3	17.7
Clothing, footwear	40– 51	128.02	336.33	2.036	3.161	2.537	12.0	18.7	15.0
Clothing	40– 47	110.03	284.83	2.046	3.475	2.666	11.1	18.9	14.5
Footwear	48– 51	17.99	51.50	1.981	2.037	2.009	17.2	17.6	17.4
Gross rent, fuel	52– 57	170.24	903.84	2.700	2.042	2.348	9.2	7.0	8.0
Gross rent	52– 53	126.12	717.46	1.827	1.688	1.756	10.4	9.6	10.0
Fuel, power	54– 57	44.12	186.38	6.060	5.106	5.563	4.6	3.9	4.3
House furnishings, operations	58– 70	86.57	343.14	5.728	1.546	2.976	16.3	4.4	8.5
Furniture	58– 60	22.58	165.64	2.920	3.361	3.133	4.1	4.7	4.4
Appliances	61– 66	18.23	56.41	18.427	13.534	15.792	2.4	1.8	2.0
Supplies, operations	67– 70	45.76	121.09	3.652	0.955	1.867	39.6	10.3	20.2
Medical care	71– 77	63.20	653.69	1.307	0.890	1.078	10.9	7.4	9.0
Transport, communications	78– 89	39.69	692.17	7.537	1.464	3.321	3.9	0.8	1.7
Equipment	78– 79	13.71	221.44	12.614	9.684	11.052	0.6	0.5	0.6
Operation costs	80– 83	3.83	338.12	5.631	5.452	5.541	0.2	0.2	0.2
Purchased transport	84– 87	19.06	40.37	1.097	0.846	0.963	55.8	43.0	49.0
Communications	88– 89	3.09	92.24	5.155	1.251	2.539	2.7	0.6	1.3
Recreation, education	90–101	133.04	783.74	2.459	0.580	1.194	29.3	6.9	14.2
Recreation	90– 96	28.86	323.24	4.479	2.775	3.526	3.2	2.0	2.5
Education	97–101	104.18	460.50	1.041	0.475	0.704	47.6	21.7	32.2
Other expenditures	102–107	120.49	628.47	3.226	1.921	2.489	10.0	5.9	7.7
Personal care	102–104	36.06	136.90	4.152	2.790	3.404	9.4	6.3	7.7
Miscellaneous services	105–107	84.43	491.57	2.968	1.696	2.243	10.1	5.8	7.7
Capital formation	109–146	660.48	1185.32	7.349	5.835	6.549	9.5	7.6	8.5
Domestic capital formation	109–145	845.52	1128.57	7.353	6.099	6.697	12.3	10.2	11.2
Construction	109–122	277.39	680.37	4.756	4.569	4.661	8.9	8.6	8.7
Residential	109–110	95.51	235.05	4.498	4.767	4.631	8.5	9.0	8.8
Nonresidential	111–118	78.46	210.33	4.391	4.185	4.287	8.9	8.5	8.7
Other	119–122	103.42	234.99	5.340	4.716	5.018	9.3	8.2	8.8
Producer durables	123–144	380.95	491.75	10.701	10.277	10.487	7.5	7.2	7.4
Transport equipment	123–129	111.79	122.69	11.860	10.741	11.286	8.5	7.7	8.1
Nonelectrical machinery	130–138	181.15	203.26	12.011	11.549	11.778	7.7	7.4	7.6
Electrical machinery	139–142	59.78	118.24	8.628	7.917	8.265	6.4	5.9	6.1
Other	143–144	28.24	47.56	7.271	8.244	7.742	7.2	8.2	7.7
Exports minus imports	146–146	− 185.04	56.75	7.275	7.275	7.275	− 44.8	− 44.8	− 44.8
Government	147–151	179.67	808.43	2.095	1.172	1.567	19.0	10.6	14.2
Compensation	147–150	96.84	419.96	0.730	0.744	0.737	31.0	31.6	31.3
Commodities	151–151	82.84	388.47	3.572	3.572	3.572	6.0	6.0	6.0
Gross domestic product	1–151	2735.42	7176.71	4.206	2.400	3.177	15.9	9.1	12.0
Aggregates									
ICP concepts[e]									
Consumption (CEP)[b,c]	1–108	1895.27	5182.96	3.816	2.170	2.878	16.9	9.6	12.7
Capital formation (GCF)[d]	109–146	660.48	1185.32	7.349	5.835	6.549	9.5	7.6	8.5
Government (PFC)	147–151	179.67	808.43	2.095	1.172	1.567	19.0	10.6	14.2
Gross domestic product	1–151	2735.42	7176.71	4.206	2.400	3.177	15.9	9.1	12.0
SNA concepts[e]									
Consumption (PFCE)	1–108	1803.48	4620.20	4.119	2.619	3.284	14.9	9.5	11.9
Capital formation (GCF)	109–146	660.48	1185.32	7.349	5.835	6.549	9.5	7.6	8.5
Government (GFCE)	1–151	260.16	1367.45	1.782	0.786	1.183	24.2	10.7	16.1
Gross domestic product	1–151	2724.11	7172.96	4.207	2.405	3.181	15.8	9.0	11.9

Note: See the end of Appendix Table 7-68 for notes.

Category	Line numbers[a]	Per capita expenditure		Purchasing power parities (zlotys/dollars)			Quantity per capita (U.S. = 100)		
		Poland (zlotys)	U.S. (dollars)	U.S. weight	Poland weight	Geometric mean	U.S. weight	Poland weight	Geometric mean
Consumption, ICP[b,c]	1–108	29570.0	5182.96	17.67	11.27	14.11	50.6	32.3	40.4
Food, beverages, tobacco	1– 39	11604.8	818.24	21.17	18.40	19.74	77.1	67.0	71.9
Food	1– 33	8479.3	658.25	20.79	15.90	18.18	81.0	62.0	70.9
Bread, cereals	1– 6	1007.1	94.81	12.13	10.39	11.23	102.2	87.6	94.6
Meat	7– 12	2526.5	163.79	16.68	17.59	17.13	87.7	92.5	90.1
Fish	13– 14	165.7	25.96	22.27	24.88	23.54	25.7	28.7	27.1
Milk, cheese, eggs	15– 17	1356.9	82.52	17.83	17.17	17.50	95.7	92.2	94.0
Oils, fats	18– 20	782.4	32.30	23.58	26.08	24.80	92.9	102.7	97.7
Fruits, vegetables	21– 26	1340.3	147.83	24.56	11.95	17.13	75.9	36.9	52.9
Coffee, tea, cocoa	27– 29	288.2	17.18	109.24	81.95	94.62	20.5	15.4	17.7
Spices, sweets, sugar	30– 33	1012.2	93.86	15.81	16.47	16.14	65.5	68.2	66.8
Beverages	34– 37	2540.1	91.02	26.07	40.80	32.61	68.4	107.1	85.6
Tobacco	38– 39	585.4	68.97	18.39	16.63	17.49	51.1	46.1	48.5
Clothing, footwear	40– 51	3777.0	336.33	23.61	24.03	23.82	46.7	47.6	47.1
Clothing	40– 47	3229.4	284.83	24.61	26.13	25.36	43.4	46.1	44.7
Footwear	48– 51	547.6	51.50	18.09	16.31	17.18	65.2	58.8	61.9
Gross rent, fuel	52– 57	2309.5	903.84	9.76	6.63	8.05	38.5	26.2	31.8
Gross rent	52– 53	1749.5	717.46	6.45	5.95	6.20	41.0	37.8	39.4
Fuel, power	54– 57	560.0	186.38	22.49	10.34	15.25	29.1	13.4	19.7
House furnishings, operations	58– 70	2605.8	343.14	19.89	15.79	17.72	48.1	38.2	42.8
Furniture	58– 60	1213.5	165.64	16.41	14.29	15.31	51.3	44.6	47.8
Appliances	61– 66	391.1	56.41	40.82	25.31	32.15	27.4	17.0	21.6
Supplies, operations	67– 70	1001.2	121.09	14.91	15.48	15.20	53.4	55.4	54.4
Medical care	71– 77	1719.7	653.69	4.48	4.02	4.24	65.4	58.8	62.0
Transport, communications	78– 89	1871.4	692.17	44.05	9.81	20.79	27.6	6.1	13.0
Equipment	78– 79	612.8	221.44	61.02	44.38	52.04	6.2	4.5	5.3
Operation costs	80– 83	380.7	338.12	45.64	35.25	40.11	3.2	2.5	2.8
Purchased transport	84– 87	716.3	40.37	5.93	4.71	5.29	376.5	299.4	335.7
Communications	88– 89	161.6	92.24	14.14	11.45	12.72	15.3	12.4	13.8
Recreation, education	90–101	3555.5	783.74	10.77	6.99	8.67	64.9	42.1	52.3
Recreation	90– 96	1717.1	323.24	18.10	10.46	13.76	50.8	29.3	38.6
Education	97–101	1838.4	460.50	5.62	5.33	5.47	74.9	71.0	72.9
Other expenditures	102–107	2126.3	628.47	13.29	10.90	12.03	31.0	25.5	28.1
Personal care	102–104	504.3	136.90	21.76	14.35	17.67	25.7	16.9	20.8
Miscellaneous services	105–107	1622.0	491.57	10.93	10.14	10.53	32.5	30.2	31.3
Capital formation	109–146	18218.5	1185.32	22.62	19.36	20.93	79.4	67.9	73.4
Domestic capital formation	109–145	21216.6	1128.57	22.76	19.43	21.03	96.7	82.6	89.4
Construction	109–122	10273.0	680.37	17.46	16.66	17.06	90.6	86.5	88.5
Residential	109–110	1848.8	235.05	18.92	15.41	17.08	51.0	41.6	46.1
Nonresidential	111–118	4622.6	210.33	18.10	19.79	18.93	111.0	121.4	116.1
Other	119–122	3801.6	234.99	15.43	14.45	14.93	111.9	104.8	108.3
Producer durables	123–144	7983.1	491.75	29.82	24.56	27.06	66.1	54.4	60.0
Transport equipment	123–129	2109.5	122.69	40.21	21.28	29.25	80.8	42.8	58.8
Nonelectrical machinery	130–138	4182.9	203.26	27.43	27.28	27.36	75.4	75.0	75.2
Electrical machinery	139–142	1534.7	118.24	23.00	22.77	22.88	57.0	56.4	56.7
Other	143–144	156.1	47.56	30.20	30.04	30.12	10.9	10.9	10.9
Exports minus imports	146–146	− 2998.1	56.75	19.92	19.92	19.92	− 265.2	− 265.2	− 265.2
Government	147–151	3715.4	808.43	12.03	11.38	11.70	40.4	38.2	39.3
Compensation	147–150	1123.2	419.96	5.98	6.01	6.00	44.5	44.7	44.6
Commodities	151–151	2592.3	388.47	18.57	18.57	18.57	35.9	35.9	35.9
Gross domestic product	1–151	51504.0	7176.71	17.85	13.24	15.37	54.2	40.2	46.7
Aggregates									
ICP concepts[e]									
Consumption (CEP)[b,c]	1–108	29570.0	5182.96	17.67	11.27	14.11	50.6	32.3	40.4
Capital formation (GCF)[d]	109–146	18218.5	1185.32	22.62	19.36	20.93	79.4	67.9	73.4
Government (PFC)	147–151	3715.4	808.43	12.03	11.38	11.70	40.4	38.2	39.3
Gross domestic product	1–151	51504.0	7176.71	17.85	13.24	15.37	54.2	40.2	46.7
SNA concepts[e]									
Consumption (PFCE)	1–108	25716.7	4620.20	19.08	14.42	16.59	38.6	29.2	33.6
Capital formation (GCF)	109–146	18218.5	1185.32	22.62	19.36	20.93	79.4	67.9	73.4
Government (GFCE)	1–151	7190.4	1367.45	9.62	6.56	7.94	80.2	54.7	66.2
Gross domestic product	1–151	51125.7	7172.96	17.86	13.38	15.46	53.3	39.9	46.1

Note: See the end of Appendix Table 7-68 for notes.

Appendix Table 7-25. Augmented Summary Binary Table: Romania/United States, 1975

Category	Line numbers[a]	Per capita expenditure		Purchasing power parities (lei/dollars)			Quantity per capita (U.S. = 100)		
		Romania (lei)	U.S. (dollars)	U.S. weight	Romania weight	Geometric mean	U.S. weight	Romania weight	Geometric mean
Consumption, ICP[b,c]	1–108	11385.4	5182.96	10.04	6.33	7.97	34.7	21.9	27.6
Food, beverages, tobacco	1– 39	4724.1	818.24	13.55	9.93	11.60	58.2	42.6	49.8
Food	1– 33	4003.8	658.25	11.18	9.43	10.27	64.5	54.4	59.2
Bread, cereals	1– 6	716.5	94.81	7.85	6.75	7.28	111.9	96.3	103.8
Meat	7– 12	1258.1	163.79	11.03	11.74	11.38	65.4	69.6	67.5
Fish	13– 14	47.7	25.96	13.32	11.97	12.62	15.3	13.8	14.5
Milk, cheese, eggs	15– 17	597.9	82.52	9.35	9.14	9.24	79.3	77.5	78.4
Oils, fats	18– 20	139.8	32.30	9.72	9.46	9.59	45.8	44.5	45.2
Fruits, vegetables	21– 26	659.9	147.83	10.78	8.31	9.47	53.7	41.4	47.2
Coffee, tea, cocoa	27– 29	58.9	17.18	37.36	35.26	36.29	9.7	9.2	9.4
Spices, sweets, sugar	30– 33	525.0	93.86	12.14	11.45	11.79	48.8	46.1	47.4
Beverages	34– 37	518.6	91.02	11.85	11.18	11.51	51.0	48.1	49.5
Tobacco	38– 39	201.7	68.97	38.47	38.76	38.62	7.5	7.6	7.6
Clothing, footwear	40– 51	1659.6	336.33	13.23	14.14	13.68	34.9	37.3	36.1
Clothing	40– 47	1365.5	284.83	13.18	14.54	13.84	33.0	36.4	34.6
Footwear	48– 51	294.0	51.50	13.52	12.55	13.03	45.5	42.2	43.8
Gross rent, fuel	52– 57	777.0	903.84	2.97	2.66	2.81	32.4	29.0	30.6
Gross rent	52– 53	492.8	717.46	1.99	1.96	1.98	35.0	34.5	34.7
Fuel, power	54– 57	284.2	186.38	6.72	6.88	6.80	22.2	22.7	22.4
House furnishings, operations	58– 70	822.6	343.14	15.06	11.34	13.07	21.1	15.9	18.3
Furniture	58– 60	356.3	165.64	11.70	10.16	10.91	21.2	18.4	19.7
Appliances	61– 66	100.7	56.41	31.87	16.65	23.04	10.7	5.6	7.8
Supplies, operations	67– 70	365.6	121.09	11.82	11.62	11.72	26.0	25.6	25.8
Medical care	71– 77	576.4	653.69	3.99	1.97	2.80	44.8	22.1	31.4
Transport, communications	78– 89	748.6	692.17	19.29	7.63	12.13	14.2	5.6	8.9
Equipment	78– 79	157.6	221.44	26.38	23.35	24.82	3.0	2.7	2.9
Operation costs	80– 83	72.0	338.12	19.42	16.42	17.86	1.3	1.1	1.2
Purchased transport	84– 87	460.6	40.37	4.66	6.10	5.33	186.9	244.8	213.9
Communications	88– 89	58.4	92.24	8.22	5.06	6.45	12.5	7.7	9.8
Recreation, education	90–101	1090.4	783.74	8.03	3.41	5.23	40.8	17.3	26.6
Recreation	90– 96	472.5	323.24	15.34	7.37	10.64	19.8	9.5	13.7
Education	97–101	617.9	460.50	2.90	2.42	2.65	55.5	46.3	50.7
Other expenditures	102–107	986.7	628.47	9.69	7.61	8.59	20.6	16.2	18.3
Personal care	102–104	131.6	136.90	16.25	12.44	14.22	7.7	5.9	6.8
Miscellaneous services	105–107	855.1	491.57	7.86	7.18	7.51	24.2	22.1	23.2
Capital formation	109–146	8482.4	1185.32	19.14	13.09	15.83	54.7	37.4	45.2
Domestic capital formation	109–145	8600.1	1128.57	19.50	13.08	15.97	58.3	39.1	47.7
Construction	109–122	3507.7	680.37	13.88	9.71	11.61	53.1	37.1	44.4
Residential	109–110	748.0	235.05	14.43	12.15	13.24	26.2	22.1	24.0
Nonresidential	111–118	1516.7	210.33	13.13	7.26	9.77	99.3	54.9	73.8
Other	119–122	1243.1	234.99	14.00	13.66	13.83	38.7	37.8	38.3
Producer durables	123–144	3501.2	491.75	26.63	21.03	23.66	33.9	26.7	30.1
Transport equipment	123–129	592.9	122.69	24.82	21.82	23.28	22.1	19.5	20.8
Nonelectrical machinery	130–138	2517.2	203.26	28.65	22.22	25.23	55.7	43.2	49.1
Electrical machinery	139–142	247.2	118.24	20.63	22.11	21.36	9.5	10.1	9.8
Other	143–144	143.9	47.56	37.60	9.68	19.07	31.3	8.0	15.9
Exports minus imports	146–146	− 117.7	56.75	12.00	12.00	12.00	− 17.3	− 17.3	− 17.3
Government	147–151	1040.6	808.43	6.59	6.20	6.39	20.8	19.5	20.1
Compensation	147–150	569.0	419.96	5.31	5.23	5.27	25.9	25.5	25.7
Commodities	151–151	471.6	388.47	7.98	7.98	7.98	15.2	15.2	15.2
Gross domestic product	1–151	20908.5	7176.71	11.15	8.00	9.44	36.4	26.1	30.8
Aggregates									
ICP concepts[e]									
Consumption (CEP)[b,c]	1–108	11385.4	5182.96	10.04	6.33	7.97	34.7	21.9	27.6
Capital formation (GCF)[d]	109–146	8482.4	1185.32	19.14	13.09	15.83	54.7	37.4	45.2
Government (PFC)	147–151	1040.6	808.43	6.59	6.20	6.39	20.8	19.5	20.1
Gross domestic product	1–151	20908.5	7176.71	11.15	8.00	9.44	36.4	26.1	30.8
SNA concepts[e]									
Consumption (PFCE)	1–108	10136.3	4620.20	10.75	8.31	9.45	26.4	20.4	23.2
Capital formation (GCF)	109–146	8482.4	1185.32	19.14	13.09	15.83	54.7	37.4	45.2
Government (GFCE)	1–151	2289.7	1367.45	5.62	3.07	4.15	54.6	29.8	40.3
Gross domestic product	1–151	20908.5	7172.96	11.16	8.00	9.45	36.4	26.1	30.9

Note: See the end of Appendix Table 7-68 for notes.

Category	Line numbers[a]	Per capita expenditures Spain (pesetas)	Per capita expenditures U.S. (dollars)	Purchasing power parities (pesetas/dollars) U.S. weight	Purchasing power parities (pesetas/dollars) Spain weight	Purchasing power parities (pesetas/dollars) Geometric mean	Quantity per capita (U.S. = 100) U.S. weight	Quantity per capita (U.S. = 100) Spain weight	Quantity per capita (U.S. = 100) Geometric mean
Consumption, ICP[b,c]	1–108	124281.2	5182.96	46.50	35.41	40.58	67.7	51.6	59.1
Food, beverages, tobacco	1– 39	40653.0	818.24	45.08	42.39	43.71	117.2	110.2	113.7
Food	1– 33	37034.9	658.25	48.52	44.48	46.45	126.5	116.0	121.1
Bread, cereals	1– 6	3486.9	94.81	43.09	36.33	39.56	101.2	85.4	93.0
Meat	7– 12	11891.8	163.79	55.96	54.88	55.42	132.3	129.7	131.0
Fish	13– 14	2928.8	25.96	40.34	41.82	41.07	269.8	279.7	274.7
Milk, cheese, eggs	15– 17	5728.1	82.52	63.09	53.85	58.29	128.9	110.0	119.1
Oils, fats	18– 20	3497.1	32.30	48.47	42.99	45.65	251.9	223.4	237.2
Fruits, vegetables	21– 26	6178.8	147.83	40.35	33.30	36.65	125.5	103.6	114.0
Coffee, tea, cocoa	27– 29	739.1	17.18	75.12	61.21	67.81	70.3	57.3	63.5
Spices, sweets, sugar	30– 33	2584.3	93.86	38.49	40.00	39.23	68.8	71.5	70.2
Beverages	34– 37	2114.0	91.02	30.36	28.33	29.33	82.0	76.5	79.2
Tobacco	38– 39	1504.2	68.97	31.71	29.05	30.35	75.1	68.8	71.9
Clothing, footwear	40– 51	11780.2	336.33	62.70	52.16	57.18	67.2	55.9	61.3
Clothing	40– 47	8952.9	284.83	68.38	66.65	67.51	47.2	46.0	46.6
Footwear	48– 51	2827.3	51.50	31.27	30.89	31.08	177.8	175.6	176.7
Gross rent, fuel	52– 57	15386.4	903.84	38.24	33.63	35.86	50.6	44.5	47.5
Gross rent	52– 53	11914.9	717.46	29.71	29.13	29.42	57.0	55.9	56.5
Fuel, power	54– 57	3471.5	186.38	71.05	71.68	71.36	26.0	26.2	26.1
House furnishings, operations	58– 70	9816.8	343.14	61.11	52.68	56.74	54.3	46.8	50.4
Furniture	58– 60	4663.0	165.64	55.63	54.74	55.18	51.4	50.6	51.0
Appliances	61– 66	1610.0	56.41	89.53	64.98	76.27	43.9	31.9	37.4
Supplies, operation	67– 70	3543.9	121.09	55.38	46.39	50.69	63.1	52.8	57.7
Medical care	71– 77	10475.9	653.69	28.86	29.34	29.10	54.6	55.5	55.1
Transport, communications	78– 89	12126.7	692.17	74.81	40.23	54.86	43.6	23.4	31.9
Equipment	78– 79	3771.4	221.44	74.72	72.46	73.58	23.5	22.8	23.1
Operation costs	80– 83	5674.2	338.12	95.68	81.67	88.40	20.5	17.5	19.0
Purchased transport	84– 87	2130.0	40.37	26.40	13.99	19.22	377.0	199.9	274.5
Communications	88– 89	551.1	92.24	19.68	19.88	19.78	30.0	30.4	30.2
Recreation, education	90–101	11109.1	783.74	35.38	23.00	28.52	61.6	40.1	49.7
Recreation	90– 96	6204.2	323.24	59.27	31.62	43.29	60.7	32.4	44.3
Education	97–101	4904.9	460.50	18.60	17.10	17.83	62.3	57.3	59.7
Other expenditures	102–107	12933.2	628.47	44.20	23.99	32.57	85.8	46.6	63.2
Personal care	102–104	2095.6	136.90	46.85	30.61	37.87	50.0	32.7	40.4
Miscellaneous services	105–107	10837.6	491.57	43.47	23.03	31.64	95.7	50.7	69.7
Capital formation	109–146	38316.2	1185.32	62.93	47.43	54.63	68.2	51.4	59.2
Domestic capital formation	109–145	44978.2	1128.57	63.21	48.68	55.47	81.9	63.1	71.8
Construction	109–122	24356.0	680.37	57.60	42.16	49.28	84.9	62.1	72.6
Residential	109–110	10381.6	235.05	56.83	42.87	49.36	103.0	77.7	89.5
Nonresidential	111–118	5585.7	210.33	44.51	38.44	41.36	69.1	59.7	64.2
Other	119–122	8388.7	234.99	70.10	44.09	55.59	81.0	50.9	64.2
Producer durables	123–144	15072.5	491.75	69.98	62.94	66.36	48.7	43.8	46.2
Transport equipment	123–129	4550.2	122.69	67.90	61.46	64.60	60.3	54.6	57.4
Nonelectrical machinery	130–138	5766.2	203.26	65.79	57.56	61.54	49.3	43.1	46.1
Electrical machinery	139–142	3714.4	118.24	68.89	68.41	68.65	45.9	45.6	45.8
Other	143–144	1041.7	47.56	95.90	94.89	95.40	23.1	22.8	23.0
Exports minus imports	146–146	– 6662.0	56.75	57.41	57.41	57.41	– 204.5	– 204.5	– 204.5
Government	147–151	6886.3	808.43	53.94	53.38	53.66	16.0	15.8	15.9
Compensation	147–150	4914.7	419.96	51.08	52.05	51.56	22.5	22.9	22.7
Commodities	151–151	1971.6	388.47	57.03	57.03	57.03	8.9	8.9	8.9
Gross domestic product	1–151	169483.7	7176.71	50.05	38.12	43.68	62.0	47.2	54.1
Aggregates									
ICP concepts[e]									
Consumption (CEP)[b,c]	1–108	124281.2	5182.98	46.50	35.41	40.58	67.7	51.6	59.1
Capital formation (GCF)[d]	109–146	38616.2	1185.32	62.93	47.43	54.63	68.2	51.4	59.2
Government (PFC)	147–151	6886.3	808.43	53.94	53.38	53.66	16.0	15.8	15.9
Gross domestic product (ICP)	1–151	189483.7	7176.71	50.05	38.12	43.68	82.0	47.2	54.1
SNA concepts[e]									
Consumption (PFCE)	1–108	115491.9	4820.20	49.16	36.57	42.40	68.4	50.8	57.0
Capital formation (GCF)	109–146	38316.2	1185.32	62.93	47.43	54.63	68.2	51.4	59.2
Government (GFCE)	1–151	15649.7	1367.45	41.96	32.68	37.03	35.0	27.2	30.9
Gross domestic product (SNA)	1–151	95255.1	3344.77	83.20	50.59	56.54	58.0	45.1	50.4

Note: See the end of Appendix Table 7-68 for notes.

Category	Line numbers[a]	Per capita expenditures		Purchasing power parities (rupees/dollars)			Quantity per capita (U.S. = 100)		
		Sri Lanka (rupees)	U.S. (dollars)	U.S. weight	Sri Lanka weight	Geometric mean	U.S. weight	Sri Lanka weight	Geometric mean
Consumption, ICP[b,c]	1–108	1689.76	5182.96	5.389	2.420	3.611	13.5	6.0	9.0
Food, beverages, tobacco	1– 39	1161.01	818.24	6.768	4.617	5.590	30.7	21.0	25.4
Food	1– 33	1022.08	658.25	6.501	4.348	5.317	35.7	23.9	29.2
Bread, cereals	1– 6	521.27	94.81	5.123	5.409	5.264	101.6	107.3	104.4
Meat	7– 12	17.34	163.79	4.116	2.359	3.116	4.5	2.6	3.4
Fish	13– 14	48.61	25.96	4.011	4.159	4.084	45.0	46.7	45.8
Milk, cheese, eggs	15– 17	45.42	82.52	5.117	4.954	5.035	11.1	10.8	10.9
Oils, fats	18– 20	9.93	32.30	4.853	4.249	4.541	7.2	6.3	6.8
Fruits, vegetables	21– 26	191.54	147.83	8.578	2.323	4.464	55.8	15.1	29.0
Coffee, tea, cocoa	27– 29	22.15	17.18	8.148	2.830	4.802	45.6	15.8	26.9
Spices, sweets, sugar	30– 33	165.83	93.86	10.955	9.278	10.082	19.0	16.1	17.5
Beverages	34– 37	44.01	91.02	7.535	8.597	8.049	5.6	6.4	6.0
Tobacco	38– 39	94.92	68.97	8.300	8.422	8.361	16.3	16.6	16.5
Clothing, footwear	40– 51	106.85	336.33	3.177	5.574	4.208	5.7	10.0	7.5
Clothing	40– 47	101.66	284.83	3.276	5.909	4.400	6.0	10.9	8.1
Footwear	48– 51	5.19	51.50	2.627	2.642	2.634	3.8	3.8	3.8
Gross rent, fuel	52– 57	84.10	903.84	2.420	1.769	2.069	5.3	3.8	4.5
Gross rent	52– 53	51.64	717.46	1.492	1.402	1.446	5.1	4.8	5.0
Fuel, power	54– 57	32.45	186.38	5.995	3.030	4.262	5.7	2.9	4.1
House furnishings, operations	58– 70	48.31	343.14	11.119	1.017	3.364	13.8	1.3	4.2
Furniture	58– 60	9.85	165.64	4.654	3.273	3.903	1.8	1.3	1.5
Appliances	61– 66	2.22	56.41	44.633	34.405	39.187	0.1	0.1	0.1
Supplies, operation	67– 70	36.23	121.09	4.350	0.816	1.884	36.7	6.9	15.9
Medical care	71– 77	43.57	653.69	1.194	0.879	1.025	7.6	5.6	6.5
Transport, communications	78– 89	104.33	692.17	12.778	1.610	4.536	9.4	1.2	3.3
Equipment	78– 79	1.93	221.44	18.751	12.850	15.523	0.1	0.0	0.1
Operation costs	80– 83	29.12	338.12	11.350	10.226	10.774	0.8	0.8	0.8
Purchased transport	84– 87	65.35	40.37	2.331	1.130	1.623	143.3	69.4	99.8
Communications	88– 89	7.93	92.24	8.246	2.008	4.069	4.3	1.0	2.1[b]
Recreation, education	90–101	94.40	783.74	3.969	0.512	1.425	23.5	3.0	8.5
Recreation	90– 96	45.05	323.24	8.337	2.122	4.206	6.6	1.7	3.3
Education	97–101	49.35	460.50	0.904	0.302	0.523	35.5	11.9	20.5
Other expenditures	102–107	61.28	628.47	3.852	1.717	2.571	5.7	2.5	3.8
Personal care	102–104	21.41	136.90	4.266	2.292	3.127	6.8	3.7	5.0
Miscellaneous services	105–107	39.86	491.57	3.736	1.513	2.377	5.4	2.2	3.4
Capital formation	109–146	141.89	1185.32	7.112	2.292	4.037	5.2	1.7	3.0
Domestic capital formation	109–145	288.97	1128.57	7.115	3.491	4.984	7.3	3.6	5.1
Construction	109–122	165.90	680.37	2.576	2.429	2.501	10.0	9.5	9.7
Residential	109–110	42.90	235.05	2.828	2.609	2.716	7.0	6.5	6.7
Nonresidential	111–118	51.20	210.33	2.860	2.865	2.862	8.5	8.5	8.5
Other	119–122	71.80	234.99	2.070	2.112	2.091	14.5	14.8	14.6
Producer durables	123–144	96.40	491.75	13.196	10.731	11.900	1.8	1.5	1.6
Transport equipment	123–129	30.16	122.69	11.961	8.787	10.252	2.8	2.1	2.4
Nonelectrical machinery	130–138	47.20	203.26	10.730	11.237	10.980	2.1	2.2	2.1
Electrical machinery	139–142	17.93	118.24	16.922	13.971	15.376	1.1	0.9	1.0
Other	143–144	1.11	47.56	17.659	16.460	17.049	0.1	0.1	0.1
Exports minus imports	146–146	− 147.08	56.75	7.050	7.050	7.050	− 36.8	− 36.8	− 36.8
Government	147–151	125.07	808.43	1.345	0.983	1.150	15.7	11.5	13.5
Compensation	147–150	78.62	419.96	0.888	0.771	0.828	24.3	21.1	22.6
Commodities	151–151	46.46	388.47	1.840	1.840	1.840	6.5	6.5	6.5
Gross domestic product	1–151	1956.73	7176.71	5.218	2.205	3.392	12.4	5.2	8.0
Aggregates									
ICP concepts[e]									
Consumption (CEP)[b,c]	1–108	1689.76	5182.96	5.389	2.420	3.611	13.5	6.0	9.0
Capital formation (GCF)[d]	109–146	141.89	1185.32	7.112	2.292	4.037	5.2	1.7	3.0
Government (PFC)	147–151	125.07	808.43	1.345	0.983	1.150	15.7	11.5	13.5
Gross domestic product (ICP)	1–151	1956.73	7176.71	5.218	2.205	3.392	12.4	5.2	8.0
SNA concepts[e]									
Consumption (PFCE)	1–108	1614.48	4620.20	5.921	3.241	4.381	10.8	5.9	8.0
Capital formation (GCF)	109–146	141.89	1185.32	7.112	2.292	4.037	5.2	1.7	3.0
Government (GFCE)	1–151	200.36	1367.45	1.211	0.612	0.861	23.9	12.1	17.0
Gross domestic product (SNA)	1–151	1956.73	7172.96	5.220	2.205	3.393	12.4	5.2	8.0

Note: See the end of Appendix Table 7-68 for notes.

Appendix Table 7-28. Augmented Summary Binary Table: Syria/United States, 1975

Category	Line numbers[a]	Per capita expenditures Syria (pounds)	Per capita expenditures U.S. (dollars)	Purchasing power parities (pounds/dollars) U.S. weight	Purchasing power parities (pounds/dollars) Syria weight	Purchasing power parities (pounds/dollars) Geometric mean	Quantity per capita (U.S. = 100) U.S. weight	Quantity per capita (U.S. = 100) Syria weight	Quantity per capita (U.S. = 100) Geometric mean
Consumption, ICP[b,c]	1–108	1778.76	5182.96	2.096	1.166	1.564	29.4	16.4	21.9
Food, beverages, tobacco	1– 39	914.88	818.24	2.398	1.315	1.776	85.0	46.6	63.0
Food	1– 33	844.98	658.25	2.361	1.296	1.749	99.1	54.4	73.4
Bread, cereals	1– 6	125.92	94.81	0.957	0.807	0.878	164.7	138.8	151.2
Meat	7– 12	101.03	163.79	3.112	2.712	2.905	22.7	19.8	21.2
Fish	13– 14	5.85	25.96	2.407	2.064	2.229	10.9	9.4	10.1
Milk, cheese, eggs	15– 17	107.15	82.52	2.655	2.747	2.701	47.3	48.9	48.1
Oils, fats	18– 20	89.20	32.30	1.827	1.644	1.733	168.0	151.2	159.3
Fruits, vegetables	21– 26	333.83	147.83	1.788	1.028	1.356	219.7	126.3	166.6
Coffee, tea, cocoa	27– 29	8.29	17.18	6.879	2.270	3.952	21.3	7.0	12.2
Spices, sweets, sugar	30– 33	73.70	93.86	2.458	2.151	2.299	36.5	31.9	34.2
Beverages	34– 37	8.29	91.02	3.015	2.912	2.963	3.1	3.0	3.1
Tobacco	38– 39	61.60	68.97	1.935	1.516	1.712	58.9	46.2	52.2
Clothing, footwear	40– 51	206.01	336.33	1.974	2.015	1.995	30.4	31.0	30.7
Clothing	40– 47	173.10	284.83	1.996	2.103	2.049	28.9	30.4	29.7
Footwear	48– 51	32.91	51.50	1.852	1.651	1.749	38.7	34.5	36.5
Gross rent, fuel	52– 57	214.99	903.84	1.497	1.393	1.444	17.1	15.9	16.5
Gross rent	52– 53	127.01	717.46	1.228	1.265	1.246	14.0	14.4	14.2
Fuel, power	54– 57	87.98	186.38	2.532	1.631	2.033	28.9	18.6	23.2
House furnishings, operations	58– 70	111.10	343.14	2.599	1.850	2.193	17.5	12.5	14.8
Furniture	58– 60	32.09	165.64	2.036	1.798	1.913	10.8	9.5	10.1
Appliances	61– 66	23.93	56.41	4.998	5.493	5.240	7.7	8.5	8.1
Supplies, operation	67– 70	55.07	121.09	2.252	1.455	1.810	31.3	20.2	25.1
Medical care	71– 77	61.06	653.69	0.860	0.884	0.872	10.6	10.9	10.7
Transport, communications	78– 89	67.58	692.17	5.027	0.807	2.014	12.1	1.9	4.8
Equipment	78– 79	12.92	221.44	8.613	1.798	3.935	3.2	0.7	1.5
Operation costs	80– 83	3.54	338.12	4.016	4.137	4.076	0.3	0.3	0.3
Purchased transport	84– 87	47.46	40.37	1.590	0.645	1.012	182.4	73.9	116.1
Communications	88– 89	3.67	92.24	1.633	1.780	1.705	2.2	2.4	2.3
Recreation, education	90–101	109.46	783.74	1.357	0.423	0.757	33.0	10.3	18.4
Recreation	90– 96	35.90	323.24	2.567	1.333	1.850	8.3	4.3	6.0
Education	97–101	73.57	460.50	0.507	0.317	0.401	50.4	31.5	39.8
Other expenditures	102–107	93.69	628.47	1.277	0.929	1.089	16.0	11.7	13.7
Personal care	102–104	39.71	136.90	2.023	1.745	1.879	16.6	14.3	15.4
Miscellaneous services	105–107	53.98	491.57	1.070	0.691	0.860	15.9	10.3	12.8
Capital formation	109–146	376.67	1185.32	3.958	1.666	2.568	19.1	8.0	12.4
Domestic capital formation	109–145	749.80	1128.57	3.971	2.293	3.018	29.0	16.7	22.0
Construction	109–122	392.17	680.37	2.662	1.896	2.247	30.4	21.7	25.7
Residential	109–110	114.63	235.05	1.918	1.943	1.931	25.1	25.4	25.3
Nonresidential	111–118	56.30	210.33	2.143	2.005	2.073	13.4	12.5	12.9
Other	119–122	221.24	234.99	3.871	1.848	2.674	51.0	24.3	35.2
Producer durables	123–144	357.63	491.75	5.715	2.977	4.125	24.4	12.7	17.6
Transport equipment	123–129	132.85	122.69	9.755	3.273	5.651	33.1	11.1	19.2
Nonelectrical machinery	130–138	163.45	203.26	3.852	2.442	3.067	32.9	20.9	26.2
Electrical machinery	139–142	42.97	118.24	5.124	4.964	5.043	7.3	7.1	7.2
Other	143–144	18.36	47.56	4.721	4.652	4.686	8.3	8.2	8.2
Exports minus imports	146–146	− 373.13	56.75	3.700	3.700	3.700	− 177.7	− 177.7	− 177.7
Government	147–151	500.68	808.43	1.885	1.835	1.860	33.7	32.8	33.3
Compensation	147–150	217.98	419.96	1.722	1.606	1.663	32.3	30.1	31.2
Commodities	151–151	282.70	388.47	2.062	2.062	2.062	35.3	35.3	35.3
Gross domestic product	1–151	2656.11	7176.71	2.380	1.312	1.767	28.2	15.6	20.9
Aggregates									
ICP concepts[e]									
Consumption (CEP)[b,c]	1–108	1778.76	5182.96	2.096	1.166	1.564	29.4	16.4	21.9
Capital formation (GCF)[d]	109–146	376.67	1185.32	3.958	1.666	2.568	19.1	8.0	12.4
Government (PFC)	147–151	500.68	808.43	1.885	1.835	1.860	33.7	32.8	33.3
Gross domestic product (ICP)	1–151	2656.11	7176.71	2.380	1.312	1.767	28.2	15.6	20.9
SNA concepts[e]									
Consumption (PFCE)	1–108	1716.07	4620.20	2.273	1.280	1.706	29.0	16.3	21.8
Capital formation (GCF)	109–146	376.67	1185.32	3.958	1.666	2.568	19.1	8.0	12.4
Government (GFCE)	1–151	563.37	1367.45	1.376	1.231	1.302	33.5	29.9	31.7
Gross domestic product (SNA)	1–151	2656.11	7172.96	2.381	1.312	1.768	28.2	15.6	20.9

Note: See the end of Appendix Table 7-68 for notes.

Category	Line numbers[a]	Per capita expenditures		Purchasing power parities (baht/dollars)			Quantity per capita (U.S. = 100)		
		Thailand (baht)	U.S. (dollars)	U.S. weight	Thailand weight	Geometric mean	U.S. weight	Thailand weight	Geometric mean
Consumption, ICP[b,c]	1–108	5187.1	5182.96	12.84	6.18	8.90	16.2	7.8	11.2
Food, beverages, tobacco	1– 39	2670.8	818.24	15.96	8.34	11.54	39.1	20.5	28.3
Food	1– 33	2240.2	658.25	16.66	8.10	11.61	42.0	20.4	29.3
Bread, cereals	1– 6	690.4	94.81	21.88	4.92	10.37	148.1	33.3	70.2
Meat	7– 12	352.7	163.79	10.00	9.07	9.52	23.7	21.5	22.6
Fish	13– 14	270.2	25.96	13.02	12.34	12.68	84.3	79.9	82.1
Milk, cheese, eggs	15– 17	145.0	82.52	23.46	16.99	19.97	10.3	7.5	8.8
Oils, fats	18– 20	55.9	32.30	27.33	15.32	20.46	11.3	6.3	8.5
Fruits, vegetables	21– 26	388.0	147.83	18.11	10.78	13.97	24.3	14.5	18.8
Coffee, tea, cocoa	27– 29	22.8	17.18	25.49	17.57	21.17	7.6	5.2	6.3
Spices, sweets, sugar	30– 33	315.1	93.86	10.45	12.11	11.25	27.7	32.1	29.8
Beverages	34– 37	298.3	91.02	12.26	8.74	10.35	37.5	26.7	31.6
Tobacco	38– 39	132.3	68.97	14.21	14.21	14.21	13.5	13.5	13.5
Clothing, footwear	40– 51	411.4	336.33	7.88	4.10	5.68	29.9	15.5	21.5
Clothing	40– 47	386.6	284.83	7.61	4.00	5.52	33.9	17.8	24.6
Footwear	48– 51	24.8	51.50	9.40	6.66	7.91	7.2	5.1	6.1
Gross rent, fuel	52– 57	302.8	903.84	14.63	7.54	10.51	4.4	2.3	3.2
Gross rent	52– 53	154.1	717.46	14.69	10.17	12.22	2.1	1.5	1.8
Fuel, power	54– 57	148.7	186.38	14.41	5.95	9.26	13.4	5.5	8.6
House furnishings, operations	58– 70	248.9	343.14	17.60	9.30	12.80	7.8	4.1	5.7
Furniture	58– 60	55.5	165.64	11.51	7.92	9.55	4.2	2.9	3.5
Appliances	61– 66	41.3	56.41	47.26	54.32	50.66	1.3	1.5	1.4
Supplies, operation	67– 70	152.1	121.09	12.10	8.01	9.85	15.7	10.4	12.8
Medical care	71– 77	302.1	653.69	6.73	6.93	6.83	6.7	6.9	6.8
Transport, communications	78– 89	360.2	692.17	21.76	3.85	9.16	13.5	2.4	5.7
Equipment	78– 79	57.0	221.44	40.45	36.51	38.43	0.7	0.6	0.7
Operation costs	80– 83	70.0	338.12	15.63	16.44	16.03	1.3	1.3	1.3
Purchased transport	84– 87	222.1	40.37	4.30	2.58	3.33	213.4	128.0	165.3
Communications	88– 89	11.1	92.24	7.02	7.61	7.31	1.6	1.7	1.6
Recreation, education	90–101	578.0	783.74	8.60	3.38	5.39	21.8	8.6	13.7
Recreation	90– 96	293.5	323.24	16.32	13.09	14.62	6.9	5.6	6.2
Education	97–101	284.6	460.50	3.18	1.92	2.47	32.3	19.4	25.0
Other expenditures	102–107	354.7	628.47	7.77	7.62	7.70	7.4	7.3	7.3
Personal care	102–104	112.3	136.90	12.34	6.80	9.16	12.1	6.6	9.0
Miscellaneous services	105–107	242.4	491.57	6.50	8.07	7.24	6.1	7.6	6.8
Capital formation	109–146	1428.2	1185.32	16.66	10.24	13.06	11.8	7.2	9.2
Domestic capital formation	109–145	1757.4	1128.57	16.47	11.29	13.64	13.8	9.5	11.4
Construction	109–122	680.0	680.37	8.56	7.38	7.95	13.5	11.7	12.6
Residential	109–110	184.3	235.05	9.30	9.12	9.21	8.6	8.4	8.5
Nonresidential	111–118	314.7	210.33	11.82	9.28	10.48	16.1	12.7	14.3
Other	119–122	181.0	234.99	4.89	4.75	4.82	16.2	15.7	16.0
Producer durables	123–144	847.6	491.75	26.82	21.37	23.94	8.1	6.4	7.2
Transport equipment	123–129	243.6	122.69	27.68	20.64	23.91	9.6	7.2	8.3
Nonelectrical machinery	130–138	309.2	203.26	24.12	20.66	22.33	7.4	6.3	6.8
Electrical machinery	139–142	107.7	118.24	33.31	25.23	28.99	3.6	2.7	3.1
Other	143–144	187.1	47.56	19.99	21.70	20.83	18.1	19.7	18.9
Exports minus imports	146–146	−329.1	56.75	20.38	20.38	20.38	−28.5	−28.5	−28.5
Government	147–151	522.8	808.43	7.22	4.93	5.97	13.1	9.0	10.8
Compensation	147–150	293.3	419.96	4.82	3.55	4.14	19.7	14.5	16.9
Commodities	151–151	229.5	388.47	9.81	9.81	9.81	6.0	6.0	6.0
Gross domestic product	1–151	7138.0	7176.71	12.84	6.58	9.19	15.1	7.7	10.8
Aggregates									
ICP concepts[e]									
Consumption (CEP)[b,c]	1–108	5187.1	5182.96	12.84	6.18	8.90	16.2	7.8	11.2
Capital formation (GCF)[d]	109–146	1428.2	1185.32	16.66	10.24	13.06	11.8	7.2	9.2
Government (PFC)	147–151	522.8	808.43	7.22	4.93	5.97	13.1	9.0	10.8
Gross domestic product (ICP)	1–151	7138.0	7176.71	12.84	6.58	9.19	15.1	7.7	10.8
SNA concepts[e]									
Consumption (PFCE)	1–108	4970.3	4620.20	13.86	6.75	9.67	15.9	7.8	11.1
Capital formation (GCF)	109–146	1428.2	1185.32	16.66	10.24	13.06	11.8	7.2	9.2
Government (GFCE)	1–151	739.5	1367.45	6.04	3.53	4.61	15.3	9.0	11.7
Gross domestic product (SNA)	1–151	7138.0	7172.96	12.83	6.58	9.19	15.1	7.8	10.8

Note: See the end of Appendix Table 7-68 for notes.

Category	Line numbers[a]	Per capita expenditures U.K. (pounds)	Per capita expenditures U.S. (dollars)	Purchasing power parities (pounds/dollars) U.S. weight	Purchasing power parities (pounds/dollars) U.K. weight	Purchasing power parities (pounds/dollars) Geometric mean	Quantity per capita (U.S. = 100) U.S. weight	Quantity per capita (U.S. = 100) U.K. weight	Quantity per capita (U.S. = 100) Geometric mean
Consumption, ICP[b,c]	1–108	1272.843	5182.96	0.4043	0.3363	0.3687	73.0	60.7	66.6
Food, beverages, tobacco	1– 39	287.044	818.24	0.4459	0.4144	0.4299	84.6	78.7	81.6
Food	1– 33	208.714	658.25	0.3966	0.3659	0.3810	86.7	79.9	83.2
Bread, cereals	1– 6	29.206	94.81	0.2911	0.2971	0.2941	103.7	105.8	104.7
Meat	7– 12	61.449	163.79	0.4374	0.4077	0.4223	92.0	85.8	88.9
Fish	13– 14	6.520	25.96	0.4710	0.4833	0.4771	52.0	53.3	52.6
Milk, cheese, eggs	15– 17	29.474	82.52	0.3367	0.3258	0.3312	109.6	106.1	107.8
Oils, fats	18– 20	8.967	32.30	0.4723	0.3481	0.4055	79.8	58.8	68.5
Fruits, vegetables	21– 26	39.478	147.83	0.4309	0.4060	0.4183	65.8	62.0	63.8
Coffee, tea, cocoa	27– 29	5.609	17.18	0.5184	0.2892	0.3872	112.9	63.0	84.3
Spices, sweets, sugar	30– 33	28.010	93.86	0.3619	0.3734	0.3676	79.9	82.5	81.2
Beverages	34– 37	28.795	91.02	0.5996	0.5453	0.5718	58.0	52.8	55.3
Tobacco	38– 39	49.535	68.97	0.7134	0.7134	0.7134	100.7	100.7	100.7
Clothing, footwear	40– 51	97.051	336.33	0.4740	0.4697	0.4718	61.4	60.9	61.2
Clothing	40– 47	80.813	284.83	0.4688	0.4725	0.4707	60.0	60.5	60.3
Footwear	48– 51	16.238	51.50	0.5025	0.4563	0.4788	69.1	62.8	65.9
Gross rent, fuel	52– 57	219.557	903.84	0.4056	0.4085	0.4070	59.5	59.9	59.7
Gross rent	52– 53	167.003	717.46	0.3695	0.3854	0.3774	60.4	63.0	61.7
Fuel, power	54– 57	52.554	186.38	0.5445	0.5043	0.5240	55.9	51.8	53.8
House furnishings, operations	58– 70	83.332	343.14	0.4534	0.3890	0.4200	62.4	53.6	57.8
Furniture	58– 60	34.655	165.64	0.3697	0.3721	0.3709	56.2	56.6	56.4
Appliances	61– 66	14.237	56.41	0.8871	0.5957	0.7269	42.4	28.4	34.7
Supplies, operation	67– 70	34.440	121.09	0.3659	0.3543	0.3601	80.3	77.7	79.0
Medical care	71– 77	75.222	653.69	0.1365	0.1197	0.1278	96.2	84.3	90.0
Transport, communications	78– 89	150.515	692.17	0.6258	0.3462	0.4655	62.8	34.7	46.7
Equipment	78– 79	33.226	221.44	0.6845	0.5590	0.6186	26.8	21.9	24.3
Operation costs	80– 83	63.325	338.12	0.5796	0.2375	0.3710	78.9	32.3	50.5
Purchased transport	84– 87	37.227	40.37	0.5937	0.4741	0.5305	194.5	155.3	173.8
Communications	88– 89	16.738	92.24	0.6686	0.5560	0.6097	32.6	27.1	29.8
Recreation, education	90–101	187.599	783.74	0.3456	0.3161	0.3305	75.7	69.3	72.4
Recreation	90– 96	95.532	323.24	0.3701	0.3418	0.3557	86.5	79.8	83.1
Education	97–101	92.067	460.50	0.3284	0.2931	0.3103	68.2	60.9	64.4
Other expenditures	102–107	172.523	628.47	0.3904	0.3615	0.3757	75.9	70.3	73.1
Personal care	102–104	32.868	136.90	0.4157	0.3634	0.3887	66.1	57.8	61.8
Miscellaneous services	105–107	139.655	491.57	0.3834	0.3610	0.3720	78.7	74.1	76.4
Capital formation	109–146	301.906	1185.32	0.5575	0.5032	0.5296	50.6	45.7	48.1
Domestic capital formation	109–145	340.651	1128.57	0.5629	0.4965	0.5287	60.8	53.6	57.1
Construction	109–122	195.727	680.37	0.5448	0.4619	0.5016	62.3	52.8	57.3
Residential	109–110	75.615	235.05	0.5281	0.4794	0.5032	67.1	60.9	63.9
Nonresidential	111–118	77.151	210.33	0.6527	0.5769	0.6136	63.6	56.2	59.8
Other	119–122	42.961	234.99	0.4648	0.3247	0.3885	56.3	39.3	47.1
Producer durables	123–144	169.861	491.75	0.5795	0.5383	0.5585	64.2	59.6	61.8
Transport equipment	123–129	52.071	122.69	0.6043	0.5136	0.5571	82.6	70.2	76.2
Nonelectrical machinery	130–138	72.971	203.26	0.5335	0.5389	0.5362	66.6	67.3	67.0
Electrical machinery	139–142	34.101	118.24	0.6720	0.6056	0.6379	47.6	42.9	45.2
Other	143–144	10.718	47.56	0.4823	0.4777	0.4800	47.2	46.7	47.0
Exports minus imports	146–146	− 38.745	56.75	0.4501	0.4501	0.4501	− 151.7	− 151.7	− 151.7
Government	147–151	287.812	808.43	0.3787	0.3247	0.3507	109.6	94.0	101.5
Compensation	147–150	192.905	419.96	0.3248	0.2882	0.3060	159.4	141.4	150.1
Commodities	151–151	94.907	388.47	0.4370	0.4370	0.4370	55.9	55.9	55.9
Gross domestic product	1–151	1862.560	7176.71	0.4267	0.3533	0.3883	73.5	60.8	66.8
Aggregates									
ICP concepts[e]									
Consumption (CEP)[b,c]	1–108	1272.843	5182.96	0.4043	0.3363	0.3687	73.0	60.7	66.6
Capital formation (GCF)[d]	109–146	301.906	1185.32	0.5575	0.5032	0.5296	50.6	45.7	48.1
Government (PFC)	147–151	287.812	808.43	0.3787	0.3247	0.3507	109.6	94.0	101.5
Gross domestic product (ICP)	1–151	1862.560	7176.71	0.4267	0.3533	0.3883	73.5	60.8	66.8
SNA concepts[e]									
Consumption (PFCE)	1–108	1095.068	4620.20	0.4180	0.3872	0.4023	61.2	56.7	58.9
Capital formation (GCF)	109–146	301.906	1185.32	0.5575	0.5032	0.5296	50.6	45.7	48.1
Government (GFCE)	1–151	446.812	1367.45	0.3432	0.2495	0.2926	130.9	95.2	111.7
Gross domestic product (SNA)	1–151	1843.786	7172.96	0.4268	0.3533	0.3883	72.8	60.2	66.2

Note: See the end of Appendix Table 7-68 for notes.

Category	Line numbers[a]	Per capita expenditures		Purchasing power parities (N.pesos/dollars)			Quantity per capita (U.S. = 100)		
		Uruguay (N.pesos)	U.S. (dollars)	U.S. weight	Uruguay weight	Geometric mean	U.S. weight	Uruguay weight	Geometric mean
Consumption, ICP[b,c]	1–108	2416.27	5182.96	1.867	0.875	1.278	53.3	25.0	36.5
Food, beverages, tobacco	1– 39	1012.85	818.24	1.603	0.960	1.241	129.0	77.2	99.8
Food	1– 33	769.63	658.25	1.499	0.875	1.145	133.7	78.0	102.1
Bread, cereals	1– 6	127.51	94.81	0.853	0.754	0.802	178.3	157.7	167.7
Meat	7– 12	203.64	163.79	1.045	0.552	0.760	225.1	119.0	163.7
Fish	13– 14	2.41	25.96	1.006	0.595	0.774	15.6	9.2	12.0
Milk, cheese, eggs	15– 17	105.89	82.52	0.969	0.914	0.941	140.4	132.4	136.4
Oils, fats	18– 20	43.90	32.30	3.342	3.171	3.255	42.9	40.7	41.8
Fruits, vegetables	21– 26	161.90	147.83	1.797	1.195	1.465	91.6	61.0	74.7
Coffee, tea, cocoa	27– 29	12.27	17.18	2.453	2.041	2.238	35.0	29.1	31.9
Spices, sweets, sugar	30– 33	112.12	93.86	2.267	1.672	1.947	71.5	52.7	61.4
Beverages	34– 37	169.94	91.02	1.378	1.238	1.306	150.9	135.5	143.0
Tobacco	38– 39	73.28	68.97	2.900	1.938	2.371	54.8	36.6	44.8
Clothing, footwear	40– 51	172.54	336.33	1.694	1.580	1.636	32.5	30.3	31.4
Clothing	40– 47	129.49	284.83	1.643	1.577	1.610	28.8	27.7	28.2
Footwear	48– 51	43.06	51.50	1.975	1.589	1.771	52.6	42.3	47.2
Gross rent, fuel	52– 57	266.19	903.84	1.085	0.889	0.982	33.1	27.1	30.0
Gross rent	52– 53	163.69	717.46	0.869	0.702	0.781	32.5	26.3	29.2
Fuel, power	54– 57	102.50	186.38	1.916	1.545	1.721	35.6	28.7	32.0
House furnishings, operations	58– 70	191.45	343.14	2.136	1.615	1.857	34.6	26.1	30.0
Furniture	58– 60	32.63	165.64	1.579	1.379	1.476	14.3	12.5	13.3
Appliances	61– 66	39.38	56.41	4.452	3.240	3.798	21.5	15.7	18.4
Supplies, operation	67– 70	119.44	121.09	1.820	1.443	1.621	68.3	54.2	60.9
Medical care	71– 77	152.54	653.69	0.717	0.548	0.627	42.6	32.5	37.2
Transport, communications	78– 89	234.39	692.17	5.051	0.872	2.099	38.8	6.7	16.1
Equipment	78– 79	34.08	221.44	8.890	8.192	8.534	1.9	1.7	1.8
Operation costs	80– 83	60.93	338.12	4.110	1.683	2.630	10.7	4.4	6.9
Purchased transport	84– 87	119.03	40.37	0.518	0.564	0.541	522.6	568.7	545.2
Communications	88– 89	20.36	92.24	1.264	1.165	1.214	18.9	17.5	18.2
Recreation, education	90–101	203.98	783.74	1.393	0.523	0.853	49.8	18.7	30.5
Recreation	90– 96	127.77	323.24	2.534	1.248	1.778	31.7	15.6	22.2
Education	97–101	76.21	460.50	0.592	0.265	0.396	62.5	28.0	41.8
Other expenditures	102–107	182.32	628.47	1.550	0.755	1.082	38.4	18.7	26.8
Personal care	102–104	41.91	136.90	3.231	1.761	2.385	17.4	9.5	12.8
Miscellaneous services	105–107	140.41	491.57	1.081	0.645	0.835	44.3	26.4	34.2
Capital formation	109–146	290.08	1185.32	2.719	1.547	2.051	15.8	9.0	11.9
Domestic capital formation	109–145	396.12	1128.57	2.740	1.695	2.155	20.7	12.8	16.3
Construction	109–122	276.78	680.37	1.684	1.419	1.546	28.7	24.2	26.3
Residential	109–110	92.45	235.05	2.057	2.094	2.076	18.8	19.1	18.9
Nonresidential	111–118	43.79	210.33	1.193	1.140	1.166	18.3	17.5	17.9
Other	119–122	140.55	234.99	1.749	1.250	1.479	47.9	34.2	40.5
Producer durables	123–144	115.02	491.75	4.084	3.235	3.635	7.2	5.7	6.4
Transport equipment	123–129	31.38	122.69	6.434	5.182	5.775	4.9	4.0	4.4
Nonelectrical machinery	130–138	57.11	203.26	3.675	3.095	3.373	9.1	7.6	8.3
Electrical machinery	139–142	8.50	118.24	2.987	3.548	3.255	2.0	2.4	2.2
Other	143–144	18.04	47.56	2.498	2.085	2.282	18.2	15.2	16.6
Exports minus imports	146–146	– 106.04	56.75	2.299	2.299	2.299	– 81.3	– 81.3	– 81.3
Government	147–151	301.90	808.43	0.843	0.476	0.634	78.5	44.3	58.9
Compensation	147–150	241.74	419.96	0.426	0.411	0.418	140.0	135.2	137.6
Commodities	151–151	60.17	388.47	1.295	1.295	1.295	12.0	12.0	12.0
Gross domestic product	1–151	3008.26	7176.71	1.893	0.840	1.261	49.9	22.1	33.3
Aggregates									
ICP concepts[e]									
Consumption (CEP)[b,c]	1–108	2416.27	5182.96	1.867	0.875	1.278	53.3	25.0	36.5
Capital formation (GCF)[d]	109–146	290.08	1185.32	2.719	1.547	2.051	15.8	9.0	11.9
Government (PFC)	147–151	301.90	808.43	0.843	0.476	0.634	78.5	44.3	58.9
Gross domestic product (ICP)	1–151	3008.26	7176.71	1.893	0.840	1.261	49.9	22.1	33.3
SNA concepts[e]									
Consumption (PFCE)	1–108	2317.03	4620.20	2.004	0.941	1.373	53.3	25.0	36.5
Capital formation (GCF)	109–146	290.08	1185.32	2.719	1.547	2.051	15.8	9.0	11.9
Government (GFCE)	1–151	401.15	1367.45	0.804	0.430	0.588	68.2	36.5	49.9
Gross domestic product (SNA)	1–151	3008.26	7172.96	1.893	0.840	1.261	50.0	22.2	33.3

Note: See the end of Appendix Table 7-68 for notes.

Category	Line numbers[a]	Per capita expenditures Yugoslavia (dinars)	U.S. (dollars)	Purchasing power parities (dinars/dollars) U.S. weight	Yugoslavia weight	Geometric mean	Quantity per capita (U.S. = 100) U.S. weight	Yugoslavia weight	Geometric mean
Consumption, ICP[b,c]	1–108	17185.4	5182.96	11.04	8.00	9.40	41.4	30.0	35.3
Food, beverages, tobacco	1– 39	6117.7	818.24	13.70	11.53	12.57	64.8	54.6	59.5
Food	1– 33	4955.5	658.25	13.64	11.26	12.39	66.9	55.2	60.7
Bread, cereals	1– 6	962.0	94.81	9.71	8.14	8.89	124.7	104.5	114.1
Meat	7– 12	1274.6	163.79	13.66	13.44	13.55	57.9	57.0	57.4
Fish	13– 14	85.4	25.96	12.00	11.53	11.76	28.5	27.4	28.0
Milk, cheese, eggs	15– 17	780.5	82.52	12.02	10.96	11.48	86.3	78.7	82.4
Oils, fats	18– 20	285.4	32.30	13.39	12.03	12.69	73.5	66.0	69.6
Fruits, vegetables	21– 26	822.8	147.83	13.06	9.90	11.37	56.2	42.6	48.9
Coffee, tea, cocoa	27– 29	222.1	17.18	48.09	32.76	39.69	39.5	26.9	32.6
Spices, sweets, sugar	30– 33	522.6	93.86	14.18	14.93	14.55	37.3	39.3	38.3
Beverages	34– 37	733.3	91.02	14.62	14.47	14.54	55.7	55.1	55.4
Tobacco	38– 39	428.9	68.97	13.02	10.86	11.89	57.3	47.8	52.3
Clothing, footwear	40– 51	1620.2	336.33	14.55	13.93	14.24	34.6	33.1	33.8
Clothing	40– 47	1280.3	284.83	14.80	14.32	14.56	31.4	30.4	30.9
Footwear	48– 51	339.9	51.50	13.14	12.65	12.89	52.2	50.2	51.2
Gross rent, fuel	52– 57	1421.6	903.84	7.12	6.60	6.85	23.8	22.1	22.9
Gross rent	52– 53	746.6	717.46	4.60	4.61	4.60	22.6	22.6	22.6
Fuel, power	54– 57	675.0	186.38	16.81	12.62	14.57	28.7	21.5	24.9
House furnishings, operations	58– 70	1651.8	343.14	15.81	13.26	14.48	36.3	30.4	33.2
Furniture	58– 60	794.1	165.64	14.14	13.15	13.64	36.5	33.9	35.2
Appliances	61– 66	323.8	56.41	25.56	17.22	20.98	33.3	22.5	27.4
Supplies, operation	67– 70	533.9	121.09	13.55	11.77	12.63	37.4	32.5	34.9
Medical care	71– 77	1262.7	653.69	4.14	3.91	4.02	49.4	46.7	48.0
Transport, communications	78– 89	1603.2	692.17	18.70	9.47	13.31	24.5	12.4	17.4
Equipment	78– 79	450.1	221.44	21.81	19.05	20.38	10.7	9.3	10.0
Operation costs	80– 83	652.1	338.12	21.03	16.10	18.40	12.0	9.2	10.5
Purchased transport	84– 87	435.6	40.37	8.15	4.55	6.08	237.4	132.5	177.3
Communications	88– 89	65.3	92.24	7.29	7.02	7.16	10.1	9.7	9.9
Recreation, education	90–101	2058.0	783.74	8.92	4.46	6.31	58.9	29.4	41.6
Recreation	90– 96	950.3	323.24	15.15	5.43	9.07	54.1	19.4	32.4
Education	97–101	1107.7	460.50	4.55	3.87	4.20	62.2	52.8	57.3
Other expenditures	102–107	1732.5	628.47	9.90	7.77	8.77	35.5	27.8	31.4
Personal care	102–104	325.2	136.90	10.93	9.16	10.01	25.9	21.7	23.7
Miscellaneous services	105–107	1407.3	491.57	9.62	7.50	8.49	38.2	29.8	33.7
Capital formation	109–146	8495.0	1185.32	18.80	17.21	17.98	41.6	38.1	39.9
Domestic capital formation	109–145	10345.4	1128.57	18.87	17.24	18.03	53.2	48.6	50.8
Construction	109–122	4615.1	680.37	17.03	17.45	17.24	38.9	39.8	39.3
Residential	109–110	1760.3	235.05	18.09	17.31	17.70	43.3	41.4	42.3
Nonresidential	111–118	1633.5	210.33	19.40	22.35	20.82	34.8	40.0	37.3
Other	119–122	1221.3	234.99	13.86	13.62	13.74	38.2	37.5	37.8
Producer durables	123–144	3457.3	491.75	21.08	18.53	19.77	37.9	33.4	35.6
Transport equipment	123–129	538.6	122.69	19.82	16.17	17.90	27.1	22.2	24.5
Nonelectrical machinery	130–138	2130.7	203.26	23.18	20.45	21.78	51.3	45.2	48.1
Electrical machinery	139–142	545.8	118.24	21.33	15.84	18.38	29.1	21.6	25.1
Other	143–144	242.2	47.56	14.74	16.57	15.63	30.7	34.5	32.6
Exports minus imports	146–146	− 1850.4	56.75	17.39	17.39	17.39	− 187.6	− 187.6	− 187.6
Government	147–151	3257.3	808.43	10.38	10.30	10.34	39.1	38.8	39.0
Compensation	147–150	1434.1	419.96	7.88	8.11	7.99	42.1	43.3	42.7
Commodities	151–151	1823.2	388.47	13.08	13.08	13.08	35.9	35.9	35.9
Gross domestic product	1–151	28937.7	7176.71	12.25	9.79	10.95	41.2	32.9	36.8
Aggregates									
ICP concepts[e]									
Consumption (CEP)[b,c]	1–108	17185.4	5182.96	11.04	8.00	9.40	41.4	30.0	35.3
Capital formation (GCF)[d]	109–146	8495.0	1185.32	18.80	17.21	17.98	41.6	38.1	39.9
Government (PFC)	147–151	3257.3	808.43	10.38	10.30	10.34	39.1	38.8	39.0
Gross domestic product (ICP)	1–151	28937.7	7176.71	12.25	9.79	10.95	41.2	32.9	36.8
SNA concepts[e]									
Consumption (PFCE)	1–108	14426.3	4620.20	11.77	10.26	10.99	30.4	26.5	28.4
Capital formation (GCF)	109–146	8495.0	1185.32	18.80	17.21	17.98	41.6	38.1	39.9
Government (GFCE)	1–151	6012.0	1367.45	8.20	5.70	6.83	77.2	53.6	64.3
Gross domestic product (SNA)	1–151	28933.4	7172.96	12.25	9.79	10.95	41.2	32.9	36.8

Note: See the end of Appendix Table 7-68 for notes.

Category	Line numbers[a]	Per capita expenditures		Purchasing power parities (kwacha/dollars)			Quantity per capita (U.S. = 100)		
		Zambia (kwacha)	U.S. (dollars)	U.S. weight	Zambia weight	Geometric mean	U.S. weight	Zambia weight	Geometric mean
Consumption, ICP[b,c]	1–108	191.106	5182.96	0.6847	0.3199	0.4680	11.5	5.4	7.9
Food, beverages, tobacco	1– 39	77.434	818.24	0.8700	0.3300	0.5358	28.7	10.9	17.7
Food	1– 33	72.255	658.25	0.7168	0.3152	0.4753	34.8	15.3	23.1
Bread, cereals	1– 6	15.599	94.81	0.5242	0.1286	0.2596	127.9	31.4	63.4
Meat	7– 12	18.832	163.79	0.6037	0.4539	0.5235	25.3	19.0	22.0
Fish	13– 14	9.938	25.96	0.6385	0.6652	0.6517	57.5	59.9	58.7
Milk, cheese, eggs	15– 17	3.152	82.52	0.6085	0.5784	0.5933	6.6	6.3	6.4
Oils, fats	18– 20	4.296	32.30	0.6754	0.6856	0.6805	19.4	19.7	19.5
Fruits, vegetables	21– 26	14.937	147.83	1.0246	0.5267	0.7346	19.2	9.9	13.8
Coffee, tea, cocoa	27– 29	1.024	17.18	0.8177	0.5334	0.6604	11.2	7.3	9.0
Spices, sweets, sugar	30– 33	4.477	93.86	0.7369	0.4697	0.5883	10.2	6.5	8.1
Beverages	34– 37	4.096	91.02	1.2697	0.9219	1.0819	4.9	3.5	4.2
Tobacco	38– 39	1.084	68.97	1.8044	1.1006	1.4092	1.4	0.9	1.1
Clothing, footwear	40– 51	12.889	336.33	0.6864	0.6638	0.6750	5.8	5.6	5.7
Clothing	40– 47	11.383	284.83	0.7479	0.7467	0.7473	5.4	5.3	5.3
Footwear	48– 51	1.506	51.50	0.3464	0.3610	0.3536	8.1	8.4	8.3
Gross rent, fuel	52– 57	18.510	903.84	0.5705	0.3742	0.4620	5.5	3.6	4.4
Gross rent	52– 53	12.568	717.46	0.5216	0.5140	0.5178	3.4	3.4	3.4
Fuel, power	54– 57	5.943	186.38	0.7587	0.2376	0.4246	13.4	4.2	7.5
House furnishings, operations	58– 70	11.162	343.14	1.0142	0.2441	0.4976	13.3	3.2	6.5
Furniture	58– 60	2.449	165.64	0.6643	0.5952	0.6288	2.5	2.2	2.4
Appliances	61– 66	0.703	56.41	2.5591	1.9526	2.2354	0.6	0.5	0.6[e]
Supplies, operation	67– 70	8.010	121.09	0.7732	0.1942	0.3875	34.1	8.6	17.1
Medical care	71– 77	10.661	653.69	0.4936	0.3108	0.3925	5.2	3.3	4.2
Transport, communications	78– 89	12.387	692.17	1.0901	0.5762	0.7926	3.1	1.6	2.3
Equipment	78– 79	6.284	221.44	1.6116	1.5437	1.5773	1.8	1.8	1.8
Operation costs	80– 83	3.935	338.12	1.0656	0.7057	0.8672	1.6	1.1	1.3
Purchased transport	84– 87	1.626	40.37	0.3482	0.1533	0.2311	26.3	11.6	17.4
Communications	88– 89	0.542	92.24	0.2528	0.4358	0.3319	1.3	2.3	1.8
Recreation, education	90–101	26.481	783.74	0.4972	0.1736	0.2938	19.5	6.8	11.5
Recreation	90– 96	6.043	323.24	0.8457	0.4805	0.6375	3.9	2.2	2.9
Education	97–101	20.438	460.50	0.2526	0.1460	0.1920	30.4	17.6	23.1
Other expenditures	102–107	20.980	628.47	0.4129	0.5397	0.4720	6.2	8.1	7.1
Personal care	102–104	1.225	136.90	0.6539	0.6676	0.6607	1.3	1.4	1.4
Miscellaneous services	105–107	19.755	491.57	0.3457	0.5334	0.4294	7.5	11.6	9.4
Capital formation	109–146	66.914	1185.32	0.7467	0.4986	0.6102	11.3	7.6	9.3
Domestic capital formation	109–145	128.950	1128.57	0.7519	0.5592	0.6484	20.4	15.2	17.6
Construction	109–122	67.858	680.37	0.5447	0.4344	0.4865	23.0	18.3	20.5
Residential	109–110	15.117	235.05	0.4921	0.4542	0.4728	14.2	13.1	13.6
Nonresidential	111–118	29.673	210.33	0.8935	0.7876	0.8389	17.9	15.8	16.8
Other	119–122	23.068	234.99	0.2851	0.2706	0.2778	36.3	34.4	35.3
Producer durables	123–144	53.062	491.75	1.0206	0.8878	0.9519	12.2	10.6	11.3
Transport equipment	123–129	18.992	122.69	1.1099	0.8131	0.9500	19.0	13.9	16.3
Nonelectrical machinery	130–138	19.574	203.26	1.0356	0.9228	0.9776	10.4	9.3	9.9
Electrical machinery	139–142	11.524	118.24	0.9945	1.0053	0.9999	9.7	9.8	9.7
Other	143–144	2.971	47.56	0.7906	0.7964	0.7935	7.8	7.9	7.9
Exports minus imports	146–146	−62.036	56.75	0.6435	0.6435	0.6435	−169.9	−169.9	−169.9
Government	147–151	60.229	808.43	0.3370	0.1988	0.2588	37.5	22.1	28.8
Compensation	147–150	22.184	419.96	0.2142	0.1000	0.1463	52.8	24.7	36.1
Commodities	151–151	38.045	388.47	0.4697	0.4697	0.4697	20.9	20.9	20.9
Gross domestic product	1–151	318.249	7176.71	0.6558	0.3076	0.4492	14.4	6.8	9.9
Aggregates									
ICP concepts[e]									
Consumption (CEP)[b,c]	1–108	191.106	5182.96	0.6847	0.3199	0.4680	11.5	5.4	7.9
Capital formation (GCF)[d]	109–146	66.914	1185.32	0.7467	0.4986	0.6102	11.3	7.6	9.3
Government (PFC)	147–151	60.229	808.43	0.3370	0.1988	0.2588	37.5	22.1	28.8
Gross domestic product (ICP)	1–151	318.249	7176.71	0.6558	0.3076	0.4492	14.4	6.8	9.9
SNA concepts[e]									
Consumption (PFCE)	1–108	163.401	4620.20	0.7312	0.3693	0.5197	9.6	4.8	6.8
Capital formation (GCF)	109–146	66.914	1185.32	0.7467	0.4986	0.6102	11.3	7.6	9.3
Government (GFCE)	1–151	87.533	1367.45	0.3228	0.1915	0.2486	33.4	19.8	25.7
Gross domestic product (SNA)	1–151	317.848	7172.96	0.6559	0.3075	0.4491	14.4	6.8	9.9

Note: See the end of Appendix Table 7-68 for notes.

Appendix Table 7-34. Augmented Summary Binary Table: Malawi/Kenya, 1975

Category	Line numbers[a]	Per capita expenditures Malawi (kwacha)	Per capita expenditures Kenya (shillings)	Purchasing power parities (kwacha/shillings) Kenya weight	Purchasing power parities Malawi weight	Purchasing power parities Geometric mean	Quantity per capita (Kenya = 100) Kenya weight	Quantity per capita Malawi weight	Quantity per capita Geometric mean
Consumption, ICP[b,c]	1–108	95.660	1370.10	0.1084	0.0776	0.0918	89.9	64.4	76.1
Food, beverages, tobacco	1– 39	55.543	602.13	0.1008	0.0723	0.0854	127.6	91.5	108.1
Food	1– 33	50.571	505.11	0.1034	0.0716	0.0860	139.9	96.9	116.4
Bread, cereals	1– 6	19.590	201.96	0.1091	0.1090	0.1090	89.0	88.9	89.0
Meat	7– 12	3.385	30.15	0.1352	0.1075	0.1206	104.4	83.0	93.1
Fish	13– 14	2.759	2.99	0.0946	0.0855	0.0899	1081.0	977.3	1027.8
Milk, cheese, eggs	15– 17	2.091	95.68	0.1210	0.1192	0.1201	18.3	18.1	18.2
Oils, fats	18– 20	0.875	15.08	0.1100	0.1086	0.1093	53.4	52.7	53.1
Fruits, vegetables	21– 26	19.739	109.26	0.0749	0.0478	0.0598	377.9	241.2	301.9
Coffee, tea, cocoa	27– 29	0.304	7.61	0.1084	0.1031	0.1057	38.7	36.8	37.8
Spices, sweets, sugar	30– 33	1.829	42.39	0.0841	0.0839	0.0840	51.4	51.3	51.4
Beverages	34– 37	4.199	63.74	0.0776	0.0779	0.0778	84.6	84.9	84.7
Tobacco	38– 39	0.773	33.29	0.1065	0.0994	0.1029	23.4	21.8	22.6
Clothing, footwear	40– 51	6.702	94.04	0.1030	0.0980	0.1005	72.7	69.2	70.9
Clothing	40– 47	6.148	80.45	0.1125	0.1089	0.1107	70.1	67.9	69.0
Footwear	48– 51	0.554	13.58	0.0470	0.0464	0.0467	87.9	86.9	87.4
Gross rent, fuel	52– 57	5.915	154.79	0.1256	0.0879	0.1051	43.5	30.4	36.4
Gross rent	52– 53	3.388	124.49	0.0984	0.0786	0.0879	34.6	27.6	31.0
Fuel, power	54– 57	2.527	30.30	0.2374	0.1045	0.1575	79.8	35.1	53.0
House furnishings, operations	58– 70	8.999	115.38	0.1882	0.0919	0.1315	84.8	41.4	59.3
Furniture	58– 60	2.085	45.68	0.1858	0.0595	0.1052	76.7	24.6	43.4
Appliances	61– 66	0.926	4.48	0.0	0.0635	0.0	325.8	0.0	0.0
Supplies, operation	67– 70	5.987	65.23	0.1900	0.1137	0.1470	80.7	48.3	62.4
Medical care	71– 77	1.835	65.68	0.0298	0.0365	0.0330	76.6	93.7	84.8
Transport, communications	78– 89	7.193	100.01	0.1261	0.1239	0.1250	58.1	57.0	57.6
Equipment	78– 79	1.618	10.60	0.1302	0.1358	0.1330	112.4	117.3	114.8
Operation costs	80– 83	4.113	42.54	0.1472	0.1230	0.1346	78.6	65.7	71.8
Purchased transport	84– 87	1.333	42.39	0.1076	0.1219	0.1146	25.8	29.2	27.5
Communications	88– 89	0.130	4.48	0.0912	0.0722	0.0811	40.2	31.8	35.7
Recreation, education	90–101	6.266	160.76	0.0550	0.0626	0.0587	62.3	70.8	66.4
Recreation	90– 96	2.548	28.81	0.1386	0.1169	0.1273	75.7	63.8	69.5
Education	97–101	3.717	131.95	0.0368	0.0475	0.0418	59.4	76.6	67.4
Other expenditures	102–107	3.206	77.32	0.1759	0.1482	0.1615	28.0	23.6	25.7
Personal care	102–104	0.481	30.30	0.2521	0.1980	0.2234	8.0	6.3	7.1
Miscellaneous services	105–107	2.725	47.02	0.1269	0.1418	0.1342	40.9	45.7	43.2
Capital formation	109–146	14.968	239.87	0.1064	0.0645	0.0829	96.7	58.6	75.3
Domestic capital formation	109–145	35.587	323.61	0.1091	0.0871	0.0975	126.2	100.8	112.8
Construction	109–122	13.272	204.05	0.1071	0.0710	0.0872	91.6	60.7	74.6
Residential	109–110	4.358	63.29	0.1099	0.1025	0.1061	67.2	62.7	64.9
Nonresidential	111–118	4.940	46.87	0.1415	0.1067	0.1229	98.8	74.5	85.8
Other	119–122	3.973	93.89	0.0881	0.0405	0.0597	104.6	48.0	70.9
Producer durables	123–144	19.143	156.58	0.1074	0.1027	0.1050	119.0	113.9	116.4
Transport equipment	123–129	8.075	47.76	0.1192	0.1147	0.1169	147.4	141.8	144.6
Nonelectrical machinery	130–138	8.710	74.04	0.1120	0.1037	0.1078	113.5	105.1	109.2
Electrical machinery	139–142	2.144	26.87	0.0863	0.0725	0.0791	110.1	92.5	100.9
Other	143–144	0.214	7.91	0.0646	0.0892	0.0759	30.4	41.9	35.7
Exports minus imports	146–146	−20.619	−83.74	0.1169	0.1169	0.1169	210.7	210.7	210.7
Government	147–151	9.169	177.03	0.1103	0.0756	0.0913	68.5	47.0	56.7
Compensation	147–150	4.347	100.01	0.1106	0.0562	0.0788	77.4	39.3	55.1
Commodities	151–151	4.822	77.02	0.1099	0.1099	0.1099	57.0	57.0	57.0
Gross domestic product	1–151	119.797	1787.00	0.1084	0.0756	0.0905	88.7	61.9	74.1
Aggregates									
ICP concepts[e]									
Consumption (CEP)[b,c]	1–108	95.660	1370.10	0.1084	0.0776	0.0918	89.9	64.4	76.1
Capital formation (GCF)[d]	109–146	14.968	239.87	0.1064	0.0645	0.0829	96.7	58.6	75.3
Government (PFC)	147–151	9.169	177.03	0.1103	0.0756	0.0913	68.5	47.0	56.7
Gross domestic product (ICP)	1–151	119.797	1787.00	0.1084	0.0756	0.0905	88.7	61.9	74.1
SNA concepts[e]									
Consumption (PFCE)	1–108	90.753	1218.15	0.1179	0.0810	0.0977	92.0	63.2	76.2
Capital formation (GCF)	109–146	14.968	239.87	0.1064	0.0645	0.0829	96.7	58.6	75.3
Government (GFCE)	1–151	13.728	328.98	0.0744	0.0598	0.0667	69.8	56.1	62.6
Gross domestic product (SNA)	1–151	119.450	1787.00	0.1084	0.0755	0.0905	88.5	61.7	73.9

Note: See the end of Appendix Table 7-68 for notes.

Category	Line numbers[a]	Per capita expenditures		Purchasing power parities (kwacha/shillings)			Quantity per capita (Kenya = 100)		
		Zambia (kwacha)	Kenya (shillings)	Kenya weight	Zambia weight	Geometric mean	Kenya weight	Zambia weight	Geometric mean
Consumption, ICP[b,c]	1–108	191.106	1370.10	0.12526	0.09144	0.10702	152.5	111.4	130.3
Food, beverages, tobacco	1– 39	77.434	602.13	0.12197	0.09859	0.10966	130.4	105.4	117.3
Food	1– 33	72.255	505.11	0.10752	0.09619	0.10169	148.7	133.0	140.7
Bread, cereals	1– 6	15.599	201.96	0.07297	0.06067	0.06654	127.3	105.8	116.1
Meat	7– 12	18.832	30.15	0.15584	0.13817	0.14674	452.0	400.8	425.6
Fish	13– 14	9.938	2.99	0.08612	0.07599	0.08090	4380.8	3865.5	4115.1
Milk, cheese, eggs	15– 17	3.152	95.68	0.12208	0.11718	0.11960	28.1	27.0	27.5
Oils, fats	18– 20	4.296	15.08	0.08451	0.09383	0.08905	303.7	337.2	320.0
Fruits, vegetables	21– 26	14.937	109.26	0.15415	0.15394	0.15405	88.8	88.7	88.7
Coffee, tea, cocoa	27– 29	1.024	7.61	0.11352	0.10058	0.10686	133.7	118.5	125.9
Spices, sweets, sugar	30– 33	4.477	42.39	0.09325	0.09510	0.09417	111.1	113.3	112.2
Beverages	34– 37	4.096	63.74	0.13409	0.13191	0.13300	48.7	47.9	48.3
Tobacco	38– 39	1.084	33.29	0.31809	0.33870	0.32823	9.6	10.2	9.9
Clothing, footwear	40– 51	12.889	94.04	0.10093	0.09719	0.09904	141.0	135.8	138.4
Clothing	40– 47	11.383	80.45	0.10912	0.10973	0.10942	128.9	129.7	129.3
Footwear	48– 51	1.506	13.58	0.05244	0.05214	0.05229	212.6	211.4	212.0
Gross rent, fuel	52– 57	18.510	154.79	0.08602	0.06935	0.07724	172.4	139.0	154.8
Gross rent	52– 53	12.568	124.49	0.08580	0.08508	0.08544	118.7	117.7	118.2
Fuel, power	54– 57	5.943	30.30	0.08692	0.04986	0.06584	393.3	225.6	297.9
House furnishings, operations	58– 70	11.162	115.38	0.20529	0.15256	0.17697	63.4	47.1	54.7
Furniture	58– 60	2.449	45.68	0.16379	0.10358	0.13025	51.8	32.7	41.2
Appliances	61– 66	0.703	4.48	0.0	0.10344	0.0	151.7	0.0	0.0
Supplies, operation	67– 70	8.010	65.23	0.23434	0.17884	0.20472	68.7	52.4	60.0
Medical care	71 77	10.661	65.68	0.09732	0.09831	0.09781	165.1	166.8	165.9
Transport, communications	78– 89	12.387	100.01	0.11774	0.10415	0.11074	118.9	105.2	111.8
Equipment	78– 79	6.284	10.60	0.10432	0.10739	0.10585	552.1	568.4	560.2
Operation costs	80– 83	3.935	42.54	0.11755	0.10508	0.11114	88.0	78.7	83.2
Purchased transport	84– 87	1.626	42.39	0.12134	0.10275	0.11166	37.3	31.6	34.4
Communications	88– 89	0.542	4.48	0.11733	0.07587	0.09435	159.5	103.2	128.3
Recreation, education	90–101	26.481	160.76	0.14527	0.11190	0.12750	147.2	113.4	129.2
Recreation	90– 96	6.043	28.81	0.15854	0.15402	0.15626	136.2	132.3	134.2
Education	97–101	20.438	131.95	0.14238	0.10352	0.12141	149.6	108.8	127.6
Other expenditures	102–107	20.980	77.32	0.13146	0.05814	0.08742	466.7	206.4	310.4
Personal care	102–104	1.225	30.30	0.20886	0.16805	0.18735	24.1	19.4	21.6
Miscellaneous services	105–107	19.755	47.02	0.08158	0.05587	0.06751	752.0	515.0	622.3
Capital formation	109–146	66.914	239.87	0.10127	0.07977	0.08988	349.7	275.5	310.4
Domestic capital formation	109–145	128.950	323.61	0.09754	0.08302	0.08998	480.0	408.5	442.8
Construction	109–122	67.858	204.05	0.11227	0.10571	0.10894	314.6	296.2	305.3
Residential	109–110	15.117	63.29	0.10501	0.09743	0.10115	245.2	227.5	236.2
Nonresidential	111–118	29.673	46.87	0.21055	0.20719	0.20886	305.6	300.7	303.1
Other	119–122	23.068	93.89	0.06810	0.06715	0.06762	365.9	360.8	363.3
Producer durables	123–144	53.062	156.58	0.08061	0.06344	0.07151	534.2	420.4	473.9
Transport equipment	123–129	18.992	47.76	0.06175	0.04829	0.05461	823.4	643.9	728.1
Nonelectrical machinery	130–138	19.574	74.04	0.09037	0.07860	0.08428	336.4	292.6	313.7
Electrical machinery	139–142	11.524	26.87	0.08909	0.07440	0.08142	576.5	481.4	526.8
Other	143–144	2.971	7.91	0.07434	0.07575	0.07504	495.8	505.2	500.5
Exports minus imports	146–146	− 62.036	− 83.74	0.08683	0.08683	0.08683	853.2	853.2	853.2
Government	147–151	60.229	177.03	0.11618	0.09693	0.10612	351.0	292.9	320.6
Compensation	147–150	22.184	100.01	0.12975	0.09427	0.11060	235.3	171.0	200.6
Commodities	151–151	38.045	77.02	0.09855	0.09855	0.09855	501.2	501.2	501.2
Gross domestic product	1–151	318.249	1787.00	0.12114	0.08964	0.10421	198.7	147.0	170.9
Aggregates									
ICP concepts[e]									
Consumption (CEP)[b,c]	1–108	191.106	1370.10	0.12526	0.09144	0.10702	152.5	111.4	130.3
Capital formation (GCF)[d]	109–146	66.914	239.87	0.10127	0.07977	0.08988	349.7	275.5	310.4
Government (PFC)	147–151	60.229	177.03	0.11618	0.09693	0.10612	351.0	292.9	320.6
Gross domestic product (ICP)	1–151	318.249	1787.00	0.12114	0.08964	0.10421	198.7	147.0	170.9
SNA concepts[e]									
Consumption (PFCE)	1–108	163.401	1218.15	0.12503	0.08948	0.10577	149.9	107.3	126.8
Capital formation (GCF)	109–146	66.914	239.87	0.10127	0.07977	0.08988	349.7	275.5	310.4
Government (GFCE)	1–151	87.533	328.98	0.12122	0.09941	0.10977	267.7	219.5	242.4
Gross domestic product (SNA)	1–151	317.848	1787.00	0.12114	0.08965	0.10421	198.4	146.8	170.7

Note: See the end of Appendix Table 7-68 for notes.

Appendix Table 7-36. Augmented Summary Binary Table: Iran/India, 1975

Category	Line numbers[a]	Per capita expenditures Iran (rials)	India (rupees)	Purchasing power parities (rials/rupees) India weight	Iran weight	Geometric mean	Quantity per capita (India = 100) India weight	Iran weight	Geometric mean
Consumption, ICP[b,c]	1–108	48847.5	877.75	16.325	11.477	13.688	484.9	340.9	406.6
Food, beverages, tobacco	1– 39	16616.6	565.34	14.108	10.091	11.932	291.3	208.3	246.3
Food	1– 33	15792.9	531.97	14.163	10.276	12.064	288.9	209.6	246.1
Bread, cereals	1– 6	4601.2	240.56	15.668	8.095	11.262	236.3	122.1	169.8
Meat	7– 12	3382.9	11.23	22.966	16.008	19.174	1881.9	1311.8	1571.2
Fish	13– 14	183.1	10.78	33.930	44.906	39.034	37.8	50.1	43.5
Milk, cheese, eggs	15– 17	1702.3	57.49	11.702	10.383	11.023	285.2	253.0	268.6
Oils, fats	18– 20	1201.2	54.77	7.788	8.792	8.275	249.5	281.6	265.1
Fruits, vegetables	21– 26	3106.5	84.64	16.585	11.388	13.743	322.3	221.3	267.1
Coffee, tea, cocoa	27– 29	559.3	8.27	22.626	23.097	22.860	292.8	298.9	295.8
Spices, sweets, sugar	30– 33	1056.3	64.23	7.026	6.793	6.908	242.1	234.1	238.1
Beverages	34– 37	169.8	7.68	10.245	5.600	7.575	394.6	215.7	291.8
Tobacco	38– 39	653.8	25.69	14.135	8.230	10.786	309.2	180.1	236.0
Clothing, footwear	40– 51	5087.5	66.32	6.992	6.790	6.890	1129.8	1097.3	1113.4
Clothing	40– 47	4113.1	61.45	6.668	6.269	6.466	1067.6	1003.9	1035.2
Footwear	48– 51	974.4	4.87	11.084	10.457	10.766	1915.2	1807.0	1860.3
Gross rent, fuel	52– 57	8223.6	53.80	22.041	13.975	17.550	1093.8	693.5	871.0
Gross rent	52– 53	6626.1	24.07	32.756	30.253	31.479	910.0	840.5	874.6
Fuel, power	54– 57	1597.5	29.73	13.367	4.324	7.603	1242.5	402.0	706.7
House furnishings, operations	58– 70	3775.8	24.43	9.174	11.488	10.266	1345.5	1684.8	1505.6
Furniture	58– 60	1985.9	3.23	9.190	14.992	11.738	4095.9	6681.8	5231.5
Appliances	61– 66	545.0	3.50	7.647	9.530	8.537	1636.0	2038.8	1826.3
Supplies, operation	67– 70	1244.9	17.70	9.473	8.954	9.210	785.5	742.5	763.7
Medical care	71– 77	3277.2	28.40	32.302	37.179	34.655	310.3	357.2	332.9
Transport, communications	78– 89	3345.3	57.20	10.633	6.808	8.508	859.0	550.0	687.3
Equipment	78– 79	1387.5	3.20	11.868	20.817	15.718	2080.1	3648.6	2754.9
Operation costs	80– 83	908.9	8.97	3.602	3.321	3.459	3051.9	2813.9	2930.5
Purchased transport	84– 87	863.1	41.92	11.917	6.736	8.960	305.7	172.8	229.8
Communications	88– 89	185.7	3.11	12.320	8.110	9.995	735.9	484.4	597.0
Recreation, education	90–101	5111.1	46.48	48.682	32.117	39.541	342.4	225.9	278.1
Recreation	90– 96	1441.0	14.64	23.172	19.697	21.364	499.6	424.7	460.6
Education	97–101	3670.1	31.83	60.416	42.686	50.783	270.1	190.8	227.0
Other expenditures	102–107	3410.5	39.74	18.206	16.668	17.420	514.9	471.4	492.7
Personal care	102–104	975.4	16.06	13.485	14.908	14.179	407.4	450.4	428.4
Miscellaneous services	105–107	2435.1	23.68	21.407	17.496	19.353	587.8	480.4	531.4
Capital formation	109–146	38661.6	247.47	16.062	10.484	12.977	1490.1	972.7	1203.9
Domestic capital formation	109–145	29096.4	250.72	15.958	11.624	13.620	998.4	727.2	852.1
Construction	109–122	16614.7	112.55	22.270	15.279	18.447	966.1	662.8	800.2
Residential	109–110	7196.1	27.59	12.194	11.755	11.972	2219.1	2139.3	2178.8
Nonresidential	111–118	5319.1	41.85	19.104	16.675	17.848	762.2	665.3	712.1
Other	119–122	4099.4	43.11	31.792	26.241	28.883	362.3	299.1	329.2
Producer durables	123–144	13921.5	88.08	10.281	9.051	9.646	1746.3	1537.4	1638.6
Transport equipment	123–129	4885.1	16.57	13.594	15.120	14.337	1950.3	2169.2	2056.9
Nonelectrical machinery	130–138	6780.4	32.42	10.340	7.349	8.717	2846.0	2022.9	2399.4
Electrical machinery	139–142	1476.5	27.00	10.204	9.346	9.766	585.2	536.0	560.0
Other	143–144	779.5	12.10	5.757	5.798	5.777	1111.5	1119.4	1115.5
Exports minus imports	146–146	9565.3	−3.25	8.075	8.075	8.075	−36495.3	−36495.3	−36495.3
Government	147–151	19855.1	94.99	37.514	19.165	26.813	1090.6	557.2	779.5
Compensation	147–150	6642.8	55.31	53.988	51.734	52.849	232.2	222.5	227.3
Commodities	151–151	13212.3	39.69	14.557	14.557	14.557	2286.9	2286.9	2286.9
Gross domestic product	1–151	107364.3	1220.21	17.921	11.956	14.638	735.9	491.0	601.1
Aggregates									
ICP concepts[e]									
Consumption (CEP)[b,c]	1–108	48847.5	877.75	16.325	11.477	13.688	484.9	340.9	406.6
Capital formation (GCF)[d]	109–146	38661.6	247.47	16.062	10.484	12.977	1490.1	972.7	1203.9
Government (PFC)	147–151	19855.1	94.99	37.514	19.165	26.813	1090.6	557.2	779.5
Gross domestic product (ICP)	1–151	107364.3	1220.21	17.921	11.956	14.638	735.9	491.0	601.1
SNA concepts[e]									
Consumption (PFCE)	1–108	43711.8	851.65	15.189	10.572	12.672	485.5	337.9	405.0
Capital formation (GCF)	109–146	38661.6	247.47	16.062	10.484	12.977	1490.1	972.7	1203.9
Government (GFCE)	1–151	24990.8	121.09	40.936	21.590	29.729	955.9	504.1	694.2
Gross domestic product (SNA)	1–151	107364.3	1220.21	17.921	11.956	14.638	735.9	491.0	601.1

Note: See the end of Appendix Table 7-68 for notes.

Appendix Table 7-37. Augmented Summary Binary Table: Japan/India, 1975

Category	Line numbers[a]	Per capita expenditures Japan (yen)	Per capita expenditures India (rupees)	Purchasing power parities (yen/rupees) India weight	Purchasing power parities (yen/rupees) Japan weight	Purchasing power parities (yen/rupees) Geometric mean	Quantity per capita (India = 100) India weight	Quantity per capita (India = 100) Japan weight	Quantity per capita (India = 100) Geometric mean
Consumption, ICP[b,c]	1–108	824902.	877.75	131.42	86.73	106.76	1083.5	715.1	880.3
Food, beverages, tobacco	1– 39	214788.	565.34	94.58	67.03	79.62	566.8	401.7	477.2
Food	1– 33	183120.	531.97	97.63	89.95	93.71	382.7	352.6	367.3
Bread, cereals	1– 6	34840.	240.56	88.57	81.57	85.00	177.6	163.5	170.4
Meat	7– 12	24721.	11.23	264.46	162.00	206.99	1358.9	832.5	1063.6
Fish	13– 14	35566.	10.78	160.60	143.77	151.95	2295.9	2055.3	2172.3
Milk, cheese, eggs	15– 17	12853.	57.49	68.62	57.23	62.67	390.6	325.8	356.7
Oils, fats	18– 20	2008.	54.77	57.23	61.83	59.49	59.3	64.1	61.6
Fruits, vegetables	21– 26	29229.	84.64	135.21	110.66	122.32	312.1	255.4	282.3
Coffee, tea, cocoa	27– 29	4446.	8.27	212.61	128.47	165.27	418.4	252.8	325.2
Spices, sweets, sugar	30– 33	39456.	64.23	87.94	60.43	72.90	1016.6	698.6	842.7
Beverages	34– 37	20320.	7.68	49.38	22.26	33.15	11880.1	5355.8	7976.7
Tobacco	38– 39	11348.	25.69	44.86	44.36	44.61	995.8	984.7	990.3
Clothing, footwear	40– 51	61264.	66.32	64.52	60.17	62.31	1535.3	1432.0	1482.7
Clothing	40– 47	55223.	61.45	61.00	57.52	59.24	1562.3	1473.1	1517.1
Footwear	48– 51	6041.	4.87	108.88	104.03	106.43	1193.7	1140.5	1166.8
Gross rent, fuel	52– 57	118701.	53.80	181.14	178.21	179.67	1238.0	1218.0	1228.0
Gross rent	52– 53	103670.	24.07	257.86	289.30	273.13	1488.9	1670.5	1577.1
Fuel, power	54– 57	15031.	29.73	119.04	48.85	76.26	1035.0	424.7	663.0
House furnishings, operations	58– 70	47990.	24.43	130.98	70.17	95.87	2799.7	1499.8	2049.1
Furniture	58– 60	17703.	3.23	99.29	96.22	97.74	5688.9	5512.7	5600.1
Appliances	61– 66	9671.	3.50	36.28	41.62	38.86	6647.4	7626.2	7120.0
Supplies, operation	67– 70	20616.	17.70	155.48	77.05	109.45	1511.8	749.2	1064.2
Medical care	71– 77	73400.	28.40	161.33	175.45	168.25	1472.9	1601.8	1536.0
Transport, communications	78– 89	72110.	57.20	146.44	52.42	87.62	2404.8	860.8	1438.8
Equipment	78– 79	14261.	3.20	43.29	30.63	36.42	14527.7	10280.7	12221.1
Operation costs	80– 83	18043.	8.97	40.58	39.71	40.14	5067.8	4958.1	5012.7
Purchased transport	84– 87	33021.	41.92	184.06	161.92	172.63	486.5	428.0	456.3
Communications	88– 89	6785.	3.11	50.94	26.96	37.06	8090.0	4280.5	5884.7
Recreation, education	90–101	119830.	46.48	519.16	108.24	237.06	2381.9	496.6	1087.6
Recreation	90– 96	59821.	14.64	112.45	67.72	87.27	6032.2	3632.8	4681.2
Education	97–101	60009.	31.83	706.25	268.22	435.24	702.8	266.9	433.1
Other expenditures	102–107	113870.	39.74	194.07	119.37	152.20	2400.6	1476.6	1882.7
Personal care	102–104	27006.	16.06	95.55	75.88	85.15	2216.5	1760.1	1975.2
Miscellaneous services	105–107	86863.	23.68	260.88	145.25	194.66	2525.5	1406.1	1884.5
Capital formation	109–146	435366.	247.47	93.75	45.96	65.64	3827.7	1876.6	2680.2
Domestic capital formation	109–145	434810.	250.72	92.99	45.98	65.39	3771.9	1865.0	2652.3
Construction	109–122	283787.	112.55	152.66	80.48	110.84	3132.9	1651.7	2274.7
Residential	109–110	100864.	27.59	222.21	207.19	214.57	1764.7	1645.4	1704.0
Nonresidential	111–118	72047.	41.85	162.45	154.79	158.57	1112.1	1059.7	1085.6
Other	119–122	110876.	43.11	98.65	43.08	65.19	5969.9	2607.0	3945.0
Producer durables	123–144	146595.	88.08	27.58	24.97	26.24	6665.7	6034.0	6342.0
Transport equipment	123–129	33424.	16.57	47.07	37.30	41.90	5408.9	4286.1	4814.9
Nonelectrical machinery	130–138	46744.	32.42	21.95	19.79	20.84	7288.1	6570.4	6920.0
Electrical machinery	139–142	35531.	27.00	21.12	22.25	21.68	5915.0	6232.0	6071.4
Other	143–144	30897.	12.10	30.43	30.43	30.43	8394.0	8394.0	8394.0
Exports minus imports	146–146	556.	−3.25	35.43	35.43	35.43	−483.2	−483.2	−483.2
Government	147–151	67691.	94.99	235.93	220.49	228.08	323.2	302.0	312.4
Compensation	147–150	53672.	55.31	330.95	312.82	321.76	310.2	293.2	301.6
Commodities	151–151	14019.	39.69	103.52	103.52	103.52	341.2	341.2	341.2
Gross domestic product	1–151	1327958.	1220.21	131.92	68.84	95.30	1580.9	825.0	1142.0
Aggregates									
ICP concepts[e]									
Consumption (CEP)[b,c]	1–108	824902.	877.75	131.42	86.73	106.76	1083.5	715.1	880.3
Capital formation (GCF)[d]	109–146	435366.	247.47	93.75	45.96	65.64	3827.7	1876.6	2680.2
Government (PFC)	147–151	67691.	94.99	235.93	220.49	228.08	323.2	302.0	312.4
Gross domestic product (ICP)	1–151	1327958.	1220.21	131.92	68.84	95.30	1580.9	825.0	1142.0
SNA concepts[e]									
Consumption (PFCE)	1–108	758018.	851.65	116.61	81.80	97.67	1088.1	763.3	911.3
Capital formation (GCF)	109–146	435366.	247.47	93.75	45.96	65.64	3827.7	1876.6	2680.2
Government (GFCE)	1–151	133473.	121.09	317.58	243.84	278.28	452.0	347.1	396.1
Gross domestic product (SNA)	1–151	1326856.	1220.21	131.92	68.80	95.26	1580.6	824.3	1141.5

Note: See the end of Appendix Table 7-68 for notes.

Category	Line numbers[a]	Per capita expenditures Korea (won)	Per capita expenditures India (rupees)	Purchasing power parities (won/rupees) India weight	Purchasing power parities (won/rupees) Korea weight	Purchasing power parities (won/rupees) Geometric mean	Quantity per capita (India = 100) India weight	Quantity per capita (India = 100) Korea weight	Quantity per capita (India = 100) Geometric mean
Consumption, ICP[b,c]	1–108	201823.	877.75	99.98	65.29	80.79	352.2	230.0	284.6
Food, beverages, tobacco	1– 39	109486.	565.34	100.60	69.16	83.42	280.0	192.5	232.2
Food	1– 33	90435.	531.97	104.98	84.75	94.33	200.6	161.9	180.2
Bread, cereals	1– 6	47229.	240.56	88.76	82.95	85.81	236.7	221.2	228.8
Meat	7– 12	6614.	11.23	139.76	132.94	136.31	443.1	421.4	432.1
Fish	13– 14	5582.	10.78	133.90	110.44	121.60	469.0	386.8	426.0
Milk, cheese, eggs	15– 17	3553.	57.49	89.88	73.77	81.43	83.8	68.8	75.9
Oils, fats	18– 20	756.	54.77	79.00	79.00	79.00	17.5	17.5	17.5
Fruits, vegetables	21– 26	13369.	84.64	142.13	65.70	96.63	240.4	111.1	163.5
Coffee, tea, cocoa	27– 29	416.	8.27	212.42	198.50	205.34	25.4	23.7	24.5
Spices, sweets, sugar	30– 33	12916.	64.23	127.73	96.33	110.92	208.8	157.5	181.3
Beverages	34– 37	10904.	7.68	43.52	50.92	47.08	2786.7	3260.6	3014.4
Tobacco	38– 39	8148.	25.69	26.99	26.99	26.99	1175.0	1175.0	1175.0
Clothing, footwear	40– 51	19097.	66.32	27.25	38.69	32.47	744.3	1056.9	887.0
Clothing	40– 47	17703.	61.45	24.01	38.06	30.23	756.9	1200.0	953.0
Footwear	48– 51	1393.	4.87	68.13	48.89	57.71	585.9	420.4	496.3
Gross rent, fuel	52– 57	15677.	53.80	162.11	74.07	109.58	393.4	179.7	265.9
Gross rent	52– 53	6342.	24.07	300.37	285.60	292.89	92.3	87.7	90.0
Fuel, power	54– 57	9335.	29.73	50.20	49.27	49.74	637.2	625.4	631.3
House furnishings, operations	58– 70	6323.	24.43	49.26	49.11	49.18	527.1	525.5	526.3
Furniture	58– 60	884.	3.23	35.50	42.69	38.93	640.5	770.3	702.4
Appliances	61– 66	3017.	3.50	46.92	50.77	48.81	1700.2	1839.6	1768.5
Supplies, operation	67– 70	2422.	17.70	52.24	49.81	51.01	274.7	261.9	268.2
Medical care	71– 77	7913.	28.40	130.94	100.76	114.87	276.5	212.7	242.5
Transport, communications	78– 89	13889.	57.20	96.64	69.73	82.09	348.2	251.2	295.8
Equipment	78– 79	633.	3.20	43.04	64.45	52.67	306.3	458.7	374.9
Operation costs	80– 83	32.	8.97	55.36	43.29	48.95	8.2	6.4	7.2
Purchased transport	84– 87	12339.	41.92	114.72	92.31	102.91	318.9	256.6	286.0
Communications	88– 89	885.	3.11	27.19	16.11	20.93	1766.4	1046.5	1359.6
Recreation, education	90–101	15777.	46.48	141.47	82.96	108.34	409.2	240.0	313.3
Recreation	90– 96	5775.	14.64	79.46	46.29	60.65	852.0	496.3	650.3
Education	97–101	10002.	31.83	169.99	152.93	161.23	205.5	184.8	194.9
Other expenditures	102–107	15387.	39.74	89.48	65.18	76.37	594.1	432.7	507.0
Personal care	102–104	6272.	16.06	69.44	75.94	72.62	514.4	562.5	537.9
Miscellaneous services	105–107	9114.	23.68	103.07	59.39	78.24	648.1	373.4	491.9
Capital formation	109–146	56894.	247.47	67.44	29.38	44.52	782.5	340.9	516.5
Domestic capital formation	109–145	81389.	250.72	67.32	34.48	48.18	941.4	482.2	673.8
Construction	109–122	38465.	112.55	85.43	63.73	73.79	536.2	400.0	463.1
Residential	109–110	12567.	27.59	81.20	80.00	80.60	569.5	561.0	565.2
Nonresidential	111–118	12867.	41.85	90.10	82.92	86.43	370.8	341.2	355.7
Other	119–122	13031.	43.11	83.61	44.74	61.16	675.6	361.5	494.2
Producer durables	123–144	33381.	88.08	48.36	20.90	31.79	1813.8	783.8	1192.3
Transport equipment	123–129	15248.	16.57	62.08	13.12	28.54	7012.9	1482.7	3224.6
Nonelectrical machinery	130–138	14991.	32.42	53.26	45.36	49.16	1019.4	868.2	940.8
Electrical machinery	139–142	2061.	27.00	46.53	37.13	41.56	205.6	164.1	183.7
Other	143–144	1082.	12.10	20.51	21.73	21.11	411.6	436.1	423.7
Exports minus imports	146–146	−24495.	−3.25	57.78	57.78	57.78	13060.6	13060.6	13060.6
Government	147–151	23352.	94.99	113.59	98.44	105.75	249.7	216.4	232.5
Compensation	147–150	11152.	55.31	135.02	121.86	128.27	165.5	149.3	157.2
Commodities	151–151	12201.	39.69	83.73	83.73	83.73	367.1	367.1	367.1
Gross domestic product	1–151	282070.	1220.21	94.44	53.58	71.13	431.5	244.8	325.0
Aggregates									
ICP concepts[e]									
Consumption (CEP)[b,c]	1–108	201823.	877.75	99.98	65.29	80.79	352.2	230.0	284.6
Capital formation (GCF)[d]	109–146	56894.	247.47	67.44	29.38	44.52	782.5	340.9	516.5
Government (PFC)	147–151	23352.	94.99	113.59	98.44	105.75	249.7	216.4	232.5
Gross domestic product (ICP)	1–151	282070.	1220.21	94.44	53.58	71.13	431.5	244.8	325.0
SNA concepts[e]									
Consumption (PFCE)	1–108	196131.	851.65	97.08	64.20	78.95	358.7	237.2	291.7
Capital formation (GCF)	109–146	56894.	247.47	67.44	29.38	44.52	782.5	340.9	516.5
Government (GFCE)	1–151	29044.	121.09	131.05	106.23	117.99	225.8	183.0	203.3
Gross domestic product (SNA)	1–151	282070.	1220.21	94.44	53.58	71.13	431.5	244.8	325.0

Note: See the end of Appendix Table 7-68 for notes.

Category	Line numbers[a]	Per capita expenditures Malaysia (ringgit)	India (rupees)	Purchasing power parities (ringgit/rupees) India weight	Malaysia weight	Geometric mean	Quantity per capita (India = 100) India weight	Malaysia weight	Geometric mean
Consumption, ICP[b,c]	1–108	1204.83	877.75	0.5448	0.4001	0.4669	343.1	251.9	294.0
Food, beverages, tobacco	1– 39	478.57	565.34	0.4400	0.3592	0.3976	235.7	192.4	212.9
Food	1– 33	406.31	531.97	0.4438	0.3682	0.4042	207.4	172.1	188.9
Bread, cereals	1– 6	117.42	240.56	0.4458	0.3524	0.3964	138.5	109.5	123.1
Meat	7– 12	70.70	11.23	0.7635	0.4123	0.5610	1527.2	824.7	1122.3
Fish	13– 14	47.94	10.78	0.7696	0.6421	0.7030	692.9	578.2	633.0
Milk, cheese, eggs	15– 17	49.16	57.49	0.5278	0.2974	0.3962	287.5	162.0	215.8
Oils, fats	18– 20	15.44	54.77	0.2293	0.2238	0.2266	126.0	122.9	124.4
Fruits, vegetables	21– 26	52.41	84.64	0.5090	0.3685	0.4331	168.1	121.7	143.0
Coffee, tea, cocoa	27– 29	8.53	8.27	0.4421	0.4895	0.4652	210.7	233.3	221.7
Spices, sweets, sugar	30– 33	44.70	64.23	0.3481	0.3431	0.3456	202.8	200.0	201.4
Beverages	34– 37	27.28	7.68	0.4119	0.2312	0.3086	1535.3	861.9	1150.3
Tobacco	38– 39	44.98	25.69	0.3694	0.4061	0.3873	431.1	474.1	452.1
Clothing, footwear	40– 51	70.25	66.32	0.3153	0.2793	0.2968	379.2	336.0	357.0
Clothing	40– 47	62.17	61.45	0.3197	0.2854	0.3021	354.5	316.5	334.9
Footwear	48– 51	8.08	4.87	0.2594	0.2399	0.2495	692.1	639.9	665.5
Gross rent, fuel	52– 57	122.93	53.80	1.0103	0.7254	0.8561	315.0	226.2	266.9
Gross rent	52– 53	99.09	24.07	0.8574	0.8334	0.8453	494.0	480.2	487.1
Fuel, power	54– 57	23.85	29.73	1.1341	0.4715	0.7313	170.1	70.7	109.7
House furnishings, operations	58– 70	71.35	24.43	0.3471	0.3333	0.3401	876.3	841.4	858.7
Furniture	58– 60	18.48	3.23	0.2454	0.3067	0.2743	1863.0	2328.2	2082.7
Appliances	61– 66	10.91	3.50	0.3153	0.3296	0.3224	947.1	990.2	968.4
Supplies, operation	67– 70	41.96	17.70	0.3720	0.3476	0.3596	682.0	637.3	659.3
Medical care	71– 77	50.74	28.40	0.9789	0.7203	0.8397	248.0	182.5	212.7
Transport, communications	78– 89	158.06	57.20	0.7809	0.3069	0.4896	900.3	353.8	564.4
Equipment	78– 79	36.51	3.20	0.4441	0.4717	0.4577	2415.5	2565.9	2489.5
Operation costs	80– 83	65.75	8.97	0.2123	0.2002	0.2062	3662.5	3453.5	3556.4
Purchased transport	84– 87	49.31	41.92	0.9535	0.5214	0.7051	225.6	123.4	166.8
Communications	88– 89	6.48	3.11	0.4406	0.4450	0.4428	468.3	473.0	470.6
Recreation, education	90–101	146.47	46.48	1.1576	0.6561	0.8715	480.4	272.2	361.6
Recreation	90– 96	58.35	14.64	0.5043	0.3598	0.4259	1107.5	790.2	935.5
Education	97–101	88.12	31.83	1.4582	1.4427	1.4504	191.9	189.8	190.9
Other expenditures	102–107	91.13	39.74	0.5177	0.5010	0.5093	457.7	443.0	450.3
Personal care	102–104	18.74	16.06	0.3609	0.3639	0.3624	320.7	323.4	322.0
Miscellaneous services	105–107	72.40	23.68	0.6240	0.5552	0.5886	550.7	490.0	519.4
Capital formation	109–146	446.40	247.47	0.3336	0.2633	0.2964	685.2	540.7	608.7
Domestic capital formation	109–145	437.93	250.72	0.3330	0.2629	0.2959	664.5	524.5	590.4
Construction	109–122	252.80	112.55	0.3072	0.2621	0.2838	856.9	731.1	791.5
Residential	109–110	69.07	27.59	0.3358	0.3130	0.3242	799.9	745.7	772.3
Nonresidential	111–118	79.41	41.85	0.4007	0.3649	0.3824	519.9	473.5	496.2
Other	119–122	104.32	43.11	0.1983	0.1983	0.1983	1220.4	1220.4	1220.4
Producer durables	123–144	217.09	88.08	0.3425	0.2758	0.3074	893.6	719.6	801.9
Transport equipment	123–129	52.63	16.57	0.3650	0.3556	0.3603	893.3	870.4	881.8
Nonelectrical machinery	130–138	129.69	32.42	0.3671	0.2409	0.2974	1661.0	1089.8	1345.4
Electrical machinery	139–142	27.72	27.00	0.3733	0.3940	0.3835	260.6	275.1	267.7
Other	143–144	7.05	12.10	0.1771	0.2330	0.2031	250.0	328.9	286.8
Exports minus imports	146–146	8.47	−3.25	0.2867	0.2867	0.2867	−910.3	−910.3	−910.3
Government	147–151	221.94	94.99	0.7115	0.7214	0.7164	323.9	328.4	326.1
Compensation	147–150	138.49	55.31	0.8576	0.9660	0.9101	259.2	292.0	275.1
Commodities	151–151	83.45	39.69	0.5080	0.5080	0.5080	413.9	413.9	413.9
Gross domestic product	1–151	1873.18	1220.21	0.5150	0.3735	0.4386	411.0	298.1	350.0
Aggregates									
ICP concepts[e]									
Consumption (CEP)[b,c]	1–108	1204.83	877.75	0.5448	0.4001	0.4669	343.1	251.9	294.0
Capital formation (GCF)[d]	109–146	446.40	247.47	0.3336	0.2633	0.2964	685.2	540.7	608.7
Government (PFC)	147–151	221.94	94.99	0.7115	0.7214	0.7164	323.9	328.4	326.1
Gross domestic product (ICP)	1–151	1873.18	1220.21	0.5150	0.3735	0.4386	411.0	298.1	350.0
SNA concepts[e]									
Consumption (PFCE)	1–108	1097.63	851.65	0.5154	0.3757	0.4401	343.0	250.0	292.9
Capital formation (GCF)	109–146	446.40	247.47	0.3336	0.2633	0.2964	685.2	540.7	608.7
Government (GFCE)	1–151	329.14	121.09	0.8823	0.8276	0.8545	328.4	308.1	318.1
Gross domestic product (SNA)	1–151	1873.18	1220.21	0.5150	0.3735	0.4386	411.0	298.1	350.0

Note: See the end of Appendix Table 7-68 for notes.

Category	Line numbers[a]	Per capita expenditures		Purchasing power parities (rupees/rupees)			Quantity per capita (India = 100)		
		Pakistan (rupees)	India (rupees)	India weight	Pakistan weight	Geometric mean	India weight	Pakistan weight	Geometric mean
Consumption, ICP[b,c]	1–108	1525.02	877.75	1.381	1.163	1.267	149.4	125.8	137.1
Food, beverages, tobacco	1– 39	905.51	565.34	1.174	1.067	1.119	150.1	136.5	143.1
Food	1– 33	866.27	531.97	1.187	1.092	1.138	149.2	137.2	143.1
Bread, cereals	1– 6	289.70	240.56	1.069	0.931	0.997	129.4	112.6	120.7
Meat	7– 12	52.04	11.23	1.093	1.270	1.178	365.0	424.1	393.5
Fish	13– 14	18.74	10.78	2.411	2.971	2.676	58.6	72.1	65.0
Milk, cheese, eggs	15– 17	191.39	57.49	1.241	1.185	1.213	280.9	268.2	274.5
Oils, fats	18– 20	122.36	54.77	0.882	0.998	0.938	223.9	253.3	238.1
Fruits, vegetables	21– 26	101.72	84.64	1.346	1.241	1.293	96.8	89.3	93.0
Coffee, tea, cocoa	27– 29	20.22	8.27	1.100	0.913	1.002	267.8	222.4	244.0
Spices, sweets, sugar	30– 33	70.10	64.23	1.450	1.497	1.473	72.9	75.3	74.1
Beverages	34– 37	2.12	7.68	1.412	1.412	1.412	19.6	19.6	19.6
Tobacco	38– 39	37.12	25.69	0.831	0.696	0.761	207.6	173.8	190.0
Clothing, footwear	40– 51	164.29	66.32	0.752	0.793	0.772	312.4	329.5	320.9
Clothing	40– 47	133.99	61.45	0.724	0.733	0.728	297.4	301.3	299.4
Footwear	48– 51	30.30	4.87	1.107	1.242	1.172	501.5	562.8	531.3
Gross rent, fuel	52– 57	175.85	53.80	3.226	2.714	2.959	120.4	101.3	110.5
Gross rent	52– 53	104.33	24.07	4.451	4.329	4.389	100.1	97.4	98.8
Fuel, power	54– 57	71.52	29.73	2.234	1.758	1.982	136.8	107.7	121.4
House furnishings, operations	58– 70	63.36	24.43	1.475	1.473	1.474	176.1	175.9	176.0
Furniture	58– 60	2.62	3.23	0.897	1.161	1.020	69.8	90.3	79.4
Appliances	61– 66	2.82	3.50	1.376	1.326	1.351	60.8	58.6	59.7
Supplies, operation	67– 70	57.93	17.70	1.600	1.499	1.549	218.4	204.6	211.4
Medical care	71– 77	71.95	28.40	2.435	1.907	2.155	132.8	104.0	117.5
Transport, communications	78– 89	29.38	57.20	1.653	1.113	1.356	46.1	31.1	37.9
Equipment	78– 79	0.11	3.20	2.069	2.048	2.058	1.7	1.7	1.7
Operation costs	80– 83	4.18	8.97	1.051	0.602	0.795	77.5	44.4	58.7
Purchased transport	84– 87	23.40	41.92	1.823	1.396	1.596	40.0	30.6	35.0
Communications	88– 89	1.68	3.11	0.669	0.638	0.654	84.6	80.6	82.6
Recreation, education	90–101	77.77	46.48	1.613	1.265	1.429	132.3	103.7	117.1
Recreation	90– 96	48.49	14.64	1.399	1.155	1.271	286.7	236.7	260.5
Education	97–101	29.28	31.83	1.712	1.501	1.603	61.3	53.7	57.4
Other expenditures	102–107	36.92	39.74	1.388	1.658	1.517	56.0	66.9	61.2
Personal care	102–104	15.90	16.06	1.503	1.495	1.499	66.2	65.9	66.0
Miscellaneous services	105–107	21.02	23.68	1.309	1.807	1.538	49.1	67.8	57.7
Capital formation	109–146	182.12	247.47	1.663	1.523	1.591	48.3	44.3	46.2
Domestic capital formation	109–145	324.07	250.72	1.657	1.354	1.498	95.4	78.0	86.3
Construction	109–122	200.68	112.55	1.821	1.571	1.691	113.5	97.9	105.4
Residential	109–110	37.83	27.59	1.359	1.359	1.359	100.9	100.9	100.9
Nonresidential	111–118	63.42	41.85	1.359	1.359	1.359	111.5	111.5	111.5
Other	119–122	99.43	43.11	2.564	1.867	2.188	123.6	89.9	105.4
Producer durables	123–144	123.38	88.08	1.640	1.107	1.347	126.6	85.4	104.0
Transport equipment	123–129	29.99	16.57	1.677	1.951	1.809	92.8	108.0	100.1
Nonelectrical machinery	130–138	72.67	32.42	1.339	0.947	1.126	236.6	167.5	199.1
Electrical machinery	139–142	17.09	27.00	1.330	1.031	1.171	61.4	47.6	54.1
Other	143–144	3.63	12.10	3.088	1.275	1.984	23.5	9.7	15.1
Exports minus imports	146–146	−141.94	−3.25	1.186	1.186	1.186	3688.6	3688.6	3688.6
Government	147–151	172.22	94.99	1.163	1.150	1.157	157.6	155.9	156.7
Compensation	147–150	91.52	55.31	1.072	1.050	1.061	157.6	154.3	156.0
Commodities	151–151	80.70	39.69	1.290	1.290	1.290	157.7	157.7	157.7
Gross domestic product	1–151	1879.36	1220.21	1.421	1.189	1.300	129.5	108.4	118.5
Aggregates									
ICP concepts[e]									
Consumption (CEP)[b,c]	1–108	1525.02	877.75	1.381	1.163	1.267	149.4	125.8	137.1
Capital formation (GCF)[d]	109–146	182.12	247.47	1.663	1.523	1.591	48.3	44.3	46.2
Government (PFC)	147–151	172.22	94.99	1.163	1.150	1.157	157.6	155.9	156.7
Gross domestic product (ICP)	1–151	1879.36	1220.21	1.421	1.189	1.300	129.5	108.4	118.5
SNA concepts[e]									
Consumption (PFCE)	1–108	1493.11	851.65	1.354	1.154	1.250	152.0	129.5	140.3
Capital formation (GCF)	109–146	182.12	247.47	1.663	1.523	1.591	48.3	44.3	46.2
Government (GFCE)	1–151	204.13	121.09	1.400	1.224	1.309	137.8	120.4	128.8
Gross domestic product (SNA)	1–151	1879.36	1220.21	1.421	1.189	1.300	129.5	108.4	118.5

Note: See the end of Appendix Table 7-68 for notes.

Category	Line numbers[a]	Per capita expenditures Philippines (pesos)	India (rupees)	Purchasing power parities (pesos/rupees) India weight	Philippines weight	Geometric mean	Quantity per capita (India = 100) India weight	Philippines weight	Geometric mean
Consumption, ICP[b,c]	1–108	1895.27	877.75	1.5308	1.0097	1.2432	213.9	141.0	173.7
Food, beverages, tobacco	1– 39	1154.03	565.34	1.6632	0.9868	1.2811	206.9	122.7	159.3
Food	1– 33	1025.98	531.97	1.7262	1.2017	1.4402	160.5	111.7	133.9
Bread, cereals	1– 6	350.24	240.56	1.9979	1.1070	1.4872	131.5	72.9	97.9
Meat	7– 12	189.99	11.23	2.0044	1.0783	1.4701	1569.2	844.1	1150.9
Fish	13– 14	210.43	10.78	2.4430	1.9812	2.2000	985.7	799.4	887.7
Milk, cheese, eggs	15– 17	25.65	57.49	2.0238	1.8144	1.9162	24.6	22.0	23.3
Oils, fats	18– 20	27.00	54.77	0.7302	0.7792	0.7543	63.3	67.5	65.4
Fruits, vegetables	21– 26	143.83	84.64	1.7823	1.5489	1.6615	109.7	95.3	102.3
Coffee, tea, cocoa	27– 29	17.66	8.27	5.1341	1.2239	2.5067	174.4	41.6	85.2
Spices, sweets, sugar	30– 33	61.18	64.23	0.6094	0.6185	0.6139	154.0	156.3	155.2
Beverages	34– 37	73.95	7.68	0.4118	0.2857	0.3430	3368.8	2336.9	2805.8
Tobacco	38– 39	54.10	25.69	0.7331	0.9521	0.8355	221.2	287.2	252.1
Clothing, footwear	40– 51	128.02	66.32	0.6568	0.6354	0.6460	303.8	293.9	298.8
Clothing	40– 47	110.03	61.45	0.6433	0.6094	0.6261	293.8	278.4	286.0
Footwear	48– 51	17.99	4.87	0.8281	0.8601	0.8439	430.0	446.6	438.2
Gross rent, fuel	52– 57	170.24	53.80	2.0372	1.3551	1.6615	233.5	155.3	190.4
Gross rent	52– 53	126.12	24.07	1.6147	1.5484	1.5812	338.4	324.5	331.4
Fuel, power	54– 57	44.12	29.73	2.3793	0.9988	1.5415	148.6	62.4	96.3
House furnishings, operations	58– 70	86.57	24.43	1.0360	0.9238	0.9783	383.6	342.1	362.2
Furniture	58– 60	22.58	3.23	0.6506	0.8449	0.7414	826.4	1073.2	941.8
Appliances	61– 66	18.23	3.50	1.0622	1.1588	1.1094	450.1	491.0	470.1
Supplies, operation	67– 70	45.76	17.70	1.1012	0.8929	0.9916	289.5	234.8	260.7
Medical care	71– 77	63.20	28.40	1.4551	1.4337	1.4444	155.2	152.9	154.1
Transport, communications	78– 89	39.69	57.20	0.9583	0.6184	0.7698	112.2	72.4	90.1
Equipment	78– 79	13.71	3.20	0.7206	1.2176	0.9367	351.5	594.0	457.0
Operation costs	80– 83	3.83	8.97	0.5237	0.4807	0.5017	88.8	81.5	85.1
Purchased transport	84– 87	19.06	41.92	1.0820	0.4558	0.7023	99.8	42.0	64.8
Communications	88– 89	3.09	3.11	0.7891	0.9825	0.8805	101.1	125.9	112.8
Recreation, education	90–101	133.04	46.48	1.5793	1.4725	1.5250	194.4	181.2	187.7
Recreation	90– 96	28.86	14.64	1.4688	1.1133	1.2787	177.0	134.2	154.1
Education	97–101	104.18	31.83	1.6302	1.6170	1.6236	202.4	200.8	201.6
Other expenditures	102–107	120.49	39.74	1.4809	1.3661	1.4223	222.0	204.7	213.2
Personal care	102–104	36.06	16.06	1.4005	1.2112	1.3024	185.4	160.3	172.4
Miscellaneous services	105–107	84.43	23.68	1.5355	1.4450	1.4896	246.7	232.2	239.4
Capital formation	109–146	660.48	247.47	1.7193	1.2951	1.4922	206.1	155.2	178.9
Domestic capital formation	109–145	845.52	250.72	1.7083	1.1694	1.4134	288.4	197.4	238.6
Construction	109–122	277.39	112.55	2.5038	1.5941	1.9978	154.6	98.4	123.4
Residential	109–110	95.51	27.59	2.0927	2.1205	2.1066	163.3	165.4	164.3
Nonresidential	111–118	78.46	41.85	1.7592	1.6092	1.6826	116.5	106.6	111.4
Other	119–122	103.42	43.11	3.4897	1.2893	2.1211	186.1	68.7	113.1
Producer durables	123–144	380.95	88.08	1.0265	0.9976	1.0120	433.5	421.4	427.4
Transport equipment	123–129	111.79	16.57	1.1140	1.1554	1.1345	584.0	605.8	594.8
Nonelectrical machinery	130–138	181.15	32.42	1.2877	1.0656	1.1714	524.4	434.0	477.1
Electrical machinery	139–142	59.78	27.00	0.8135	0.8113	0.8124	273.0	272.2	272.6
Other	143–144	28.24	12.10	0.6819	0.6819	0.6819	342.3	342.3	342.3
Exports minus imports	146–146	−185.04	−3.25	0.8685	0.8685	0.8685	6564.5	6564.5	6564.5
Government	147–151	179.67	94.99	1.0855	0.8970	0.9868	210.9	174.2	191.7
Compensation	147–150	96.84	55.31	0.9637	0.7210	0.8336	242.8	181.7	210.0
Commodities	151–151	82.84	39.69	1.2551	1.2551	1.2551	166.3	166.3	166.3
Gross domestic product	1–151	2735.42	1220.21	1.5344	1.0572	1.2736	212.0	146.1	176.0
Aggregates									
ICP concepts[e]									
Consumption (CEP)[b,c]	1–108	1895.27	877.75	1.5308	1.0097	1.2432	213.9	141.0	173.7
Capital formation (GCF)[d]	109–146	660.48	247.47	1.7193	1.2951	1.4922	206.1	155.2	178.9
Government (PFC)	147–151	179.67	94.99	1.0855	0.8970	0.9868	210.9	174.2	191.7
Gross domestic product (ICP)	1–151	2735.42	1220.21	1.5344	1.0572	1.2736	212.0	146.1	176.0
SNA concepts[e]									
Consumption (PFCE)	1–108	1803.48	851.65	1.5281	0.9917	1.2310	213.5	138.6	172.0
Capital formation (GCF)	109–146	660.48	247.47	1.7193	1.2951	1.4922	206.1	155.2	178.9
Government (GFCE)	1–151	260.16	121.09	1.2009	1.0356	1.1152	207.5	178.9	192.6
Gross domestic product (SNA)	1–151	2724.11	1220.21	1.5344	1.0559	1.2729	211.4	145.5	175.4

Note: See the end of Appendix Table 7-68 for notes.

Category	Line numbers[a]	Per capita expenditures — Sri Lanka (rupees)	Per capita expenditures — India (rupees)	Purchasing power parities (rupees/rupees) — India weight	Purchasing power parities (rupees/rupees) — Sri Lanka weight	Purchasing power parities (rupees/rupees) — Geometric mean	Quantity per capita (India = 100) — India weight	Quantity per capita (India = 100) — Sri Lanka weight	Quantity per capita (India = 100) — Geometric mean
Consumption, ICP[b,c]	1–108	1689.76	877.75	1.4436	1.2654	1.3515	152.1	133.4	142.4
Food, beverages, tobacco	1– 39	1161.01	565.34	1.5798	1.4029	1.4887	146.4	130.0	137.9
Food	1– 33	1022.08	531.97	1.6078	1.4509	1.5273	132.4	119.5	125.8
Bread, cereals	1– 6	521.27	240.56	1.9425	1.6279	1.7783	133.1	111.5	121.9
Meat	7– 12	17.34	11.23	1.5575	1.3433	1.4465	114.9	99.1	106.7
Fish	13– 14	48.61	10.78	1.9526	1.7611	1.8544	256.1	231.0	243.3
Milk, cheese, eggs	15– 17	45.42	57.49	0.8361	0.7902	0.8128	100.0	94.5	97.2
Oils, fats	18– 20	9.93	54.77	0.6987	0.6704	0.6844	27.0	25.9	26.5
Fruits, vegetables	21– 26	191.54	84.64	1.4716	1.2100	1.3344	187.0	153.8	169.6
Coffee, tea, cocoa	27– 29	22.15	8.27	0.7372	0.8375	0.7858	319.8	363.3	340.9
Spices, sweets, sugar	30– 33	165.83	64.23	2.0626	1.9129	1.9863	135.0	125.2	130.0
Beverages	34– 37	44.01	7.68	1.0957	1.0269	1.0607	557.8	522.8	540.0
Tobacco	38– 39	94.92	25.69	1.1460	1.1823	1.1640	312.5	322.4	317.4
Clothing, footwear	40– 51	106.85	66.32	0.7530	0.7423	0.7477	217.0	214.0	215.5
Clothing	40– 47	101.66	61.45	0.7209	0.7294	0.7251	226.8	229.5	228.1
Footwear	48– 51	5.19	4.87	1.1583	1.1382	1.1482	93.7	92.0	92.8
Gross rent, fuel	52– 57	84.10	53.80	1.0503	1.1243	1.0867	139.0	148.8	143.8
Gross rent	52– 53	51.64	24.07	1.3544	1.5226	1.4360	140.9	158.4	149.4
Fuel, power	54– 57	32.45	29.73	0.8042	0.7939	0.7990	137.5	135.7	136.6
House furnishings, operations	58– 70	48.31	24.43	1.2064	0.8832	1.0322	223.9	163.9	191.6
Furniture	58– 60	9.85	3.23	0.9556	0.8486	0.9005	359.1	318.9	338.4
Appliances	61– 66	2.22	3.50	2.5835	2.6149	2.5992	24.3	24.6	24.5
Supplies, operation	67– 70	36.23	17.70	0.9802	0.8578	0.9170	238.6	208.9	223.3
Medical care	71– 77	43.57	28.40	1.2361	1.2745	1.2551	120.4	124.1	122.2
Transport, communications	78– 89	104.33	57.20	1.5226	1.1981	1.3507	152.2	119.8	135.0
Equipment	78– 79	1.93	3.20	2.0650	2.0641	2.0645	29.1	29.1	29.1
Operation costs	80– 83	29.12	8.97	0.7848	0.8524	0.8179	381.0	413.8	397.0
Purchased transport	84– 87	65.35	41.92	1.6660	1.6400	1.6529	95.1	93.6	94.3
Communications	88– 89	7.93	3.11	1.1582	0.6536	0.8701	389.8	220.0	292.9
Recreation, education	90–101	94.40	46.48	1.3708	1.1953	1.2800	169.9	148.2	158.7
Recreation	90– 96	45.05	14.64	1.5975	1.1596	1.3610	265.3	192.6	226.0
Education	97–101	49.35	31.83	1.2665	1.2299	1.2481	126.0	122.4	124.2
Other expenditures	102–107	61.28	39.74	1.3951	1.2052	1.2967	127.9	110.5	118.9
Personal care	102–104	21.41	16.06	1.1153	1.2405	1.1762	107.5	119.6	113.4
Miscellaneous services	105–107	39.86	23.68	1.5849	1.1871	1.3717	141.8	106.2	122.7
Capital formation	109–146	141.89	247.47	1.1937	1.1431	1.1681	50.2	48.0	49.1
Domestic capital formation	109–145	288.97	250.72	1.1891	0.9669	1.0723	119.2	96.9	107.5
Construction	109–122	165.90	112.55	0.9581	0.8804	0.9184	167.4	153.8	160.5
Residential	109–110	42.90	27.59	1.3126	1.2828	1.2976	121.2	118.5	119.9
Nonresidential	111–118	51.20	41.85	0.9960	0.9449	0.9701	129.5	122.8	126.1
Other	119–122	71.80	43.11	0.6946	0.7122	0.7033	233.8	239.8	236.8
Producer durables	123–144	96.40	88.08	1.4851	1.0957	1.2757	99.9	73.7	85.8
Transport equipment	123–129	30.16	16.57	1.0303	0.9427	0.9856	193.1	176.7	184.7
Nonelectrical machinery	130–138	47.20	32.42	1.6006	1.1019	1.3280	132.1	91.0	109.6
Electrical machinery	139–142	17.93	27.00	1.5875	1.4315	1.5075	46.4	41.8	44.1
Other	143–144	1.11	12.10	1.5700	1.7757	1.6697	5.2	5.9	5.5
Exports minus imports	146–146	− 147.08	− 3.25	0.8417	0.8417	0.8417	5384.1	5384.1	5384.1
Government	147–151	125.07	94.99	0.8880	0.8625	0.8751	152.7	148.3	150.5
Compensation	147–150	78.62	55.31	1.0613	1.0746	1.0679	132.3	133.9	133.1
Commodities	151–151	46.46	39.69	0.6465	0.6465	0.6465	181.1	181.1	181.1
Gross domestic product	1–151	1956.73	1220.21	1.3496	1.2195	1.2829	131.5	118.8	125.0
Aggregates									
ICP concepts[e]									
Consumption (CEP)[b,c]	1–108	1689.76	877.75	1.4436	1.2654	1.3515	152.1	133.4	142.4
Capital formation (GCF)[d]	109–146	141.89	247.47	1.1937	1.1431	1.1681	50.2	48.0	49.1
Government (PFC)	147–151	125.07	94.99	0.8880	0.8625	0.8751	152.7	148.3	150.5
Gross domestic product (ICP)	1–151	1956.73	1220.21	1.3496	1.2195	1.2829	131.5	118.8	125.0
SNA concepts[e]									
Consumption (PFCE)	1–108	1614.48	851.65	1.4451	1.2687	1.3540	149.4	131.2	140.0
Capital formation (GCF)	109–146	141.89	247.47	1.1937	1.1431	1.1681	50.2	48.0	49.1
Government (GFCE)	1–151	200.36	121.09	0.9972	0.9641	0.9805	171.6	165.9	168.7
Gross domestic product (SNA)	1–151	1956.73	1220.21	1.3496	1.2195	1.2829	131.5	118.8	125.0

Note: See the end of Appendix Table 7-68 for notes.

Category	Line numbers[a]	Per capita expenditures Syria (pounds)	Per capita expenditures India (rupees)	Purchasing power parities (pounds/rupees) India weight	Purchasing power parities (pounds/rupees) Syria weight	Purchasing power parities (pounds/rupees) Geometric mean	Quantity per capita (India = 100) India weight	Quantity per capita (India = 100) Syria weight	Quantity per capita (India = 100) Geometric mean
Consumption, ICP[b,c]	1–108	1778.76	877.75	0.6883	0.4132	0.5333	490.4	294.4	380.0
Food, beverages, tobacco	1– 39	914.88	565.34	0.4638	0.3709	0.4148	436.3	348.9	390.2
Food	1– 33	844.98	531.97	0.4643	0.3741	0.4167	424.6	342.1	381.2
Bread, cereals	1– 6	125.92	240.56	0.4254	0.2589	0.3318	202.2	123.1	157.7
Meat	7– 12	101.03	11.23	1.6292	0.9160	1.2216	982.2	552.3	736.5
Fish	13– 14	5.85	10.78	1.2148	0.6338	0.8774	85.6	44.7	61.8
Milk, cheese, eggs	15– 17	107.15	57.49	0.3859	0.4408	0.4124	422.8	483.0	451.9
Oils, fats	18– 20	89.20	54.77	0.2658	0.2552	0.2604	638.3	612.7	625.4
Fruits, vegetables	21– 26	333.83	84.64	0.5173	0.3834	0.4454	1028.7	762.4	885.6
Coffee, tea, cocoa	27– 29	8.29	8.27	0.5257	0.6631	0.5904	151.2	190.8	169.9
Spices, sweets, sugar	30– 33	73.70	64.23	0.4419	0.4161	0.4288	275.8	259.7	267.6
Beverages	34– 37	8.29	7.68	0.4763	0.2996	0.3778	360.3	226.7	285.8
Tobacco	38– 39	61.60	25.69	0.4497	0.3426	0.3925	699.8	533.2	610.8
Clothing, footwear	40– 51	206.01	66.32	0.3383	0.3899	0.3632	796.7	918.3	855.3
Clothing	40– 47	173.10	61.45	0.3061	0.3600	0.3320	782.5	920.3	848.6
Footwear	48– 51	32.91	4.87	0.7452	0.6924	0.7183	976.9	907.7	941.6
Gross rent, fuel	52– 57	214.99	53.80	0.9741	0.3983	0.6229	1003.2	410.2	641.5
Gross rent	52– 53	127.01	24.07	1.1667	1.1276	1.1470	468.0	452.3	460.1
Fuel, power	54– 57	87.98	29.73	0.8181	0.2060	0.4105	1436.5	361.7	720.8
House furnishings, operations	58– 70	111.10	24.43	0.7366	0.5310	0.6254	856.4	617.4	727.2
Furniture	58– 60	32.09	3.23	0.6142	0.4981	0.5531	1992.0	1615.5	1793.9
Appliances	61– 66	23.93	3.50	0.5294	0.5440	0.5367	1258.5	1293.1	1275.7
Supplies, operation	67– 70	55.07	17.70	0.7998	0.5464	0.6610	569.5	389.0	470.7
Medical care	71– 77	61.06	28.40	0.7906	0.5967	0.6868	360.3	271.9	313.0
Transport, communications	78– 89	67.58	57.20	2.6655	0.5139	1.1704	229.9	44.3	100.9
Equipment	78– 79	12.92	3.20	0.1854	0.3145	0.2415	1281.8	2174.4	1669.5
Operation costs	80– 83	3.54	8.97	0.6354	0.3323	0.4595	118.7	62.1	85.8
Purchased transport	84– 87	47.46	41.92	3.4509	0.6853	1.5379	165.2	32.8	73.6
Communications	88– 89	3.67	3.11	0.4883	0.3483	0.4124	338.8	241.6	286.1
Recreation, education	90–101	109.46	46.48	0.9998	0.8994	0.9483	261.9	235.6	248.4
Recreation	90– 96	35.90	14.64	0.5657	0.6159	0.5903	398.0	433.3	415.3
Education	97–101	73.57	31.83	1.1995	1.1599	1.1795	199.2	192.7	195.9
Other expenditures	102–107	93.69	39.74	0.7430	0.4557	0.5819	517.3	317.3	405.2
Personal care	102–104	39.71	16.06	0.7468	0.5187	0.6224	476.7	331.1	397.3
Miscellaneous services	105–107	53.98	23.68	0.7405	0.4184	0.5566	544.9	307.9	409.6
Capital formation	109–146	376.67	247.47	0.6701	0.4876	0.5716	312.1	227.1	266.3
Domestic capital formation	109–145	749.80	250.72	0.6672	0.4637	0.5562	645.0	448.3	537.7
Construction	109–122	392.17	112.55	0.8829	0.6891	0.7800	505.7	394.6	446.7
Residential	109–110	114.63	27.59	0.9018	0.8469	0.8739	490.7	460.8	475.5
Nonresidential	111–118	56.30	41.85	0.7619	0.7640	0.7630	176.1	176.5	176.3
Other	119–122	221.24	43.11	0.9883	0.6144	0.7792	835.2	519.2	658.5
Producer durables	123–144	357.63	88.08	0.4722	0.3413	0.4014	1189.8	859.9	1011.5
Transport equipment	123–129	132.85	16.57	0.7228	0.4916	0.5961	1631.3	1109.6	1345.4
Nonelectrical machinery	130–138	163.45	32.42	0.3568	0.2514	0.2995	2005.4	1413.3	1683.5
Electrical machinery	139–142	42.97	27.00	0.4885	0.4843	0.4864	328.6	325.8	327.2
Other	143–144	18.36	12.10	0.4018	0.4716	0.4353	321.8	377.6	348.6
Exports minus imports	146–146	−373.13	-3.25	0.4417	0.4417	0.4417	26025.3	26025.3	26025.3
Government	147–151	500.68	94.99	1.6083	1.0177	1.2793	517.9	327.7	412.0
Compensation	147–150	217.98	55.31	2.2424	2.1402	2.1907	184.2	175.8	179.9
Commodities	151–151	282.70	39.69	0.7246	0.7246	0.7246	983.0	983.0	983.0
Gross domestic product	1–151	2656.11	1220.21	0.7563	0.4769	0.6006	456.4	287.8	362.5
Aggregates									
ICP concepts[c]									
Consumption (CEP)[b,c]	1–108	1778.76	877.75	0.6883	0.4132	0.5333	490.4	294.4	380.0
Capital formation (GCF)[d]	109–146	376.67	247.47	0.6701	0.4876	0.5716	312.1	227.1	266.3
Government (PFC)	147–151	500.68	94.99	1.6083	1.0177	1.2793	517.9	327.7	412.0
Gross domestic product (ICP)	1–151	2656.11	1220.21	0.7563	0.4769	0.6006	456.4	287.8	362.5
SNA concepts[e]									
Consumption (PFCE)	1–108	1716.07	851.65	0.6686	0.4042	0.5198	498.6	301.4	387.6
Capital formation (GCF)	109–146	376.67	247.47	0.6701	0.4876	0.5716	312.1	227.1	266.3
Government (GFCE)	1–151	563.37	121.09	1.5489	1.0227	1.2586	454.9	300.4	369.6
Gross domestic product (SNA)	1–151	2656.11	1220.21	0.7563	0.4769	0.6006	456.4	287.8	362.5

Note: See the end of Appendix Table 7-68 for notes.

Category	Line numbers[a]	Per capita expenditures Thailand (baht)	Per capita expenditures India (rupees)	Purchasing power parities (baht/rupees) India weight	Purchasing power parities (baht/rupees) Thailand weight	Purchasing power parities (baht/rupees) Geometric mean	Quantity per capita (India = 100) India weight	Quantity per capita (India = 100) Thailand weight	Quantity per capita (India = 100) Geometric mean
Consumption, ICP[b,c]	1–108	5187.1	877.75	3.826	2.564	3.132	230.5	154.4	188.7
Food, beverages, tobacco	1– 39	2670.8	565.34	3.460	2.152	2.729	219.5	136.5	173.1
Food	1– 33	2240.2	531.97	3.507	2.423	2.915	173.8	120.1	144.5
Bread, cereals	1– 6	690.4	240.56	3.082	1.501	2.151	191.3	93.1	133.5
Meat	7– 12	352.7	11.23	4.043	2.960	3.460	1060.9	776.9	907.8
Fish	13– 14	270.2	10.78	5.861	7.652	6.697	327.6	427.8	374.4
Milk, cheese, eggs	15– 17	145.0	57.49	4.282	2.667	3.379	94.6	58.9	74.6
Oils, fats	18– 20	55.9	54.77	4.235	4.147	4.191	24.6	24.1	24.4
Fruits, vegetables	21– 26	388.0	84.64	4.337	2.864	3.525	160.1	105.7	130.1
Coffee, tea, cocoa	27– 29	22.8	8.27	3.673	4.068	3.865	67.9	75.2	71.4
Spices, sweets, sugar	30– 33	315.1	64.23	2.180	3.116	2.606	157.4	225.0	188.2
Beverages	34– 37	298.3	7.68	0.897	1.082	0.985	3586.4	4328.6	3940.1
Tobacco	38– 39	132.3	25.69	3.248	3.248	3.248	158.6	158.6	158.6
Clothing, footwear	40– 51	411.4	66.32	2.319	2.153	2.235	288.1	267.5	277.6
Clothing	40– 47	386.6	61.45	2.211	2.110	2.160	298.2	284.5	291.3
Footwear	48– 51	24.8	4.87	3.687	3.173	3.420	160.7	138.3	149.1
Gross rent, fuel	52– 57	302.8	53.80	7.128	3.144	4.734	179.0	79.0	118.9
Gross rent	52– 53	154.1	24.07	13.394	7.849	10.253	81.6	47.8	62.5
Fuel, power	54– 57	148.7	29.73	2.056	1.939	1.997	257.9	243.2	250.4
House furnishings, operations	58– 70	248.9	24.43	2.796	2.546	2.668	400.1	364.4	381.8
Furniture	58– 60	55.5	3.23	2.259	1.976	2.113	868.3	759.4	812.0
Appliances	61– 66	41.3	3.50	2.682	2.531	2.605	466.7	440.5	453.4
Supplies, operation	67– 70	152.1	17.70	2.916	2.851	2.883	301.4	294.7	298.0
Medical care	71– 77	302.1	28.40	6.401	4.343	5.273	244.9	166.1	201.7
Transport, communications	78– 89	360.2	57.20	3.085	2.682	2.877	234.7	204.1	218.9
Equipment	78– 79	57.0	3.20	4.492	4.589	4.540	387.9	396.3	392.1
Operation costs	80– 83	70.0	8.97	1.588	1.415	1.499	551.3	491.2	520.4
Purchased transport	84– 87	222.1	41.92	3.347	3.275	3.311	161.8	158.3	160.1
Communications	88– 89	11.1	3.11	2.426	2.413	2.419	147.3	146.5	146.9
Recreation, education	90–101	578.0	46.48	6.655	5.280	5.928	235.5	186.9	209.8
Recreation	90– 96	293.5	14.64	5.121	4.517	4.810	443.6	391.3	416.7
Education	97–101	284.6	31.83	7.361	6.393	6.860	139.8	121.4	130.3
Other expenditures	102–107	354.7	39.74	3.503	3.511	3.507	254.2	254.8	254.5
Personal care	102–104	112.3	16.06	3.228	3.588	3.403	195.0	216.7	205.5
Miscellaneous services	105–107	242.4	23.68	3.690	3.476	3.581	294.5	277.4	285.8
Capital formation	109–146	1428.2	247.47	2.787	2.376	2.573	242.9	207.0	224.3
Domestic capital formation	109–145	1757.4	250.72	2.783	2.386	2.577	293.7	251.9	272.0
Construction	109–122	680.0	112.55	3.376	2.901	3.130	208.2	179.0	193.0
Residential	109–110	184.3	27.59	4.320	4.312	4.316	155.0	154.7	154.8
Nonresidential	111–118	314.7	41.85	4.590	3.760	4.154	200.0	163.8	181.0
Other	119–122	181.0	43.11	1.594	1.677	1.635	250.3	263.3	256.7
Producer durables	123–144	847.6	88.08	2.265	2.094	2.178	459.5	424.9	441.9
Transport equipment	123–129	243.6	16.57	2.166	2.073	2.119	709.2	678.9	693.9
Nonelectrical machinery	130–138	309.2	32.42	2.252	2.035	2.141	468.8	423.5	445.6
Electrical machinery	139–142	107.7	27.00	2.340	2.638	2.485	151.2	170.5	160.6
Other	143–144	187.1	12.10	2.265	1.981	2.118	780.9	683.0	730.3
Exports minus imports	146–146	− 329.1	− 3.25	2.433	2.433	2.433	4168.1	4168.1	4168.1
Government	147–151	522.8	94.99	4.063	4.036	4.050	136.3	135.4	135.9
Compensation	147–150	293.3	55.31	4.505	4.658	4.581	113.9	117.7	115.8
Commodities	151–151	229.5	39.69	3.448	3.448	3.448	167.7	167.7	167.7
Gross domestic product	1–151	7138.0	1220.21	3.634	2.592	3.069	225.7	161.0	190.6
Aggregates									
ICP concepts[e]									
Consumption (CEP)[b,c]	1–108	5187.1	877.75	3.826	2.564	3.132	230.5	154.4	188.7
Capital formation (GCF)[d]	109–146	1428.2	247.47	2.787	2.376	2.573	242.9	207.0	224.3
Government (PFC)	147–151	522.8	94.99	4.063	4.036	4.050	136.3	135.4	135.9
Gross domestic product (ICP)	1–151	7138.0	1220.21	3.634	2.592	3.069	225.7	161.0	190.6
SNA concepts[e]									
Consumption (PFCE)	1–108	4970.3	851.65	3.691	2.497	3.036	233.7	158.1	192.3
Capital formation (GCF)	109–146	1428.2	247.47	2.787	2.376	2.573	242.9	207.0	224.3
Government (GFCE)	1–151	739.5	121.09	4.967	4.564	4.761	133.8	123.0	128.3
Gross domestic product (SNA)	1–151	7138.0	1220.21	3.634	2.592	3.069	225.7	161.0	190.6

Note: See the end of Appendix Table 7-68 for notes.

Appendix Table 7-45. Augmented Summary Binary Table: Belgium/Austria, 1975

Category	Line numbers[a]	Per capita expenditures Belgium (francs)	Per capita expenditures Austria (schillings)	Purchasing power parities (francs/schillings) Austria weight	Purchasing power parities (francs/schillings) Belgium weight	Purchasing power parities (francs/schillings) Geometric mean	Quantity per capita (Austria = 100) Austria weight	Quantity per capita (Austria = 100) Belgium weight	Quantity per capita (Austria = 100) Geometric mean
Consumption, ICP[b,c]	1–108	152538.6	55940.8	2.652	2.391	2.518	114.0	102.8	108.3
Food, beverages, tobacco	1– 39	34401.6	13873.4	2.225	2.015	2.117	123.1	111.4	117.1
Food	1– 33	28668.2	9957.3	2.213	1.999	2.104	144.0	130.1	136.9
Bread, cereals	1– 6	3630.7	1294.0	2.184	2.130	2.157	131.7	128.5	130.1
Meat	7– 12	11250.5	3098.7	2.019	1.734	1.871	209.4	179.9	194.1
Fish	13– 14	1214.6	147.9	2.589	2.564	2.576	320.4	317.3	318.8
Milk, cheese, eggs	15– 17	3101.6	1467.8	2.248	2.297	2.272	92.0	94.0	93.0
Oils, fats	18– 20	1957.7	694.7	2.357	2.307	2.332	122.1	119.6	120.8
Fruits, vegetables	21– 26	4360.2	1936.6	2.556	2.320	2.435	97.1	88.1	92.5
Coffee, tea, cocoa	27– 29	870.7	244.9	1.918	1.942	1.930	183.0	185.3	184.2
Spices, sweets, sugar	30– 33	2282.3	1072.7	2.066	1.994	2.030	106.7	103.0	104.8
Beverages	34– 37	3150.4	2707.3	2.422	2.314	2.367	50.3	48.0	49.2
Tobacco	38– 39	2583.0	1208.8	1.882	1.882	1.882	113.6	113.6	113.6
Clothing, footwear	40– 51	11738.8	6078.5	2.914	2.792	2.853	69.2	66.3	67.7
Clothing	40– 47	9916.3	5059.6	2.868	2.740	2.803	71.5	68.3	69.9
Footwear	48– 51	1822.5	1018.9	3.145	3.113	3.129	57.5	56.9	57.2
Gross rent, fuel	52– 57	22203.2	6743.4	3.694	3.283	3.482	100.3	89.1	94.6
Gross rent	52– 53	13937.9	4641.0	4.258	4.602	4.427	65.3	70.5	67.8
Fuel, power	54– 57	8265.4	2102.4	2.449	2.213	2.328	177.7	160.6	168.9
House furnishings, operations	58– 70	17559.8	4898.8	2.230	2.093	2.160	171.3	160.7	165.9
Furniture	58– 60	6675.5	2614.4	1.935	1.603	1.761	159.3	132.0	145.0
Appliances	61– 66	2315.6	1102.3	2.506	2.553	2.529	82.3	83.8	83.1
Supplies, operation	67– 70	8568.7	1182.2	2.628	2.582	2.605	280.8	275.8	278.3
Medical care	71– 77	12290.3	5603.6	2.228	2.151	2.189	102.0	98.5	100.2
Transport, communications	78– 89	15936.4	7383.0	2.308	1.927	2.109	112.0	93.5	102.4
Equipment	78– 79	5056.3	1583.8	1.638	1.609	1.623	198.4	194.9	196.7
Operation costs	80– 83	8009.2	4142.3	1.938	1.913	1.926	101.1	99.8	100.4
Purchased transport	84– 87	1722.9	1014.6	2.956	2.634	2.790	64.5	57.5	60.9
Communications	88– 89	1148.0	642.3	5.323	4.005	4.617	44.6	33.6	38.7
Recreation, education	90–101	20373.5	6332.4	2.924	3.022	2.973	106.5	110.0	108.2
Recreation	90– 96	7656.1	3400.3	2.267	2.310	2.288	97.5	99.3	98.4
Education	97–101	12717.5	2932.2	3.686	3.711	3.699	116.9	117.7	117.3
Other expenditures	102–107	18034.9	8819.0	2.710	2.721	2.715	75.2	75.5	75.3
Personal care	102–104	4065.8	1658.1	2.886	2.344	2.601	104.6	85.0	94.3
Miscellaneous services	105–107	13969.1	7160.9	2.669	2.855	2.760	68.3	73.1	70.7
Capital formation	109–146	53393.9	23300.7	2.111	1.794	1.946	127.8	108.5	117.8
Domestic capital formation	109–145	50894.2	22739.5	2.111	1.781	1.939	125.7	106.0	115.4
Construction	109–122	32412.2	14379.1	2.069	1.676	1.862	134.5	109.0	121.1
Residential	109–110	13178.8	5183.2	1.706	1.656	1.681	153.5	149.0	151.3
Nonresidential	111–118	13323.4	5484.0	2.646	2.043	2.325	118.9	91.8	104.5
Other	119–122	5910.0	3711.8	1.721	1.217	1.447	130.8	92.5	110.0
Producer durables	123–144	19740.2	8942.8	2.182	2.007	2.093	110.0	101.2	105.5
Transport equipment	123–129	4318.6	1460.1	1.787	2.139	1.955	138.3	165.6	151.3
Nonelectrical machinery	130–138	8819.1	4683.6	2.086	1.903	1.992	99.0	90.2	94.5
Electrical machinery	139–142	5272.0	1936.3	2.901	2.174	2.511	125.2	93.9	108.4
Other	143–144	1330.5	862.8	1.754	1.763	1.758	87.5	87.9	87.7
Exports minus imports	146–146	2499.7	561.2	2.112	2.112	2.112	210.9	210.9	210.9
Government	147–151	25706.3	8026.6	2.878	2.848	2.863	112.4	111.3	111.9
Compensation	147–150	18271.4	6157.3	2.994	3.021	3.008	98.2	99.1	98.7
Commodities	151–151	7434.9	1869.3	2.497	2.497	2.497	159.3	159.3	159.3
Gross domestic product	1–151	231638.8	87268.1	2.528	2.528	2.389	117.5	105.0	111.1
Aggregates									
ICP concepts[e]									
Consumption (CEP)[b,c]	1–108	152538.6	55940.8	2.652	2.391	2.518	114.0	102.8	108.3
Capital formation (GCF)[d]	109–146	53393.9	23300.7	2.111	1.794	1.946	127.8	108.5	117.8
Government (PFC)	147–151	25706.3	8026.6	2.878	2.848	2.863	112.4	111.3	111.9
Gross domestic product (ICP)	1–151	231638.8	87268.1	2.528	2.258	2.389	117.5	105.0	111.1
SNA concepts[e]									
Consumption (PFCE)	1–108	139736.0	48900.9	2.630	2.314	2.467	123.5	108.7	115.8
Capital formation (GCF)	109–146	53393.9	23300.7	2.111	1.794	1.946	127.8	108.5	117.8
Government (GFCE)	1–151	38127.2	15066.5	2.844	3.089	2.964	81.9	89.0	85.4
Gross domestic product (SNA)	1–151	231257.1	87268.1	2.528	2.256	2.388	117.5	104.8	111.0

Note: See the end of Appendix Table 7-68 for notes.

Category	Line numbers[a]	Per capita expenditures		Purchasing power parities (kroner/schillings)			Quantity per capita (Austria = 100)		
		Denmark (kroner)	Austria (schillings)	Austria weight	Denmark weight	Geometric mean	Austria weight	Denmark weight	Geometric mean
Consumption, ICP[b,c]	1–108	28212.05	55940.8	0.5085	0.4429	0.4746	113.9	99.2	106.3
Food, beverages, tobacco	1– 39	6627.47	13873.4	0.5598	0.4573	0.5059	104.5	85.3	94.4
Food	1– 33	4452.77	9957.3	0.4833	0.3819	0.4296	117.1	92.5	104.1
Bread, cereals	1– 6	595.26	1294.0	0.4225	0.4077	0.4150	112.8	108.9	110.8
Meat	7– 12	1362.45	3098.7	0.4157	0.2866	0.3452	153.4	105.8	127.4
Fish	13– 14	208.89	147.9	0.4955	0.4963	0.4959	284.6	285.1	284.9
Milk, cheese, eggs	15– 17	544.66	1467.8	0.4048	0.4125	0.4086	89.9	91.7	90.8
Oils, fats	18– 20	248.02	694.7	0.4958	0.4419	0.4681	80.8	72.0	76.3
Fruits, vegetables	21– 26	574.90	1936.6	0.6573	0.5688	0.6114	52.2	45.2	48.6
Coffee, tea, cocoa	27– 29	272.53	244.9	0.3984	0.3867	0.3925	287.7	279.3	283.5
Spices, sweets, sugar	30– 33	646.05	1072.7	0.5548	0.4526	0.5011	133.1	108.6	120.2
Beverages	34– 37	1237.75	2707.3	0.6927	0.6939	0.6933	65.9	66.0	65.9
Tobacco	38– 39	936.96	1208.8	0.8924	0.8924	0.8924	86.9	86.9	86.9
Clothing, footwear	40– 51	1510.67	6078.5	0.5006	0.4973	0.4989	50.0	49.6	49.8
Clothing	40– 47	1283.20	5059.6	0.4843	0.4844	0.4843	52.4	52.4	52.4
Footwear	48– 51	227.47	1018.9	0.5816	0.5850	0.5833	38.2	38.4	38.3
Gross rent, fuel	52– 57	5515.61	6743.4	0.4520	0.4353	0.4436	187.9	181.0	184.4
Gross rent	52– 53	4038.54	4641.0	0.5029	0.5147	0.5087	169.1	173.0	171.1
Fuel, power	54– 57	1477.07	2102.4	0.3396	0.3062	0.3225	229.5	206.9	217.9
House furnishings, operations	58– 70	2162.25	4898.8	0.3908	0.3575	0.3738	123.5	113.0	118.1
Furniture	58– 60	1002.57	2614.4	0.3161	0.3040	0.3100	126.1	121.3	123.7
Appliances	61– 66	297.23	1102.3	0.4836	0.4080	0.4442	66.1	55.8	60.7
Supplies, operation	67– 70	862.45	1182.2	0.4694	0.4265	0.4474	171.0	155.4	163.1
Medical care	71– 77	1453.75	5603.6	0.2972	0.2693	0.2829	96.3	87.3	91.7
Transport, communications	78– 89	3359.09	7383.0	0.4221	0.3717	0.3961	122.4	107.8	114.9
Equipment	78– 79	1050.59	1583.8	0.5765	0.5739	0.5752	115.6	115.1	115.3
Operation costs	80– 83	1646.64	4142.3	0.3041	0.2893	0.2966	137.4	130.7	134.0
Purchased transport	84– 87	423.52	1014.6	0.6113	0.5498	0.5797	75.9	68.3	72.0
Communications	88– 89	238.34	642.3	0.5032	0.3199	0.4013	116.0	73.7	92.5
Recreation, education	90–101	5446.24	6332.4	0.6505	0.6022	0.6259	142.8	132.2	137.4
Recreation	90– 96	2007.90	3400.3	0.4653	0.4522	0.4587	130.6	126.9	128.7
Education	97–101	3438.34	2932.2	0.8653	0.7469	0.8039	157.0	135.5	145.9
Other expenditures	102–107	2136.96	8819.0	0.5699	0.5391	0.5543	44.9	42.5	43.7
Personal care	102–104	600.20	1658.1	0.6443	0.5597	0.6005	64.7	56.2	60.3
Miscellaneous services	105–107	1536.76	7160.9	0.5527	0.5315	0.5420	40.4	38.8	39.6
Capital formation	109–146	8209.49	23300.7	0.3499	0.2587	0.3009	136.2	100.7	117.1
Domestic capital formation	109–145	8771.54	22739.5	0.3504	0.2623	0.3032	147.1	110.1	127.2
Construction	109–122	6300.39	14379.1	0.3371	0.2546	0.2930	172.1	130.0	149.6
Residential	109–110	2917.00	5183.2	0.2654	0.2661	0.2657	211.5	212.1	211.8
Nonresidential	111–118	2346.24	5484.0	0.4734	0.3011	0.3775	142.1	90.4	113.3
Other	119–122	1037.15	3711.8	0.2360	0.1731	0.2021	161.4	118.4	138.2
Producer durables	123–144	3061.66	8942.8	0.3755	0.3018	0.3366	113.4	91.2	101.7
Transport equipment	123–129	1000.40	1460.1	0.4723	0.3420	0.4019	200.3	145.1	170.5
Nonelectrical machinery	130–138	1343.28	4683.6	0.3217	0.2832	0.3018	101.3	89.2	95.0
Electrical machinery	139–142	394.27	1936.3	0.4765	0.2787	0.3644	73.0	42.7	55.9
Other	143–144	323.72	862.8	0.2770	0.3047	0.2905	123.1	135.5	129.2
Exports minus imports	146–146	− 562.06	561.2	0.3299	0.3299	0.3299	− 303.6	− 303.6	− 303.6
Government	147–151	6665.61	8026.6	0.4247	0.4378	0.4312	189.7	195.5	192.6
Compensation	147–150	5513.44	6157.3	0.4265	0.4421	0.4342	202.6	210.0	206.2
Commodities	151–151	1152.17	1869.3	0.4187	0.4187	0.4187	147.2	147.2	147.2
Gross domestic product	1–151	43087.15	87268.1	0.4585	0.3894	0.4225	126.8	107.7	116.9
Aggregates									
ICP concepts[e]									
Consumption (CEP)[b,c]	1–108	28212.05	55940.8	0.5085	0.4429	0.4746	113.9	99.2	106.3
Capital formation (GCF)[d]	109–146	8209.49	23300.7	0.3499	0.2587	0.3009	136.2	100.7	117.1
Government (PFC)	147–151	6665.61	8026.6	0.4247	0.4378	0.4312	189.7	195.5	192.6
Gross domestic product (ICP)	1–151	43087.15	87268.1	0.4585	0.3894	0.4225	126.8	107.7	116.9
SNA concepts[e]									
Consumption (PFCE)	1–108	23251.18	48900.9	0.4985	0.4343	0.4653	109.5	95.4	102.2
Capital formation (GCF)	109–146	8209.49	23300.7	0.3499	0.2587	0.3009	136.2	100.7	117.1
Government (GFCE)	1–151	11483.99	15066.5	0.4965	0.4578	0.4768	166.5	153.5	159.9
Gross domestic product (SNA)	1–151	42944.66	87268.1	0.4585	0.3891	0.4224	126.5	107.3	116.5

Note: See the end of Appendix Table 7-68 for notes.

Category	Line numbers[a]	Per capita expenditures		Purchasing power parities (francs/schillings)			Quantity per capita (Austria = 100)		
		France (francs)	Austria (schillings)	Austria weight	France weight	Geometric mean	Austria weight	France weight	Geometric mean
Consumption, ICP[b,c]	1–108	18015.41	55940.8	0.3136	0.2773	0.2949	116.1	102.7	109.2
Food, beverages, tobacco	1– 39	4118.37	13873.4	0.2719	0.2643	0.2680	112.3	109.2	110.8
Food	1– 33	3402.35	9957.3	0.2786	0.2747	0.2767	124.4	122.6	123.5
Bread, cereals	1– 6	434.94	1294.0	0.2591	0.2520	0.2556	133.4	129.7	131.5
Meat	7– 12	1162.09	3098.7	0.2638	0.2807	0.2721	133.6	142.1	137.8
Fish	13– 14	181.37	147.9	0.3296	0.3114	0.3204	393.9	372.1	382.9
Milk, cheese, eggs	15– 17	451.83	1467.8	0.2463	0.2538	0.2500	121.3	125.0	123.1
Oils, fats	18– 20	211.02	694.7	0.3219	0.2846	0.3026	106.7	94.4	100.4
Fruits, vegetables	21– 26	578.22	1936.6	0.3296	0.2962	0.3124	100.8	90.6	95.6
Coffee, tea, cocoa	27– 29	85.67	244.9	0.2143	0.2126	0.2134	164.5	163.2	163.9
Spices, sweets, sugar	30– 33	297.21	1072.7	0.2768	0.2805	0.2786	98.8	100.1	99.4
Beverages	34– 37	525.54	2707.3	0.2706	0.2257	0.2471	86.0	71.7	78.6
Tobacco	38– 39	190.49	1208.8	0.2188	0.2188	0.2188	72.0	72.0	72.0
Clothing, footwear	40– 51	1344.15	6078.5	0.3933	0.3930	0.3931	56.3	56.2	56.2
Clothing	40– 47	1090.32	5059.6	0.3798	0.3805	0.3801	56.6	56.7	56.7
Footwear	48– 51	253.83	1018.9	0.4604	0.4574	0.4589	54.5	54.1	54.3
Gross rent, fuel	52– 57	2579.21	6743.4	0.4003	0.4059	0.4031	94.2	95.6	94.9
Gross rent	52– 53	1951.51	4641.0	0.4583	0.4824	0.4702	87.2	91.8	89.4
Fuel, power	54– 57	627.70	2102.4	0.2722	0.2720	0.2721	109.8	109.7	109.7
House furnishings, operations	58– 70	1796.58	4898.8	0.2699	0.2460	0.2577	149.1	135.9	142.3
Furniture	58– 60	776.64	2614.4	0.2306	0.1896	0.2091	156.7	128.8	142.1
Appliances	61– 66	240.84	1102.3	0.3115	0.3277	0.3195	66.7	70.1	68.4
Supplies, operation	67– 70	779.10	1182.2	0.3180	0.3153	0.3167	209.0	207.2	208.1
Medical care	71– 77	1903.94	5603.6	0.3104	0.2440	0.2752	139.2	109.5	123.4
Transport, communications	78– 89	2055.79	7383.0	0.2631	0.1978	0.2281	140.8	105.8	122.1
Equipment	78– 79	481.80	1583.8	0.2563	0.2588	0.2576	117.5	118.7	118.1
Operation costs	80– 83	1142.94	4142.3	0.2210	0.1650	0.1910	167.2	124.8	144.5
Purchased transport	84– 87	304.86	1014.6	0.3158	0.2379	0.2741	126.3	95.1	109.6
Communications	88– 89	126.18	642.3	0.4677	0.3899	0.4270	50.4	42.0	46.0
Recreation, education	90–101	2112.63	6332.4	0.3189	0.3109	0.3149	107.3	104.6	106.0
Recreation	90– 96	1098.79	3400.3	0.2940	0.2771	0.2854	116.6	109.9	113.2
Education	97–101	1013.84	2932.2	0.3478	0.3582	0.3530	96.5	99.4	98.0
Other expenditures	102–107	2104.74	8819.0	0.2936	0.2877	0.2906	82.9	81.3	82.1
Personal care	102–104	577.44	1658.1	0.3615	0.3538	0.3576	98.4	96.3	97.4
Miscellaneous services	105–107	1527.30	7160.9	0.2779	0.2688	0.2733	79.4	76.8	78.0
Capital formation	109–146	6530.31	23300.7	0.2408	0.1907	0.2143	147.0	116.4	130.8
Domestic capital formation	109–145	6341.26	22739.5	0.2407	0.1894	0.2135	147.2	115.9	130.6
Construction	109–122	4038.56	14379.1	0.2335	0.1747	0.2020	160.8	120.3	139.1
Residential	109–110	2094.22	5183.2	0.1636	0.1649	0.1643	244.9	247.0	246.0
Nonresidential	111–118	1309.41	5484.0	0.3299	0.2421	0.2826	98.6	72.4	84.5
Other	119–122	634.92	3711.8	0.1887	0.1266	0.1546	135.1	90.6	110.7
Producer durables	123–144	2371.77	8942.8	0.2531	0.2232	0.2377	118.8	104.8	111.6
Transport equipment	123–129	559.43	1460.1	0.2491	0.2282	0.2384	167.9	153.8	160.7
Nonelectrical machinery	130–138	1440.04	4683.6	0.2485	0.2249	0.2364	136.7	123.7	130.0
Electrical machinery	139–142	240.01	1936.3	0.2973	0.2266	0.2595	54.7	41.7	47.8
Other	143–144	132.29	862.8	0.1858	0.1854	0.1856	82.7	82.5	82.6
Exports minus imports	146–146	189.05	561.2	0.2461	0.2461	0.2461	136.9	136.9	136.9
Government	147–151	3009.19	8026.6	0.2791	0.2740	0.2766	136.8	134.3	135.6
Compensation	147–150	1969.44	6157.3	0.2810	0.2746	0.2778	116.5	113.8	115.2
Commodities	151–151	1039.76	1869.3	0.2729	0.2729	0.2729	203.8	203.8	203.8
Gross domestic product	1–151	27554.92	87268.1	0.2910	0.2501	0.2697	126.3	108.5	117.1
Aggregates									
ICP concepts[e]									
Consumption (CEP)[b,c]	1–108	18015.41	55940.8	0.3136	0.2773	0.2949	116.1	102.7	109.2
Capital formation (GCF)[d]	109–146	6530.31	23300.7	0.2408	0.1907	0.2143	147.0	116.4	130.8
Government (PFC)	147–151	3009.19	8026.6	0.2791	0.2740	0.2766	136.8	134.3	135.6
Gross domestic product (ICP)	1–151	27554.92	87268.1	0.2910	0.2501	0.2697	126.3	108.5	117.1
SNA concepts[e]									
Consumption (PFCE)	1–108	16991.35	48900.9	0.3105	0.2733	0.2913	127.1	111.9	119.3
Capital formation (GCF)	109–146	6530.31	23300.7	0.2408	0.1907	0.2143	147.0	116.4	130.8
Government (GFCE)	1–151	3976.97	15066.5	0.3052	0.2909	0.2980	90.7	86.5	88.6
Gross domestic product (SNA)	1–151	27498.63	87268.1	0.2910	0.2498	0.2696	126.1	108.3	116.9

Note: See the end of Appendix Table 7-68 for notes.

Category	Line numbers[a]	Per capita expenditures Germany (DM)	Per capita expenditures Austria (schillings)	Purchasing power parities (DM/schillings) Austria weight	Purchasing power parities (DM/schillings) Germany weight	Purchasing power parities (DM/schillings) Geometric mean	Quantity per capita (Austria = 100) Austria weight	Quantity per capita (Austria = 100) Germany weight	Quantity per capita (Austria = 100) Geometric mean
Consumption, ICP[b,c]	1–108	10845.56	55940.8	0.1904	0.1736	0.1818	111.7	101.8	106.6
Food, beverages, tobacco	1– 39	2164.81	13873.4	0.1868	0.1671	0.1766	93.4	83.6	88.3
Food	1– 33	1650.05	9957.3	0.1717	0.1558	0.1636	106.3	96.5	101.3
Bread, cereals	1– 6	297.95	1294.0	0.1760	0.1755	0.1758	131.2	130.8	131.0
Meat	7– 12	439.68	3098.7	0.1657	0.1223	0.1423	116.1	85.6	99.7
Fish	13– 14	25.80	147.9	0.1920	0.1746	0.1831	99.9	90.9	95.3
Milk, cheese, eggs	15– 17	189.23	1467.8	0.1652	0.1662	0.1657	77.5	78.0	77.8
Oils, fats	18– 20	161.88	694.7	0.1739	0.1724	0.1732	135.1	134.0	134.6
Fruits, vegetables	21– 26	250.43	1936.6	0.1801	0.1642	0.1719	78.8	71.8	75.2
Coffee, tea, cocoa	27– 29	129.66	244.9	0.2080	0.2086	0.2083	253.8	254.5	254.1
Spices, sweets, sugar	30– 33	155.41	1072.7	0.1652	0.1682	0.1667	86.1	87.7	86.9
Beverages	34– 37	319.87	2707.3	0.2336	0.2251	0.2293	52.5	50.6	51.5
Tobacco	38– 39	194.89	1208.8	0.2056	0.2056	0.2056	78.4	78.4	78.4
Clothing, footwear	40– 51	940.40	6078.5	0.1757	0.1778	0.1768	87.0	88.0	87.5
Clothing	40– 47	786.69	5059.6	0.1721	0.1768	0.1744	88.0	90.3	89.1
Footwear	48– 51	153.71	1018.9	0.1935	0.1833	0.1883	82.3	78.0	80.1
Gross rent, fuel	52– 57	1587.28	6743.4	0.2567	0.2462	0.2514	95.6	91.7	93.6
Gross rent	52– 53	1177.59	4641.0	0.3038	0.3136	0.3087	80.9	83.5	82.2
Fuel, power	54– 57	409.69	2102.4	0.1527	0.1522	0.1525	128.0	127.6	127.8
House furnishings, operations	58– 70	1045.61	4898.8	0.1535	0.1446	0.1490	147.6	139.0	143.2
Furniture	58– 60	444.95	2614.4	0.1426	0.1236	0.1328	137.7	119.4	128.2
Appliances	61– 66	155.70	1102.3	0.1582	0.1544	0.1563	91.5	89.3	90.4
Supplies, operation	67– 70	444.95	1182.2	0.1733	0.1697	0.1715	221.7	217.2	219.5
Medical care	71– 77	1371.48	5603.6	0.2084	0.1909	0.1994	128.2	117.4	122.7
Transport, communications	78– 89	1321.35	7383.0	0.1483	0.1368	0.1424	130.8	120.7	125.6
Equipment	78– 79	331.28	1583.8	0.1176	0.1186	0.1181	176.4	177.9	177.2
Operation costs	80– 83	628.41	4142.3	0.1206	0.1180	0.1193	128.5	125.8	127.2
Purchased transport	84– 87	196.02	1014.6	0.2246	0.2114	0.2179	91.4	86.0	88.7
Communications	88– 89	165.63	642.3	0.2822	0.2704	0.2763	95.4	91.4	93.3
Recreation, education	90–101	1398.08	6332.4	0.1924	0.1809	0.1865	122.1	114.8	118.4
Recreation	90– 96	731.78	3400.3	0.1465	0.1491	0.1478	144.3	146.9	145.6
Education	97–101	666.31	2932.2	0.2456	0.2362	0.2409	96.2	92.5	94.3
Other expenditures	102–107	1016.55	8819.0	0.1773	0.1697	0.1735	67.9	65.0	66.4
Personal care	102–104	237.02	1658.1	0.2166	0.1969	0.2065	72.6	66.0	69.2
Miscellaneous services	105–107	779.52	7160.9	0.1682	0.1629	0.1655	66.8	64.7	65.8
Capital formation	109–146	4064.03	23300.7	0.1408	0.1115	0.1253	156.5	123.8	139.2
Domestic capital formation	109–145	3448.95	22739.5	0.1408	0.1074	0.1230	141.2	107.7	123.3
Construction	109–122	2099.53	14379.1	0.1377	0.0958	0.1148	152.5	106.1	127.2
Residential	109–110	863.58	5183.2	0.1259	0.1222	0.1240	136.4	132.3	134.3
Nonresidential	111–118	441.62	5484.0	0.1757	0.1385	0.1560	58.2	45.8	51.6
Other	119–122	794.34	3711.8	0.0978	0.0681	0.0816	314.4	218.7	262.2
Producer durables	123–144	1370.44	8942.8	0.1465	0.1328	0.1395	115.4	104.6	109.8
Transport equipment	123–129	290.53	1460.1	0.1202	0.1108	0.1154	179.6	165.5	172.4
Nonelectrical machinery	130–138	558.41	4683.6	0.1445	0.1299	0.1370	91.8	82.5	87.0
Electrical machinery	139–142	420.34	1936.3	0.1775	0.1585	0.1677	137.0	122.3	129.4
Other	143–144	101.17	862.8	0.1326	0.1365	0.1346	85.9	88.4	87.1
Exports minus imports	146–146	615.08	561.2	0.1413	0.1413	0.1413	775.9	775.9	775.9
Government	147–151	1814.50	8026.6	0.1776	0.1749	0.1762	129.3	127.3	128.3
Compensation	147–150	1419.61	6157.3	0.1826	0.1791	0.1808	128.7	126.3	127.5
Commodities	151–151	394.90	1869.3	0.1613	0.1613	0.1613	131.0	131.0	131.0
Gross domestic product	1–151	16724.10	87268.1	0.1760	0.1530	0.1641	125.3	108.9	116.8
Aggregates									
ICP concepts[e]									
Consumption (CEP)[b,c]	1–108	10845.56	55940.8	0.1904	0.1736	0.1818	111.7	101.8	106.6
Capital formation (GCF)[d]	109–146	4064.03	23300.7	0.1408	0.1115	0.1253	156.5	123.8	139.2
Government (PFC)	147–151	1814.50	8026.6	0.1776	0.1749	0.1762	129.3	127.3	128.3
Gross domestic product (ICP)	1–151	16724.10	87268.1	0.1760	0.1530	0.1641	125.3	108.9	116.8
SNA concepts[e]									
Consumption (PFCE)	1–108	10225.54	48900.9	0.1848	0.1706	0.1776	122.6	113.1	117.8
Capital formation (GCF)	109–146	4064.03	23300.7	0.1408	0.1115	0.1253	156.5	123.8	139.2
Government (GFCE)	1–151	2420.77	15066.5	0.2017	0.1879	0.1947	85.5	79.6	82.5
Gross domestic product (SNA)	1–151	16710.35	87268.1	0.1760	0.1529	0.1641	125.2	108.8	116.7

Note: See the end of Appendix Table 7-68 for notes.

Category	Line numbers[a]	Per capita expenditures		Purchasing power parities (forint/schillings)			Quantity per capita (Austria = 100)		
		Hungary (forint)	Austria (schillings)	Austria weight	Hungary weight	Geometric mean	Austria weight	Hungary weight	Geometric mean
Consumption, ICP[b,c]	1–108	26761.1	55940.8	0.803	0.646	0.720	74.1	59.6	66.4
Food, beverages, tobacco	1– 39	9798.6	13873.4	0.928	0.830	0.878	85.1	76.1	80.5
Food	1– 33	7049.9	9957.3	0.852	0.766	0.808	92.5	83.1	87.6
Bread, cereals	1– 6	777.7	1294.0	0.514	0.367	0.434	163.7	117.0	138.4
Meat	7– 12	2008.5	3098.7	0.633	0.669	0.651	96.8	102.3	99.5
Fish	13– 14	62.0	147.9	1.112	0.581	0.803	72.3	37.7	52.2
Milk, cheese, eggs	15– 17	948.1	1467.8	0.970	0.994	0.982	65.0	66.6	65.8
Oils, fats	18– 20	565.5	694.7	0.998	1.162	1.077	70.0	81.6	75.6
Fruits, vegetables	21– 26	1241.5	1936.6	1.047	0.939	0.992	68.2	61.2	64.6
Coffee, tea, cocoa	27– 29	389.2	244.9	1.741	1.777	1.759	89.4	91.3	90.3
Spices, sweets, sugar	30– 33	1057.2	1072.7	1.048	1.056	1.052	93.3	94.0	93.7
Beverages	34– 37	2152.9	2707.3	1.326	1.358	1.342	58.6	60.0	59.3
Tobacco	38– 39	595.8	1208.8	0.655	0.592	0.623	83.2	75.2	79.1
Clothing, footwear	40– 51	2850.3	6078.5	1.066	1.019	1.042	46.0	44.0	45.0
Clothing	40– 47	2330.9	5059.6	1.073	1.011	1.042	45.5	42.9	44.2
Footwear	48– 51	519.4	1018.9	1.034	1.054	1.044	48.4	49.3	48.8
Gross rent, fuel	52– 57	1985.2	6743.4	0.975	0.646	0.794	45.6	30.2	37.1
Gross rent	52– 53	1117.7	4641.0	1.093	0.807	0.939	29.9	22.0	25.7
Fuel, power	54– 57	867.5	2102.4	0.716	0.514	0.607	80.2	57.6	68.0
House furnishings, operations	58– 70	2436.0	4898.8	1.049	0.980	1.014	50.7	47.4	49.0
Furniture	58– 60	1047.4	2614.4	0.965	0.945	0.955	42.4	41.5	41.9
Appliances	61– 66	303.9	1102.3	1.264	1.299	1.281	21.2	21.8	21.5
Supplies, operation	67– 70	1084.7	1182.2	1.036	0.949	0.992	96.6	88.5	92.5
Medical care	71– 77	1576.1	5603.6	0.307	0.299	0.303	94.0	91.5	92.8
Transport, communications	78– 89	1964.8	7383.0	0.925	0.597	0.743	44.6	28.8	35.8
Equipment	78– 79	651.0	1583.8	1.065	1.090	1.078	37.7	38.6	38.1
Operation costs	80– 83	566.3	4142.3	0.999	0.950	0.974	14.4	13.7	14.0
Purchased transport	84– 87	633.7	1014.6	0.453	0.356	0.402	175.5	137.8	155.5
Communications	88– 89	113.8	642.3	0.845	0.359	0.551	49.3	21.0	32.2
Recreation, education	90–101	3360.2	6332.4	0.676	0.471	0.565	112.6	78.5	94.0
Recreation	90– 96	1897.0	3400.3	0.858	0.490	0.649	113.7	65.0	86.0
Education	97–101	1463.2	2932.2	0.465	0.449	0.457	111.2	107.3	109.2
Other expenditures	102–107	2789.9	8819.0	0.625	0.499	0.559	63.4	50.6	56.6
Personal care	102–104	716.8	1658.1	1.033	0.736	0.872	58.8	41.9	49.6
Miscellaneous services	105–107	2073.0	7160.9	0.531	0.449	0.488	64.5	54.5	59.3
Capital formation	109–146	13718.1	23300.7	0.852	0.635	0.736	92.7	69.1	80.0
Domestic capital formation	109–145	17101.3	22739.5	0.844	0.699	0.768	107.5	89.1	97.9
Construction	109–122	8529.4	14379.1	0.635	0.590	0.612	100.6	93.4	96.9
Residential	109–110	2598.2	5183.2	0.467	0.449	0.458	111.7	107.3	109.5
Nonresidential	111–118	3165.6	5484.0	0.852	0.895	0.873	64.5	67.8	66.1
Other	119–122	2765.5	3711.8	0.550	0.539	0.544	138.4	135.5	136.9
Producer durables	123–144	6628.5	8942.8	1.180	0.865	1.010	85.7	62.8	73.4
Transport equipment	123–129	1273.4	1460.1	0.852	0.496	0.650	175.9	102.4	134.2
Nonelectrical machinery	130–138	3827.3	4683.6	1.472	1.276	1.371	64.0	55.5	59.6
Electrical machinery	139 142	770.4	1936.3	0.917	0.995	0.955	40.0	43.4	41.7
Other	143–144	757.3	862.8	0.735	0.574	0.649	153.0	119.4	135.2
Exports minus imports	146–146	−3383.3	561.2	1.186	1.186	1.186	−508.3	−508.3	−508.3
Government	147–151	3414.0	8026.6	0.464	0.581	0.519	73.2	91.7	81.9
Compensation	147–150	917.8	6157.3	0.350	0.316	0.333	47.1	42.6	44.8
Commodities	151–151	2496.2	1869.3	0.840	0.840	0.840	158.9	158.9	158.9
Gross domestic product	1–151	43893.2	87268.1	0.785	0.637	0.707	79.0	64.1	71.1
Aggregates									
ICP concepts[e]									
Consumption (CEP)[b,c]	1–108	26761.1	55940.8	0.803	0.646	0.720	74.1	59.6	66.4
Capital formation (GCF)[d]	109–146	13718.1	23300.7	0.852	0.635	0.736	92.7	69.1	80.0
Government (PFC)	147–151	3414.0	8026.6	0.464	0.581	0.519	73.2	91.7	81.9
Gross domestic product (ICP)	1–151	43893.2	87268.1	0.785	0.637	0.707	79.0	64.1	71.1
SNA concepts[e]									
Consumption (PFCE)	1–108	23146.7	48900.9	0.861	0.728	0.792	65.0	54.9	59.8
Capital formation (GCF)	109–146	13718.1	23300.7	0.852	0.635	0.736	92.7	69.1	80.0
Government (GFCE)	1–151	6695.6	15066.5	0.433	0.440	0.436	101.1	102.7	101.9
Gross domestic product (SNA)	1–151	43560.3	87268.1	0.785	0.635	0.706	78.7	63.6	70.7

Note: See the end of Appendix Table 7-68 for notes.

Category	Line numbers[a]	Per capita expenditures		Purchasing power parities (pounds/schillings)			Quantity per capita (Austria = 100)		
		Ireland (pounds)	Austria (schillings)	Austria weight	Ireland weight	Geometric mean	Austria weight	Ireland weight	Geometric mean
Consumption, ICP[b,c]	1–108	876.260	55940.8	0.02602	0.02159	0.02370	72.5	60.2	66.1
Food, beverages, tobacco	1– 39	258.186	13873.4	0.02982	0.02177	0.02548	85.5	62.4	73.0
Food	1– 33	202.141	9957.3	0.02457	0.01947	0.02187	104.3	82.6	92.8
Bread, cereals	1– 6	27.393	1294.0	0.02281	0.01902	0.02083	111.3	92.8	101.6
Meat	7– 12	69.584	3098.7	0.02026	0.01707	0.01860	131.5	110.8	120.7
Fish	13– 14	5.668	147.9	0.02759	0.02393	0.02569	160.1	138.9	149.2
Milk, cheese, eggs	15– 17	26.763	1467.8	0.02371	0.02146	0.02255	85.0	76.9	80.8
Oils, fats	18– 20	11.020	694.7	0.02561	0.01991	0.02258	79.7	61.9	70.2
Fruits, vegetables	21– 26	33.375	1936.6	0.03502	0.02812	0.03138	61.3	49.2	54.9
Coffee, tea, cocoa	27– 29	4.408	244.9	0.01510	0.00775	0.01082	232.3	119.2	166.4
Spices, sweets, sugar	30– 33	23.929	1072.7	0.02252	0.02229	0.02240	100.1	99.1	99.6
Beverages	34– 37	14.798	2707.3	0.04574	0.03943	0.04247	13.9	12.0	12.9
Tobacco	38– 39	41.247	1208.8	0.03741	0.03741	0.03741	91.2	91.2	91.2
Clothing, footwear	40– 51	63.602	6078.5	0.02730	0.02766	0.02748	37.8	38.3	38.1
Clothing	40– 47	52.897	5059.6	0.02626	0.02682	0.02653	39.0	39.8	39.4
Footwear	48– 51	10.705	1018.9	0.03247	0.03278	0.03263	32.1	32.4	32.2
Gross rent, fuel	52– 57	88.476	6743.4	0.03030	0.02977	0.03003	44.1	43.3	43.7
Gross rent	52– 53	49.433	4641.0	0.03236	0.03257	0.03247	32.7	32.9	32.8
Fuel, power	54– 57	39.043	2102.4	0.02575	0.02685	0.02630	69.2	72.1	70.6
House furnishings, operations	58– 70	59.824	4898.8	0.02659	0.02446	0.02550	49.9	45.9	47.9
Furniture	58– 60	24.559	2614.4	0.02830	0.02751	0.02790	34.1	33.2	33.7
Appliances	61– 66	9.761	1102.3	0.02551	0.02413	0.02481	36.7	34.7	35.7
Supplies, operation	67– 70	25.504	1182.2	0.02382	0.02221	0.02300	97.2	90.6	93.8
Medical care	71– 77	78.715	5603.6	0.02228	0.01710	0.01952	82.1	63.1	72.0
Transport, communications	78– 89	75.567	7383.0	0.02429	0.02052	0.02233	49.9	42.1	45.8
Equipment	78– 79	25.189	1583.8	0.02939	0.02835	0.02886	56.1	54.1	55.1
Operation costs	80– 83	33.060	4142.3	0.01727	0.01542	0.01632	51.7	46.2	48.9
Purchased transport	84– 87	12.594	1014.6	0.03522	0.02705	0.03087	45.9	35.2	40.2
Communications	88– 89	4.723	642.3	0.03978	0.02562	0.03192	28.7	18.5	23.0
Recreation, education	90–101	114.295	6332.4	0.02148	0.01930	0.02036	93.5	84.0	88.7
Recreation	90– 96	48.489	3400.3	0.02001	0.01583	0.01780	90.1	71.3	80.1
Education	97–101	65.806	2932.2	0.02319	0.02301	0.02310	97.5	96.8	97.1
Other expenditures	102–107	137.594	8819.0	0.02258	0.02024	0.02138	77.1	69.1	73.0
Personal care	102–104	13.224	1658.1	0.03005	0.02271	0.02612	35.1	26.5	30.5
Miscellaneous services	105–107	124.370	7160.9	0.02084	0.02001	0.02042	86.8	83.3	85.0
Capital formation	109–146	183.879	23300.7	0.02394	0.01448	0.01862	54.5	33.0	42.4
Domestic capital formation	109–145	253.778	22739.5	0.02389	0.01648	0.01984	67.7	46.7	56.3
Construction	109–122	164.673	14379.1	0.02163	0.01493	0.01797	76.7	53.0	63.7
Residential	109–110	72.103	5183.2	0.01489	0.01548	0.01518	89.9	93.4	91.6
Nonresidential	111–118	44.081	5484.0	0.03037	0.02157	0.02560	37.3	26.5	31.4
Other	119–122	48.489	3711.8	0.01810	0.01121	0.01425	116.5	72.2	91.7
Producer durables	123–144	101.071	8942.8	0.02746	0.02062	0.02380	54.8	41.2	47.5
Transport equipment	123–129	24.874	1460.1	0.02631	0.02481	0.02555	68.7	64.7	66.7
Nonelectrical machinery	130–138	56.360	4683.6	0.02146	0.01938	0.02040	62.1	56.1	59.0
Electrical machinery	139–142	9.131	1936.3	0.04646	0.02004	0.03052	23.5	10.1	15.5
Other	143–144	10.705	862.8	0.01937	0.02000	0.01968	62.0	64.0	63.0
Exports minus imports	146–146	−69.899	561.2	0.02584	0.02584	0.02584	−482.0	−482.0	−482.0
Government	147–151	124.370	8026.6	0.02068	0.01844	0.01953	84.0	74.9	79.3
Compensation	147–150	75.567	6157.3	0.02249	0.02202	0.02226	55.7	54.6	55.1
Commodities	151–151	48.804	1869.3	0.01472	0.01472	0.01472	177.3	177.3	177.3
Gross domestic product	1–151	1184.509	87268.1	0.02497	0.01973	0.02220	68.8	54.4	61.1
Aggregates									
ICP concepts[e]									
Consumption (CEP)[b,c]	1–108	876.260	55940.8	0.02602	0.02159	0.02370	72.5	60.2	66.1
Capital formation (GCF)[d]	109–146	183.879	23300.7	0.02394	0.01448	0.01862	54.5	33.0	42.4
Government (PFC)	147–151	124.370	8026.6	0.02068	0.01844	0.01953	84.0	74.9	79.3
Gross domestic product (ICP)	1–151	1184.509	87268.1	0.02497	0.01973	0.02220	68.8	54.4	61.1
SNA concepts[e]									
Consumption (PFCE)	1–108	750.000	48900.9	0.02630	0.02176	0.02392	70.5	58.3	64.1
Capital formation (GCF)	109–146	183.879	23300.7	0.02394	0.01448	0.01862	54.5	33.0	42.4
Government (GFCE)	1–151	241.184	15066.5	0.02226	0.01911	0.02063	83.8	71.9	77.6
Gross domestic product (SNA)	1–151	1175.063	87268.1	0.02497	0.01965	0.02215	68.5	53.9	60.8

Note: See the end of Appendix Table 7-68 for notes.

Category	Line numbers[a]	Per capita expenditures		Purchasing power parities (lire/schillings)			Quantity per capita (Austria = 100)		
		Italy (lire)	Austria (schillings)	Austria weight	Italy weight	Geometric mean	Austria weight	Italy weight	Geometric mean
Consumption, ICP[b,c]	1–108	1554899.	55940.8	36.53	34.54	35.52	80.5	76.1	78.2
Food, beverages, tobacco	1– 39	530127.	13873.4	39.07	36.76	37.90	103.9	97.8	100.8
Food	1– 33	451299.	9957.3	39.65	37.95	38.79	119.4	114.3	116.8
Bread, cereals	1– 6	60165.	1294.0	35.98	34.03	34.99	136.6	129.2	132.9
Meat	7– 12	150690.	3098.7	38.71	39.76	39.23	122.3	125.6	124.0
Fish	13– 14	15458.	147.9	50.41	51.50	50.95	203.0	207.4	205.2
Milk, cheese, eggs	15– 17	57693.	1467.8	40.48	41.93	41.20	93.7	97.1	95.4
Oils, fats	18– 20	35536.	694.7	44.01	37.50	40.63	136.4	116.2	125.9
Fruits, vegetables	21– 26	102364.	1936.6	36.20	34.04	35.10	155.3	146.0	150.6
Coffee, tea, cocoa	27– 29	7917.	244.9	42.47	42.08	42.27	76.8	76.1	76.5
Spices, sweets, sugar	30– 33	21476.	1072.7	46.89	41.80	44.27	47.9	42.7	45.2
Beverages	34– 37	45262.	2707.3	41.78	33.76	37.56	49.5	40.0	44.5
Tobacco	38– 39	33566.	1208.8	28.25	28.25	28.25	98.3	98.3	98.3
Clothing, footwear	40– 51	130163.	6078.5	36.63	36.92	36.77	58.0	58.5	58.2
Clothing	40– 47	106681.	5059.6	36.67	37.74	37.21	55.9	57.5	56.7
Footwear	48– 51	23482.	1018.9	36.38	33.60	34.96	68.6	63.3	65.9
Gross rent, fuel	52– 57	194232.	6743.4	45.40	49.43	47.37	58.3	63.4	60.8
Gross rent	52– 53	149704.	4641.0	52.50	63.75	57.85	50.6	61.4	55.8
Fuel, power	54– 57	44528.	2102.4	29.72	28.17	28.94	75.2	71.3	73.2
House furnishings, operations	58– 70	91599.	4898.8	37.11	35.78	36.44	52.3	50.4	51.3
Furniture	58– 60	36092.	2614.4	32.91	30.29	31.57	45.6	41.9	43.7
Appliances	61– 66	13290.	1102.3	44.07	45.46	44.76	26.5	27.4	26.9
Supplies, operation	67– 70	42217.	1182.2	39.92	39.23	39.57	91.0	89.5	90.2
Medical care	71– 77	124646.	5603.6	30.54	28.55	29.53	77.9	72.8	75.3
Transport, communications	78– 89	158606.	7383.0	31.72	24.81	28.06	86.6	67.7	76.6
Equipment	78– 79	38349.	1583.8	31.42	31.94	31.68	75.8	77.1	76.4
Operation costs	80– 83	83056.	4142.3	31.79	24.68	28.01	81.3	63.1	71.6
Purchased transport	84– 87	22067.	1014.6	23.85	17.26	20.29	126.0	91.2	107.2
Communications	88– 89	15135.	642.3	44.51	27.62	35.06	85.3	52.9	67.2
Recreation, education	90–101	181354.	6332.4	37.69	35.14	36.39	81.5	76.0	78.7
Recreation	90– 96	81085.	3400.3	39.60	34.77	37.11	68.6	60.2	64.3
Education	97–101	100269.	2932.2	35.47	35.44	35.46	96.5	96.4	96.4
Other expenditures	102–107	144170.	8819.0	32.77	30.94	31.84	52.8	49.9	51.3
Personal care	102–104	51245.	1658.1	40.90	38.00	39.43	81.3	75.6	78.4
Miscellaneous services	105–107	92925.	7160.9	30.89	28.06	29.44	46.2	42.0	44.1
Capital formation	109–146	428139.	23300.7	29.84	23.03	26.22	79.8	61.6	70.1
Domestic capital formation	109–145	455347.	22739.5	29.66	23.58	26.44	84.9	67.5	75.7
Construction	109–122	281426.	14379.1	24.59	20.24	22.31	96.7	79.6	87.7
Residential	109–110	139584.	5183.2	18.32	18.41	18.36	146.3	147.0	146.6
Nonresidential	111–118	87856.	5484.0	32.59	29.00	30.75	55.2	49.2	52.1
Other	119–122	53985.	3711.8	21.50	16.39	18.77	88.7	67.6	77.5
Producer durables	123–144	180226.	8942.8	38.04	32.19	34.99	62.6	53.0	57.6
Transport equipment	123–129	46713.	1460.1	33.78	31.10	32.41	102.9	94.7	98.7
Nonelectrical machinery	130–138	80226.	4683.6	37.25	32.88	35.00	52.1	46.0	48.9
Electrical machinery	139–142	34515.	1936.3	48.64	36.51	42.14	48.8	36.7	42.3
Other	143–144	18771.	862.8	25.76	26.39	26.07	82.5	84.5	83.5
Exports minus imports	146–146	– 27208.	561.2	37.48	37.48	37.48	– 129.3	– 129.3	– 129.3
Government	147–151	262672.	8026.6	31.68	33.00	32.34	99.2	103.3	101.2
Compensation	147–150	161311.	6157.3	30.68	31.88	31.27	82.2	85.4	83.8
Commodities	151–151	101361.	1869.3	34.97	34.97	34.97	155.0	155.0	155.0
Gross domestic product	1–151	2245710.	87268.1	34.30	31.38	32.81	82.0	75.0	78.4
Aggregates									
ICP concepts[e]									
Consumption (CEP)[b,c]	1–108	1554899.	55940.8	36.53	34.54	35.52	80.5	76.1	78.2
Capital formation (GCF)[d]	109–146	428139.	23300.7	29.84	23.03	26.22	79.8	61.6	70.1
Government (PFC)	147–151	262672.	8026.6	31.68	33.00	32.34	99.2	103.3	101.2
Gross domestic product (ICP)	1–151	2245710.	87268.1	34.30	31.38	32.81	82.0	75.0	78.4
SNA concepts[e]									
Consumption (PFCE)	1–108	1459556.	48900.9	36.74	34.45	35.58	86.6	81.2	83.9
Capital formation (GCF)	109–146	428139.	23300.7	29.84	23.03	26.22	79.8	61.6	70.1
Government (GFCE)	1–151	358015.	15066.5	33.26	33.75	33.50	70.4	71.4	70.9
Gross domestic product (SNA)	1–151	2245710.	87268.1	34.30	31.38	32.81	82.0	75.0	78.4

Note: See the end of Appendix Table 7-68 for notes.

Category	Line numbers[a]	Per capita expenditures Luxembourg (francs)	Austria (schillings)	Purchasing power parities (francs/schillings) Austria weight	Luxembourg weight	Geometric mean	Quantity per capita (Austria = 100) Austria weight	Luxembourg weight	Geometric mean
Consumption, ICP[b,c]	1–108	149966.7	55940.8	2.524	2.376	2.449	112.8	106.2	109.5
Food, beverages, tobacco	1– 39	33419.4	13873.4	2.363	2.231	2.296	108.0	101.9	104.9
Food	1– 33	28169.4	9957.3	2.469	2.297	2.382	123.1	114.6	118.8
Bread, cereals	1– 6	3977.8	1294.0	2.311	2.314	2.312	132.9	133.0	132.9
Meat	7– 12	9127.8	3098.7	2.201	2.000	2.098	147.3	133.8	140.4
Fish	13– 14	755.6	147.9	2.914	2.896	2.905	176.4	175.3	175.9
Milk, cheese, eggs	15– 17	4080.6	1467.8	2.529	2.532	2.530	109.8	109.9	109.9
Oils, fats	18– 20	2258.3	694.7	2.337	2.344	2.341	138.7	139.1	138.9
Fruits, vegetables	21– 26	4877.8	1936.6	3.033	2.680	2.851	94.0	83.1	88.4
Coffee, tea, cocoa	27– 29	1030.6	244.9	2.134	2.151	2.142	195.6	197.2	196.4
Spices, sweets, sugar	30– 33	2061.1	1072.7	2.432	2.447	2.440	78.5	79.0	78.8
Beverages	34– 37	3180.6	2707.3	2.293	2.173	2.232	54.1	51.2	52.6
Tobacco	38– 39	2069.4	1208.8	1.648	1.648	1.648	103.9	103.9	103.9
Clothing, footwear	40– 51	12405.6	6078.5	2.968	2.954	2.961	69.1	68.8	68.9
Clothing	40– 47	10638.9	5059.6	3.006	2.985	2.995	70.5	69.9	70.2
Footwear	48– 51	1766.7	1018.9	2.780	2.782	2.781	62.3	62.4	62.3
Gross rent, fuel	52– 57	25402.8	6743.4	3.428	3.404	3.416	110.7	109.9	110.3
Gross rent	52– 53	18122.2	4641.0	4.057	4.891	4.455	79.8	96.3	87.7
Fuel, power	54– 57	7280.6	2102.4	2.039	1.938	1.988	178.7	169.8	174.2
House furnishings, operations	58– 70	15002.8	4898.8	2.378	2.180	2.277	140.5	128.8	134.5
Furniture	58– 60	6344.4	2614.4	2.207	1.981	2.091	122.5	109.9	116.0
Appliances	61– 66	2061.1	1102.3	2.594	2.620	2.607	71.4	72.1	71.7
Supplies, operation	67– 70	6597.2	1182.2	2.552	2.280	2.412	244.7	218.7	231.4
Medical care	71– 77	9022.2	5603.6	1.821	1.705	1.762	94.4	88.4	91.4
Transport, communications	78– 89	18302.8	7383.0	2.017	1.787	1.898	138.7	122.9	130.6
Equipment	78– 79	6363.9	1583.8	1.663	1.616	1.639	248.6	241.7	245.1
Operation costs	80– 83	8236.1	4142.3	1.796	1.790	1.793	111.1	110.7	110.9
Purchased transport	84– 87	2366.7	1014.6	2.810	2.305	2.545	101.2	83.0	91.7
Communications	88– 89	1336.1	642.3	3.059	1.975	2.458	105.3	68.0	84.6
Recreation, education	90–101	16197.2	6332.4	2.940	3.035	2.987	84.3	87.0	85.6
Recreation	90– 96	5627.8	3400.3	1.915	1.976	1.945	83.8	86.4	85.1
Education	97–101	10569.4	2932.2	4.128	4.247	4.187	84.9	87.3	86.1
Other expenditures	102–107	20213.9	8819.0	2.259	2.319	2.289	98.8	101.4	100.1
Personal care	102–104	4905.6	1658.1	2.868	2.508	2.682	118.0	103.2	110.3
Miscellaneous services	105–107	15308.3	7160.9	2.118	2.264	2.190	94.4	100.9	97.6
Capital formation	109–146	63100.0	23300.7	2.108	1.744	1.918	155.2	128.5	141.2
Domestic capital formation	109–145	67666.7	22739.5	2.108	1.765	1.929	168.6	141.2	154.3
Construction	109–122	47850.0	14379.1	2.069	1.670	1.858	199.3	160.9	179.1
Residential	109–110	18519.4	5183.2	1.706	1.703	1.704	209.9	209.4	209.6
Nonresidential	111–118	20316.7	5484.0	2.646	1.980	2.289	187.1	140.0	161.9
Other	119–122	9013.9	3711.8	1.721	1.199	1.436	202.6	141.1	169.1
Producer durables	123–144	18755.6	8942.8	2.182	2.037	2.108	102.9	96.1	99.5
Transport equipment	123–129	4522.2	1460.1	1.787	2.263	2.011	136.9	173.4	154.0
Nonelectrical machinery	130–138	8138.9	4683.6	2.086	1.905	1.994	91.2	83.3	87.2
Electrical machinery	139–142	4866.7	1936.3	2.901	2.174	2.511	115.6	86.6	100.1
Other	143–144	1227.8	862.8	1.754	1.763	1.759	80.7	81.1	80.9
Exports minus imports	146–146	−4566.7	561.2	2.112	2.112	2.112	−385.3	−385.3	−385.3
Government	147–151	23677.8	8026.6	3.011	2.862	2.935	103.1	98.0	100.5
Compensation	147–150	15305.6	6157.3	3.194	3.191	3.193	77.9	77.8	77.9
Commodities	151–151	8372.2	1869.3	2.408	2.408	2.408	186.0	186.0	186.0
Gross domestic product	1–151	236744.4	87268.1	2.458	2.201	2.326	123.2	110.4	116.6
Aggregates									
ICP concepts[e]									
Consumption (CEP)[b,c]	1–108	149966.7	55940.8	2.524	2.376	2.449	112.8	106.2	109.5
Capital formation (GCF)[d]	109–146	63100.0	23300.7	2.108	1.744	1.918	155.2	128.5	141.2
Government (PFC)	147–151	23677.8	8026.6	3.011	2.862	2.935	103.1	98.0	100.5
Gross domestic product (ICP)	1–151	236744.4	87268.1	2.458	2.201	2.326	123.2	110.4	116.6
SNA concepts[e]									
Consumption (PFCE)	1–108	139786.1	48900.9	2.506	2.299	2.401	124.3	114.1	119.1
Capital formation (GCF)	109–146	63100.0	23300.7	2.108	1.744	1.918	155.2	128.5	141.2
Government (GFCE)	1–151	33858.3	15066.5	2.842	3.197	3.014	70.3	79.1	74.6
Gross domestic product (SNA)	1–151	236744.4	87268.1	2.458	2.201	2.326	123.2	110.4	116.6

Note: See the end of Appendix Table 7-68 for notes.

Category	Line numbers[a]	Per capita expenditures		Purchasing power parities (guilders/schillings)			Quantity per capita (Austria = 100)		
		Netherlands (guilders)	Austria (schillings)	Austria weight	Netherlands weight	Geometric mean	Austria weight	Netherlands weight	Geometric mean
Consumption, ICP[b,c]	1–108	9744.07	55940.8	0.1917	0.1744	0.1828	99.9	90.9	95.3
Food, beverages, tobacco	1– 39	2110.40	13873.4	0.1627	0.1505	0.1565	101.1	93.5	97.2
Food	1– 33	1623.57	9957.3	0.1607	0.1474	0.1539	110.6	101.5	106.0
Bread, cereals	1– 6	212.30	1294.0	0.1431	0.1353	0.1392	121.2	114.6	117.9
Meat	7– 12	447.29	3098.7	0.1536	0.1322	0.1425	109.2	94.0	101.3
Fish	13– 14	51.98	147.9	0.1770	0.1580	0.1672	222.4	198.6	210.2
Milk, cheese, eggs	15– 17	273.72	1467.8	0.1610	0.1703	0.1656	109.5	115.8	112.6
Oils, fats	18– 20	74.67	694.7	0.1847	0.1844	0.1845	58.3	58.2	58.2
Fruits, vegetables	21– 26	320.64	1936.6	0.1809	0.1676	0.1741	98.8	91.5	95.1
Coffee, tea, cocoa	27– 29	83.38	244.9	0.1202	0.1173	0.1187	290.3	283.1	286.7
Spices, sweets, sugar	30– 33	159.59	1072.7	0.1566	0.1454	0.1509	102.3	95.0	98.6
Beverages	34– 37	284.04	2707.3	0.1766	0.1732	0.1749	60.6	59.4	60.0
Tobacco	38– 39	202.78	1208.8	0.1483	0.1483	0.1483	113.1	113.1	113.1
Clothing, footwear	40– 51	800.95	6078.5	0.1807	0.1676	0.1740	78.6	72.9	75.7
Clothing	40– 47	683.82	5059.6	0.1824	0.1666	0.1743	81.1	74.1	77.5
Footwear	48– 51	117.13	1018.9	0.1719	0.1738	0.1728	66.1	66.9	66.5
Gross rent, fuel	52– 57	1203.51	6743.4	0.2159	0.2006	0.2081	89.0	82.7	85.8
Gross rent	52– 53	833.09	4641.0	0.2523	0.2590	0.2556	69.3	71.2	70.2
Fuel, power	54– 57	370.42	2102.4	0.1354	0.1330	0.1342	132.5	130.1	131.3
House furnishings, operations	58– 70	898.83	4898.8	0.1498	0.1394	0.1445	131.7	122.5	127.0
Furniture	58– 60	473.21	2614.4	0.1298	0.1222	0.1259	148.1	139.4	143.7
Appliances	61– 66	124.23	1102.3	0.1640	0.1648	0.1644	68.4	68.7	68.6
Supplies, operation	67– 70	301.39	1182.2	0.1806	0.1653	0.1728	154.2	141.2	147.5
Medical care	71– 77	1002.27	5603.6	0.2499	0.2304	0.2400	77.6	71.6	74.5
Transport, communications	78– 89	941.65	7383.0	0.1582	0.1424	0.1501	89.5	80.6	85.0
Equipment	78– 79	324.30	1583.8	0.1472	0.1483	0.1478	138.1	139.1	138.6
Operation costs	80– 83	432.72	4142.3	0.1355	0.1252	0.1302	83.5	77.1	80.2
Purchased transport	84– 87	68.23	1014.6	0.1853	0.1765	0.1809	38.1	36.3	
Communications	88– 89	116.40	642.3	0.2889	0.2006	0.2408	90.3	62.7	75.3
Recreation, education	90–101	1797.51	6332.4	0.2249	0.2138	0.2192	132.8	126.2	129.5
Recreation	90– 96	804.47	3400.3	0.1499	0.1543	0.1521	153.3	157.8	155.6
Education	97–101	993.05	2932.2	0.3118	0.3107	0.3113	109.0	108.6	108.8
Other expenditures	102–107	988.95	8819.0	0.1967	0.1881	0.1924	59.6	57.0	58.3
Personal care	102–104	202.93	1658.1	0.2319	0.2096	0.2204	58.4	52.8	55.5
Miscellaneous services	105–107	786.02	7160.9	0.1886	0.1832	0.1859	59.9	58.2	59.0
Capital formation	109–146	3767.42	23300.7	0.1785	0.1215	0.1473	133.0	90.6	109.8
Domestic capital formation	109–145	3157.61	22739.5	0.1793	0.1178	0.1454	117.8	77.4	95.5
Construction	109–122	1768.01	14379.1	0.1507	0.1032	0.1247	119.2	81.6	98.6
Residential	109–110	728.70	5183.2	0.0960	0.0893	0.0926	157.4	146.5	151.8
Nonresidential	111–118	645.90	5484.0	0.2253	0.1523	0.1853	77.3	52.3	63.6
Other	119–122	393.41	3711.8	0.1169	0.0831	0.0986	127.6	90.7	107.5
Producer durables	123–144	1421.82	8942.8	0.2231	0.1438	0.1791	110.5	71.3	88.8
Transport equipment	123–129	396.19	1460.1	0.1470	0.1451	0.1460	187.0	184.6	185.8
Nonelectrical machinery	130–138	555.49	4683.6	0.1504	0.1406	0.1454	84.4	78.9	81.6
Electrical machinery	139–142	319.99	1936.3	0.4998	0.1575	0.2806	104.9	33.1	58.9
Other	143–144	150.15	862.8	0.1260	0.1280	0.1270	135.9	138.1	137.0
Exports minus imports	146–146	609.81	561.2	0.1452	0.1452	0.1452	748.3	748.3	748.3
Government	147–151	1819.40	8026.6	0.2136	0.2081	0.2109	108.9	106.1	107.5
Compensation	147–150	1294.66	6157.3	0.2290	0.2344	0.2317	89.7	91.8	90.8
Commodities	151–151	524.74	1869.3	0.1631	0.1631	0.1631	172.2	172.2	172.2
Gross domestic product	1–151	15330.89	87268.1	0.1902	0.1603	0.1746	109.6	92.4	100.6
Aggregates									
ICP concepts[e]									
Consumption (CEP)[b,c]	1–108	9744.07	55940.8	0.1917	0.1744	0.1828	99.9	90.9	95.3
Capital formation (GCF)[d]	109–146	3767.42	23300.7	0.1785	0.1215	0.1473	133.0	90.6	109.8
Government (PFC)	147–151	1819.40	8026.6	0.2136	0.2081	0.2109	108.9	106.1	107.5
Gross domestic product (ICP)	1–151	15330.89	87268.1	0.1902	0.1603	0.1746	109.6	92.4	100.6
SNA concepts[e]									
Consumption (PFCE)	1–108	8701.32	48900.9	0.1774	0.1657	0.1714	107.4	100.3	103.8
Capital formation (GCF)	109–146	3767.42	23300.7	0.1785	0.1215	0.1473	133.0	90.6	109.8
Government (GFCE)	1–151	2793.34	15066.5	0.2496	0.2358	0.2426	78.6	74.3	76.4
Gross domestic product (SNA)	1–151	15262.08	87268.1	0.1902	0.1601	0.1745	109.3	92.0	100.2

Note: See the end of Appendix Table 7-68 for notes.

Category	Line numbers[a]	Per capita expenditures		Purchasing power parities (zlotys/schillings)			Quantity per capita (Austria = 100)		
		Poland (zlotys)	Austria (schillings)	Austria weight	Poland weight	Geometric mean	Austria weight	Poland weight	Geometric mean
Consumption, ICP[b,c]	1–108	29570.0	55940.8	1.072	0.763	0.905	69.3	49.3	58.4
Food, beverages, tobacco	1– 39	11604.8	13873.4	1.335	1.047	1.182	79.9	62.7	70.8
Food	1– 33	8479.3	9957.3	1.145	0.911	1.021	93.5	74.3	83.4
Bread, cereals	1– 6	1007.1	1294.0	0.758	0.647	0.700	120.4	102.6	111.2
Meat	7– 12	2526.5	3098.7	0.803	0.713	0.756	114.4	101.5	107.8
Fish	13– 14	165.7	147.9	1.628	1.302	1.456	86.1	68.8	77.0
Milk, cheese, eggs	15– 17	1356.9	1467.8	1.145	1.155	1.150	80.0	80.7	80.4
Oils, fats	18– 20	782.4	694.7	1.382	1.392	1.387	80.9	81.5	81.2
Fruits, vegetables	21– 26	1340.3	1936.6	1.550	0.971	1.227	71.3	44.7	56.4
Coffee, tea, cocoa	27– 29	288.2	244.9	3.156	2.695	2.916	43.7	37.3	40.4
Spices, sweets, sugar	30– 33	1012.2	1072.7	1.194	1.182	1.188	79.8	79.0	79.4
Beverages	34– 37	2540.1	2707.3	2.250	2.455	2.350	38.2	41.7	39.9
Tobacco	38– 39	585.4	1208.8	0.844	0.792	0.818	61.1	57.4	59.2
Clothing, footwear	40– 51	3777.0	6078.5	1.274	1.195	1.234	52.0	48.8	50.4
Clothing	40– 47	3229.4	5059.6	1.319	1.228	1.272	52.0	48.4	50.2
Footwear	48– 51	547.6	1018.9	1.051	1.034	1.043	52.0	51.2	51.6
Gross rent, fuel	52– 57	2309.5	6743.4	0.757	0.588	0.667	58.3	45.2	51.3
Gross rent	52– 53	1749.5	4641.0	0.739	0.660	0.699	57.1	51.0	54.0
Fuel, power	54– 57	560.0	2102.4	0.797	0.437	0.590	60.9	33.4	45.1
House furnishings, operations	58– 70	2605.8	4898.8	1.111	1.000	1.054	53.2	47.9	50.5
Furniture	58– 60	1213.5	2614.4	1.146	1.068	1.106	43.5	40.5	42.0
Appliances	61– 66	391.1	1102.3	1.233	1.238	1.236	28.7	28.8	28.7
Supplies, operation	67– 70	1001.2	1182.2	0.918	0.869	0.893	97.5	92.2	94.8
Medical care	71– 77	1719.7	5603.6	0.402	0.367	0.384	83.7	76.4	79.9
Transport, communications	78– 89	1871.4	7383.0	1.541	0.506	0.883	50.1	16.4	28.7
Equipment	78– 79	612.8	1583.8	2.300	2.019	2.155	19.2	16.8	18.0
Operation costs	80– 83	380.7	4142.3	1.569	1.516	1.543	6.1	5.9	6.0
Purchased transport	84– 87	716.3	1014.6	0.627	0.255	0.400	277.0	112.6	176.6
Communications	88– 89	161.6	642.3	0.935	0.486	0.674	51.8	26.9	37.3
Recreation, education	90–101	3555.5	6332.4	0.752	0.557	0.647	100.8	74.7	86.8
Recreation	90– 96	1717.1	3400.3	0.941	0.639	0.775	79.0	53.7	65.1
Education	97–101	1838.4	2932.2	0.532	0.497	0.514	126.1	117.8	121.9
Other expenditures	102–107	2126.3	8819.0	1.032	0.666	0.829	36.2	23.4	29.1
Personal care	102–104	504.3	1658.1	1.463	0.949	1.178	32.0	20.8	25.8
Miscellaneous services	105–107	1622.0	7160.9	0.933	0.609	0.754	37.2	24.3	30.1
Capital formation	109–146	18218.5	23300.7	0.888	0.804	0.845	97.2	88.0	92.5
Domestic capital formation	109–145	21216.6	22739.5	0.882	0.839	0.860	111.1	105.8	108.4
Construction	109–122	10273.0	14379.1	0.686	0.720	0.703	99.3	104.1	101.7
Residential	109–110	1848.8	5183.2	0.627	0.588	0.607	60.7	56.9	58.8
Nonresidential	111–118	4622.6	5484.0	0.757	0.788	0.772	107.0	111.3	109.1
Other	119–122	3801.6	3711.8	0.664	0.722	0.693	141.8	154.1	147.9
Producer durables	123–144	7983.1	8942.8	1.203	1.005	1.100	88.8	74.2	81.2
Transport equipment	123–129	2109.5	1460.1	1.728	0.845	1.208	171.0	83.6	119.6
Nonelectrical machinery	130–138	4182.9	4683.6	1.197	1.188	1.193	75.2	74.6	74.9
Electrical machinery	139–142	1534.7	1936.3	0.849	0.857	0.853	92.5	93.4	92.9
Other	143–144	156.1	862.8	1.138	1.168	1.153	15.5	15.9	15.7
Exports minus imports	146–146	– 2998.1	561.2	1.144	1.144	1.144	– 467.1	– 467.1	– 467.1
Government	147–151	3715.4	8026.6	0.482	0.609	0.542	76.0	96.1	85.5
Compensation	147–150	1123.2	6157.3	0.338	0.331	0.334	55.1	54.0	54.5
Commodities	151–151	2592.3	1869.3	0.956	0.956	0.956	145.0	145.0	145.0
Gross domestic product	1–151	51504.0	87268.1	0.969	0.763	0.860	77.3	60.9	68.6
Aggregates									
ICP concepts[e]									
Consumption (CEP)[b,c]	1–108	29570.0	55940.8	1.072	0.763	0.905	69.3	49.3	58.4
Capital formation (GCF)[d]	109–146	18218.5	23300.7	0.888	0.804	0.845	97.2	88.0	92.5
Government (PFC)	147–151	3715.4	8026.6	0.482	0.609	0.542	76.0	96.1	85.5
Gross domestic product (ICP)	1–151	51504.0	87268.1	0.969	0.763	0.860	77.3	60.9	68.6
SNA concepts[e]									
Consumption (PFCE)	1–108	25716.7	48900.9	1.155	0.855	0.994	61.5	45.5	52.9
Capital formation (GCF)	109–146	18218.5	23300.7	0.888	0.804	0.845	97.2	88.0	92.5
Government (GFCE)	1–151	7190.4	15066.5	0.487	0.505	0.496	94.5	98.1	96.2
Gross domestic product (SNA)	1–151	51125.7	87268.1	0.969	0.764	0.860	76.7	60.5	68.1

Note: See the end of Appendix Table 7-68 for notes.

Category	Line numbers[a]	Per capita expenditures		Purchasing power parities (lei/schillings)			Quantity per capita (Austria = 100)		
		Romania (lei)	Austria (schillings)	Austria weight	Romania weight	Geometric mean	Austria weight	Romania weight	Geometric mean
Consumption, ICP[b,c]	1–108	11385.4	55940.8	0.6138	0.4796	0.5425	42.4	33.2	37.5
Food, beverages, tobacco	1– 39	4724.1	13873.4	0.7889	0.6242	0.7017	54.6	43.2	48.5
Food	1– 33	4003.8	9957.3	0.6509	0.5961	0.6229	67.5	61.8	64.5
Bread, cereals	1– 6	716.5	1294.0	0.4921	0.4945	0.4933	112.0	112.5	112.3
Meat	7– 12	1258.1	3098.7	0.5561	0.5962	0.5758	68.1	73.0	70.5
Fish	13– 14	47.7	147.9	0.9367	0.5660	0.7281	57.0	34.4	44.3
Milk, cheese, eggs	15– 17	597.9	1467.8	0.5950	0.6052	0.6001	67.3	68.5	67.9
Oils, fats	18– 20	139.8	694.7	0.6420	0.5409	0.5893	37.2	31.4	34.2
Fruits, vegetables	21– 26	659.9	1936.6	0.7136	0.6521	0.6822	52.3	47.7	50.0
Coffee, tea, cocoa	27– 29	58.9	244.9	1.1028	1.1305	1.1166	21.3	21.8	21.5
Spices, sweets, sugar	30– 33	525.0	1072.7	0.9432	0.6886	0.8059	71.1	51.9	60.7
Beverages	34– 37	518.6	2707.3	0.7873	0.6937	0.7390	27.6	24.3	25.9
Tobacco	38– 39	201.7	1208.8	1.9288	1.9300	1.9294	8.6	8.7	8.6
Clothing, footwear	40– 51	1659.6	6078.5	0.7415	0.7067	0.7239	38.6	36.8	37.7
Clothing	40– 47	1365.5	5059.6	0.7285	0.6896	0.7088	39.1	37.0	38.1
Footwear	48– 51	294.0	1018.9	0.8060	0.7985	0.8023	36.1	35.8	36.0
Gross rent, fuel	52– 57	777.0	6743.4	0.2381	0.2311	0.2346	49.9	48.4	49.1
Gross rent	52– 53	492.8	4641.0	0.2201	0.2200	0.2201	48.3	48.2	48.3
Fuel, power	54– 57	284.2	2102.4	0.2779	0.2533	0.2653	53.4	48.6	50.9
House furnishings, operations	58– 70	822.6	4898.8	0.8452	0.7544	0.7985	22.3	19.9	21.0
Furniture	58– 60	356.3	2614.4	0.8734	0.8743	0.8739	15.6	15.6	15.6
Appliances	61– 66	100.7	1102.3	0.8824	0.8595	0.8709	10.6	10.4	10.5
Supplies, operation	67– 70	365.6	1182.2	0.7480	0.6463	0.6953	47.8	41.3	44.5
Medical care	71– 77	576.4	5603.6	0.2565	0.2217	0.2385	46.4	40.1	43.1
Transport, communications	78– 89	748.6	7383.0	0.6952	0.5405	0.6130	18.8	14.6	16.5
Equipment	78– 79	157.6	1583.8	0.9684	0.9584	0.9634	10.4	10.3	10.3
Operation costs	80– 83	72.0	4142.3	0.6338	0.6844	0.6586	2.5	2.7	2.6
Purchased transport	84– 87	460.6	1014.6	0.7519	0.5253	0.6285	86.4	60.4	72.2
Communications	88– 89	58.4	642.3	0.3278	0.2449	0.2833	37.1	27.7	32.1
Recreation, education	90–101	1090.4	6332.4	0.5255	0.3290	0.4158	52.3	32.8	41.4
Recreation	90– 96	472.5	3400.3	0.7369	0.4765	0.5926	29.2	18.9	23.4
Education	97–101	617.9	2932.2	0.2804	0.2660	0.2731	79.2	75.2	77.2
Other expenditures	102–107	986.7	8819.0	0.6634	0.4762	0.5620	23.5	16.9	19.9
Personal care	102–104	131.6	1658.1	1.0161	0.8657	0.9379	9.2	7.8	8.5
Miscellaneous services	105–107	855.1	7160.9	0.5817	0.4453	0.5090	26.8	20.5	23.5
Capital formation	109–146	8482.4	23300.7	0.7613	0.5685	0.6579	64.0	47.8	55.3
Domestic capital formation	109–145	8600.1	22739.5	0.7631	0.5698	0.6594	66.4	49.6	57.4
Construction	109–122	3507.7	14379.1	0.4935	0.4095	0.4496	59.6	49.4	54.3
Residential	109–110	748.0	5183.2	0.4763	0.4530	0.4645	31.9	30.3	31.1
Nonresidential	111–118	1516.7	5484.0	0.4640	0.3015	0.3740	91.7	59.6	73.9
Other	119–122	1243.1	3711.8	0.5613	0.6600	0.6087	50.7	59.7	55.0
Producer durables	123–144	3501.2	8942.8	1.1861	0.9009	1.0337	43.5	33.0	37.9
Transport equipment	123–129	592.9	1460.1	0.9333	0.8114	0.8702	50.0	43.5	46.7
Nonelectrical machinery	130–138	2517.2	4683.6	1.2552	1.0261	1.1349	52.4	42.8	47.4
Electrical machinery	139–142	247.2	1936.3	0.9200	0.8474	0.8829	15.1	13.9	14.5
Other	143–144	143.9	862.8	1.8356	0.3503	0.8019	47.6	9.1	20.8
Exports minus imports	146–146	-117.7	561.2	0.6890	0.6890	0.6890	-30.4	-30.4	-30.4
Government	147–151	1040.6	8026.6	0.3292	0.3214	0.3253	40.3	39.4	39.9
Compensation	147–150	569.0	6157.3	0.3043	0.2722	0.2878	34.0	30.4	32.1
Commodities	151–151	471.6	1869.3	0.4111	0.4111	0.4111	61.4	61.4	61.4
Gross domestic product	1–151	20908.5	87268.1	0.6270	0.4990	0.5593	48.0	38.2	42.8
Aggregates									
ICP concepts[c]									
Consumption (CEP)[b,c]	1–108	11385.4	55940.8	0.6138	0.4796	0.5425	42.4	33.2	37.5
Capital formation (GCF)[d]	109–146	8482.4	23300.7	0.7613	0.5685	0.6579	64.0	47.8	55.3
Government (PFC)	147–151	1040.6	8026.6	0.3292	0.3214	0.3253	40.3	39.4	39.9
Gross domestic product (ICP)	1–151	20908.5	87268.1	0.6270	0.4990	0.5593	48.0	38.2	42.8
SNA concepts[c]									
Consumption (PFCE)	1–108	10136.3	48900.9	0.6651	0.5483	0.6039	37.8	31.2	34.3
Capital formation (GCF)	109–146	8482.4	23300.7	0.7613	0.5685	0.6579	64.0	47.8	55.3
Government (GFCE)	1–151	2289.7	15066.5	0.2956	0.2697	0.2823	56.4	51.4	53.8
Gross domestic product (SNA)	1–151	20908.5	87268.1	0.6270	0.4990	0.5593	48.0	38.2	42.8

Note: See the end of Appendix Table 7-68 for notes.

Category	Line numbers[a]	Per capita expenditures Spain (pesetas)	Per capita expenditures Austria (schillings)	Purchasing power parities (pesetas/schillings) Austria weight	Purchasing power parities (pesetas/schillings) Spain weight	Purchasing power parities (pesetas/schillings) Geometric mean	Quantity per capita (Austria = 100) Austria weight	Quantity per capita (Austria = 100) Spain weight	Quantity per capita (Austria = 100) Geometric mean
Consumption, ICP[b,c]	1–108	124281.2	55940.8	2.760	2.439	2.595	91.1	80.5	85.6
Food, beverages, tobacco	1– 39	40653.0	13873.4	2.621	2.430	2.523	120.6	111.8	116.1
Food	1– 33	37034.9	9957.3	2.924	2.546	2.728	146.1	127.2	136.3
Bread, cereals	1– 6	3486.9	1294.0	2.357	2.252	2.304	119.7	114.3	116.9
Meat	7– 12	11891.8	3098.7	2.798	2.574	2.683	149.1	137.2	143.0
Fish	13– 14	2928.8	147.9	2.101	2.077	2.089	953.8	942.9	948.3
Milk, cheese, eggs	15– 17	5728.1	1467.8	4.068	3.387	3.712	115.2	95.9	105.1
Oils, fats	18– 20	3497.1	694.7	3.709	2.497	3.043	201.6	135.7	165.4
Fruits, vegetables	21– 26	6178.8	1936.6	2.686	2.393	2.535	133.3	118.8	125.8
Coffee, tea, cocoa	27– 29	739.1	244.9	2.196	2.221	2.208	135.9	137.4	136.6
Spices, sweets, sugar	30– 33	2584.3	1072.7	2.605	2.689	2.646	89.6	92.5	91.0
Beverages	34– 37	2114.0	2707.3	2.051	1.881	1.964	41.5	38.1	39.8
Tobacco	38– 39	1504.2	1208.8	1.400	1.418	1.409	87.8	88.9	88.3
Clothing, footwear	40– 51	11780.2	6078.5	3.463	2.946	3.194	65.8	56.0	60.7
Clothing	40– 47	8952.9	5059.6	3.755	3.476	3.613	50.9	47.1	49.0
Footwear	48– 51	2827.3	1018.9	2.011	1.985	1.998	139.8	138.0	138.9
Gross rent, fuel	52– 57	15386.4	6743.4	3.061	3.306	3.181	69.0	74.5	71.7
Gross rent	52– 53	11914.9	4641.0	3.173	3.478	3.322	73.8	80.9	77.3
Fuel, power	54– 57	3471.5	2102.4	2.812	2.826	2.819	58.4	58.7	58.6
House furnishings, operations	58– 70	9816.8	4898.8	3.942	3.468	3.697	57.8	50.8	54.2
Furniture	58– 60	4663.0	2614.4	4.364	3.998	4.177	44.6	40.9	42.7
Appliances	61– 66	1610.0	1102.3	3.495	3.148	3.317	46.4	41.8	44.0
Supplies, operation	67– 70	3543.9	1182.2	3.424	3.074	3.244	97.5	87.6	92.4
Medical care	71– 77	10475.9	5603.6	2.451	2.256	2.352	82.9	76.3	79.5
Transport, communications	78– 89	12126.7	7383.0	2.705	1.884	2.258	87.2	60.7	72.8
Equipment	78– 79	3771.4	1583.8	2.742	2.702	2.722	88.1	86.9	87.5
Operation costs	80– 83	5674.2	4142.3	3.183	3.193	3.188	42.9	43.0	43.0
Purchased transport	84– 87	2130.0	1014.6	1.456	0.947	1.174	221.6	144.2	178.8
Communications	88– 89	551.1	642.3	1.508	0.543	0.905	158.0	56.9	94.8
Recreation, education	90–101	11109.1	6332.4	2.443	2.075	2.251	84.6	71.8	
Recreation	90– 96	6204.2	3400.3	3.049	2.423	2.718	75.3	59.8	67.1
Education	97–101	4904.9	2932.2	1.739	1.756	1.747	95.3	96.2	95.7
Other expenditures	102–107	12933.2	8819.0	2.309	2.054	2.178	71.4	63.5	67.3
Personal care	102–104	2095.6	1658.1	3.106	1.991	2.487	63.5	40.7	50.8
Miscellaneous services	105–107	10837.6	7160.9	2.125	2.067	2.095	73.2	71.2	72.2
Capital formation	109–146	38316.2	23300.7	2.385	1.865	2.109	88.2	69.0	78.0
Domestic capital formation	109–145	44978.2	22739.5	2.362	1.993	2.170	99.2	83.7	91.2
Construction	109–122	24356.0	14379.1	2.110	1.658	1.870	102.2	80.3	90.6
Residential	109–110	10381.6	5183.2	1.852	1.646	1.746	121.6	108.2	114.7
Nonresidential	111–118	5585.7	5484.0	1.828	1.431	1.617	71.2	55.7	63.0
Other	119–122	8388.7	3711.8	2.888	1.871	2.325	120.8	78.3	97.2
Producer durables	123–144	15072.5	8942.8	2.780	2.644	2.711	63.8	60.6	62.2
Transport equipment	123–129	4550.2	1460.1	2.717	2.582	2.648	120.7	114.7	117.7
Nonelectrical machinery	130–138	5766.2	4683.6	2.554	2.607	2.581	47.2	48.2	47.7
Electrical machinery	139–142	3714.4	1936.3	2.722	2.573	2.646	74.6	70.5	72.5
Other	143–144	1041.7	862.8	4.245	3.673	3.949	32.9	28.4	30.6
Exports minus imports	146–146	– 6662.0	561.2	3.296	3.296	3.296	– 360.2	– 360.2	– 360.2
Government	147–151	6886.3	8026.6	2.884	2.914	2.899	29.4	29.8	29.6
Compensation	147–150	4914.7	6157.3	2.868	2.905	2.886	27.5	27.8	27.7
Commodities	151–151	1971.6	1869.3	2.937	2.937	2.937	35.9	35.9	35.9
Gross domestic product	1–151	169483.7	87268.1	2.671	2.295	2.476	84.6	72.7	78.4
Aggregates									
ICP concepts[e]									
Consumption (CEP)[b,c]	1–108	124281.2	55940.8	2.760	2.439	2.595	91.1	80.5	85.6
Capital formation (GCF)[d]	109–146	38316.2	23300.7	2.385	1.865	2.109	88.2	69.0	78.0
Government (PFC)	147–151	6886.3	8026.6	2.884	2.914	2.899	29.4	29.8	29.6
Gross domestic product (ICP)	1–151	169483.7	87268.1	2.671	2.295	2.476	84.6	72.7	78.4
SNA concepts[e]									
Consumption (PFCE)	1–108	115491.9	48900.9	2.861	2.469	2.658	95.6	82.5	88.9
Capital formation (GCF)	109–146	38316.2	23300.7	2.385	1.865	2.109	88.2	69.0	78.0
Government (GFCE)	1–151	15649.7	15066.5	2.498	2.395	2.446	43.4	41.6	42.5
Gross domestic product (SNA)	1–151	169457.8	87268.1	2.671	2.295	2.476	84.6	72.7	78.4

Note: See the end of Appendix Table 7-68 for notes.

Category	Line numbers[a]	Per capita expenditures		Purchasing power parities (pounds/schillings)			Quantity per capita (Austria = 100)		
		U.K. (pounds)	Austria (schillings)	Austria weight	U.K. weight	Geometric mean	Austria weight	U.K. weight	Geometric mean
Consumption, ICP[b,c]	1–108	1272.843	55940.8	0.02571	0.02202	0.02379	103.3	88.5	95.6
Food, beverages, tobacco	1– 39	287.044	13873.4	0.02854	0.02201	0.02506	94.0	72.5	82.6
Food	1– 33	208.714	9957.3	0.02385	0.01942	0.02152	107.9	87.9	97.4
Bread, cereals	1– 6	29.206	1294.0	0.01851	0.01663	0.01754	135.7	121.9	128.6
Meat	7– 12	61.449	3098.7	0.02175	0.01643	0.01890	120.7	91.2	104.9
Fish	13– 14	6.520	147.9	0.02513	0.02423	0.02468	182.0	175.4	178.7
Milk, cheese, eggs	15– 17	29.474	1467.8	0.02200	0.02161	0.02180	92.9	91.3	92.1
Oils, fats	18– 20	8.967	694.7	0.02288	0.01675	0.01958	77.1	56.4	65.9
Fruits, vegetables	21– 26	39.478	1936.6	0.03237	0.02759	0.02989	73.9	63.0	68.2
Coffee, tea, cocoa	27– 29	5.609	244.9	0.01533	0.01006	0.01242	227.7	149.4	184.4
Spices, sweets, sugar	30– 33	28.010	1072.7	0.02586	0.02561	0.02573	102.0	101.0	101.5
Beverages	34– 37	28.795	2707.3	0.04336	0.03449	0.03867	30.8	24.5	27.5
Tobacco	38– 39	49.535	1208.8	0.03397	0.03397	0.03397	120.6	120.6	120.6
Clothing, footwear	40– 51	97.051	6078.5	0.02519	0.02558	0.02538	62.4	63.4	62.9
Clothing	40– 47	80.813	5059.6	0.02463	0.02502	0.02482	63.8	64.9	64.3
Footwear	48– 51	16.238	1018.9	0.02801	0.02875	0.02838	55.4	56.9	56.2
Gross rent, fuel	52– 57	219.557	6743.4	0.03659	0.03664	0.03661	88.9	89.0	88.9
Gross rent	52– 53	167.003	4641.0	0.04418	0.04830	0.04619	74.5	81.5	77.9
Fuel, power	54– 57	52.554	2102.4	0.01982	0.02074	0.02028	120.5	126.1	123.3
House furnishings, operations	58– 70	83.332	4898.8	0.02459	0.02350	0.02404	72.4	69.2	70.8
Furniture	58– 60	34.655	2614.4	0.02447	0.02632	0.02538	50.4	54.2	52.2
Appliances	61– 66	14.237	1102.3	0.02776	0.02617	0.02695	49.4	46.5	47.9
Supplies, operation	67– 70	34.440	1182.2	0.02192	0.02043	0.02117	142.6	132.9	137.6
Medical care	71– 77	75.222	5603.6	0.01554	0.01132	0.01326	118.6	86.4	101.2
Transport, communications	78– 89	150.515	7383.0	0.02097	0.01633	0.01850	124.9	97.2	110.2
Equipment	78– 79	33.226	1583.8	0.02277	0.02211	0.02244	94.9	92.1	93.5
Operation costs	80– 83	63.325	4142.3	0.01652	0.01158	0.01383	132.0	92.5	110.5
Purchased transport	84– 87	37.227	1014.6	0.03320	0.02308	0.02768	159.0	110.5	132.6
Communications	88– 89	16.738	642.3	0.02588	0.02647	0.02617	98.4	100.7	99.6
Recreation, education	90–101	187.599	6332.4	0.02503	0.02305	0.02402	128.5	118.4	123.3
Recreation	90– 96	95.532	3400.3	0.01920	0.01821	0.01870	154.3	146.3	150.3
Education	97–101	92.067	2932.2	0.03178	0.03185	0.03182	98.6	98.8	98.7
Other expenditures	102–107	172.523	8819.0	0.02492	0.02321	0.02405	84.3	78.5	81.3
Personal care	102–104	32.868	1658.1	0.02899	0.02421	0.02649	81.9	68.4	74.8
Miscellaneous services	105–107	139.655	7160.9	0.02398	0.02298	0.02347	84.9	81.3	83.1
Capital formation	109–146	301.906	23300.7	0.02487	0.01854	0.02148	69.9	52.1	60.3
Domestic capital formation	109–145	340.651	22739.5	0.02485	0.01916	0.02182	78.2	60.3	68.7
Construction	109–122	195.727	14379.1	0.02457	0.01769	0.02085	76.9	55.4	65.3
Residential	109–110	75.615	5183.2	0.01821	0.01818	0.01820	80.2	80.1	80.2
Nonresidential	111–118	77.151	5484.0	0.03315	0.02118	0.02650	66.4	42.4	53.1
Other	119–122	42.961	3711.8	0.02077	0.01317	0.01654	87.9	55.7	70.0
Producer durables	123–144	169.861	8942.8	0.02518	0.02178	0.02342	87.2	75.4	81.1
Transport equipment	123–129	52.071	1460.1	0.02376	0.02168	0.02270	164.5	150.1	157.1
Nonelectrical machinery	130–138	72.971	4683.6	0.02453	0.02270	0.02360	68.6	63.5	66.0
Electrical machinery	139–142	34.101	1936.3	0.03054	0.02094	0.02529	84.1	57.7	69.6
Other	143–144	10.718	862.8	0.01903	0.01933	0.01918	64.3	65.3	64.8
Exports minus imports	146–146	−38.745	561.2	0.02584	0.02584	0.02584	−267.2	−267.2	−267.2
Government	147–151	287.812	8026.6	0.01823	0.01796	0.01809	199.7	196.7	198.2
Compensation	147–150	192.905	6157.3	0.01693	0.01634	0.01663	191.8	185.1	188.4
Commodities	151–151	94.907	1869.3	0.02251	0.02251	0.02251	225.6	225.6	225.6
Gross domestic product	1–151	1862.560	87268.1	0.02480	0.02067	0.02264	103.3	86.1	94.3
Aggregates									
ICP concepts[e]									
Consumption (CEP)[b,c]	1–108	1272.843	55940.8	0.02571	0.02202	0.02379	103.3	88.5	95.6
Capital formation (GCF)[d]	109–146	301.906	23300.7	0.02487	0.01854	0.02148	69.9	52.1	60.3
Government (PFC)	147–151	287.812	8026.6	0.01823	0.01796	0.01809	199.7	196.7	198.2
Gross domestic product (ICP)	1–151	1862.560	87268.1	0.02480	0.02067	0.02264	103.3	86.1	94.3
SNA concepts[e]									
Consumption (PFCE)	1–108	1095.068	48900.9	0.02579	0.02266	0.02418	98.8	86.8	92.6
Capital formation (GCF)	109–146	301.906	23300.7	0.02487	0.01854	0.02148	69.9	52.1	60.3
Government (GFCE)	1–151	446.812	15066.5	0.02146	0.01775	0.01952	167.1	138.2	152.0
Gross domestic product (SNA)	1–151	1843.786	87268.1	0.02480	0.02054	0.02257	102.9	85.2	93.6

Note: See the end of Appendix Table 7-68 for notes.

Category	Line numbers[a]	Per capita expenditures Yugoslavia (dinars)	Per capita expenditures Austria (schillings)	Purchasing power parities (dinars/schillings) Austria weight	Purchasing power parities (dinars/schillings) Yugoslavia weight	Purchasing power parities (dinars/schillings) Geometric mean	Quantity per capita (Austria = 100) Austria weight	Quantity per capita (Austria = 100) Yugoslavia weight	Quantity per capita (Austria = 100) Geometric mean
Consumption, ICP[b,c]	1–108	17185.4	55940.8	0.6659	0.5744	0.6185	53.5	46.1	49.7
Food, beverages, tobacco	1– 39	6117.7	13873.4	0.7995	0.6979	0.7470	63.2	55.2	59.0
Food	1– 33	4955.5	9957.3	0.7707	0.6877	0.7280	72.4	64.6	68.4
Bread, cereals	1– 6	962.0	1294.0	0.5718	0.5056	0.5377	147.0	130.0	138.3
Meat	7– 12	1274.6	3098.7	0.6980	0.6326	0.6645	65.0	58.9	61.9
Fish	13– 14	85.4	147.9	0.6289	0.6223	0.6256	92.8	91.8	92.3
Milk, cheese, eggs	15– 17	780.5	1467.8	0.7709	0.7539	0.7623	70.5	69.0	69.7
Oils, fats	18– 20	285.4	694.7	0.8322	0.7295	0.7792	56.3	49.4	52.7
Fruits, vegetables	21– 26	822.8	1936.6	0.8435	0.8109	0.8270	52.4	50.4	51.4
Coffee, tea, cocoa	27– 29	222.1	244.9	1.3108	1.0940	1.1975	82.9	69.2	75.7
Spices, sweets, sugar	30– 33	522.6	1072.7	0.9456	1.0300	0.9869	47.3	51.5	49.4
Beverages	34– 37	733.3	2707.3	1.0072	1.0026	1.0049	27.0	26.9	27.0
Tobacco	38– 39	428.9	1208.8	0.5714	0.5175	0.5438	68.6	62.1	65.3
Clothing, footwear	40– 51	1620.2	6078.5	0.7735	0.7004	0.7360	38.1	34.5	36.2
Clothing	40– 47	1280.3	5059.6	0.7632	0.6723	0.7163	37.6	33.2	35.3
Footwear	48– 51	339.9	1018.9	0.8249	0.8310	0.8280	40.1	40.4	40.3
Gross rent, fuel	52– 57	1421.6	6743.4	0.5349	0.4806	0.5070	43.9	39.4	41.6
Gross rent	52– 53	746.6	4641.0	0.5037	0.4407	0.4711	36.5	31.9	34.1
Fuel, power	54– 57	675.0	2102.4	0.6039	0.5340	0.5679	60.1	53.2	56.5
House furnishings, operations	58– 70	1651.8	4898.8	0.9357	0.8416	0.8874	40.1	36.0	38.0
Furniture	58– 60	794.1	2614.4	1.0304	1.0101	1.0202	30.1	29.5	29.8
Appliances	61– 66	323.8	1102.3	0.8611	0.8450	0.8530	34.8	34.1	34.4
Supplies, operation	67– 70	533.9	1182.2	0.7958	0.6730	0.7318	67.1	56.7	61.7
Medical care	71– 77	1262.7	5603.6	0.4284	0.3734	0.3999	60.4	52.6	56.3
Transport, communications	78– 89	1603.2	7383.0	0.6745	0.5149	0.5893	42.2	32.2	36.8
Equipment	78– 79	450.1	1583.8	0.8133	0.8090	0.8112	35.1	34.9	35.0
Operation costs	80– 83	652.1	4142.3	0.6620	0.6304	0.6460	25.0	23.8	24.4
Purchased transport	84– 87	435.6	1014.6	0.4461	0.3646	0.4033	117.8	96.2	106.5
Communications	88– 89	65.3	642.3	0.7736	0.1995	0.3928	51.0	13.2	25.9
Recreation, education	90–101	2058.0	6332.4	0.6277	0.4396	0.5253	73.9	51.8	61.9
Recreation	90– 96	950.3	3400.3	0.7916	0.4587	0.6025	60.9	35.3	46.4
Education	97–101	1107.7	2932.2	0.4377	0.4244	0.4310	89.0	86.3	87.6
Other expenditures	102–107	1732.5	8819.0	0.6459	0.5731	0.6084	34.3	30.4	32.3
Personal care	102–104	325.2	1658.1	0.6933	0.6298	0.6608	31.1	28.3	29.7
Miscellaneous services	105–107	1407.3	7160.9	0.6349	0.5614	0.5970	35.0	31.0	32.9
Capital formation	109–146	8495.0	23300.7	0.7584	0.6779	0.7170	53.8	48.1	50.8
Domestic capital formation	109–145	10345.4	22739.5	0.7525	0.7192	0.7357	63.3	60.5	61.8
Construction	109–122	4615.1	14379.1	0.6674	0.6631	0.6652	48.4	48.1	48.2
Residential	109–110	1760.3	5183.2	0.6171	0.6172	0.6171	55.0	55.0	55.0
Nonresidential	111–118	1633.5	5484.0	0.7891	0.8488	0.8184	35.1	37.7	36.4
Other	119–122	1221.3	3711.8	0.5578	0.5594	0.5586	58.8	59.0	58.9
Producer durables	123–144	3457.3	8942.8	0.8892	0.7874	0.8368	49.1	43.5	46.2
Transport equipment	123–129	538.6	1460.1	0.7955	0.6247	0.7050	59.0	46.4	52.3
Nonelectrical machinery	130–138	2130.7	4683.6	1.0322	0.9505	0.9905	47.9	44.1	45.9
Electrical machinery	139–142	545.8	1936.3	0.7610	0.6157	0.6845	45.8	37.0	41.2
Other	143–144	242.2	862.8	0.5592	0.6048	0.5816	46.4	50.2	48.3
Exports minus imports	146–146	− 1850.4	561.2	0.9982	0.9982	0.9982	− 330.3	− 330.3	− 330.3
Government	147–151	3257.3	8026.6	0.4976	0.5304	0.5138	76.5	81.6	79.0
Compensation	147–150	1434.1	6157.3	0.4441	0.4175	0.4306	55.8	52.4	54.1
Commodities	151–151	1823.2	1869.3	0.6738	0.6738	0.6738	144.8	144.8	144.8
Gross domestic product	1–151	28937.7	87268.1	0.6751	0.5956	0.6341	55.7	49.1	52.3
Aggregates									
ICP concepts[e]									
Consumption (CEP)[b,c]	1–108	17185.4	55940.8	0.6659	0.5744	0.6185	53.5	46.1	49.7
Capital formation (GCF)[d]	109–146	8495.0	23300.7	0.7584	0.6779	0.7170	53.8	48.1	50.8
Government (PFC)	147–151	3257.3	8026.6	0.4976	0.5304	0.5138	76.5	81.6	79.0
Gross domestic product (ICP)	1–151	28937.7	87268.1	0.6751	0.5956	0.6341	55.7	49.1	52.3
SNA concepts[e]									
Consumption (PFCE)	1–108	14426.3	48900.9	0.6902	0.6340	0.6615	46.5	42.7	44.6
Capital formation (GCF)	109–146	8495.0	23300.7	0.7584	0.6779	0.7170	53.8	48.1	50.8
Government (GFCE)	1–151	6012.0	15066.5	0.4973	0.4522	0.4742	88.2	80.2	84.1
Gross domestic product (SNA)	1–151	28933.4	87268.1	0.6751	0.5956	0.6341	55.7	49.1	52.3

Note: See the end of Appendix Table 7-68 for notes.

Category	Line numbers[a]	Per capita expenditures		Purchasing power parities (pesos/cruzeiros)			Quantity per capita (Brazil = 100)		
		Colombia (pesos)	Brazil (cruzeiros)	Brazil weight	Colombia weight	Geometric mean	Brazil weight	Colombia weight	Geometric mean
Consumption, ICP[b,c]	1–108	13745.7	6729.29	2.432	1.932	2.168	105.7	84.0	94.2
Food, beverages, tobacco	1– 39	5368.9	2476.69	2.615	2.237	2.419	96.9	82.9	89.6
Food	1– 33	4655.4	2283.74	2.696	2.452	2.571	83.2	75.6	79.3
Bread, cereals	1– 6	720.2	506.19	3.452	4.199	3.807	33.9	41.2	37.4
Meat	7– 12	1613.3	617.70	2.623	2.490	2.556	104.9	99.6	102.2
Fish	13– 14	95.0	72.63	3.338	3.357	3.347	39.0	39.2	39.1
Milk, cheese, eggs	15– 17	513.2	231.09	2.914	2.923	2.918	76.0	76.2	76.1
Oils, fats	18– 20	210.4	159.20	2.741	2.706	2.724	48.8	48.2	48.5
Fruits, vegetables	21– 26	766.1	464.38	1.994	1.697	1.840	97.2	82.7	89.7
Coffee, tea, cocoa	27– 29	199.6	102.70	1.512	1.747	1.625	111.2	128.5	119.6
Spices, sweets, sugar	30– 33	537.6	129.85	2.746	2.315	2.521	178.8	150.8	164.2
Beverages	34– 37	531.3	40.36	2.844	2.861	2.853	460.3	462.9	461.6
Tobacco	38– 39	182.1	152.59	1.343	0.578	0.881	206.4	88.9	135.4
Clothing, footwear	40– 51	1266.0	629.43	1.808	1.746	1.777	115.2	111.3	113.2
Clothing	40– 47	947.7	526.73	1.793	1.763	1.778	102.0	100.3	101.2
Footwear	48– 51	318.3	102.69	1.882	1.697	1.787	182.7	164.7	173.5
Gross rent, fuel	52– 57	1064.2	717.36	1.610	1.248	1.418	118.9	92.1	104.7
Gross rent	52– 53	830.0	454.73	2.292	2.439	2.364	74.8	79.6	77.2
Fuel, power	54– 57	234.2	262.63	0.430	0.457	0.443	195.1	207.2	201.1
House furnishings, operations	58– 70	854.6	558.27	2.446	1.797	2.097	85.2	62.6	73.0
Furniture	58– 60	176.5	207.61	1.723	1.691	1.707	50.3	49.3	49.8
Appliances	61– 66	104.0	90.22	4.507	4.187	4.344	27.5	25.6	26.5
Supplies, operation	67– 70	574.2	260.44	2.308	1.658	1.956	133.0	95.5	112.7
Medical care	71– 77	716.7	362.27	3.056	1.628	2.230	121.5	64.7	88.7
Transport, communications	78– 89	1272.9	721.02	2.766	1.882	2.282	93.8	63.8	77.4
Equipment	78– 79	131.5	194.31	5.011	6.083	5.521	11.1	13.5	12.3
Operation costs	80– 83	80.3	322.79	2.147	1.700	1.910	14.6	11.6	13.0
Purchased transport	84– 87	973.2	173.12	1.739	1.951	1.842	288.1	323.3	305.2
Communications	88– 89	87.9	30.81	0.863	0.810	0.836	352.3	330.9	341.5
Recreation, education	90–101	1605.1	593.74	2.625	2.098	2.347	128.9	103.0	115.2
Recreation	90– 96	485.3	346.63	2.201	1.382	1.744	101.3	63.6	80.3
Education	97–101	1119.8	247.10	3.219	2.705	2.951	167.5	140.8	153.6
Other expenditures	102–107	1597.4	670.52	2.337	2.052	2.190	116.1	101.9	108.8
Personal care	102–104	309.1	152.58	3.339	2.678	2.991	75.6	60.7	67.7
Miscellaneous services	105–107	1288.3	517.94	2.042	1.943	1.992	128.0	121.8	124.9
Capital formation	109–146	3201.1	2013.05	3.509	1.671	2.422	95.1	45.3	65.7
Domestic capital formation	109–145	3108.6	2388.38	3.549	1.644	2.416	79.2	36.7	53.9
Construction	109–122	1913.6	1183.77	1.357	1.124	1.235	143.8	119.1	130.9
Residential	109–110	396.1	249.05	2.178	1.966	2.069	80.9	73.0	76.9
Nonresidential	111–118	121.8	297.86	1.455	1.323	1.387	30.9	28.1	29.5
Other	119–122	1395.7	636.86	0.991	0.991	0.991	221.2	221.2	221.2
Producer durables	123–144	1362.8	1204.61	5.703	4.971	5.325	22.8	19.8	21.2
Transport equipment	123–129	467.9	249.33	4.858	5.087	4.971	36.9	38.6	37.7
Nonelectrical machinery	130–138	236.8	550.77	6.009	4.398	5.141	9.8	7.2	8.4
Electrical machinery	139–142	593.5	191.64	5.784	5.079	5.420	61.0	53.5	57.1
Other	143–144	64.5	212.87	5.829	5.641	5.734	5.4	5.2	5.3
Exports minus imports	146–146	92.5	− 375.32	3.763	3.763	3.763	− 6.5	− 6.5	− 6.5
Government	147–151	489.7	680.40	2.535	1.883	2.184	38.2	28.4	32.9
Compensation	147–150	400.7	468.79	2.672	1.819	2.205	47.0	32.0	38.8
Commodities	151–151	89.1	211.61	2.231	2.231	2.231	18.9	18.9	18.9
Gross domestic product	1–151	17436.6	9422.75	2.669	1.877	2.239	98.6	69.3	82.7
Aggregates									
ICP concepts[e]									
Consumption (CEP)[b,c]	1–108	13745.7	6729.29	2.432	1.932	2.168	105.7	84.0	94.2
Capital formation (GCF)[d]	109–146	3201.1	2013.05	3.509	1.671	2.422	95.1	45.3	65.7
Government (PFC)	147–151	489.7	680.40	2.535	1.883	2.184	38.2	28.4	32.9
Gross domestic product (ICP)	1–151	17436.6	9422.75	2.669	1.877	2.239	98.6	69.3	82.7
SNA concepts[e]									
Consumption (PFCE)	1–108	12950.4	6480.32	2.403	1.909	2.142	104.7	83.2	93.3
Capital formation (GCF)	109–146	3201.1	2013.05	3.509	1.671	2.422	95.1	45.3	65.7
Government (GFCE)	1–151	1285.1	927.28	2.709	2.176	2.428	63.7	51.2	57.1
Gross domestic product (SNA)	1–151	17436.6	9420.66	2.669	1.877	2.239	98.6	69.3	82.7

Note: See the end of Appendix Table 7-68 for notes.

Category	Line numbers[a]	Per capita expenditures		Purchasing power parities (dollars/cruzeiros)			Quantity per capita (Brazil = 100)		
		Jamaica (dollars)	Brazil (cruzeiros)	Brazil weight	Jamaica weight	Geometric mean	Brazil weight	Jamaica weight	Geometric mean
Consumption, ICP[b,c]	1–108	918.799	6729.29	0.1495	0.1219	0.1350	112.0	91.3	101.1
Food, beverages, tobacco	1– 39	384.013	2476.69	0.1753	0.1429	0.1583	108.5	88.5	98.0
Food	1– 33	300.143	2283.74	0.1772	0.1429	0.1592	91.9	74.2	82.6
Bread, cereals	1– 6	87.629	506.19	0.1598	0.1454	0.1525	119.0	108.3	113.5
Meat	7– 12	36.837	617.70	0.2185	0.1881	0.2027	31.7	27.3	29.4
Fish	13– 14	24.476	72.63	0.1701	0.1656	0.1678	203.5	198.1	200.8
Milk, cheese, eggs	15– 17	35.896	231.09	0.1830	0.1101	0.1419	141.1	84.9	109.5
Oils, fats	18– 20	8.857	159.20	0.1371	0.1282	0.1326	43.4	40.6	42.0
Fruits, vegetables	21– 26	83.154	464.38	0.1539	0.1386	0.1461	129.2	116.3	122.6
Coffee, tea, cocoa	27– 29	2.653	102.70	0.1975	0.1829	0.1901	14.1	13.1	13.6
Spices, sweets, sugar	30– 33	20.642	129.85	0.1589	0.1436	0.1511	110.7	100.0	105.2
Beverages	34– 37	43.838	40.36	0.1671	0.1727	0.1699	629.0	650.0	639.4
Tobacco	38– 39	40.031	152.59	0.1481	0.1201	0.1334	218.4	177.1	196.7
Clothing, footwear	40– 51	36.965	629.43	0.1055	0.1091	0.1073	53.8	55.7	54.7
Clothing	40– 47	18.467	526.73	0.1006	0.0982	0.0994	35.7	34.9	35.3
Footwear	48– 51	18.497	102.69	0.1307	0.1227	0.1266	146.8	137.8	142.2
Gross rent, fuel	52– 57	97.715	717.36	0.1777	0.1399	0.1576	97.4	76.7	86.4
Gross rent	52– 53	73.897	454.73	0.2279	0.1931	0.2098	84.1	71.3	77.5
Fuel, power	54– 57	23.818	262.63	0.0907	0.0754	0.0827	120.3	100.0	109.7
House furnishings, operations	58– 70	52.905	558.27	0.1154	0.0939	0.1041	101.0	82.1	91.0
Furniture	58– 60	21.003	207.61	0.1052	0.1088	0.1070	93.0	96.2	94.6
Appliances	61– 66	5.225	90.22	0.1617	0.1641	0.1629	35.3	35.8	35.6
Supplies, operation	67– 70	26.677	260.44	0.1075	0.0788	0.0920	130.1	95.3	111.3
Medical care	71– 77	39.875	362.27	0.1509	0.1116	0.1298	98.6	72.9	84.8
Transport, communications	78– 89	106.338	721.02	0.1443	0.1274	0.1356	115.8	102.2	108.8
Equipment	78– 79	10.786	194.31	0.1569	0.1586	0.1578	35.0	35.4	35.2
Operation costs	80– 83	48.990	322.79	0.1214	0.0990	0.1096	153.3	125.1	138.5
Purchased transport	84– 87	40.740	173.12	0.1888	0.1886	0.1887	124.8	124.7	124.7
Communications	88– 89	5.822	30.81	0.0557	0.1038	0.0761	182.1	339.0	248.5
Recreation, education	90–101	80.664	593.74	0.1420	0.0956	0.1165	142.1	95.7	116.6
Recreation	90– 96	33.285	346.63	0.1161	0.0560	0.0806	171.6	82.7	119.1
Education	97–101	47.379	247.10	0.1783	0.1903	0.1842	100.8	107.6	104.1
Other expenditures	102–107	154.601	670.52	0.1054	0.1014	0.1034	227.3	218.7	223.0
Personal care	102–104	39.883	152.58	0.1099	0.1053	0.1076	248.1	237.9	242.9
Miscellaneous services	105–107	114.719	517.94	0.1041	0.1001	0.1021	221.2	212.7	216.9
Capital formation	109–146	193.717	2013.05	0.1611	0.1870	0.1735	51.5	59.7	55.5
Domestic capital formation	109–145	331.896	2388.38	0.1532	0.1454	0.1492	95.6	90.7	93.1
Construction	109–122	146.331	1183.77	0.1518	0.1645	0.1580	75.1	81.4	78.2
Residential	109–110	89.023	249.05	0.2080	0.1833	0.1953	195.0	171.8	183.1
Nonresidential	111–118	45.874	297.86	0.1676	0.1478	0.1574	104.2	91.9	97.9
Other	119–122	11.434	636.86	0.1225	0.1225	0.1225	14.7	14.7	14.7
Producer durables	123–144	155.252	1204.61	0.1545	0.1321	0.1429	97.6	83.4	90.2
Transport equipment	123–129	47.420	249.33	0.1342	0.1401	0.1371	135.7	141.7	138.7
Nonelectrical machinery	130–138	65.707	550.77	0.1712	0.1275	0.1477	93.6	69.7	80.8
Electrical machinery	139–142	20.897	191.64	0.1373	0.1113	0.1236	98.0	79.4	88.2
Other	143–144	21.228	212.87	0.1508	0.1590	0.1548	62.7	66.1	64.4
Exports minus imports	146–146	−138.179	−375.32	0.1108	0.1108	0.1108	332.2	332.2	332.2
Government	147–151	165.510	680.40	0.2107	0.1645	0.1861	147.9	115.5	130.7
Compensation	147–150	104.346	468.79	0.2367	0.1720	0.2018	129.4	94.0	110.3
Commodities	151–151	61.164	211.61	0.1530	0.1530	0.1530	188.9	188.9	188.9
Gross domestic product	1–151	1278.025	9422.75	0.1564	0.1334	0.1444	101.7	86.7	93.9
Aggregates									
ICP concepts[e]									
Consumption (CEP)[b,c]	1–108	918.799	6729.29	0.1495	0.1219	0.1350	112.0	91.3	101.1
Capital formation (GCF)[d]	109–146	193.717	2013.05	0.1611	0.1870	0.1735	51.5	59.7	55.5
Government (PFC)	147–151	165.510	680.40	0.2107	0.1645	0.1861	147.9	115.5	130.7
Gross domestic product (ICP)	1–151	1278.025	9422.75	0.1564	0.1334	0.1444	101.7	86.7	93.9
SNA concepts[e]									
Consumption (PFCE)	1–108	849.750	6480.32	0.1483	0.1201	0.1334	109.2	88.4	98.3
Capital formation (GCF)	109–146	193.717	2013.05	0.1611	0.1870	0.1735	51.5	59.7	55.5
Government (GFCE)	1–151	234.558	927.28	0.2030	0.1597	0.1800	158.4	124.6	140.5
Gross domestic product (SNA)	1–151	1278.025	9420.66	0.1564	0.1334	0.1444	101.7	86.7	93.9

Note: See the end of Appendix Table 7-68 for notes.

Category	Line numbers[a]	Per capita expenditures		Purchasing power parities (pesos/cruzeiros)			Quantity per capita (Brazil = 100)		
		Mexico (pesos)	Brazil (cruzeiros)	Brazil weight	Mexico weight	Geometric mean	Brazil weight	Mexico weight	Geometric mean
Consumption, ICP[b,c]	1–108	13561.6	6729.29	1.546	1.230	1.379	163.9	130.4	146.2
Food, beverages, tobacco	1– 39	5306.2	2476.69	1.714	1.349	1.521	158.8	125.0	140.9
Food	1– 33	5093.9	2283.74	1.795	1.413	1.593	157.9	124.2	140.0
Bread, cereals	1– 6	1217.5	506.19	1.848	1.595	1.717	150.8	130.1	140.1
Meat	7– 12	1293.9	617.70	2.523	2.048	2.273	102.3	83.0	92.2
Fish	13– 14	86.6	72.63	1.408	1.318	1.362	90.5	84.6	87.5
Milk, cheese, eggs	15– 17	927.1	231.09	1.674	1.204	1.419	333.3	239.6	282.6
Oils, fats	18– 20	382.0	159.20	1.618	1.673	1.645	143.5	148.3	145.9
Fruits, vegetables	21– 26	738.6	464.38	0.963	0.882	0.921	180.4	165.2	172.6
Coffee, tea, cocoa	27– 29	147.7	102.70	2.294	1.985	2.134	72.4	62.7	67.4
Spices, sweets, sugar	30– 33	300.6	129.85	1.360	1.285	1.322	180.1	170.2	175.1
Beverages	34– 37	116.7	40.36	2.146	1.431	1.752	202.1	134.8	165.1
Tobacco	38– 39	95.5	152.59	0.389	0.388	0.388	161.4	161.0	161.2
Clothing, footwear	40– 51	1366.7	629.43	1.261	1.228	1.244	176.8	172.2	174.5
Clothing	40– 47	1034.6	526.73	1.262	1.221	1.241	160.9	155.6	158.2
Footwear	48– 51	332.1	102.69	1.252	1.252	1.252	258.3	258.4	258.3
Gross rent, fuel	52– 57	1312.6	717.36	0.902	0.912	0.907	200.6	202.9	201.7
Gross rent	52– 53	704.7	454.73	0.827	0.829	0.828	186.9	187.4	187.1
Fuel, power	54– 57	607.9	262.63	1.032	1.032	1.032	224.4	224.4	224.4
House furnishings, operations	58– 70	1489.9	558.27	1.117	1.024	1.069	260.7	239.0	249.6
Furniture	58– 60	257.8	207.61	0.791	0.757	0.774	164.1	156.9	160.5
Appliances	61– 66	291.0	90.22	1.660	1.642	1.651	196.4	194.3	195.3
Supplies, operation	67– 70	941.1	260.44	1.188	1.004	1.092	360.1	304.3	331.0
Medical care	71– 77	803.9	362.27	2.467	1.687	2.040	131.5	89.9	108.8
Transport, communications	78– 89	1096.0	721.02	1.258	1.009	1.126	150.6	120.9	134.9
Equipment	78– 79	296.4	194.31	1.655	1.487	1.569	102.6	92.2	97.2
Operation costs	80– 83	386.5	322.79	1.271	0.971	1.111	123.3	94.2	107.8
Purchased transport	84– 87	344.2	173.12	0.847	0.833	0.840	238.5	234.8	236.7
Communications	88– 89	69.0	30.81	0.920	0.909	0.915	246.6	243.5	245.1
Recreation, education	90–101	1205.2	593.74	2.191	1.753	1.960	115.8	92.7	103.6
Recreation	90– 96	408.0	346.63	1.477	1.191	1.326	98.9	79.7	88.7
Education	97–101	797.2	247.10	3.192	2.312	2.716	139.6	101.1	118.8
Other expenditures	102–107	1251.4	670.52	1.478	1.236	1.352	151.0	126.2	138.1
Personal care	102–104	395.4	152.58	1.693	1.238	1.448	209.4	153.1	179.0
Miscellaneous services	105–107	855.9	517.94	1.415	1.235	1.322	133.8	116.8	125.0
Capital formation	109–146	3834.6	2013.05	2.074	1.368	1.684	139.3	91.8	113.1
Domestic capital formation	109–145	4413.7	2388.38	1.988	1.386	1.660	133.3	93.0	111.3
Construction	109–122	2354.5	1183.77	1.611	1.179	1.378	168.7	123.4	144.3
Residential	109–110	1146.1	249.05	1.535	1.512	1.524	304.4	299.7	302.1
Nonresidential	111–118	477.6	297.86	1.167	1.141	1.154	140.5	137.4	138.9
Other	119–122	730.8	636.86	1.849	0.890	1.283	128.9	62.1	89.4
Producer durables	123–144	1625.2	1204.61	2.358	1.895	2.114	71.2	57.2	63.8
Transport equipment	123–129	397.8	249.33	1.817	1.421	1.607	112.3	87.8	99.3
Nonelectrical machinery	130–138	566.8	550.77	2.275	2.016	2.141	51.1	45.2	48.1
Electrical machinery	139–142	315.3	191.64	3.363	2.290	2.776	71.8	48.9	59.3
Other	143–144	345.3	212.87	2.302	2.171	2.236	74.7	70.5	72.6
Exports minus imports	146–146	− 579.0	− 375.32	1.524	1.524	1.524	101.3	101.3	101.3
Government	147–151	915.7	680.40	2.267	1.635	1.925	82.3	59.4	69.9
Compensation	147–150	707.8	468.79	2.670	1.732	2.151	87.2	56.5	70.2
Commodities	151–151	207.9	211.61	1.373	1.373	1.373	71.5	71.5	71.5
Gross domestic product	1–151	18311.9	9422.75	1.711	1.273	1.476	152.7	113.6	131.7
Aggregates									
ICP concepts[e]									
Consumption (CEP)[b,c]	1–108	13561.6	6729.29	1.546	1.230	1.379	163.9	130.4	146.2
Capital formation (GCF)[d]	109–146	3834.6	2013.05	2.074	1.368	1.684	139.3	91.8	113.1
Government (PFC)	147–151	915.7	680.40	2.267	1.635	1.925	82.3	59.4	69.9
Gross domestic product (ICP)	1–151	18311.9	9422.75	1.711	1.273	1.476	152.7	113.6	131.7
SNA concepts[e]									
Consumption (PFCE)	1–108	12568.3	6480.32	1.490	1.195	1.335	162.3	130.1	145.3
Capital formation (GCF)	109–146	3834.6	2013.05	2.074	1.368	1.684	139.3	91.8	113.1
Government (GFCE)	1–151	1887.0	927.28	2.464	1.807	2.110	112.6	82.6	96.4
Gross domestic product (SNA)	1–151	18289.9	9420.66	1.711	1.273	1.476	152.5	113.5	131.5

Note: See the end of Appendix Table 7-68 for notes.

Category	Line numbers[a]	Per capita expenditures		Purchasing power parities (N.pesos/cruzeiros)			Quantity per capita (Brazil = 100)		
		Uruguay (N.pesos)	Brazil (cruzeiros)	Brazil weight	Uruguay weight	Geometric mean	Brazil weight	Uruguay weight	Geometric mean
Consumption, ICP[b,c]	1–108	2416.27	6729.29	0.2590	0.1864	0.2197	192.6	138.7	163.4
Food, beverages, tobacco	1– 39	1012.85	2476.69	0.2292	0.1785	0.2022	229.1	178.4	202.2
Food	1– 33	769.63	2283.74	0.2286	0.1665	0.1951	202.4	147.4	172.8
Bread, cereals	1– 6	127.51	506.19	0.1780	0.1617	0.1696	155.8	141.5	148.5
Meat	7– 12	203.64	617.70	0.1888	0.1467	0.1664	224.7	174.6	198.1
Fish	13– 14	2.41	72.63	0.2013	0.0836	0.1297	39.6	16.4	25.5
Milk, cheese, eggs	15– 17	105.89	231.09	0.1791	0.1679	0.1734	273.0	255.8	264.3
Oils, fats	18– 20	43.90	159.20	0.4010	0.4286	0.4146	64.3	68.8	66.5
Fruits, vegetables	21– 26	161.90	464.38	0.1809	0.1262	0.1511	276.3	192.7	230.8
Coffee, tea, cocoa	27– 29	12.27	102.70	0.3909	0.3524	0.3712	33.9	30.6	32.2
Spices, sweets, sugar	30– 33	112.12	129.85	0.5496	0.3059	0.4100	282.3	157.1	210.6
Beverages	34– 37	169.94	40.36	0.2314	0.2226	0.2269	1891.9	1820.0	1855.6
Tobacco	38– 39	73.28	152.59	0.2373	0.2543	0.2457	188.9	202.4	195.5
Clothing, footwear	40– 51	172.54	629.43	0.2129	0.1994	0.2060	137.5	128.8	133.1
Clothing	40– 47	129.49	526.73	0.1996	0.1849	0.1921	133.0	123.2	128.0
Footwear	48– 51	43.06	102.69	0.2809	0.2607	0.2706	160.8	149.2	154.9
Gross rent, fuel	52– 57	266.19	717.36	0.1832	0.1415	0.1610	262.3	202.5	230.5
Gross rent	52– 53	163.69	454.73	0.1838	0.1480	0.1650	243.2	195.8	218.2
Fuel, power	54– 57	102.50	262.63	0.1821	0.1321	0.1551	295.4	214.3	251.6
House furnishings, operations	58– 70	191.45	558.27	0.3231	0.3179	0.3205	107.9	106.1	107.0
Furniture	58– 60	32.63	207.61	0.1692	0.1711	0.1701	91.9	92.9	92.4
Appliances	61– 66	39.38	90.22	0.3960	0.2957	0.3422	147.6	110.2	127.6
Supplies, operation	67– 70	119.44	260.44	0.4205	0.4292	0.4248	106.9	109.1	108.0
Medical care	71– 77	152.54	362.27	0.2201	0.1313	0.1700	320.7	191.3	247.7
Transport, communications	78– 89	234.39	721.02	0.4117	0.2832	0.3415	114.8	79.0	95.2
Equipment	78– 79	34.08	194.31	0.6912	0.6851	0.6882	25.6	25.4	25.5
Operation costs	80– 83	60.93	322.79	0.3210	0.2518	0.2843	75.0	58.8	66.4
Purchased transport	84– 87	119.03	173.12	0.2916	0.2628	0.2768	261.7	235.8	248.4
Communications	88– 89	20.36	30.81	0.2734	0.2455	0.2591	269.2	241.6	255.0
Recreation, education	90–101	203.98	593.74	0.2863	0.2265	0.2546	151.7	120.0	134.9
Recreation	90– 96	127.77	346.63	0.2545	0.1894	0.2195	194.6	144.8	167.9
Education	97–101	76.21	247.10	0.3309	0.3373	0.3341	91.4	93.2	92.3
Other expenditures	102–107	182.32	670.52	0.2725	0.1741	0.2178	156.2	99.8	124.9
Personal care	102–104	41.91	152.58	0.3604	0.2943	0.3257	93.3	76.2	84.3
Miscellaneous services	105–107	140.41	517.94	0.2466	0.1551	0.1956	174.7	109.9	138.6
Capital formation	109–146	290.08	2013.05	0.4859	0.3492	0.4119	41.3	29.7	35.0
Domestic capital formation	109–145	396.12	2388.38	0.4535	0.3276	0.3855	50.6	36.6	43.0
Construction	109–122	276.78	1183.77	0.4409	0.2972	0.3620	78.7	53.0	64.6
Residential	109–110	92.45	249.05	0.4853	0.4753	0.4803	78.1	76.5	77.3
Nonresidential	111–118	43.79	297.86	0.2053	0.1832	0.1940	80.2	71.6	75.8
Other	119–122	140.55	636.86	0.5337	0.2824	0.3882	78.1	41.4	56.8
Producer durables	123–144	115.02	1204.61	0.4660	0.4474	0.4566	21.3	20.5	20.9
Transport equipment	123–129	31.38	249.33	0.6364	0.5232	0.5770	24.1	19.8	21.8
Nonelectrical machinery	130–138	57.11	550.77	0.4247	0.4639	0.4439	22.4	24.4	23.4
Electrical machinery	139–142	8.50	191.64	0.4992	0.3798	0.4354	11.7	8.9	10.2
Other	143–144	18.04	212.87	0.3435	0.3492	0.3463	24.3	24.7	24.5
Exports minus imports	146–146	− 106.04	− 375.32	0.2802	0.2802	0.2802	100.8	100.8	100.8
Government	147–151	301.90	680.40	0.2221	0.1472	0.1808	301.4	199.7	245.4
Compensation	147–150	241.74	468.79	0.2297	0.1375	0.1777	374.9	224.5	290.1
Commodities	151–151	60.17	211.61	0.2054	0.2054	0.2054	138.4	138.4	138.4
Gross domestic product	1–151	3008.26	9422.75	0.3084	0.1899	0.2406	168.1	104.7	132.7
Aggregates									
ICP concepts[e]									
Consumption (CEP)[b,c]	1–108	2416.27	6729.29	0.2590	0.1864	0.2197	192.6	138.7	163.4
Capital formation (GCF)[d]	109–146	290.08	2013.05	0.4859	0.3492	0.4119	41.3	29.7	35.0
Government (PFC)	147–151	301.90	680.40	0.2221	0.1472	0.1808	301.4	199.7	245.4
Gross domestic product (ICP)	1–151	3008.26	9422.75	0.3048	0.1899	0.2406	168.1	104.7	132.7
SNA concepts[e]									
Consumption (PFCE)	1–108	2317.03	6480.32	0.2571	0.1852	0.2182	193.1	139.1	163.9
Capital formation (GCF)	109–146	290.08	2013.05	0.4859	0.3492	0.4119	41.3	29.7	35.0
Government (GFCE)	1–151	401.15	927.28	0.2452	0.1605	0.1984	269.6	176.5	218.1
Gross domestic product (SNA)	1–151	3008.26	9420.66	0.3048	0.1899	0.2406	168.2	104.8	132.7

Note: See the end of Appendix Table 7-68 for notes.

Category	Line numbers[a]	Per capita expenditures		Purchasing power parities (cruzeiros/shillings)			Quantity per capita (Kenya = 100)		
		Brazil (cruzeiros)	Kenya (shillings)	Kenya weight	Brazil weight	Geometric mean	Kenya weight	Brazil weight	Geometric mean
Consumption, ICP[b,c]	1–108	6729.29	1370.10	1.434	1.001	1.198	490.4	342.5	409.8
Food, beverages, tobacco	1– 39	2476.69	602.13	1.520	1.158	1.326	355.3	270.7	310.1
Food	1– 33	2283.74	505.11	1.552	1.133	1.326	399.2	291.3	341.0
Bread, cereals	1– 6	506.19	201.96	2.014	1.539	1.761	162.9	124.4	142.4
Meat	7– 12	617.70	30.15	1.284	1.110	1.194	1845.1	1595.3	1715.6
Fish	13– 14	72.63	2.99	0.708	0.631	0.668	3856.6	3434.9	3639.6
Milk, cheese, eggs	15– 17	231.09	95.68	1.074	1.040	1.057	232.2	225.0	228.5
Oils, fats	18– 20	159.20	15.08	0.874	0.869	0.871	1215.6	1207.8	1211.7
Fruits, vegetables	21– 26	464.38	109.26	1.692	1.550	1.620	274.2	251.1	262.4
Coffee, tea, cocoa	27– 29	102.70	7.61	1.337	0.973	1.141	1385.9	1009.1	1182.6
Spices, sweets, sugar	30– 33	129.85	42.39	0.600	0.632	0.616	485.0	510.2	497.4
Beverages	34– 37	40.36	63.74	0.775	0.651	0.710	97.2	81.7	89.1
Tobacco	38– 39	152.59	33.29	2.450	2.514	2.481	182.4	187.1	184.7
Clothing, footwear	40– 51	629.43	94.04	1.262	1.168	1.214	572.9	530.4	551.3
Clothing	40– 47	526.73	80.45	1.363	1.392	1.378	470.3	480.3	475.3
Footwear	48– 51	102.69	13.58	0.662	0.640	0.651	1180.8	1141.9	1161.2
Gross rent, fuel	52– 57	717.36	154.79	0.850	0.727	0.786	637.5	545.0	589.4
Gross rent	52– 53	454.73	124.49	0.836	0.781	0.808	468.0	436.8	452.1
Fuel, power	54– 57	262.63	30.30	0.908	0.650	0.768	1334.1	954.2	1128.3
House furnishings, operations	58– 70	558.27	115.38	2.793	1.541	2.074	314.1	173.2	233.3
Furniture	58– 60	207.61	45.68	2.242	1.560	1.870	291.4	202.7	243.0
Appliances	61– 66	90.22	4.48	0.0	1.590	0.0	1267.2	0.0	0.0
Supplies, operation	67– 70	260.44	65.23	3.178	1.524	2.201	262.0	125.6	181.4
Medical care	71– 77	362.27	65.68	0.577	0.550	0.563	1002.2	956.6	979.1
Transport, communications	78– 89	721.02	100.01	1.316	1.053	1.177	684.8	547.9	612.5
Equipment	78– 79	194.31	10.60	0.931	0.969	0.950	1891.5	1970.3	1930.5
Operation costs	80– 83	322.79	42.54	1.580	1.161	1.354	653.8	480.1	560.2
Purchased transport	84– 87	173.12	42.39	1.173	1.065	1.118	383.3	348.2	365.3
Communications	88– 89	30.81	4.48	1.069	0.703	0.867	978.2	643.6	793.4
Recreation, education	90–101	593.74	160.76	1.105	1.121	1.113	329.6	334.3	332.0
Recreation	90– 96	346.63	28.81	2.062	1.693	1.868	710.9	583.6	644.1
Education	97–101	247.10	131.95	0.896	0.760	0.825	246.4	209.0	226.9
Other expenditures	102–107	670.52	77.32	1.685	0.818	1.174	1060.1	514.7	738.6
Personal care	102–104	152.58	30.30	2.404	1.497	1.897	336.5	209.5	265.5
Miscellaneous services	105–107	517.94	47.02	1.222	0.722	0.939	1526.4	901.7	1173.2
Capital formation	109–146	2013.05	239.87	0.814	0.632	0.717	1327.8	1030.4	1169.7
Domestic capital formation	109–145	2388.38	323.61	0.890	0.678	0.777	1089.0	829.1	950.2
Construction	109–122	1183.77	204.05	1.086	0.767	0.913	756.0	534.3	635.5
Residential	109–110	249.05	63.29	0.954	1.177	1.059	334.5	412.6	371.5
Nonresidential	111–118	297.86	46.87	1.518	1.346	1.429	472.2	418.6	444.6
Other	119–122	636.86	93.89	0.959	0.574	0.742	1181.7	707.2	914.2
Producer durables	123–144	1204.61	156.58	0.750	0.608	0.675	1265.5	1025.6	1139.3
Transport equipment	123–129	249.33	47.76	0.622	0.464	0.537	1125.4	839.0	971.7
Nonelectrical machinery	130–138	550.77	74.04	0.828	0.711	0.767	1046.9	898.0	969.6
Electrical machinery	139–142	191.64	26.87	0.814	0.632	0.717	1128.8	876.4	994.6
Other	143–144	212.87	7.91	0.573	0.582	0.578	4621.1	4693.1	4657.0
Exports minus imports	146–146	− 375.32	− 83.74	1.107	1.107	1.107	404.9	404.9	404.9
Government	147–151	680.40	177.03	1.678	1.425	1.546	269.8	229.0	248.6
Compensation	147–150	468.79	100.01	1.952	1.476	1.697	317.6	240.2	276.2
Commodities	151–151	211.61	77.02	1.323	1.323	1.323	207.7	207.7	207.7
Gross domestic product	1–151	9422.75	1787.00	1.375	0.908	1.117	581.0	383.4	472.0
Aggregates									
ICP concepts[e]									
Consumption (CEP)[b,c]	1–108	6729.29	1370.10	1.434	1.001	1.198	490.4	342.5	409.8
Capital formation (GCF)[d]	109–146	2013.05	239.87	0.814	0.632	0.717	1327.8	1030.4	1169.7
Government (PFC)	147–151	680.40	177.03	1.678	1.425	1.546	269.8	229.0	248.6
Gross domestic product (ICP)	1–151	9422.75	1787.00	1.375	0.908	1.117	581.0	383.4	472.0
SNA concepts[e]									
Consumption (PFCE)	1–108	6480.32	1218.15	1.514	1.021	1.244	520.8	351.4	427.8
Capital formation (GCF)	109–146	2013.05	239.87	0.814	0.632	0.717	1327.8	1030.4	1169.7
Government (GFCE)	1–151	927.28	328.98	1.270	1.090	1.177	258.5	221.9	239.5
Gross domestic product (SNA)	1–151	9420.66	1787.00	1.375	0.908	1.117	580.8	383.4	471.9

Note: See the end of Appendix Table 7-68 for notes.

Category	Line numbers[a]	Per capita expenditures		Purchasing power parities (rupees/shillings)			Quantity per capita (Kenya = 100)		
		India (rupees)	Kenya (shillings)	Kenya weight	India weight	Geometric mean	Kenya weight	India weight	Geometric mean
Consumption, ICP[b,c]	1–108	877.75	1370.10	0.783	0.554	0.659	115.7	81.8	97.3
Food, beverages, tobacco	1– 39	565.34	602.13	1.029	0.809	0.913	116.0	91.3	102.9
Food	1– 33	531.97	505.11	0.928	0.811	0.867	129.9	113.5	121.4
Bread, cereals	1– 6	240.56	201.96	0.923	1.031	0.976	115.5	129.1	122.1
Meat	7– 12	11.23	30.15	0.616	0.759	0.684	49.1	60.4	54.4
Fish	13– 14	10.78	2.99	0.454	0.172	0.279	2102.5	794.2	1292.2
Milk, cheese, eggs	15– 17	57.49	95.68	1.406	1.231	1.316	48.8	42.7	45.7
Oils, fats	18– 20	54.77	15.08	0.825	0.793	0.808	458.3	440.6	449.4
Fruits, vegetables	21– 26	84.64	109.26	0.605	0.644	0.624	120.2	128.1	124.1
Coffee, tea, cocoa	27– 29	8.27	7.61	0.868	0.858	0.863	126.6	125.2	125.9
Spices, sweets, sugar	30– 33	64.23	42.39	1.007	0.726	0.855	208.6	150.5	177.2
Beverages	34– 37	7.68	63.74	1.598	0.733	1.082	16.4	7.5	11.1
Tobacco	38– 39	25.69	33.29	1.471	0.804	1.088	96.0	52.5	71.0
Clothing, footwear	40– 51	66.32	94.04	0.726	0.768	0.747	91.8	97.1	94.4
Clothing	40– 47	61.45	80.45	0.791	0.843	0.816	90.6	96.6	93.5
Footwear	48– 51	4.87	13.58	0.343	0.362	0.352	99.0	104.5	101.7
Gross rent, fuel	52– 57	53.80	154.79	0.297	0.275	0.286	126.2	116.9	121.5
Gross rent	52– 53	24.07	124.49	0.157	0.159	0.158	121.6	123.3	122.4
Fuel, power	54– 57	29.73	30.30	0.874	0.675	0.768	145.3	112.2	127.7
House furnishings, operations	58– 70	24.43	115.38	1.005	0.656	0.812	32.3	21.1	26.1
Furniture	58– 60	3.23	45.68	1.233	0.951	1.083	7.4	5.7	6.5
Appliances	61– 66	3.50	4.48	0.0	0.777	0.0	100.4	0.0	0.0
Supplies, operation	67– 70	17.70	65.23	0.846	0.620	0.724	43.8	32.1	37.5
Medical care	71– 77	28.40	65.68	0.150	0.155	0.152	279.5	287.9	283.6
Transport, communications	78– 89	57.20	100.01	0.847	0.406	0.586	140.9	67.5	97.5
Equipment	78– 79	3.20	10.60	0.633	0.584	0.608	51.8	47.8	49.7
Operation costs	80– 83	8.97	42.54	1.171	1.067	1.118	19.8	18.0	18.9
Purchased transport	84– 87	41.92	42.39	0.599	0.342	0.452	289.4	165.0	218.5
Communications	88– 89	3.11	4.48	0.629	0.709	0.668	97.9	110.4	104.0
Recreation, education	90–101	46.48	160.76	0.436	0.274	0.346	105.5	66.3	83.6
Recreation	90– 96	14.64	28.81	0.985	0.644	0.797	78.9	51.6	63.8
Education	97–101	31.83	131.95	0.316	0.217	0.262	111.3	76.3	92.2
Other expenditures	102–107	39.74	77.32	0.759	0.513	0.624	100.2	67.7	82.4
Personal care	102–104	16.06	30.30	1.258	0.614	0.879	86.4	42.1	60.3
Miscellaneous services	105–107	23.68	47.02	0.437	0.462	0.449	109.0	115.3	112.1
Capital formation	109–146	247.47	239.87	0.501	0.590	0.544	174.7	205.7	189.6
Domestic capital formation	109–145	250.72	323.61	0.664	0.594	0.628	130.4	116.7	123.3
Construction	109–122	112.55	204.05	0.584	0.478	0.529	115.4	94.4	104.4
Residential	109–110	27.59	63.29	0.483	0.502	0.492	86.9	90.3	88.6
Nonresidential	111–118	41.85	46.87	0.535	0.499	0.517	178.8	166.8	172.7
Other	119–122	43.11	93.89	0.677	0.446	0.550	103.0	67.8	83.6
Producer durables	123–144	88.08	156.58	0.800	0.711	0.754	79.1	70.3	74.6
Transport equipment	123–129	16.57	47.76	0.541	0.438	0.487	79.2	64.1	71.2
Nonelectrical machinery	130–138	32.42	74.04	0.935	0.848	0.890	51.6	46.9	49.2
Electrical machinery	139–142	27.00	26.87	0.846	0.772	0.808	130.2	118.7	124.3
Other	143–144	12.10	7.91	0.948	0.943	0.945	162.2	161.3	161.8
Exports minus imports	146–146	− 3.25	− 83.74	1.130	1.130	1.130	3.4	3.4	3.4
Government	147–151	94.99	177.03	0.623	0.569	0.596	94.2	86.1	90.1
Compensation	147–150	55.31	100.01	0.643	0.551	0.595	100.4	86.0	92.9
Commodities	151–151	39.69	77.02	0.597	0.597	0.597	86.3	86.3	86.3
Gross domestic product	1–151	1220.21	1787.00	0.730	0.562	0.640	121.5	93.6	106.6
Aggregates									
ICP concepts[e]									
Consumption (CEP)[b,c]	1–108	877.75	1370.10	0.783	0.554	0.659	115.7	81.8	97.3
Capital formation (GCF)[d]	109–146	247.47	239.87	0.501	0.590	0.544	174.7	205.7	189.6
Government (PFC)	147–151	94.99	177.03	0.623	0.569	0.596	94.2	86.1	90.1
Gross domestic product (ICP)	1–151	1220.21	1787.00	0.730	0.562	0.640	121.5	93.6	106.6
SNA concepts[e]									
Consumption (PFCE)	1–108	851.65	1218.15	0.848	0.598	0.712	116.9	82.4	98.1
Capital formation (GCF)	109–146	247.47	239.87	0.501	0.590	0.544	174.7	205.7	189.6
Government (GFCE)	1–151	121.09	328.98	0.457	0.368	0.410	99.9	80.6	89.7
Gross domestic product (SNA)	1–151	1220.21	1787.00	0.730	0.562	0.640	121.5	93.6	106.6

Note: See the end of Appendix Table 7-68 for notes.

Category	Line numbers[a]	Per capita expenditures		Purchasing power parities (cruzeiros/rupees)			Quantity per capita (India = 100)		
		Brazil (cruzeiros)	India (rupees)	India weight	Brazil weight	Geometric mean	India weight	Brazil weight	Geometric mean
Consumption, ICP[b,c]	1–108	6729.29	877.75	2.0413	1.6665	1.8444	460.0	375.6	415.7
Food, beverages, tobacco	1– 39	2476.69	565.34	1.7266	1.3181	1.5086	332.4	253.7	290.4
Food	1– 33	2283.74	531.97	1.7186	1.3557	1.5264	316.7	249.8	281.2
Bread, cereals	1– 6	506.19	240.56	1.8609	1.4083	1.6189	149.4	113.1	130.0
Meat	7– 12	617.70	11.23	2.2524	1.5935	1.8945	3452.2	2442.3	2903.7
Fish	13– 14	72.63	10.78	3.2535	2.0171	2.5618	334.2	207.2	263.1
Milk, cheese, eggs	15– 17	231.09	57.49	0.8751	0.8739	0.8745	459.9	459.3	459.6
Oils, fats	18– 20	159.20	54.77	1.0330	1.0358	1.0344	280.6	281.4	281.0
Fruits, vegetables	21– 26	464.38	84.64	2.6022	2.3980	2.4980	228.8	210.8	219.6
Coffee, tea, cocoa	27– 29	102.70	8.27	1.8128	1.0723	1.3942	1157.9	684.9	890.6
Spices, sweets, sugar	30– 33	129.85	64.23	0.9981	0.6697	0.8176	301.9	202.6	247.3
Beverages	34– 37	40.36	7.68	0.5075	0.3971	0.4490	1322.5	1034.9	1169.9
Tobacco	38– 39	152.59	25.69	2.2569	1.6430	1.9256	361.5	263.2	308.4
Clothing, footwear	40– 51	629.43	66.32	1.2469	1.9401	1.5553	489.2	761.2	610.3
Clothing	40– 47	526.73	61.45	1.1257	1.8386	1.4387	466.2	761.4	595.8
Footwear	48– 51	102.69	4.87	2.7766	2.7059	2.7410	780.1	760.2	770.1
Gross rent, fuel	52– 57	717.36	53.80	3.2217	2.8373	3.0234	469.9	413.9	441.0
Gross rent	52– 53	454.73	24.07	4.7636	4.7211	4.7423	400.2	396.6	398.4
Fuel, power	54– 57	262.63	29.73	1.9736	1.6781	1.8198	526.4	447.6	485.4
House furnishings, operations	58– 70	558.27	24.43	1.9039	1.7664	1.8338	1293.8	1200.4	1246.2
Furniture	58– 60	207.61	3.23	2.0393	2.0836	2.0613	3080.9	3147.9	3114.2
Appliances	61– 66	90.22	3.50	0.8709	0.9962	0.9315	2590.8	2963.5	2770.9
Supplies, operation	67– 70	260.44	17.70	2.0831	2.0695	2.0763	711.1	706.4	708.7
Medical care	71– 77	362.27	28.40	3.3763	3.3581	3.3672	379.8	377.8	378.8
Transport, communications	78– 89	721.02	57.20	2.6027	1.2566	1.8084	1003.1	484.3	697.0
Equipment	78– 79	194.31	3.20	2.0254	1.4938	1.7394	4059.4	2993.9	3486.2
Operation costs	80– 83	322.79	8.97	1.1069	0.9488	1.0248	3794.1	3252.1	3512.6
Purchased transport	84– 87	173.12	41.92	3.0713	2.4626	2.7502	167.7	134.5	150.2
Communications	88– 89	30.81	3.11	1.1944	0.9272	1.0524	1067.8	829.0	940.9
Recreation, education	90–101	593.74	46.48	3.1550	2.2419	2.6595	569.8	404.9	480.3
Recreation	90– 96	346.63	14.64	3.2181	2.0347	2.5589	1163.4	735.6	925.1
Education	97–101	247.10	31.83	3.1259	2.6154	2.8593	296.8	248.3	271.5
Other expenditures	102–107	670.52	39.74	3.1601	2.1011	2.5768	803.1	534.0	654.8
Personal care	102–104	152.58	16.06	3.0669	1.7279	2.3020	549.9	309.8	412.8
Miscellaneous services	105–107	517.94	23.68	3.2233	2.2439	2.6894	974.8	678.6	813.3
Capital formation	109–146	2013.05	247.47	1.5263	0.9208	1.1855	883.4	532.9	686.1
Domestic capital formation	109–145	2388.38	250.72	1.5193	0.9296	1.1884	1024.8	627.0	801.6
Construction	109–122	1183.77	112.55	1.8989	1.1358	1.4686	926.0	553.9	716.1
Residential	109–110	249.05	27.59	2.0444	1.8996	1.9707	475.2	441.6	458.1
Nonresidential	111–118	297.86	41.85	2.7569	2.5686	2.6611	277.1	258.1	267.4
Other	119–122	636.86	43.11	0.9729	0.8009	0.8827	1844.3	1518.3	1673.4
Producer durables	123–144	1204.61	88.08	0.9410	0.7888	0.8616	1733.8	1453.4	1587.4
Transport equipment	123–129	249.33	16.57	1.2577	0.9809	1.1107	1534.4	1196.7	1355.1
Nonelectrical machinery	130–138	550.77	32.42	1.0733	0.7715	0.9100	2202.2	1583.1	1867.1
Electrical machinery	139–142	191.64	27.00	0.7317	0.7473	0.7394	949.9	970.1	960.0
Other	143–144	212.87	12.10	0.6201	0.7036	0.6605	2501.2	2838.0	2664.3
Exports minus imports	146–146	−375.32	−3.25	0.9795	0.9795	0.9795	11806.3	11806.3	11806.3
Government	147–151	680.40	94.99	2.6635	2.5206	2.5910	284.2	268.9	276.4
Compensation	147–150	468.79	55.31	2.9850	2.6877	2.8324	315.4	284.0	299.3
Commodities	151–151	211.61	39.69	2.2154	2.2154	2.2154	240.7	240.7	240.7
Gross domestic product	1–151	9422.75	1220.21	1.9853	1.4510	1.6973	532.2	389.0	455.0
Aggregates									
ICP concepts[e]									
Consumption (CEP)[b,c]	1–108	6729.29	877.75	2.0413	1.6665	1.8444	460.0	375.6	415.7
Capital formation (GCF)[d]	109–146	2013.05	247.47	1.5263	0.9208	1.1855	883.4	532.9	686.1
Government (PFC)	147–151	680.40	94.99	2.6635	2.5206	2.5910	284.2	268.9	276.4
Gross domestic product (ICP)	1–151	9422.75	1220.21	1.9853	1.4510	1.6973	532.2	389.0	455.0
SNA concepts[e]									
Consumption (PFCE)	1–108	6480.32	851.65	1.9854	1.6402	1.8045	463.9	383.3	421.7
Capital formation (GCF)	109–146	2013.05	247.47	1.5263	0.9208	1.1855	883.4	532.9	686.1
Government (GFCE)	1–151	927.28	121.09	2.9228	2.6011	2.7573	294.4	262.0	277.7
Gross domestic product (SNA)	1–151	9420.66	1220.21	1.9853	1.4508	1.6971	532.2	388.9	454.9

Note: See the end of Appendix Table 7-68 for notes.

Category	Line numbers[a]	Per capita expenditures		Purchasing power parities (shillings/schillings)			Quantity per capita (Austria = 100)		
		Kenya (shillings)	Austria (schillings)	Austria weight	Kenya weight	Geometric mean	Austria weight	Kenya weight	Geometric mean
Consumption, ICP[b,c]	1–108	1370.10	55940.8	0.4523	0.1904	0.2934	12.9	5.4	8.3
Food, beverages, tobacco	1– 39	602.13	13873.4	0.4275	0.2761	0.3435	15.7	10.2	12.6
Food	1– 33	505.11	9957.3	0.3779	0.2723	0.3208	18.6	13.4	15.8
Bread, cereals	1– 6	201.96	1294.0	0.2998	0.2358	0.2659	66.2	52.1	58.7
Meat	7– 12	30.15	3098.7	0.2313	0.1914	0.2104	5.1	4.2	4.6
Fish	13– 14	2.99	147.9	0.4746	0.4588	0.4667	4.4	4.3	4.3
Milk, cheese, eggs	15– 17	95.68	1467.8	0.3880	0.3288	0.3572	19.8	16.8	18.3
Oils, fats	18– 20	15.08	694.7	0.4190	0.4455	0.4320	4.9	5.2	5.0
Fruits, vegetables	21– 26	109.26	1936.6	0.5885	0.3041	0.4230	18.6	9.6	13.3
Coffee, tea, cocoa	27– 29	7.61	244.9	0.2242	0.1679	0.1940	18.5	13.9	16.0
Spices, sweets, sugar	30– 33	42.39	1072.7	0.4966	0.4032	0.4475	9.8	8.0	8.8
Beverages	34– 37	63.74	2707.3	0.7251	0.6156	0.6681	3.8	3.2	3.5
Tobacco	38– 39	33.29	1208.8	0.1695	0.1495	0.1592	18.4	16.2	17.3
Clothing, footwear	40– 51	94.04	6078.5	0.3857	0.2901	0.3345	5.3	4.0	4.6
Clothing	40– 47	80.45	5059.6	0.3396	0.2666	0.3009	6.0	4.7	5.3
Footwear	48– 51	13.58	1018.9	0.6148	0.6062	0.6105	2.2	2.2	2.2
Gross rent, fuel	52– 57	154.79	6743.4	0.7112	0.3689	0.5122	6.2	3.2	4.5
Gross rent	52– 53	124.49	4641.0	0.7841	0.7539	0.7689	3.6	3.4	3.5
Fuel, power	54– 57	30.30	2102.4	0.5502	0.1190	0.2559	12.1	2.6	5.6
House furnishings, operations	58– 70	115.38	4898.8	0.3475	0.0640	0.1492	36.8	6.8	15.8
Furniture	58– 60	45.68	2614.4	0.3168	0.2762	0.2958	6.3	5.5	5.9
Appliances	61– 66	4.48	1102.3	0.4621	0.0	0.0	0.0	0.0	0.0
Supplies, operation	67– 70	65.23	1182.2	0.3899	0.0416	0.1274	132.5	14.2	43.3
Medical care	71– 77	65.68	5603.6	0.6325	0.4531	0.5353	2.6	1.9	2.2
Transport, communications	78– 89	100.01	7383.0	0.3657	0.2241	0.2863	6.0	3.7	4.7
Equipment	78– 79	10.60	1583.8	0.5255	0.5128	0.5192	1.3	1.3	1.3
Operation costs	80– 83	42.54	4142.3	0.3320	0.2444	0.2849	4.2	3.1	3.6
Purchased transport	84– 87	42.39	1014.6	0.1800	0.1761	0.1781	23.7	23.2	23.5
Communications	88– 89	4.48	642.3	0.4825	0.4084	0.4439	1.7	1.4	1.6
Recreation, education	90–101	160.76	6332.4	0.2810	0.1067	0.1732	23.8	9.0	14.7
Recreation	90– 96	28.81	3400.3	0.3359	0.2296	0.2777	3.7	2.5	3.1
Education	97–101	131.95	2932.2	0.2173	0.0955	0.1441	47.1	20.7	31.2
Other expenditures	102–107	77.32	8819.0	0.4672	0.2074	0.3113	4.2	1.9	2.8
Personal care	102–104	30.30	1658.1	0.2224	0.2048	0.2135	8.9	8.2	8.6
Miscellaneous services	105–107	47.02	7160.9	0.5238	0.2091	0.3309	3.1	1.3	2.0
Capital formation	109–146	239.87	23300.7	0.3203	0.1888	0.2459	5.5	3.2	4.2
Domestic capital formation	109–145	323.61	22739.5	0.3177	0.2205	0.2647	6.5	4.5	5.4
Construction	109–122	204.05	14379.1	0.1653	0.1540	0.1596	9.2	8.6	8.9
Residential	109–110	63.29	5183.2	0.1448	0.1449	0.1449	8.4	8.4	8.4
Nonresidential	111–118	46.87	5484.0	0.1944	0.1451	0.1680	5.9	4.4	5.1
Other	119–122	93.89	3711.8	0.1511	0.1661	0.1584	15.2	16.7	16.0
Producer durables	123–144	156.58	8942.8	0.5583	0.5402	0.5492	3.2	3.1	3.2
Transport equipment	123–129	47.76	1460.1	0.6937	0.7086	0.7011	4.6	4.7	4.7
Nonelectrical machinery	130–138	74.04	4683.6	0.5483	0.5022	0.5247	3.1	2.9	3.0
Electrical machinery	139–142	26.87	1936.3	0.5408	0.4705	0.5044	2.9	2.6	2.8
Other	143–144	7.91	862.8	0.4226	0.4419	0.4322	2.1	2.2	2.1
Exports minus imports	146–146	−83.74	561.2	0.4255	0.4255	0.4255	−35.1	−35.1	-35.1
Government	147–151	177.03	8026.6	0.1291	0.1261	0.1276	17.5	17.1	17.3
Compensation	147–150	100.01	6157.3	0.0938	0.0917	0.0928	17.7	17.3	17.5
Commodities	151–151	77.02	1869.3	0.2454	0.2454	0.2454	16.8	16.8	16.8
Gross domestic product	1–151	1787.00	87268.1	0.3873	0.1810	0.2648	11.3	5.3	7.7
Aggregates									
ICP concepts[e]									
Consumption (CEP)[b,c]	1–108	1370.10	55940.8	0.4523	0.1904	0.2934	12.9	5.4	8.3
Capital formation (GCF)[d]	109–146	239.87	23300.7	0.3203	0.1888	0.2459	5.5	3.2	4.2
Government (PFC)	147–151	177.03	8026.6	0.1291	0.1261	0.1276	17.5	17.1	17.3
Gross domestic product (ICP)	1–151	1787.00	87268.1	0.3873	0.1810	0.2648	11.3	5.3	7.7
SNA concepts[e]									
Consumption (PFCE)	1–108	1218.15	48900.9	0.4712	0.2044	0.3103	12.2	5.3	8.0
Capital formation (GCF)	109–146	239.87	23300.7	0.3203	0.1888	0.2459	5.5	3.2	4.2
Government (GFCE)	1–151	328.98	15066.5	0.2190	0.1246	0.1651	17.5	10.0	13.2
Gross domestic product (SNA)	1–151	1787.00	87268.1	0.3873	0.1810	0.2648	11.3	5.3	7.7

Note: See the end of Appendix Table 7-68 for notes.

Category	Line numbers[a]	Per capita expenditures		Purchasing power parities (cruzeiros/schillings)			Quantity per capita (Austria = 100)		
		Brazil (cruzeiros)	Austria (schillings)	Austria weight	Brazil weight	Geometric mean	Austria weight	Brazil weight	Geometric mean
Consumption, ICP[b,c]	1–108	6729.29	55940.8	0.4229	0.3063	0.3599	39.3	28.4	33.4
Food, beverages, tobacco	1– 39	2476.69	13873.4	0.4257	0.3160	0.3668	56.5	41.9	48.7
Food	1– 33	2283.74	9957.3	0.4315	0.3129	0.3674	73.3	53.2	62.4
Bread, cereals	1– 6	506.19	1294.0	0.2897	0.3351	0.3116	116.7	135.0	125.5
Meat	7– 12	617.70	3098.7	0.3184	0.2427	0.2780	82.1	62.6	71.7
Fish	13– 14	72.63	147.9	0.3225	0.3231	0.3228	152.0	152.3	152.2
Milk, cheese, eggs	15– 17	231.09	1467.8	0.4057	0.3490	0.3763	45.1	38.8	41.8
Oils, fats	18– 20	159.20	694.7	0.4295	0.4498	0.4395	51.0	53.4	52.1
Fruits, vegetables	21– 26	464.38	1936.6	0.7503	0.5060	0.6162	47.4	32.0	38.9
Coffee, tea, cocoa	27– 29	102.70	244.9	0.1999	0.1790	0.1892	234.2	209.8	221.7
Spices, sweets, sugar	30– 33	129.85	1072.7	0.4581	0.2541	0.3412	47.6	26.4	35.5
Beverages	34– 37	40.36	2707.3	0.4192	0.4165	0.4178	3.6	3.6	3.6
Tobacco	38– 39	152.59	1208.8	0.3930	0.3446	0.3680	36.6	32.1	34.3
Clothing, footwear	40– 51	629.43	6078.5	0.4556	0.3907	0.4219	26.5	22.7	24.5
Clothing	40– 47	526.73	5059.6	0.4670	0.3939	0.4289	26.4	22.3	24.3
Footwear	48– 51	102.69	1018.9	0.3991	0.3750	0.3869	26.9	25.3	26.1
Gross rent, fuel	52– 57	717.36	6743.4	0.5333	0.5807	0.5565	18.3	19.9	19.1
Gross rent	52– 53	454.73	4641.0	0.5489	0.6798	0.6109	14.4	17.8	16.0
Fuel, power	54– 57	262.63	2102.4	0.4988	0.4637	0.4809	26.9	25.0	26.0
House furnishings, operations	58– 70	558.27	4898.8	0.5822	0.3405	0.4452	33.5	19.6	25.6
Furniture	58– 60	207.61	2614.4	0.6546	0.6086	0.6312	13.0	12.1	12.6
Appliances	61– 66	90.22	1102.3	0.5967	0.5284	0.5615	15.5	13.7	14.6
Supplies, operation	67– 70	260.44	1182.2	0.4084	0.2310	0.3071	95.4	53.9	71.7
Medical care	71– 77	362.27	5603.6	0.3686	0.2671	0.3138	24.2	17.5	20.6
Transport, communications	78– 89	721.02	7383.0	0.3821	0.2479	0.3077	39.4	25.6	31.7
Equipment	78– 79	194.31	1583.8	0.4781	0.5006	0.4892	24.5	25.7	25.1
Operation costs	80– 83	322.79	4142.3	0.4047	0.3543	0.3786	22.0	19.3	20.6
Purchased transport	84– 87	173.12	1014.6	0.1823	0.1271	0.1522	134.2	93.6	112.1
Communications	88– 89	30.81	642.3	0.3153	0.1241	0.1978	38.6	15.2	24.2
Recreation, education	90–101	593.74	6332.4	0.3327	0.1990	0.2573	47.1	28.2	36.4
Recreation	90– 96	346.63	3400.3	0.4899	0.4403	0.4645	23.2	20.8	21.9
Education	97–101	247.10	2932.2	0.1504	0.1125	0.1301	74.9	56.0	64.8
Other expenditures	102–107	670.52	8819.0	0.3773	0.2794	0.3247	27.2	20.2	23.4
Personal care	102–104	152.58	1658.1	0.4670	0.4193	0.4425	21.9	19.7	20.8
Miscellaneous services	105–107	517.94	7160.9	0.3565	0.2544	0.3012	28.4	20.3	24.0
Capital formation	109–146	2013.05	23300.7	0.2846	0.1974	0.2370	43.8	30.4	36.5
Domestic capital formation	109–145	2388.38	22739.5	0.2800	0.2172	0.2466	48.4	37.5	42.6
Construction	109–122	1183.77	14379.1	0.2053	0.1638	0.1834	50.3	40.1	44.9
Residential	109–110	249.05	5183.2	0.1585	0.1685	0.1635	28.5	30.3	29.4
Nonresidential	111–118	297.86	5484.0	0.2857	0.2158	0.2483	25.2	19.0	21.9
Other	119–122	636.86	3711.8	0.1518	0.1457	0.1488	117.7	113.0	115.3
Producer durables	123–144	1204.61	8942.8	0.4075	0.3196	0.3609	42.1	33.1	37.3
Transport equipment	123–129	249.33	1460.1	0.4910	0.3619	0.4215	47.2	34.8	40.5
Nonelectrical machinery	130–138	550.77	4683.6	0.4238	0.3191	0.3678	36.8	27.7	32.0
Electrical machinery	139–142	191.64	1936.3	0.3587	0.3218	0.3397	30.8	27.6	29.1
Other	143–144	212.87	862.8	0.2866	0.2807	0.2836	87.9	86.1	87.0
Exports minus imports	146–146	− 375.32	561.2	0.4710	0.4710	0.4710	−142.0	−142.0	−142.0
Government	147–151	680.40	8026.6	0.2273	0.1556	0.1881	54.5	37.3	45.1
Compensation	147–150	468.79	6157.3	0.1978	0.1260	0.1579	60.4	38.5	48.2
Commodities	151–151	211.61	1869.3	0.3247	0.3247	0.3247	34.9	34.9	34.9
Gross domestic product	1–151	9422.75	87268.1	0.3680	0.2578	0.3080	41.9	29.3	35.1
Aggregates									
ICP concepts[e]									
Consumption (CEP)[b,c]	1–108	6729.29	55940.8	0.4229	0.3063	0.3599	39.3	28.4	33.4
Capital formation (GCF)[d]	109–146	2013.05	23300.7	0.2846	0.1974	0.2370	43.8	30.4	36.5
Government (PFC)	147–151	680.40	8026.6	0.2273	0.1556	0.1881	54.5	37.3	45.1
Gross domestic product (ICP)	1–151	9422.75	87268.1	0.3680	0.2578	0.3080	41.9	29.3	35.1
SNA concepts[e]									
Consumption (PFCE)	1–108	6480.32	48900.9	0.4488	0.3232	0.3809	41.0	29.5	34.8
Capital formation (GCF)	109–146	2013.05	23300.7	0.2846	0.1974	0.2370	43.8	30.4	36.5
Government (GFCE)	1–151	927.28	15066.5	0.2348	0.1473	0.1860	41.8	26.2	33.1
Gross domestic product (SNA)	1–151	9420.66	87268.1	0.3680	0.2578	0.3080	41.9	29.3	35.0

Note: See the end of Appendix Table 7-68 for notes.

Category	Line numbers[a]	Per capita expenditures India (rupees)	Per capita expenditures Austria (schillings)	Purchasing power parities (rupees/schillings) Austria weight	Purchasing power parities (rupees/schillings) India weight	Purchasing power parities (rupees/schillings) Geometric mean	Quantity per capita (Austria = 100) Austria weight	Quantity per capita (Austria = 100) India weight	Quantity per capita (Austria = 100) Geometric mean
Consumption, ICP[b,c]	1–108	877.75	55940.8	0.2438	0.1446	0.1877	10.9	6.4	8.4
Food, beverages, tobacco	1– 39	565.34	13873.4	0.4515	0.2411	0.3299	16.9	9.0	12.4
Food	1– 33	531.97	9957.3	0.2841	0.2340	0.2579	22.8	18.8	20.7
Bread, cereals	1– 6	240.56	1294.0	0.2541	0.2219	0.2375	83.8	73.2	78.3
Meat	7– 12	11.23	3098.7	0.1641	0.1989	0.1807	1.8	2.2	2.0
Fish	13– 14	10.78	147.9	0.1954	0.0990	0.1391	73.6	37.3	52.4
Milk, cheese, eggs	15– 17	57.49	1467.8	0.4251	0.4589	0.4417	8.5	9.2	8.9
Oils, fats	18– 20	54.77	694.7	0.3328	0.3420	0.3374	23.1	23.7	23.4
Fruits, vegetables	21– 26	84.64	1936.6	0.3192	0.1872	0.2444	23.4	13.7	17.9
Coffee, tea, cocoa	27– 29	8.27	244.9	0.1648	0.1130	0.1365	29.9	20.5	24.7
Spices, sweets, sugar	30– 33	64.23	1072.7	0.4185	0.3019	0.3554	19.8	14.3	16.8
Beverages	34– 37	7.68	2707.3	1.1662	0.4807	0.7487	0.6	0.2	0.4
Tobacco	38– 39	25.69	1208.8	0.2292	0.4620	0.3254	4.6	9.3	6.5
Clothing, footwear	40– 51	66.32	6078.5	0.2198	0.1922	0.2055	5.7	5.0	5.3
Clothing	40– 47	61.45	5059.6	0.2336	0.1971	0.2145	6.2	5.2	5.7
Footwear	48– 51	4.87	1018.9	0.1513	0.1464	0.1488	3.3	3.2	3.2
Gross rent, fuel	52– 57	53.80	6743.4	0.1469	0.1228	0.1343	6.5	5.4	5.9
Gross rent	52– 53	24.07	4641.0	0.1154	0.1140	0.1147	4.5	4.5	4.5
Fuel, power	54– 57	29.73	2102.4	0.2165	0.1310	0.1684	10.8	6.5	8.4
House furnishings, operations	58– 70	24.43	4898.8	0.3274	0.1482	0.2203	3.4	1.5	2.3
Furniture	58– 60	3.23	2614.4	0.3154	0.3166	0.3160	0.4	0.4	0.4
Appliances	61– 66	3.50	1102.3	0.4388	0.6832	0.5475	0.5	0.7	0.6
Supplies, operation	67– 70	17.70	1182.2	0.2502	0.1184	0.1721	12.6	6.0	8.7
Medical care	71– 77	28.40	5603.6	0.0570	0.0820	0.0684	6.2	8.9	7.4
Transport, communications	78– 89	57.20	7383.0	0.3419	0.0652	0.1493	11.9	2.3	5.2
Equipment	78– 79	3.20	1583.8	0.3296	0.2814	0.3046	0.7	0.6	0.7
Operation costs	80– 83	8.97	4142.3	0.4179	0.3600	0.3879	0.6	0.5	0.6
Purchased transport	84– 87	41.92	1014.6	0.0742	0.0507	0.0614	81.4	55.6	67.3
Communications	88– 89	3.11	642.3	0.3052	0.2107	0.2536	2.3	1.6	1.9
Recreation, education	90–101	46.48	6332.4	0.1564	0.0420	0.0811	17.5	4.7	9.1
Recreation	90– 96	14.64	3400.3	0.2407	0.1454	0.1871	3.0	1.8	2.3
Education	97–101	31.83	2932.2	0.0586	0.0317	0.0431	34.3	18.5	25.2
Other expenditures	102–107	39.74	8819.0	0.1625	0.0869	0.1188	5.2	2.8	3.8
Personal care	102–104	16.06	1658.1	0.2124	0.1325	0.1678	7.3	4.6	5.8
Miscellaneous services	105–107	23.68	7160.9	0.1509	0.0705	0.1031	4.7	2.2	3.2
Capital formation	109–146	247.47	23300.7	0.2377	0.1425	0.1840	7.5	4.5	5.8
Domestic capital formation	109–145	250.72	22739.5	0.2317	0.1438	0.1825	7.7	4.8	6.0
Construction	109–122	112.55	14379.1	0.0990	0.0881	0.0934	8.9	7.9	8.4
Residential	109–110	27.59	5183.2	0.0818	0.0717	0.0766	7.4	6.5	6.9
Nonresidential	111–118	41.85	5484.0	0.0990	0.0842	0.0913	9.1	7.7	8.4
Other	119–122	43.11	3711.8	0.1229	0.1091	0.1158	10.6	9.5	10.0
Producer durables	123–144	88.08	8942.8	0.4430	0.4059	0.4240	2.4	2.2	2.3
Transport equipment	123–129	16.57	1460.1	0.3560	0.3216	0.3384	3.5	3.2	3.4
Nonelectrical machinery	130–138	32.42	4683.6	0.4892	0.4329	0.4602	1.6	1.4	1.5
Electrical machinery	139–142	27.00	1936.3	0.4060	0.4128	0.4094	3.4	3.4	3.4
Other	143–144	12.10	862.8	0.4225	0.4801	0.4504	2.9	3.3	3.1
Exports minus imports	146–146	− 3.25	561.2	0.4809	0.4809	0.4809	−1.2	−1.2	−1.2
Government	147–151	94.99	8026.6	0.0722	0.0667	0.0694	17.7	16.4	17.0
Compensation	147–150	55.31	6157.3	0.0497	0.0480	0.0488	18.7	18.1	18.4
Commodities	151–151	39.69	1869.3	0.1466	0.1466	0.1466	14.5	14.5	14.5
Gross domestic product	1–151	1220.21	87268.1	0.2264	0.1322	0.1730	10.6	6.2	8.1
Aggregates									
ICP concepts[e]									
Consumption (CEP)[b,c]	1–108	877.75	55940.8	0.2438	0.1446	0.1877	10.9	6.4	8.4
Capital formation (GCF)[d]	109–146	247.47	23300.7	0.2377	0.1425	0.1840	7.5	4.5	5.8
Government (PFC)	147–151	94.99	8026.6	0.0722	0.0667	0.0694	17.7	16.4	17.0
Gross domestic product (ICP)	1–151	1220.21	87268.1	0.2264	0.1322	0.1730	10.6	6.2	8.1
SNA concepts[e]									
Consumption (PFCE)	1–108	851.65	48900.9	0.2717	0.1600	0.2085	10.9	6.4	8.4
Capital formation (GCF)	109–146	247.47	23300.7	0.2377	0.1425	0.1840	7.5	4.5	5.8
Government (GFCE)	1–151	121.09	15066.5	0.0618	0.0558	0.0587	14.4	13.0	13.7
Gross domestic product (SNA)	1–151	1220.21	87268.1	0.2264	0.1322	0.1730	10.6	6.2	8.1

Note: See following page for notes.

Notes for Appendix Tables 7-1 to 7-68.

a. Line numbers refer to Appendix Table 6-1 and show the detailed categories that are included in each aggregation.

b. Consumption, ICP, includes both household and government expenditures. The latter are shown separately in Table 2-1. Consumption, SNA, excludes these governmental expenditures.

c. The consumption aggregate (lines 1–108) includes net expenditure of residents abroad (line 108), not shown separately in these tables.

d. The capital formation aggregate (lines 109–146) includes increase in stocks (line 145) not shown separately in these tables.

e. Letters in parentheses are: CEP, consumption expenditures of the population; GCF, gross capital formation; PFC, public final consumption expenditure; PFCE, private final consumption expenditure; GFCE, government final consumption expenditure. See Glossary for definitions.

8

Gross Domestic Product and Gross Domestic Income for Nonbenchmark Years and Places

THE LONG-RUN OBJECTIVE OF THE ICP is to provide a system of annual comparisons, for at least GDP and its three main subaggregates, that includes virtually all countries. This objective is impractical through annual benchmark comparisons of the type described in the preceding chapters for all of the 150-plus countries and areas that report national-accounts data to the United Nations. Even among the countries that have participated in the ICP, not all would be willing to accept the burdens of participation every year, and many countries lack the interest or the statistical resources to participate in a benchmark comparison. Clearly, less burdensome methods must be found for extending the estimates to countries for which benchmark studies cannot be done soon or at all. And ways must be found to extrapolate from a benchmark year to successive years until a new benchmark study can be made, perhaps five years later.

This chapter sets out the methodology for filling these gaps in benchmark data and provides actual estimates, necessarily approximate, for nonbenchmark years for the thirty-four Phase III countries and global estimates for the other countries of the world.[1] Work of a similar nature already published was based on a methodology still in a relatively early stage of development and drew on a smaller data set than is now available in Phase III.[2] Future research should produce yet better estimates. The estimates reported here are advanced much more tentatively than the benchmark estimates reported on in the earlier chapters.

1. This chapter extends the materials in Chapters 1 through 7 of this report; as such, it is done on the responsibility of the authors, and not the U.N. Statistical Office or the World Bank.

2. Summers, Kravis, Heston (1980).

GDP and GDY for Thirty-four Countries, 1950–79

A table comparing the real GDPs for various countries in different years (including nonbenchmark years) can be presented where relative positions of countries are (1) comparable across countries within years but not across years or (2) comparable year to year as well as within years. As long as the concern is with the first criterion it is not necessary to worry about the difference between a country's GDP and its GDY (gross domestic income).[3]

In expressing results for different years in the prices of a selected year, GDP and GDY may differ because of changes in the terms of trade. These differences are elaborated in the following section.

Benchmark-type Estimates for Nonbenchmark Years

ICP benchmark studies produce estimates of the first of these types. Thus ICP results for two or more benchmark years do not provide directly comparable dollar figures for the GDPs of different years. The fact that the comparisons for each benchmark year are based

3. The ICP assumes that for each country GDP and GDY are equal in any given benchmark year when current prices are used. This implicitly assumes that countries exporting the same bundle of goods experience the same terms of trade. If two countries produced identical baskets of goods and exported identical bundles, but one received more imports in exchange, the GDPs of the two would be equal but their GDYs would not be. GDP and GDY could not therefore be equal for each of the two countries. Attention was drawn to this point by Lazlo Drechsler.

on current prices means that both the level and the structure of prices that are used to value the quantities of goods in each country's GDP differ from one year to another. With respect to price levels, the 1970 and 1975 benchmark comparisons, for example, are geared to U.S. per capita GDPs of $4,814 and $7,176, respectively. Most of the difference represented inflation, but the structure of prices used to value the quantities also differed between the two years with energy prices, to take one example, being much higher relative to other prices in the later year.

Although the extrapolation might have been carried out for each category separately, the purchasing power parities (PPPs) were obtained for domestic absorption (DA)—that is, for the aggregate of all the categories except the net foreign balance (NFB).[4] The NFB was treated separately. The formula for extrapolating the PPPs for DA is as follows:

$$(8.1) \qquad \mathrm{PPP}_{j,t}^{DA} = \mathrm{PPP}_{j,t_0}^{DA} \cdot \frac{P_{j,t}^{DA}/P_{j,t_0}^{DA}}{P_{US,t}^{DA}/P_{US,t_0}^{DA}}$$

where $\mathrm{PPP}_{j,t}^{DA}$ is country j's PPP (relative to the numéraire country, the United States) for DA in the extrapolation year t, t_0 is the benchmark year, and P is an implicit deflator derived by dividing the country's expenditure on DA in current prices by its expenditures on DA in constant prices.[5] Each country's extrapolation-year (t) per capita DA in own current prices was converted to extrapolation-year international dollars by dividing it by $\mathrm{PPP}_{j,t}^{DA}$.

4. A more satisfying way to approximate closely the results for a nonbenchmark year that would be obtained by a benchmark study would be actually to perform a Geary-Khamis calculation, not for the 151 detailed categories (that would be a whole benchmark study) but for the 35 summary categories. The allocation of expenditures on GDP of the selected extrapolation year to the 35 ICP categories should not be a large task; if necessary, part of the breakdowns could be patterned on those found in the benchmark year, especially if the interval between the two years was short. The price data could be obtained by extrapolating the prices of the benchmark year to the new year on the basis of price indexes from the participating countries. These extrapolations would yield a PPP for each summary category that, when divided into the corresponding expenditure in own currency, would yield the expenditure for the given categories in international prices of the extrapolation year. (The statement is not completely accurate because each country's index used for extrapolation embodies its own weights.)

5. The expenditure aggregate used here is what is referred to as "final consumption and gross capital formation" in the U.N. *Yearbook of National Accounts*. It includes government final-consumption expenditure, private final-consumption expenditure, and gross fixed-capital formation. It excludes exports and imports. The advantage of deriving $\mathrm{PPP}_{j,t}^{DA}$ by relying on the price indexes for individual categories would have been that the relative importance of categories in the benchmark year would be preserved, whereas this is not true when $\mathrm{PPP}_{j,t}^{DA}$ is derived from aggregate price indexes for DA as is done here.

There is no fully satisfactory way to deal with the NFB in the context either of the intertemporal deflation of the national accounts of individual countries or of international comparisons.[6] For ICP purposes a method has been adopted that replicates for the extrapolation year as closely as possible the procedure that is used for the benchmark year. First, the per capita NFB for the extrapolation year is converted to dollars at the current exchange rate. Then the NFB expressed in U.S. dollars is multiplied by the international price of the NFB for the extrapolation year (Π_t^{NFB}). Π_t^{NFB} is defined as the average exchange-rate–deviation index of the countries included in the extrapolation for the year t. The exchange-rate–deviation index used here is the ratio of real per capita DA in international dollars (obtained by dividing own-currency expenditures by PPP_t^{DA}) to per capita DA calculated through the exchange-rate conversion to dollars. This procedure approximately matches the ICP method of incorporating the NFB in the benchmark year.[7] The reason for this treatment of the NFB in both benchmark and extrapolation years is that it corresponds to the way that international prices are derived for other categories; that is, the international price for a given country is the average across the countries of the ratio of the PPP for the category to the PPP for GDP as a whole.[8]

The final step in obtaining the benchmark-type real GDP per capita for the extrapolation year is to add together the DA and NFB components, each expressed in international dollars. Indexes of real income per capita are then formed by dividing the international-dollar total in a given year for each country by that for the numéraire country.

Comparison of Benchmark Estimates and Extrapolated Estimates of Real Income Per Capita

Table 8-1 shows how closely extrapolations based on the method of the last section compare with actual benchmark estimates. The benchmark estimates for the three years 1970, 1973, and 1975 are given for the

6. For a discussion of alternative methods of treating the NFB in intertemporal comparisons, see Kurabayashi (1971) and references to the literature offered there.

7. Since Π_t^{NFB} is computed for a different set of countries from that which is used to compute the benchmark international price of the NFB (Π_b^{NFB}), and Π_b^{NFB} is also supercountry-weighted, the Π_t^{NFB} actually used is adjusted to make it comparable with Π_b^{NFB}. Because the NFB is one of the three possibly negative categories in the Geary-Khamis estimates for benchmark countries, the actual benchmark NFB international price is based on the PPP for the composite of all non-negative categories (changes in stocks and net expenditure of residents abroad may also be negative).

8. See equation 3.14. For the NFB, the PPP is the exchange rate, and the denominator of the ratio is $\mathrm{PPP}_{j,t}^{DA}$ rather than $\mathrm{PPP}_{j,t}^{GDP}$.

Table 8-1. Indexes of GDP per Capita for Sixteen Countries, 1970, 1973, and 1975
(U.S. = 100 in each year)

	Benchmark indexes[a]			1975 extrapolated from 1970[b]	1970 extrapolated from 1975[b]	1975 extrapolated estimate ÷ benchmark estimate
	1970	1973	1975			
Country	(1)	(2)	(3)	(4)	(5)	(6) = (4) ÷ (3)
Kenya	5.88	5.94	6.56	5.2	7.4	0.79
India	6.45	6.05	6.56	6.3	6.8	0.96
Philippines	11.7	12.0	13.2	12.9	12.1	0.98
Korea	11.8	14.6	20.7	15.1	16.4	0.73
Malaysia	15.6	19.7	21.5	17.6	19.1	0.82
Colombia	17.2	17.8	22.4	19.2	20.4	0.86
Iran	19.4	28.1	37.7	42.8	16.8	1.14
Hungary[c]	41.4	44.0	49.6	—	—	—
Italy	48.0	47.4	53.8	46.7	55.9	0.87
U.K.	62.7	60.7	63.9	61.7	65.6	0.97
Japan	58.5	63.7	68.4	63.7	63.4	0.93
Netherlands	68.3	69.3	75.2	72.0	72.2	0.96
Belgium	72.3	76.5	77.7	79.4	71.1	1.02
Germany	76.5	76.0	83.0	79.5	80.2	0.96
France	71.9	75.4	81.9	78.8	75.5	0.96
U.S.	100.0	100.0	100.0	100.0	100.0	1.00

a. The indexes for any given year may equally be interpreted as indexes of GDY.
b. Includes adjustment for changes in the terms of trade.
c. Information for extrapolations not available.

Phase II countries along with the estimates that are produced if the benchmark per capita GDPs for 1975 are extrapolated to 1970 and vice versa. The 1970 and 1973 benchmark estimates are the Phase III revisions for those years, while the 1975 estimates are reproduced from Table 1-2. The indexes in columns 4 and 5 were obtained by the methods for benchmark-type extrapolations described above.

The differences for the developed countries, except Italy, are all 7 percent or less, but there are some large deviations for developing countries, ranging up to 27 percent. The number of countries is too small to make any firm generalization, but it is noteworthy that twelve of the fourteen extrapolations imply less growth than do the 1970 and 1975 benchmarks, and that developing

countries with longer traditions in statistical services, namely India and the Philippines, show relatively small differences. In interpreting column 6, it should be kept in mind that any difference from unity may be attributable to errors in the deflators of the numéraire country as well as the given country.[9]

Before an assessment is made of the various possible explanations for entries in column 6, a longer term comparison can be made. The 1970–75 differences are large relative to those obtained by extrapolating the 1970 and 1975 ICP results back to 1950 and then com-

9. A comparison of the 1970 benchmarks with extrapolations from 1975 back to 1970 (columns 1 and 5) leads to the same conclusions.

Table 8-2. Comparison of 1950 OEEC Price Levels as Estimated in Benchmark Study and as Extrapolated from 1970 and 1975

	1950 price level				
	OEEC benchmark	Extrapolated from		Ratios	
		1970	1975		
Country	(1)	(2)	(3)	(4) = (2) ÷ (1)	(5) = (3) ÷ (1)
Belgium	79.6	74.5	76.1	94	96
Denmark	66.2	61.8	63.3	93	96
France	73.7	73.9	70.8	100	96
Germany	69.1	66.2	63.4	96	92
Italy	66.9	66.9	57.7	100	86
Netherlands	59.9	50.8	48.4	85	81
U.K.	64.4	65.5	62.9	102	98
U.S.	100.0	100.0	100.0	100	100

paring them with the OEEC benchmark estimates[10] for seven Western European countries relative to the United States (see Table 8-2). The extrapolations from 1970 are somewhat closer to the 1950 benchmarks than the extrapolations based on 1975. Both sets of extrapolations tend to place price levels lower and therefore incomes higher in 1950 than the 1950 benchmarks. To put it another way, the real growth in output relative to the United States as estimated by national growth rates was less than implied by the two benchmarks. It would be interesting to examine systematically the reasons for these differences.

Much work also remains to be done in investigating the discrepancy between the growth rate implied by the 1970 and 1975 benchmark comparisons and the internal growth rates of the individual countries. Both conceptual differences and errors in the data of both kinds must be explored more thoroughly than can be done here.

The conceptual differences lie in the fact that the two sets of intertemporal comparisons involve the evaluation of quantities at different relative prices. Furthermore, the quantities are not valued so as to achieve comparability within either set. The growth rates of each country are based on constant price expenditure series, which are usually obtained by deflating current expenditures for detailed categories by price indexes of similar commodity coverage, and then summing the deflated expenditures. The latter may then be regarded as constituting a quantity index. The 1975 extrapolations in column 4, for example, are thus in part the quotient of two quantity indexes, one for the given country and the other for the numéraire country. This quotient is then multiplied by the 1970 benchmark estimate for the given country (column 1) to derive the 1975 estimates. Note that each quantity index is based on each country's (j's and the United States') own price weights and that the actual base year for the underlying price indexes may be different for the two countries. (The shifting of the original series to a common base year by dividing each series by its value for the chosen year makes the series much more comparable but does not eliminate the conceptual and empirical difference.)

The benchmark estimates are constructed in an entirely different way. Average international prices for the given year (1970 or 1975) are used to value the quantities of each final product in the GDP of each country. The entries in a benchmark column reflect the ratio of the aggregate of these values for the given country to that of the numéraire country. Thus one set of international prices enters into the determination of the 1970 benchmark estimates and another set into the determination of those for 1975.

As for the data problems, both the benchmark estimates and the growth rates computed from national data have obvious sources of error. The benchmark estimates rely on place-to-place comparisons based on samples of prices that are, at least for the developed countries, smaller than the samples used in the national time-to-time comparisons of prices. It is inherently easier to measure time-to-time changes, at least for items sold off the shelf, because it is possible simply to trace the price of a particular item found in a particular outlet from month to month or year to year. (New products are an exception; their introduction into later benchmark comparisons are likely to be more accurate than their treatment in time-to-time indexes.) The price change for a commodity can then be averaged from these changes for individual samples of the commodity. If there is a little variation in quality from one outlet to another, that does not matter so long as the same quality in a given outlet is priced in each period. It is much more difficult to get the average national price for a particular specification of a good in any one country. Then it is necessary to ensure that the same quality of each good is priced in every outlet. Further possibilities of error are introduced in place-to-place comparisons by the need to hold quality constant not only within each country, but across countries as well.

However, the growth rates computed from the national data are not without their statistical difficulties. For one thing, even for goods sold from the shelf, a significant fraction of the items that are priced at any given time will not be available in exactly the same form a year later. In one recent survey it was found, for example, that one-sixth of the goods had disappeared from retail outlets between two years. This problem confronts every country to a major extent, and it must be expected that the statistical practices regarding substitutions and, more important, the way prices for the substitute items are linked, will not be the same in different countries. The intercountry comparability of price indexes is even more questionable for items that are not sold off the shelf, including such important categories as sophisticated durable goods (especially producer durables), construction, medical care, education, and government services. These represent difficult problems in the construction of intertemporal price indexes, and there are no internationally standard ways of handling them. The international comparability of intertemporal price indexes is thus

---

10. For an earlier extrapolation of the 1970 figure, see Summers, Kravis, Heston (1980), p. 30. The minor differences of the present figures from the earlier ones are due mainly to data revisions. The OEEC benchmark figures in column 1 are adjusted to a multilateral basis as described in the same article.

Table 8-3. Comparisons of Real GDY per Capita, Thirty Countries, 1950–80

Country	1950	1951	1952	1953	1954	1955	1956	1957	1958	1959
Malawi	3.69	—	—	—	3.93	3.97	4.40	4.40	4.50	3.99
Kenya	7.77	7.97	7.03	6.52	7.45	7.44	7.50	7.39	7.22	6.64
India	7.08	6.86	6.75	6.86	7.31	6.98	7.16	7.00	7.57	7.23
Pakistan	9.03	8.33	7.88	7.81	8.07	7.34	7.57	7.54	7.58	7.66
Sri Lanka	11.4	11.3	10.0	9.73	10.7	10.8	9.62	9.79	10.1	10.0
Zambia	11.0	—	—	—	—	15.0	16.1	13.7	12.7	15.0
Philippines	10.3	9.36	9.73	10.7	11.6	11.4	11.9	12.0	12.6	12.6
Thailand	9.89	8.89	8.57	7.73	8.45	7.57	7.53	8.25	8.52	8.84
Korea	7.55	—	—	7.74	7.98	7.87	7.77	8.55	8.94	8.58
Malaysia	14.6	—	—	—	—	15.5	15.2	14.4	14.0	15.5
Colombia	18.5	16.9	17.1	17.9	20.0	18.7	18.6	17.9	17.7	17.3
Syria	17.1	—	—	—	—	—	—	—	—	—
Jamaica	12.6	—	—	15.6	17.9	18.2	19.1	21.8	22.2	22.4
Brazil	15.2	14.1	14.4	14.2	15.9	15.5	15.4	16.3	17.4	17.3
Mexico	25.5	25.0	24.9	23.1	25.8	25.6	26.5	27.6	28.6	27.3
Iran	11.9			—	—	13.5	14.1	15.2	16.3	15.8
Uruguay	54.9	60.9	53.6	54.0	63.0	60.5	58.6	60.9	56.0	52.4
Ireland	33.0	30.3	31.3	32.4	33.8	32.9	32.4	32.2	33.4	34.2
Spain	26.5	28.3	28.9	27.0	31.6	31.4	33.4	34.6	36.8	34.4
Italy	27.5	27.1	27.4	28.8	31.9	31.4	32.5	33.9	36.5	37.1
U.K.	59.1	55.3	56.0	57.5	61.3	59.6	60.8	61.6	63.8	63.3
Japan	17.1	17.6	19.0	19.4	20.8	21.2	22.6	24.0	25.8	26.8
Austria	37.9	37.2	36.6	36.6	41.2	43.4	45.2	48.2	50.9	50.3
Netherlands	50.2	46.1	46.7	48.7	53.3	53.8	55.4	55.8	55.8	55.6
Belgium	54.8	53.7	53.5	52.4	55.8	55.9	57.4	57.8	59.3	57.4
Denmark	61.9	55.2	56.1	58.2	61.9	58.4	59.5	61.6	64.8	67.7
Germany	40.8	41.2	44.4	46.3	50.8	53.5	56.2	58.5	62.1	63.5
France	48.2	46.2	47.4	47.7	50.9	50.1	52.1	53.9	56.6	56.5
Luxembourg	59.7	67.5	70.5	62.8	65.2	67.1	71.8	74.1	74.1	72.8
U.S.	100.0	100.0	100.0	100.0	100.0	100.0	100.0	100.0	100.0	100.0

(Table continues on the following page.)

open to serious question. These incomparabilities in the price indexes in turn carry over to incomparabilities in growth rates.

The upshot is that although the extrapolation results seem too far from the benchmark results to be explicable by conceptual differences, it is not possible to say which is more trustworthy, given this very preliminary assessment of sources of error.[11] In the present state of our knowledge it appears that national growth rates should be used for growth comparisons over time and the benchmark results for place-to-place comparisons in a given year where available. In the absence of benchmark estimates for a year of interest, there is no choice but to use extrapolations. Certainly the evidence of inaccuracy of exchange-rate conversions given in

11. More light might be shed on the differences by comparing the two sets of estimates for disaggregations. The internal growth rates might be given more credibility for easy-to-specify shelf-goods categories such as food, while the benchmark estimates might be trusted more where national price indexes tend to be poor for categories such as producer durables and construction.

Table 1-2—substantially in excess of what is displayed in Table 8-1—shows that they are a worse alternative, to say the least.

Table 8-3 presents benchmark-type estimates of real income per capita for thirty countries annually for 1950–80. Hungary, Poland, Romania, and Yugoslavia are not included because GDP expenditure data are not available from the standard international sources for these countries. Where available, benchmark data are entered in the table; this includes estimates for fifteen Phase II countries for 1970 and 1973 and for thirty Phase III countries for 1975. The rest of the data in the table are extrapolated from these benchmark figures. For the fifteen Phase II countries the estimates for the years 1950–69 are extrapolated backward from the 1970 benchmark estimates; for the years 1976–79 they are extrapolated forward from the 1975 benchmark estimate; and for 1972 and 1971, the average of the extrapolations forward from 1970 and backward from 1973 are used, while 1974 is the average of the extrapolation from that year forward from 1973 and backward from 1975. For the fifteen new countries of Phase III (eighteen new

Table 8-3 *(continued)*

Country	1960	1961	1962	1963	1964	1965	1966	1967	1968	1969
Malawi	4.35	4.72	4.12	3.98	3.69	4.01	4.21	4.27	4.15	4.33
Kenya	6.81	5.82	5.73	5.87	5.60	5.20	5.47	5.55	5.50	5.47
India	7.50	7.04	6.87	6.92	7.03	6.38	5.93	6.17	5.98	6.14
Pakistan	7.75	8.03	8.09	8.24	8.47	8.99	8.88	9.10	8.94	8.52
Sri Lanka	10.2	9.81	9.49	9.32	9.27	8.84	8.66	8.65	8.72	9.01
Zambia	15.3	14.4	13.0	12.8	13.8	15.0	15.5	15.6	15.8	17.4
Philippines	12.3	12.3	12.3	12.3	11.8	11.5	11.1	11.4	11.5	11.6
Thailand	9.50	9.63	9.55	9.72	9.84	10.1	10.7	10.7	10.8	11.3
Korea	8.15	8.42	8.12	8.47	8.62	8.53	9.05	9.30	9.95	11.0
Malaysia	16.7	16.3	16.1	15.9	15.7	15.9	15.5	15.0	14.6	15.0
Colombia	17.5	17.7	17.4	16.9	17.1	16.0	15.9	15.5	15.7	16.0
Syria	16.5	17.0	19.3	18.0	18.1	17.0	15.8	15.6	15.4	17.6
Jamaica	23.3	23.4	22.9	22.7	22.9	23.0	23.5	23.8	24.8	26.1
Brazil	18.2	19.2	18.7	18.0	17.5	16.5	15.8	15.9	16.5	17.3
Mexico	29.0	29.1	28.3	29.0	30.1	29.8	29.4	29.9	30.4	30.7
Iran	16.5	16.2	12.6	13.1	13.9	14.9	15.2	16.2	17.0	17.7
Uruguay	54.2	53.4	50.8	48.1	47.6	42.9	43.6	40.6	38.7	40.8
Ireland	35.5	36.9	36.7	37.1	37.2	36.2	35.2	36.7	37.8	40.0
Spain	33.7	37.5	39.3	41.7	41.8	42.7	43.7	44.2	44.4	46.6
Italy	38.5	41.2	41.7	42.6	41.9	41.1	41.0	43.1	44.0	45.6
U.K.	64.2	65.7	61.7	63.5	64.0	62.4	60.7	61.1	60.8	60.6
Japan	29.8	33.4	34.1	36.3	39.1	38.8	40.5	44.4	48.4	52.5
Austria	53.4	55.9	54.7	55.0	56.1	54.7	55.0	55.3	55.8	57.5
Netherlands	59.3	59.8	59.3	59.4	61.1	60.9	58.9	60.7	62.6	64.7
Belgium	59.9	62.0	62.6	62.9	64.5	63.7	62.3	63.6	63.7	67.2
Denmark	70.2	72.9	73.9	72.4	76.0	75.6	73.5	75.1	75.0	79.3
Germany	68.0	70.0	69.4	68.8	69.8	69.4	67.5	66.4	67.7	71.4
France	59.2	61.2	61.4	62.3	63.2	62.6	62.3	63.9	64.3	68.3
Luxembourg	81.4	82.0	76.9	76.6	79.9	77.1	73.6	73.5	75.3	82.9
U.S.	100.0	100.0	100.0	100.0	100.0	100.0	100.0	100.0	100.0	100.0

countries minus the three excluded), all years before and after 1975 were extrapolated from 1975 in the same ways described above for the Phase II countries.

Note that the relationships between 1970 and earlier years are consistent with and, indeed, depend on the growth-rate data of the individual countries. The same is true for the relationships between 1975 and later years. Comparisons for Phase II countries between any year before 1970 and after 1975 are not consistent with corresponding growth-rate data. The figures are presented in this way, unsatisfactory though it may be, because these are the best estimates of the *interspatial* relationships in the given years. For those who want interspatial data for the Phase II countries for different years that are fully consistent with growth-rate data, a choice must be made between using 1970 as the starting date and extrapolating forward and backward, or using 1975 as the beginning point for the extrapolations in both directions.

Fortunately, the gross changes shown in Table 8-3 are similar by any extrapolation procedure. In general, the affluence of the countries has risen relative to the United States. As can be observed in Table 8-3, the incomes of the Western European countries have risen from 27 to 62 percent of the United States in the 1950s to 42 to 88 percent in 1980. The middle-income developing countries have also improved their position with respect to the United States. Some, such as Iran and the Republic of Korea, have risen substantially. But the most remarkable growth story is the rise of Japan from a per capita income of under 20 percent of the United States in 1950 to nearly 75 percent in 1980. The lowest income countries, however, have remained in the same relative position to the United States. Some have even declined; relative to the middle- and high-income countries other than the United States, their relative incomes have declined more consistently.

Comparison of GDP Over Space and Time Simultaneously for ICP Countries

Before estimates of GDP over time are presented, it may be worth returning to the difference between GDP and GDY produced by different valuations of the NFB. Imagine that an important exporter of some raw

Table 8-3 (*continued*)

Country	1970	1971	1972	1973	1974	1975	1976	1977	1978	1979	1980
Malawi	4.40	4.73	4.64	4.44	4.61	4.90	4.66	4.80	4.49[a]	4.43[a]	4.36[a]
Kenya	5.88	6.19	5.98	5.93	6.46	6.56	6.56	6.90	6.34[a]	6.20[a]	6.26[a]
India	6.46	6.51	6.13	6.05	6.11	6.56	6.15	6.29	6.23[a]	5.68[a]	—
Pakistan	8.45	8.11	8.00	7.97	8.00	8.23	8.07	8.08	7.75[a]	7.60[a]	7.99[a]
Sri Lanka	9.51	9.03	8.75	8.60	8.99	9.30	9.36	10.0	8.86[a]	9.04[a]	9.49[a]
Zambia	15.5	13.4	13.2	12.9	13.8	10.3	10.3	8.35	8.76[a]	7.55[a]	—
Philippines	11.7	11.8	11.6	12.0	12.9	13.2	13.0	12.7	13.2[a]	13.3[a]	13.7[a]
Thailand	11.7	11.7	11.6	12.3	12.7	13.0	13.0	13.0	13.3[a]	13.4[a]	13.9[a]
Korea	11.8	13.1	13.6	14.6	18.0	20.7	22.3	23.6	24.1[a]	24.8[a]	23.7[a]
Malaysia	15.6	16.4	17.0	19.7	22.7	21.5	23.2	24.1	22.5[a]	23.2[a]	24.7[a]
Colombia	17.3	17.7	17.8	17.8	21.2	22.4	23.9	23.6	22.5[a]	22.5[a]	23.1[a]
Syria	17.1	18.3	18.3	17.5	22.0	25.0	24.4	24.9	23.8[a]	23.7[a]	25.4[a]
Jamaica	28.6	28.3	28.1	25.2	24.5	24.0	21.7	20.3	19.0[a]	18.0[a]	17.0[a]
Brazil	18.6	20.3	21.0	22.2	24.3	25.2	25.9	25.7	25.4[a]	25.6[a]	27.2[a]
Mexico	32.4	31.8	31.6	31.8	33.9	34.7	32.5	31.1	31.3[a]	32.3[a]	34.2[a]
Iran	19.4	22.6	24.5	28.1	37.5	37.7	40.4	38.3	—	—	—
Uruguay	43.6	43.4	40.5	39.8	39.4	39.6	38.0	38.0	38.1[a]	40.0[a]	42.0[a]
Ireland	41.4	42.3	43.3	44.2	41.9	42.5	42.4	41.9	41.3[a]	40.9[a]	41.6[a]
Spain	49.0	49.8	51.6	53.4	56.3	55.9	54.3	53.1	51.7[a]	50.3[a]	51.0[a]
Italy	48.0	48.1	47.3	47.4	52.4	53.8	54.7	53.5	51.5	52.2	54.6
U.K.	62.7	62.9	61.0	60.7	61.3	63.9	63.7	62.7	63.9	64.0	65.7
Japan	58.5	60.1	62.1	63.7	65.6	68.4	68.6	69.3	71.3	70.9	74.1
Austria	62.2	64.5	65.1	65.5	69.6	69.6	69.7	69.4	68.8	70.0	72.5
Netherlands	68.3	69.4	68.9	69.3	73.6	75.2	74.9	73.3	71.6[a]	71.1[a]	72.1[a]
Belgium	72.3	73.7	75.0	76.5	80.1	77.7	78.0	76.3	75.5[a]	74.9[a]	77.0[a]
Denmark	81.8	82.0	83.5	82.2	81.2	82.4	82.2	81.1	79.6[a]	80.0[a]	80.6[a]
Germany	76.5	77.5	76.4	76.0	81.0	83.0	83.4	83.3	85.3	85.9	87.7
France	71.9	74.4	75.2	75.4	78.6	81.9	81.5	81.3	81.5	81.8	83.6
Luxembourg	88.9	84.3	84.4	94.1	104.3	82.0	80.6	77.7	79.1[a]	80.7[a]	82.0[a]
U.S.	100.0	100.0	100.0	100.0	100.0	100.0	100.0	100.0	100.0	100.0	100.0

a. Extrapolation of GDP.

material (say, petroleum) has enjoyed a substantial improvement in the price of its main export relative to the price of its imported products between the benchmark year and the extrapolation year. If the country has taken all of its increased purchasing power abroad in the form of imports, its net foreign balance in current prices would be zero. The improved terms of trade would be reflected in the increased quantities of goods and services absorbed in the country, whether in the form of household consumption, government consumption, or capital formation; by the method used here, no further adjustment would be made. However, the constant price GDP of a country would show a negative foreign balance, and there would have been a compensating reduction for the increased quantities absorbed. Thus the enhanced power to command goods overseas resulting from the rise in the export price will not be captured in the constant-price measure of GDP.

It follows that if the aim is to extrapolate benchmark estimates in order to compare relative *production* (GDP) in the different countries, the procedure can be simple. It is necessary only to apply to the benchmark estimate the relative change in the real GDP per capita of the given country and the numéraire country. That is, real per capita GDP in the currency of the numéraire country in the base year, 1975, for country j for a non-benchmark year ($\text{RGDP}_{j,t}$) is given by

$$(8.2) \qquad \text{RGDP}_{j,t} = \text{RGDP}_{j,75} \cdot \frac{\overline{\text{GDP}}_{j,t}/Pop_{j,t}}{\overline{\text{GDP}}_{j,75}/Pop_{j,75}}$$

where $\overline{\text{GDP}}$ is a constant price series of gross domestic product, *Pop* refers to population, and the benchmark year is 1975.[12]

If the aim is to trace the changes in relative *income* (GDY) from a benchmark year, separate treatment is necessary for domestic absorption and the net foreign balance as was used in the earlier benchmark-type extrapolations. The current year per capita GDY relative to the United States as the numéraire country, when multiplied by the value for that year of U.S. real per capita GDP (in base year prices), provides one type

12. A better procedure would be to extrapolate each final expenditure component of GDP separately. See note 4 in this chapter.

Table 8-4. Comparisons of Real Per Capita GDP and GDY in 1975 Prices for Thirty Countries, 1950–1977, Extrapolated From 1975 Phase III Results

Country	1950			1951			1952			1953		
	GDP	GDY	Ratio	GDP	GDY	Ratio	GDP	GDY	Ratio	GDP	GDY	Ratio
1 Malawi	153	164	1.07	n.a.	n.a.	n.a.	n.a.	n.a.	n.a.	n.a.	n.a.	n.a.
2 Kenya	385	439	1.14	419	493	1.18	391	441	1.13	366	419	1.14
3 India	345	333	0.96	352	349	0.99	359	348	0.97	374	362	0.97
4 Pakistan	345	404	1.17	339	404	1.19	347	387	1.12	376	392	1.04
5 Sri Lanka	381	509	1.34	401	546	1.36	408	493	1.21	387	491	1.27
6 Zambia	415	495	1.19	n.a.	n.a.	n.a.	n.a.	n.a.	n.a.	n.a.	n.a.	n.a.
7 Thailand	499	443	0.89	463	431	0.93	443	421	0.95	392	388	0.99
8 Philippines	425	472	1.11	430	467	1.09	473	492	1.04	496	549	1.11
9 Korea	423	459	1.09	n.a.	n.a.	n.a.	n.a.	n.a.	n.a.	524	538	1.03
10 Malaysia	649	784	1.21	n.a.	n.a.	n.a.	n.a.	n.a.	n.a.	n.a.	n.a.	n.a.
11 Colombia	931	972	1.04	935	955	1.02	967	983	1.02	1,006	1,052	1.05
12 Jamaica	556	565	1.02	n.a.	n.a.	n.a.	n.a.	n.a.	n.a.	754	783	1.04
13 Syria	735	766	1.04	699	n.a.	n.a.	868	n.a.	n.a.	930	n.a.	n.a.
14 Brazil	668	679	1.02	679	684	1.01	711	707	0.99	706	713	1.01
15 Mexico	1,142	1,142	1.00	1,196	1,212	1.01	1,206	1,224	1.01	1,173	1,157	0.99
16 Iran	659	469	0.71	n.a.	n.a.	n.a.	n.a.	n.a.	n.a.	n.a.	n.a.	n.a.
17 Uruguay	2,369	2,449	1.03	2,675	2,952	1.10	2,583	2,630	1.02	2,702	2,710	1.00
18 Ireland	1,498	1,477	0.99	1,556	1,471	0.95	1,584	1,537	0.97	1,637	1,628	0.99
19 Italy	1,373	1,427	1.04	1,478	1,526	1.03	1,526	1,559	1.02	1,632	1,680	1.03
20 Spain	1,179	1,187	1.01	1,374	1,372	1.00	1,428	1,420	0.99	1,364	1,359	1.00
21 U.K.	2,739	2,750	1.00	2,841	2,791	0.98	2,855	2,863	1.00	2,973	3,006	1.01
22 Japan	828	824	0.99	916	919	1.00	1,010	1,004	0.99	1,051	1,049	1.00
23 Austria	1,726	1,698	0.98	1,860	1,801	0.97	1,808	1,795	0.99	1,865	1,839	0.99
24 Netherlands	2,439	2,361	0.97	2,423	2,346	0.97	2,421	2,399	0.99	2,611	2,565	0.98
25 Belgium	2,438	2,398	0.98	2,508	2,543	1.01	2,527	2,568	1.02	2,597	2,570	0.99
26 France	2,263	2,251	0.99	2,378	2,337	0.98	2,454	2,429	0.99	2,502	2,501	1.00
27 Luxembourg	3,236	2,669	0.83	3,045	3,274	1.08	3,038	3,459	1.14	3,262	3,151	0.97
28 Denmark	2,810	2,770	0.99	2,741	2,678	0.98	2,777	2,754	0.99	2,938	2,922	0.99
29 Germany	1,989	1,908	0.96	2,160	2,085	0.97	2,347	2,277	0.97	2,485	2,426	0.98
30 U.S.	4,472	4,473	1.00	4,834	4,846	1.00	4,906	4,908	1.00	5,032	5,021	1.00

n.a. Not available.

Note: All GDP and GDY figures in the table are expressed in 1975 U.S. dollars.

of estimate. The resulting dollar figure would express the real income of a country in a given year, relative to the numéraire country in the base year (say, the United States in 1975).[13]

This approach, which defines GDY as GDP for the base country in each year, has the disadvantage of ignoring the changes in the terms of trade of the numéraire country. An alternative is to define the real GDY of the numéraire country, so it may also differ from its real GDP.[14] The definition used here is:

$$(8.3) \quad \overline{GDY}_{US,t} = (GDY_{US,t}/GDP_{US,t}) \cdot \overline{GDP}_{US,t}$$

---

13. In the ICP treatment there are in fact three factors affecting differences between GDY and GDP. First, and quantitatively probably most important, are changes in the terms of trade. When the terms of trade improve for a country, the net foreign balance relative to GDP in current prices will be greater than in constant prices, and the valuation method used here would in this case appropriately lead to GDY being larger than GDP.

A second influence will be the relative price of domestic absorption and the net foreign balance. The price level of the net foreign balance is at the average for all of the countries, while that for domestic absorption is at the price level for each country. (That is, each country's domestic absorption is converted to international dollars at its own PPP.) If the price level of the net foreign balance rose relative to the price level for domestic absorption between two years, then it would raise GDY relative to GDP for a country with a positive net foreign balance. (The opposite would occur for import surplus.)

The third factor is the size of the net foreign balance. If the net foreign balance rises in current prices, with terms of trade unchanged, then GDY will tend to rise above GDP for countries with price levels for domestic absorption which are above the world average, and the opposite for countries below the world average. The sense of this is that countries choosing to accumulate purchasing power abroad are credited with more income if their domestic price level is above the world average.

14. Another method of producing constant-price estimates of GDY for other years is to extrapolate domestic absorption in the base year for each country and add on the net foreign balance in constant prices. (The latter takes net foreign balance in current prices divided by the exchange rate brought to constant prices by a world or numéraire country index of traded-goods prices, all multiplied by the international price for the year.) This experiment was explored in Kravis, Heston, Summers (1978a), p. 131. Although it produces differences between GDP and GDY for the numéraire country in nonbenchmark years, it is not consistent with the use of international prices to value all quantities.

Table 8-4 *(continued)*

	1954			1955			1956			1957		
Country	GDP	GDY	*Ratio*	GDP	GDY	*Ratio*	GDP	GDY	*Ratio*	GDP	GDY	*Ratio*
1 Malawi	196	191	0.97	200	201	1.00	203	210	1.04	213	226	1.06
2 Kenya	379	461	1.22	395	487	1.23	419	486	1.16	417	479	1.15
3 India	382	373	0.98	384	374	0.98	391	385	0.98	384	376	0.98
4 Pakistan	363	392	1.08	360	375	1.04	367	387	1.05	366	385	1.05
5 Sri Lanka	396	519	1.31	403	554	1.37	351	492	1.40	373	500	01.34
6 Zambia	n.a.	n.a.	n.a.	514	767	1.49	561	825	1.47	570	702	1.23
7 Thailand	415	410	0.99	378	387	1.02	382	385	1.01	423	421	1.00
8 Philippines	532	579	1.09	536	596	1.11	597	625	1.05	580	630	1.09
9 Korea	544	537	0.99	571	562	0.98	570	559	0.98	600	611	1.02
10 Malaysia	n.a.	n.a.	n.a.	790	938	1.19	800	928	1.16	793	886	1.12
11 Colombia	1,048	1,134	1.08	1,058	1,121	1.06	1,062	1,115	1.05	1,042	1,071	1.03
12 Jamaica	821	870	1.06	890	929	1.04	968	979	1.01	1,070	1,112	1.04
13 Syria	1,032	n.a.	n.a.	967	n.a.	n.a.	1,069	n.a.	n.a.	1,044	n.a.	n.a.
14 Brazil	766	775	1.01	786	790	1.00	784	787	1.00	830	834	1.01
15 Mexico	1,255	1,251	1.00	1,322	1,310	0.99	1,369	1,357	0.99	1,426	1,408	0.99
16 Iran	n.a.	n.a.	n.a.	730	606	0.83	770	634	0.82	850	685	0.81
17 Uruguay	2,851	3,062	1.07	2,898	3,092	1.07	2,885	2,997	1.04	2,924	3,111	1.06
18 Ireland	1,652	1,639	0.99	1,712	1,685	0.98	1,693	1,657	0.98	1,695	1,649	0.97
19 Italy	1,683	1,747	1.04	1,790	1,857	1.04	1,857	1,925	1.04	1,924	2,005	1.04
20 Spain	1,537	1,536	1.00	1,605	1,602	1.00	1,708	1,707	1.00	1,765	1,766	1.00
21 U.K.	3,066	3,100	1.01	3,143	3,168	1.01	3,177	3,235	1.02	3,218	3,277	1.02
22 Japan	1,086	1,092	1.01	1,163	1,169	1.01	1,239	1,247	1.01	1,316	1,320	1.00
23 Austria	2,036	2,002	0.98	2,238	2,217	0.99	2,331	2,311	0.99	2,491	2,465	0.99
24 Netherlands	2,788	2,720	0.98	2,937	2,884	0.98	3,055	2,977	0.97	3,089	2,996	0.97
25 Belguim	2,691	2,649	0.98	2,791	2,792	1.00	2,849	2,870	1.01	2,891	2,888	1.00
26 France	2,554	2,578	1.01	2,646	2,670	1.01	2,805	2,783	0.99	2,912	2,880	0.99
27 Luxembourg	3,217	3,164	0.98	3,444	3,427	0.99	3,480	3,669	1.05	3,702	3,783	1.02
28 Denmark	3,026	3,008	0.99	2,979	2,982	1.00	3,040	3,041	1.00	3,163	3,148	1.00
29 Germany	2,646	2,576	0.97	2,943	2,853	0.97	3,087	2,996	0.97	3,216	3,119	0.97
30 U.S.	4,862	4,856	1.00	5,114	5,107	1.00	5,108	5,112	1.00	5,094	5,108	1.00

(Table continues on the following page.)

where $\overline{GDY}_{US,t}$ is the value of gross domestic income of the United States in year t in the prices of a base year. $GDY_{US,t}$ is the value of U.S. GDY extrapolated from a benchmark year in the prices of the current year (t); $GDP_{US,t}$ is current year GDP; and $\overline{GDP}_{US,t}$ is constant price GDP. The gross domestic income of the United States and its gross domestic product are the same in the base year but may differ in year t. One reason is that the terms of trade may differ between the two years. Another possible reason is that international prices of the net foreign balance (Π^{NFB}) may differ. The extrapolations involve base year prices in the case of GDP and current year prices for exports, imports, and Π^{NFB} in the case of GDY (see note 13).

Estimates of Constant-price GDP and GDY

Since the intertemporal and interspatial aspects are clearly of equal importance in constant-price estimates, it seems desirable to present estimates consistent with domestic growth rates. For any constant-price series a base year must be chosen. In Table

8-4, 1975 is used, because it is the focus of this study. However, since the 1970 and 1975 benchmarks are not consistent with the growth rates, only the 1975 benchmarks are presented in Table 8-4. The entries in Table 8-4 are all in 1975 U.S. dollars and may be compared directly within and between years for either GDY or GDP.

Comparisons of GDY and GDP

The constant-price GDP and GDY series in 1975 international dollars with the United States in 1975 equalling 100, or $7,176, are compared in Table 8-4. By examining the ratio of the index of GDY to the index of GDP over time it is possible to trace the effect on income of changes in a country's terms of trade and in related aspects of its net foreign balance (see note 13). For large countries with relatively small ratios of exports and imports to GDP, changes originating in the net foreign balance tend to have but little effect on income, usually 5 percent or less. This is true even

Table 8-4 (continued)

	1958			1959			1960			1961		
Country	GDP	GDY	Ratio	GDP	GDY	Ratio	GDP	GDY	Ratio	GDP	GDY	Ratio
1 Malawi	210	224	1.07	203	206	1.02	212	227	1.07	248	248	1.00
2 Kenya	403	450	1.12	382	429	1.12	396	445	1.12	332	381	1.15
3 India	401	394	0.98	399	391	0.98	416	411	0.99	395	388	0.98
4 Pakistan	368	375	1.02	359	395	1.10	370	404	1.09	377	421	1.12
5 Sri Lanka	370	499	1.35	374	514	1.37	392	531	1.35	406	515	1.27
6 Zambia	542	629	1.16	637	773	1.21	670	798	1.19	653	755	1.16
7 Thailand	413	422	1.02	445	455	1.02	482	495	1.03	491	505	1.03
8 Philippines	609	642	1.05	652	667	1.02	651	660	1.01	670	665	0.99
9 Korea	610	613	1.01	614	609	0.99	599	590	0.98	616	607	0.99
10 Malaysia	767	836	1.09	827	952	1.15	860	1,040	1.21	908	1,035	1.14
11 Colombia	1,029	1,022	0.99	1,067	1,038	0.97	1,084	1,067	0.98	1,099	1,091	0.99
12 Jamaica	1,076	1,100	1.02	1,138	1,154	1.01	1,194	1,213	1.02	1,230	1,229	1.00
13 Syria	972	n.a.	n.a.	925	n.a.	n.a.	942	858	0.91	986	893	0.91
14 Brazil	861	865	1.00	886	893	1.01	934	949	1.02	1,006	1,007	1.00
15 Mexico	1,453	1,418	0.98	1,446	1,405	0.97	1,557	1,509	0.97	1,579	1,524	0.97
16 Iran	926	709	0.77	981	714	0.73	1,062	756	0.71	1,090	748	0.69
17 Uruguay	2,757	2,776	1.01	2,650	2,702	1.02	2,715	2,824	1.04	2,712	2,801	1.03
18 Ireland	1,674	1,654	0.99	1,761	1,764	1.00	1,856	1,850	1.00	1,953	1,937	0.99
19 Italy	1,999	2,095	1.05	2,125	2,215	1.04	2,284	2,323	1.02	2,456	2,503	1.02
20 Spain	1,825	1,825	1.00	1,772	1,773	1.00	1,771	1,758	0.99	1,967	1,964	1.00
21 U.K.	3,208	3,287	1.02	3,314	3,391	1.02	3,406	3,485	1.02	3,500	3,588	1.03
22 Japan	1,365	1,376	1.01	1,471	1,489	1.01	1,649	1,676	1.02	1,868	1,893	1.01
23 Austria	2,540	2,521	0.99	2,617	2,590	0.99	2,809	2,786	.99	2,942	2,930	1.00
24 Netherlands	2,965	2,896	0.98	3,055	3,001	0.98	3,302	3,241	0.98	3,362	3,291	0.98
25 Belgium	2,848	2,871	1.01	2,920	2,889	0.99	3,065	3,055	1.00	3,215	3,181	0.99
26 France	2,950	2,930	0.99	3,040	3,038	1.00	3,209	3,219	1.00	3,343	3,349	1.00
27 Luxembourg	3,731	3,668	0.98	3,828	3,750	0.98	3,946	4,243	1.08	4,263	4,298	1.01
28 Denmark	3,204	3,211	1.00	3,454	3,486	1.01	3,658	3,662	1.00	3,840	3,825	1.00
29 Germany	3,305	3,212	0.97	3,520	3,415	0.97	3,809	3,699	0.97	3,934	3,833	0.97
30 U.S.	4,957	4,953	1.00	5,162	5,151	1.00	5,210	5,214	1.00	5,240	5,245	1.00

over a long and eventful period, such as that represented by 1950–77. This observation applies equally to India, a large developing country, and to the United States, a large developed country. For other advanced economies, including small ones with a variety of exports and imports, such as Denmark and Belgium, net foreign balance influences between 1950 and 1975 produced only small differences between real GDP and real GDY.

In contrast to the stability (despite substantial changes in relative prices) of relative incomes of all large countries and of small ones with varied exports and imports, other small countries and medium countries with concentrated exports in one or a few commodities are subject to wide fluctuations in income relative to the fluctuations in their production. Again, the generalization applies to both developing and developed countries (for example, Zambia and Luxembourg).

Extensions beyond the ICP Countries

This section describes the methods by which benchmark estimates of real GDP per capita are extended to nonbenchmark countries. The shortcut procedure used entails estimating, with the use of the data of the ICP countries, a functional relationship between real GDP per capita and various variables that are available for all or most other countries. The specific equations dealt with, in their various forms, are given in Tables 8-6 to 8-9. As with the extensions to other years, the estimates offered here are much more tentative than those reported in Chapters 1 through 7.

The rationale for the equations is the same in the main as that motivating earlier efforts.[15] Here as in those studies, the productivity-differential model is the basis for thinking that the relationship of real (r, based on PPP conversion) to nominal (n, based on exchange-rate conversion) GDP per capita will depend on the level of r and on the degree of exposure of a country's price system to external influences. The gap between n and r (each scaled to U.S. = 1.00) will be great when a country's exchange-rate–converted prices are

15. Kravis, Heston, Summers (1978b), and Summers, Kravis, Heston (1980).

Table 8-4. *(continued)*

	1962			1963			1964			1965		
Country	GDP	GDY	*Ratio*	GDP	GDY	*Ratio*	GDP	GDY	*Ratio*	GDP	GDY	*Ratio*
1 Malawi	220	225	1.02	210	223	1.06	214	214	1.00	232	243	1.05
2 Kenya	349	390	1.12	377	409	1.09	374	405	1.08	362	395	1.09
3 India	399	394	0.99	415	407	0.98	437	429	0.98	413	407	0.99
4 Pakistan	395	441	1.12	411	461	1.12	448	492	1.10	520	546	1.05
5 Sri Lanka	393	517	1.32	429	521	1.21	451	539	1.20	459	537	1.17
6 Zambia	630	709	1.13	626	714	1.14	690	803	1.16	794	913	1.15
7 Thailand	517	521	1.01	543	544	1.00	609	572	0.94	582	612	1.15
8 Philippines	720	693	0.96	762	710	0.93	743	707	0.95	766	716	0.93
9 Korea	613	611	1.00	652	659	1.01	698	688	0.99	720	710	0.99
10 Malaysia	942	1,067	1.13	987	1,083	1.10	1,013	1,110	1.10	1,062	1,170	1.10
11 Colombia	1,122	1,110	0.99	1,116	1,107	0.99	1,147	1,169	1.02	1,151	1,136	0.99
12 Jamaica	1,268	1,250	0.99	1,259	1,271	1.01	1,342	1,329	0.99	1,454	1,398	0.96
13 Syria	1,226	1,052	0.86	1,191	1,007	0.85	1,242	1,051	0.85	1,218	1,033	0.85
14 Brazil	1,027	1,021	0.99	1,017	1,008	0.99	1,020	1,014	0.99	1,011	999	0.99
15 Mexico	1,599	1,543	0.96	1,671	1,620	0.97	1,807	1,750	0.97	1,861	1,807	0.97
16 Iran	1,016	609	0.60	1,063	648	0.61	1,121	714	0.64	1,259	800	0.64
17 Uruguay	2,633	2,771	1.05	2,619	2,690	1.03	2,660	2,766	1.04	2,616	2,607	1.00
18 Ireland	2,012	2,001	0.99	2,082	2,072	1.00	2,146	2,163	1.01	2,192	2,198	1.00
19 Italy	2,585	2,637	1.02	2,694	2,763	1.03	2,745	2,821	1.03	2,808	2,883	1.00
20 Spain	2,131	2,140	1.00	2,299	2,329	1.01	2,396	2,430	1.01	2,535	2,593	1.02
21 U.K.	3,290	3,503	1.00	3,605	3,698	1.03	3,775	3,870	1.02	3,841	3,940	1.03
22 Japan	1,980	2,004	1.01	2,160	2,190	1.01	2,412	2,451	1.02	2,493	2,539	1.02
23 Austria	3,008	2,984	0.99	3,094	3,075	0.99	3,272	3,261	1.00	3,333	3,322	1.00
24 Netherlands	3,460	3,391	0.98	3,546	3,489	0.98	3,796	3,730	0.98	3,927	3,884	0.99
25 Belgium	3,371	3,336	0.99	3,505	3,441	0.98	3,714	3,667	0.99	3,812	3,778	0.99
26 France	3,503	3,497	1.00	3,638	3,636	1.00	3,832	3,833	1.00	3,967	3,967	1.00
27 Luxembourg	4,300	4,191	0.97	4,431	4,283	0.97	4,754	4,644	0.98	4,824	4,681	0.97
28 Denmark	4,043	4,191	1.00	4,014	4,047	1.01	4,375	4,415	1.01	4,451	4,587	1.01
29 Germany	4,059	3,953	0.97	4,127	4,016	0.97	4,349	4,237	0.97	4,541	4,401	0.97
30 U.S.	5,452	5,453	1.00	5,589	5,593	1.00	5,801	5,811	1.00	6,067	6,070	1.00

(Table continues on the following page.)

low for the goods entering into its final expenditures. Low-income countries tend to have low prices because the low wages reflecting low productivity in commodity-producing industries carry over to service industries, in which productivity is not so low.

In high-income countries the general level of wages is pulled up by the greater weight of capital- and technology-intensive, high-productivity, high-wage industries. The high wages of these industries, which are mainly commodity producing, carry over to other industries, in which productivity is not so high.

The resulting national price structures are differentiated by relatively high service prices in the rich countries compared with the poor ones. Since the link between the final-product price structures of different countries is stronger for tradable commodities than for nontradable services, the prices of commodities are more nearly drawn to a common level in low- and high-income countries.

These two characteristics of the service industries—a smaller productivity gap between low- and high-income countries and limited tradability—apply to intermediate services (for example, wholesale and retail

trade) as well as to final-product services. They thus operate to make the GDP price level of low-income countries lower than that of high-income countries in two ways: directly, in the form of low prices for final-product services, and indirectly, in the form of low-cost service components (for example, trade and transport) in the domestic final-product prices of tradable commodities.[16]

That the behavior of price levels for services, commodities, and GDP as a whole corresponds to the above account is readily seen by figures in Table 8-5. Since the exchange-rate–deviation index, the ratio of the nominal to the real GDP, is the reciprocal of the price level, the systematic association of price levels with real per capita GDP means that nominal per capita GDP (n) is a function of real GDP per capita (r). However, because the functional relationship is to be used for "forecasting" r for countries for which it is unknown on the basis of known n, the functional relationship

---

16. More detailed support for this proposition is presented in Kravis, Heston, Summers (1982).

Table 8-4. *(continued)*

	1966			1967			1968			1969		
Country	GDP	GDY	*Ratio*	GDP	GDY	*Ratio*	GDP	GDY	*Ratio*	GDP	GDY	*Ratio*
1 Malawi	255	267	1.05	274	275	1.00	265	275	1.04	283	291	1.03
2 Kenya	395	434	1.10	406	447	1.10	423	456	1.08	434	460	1.06
3 India	402	396	0.99	424	418	0.99	429	417	0.97	446	434	0.97
4 Pakistan	518	564	1.09	540	586	1.08	570	593	1.04	583	573	0.98
5 Sri Lanka	469	550	1.17	497	557	1.12	498	578	1.16	524	606	1.16
6 Zambia	729	985	1.35	764	1,001	1.31	752	1,046	1.39	727	1,172	1.61
7 Thailand	631	679	1.08	662	687	1.04	699	717	1.03	721	761	1.06
8 Philippines	771	723	0.94	786	755	0.96	782	780	1.00	795	802	1.01
9 Korea	790	791	1.00	818	826	1.01	889	914	1.03	992	1,027	1.04
10 Malaysia	1,117	1,194	1.07	1,130	1,174	1.04	1,192	1,177	0.99	1,211	1,214	1.00
11 Colombia	1,172	1,188	1.01	1,197	1,171	0.98	1,234	1,221	0.99	1,276	1,265	0.99
12 Jamaica	1,511	1,491	0.99	1,544	1,532	0.99	1,730	1,641	0.95	1,823	1,752	0.96
13 Syria	1,149	1,000	0.87	1,166	1,001	0.86	1,192	1,020	0.86	1,337	1,182	0.88
14 Brazil	1,018	1,002	0.98	1,036	1,023	0.99	1,117	1,096	0.98	1,191	1,166	0.98
15 Mexico	1,924	1,864	0.97	1,980	1,924	0.97	2,076	2,014	0.97	2,137	2,062	0.97
16 Iran	1,343	853	0.64	1,456	919	0.63	1,592	991	0.62	1,733	1,052	0.61
17 Uruguay	2,708	2,766	1.02	2,551	2,610	1.02	2,558	2,566	1.00	2,687	2,747	1.02
18 Ireland	2,214	2,237	1.01	2,327	2,362	1.02	2,469	2,508	1.02	2,619	2,689	1.03
19 Italy	2,945	3,016	1.02	3,136	3,211	1.02	3,307	3,374	1.02	3,464	3,550	1.02
20 Spain	2,708	2,772	1.02	2,794	2,845	1.02	2,910	2,941	1.01	3,100	3,132	1.01
21 U.K.	3,902	4,010	1.03	3,982	4,096	1.03	4,105	4,198	1.02	4,153	4,242	1.02
22 Japan	2,725	2,771	1.02	3,031	3,083	1.02	3,403	3,456	1.02	3,679	3,804	1.03
23 Austria	3,512	3,492	0.99	3,588	3,557	0.99	3,729	3,698	0.99	3,927	3,869	0.99
24 Netherlands	3,979	3,927	0.99	4,142	4,101	0.99	4,363	4,357	1.00	4,591	4,568	1.00
25 Belgium	3,906	3,864	0.99	4,039	3,999	0.99	4,189	4,131	0.99	4,446	4,417	0.99
26 France	4,141	4,130	1.00	4,306	4,296	1.00	4,476	4,453	0.99	4,830	4,796	0.99
27 Luxembourg	4,810	4,671	0.97	4,780	4,728	0.99	5,079	4,993	0.98	5,452	5,573	1.02
28 Denmark	4,613	4,668	1.01	4,782	4,830	1.01	4,956	4,970	1.00	5,274	5,335	1.01
29 Germany	4,608	4,473	0.97	4,575	4,457	0.97	4,835	4,684	0.97	5,183	5,013	0.97
30 U.S.	6,353	6,348	1.00	6,443	6,436	1.00	6,646	6,630	1.00	6,741	6,726	1.00

is estimated with the dependent and independent variable roles of r and n reversed. The possible econometric distortion resulting from this is mitigated by the very high $\overline{R}^2$ of the relationship. How much difference the reversal makes in the quadratic-in-the-logs functional form used can be seen in Tables 8-8 and 8-9.[17]

The productivity-differential model is not advanced as a complete explanation of all the factors at work affecting the relationship of real to nominal GDP. When there are very large differences in per capita real incomes there are correspondingly large differences in economic structures, and the factors set out in the productivity-differential model dominate the result. Thus the model performs very well in explaining the r/n ratio for the range of countries with per capita real GDP falling below 75 to 80 percent of that of the United States. Among these countries the lowest per capita GDP is less than 10 percent of that of the United States,

and there is room for several doublings in r as the countries rise on the income scale (for example, from 7 percent to 15 percent, 15 percent to 30 percent, and so on). Once the 75 or 80 percent level is reached, differences in economic structure are not so great, and other factors, particularly financial influences, may play a larger role.[18] This may be the reason that in 1975 the price levels above that of the United States are found for several high-income countries in Group 5 (see Chapter 6, under the section "Comparison of the Structures of Expenditures, Prices, and Quantities for Six Groups of Countries").

The task of incorporating all these variables could not be performed for the present volume, but the exposure variables used in previous work have been investigated. The rationale for these variables is this: between two countries with the same r, the more open economy—the one that is more exposed to external price influences—will tend to have prices that conform more closely to those of its trading partners. For the

17. A priori, the best functional form seemed to be a logarithmic one. Applying the Box-Tidwell procedure (Maddala, 1977, pp. 314–17) verified that indeed such a form was preferable to a linear equation. (The diagnostic statistic $\hat{\lambda}$ was equal to 0.16.)

18. For other suggestions about filling out the model see Clague (1980) and Isenman (1980).

Table 8-4. *(continued)*

	1970			1971			1972			1973		
Country	GDP	GDY	*Ratio*	GDP	GDY	*Ratio*	GDP	GDY	*Ratio*	GDP	GDY	*Ratio*
1 Malawi	276	291	1.05	309	318	1.03	313	328	1.05	331	328	0.99
2 Kenya	445	492	1.11	456	511	1.12	468	500	1.07	486	508	1.05
3 India	463	454	0.98	462	453	0.98	448	438	0.98	455	447	0.98
4 Pakistan	567	561	0.99	556	546	0.98	573	564	0.98	580	590	1.02
5 Sri Lanka	560	632	1.13	559	608	1.09	572	617	1.08	612	637	1.04
6 Zambia	738	1,027	1.39	723	901	1.25	768	934	1.22	730	954	1.31
7 Thailand	740	774	1.05	791	785	0.99	831	819	0.99	863	912	1.06
8 Philippines	815	805	0.99	823	805	0.98	841	813	0.97	892	863	0.97
9 Korea	1,054	1,088	1.03	1,130	1,183	1.05	1,210	1,227	1.01	1,325	1,342	1.01
10 Malaysia	1,246	1,266	1.02	1,285	1,286	1.00	1,382	1,334	0.97	1,495	1,530	1.02
11 Colombia	1,330	1,351	1.02	1,371	1,400	1.02	1,451	1,470	1.01	1,553	1,546	1.01
12 Jamaica	1,966	1,899	0.97	1,997	1,903	0.95	2,114	1,979	0.94	2,018	1,869	0.93
13 Syria	1,312	1,139	0.87	1,383	1,230	0.89	1,468	1,292	0.88	1,455	1,295	0.90
14 Brazil	1,261	1,238	0.98	1,382	1,369	0.99	1,504	1,482	0.99	1,664	1,642	0.99
15 Mexico	2,210	2,152	0.97	2,212	2,145	0.97	2,303	2,229	0.97	2,406	2,353	0.98
16 Iran	1,898	1,114	0.59	2,082	1,359	0.65	2,367	1,569	0.66	2,565	1,935	0.75
17 Uruguay	2,796	2,892	1.03	2,766	2,923	1.06	2,707	2,857	1.06	2,736	2,950	1.08
18 Ireland	2,678	2,746	1.03	2,765	2,849	1.03	2,892	3,053	1.06	3,002	3,277	1.09
19 Italy	3,587	3,711	1.03	3,612	3,728	1.03	3,682	3,811	1.04	3,918	3,992	1.02
20 Spain	3,236	3,254	1.01	3,352	3,358	1.00	3,595	3,635	1.01	3,883	3,952	1.02
21 U.K.	4,243	4,354	1.03	4,333	4,456	1.03	4,418	4,568	1.03	4,755	4,828	1.02
22 Japan	4,120	4,205	1.02	4,278	4,357	1.02	4,605	4,712	1.02	4,968	5,075	1.02
23 Austria	4,195	4,127	0.98	4,416	4,347	0.98	4,649	4,588	0.99	4,850	4,852	1.00
24 Netherlands	4,839	4,791	0.99	4,983	4,910	0.99	5,102	5,093	1.00	5,348	5,373	1.00
25 Belgium	4,720	4,716	1.00	4,892	4,842	0.99	5,144	5,145	1.00	5,440	5,494	1.01
26 France	5,040	5,010	0.99	5,243	5,221	1.00	5,497	5,511	1.00	5,745	5,796	1.01
27 Luxembourg	5,469	5,903	1.08	5,570	5,678	1.02	5,907	5,951	1.01	6,458	6,968	1.08
28 Denmark	5,362	5,429	1.01	5,462	5,522	1.01	5,737	5,886	1.03	5,979	6,089	1.02
29 Germany	5,461	5,324	0.98	5,581	5,467	0.98	5,745	5,660	0.99	6,009	5,935	0.99
30 U.S.	6,646	6,636	1.00	6,755	6,736	1.00	7,706	7,049	1.00	7,420	7,404	1.00

(Table continues on the following page.)

empirical work, openness (OP) has been defined as the ratio of the sum of exports and imports to GDP.[19] For low-income countries, trading partners are rich countries, and a high degree of openness should raise the level of prices and produce a larger n relative to r. In the equations with r as the dependent variable, the coefficient of openness should be negative for these countries. For rich countries, much of whose trade is with each other, the effect of high openness is less clear cut, especially since the shift toward more capital-intensive, more technology-intensive production may be attenuated after a certain level of income is reached. Some higher income countries will find themselves with trading partners whose average price level is lower than theirs and others with partners whose average price level is higher than theirs. Thus as between two countries with the same high n, the effect of a high openness ratio is more difficult to predict.

It may therefore be expected that the coefficient of openness will be a less powerful explanatory variable for the rich countries.[20]

In a work referred to above, another measure of exposure, price isolation (PI), was included not merely to capture the opportunity for exposure at which OP is aimed, but also to discern the actual effect on prices.

20. A rough test of this expectation was carried out by creating separate OP variables for poor (Groups I through IV) and rich (Groups V and VI) countries. The equation for thirty-four countries in 1975 was:

$$\ln r = -0.0862 + 0.4931 \ln n - 0.0474 (\ln n)^2$$
$$\quad\quad (0.1014) \quad (0.1144) \quad\quad (0.0258)$$

$$-0.0914 \ln OP \cdot D_1 - 0.0526 \ln OP \cdot D_2$$
$$\quad (0.0516) \quad\quad\quad (0.0619)$$

$$\bar{R}^2 = 0.967 \quad\quad SEE = 0.1566$$

where D_1 was a dummy variable that took on a value of 1 if the country was in Group I through IV and zero otherwise, and D_2 a dummy variable that took on a value of 1 if the country was in Group V or VI and zero otherwise. The coefficient of OP for the low- and middle-income countries is larger than that for the high-income countries, though the difference is not significant.

19. The average ratio for the years 1971–75 was used. Data were from a U.N. national accounts tape supplied by Douglas Walker, of the Projections and Perspective Studies Branch of the Department of International Economic and Social Affairs.

Table 8-4 (continued)

Country	1974			1975			1976			1977		
	GDP	GDY	Ratio	GDP	GDY	Ratio	GDP	GDY	Ratio	GDP	GDY	Ratio
1 Malawi	381	336	0.88	352	352	1.00	389	349	0.90	393	372	0.95
2 Kenya	504	505	1.00	471	471	1.00	500	491	0.98	516	535	1.04
3 India	461	444	0.97	471	471	1.00	484	461	0.95	505	488	0.97
4 Pakistan	592	583	0.98	591	591	1.00	593	604	1.02	612	626	1.02
5 Sri Lanka	750	655	0.87	667	667	1.00	760	701	0.92	765	774	1.01
6 Zambia	752	1,006	1.34	738	738	1.00	756	773	1.02	711	647	0.91
7 Thailand	889	929	1.05	936	936	1.00	966	975	1.01	1,002	1,006	1.00
8 Philippines	954	925	0.97	947	947	1.00	1,048	974	0.93	1,083	982	0.91
9 Korea	1,402	1,457	1.04	1,484	1,484	1.00	1,647	1,667	1.01	1,783	1,830	1.03
10 Malaysia	1,570	1,693	1.08	1,541	1,541	1.00	1,686	1,738	1.03	1,749	1,865	1.07
11 Colombia	1,602	1,665	1.04	1,609	1,609	1.00	1,751	1,792	1.02	1,727	1,830	1.06
12 Jamaica	1,893	1,788	0.94	1,723	1,723	1.00	1,622	1,625	1.00	1,551	1,570	1.01
13 Syria	1,593	1,601	1.00	1,794	1,794	1.00	1,830	1,831	1.00	1,830	1,930	1.05
14 Brazil	1,803	1,771	0.98	1,811	1,811	1.00	1,985	1,939	0.98	2,042	1,993	0.98
15 Mexico	2,716	2,473	0.91	2,487	2,487	1.00	2,684	2,431	0.91	2,664	2,413	0.91
16 Iran	2,667	2,636	0.99	2,705	2,705	1.00	2,904	3,024	1.04	2,854	2,966	1.04
17 Uruguay	2,840	2,868	1.01	2,845	2,845	1.00	2,929	2,844	0.97	2,985	2,942	0.99
18 Ireland	3,065	3,053	1.00	3,049	3,049	1.00	3,107	3,161	1.02	3,207	3,250	1.01
19 Italy	4,479	4,065	0.91	3,861	3,861	1.00	4,499	4,095	0.91	4,519	4,144	0.92
20 Spain	4,175	4,102	0.98	4,010	4,010	1.00	4,147	4,069	0.98	4,201	4,114	0.98
21 U.K.	4,764	4,625	0.97	4,588	4,588	1.00	4,849	4,772	0.98	4,907	4,863	0.99
22 Japan	4,862	4,957	1.02	4,907	4,907	1.00	5,125	5,138	1.00	5,317	5,371	1.01
23 Austria	5,077	5,075	1.00	4,994	4,994	1.00	5,257	5,217	0.99	5,478	5,379	0.98
24 Netherlands	5,510	5,486	1.00	5,397	5,397	1.00	5,615	5,611	1.00	5,712	5,679	0.99
25 Belgium	5,620	5,746	1.02	5,574	5,574	1.00	5,793	5,841	1.01	5,854	5,918	1.01
26 France	5,912	5,834	0.99	5,877	5,877	1.00	6,142	6,104	0.99	6,308	6,299	1.00
27 Luxembourg	6,570	7,602	1.16	5,884	5,884	1.00	6,101	6,035	0.99	6,131	6,022	0.98
28 Denmark	6,072	5,917	0.97	5,911	5,911	1.00	6,343	6,157	0.97	6,450	6,284	0.97
29 Germany	6,082	6,057	1.00	5,952	5,952	1.00	6,322	6,250	0.99	6,511	6,457	0.99
30 U.S.	7,311	7,287	1.00	7,176	7,176	1.00	7,515	7,490	1.00	7,802	7,751	0.99

It was posited that the greater the isolation—that is, the larger the differences between the time-to-time movements of a given country's prices and world prices—the less will that country's prices be influenced by the price levels of other countries. The role of PI has been subordinated in the present exercise mainly because of uncertainties about the underlying data required to construct the variable. United Nations and World Bank sources produce different implicit deflators—the price indexes used in PI—for several countries. In some cases there are also differences in exchange rates.[21]

21. An experiment was carried out to see what the effect of "reliable" PI would be in the 1975 data. It involved the twenty-two out of the thirty-four countries for which U.N. and World Bank sources yielded similar (within 5 percent for each year in 1971–75) dollar-converted implicit deflators. An equation using 1975 benchmark data for these twenty-two countries and including both OP and PI (that is, of the D type in terms of the symbols used to identify equations with different sets of independent variables in the Kravis, Heston, Summers [1978b] article referred to earlier) was about as good as the corresponding equation for 1970. However, OP was stronger than PI, relative to the 1970 equation, both in the size of the coefficient and in its t ratio.

The Choice between 1970 and 1975
as the Basis for Extrapolation
to Other Countries

An important question has to be faced in applying the productivity-differential model as amended by one or more exposure variables. That is whether to place main reliance on the n/r relationship of 1970 or that of 1975. The 1970 benchmark data imply lower r's for most countries relative to the United States in 1975 than the 1975 benchmark data, after adjustments are made for the differences in reference years.[22]

Three sets of considerations are relevant to this issue. One is whether there is any reason to believe that the 1970 benchmark comparisons are superior to those of 1975 or vice versa. On balance, the judgment of the staff is that if there is any difference in the quality of the basic data, the margin of superiority is in favor of 1975 but that the quality difference cannot be very great on the average. The 1975 price comparisons in

22. See column 6, Table 8-1.

Table 8-5. Price Level for Services, Commodities, and GDP and Exchange-rate–Deviation Index, 1975

Group	Real per capita GDP (U.S. = 100)	Number of countries (1)	Price indexes (U.S. = 100) Commodities (2)	Services (3)	GDP (4)	Exchange-rate– deviation index (5)
I	Less than 15	8	57.2	20.7	40.6	2.64
II	15–29.9	6	65.9	34.1	51.7	2.11
III	30–49.9	6	83.1	41.2	64.7	1.61
IV	50–64.9	4	94.0	46.3	73.5	1.39
V	65–89.9	9	119.0	94.6	107.5	1.05
VI	90 and over	1	100.0	100.0	100.0	1.00

Sources: Table 6-12. The exchange-rate–deviation indexes are from Table 1-10.

Europe were probably better on average than the earlier ones, but the opposite may have been true for those involving other countries, including some for which very large discrepancies are shown between the 1970 and the 1975 estimates. The fact that thirty-four countries are included in the 1975 benchmarks as against only sixteen in 1970 is a clearer factor in favor of the use of 1975. However, by extrapolation it is also possible to use the 1975 estimate for the new countries in conjunction with 1970 estimates for the Phase II countries.

A second consideration is whether the long-run structural relationship between n and r was better reflected in the data of one year or the other. It might be argued that the system of mainly fixed exchange rates that still prevailed in 1970 better captured this relationship. In this view the variability of exchange rates in the subsequent years, including 1973 and 1975, was too large, too frequent, and perhaps even too erratic to reflect the underlying forces at work as summarized in the productivity differential model. More fundamentally, the full effects of the shock of large increases in oil prices may not have worked themselves out by 1975. Of course, if the PPP theory of exchange rates worked, the fluctuations of exchange rates since 1970 would be offset by price-level changes and the 1970 relationship of n to r would still be observable. On this basis any differences in the relation of n to r between the two years for any country would betoken

a measurement error in the r for one or both years. In point of fact, the PPP theory of exchange rates, though the subject of a recent revival by advocates of the monetary approach to the balance of payments, has not won wide allegiance. Also, at least as it is most often propounded, the theory excludes the possibility of a structural shift in relative price levels associated with rising r's.

There are some strong arguments against the proposition that the 1970 data better reflect the basic relationship between n and r than the 1975 data. In the first place, 1970 can hardly be regarded as an equilibrium period; it was the last year before the accumulating disequilibriums of the old system finally destroyed it.

Instead of being a system of infrequently adjusted pegged rates as previously, the new system is a mixed one in which major currencies are in a managed float and other currencies are pegged to the major currencies or some combination of them. It cannot be presumed that the long-run relationships between n and r will remain the same under the new system as under the old one. The relationship between n and r for the three ICP benchmark years is consistently strong, as is indicated by the equations in Table 8-6.

Also, the mechanism through which price influences are transmitted from one country to another may work differently under the new system. This is at least hinted at by the changes in PI and OP. For what it is worth,

Table 8-6. Relationship between Nominal (n) and Real (r) GDP per Capita, 1970, 1973, and 1975

Equation number	$\ln r$	$(\ln r)^2$	Constant	$\bar{R}^2$ (SEE)	n
A_{75}	1.8937 (0.1632)	0.1631 (0.0555)	0.2546 (0.0927)	0.970 (0.2193)	34
A_{73}	1.9157 (0.1734)	0.1792 (0.0599)	0.2507 (0.905)	0.986 (0.1606)	16
A_{70}	1.7972 (0.1692)	0.1692 (0.0505)	0.0107 (0.0736)	0.990 (0.1259)	16

Note: The dependent variable is $\ln n$.

Table 8-7. Relationship between Nominal (*n*) and Real (*r*) GDP per Capita and Openness (OP)

Equation number	ln r	(ln r)²	OP	Constant	$\overline{R}^2$ (SEE)	n
B₇₅	1.8668 (0.1566)	0.1573 (0.0532)	0.1125 (0.0566)	0.1092 (0.1148)	0.972 (0.2095)	34
B₇₃	2.0262 (0.1551)	0.2211 (0.0541)	0.1433 (0.0595)	0.1107 (0.0930)	0.989 (0.1372)	16
B₇₀	1.8480 (0.1478)	0.1881 (0.0520)	0.0646 (0.0531)	−0.0513 (0.0885)	0.991 (0.1236)	16

Note: The dependent variable is ln *n*.

given the uncertainties of the data, the PI tended to be larger in the rich countries and smaller in the poor countries in 1971–75 than in 1963–70 (using United Nations data). That is, the time-to-time changes in the implicit deflators of the different countries tended to be less similar for the rich countries in the later period than in the earlier, while the opposite tended to be true for the poor countries. There was also a substantial increase in the relative volume of world trade, probably owing to relatively higher oil prices and to the need for most countries to export more to pay higher petroleum bills. The 1971–75 average ratio of $X + M$ to GDP was 21 percent higher than the 1963–70 average for all thirty-four Phase III countries and 30 percent higher for the sixteen Phase II countries.[23] When OP is added to the previous set of equations, its coefficient is larger and more significant in 1973 and 1975 than in 1970 (see Table 8-7).

Thus on general considerations of the two periods, a case can be made that the *r/n* relationship for 1970, as used in earlier work, or for 1973 and 1975, might be used for estimation for nonbenchmark countries. Because the 1973 benchmarks were partly dependent on the 1970 results, and because 1973 relationships tend to be in between those for 1970 and 1975, the remainder of this chapter will be based on these two years.

Shortcut Strategies

The addition of eighteen countries in Phase III provides an opportunity to examine the predictive characteristics of the 1970 and 1975 relationships. The reader may imagine that the 1975 benchmark data for the eighteen additional countries are not available, and it is necessary to determine which of several ways of estimating their 1975 real GDPs (*r*'s) comes closest to the benchmark estimates. There are three broad strategies of estimation:

1. The most direct is to base the estimates on the 1975 benchmark data for the sixteen countries that were included in Phase II. This involves (a) a Geary-Khamis calculation for 1975 for these sixteen countries;[24] (b) fitting an equation to the *r*'s produced by this calculation, the equation reflecting one of the relationships between *n*, *r*, and the exposure variables discussed below; and (c) using this equation to estimate the *r*'s for the eighteen additional countries.

This approach implicitly assumes that the 1975 relationships of *n* to *r* can best be gauged from 1975 data, even though by 1975 the exchange-rate regime represented a mixed system of managed floats for the major currencies and pegged rates for most others. A variant of the direct approach is to calculate the *r/n* relationship on the basis of an average for the years 1974–76. That was intended to offset the possible disturbing effects of highly variable exchange rates. However, as the results of this method are virtually identical with 1975, they will not be further discussed.

2. The roundabout strategy, as well as the intermediate one that follows it, is based on the assumption that the long-run relationships between *r* and the other variables can best be measured by data of 1970, when the exchange regime was one of mainly pegged rates. The roundabout method seeks to take advantage of the possibility that the Phase III set of specifications and prices might provide a basis for more accurate extrapolation from the old sixteen to the eighteen additional countries. In this approach the first step (a) is the same as in the direct method; that is, 1975 benchmark *r*'s are obtained from a sixteen-country Geary-Khamis calculation. Next (b) these *r*'s are extrapolated back to 1970 by methods explained in the first part of this chapter. Then (c) an equation is fitted to these

---

23. Note that the ratio referred to in this sentence is $(X + M)/$ GDP for each country. The OP used in the equations is this ratio taken relative to that of the United States. The U.S. ratio $(X + M)/$ GDP was 41 percent higher in the later period than in the earlier one.

24. The five-tier supercountry weighting system of Phase II was used. See Kravis, Heston, Summers (1978a), p. 77. For an explanation of supercountry weights see Chapter 3 under the section "Supercountry Weighting."

1970 sixteen-country data, and (d) used to estimate 1970 *r*'s for the fifteen new countries.[25] Finally, (e) the 1970 *r*'s are extrapolated to 1975 by the methods referred to in (b).

3. The intermediate approach does not seek to take advantage of the 1975 data commonality between the sixteen old and eighteen additional countries. It is, however, like the roundabout method in that it relies on 1970 relationships. The sacrifice of commonality is offset by the avoidance of the initial extrapolation of 1975 data to 1970, step (b) of the roundabout method. The starting point (a) thus is the 1970 set of benchmark estimates for the sixteen Phase II countries. (Phase III revisions of the 1970 data are used.) An equation (b) is fitted linking the *r*'s and *n*'s of these data and the exposure variables, and (c) the equation is used to produce 1970 *r*'s for the fifteen new countries. Finally, (d) these *r*'s are extrapolated to 1975.

In each of these approaches several differently specified equations were tried. Four are reported in Table 8-8. The dependent variable in all the equations is ln *r*. The independent variables are successively (Λ) ln *r* and $(\ln r)^2$; (B) ln *r*, $(\ln r)^2$, and OP; (BI) ln *r*, $(\ln r)^2$, and $(\ln r \cdot \ln OP)$; and (D) ln *r*, $(\ln r)^2$, OP, and PI. The squared term for *r* is included simply to capture the curvilinearity that is found in the double log relationship between *n* and *r*. The term $(\ln n \cdot \ln OP)$ is an interaction term that takes account of the attenuated influence of OP as *r* rises.

The corresponding equations of the three sets are generally similar. The most notable difference is the larger size and greater statistical significance of the openness coefficient in the 1975 equation B compared with the 1970 equations.[26]

The dependent variable in Table 8-8 is the natural log of the nominal index of per capita income, and the real GDP per capita is treated as an independent variable. This is a more nearly "structural" equation than would be obtained by reversing the positions of *r* and *n*, since the underlying explanation of the relationships set out earlier makes *n* dependent on *r*. However, for use as an estimating equation, there is, as was mentioned earlier, no choice but to reverse the

positions of *n* and *r*, since the former is known for non-ICP countries and the latter is not. In Table 8-9, *n* is treated as an independent variable, and the dependent variable is *r*.

The performance of the twelve equations set out in Table 8-9 is measured against the 1975 actual benchmark *r*'s for the fifteen new Phase III countries in Table 8-10.[27] For the fifteen new Phase III countries that can be tested, Table 8-10 summarizes the results for the three sets of equations with respect to five characteristics of the errors of estimation. The low and high estimates relative to the 1975 benchmarks are given, along with the mean ratio of the estimated value to the benchmark value, the mean deviation between the estimated and benchmark figures, and the mean deviation squared. The highs and lows and other measures can be heavily influenced by one or two countries. One measure in the table is called the country deviation rank; it ranks each equation by the closeness of its prediction for each country, and then sums these ranks. Similarly, summed ranks have been computed for the mean deviation and the squared deviation. The last five rows of the table, therefore, are the most relevant.

Overall, these performance measures seem to point to a small margin of superiority for equation BI in the direct method. However, the superiority of BI does not carry over to the other two approaches. If the roundabout approach were chosen, equation D would seem slightly better, and if the intermediate approach were favored, equation A would merit preference.

Although the choice among the equations is thus reduced to very narrow ground, BI has been selected for the extrapolations reported on here. Because of the differences between the real GDP levels estimated from the 1970 and 1975 benchmarks, discussed in a previous section, a compromise has been followed in which real GDP per capita for each non-ICP country has first been estimated for 1970 from a BI equation and then extrapolated to 1975 and, second, been estimated directly from a BI equation for 1975. The two estimates of 1975 real per capita GDP have been averaged to produce the estimate included in the figures reported here.

For both 1970 and 1975, the BI equations used in the extrapolations were estimated from the full com-

25. It is not possible to perform these extrapolations on a strictly comparable basis for Poland, Romania, and Yugoslavia, so these countries are not included in the comparisons.

26. The standard analysis of covariance test for the difference between pairs of A, pairs of B, pairs of BI, and pairs of D equations shows that none of the differences was statistically significant. However, the test is not completely appropriate here, since the assumption of uncorrelated error terms for each pair of equations may not be warranted. When ln OP was included with the independent variables in the BI equations its coefficient was never significantly different from zero.

27. There are eighteen new Phase III countries, but because it has not been possible to extrapolate the results for Romania and only rough extrapolations could be made for Poland and Yugoslavia between 1970 and 1975—an operation necessary for the intermediate and roundabout methods—the test has been attempted for only fifteen new countries. In the final estimating equation for 1970 discussed below, the observations for Poland and Yugoslavia were included.

Table 8-8. "Structural" Equations Relating Nominal per Capita GDP to Real per Capita GDP and Exposure Variables

Equation number	ln r	$(\ln r)^2$	ln OP	ln PI	(ln OP)(ln r)	Constant	$\overline{R}^2$ (SEE)
Direct approach							
A$_{75}$	1.8970 (0.1659)	0.1612 (0.0569)	—	—	—	0.2526 (0.0936)	0.969 (0.2216)
B$_{75}$	1.8661 (0.1586)	0.1541 (0.0543)	0.1168 (0.0570)	—	—	0.1007 (0.1159)	0.972 (0.2109)
BI$_{75}$	1.9836 (0.1583)	0.1581 (0.0529)	—	—	0.0947 (0.0391)	0.2426 (0.0871)	0.973 (0.2059)
D$_{75}$	1.8644 (0.1607)	0.1550 (0.0550)	0.1144 (0.0579)	−0.0174 (0.0341)	—	0.0876 (0.1201)	0.971 (0.2136)
Roundabout approach							
A$'_{70}$	1.9253 (0.1513)	0.2017 (0.0571)	—	—	—	−0.0348 (0.0701)	0.990 (0.1239)
B$'_{70}$	1.9886 (0.1579)	0.2272 (0.0600)	0.0641 (0.0534)	—	—	−0.0941 (0.0848)	0.991 (0.1218)
BI$'_{70}$	2.0803 (0.1476)	0.2337 (0.0514)	—	—	−0.0706 (0.0307)	−0.0211 (0.0610)	0.993 (0.1074)
D$_{70}$	1.9184 (0.1790)	0.2119 (0.0632)	0.0569 (0.0546)	−0.0195 (0.0225)	—	−0.0769 (0.0880)	0.991 (0.1231)
Intermediate approach							
A$_{70}$	1.7973 (0.1444)	0.1692 (0.0505)	—	—	—	0.0107 (0.0736)	0.990 (0.1259)
B$_{70}$	1.8480 (0.1478)	0.1881 (0.0520)	0.0646 (0.0531)	—	—	−0.0513 (0.0885)	0.991 (0.1236)
BI$_{70}$	1.9324 (0.1285)	0.1900 (0.0421)	—	—	−0.0729 (0.0269)	0.0189 (0.0604)	0.993 (0.1032)
D$_{70}$	1.7540 (0.1603)	0.1695 (0.0523)	0.0549 (0.0520)	−0.0286 (0.0217)	—	−0.0281 (0.0876)	0.991 (0.1200)

Note: The dependent variable is ln n; number = 16.

plement of Phase III countries. The 1970 equation, based on thirty-three countries (Romanian data could not be extrapolated back from 1975 to 1970), is:

$$\ln r = -0.0198 + 0.5066 \ln n - 0.0539 (\ln n)^2$$
$$(0.0661) \quad (0.0809) \quad (0.0187)$$
$$+ 0.0271 \ln n \cdot \ln \text{OP}$$
$$(0.0172)$$
$$\overline{R}^2 = 0.980 \quad \text{SEE} = 0.1264$$

The 1975 equation based on thirty-four countries is:

$$\ln r = -0.1572 + 0.4569 \ln n - 0.0469 (\ln n)^2$$
$$(0.0541) \quad (0.0791) \quad (0.0190)$$
$$+ 0.0464 \ln n \cdot \ln \text{OP}$$
$$(0.0202)$$
$$\overline{R}^2 = 0.969 \quad \text{SEE} = 0.151$$

Fortunately, while the different equations do produce some very divergent estimates of r for individual countries, the differences are much smaller when the objective, as in the present content, is the estimation of real GDP for groups of countries. For example, in Table 8-11 the distribution of income for 118 market economies is estimated from equations BI based on

33 countries for 1970, and 34 countries for 1975; each country is estimated for 1975, and the two estimates averaged.

Choice of other equations would produce a different distribution, but the difference would be modest. The ranges produced by the eight alternative equations in the percentage distribution of total real GDP are:

Low income   8.6 to 9.4 percent
Middle income 24.2 to 25.3 percent
Industrialized 65.3 to 67.2 percent

For definitions of country groups see notes to Table 8-12.

World Income and Product

The methods set out in the preceding parts of this chapter make it possible to produce estimates of the distribution of the world income and product among the various countries. Although the building blocks of these figures were estimates for individual countries, only data for groups of countries are presented here. It is hoped that future work will make possible the reduction of errors entailed in the estimates for indi-

Table 8-9. "Estimating" Equations Relating Real to Nominal per Capita GDP and Exposure Variables

Equation number	ln n	$(\ln n)^2$	ln OP	ln PI	$(\ln OP)(\ln n)$	Constant	$\bar{R}^2$ (SEE)
Direct approach							
A$_{75}$	0.4331 (0.0897)	−0.0640 (0.0250)	—	—	—	−0.1505 (0.0563)	0.979 (0.1285)
B$_{75}$	0.4228 (0.0810)	−0.0711 (0.0228)	−0.0828 (0.0414)	—	—	−0.0434 (0.0738)	0.983 (0.1158)
D$_{75}$	0.3821 (0.0784)	−0.0790 (0.0216)	−0.0525 (0.0420)	0.0705 (0.0403)	—	−0.0360 (0.0683)	0.985 (0.1070)
BI$_{75}$	0.4537 (0.0781)	−0.0453 (0.0187)	—	—	0.0498 (0.0209)	−0.1558 (0.0534)	0.970 (0.1493)
Roundabout approach							
A$'_{70}$	0.4772 (0.0940)	−0.0581 (0.0239)	—	—	—	0.0053 (0.0672)	0.987 (0.1015)
B$'_{70}$	0.4147 (0.1049)	0.0747 (0.0270)	−0.0583 (0.0469)	—	—	0.0441 (0.0729)	0.988 (0.0944)
D$'_{70}$	0.4417 (0.1109)	−0.0724 (0.0275)	−0.0543 (0.0477)	0.0156 (0.0185)	—	0.0316 (0.0753)	0.987 (0.1006)
BI$'_{70}$	0.3596 (0.1022)	−0.0791 (0.0238)	—	—	0.0380 (0.0187)	−0.0235 (0.0620)	0.990 (0.0910)
Intermediate approach							
A$_{70}$	0.5474 (0.1053)	−0.0507 (0.0268)	—	—	—	−0.0035 (0.0753)	0.986 (0.1138)
B$_{70}$	0.4790 (0.1180)	−0.0689 (0.0304)	−0.0638 (0.0528)	—	—	0.0388 (0.0820)	0.986 (0.1118)
D$_{70}$	0.5203 (0.1214)	−0.0654 (0.0300)	−0.0577 (0.0522)	0.0238 (0.0202)	—	0.0198 (0.0823)	0.987 (0.1101)
BI$_{70}$	0.3959 (0.1080)	−0.0777 (0.0251)	—	—	0.0490 (0.0198)	−0.0406 (0.0655)	0.990 (0.0962)

Note: The dependent variable is ln r; number = 16.

Table 8-10. Comparison of Accuracy of Various Methods in Estimating 1975 Real per Capita GDPs for Fifteen New Countries

Item	Direct				Roundabout				Intermediate			
	A	B	D	BI	A	B	D	BI	A	B	D	BI
Ratio of estimated to benchmark r												
Low range	0.86	0.89	0.91	0.81	0.87	0.75	0.74	0.67	0.78	0.65	0.40	0.63
High range	1.65	1.55	1.89	1.40	1.53	1.28	1.26	1.21	1.33	1.09	1.09	1.11
Mean	1.11	1.09	1.15	1.05	1.08	0.99	0.97	0.94	0.98	0.87	0.84	0.79
Deviation from unity of ratio of estimated to benchmark r												
Mean deviation	0.15	0.15	0.17	0.12	0.15	0.14	0.14	0.16	0.13	0.17	0.17	0.23
Mean squared deviation	0.23	0.21	0.30	0.16	0.20	0.17	0.16	0.19	0.16	0.20	0.22	0.30
Ranks												
Country deviation rank[a]	5½	3	2	1	7	8	4	9	5½	10	11	12
Mean deviation[b]	6	6	10	1	6	3½	3½	8	2	6½	10	12
Squared deviation[b]	10	8	11½	2	6½	4	2	2	2	6½	9	11½

a. Sum of ranks, based on each individual country.
b. The country with the lowest absolute deviation from 1 is assigned the rank of 1; for example, the lowest mean deviation is 0.12 for direct equation BI.

Table 8-11. 1975 Distribution of Population and GDP for 118 Market Economies from Equations BI for 1970 and 1975

Country group	Number of countries	Population 1975 (millions)	Percent	GDP per capita, 1975 (I$)	Total GDP (million I$)	Percent
Low income	32	1,152	43.5	459	529	9.1
Middle income	66	817	30.8	1,777	1,452	24.7
Industrialized	20	679	25.7	5,737	3,895	66.2
Total	118	2,649	100.0	2,220	5,881	100.0

Note: For definitions of country groups see Table 8-12.

vidual countries.[28] Success in such an effort can be expected to have a smaller effect on group averages such as those presented here.

The distribution of world GDY excluding the socialist economies is shown in Table 8-12 for selected dates in the period 1950–77. The classification of countries is based on a mixture of income level and form of economic organization. As was discussed above, the 1975 figures have been derived by extrapolating the 1975 benchmark estimates to other countries by the use of results averaged from those produced by equations BI_{75} and BI_{70}. These 1975 estimates were then extrapolated in a way that obtains benchmark-type estimates for each of the 118 countries for the other years in the table. These benchmark-type estimates can be expressed in current or constant prices of the numéraire country, both of which are shown in panels D, E, F, and G of Table 8-12. Because the distributions within each year are unaffected by whether the income of a country relative to the United States is multiplied by the current- or constant-price U.S. total, panels A and B are not affected by the choice of the numéraire country even in a scaling sense.

In each of the years the shares of low- and middle-income countries in real-world GDP are much higher than is indicated by the exchange-rate–converted figures. In the last year, 1977, the quarter of the population of the market economies living in middle-income non–oil-exporting countries produced and received 19 percent of the real aggregate output of all

market economies, rather than 13 percent as the nominal figures suggest. The 44 percent of the population of the market economies living in low-income countries had real per capita incomes of nearly $500, very low but still more than twice as much as the exchange-rate conversions suggest.

The development of the income and population of the market economies over the twenty-seven–year period shown in the table depends on the application of each country's growth rates for domestic absorption to the 1975 real per capita domestic absorption and on the valuation in each year of the country's net foreign balance. The extrapolations back to 1950 are particularly suspect because, in many cases, the data needed for the separate treatment of the net foreign balance were not available. However, the overall trends shown in Table 8-12 do not differ much whether the 1950 data or the more reliable 1960 data are taken as the starting point. For the twenty-seven–year period in the low-income countries, the population share rises from 41 to 44 percent, while the share in real GDY dips slightly. For the middle-income non–oil exporters, the population share also rises by about 10 percent, but there is a larger rise in the share in real GDP; it increases by one-third. The industrial countries experience notable declines in both population and real GDY shares.

The extension of these distributions to the entire world inclusive of the socialist economies can be done only on a still more approximate basis. Most socialist economies do not publish estimates of GDP on either a current- or constant-price basis; rather, they use the somewhat different material-product system of accounts. Given the purposes at hand, and the conceptual problems with the data, the method of linking the socialist economies of Europe into the world system has been kept simple. The Economic Commission for Europe (ECE) has published a series of estimates for the socialist economies based on physical indicators and related measures, with a base year of 1970 and

---

28. The range of the errors of estimate of the individual countries is generally much larger than the errors for the group. Excluding the thirty Phase III countries, the coefficient of variation was above 20 percent for twenty countries, 10 to 20 percent for twenty-eight countries, and under 10 percent for the remaining forty countries across the eight estimates for each country. While such variation means that estimates for individual countries are subject to substantial error, it will still be less than the error associated with exchange-rate conversions.

Table 8-12. Distribution of World GDY of Market Economies by Type of Country, 1950, 1960, 1965, 1970, 1975, and 1977

Type of country	1950	1960	1965	1970	1975	1977
A. Distribution of nominal GDP (percent)						
Low income[a]	7	5	5	4	4	4
Middle income[b]	17	14	13	13	17	18
Oil exporters[c]	3	3	3	3	5	5
Other	15	11	10	10	12	13
Industrial[d]	76	81	82	82	79	79
Total	100	100	100	100	100	100
B. Distribution of real GDY (percent)						
Low income	10	10	9	9	9	9
Middle income	17	19	19	20	25	25
Oil exporters	3	4	4	4	7	6
Other	14	15	15	16	18	19
Industrial	73	71	72	71	66	66
Total	100	100	100	100	100	100
C. Distribution of population (percent)						
Low income	41	41	42	43	43	44
Middle income	27	29	29	30	31	31
Oil exporters	4	5	5	5	6	6
Other	23	24	24	25	25	25
Industrial	32	30	29	27	26	25
Total	100	100	100	100	100	100
D. Real per capita GDY (1975 international dollars [I$])						
Low income	299	362	374	421	459	484
Middle income	740	983	1,142	1,361	1,777	1,863
Oil exporters	820	1,207	1,377	1,674	2,703	2,564
Other	725	937	1,093	1,294	1,571	1,705
Industrial	2,687	3,592	4,343	5,210	5,737	6,187
Total	1,183	1,511	1,741	2,007	2,220	2,337
E. Real per capita GDY (current I$)						
Low income	125	194	217	302	459	534
Middle income	310	527	664	976	1,777	2,056
Oil exporters	344	648	800	1,200	2,703	2,829
Other	304	503	635	928	1,571	1,881
Industrial	1,127	1,927	2,523	3,735	5,737	6,827
Total	496	810	1,011	1,438	2,220	2,579
F. All market economies (1975 I$)						
Total						
Nominal GDY (billion US$)	1,466,455	2,126,906	2,850,749	3,462,353	4,996,840	5,472,041
Real GDY (billion I$)	1,901,604	2,928,234	3,748,147	4,791,834	5,878,209	6,450,775
Population (millions)	1,607	1,938	2,153	2,388	2,648	2,760
Per capita						
Nominal GDY (US$)	913	1,097	1,324	1,450	1,887	1,983
Real GDY (I$)	1,183	1,511	1,741	2,007	2,220	2,337
G. All market economies (current I$)						
Total						
Nominal GDY (billion US$)	614,862	1,141,103	1,655,884	2,481,872	4,996,837	6,038,034
Real GDY (billion I$)	797,314	1,571,032	2,177,143	3,434,865	5,878,205	7,118,003
Population (millions)	1,607	1,938	2,153	2,388	2,648	2,760
Per capita						
Nominal GDY (US$)	383	589	769	1,039	1,887	2,188
Real GDY (I$)	496	810	1,011	1,438	2,220	2,579

a. 1976 nominal GDP of US$250 or less. Thirty-two countries.

b. All nonsocialist countries other than low income and industrialized. Includes Greece, Portugal, Spain, and Turkey. Fifty-seven countries.

c. Kuwait, Libya, Saudi Arabia, Algeria, Iran, Iraq, Mexico, Ecuador, and Venezuela. Nine countries. Note that the definitions of countries follows the World Bank (1978), p. ix. Other oil-exporting countries (where oil is important), such as Indonesia, Mexico, and Nigeria, are included with other low- and middle-income countries.

d. Members of Organisation for Economic Co-operation and Development, excluding the four countries mentioned in note *b* but including South Africa, Australia, and New Zealand. Twenty countries.

Table 8-13. Real World GDP, Selected Years in Current Prices

	Population (millions)			GDP (billion current I$)		
	World	Market economies	Socialist economies	World	Market economies	Socialist economies
1950	2,448	1,607	841	1,055.3	822.0	233.3
1960	2,949	1,938	1,011	2,169.3	1,628.2	537.1
1965	3,258	2,153	1,105	3,028.2	2,267.0	761.2
1970	3,583	2,388	1,195	4,780.5	3,583.6	1,169.9
1975	3,925	2,648	1,277	7,919.8	5,878.2	2,041.6
1977	4,069	2,760	1,309	9,784.2	7,253.2	2,531.0

Sources: 1. Population data from U.N. Tape and from *National Yearbook for Romania*, the total covering about 97 percent of the world.

2. Real-income estimates for the Peoples Republic of China are from Kravis (1981) p. 73, which puts 1975 GDP per capita of China at 12.3 percent of the United States. Extrapolations to other years are described in Summers, Kravis, Heston (1981).

3. Real-income estimates for the Union of Soviet Socialist Republics, Bulgaria, Czechoslovakia, Federal Republic of Germany, Hungary, Poland, Romania, and Yugoslavia are estimated or extrapolated as discussed in text. In 1975 the populations and GDP were:

	Population	Real GDP
Union of Soviet Socialist Republics	254	876.7
Seven European socialist economies	128	374.9
People's Republic of China	895	790.0
Total	1,277	2,041.6

4. The estimates for the market economies are based on GDP, not GDY, extrapolations; hence, totals will differ slightly from those in Table 8-12.

including 1950, 1955, 1960, 1965, and 1973.[29] Estimates from these series were extrapolated to 1975 from both 1970 and 1973. Each extrapolation was compared with the ICP estimates for Hungary, Poland, Romania, and Yugoslavia. The extrapolations from 1973 for these countries averaged 101 percent of the ICP estimates, with a range of 93 percent for Hungary to 114 percent for Romania. The procedure adapted was to extrapolate the other socialist economies in Europe from 1973 to 1975 (divided by 1.01) and to use these along with the benchmark estimates for the remaining four countries. This provided coverage for that year of all socialist economies except Albania, Cuba, and the People's Republic of China, the last of which is mentioned below.[30]

The claim for using the ECE estimates is that they roughly fit the 1975 benchmark data. However, little claim can be made for using the ECE data over time since it is not clear that a set of indicators will necessarily reflect real-product changes. The alternative chosen has been to use a series that attempts to put the reported net material product (NMP) for the eight

socialist economies in Europe on a basis of real GDP growth. These real GDP series have been used to extrapolate 1975 estimates for the individual countries to other years. The resulting estimates for the individual years have been summed and an independent estimate for China added[31] to provide the totals for the socialist economies reported in Table 8-13.

The resulting indexes of GDP relative to the United States have been weighted by populations of the countries as provided by the United Nations.[32] They have been expressed in current prices in each year by multiplying the ratios times the U.S. GDP in the selected years, summed over the nine socialist economies considered, and the total given in Table 8-13. The total for the market economies are also given in current prices on a GDP basis (not GDY as in Table 8-12). The estimates for the socialist economies are less reliable than those for the market economies because there have been fewer benchmark studies, and because the time-to-time extrapolations are not on a comparable basis. The reader is therefore reminded that these estimates are subject to a wider range of error. For what they are worth, the data suggest that the real GDP of the socialist economies has been about one-fourth the world total since 1960.

Quite another principle of classification—geographical—is employed in organizing the same data in Table 8-14, which again refers only to the market economies and presents GDP extrapolations.[33] The results are ex-

29. The ECE estimates use 1970 as a base year and provide one set of estimates for that year. For other years, two series are presented: one based on a standard set of physical indicators available for all countries, and another including all available indicators available for a country in a year. The estimates based on standard indicators have been used here. See U.N. Economic Commission for Europe (1980). For a review of these methods, see Heston (1973).

30. The indexes used to move the socialist economies from time to time are approximations because GDP deflators are not a price index usually produced by material-product–system countries. The indexes used are from Alton (1970, 1977, and 1979); and IMF (1978). For a fuller description of their use see Summers, Kravis, Heston (1981), appendix.

31. Kravis (1981).

32. U.N. *Monthly Bulletin of Statistics* (October 1980).

33. These estimates are based on extrapolations of 1975 GDP-GDY estimates for each of the 118 countries to other years on the basis of growth in each country's real GDP.

Table 8-14. Distribution of World GDP of Market Economies by Continent, 1950, 1960, 1965, 1970, 1975, and 1977

Continent	1950	1960	1965	1970	1975	1977
A. Distribution of nominal GDP						
Africa	4	3	3	3	4	4
Asia	9	10	12	14	17	18
Europe	25	30	32	32	36	34
North America	47	44	42	39	31	31
Latin America and Caribbean	13	10	10	10	11	10
Oceania	2	2	2	2	3	3
Total	100	100	100	100	100	100
B. Distribution of real GDP						
Africa	5	5	5	6	6	6
Asia	15	17	18	21	22	22
Europe	31	32	32	31	30	30
North America	35	31	31	28	26	26
Latin America and Caribbean	11	12	12	12	13	14
Oceania	3	3	3	3	3	3
Total	100	100	100	100	100	100
C. Distribution of population						
Africa	14	14	14	15	15	15
Asia	42	42	43	43	44	44
Europe	19	17	16	15	15	14
North America	9	9	9	9	8	8
Latin America and Caribbean	11	12	12	12	13	13
Oceania	5	6	6	6	6	6
Total	100	100	100	100	100	100
D. Real per capita GDP (1975 I$)						
Africa	451	592	685	793	817	862
Asia	441	627	758	992	1,124	1,179
Europe	1,944	2,856	3,453	4,181	4,585	4,943
North America	4,485	5,225	6,085	6,666	7,170	7,795
Latin America and Caribbean	1,257	1,558	1,782	2,069	2,341	2,514
Oceania	646	784	829	966	1,099	1,134
Total	1,211	1,555	1,800	2,074	2,220	2,348
E. Real per capita GDP (current I$)						
Africa	191	320	401	574	817	965
Asia	186	339	443	718	1,124	1,320
Europe	821	1,543	2,021	3,024	4,585	5,532
North America	1,895	2,823	3,561	4,822	7,170	8,725
Latin America and Caribbean	531	842	1,043	1,497	2,341	2,813
Oceania	273	423	485	699	1,099	1,269
Total	512	840	1,053	1,501	2,220	2,628
F. All market economies (1975 I$)						
Total						
Nominal GDP (billion US$)	1,466,455	2,126,906	2,850,749	3,462,353	4,996,840	5,472,041
Real GDP (billion I$)	1,945,634	3,013,426	3,874,549	4,953,862	5,878,209	6,480,711
Population (millions)	1,607	1,938	2,153	2,388	2,648	2,760
Per capita						
Nominal GDP (US$)	913	1,097	1,324	1,450	1,887	1,983
Real GDP (I$)	1,211	1,555	1,800	2,074	2,220	2,348
G. All market economies (current I$)						
Total						
Nominal GDP (billion US$)	619,580	1,149,163	1,667,973	2,504,662	4,996,840	6,124,304
Real GDP (billion I$)	822,033	1,628,156	2,266,991	3,583,623	5,878,209	7,253,213
Population (millions)	1,607	1,938	2,153	2,388	2,648	2,760
Per capita						
Nominal GDP (US$)	386	593	775	1,049	1,887	2,219
Real GDP (I$)	512	840	1,053	1,501	2,220	2,628

Table 8-15. Ratio of GDY to GDP, Selected years, 118 market economies

Country group	1950	1960	1965	1970	1975	1977
Low income	91	91	91	94	100	99
Middle income	96	93	90	89	100	99
Petroleum exporting	81	76	70	68	100	95
Other	100	99	98	99	100	101
Industrial	99	99	99	100	100	100
Total	98	97	97	97	100	100

plicable by the geographical distribution of the various types of countries considered in Table 8-12. North America has lower shares in real GDP than in nominal GDP, and so has Europe in the 1970s, though not earlier. For Africa, Asia, and Latin America, where the developing countries are found, real shares of production are larger than nominal shares. As in Table 8-12, the results are presented in constant and current prices. The implicit price index in both tables is simply the U.S. deflator and is therefore not base-country invariant.

When the estimates for the socialist economies are assigned to continents, the resulting distribution for 1975 is:

	Population		GDP *or* GDY		
	Total	Percent	Total (billion I$)	Per-cent	Per capita (I$)
Africa	397	10.1	324	4.1	817
Asia	2,048	52.1	2.086	26.3	1,019
Europe	765	19.5	3,009	38.0	3,933
North America	212	5.4	1,520	19.2	7,170
Latin America and Caribbean	344	8.8	806	10.2	2,341
Oceania	159	4.1	175	2.2	1,099
Total	3,925	100.0	7,920	100.0	2,018

The estimates underlying Tables 8-12 and 8-14 allow comparisons of GDP and GDY by groups of countries. The figures in Table 8-15 express GDY as a percent of GDP in each selected year, where the 1975 relationship is taken as 100. Values above 100 mean the net foreign balance was more helpful in that year than in 1975, and vice versa for entries less than 100.[34] As was noted earlier, the differences between GDY and GDP may be due to changes in the terms of trade, in the relative prices of domestic absorption and the net foreign balance, or in the size of the net foreign balance (see

note 13, this chapter, for further explanation). An examination of the GDY/GDP ratios does reveal a substantial rise in the absorption capabilities of the low-income countries, relative to production in the twenty-five years before 1975 (see Table 8-15). The petroleum exporters show a large decline in their absorptive capacity through 1970, followed by a very dramatic rise, both movements probably being dominated by terms-of-trade movements. While there are large movements in the GDY/GDP ratio for individual countries within the other middle-income and the industrial-income countries, there are no major trends for groups.

Summary

This chapter, concerned with the extension of benchmark estimates to other years and other countries, is necessarily more tentative than those dealing with the benchmark estimates. Further work on the methods of the extrapolations may improve the estimates for nonbenchmark years and countries, but estimates of the general character offered here will continue to provide the only means to broad-coverage, comparative estimates of per capita GDPs for past years that avoid the clear biases of GDPs arrived at through the use of exchange rates. The errors and uncertainties of the extrapolations, troublesome though they are, are small relative to the differences that are known to exist between nominal and real GDP in the cases of low- and middle-income countries.

The period 1950–77, it seems clear, has been marked by important shifts in the world distribution of production and income. Developing countries as a whole gained relative to developed countries, but the lowest income developing countries did not share in these gains. Their share edged down from 1950 through 1965 and has remained constant since. The share of the socialist economies in real-world GDP has probably remained fixed at about one-fourth in the last two decades.

---

34. The method of extrapolation for countries without complete 1950 data is to preserve the GDY/GDP ratio of 1960 in 1950.

9

Interspatial Demand Analysis

ARE TASTES THE SAME THE WORLD ROUND? In this concluding chapter, the income and disaggregate quantity and price data of Chapters 6 and 7 are examined to illuminate this question, and more generally to find structural patterns in the data.[1]

In any absolute sense the answer to the question is no, just as it surely is not true that *any* two persons have exactly the same tastes. Physiology may determine a floor to elementary needs, which in turn contribute to a definition of tastes. But it is clear that, with regard to the consumption of inhabitants of the thirty-four countries studied in the ICP, tastes are not so narrowly determined. It is likely that an Indian born in Bombay would, if raised in Boston, consume more like Bostonians than like Bombaywallas, prices and incomes being equal—and vice versa. But would a person raised in Bombay facing the same prices and with the same income as a Bostonian want the same goods and services as the Bostonian? Surely not, at a very fine level of detail of goods and services. To take the most obvious examples, differences in religion would almost certainly dictate differences in meat consumption, and differences in climate would lead to differences in clothing. A plausible possibility, however, is that at a higher level of aggregation—say, food, clothing, and shelter—tastes would be similar, but with food or clothing or shelter requirements being satisfied in different ways in different countries. These matters are discussed below.

The operational significance of "same tastes" in the context of this chapter is this: if in two situations a market choice is made on the basis of the same tastes about what to consume and in what quantities, the actual choices will be determined by the available consumption opportunities defined by prevailing prices and the consuming units' income. The degree to which it is useful to speak of tastes being the same in different countries turns on the extent to which prices and income explain differences in consumption patterns in the countries.

This chapter undertakes to quantify the role of economic variables in determining consumption patterns, starting with a watered-down variation of the theme question above: Are the observed quantity-price-income data demonstrably inconsistent with the identity (or, less strongly stated, similarity) of tastes among the thirty-four ICP countries?

Demand analysis findings in Phase I based on ten countries were checked in Phase II with data on six new countries. Now the addition of eighteen countries in Phase III makes possible a reexamination of the earlier conclusions and an extension of the analysis in new directions. The relationship between quantities, prices, and income is investigated in four increasingly sophisticated ways: (1) through a similarity analysis, which draws only in the loosest way on theoretical demand analysis; (2) through a check of the consistency of observed quantity and price patterns with the implications of common tastes for revealed preference; (3) through relatively crude ad hoc demand equations; and (4) through submission of the data to the rigorous requirements of a more theoretically acceptable linear expenditure system (LES) of demand equations.[2]

---

1. This chapter is an extension of the materials in Chapters 1 through 7 of this report; as such, it is done on the responsibility of the authors, and not the U.N. Statistical Office or the World Bank.

2. The analysis and, indeed, exposition for (1) and much of (3) follow the same lines as in the previous ICP volumes. In addition, the similarity definitions presented in Chapter 4 in connection with regionalization are repeated here to make it unnecessary for the reader to refer back.

In addition, a by-product of the linear expenditure analysis is examined with a view to comparing the multilateral results of Chapter 6 with estimates based on utility maximization. An empirical estimate of the so-called expenditure function associated with the LES utility function is used to estimate the relative levels of real per capita consumption of the thirty-four Phase III countries. These quantity indexes, based on true-cost-of-living indexes, are then compared with the Geary-Khamis estimates that are given in Chapters 1 and 6.

The Similarity of Quantity and Price Structures

If the world works the way economists' models suggest—such that quantities consumed depend on opportunities as defined by prices and income—then countries that have similar price structures and similar incomes should have similar quantity structures. That is, they ought to absorb the various categories of goods in the same proportions.

To verify this proposition, measures of the similarity of the price and of the quantity structures of the different countries were formulated. As in the earlier ICP reports, the measure of similarity between the vectors of quantities (or prices) referring to any pair of countries is their weighted raw-correlation coefficient. This is defined as the ratio of the weighted cross moment to the square root of the product of the two weighted second moments, each moment being computed relative to the origin rather than to the mean. The formulas are:

$$(9.1) \qquad S_{jk}^q = \frac{\sum\limits_{i=1}^{m} q_{ij}\, q_{ik}}{\sqrt{\sum\limits_{i=1}^{m} q_{ij}{}^2 \sum\limits_{i=1}^{m} q_{ik}{}^2}}$$

$$(9.2) \qquad S_{jk}^p = \frac{\sum\limits_{i=1}^{m} w_i R_{ij} R_{ik}}{\sqrt{\sum\limits_{i=1}^{m} w_i R_{ij}{}^2 \sum\limits_{i=1}^{m} w_i R_{ik}{}^2}}$$

where

S_{jk}^q = quantity similarity index between countries j and k

S_{jk}^p = price similarity index between countries j and k

q_{ij} = quantity valued in international dollars of the ith category in the jth country

R_{ij} = ratio of the percentage of expenditure on the ith category in country j measured in domestic-currency units to the corresponding percentage measured in international dollars

m = number of categories

w = weight

The similarity measure is equal to the cosine of the angle between the m dimensional quantity (or price) vectors. No w's appear in the S_{jk}^q formula because the category quantities, expressed in international dollars, were self-weighting in the sense that the quantities in important categories would already be large compared with the quantities in unimportant categories.[3] Category R's were weighted by the ratio of the total world output in the category to total world GDP, both valued in international prices.[4] These weights were obtained through the use of the supercountry method.

The R's serve as measures of relative price structures. As was pointed out in Chapter 6, the value of R_{ij} for GDP as a whole is 1. A value above 1 for a given i for a particular country indicates that relative to the relationship of the country's prices to international prices for GDP as a whole, its price for i is high.[5]

Similarity indexes were computed for each pair of countries for each of four different vectors of price indexes and four vectors of quantity indexes. The vectors consisted of indexes referring to 34 summary categories of GDP, 148 detailed categories of GDP,[6] 25 summary categories of consumption, and 108 detailed categories of consumption. For each of the four vectors, there are 561 quantity- and 561 price-similarity indexes ($n[n-1]/2$), one for each possible pair among the 34 countries.

The relationship between quantity and price similarity cannot be satisfactorily explored without one's

3. The summary category quantities are from Summary Multilateral Table 6-5; those for the detailed categories are from Appendix Table 6-5.

4. The summary category R's are derived from Summary Multilateral Tables 6-1 and 6-5. Those for the detailed categories are derived from Appendix Tables 6-1 and 6-5.

5. Note that in Kravis, Kenessey, Heston, Summers (1975) the price similarity indexes were based on category purchasing power parities (PPPs) with the United States as base. The formulation using R's is superior in that relative price structures are expressed in terms of the average international price structure rather than that of the United States. This is preferable conceptually, though it makes little difference in the empirical results. It should be noted also that the Phase I similarity indexes were based on U.S.-weighted binary indexes, while those presented here and in the Phase II report are based on multilateral price and quantity indexes.

6. Categories in which expenditures can be negative—net expenditure of residents abroad, exports minus imports, and increase in stocks—were omitted.

taking account of the similarity of incomes. With y representing per capita income relative to the United States, income similarity, S_{jk}^y, is defined as:

$$(9.3) \qquad S_{jk}^y = \frac{2 \cdot min \ (y_j, \ y_k)}{y_j + y_k}$$

so it takes on values between 0 (approached when the two incomes are far apart) and 1 (when the incomes are identical).[7] (The values of y_j and y_k that are used in calculating S_{jk}^y are taken from Table 1-2.) Equation 9.4 is the primary basis for the empirical relationship between S_{jk}^q, S_{jk}^p, and S_{jk}^y.

$$(9.4) \qquad S_{jk}^q = \alpha S_{jk}^p + \beta S_{jk}^y + \gamma + u_{jk}$$

where u_{jk} is a random disturbance. It is to be expected that α and β will both be greater than 0. Furthermore, if prices and incomes alone were the only systematic determinants of quantities, then $\alpha + \beta + \gamma$ should equal 1. (When $S_{jk}^p = S_{jk}^y = 1$, then $S_{jk}^q = 1$.) The parameters of equation 9.4 have been estimated for the p's and q's of four sets of data (GDP summary categories, GDP detailed categories, consumption summary categories, and consumption detailed categories). The same S_{jk}^y's are used with all four data sets. Before these regressions are discussed, the similarity measurements themselves are described.

Similarity Indexes

The similarity indexes for quantities and prices are set out for the thirty-four summary categories of GDP in Table 9-1. (The indexes, entered into the regressions as decimals, are multiplied by 1,000 for use in text and tables.) The countries are arrayed in both the rows and the columns in order of increasing size of real GDP per capita. The impact of real per capita income on the similarity of quantity compositions is evident. There is a distinct tendency for the size of the similarity indexes to increase as the proximity to the principal diagonal (from upper left to lower right) increases along any row or column. That is, the similarity of quantity composition increases as the per capita incomes of countries become more similar.[8] The

association is summarized by the regression results of equation 9.5:[9]

$$(9.5) \quad S_{jk}^q = 0.5693 \quad + 0.3353 \ S_{jk}^y$$
$$(0.0086) \quad (0.0134)$$
$$\overline{R}^2 = 0.526 \quad \text{SEE} = 0.081$$

A comparison of the matrix of price-similarity indexes with that of the quantity indexes indicates that price structures are generally more similar than quantity compositions. The mean of the 561 similarity indexes is 766 for quantities and 874 for prices, with much less dispersion around the latter. This is to be expected, since there are more direct links between prices in different countries than between quantities. The similarity indexes for the R's also show some tendency for figures near the principal diagonal to be larger than figures distant from it. However, the correlation between price similarity and income similarity is weaker than that between quantity similarity and income similarity:

$$(9.6) \ S_{jk}^p = 0.7819 \quad + 0.1572 \ S_{jk}^y$$
$$(0.0052) \quad (0.0082)$$
$$\overline{R}^2 = 0.397 \quad \text{SEE} = 0.049.$$

The larger coefficient of S_{jk}^y in equation 9.5 relative to that in equation 9.6 means that quantity structures are more sharply differentiated by income levels than price structures. The greater rise in quantity similarity as income rises emerges even more clearly from a regression of the ratio of S_{jk}^q to S_{jk}^p on S_{jk}^y:

$$(9.7) \ S_{jk}^q/S_{jk}^p = 0.7402 \quad + 0.2284 \ S_{jk}^y$$
$$(0.0091) \quad (0.0141)$$
$$\overline{R}^2 = 0.317 \quad \text{SEE} = 0.085$$

Essentially the same relationships hold for GDP detailed categories and for consumption at both summary and detailed levels. However, detailed-level similarities are smaller than summary-level ones (especially for quantities). The means (and standard deviations) of similarity indexes are shown below:

	Summary categories		Detailed categories	
	S_{jk}^q	S_{jk}^p	S_{jk}^q	S_{jk}^p
Consumption	769	881	593	769
	(139)	(3)	(194)	(8)
GDP	766	874	592	772
	(118)	(4)	(164)	(8)

(Note that the mean of S_{jk}^y is 588 [255].) The fact that quantity patterns throughout the world are more sim-

---

7. Alternative plausible measures of income similarity are essentially equivalent. For example, suppose the measure were defined in terms of the absolute value of the difference between the countries' incomes expressed as a fraction of their average income: $|y_j - y_k|/(y_j + y_k)$. Standardizing this quantity through a linear transformation so that it takes on a value of 0 when y_j and y_k are far apart and a value of 1 when they are equal leads precisely to S_{jk}^y. The difference divided by the average was used as an index of dissimilarity of incomes in Kravis (1958).

8. For a similar conclusion based on a comparison of family budgets, see Kravis (1958), p. 333.

9. However, in interpreting the standard errors in parentheses beneath the coefficients of equation 9.5, the caveat of note 10 should be considered.

Table 9-1. Index of Similarity for Quantity Structures and Price Structures for Thirty-four Summary Categories of GDP, 1975

Country	Malawi	Kenya	India	Paki-stan	Sri Lanka	Zambia	Thai-land	Philip-pines	Korea	Malay-sia	Colom-bia	Jamaica	Syria	Brazil	Roma-nia	Mexico	Yugo-slavia
						A. Quantity Structures											
Malawi	1,000	769	814	757	853	662	757	712	704	634	489	631	841	642	523	640	609
Kenya	769	1,000	897	861	913	803	842	855	803	802	658	752	723	780	638	804	752
India	814	897	1,000	936	970	798	911	872	859	777	573	737	750	735	616	720	713
Pakistan	757	861	936	1,000	928	812	909	847	853	781	569	702	753	772	641	757	748
Sri Lanka	853	913	970	928	1,000	823	917	894	884	826	640	766	802	776	654	770	764
Zambia	662	803	798	812	823	1,000	783	833	807	894	680	776	733	866	683	736	807
Thailand	757	842	911	909	917	783	1,000	888	916	780	647	736	717	773	663	746	752
Philippines	712	855	872	847	894	833	888	1,000	816	826	694	801	702	849	720	762	811
Korea	704	803	859	853	884	807	916	816	1,000	843	672	812	787	772	699	778	810
Malaysia	634	802	777	781	826	894	780	826	843	1,000	772	849	750	902	834	887	906
Colombia	489	658	573	569	640	680	647	694	672	772	1,000	679	597	849	844	828	723
Jamaica	631	752	737	702	766	776	736	801	812	849	679	1,000	708	818	712	793	882
Syria	841	723	750	753	802	733	717	702	787	750	597	708	1,000	723	650	748	787
Brazil	642	780	735	772	776	866	773	849	772	902	849	818	723	1,000	804	878	893
Romania	523	638	616	641	654	683	663	720	699	834	644	712	650	804	1,000	771	866
Mexico	640	804	720	757	770	736	746	762	778	887	828	793	748	878	771	1,000	848
Yugoslavia	609	752	713	748	764	807	752	811	810	906	723	882	787	893	866	848	1,000
Iran	489	624	625	650	645	738	629	646	749	814	508	736	761	666	696	732	813
Uruguay	609	697	684	741	724	750	722	832	656	740	758	748	613	868	697	768	792
Ireland	521	635	595	633	657	742	652	738	724	853	784	890	688	894	803	826	941
Hungary	548	659	619	648	684	775	711	718	797	890	774	853	724	868	834	826	950
Poland	548	678	625	652	683	779	680	728	758	901	731	770	726	865	945	815	935
Italy	637	700	665	700	725	759	692	777	762	893	709	856	791	874	841	885	950
Spain	531	602	581	590	635	644	630	739	689	845	775	830	691	843	848	872	893
U.K.	511	646	621	675	686	772	627	763	708	844	658	866	677	852	797	771	937
Japan	460	582	569	563	642	696	638	665	729	867	727	741	616	820	786	777	847
Austria	492	600	554	590	621	656	628	714	700	830	692	834	656	824	876	795	928
Netherlands	516	647	562	609	639	698	629	698	723	858	669	822	700	825	814	838	937
Belgium	515	647	568	608	630	716	638	717	713	862	695	834	678	860	861	849	939
France	485	608	541	576	600	689	591	682	677	860	625	828	662	818	822	825	928
Luxembourg	477	599	540	568	598	697	598	660	701	870	683	832	662	814	859	844	906
Denmark	463	649	577	602	636	719	582	727	659	862	614	776	614	813	844	801	888
Germany	498	637	568	615	649	726	620	698	695	872	717	774	669	851	791	836	919
U.S.	464	600	546	570	619	689	578	684	671	823	640	810	689	791	792	763	917

ilar when broad categories are considered suggests that substitutions in the form in which GDP is absorbed are more extensive at detailed-category levels than at the more aggregative levels of the summary categories.

Between 1970 and 1975 the similarity of economic structure did not change much on average for the 120 pairs formed by the 16 Phase II countries: paired quantity bundles became less similar, paired price vectors became a little less similar, and paired income became more similar. This can be seen by examining the following similarity averages and standard deviations for GDP summary categories:

	1970	1975
S^q	849	774
	(102)	(122)
S^p	898	875
	(5)	(5)
S^y	554	582
	(277)	(270)

Regression Analysis

The dependence of similarity of quantities on both similarity of prices and incomes considered together has been examined by estimating the parameters of equation 9.4 and of equations incorporating additional independent variables. The investigation is based on the simple interpretation of conventional demand theory, which asserts that the extent of similarity in quantity composition for various pairs of countries (S^q_{jk}) should be directly related to the extent of similarity of price structures (S^p_{jk}) and similarity of real per capita income level (S^y_{jk}).

Parameter estimates for equation 9.4 appear in Table 9-2 in rows A, C, E, and G. The values of $\overline{R}^2$ indicate that about 60 percent of the variation in similarity of quantity composition is explained by similarity in price structure and income level. The coefficients of S^p_{jk} and S^y_{jk} are uniformly of the right sign and well in

Table 9-1 *(continued)*

Iran	Uruguay	Ireland	Hungary	Poland	Italy	Spain	U.K.	Japan	Austria	Netherlands	Belgium	France	Luxembourg	Denmark	Germany	U.S.
						A. Quantity Structures										
489	609	521	548	548	637	531	511	460	492	516	515	485	477	463	498	464
624	697	635	659	678	700	602	646	582	600	647	647	608	599	649	637	600
625	684	595	619	625	665	581	621	569	554	562	568	541	540	577	568	546
650	741	633	648	652	700	590	675	563	590	609	608	576	568	602	615	570
645	724	657	684	683	725	635	686	642	621	639	630	600	598	636	649	619
738	750	742	775	779	759	644	772	696	656	698	716	689	697	719	726	689
629	722	652	711	680	692	630	627	638	628	629	638	591	598	582	620	578
646	832	738	718	728	777	739	763	665	714	698	717	682	660	727	698	684
749	656	724	797	758	762	689	708	729	700	723	713	677	701	659	695	671
814	740	853	890	901	893	845	844	867	830	858	862	860	870	862	872	823
508	758	784	774	731	709	775	658	727	692	669	695	625	683	614	717	640
736	748	890	853	770	856	830	866	741	834	822	834	828	832	776	774	810
761	613	688	724	726	791	691	677	616	656	700	678	662	662	614	669	689
666	868	894	868	865	874	843	852	820	824	825	860	818	814	813	851	791
696	697	803	834	945	841	848	797	786	876	814	861	822	859	844	791	792
732	768	826	826	815	885	872	771	777	795	838	849	825	844	801	836	763
813	792	941	950	935	950	893	937	847	928	937	939	928	906	888	919	917
1,000	530	711	753	751	824	702	716	631	690	782	764	797	782	743	699	752
530	1,000	792	725	704	801	749	821	586	740	705	737	703	677	742	718	679
711	792	1,000	942	869	909	918	923	826	914	897	926	902	906	828	889	884
753	725	942	1,000	938	905	889	874	892	892	910	913	897	900	822	902	856
751	704	869	938	1,000	891	878	856	888	900	892	911	879	899	869	890	856
824	801	909	905	891	1,000	928	919	810	918	945	949	955	932	917	922	915
702	749	918	889	878	928	1,000	857	837	923	905	922	902	926	860	887	873
716	821	923	874	856	919	857	1,000	800	923	915	914	907	885	917	918	934
631	586	826	892	888	810	837	800	1,000	855	853	837	827	839	804	899	819
690	740	914	892	900	918	923	923	855	1,000	939	952	933	947	907	936	933
782	705	897	910	892	945	905	915	853	939	1,000	969	968	947	940	958	941
764	737	926	913	911	949	922	914	837	952	969	1,000	972	979	927	943	938
797	703	902	897	879	955	902	907	827	933	968	972	1,000	957	944	942	921
782	677	906	900	899	932	926	885	839	947	947	979	957	1,000	911	927	932
743	742	828	822	869	917	860	917	804	907	940	927	944	911	1,000	926	911
699	718	889	902	890	922	887	918	899	936	958	943	942	927	926	1,000	936
752	679	884	856	856	915	873	934	819	933	941	938	921	932	911	936	1,000

(Table continues on the following page.)

excess of twice their standard errors.[10] The sums of the coefficients (column 5) are fairly close to unity, but when formal F tests are applied, the hypothesis that the sum is equal to 1 passes at the 5 percent level in only the case of the summary consumption categories.[11] (With 561 observations, the F test is a sharp one!)

Unfortunately, it cannot be claimed that equation 9.4 is stable either interspatially or intertemporally. The standard analysis of covariance tests[12] led to the rejection of the hypothesis that the coefficients of equation 9.4, applied to the sixteen Phase II countries, would be the same as those for the equation fitted to the eighteen additional countries, the 1975 data being used in both cases. Similarly the hypothesis of equality of coefficients for 1970 and 1975 data for the sixteen Phase II countries had to be rejected. However, the estimates of the parameters of the three sets of equations[13] always conform to expectations with re-

10. The usual multiple-regression assumption of independent disturbances may not be justified in this similarity-index regression. If one country is an outlier, the residuals for the observations involving that country and each of the other countries all will be affected. Therefore, the computed standard errors are probably smaller than the true ones.

11. The possible clustering of residuals referred to in note 10 may make the usual F test misleading in this case because it assumes that the disturbances within each of the regressions are independent. Clustering probably would make the critical values of the test statistic larger than those found in the F table. Also, it should be emphasized that the four regressions are not independent; there is

overlap between the summary and the detailed sets and between the GDP and the consumption data.

12. See Johnston (1972), p. 199.

13. The sets are the sixteen Phase II countries in 1975, the eighteen additional new Phase III countries in 1975, and the sixteen Phase II countries in 1970. For each set there are A, C, E, and G equations.

Table 9-1 (continued)

Country	Malawi	Kenya	India	Paki-stan	Sri Lanka	Zambia	Thai-land	Philip-pines	Korea	Malay-sia	Colom-bia	Jamaica	Syria	Brazil	Roma-nia	Mexico	Yugo-slavia
						B. Price Structures											
Malawi	1,000	912	898	941	869	877	914	890	877	914	875	883	841	897	835	866	865
Kenya	912	1,000	855	902	839	922	937	855	889	903	884	907	858	910	823	917	878
India	898	855	1,000	936	942	379	889	918	873	923	846	859	890	889	879	868	888
Pakistan	941	902	936	1,000	899	864	898	898	875	913	851	860	865	866	806	833	848
Sri Lanka	869	839	942	899	1,000	829	869	888	853	906	913	844	834	837	852	856	845
Zambia	877	922	879	864	829	1,000	960	862	883	914	837	930	880	942	877	897	911
Thailand	914	937	889	898	869	960	1,000	904	907	938	888	925	896	926	875	921	912
Philippines	890	855	918	898	888	862	904	1,000	887	903	868	890	865	892	871	873	902
Korea	877	889	873	875	853	883	907	887	1,000	917	887	942	890	893	829	905	908
Malaysia	914	903	923	913	906	914	938	903	917	1,000	901	945	920	937	887	943	933
Colombia	875	884	846	851	913	837	888	868	887	901	1,000	890	795	867	803	921	830
Jamaica	883	907	859	860	844	930	925	890	942	945	890	1,000	910	959	875	922	939
Syria	841	858	890	865	834	880	896	865	890	920	795	910	1,000	874	871	890	944
Brazil	897	910	889	866	837	942	926	892	893	937	867	959	874	1,000	877	932	928
Romania	835	823	879	806	852	877	875	871	829	887	803	875	871	877	1,000	846	915
Mexico	866	917	868	833	856	897	921	873	905	943	921	922	890	932	846	1,000	931
Yugoslavia	865	878	888	848	845	911	912	902	908	933	830	939	944	928	915	931	1,000
Iran	814	880	812	843	782	867	904	871	867	902	858	897	910	865	837	899	893
Uruguay	912	868	870	877	847	886	928	873	826	888	872	859	827	884	888	863	881
Ireland	822	848	798	770	775	892	865	802	843	914	799	930	878	906	901	885	930
Hungary	888	877	909	867	849	937	923	889	916	929	818	927	927	924	896	905	971
Poland	882	871	913	872	869	912	904	876	911	920	837	896	909	901	905	897	947
Italy	845	880	826	801	790	903	905	846	912	942	848	940	919	924	865	958	951
Spain	844	861	860	830	807	871	883	851	887	933	836	933	947	928	863	941	950
U.K.	805	831	778	751	756	886	856	795	842	895	781	918	862	888	890	873	921
Japan	796	846	772	762	733	874	865	813	907	895	801	939	898	895	815	921	934
Austria	817	857	812	785	781	867	872	841	868	919	816	931	922	907	889	930	963
Netherlands	721	803	704	680	677	821	811	716	797	867	757	869	853	831	795	892	882
Belgium	760	811	727	704	691	829	821	742	818	882	759	889	871	858	815	893	902
France	802	851	769	741	742	867	854	781	856	908	808	919	875	901	846	926	925
Luxembourg	732	773	701	677	676	803	795	725	809	860	750	875	853	824	790	876	888
Denmark	766	811	742	709	734	856	839	757	826	890	787	901	850	868	858	889	906
Germany	778	837	756	727	735	859	847	765	851	903	795	912	876	879	846	912	916
U.S.	748	846	734	728	711	853	836	756	853	876	803	899	855	867	805	915	896

spect to signs. They have coefficients that sum to near 1 in all cases and differ from 1 insignificantly always in the consumption equations.

The reasons for the differences in the coefficients have not been fully investigated, and it is not intended to try to resolve this question here. However, the highly simplified explanation of S_{jk}^q given by equations A, C, E, and G has been extended in some obvious directions.

The Phase I and II results suggested that the absolute income of country pairs as well as their price and income similarities affected S_{jk}^q. Consider, specifically, two pairs of countries: Pair I consists of countries 1 and 2; and Pair II consists of countries 3 and 4. If $S_{12}^p \doteq S_{34}^p$ and $S_{12}^y \doteq S_{34}^y$ but y_1 and y_2 are both much greater than y_3 and y_4, S_{12}^q would be greater than S_{34}^q. That is, among pairs of countries with the same price and income similarities, the pairs with high incomes (at a more advanced stage of development) will have more similar quantity-bundles. This finding is reaffirmed on the basis of the thirty-four–country data for 1975 in equations B, D, F, and H. The variable $\bar{y}$, the mean real per capita GDP of each pair of countries, has been added to the right-hand side of equation 9.4.[14] The coefficient of $\bar{y}$ is positive and highly significant in all four equations. Thus quantity structures of developed countries with similar prices and incomes are more alike than quantity structures of developing countries with similar prices and incomes. Perhaps the explanation is that low-income countries are still closer to their traditional patterns of production and consumption, which may differ from culture to culture,

14. In Phase II a somewhat complex system of income dummy variables was used to explore the independent role of the countries' incomes over and above the S_{jk}^y. $\bar{y}$ is a much simpler way of capturing this effect. (Observe that in effect $(y_j - y_k)$ and $(y_j + y_k)$ are used to explain S_{jk}^q.)

Table 9-1 (continued)

Iran	Uruguay	Ireland	Hungary	Poland	Italy	Spain	U.K.	Japan	Austria	Netherlands	Belgium	France	Luxembourg	Denmark	Germany	U.S.
							B. Price Structures									
814	912	822	888	882	845	844	805	796	817	721	760	802	732	766	778	748
880	868	848	877	871	880	861	831	846	857	803	811	851	773	811	837	846
812	870	798	909	913	826	860	778	772	812	704	727	769	701	742	756	734
843	877	770	867	872	801	830	751	762	785	680	704	741	677	709	727	728
782	847	775	849	869	790	807	756	733	781	677	691	742	676	734	735	711
867	886	892	937	912	903	871	886	874	867	821	829	867	803	856	859	853
904	928	865	923	904	905	883	856	865	872	811	821	854	795	839	847	836
871	873	802	889	876	846	851	795	813	841	716	742	781	725	757	765	756
867	826	843	916	911	912	887	842	907	868	797	818	856	809	826	851	853
902	888	914	929	920	942	933	895	895	919	867	882	908	860	890	903	876
858	872	799	818	837	848	836	781	801	818	757	759	808	750	787	795	803
897	859	930	927	896	940	933	918	939	931	869	889	919	875	901	912	899
910	827	878	927	909	919	947	862	898	922	853	871	875	853	850	876	855
865	884	906	924	901	924	928	888	895	907	831	858	901	824	868	879	867
837	888	901	896	905	865	863	890	815	889	795	815	846	790	858	846	805
899	863	885	905	897	958	941	873	921	930	892	893	926	876	889	912	915
893	881	930	971	947	951	950	921	934	963	882	902	925	888	906	916	896
1,000	863	843	861	865	901	909	827	863	896	852	848	854	833	834	847	864
863	1,000	830	888	880	831	847	812	774	836	743	766	802	739	790	783	766
843	830	1,000	901	868	945	914	990	918	967	947	962	975	943	977	977	944
861	888	901	1,000	968	930	919	903	899	909	840	869	894	855	874	882	855
865	880	868	968	1,000	907	895	858	871	885	799	824	857	808	847	848	820
901	831	945	930	907	1,000	958	945	968	967	949	963	977	952	954	968	960
909	847	914	919	895	958	1,000	895	931	965	914	931	941	913	904	931	923
827	812	990	903	858	945	895	1,000	924	955	944	961	971	953	980	971	948
863	774	918	899	871	968	931	924	1,000	951	924	938	949	934	935	946	945
896	836	967	909	885	967	965	955	951	1,000	955	966	974	953	957	974	958
852	743	947	840	799	949	914	944	924	955	1,000	990	979	984	973	984	978
848	766	962	869	824	963	931	961	938	966	990	1,000	990	990	979	989	973
854	802	975	894	857	977	941	971	949	974	979	990	1,000	976	983	993	978
833	739	943	855	808	952	913	953	934	953	984	990	976	1,000	975	976	967
834	790	977	874	847	954	904	980	935	957	973	979	983	975	1,000	984	963
847	783	977	882	848	968	931	971	946	974	984	989	993	976	984	1,000	980
864	766	944	855	820	960	923	948	945	958	978	973	978	967	963	980	1,000

while the higher income countries show the homogenizing effects of industrialization.

Another commonality among countries that may produce more quantity similarity than can be accounted for by S^p_{jk} and S^y_{jk} alone is geographical location. The effect of a common location was tested by adding to equations A, C, E, and G a dummy variable for each continent which took on a value of 1 when the similarity indexes referred to a pair of countries, both of which were in the given continent, and a 0 otherwise. The coefficients were generally positive; the occasional negative one (for Africa) was not significant at the 5 percent level. The coefficient for Europe was consistently the largest and was significant at the 1 percent level in all four sets of data. The only other continental dummy that was significant rather consistently was that for Asia (at the 5 percent level in three of the four sets, the exception being detailed consumption). The strong result for Europe raises the possibility that income influences not fully measured by $S^{\bar{y}}_{jk}$ may be at work; that is, pairs of European countries may have higher S^q_{jk}'s because they have higher incomes rather than because they are European. This possibility was tested by adding dummy variables to equations B, D, F, and H that served to distinguish continental differences in the slope coefficients for $\bar{y}$.[15] Once again, almost all the signs were positive, with the coefficients for Europe exceeding twice their standard errors in all four cases and those for Asia in three cases.

Thus there is a clear tendency for the similarity in quantity structure to be greater, holding prices and income similarities constant, within a region. That this tendency is most marked among the European coun-

15. The variable for Europe, for example, took on the value of $\bar{y}$ if both members of a given pair were European, and 0 otherwise.

Table 9-2. Coefficients of Regressions Relating Quantity Similarity to Price and Income Similarity, 1975

$$S^q_{jk} = \alpha S^p_{jk} + \beta S^y_{jk} + \delta \bar{y}_{jk} + \gamma + u_{jk}$$

Equation	S^p_{jk} (1)	S^y_{jk} (2)	$\bar{y}_{jk}$ (3)	Constant (4)	$\bar{R}^2$ (5)	Sum of coefficients (6)
	GDP: *34 summary categories*					
A	0.7151	0.2229	—	0.0102	0.615	0.9482
	(0.0626)	(0.0156)	—	(0.0496)	(0.073)	
B	0.6981	0.2051	0.1138	−0.0122	0.647	0.8975:9951[a]
	(0.0601)	(0.0152)	(0.0159)	(0.0476)	(0.070)	
	GDP: *148 detailed categories*					
C	0.7154	0.2885	—	−0.1300	0.572	0.8739
	(0.0696)	(0.0238)	—	(0.0458)	(0.107)	
D	0.5863	0.2799	0.2111	−0.1138	0.626	0.7644:0.9456[a]
	(0.0666)	(0.0223)	(0.0233)	(0.0429)	(0.100)	
	Consumption: *25 summary categories*					
E	0.5137	0.3795	—	0.0928	0.690	0.9860[b]
	(0.0680)	(0.0154)	—	(0.0555)	(0.078)	
F	0.4984	0.3685	0.0715	0.0827	0.699	0.9537:1.015[a]
	(0.0671)	(0.0154)	(0.0174)	(0.0548)	(0.076)	
	Consumption: *108 detailed categories*					
G	0.6792	0.4332	—	−0.1843	0.635	0.9281
	(0.0714)	(0.0247)	—	(0.0476)	(0.117)	
H	0.5413	0.4229	0.2200	−0.1646	0.676	0.8121:1.0009[a]
	(0.0691)	(0.0232)	(0.0258)	(0.0449)	(0.110)	

Note: Numbers in parentheses in columns 1–4 are coefficient standard errors. Numbers in parentheses in column 5 are standard errors of estimate (SEE).

a. Lower limit is for lowest observed $\bar{y}$ (0.057) and upper limit is for highest observed $\bar{y}$ (0.915). (Lower limit: $\hat{\alpha} + \hat{\beta} + \hat{\gamma} + \hat{\delta} \cdot [0.057]$. Upper limit: $\hat{\alpha} + \hat{\beta} + \hat{\gamma} + \hat{\delta} \cdot [0.915]$.)

b. Insignificantly different from 1 at the 0.05 level of significance.

tries may reflect the closer cultural and economic ties that have marked the history of the countries of that continent over the centuries.

The parameter estimates of equations A, C, E, and G support the notion of commonality of world tastes. The estimates of B, D, F, and G suggest, however, that the commonality hypothesis is more tenable for developed countries than developing ones. Geographic differences can be discerned that are statistically significant but are relatively small.[16]

Revealed Preference

The similarity analysis above drew from demand theory only the propositions that prices and income

16. Among other possible explanatory variables for S^q_{jk}, climate, degree of income inequality, and trading-partner associations (for example, the British Commonwealth and the European Common Market) were briefly explored in connection with the Phase II report. Failure to find significant relationships may well have been due to the difficulty of devising, within the limited attention that could be given to the task, adequate measures of the relevant variables.

are what count in determining quantities. The exact aggregation theory implicit in making judgments about tastes of individuals in different countries from the per capita quantities was left vague. The simplest extension explicitly assumes that each consumer in a country consumes the country's per capita quantity of each good and that the per capita quantities were selected on the basis of a budget constraint, defined by the country's prices and per capita income, facing an ordinal utility function. Tastes being the same means that the utility function is the same for all countries.

An empirical check on whether the observed ICP quantity and price data are consistent with a common utility function is available through revealed preference theory.[17] Suppose that in a two-good world, the representative consumer of country a—to be referred to as consumer a—with income y_a paying prices p_{1a} and p_{2a} maximizes his satisfactions by selecting q_{1a} and q_{2a}, depicted as a point on a's budget constraint in each panel of Figure 9-1. Similarly, the representative

17. See Samuelson (1948), pp. 111–12, or Henderson and Quandt (1971), pp. 39–42. A quantity bundle is said to be revealed preferred to another bundle by a chooser if, when the chooser has resources sufficient to purchase either bundle, he in fact chooses the first.

Figure 9-1. Possible Configurations for the Budget Constraints and Consumption Points of Two Countries

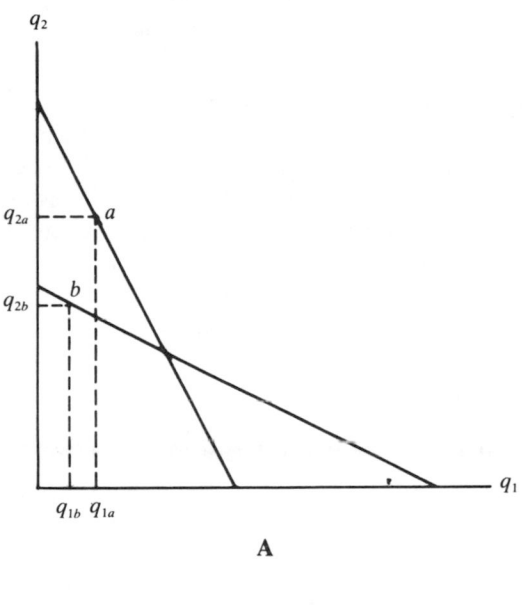

A

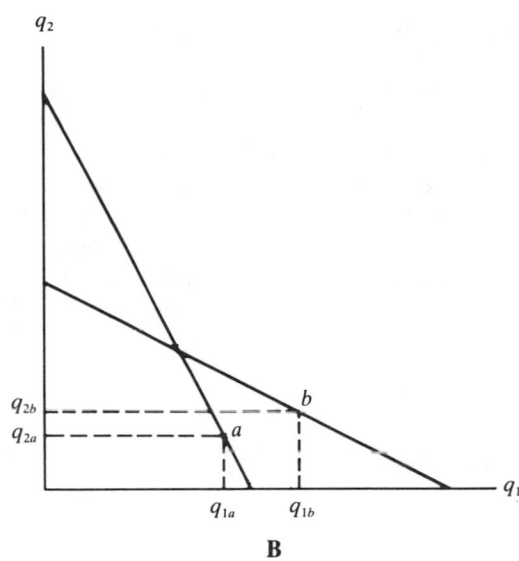

B

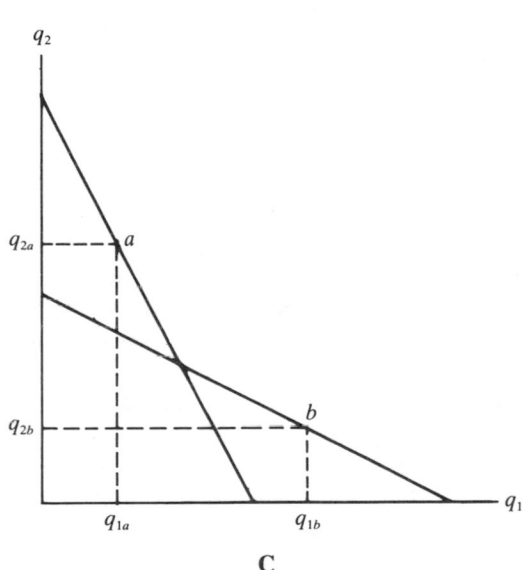

C

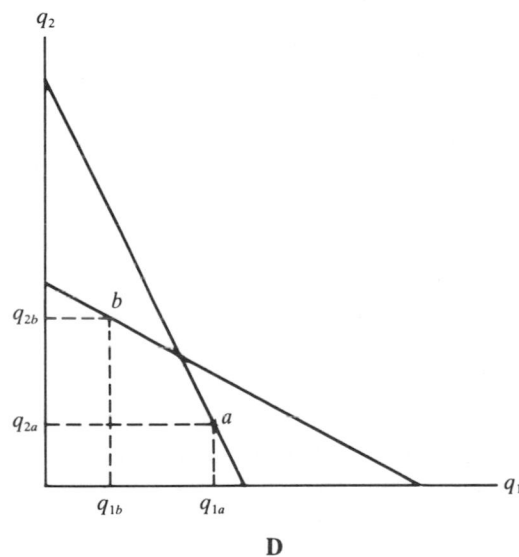

D

consumer of country b—consumer b—reacts to the b budget constraint by selecting q_{1b} and q_{2b}. The four panels of Figure 9-1 show all the possible distinct configurations of (q_{1a}, q_{2a}) and (q_{1b}, q_{2b}). If there is a set of indifference curves with the usual properties common to a and b they will be tangent to the a and b budget lines at (q_{1a}, q_{2a}) and (q_{1b}, q_{2b}), respectively. The configurations compatible with an acceptable indifference map (that is, one made up of convex indifference curves) are shown in panels A, B, and C. The configuration of panel D, however, could not re-

sult from utility maximization based on the same indifference map. In the language of revealed-preference theory, the configuration of panel D violates the Weak Axiom of Revealed Preference while the other three configurations are consistent with it. The Weak Axiom asserts that if one commodity bundle is revealed preferred to another, the converse may not also hold.

The violation can be explained as follows: the (q_{1a}, q_{2a}) and (q_{1b}, q_{2b}) points in panel D are characterized by expressions 9.8 and 9.9:

(9.8) $p_{1a}q_{1a} + p_{2a}q_{2a} > p_{1a}q_{1b} + p_{2a}q_{2b}$ and

(9.9) $p_{1b}q_{1a} + p_{2b}q_{2a} < p_{1b}q_{1b} + p_{2b}q_{2b}.$

The bundle (q_{1a}, q_{2a}) is said to be revealed preferred to (q_{1b}, q_{2b}) because consumer a could have purchased either bundle but chose the former. The inequality of 9.8 asserts that at the prices faced by a the cost of a's quantity selection was greater than the cost of (q_{1b}, q_{2b}). Therefore, (q_{1b}, q_{2b}) could have been purchased. However, (q_{1b}, q_{2b}) is revealed preferred to (q_{1a}, q_{2a}) because consumer b, having the opportunity to consume either, chose the former. (The inequality of 9.9 ensures b's opportunity to buy either bundle.) The condition of two quantity points each being preferred to the other is precisely what constitutes a violation of the Weak Axiom of Revealed Preference. In the cases covered by the other panels, either (q_{1a}, q_{2a}) is revealed preferred to (q_{1b}, q_{2b}) only (panel A) or the reverse (panel B), or neither is revealed preferred to the other (panel C).[18] If the Weak Axiom of Revealed Preference did not hold, the quantity points could not have come forth from the maximization of satisfactions based on the same utility function.

If the number of goods is generalized to m (108 consumption goods and services in the empirical work to be described), the $(q_{1a}, \ldots ,q_{ma})$, $(q_{1b}, \ldots ,q_{mb})$, configurations cannot be displayed graphically, but there is an algebraic representation that is a simple generalization of the two-good case. Inequalities 9.8' and 9.9' together imply a violation of the Weak Axiom:

(9.8') $$\sum_{i=1}^{m} p_{ia}q_{ia} > \sum_{i=1}^{m} p_{ia}q_{ib} \quad \text{and}$$

(9.9') $$\sum_{i=1}^{m} p_{ib}q_{ia} < \sum_{i=1}^{m} p_{ib}q_{ib}.$$

These inequalities can be rewritten in the form of binary quantity indexes described in Chapter 7:

(9.8'') $$\frac{\sum p_{ia}q_{ia}}{\sum p_{ia}q_{ib}} > 1 \quad \text{and}$$

(9.9'') $$\frac{\sum p_{ib}q_{ia}}{\sum p_{ib}q_{ib}} < 1.$$

Inequalities 9.8'' and 9.9'' say that the Paasche quantity index for a and b is greater than unity and the Laspeyres quantity index is less than unity.

---

18. Since (q_{1b}, q_{2b}) is not among the quantity bundles a could buy (that is, it does not lie on or within the triangle formed by the axes and the line representing a's budget constraint), the point (q_{1a}, q_{2a}) is not revealed preferred to (q_{1b}, q_{2b}). In the same way, since (q_{1a}, q_{2a}) is outside the set of possible purchases made when (q_{1b}, q_{2b}) was choosen, (q_{1b}, q_{2b}) is not revealed preferred to (q_{1a}, q_{2a}).

The Laspeyres and Paasche indexes covering the 108 categories of consumption for all 561 pairs of Phase III countries are given in Table 7-5. By examining this table, one can easily see if there are any cases analogous to panel D. There are none. Exactly 514 cases are of the panel-A or -B types, while 47 are of the panel-C type. This way of testing whether tastes are the same has little power to detect taste differences if the incomes of the paired countries are very different. No panel-D cases would be expected even if tastes were not the same for pairs of countries where incomes are far apart. If one country's budget constraint lay inside another's everywhere, there could not be a violation of the Weak Axiom, no matter what. (With regard to panel D, this would mean that a's budget constraint would not cross b's, so there would be no possibility of both being on their "inner segments.") In the ICP data set, of the 561 country pairs, in 74 cases (13 percent of the total), the two countries had income similarity indexes greater than 0.90—that is, their incomes differed by less than 22 percent of the lower of the two. Thus the test was not without power.

A more stringent restriction on commodity bundles selected on the basis of budget constraints is that the Strong Axiom of Revealed Preference must be complied with. The Strong Axiom asserts that if a_1 is revealed preferred to a_2, a_2 is revealed preferred to a_3, $\ldots$, and a_{n-1} is revealed preferred to a_n, a_n may not be revealed preferred to a_1.[19] Transitivity of revealed preference follows from the Strong Axiom. The test of whether or not the Strong Axiom holds for the thirty-four ICP countries appears to require the inspection of a great many combinations (over 17 billion in all, if every possible pair, triplet, and the like, had to be considered). However, in an elegant nonparametric approach to demand analysis, Varian (1981) has developed an algorithm in which he can thread his way through the data in such a way that not all combinations need be examined. In the present work it turns out, though, that the thirty-four country quantity bundles can be shown to obey the Strong Axiom without even having recourse to the Varian algorithm. The countries were ordered by real income per capita as determined by the Geary-Khamis calculations of Chapter 6. An examination of just the 561 possible pairs demonstrated that no country's quantity bundle was revealed preferred to that of any country above it in the ordering. Therefore, there can be no chain of countries of any length—starting anywhere but extending to countries successively lower on the list—that culminates in the last country's quantity bundle

---

19. See Houthakker (1950).

being revealed preferred to the first country of the chain. Therefore, the Strong Axiom cannot be violated.

The compliance of the quantity bundles of the thirty-four diverse ICP countries with the revealed-preference requirements supports the hypothesis of commonality of tastes, but it is hardly conclusive.

Log-linear Demand Analysis

In this section a simple kind of demand analysis is carried out. The various quantities absorbed by different countries expressed in international dollars, the q_{ij}'s, are treated as log-linear functions of prices and incomes.[20] At the end of this section a very minor effort at estimating a complete demand system is attempted.[21] The basic regression equation investigated is:

$$(9.10) \quad \ln q_{ij} = \beta_{i1} \ln \frac{p_{ij}}{p_{Cj}} + \beta_{i2} \ln C_j + \beta_{i0} + u_{ij}$$
$$i = 1, \ldots, m; j = 1, \ldots, 34,$$

where

ln   = natural logarithm

q_{ij} = real quantity per capita of the ith good consumed in the jth country (denominated in international dollars and given in either Summary Multilateral Table 6-5 or Appendix Table 6-5)

p_{ij} = PPP for the ith good in the jth country (as given in either Summary Multilateral Table 6-3 or Appendix Table 6-3, the latter being derivable, as indicated in Chapter 6, from Appendix Tables 6-1 and 6-5)

p_{Cj} = PPP for consumption in the jth country (denominated in international dollars and given in line 1 of Summary Multilateral Table 6-3)

C_j = real consumption per capita in the jth country (denominated in international dollars and given in line 1 of Summary Multilateral Table 6-5).

Since p_{ij} and p_{Cj} appear in ratio form and C is expressed on a scale unrelated to the p's, the demand function is the equivalent of homogeneous of degree zero. That is, the quantities demanded do not depend upon currency units. The regression coefficients β_{i1} and β_{i2} can

be interpreted as price and income elasticities. Here they have been estimated by the ordinary least squares (OLS) method, one equation at a time, for each of the subaggregate groupings defined in the summary multilateral tables of Chapter 6, and also for most of the detailed categories.[22]

Price is introduced as a right-hand side exogenous variable in equation 9.10. There are reasons for thinking that simultaneity arising from prices possibly being endogenous may not be a major problem. Price differences between countries for a given category may be attributable not to the influence of quantities but to varying income levels and to differences in transfer costs and in government policies. Also, it is possible that differing factor intensities from country to country may lead to price differences that are not completely eradicated by competitive forces. Finally, in the Phase I investigation, several different instrumental variables were used in a treatment of price as endogenous. Depending upon which instrument or combination of instruments was used, the price elasticity estimates varied over a wide range, but the consumption elasticities were fairly robust.

In the next two subsections, the demand analysis is carried out at the summary-category and detailed-category levels of aggregation. Subsequently, groupings at a higher level of aggregation are examined.

Summary Categories

The regression equations of the form given in equation 9.10 are set out in Table 9-3 for the twenty-five summary categories of consumption. The equations taken as a group are well behaved. Relative prices and incomes (that is, consumption levels) explain the variations in quantities consumed among the thirty-four countries very well; for seventeen of the categories, the $\overline{R}^2$'s exceed 0.75 and only two (bread and cereals, and fish) fail to produce substantial explanatory power. It is no coincidence that bread and cereals does not have a high $\overline{R}^2$. Its very low income elasticity makes it likely that its income coefficient will be small relative to its standard error.

The coefficient of the price variable is negative with but two exceptions (spices, sweets, and sugar, and

20. Application of the Box-Tidwell procedure to this demand relationship (see note 20, Chapter 8) through use of selected detailed and summary categories indicated that linear-in-the-logs is a better specification than linear.

21. The so-called seemingly unrelated regression technique is applied below. See Zellner (1962).

22. In countries as diverse as the thirty-four under study here, one would expect climate to play a role in determining tastes. As in the case of the similarity analyses of the previous section, attempts in Phase II to allow climate to help in the explanation of quantities consumed were not successful. When various climatic variables, such as mean temperature and rainfall of the capital city, were introduced as additional independent variables, their coefficients were insignificant for most categories. When the coefficient was significant, it was not always of the right sign.

Table 9-3. Regressions of Real per Capita Quantities on Relative Prices and per Capita Consumption, 1975, Twenty-five Summary Categories

Category	Natural log of relative price (SE)	Natural log of per capita consumption (SE)	Constant (SE)	$\bar{R}^2$ (SEE)
Bread, cereals	−0.4558 (0.1920)	0.0595 (0.0663)	4.0739 (0.4892)	0.1174 (0.3158)
Meat	−0.8119 (0.3868)	1.2351 (0.1190)	−4.4957 (0.8754)	0.7653 (0.5655)
Fish	−0.5472 (0.6391)	0.4720 (0.2271)	−0.6299 (1.7570)	0.1377 (1.0105)
Milk, cheese, eggs	−1.2103 (0.3281)	0.7409 (0.1502)	−1.2417 (1.1690)	0.7965 (0.5001)
Oils, fats	−1.1731 (0.5079)	0.7385 (0.1964)	−1.9239 (1.5687)	0.5975 (0.7238)
Fruits, vegetables	−1.2233 (0.2652)	0.4589 (0.0760)	1.2428 (0.5821)	0.7439 (0.3295)
Coffee, tea, cocoa	−1.0305 (0.1889)	0.9656 (0.1133)	−4.0717 (0.8562)	0.7619 (0.5393)
Spices, sweets, sugar	0.0296 (0.2350)	0.8740 (0.0881)	−2.6146 (0.6605)	0.8065 (0.3503)
Beverages	−1.3446 (0.5720)	1.0849 (0.2616)	−3.9579 (2.0601)	0.6518 (0.9325)
Tobacco	−0.5885 (0.1978)	0.9963 (0.1123)	−3.7319 (0.8415)	0.7461 (0.5280)
Clothing	−0.7355 (0.2495)	1.0197 (0.0656)	−2.7109 (0.5015)	0.8949 (0.3055)
Footwear	−0.5184 (0.2904)	1.2218 (0.1032)	−6.0151 (0.7553)	0.8092 (0.4751)
Gross rent	−0.6122 (0.1476)	1.3979 (0.0747)	−5.6205 (0.5473)	0.9252 (0.3499)
Fuel, power	−0.7570 (0.1541)	1.1495 (0.0651)	−4.3690 (0.4894)	0.9156 (0.3085)
Furniture, appliances	−1.3824 (0.3599)	1.4543 (0.1528)	−6.4798 (1.2264)	0.9202 (0.4724)
Supplies, operation	−0.6162 (0.2301)	0.9468 (0.0790)	−3.0062 (0.5822)	0.8151 (0.3493)
Medical care	−0.5199 (0.0948)	1.4002 (0.0432)	−5.9500 (0.3267)	0.9698 (0.2056)
Personal transport equipment	−0.9697 (0.4021)	1.9135 (0.2854)	−10.5675 (2.3659)	0.7915 (1.0238)
Operation costs	−2.2089 (0.7477)	1.2394 (0.3731)	−4.5798 (3.1074)	0.6966 (1.1832)
Purchased transport	−1.1005 (0.2555)	0.8383 (0.1495)	−3.0878 (1.1426)	0.4890 (0.5950)
Communication	−1.0215 (0.1464)	1.6506 (0.0856)	−10.1065 (0.6316)	0.9270 (0.4080)
Recreation	−1.1966 (0.2320)	1.4024 (0.0647)	−6.0137 (0.4833)	0.9427 (0.3046)
Education	0.0202 (0.1298)	0.5417 (0.0940)	0.6714 (0.7748)	0.8122 (0.2197)
Personal care	−1.6554 (0.2528)	1.3136 (0.0713)	−5.9832 (0.5323)	0.9243 (0.3389)
Miscellaneous services	−0.6169 (0.2792)	1.4203 (0.0843)	−5.8875 (0.6267)	0.8954 (0.3958)

Note: The basic equation for these regressions is equation 9.10 in the text. $\bar{R}^2$ is the coefficient of determination. The numbers in parentheses in the first three columns are coefficient standard errors (SE); in the fourth column, standard errors of estimate (SEE).

education) and is significant at the 5 percent level in twenty-one of the categories. Operation of transport equipment, personal care, and furniture and appliances have high price elasticities. Medical care, provided out of the public purse to varying degrees, has a low one as do bread and cereals, tobacco, and footwear.

The coefficient of the income variable is positive in every case. Categories for which elasticities are significantly above unity are footwear, rents, fuel and power, furniture and appliances, medical care, personal transport, communications, recreation, personal care, and miscellaneous services. They are significantly below unity for bread and cereals, fish, fruits and vegetables, and education.

The income coefficients estimated for thirty-four countries in 1975 are very similar to the estimates of Phase II based on sixteen countries in 1970. The price elasticities differ more, though their general pattern remains similar.[23] The differences between the two sets of price elasticities are not surprising, given their standard errors. (Compare the standard errors of the price coefficients with those of the income coefficients in Table 9-3.) The difference between the price and income elasticities in this respect may reflect the relatively narrower range of variation and the possibly larger measurement errors of the price observations. These findings resemble a 1950–70 comparison presented in the Phase I report.[24]

Detailed Categories

The results of the demand equations for the detailed categories in Table 9-4 are similar in broad pattern to those for the summary categories. The table covers 103 detailed consumption categories. Five categories in which direct price comparisons were not made for any or for most countries were excluded.

The proportion of variance in quantities explained tends to be smaller than for the summary categories. Although over 70 percent of the $\bar{R}^2$'s are 0.50 or higher, only about one-third exceed 0.75. In all but five of the equations, the price coefficients are negative; about two-thirds of the coefficients are significantly different from zero at the 5 percent level. A little under 10

percent are significantly elastic, and a somewhat smaller proportion are significantly inelastic. All of the consumption coefficients are positive, except those for rice and for meal and other cereals. The negative coefficients of these two categories in fact were statistically significant. About 35 percent are significantly above 1—that is, these categories are income elastic.

An Alternative Log-linear Specification: Variable Parameters

The demand equations of the 9.10 form were written with an added-on stochastic shock term, u_{ij}, which was assumed to have constant variance, independent of the levels of either p_{ij}/p_{Cj} or C_j. A possibly more structural way of specifying equation 9.10 that implies heteroskedasticity of the stochastic term was also examined.

Let each country have its own price and income elasticities, β_{i1}^j and β_{i2}^j, for the ith good. Suppose that the collection of country β_{i1}^j's are clustered around a central value, β_{i1}, with a dispersion, and that a corresponding supposition is made for the β_{i2}'s. If the collections of country price and income elasticities are assumed to have the characteristics of independent random variables, then equation 9.10 can be replaced by 9.10':

$$(9.10') \quad \ln q_{ij} = (\beta_{i1} + \varepsilon_{ij}) \ln \frac{p_{ij}}{p_{Cj}} + (\beta_{i2} + \delta_{ij}) \ln C_j + (\beta_{i0} + \xi_{ij})$$

where the stochastic terms (ε_{ij}, δ_{ij}, and ξ_{ij}) are independently normally distributed variables with expected values all equal to zero and variances equal to ($\sigma_{\varepsilon i}^2$, $\sigma_{\delta i}^2$, and $\sigma_{\xi i}^2$).[25] In the spirit of the last section, the parameters of interest are the average price and income elasticities of the countries. But the concern about similarity of tastes leads to a special interest in $\sigma_{\varepsilon i}$, $\sigma_{\delta i}$, $\sigma_{\xi i}$, because they provide a basis for judging just how close together price and income elasticities are around the world. (The smaller they are, the more tenable becomes the hypotheses that tastes are common.)

Collecting the stochastic terms, equation 9.10' can be rewritten as 9.10'':

$$(9.10'') \quad \ln q_{ij} = \beta_{i1} \ln \frac{p_{ij}}{p_{Cj}} + \beta_{i2} \ln C_j + \beta_{i0} + u_{ij},$$

23. The rank correlation between the Phase II and the present 1975 price elasticities is 0.58, which is significant at the 1 percent level.

24. In Kravis, Kenessey, Heston, Summers (1975), pp. 280, 283, price and income elasticities based upon ten countries in 1970 were compared with corresponding estimates reported in Gilbert and associates (1958), pp. 63–74, for eight OEEC countries in 1950. Twenty years later the 1950 estimates had not changed much.

25. These variances are related to the coefficient parameters of equation 9.10' and are not to be confused with the standard errors of the parameters. For a well-rounded textbook treatment of this model see Maddala (1977), pp. 390–93.

Table 9-4. Regressions of Real per Capita Quantities on Relative Price and per Capita Consumption, 1975, 103 Detailed Categories

Code	Category	Natural log of relative price (SE)	Natural log of consumption (SE)	Constant (SE)	$\overline{R}^2$ (SEE)	Number of observations
1101	Rice	−0.2349 (0.8363)	−0.7994 (0.3555)	7.6623 (2.6482)	0.0848 (1.6770)	34
1102	Meal, other cereals	−0.7869 (0.4832)	−0.9103 (0.2433)	9.1448 (1.8008)	0.2691 (1.0914)	34
1103	Bread	−1.6441 (0.3435)	1.2587 (0.1962)	−6.7109 (1.4350)	0.7044 (0.9142)	34
1104	Biscuits, cakes, etc.	−2.1061 (0.6270)	1.1509 (0.3065)	−5.6929 (2.4954)	0.7926 (0.8720)	34
1105	Cereal preparations	−0.9866 (0.3439)	1.1333 (0.2565)	−8.4334 (1.9212)	0.5043 (1.1729)	27
1106	Macaroni, spaghetti	−2.2788 (0.7952)	1.2913 (0.3903)	−8.5517 (3.0362)	0.5521 (1.5658)	33
1111	Fresh beef, veal	−1.3596 (0.4077)	1.2156 (0.2142)	−5.8694 (1.5751)	0.4966 (0.9632)	34
1112	Fresh lamb, mutton	0.5045 (1.0449)	0.4648 (0.3675)	−2.5328 (2.7408)	−0.0100 (1.6780)	29
1113	Fresh pork	0.9455 (1.0846)	1.4534 (0.2175)	−8.4371 (1.6425)	0.5873 (0.9940)	31
1114	Chicken	−0.6419 (1.0074)	0.8805 (0.2893)	−3.8634 (2.5019)	0.3142 (1.1461)	34
1115	Other fresh meat	−1.2091 (0.4419)	1.6552 (0.2464)	−10.8207 (1.8659)	0.6292 (1.1658)	34
1116	Frozen, salted meat	−2.2615 (1.0360)	2.2936 (0.3377)	−13.8686 (2.8062)	0.8250 (1.0683)	33
1121	Fresh, frozen fish	−0.6812 (0.5166)	0.4622 (0.2422)	−0.9755 (1.8437)	0.1317 (1.1204)	34
1122	Canned fish	−2.3910 (0.6350)	0.4754 (0.2621)	−1.4712 (1.9982)	0.4014 (1.1864)	34
1131	Fresh milk	−1.9387 (0.3192)	0.3755 (0.2270)	0.4716 (1.7205)	0.7241 (0.8324)	34
1132	Milk products	−1.1873 (0.5166)	1.0245 (0.2366)	−4.5387 (1.8612)	0.7047 (0.7783)	34
1133	Eggs, egg products	−0.3353 (0.3142)	0.9935 (0.1280)	−4.7516 (1.0311)	0.7258 (0.5372)	34
1141	Butter	−2.2020 (0.6503)	1.2352 (0.2844)	−6.2219 (2.3630)	0.6423 (1.1735)	33
1142	Margarine, edible oil	−1.6366 (0.5536)	0.5935 (0.2374)	−1.4962 (1.8800)	0.5115 (0.9120)	34
1143	Lard, edible fat	−0.9602 (1.1719)	0.1854 (0.5883)	−0.6359 (4.6248)	−0.0081 (1.7637)	27
1151	Fresh fruits, tropical	−1.9297 (0.2953)	0.5065 (0.1780)	−0.6076 (1.3004)	0.5736 (0.8395)	34
1152	Fresh fruits, other	−1.6874 (0.9445)	1.7370 (0.4778)	−10.6909 (3.7400)	0.5284 (1.8007)	34
1153	Fresh vegetables	−1.4857 (0.3333)	0.1551 (0.0999)	1.7516 (0.7181)	0.4388 (0.4597)	34
1161	Fruit other than fresh	−1.3539 (0.4498)	1.2537 (0.2697)	−7.7083 (2.2226)	0.8302 (0.7366)	34
1162	Vegetables other than fresh	−1.5107 (0.8240)	1.1977 (0.3961)	−6.6480 (3.2599)	0.4999 (1.4207)	34
1170	Tubers, including potatoes and manioc	−1.2044 (0.2992)	0.2865 (0.1791)	0.6266 (1.3611)	0.4871 (0.7385)	33
1191	Coffee	−1.0618 (0.4564)	1.7077 (0.3010)	−10.3226 (2.3671)	0.5787 (1.3880)	34
1192	Tea	−1.7584 (0.3641)	0.2538 (0.2576)	−1.0343 (1.8858)	0.3936 (1.2154)	34
1193	Cocoa	−1.3256 (0.4713)	0.6419 (0.3548)	−5.2628 (2.6996)	0.4076 (1.2690)	30
1180	Sugar	−0.7285 (0.2164)	0.1997 (0.1167)	1.2279 (0.8592)	0.3809 (0.5111)	34

Table 9-4 *(continued)*

Code	Category	Natural log of relative price (SE)	Natural log of consumption (SE)	Constant (SE)	$\bar{R}^2$ (SEE)	Number of observations
1201	Jam, syrup, honey	−2.0343 (0.7010)	1.0938 (0.3567)	−6.9280 (2.7471)	0.6809 (1.1171)	34
1202	Chocolate, ice cream	−0.4095 (0.4903)	2.0515 (0.2459)	−13.2497 (1.9378)	0.8171 (0.8568)	34
1203	Salt, spices, sauces	−0.8642 (0.6635)	0.5830 (0.3163)	−1.9894 (2.4432)	0.2738 (1.1389)	34
1310	Nonalcoholic beverages	−1.0690 (0.3149)	1.0576 (0.2292)	−5.3427 (1.7658)	0.7634 (0.7769)	34
1321	Spirits	−0.4304 (0.3970)	1.0656 (0.2613)	−5.3531 (2.0328)	0.4095 (1.1195)	33
1322	Wine, cider	−2.6737 (0.4920)	1.0249 (0.4351)	−4.9575 (3.4783)	0.8591 (1.0469)	29
1323	Beer	−1.5683 (0.7533)	0.8189 (0.3646)	−3.4177 (2.8557)	0.4484 (1.2444)	32
1410	Cigarettes	−0.6103 (0.2085)	1.1585 (0.1234)	−5.1955 (0.9202)	0.7615 (0.5817)	34
1420	Cigars, tobacco, snuff	−0.9641 (0.4726)	0.5128 (0.3833)	−2.0799 (3.0368)	0.1729 (1.7037)	32
2110	Clothing materials	−0.2127 (0.5796)	0.2077 (0.2247)	1.2325 (1.7545)	−0.0301 (1.0513)	33
2121	Men's clothing	−0.5820 (0.4841)	1.2705 (0.1652)	−6.3701 (1.2612)	0.7054 (0.7215)	34
2122	Women's clothing	0.3257 (0.3440)	1.5217 (0.1221)	−8.6080 (0.9169)	0.8231 (0.5818)	34
2123	Boys', girls' clothing	0.4394 (0.6013)	1.5654 (0.2019)	−9.8406 (1.5070)	0.6398 (0.9624)	34
2131	Mens, boys underwear	−0.1099 (0.6020)	1.9228 (0.1922)	−12.4634 (1.5111)	0.7593 (0.8935)	34
2132	Women's, girls' underwear	−0.2615 (0.4706)	1.9707 (0.1667)	−12.5606 (1.2483)	0.8120 (0.7872)	34
2150	Other clothing	−0.7903 (0.7771)	1.5869 (0.2087)	−9.8858 (1.5482)	0.6330 (0.9950)	34
2160	Clothing rental, repair	−1.4557 (0.5616)	1.1348 (0.3547)	−8.8681 (2.8451)	0.2140 (1.1464)	32
2211	Men's footwear	−0.7567 (0.3173)	1.0988 (0.1170)	−6.2704 (0.8636)	0.7510 (0.5527)	34
2212	Women's footwear	−0.7089 (0.2878)	1.4249 (0.1445)	−8.4169 (1.0390)	0.7694 (0.5521)	33
2213	Children's footwear	−0.5417 (0.3371)	1.2401 (0.1358)	−7.8889 (1.0247)	0.7422 (0.5497)	32
2220	Footwear repairs	−0.3382 (0.6213)	1.1224 (0.2270)	−8.2591 (1.6698)	0.4395 (1.0426)	33
3110	Gross rents	−0.7113 (0.1461)	1.3638 (0.0893)	−5.5676 (0.6514)	0.9063 (0.4096)	34
3120	Indoor repair, upkeep	−1.0210 (0.3224)	1.6489 (0.1786)	−9.4881 (1.3161)	0.7318 (0.8213)	33
3210	Electricity	−0.8747 (0.1242)	1.6578 (0.0754)	−9.3827 (0.5662)	0.9488 (0.3531)	34
3220	Gas	−1.0022 (0.2512)	2.3638 (0.2004)	−15.5665 (1.5507)	0.8736 (0.8831)	33
3230	Liquid fuels	−2.0968 (0.5446)	0.9399 (0.3145)	−3.7245 (2.5022)	0.5374 (1.3740)	33
3240	Other fuels, ice	−1.2763 (0.2648)	0.4057 (0.1676)	−0.5915 (1.2367)	0.4562 (0.7967)	32
4110	Furniture, fixtures	−0.9532 (0.3783)	1.6997 (0.2186)	−9.9482 (1.5710)	0.7904 (0.8709)	34
4120	Floor coverings	−0.6073 (0.6287)	2.2952 (0.2727)	−15.7754 (2.1083)	0.7192 (1.2502)	32
4200	Household textiles, etc.	−0.7357 (0.6264)	1.5817 (0.1780)	−9.3117 (1.4276)	0.7565 (0.7809)	34

(Table continues on the following page.)

Table 9-4 (continued)

Code	Category	Natural log of relative price (SE)	Natural log of consumption (SE)	Constant (SE)	$\bar{R}^2$ (SEE)	Number of observations
4310	Refrigerators, freezers	−1.0264 (0.2950)	1.4474 (0.2566)	−8.8861 (2.1169)	0.9205 (0.5355)	33
4320	Washing appliances	−0.7753 (0.5785)	2.4074 (0.5475)	−16.9469 (4.6089)	0.7134 (0.7946)	21
4330	Cooking appliances	−1.0011 (0.7005)	1.8567 (0.4311)	−12.5819 (3.5171)	0.7406 (1.1218)	33
4340	Heating appliances	−0.7148 (0.2528)	2.1218 (0.2398)	−15.4594 (1.9073)	0.8382 (0.8798)	32
4350	Cleaning appliances	−0.9835 (0.2818)	1.9080 (0.2518)	−13.8101 (2.0807)	0.8474 (0.6330)	23
4360	Other household appliances	−2.0418 (0.5687)	0.3557 (0.3952)	0.6209 (3.7286)	0.7511 (0.8212)	31
4400	Household utensils	−0.9577 (0.5816)	1.2556 (0.2151)	−6.5361 (1.6658)	0.7104 (0.7982)	33
4510	Nondurable household goods	−0.1468 (0.3625)	1.2083 (0.1184)	−6.1462 (0.9738)	0.8790 (0.3815)	34
4520	Domestic services	−1.0556 (0.4302)	0.7421 (0.4495)	−4.7603 (3.5976)	0.1286 (1.3599)	29
4530	Household services	−1.6262 (0.3822)	1.3309 (0.1849)	−7.9545 (1.3794)	0.6053 (0.7734)	34
5110	Drugs, medical preparations	−0.9357 (0.2911)	1.3012 (0.1007)	−6.4885 (0.7429)	0.8497 (0.4772)	34
5120	Medical supplies	−1.8723 (0.4994)	0.8164 (0.2031)	−4.4187 (1.5083)	0.4426 (0.9655)	34
5200	Therapeutic equipment	−0.7681 (0.3060)	1.4256 (0.2065)	−9.8460 (1.5592)	0.5897 (0.8989)	33
5310	Physician's services	−0.4482 (0.0885)	1.6613 (0.0869)	−9.6139 (0.6422)	0.9236 (0.4140)	34
5320	Dentists' services	−0.3354 (0.1027)	2.2710 (0.1423)	−15.8364 (1.0651)	0.8854 (0.6739)	34
5330	Nurses' services	−0.2691 (0.0875)	1.4940 (0.1089)	−8.5364 (0.7877)	0.8762 (0.5012)	34
5400	Hospitals	−0.4088 (0.1244)	1.4787 (0.1338)	−8.0568 (1.0180)	0.7877 (0.6298)	34
6110	Personal cars	−1.2368 (0.4748)	2.0658 (0.3641)	−11.6209 (3.0638)	0.7746 (1.2466)	34
6120	Other personal transport	−1.2986 (0.3901)	1.3727 (0.2678)	−8.7425 (2.0822)	0.6710 (1.1229)	34
6210	Tires, tubes, accessories	−2.4886 (0.7199)	0.9906 (0.4014)	−4.8997 (3.2664)	0.6697 (1.2781)	34
6220	Repair charges	−1.4104 (0.4846)	1.7614 (0.3791)	−11.5064 (2.7636)	0.6363 (1.5104)	33
6230	Gasoline, oil, grease	−1.4383 (0.6304)	1.5803 (0.3306)	−7.8069 (2.8528)	0.6241 (1.3354)	33

where $u_{ij} = \varepsilon_{ij} \cdot \ln(p_{ij}/p_{Cj}) + \delta_{ij} \cdot \ln C_j + \xi_{ij}$. It follows that the variance of u_{ij} is a linear combination of the variances of ε_{ij}, δ_{ij}, and ξ_{ij}; but more to the point, that the variance of u_{ij} is a linear combination of $(\ln[p_{ij}/p_{Cj}])^2$ and $(\ln C_j)^2$ with *positive* weights, namely the variances of ε_{ij} and δ_{ij}. Unfortunately for the applicability of this model in the present context, the quantity, price, and income data did not support the expectation that the variance of the disturbance term increases when $\ln C_j$ increases, at least in the two summary categories that were studied intensively: bread and cereals, and meat. To the contrary, the observed heteroskedasticity went the other way. The hill-climbing algorithm used in maximizing the likelihood function derived from equation 9.10″ broke down when in successive iterations the trial values of $\sigma^2_{\delta i}$ persistently penetrated the negative range. As a consequence, no admissable estimates of $\sigma_{\varepsilon i}$, $\sigma_{\delta i}$, and $\sigma_{\xi i}$ could be obtained. Though in advance the variable parameters model seemed to be a plausible maintained hypothesis within which common tastes represented a possible case (that is, common tastes represented by $\sigma_{\varepsilon i} = \sigma_{\delta i} = \sigma_{\xi i} = 0$ was nested within the variable-parameters model), in fact the nature of the

Table 9-4 *(continued)*

Code	Category	Natural log of relative price (SE)	Natural log of consumption (SE)	Constant (SE)	$\bar{R}^2$ (SEE)	Number of observations
6240	Parking, tolls, etc.	−0.2243 (0.7399)	2.4736 (0.3960)	−17.3631 (2.9612)	0.6000 (1.5904)	32
6310	Local transport	−1.4028 (0.2905)	1.0034 (0.2015)	−5.7782 (1.5583)	0.4918 (0.8723)	34
6321	Rail transport	−0.5784 (0.3533)	1.2813 (0.2901)	−9.0590 (2.2665)	0.3574 (1.2898)	33
6322	Bus transport	−0.4061 (0.3953)	0.0037 (0.2489)	1.3778 (2.0748)	−0.0186 (0.9808)	33
6323	Air transport	−0.9550 (0.3100)	1.2063 (0.2348)	−7.9623 (1.7493)	0.4748 (1.0014)	32
6410	Postal communication	−0.6784 (0.3842)	1.3320 (0.1704)	−9.1096 (1.2562)	0.6833 (0.7942)	34
6420	Telephone, telegraph	−1.0695 (0.1247)	1.8495 (0.0936)	−11.9783 (0.6910)	0.9343 (0.4461)	34
7110	Radio, TV, phonograph	−1.7237 (0.4955)	1.3448 (0.3278)	−6.9125 (2.6898)	0.7551 (1.0800)	34
7120	Major durable recreation equipment	−2.0217 (0.5046)	1.5140 (0.3403)	−9.4066 (2.8392)	0.7911 (1.1285)	34
7130	Other recreation equipment	−1.0543 (0.7356)	2.7127 (0.2698)	−18.0845 (2.2038)	0.8241 (1.1143)	34
7210	Public entertainment	−1.0940 (0.3899)	1.3185 (0.2052)	−8.3190 (1.5871)	0.5612 (0.8628)	34
7230	Other recreation, cultural	−0.8738 (0.3571)	1.0920 (0.1633)	−5.4599 (1.2056)	0.5669 (0.7504)	34
7310	Books, papers, magazines	−0.9927 (0.2838)	1.5840 (0.1235)	−9.2990 (0.9188)	0.8709 (0.5610)	34
7320	Stationery	−0.5321 (0.9580)	1.2531 (0.3415)	−8.2957 (2.7571)	0.3980 (1.3384)	34
7411	Teachers, 1st and 2nd level	−0.0528 (0.0871)	0.3774 (0.0825)	1.3789 (0.7015)	0.6471 (0.2023)	34
7412	College teachers	−0.2306 (0.1341)	1.0134 (0.1096)	−5.3968 (0.8389)	0.7179 (0.5043)	34
8100	Barber, beauty shops	−1.4101 (0.2636)	1.6895 (0.1624)	−11.3462 (1.2432)	0.7769 (0.7517)	34
8210	Toilet articles	−1.0218 (0.3130)	1.1439 (0.1367)	−5.6974 (1.0851)	0.8490 (0.5098)	34
8220	Other personal-care goods	−1.5927 (0.3566)	1.4774 (0.1628)	−8.2340 (1.2009)	0.7448 (0.7751)	34
8310	Restaurants, cafés	0.3683 (0.4309)	1.8805 (0.1940)	−10.0281 (1.4355)	0.7422 (0.8927)	34
8320	Hotels, lodging	−1.3602 (0.5027)	1.3871 (0.2425)	−8.5394 (1.7048)	0.7162 (0.8887)	30

Note: The basic equation for these regressions is equation 9.10 in the text. $\bar{R}^2$ is the coefficient of determination. The numbers in parentheses in the first three columns are coefficient standard errors (SE); in the fourth column, standard errors of estimate (SEE).

observed heteroskedasticity of the disturbance term of equation 9.10″ ruled out the model, so it was dropped.

Log-linear Demand Equations Estimated Simultaneously

Equation 9.10 refers to a system of m equations. When it is applied to the detailed categories, m equals 103; when it is applied to the summary categories, m equals 25. The coefficient estimates ($\hat{\beta}_{i1}$, $\hat{\beta}_{i2}$, $\hat{\beta}_{i0}$) for each equation of the system that appear in Tables 9-3 and 9-4 were obtained through the use of ordinary least squares (OLS) applied one equation at a time. However, it has been shown that under fairly general circumstances more efficient estimates can be obtained by estimating all of the parameters of all of the equations simultaneously by a generalized–least-squares (GLS) procedure.[26] The small number of observations

26. Zellner (1962). The value of the system-estimation procedure stems from the fact that it can be expected that the disturbances of each equation will be correlated with the disturbances of all other equations. OLS, equation by equation, ignores these correlations. Zellner's "seemingly unrelated equation" approach exploits these correlations.

Table 9-5. A Comparison of Estimates of Demand Elasticities Obtained Through Use of Ordinary Least Squares and Generalized Least Squares, 1975

	Demand elasticities						$\bar{R}^2/$ (SEE)[d] (7)
	Price			Consumption			
	OLS[a] (1)	GLS$^b_4$ (2)	GLS$^c_7$ (3)	OLS[a] (4)	GLS$^b_4$ (5)	GLS$^c_7$ (6)	
Food	− 0.0216 (0.2322)	− 0.1147 (0.1638)	− 0.2835 (0.1488)	0.6925 (0.0386)	0.6840 (0.0343)	0.6688 (0.0337)	0.933 (0.1544)
Clothing	− 0.7704 (0.2172)	− 0.6107 (0.1712)	− 0.8314 (0.1666)	1.0424 (0.0552)	1.0488 (0.0525)	1.0399 (0.0525)	0.924 (0.2598)
Shelter	− 0.5474 (0.1809)	− 0.4421 (0.1349)	− 0.4921 (0.1451)	1.2772 (0.0423)	1.2808 (0.0402)	1.2791 (0.0402)	0.967 (0.1993)
All other	− 0.1499 (0.1881)	− 0.0554 (0.1209)	—	1.1932 (0.0461)	1.1786 (0.0389)	—	0.970 (0.1702)
Medical care	− 0.5200 (0.0948)	—	− 0.4931 (0.0798)	1.4002 (0.0432	—	1.3994 (0.0412)	0.970 (0.2055)
Transportation and communication	− 0.4524 (0.2066)	—	− 0.3442 (0.1582)	1.3554 (0.0724)	—	1.3617 (0.0688)	0.920 (0.3403)
Recreational and education	− 0.1793 (0.1866)	—	− 0.2413 (0.1296)	0.9361 (0.0858)	—	0.9607 (0.0661)	0.923 (0.2078)
Other	− 0.6303 (0.3136)	—	− 0.5643 (0.2673)	1.3660 (0.0716)	—	1.3612 (0.0676)	0.920 (0.3235)

Note: The standard errors of the elasticities appear in parentheses.
a. Elasticities obtained through use of ordinary least squares, one equation at a time.
b. Elasticities obtained through use of generalized least squares on four categories.
c. Elasticities obtained through use of generalized least squares on seven categories.
d. Coefficient of determination and standard error of estimate obtained through use of OLS.

(34) relative to the number of equations (103 for the detailed categories, and 25 for the summary categories) made it necessary to confine simultaneous system estimation to a smaller set of consumption groups. As a consequence, total consumption was divided into two alternative sets of more gross groupings. One set comprised four "major" categories: food, clothing, shelter, and all other. The second set comprised seven "grand" categories where "all other" is divided four ways: food; clothing; shelter; medical care; transportation and communication; recreation and education; and other.[27] Computation of the quantities and prices for these groupings were derived from Summary Tables 6-1, 6-3, and 6-5 in the same way that quantities and prices were derived for the summary and detailed categories.

Table 9-5 gives the prices and consumption elasticities obtained first using OLS one equation at a time, and then from the application of the GLS procedure to both the four-category and seven-category systems. Most GLS estimates of the consumption elasticities were virtually the same as the OLS estimates, whether the four-category or seven-category breakdown was used.

27. These groupings are defined in the lines of Table 6-1: food, lines 1–33; clothing, lines 40–51; shelter, lines 52–70; medical care, lines 71–77; transportation and communication, lines 78–89; recreation and education, lines 90–101; other, lines 102–07; and all other, the last four sets of lines. The four-category breakdown is also used in the linear expenditure system analysis of the next section.

The estimates of the price elasticities varied much more in percentage terms, but, with the exception of food, the absolute differences between the elasticities was substantively unimportant. There is no systematic pattern to the differences between the OLS and GLS price-elasticity estimates. The GLS estimates of the price elasticities in the seven-category case are larger than those in the four-category case, while the reverse is true for the consumption elasticities. The estimated standard errors of the GLS estimates are all lower than the OLS-estimated standard errors, probably reflecting the greater efficiency of GLS.[28]

All of the price elasticities are low. As was indicated in the discussion of the summary and detailed categories, the price elasticities are much less robust than the consumption ones to considerations of endogeneity of prices. The shelter consumption elasticity is right in line with the consumption elasticities of the sub-aggregates of shelter that are detailed in Table 9-3.

Asia versus Europe: The Same Demand Functions?

The demand coefficients of Tables 9-3, 9-4, and 9-5 are based on data for thirty-four countries highly

28. The tentative quality of this remark reflects the uncertainties arising from the fact that the GLS-estimated standard errors are only asymptotically correct.

varied not only in income levels but also in cultural heritage. To what extent would the same demand relationships hold if they were estimated for relatively homogeneous subsets of countries? An attempt was made to gain insight into this question by estimating the demand equations separately for countries in the two regions for which the largest number of countries are available: Europe with fifteen countries and Asia with ten.

Of course, one should not expect literally identical tastes in Asia and Europe. The question under consideration here is better stated: At what level of aggregation are the quantities, prices, and consumption levels consistent with the hypothesis of the same demand coefficients?

The standard analysis of covariance was used to judge whether the demand coefficients were the same in the two continents. The example of the clothing summary category illustrates the nature of the test.[29] Equations 9.11, 9.12, and 9.13 give the clothing demand coefficients for the ten countries of Asia, the fifteen countries of Europe, and the pooled twenty-five countries of both continents:

(9.11) Asia:
$$\ln q = -0.9986 \ln p/p_C + 1.0374 \ln C - 2.6874$$
$$\quad\quad\quad (0.4201) \quad\quad\quad (0.1518) \quad\quad (1.0537)$$

(9.12) Europe:
$$\ln q = -0.4762 \ln p/p_C + 0.6680 \ln C + 0.0538$$
$$\quad\quad\quad (0.3520) \quad\quad\quad (0.1852) \quad\quad (1.5348)$$

(9.13) Pooled:
$$\ln q = -0.6933 \ln p/p_C + 0.9606 \ln C - 2.2059$$
$$\quad\quad\quad (0.2143) \quad\quad\quad (0.0600) \quad\quad (0.4492)$$

In this case, the differences between the Asian and European coefficients are within the bounds of what may be expected from chance at the 0.10 level. The F statistic based on the reduction in the sum of squared residuals from dividing the twenty-five observations into the two continent sets is 2.28. The probability of obtaining 2.28 or greater if the demand for clothing is the same in Asia as in Europe is 0.11.[30]

An analysis of covariance was performed for each of the following: the first 21 of the 103 detailed categories; each of the 25 summary categories; each of the 7 grand categories; and each of the 4 major categories. The results of the 57 individual tests of hypothesis were (percentages in parentheses):

	21 detailed categories	25 summary categories	7 grand categories	4 major categories
Pass at 0.10 level	14 (67)	19 (76)	6 (86)	4 (100)
Pass at 0.05 level	2 (10)	1 (4)	—	—
Pass at 0.01 level	1 (5)	3 (12)	1 (14)	—
Fail at 0.01 level	4 (19)	2 (8)	—	—

It appears that the higher the level of aggregation, the more tenable becomes the hypothesis that the Asian and European demands are the same. The probable explanation for this is that the desire for broad classes of products is likely to be widely shared even if there is variation among people in their choice of which particular products they consume to satisfy each such class of desires. Warm beverages may be wanted in similar quantities everywhere, but in some places people meet the desire by consuming coffee, while in others they meet it by consuming tea.

Three caveats must be considered in connection with this finding. The first, relating to the F tests, is that the maintained hypothesis underlying the analysis of covariance requires that the variance of the disturbances be the same in Asia and Europe.[31] In the present case, however, the variances of the disturbances of the Asian equations are definitely larger than the variance in the European equations.[32]

The second caveat is that what is called for in the four sets of F tests (twenty-one tests, twenty-five tests, seven tests, and four tests) is four joint tests.[33] Two different kinds of joint tests were applied.[34] The primary one drew on a χ^2 tests developed by R. A. Fisher.[35]

---

29. This is not the same as the clothing major category of Table 9-5, which also includes footwear.

30. For 3 and 19 degrees of freedom, the tabled critical F values are: $F_{0.10} = 2.40$, $F_{0.05} = 3.13$, and $F_{0.01} = 5.01$.

31. Fortunately, the analysis of covariance is fairly robust to unequal variances if the sample sizes are not very different. See Box (1953).

32. In the similarity analysis above, this conclusion was foreshadowed by the observation that q's appeared to be less dependent on prices and income in poor countries than in rich.

33. That a joint test is required is easy to see from the following example. Suppose an F value were obtained such that under the null hypothesis the probability was 0.15 that such a value or larger would be observed. Then at the 0.10 level the null hypothesis would be accepted. But what if in twenty-five cases all F's had a probability of precisely 0.15 associated with them? Following the one-test-at-a-time strategy, one would accept all eighteen hypotheses at the 0.10 level. However, the fact that all of the F's are pretty far into the right tail of the F distribution means that the probability is very low that they would all be out there for chance reasons alone.

34. A likelihood-ratio test covering all of the categories of a set could be used only if the sample sizes were large enough to justify the assumption that the distribution of the likelihood-ratio statistic had its asymptotic shape. For any single category, the analysis-of-covariance F test is equivalent to the likelihood-ratio test. It was found that the likelihood-ratio test led to smaller probabilities than the F test, so it was not used for the joint tests.

35. See Bancroft, Anderson (1952), pp. 140–41. Under the null

(Note continues on following page.)

The other was a Kolmogorov-Smirnov test.[36] In the former case, the joint test results confirm the proposition that the demands of Asians and Europeans are more alike the higher the level of aggregation. In the latter, the differences in tastes are shown to be not gross even at the summary-category level.

The third caveat is that the demand equations for Asia were not in every case based on ten observations because q and p were not available for every Asian country. In the seven cases of this sort, the regressions were based on only the countries for which data were available;[37] the others probably consumed only very small quantities of the missing categories. Thus excluding them was equivalent to truncation on the basis of the value of the dependent variable, and this may lead to biased coefficients. Moreover, if indeed the absence of observations from some countries is a reflection of the product's not being consumed internally, then those countries not represented in the data set might well have had different tastes.

Overall the Asia-Europe comparisons offer some support for the hypothesis of the similarity of tastes the world round at high levels of aggregation. However, the tests are not very discriminating in the sense

that they lump together statistical estimates of elasticities that one would regard as very different in substantive economic terms. For example, although the same-taste hypothesis was accepted for meat at the 5 percent level, the consumption elasticity (coefficient of ln C) is 1.74 for Asia and 0.50 for Europe. However, at the level of the four major categories, the Asian consumption elasticities are much closer to their European counterparts.

	Price elasticity		Consumption elasticity	
	Asia	Europe	Asia	Europe
Food	−0.353	−0.250	0.646	0.535
Clothing	−0.921	−0.476	1.070	0.636
Shelter	−0.362	−1.024	1.352	1.599
All other	−0.225	−0.490	1.219	1.226

Summary of Log-linear Demand Analysis

Results of the log-linear demand analysis clearly confirm the Phase II conclusion that price and incomes go far toward an explanation of consumption patterns. This conclusion appears to hold over a diverse set of countries and at least for periods of time not far apart. In addition, dividing the ICP countries along continental lines made it possible to see that the higher the level of aggregation, the more similar the demand equations were for Asian and European countries, and therefore the more similar tastes could be considered to be.

The Linear Expenditure System

The above similarity analysis, revealed-preference discussion, and log-linear demand analysis drew upon the formal theory of consumer behavior only in the most casual way. The empirical results so far presented suggest that the broad assumption of commonality of tastes has a plausibility that justifies more sophisticated investigation. Consequently, two further lines of work have been pursued: (1) a generalized–demand-system analysis drawing specifically on the satisfaction-maximizing calculus and (2) a kind of true-cost-of-living–index approach to the estimation of comparative levels of affluence implied by the ICP prices and expenditures.[38]

The information about price and income elasticities has been provided in the previous sections in two different forms. The magnitude of the coefficients of the price- and income-similarity indexes in Table 9-2 reflect in an overall way the elasticities. That is, higher coefficients indicate a greater response of quantities

---

hypothesis that Asian and European demands for a product are the same, the probabilities derived from the analysis of covariance will be distributed uniformly on the unit interval, and the negative of twice the natural logarithm of the probability is distributed as χ^2 with two degrees of freedom. If

$$Z = \sum_{i=1}^{n} (-2 \ln \Pi_i) = -2n \cdot \ln \text{GM}(\Pi)$$

where $\text{GM}(\Pi)$ is the geometric mean of the probabilities associated with n independent events, then Z is distributed as χ^2 with $2n$ degrees of freedom. By calculating the probabilities associated with each of the F statistics in each of the sets and computing Z for each set, it is possible to find the probability of getting such sets of F values. The Z's and their probabilities are: twenty-one detailed categories: $Z_{42} = 82.92$, $Pr (\chi_{42}^2 > 82.92) = 0.00017$; twenty-five summary categories: $Z_{50} = 105.60$, $Pr (\chi_{50}^2 > 105.60) = 0.000007$; seven grand categories: $Z_{14} = 23.12$, $Pr (\chi_{14}^2 > 23.12) = 0.058$; and four major categories: $Z_8 = 7.62$, $Pr (\chi_8^2 > 7.62) = 0.471$.

36. Not all Asian countries supplied quantity and price data for every one of the twenty-five summary categories, but, in eighteen of the twenty-five, all of the Asian countries were represented. Under the null hypothesis that Asia and Europe have the same demand coefficients, the eighteen F statistics can be regarded as a sample of eighteen random observations from the $F(3,19)$ density function. The Kolmogorov-Smirnov test (Hays, Winkler [1971], pp. 817–21) was used to see if the differences between the empirical frequency distribution of the eighteen observed F's differed from the theoretical $F(3, 19)$ more than the amount that could be attributed to chance. The null hypothesis could be accepted at the 0.01 level but had to be rejected at the 0.05 level.

37. With the exception of beverages, the analysis of covariance F's for the seven categories were not large: 0.95 (seven), 1.88 (seven), 2.51 (nine), 2.59 (nine), 2.98 (seven), and 5.78 (nine). (The number of Asian observations is in parentheses.)

38. This analysis will provide estimates of comparative consumption rather than GDP.

Figure 9-2.   An Indifference Map for a Member of the Utility-function Family.

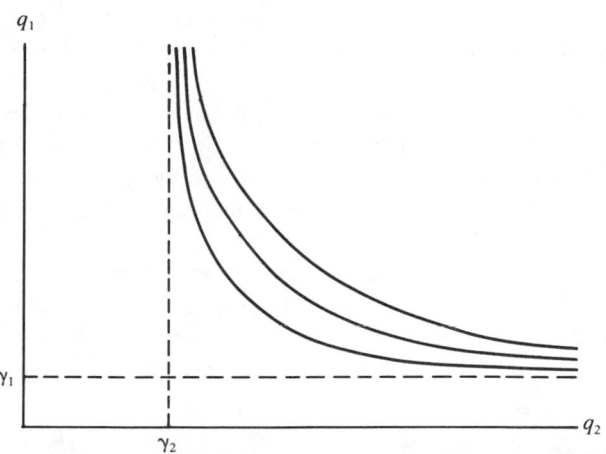

to differences in prices and income. It is not surprising to find the coefficients higher—in seven of the eight possible comparisons—for the regressions relating to the detailed categories than for those relating to the summary categories.

The coefficients of the demand-type equations given in Tables 9-3, 9-4, and 9-5 provide estimates for specific goods, but under a simple specification of the demand relationship. The limitations of the specification arise from the omission of the obviously relevant prices of substitutes and complements; the rigid form of the equations, which does not permit the elasticities to vary with prices and incomes; and the failure to take into account the adding-up requirement and the Slutsky conditions that are implied by the consumer-behavior model.[39]

The simplest representation of a demand system meeting these theoretical conditions is the linear expenditure system (LES).[40] Its attractiveness as a demand model is enhanced by its suitability for the true-cost-of-living approach to income comparisons, which will be explored below.

The linear expenditure system is based on the specifications of a utility function as given by equation 9.14:

$$(9.14)\quad U = F(q_1, q_2, \ldots, q_m)$$
$$= A \cdot (q_1 - \gamma_1)^{\beta_1} \cdot (q_2 - \gamma_2)^{\beta_2}$$
$$\cdots \cdot (q_m - \gamma_m)^{\beta_m}$$
$$q_i > \gamma_i;\ \beta_i > 0$$

where q_i refers to the quantity consumed of the ith good, γ_i is the minimum quantity of the ith good for the consumer's existence, and β_i is the marginal budget share of the ith good. The function F is normalized by setting $A = 1$ and requiring the β's to sum to unity.[41] Figure 9-2 depicts in two dimensions an indifference map for a member of the utility-function family. The first-order demand equations implied by the maximization of U in equation 9.14 subject to the budget constraint

$$\sum_{i=1}^{m} p_i q_i = E \text{ are:}$$

$$p_1 q_1 = \gamma_1 p_1 + \beta_1 \left(E - \sum_{i=1}^{m} p_i \gamma_i \right)$$

(9.15)

$$p_m q_m = \gamma_m p_m + \beta_m \left(E - \sum_{i=1}^{m} p_i \gamma_i \right),$$

where p_i is the price paid for the ith good, q_i is the quantity of it purchased, and E is total expenditure. (The origin of the name of the demand system is now apparent: expenditure on each good is a linear function of total expenditure and all prices.) For a person with a utility function like that given in equation 9.14, who is motivated by maximization of satisfaction, the demand function will have price and consumption elasticities given by equations 9.16 and 9.17:

$$(9.16)\qquad \eta_i^p = -1 + \frac{\gamma_i(1 - \beta_i)}{q_i}$$

$$(9.17)\qquad \eta_i^E = \beta_i \Big/ \frac{p_i q_i}{E}.$$

Observe that the elasticities are not constant in the sense that they depend on quantities and prices as well as the parameters of the utility function. However, the connection between the elasticities and the market prices, quantities, and total expenditure is quite special. (For example, no inferior goods are possible, and consumption elasticities less than 1 must increase with increasing expenditure.[42])

---

41. Alternatively, the utility function can be written in logarithmic form:

$$U = \sum_{i=1}^{m} \beta_i \ln (q_i - \gamma_i).$$

42. This latter feature of the LES consumption elasticities seems implausible in the case of, say, the demand for food. This matter was examined briefly by introducing into the demand equation for food (equation 9.10) a $(\ln C_j)^2$ term. The estimate of the coefficient of the new term was negative (and almost significantly so), indicating that the elasticity falls with rising affluence. The inconsistency between this empirical finding and the LES structural requirement that the elasticity increase with rising affluence must be regarded as a serious flaw in the LES.

---

39. But see the references below (note 45), in which the applicability of such conditions to group data is called into question.

40. Klein and Rubin (1947–48), Samuelson (1947–48), Geary (1950–51), Stone (1954). For a convenient review of the theoretical and empirical literature on the linear expenditure system, see Phlips (1974), pp. 121–31, 135–39.

While neither the indirect utility function nor expenditure function associated with the linear expenditure system is needed in this study, the true-cost-of-living–index conception based on them will be used in the next section. For completeness here, the formula for a constant-utility index is given in equation 9.18. This index provides the answer to the question: By how much must a person's income be changed if he is faced with a certain set of prices in order to provide him with the same level of satisfaction as he enjoyed in another situation when his income and the prices he faced were different? If j refers to the first situation and b (base) to the second, the ratio of the person's income in j ($\overline{E}_j$) to his actual income, $I_j = \overline{E}_j/E_j$, to make him as well off as in b is given by equation 9.18.[43]

$$(9.18) \quad I_j = \left\{ \frac{\sum\limits_{i=1}^{m} p_{ij} \gamma_i}{E_b} + \left(1 - \frac{\sum\limits_{i=1}^{m} p_{ib} \gamma_i}{E_b} \right) \prod_{i=1}^{m} \left(\frac{p_{ij}}{p_{ib}} \right)^{\beta_i} \right\} \cdot \left(\frac{E_b}{E_j} \right).$$

The econometric problem of empirically characterizing the demand of an LES person is to estimate his parameters β_i and γ_i and from these numbers to estimate his price and income elasticities and his direct or indirect utility function.

The Data

Estimation of the β's and γ's for an individual can be carried out easily with high-speed computers if data on his quantity responses to a broad range of $(p_1, \ldots, p_m; E)$ situations are available. Virtually never are sufficiently varying data on individuals available, but many empirical investigations have been carried out that were based on the quantity responses of a set of different individuals (or households) who are assumed to share the same utility function and therefore the same β's and γ's. How the econometric estimation proceeds depends, for example, on the pattern of variation and covariation of prices and income across individuals. One can rarely find data in which similar individuals with different incomes are exposed to prices that vary.[44]

Many, perhaps most, demand studies apply micro-demand relationships appropriate to individuals to the average quantities, prices, and incomes of groups of individuals. The aggregation of individuals with different incomes facing different prices gives rise to group demand relationships that are more complicated (and more information demanding) than the microrelationships applicable to the data of individuals.[45] Even so, it is commonly believed that the demand equations for individuals constitute a convenient framework for illuminating the group quantity-price-income relationships.[46] The present work has been carried out from this point of view.

The representative-person notion inherent in this ICP application was referred to in the revealed-preference discussion above. Each person in each of the thirty-four ICP countries is assumed to have the same utility function, and to receive an income equal to the per capita consumption of his own country. Faced with the prices of his country for the various goods that could be bought, he spends his country's per capita expenditure on each of the goods. (The terms "country" and "consumer" will be used interchangeably in the following discussion.)

The linear expenditure system parameters have been estimated with the use of ICP data on the four major groupings (food, clothing, shelter, and all other) that were defined above. The quantity units for each of these major groupings are the quantities that could be purchased for US$1 in the United States. The prices in each country for each good, p_{ij}, are then the country's PPP_{ij} for the good. The PPPs for these aggregates are augmented binary Fisher indexes based entirely on relative item prices in each country and in the United States.

A country's quantity of one of the goods, q_{ij}, is given by the ratio of its expenditure on the good to its PPP for the good: $E_{ij} \div PPP_{ij}$. (If $E_{i,Fr} = F20$ and $PPP_{i,Fr} = F5/\$1$, $q_{i,Fr} = F20 \div F5/\$1 = 4$.) Observe that $p_{ij} \cdot q_{ij} = (PPP_{ij}) \cdot (E_{ij}/PPP_{ij}) = E_{ij}$.[47]

---

43. See the development of this relationship in Phlips (1974), pp. 136–37. (The Phlips treatment uses different notation and addresses the slightly different true-cost-of-living–index problem.)

44. In household-budget studies, incomes vary across individuals, but usually all individuals face the same set of prices.

45. This point was made earlier in Chapter 2. In addition to the references given there, see Debreu (1974); Sonnenschein (1972); Mantel (1977); or Wold and Jureen (1953), p. 120.

46. The pragmatic reason given in Pollak and Wales (1969), pp. 611–12, for imposing the consumer-behavior conditions is the justification for the present treatment: the restrictions provide a basis for taking account of all cross-price elasticities in a way that economizes on scarce degrees of freedom.

47. Note that unlike the log-linear demand analysis of the previous section, neither the p's nor the q's are obtained from the Geary-Khamis multilateral calculations embedded in Tables 6-3 and 6-5. This linear expenditure-system analysis is entirely independent of any of the calculations underlying the multilateral work described in Chapter 3, reported on in full in Chapter 6, and summarized in Chapter 1.

Estimation of the System

How the demand equations of 9.15 are made stochastic determines how the β's and γ's are estimated. The forming of the likelihood function, which must be maximized, depends on the way disturbance terms are introduced into the equations. Moreover, the restrictions, if any, that must be complied with as the likelihood function is maximized also depend on the role of the disturbances. First, the stochasticizing will be discussed, and then a complication in the estimation process will be explained.

MAKING THE LINEAR EXPENDITURE SYSTEM STOCHASTIC. There is no set of β's and γ's such that the (q_{ij}, p_{ij}, E_j) will satisfy equation system 9.15 for all thirty-four countries. To allow for missing influences, errors in measurement, possible failure of consumers to maximize their satisfactions precisely, or other possible considerations, it is necessary to introduce stochastic terms into the equations.

Observe that the deterministic version of the linear expenditure system can be expressed in three ways: with expenditure on the good appearing as the left-hand side variable, as in equation 9.15, or alternatively with either quantity or budget share on the left. Equations 9.19 and 9.20 give these other versions:

$$(9.19) \quad q_{ij} = \gamma_i + \beta_i \left[\frac{E_j}{p_{ij}} - \sum_{k=1}^{4} \gamma_k \frac{p_{kj}}{p_{ij}} \right] \quad \begin{array}{l} i=1,\ldots,4; \\ j=1,\ldots,n \end{array}$$

$$(9.20) \quad \frac{p_{ij}q_{ij}}{E_j} = \frac{\gamma_i p_{ij}}{E_j} + \beta_i \left[1 - \sum_{k=1}^{4} \frac{\gamma_k p_{kj}}{E_j} \right]. \quad \begin{array}{l} i=1,\ldots,4; \\ j=1,\ldots,n \end{array}$$

The three versions are entirely equivalent until a stochastic specification is introduced. It is conventionally assumed that the stochastic character of the real world with respect to consumption of food, clothing, shelter, and all other is adequately captured by additive independent normally distributed disturbances.[48] Under this assumption, the differences between the three versions turn on assumptions about homoskedasticity for the disturbance terms in the equations.

Since in the ICP application of the LES the currency units are not the same, the expenditure version is inappropriate for econometric estimation. The Share version, given by equation 9.20 is the preferred form

because the data units are pure numbers and do not rely on any arbitrary scaling.[49] Subsequently, a test for homoskedasticity of the residuals of the Share equations verified that the Share version is the appropriate one to use. To get a reading on robustness of this specification, the parameters were estimated also through the use of the Quantity version, equation 9.19.

RESTRICTIONS IN MAXIMIZING THE LIKELIHOOD FUNCTION. The inequalities $q_i \geqslant \gamma_i$ attached to equation 9.14 are required because, in the region where q does not satisfy the inequalities, either U is not defined or, if defined, the function cannot serve as a well-behaved utility function because one or more of the marginal utilities is negative. However, suppose these considerations are ignored in maximizing the likelihood function to estimate the β's and γ's. What is the consequence of discovering that one or more of the $\hat{\gamma}$'s is greater than some countries' q's? Provided each consumer's total income is sufficient to enable him to purchase the quantity $(\hat{\gamma}_1, \hat{\gamma}_2, \hat{\gamma}_3, \hat{\gamma}_4)$, the minimum necessary bundle, the fact that one or more of the q's is less than its corresponding $\hat{\gamma}$ makes no essential difference. (Recall that part of the motivation for introducing disturbance terms in equation 9.15 was to take account of the possibility that consumers may not maximize their satisfactions precisely. Therefore, the difference between q_{ij} and $\hat{\gamma}_i$ may simply be stochastic.) It should not be inferred that a country does not share the tastes of the others simply because it has a q outside the $q > \gamma$ region.

But something has gone awry if the $\hat{\gamma}$ quantities are not attainable by all of the consumers. In that case the process of maximizing the likelihood function was not carried out properly. For any set of parameter values (β, γ), the likelihood function is valued by a summing of the weighted squared disturbances. Loosely speaking, this can be thought of as summing a set of squared distances, each one being the distance of a consumption point q from the point where the indifference map defined by $\{\beta, \gamma\}$ is tangent to the budget constraint on which q is located. The maximization process consists of searching out, through use of a hill-climbing computational algorithm, the $\{\beta, \gamma\}$ combination for which the sum of squared "distances" is smallest. But consider a case in which, at any stage, the γ's are such that some consumer had insufficient income to purchase the $\hat{\gamma}$ bundles. In such an instance, the tangency point on the consumer's budget constraint used to determine the distance that is then

---

48. An exception is the habit-formation treatment of the disturbance term in Pollak and Wales (1969).

49. S_{ij} itself is units free. $\gamma_i p_{ij}/E_j$ is the proportion of total expenditure in the jth country that must be paid for the minimum quantity, γ_i, of the ith good, so it, too, is units free.

Table 9-6. Estimates of the Parameters of the Linear Expenditure System in Quantity and in Share Form, 1975

Quantity: $q_{ij} = \gamma_i + \beta_i \left(\dfrac{E_j}{p_{ij}} - \sum_{k=1}^{4} \gamma_k \dfrac{p_{kj}}{p_{ij}} \right) + u_{ij}$ $i = 1,\ldots,4$

$j = 1,\ldots,34$

Share: $\dfrac{p_{ij}q_{ij}}{E_j} = \gamma_i \dfrac{p_{ij}}{E_j} + \beta_i \left(1 - \sum_{k=1}^{4} \gamma_k \dfrac{p_{kj}}{E_j} \right) + u_{ij}$ $i = 1,\ldots,4$

$j = 1,\ldots,34$

Parameter[a]	Quantity equation (unconstrained)[b]	Share equation Unconstrained[b]	Share equation Constrained[c]
γ_1	251.5[d]	152.8[d]	133.6
	(55.0)	(19.3)	(7.5)
γ_2	33.6	18.4[d]	12.8[d]
	(17.5)	(7.3)	(3.3)
γ_3	−23.4	40.1	22.2[d]
	(101.2)	(25.4)	(4.9)
γ_4	−84.1	99.5	45.1[d]
	(185.1)	(68.6)	(13.1)
β_1	0.170[d]	0.277[d]	0.275[d]
	(0.014)	(0.021)	(0.021)
β_2	0.071[d]	0.091[d]	0.090[d]
	(0.004)	(0.006)	(0.006)
β_3	0.252[d]	0.215[d]	0.214[d]
	(0.011)	(0.010)	(0.010)
β_4	0.507[d]	0.416[d]	0.421[d]
	(0.014)	(0.019)	(0.019)

Note: Standard errors are presented in parentheses.

a. γ_1, β_1: food.

γ_2, β_2: clothing.

γ_3, β_3: shelter.

γ_4, β_4: all other.

b. Inability of some countries to purchase the estimated minimum consumption bundle $\{\hat{\gamma}_1, \hat{\gamma}_2, \hat{\gamma}_3, \hat{\gamma}_4\}$ ignored.

c. $\hat{\gamma}_i$'s estimated subject to the constraint that all countries are able to purchase the minimum consumption bundle.

d. Significant at the 0.05 level.

squared and added to the other squared distances is a tangency point on the unacceptable part of the utility function. This is not simply a matter of intellectual interest and of no empirical concern. In fact, two countries—Malawi and India—had too little income to buy the $\hat{\gamma}$ bundle.[50] (Two other countries had one or more q's less than corresponding $\hat{\gamma}$'s.)

This problem was handled by imposing the requirement that the $\hat{\gamma}$ bundle be attainable by every country.[51] (In the general case of many countries' not being able to buy $\hat{\gamma}$, imposing this requirement requires application of mathematical programing techniques in addition to the standard nonlinear maximum-likelihood estimation procedure. With only two countries falling short, it was easy to determine that it was Malawi's deficient income that set the binding restriction.

The maximization of the likelihood function then was carried out subject to the restriction that

$$\sum_{i=1}^{4} p_{i,Mal} \gamma_i = E_{Mal}.$$

Results

Table 9-6 gives the LES parameter estimates with their (asymptotic) standard errors for the constrained Share version and, for comparison purposes, the unconstrained Share version and unconstrained Quantity version. The parameters of the constrained and unconstrained Share forms are quite similar. As is to be expected, the constrained $\hat{\gamma}$'s are smaller; the $\hat{\beta}$'s, it turns out, are virtually the same for the two forms. However, while the unconstrained Quantity form yields rather similar $\hat{\beta}$ estimates, the $\hat{\gamma}$'s are distinctly dif-

50. It is to be expected that any problems in this area would almost certainly involve the poorest countries. The expenditure shortfalls of Malawi and India preventing them from purchasing the $\hat{\gamma}$ bundle were respectively, 25 percent and 14 percent.

51. The linear-expenditure system is defective in being based on a utility function that is not defined for every commodity bundle. The procedure adopted here consists of requiring that the γ's be such that the utility function be defined for all relevant bundles.

(Note that the utility function need not be defined for all thirty-four selected bundles.) Two alternative approaches were possible: (1) throw out any observations involving budget constraints that do not permit the purchase of the γ bundle; and (2) add another component to the utility function that provides well-behaved indifference curves in the regions left uncovered by the LES utility function. See McElroy (1975).

Table 9-7. Estimates of Own-price and Consumption Expenditure Elasticities: Linear Expenditure System (Quantity and Share Forms) Compared with Log-linear Form, 1975

Elasticities[a]	Quantity (unconstrained)	Share Unconstrained[c]	Share Constrained[d]	Log-linear[e]
Price (p)[b]				
η_{Food}	−0.60	−0.81	−0.83	−0.02
	(0.08)	(0.03)	(0.02)	(0.23)
$\eta_{Clothing}$	−0.77	−0.88	−0.92	−0.77[g]
	(0.12)	(0.05)	(0.02)	(0.22)
$\eta_{Shelter}$	−1.04	−0.92	−0.96	−0.55[g]
	(0.17)	(0.05)	(0.01)	(0.18)
$\eta_{All\ other}$	−1.05	−0.93	−0.99	−0.15
	(0.10)	(0.05)	(0.00)[h]	(0.19)
Consumption expenditure (E)[f]				
η_{Food}	0.38	0.73	0.72	0.69[g]
	(0.06)	(0.04)	(0.04)	(0.04)
$\eta_{Clothing}$	0.75	1.09	1.07	1.04[g]
	(0.14)	(0.06)	(0.06)	(0.06)
$\eta_{Shelter}$	1.59	1.19	1.17	1.28[g]
	(0.37)	(0.04)	(0.04)	(0.04)
$\eta_{All\ other}$	1.70	1.18	1.27	1.19[g]
	(0.28)	(0.05)	(0.02)	(0.05)

Note: Standard errors are presented in parentheses.

a. The price elasticities have been evaluated at the average of the estimated q's of the thirty-four countries. The consumption expenditure elasticities have been evaluated at the average of the estimated shares of the thirty-four countries.

b. $\eta_i^p = -1 + \dfrac{\hat{\gamma}_i(1-\hat{\beta}_i)}{\bar{q}_i}$ where $\bar{q}_i = \sum\limits_{j=1}^{34} \hat{q}_{ij}/34$.

c. Inability of some countries to purchase the estimated minimum consumption bundle $\{\hat{\gamma}_1, \hat{\gamma}_2, \hat{\gamma}_3, \hat{\gamma}_4\}$ is ignored.

d. $\hat{\gamma}$'s estimated subject to the constraint that all countries are able to purchase the minimum consumption bundle.

e. Source: Table 9-4, OLS elasticities.

f. $\eta_i^E = \hat{\beta}_i/\bar{S}_i$ where $\bar{S}_i = \sum\limits_{j=1}^{34} \hat{S}_{ij}/34$.

g. Significant at the 0.05 level.

h. Less than 0.01.

ferent. The standard errors of the $\hat{\beta}_i$'s are small enough to make the $\hat{\beta}$'s significantly different from zero in every case. In the constrained Share form, all of the $\hat{\gamma}$'s are also significant.[52]

DEMAND ELASTICITIES. The substantive interest in these parameter estimates stems from the fact that they determine the price and income elasticities for the four categories. (As will be seen, they also are instrumental in providing an LES version of real per capita consumption comparisons across countries.) Table 9-7 presents the price and expenditure elasticity estimates obtained from the parameter estimates in Table 9-6. As would be expected from the similarity of their parameter estimates, the unconstrained and constrained Share forms exhibit very similar elasticities. The price elasticities derived from the unconstrained Quantity form, while different in magnitude, are in the same rank order as those of the Share forms.[53]

52. Non-zero γ's mean that the utility function is not homothetic.

53. The LES requires that negative γ's lead to price inelasticity and positive γ's lead to price elasticity. The price elasticity entries in Table 9-7 of course reflect this.

Perhaps the most remarkable finding displayed in the table is the very small differences between the expenditure elasticities of the Share forms and those obtained from the log-linear demand analysis of the last section. (Compare the second and third columns with the fourth one.) The price elasticities, however, are quite different. Perhaps this is just one more example of the lack of robustness of the price-elasticity estimates.

LES ESTIMATES OF COMPARATIVE LEVELS OF REAL PER CAPITA CONSUMPTION. With the use of equation 9.18, estimates of relative real per capita consumption have been computed to get a second reading, based on a different methodology from that produced by the procedures of Chapter 3. (I_j in equation 9.18 gives the factor by which the jth country consumption expenditure must be multiplied to enable the representative consumer in j to enjoy the level of satisfaction of the representative consumer in the United States. The relative per capita consumption would then be the reciprocal of 100 I_j.) Columns 4 and 5 of Table 9-8 contain real per capita consumption estimates based on

Table 9-8. Comparison of Estimates of Real per Capita Consumption Expenditures: Exchange-rate–Converted, Geary-Khamis, and Linear Expenditure System, 1975
(U.S. = 100)

Country	Exchange-rate converted (1)	Geary-Khamis Supercountry weights (2)	Geary-Khamis Equal weights (3)	Linear expenditure system Share unconstrained (4)	Linear expenditure system Share constrained (5)
Group I[a]					
Malawi	2.13	5.52	4.76	4.48	4.49
Kenya	3.57	7.32	6.09	6.66	6.67
India	2.02	6.77	5.86	6.49	6.51
Pakistan	2.96	8.86	7.81	8.29	8.31
Sri Lanka	3.05	10.20	8.75	10.48	10.50
Zambia	5.73	8.37	7.25	7.45	7.46
Thailand	4.91	14.00	12.79	11.51	11.52
Philippines	5.02	13.98	12.14	14.06	14.09
Group II					
Korea	8.04	20.36	18.69	17.91	17.95
Malaysia	9.68	19.01	17.14	18.31	18.33
Colombia	8.64	25.38	22.21	22.36	22.38
Jamaica	19.50	25.78	23.92	26.66	26.70
Syria	9.27	25.99	23.66	23.19	23.22
Brazil	15.83	24.46	22.21	22.80	22.82
Group III					
Romania	18.31	28.80	26.00	27.85	27.89
Mexico	20.93	36.35	33.66	37.03	37.04
Yugoslavia	19.07	33.95	31.78	34.64	34.68
Iran	13.93	26.99	24.64	25.11	25.12
Uruguay	20.28	44.82	39.92	36.82	36.83
Ireland	38.15	46.13	43.70	44.36	44.38
Group IV					
Hungary	24.99	46.41	42.81	44.01	44.09
Poland	28.64	43.23	39.63	40.07	40.12
Italy	45.95	52.89	49.05	53.16	53.19
Spain	41.67	60.21	57.70	58.86	58.90
Group V					
U.K.	54.50	63.68	61.03	62.65	62.70
Japan	53.62	58.69	55.34	55.90	55.96
Austria	61.97	69.09	72.01	74.95	74.95
Netherlands	74.33	68.18	66.11	68.36	68.35
Belgium	80.02	74.54	71.90	73.96	73.99
France	81.09	75.15	71.58	74.34	74.37
Luxembourg	79.11	78.94	71.69	77.66	77.71
Denmark	94.73	77.99	75.48	74.15	74.16
Germany	85.05	75.10	72.98	74.97	74.98
Group VI					
U.S.	100.00	100.00	100.00	100.00	100.00

a. Groups and rank order defined on the basis of ICP's Geary-Khamis estimates of per capita GDP.
Sources: Column 1: ([Table 6-1, row 1]$_j$ /exchange rate$_j$) ÷ (Table 6-1, row 1)$_{US}$.
Column 2: Table 6-4, row 1.
Column 3: special calculation for this table.

the unconstrained and constrained Share forms of LES.[54] As in the case of price and expenditure elasticities, the unconstrained and constrained versions give almost identical results. When they each are compared with the Phase III ICP per capita consumption esti-

mates in column 2 (reported from Chapters 1 and 6), differences as large as 19 percent show up in the least affluent group of countries. The largest difference in Group II is 12 percent, but, except for Uruguay, the differences are all much smaller in the remaining groups.

The estimates given in column 3 are also based on the Geary-Khamis method described in Chapter 3, but only consumption data were used—instead of all of GDP as in the case of column 2—and equal weights

54. In Table 9-8 the thirty-four ICP countries are arranged in the six income groups that were defined in Chapter 6 on the basis of ICP's estimates of per capita real GDP.

were substituted for supercountry weights.[55] One would expect that since the data and the weighting underlying column 3 and the LES columns were identical, the LES estimates would be closer to the entries in column 3 than to those in column 2. This is in fact so in most of the thirty-four cases. (If column 5 is taken as the reference, the root-mean-square error, expressed in percentages, is 6.5 percent for column 3 and 8.8 percent for column 2. Only five of the column 3 entries differ from the corresponding column 5 entries by more than 10 percent and only two differ by more than 11 percent.)

In passing, two comments should be made that add perspective to the LES results detailed in Table 9-8. First, the comparisons of columns 1, 2, and 3 are base-country invariant, but in the deep sense of that term those of columns 4 and 5 are not. The latter all refer to how much the expenditures of the various countries would have to be increased in order to raise the level of satisfaction of the individual representative consumers to that of the representative U.S. consumer. However, turning around the question underlying the comparison yields different answers. How much can be taken from a U.S. representative consumer and still leave him with the same level of satisfaction as the *j*th country representative consumer? This is not answered in the LES approach by computations that lead to the same answers as given in the LES columns. The answers would be the same only if the utility function were homothetic, a possibility denied by the significance of the $\hat{\gamma}$'s given in Table 9-6. If one were to take seriously the LES specification of consumption behavior in this interspatial context, this observation would put on shaky ground the insistence running through the earlier chapters on base-country invariance. It would appear that the relevant comparison question has two distinct answers, depending on how the question is framed, and not just one. However, close checking has revealed that the observed difference between the compensating and equivalent variations in fact are quite small: in 88 percent of the cases (all those not involving countries with *q*'s less than *γ*'s) the difference between the two variations is smaller than 5 percent, 96 percent are smaller than 10 percent, and none are greater than 15 percent. This indicates that no significant distortion results from imposing the base-country–invariance criterion.

The second comment is that the LES comparisons

in columns 4 and 5 are based on estimated quantities for each country as derived from LES parameter estimates rather than the actual country quantities consumed. It is the latter on which the Geary-Khamis comparisons are based. In some cases this can make a difference of a few percentages. Note that, here and above, what is referred to is percentage differences, not percentage points.

It should be no surprise that the differences between LES and Geary-Khamis estimates, notable as they are for some poor countries, are trivial in comparison with differences between exchange-rate–converted and Geary-Khamis estimates. Column 1 set along columns 2 and 3 make this easy to verify. Added perspective on these various comparisons can be gotten by looking back at Table 3-6, where Geary-Khamis estimates for real per capita GDP were compared with estimates obtained through use of several other multilateral but not basically stochastic methods. The differences between LES and Geary-Khamis for consumption are of the orders of magnitude appearing in that table.

LES CONCLUSIONS. All in all, the LES analysis is consistent with the more ad hoc empirical work that preceded it in this chapter. The conclusions with respect to expenditure elasticities appear to be robust to the particular way in which the demand analysis is carried out. The comparisons of the real per capita consumption levels of the various ICP countries, obtained through use of the LES theoretically based approach, generally confirm the results obtained through use of the ICP multilateral methods in Chapters 3 and 6. With respect to the proposition "Tastes are the same. . . ," since it was a maintained hypothesis in computing LES estimates, the analysis can barely help the reader to judge its plausibility.[56] Only LES results that were patently wrong as a description of the thirty-four countries—that is, positive price elasticities, the food-expenditure elasticity much greater than unity, and so forth—would make an adverse judgment possible. Commonality of tastes passes this (weak) test. The need to constrain the Share form to ensure that Malawi and Kenya could enjoy the minimum bundle

55. In the maximum-likelihood estimation process, the LES Shares form assigns equal weight to each country observation. The corresponding weighting process in Geary-Khamis requires that each country's total consumption be scaled so that all thirty-four are equal.

56. It would have been desirable to perform the equivalent of the Asia-versus-Europe analysis of covariance on the LES approach. The obvious statistic, the likelihood ratio, cannot be relied upon to have a distribution close to its asymptotic form, however. This can be seen by comparing the Asia-versus-Europe results for the individual summary and detailed-category log-linear regressions based upon the analysis of covariance F tests with the results based upon corresponding likelihood-ratio statistics. The likelihood-ratio test rejected the null hypothesis of no difference between Asia and Europe in many of the cases where the F test called for acceptance. The χ^2 approximation for $(-2 \ln \lambda)$ has too thin a tail.

might cast doubt on the applicability of LES, but the fact that the constraint makes so little difference can be taken as a positive sign that the LES approach captured the essence of the data.

Summary

Unmistakably, the differences in quantities of goods and services consumed by representative people in diverse parts of the world can be explained in large part by differences in their incomes and the prices they face. The similarity and log-linear regressions and the more complicated LES analysis make this clear. This leads to the conclusion that for most practical purposes the proposition "Tastes are the same. . . ." is supported. The question of the commonality of tastes in the more basic sense of identical preference functions is left more equivocal. However, the revealed-preference analysis and Asia-versus-Europe comparisons suggest that at least at a high level of aggregation the generalization is not inconsistent with the observed data.

The last part of the chapter confirms the general robustness of the comparisons appearing in Chapter 1 to differences in methodology of estimation. The stochastic multilateral approach to international comparisons embodied in the LES differs from the Geary-Khamis multilateral approach, but still produces remarkably similar estimates.

References

The word "processed" describes works that are reproduced from typescript by mimeograph, xerography, or similar means; such works may not be cataloged or commonly available through libraries, or may be subject to restricted circulation.

Aiken, L. H., and others. 1970. The contribution of specialists to the delivery of primary care: A new perspective. *New England journal of medicine* 300(24).

Allen, R. G. D. 1975. *Index Numbers in Theory and Practice*. Chicago: Aldine Publishing Co.

Alton, T. P. 1970. Economic structure and growth in Eastern Europe. In *Economic Developments in Countries of Eastern Europe*. U.S. Congress, Joint Economic Committee. Washington, D.C.

————. 1977. Comparative structure and growth of economic activity in Eastern Europe. In *East European Economies Post-Helsinki*. U.S. Congress, Joint Economic Committee. Washington, D.C.

————, and others. 1979. Economic growth in Eastern Europe, 1965–78. Occasional Paper no. 54. Research Project in East Central Europe. New York: I. W. International Financial Research, Inc.

Anderson, C. Arnold. 1969. The international comparative study of achievement in mathematics. In Max A. Eckstein and Harold J. Noah, eds. *Scientific Investigations in Comparative Education*. New York: Macmillan.

Balassa, Bela. 1964. The purchasing power parity doctrine: A reappraisal. *Journal of political economy*. December.

Balassa, Bela, and associates. 1971. *The Structure of Protection in Developing Countries*. Baltimore, Md.: Johns Hopkins University Press.

Bancroft, T. A., and R. L. Anderson. 1952. *Statistical Theory in Research*. New York: McGraw-Hill.

Box, G. E. P. 1953. Non-normality and tests on variances. *Biometrika* 40.

Brady, D., and A. Hurwitz. 1957. Measuring comparative purchasing power. In *Problems in the International Comparison of Economic Accounts*. Studies in Income and Wealth. Vol. 20. Princeton, N.J.: Princeton University Press.

Central Statistical Office of Austria and Central Statistical Office of Poland. 1980. *Comparison of Prices and Levels of Gross Domestic Expenditure between Austria and Poland, 1975 and 1978*. Vienna and Warsaw.

Chenery, Hollis, and others. 1974. *Redistribution with Growth*. London: Oxford University Press.

Chenery, Hollis, and others. 1979. *Structural Change and Development Policy*. New York: Oxford University Press.

Chenery, Hollis, and Moises Syrquin. 1975. *Patterns of Development, 1950–70*. Oxford: Oxford University Press.

Christensen, L. R., D. Cummings, and D. W. Jorgenson. 1980. Economic growth, 1947–1973: An international comparison. In J. W. Kendrick and B. Vaccara, eds. *New Developments in Productivity Measurement and Analysis*. Chicago: University of Chicago Press.

Clague, C. 1980. Short-cut methods of estimating real income: An interim report. Report prepared for the World Bank. Washington, D.C. Processed.

Clark, Colin, 1940. *The Conditions of Economic Progress*. 2d ed, 1951. London: Macmillan.

————. 1979. Productivity in the service industries. In C. H. Hanamantha Rao and P. C. Joshi, eds. *Reflections of Economic Development and Social Change: Essays in Honor of Professor V. K. R. V. Rao*. New Delhi: Allied Publishers Private Ltd.

Cochrane, Susan H., Donald O'Hara, and Joanne Leslie. 1980. *The Effects of Education on Health*. World Bank Staff Working Paper no. 405. Washington, D.C.

Cohn, E. 1972. *The Economics of Education*. Lexington, Mass.: D. C. Heath.

Conference of European Statisticians. 1968. *Comparison of Levels of Consumption in Austria and Poland*. Document WG. 22/19. New York: United Nations. Processed.

Cremeans, John E. 1979. Consumer services provided by business through advertising-supported media in the U.S. 16th General Conference of the International Association for Research in Income and Wealth. Processed.

Debreu, G. 1974. Excess demand functions. *Journal of mathematical economics* 1(1).

DeAmico, Gerald, and Robert S. Ingle. 1969. The effect of physical conditions of the test room in standardized achievement test scores. *Journal of educational measurement* 6(4).

Denison, E. F. 1957. Theoretical aspects of quality change, capital consumption, and net capital formation. In *Problems of Capital Formation*. Studies in Income and Wealth. Vol. 19. Princeton, N.J.: Princeton University Press.

———. 1965. Improved allocation of labor as a source of higher European growth rate. In M. J. Brennan, ed. *Patterns of Market Behavior*. Providence, R.I.: Brown University Press.

———. 1967. *Why Growth Rates Differ*. Washington, D.C.: Brookings Institution.

Doan, Jean Bui-Dang-Na. 1977. Specialization of physicians: Levels and trends in some industrialized countries. *World health statistics report* 30(3). Geneva: World Health Organization.

Drechsler, L. 1966. *Ertekbeni Mutatoszamok Nemzetkozi Osszehasonlitasanak Modszertag*. Budapest: Kozgazdasagi es Jogi Konyvkiado.

———. 1975. Weighting of index numbers in multilateral international comparisons. *Review of income and wealth*. March.

Duncan, Beverly, and Wilbert E. Moore, eds. 1968. *Indicators of Social Change, Concepts and Measurements*. New York: Russell Sage.

Dyckman, Zachary Y. 1978. *Physicians: A Study of Physicians' Fees*. Washington, D.C.: Council on Wage and Price Stability.

Educational Commission for Foreign Medical Graduates. 1977. *Annual Report 1975*. Philadelphia.

European Coal and Steel Community. 1960. Revenue réels CECA, 1954–58. *Statistique Sociales* (3).

European Communities Statistical Office. 1977. Comparison in real values of the aggregates of ESA, 1975. Luxembourg.

———. 1979. *Price and Volume Measures for Non-Market Services*. Luxembourg.

Eurostat news. 1978. Aggregation methods in international comparisons of real product. Special number.

Feldsteen, Paul J. 1974. A review of productivity in dentistry. In John Rafferty, ed. *Health, Manpower and Productivity*. Lexington, Mass.: D. C. Heath.

Fisher, I. 1922. *The Making of Index Numbers*. Boston, Mass.: Houghton Mifflin.

Fisher, F. M., and K. Shell, 1972. *The Economic Theory of Price Indexes*. New York: Academic Press.

Frisch, R. 1936. Annual survey of general economic theory: The problem of index numbers. *Econometrica* 4.

Fuchs, V. 1968. *The Service Economy*. New York: National Bureau of Economic Research.

———. 1979. The economics of health in a post-industrial society. *Public interest*. Summer.

Geary, R. C. 1950–51. A note on "A constant utility index of the cost of living." *Review of economic studies* 18.

———. 1958. A note on comparisons of exchange rates and purchasing power between countries. *Journal of the Royal Statistical Society* 121, pt. 1.

General Agreement on Tariffs and Trade (GATT). 1976. *International Trade 1975/76*. Geneva.

Gilbert, M., and associates. 1958. *Comparative National Products and Price Levels*. Paris: Organisation for European Economic Co-operation.

Gilbert, M., and Kravis, I. B. 1954. *An International Comparison of National Products and the Purchasing Power of Currencies: A Study of the United States, the United Kingdom, France, Germany, and Italy*. Paris: Organisation for European Economic Co-operation.

Gilliand, Pierre, and René Galland. 1977. Outline on international comparison of public health. Based on data collected by the World Health Organization. *World Health Statistics Report* 30(3).

Greenslade, R. V. 1976. The real gross national product of the U.S.S.R., 1950–75. In *Soviet Economy in a New Perspective*. U.S. Congress, Joint Economic Committee. Washington, D.C.

Griliches, Z., ed. 1971. *Price Indexes and Quality Change*. Cambridge, Mass.: Harvard University Press.

Hanushek, E. 1979. Conceptual issues in estimation of educational production functions. *Journal of human resources*. Summer.

Harrod, R. F. 1947. *International Economics*. New York and London: Pitman.

Hays, W. L., and R. L. Winkler. 1971. *Statistics Probability Inference and Decision*. New York: Holt, Rinehart, and Winston.

Henderson, J. M., and R. E. Quandt. 1971. *Microeconomics Theory: A Mathematical Approach*. 2d ed. New York: McGraw-Hill.

Heston, Alan W. 1973. A comparison of some short-cut methods of estimating real product per capita. *Review of income and wealth*. March.

Hicks, J. R. 1946. *Value and Capital*. 2d ed. London: Oxford University Press.

Hill, P. 1977. On goods and services. *Review of income and wealth*. December.

———. 1981. Multilateral measurements of purchasing power and real GDP. Report prepared for the European Communities Statistical Office and the Economic Commission for Europe. Luxembourg. Processed.

Houthakker, H. S. 1950. Revealed preference and the utility function. *Economica*. May.

Houthakker, H. S., and L. D. Taylor. 1966. *Consumer Demand in the United States*. Cambridge, Mass.: Harvard University Press.

Hsiso, W. C., and W. E. Stason. 1979. Toward developing a relative value scale for medical and surgical services. *Health care financing review*. Fall.

Hungarian Central Statistical Office. 1980. *Measures for Improving the Quality of International Comparisons of Real Product and Purchasing-Power Parities*. Working paper no. 5. Geneva: Economic Commission for Europe.

International Labour Organisation. *Yearbook of Labour Statistics*. Various years.

———. 1969. *International Standard Classification of Occupations*. Rev. 1968. Geneva.

International Monetary Fund (IMF). 1977. *International Financial Statistics*. February.

———. 1978. *International Financial Statistics*. May.

Isenman, Paul. 1980. Inter-country comparisons of "real" (PPP) incomes: Revised estimates and unresolved questions. *World development* 8.

Japan, Administrative Management Agency. 1977. Report of the data for ICP Phase III, 1975. Tokyo. Processed.

Johnson, S. C. 1967. Hierarchical clustering schemes. *Psychometrika*. 32(3).

Johnson, Samuel. 1775. *The Works of Samuel Johnson*. Arthur Murphy, ed. London: Jones & Co., 1825. Vol. 2, *A Journey to the Western Islands of Scotland*.

Johnston, J. 1972. *Econometric Methods*. New York: McGraw-Hill.

Jorgenson, D. W., and Z. Griliches, 1967. The explanation of productivity change. *Review of economic studies* 34 (July).

Kawakatsu, S. 1970. International average prices and comparisons of national aggregate production of agriculture. *Review of income and wealth*. June.

Kendrick, J. W. 1973. *Postwar Productivity Trends in the U.S., 1948–1964*. New York: National Bureau of Economic Research.

Keynes, J. M. 1930. *A Treatise on Money*. Vol. 1. London: Macmillan.

Khamis, S. H. 1967. Some problems relating to international comparability and fluctuating of production volume indicators. *Bulletin of International Statistical Institute* 42.

———. 1970. Properties and conditions for the existence of a new type of index number. *Sankhya* 32.

———. 1972. A new system of index numbers for national and international purposes. *Journal of the Royal Statistical Society* 135(1).

Klein, L. R., and H. Rubin. 1947–48. A constant-utility index of the cost of living. *Review of economic studies* 15(38).

Kohn, Robert, and Kerr L. White, eds. 1976. *Health Care: An International Study*. Report of the World Health Organization, International Collaboration Study of Medical Care Utilization. Oxford: Oxford University Press.

Kravis, Irving B. 1956. "Availability" and other influences on the commodity composition of trade. *The journal of political economy* 64(2).

———. 1958. International and intertemporal comparisons in the structure of consumption. In L. Clark, ed. *Consumer Behavior*. New York: Harper and Harper.

———. 1976. A survey of international comparisons of productivity. *Economic journal* 86(March).

Kravis, Irving B., Zoltan Kenessey, Alan W. Heston, and Robert Summers. 1975. *A System of International Comparisons of Gross Product and Purchasing Power*. Baltimore, Md.: Johns Hopkins University Press.

Kravis, Irving B., Alan W. Heston, and Robert Summers. 1978a. *International Comparisons of Real Product and Purchasing Power*. Baltimore, Md.: Johns Hopkins University Press.

———. 1978b. Real GDP per capita for more than one hundred countries. *Economic journal* 88(June).

———. 1978c. Aggregation methods in international comparisons of real products. *Eurostat news*. Special number.

———. 1979. The role of regionalization in a world-wide system of international product comparison. Paper presented at the Conference on Purchasing Power and Real Product of Programa de Estudios Conjuntos Sobre la Integración Económica Latinamericana (ECIEL). Rio de Janeiro.

———. 1982, forthcoming. The share of services in economic growth. In B. G. Hickman and F. G. Adams, eds. *Global Econometrics: Essays in Honor of Lawrence R. Klein*. Cambridge, Mass.: M.I.T. Press.

Krzeczkowska, Eugenia. 1967. On the international comparison of consumption level carried out by the Polish Central Statistical Office. *Review of income and wealth*. December.

———. 1978. Some problems of international comparisons. Oeconomica Polona, *Journal of the economic committee of the Polish Academy of Sciences and of the Polish Economic Society* (2). Translation of an article published in *Ekonomista* (5), 1977.

Kurabayashi, Y. 1971. The impact of the terms of trade on a system of national accounts: An attempted synthesis. *Review of income and wealth*. September.

Kuznets, S. 1972. Problems in comparing recent growth rated for developed and less developed countries. *Economic development and cultural change*. January.

Levin, Henry M. 1976. Concepts of efficiency and educational production. In J. T. Froomkin, D. T. Jamison, and R. Radnor, eds. *Education as an Industry*. Cambridge, Mass.: Ballinger.

Little, I., T. Scitovsky, and M. Scott. 1970. *Industry and Trade in Some Developing Countries*. London: Oxford University Press.

Lluch, Constantino, Alan A. Powell, and Ross A. Williams. 1977. *Patterns in Household Demand and Saving*. New York: Oxford University Press.

Maddala, G. S. 1977. *Econometrics*. New York: McGraw-Hill.

Mantel. R. 1977. Implications of microeconomic theory for community excess demand functions. In M. Intriligator, ed. *Frontiers of Quantitative Economics*, vol. IIIA.

Marris, R. 1980. The sensitivity of real product estimation to assumptions about services output. Draft staff working paper. World Bank, Washington, D.C. Processed.

McElroy, M. B. 1975. A spliced CES expenditure system. *International economic review* 16(3).

Morris, Morris David. 1979. *Measuring the Condition of the*

World's Poor: The Physical Quality of Life Index. Pergamon Policy Studies no. 42. Washington, D.C.: Overseas Development Council.

Musgrave, R. 1969. Provision for social goods. In J. Margolis and H. Guitton, eds. *Public Economics*. London: Macmillan.

Orlando, Frank. 1979. A theoretical and empirical analysis of index number formulas for multilateral purchasing power and real product comparisons. ECIEL Conference on Purchasing Power and Real Product Comparisons for Latin America, Rio de Janeiro.

Paige, D., and G. Bombach. 1959. *A Comparison of National Output and Productivity of the United Kingdom and the United States*. Paris: Organization for European Economic Cooperation.

Paretti, V., H. Krijnse Locker, and Ph. Goybet. 1974. Comparison réelle du produit intérieur brut des pays de la Communauté Européenne: Parités de prix et rapports de volume, 1970. *Analyse et previson* 17(16).

Phelps-Brown, Henry. 1977. *The Inequality of Pay*. Oxford: Oxford University Press.

Phlips, L. 1974. *Applied Consumption Analysis*. Amsterdam: North-Holland.

Pollak, R. A., and T. J. Wales, 1969. Estimation of the linear expenditure system. *Econometrica* 37(4). October

Postlethwaite, Neville T. 1973. A résumé of the surveys of the evaluation of educational achievement. Paris: Organisation for Economic Co-operation and Development (OECD). Processed.

Rao, D. S. Prasada. 1972. Contributions to methodology of construction of consistent index numbers. Ph.D. dissertation. Indian Statistical Institute, Calcutta.

Relman, Arnold S. 1980. Intensive care units: Who needs them? *New England journal of medicine*. April 24.

Ricardo, R. 1911. *The Principles of Political Economy and Taxation*. London: J. M. Dent.

Ruggles, R. 1967. Price indexes and international price comparisons. *Ten Economic Studies in the Tradition of Irving Fisher*. New York: John Wiley.

Russell, Louise B. 1979. *Technology in Hospitals*. Washington, D.C.: Brookings Institution.

Salazar-Carillo, J. 1973. Price, purchasing power, and real product comparisons in Latin America. *Review of income and wealth* Ser. 19(1). March.

———. 1978. *Prices and Purchasing Power Parities in Latin America, 1960–1972*. An ECIEL Study. Washington, D.C.: Organization of American States.

Samuelson, P. A. 1947–48. Some implications of linearity. *Review of economic studies* 15(38).

———. 1948. *The Foundations of Economic Analysis*. Cambridge, Mass.: Harvard University Press.

———. 1969. Pure theory of public expenditure and taxation. In J. Margolis and H. Guitton, eds. *Public Economics*. London: Macmillan.

Sonnenschein, H. 1972. Market excess demand functions. *Econometrica* 40(3). May.

———. 1973. Do Walras' identity and continuity characterize the case of community excess demand functions? *Journal of economic theory* 6.

Stone, J. R. N. 1954. Linear expenditure systems and demand analysis: An application to the pattern of British demand. *Economic journal* 64(September).

Summers, Anita A., and Barbara L. Wolfe. 1977. Do schools make a difference? *American economic review* 67(4). September.

Summers, Robert, Irving B. Kravis, and Alan W. Heston. 1980. International comparison of real product and its composition: 1950–77. *Review of income and wealth*. March.

———. 1981. Inequality among nations: 1950 and 1975. In P. Bairoch and M. Levy-Leboyer, eds. *Disparities in Economic Development since the Industrial Revolution*. London: Macmillan.

Summers, Robert. 1973. International comparisons with incomplete data. *Review of income and wealth*. March.

Survey of Current Business 49(May 1969, pt. 3). Some major issues in productivity analysis: An examination of estimates by Jorgenson and Griliches.

——— 52(May 1972, pt. 2). Issues in growth accounting: A reply to Edward F. Denison; and Final comments.

United Nations. 1954. *Report on International Definition and Measurement of Standards and Levels of Living*. New York.

U.N. Economic Commission for Latin America. 1967. The measurement of Latin American real income in U.S. dollars. *Economic Bulletin for Latin America 12* (October).

U.N. Economic Commission for Europe. 1980. *Economic Bulletin for Europe* 31(2), New York: United Nations.

U.N. Statistical Commission. 1979. Twentieth session. *Progress Report on Public Sector Statistics*. New York: United Nations.

U.N. Statistical Office. 1968a. *International Standard Industrial Classification of All Economic Activities*. Statistical papers, series M, No. 4, rev. 2. New York.

———. 1968b. *A System of National Accounts, Studies in Methods*. Series F, No. 2, rev. 3. New York.

———. 1976. *Yearbook of National Accounts 1976*. Vol. 2. New York.

———. 1980a. Treatment of services provided or priced by government in international product comparisons. Expert Group meeting, Bellagio, Italy, December 6–10.

———. 1980b. *Compendium of Housing Statistics, 1955–77*. New York: Department of International Economic and Social Affairs.

U.S. Congress, Joint Economic Committee. 1972. *Measuring and Enhancing Productivity in the Federal Sector*. Washington, D.C.: Government Printing Office.

Van Yzeren, J. 1946. Three methods of comparing the purchasing power of currencies. Netherlands Central Bureau of Statistics, *Statistical Studies*. December.

Varian, H. R. 1980. The new non-parametric approach to demand analysis. C-22. March (rev. July 1980). University of Michigan. Processed.

Viner, J. 1937. *Studies in the Theory of International Trade.* New York: Harper & Brothers.

Walsh, Correa M. 1910. *The Measurement of General Exchange Values.* New York: Macmillan.

Wells, L. T. 1969. Test of a product cycle model of international trade: U.S. exports of consumer durables. *Quarterly journal of economics.* February.

Wold, H., and L. Jureen. 1953. *Demand Analysis.* New York: John Wiley.

World Bank. 1977. *World Bank Atlas.* Washington, D.C.

Zellner, A. 1962. An efficient method of estimating seemingly unrelated regressions and tests for aggregation bias. *Journal of the American Statistical Association* 57. June.

Glossary

Additivity: Used in the Phase I and Phase II reports in the sense that **matrix consistency** is used in this report. "Full" additivity is used here to denote consistency between (1) the sum of the components of GDP, each component being estimated in a separate aggregation procedure; and (2) GDP obtained by applying the aggregation procedure to all categories at once.

Augmented price tableau: A price tableau in which the missing prices have been filled in by estimating each from a CPD equation.

Base-country invariance: The index-number property that involves the symmetrical treatment of all countries, with the result that the relative index-number standings of the countries are not affected by the choice of the reference (numéraire) country.

Binary comparison: A price or quantity comparison between two countries that draws upon data only for those two countries, though augmented binary comparisons include some prices influenced by other countries.

Augmented binary comparison: Includes prices drawn from an augmented price tableau in cases in which one country has priced an item and the other has not.

Bridge-country binary comparison: A price or quantity comparison between a pair of countries derived from the comparison of each country with a third country. For example, given $I_{j/k}$ and $I_{l/k}$, the bridge-country method of obtaining $I_{j/l}$ is to divide $I_{j/k}$ by $I_{l/k}$ where I is a price or quantity index and j, k, and l are countries.

Original-country binary comparison: A price or quantity comparison between countries based on the data of the two countries, possibly augmented by prices from an augmented price tableau. (In contrast to bridge-country binary comparisons.)

CEP (consumption expenditures of the population): The ICP concept of "consumption" that includes both household expenditures and expenditures of government on such categories as health and education (see Table 2-1).

Characteristicity: The property whereby the sample of prices or quantities and the weights used in an international comparison conform closely to a representative sample of items and to the weights of each of the countries included in the comparison.

Circularity or transitivity: The property of indexes when the price or quantity relationship among any two or three countries is the same, whether derived from an original-country comparison between them or from the comparison of each country with any third country. In the case of three countries, where I is a price or quantity index and j, k, and l are countries, the circularity test is satisfied if $I_{jk} = I_{jl} \div I_{kl}$. When this test is satisfied, there is a unique cardinal scaling of countries with respect to relative quantities and prices.

Country-product-dummy (CPD) method: A generalized bridge-country method in which regression analysis is used to obtain transitive price comparisons for each detailed category. The basic data for a given category consist of all the prices available for the various specifications for the entire collection of countries. The prices are regressed against two sets of dummy variables: one set contains a dummy for each specification; the second set, a dummy for each country other than the numéraire country. The transitive price comparisons are derived from the coefficients of the country dummies (see Chapter 3).

> **Filler:** A weighted CPD method in which the weights are the products of (1) the importance of each cell in the column in which it falls (the percentage of the country's expenditure); and (2) the importance of the cell in the row in which it falls (the percentage of the total quantity of the category in the thirty-four countries). The double-weighted CPD is used as a hole-filling procedure to obtain PPPs for categories for which no price comparisons were made. The CPD method is applied in this case to the matrix of PPPs in which the columns represent countries and the rows detailed categories.
> **One-stage (universal) CPD:** A CPD calculation in which all countries are included. Regionalization is omitted.
> **Two-stage CPD:** A first-stage CPD regression is applied to each region to obtain PPPs for the countries of the region relative to the regional numéraire currency. A second-stage CPD regression is then used to link the regions (or the countries in different regions) so that the PPP for each country can be expressed relative to the world numéraire. In generating the final indexes of this report, the first-stage CPD regression was used to fill in the missing prices in each regional price tableau, and the second-stage CPD regression was applied to all the countries. The country entries in the second stage include the full set of the prices for all the items priced by at least two countries in the region.

Country-reversal test: This test is satisfied if, when country j is taken as the base country, the price or quantity index for countries j and k is the reciprocal of the index when country k is the base country. For example, $I_{j/k} \cdot I_{k/j} = 1$, where I is a price or quantity index.

Detailed categories: The subdivisions of final expenditure which correspond to the first aggregation of price (or quantity) ratios for individual specifications or items. (For the list of categories, see the appendix to Chapter 2 or Appendix Tables 6-1–6-5.)

Direct price or quantity comparison: Made by comparing for two or more countries the prices or quantities for a representative sample of equivalent commodities. (See also **Indirect price or quantity comparison.**)

Exchange-rate–deviation index: The ratio of the real GDP per capita relative to the United States as estimated by the ICP to the GDP per capita relative to the United States when the exchange rate is used to con-

vert nondollar currencies to dollars. Alternatively, it is the ratio of the exchange rate to the PPP for GDP.

Factor-reversal test: The condition that, for any given item, category, or aggregate and for any given pair of countries, the product of the price ratio (or index) and the quantity ratio (or index) be equal to the expenditure ratio.

Filler: See entry under **Country-product-dummy method.**

Final products: Products purchased for own use and not for resale or for embodiment in a product for resale; those purchased by households, by government, or by business on capital account.

Fisher, or "ideal," index: The geometric mean of two indexes: one, the harmonic mean of price (or quantity) relatives weighted by the numerator country's expenditures; the other, the arithmetic mean weighted by the denominator country's expenditures. (The more usual definition is the geometric mean of 'the own-weighted and base-country–weighted indexes.)

GCF (gross capital formation): Includes fixed capital formation, change in stocks, and net exports. Definitions of these three components correspond to SNA concepts, although the SNA does not include net exports in its definition of GCF.

GDP: Gross domestic product.

Geary-Khamis method: An aggregation method in which category international prices (reflecting relative category values) and country PPPs (depicting relative country price levels) are estimated simultaneously from a system of linear equations.

> **First-stage Geary-Khamis:** A Geary-Khamis calculation for each region of the world in which the inputs are the expenditures and prices of countries, the prices being PPPs from a first-stage CPD. The outputs are intraregional quantity and price comparisons.
> **Second-stage Geary-Khamis:** A Geary-Khamis calculation in which the inputs are the expenditures and prices of regions. Each region's expenditures are obtained by aggregating expenditures derived from the regional first-stage Geary-Khamis calculation; each region's prices are PPPs obtained either from a universal CPD or a second-stage CPD. The immediate outputs are quantity and price comparisons of regions, which make possible interregional country comparisons when combined with the first-stage Geary-Khamis comparisons.
> **Single-stage (universal) Geary-Khamis:** A Geary-Khamis calculation applied to the detailed-category expenditures and prices (that is, PPPs) of all the representative countries.

GFCE (government final consumption expenditure): The SNA concept of "government" that includes public expenditures on education, health, and similar categories (see Table 2-1).

ICP: International Comparison Project.

"Ideal" index: See **Fisher, or "ideal," index.**

Indirect price or quantity comparison: A comparison made by dividing the price or quantity ratio into the expenditure ratio. That is, the indirect quantity comparison between country j and country k for commodity i, q_{ij}/q_{ik}, is obtained from $p_{ij}q_{ij}/p_{ik}q_{ik} \div p_{ij}/p_{ik} = q_{ij}/q_{ik}$, where the p's are the commodity prices. (See also **Direct price or quantity comparison.**)

International dollars (I\$): Dollars with the same purchasing power over total U.S. GDP as the U.S. dollar in a given year, but with a purchasing power over subaggregates and over detailed categories determined by average international prices rather than by U.S. relative prices.

International price (Π): Π_i is the average international price of category i, defined as the quantity-weighted average of the purchasing-power–adjusted prices in the n countries (see equation 3.12). The symbol $\overline{\Pi}$ is the ICP version of Geary's original Π.

Matrix consistency: The property that makes it possible to have correct country-to-country quantity relationships for each detailed category and, at the same time, to obtain the correct country-to-country quantity relationships for any desired aggregation of categories simply by summing the quantities for the included categories. This requires that the quantities be stated in value terms so that (1) the values for any category are directly comparable between countries and (2) the values for any country are directly comparable between categories.

Multilateral comparison: A price or quantity comparison of more than two countries simultaneously that produces consistent relations among all pairs; that is, one that satisfies the circular test or the transitivity requirement.

Own weights: The weights of the numerator country; that is, the weights of country j in the index $I_{j/k}$. The term is used, for example, to refer to the weights of the country other than the United States in a binary comparison in which the United States is the base country, k.

PLS (Paasche-Laspeyres spread): The ratio of an index using own-country weights in a binary comparison to an index using base-country weights.

PFC (public final consumption expenditure): The ICP concept of "government" that excludes public expenditures for education, health, and similar categories (see Table 2-1).

PFCE (private final consumption expenditure): The SNA concept of "consumption" that excludes public expenditures on education, health, and similar categories (see Table 2-1).

PPP: See **Purchasing-power parity**.

Price index: The price level for a category or aggregate of goods in one country expressed as a percentage of the price level for the same category or aggregate in another country, when prices in both countries are expressed in a common currency, usually the U.S. dollar, with the official exchange rate being used for currency conversions. A price index may be derived from a purchasing-power parity by dividing by the exchange rate. (See **Purchasing-power parity**.)

Price tableau: A matrix of prices for a detailed category in which the rows represent different items and the columns the various countries.

Purchasing-power parity (PPP): The number of currency units required to buy goods equivalent to what can be bought with one unit of the currency of the base country, usually the U.S. dollar in the present study.

Quantity index: The quantity per capita of a category or aggregate of goods in one country expressed as a percentage of the quantity per capita in another country.

Quantity ratio: The quantity of a particular commodity in one country as a proportion of the quantity of the same commodity in another country.

Real product or real quantity: The final product or quantity in two or more countries that is valued at common prices and, therefore, valued in comparable terms internationally.

Representative country: One of the thirty-four included countries regarded as a representative of a larger group of countries that together with it form a supercountry. All the countries in the world are assigned to one of the thirty-four supercountries. (See also **Supercountry.**)

Similarity indexes for prices and for quantities: The similarity index for quantities is the weighted "raw correlation" coefficient between the quantity vectors of two countries. The coefficient is the ratio of the cross moment to the square root of the product of the two second moments, where each moment is computed relative to the origin rather than to the mean. The similarity index for prices is the corresponding measure for the price vectors of two countries, with the category prices weighted by the relative importance of each category in total world GDP.

Similarity index for per capita income: The similarity index for a pair of countries is the ratio of (1) twice the index of the real GDP per capita (with the United States equal to 100) of the member of the pair with the smaller index to (2) the sum of the indexes of the two members of the pair.

SNA: The U.N. System of National Accounts.

Specification: A description of an item for which a price comparison is to be made. The description is designed to ensure that goods of equivalent quality are compared.

Supercountry: A group of countries assumed to have the price and quantity structure of the representative country. The aggregate GDP of the supercountry is used to weight the prices of the representative country in the process of deriving average international prices. (See also **Representative country**.)

Transactions equality: The index number property that makes the relative importance of each transaction involving the purchase of a final product dependent solely on its magnitude and not on the size of the country in which it occurred.

Transitivity requirements: See **Circularity or transitivity**.

Index

Accounting, problems with, 35–36

Additive consistency, 72n7

Additivity, full, 72n7; Geary-Khamis method and, 92

Aggregation method, 74, 99; for category expenditures and prices, 89–94; at detailed category level, 82–89, 116–17; methodology and, 6–7, 98; regionalization and, 127

Aggregations: binary comparisons results and, 225; procedure used to produce, 172

Asia, demand function and, 364–66

Augmented binary price comparisons. *See* Binary comparisons

Austria, price data collection in, 40

Automobiles, price data on, 50–54

Average-price-weight index, 77–79

Base country, 74; detailed category aggregation and, 85, 117; star system of binary comparisons and, 111, 112, 114

Base-country invariance, 71–72; Geary-Khamis method and, 94. *See also* Homotheticity

Benchmark years: choice of (1970 or 1975), 336–46; ICP objectives and, 23–24; nonbenchmark years estimate and, 323–24; real income per capita and, 324–28

Binary comparisons: augmented (compared with multilateral and traditional binary results), 230–33; augmented (method), 225–26; augmented (results), 226–30; disadvantage of, 6; intraregional comparisons and, 101–02; involving only weights and specifications of included countries, 8; methods of, 74–75; multilateral comparisons and, 75–77, 99; Phase III and, 5; PLS and, 105; regional groupings and selective sets of, 111–15; regionalization and multilateral methods based on, 115–16; traditional, 225; transitivity criterion and, 85; unique goods and, 40

Bombach, G., 27

Brazil, price data collection in, 40

Bridge-country binary comparisons, 85, 86, 111, 112–15

Capital: adjustment (for government employee compensation), 159; educational inputs and, 156; medical care inputs and, 141–44; as omitted input (Phases I and II), 134; Phase III methodology and, 159–60, 161

Capital formation: ICP concept and, 35; ICP results and, 18–20; output and, 29–30. *See also* Gross capital formation

Categories. *See* Detailed categories; Summary categories; *and names of specific categories*

Category-control-total method, 122–23

CEP. *See* Consumption expenditure of the population

Chain indexes, 76

Characteristicity, 105; augmented binaries and, 226; multilateral methods and, 73; regionalization and, 101–03, 104, 128

Chenery, Hollis, 137

Circularity or transitivity, 72, 74, 94, 101; detailed category aggregation and, 84–86, 87; regionalization data and, 105

Clark, Colin, 139

Classification system (ICP), 60–69

Clothing and footwear category, 61–62

Cobb-Douglas production function, 141

Colombia, price data collection in, 40–41

Commodities: comparisons for, 191–95; component of GDP (ICP study results), 21–23; defined, 193

Compensation. *See* Employee compensation (government)

Construction: defined, 193; ICP category for, 64–65; prices for, 47–49

Consumer goods specifications, 45–47. *See also* Specifications

Consumption: expenditure data and, 33, 35; ICP results and, 20–21; real per capita, 371–73

Consumption expenditure of the population (CEP), 33, 35; ICP classification system and, 60–64, 67

Consumption goods prices, 44–47

Country-product-dummy method (CPD), 51, 98, 99; augmented binary method and,

226; detailed category aggregation and, 86–87, 116–20; versus EKS, 88–89; as a filler technique, 87–88; government expenditures and, 33; methodology and, 6, 7; regionalization and, 9, 123–25, 127; rent estimates and, 57, 58

Country reversal test, 72

CPD. *See* Country-product-dummy method

DA. *See* Domestic absorption component

Data base of ICP, 6

Demand analysis: linear expenditure system and, 366–74; log-linear, 357–66; Phases I and II and, 347; price and quantity similarity and, 348–54; revealed preference and, 354–57; taste and, 347, 354

Demand function (reverse), missing PPPs and, 88

Detailed categories: aggregation methods and, 82–89, 116–17; components of GDP and, 35; log-linear demand analysis and, 359; methodology and, 6, 7; Phase III results and, 163–73; PPPs and, 163–72; quantity comparisons for, 172–73

Divisia index, 75–76

Domestic absorption component (DA), 324, 329, 330n13

Drechsler, Lazlo, 323n3

Durable furnishings and equipment, other, category, 66

Education category, 50, 94; measuring inputs in, 154–56; methodological changes in measuring (Phase III), 159–60; methodology for measuring, 156–59; in Phases I and II, 132

EEC. *See* European Economic Community

EKS (Elteto, Koves, and Szulc) method, 76, 95; versus CPD, 88–89; regionalization and, 116, 117, 127

Electrical machinery and appliances category, 66

Employee compensation category, 66

Employee compensation (government), 21, 50, 175; capital adjustment in methodology and, 159; in Phases I and II, 132–33

The full range of World Bank publications, both free and for sale, is described in the *Catalog of World Bank Publications;* the continuing research program is outlined in *World Bank Research Program: Abstracts of Current Studies*. Both booklets are updated annually; the most recent edition of each is available without charge from the Publications Unit, World Bank, 1818 H Street, N.W., Washington, D.C. 20433, U.S.A.

Irving B. Kravis and Robert Summers are professors of economics, and Alan Heston is professor of South Asian economics, at the University of Pennsylvania.